Consumer
Behavior

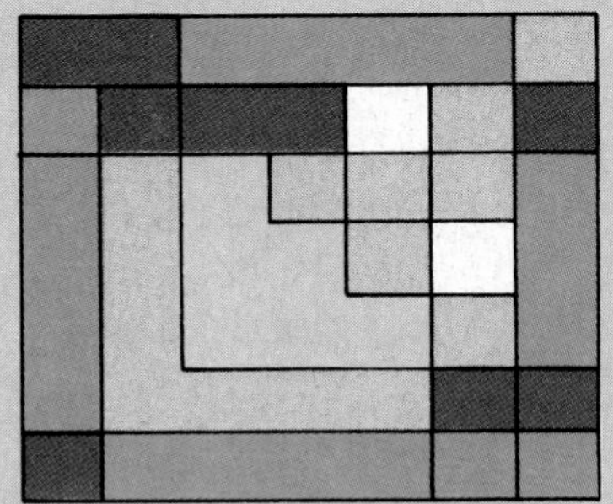

# CONSUMER

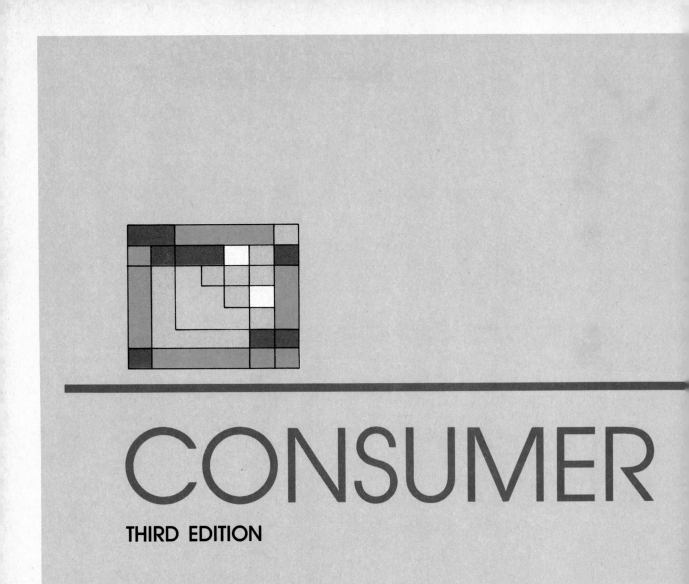

THIRD EDITION

*Leon G. Schiffman*
Baruch College
City University of New York

*Leslie Lazar Kanuk*
Baruch College
City University of New York

# BEHAVIOR

PRENTICE-HALL, INC.
Englewood Cliffs, New Jersey 07632

*Library of Congress Cataloging-in-Publication Data*

SCHIFFMAN, LEON G.
Consumer behavior.

Includes index.
1. Consumers. 2. Motivation research (Marketing)
I. Kanuk, Leslie Lazar. II. Title.
HF5415.3.S29 1987 658.8'342 86-25224
ISBN 0-13-169020-5

TO
ELAINE, JANET, AND DAVID SCHIFFMAN
AND
JACK, RANDI, AND ALAN KANUK

Editorial/production supervision: Pamela Wilder
Cover and interior design: Suzanne Behnke
Artistic supervisor: Christine Gehring-Wolf
Manufacturing buyer: Ed O'Dougherty

CONSUMER BEHAVIOR, Third Edition
by Leon G. Schiffman and Leslie Lazar Kanuk



Printed in the United States of America

10 9 8 7 6 5 4 3 2 1

ISBN 0-13-169020-5 01

Prentice-Hall International (UK) Limited, *London*
Prentice-Hall of Australia Pty. Limited, *Sydney*
Prentice-Hall Canada Inc., *Toronto*
Prentice-Hall Hispanoamericana, S.A., *Mexico*
Prentice-Hall of India Private Limited, *New Delhi*
Prentice-Hall of Japan, Inc., *Tokyo*
Prentice-Hall of Southeast Asia Pte. Ltd., *Singapore*
Editora Prentice-Hall do Brasil, Ltda., *Rio de Janeiro*

# Contents

## PART II THE CONSUMER AS AN INDIVIDUAL

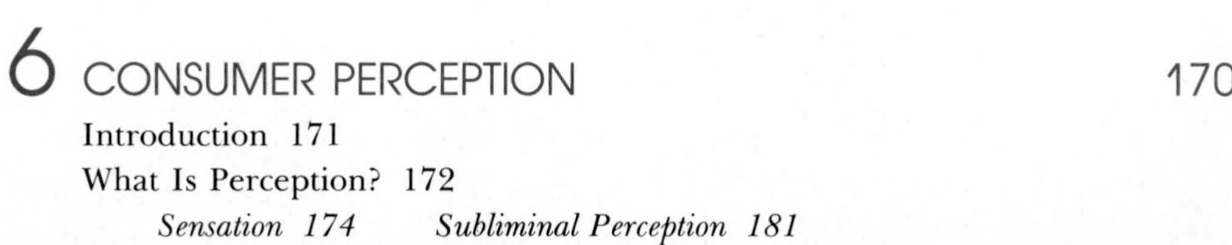

## PART III CONSUMERS IN THEIR SOCIAL AND CULTURAL SETTINGS

## 13 SOCIAL CLASS AND CONSUMER BEHAVIOR 434



## 14 THE INFLUENCE OF CULTURE ON CONSUMER BEHAVIOR 472

# Preface

As we labored over the first and second editions of *Consumer Behavior,* we took comfort from the reassurances of friends in the academic and publishing communities who told us that future editions would be a "snap." Now that we have completed the third edition, we would like to suggest that the statement "Revisions are easy" be placed alongside such academic exaggerations as: "The term paper got lost in my computer," "My printer broke down," and "You'll have an advance copy of the paper three weeks before the conference."

Part of the difficulty in preparing this revision was the fact that the field of consumer behavior is so dynamic and its researchers so prolific. Given the number and diversity of consumer behavior studies today, it was difficult to decide when to cut off the review of new articles, which new streams of research to include, and where to include them, since they often fit into more than one topical area. Indeed, the temptation right through the "galley" stage of this edition was to keep adding new research findings to the manuscript.

As true believers in the marketing concept, we have tried our best to meet the needs of our consumers—students, practitioners, and professors of consumer behavior—by providing a text that is highly readable and that clearly explains the relevant concepts upon which the discipline of consumer behavior is based. We have supplemented this material with "real-world" and high tech examples that illustrate how consumer behavior concepts are used by marketing practitioners to develop and implement effective marketing strategies.

Our aim in the third edition, as it was in the earlier editions, was to write a book that was complete and comprehensive without being encyclopedic. To make it as useful as possible to both graduate and undergraduate students, we sought to maintain a firm balance of basic behavioral concepts, research findings, and applied marketing examples.

We continue to be convinced that the major contribution of consumer behavior studies to the practice of marketing is the provision of structure and direction for effective market segmentation. To this end, we have included a greatly expanded discussion of market segmentation in this edition. We have also increased the number of market segmentation examples throughout the book.

This third edition of *Consumer Behavior* is divided into five parts, consisting of twenty chapters. Part I introduces the reader to the study of consumer behavior and its applications to strategic planning and strategic marketing. It shows how consumer behavior principles provide the conceptual framework and strategic direction for profit and not-for-profit organizations in segmenting markets, targeting, and positioning.

Part II discusses the consumer as an individual. It begins with an exploration of consumer needs and motivations, recognizing both the rational and emotional bases of many consumer actions. A discussion of personality and psychographics follows, including an expanded discussion of SRI VALS. A comprehensive examination of the impact of consumer perception on marketing strategies includes a discussion of product positioning and repositioning. The discussion of consumer learning focuses on limited and extensive information processing, including a new and comprehensive evaluation of involvement theory and its applications to marketing practice. After an in-depth examination of consumer attitudes, Part II concludes with a discussion of communication and media strategy and links consumers as individuals to the world and people around them.

Part III is concerned with the social and cultural dimensions of consumer behavior. It begins with a discussion of group dynamics and consumer reference groups, followed by an examination of new family role orientations and changing family lifestyles. It presents consumers in their social and cultural milieus, and investigates the impact of societal and subcultural values, beliefs, and customs on consumer behavior. This section includes an in-depth discussion of geodemographic clustering and such subcultures as the baby boomer, the affluent, and the elderly, and concludes with an exploration of consumer behavior in other countries and a discussion of the need for careful cross-cultural analyses in an era of increasing multinational marketing.

Part IV provides a greatly expanded treatment of various aspects of consumer decision making. It begins with a discussion of personal influence and opinion leadership, followed by an examination of the diffusion of innovations. Next, it describes how consumers make product decisions and offers the reader a simple model of consumer decision making which ties together the psychological, social, and cultural concepts examined throughout the book. Because some professors like to discuss the evolution of consumer theory in their classes, we have included in this section an overview of various models of consumer behavior that have received attention in the literature in previous years.

Part V presents an all-new analysis of consumer behavior applications to the marketing of services, including political marketing and health care marketing, and concludes with a discussion of the application of consumer behavior research to public policy issues.

Of the many people who have been enormously helpful in the preparation of this new edition of *Consumer Behavior,* we are especially grateful to our own consumers—the graduate and undergraduate students of consumer behavior and their professors—who have provided us with invaluable experiential feedback to our earlier editions.

We would particularly like to thank our close friend and colleague, Professor Conrad Berenson, Chairman of the Department of Marketing at Baruch College, for his continued encouragement, his friendship, and his unfailing support. We are grateful to the following professors for their useful suggestions and highly constructive comments: Steve Schnaars, Baruch College; Benny Barak, Hofstra University; Elaine Sherman, Hofstra University; Marty Topol, Pace University; Jerry Greenberg, Rutgers University; Hal Kassarjian, UCLA; David Brinberg, SUNY, Albany; John Holmes, Bowling Green State University; Joel Saegert, The University of Texas at San Antonio; Havva J. Meric, East Carolina University; Ron Goldsmith, Florida State University; Richard Yalch, University of Washington; Mark Young, Winona State University; Michael Taylor, Marietta College; Daniel Johnson, Radford University; Bob Settle, San Diego State University; Gerald Cavallo, Fairfield University; and Kristina Cannon-Bonventre, Northeastern University.

We would like to give special recognition to Professors Stanley Garfunkel of CUNY and Joseph Wisenblit of Seton Hall University for their invaluable advice, assistance, and support throughout the preparation of this edition. We would also like to acknowledge Ross Cooper of D'Arcy Masius Benton & Bowles, Jerry Lott of Warner-Lambert, and Robert Atkyns, Marilyn Fox, John Veltri, and Skip West of AT&T, who provided us with important practical applications of the concepts explored throughout the text. We are grateful to Whitney Blake and Pam Wilder of Prentice-Hall for their hard work on our behalf.

Finally, we would like to express special thanks to Robyn Lindner, Carol Bergman-George, and Randi Dauler for the close attention to detail and careful follow-through so necessary to turning a manuscript into a book. To the many others whom we have not specifically named, we think of you, we thank you, and we love you nonetheless.

LEON G. SCHIFFMAN
LESLIE LAZAR KANUK

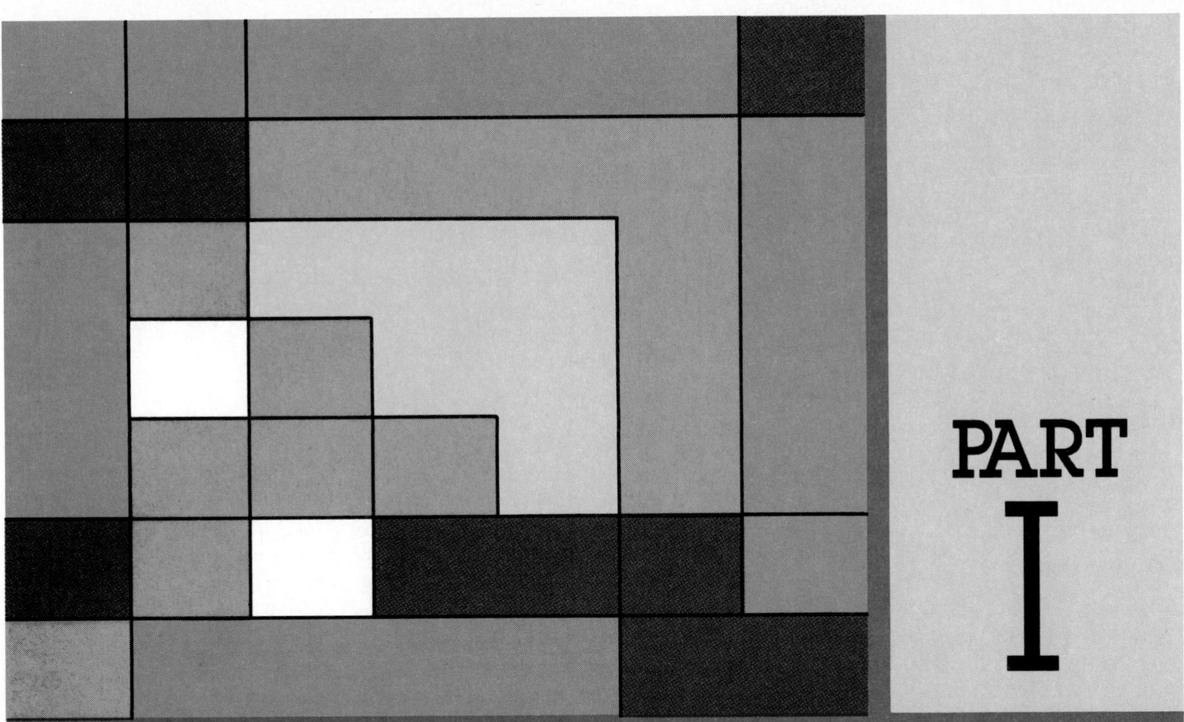

# PART I

# INTRODUCTION

Part I is designed to introduce the reader to the study of consumer behavior. Chapter 1 sets the stage for the remainder of the book by focusing on what consumer behavior is, why we study it, how and why consumer behavior developed as a theoretical and applied discipline, and how firms apply consumer behavior principles to strategic marketing. Chapter 2 discusses the theory and practice of market segmentation and demonstrates how consumer behavior provides both the conceptual framework and the strategic direction for the practical segmentation of markets.

# 1

# Consumer Behavior: Introduction

## *introduction*

COSMETICS for men? A flourishing business today, but ten, or even five years ago no self-respecting cosmetics manufacturer would have attempted anything so foolhardy as marketing a line of cosmetics or skin-care products for men.

What has happened to make such products acceptable today? Have men become more vain? Have they become less masculine? Have sex roles become so blurred as to obscure the market for gender-specific products?

More to the point: What cues were there in the environment to signal marketers that the time was ripe to develop male-targeted skin-care products? What elements in a man's personality or lifestyle made ads for cosmetics suddenly acceptable (see Figure 1-1). What needs do male skin-care products fulfill? How do they affect his self-image? How does a man "learn" to use cosmetics? What influence do his family, his friends, or his social class have on his willingness to try or to buy cosmetics?

These are the types of questions that consumer behaviorists address as they try to understand what it is that influences consumers in their consumption-related decisions.

This book is designed to give the reader a strong understanding of the basic principles of consumer behavior, an insight into the scientific investigations on which our knowledge of consumer behavior is based, and an awareness of how consumer behavior findings can be practically applied to the professional practice of marketing.

One of the few common denominators among all of us—no matter what our education, our politics, or our commitments—is that, above all, we are consumers. That is, we use or consume—on a regular basis—food, clothing, shel-

> *Behavior is a mirror in which everyone displays his own image.*
>
> *GOETHE*
> *Elective Affinities, 1809*

FIGURE 1-1 Advertisement for Male Fragrance

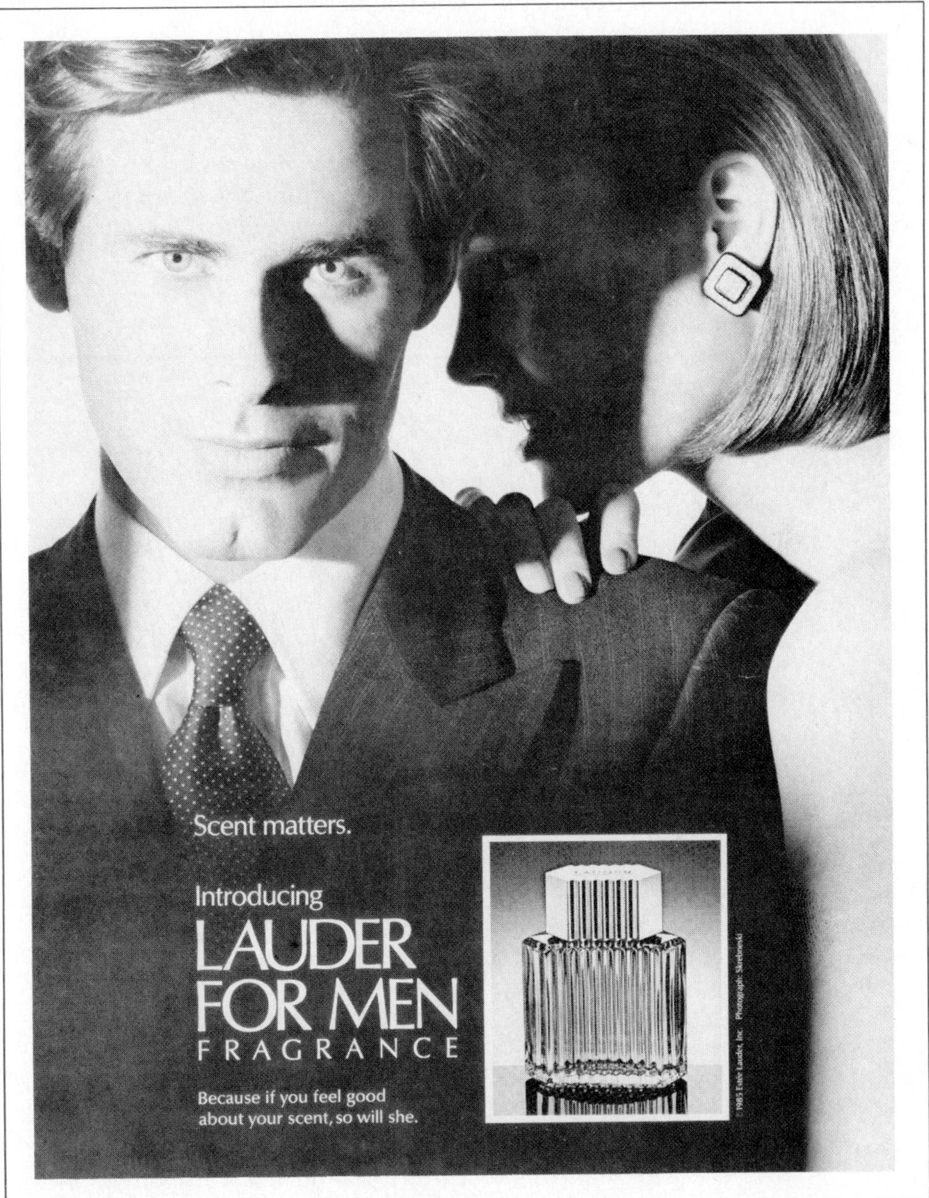


Courtesy of Estee Lauder Inc.

ter, transportation, education, brooms, dishes, vacations, necessities, luxuries, services, even ideas. As consumers, we play a vital role in the health of the economy—local, national, and international. The decisions we make concerning our consumption behavior affect the demand for basic raw materials, for transportation, for production, for banking; they affect the employment of workers and the deployment of resources, the success of some industries and the failure of others. Thus, **consumer behavior** is an integral factor in the ebb and flow of *all* business in a consumer-oriented society such as our own.

This chapter introduces the reader to the notion of consumer behavior as an interdisciplinary science that investigates the decision-making activities of individuals in their consumption roles. It describes the reasons for the development of consumer behavior as an academic discipline and an applied science. The role and scope of the research process in the study of consumer behavior is considered. The chapter discusses the evolution of marketing in this country from a production and product orientation to a selling orientation to a consumer orientation, and briefly examines the importance of the application of consumer behavior principles to strategic market planning.

## CONSUMER BEHAVIOR AS A MARKETING DISCIPLINE

### What Is Consumer Behavior?

The term *consumer behavior* can be defined as *the behavior that consumers display in searching for, purchasing, using, evaluating, and disposing of products, services and ideas which they expect will satisfy their needs.* The study of consumer behavior is the study of how individuals make decisions to spend their available resources (money, time, effort) on consumption-related items. It includes the study of *what* they buy, *why* they buy it, *how* they buy it, *when* they buy it, *where* they buy it, and *how often* they buy it. Thus the study of an individual's consumption behavior in the area of toothpaste products might include a study of why he uses toothpaste (e.g., to whiten his teeth), which brand of toothpaste he buys (e.g., Close-Up), why he buys it (because he believes that it will whiten his teeth better than competing brands), how he buys it (for cash and coupon), when he buys it (when he does the food shopping), where he buys it (in a supermarket), and how often he buys it (approximately every three weeks).

A study of another individual's consumption behavior regarding a more durable item, such as a rug, might include a study of what kind of rug she buys (e.g., a handloomed six-by-nine-foot rug), why she buys it (to give physical and visual warmth to her living room and to impress her friends), how she buys it (on credit), when she buys it (on home-furnishings sale days), where she buys it (in a well-known department store), how often she buys or replaces it (when it is worn or when she refurnishes her living room), and where she discards it (in a hospital thrift shop).

Although this text will focus on how and why consumers make decisions to buy goods and services, consumer behavior research today goes far beyond these facets of consumer behavior. Research also considers the uses consumers make of the goods they buy and their evaluations of these goods after use. What happens after the consumer makes a purchase can have many repercussions. For example, a woman may feel remorse or dissatisfaction with her choice of a particular automobile—perhaps because she had to forgo an equally attractive purchase in order to pay for it, or because it has continuing service problems. She may communicate her dissatisfaction to a friend and may in turn influence his next purchase of an automobile. She may vow never to buy the same make or model again. Each of these possible consequences of consumer postpurchase dissatisfaction has significant ramifications for the marketer.

In addition to studying consumers' use and postpurchase evaluations of the products they buy, consumer researchers are also interested in how individuals dispose of their once-new purchases. For example, after consumers have used a product, do they store it, throw it or give it away, sell it, rent it, or lend it out? The answer to this question is important to marketers because they must match their production to the frequency with which consumers buy replacements. But it is also important to society as a whole, because scarce resources (both economic and natural resources) are forcing all of us to reevaluate our use of products and services, and because solid waste disposal is a troubling environmental problem. Research into current disposal practices enables marketers to develop and promote environmentally sound and economically efficient consumer products.

## PERSONAL CONSUMERS VERSUS ORGANIZATIONAL CONSUMERS

The term **consumer** is often used to describe two different kinds of consuming entities: the personal consumer and the organizational consumer. The *personal consumer* is the individual who buys goods and services for his or her own use (e.g., shaving cream or lipstick), for the use of the household (a cake mix), for just one member of the household (a shirt), or as a gift for a friend (a book). In all these contexts, the goods are bought for final use by individuals, who are referred to as "end users" or "ultimate consumers."

The second category of consumer, the *organizational consumer,* encompasses private businesses, government agencies (local, state, and national), and institutions (schools, churches, prisons), all of which must buy products, equipment, and services in order to run their organizations—whether for profit or not-for-profit. Manufacturing companies must buy the raw materials and other components to manufacture and sell their own products; service companies must buy the equipment necessary to render the services they sell; government agencies must buy the variety of products they need to operate agencies and offices; and institutions must buy the materials they need to maintain themselves and their populations.

Despite the importance of both categories of consumers—individuals and organizations—this book will focus on the individual consumer, who purchases for his or her own personal use or for household use. End-use consumption is perhaps the most pervasive of all types of consumer behavior, since it involves every individual, of every age and every background, in the role of either buyer or user, or both.

## BUYERS AND USERS

Inherent in the notion that individuals buy products for themselves and their families is the distinction that exists between *buyers* and *users*. The person who makes the actual purchase is not always the user, or the only user, of the product in question. Nor is the purchaser necessarily the person who makes the product decision. A mother may buy toys for her children (who are the users); she may buy food for dinner (and be one of the users); she may buy a handbag (and be the only user). She may buy a record that one of her teenagers requested, or a magazine that her husband requested, or she and her husband together may buy a car that they both selected. The various influences on family product-related decisions are discussed in detail in Chapter 12; suffice it here to stress the fact that buyers are not always the users, or the only users, of the products they buy, nor are they necessarily the persons who make the product selection decisions.

Marketers must decide at whom to direct their promotional efforts; in so doing, they must identify the best *prospect* for the product they want to sell. Some marketers believe that the buyer of the product is the best prospect, others believe it is the user of the product, while still others play it safe by directing their promotional efforts to both buyers and users. For example, some toy manufacturers advertise their products on children's television shows to reach the users, others advertise in *Parents' Magazine* to reach the buyers, while still others run dual campaigns designed to reach both children and their parents. Because such toy marketers are uncertain as to how much influence children exert on their parents, they try to favorably influence parents in an effort to make them more receptive to their children's requests for particular toys.

### CONSUMER BEHAVIOR AND CONSUMERISM

Many people confuse the terms **consumer behavior** with **consumerism,** and **consumer researchers** with **consumer advocates** or **consumer activists.** As we noted above, *consumer behavior* is the study of how individuals make consumption decisions; *consumer researchers* are behavioral scientists who undertake such studies. *Consumerism,* on the other hand, is a movement by consumers (i.e., *consumer advocates*) designed to ensure fair and ethical practices toward consumers by manufacturers, retailers, and other selling intermediaries. As discussed later in this chapter, a knowledge of consumer behavior assists consumer advocates in identifying areas for needed consumer protection legislation.

## Why We Study Consumer Behavior

The study of consumer behavior holds great interest for us as consumers, as students and scientists, and as marketers. As consumers, we need insights into our own consumption-related decisions: what we buy, why we buy, and how we buy. The study of consumer behavior makes us aware of the subtle influences that persuade us to make the product or service choices we do.

As students of human behavior, it is important for us to understand the internal and external influences that impel individuals to act in certain consumption-related ways. Consumer behavior is simply a subset of the larger field of human behavior. As scientists, we are interested in understanding every aspect of human behavior. Certainly, as scientists, we should also want to understand the special aspect of human behavior known as consumer behavior. As marketers (and future marketers), it is important for us to recognize why and how individuals make their consumption decisions so that we can make better strategic marketing decisions. Without doubt, marketers who understand consumer behavior have a great competitive advantage in the marketplace.

## HOW AND WHY THE FIELD OF CONSUMER BEHAVIOR DEVELOPED

There are a number of reasons why the study of consumer behavior developed as a separate marketing discipline. Marketing scientists had long noted that consumers did not always act or react as economic theory would suggest. The size of the consumer market in this country was vast and constantly expanding. Billions of dollars were being spent on goods and services by tens of millions of people. Consumer preferences were changing and becoming highly diversified. Even in industrial markets, where needs for goods and services were always more homogeneous than in consumer markets, buyers were exhibiting diversified preferences and less predictable purchase behavior.

As marketing researchers began to study the buying behavior of consumers, they soon realized that despite overriding similarities, consumers were not all alike. Despite a sometimes "me-too" approach to fads and fashions, many consumers rebelled at using the identical products everyone else used. Instead, they preferred differentiated products which they felt closely reflected their own special needs, personalities, and lifestyles. To better meet the needs of specific groups of consumers, "enlightened" marketers adopted a policy of **market segmentation,** which called for the division of their total potential market into smaller, homogeneous segments for which they could design a specific product and/or promotional campaign. A market segmentation strategy requires a great deal of insight into the consumption habits of selected market segments. The collection and analysis of such information is the province of the field of consumer behavior. (See Chapter 2 for an in-depth discussion of market segmentation.)

At the same time, the technological explosion that hit this country resulted in the rapid introduction of new products at an ever-increasing rate. Many of these new products—some experts estimate over 80 percent—proved to be marketing disasters. To increase the likelihood of successful new product introductions, marketers realized that they needed better information about consumers—their wishes, their preferences, their changing lifestyles—to guide in new product development. Table 1-1 lists several new products that failed because they did not appeal to consumer needs, and several that succeeded handsomely because they did.

In addition to the fast pace of new product introduction, other factors that contributed to the development of consumer behavior as a marketing discipline include shorter product life cycles, environmental concerns, increased interest in consumer protection and public policy legislation, the growth of services marketing and nonprofit marketing, the growth of international marketing, and the development of computers and sophisticated methods of statistical analysis.

**TABLE 1-1 The Success or Failure of New Products Depends on Consumer Need Satisfaction**

1. Low-calorie beers were unsuccessful until Miller Lite positioned itself as a beer that didn't leave the drinker "feeling full". Consumer behavior research would have pointed out that diet-conscious consumers were not beer drinkers, and that heavy beer drinkers—the prime target group for most beer marketers—were not diet conscious. The appeal they did respond to was the notion that they could drink even more beer with no discomfort.
2. Frank Purdue tells consumers in a television commercial that he "hates pudgy poultry" and removes all fat from his chickens, "even flab from the chicken's belly." This is a direct appeal to diet-conscious consumers. The company took a relatively undifferentiated commodity and developed strong brand identification by advertising quality and guaranteeing satisfaction or a full refund. Purdue's appearance as the company spokesman conveys sincerity as well as humor.
3. When Apple Computer entered the personal computer market, interest in computers was growing among the general public. Apple promised simplified, reliable operation to consumers who had no programming knowledge, and quickly garnered a large share of the market.
4. DuPont's Corfam failed because consumers didn't want shoes that would last forever, as the Corfam ads suggested. Furthermore, the company paid too little attention to marketing research which indicated that some consumers experienced discomfort with the material.

SHORTER PRODUCT LIFE CYCLES. Because of the fast pace of new product introductions, many product life cycles are necessarily compressed as products are modified, improved, or replaced by new and substitute products. Faced with a much shorter product life cycle, companies need a constant supply of new product ideas to satisfy the needs of their target segments. Research into present and evolving consumer lifestyles and unsatisfied (or unfelt) consumer needs provides the basis for a steady stream of new product concepts and complementary promotional appeals. At the same time, research into consumer media habits provides the necessary insights into how best to reach consumer prospects in order to influence their purchase behavior.

ENVIRONMENTAL CONCERNS. Increased public concern regarding environmental deterioration, resource shortages, and the population explosion made both marketers and public policy makers aware of the potentially negative impact of such products as high-suds detergents, aerosol sprays, and disposable bottles. Research into consumer interests and practices enables marketers to develop and effectively promote environmentally sound product modifications for socially concerned consumers. Table 1-2 lists some consumer products that have been modified to meet environmental concerns.

INCREASED INTEREST IN CONSUMER PROTECTION. The growth of the consumer protection movement created an urgent need to understand how consumers make their consumption decisions. For example, in order to identify sources of consumer confusion and deception, consumer advocates have sought to under-

**TABLE 1-2 Products Modified to Meet Environmental Concerns**

- Greeting cards and stationery made of recycled paper.
- Disposable diapers that are biodegradable.
- Automobiles that use lead-free gasoline.
- Low-suds detergents.
- Trash compactors.
- Recycled soda bottles and cans.

stand how consumers perceive and interpret various marketing and promotional information (e.g., promotional appeals, package labels, warranties). Consumer research has provided the basis for a number of recommendations concerning consumer protection legislation.

PUBLIC POLICY CONCERNS. Parallel with the growth of the consumer protection movement, policy makers at the local, state and federal levels became more aware of their responsibility to protect the consumer interests and well-being of their constituents. At the federal level, such agencies as the Federal Trade Commission and the Food and Drug Administration began to sponsor research to discover the impact of various products and advertisements on the consuming public.

GROWTH OF SERVICES MARKETING. As the United States turned to a service economy, it became apparent to many service providers that marketing their intangible "products" was becoming more and more difficult. Services cannot be seen, heard, examined, or felt in advance of purchase, nor is employee-dependent quality consistent over time. In some industries, such as transportation or broadcasting, services are "perishable" in the sense that they are lost forever to the marketer if not consumed at the time scheduled (e.g., the revenues lost from flying a half-empty plane can never be recouped.) Not only did service providers need to market, but they realized that knowledge of consumer needs and interests was essential to the development of effective marketing strategies. Figure 1-2 presents an example of service advertising that attempts to "humanize" the services offered.

GROWTH OF NONPROFIT MARKETING. Organizations in the public and private nonprofit sectors began to recognize the need to use marketing strategies to bring their services to the attention of their relevant publics. For example, private and public colleges experiencing enrollment declines have developed marketing campaigns to attract students; museums dependent on public support now use marketing programs to enlist private contributions.

FIGURE 1-2 Service Marketing

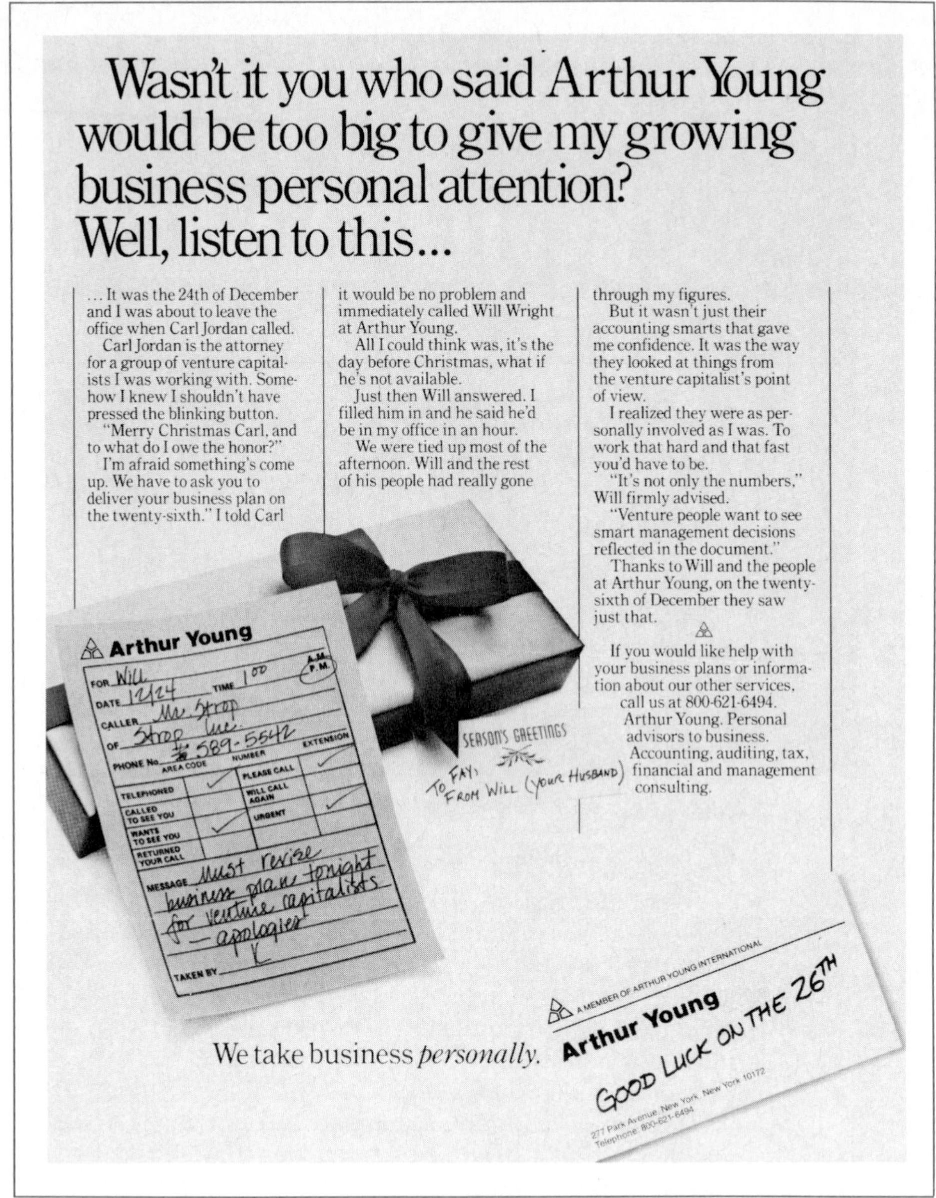


Courtesy of Arthur Young

GROWTH OF INTERNATIONAL MARKETING. In an effort to seek new and expanded markets, most large companies in the United States promote their products abroad. Indeed, in an effort to correct the balance of trade deficit, the federal government is trying to encourage small and medium-sized companies to sell their products abroad as well. A major stumbling block to many international marketing efforts has been the general lack of familiarity with the needs, preferences, and consumption habits of consumers in targeted foreign markets. Assumptions that foreign consumers are similar to United States con-

FIGURE 1-3 International Marketing

Courtesy of AT&T

sumers have led to frequent international marketing failures. Marketers have come to realize the importance of understanding consumer behavior in foreign markets so they can tailor their products and/or promotional strategies to meet the needs of targeted foreign consumers (see Figure 1-3).

COMPUTER AND STATISTICAL TECHNIQUES. The development of microcomputers and sophisticated analytical techniques has encouraged and facilitated research into consumer behavior. The computer enables consumer researchers to process and store vast amounts of data concerning consumers—their characteristics, attitudes, interests, activities, etc.—and the use of advanced statistical techniques enables them to analyze these data and to delineate homogeneous market segments.

## CONSUMER BEHAVIOR IS AN INTERDISCIPLINARY SCIENCE

Consumer behavior was a relatively new field of study in the mid to late 1960s. With no history or body of research of its own, the new discipline borrowed heavily from concepts developed in other scientific disciplines, such as psychology, sociology, social psychology, cultural anthropology, and economics.

PSYCHOLOGY. Psychology is the study of the individual. It includes the study of motivation, perception, attitudes, personality, and learning patterns. All these factors are integral to an understanding of consumer behavior. They enable us to understand the various consumption needs of individuals, their actions and reactions in response to different products and product messages, and the way personality characteristics and previous experiences affect their product choices.

SOCIOLOGY. Sociology is the study of groups. Group behavior—the actions of individuals in groups—often differs from the actions of individuals operating alone. The influence of group memberships, family structure, and social class on consumer behavior are all relevant to the study of consumer segments in the marketplace.

SOCIAL PSYCHOLOGY. Social psychology is an amalgam of sociology and psychology. It is the study of how an individual operates in a group. The study of consumer behavior is not only the study of how groups operate in terms of market behavior; it is also the study of how individuals are influenced in their personal consumption behavior by those whose opinions they respect: their peers, their reference groups, their families, and opinion leaders.

CULTURAL ANTHROPOLOGY. The study of human beings in society is the study of cultural anthropology. It traces the development of the core beliefs, values, and customs that are passed down to individuals from their parents and grandparents and influence their purchase and consumption behavior. It also includes the study of subcultures (subgroups within the larger society) and lends itself to a comparison of consumers of different nationalities with diverse cultures and customs.

ECONOMICS. An important component of the study of economics is the study of consumers: how they spend their funds, how they evaluate alternatives, and how they make decisions to maximize satisfaction. Many early theories concerning consumer behavior were based on economic theory. For example, the *economic man* theory postulates that individuals act rationally to maximize their utilities (i.e., their benefits) in the purchase of goods and services. More recent consumer studies have indicated that individuals often act less than rationally (i.e., emotionally) to fulfill their psychological needs.

The **interdisciplinary** nature of consumer behavior is perhaps its greatest strength: it serves to integrate existing knowledge from other fields into a comprehensive body of information about individuals in their consumption roles. Thus, despite the fact that the study of consumer behavior is of relatively recent origin, its underpinnings are rooted in scientific evidence that has emerged from many years of research by scientists specializing in the study of human behavior.

Since its beginnings as a "borrowed" science, the field of consumer behavior has grown enormously, and has become the backbone of most programs of marketing study. As students of consumer behavior moved into marketing management positions throughout industry, they brought with them a knowledge and appreciation of consumer behavior principles as an applied science, opening up new areas for needed research. At the same time, new scholarly journals were established to report on such research, and new professional associations organized to provide forums for the dissemination of consumer research findings. The field of consumer behavior has now become a full-blown discipline on its own, buttressed by a strong and growing body of meaningful research. Figure 1-4 depicts the increasing and proliferating streams of consumer behavior research reported in the marketing literature.

## The Role of Consumer Research

Consumer research is the **methodology** used to study consumer behavior. As in any science, consumer behavior theories must be tested and either supported or rejected before conclusions can be generalized as principles applicable to marketing practice. Some consumer behavior research is conducted on the basis of observations of actual behavior in the marketplace; other research is conducted under controlled conditions in the laboratory; still other research is based on the manipulation of marketing variables within a simulated marketing context. Only through constant testing, evaluation, rejection, and support of related hypotheses can behavioral principles be developed to provide marketers with meaningful insights into psychological and environmental factors that influence consumer decision making. Consumer behavior research also enables marketers to carve out new market segments based on variables that emerge as important discriminators among consumers for a specific product or product category.

**FIGURE 1-4** **Occurrence of Major Streams of Consumer Research Reported in Marketing Journals over Time** Source: Adapted from James G. Helgeson, E. Alan Kluge, John Mager, Cheri Taylor, "Trends in Consumer Behavior Literature: A Content Analysis," *Journal of Consumer Research,* 10 (March 1984), 452.

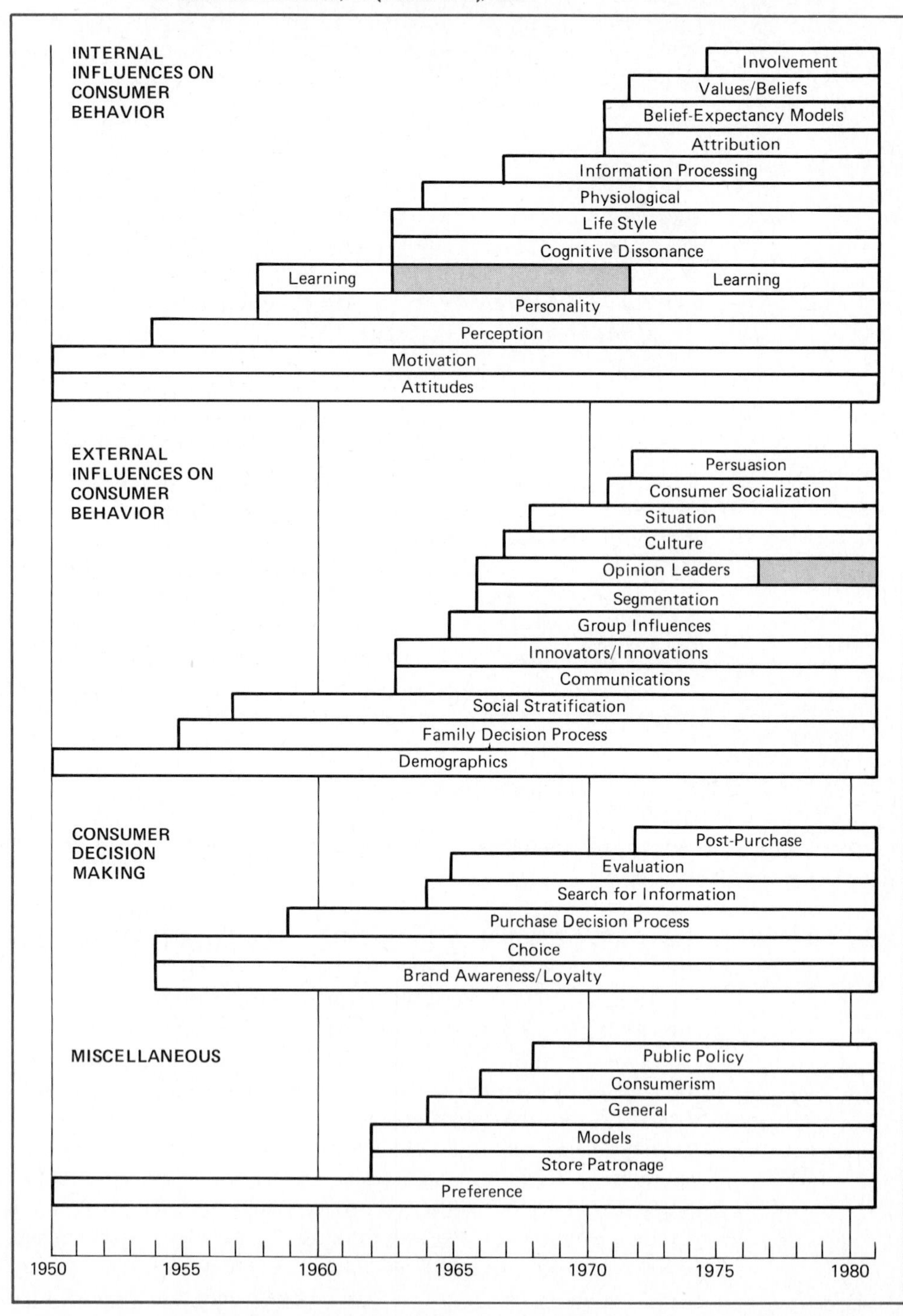

### SCOPE OF CONSUMER RESEARCH

Consumer behavior research is conducted for every phase of the consumption process: from *before* the purchase takes place (when the consumer first becomes aware of a need), to the *search and evaluation* of product alternatives (ranging from simple to extensive information search), to the *actual purchase decision* (including such factors as product and brand choice, store choice, and method of payment), to *after* the purchase takes place (through any periods of uncertainty, satisfaction, dissatisfaction, repurchase, or further search in the marketplace).

### CONSUMER RESEARCH AND THE MARKETING MIX

Consumer research is relevant to each variable in the marketing mix: product, price, promotion and distribution.

**Product.** Consumer research enables the marketer to build consumer "meaning" into the product by discovering which attributes are most important to the target market and integrating them into the design of the product. It provides the basis for the development of new product concepts and families of products to meet targeted consumer needs.

**Price.** Consumer research assists the marketer in establishing psychological pricing levels that consumers would be willing to pay.

**Promotion.** Consumer research is used to determine persuasive advertising appeals and to identify appropriate media choices to reach selected target markets.

**Distribution.** Consumer research identifies where consumers shop and how they perceive various distribution outlets, and provides the basis for an effective distribution strategy.

# THE APPLICATION OF CONSUMER BEHAVIOR PRINCIPLES TO STRATEGIC MARKETING

To operate successfully, marketing firms must have a thorough understanding—explicit rather than implicit—of what makes consumers buy. They have to know *why* they buy, what *needs* they are trying to fulfill, and what outside *influences* affect their product choices in order to design marketing strategies that will favorably influence related consumer decisions.

## Development of the Marketing Concept

The field of consumer behavior is rooted in the **marketing concept**, a marketing strategy that evolved after World War II. When the war was over, marketers found they could sell almost any goods they could produce to consumers who had done without while the nation's manufacturing facilities were dedicated to the production of war materiél. The marketing objective implicit in this **production orientation** was cheap, efficient production and intensive distribution. A production orientation is a feasible marketing strategy when demand exceeds supply, and when consumers are more interested in obtaining the product than in its specific features. For example, when World War II was over, automobile-hungry consumers sometimes waited six to twelve months for delivery of a new car. When the dealer notified a consumer that a new car was available, the consumer grabbed it, regardless of style, color, or accessories.

After consumer production had been resumed for a number of years, competition intensified and marketers moved from a production orientation to a **product orientation**. The assumption underlying the product orientation is that consumers will buy the product which offers them the highest quality, the best performance, and the most features. A product orientation leads the company to constantly strive to improve the quality of its product, with a result often referred to as *marketing myopia* (that is, a focus on the product rather than on the consumer need it presumes to satisfy). A marketer "in love" with its own product may improve it far beyond its worth to the consumer, passing the cost of unneeded quality or features through to the public. For example, an office equipment manufacturer can make a file cabinet so strong that it will remain intact when dropped from a fourth story window. Its durability may be noteworthy, but the likelihood of having to withstand a four-story drop is not high. On the other hand, given the rough treatment that suitcases receive from airline baggage handling facilities, crash-resistant strength in luggage may realistically fulfill consumer needs.

When the public's appetite for consumer goods had become somewhat sated and consumers began to exercise discrimination in their selection of products, many companies switched to a **selling orientation**; that is, they changed their primary focus from *improving* the product to *selling* the product. During this period, companies exerted a tremendous "hard sell" on consumers in order to move the goods they had unilaterally decided to produce. The implicit assumption in the selling orientation is that consumers are unlikely to buy a product unless they are actively and aggressively persuaded to do so. The problem with the selling orientation is that it does not take consumer satisfactions into account. If a consumer is induced to buy a product that he doesn't want or doesn't need, his unhappiness is likely to be communicated through negative word-of-mouth that is likely to dissuade other potential consumers. The only kinds of goods and services that are possible candidates for a selling orientation are *unsought* goods, such as life insurance and encyclopedias, and non-profit marketing activities like fund-raising and political campaigns. However, even in these cases, if the product (or service or political candidate) does not fulfill a consumer need, it is unlikely that a repeat purchase (or donation or vote) will be forthcoming.

In the mid-1950s, many marketers began to realize they could sell more goods, more easily, if they produced only those goods they had predetermined that consumers would buy. Instead of trying to persuade customers to buy what the firm had already produced, marketing-oriented firms endeavored to produce only what they had predetermined consumers were willing to buy. Consumer *needs* became the firm's primary focus. This consumer-oriented marketing philosophy came to be known as the **marketing concept**. The key assumption underlying the marketing concept is that to be successful, a company must determine the needs and wants of specific target markets and deliver the desired satisfactions better than the competition.

The marketing concept is based upon the premise that a marketer should make what it can sell instead of trying to sell what it can make. While the selling concept focused on the needs of the seller, the marketing concept focuses on the needs of the buyer. The marketing concept is embodied in such corporate slogans as Burger King's "Have it *your way*" and United Airlines' "*You're* the boss." Figure 1-5 illustrates the application of the marketing concept.

**FIGURE 1-5 Illustration of the Marketing Concept**

Courtesy of Minolta Corporation

The widespread adoption of the marketing concept by American business provided the impetus for the study of consumer behavior. To identify unsatisfied consumer needs, companies had to engage in extensive marketing research. In so doing, they discovered that consumers were highly complex individuals, subject to a variety of psychological and social needs quite apart from their survival needs. They discovered that the needs and priorities of different consumer segments differed dramatically. And they discovered that in order to design new products and marketing strategies that would fulfill consumer needs, they had to study consumers and their consumption behavior in depth. Thus market segmentation and the marketing concept laid the groundwork for the application of consumer behavior principles to marketing strategy.

## Product-Oriented Versus Market-Oriented Definitions of the Firm's Business Domain

A company that defines itself according to the needs of the market it serves is likely to remain in business long after the product-oriented company has perished. For example, if buggy whip manufacturers had defined their business as fulfilling consumer transportation needs, chances are they would still be in business—even if space shuttles were the prevailing mode. They would simply have had to adapt their product lines to the evolving needs of transportation consumers. Companies that focus on *need satisfaction* rather than product manufacture are likely to survive over the long term, since generic needs tend to remain; only the products needed to satisfy them change. Another example: If Atari had viewed itself as a supplier of family entertainment rather than as a producer of video games, it might still be around today. As it turned out, however, when the video game fad was over, the company went under. Table 1-3 lists product-oriented versus market-oriented definitions of some well-known companies.

## Market Segmentation, Targeting, and Product Positioning

The marketing concept is a philosophy which is reflected in a marketing strategy based on **market segmentation, targeting,** and **product positioning.**

### MARKET SEGMENTATION

Market segmentation is the first step in the development of a successful marketing strategy. Consumer behavior research enables the marketer to identify consumers' needs in relation to the product category, and to group consumers according to these needs or some other relevant characteristic. The resulting

TABLE 1-3 **Product-Oriented Versus Market-Oriented Definitions of a Business**

| COMPANY | PRODUCT-ORIENTED DEFINITION | MARKET-ORIENTED DEFINITION |
|---|---|---|
| Revlon | We make cosmetics | We sell hope |
| Missouri-Pacific Railroad | We run a railroad | We are a people-and-goods mover |
| Xerox | We make copying equipment | We improve office productivity |
| International Minerals and Chemicals | We sell fertilizer | We help improve agricultural productivity |
| Standard Oil | We sell gasoline | We supply energy |
| Columbia Pictures | We make movies | We market entertainment |
| Encyclopedia Britannica | We sell encyclopedias | We are in the information-production and distribution business |
| Carrier | We make air conditioners and furnaces | We provide a comfortable climate in the home |

Source: Philip Kotler, *Marketing Management:* Analysis, Planning, and Control, 5th ed. (Englewood Cliffs, N.J.: Prentice-Hall, 1984), 48.

market division provides a "map" of the market broken into consumer segments.

## SELECTING TARGET MARKETS

After considering the size and potential of each of the segments identified, and further considering the firm's own expertise and objectives, the marketer selects one or more segments as its *target market*(s). Companies generally do not have the capability to target *all* potential segments, nor do all segments have the same profit potential.

## PRODUCT POSITIONING

The marketer must persuade the selected target markets that its product will satisfy their needs better than competitive products. To do so, the marketer attempts to develop a special image for its product in the consumer's mind relative to competitive products; that is, it tries to *position* its product as filling a special niche in the marketplace. For example, AT&T, since its breakup, has tried to position itself as far superior to competing phone companies with the line, "The more you hear, the better we sound." Similarly, to reflect consumer interests in natural foods, the Thomas J. Lipton Company has positioned its dry soup mixes as healthy soups "made with no artificial ingredients." Figure 1-6 illustrates the positioning of Grey Poupon mustard as an elegant enhancement to quality foods.

FIGURE 1-6 Positioning Strategy

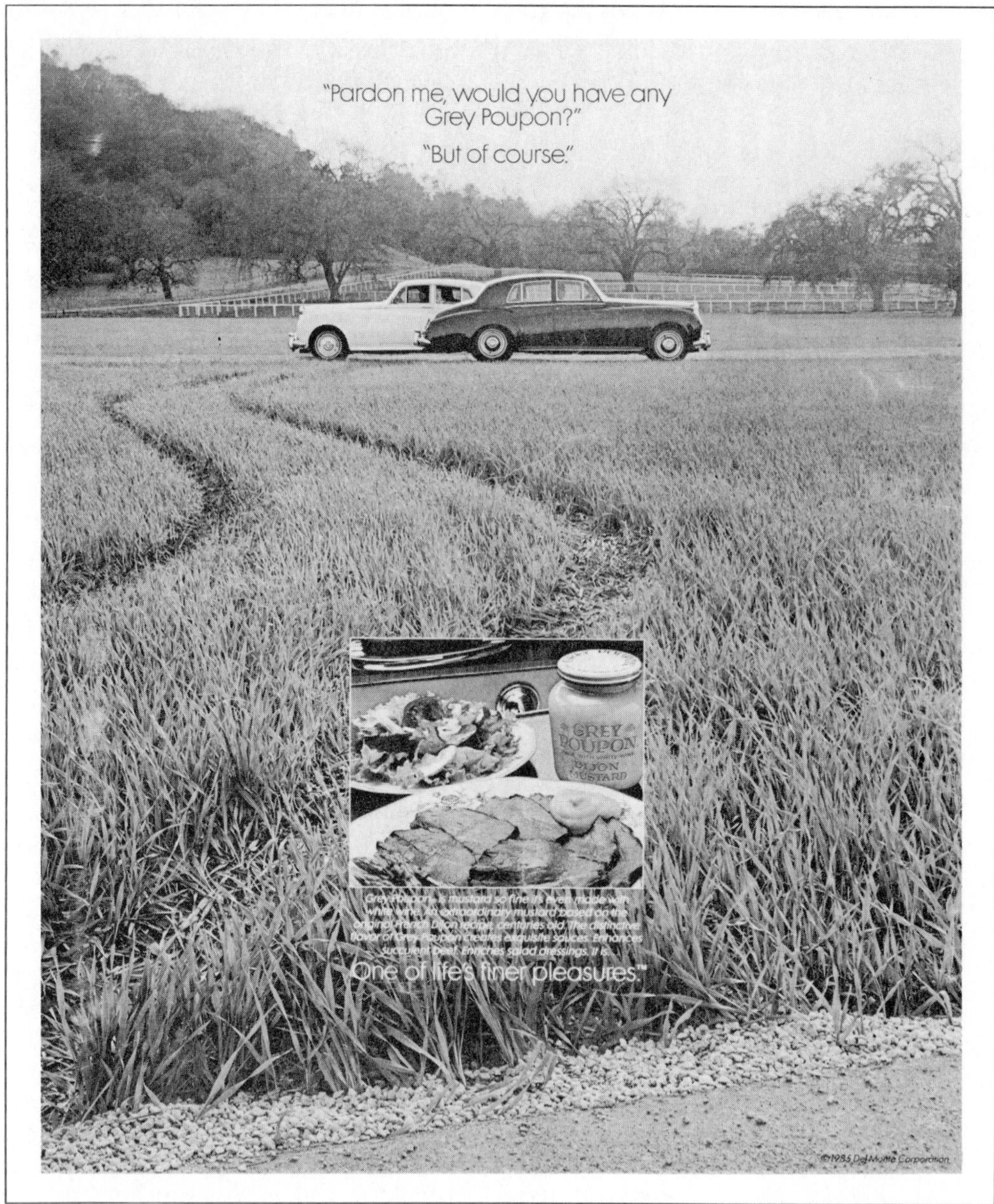


Courtesy of Nabisco Brands USA

## MARKETING STRATEGY REFLECTS POSITIONING STRATEGY

The marketer uses the marketing variables under its control—product, price, promotion, and distribution (i.e., the marketing mix)—to operationalize its marketing strategy. Thus research into consumer needs enables marketers to segment their markets, to target profitable market segments, and to position

FIGURE 1-7 Knowledge of Consumer Behavior Facilitates Development of Successful Marketing Strategies

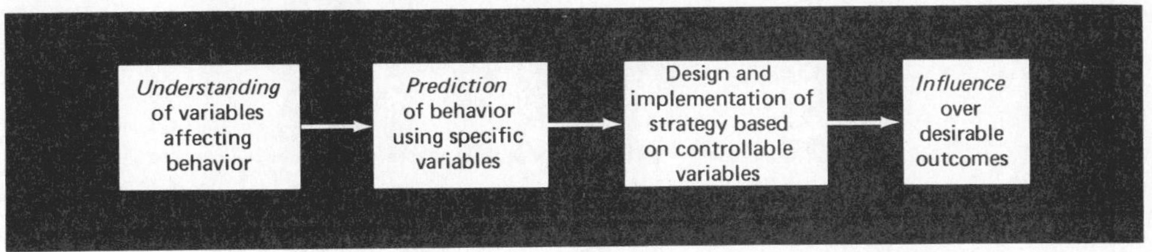


their products as a unique way to fulfill identified consumer needs.

Knowledge and understanding of consumer behavior principles enables marketers to design effective marketing mixes to operationalize their positioning strategies. As depicted in Figure 1-7, *understanding* (and this is true of any human phenomenon) leads to *prediction,* which in turn leads to the development of strategies designed to *achieve favorable outcomes.*

## The Role of Consumer Behavior in Strategic Planning

**Strategic planning** is a management approach that stresses organizational adaptability—the adjustment of the firm's objectives, its use of resources, and its operations—to the changing environment. The purpose of strategic planning is to develop a long-range game plan to ensure the company's survival, its profitability, its growth, and its perpetuity. By means of strategic planning, a company can be one that *makes* things happen (e.g., IBM or Kodak), rather than a company that *watches* things happen—or worse, one that *wonders* what happened.

A recent survey of chief executive officers and other top executives found that companies are adopting a strategic marketing approach by integrating marketing plans into their firms' overall strategic plans.[1] As the following discussion indicates, consumer behavior principles are applicable to each step of the strategic market planning process.

STEP 1. DEFINE THE FIRM'S BUSINESS DOMAIN. Here, consumer behavior and the marketing concept dictate that definitions of the firm's business domain must be market-oriented (i.e., satisfying consumer needs) rather than product- or sales-oriented (satisfying the firm's needs).

STEP 2. ENVIRONMENTAL SCANNING (OPPORTUNITIES AND THREATS ANALYSIS). If diagnosed in time, most environmental "threats" can be turned into marketing opportunities. In consumer behavior terms, a company that closely monitors evolving lifestyles and trends can anticipate changing consumer needs and respond promptly with new or revised products or promotional programs to meet those needs. Figure 1-8 illustrates the adaption of Chivas Regal's promotional strategy to the fact that the consumption of alcoholic drinks has dimin-

FIGURE 1-8 Adapting Product Promotion to Evolving Lifestyles

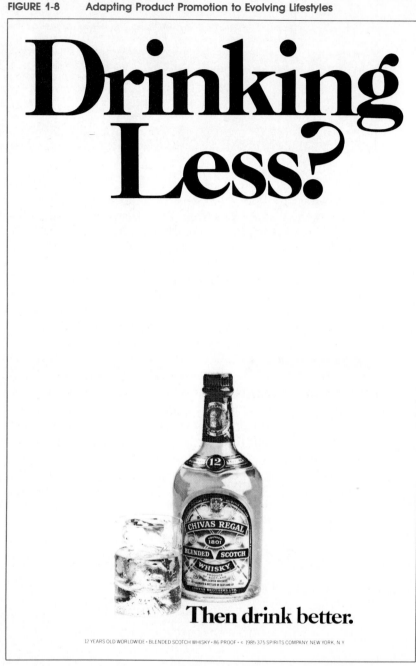

Drinking Less?
CHIVAS REGAL
1801
BLENDED SCOTCH
WHISKY
Then drink better.
12 YEARS OLD WORLDWIDE • BLENDED SCOTCH WHISKY • 86 PROOF • © 1985 375 SPIRITS COMPANY NEW YORK, N.Y.


Courtesy of 375 Spirits Co.

ished significantly of recent years in response to health, fitness, and safety campaigns.

STEP 3. ESTABLISH GOALS AND OBJECTIVES. Company objectives should be realistic in terms of its resources—technological, financial, and human. The company should establish objectives consistent with its image in the marketplace. For example, a sales penetration objective to be achieved through a relaxation of quality and a decrease in price would be inappropriate for a company which enjoys a high quality image (e.g., Hewlett-Packard).

STEP 4. ANALYZE THE COMPANY'S EXISTING PRODUCT PORTFOLIO. Management should determine through sales analyses and consumer research which products still satisfy consumer needs and which are on their way out (i.e., where each product stands in terms of its product life cycle).

STEP 5. DEVELOP A NEW BUSINESS PLAN. In consumer behavior terms, management should develop plans for new product concepts that correspond to changing lifestyles (see Figure 1-8) and emerging consumer needs, and should consider modifying or repositioning existing products to better fit changing needs. It should evaluate and select market segments with good profitability and growth potential. Table 1-4 gives examples of products developed or adapted to meet consumer needs.

STEP 6. DEVELOP A MARKETING STRATEGY CONGRUENT WITH THE FIRM'S STRATEGIC PLAN. In consumer behavior terms, the company should develop a positioning strategy congruent with its objectives and operationalize it through its marketing mix. (Figure 1-9 presents two examples of how Corum operationalizes its positioning strategy based on its segmentation strategy.)

STEP 7. MEASURING MARKETING PERFORMANCE. The company should closely monitor actual consumer behavior in the marketplace to measure the success or failure of its marketing strategy and modify or change the marketing plan as needed.

As an input to the strategic planning process, consumer behavior *affects* marketing strategy; as a measure of marketing performance, consumer behavior *reflects* marketing strategy and signals the need for timely adjustment or change.

**TABLE 1-4 Products Developed or Adapted to Meet Consumer Needs**

- Medical home test kits meet the needs of the educated, health-oriented consumer.
- Disposable diapers and pre-mixed baby formulas in sterilized, disposable bottles take the drudgery out of infant care.
- Microwave ovens with a browning device bring food to the "color" preferred by users of conventional ovens.
- A phone answering machine with a built-in telephone and radio alarm clock provides convenience to the consumer with minimal bedside table space.
- Television sets with built-in videocassette recorders save space for apartment dwellers.
- Cordless telephone sets provide convenience for people who wish to speak beyond the confines set by the length of a telephone wire.

FIGURE 1-9 Corum Segments Its Upscale Market

Courtesy of Corum Watch Corporation

## PLAN OF THE BOOK

In order to build a useful conceptual framework that both enhances understanding and permits practical application of consumer behavior principles, this book is divided into five parts. The following chapter supplements this introduction by describing market segmentation as an effective marketing strategy and illustrates how consumer behavior research can be used to identify homogeneous target markets. Market segmentation is the basic theme that underlies the balance of the book.

Part II explores the consumer as an individual. It discusses how individuals are motivated (Chapter 3); the impact of individual personality characteristics (Chapter 4) and lifestyles (Chapter 5) on consumer behavior; and the process and importance of perception (Chapter 6) and learning (Chapter 7) on consumer attitudes (Chapters 8 and 9). This part concludes with an examination of the communication process as it influences consumer behavior (Chapter 10).

Part III focuses on consumers as members of society, subject to varying external influences on their buying behavior, such as their group memberships (Chapter 11), families (Chapter 12), social class (Chapter 13), and the broad cultural and specific subcultural groups to which they belong (Chapters 14 and 15).

Part IV examines the consumer decision-making process. It explores the impact of respected "others" whose product opinions influence consumer choices (Chapter 16) and describes the process by which new products are adopted by consumers and diffused throughout the target population (Chapter 17). The various steps in the consumer decision-making process are presented in Chapter 18, and various models of this process are examined in Chapter 19.

Part V discusses the broad application of consumer behavior research to profit and nonprofit services marketing and concludes with an examination of consumer protection and public policy issues (Chapter 20).

## *summary*

Consumer behavior can be defined as the behavior that consumers display in searching for, purchasing, using, evaluating, and disposing of products, services, and ideas which they expect will satisfy their needs. The study of consumer behavior is concerned not only with *what* consumers buy, but with why they buy it, when, where, and how they buy it, and how often they buy it. Consumer behavior research takes place at every phase of the consumption process: before the purchase, during the purchase, and after the purchase.

There are two kinds of consumers: personal (or ultimate) consumers, who buy goods and services for their own use or for household use, and organizational consumers, who buy products, equipment, and services in order to run their organizations, which may be operated for profit (e.g., commercial enterprises) or not-for-profit (e.g., governmental agencies, museums, or hospitals).

Consumer behavior is interdisciplinary; that is, it is based on concepts and theories about people which have been developed by scientists in such diverse disciplines as psychology, sociology, social psychology, cultural anthropology, and economics. Consumer research is the methodology used to study consumer behavior.

Marketing firms use their knowledge of consumer behavior to segment markets, to design marketing strategies, and to measure marketing performance. The development of consumer behavior studies was an outgrowth of the evolution of marketing philosophy from a production and product orientation to a selling orientation to a marketing orientation (the marketing concept). Other factors that have contributed to the development of consumer behavior studies include the fast pace of new product introduction, shorter product life cycles, the high rate of new-product failures, increased interest in consumer protection by private groups and public policy decision makers, concern over the environment, the adoption of marketing practices by service and nonprofit organizations, the availability of computers and sophisticated statistical techniques, and the growth of segmentation as a marketing strategy. Consumer behavior has become an integral part of strategic market planning.

## *discussion questions*

1. Mrs. Jones is buying a can of Campbell's soup. Mr. Jones, her husband, a buyer for a quality men's store, is ordering a new line of men's leisure suits. Describe the consumer behavior aspects of each purchase in terms of
   a. What, why, how, when, how often
   b. Personal versus organizational buying
   c. Buyer versus user
2. In the 1920s, Henry Ford remarked that his customers could have any color car they wanted as long as it was black. Why won't the president of Ford Motor Company make the same statement today? In your answer, discuss the changes in marketing philosophy that have occurred since the 1920s.
3. You are the product manager of a line of toys for preschool children. Describe how an understanding of consumer behavior can be useful to you in terms of
   a. Market segmentation strategy
   b. New product introduction
   c. Product life cycle
   d. Consumer protection

4. Name three ways in which an understanding of consumer behavior can help the marketer design effective marketing strategies.
5. Consumer behavior has been said to both *affect* and *reflect* marketing strategy. Discuss.
6. Consumer behavior is based on principles "borrowed" from other disciplines. Name five such disciplines and explain how they contribute to the study of consumer behavior.
7. "Consumers don't need more laws to protect them; they need more knowledge." Discuss.
8. An argument often used against the application of consumer behavior principles in promoting social causes is that "You can't sell 'brotherhood' like you do soap." Do you agree? Why or why not?

## *endnote*


1. "Strategic Marketing Top Priority of Chief Execs," *Marketing News,* January 31, 1986, 1.

# 2

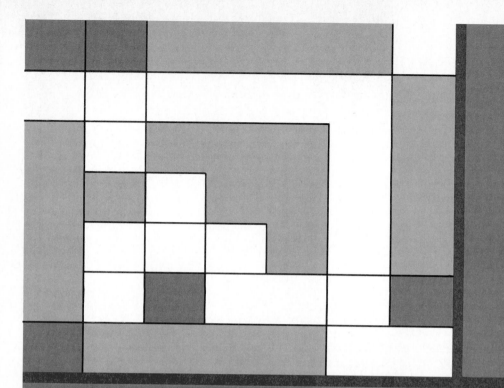

# Market Segmentation

## *introduction*

THE development of the marketing concept gave impetus to the study of consumer behavior. As marketers began to study the behavior of consumers, they soon realized that despite overriding similarities, consumers were not all alike; nor did they wish to use the identical products that everyone else used. Rather, many consumers preferred differentiated products that they felt more closely reflected their own personal needs, personalities, lifestyles, and so forth. To better satisfy the specialized needs of selected groups of consumers, marketers adopted a strategy of **market segmentation.**

Though the concept of segmentation is relatively new, it has spread very fast. As evidence, we need only point to the great variety of automobiles of every color and style that can be found on the street, or note the vast array of magazines—for every conceivable interest from tennis to auto repair to astrology—that can be found at the corner news stand.

Consumer behavior findings have direct application to effective market segmentation. In this chapter we examine some of the major elements of segmentation strategy and explore the criteria marketers use to determine when and if a segmentation approach is feasible. The chapter concludes with an evaluation of the strengths and weaknesses of this key marketing strategy.

## WHAT IS MARKET SEGMENTATION?

If you're under twenty-five years of age, chances are that you've got a Swatch watch (or more than one) strapped to your wrist. The probability is high that

> *By nature, men are nearly alike; by practice, they get to be wide apart.*
>
> *CONFUCIUS*
> *Analects, 5th c. BC*

your younger brothers and sisters wear Swatch watches, but that your parents do not. In the relatively short time that this brand of watch, which takes it name from the words "Swiss" and "watch," has been available, it has built a following among young adults and teenagers. This is the portion of the watch market that the Swatch Watch Company has targeted.

Swatch is not trying to attract all potential watch purchasers; it knows that the person who wants a Concord or Rolex is not going to buy a Swatch watch instead. The low price tag and colorful styling of the Swatch line (most styles are priced at about $30) appeal primarily to teenagers and young adults. To reach this market, Swatch advertises on MTV (the music video channel) and in such magazines as *Glamour, GQ, Vogue,* and *Rolling Stone.* The overwhelming majority of its ads are aimed at young adults and teenagers. Swatch is effectively practicing market segmentation.[1]

Before the widespread adoption of the marketing concept and market segmentation, the prevailing way of doing business with consumers was through **mass marketing;** that is, offering the identical product to all consumers. The essence of this strategy was summed up by entrepreneur Henry Ford, who offered the Model T automobile to the public "in any color it wanted, as long as it was black." The public could also have any refrigerator it wanted, as long as it was white, and any boots it wanted, as long as they were high-buttoned.

If all potential customers did indeed have the same needs, *mass marketing*—the practice of offering a single product or marketing mix to everyone—would be a logical strategy. A few companies, primarily those that deal in agricultural products or very simple manufactured goods, do use a mass–marketing approach. The primary advantage of mass marketing is that it saves money. One advertising campaign is all that is needed; one marketing strategy is all that is developed; and usually, one standardized product is all that is offered.

There are, of course, drawbacks to such a strategy for both producers and consumers. In trying to sell their products to every prospect by using a single advertising campaign, marketers must try to represent their products as being all things to all people, and may end up appealing to no one. Without market differentiation, the bachelor and the family of six would have to make do with the same standard-size refrigerator.

Segmentation developed as an answer to the problems of both marketers and consumers. A good statement of the essence of segmentation strategy is the slogan General Motors used for years—"A car for every price, purpose, and personality." More formally, *market segmentation* is *the process of dividing a potential market into distinct subsets of consumers and selecting one or more segments as a target to be reached with a distinct marketing mix.*

The strategy of segmentation allows producers to avoid head-on competition in the marketplace by differentiating their offerings, not just on the basis of price, but through styling, packaging, promotional appeal, or method of distribution. By offering distinctively styled cars with many options, for example, General Motors no longer has to undercut the price of Ford to have a wide market appeal. Manufacturing many different models does, of course, raise costs, because engineering costs are higher and production runs are shorter. But sales are likely to increase, offsetting the higher costs, because many more consumers can find just what they want. Consumers are thereby better off.

## Users of Segmentation

Because the strategy of market segmentation benefits both sides of the marketplace, it has caught on quickly. Manufacturers of consumer goods are eager practitioners; today nearly every product category in the consumer market is highly segmented. To take just one example, the $1.3 billion vitamin market is subdivided by age (adults, children), place of distribution (drugstores, supermarkets, health food stores, mail order), and formulation (multivitamins, special combinations of vitamins, liquids, tablets).[2]

But the makers of consumer goods are not the only users of segmentation. Manufacturers of products used by business and industry also segment their markets. Pitney-Bowes produces different postage meters to meet the needs of small-, medium-, and large-size firms. Mack Truck produces different models to meet the needs of manufacturers, distributors, retailers, and trucking companies.

The concept of market segmentation has also been adopted by retailers. The median annual income of Neiman-Marcus customers is $50,000 to $65,000, and the store purposely carries the high-priced and high-fashion clothing sought by affluent consumers. In contrast, Kmart shoppers tend to be blue-collar consumers looking for economy and practicality. To these shoppers, a $175 Neiman-Marcus blouse might sound like a distasteful joke. Restaurants also segment their markets. Pillsbury's two restaurant groups, Burger King and S&A, target their respective outlets to different audiences. Burger King is positioned to service the low-income consumer; Bennigan's, a chain operated by the S&A group, focuses on the more upscale portion of the baby-boomer market.[3]

The nonprofit sector has recently begun to realize the importance of marketing, and it too has adopted segmentation strategies. Charities such as the March of Dimes frequently concentrate their fund raising efforts on heavy givers. Theater companies, such as the American Conservatory Theatre of San Francisco, have been able to segment their subscribers on the basis of benefits sought in subscribing, and have succeeded in increasing attendance through specialized promotional appeals.[4]

Various media vehicles—magazines, cable TV stations, radio stations—deliberately single out highly specific target segments to whom they appeal through special-interest programming. For example, classical music stations, disco stations, and all-news stations appeal to very different radio audiences. The major advantage of capturing a specialized or unique audience segment is that the medium can then "sell" that audience to advertisers interested in reaching the same segment.

## Uses of Segmentation

Basically, segmentation strategies are designed to discover the needs and wants of specific groups of consumers so that specialized goods and services can be developed and promoted to satisfy their needs. Many new products have been developed to fill gaps in the marketplace revealed through segmentation research. Segmentation studies are also used to guide the redesign or *repositioning* of old products as sales of a brand begin to taper off. Very often all that is needed is to find a new market segment for the product. Repositioning the product can be accomplished by changing some features of the product itself, or by changing its promotion, distribution, or price. For example, now that Diet Coke is so popular, Coke has repositioned its Tab brand of diet soda. Rather than using a weight control theme and a beach scene featuring a slender, bikini-clad woman, the new emphasis in Tab advertisements is on the product's "crisp, sassy, not-too-sweet taste."[5]

Advertising, aided by segmentation research, plays a major role in the positioning of any product. Advertisers can tailor their messages better if they know exactly whom they are targeting and what these consumers are seeking in the way of product benefits. Segmentation studies reveal the characteristics and needs of potential product and service users. For example, segmentation research revealed a distinctive segment in the retail banking market, the so-called *conservators,* who want personal service, privacy, and one-stop shopping for financial investments. The members of this segment tend to maintain high account balances and cash most of their checks at their banks.[6] If a bank decided to target this segment, it might develop advertising that features auto and boat loans, mortgages, life insurance, in-bank express lines, and money-market funds. It would not stress such services as automatic banking machines or computerized at-home banking. These latter services are unlikely to appeal to conservators, who want more personal service and financial investment advice.

In addition to shaping advertising messages, segmentation research is used by advertisers to identify the most appropriate media in which to place advertisements. Almost all media vehicles—from TV and radio stations to newspapers and magazines—use segmentation research to determine the characteristics of their audiences. They then publicize their findings to attract advertisers seeking a similar audience (see Figure 2-1).

Academic researchers are also interested in discovering the audience characteristics of various media. For example, a study of Cincinnati area women aged eighteen to forty-nine revealed three distinct segments of TV viewers. These groups were identified by the researchers as (1) *embracers* (consisting primarily of low income eighteen- to twenty-nine-year-old women employed in clerical or sales jobs); (2) *accommodators* (consisting primarily of middle-income women aged forty to forty-nine employed in managerial positions); and (3) *protestors* (mostly women in their thirties with technical or professional careers, and half in the high-income category).[7]

The TV program choices of these three segments are compared in Table 2-1. The results suggest that a marketer of pantyhose, like Hanes, wishing to appeal to the broadest possible number of eighteen- to forty-nine-year-old

FIGURE 2-1 Advertisement Promoting a Radio Station by Market Segment

When I Became A Man I Didn't Put Away My Rock & Roll.

If your idea of a rocker is a spaced-out hippy in Earth Shoes, you'd better get with it.

The rockers of the eighties are a social phenomenon. Everything about them has changed, except their music.

They're into making money. And spending it.

WRXL ranks number one in Richmond in reaching 25-34 male listeners with individual employment incomes exceeding $30,000.*

If you sell fast cars, plane tickets, premium beer, good food, banking services or the latest fashions, you'd better get to know your local rocker.

**WRXL102 FM**

**A Generation Of Rock & Roll.**

3245 Basie Road, Richmond, Virginia 23228 (804) 282-9731

*Source: Arbitron Spring 1985/Simmons 1984 Study of Media & Markets/M-F, 6am-7pm/AQH Listening

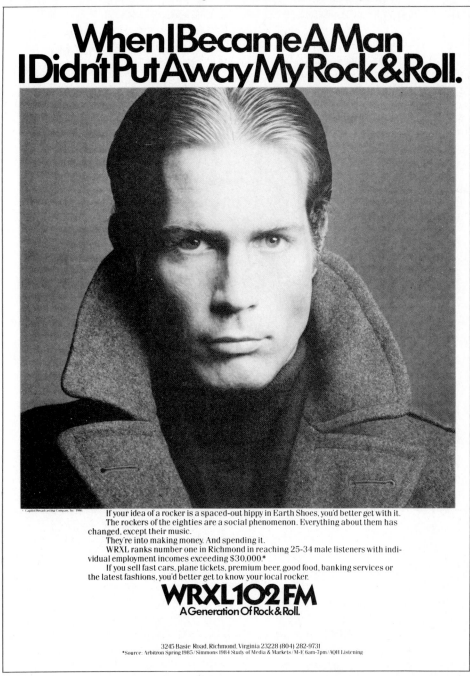

Courtesy of WRXL102FM

**TABLE 2-1** Program Choice (Viewing Intention) by Segment

| PROGRAM | SEGMENT 1 EMBRACERS | SEGMENT 2 ACCOMMODATORS | SEGMENT 3 PROTESTORS |
|---|---|---|---|
| Dallas | Regularly | Occasionally | Occasionally |
| Dukes of Hazzard | Occasionally | Occasionally | Never |
| 60 Minutes | Regularly | Regularly | Regularly |
| Dynasty | Occasionally | Occasionally | Never |
| Nero Wolfe | Occasionally | Occasionally | Occasionally |
| M*A*S*H | Regularly | Regularly | Regularly |
| Hill Street Blues | Occasionally | Occasionally | Never |
| Paper Chase | Occasionally | Occasionally | Occasionally |
| Taxi | Occasionally | Regularly | Occasionally |
| Fantasy Island | Occasionally | Occasionally | Never |
| Jeffersons | Regularly | Occasionally | Occasionally |
| Real People | Occasionally | Occasionally | Never |
| Quincy | Regularly | Regularly | Occasionally |
| 20/20 | Occasionally | Regularly | Occasionally |
| Those Amazing Animals | Occasionally | Occasionally | Never |
| Lou Grant | Occasionally | Regularly | Regularly |
| Benson | Occasionally | Occasionally | Never |
| Little House on the Prairie | Regularly | Occasionally | Occasionally |
| Love Boat | Regularly | Occasionally | Never |
| Buck Rogers | Never | Never | Never |

Source: Teresa J. Domzal and Jerome B. Kernan, "Television Audience Segmentation According to Need Gratification," *Journal of Advertising Research,* 23 (October–November 1983), 42.

women, might consider advertising on "Dallas" or reruns of "M*A*S*H." On the other hand, Revlon, a leading marketer of popularly priced lipsticks purchased primarily by the younger, less affluent members of this age category, might spend its advertising money on "The Love Boat."

## DEFINING THE OVERALL MARKET

A logical first step in segmenting a market is for marketers to define the boundaries (the parameters) of the market they desire to segment. To demonstrate the importance of this initial effort, consider the problem of defining the market for coffee. If General Foods product managers wished to rethink their prior segmentation of the coffee market, they might begin by redefining the boundaries of what they mean by the term "coffee market." For instance, it could include all drinkers of coffee; or it might include or exclude the following: all regular ground coffee drinkers, Colombian-only coffee drinkers, all decaffeinated coffee drinkers, all instant coffee drinkers, all instant decaffeinated coffee drinkers, and all freeze-dried coffee drinkers. Still further, it could include or exclude in-home, in-office, in-military, in-institutional, and in-restaurant coffee drinkers. This listing still does not exhaust all possible types of coffee drinkers. For instance, we have not considered coffee drinkers in terms of motivations for drinking or not drinking specific types of coffees.

Clearly, defining the market to be segmented is not easy. To accomplish this task, brand or product managers at General Foods would have to consider the pros and cons of adopting various alternative definitions of the coffee market. It is likely they would undertake consumer research to help define the boundaries of the overall market, so that their eventual definition takes into consideration the perceptions, attitudes, and behavior of coffee drinkers. Ultimately, the decision as to how broadly or narrowly to define the coffee market will be a management decision. It is this strategic decision that is the real starting point for market segmentation.

## BASES FOR SEGMENTATION

In searching for appropriate market segments, it is critical for a marketer to decide which bases for defining segments would be most fruitful in creating a winning marketing strategy. Six major categories of consumer characteristics or variables can be distinguished as bases for segmentation; they are shown in Table 2-2. These segmentation bases include **geographic** characteristics, **demographic** factors, **psychological** characteristics, **sociocultural** variables, **user behavior** characteristics, and **usage situation** factors surrounding the purchase decision.

### Geographic Segmentation

In *geographic segmentation,* the market is divided in terms of different locations. The theory behind this strategy is that people who live in the same locale have similar needs and wants, and that these needs and wants differ from those of people in other areas. That assumption may not be as valid today as it was in the past when, lacking good transportation, television, and other means of communication, communities tended to grow up in isolation from one another and developed distinctive tastes and customs. Beer, for example, was once brewed almost entirely on a local basis. In contrast, today national or regional beer brands dominate the market.

Although Americans, as a people, are much more unified today, regional differences still exist. Certain food products sell better in one region than in others (e.g., cream cheese and frozen waffles tend to sell better in the Northeast, Japanese food and soy sauce in the Northwest, and cake mixes and cottage cheese in the Midwest and Mountain states). Other product categories that show regional differences are appliances (home freezers sell best in the Southeast, garbage disposals on the West Coast); automotive products (snow tires in the Northeast, power house trailers in the Northwest, motorcycles and foreign cars on the West Coast); and clothing.[8]

Some of the regional differences can be accounted for by climate. The Sunbelt regions of the South and West represent better opportunities for selling bathing suits and central air-conditioning systems than the Snowbelt regions of the North and East, where electric blankets and children's sleds are likely to be better sellers. But beyond regional and climatic differences, market

**TABLE 2-2 Market Segmentation Categories and Selected Segmentation Variables**

| VARIABLES | EXAMPLES |
|---|---|
| **geographic characteristics** | |
| Region | North, South, East, West |
| City size | Major metropolitan areas, small cities, towns |
| Density of area | Urban, suburban, exurban, rural |
| Climate | Temperate, hot, humid |
| **demographic characteristics** | |
| Age | Under 11, 12–17, 18–34, 35–49, 50–64, 65–74, 75+ |
| Sex | Male, female |
| Marital status | Single, married, divorced |
| Income | Under $10,000, $10,000–$14,999, $15,000–$24,999, $25,000–$39,999, $40,000–$64,999, over $65,000 |
| Occupation | Professional, blue-collar, white-collar, agricultural |
| Education | Some high school, high school graduate, some college, college graduate, postgraduate |
| **psychological characteristics** | |
| Personality | Extroverts, introverts, aggressives, compliants |
| Lifestyle | Swingers, straights, conservatives, status seekers |
| Benefits sought | Convenience, prestige, economy |
| **sociocultural characteristics** | |
| Culture | American, Italian, Chinese, Mexican |
| Subculture | |
| Religion | Jewish, Catholic, Protestant, other |
| Race | Black, Caucasian, Oriental, Hispanic |
| Social class | Lower, middle, upper |
| Family life cycle | Bachelors, young marrieds, empty nesters |
| **user behavior characteristics** | |
| Usage rate | Heavy, medium, light users, nonusers |
| Brand loyalty status | None, medium, strong |
| **usage situation characteristics** | |
| Time | Leisure, work, rush, morning, night |
| Objective | Personal, gift, snack, fun, achievement |
| Location | Home, work, friend's home, in-store |
| Person | Self, friend, boss, peer |

researchers have found that product usage frequently differs between major metropolitan areas. Some of these differences are listed in Table 2–3. Such findings are important to marketers, especially in making distribution or advertising decisions. Many companies that market nationally would prefer to allocate their advertising dollars to those areas where they are likely to achieve the best results. Some advertising agencies now offer their clients just such an option in market-by-market ad plans. Thus a Scotch whiskey brand like J & B might devote more of its advertising budget to New York (the best market for Scotch whiskey, according to Table 2-3) than to St. Louis (the worst market for Scotch whiskey).

Sometimes brand shares within a product category fluctuate widely among different geographic markets. For example, Yoplait has so far captured a 25 percent share of the Los Angeles yogurt market, but only a 6 percent market share in New York, where consumers seem to prefer Dannon. In Chicago, these two brands together account for 60 percent of all yogurt sales.[9]

Besides differences among cities, marketers are also conscious of diver-

TABLE 2-3 Product Purchase/Usage by Leading Metropolitan Market—the Best and the Worst

| PRODUCT/ACTIVITY | THE BEST | THE WORST |
|---|---|---|
| Scotch Whiskey | New York | St. Louis |
| New Domestic Car | Detroit | San Francisco |
| New Imported Car | Los Angeles | Detroit |
| Have Life Insurance | Cleveland | Los Angeles |
| Purchased Men's Jeans in past 12 months | Detroit | Boston |
| Have a Video Cassette Recorder | San Francisco | Cleveland |
| Bicycled in past 12 months | Chicago | St. Louis |
| Did Needlework in past 12 months | Boston | New York |
| Attended 2-plus Movies in past 30 days | Detroit | Cleveland |
| Used Cough Syrup 2-plus times in past 30 days | New York | Los Angeles |
| Popcorn, 2-plus bowls in past 30 days | Cleveland | New York |

Source: *10 Mediamarket Summary* (New York: Mediamark Research Inc., 1985).

gent consumer purchasing patterns among rural, suburban, and urban areas. Throughout the United States, more furs and expensive jewelry are sold in cities than in small towns. Even within a large metropolitan area, different types of household furnishings and leisure products are sold in the central city and in the suburbs. Convertible sofas and small appliances are more likely to be bought by the city apartment dweller than the suburban homeowner, who may in turn call for more barbecue grills and large home freezers. This, of course, is a function of available living space and lifestyle, both characteristics that lend themselves to segmentation.

Geographic segmentation, therefore, can be a useful beginning point. It is relatively easy to find geographically-based differences for some products; in addition, geographic segments are usually readily accessible through local media, including newspapers, TV, and radio, and through regional editions of magazines.

## Demographic Segmentation

Demographic characteristics, such as age, sex, marital status, income, occupation, and education, are most often used as the basis for market segmentation. **Demography** refers to the vital and measurable statistics of a population. Demographic characteristics are generally easy to identify and to measure; furthermore, they can often be associated—either singly or in composite—with the usage of specific products and with specific media.

### AGE

Because product needs often vary with age, marketers have found age to be a useful variable in distinguishing segments. Many producers have carved out a place in the market by concentrating on a specific age segment. For example, Selchow & Righter, in addition to marketing its standard and topical versions of Trivial Pursuit, also markets a Trivial Pursuit "Baby Boomer Edition" to attract the twenty-five to forty-year-old market, and a "Young Players Edition" for children age seven and up. Similarly, many gum, candy, and even over-the-counter pharmaceutical marketers have specific brands targeted to specific age categories. However, sometimes astute marketers want to break down traditional age barriers to have their products appeal to a broader or distinctly different age category. To illustrate, Figure 2-2 shows an ad for Sugarless BUBBLE YUM that depicts a sophisticated looking woman blowing a bubble (a feat usually associated with children). The headline states: "If you've outgrown the sugar, but not the fun." The Sugarless BUBBLE YUM ad points up the usefulness of sometimes defining age in other than chronological terms.[10]

**FIGURE 2-2** **Advertisement Appealing to a Broader Target Market** BUBBLE YUM is a registered trademark owned and used exclusively by NABISCO BRANDS, INC.

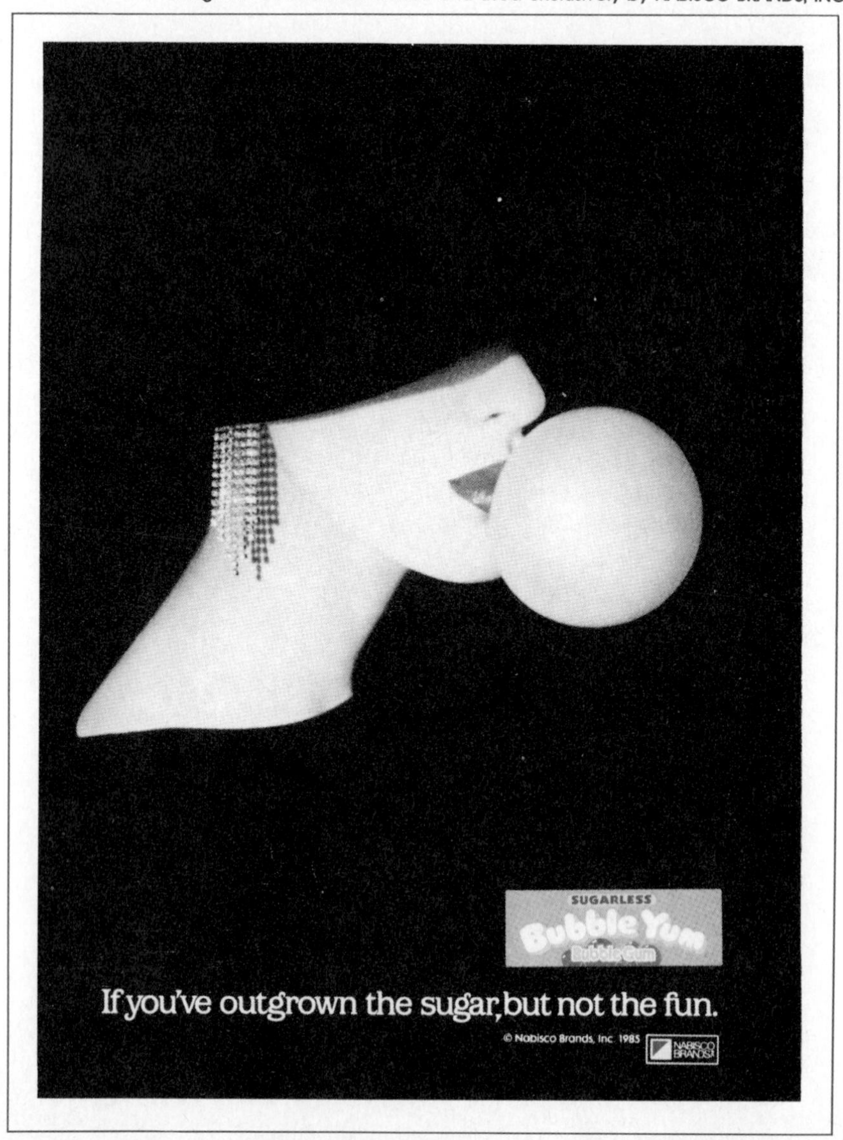


Courtesy of NABISCO BRANDS, INC.

## SEX

Gender has always been a distinguishing segmentation variable. Women have traditionally been the main users of such products as hair coloring and cosmetics; and men, of cigars and shaving preparations. In recent years, however, sex roles have been breaking down, and gender may no longer be an accurate way to distinguish consumers in some product categories. The hair-care market, which used to be divided strictly along sex lines, with barbershops for men and beauty salons for women, is becoming much more homogeneous with the advent of unisex beauty shops and unisex hair products.

Role changes may have limited gender as a segmentation variable in some markets, but they have created new opportunities in others. For example, the market for men's fragrances and skin-care products has grown tremendously in the past ten years, as has the market for life insurance for women.

Much of the change in sex roles has come about because of the upsurge in the number of working women (see Chapter 15). One consequence for marketers is that women are not as readily accessible through traditional media as they once were. Since working women do not have as much time to watch TV or listen to the radio as those who do not work, many advertisers now emphasize magazines in their media schedules, especially those specifically aimed at working women (such as *Savvy, Self,* and *New Women*).

Working women who do watch TV may be using videocassette recorders to record programs while they are at work, and then watching these shows during the evening hours. Such "time shifting" has made advertisers unsure of exactly what type of audience a particular TV program enjoys. A 12 noon soap opera may now be viewed at 9 P.M; should the advertising on this show be directed at homemakers or at working women?

Two of the many product categories affected by the increased number of women in the labor force have been automobiles and fur coats. Some 50 percent of Buick Regal coupe buyers are female, and Buick has developed advertisements specifically targeted to women. With respect to fur coats, no longer is it only the husband buying the coat as a gift for his wife. He may be buying it for himself. Executive and professional women purchase their own fur coats, and a number of furriers, such as New York's "Fred the Furrier," aim their advertising directly to women.

## MARITAL STATUS

Marital status is an increasingly important variable for segmenting markets, now that more and more people are choosing to remain single or are divorcing. In the past, the focus of most marketing efforts was the family, but marketers are gradually discovering the benefits of targeting special promotional efforts to singles, especially one-person households. To provide some idea as to just what type of consumers they are, Table 2-4 lists a number of supermarket and packaged goods products, together with usage factors, for one-person households with $20,000+ income. As the table indicates, this market segment is

**TABLE 2-4 Package-Goods Usage Patterns of $20,000-Plus Single-Person Households**

| ABOVE AVERAGE USAGE | | BELOW AVERAGE USAGE | |
|---|---|---|---|
| Shaving creams or gels* | +146 | Ketchup | −93 |
| Pressed powder | +110 | Frankfurters/weiners | −91 |
| Lipstick/lipgloss | +94 | Peanut butter | −87 |
| Cognac | +84 | Mayonnaise | −82 |
| Foundation makeup | +77 | Potato chips | −81 |
| Frozen main courses | +73 | Soaps/detergents | |
| Imported beer | +67 | regular laundry | −81 |
| Razor blades | +63 | Fabric softeners | −81 |
| Books | +62 | Salt | −85 |
| Cordials/liqueurs | +63 | Pizza mixes | −80 |
| Brandy | +65 | Beans prepared in sauce | −78 |
| Scotch | +60 | Canned tomatoes | −78 |
| Blusher | +60 | Bacon | −78 |
| Regular loose tea | +60 | Margarine | −77 |

*This should be read that one-person households with $20,000-plus income are 146 percent greater in their incidence of shaving creams or gels than the population as a whole.

Source: "High Income Level Is Shared but Tastes Are Certainly Not," *Supermarket Business* (June 1985), p. 31.

above average in its usage of products not traditionally associated with supermarkets, and below average in consumption of traditional supermarket products. For a supermarket operating in a one-person household neighborhood of Atlanta, Chicago, New York, or San Francisco, such insights can be particularly useful in deciding on the merchandise mix for the store.

Some food marketers deliberately appeal to the singles or one-person household. Campbell's has a line of Soups-for-One and Stouffer's has promoted a line of frozen entrees to people living away from home for the first time. Marketers are also offering "mini-appliances," such as small microwave ovens and two-cup coffee makers, to singles. To reach this growing segment, special magazines (e.g., *Your Place*) have emerged.

## INCOME

Income has long been an important variable for distinguishing market segments. Marketers are usually interested in affluent consumers—and for good reason. Twenty percent of those families at the highest income levels in this country receive more than 40 percent of the nation's total money income. Moreover, the number of families with household incomes of $40,000+ is forecasted to increase by over 85 percent between 1980 and 1990.[11]

Although affluence by itself is frequently a desirable segmentation characteristic, marketers often combine high income with some other demographic variable when pinpointing a target market for products or services. For instance, high incomes have been combined with age to produce the newly recognized *affluent elderly*; it has also been combined with age and occupational status to produce a much-sought-after subgroup of the baby-boomer market—the so-called *Yuppies* (i.e., young upwardly mobile professionals).

### OCCUPATION AND EDUCATION

Marketers have found that occupational category (white-collar, blue-collar, etc.) and educational level can also be used to distinguish market segments. These two socioeconomic variables are useful to marketers because they seem to reflect values, attitudes, tastes, or more broadly, *lifestyles*. For example, beer is more likely to be marketed to less-educated blue-collar workers; Scotch and fine wines, on the other hand, are generally targeted at college-educated white-collar workers or professionals.

The composition of the work force is changing as the amount of education rises. Today over 50 percent of the work force is engaged in white-collar occupations (in schools, offices, banks, etc.), and that percentage is expected to increase. Cultural organizations such as museums, operas, and theaters—which have traditionally catered to upper-income groups—now broaden their appeals to reach new segments.

## Combining Geodemographic Variables

Although some marketers rely on a single demographic variable to define significant market segments, many marketers combine several geographic or demographic characteristics to identify their target markets. For instance, Fanny Farmer, which operates some 300 candy shops, defines its target market in terms of three demographic variables: sex, age, and income—women between the ages of twenty-two and forty, with incomes in excess of $30,000.[12] With this target market in mind, the chain is redesigning its stores and its packaging.

To help marketers who want to define their markets in terms of a composite of demographic variables, a variety of syndicated geodemographic data-clustering services have developed. They offer subscribers population information that allows them to identify potential market segments by combining geographic variables (zip codes, neighborhoods, or blocks) and demographic factors (income, occupational status, and value of family dwelling).[13] These *geodemographic segmentation* schemes are particularly useful because they can be further combined with product or service usage data and media exposure information to develop a highly comprehensive **consumer profile** (see Chapter 13 for a more detailed discussion of geodemographic clustering).

Composite geodemographic variables are not only used to pinpoint target markets directly; they are also used to identify stages in the family life cycle and social class (see Chapters 12 and 13). However, geodemographic variables do not always provide sufficient information to fine-tune a marketing effort. Two individuals with the same demographic profile may still purchase different brands. To understand why, marketers often have to turn to other consumer characteristics, such as psychological makeup.

## Psychological Segmentation

*Psychological* characteristics refer to the *intrinsic qualities of the individual consumer.* Such qualities are often used as segmentation variables. This section will briefly examine the potential of several psychological variables as a basis for market segmentation. Other psychological factors used for market segmentation will be discussed in later chapters of this text.

### PERSONALITY AND PSYCHOGRAPHICS

The earliest psychological segmentation studies concentrated on the relationship between personality characteristics and product choice. The object was to find one or more personality traits that could reliably predict the selection of one brand over another. Consumers were given standard personality tests that measured such traits as *dominance* or *aggression* and were also asked—in an addendum, as it were—to specify their brand preferences in certain product categories. Researchers then looked for correlations between personality traits and brand preferences. Much of this early consumer research was disappointing. However, more recent personality research has moved away from standardized personality tests (which were frequently developed to pinpoint broad personality maladjustments) and consequently have done better. For instance, armed with more focused and consumer-relevant personality traits, such as *innovativeness, novelty* or *variety seeking, inner-* or *other-directedness, optimum stimulation level,* and various cognitive personality traits, consumer researchers have made strides in using personality as a basis for segmentation.

Since the early 1970s, **psychographics** (alternatively known as **lifestyles**) has been growing in popularity as a psychological basis for segmentation. Psychographic tests (i.e., *inventories*) appear similar in composition to personality tests because they often consist of a battery of brief statements designed to capture selected dimensions of consumers' inner feelings and their predispositions to behave in certain ways.

There are three principal indicators of lifestyle: *activities,* or how consumers spend their time; *interests,* or what preferences consumers have; and *opinions,* or where consumers stand on social issues, products, or a variety of other issues. Researchers conduct psychographic research by asking consumers to express agreement or disagreement with statements covering their activities, interests, and opinions. Statistical techniques are then used to group together consumers with similar responses and to contrast them with groups of consumers who hold dissimilar views.

Psychographic studies can be either **generic** or **product-specific.**[14] A *product-specific* study, as the name implies, is used to determine the psychological profile of users or potential users of a specific product. For example, a study conducted among female readers of paperback historical romances divided them into four distinct segments: (1) *movers and shakers,* (2) *isolated readers,* (3) *young swingers,* and (4) *laggards.*[15] As depicted in Table 2-5, many of the differences among these four groups could have significant impact on a publisher's marketing mix. For example, the price of a romance novel would be a more important criterion in the purchasing process for *laggards* than it would be for *movers and shakers.*

**TABLE 2-5 Segment Profiles of the Historical Romance Novel Market**

| MEASURE | MOVERS AND SHAKERS | ISOLATED READERS | YOUNG SWINGERS | LAGGARDS |
|---|---|---|---|---|
| **Activities** | Heaviest movie attendance | Least frequent movie attendance | Frequent movie attendance | Low movie attendance |
| | Heaviest letter writer | Least letter writer | Infrequent letter writer | |
| | Least bowling activity | Little bowling activity | | Most frequent bowlers |
| | | Least record purchases | Most record purchases | |
| **Product-specific items** | Most innovative | Moderately innovative | Not innovative | Least innovative |
| | Most interest in romance | | Least interest in romance | |
| | | | Tired of reading romance novels | |
| **General psychographic items** | Least price consciousness | Low price consciousness | | Most price consciousness |
| | | | Most likely to be swingers | |
| | | Most likely to prefer a quiet evening at home | Least likely to prefer a quiet evening at home | |
| | Least religious | Most religious | Most fashion interest | Highly religious |
| | | Least fashion interest | Greatest word of mouth communication | Least word of mouth communication |
| | | Least opinion leadership | | |
| | | Low opinion seeking | Most independent | |
| **Demographics** | Average age 30–40 | Average age 40–50 | Average age under 30 years | Average age over 50 years |
| | One or no children | At least one child | Most have no children | Most have grown child |
| | High school education | High school education | One-third have college degree | Least education |
| | Most employed | Half are employed | Most employed | More unemployed |
| | Family income of $20,000 | Family income of $20,000 | Income less than $20,000 | Lowest income |

Source: Steven P. Schnaars and Leon G. Schiffman, "An Application of a Segmentation Design Based on a Hybrid of Canonical Correlation and Simple Crosstabulation," *Journal of the Academy of Marketing Science*, 12 (Fall 1984), 187.

Unlike product-specific studies, *generic studies* are conducted with no specific product in mind. Their purpose is to reveal broad-based patterns in the marketplace, and they are used by marketers to uncover new product opportunities or new ways to promote existing products.

Consider, for example, the study of the television viewing habits of Cincinnati-area women discussed earlier in this chapter. This research provides clues for television advertisers as to the type of woman who watches different kinds of TV programs. When program choices (Table 2-1), are examined in conjunction with demographic and psychographic profiles (see Table 2-6), the

**TABLE 2-6 Profiles of the Cincinnati Female Television Audience**

| | PROFILE FOR SEGMENT 1 EMBRACERS | PROFILE FOR SEGMENT 2 ACCOMMODATORS | PROFILE FOR SEGMENT 3 PROTESTERS |
|---|---|---|---|
| **Television viewing** | 30 hours and 6 minutes per week | 24 hours and 54 minutes per week | 19 hours and 30 minutes per week |
| **Need gratification** | Relaxing and forget problems<br>Be entertained<br>Having emotional experiences | Watch to be with other people<br>Avoid boredom<br>Having friends and social interaction | Know what's going on in the world<br>Learn something new<br>Knowing things as they really exist |
| **Attitudes toward television** | In good taste<br>Interesting<br>Getting better<br>Important<br>Relaxing<br>Satisfied the majority of the American public<br>Good and bad points balance each other | In bad taste<br>No imagination<br>All the same<br>Boring<br>Too liberal in its programming<br>Good and bad points balance each other<br>Exerts a strong influence on people<br>Will be vastly improved in cable TV | In bad taste<br>Dull<br>All the same<br>Simple-minded<br>Not educational<br>Boring<br>Does more harm than good<br>Gives the viewer no opportunity for self-expression<br>Interferes with social activities |
| **Feelings about watching TV** | Can identify with what is seen on television<br>Accept most of what is seen on television<br>Enjoy programs with characters they can relate to<br>Watching TV is worthwhile<br>Easily become involved with a TV series<br>Have a strong loyalty to programs viewed<br>Most satisfied with the *types* of programs on network TV<br>Most satisfied with the *variety* of programs on network TV<br>Irresistibly attracted to watching TV | Enjoy programs with characters they can relate to<br>The more they watch the less they enjoy TV<br>Are very selective about what they watch<br>Do not find most of what they see on TV acceptable | The more they watch, the less they enjoy<br>Are very critical about what they see on television<br>Are very selective about what they watch<br>Are least satisfied with *types* of shows on network TV<br>Are least satisfied with *variety* of shows on network TV |
| **Activities** | Baseball<br>Watching television<br>Bowling<br>Dancing<br>Listening to the radio<br>Basketball | Local cultural activities<br>Ballet<br>Bicycling<br>Community social functions<br>Gourmet cooking<br>Hiking<br>Backpacking<br>Movies | Antiques<br>Classical music<br>Literature<br>Live theater<br>Paintings<br>Visiting friends |

| | | | |
|---|---|---|---|
| **Interests** | Religion; Right-to-life; Career guidance; Child rearing; Health and nutrition; Sex education | Right-to-life issues; Conservation; Ecology; Education and schools; Consumerism; Rights of minority groups | Arms race; Balance of trade; Conflict in the Middle East; Election campaigns; National economy; Nuclear energy |
| **Opinions** | Traditional opinions on feminine lifestyle | Moderate opinions on feminine lifestyle (more feminist) | Most modern (feminist) in opinions on feminine lifestyle |
| **Radio** | 8 hours and 43 minutes per week<br>AM and FM about equally<br>Popular music, rock and top hits of the week | 6 hours and 30 minutes per week<br>Mostly FM<br>Popular music, '50s and '60s oldies | 6 hours and 22 minutes per day<br>Mostly or only to FM |
| **Newspapers** | Local news, gardening, travel, advertising, social news, entertainment, comics, personal advice, and sports | World news, national news, business, and real estate | Editorial section most, sports least |
| **Books** | Light readers: mostly mysteries, humor, and other fiction | Medium to heavy readers: mostly mystery, historical novel, psychology and self-help, and humor books | Fiction, autobiography, "how-to" books |
| **Movies** | Love and romance, horror, disaster movies | Heaviest attendance: comedies, science fiction, musicals, crime-spy thrillers, historical-adventures | Comedies, love and romance, science fiction, crime-spy thrillers |
| **Magazines** | Heaviest readers of fashion magazines and women's magazines: *Glamour, Family Circle, Good Housekeeping* | General types: *Reader's Digest, TV Guide, Smithsonian, Better Homes and Gardens* | Heaviest readers of news magazines: *Newsweek, Time,* and *MS* |
| **Cable TV** | Think it's too expensive and are satisfied with network TV | Highest percentage of interest in this group, but would like more information | Moderately interested in subscribing |
| **Demographics** | Age: 30. Education: More than half attended college; 10 percent, graduate school. 37 percent work full-time. Occupation: sales/clerical. Income: 33 percent (less than \$14,999); 26 percent (\$15,000–24,999); 40 percent (over \$25,000) | Age: 30. Education: 73 percent attended college. 34 percent work full-time. Occupation: sales/clerical and professional/technical. Income: 30.6 percent (less than \$14,999); 27.8 percent (\$15,000 to 24,999); 41.7 percent (over \$25,000) | Age: 32. Education: 63 percent attended college: 24.2 percent attended graduate school. 27 percent work full-time. Occupation: professional/technical. Income: 12.1 percent (less than \$14,999); 18.2 percent (\$15,000 to \$24,999); and 69.7 percent (over \$25,000) |

Source: Teresa J. Domzal and Jerome B. Kernan, "Television Audience Segmentation According to Need Gratification," *Journal of Advertising Research,* 23 (October–November 1983), 46–48.

advertiser can determine where advertising dollars should be spent. For example, an outdoor equipment manufacturer like Coleman (hiking boots, lanterns, sleeping bags) might best target *accommodators,* and reach them with commercials on shows like "20/20" and "Taxi."

### BENEFITS SOUGHT

Another form of psychological segmentation is based on the kinds of benefits consumers seek in products. The classic case of successful segmentation on the basis of *benefits sought* is the market for toothpaste. Research has discovered that children look for flavor or product appearance; teens and young marrieds look for brighteners; large families, for decay-prevention qualities; and men, for a good deal on price. Marketers of brands that have been introduced since that study was published have generally gone after one or more of these segments. For example, Crest tartar control formulation, introduced in the mid-1980s, stresses both reduced tartar buildup and tooth-decay prevention in its commercials—a benefits appeal targeted to overall family use (see Figure 2-3).[16]

**Benefit segmentation** has been used not only to find a niche for new products, but to reposition established brands. Research done by Colgate Palmolive for Irish Spring soap provides a case in point. The research uncovered three segments for deodorant soap: (1) males who wanted a light-fragrance deodorant soap; (2) females who wanted a gentle, mild-fragrance bar; and (3) a mixed segment (predominantly male) who looked for a strong-fragrance, refreshing deodorant soap. Irish Spring was found to do well with the last segment, but the company saw a bigger sales opportunity in the second segment. As a result, the soap was reformulated and ads began to stress a family appeal for the product.

Benefits are used as a segmentation basis for many consumer product categories. For example, Preference, by L'Oreal, emphasizes its conditioning benefits in TV commercials, whereas Clairol's Loving Care stresses that it can color gray hair without damaging the hair or changing its color.[17] Another product group that lends itself to market segmentation on the basis of benefits is soft drinks. For instance, the phrase "no preservatives" is emphasized in a new Seven-Up campaign.[18] Figure 2-4 presents an ad for Match Light Instant Lighting Charcoal, which offers the benefit of *convenience*—not requiring the use of lighter fluid.

Benefit segmentation, like other types of psychological segmentation, is a useful way of identifying new market segments. However, some consumer researchers prefer related but different types of psychological segmentation for new product development. For instance, **problem segmentation** (i.e., segmentation of the market according to problems uncovered in talking to consumers) may be a promising alternative.[19] A recent study of dog food purchasers examined three alternative segmentation variables (attitudes, benefits, and problems) and concluded that problems (e.g., does not smell good) and benefits (e.g., easy to prepare) are contextually independent constructs, and that either would serve as a useful market segmentation criterion.[20]

Because the field of psychological segmentation is relatively new, disputes

FIGURE 2-3 Advertisement Depicting Benefit Segmentation

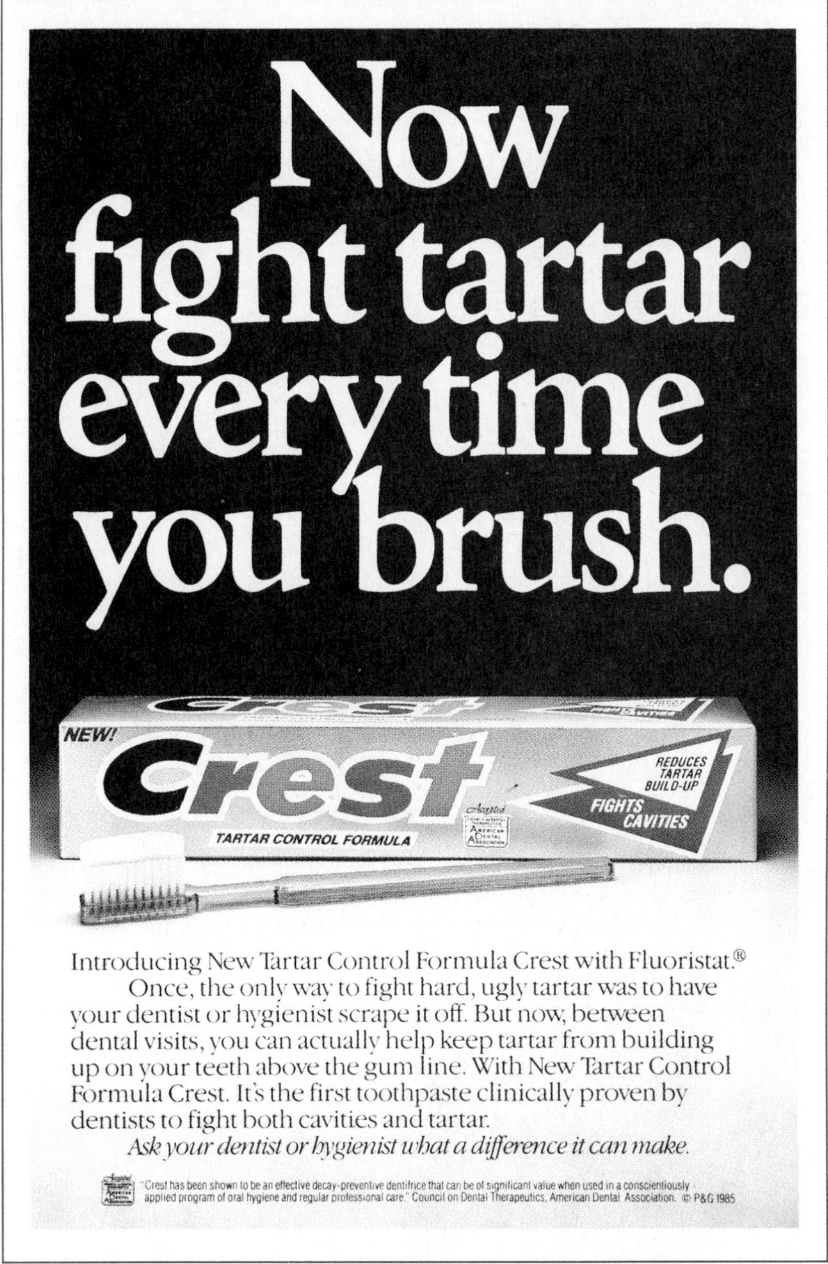


Courtesy of The Procter & Gamble Company

about its most effective form will no doubt continue for some time. In the real world of consumer segmentation, demographic, psychological, and sociocultural factors are frequently explored concurrently to develop fine-tuned consumer profiles for use in a market segmentation strategy.

FIGURE 2-4 Advertisement Stressing a Product Benefit

Courtesy of The Kingsford Co.

## Sociocultural Segmentation

*Sociological* (i.e., group) and *anthropological* (i.e., cultural) variables provide further bases for market segmentation. For example, consumer markets have been successfully subdivided into segments on the basis of cultural and subcultural membership, social class membership, and stage in the family life cycle.

### CULTURE

Some marketers have found it useful to segment their markets on the basis of cultural heritage, since members of the same society tend to share the same values, beliefs, and customs. This strategy is particularly successful if marketing takes place in an international context.

Very often a product must be altered or reformulated in some way in order for it to do well in several cultures. For example, Nestlé sells coffee worldwide, but the Italian segment of its coffee market (which prefers a strong, black brew) would not buy the same blend that is sold in the United States. Both American cigarette and soup companies have discovered that taste preferences in the United Kingdom do not parallel those of United States consumers. Sometimes it is merely custom that divides cultural segments. Greeting cards, usually sold with a verse in the United States, are sold without one in Europe.

Culturally distinct segments may be prospects for the same product, but it may be necessary to promote the product in quite different ways. For example, outboard motors might be promoted as an efficient means of transportation in Asia and as a leisure-time product in the United States. International marketers who engage in segmentation studies are likely to better target their products and their promotional efforts than those who use a standardized marketing approach.

### SUBCULTURE

Within a particular culture there are sometimes distinct groups or **subcultures** that are united by certain experiences, values, or beliefs. Such groups can also provide fertile segments for selected marketing efforts. For example, various religious, racial, and ethnic subcultures have served as bases for market segmentation.

Some marketers give a great deal of attention to the black subculture. Although the income of blacks tends to be lower than that of whites, blacks account for a disproportionate share of market in some product categories (e.g., over 40 percent of the shaver and rice markets). In such product categories, it pays to target blacks for special marketing efforts.

Cigarette companies have been especially diligent in focusing attention on subcultural segments. For example, Liggett and Myers' Dorado brand is targeted to Hispanic smokers. Philip Morris' Rio is aimed at blacks—the principal smokers of menthol cigarettes. In the cigarette marketplace, it requires only a half of one percent market share to have a successful brand. Market segmentation is how the industry copes with the shrinking cigarette market.[21]

### SOCIAL CLASS

Social class has been particularly amenable to treatment as a market segmentation variable. It is sometimes measured by income alone, or by an index composed of several demographic variables, such as education, income, and occupation.

The concept of social class implies that there are people higher or lower on the social status scale. Studies have shown that consumers in different social classes vary in terms of values, product preferences, and buying habits. It is doubtful, for example, that Toyota expects a prospective auto buyer to spend sleepless nights deciding whether to purchase its Tercel or its Cressida, as these models are likely to appeal to members of different social classes.

Marketers have regularly used their knowledge of social class differences to appeal to specific social classes. Many large commercial banks, for example, offer a variety of distinctive levels of service for people from different social classes. Bankers Trust Company, in an effort to secure the patronage of particularly well-off people for its private banking group, promises: "We make money for people who make money." This ad theme simply and directly identifies the market segment that the private banking group at Bankers Trust is interested in servicing.

### FAMILY LIFE CYCLE

Another frequently used sociological basis for market segmentation is **stage in the family life cycle.** The life cycle concept is based on the premise that families pass through several phases in their formation, growth, and final dissolution. At each phase the family unit needs different products. Young marrieds, for example, need basic furniture to start a home; older, more established families may want more elaborate furnishings. Each of the family life cycle categories may be a distinct segment for a particular marketer.

The family life cycle concept is used successfully by cereal marketers. For example, Kellogg targets a variety of breakfast cereals to different segments of the market: Froot Loops is aimed at the children in the family, Corn Flakes at older children and adults, Special K at adults who want a cereal to help them stay fit and healthy, and All Bran to older people who perceive the need for fiber in their diets. As this illustration points up, several bases for segmenting a market are often combined to produce a sharper picture of the target audience. In the case of cereal, *stage in the family life cycle* and *benefits sought* both serve to delineate likely segments.

## User Behavior Segmentation

Markets can also be segmented by the **rate of usage** of a particular product category and by the degree of **loyalty** to a particular brand.

*Rate of usage* refers to the volume of purchases a consumer makes of a particular product, and it generally differentiates between heavy users, light users, and nonusers. Marketers who rely on usage rate to segment their markets also seek demographic or psychological information to distinguish subgroups. For example, one study of male beer drinkers utilized psychographic variables to distinguish heavy drinkers from nondrinkers and light drinkers. Compared with the other two segments, heavy drinkers were found to be more self-indulgent, less accepting of responsibility, more sports minded, and to have a very masculine view of life.[22]

Research has consistently indicated that between 25 and 35 percent of the beer drinkers account for more than 70 percent of all beer consumed. In a similar manner, many other marketers have found that a relatively small group of heavy users accounts for a disproportionately large percentage of product usage. For this reason, most marketers would prefer to target campaigns to the heavy users (e.g., "The one beer to have, when you're having more than one"), rather than spend considerably more money trying to attract light users.

Sometimes *brand loyalty* is a useful basis for segmentation. Marketers often try to identify the characteristics of their brand-loyal consumers so that they can direct their promotional efforts to people with similar characteristics in the larger population. Or they may decide to go after consumers who show no brand loyalty, since such people may represent greater market potential than consumers who are loyal to competing brands. Non-brand-loyal consumers also suggest a different type of marketing mix to the marketing practitioner (low price, consumer "deals," point-of-purchase displays, etc.) Identifying brand-loyal consumers and distinguishing them from those who are not brand loyal by means of demographic, psychological or sociocultural characteristics is seldom easy. For this reason, *brand loyalty* is used less frequently than *usage rate* to differentiate market segments.

## Usage Situation Segmentation

"I don't have time for a formal lunch. Let's go downstairs to Burger King." "I'm sorry, I know you love Cheerios in the morning, but the supermarket was out of it." "I use Lipton Onion Soup for chip-dips when I have friends over." "When I'm away on business I always stay at a Marriott; however, when I take the whole family on vacation, we stay at Days Inn."

What do each of these statements have in common? They describe a consumer's behavior within the context of a particular situation in which the consumer made a specific choice. Under other circumstances, in other situations, and on other specific occasions, the same consumer might make other choices.

Relatively recent evidence suggests that particular **usage situations** are viable bases for segmentation. For example, one study found that the evaluation of specific fruit varied according to whether the fruit was viewed as (1) part of breakfast, (2) a daytime snack, or (3) a supper dessert.[23] Other research found that behavior differs between gift-giving situations which are obligatory in nature and those that are voluntary.[24]

*Time pressure* has been found to be a determinant in store choice. Consumers who are in rush are less likely to visit department stores, and will select some other type of store that they feel they can get in and out of quickly.[25] It is likely that future research will continue to examine the role of situational factors as bases for segmentation.

## CRITERIA FOR EFFECTIVE MARKET SEGMENTATION

Five criteria must be met if a market segmentation strategy is to be successful: (1) **identification**—the market segment(s) must be able to be characterized in terms of distinctive needs, geodemographics, or psychosocial traits; (2) **responsiveness**—members of the selected market segment(s) must give evidence of a positive reaction to the product; (3) **adequate market potential**—the selected market segment(s) must be large enough to be profitable; (4) **accessibility**—the selected market segment(s) must be able to be reached economically; and (5) **stability** or **growth**—the selected market segment(s) must at least be able to replace itself in size or composition or, preferably, grow in size.

### Identification

Segments must be capable of *identification;* that is, a portion of the firm's potential market must have a common need or, upon examination, possess one or more characteristics that set it apart from the rest of the market. For example, are there young families in the audiocassette market that have elementary school children who listen to children's tapes? If "yes," are these parents a feasible market segment for a special Sharp cassette deck designed for simple operation and rugged use? If "yes" again, the product might be promoted through a campaign carefully tailored to the special needs, interests and media habits of this group (e.g., *Parent* magazine). Similarly, if there is a concentration of families in a Baltimore-area community that own homes in the $175,000 to $350,000 range, these homeowners might be a feasible market segment for a lawn maintenance service.

Some segmentation characteristics are easily identifiable, such as *age, occupation, race,* or *geographic location.* Others can be determined through questionnaires, such as *education, income,* or *marital status.* Still other characteristics are more difficult to identify, such as *attitudes, personality,* or *lifestyle.* A knowledge of consumer behavior is especially useful to marketers who wish to segment markets on the basis of such elusive or intangible consumer characteristics.

### Responsiveness

For marketers, identifying a group of consumers with a potential need for a specific product (e.g., a high quality child-proof cassette deck) or a specific service (lawn maintenance care) is only a first step. The next step is to determine if the identified group of consumers is likely to respond favorably enough to the firm's product or service to justify being singled out for special treatment.

To actually establish if the product (or service), ads or other promotional materials designed to persuade the potential target market are likely to be effective, marketers frequently conduct *focus group* sessions. These discussions with small numbers of consumers drawn from the potential target market provide an initial assessment of likely reactions. As a followup, marketers sometimes conduct *test markets* or *special trial offers* to monitor the target segment's reactions in a "natural" market environment.

## Adequate Market Potential

For a market segmentation strategy to be worthwhile, there must be a sufficient number of people in the potential market with the same characteristics or needs. For example, Sharp is unlikely to be interested in producing a child-proof cassette deck unless it estimates that the size of the potential target market is large enough to be profitable. Similarly, the Baltimore lawn maintenance service would want to know if the number of upscale homes in the designated community is large enough to warrant putting together a special crew to service this target market.

For both examples, it is likely that *secondary demographic data* (e.g., United States Census data available at a local library) would be helpful in estimating the potential size and concentration of the target markets.

## Accessibility

A fourth requirement for effective market segmentation is *accessibility,* which means that marketers must be able to reach the market segment or segments they have selected economically. Today, with so many special interest magazines and a great variety of special interest cable TV shows, there are few market segments that cannot be reached by one or more forms of print or broadcast media. The marketer can also use direct mail, an extremely powerful way of reaching individual consumers in a selected target market.

It may not be worthwhile for advertisers to use mass media to reach a specific market segment, because they would have to pay for waste circulation coverage. For example, manufacturers of expensive automobiles may be able to reach wealthy individuals by advertising in *TV Guide,* but they are also paying good advertising dollars to reach many readers who cannot afford the product. In the case of luxury cars, manufacturers might consider placing ads in upscale publications such as *Town and Country.*

## Stability

Because the "marketing muscle" required to penetrate a market segment typically involves large amounts of money and risk, marketers do not wish to commit such resources until they determine that the segment is unlikely to contract in size in the near future. Similarly, marketers do not want the composition of the segment to change without adequate warning which allows them to adjust their marketing mix commitments and to retarget their communications.

Large marketers are usually most comfortable targeting consumer segments that are relatively stable in terms of needs and demographic and psychological factors. They want their target markets to grow larger over time, or at the very least, to remain constant in size.

The amount of research needed to implement a segmentation strategy depends on the bases used for segmentation. If the basis is *demographic,* the task may be relatively easy, since secondary sources for such information are often readily available. If bases other than demographic are utilized, then **primary research** involving focus groups, depth interviews, and survey questionnaires may be warranted. A decision must be made at the completion of such studies as to whether to pursue just one or several of the segments uncovered by the research.

Figure 2-5 presents an overview of the **multistep market segmentation process.** The first step of the process requires marketing management to define the boundaries of the specific market it wants to segment. In step two, marketing management and researchers explore various alternative bases for segmenting the defined market—*geographic, demographic, psychological, sociocultural, user behavior,* or *usage situation.*

In step three, the market is divided up in terms of the selected segmentation bases and the resulting segments are profiled in terms of still other consumer behavior variables. In other words, some consumer behavior variables are used to segment the market (e.g., demographic factors such as *age, sex,* and *income*); then other consumer behavior variables (e.g., *psychographics* and *usage rates*) are used to profile the segments created by the three demographic factors. Segmentation research for other products or services might reverse this pattern; that is, a market might be segmented in terms of *psychographics* and *usage* and profiled in terms of a group of *geodemographic* factors.

After this research task is completed, marketing management must evaluate, on the basis of the five criteria discussed above (identification, responsiveness, market potential, accessibility and stability) which if any of the potential market segments to *target* (step four). After selection of attractive target markets (step five), the company must design and implement appropriate marketing strategies (steps six and seven). Remember, a unique marketing mix for each targeted segment is the core of market segmentation strategy. For example, an Olympus camera ad aimed at amateur photographers might contain a large amount of technical body copy and be placed in *Modern Photography Magazine.* To appeal to individuals with little photographic knowledge, promotion for the same model might take the form of a television commercial that stresses

**FIGURE 2-5** **An Overview of the Multistep Market Segmentation Process**

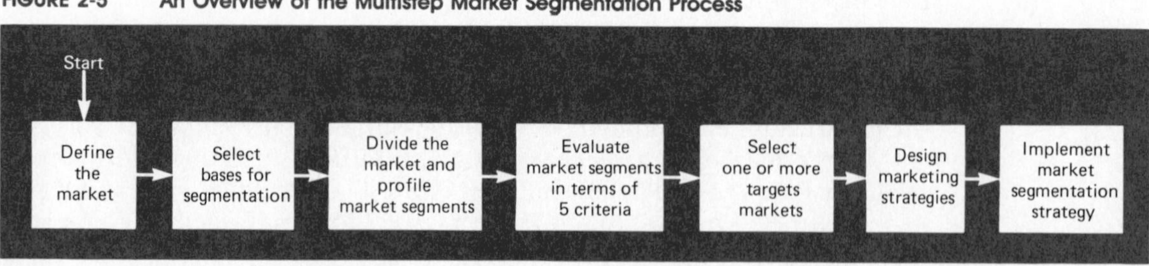

how easy the camera is to use. It might even employ a celebrity to point up its simplicity and other selected attributes.

## Conducting a Segmentation Study

To provide a sense of the basic elements of segmentation research, let us briefly consider the role of secondary and primary data collection.

### LOCATING SECONDARY DATA

A great deal of geographic, demographic, and sociocultural information is available from government sources. For example, the U.S. Census of Housing and Population collects data on the age, education, occupation, and income of residents of areas as small as a city block. Additional information on rents, places of work, automobile ownership, and patterns of migration is provided by the government in studies of census tracts within major metropolitan areas.

A host of private population data firms, marketing research companies, and advertising agencies are also important sources of **secondary market data.** For instance, the A. C. Nielsen Company regularly supplies subscribers (such as General Foods, Nabisco, Beatrice, Procter & Gamble) with brand-by-brand sales data for their products sold by food and drug retailers. Other marketing information is routinely published by data/market research firms that show annual changes in key demographic data by census tracts (e.g., Census Update), or break down such data by ZIP code areas (ZIProfile).[26]

Retailers and nonprofit organizations often have directly relevant demographic, sociocultural, and usage information available in their own customer or client records. For example, retailers can use their own credit and charge account data or mail order records to identify just who their customers are and what products and brands they have purchased. Subscription and donor lists serve the same purpose for nonprofit organizations and charities.

### COLLECTING PRIMARY DATA

If more detailed information on purchasing patterns and product attitudes is needed—for example, when psychological and usage behavior are used as segmentation bases—then **primary data** (data collected for the specific purpose of the study) must be gathered. Research to secure such information is more costly than secondary data, but often yields a more accurate picture of potential segments than studies based on generally available data.

Detailed segmentation studies are often conducted in three phases, as summarized in Table 2-7. In the **exploratory qualitative** phase, researchers conduct depth interviews and focus group discussions to gather ideas about consumers' motivations, perceptions, and attitudes towards specific brands

**TABLE 2-7 Phases of a Segmentation Study**

| | | |
|---|---|---|
| phase 1 | Exploratory qualitative | Examines the usage patterns, buying habits, benefits sought, and attitudes about a product class |
| phase 2 | Exploratory quantitative | Measures brand similarities, attitudes, perceptions of brand images, and preferences |
| phase 3 | Quantitative probability | Identifies the prime segments to be pursued in terms of members' behavior, attitudes, demographic characteristics, and media habits. |

Source: Adapted from Larry Percy, "How Market Segmentation Guides Advertising Strategy," *Journal of Advertising Research*, 16 (October 1976), 11–22

within a given product category. They also look for the principal benefits sought by consumers. This research is *qualitative* rather than quantitative, because it seeks to gather ideas and tentative generalizations about the product qualities consumers prefer, without attaching hard numbers or percentages to the ideas obtained.

In the **exploratory quantitative** phase, numbers are sought to support or refute the findings that emerged from the first phase. Representative consumers are interviewed concerning the similarities they see among various brands, their perceptions of different brand images, their attitudes, and their preferences. Researchers then apply appropriate statistical techniques to analyze and synthesize the information gathered. On the basis of this analysis, researchers identify prime segments for a new product idea or a revised marketing mix.

In the **quantitative probability** phase, individuals are grouped together into likely segments, not only on the basis of various demographic traits, but also by media habits, attitudes, perceptions, and personality characteristics.

## Implementing Segmentation Strategies

Firms that employ market segmentation can pursue a **concentrated marketing** strategy or a **differentiated marketing** strategy.

### CONCENTRATED VERSUS DIFFERENTIATED MARKETING

Once an organization has identified its most promising market segments, it must then decide whether to pursue several segments or just one. Marketing to several segments, using a distinct product, promotional appeal, price, and/or method of distribution for each, is called *differentiated marketing*. Marketing to a single segment with a unique marketing mix is called *concentrated marketing.*

Examples of firms that practice differentiated marketing are not difficult to find. Coca-Cola appeals to select components of the overall calorie-conscious segment of the soft drink market with both Diet Coke and Tab, and aims at the regular cola market with Coke, Classic Coke, and Cherry Coke. Some of these products are even offered in two versions—with and without caffeine. Ford Motor Company targets the Escort to economy-minded shoppers, the Mustang to the "young at heart," LTDs to the middle-income car-buying family, and Lincoln Continentals to the more affluent end of the car-buying public.

Differentiated marketing is an especially appropriate segmentation strategy for financially strong companies that are well established in a product category and competitive with other firms that are also strong in the category. However, if a company is small or new to a field, concentrated marketing is probably a better bet. By finding a niche not occupied by stronger competitors, such a company can survive and prosper. As an example, for a fairly long time Topol toothpaste was basically alone in targeting smokers with teeth discolored from smoking. Today, Topol enjoys a market leadership position in a small but increasingly important submarket of the overall toothpaste market.

## PRODUCT POSITIONING

Once a firm has defined the market, determined which segments exist in the marketplace and which segment or segments it wishes to target, it must then *position* its product or service. As Chapter 1 has pointed out, positioning is *not* something that a company does *to* its product, but how it wants targeted consumers to *perceive* the product. A recent study, for example, found that consumers associated a specific brand with each of several product categories: (1) soft drinks—Coca-Cola; (2) beer—Budweiser (3) orange juice—Minute Maid; (4) coffee—Maxwell House; and (5) tea—Lipton.[27] A major reason for some of these product-brand associations is that often the first brand to find success in a market comes to "own" the leadership position.[28]

Marketers must decide, therefore, how to position their products in the consumer's mind. If research determines that the brand is communicating the wrong image to the desired target market—then the brand must be *repositioned.* Consider a few recent examples. Sanka brand decaffeinated coffee was positioned for decades as most appropriate for elderly consumers; the new Sanka advertising targets active achievers of all ages, and portrays them in a number of adventurous activities.[29] Benetton, the Italian clothing manufacturer and retail franchiser that has had great success in the United States, is attempting to shift its male/female sales ratio from 70 percent female to a 50-50 mix; a new multimillion-dollar advertising campaign is being employed in this repositioning effort.[30] Finally, *TeenAge Magazine,* formerly aimed at both male and female teens, has repositioned itself to appeal only to female teenagers—they read more.[31]

## summary

Before the widespread adoption of the marketing concept, mass marketing—offering the same product or marketing mix to everyone—was the marketing strategy most widely used. Market segmentation followed as a more logical way to meet the specific needs of subsets of consumers.

Segmentation research is designed to identify such subsets within a larger consumer market and to identify the needs and wants of one or more groups so that specific goods and services can be developed to satisfy their needs. Besides aiding in the development of new products, segmentation studies assist in the redesign and repositioning of existing products, as well as in the creation of advertising appeals and the selection of advertising media.

Since segmentation strategies benefit both marketers and consumers, they have received wide support from both sides of the marketplace. Market segmentation is now widely used by manufacturers, by retailers, and by the nonprofit sector. Important criteria for the successful use of market segmentation strategies are the ability to identify, measure, evaluate and reach significant subgroups of the total potential market.

Six major classes of consumer characteristics serve as the most common bases for market segmentation. These include geographic variables (e.g., region, density, climate); demographic variables (e.g., age, sex, education); psychological variables (e.g., personality, lifestyle); sociocultural variables (e.g., race, religion, social class); user behavior variables (usage rate and brand loyalty); and usage situation variables (factors that define the situational context of purchase or usage, such as the availability of time, the purpose of a gift, or the availability of credit).

The methodologies used in segmentation research depend upon the segmentation bases used. For example demographic data are often available through secondary sources (that is, from data that have been collected for other purposes), while psychological segmentation usually requires primary research, such as interviews or questionnaires specifically designed for the study in question.

Once an organization has identified promising market segments, it must decide whether to pursue several segments (differentiated marketing) or just one segment (concentrated marketing). It then selects a positioning strategy for each targeted segment.

## discussion questions

1. Define *market segmentation.* What are the major advantages and disadvantages of this marketing strategy for marketers and for consumers?
2. From a market segmentation viewpoint, in what ways are the marketing strategies of IBM and Radio Shack personal computers similar, and in what ways are they different?

3. Describe the relative importance of each of the six segmentation bases in marketing the following products: lawnmowers, health spas for citizens over fifty-five years of age, home computers, and videocassettes.
4. Since the Coca-Cola Company for years had offered Tab to the diet-conscious segment of the market, why should it have found it necessary to introduce Diet Coke?
5. As vice-president of marketing for Burger King, what bases might you use to segment the fast-food market?
6. Could you segment a market for novels based on situational factors? Explain your answer.
7. What is psychographic segmentation, and on what variables is it based?
8. Can your college use market segmentation to increase enrollment? Discuss.

## endnotes


1. Pamela G. Hollie, "Swatch's Total Look Campaign," *The New York Times,* August 13, 1985, D21.
2. "The Vitamin and Nutrient Market: Current Performance And Future Prospects," *Marketing Review,* September–October 1983, 11.
3. Bruce Steinberg, "The Mass Market Is Splitting Apart," *Fortune,* November 28, 1983.
4. Gloria Bordeaux Mitchel, "America Conservatory Theatre: A Case Study" (Unpublished paper, 1979).
5. Ronald Alsop, "To Revive Tab, Coke Stresses 'Sassy' Taste Over Sex Appeal," *The Wall Street Journal,* March 14, 1985, 33.
6. Bill Abrams, "Measuring Markets by Hopes and Fears," *The Wall Street Journal,* June 3, 1982, 27.
7. Teresa J. Domzal and Jerome B. Kernan, "Television Audience Segmentation According to Need Gratification," *Journal of Advertising Research,* 23 (October–November 1983), 37–49.
8. S. Baker, *Advertising Creativity* (New York: McGraw-Hill, 1979), 44–45.
9. Philip H. Dougherty, "Yoplait Yogurt on the Move," *The New York Times,* July 31, 1985.
10. See, for example, Benny Barak and Steven Gould, "Alternative Age Measures: A Research Agenda," in Elizabeth C. Hirschman and Morris B. Holbrook, eds., *Advances in Consumer Research* (Provo, Ut.: Association for Consumer Research, 1985), 12, 53–55; and Benny Barak and Barbara Stern, "SFantastic at Forty," *The Journal of Consumer Marketing,* 2 (Spring 1985), 41–54.
11. Steinberg, "The Mass Market Is Splitting Apart", and "Affluent Market Growing But Elusive,"*Marketing News,* January 4, 1985.
12. "Consumers Give Fanny Farmer the Recipe for Sweet Comeback," *Marketing News,* January 31, 1986, 12.
13. Dentiny Kinal, "Dip into Several Segmentation Schemes to Paint Accurate Picture of Marketplace," *Marketing Review,* September 14, 1984, 32; James Atlas, "Beyond Demographics," *Atlantic Monthly,* October 1984, 49–58; and "Segmentation System Debuts in U.S., Europe," *Marketing News,* May 24, 1985, 35, 41.

14. For a discussion of this distinction and the relative merits of each type, see William D. Wells, "Psychographics: A Critical Review," *Journal of Marketing Research,* 12 (May 1975), 196–213; and Stuart Van Auken, "General versus Product-Specific Life Style Segmentations," *Journal of Advertising,* 7 (Fall 1978), 31–35.

15. Steven P. Schnaars and Leon G. Schiffman, "An Application of a Segmentation Design Based on a Hybrid of Canonical Correlation and Simple Crosstabulation," *Journal of the Academy of Marketing Science,* 12 (Fall 1984), 177–89.

16. Russell I. Haley, "Benefit Segmentation: A Decision-Oriented Research Tool," *Journal of Marketing,* 32 (July 1968); 30–35; "Benefit Segmentation—20 Years Later," *Journal of Consumer Marketing,* 1 (1984), 5–13; and "Benefit Segments: Backwards and Forwards," *Journal of Advertising Research,* 24 (February–March, 1984), 19–25.

17. Pat Sloan, "Clairol Ultresse Adds Color to Dull Market," *Advertising Age,* April 1, 1985, 66.

18. Scott Hume, "An Un-happy Seven-Up Returns to Old Theme," *Advertising Age,* March 11, 1985, 10.

19. Richard H. Evans, "Benefit Analysis or Problem Analysis," *Journal of Advertising,* 9 (Winter 1980), 27–31.

20. Stuart Van Auken and Subhash C. Lonial, "Assessing Mutual Association Between Alternative Market Segmentation Bases," *Journal of Advertising,* 13 (1984), 11–16.

21. Pamela G. Hollie, "Segmented Cigarette Market," *The New York Times,* March 23, 1985, 31.

22. J. T. Plummer, "Life Style and Advertising: Case Studies," in Fred Allvine, ed., *1971 Proceedings of the American Marketing Association* (Chicago: American Marketing Association, 1971), 294.

23. Peter R. Dickson, "Person-Situation: Segmentation's Missing Link," *Journal of Marketing,* 46 (Fall 1982), 56–64.

24. Debra L. Scammon, Roy T. Shaw, and Gary Bemossy, "Is a Gift Always a Gift? An Investigation of Flower Purchasing Behavior Across Situations," in Andrew Mitchell, ed., *Advances in Consumer Research* (Ann Arbor, Mich.: Association for Consumer Research, 1982), 9, 531–36.

25. Bruce E. Mattson, "Situational Influences on Store Choice," *Journal of Retailing,* 58 (Fall 1982), 46–58.

26. "Census Update & ZIProfile Offer Detailed Demographics," *Marketing News,* November 30, 1979, 5, and Atlas, "Beyond Demographics."

27. "Top-of-Mind Usually Top-of-Line," *Marketing News,* September 27, 1985, 13.

28. For a detailed discussion of positioning, see Al Ries and Jack Trout, *Positioning: The Battle for Your Mind* (New York: McGraw-Hill, 1981); and *Marketing Warfare* (New York: McGraw-Hill, 1985).

29. Bickley Townsend, "Psychographic Glitter and Gold," *American Demographics,* November 1985, 23.

30. Miriam Rozen, "Can Benetton Sustain Its Momentum," *Adweek,* December 16, 1985, 10.

31. Stuart J. Elliott, "TeenAge Decides It's Girls That Count," *Advertising Age,* October 28, 1985, 68.

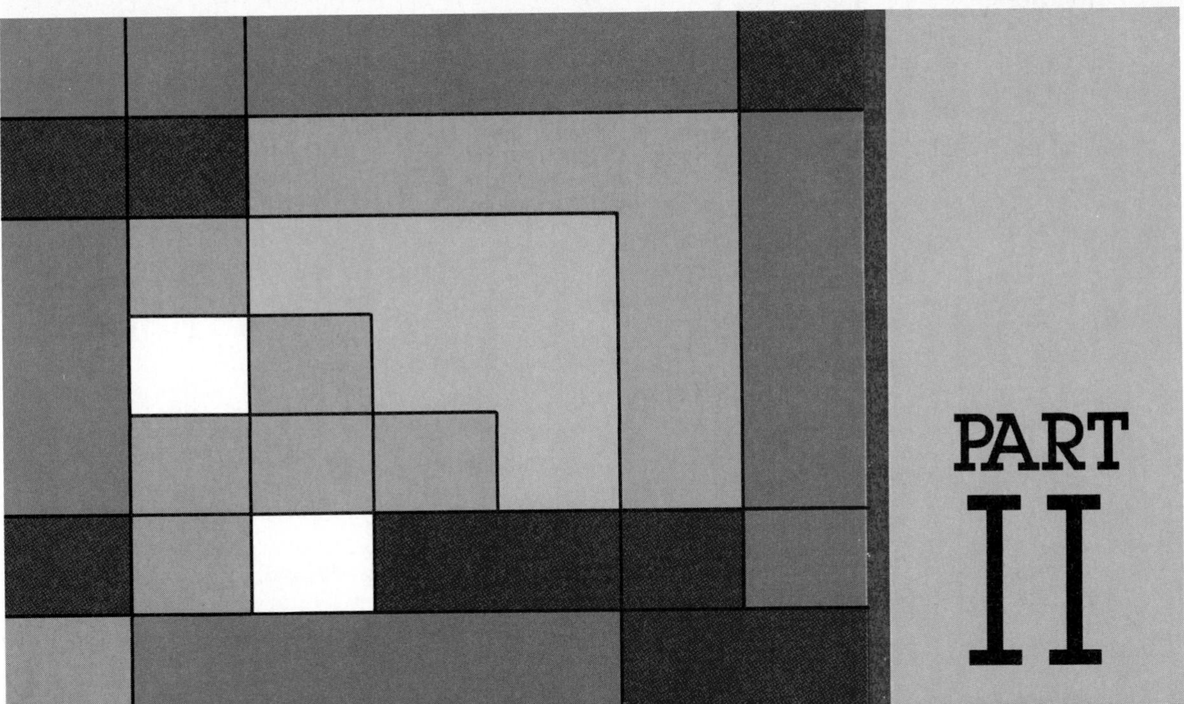

# PART II

# THE CONSUMER AS AN INDIVIDUAL

Chapters 3 through 10 are designed to provide the reader with a comprehensive picture of consumer psychology. The objectives of these chapters are (1) to explain the basic psychological concepts that account for individual behavior, and (2) to show how these concepts influence the individual's consumption-related behavior. Chapter 10, "Communication and Consumer Behavior," provides the bridge between the individual and his or her connection with the outside world.

# 3

# Consumer Needs and Motivation

## *introduction*

We have all grown up "knowing" that people are different. They seek different pleasures, spend their money in different ways. One couple may spend their vacation traveling in Europe; their friends may prefer to lie on a beach and watch the sea. One father may buy his young son a set of electric trains; another may buy his son a personal computer. One woman may spend her Christmas bonus on a microwave oven; her neighbor may spend hers to join a health club.

Different modes of consumer behavior—different ways of spending money—do not surprise us. We have been brought up to believe that the differences in people are what makes life interesting. However, this apparent diversity in human behavior often causes us to overlook the fact that people are really very much alike. There are underlying similarities—*constants* that tend to operate across many types of people—which serve to explain and to clarify their consumption behavior. Psychologists and consumer behaviorists agree that basically most people experience the same kinds of needs and motives; they simply express these motives in different ways. For this reason, an understanding of human motives is very important to marketers; it enables them to understand, and even anticipate, human behavior in the marketplace.

Human **needs**—consumer needs—are the basis of all modern marketing. Needs are the essence of the marketing concept. The key to a company's survival, profitability, and growth in a highly competitive market environment is its ability to identify and satisfy unfulfilled consumer needs better and sooner than the competition.

Marketers do not create needs, though in some instances they may make consumers more keenly aware of unfelt needs. Successful marketers define

> *Understanding human needs is half the job of meeting them.*
>
> *ADLAI STEVENSON*
> *Speech, Columbus, Ohio (October 3, 1952)*

their markets in terms of the needs they are trying to satisfy, rather than in terms of the products they sell. This is a market-oriented, rather than a product-oriented, approach to marketing. A marketing orientation focuses on the needs of the buyer; a product orientation focuses on the needs of the seller. The marketing concept implies that the manufacturer will make what it can sell; a product orientation implies that the manufacturer will try to sell what it can make.

A product-oriented approach spelled doom for many small computer companies that tried to sell home computers to a nonbusiness market which had little need for the product. As one analyst put it: "Home computers are a wonderful solution looking for a problem."[1] Rather than try to understand and satisfy consumers' unfulfilled needs, computer makers tried to unload onto individual households sophisticated technology that served no purpose for them. Recognizing this problem, Hewlett-Packard recently shifted its marketing strategy to focus on consumer needs and user benefits in the design and marketing of a new line of computers.[2]

Marketers who base their offerings on a recognition of consumer needs find a ready market for their products. The recent popularity of farmers' markets in the United States is grounded in their appeal to consumers' needs for flavor, quality, and freshness, needs that too often are not met by large food marketers who focus on appearance and convenience.[3] The success of Merrill Lynch's new Cash Management Account is based on its satisfaction of consumers' expressed needs for a bank account that eliminated idle funds, provided access to credit, and compiled consolidated information about their total financial picture.[4]

There are unlimited examples of products that have succeeded in the marketplace because they fulfilled consumer needs; there are even more examples of products and companies that have failed because they didn't recognize or understand consumer needs.

This chapter will discuss basic needs that operate in most people to motivate behavior. It explores the influence such needs have on consumption behavior. Later chapters in this section explain why and how these basic human motives are expressed in so many diverse ways.

## WHAT IS MOTIVATION?

Several basic concepts are integral to an understanding of human motivation. Before we discuss these, it is necessary to agree on some basic definitions.

### Motivation

*Motivation* can be described as *the driving force within individuals that impels them to action.* This driving force is produced by a state of tension, which exists as the result of an unfilled need. Individuals strive—both consciously and subconsciously—to reduce this tension through behavior that they anticipate will fulfill their needs and thus relieve them of the stress they feel. The specific goals they select and the patterns of action they undertake to achieve their goals are the results of individual thinking and learning. Figure 3-1 presents a model of the motivational process. It portrays motivation as a state of need-induced tension, which exerts a "push" on the individual to engage in behavior that he or she expects will gratify needs and thus reduce tension. Whether gratification is actually achieved depends on the course of action pursued. (If a high school girl pins her hopes of being asked to the senior prom on her switch to a highly advertised "sexy" toothpaste, she may be disappointed.)

The specific courses of action undertaken by consumers and the specific goals chosen are selected on the basis of their thinking processes (i.e., cognition) and previous learning. For that reason, marketers who understand motivational theory attempt to influence the consumer's cognitive processes.

## Needs

Every individual has needs; some are innate, others are acquired. Innate needs are *physiological* (i.e., biogenic); they include the needs for food, for water, for air, for clothing, for shelter, and for sex. Because they are needed to sustain biological life, the biogenic needs are considered **primary needs** or motives.

Acquired needs are needs we learn in response to our culture or environment. These may include needs for esteem, for prestige, for affection, for power, and for learning. Because acquired needs are generally *psychological* (i.e., psychogenic), they are considered **secondary needs** or motives. They result from the individual's subjective psychological state and from relationships with others. For example, all individuals need shelter from the elements; thus, finding a place to live fulfills an important primary need for a newly transferred executive. However, the kind of house she buys may be the result of secondary needs. She may seek a house where she can entertain large groups of people (and fulfill her social needs); furthermore, she may want to buy a house in an

**FIGURE 3-1** **Model of the Motivation Process**

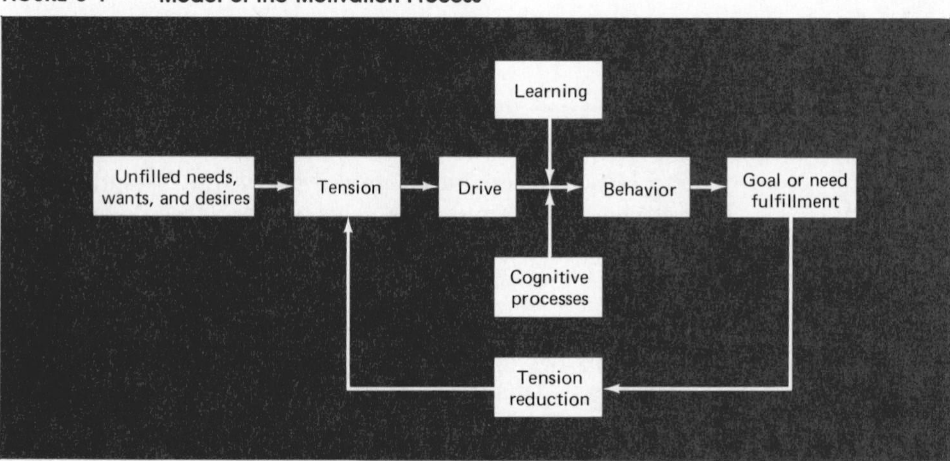

exclusive community in order to impress her friends and family (and fulfill her ego needs). The house an individual ultimately purchases thus may serve to fulfill both primary and secondary needs.

## Goals

Goals are the sought-after results of motivated behavior. As Figure 3-1 indicates, all behavior is goal-oriented. Our discussion of motivation in this chapter is in part concerned with **generic goals**; that is, the general classes or categories of goals consumers select to fulfill their needs. Marketers are even more concerned with consumers' **product-specific goals;** that is, the specifically branded or labeled products they select to fulfill their needs. For example, the Thomas J. Lipton Company wants consumers to view iced tea as a good way to quench summer thirst (i.e., as a generic goal). However, it is even more interested in having consumers view *Lipton's* iced tea as the *best* way to quench summer thirst (i.e., as a product-specific goal). As trade association advertising indicates, marketers recognize the importance of promoting both types of goals. The American Dairy Association advertises that "milk is a natural," while Borden's, a member of the association, advertises its own brand of milk.

### THE SELECTION OF GOALS

For any given need, there are many different and appropriate **goals**. The goals selected by individuals depend on their personal experiences, physical capacity, prevailing cultural norms and values, and the goal's accessibility in the physical and social environment. For example, an individual may have a strong hunger need. If he is a young American athlete, he may envision a rare sirloin steak as his goal-object; if he is also an orthodox Jew, he may require that the steak be kosher to conform to dietary laws. If the individual is old or infirm, he may not have the physical capacity to chew or digest a steak; therefore, he may select hamburger instead. If he has never tasted steak—if it is outside of his realm of personal experience—he will probably not even think of steak, but instead will select a food that has previously satisfied his hunger (perhaps fish or chicken).

Finally, the goal-object has to be both physically and socially accessible. If the individual was shipwrecked on an island with no food provisions or living animals, he could not realistically select steak as his goal-object, though he might fantasize about it. If he were in India where cows are considered sacred, he would not be able to consume steak, because to do so would be considered sacrilegious. He would have to select a substitute goal more appropriate to the social environment.

The individual's own perception of himself or herself also serves to influence the specific goals selected. The products a person owns, would like to own, or would not like to own are often perceived in terms of how closely they reflect (are congruent with) the person's **self-image**. A product that is perceived as fitting an individual's self-image has a greater probability of being selected than one that is not. Thus a man who perceives himself as young and "swinging" may drive a Porsche; a woman who perceives herself as rich and conservative may drive a Mercedes. The types of houses people live in, the cars they drive, the clothes they wear, the very foods they eat—these specific goal-objects are often chosen because symbolically they reflect the individual's self-image while they satisfy specific needs. (The relationship of self-concept to product choice is explained more fully in Chapter 6.)

### INTERDEPENDENCE OF NEEDS AND GOALS

Needs and goals are interdependent; one does not exist without the other. However, people are often not as aware of their needs as they are of their goals. For example, a teenager may not consciously be aware of her social needs but may join many clubs to meet new friends. A local politician may not consciously be aware of a power need but may regularly run for public office. A woman may not recognize her ego needs but may strive to have the most successful real estate office in town.

Individuals are usually somewhat more aware of their physiological needs than they are of their psychological needs. Most people know when they are hungry or thirsty or cold, and they take appropriate steps to satisfy these needs. Sometimes they may subconsciously engage in behavior designed to fulfill their bodily needs, even though they are not consciously aware of such needs. Medical researchers have reported the case of a young child who had an overwhelming craving for salt almost from the time of his birth. All the foods he liked were salty; in addition, he ate about a teaspoonful of salt daily. When he was about three and one-half years old, he was placed in a hospital for observation and was restricted to a routine hospital diet. Within seven days he was dead. A postmortem examination revealed a glandular deficiency which had caused excessive loss of salt from his body through urination. The boy had literally kept himself alive for three and one-half years by eating great quantities of salt to compensate for his salt deficiency. When he no longer had free access to salt, he died.[5]

## Positive and Negative Motivation

Motivation can be positive or negative in direction. We may feel a driving force *toward* some object or condition, or a driving force *away* from some object or condition. For example, a person may be impelled toward a restaurant to fulfill a hunger need and away from motorcycle transportation to fulfill a safety need. Some psychologists refer to positive drives as *needs, wants,* or *desires,* and to negative drives as *fears* or *aversions*. However, though negative and positive motivational forces seem to differ dramatically in terms of physical (and sometimes emotional) activity, they are basically similar in that both serve to initiate and sustain human behavior. For this reason, researchers often refer to both kinds of drives or motives as **needs, wants,** and **desires**.

Goals, too, can be positive or negative. A positive goal is one toward which behavior is directed, and thus it is often referred to as an *approach* object. A negative goal is one from which behavior is directed away, and thus it is sometimes referred to as an *avoidance* object. Since both approach and avoidance goals can be considered objectives of motivated behavior, most researchers refer to both types simply as **goals**. Consider this example. A middle-aged woman may wish to remain as attractive as possible to male acquaintances. Her positive goal is to appear desirable, and therefore she uses a perfume advertised to make her "irresistible." A negative goal may be aging skin, and so she buys and uses face creams advertised to prevent wrinkles. In the former case, she uses perfume to help her achieve her positive goal—sexual attractiveness; in the latter case, she uses face creams to help avoid a negative goal—wrinkled skin. Figure 3-2 presents a negative situation with which most people could identify, and copy that explains how its effects could be mitigated.

## Rational Versus Emotional Motives

Some consumer researchers distinguish between so-called **rational motives** and **emotional** (or nonrational) **motives**. They use the term *rationality* in the traditional economic sense which assumes that consumers behave rationally when they carefully consider all alternatives and choose those that give them the greatest utility (i.e., satisfaction).[6] In a marketing context, the term *rationality* implies that the consumer selects goals based on totally objective criteria, such as size, weight, price, or miles per gallon. *Emotional motives* imply the selection of goals according to personal or subjective criteria (the desire for individuality, pride, fear, affection, status).

The assumption underlying this distinction is that subjective or emotional criteria do not maximize utility or satisfaction. However, it is reasonable to assume that consumers always attempt to select alternatives that, *in their view,* serve to maximize satisfaction. Obviously, assessment of satisfaction is a very personal process, based upon the individual's own need structure as well as on past behavioral, social, and learning experiences. What may appear irrational to an outside observer may be perfectly rational within the context of the consumer's own psychological field. For example, a product purchased to enhance self-image (such as a fragrance) is a perfectly rational form of consumer behavior.

If behavior did not appear rational to the person who undertakes it at the time it is undertaken, obviously he or she would not do it. Therefore the distinction between rational and emotional *motives* does not appear to be warranted, though some *consumers* may be more emotional than others. Indeed, research suggests that impulse buyers react more emotionally than others to stimuli in the buying situation.[7]

Some researchers go so far as to suggest that emphasis on needs obscures the rational, or conscious, nature of most consumer motivation. They claim that consumers act consciously to maximize gains and minimize losses; that they act not from subconscious drives but from rational preferences, or what they perceive to be in their own best interests.

Marketers who agree with this view are reluctant to spend either time or money to uncover subconscious buyer motives. Instead, they try to identify problems that consumers experience with products on the market.[8] For exam-

FIGURE 3-2 Negative Motivation

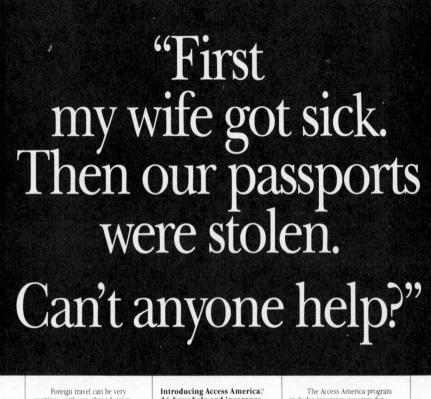

"First
my wife got sick.
Then our passports
were stolen.

Can't anyone help?"

Foreign travel can be very exciting, until something foreign happens to you.

It could be an accident or sudden illness. Missing luggage. Cancelled trip. Lost passport or legal problem.

Most people think their ordinary insurance will cover them.

But ordinary insurance—even travel insurance—won't help solve your problems overseas. At best, it may only reimburse you for expenses once you've returned home.

That's not much help when home is 3,000 miles away.

**Introducing Access America.[SM] 24-hour help and insurance—double protection—for emergencies overseas.**

Access America starts with a 24-hour, free telephone Hotline. It connects you to English-speaking emergency assistance experts around the world. Coordinated through Washington, D.C., Access America is a subsidiary of the Blue Cross and Blue Shield Plans of the New York City and Washington, D.C., areas.

These experts from Access America can help you recover passports, tickets or luggage. Help you replace prescription medicine. Refer you to a doctor. Get you into a hospital. Help find you a legal advisor. Help post bail. Even fly you and your family home, if necessary.

The Access America program includes insurance coverage for accidents, illnesses, medical treatment, lost luggage, protection against cancelled or interrupted trips or charters, and much more.

So why take a chance when you take a trip? Learn more about Access America. For a free brochure call toll-free **1-800-228-2028** Extension 41. Or visit any of the locations listed below.

**Access America**[SM]

plans of the New York and Washington, D.C., areas

Insurance benefits are underwritten by BCS Life Insurance Company and BCS Insurance Company.



**Chase Manhattan Bank, N.A. TWA Participating AAA Clubs**

Courtesy of Access America Inc.

ple, instead of trying to identify any special needs that consumers may have in connection with clothing maintenance, a manufacturer of electric irons may try to discover what problems, if any, consumers are experiencing with irons presently on the market. Such problem identification resulted in the development of a cordless electric iron safe from children and pets, and in the introduction of a steamer which could be used horizontally as well as vertically to remove wrinkles from hanging draperies and clothes.

## Needs and Goals Are Constantly Changing

Needs and goals are constantly growing and changing in response to an individual's physical condition, environment, interactions with others, and experiences. As individuals attain their goals, they develop new ones. If they do not attain their goals, they continue to strive for old goals, or they develop substitute goals. Some of the reasons why need-driven human activity never ceases include the following: (1) existing needs are never completely satisfied and thus constantly require activity designed to attain or maintain fulfillment; (2) as needs become satisfied, new, higher-order needs emerge which must be fulfilled; and (3) people who achieve their goals set new and higher goals for themselves.

### NEEDS ARE NEVER FULLY SATISFIED

Most human needs are never completely, or fully, satisfied. For example, at regular intervals people experience hunger needs that must be satisfied by eating. Most people regularly seek companionship and approval from others to satisfy their social needs. Even more complex psychological needs are rarely satisfied. For example, a person may partially or temporarily satisfy a power need by serving on the town council, but this small taste of power may not sufficiently satisfy her need, so she may run for successively higher public office. In this instance, temporary goal achievement does not fully satisfy the need for power, and the individual keeps striving to satisfy that need more fully.

### NEW NEEDS EMERGE AS OLD NEEDS ARE SATISFIED

Some motivational theorists believe that a **hierarchy of needs** exists and that new, higher-order needs emerge as lower-order needs are fulfilled.[9] For example, a man who has largely satisfied his basic physiological needs may turn his efforts to achieving acceptance among his new neighbors by joining their clubs and supporting their candidates. Having achieved such acceptance, he may then seek recognition by winning tennis trophies or giving lavish parties.

Marketers must stay attuned to changing needs. Car manufacturers who stress the prestige value of their products fail to recognize that many consumers now look elsewhere to satisfy needs for prestige—for example, by installing tennis courts in their backyards or taking exotic trips abroad. For this reason, manufacturers of prestige cars may do better if they were to stress other need satisfactions (e.g., reliability or safety) as reasons for buying a new model.

### SUCCESS AND FAILURE INFLUENCE GOALS

A number of researchers have explored the nature of the goals that individuals set for themselves.[10] In general, they have concluded that individuals who successfully achieve their goals usually set new and higher goals for themselves;

that is, they *raise* their **levels of aspiration**. This is probably due to the fact that they become more confident of their ability to reach their goals. Conversely, those who do not reach their goals sometimes *lower* their levels of aspiration. Thus goal selection is often a function of success and failure. For example, a college senior who is not accepted into medical school may try instead to go to dental school; failing that, he may train to be a pharmacist.

The nature and persistence of an individual's behavior are often influenced by expectations of success or failure in reaching certain goals. Those expectations, in turn, are often based upon past **experience**. A person who takes good snapshots with an inexpensive camera may be motivated to buy a more sophisticated camera in the belief that it will enable her to take even better photographs. In this way, she may eventually upgrade her camera by several hundred dollars. On the other hand, a person who cannot take good pictures is just as likely to keep the same camera or may even lose all interest in photography.

These effects of success and failure on goal selection have strategy implications for the marketer. Goals should be reasonably attainable. Advertisements should not promise more than the product will deliver. Even a good product will not be repurchased if it fails to live up to expectations. Research shows that a disappointed consumer will regard a product that has not lived up to expectations with even less satisfaction than its objective performance warrants.[11] Advertisers who create unrealistic expectations for their products are likely to cause dissatisfaction among consumers. It has been suggested that the frustration and disappointment which result from such consumer dissatisfaction have been the driving force behind consumerism.[12]

SUBSTITUTE GOALS. When, for one reason or another, an individual cannot attain a particular goal or type of goal that he or she anticipates will satisfy certain needs, behavior may be directed to a **substitute goal**. Although the substitute goal may not be as satisfactory as the primary goal, it may be sufficient to dispel uncomfortable tension. Continued deprivation of a primary goal may result in the substitute goal assuming primary-goal status. A man who has stopped drinking whole milk because he is dieting may actually begin to prefer skimmed milk. A woman who cannot afford a Mercedes may convince herself that a Cadillac has an image she clearly prefers. Of course, in this latter instance, the substitute goal may be a defensive reaction to frustration.

FRUSTRATION. Failure to achieve a goal often results in feelings of frustration. Everyone has at one time or another experienced the frustration that comes from inability to attain a goal. The barrier that prevents attainment of a goal may be personal to the individual (i.e., it can be a physical or financial limitation, or a psychological barrier such as conflicting goals), or it can be an obstacle in the physical or social environment. Regardless of the cause, individuals react differently to frustrating situations. Some people are adaptive and manage to cope by finding their way around the obstacle or, if that fails, by selecting a substitute goal. Others are less adaptive and may regard their inability to achieve a goal as a personal failure and experience feelings of anxiety. An example of adaptive behavior would be the college student who would prefer a sports car but settles for a secondhand Volkswagen. If he cannot afford the insurance for a used car, he may settle for a bike on which to ride around campus.

People who cannot cope with frustration often mentally redefine the frustrating situation in order to protect their self-image and defend their self-esteem. For example, a young wife may yearn for a full-length mink coat she cannot afford. The coping individual may select a less expensive fur, such as muskrat, or a cloth coat, or even a fake fur. The person who cannot cope may react with anger toward her husband for not making enough money to buy her a mink, or she may decide that wearing the fur of animals is a barbaric custom in which she will not participate. These last two possibilities are examples, respectively, of *aggression* and *rationalization,* **defense mechanisms** people sometimes adopt to protect their egos from feelings of failure when they cannot attain their goals. Other defense mechanisms include *regression, withdrawal, projection, autism, identification,* and *repression.*

AGGRESSION. Individuals who experience frustration may resort to aggressive behavior in an attempt to protect their self-esteem. This was aptly illustrated by two British yachtsmen who, disappointed at their poor showing in a sailing competition, burned their boat and swam ashore. Frustrated consumers have boycotted manufacturers in efforts to improve product quality, and boycotted retailers in efforts to have prices lowered.

RATIONALIZATION. Sometimes individuals redefine the frustrating situation by inventing plausible reasons for not being able to attain their goals. Or they may decide that the goal really wasn't worth pursuing. Rationalizations are not deliberate lies, since the individual is not fully aware of the cognitive distortion that arises as a result of the frustrating situation. Thus a consumer who cannot give up smoking may convince herself she is smoking less if she smokes fewer (though longer) cigarettes each day.

REGRESSION. Sometimes people react to frustrating situations with childish or immature behavior. A woman attending a bargain sale, for example, may fight over merchandise and resort to tearing a garment that another woman will not relinquish, rather than allow her to have it.

WITHDRAWAL. Frustration is often resolved by simply withdrawing from the situation. A person who has difficulty using a sewing machine may simply stop sewing. Furthermore, she may rationalize her withdrawal by deciding that it really is cheaper to buy ready-made clothing; in addition, she may decide she can use her time more constructively in other activities.

PROJECTION. The individual may redefine the frustrating situation by projecting blame for his or her own failures and inabilities on other objects or persons. Thus the golfer who misses a stroke may blame his caddy or his ball; the driver who has an automobile accident may blame the other driver or the condition of the road.

AUTISM. Autism, or autistic thinking, refers to thinking that is almost completely dominated by needs and emotions, with little effort made to relate to reality. Such daydreaming, or fantasizing, enables the individual to attain imaginary gratification of unfulfilled needs. A person who is dieting may daydream about gorging with ice cream and candy bars; a middle-aged housewife may fantasize about a passionate love affair (see Figure 3-3).

IDENTIFICATION. Sometimes people resolve their feelings of frustration by subconsciously identifying with other persons or situations they consider relevant. Marketers have long recognized the importance of this defense mechanism and often use it as the basis for advertising appeals. That is why *slice-of-life* commercials or advertisements are so popular. Such advertisements usually portray a stereotypical situation in which an individual experiences a frustration and then overcomes the problem which has caused the frustration by using the advertised product (see Figure 3-4). If the viewer can identify with the frus-

**FIGURE 3-3** **Autism Appeal**

Courtesy of Evyan Perfums, Inc.

**FIGURE 3-4** Identification Appeal

**"You know the feeling. I thought everyone was staring at my hands."**

"Those horrid weathered age spots made me so self-conscious I hated to play cards. Then the girls told me about this cream Esoterica. What a blessing. It's just made to fade age spots. And it creams your hands beautiful besides. You'll see."

**Esoterica.**
**It's made to fade age spots**
(and it creams your hands beautiful besides).

ESOTERICA HAND LOTION

Original ESOTERICA

Cream and Lotion

Courtesy of Norcliff Thayer, Inc.

trating situation, he or she may very likely adopt the proposed solution and buy the product advertised. For example, a fellow who has difficulty attracting a girl he likes may decide to use the same mouthwash or shampoo or deodorant that "worked" for the man in the commercial. Interestingly enough, use of the product may increase his self-confidence sufficiently to enable him to achieve his goal.

**REPRESSION.** Another way that the individual avoids the tension arising from frustration is by repressing the unsatisfied need. Thus individuals may "forget" a need; that is, they force the need out of their conscious awareness. Sometimes repressed needs manifest themselves indirectly. A couple who cannot have children may surround themselves with plants or pets. The wife may teach school or work in a library; the husband may do volunteer work in a boys' club. The manifestation of repressed needs in a socially acceptable form of behavior is called *sublimation,* another type of defense mechanism.

This listing of defense mechanisms is far from exhaustive. People have virtually limitless ways of redefining frustrating situations so they can protect their self-esteem from the anxieties that result from experiencing failure. Based on their early experiences, individuals tend to develop their own characteristic ways of handling frustration. Marketers often consider this fact in their selection of advertising appeals. For example, a flour manufacturer may convince consumers that baking failures were caused by the ingredients they used, rather than the ineptness of their efforts.

### MULTIPLICITY OF NEEDS

Consumer behavior is often designed to fulfill more than one need. In fact, it is more likely that specific goals are selected because they fulfill several needs. We buy clothing for protection and for modesty; in addition, our clothing fulfills an enormous range of personal and social needs. Usually, however, there is one overriding (i.e., *prepotent*) need that initiates behavior. For example, a man may stop smoking because he wants to rid himself of a chronic cough; he may also be concerned about the cigarette-cancer controversy. In addition, his girlfriend may be "turned off" by the smell of cigarette smoke. If the cumulative amount of tension produced by each of these three reasons is sufficiently strong, he will stop smoking; however, just one of the reasons (e.g., his girlfriend's influence) may serve as the triggering mechanism. That one would be called the *prepotent* need.

### NEEDS AND GOALS VARY AMONG INDIVIDUALS

One cannot accurately infer motives from behavior. People with different needs may seek fulfillment through selection of the same goals, while people with the same needs may seek fulfillment through different goals. Consider the following examples. Five people who are active in a consumer organization may each belong for a different reason. The first may be genuinely concerned with protecting consumer interests, the second may be concerned about an increase in shoddy merchandise, the third may seek the social contacts that derive from organizational meetings, the fourth may enjoy the power inherent in directing a large group, and the fifth may enjoy the status provided by membership in a powerful organization.

Similarly, five people may be driven by the same need (e.g., an ego need) to seek fulfillment in different ways. The first may seek advancement and recognition through a professional career, the second may become active in the League of Women Voters, the third may join a health club, the fourth may become a gang leader, and the fifth may seek attention by monopolizing classroom discussions.

## Arousal of Motives

Most of the specific needs of an individual are dormant much of the time. The arousal of any particular set of needs at a specific point in time may be caused by internal stimuli found in the individual's physiological condition, emotional or cognitive processes, or by external stimuli in the outside environment.

### PHYSIOLOGICAL AROUSAL

Bodily needs at any one specific moment are rooted in an individual's physiological condition at that moment. A drop in blood sugar level or stomach contractions will trigger awareness of a hunger need. Secretion of sex hormones will awaken the sex need. A decrease in body temperature will induce shivering, which makes the individual aware of the need for warmth. Most of these physiological cues are involuntary; however, they arouse related needs which cause uncomfortable tensions until they are satisfied. For example, a shivering man may turn up the heat in his home to relieve his discomfort; he may also make a mental note to buy flannel pajamas.

### EMOTIONAL AROUSAL

Sometimes thinking or daydreaming results in the arousal or stimulation of *latent* needs. People who are bored or frustrated in attempts to achieve their goals often engage in daydreaming (autistic thinking), in which they imagine themselves in all sorts of desirable situations. These thoughts tend to arouse dormant needs, which may produce uncomfortable tensions that "push" them into goal-oriented behavior. A young girl who dreams of becoming a writer may identify with her favorite author and enroll in a writing course. Similarly, a young man who wants to play football professionally may identify with a major league player and use the products he endorses commercially.

A recent advertising campaign for Calvin Klein's new perfume, Obsession, relies on the emotional arousal of needs. The four 30-second TV commercials are based on "obsession" with a tempestuous woman, and portray men and women in situations of feverish, all-consuming intensity. Though most perfume advertising talks about the fragrance or scent of the product, these commercials are capped with the phrase "Ahhh . . . the smell of it," further stressing the all-consuming lust portrayed.[13]

### COGNITIVE AROUSAL

Sometimes a stimulus in the environment—such as a friend's remark, a news report, or an advertisement—will trigger thoughts that result in a cognitive awareness of needs. Thus an advertisement reporting low long distance rates can arouse a cognitive need to speak to friends or relatives in a foreign land. This is the basis for an AT&T campaign underscoring their inexpensive international long distance rates to many countries.

### ENVIRONMENTAL AROUSAL

The set of needs activated at a particular time are often determined by specific cues in the environment. Without these cues, the needs would remain dormant. Thus the six o'clock news, the sight or smell of food, food commercials on television, the children's return from school—all these may arouse the "need" for food. In such cases, modification of the environment may be necessary in order to reduce the arousal of hunger.

A most potent form of situational cue is the goal-object itself. A couple may experience an overwhelming need for a new dishwasher when they see their neighbor's new dishwasher; a person may suddenly experience a need for a new car when passing a dealer's display window. Sometimes an advertisement or other environmental cue produces a psychological imbalance in the viewer's mind. For example, a man who prides himself on his gardening may see an advertisement for a tractor mower that apparently works more efficiently than his own rotary mower. The ad may make him so unhappy with his old mower that he experiences severe tension until he buys himself a new tractor model.

When people live in a complex and highly varied environment, they experience many opportunities for need arousal. Conversely, when their environment is poor or deprived, fewer needs are activated. This explains why television has had such a mixed effect on the lives of the ghetto poor. It exposes them to various lifestyles and expensive products that they would not otherwise see, and it awakens wants and desires they have little opportunity or even hope of attaining. Thus, while it enriches their lives, television may also serve to frustrate their lives and sometimes results in the adoption of antisocial defense mechanisms such as aggression.

There are two opposing philosophies concerned with the arousal of human motives. The *behaviorist* school considers motivation to be a mechanical process; behavior is seen as the response to a stimulus, and elements of conscious thought are ignored. An extreme example of this **stimulus-response** theory of motivation is the impulse buyer, who largely reacts to external stimuli in the buying situation. The consumer's cognitive control is limited; he or she does not act, but *reacts* to stimuli in the marketplace.[14] The *cognitive* school believes that all behavior is directed at goal achievement. Needs and past experiences are reasoned, categorized, and transformed into attitudes and beliefs which act as predispositions to behavior. These predispositions are aimed at helping the person to satisfy needs and they determine the direction that the individual takes to achieve this satisfaction.[15]

## Diversity of Need Systems

For many years, psychologists and others interested in human behavior have attempted to develop exhaustive lists of human needs or motives. These lists have proved to be as diverse in content as they have been in length. Although there is little disagreement about specific *physiological* needs, there is considerable disagreement about specific *psychogenic* needs. For example, in 1923 Professor Daniel Starch of the Harvard Business School compiled a list of forty-four human motives for use as copy appeals (see Table 3-1).

In 1938, psychologist Henry Murray prepared a detailed list of twenty-eight psychogenic needs which have served as the basic constructs for a number of widely used personality tests (for example, the Thematic Apperception Technique and Edwards Personal Preference Schedule). Murray believed that everyone has the same basic set of needs, but that individuals differ in their priority ranking of these needs. Murray's basic needs include many motives that are assumed to play an important role in consumer behavior, such as *acquisition, achievement, recognition,* and *exhibition* (see Table 3-2).

Lists of human motives are often too long to be of practical use to marketers. The most useful kind of list is a limited one in which needs are sufficiently generic in title to subsume more detailed human needs. For example, one con-

**TABLE 3-1 Motives in Male and Female Adults**

| | |
|---|---|
| Appetite—Hunger | Respect for Deity |
| Love of Offspring | Sympathy for Others |
| Health | Protection of Others |
| Sex Attraction | Domesticity |
| Parental Affection | Social Distinction |
| Ambition | Devotion to Others |
| Pleasure | Hospitality |
| Bodily Comfort | Warmth |
| Possession | Imitation |
| Approval of Others | Courtesy |
| Gregariousness | Play—Sport |
| Taste | Managing Others |
| Personal Appearance | Coolness |
| Safety | Fear—Caution |
| Cleanliness | Physical Activity |
| Rest—Sleep | Manipulation |
| Home Comfort | Construction |
| Economy | Style |
| Curiosity | Humor |
| Efficiency | Amusement |
| Competition | Shyness |
| Cooperation | Teasing |

Source: Daniel Starch, Principles of Advertising (Chicago: A.W. Shaw & Co., 1923), 273.

**TABLE 3-2 Murray's List of Psychogenic Needs**

*Needs Associated with Inanimate Objects*
- Acquisition
- Conservance
- Order
- Retention
- Construction

*Needs That Reflect Ambition, Power, Accomplishment, and Prestige*
- Superiority
- Achievement
- Recognition
- Exhibition
- Inviolacy (inviolate attitude)
- Infavoidance (to avoid shame, failure, humiliation, ridicule)
- Defendance (defensive attitude)
- Counteraction (counteractive attitude)

*Needs Concerned with Human Power*
- Dominance
- Deference
- Similance (suggestible attitude)
- Autonomy
- Contrarience (to act differently from others)

*Sado-Masochistic Needs*
- Aggression
- Abasement

*Needs Concerned with Inhibition*
- Blamavoidance (to avoid blame)

*Needs Concerned with Affection between People*
- Affiliation
- Rejection
- Nurturance (to nourish, aid, or protect the helpless)
- Succorance (to seek aid, protection, or sympathy)
- Play

*Needs Concerned with Social Intercourse (the Needs to Ask and Tell)*
- Cognizance (inquiring attitude)
- Exposition (expositive attitude)

Source: Adapted from Henry A. Murray, "Types of Human Needs," in David C. McClelland, Studies in Motivation (New York: Appleton-Century-Crofts, 1955), 63–66. Reprinted by permission of Irvington Publishers, Inc.

sumer behaviorist grouped the various lists of psychogenic needs into just three broad categories: affectional needs, ego-bolstering needs, and ego-defensive needs.[16]

**Affectional needs** are described as the needs to form and maintain warm, harmonious, and emotionally satisfying relations with others.

**Ego-bolstering needs** are the needs to enhance or promote the personality (to achieve, to gain prestige and recognition, and to satisfy the ego through domination of others).

**Ego-defensive needs** are the needs to protect the personality (to avoid physical and psychological harm, to avoid ridicule and "loss of face," to prevent loss of prestige, and to avoid or obtain relief from anxiety).

While some psychologists have suggested that people have different need priorities based on their personalities, their experiences, their environments, and so forth, others believe that most human beings assign a similar priority ranking to their basic needs.

## HIERARCHY OF NEEDS

The first proponent of the theory of a universal **hierarchy of human needs** was Dr. Abraham Maslow, a psychologist who formulated a widely accepted theory of human motivation after some twenty years of clinical practice.[17] Maslow's theory postulates five basic levels of human needs, which rank in order of importance from low-level (*biogenic*) needs to higher-level *(psychogenic)* needs. It suggests that individuals seek to satisfy lower-level needs before higher-level needs emerge. The lowest level of chronically unsatisfied need an individual experiences serves to motivate his or her behavior; when that need is fairly well satisfied, a new (and higher) need emerges which the individual is motivated to fulfill. When this need is satisfied, a new (and still higher) need emerges, and so on. Of course, if a lower-level need experiences some renewed deprivation, it may temporarily become dominant again. Figure 3-5 presents Maslow's *hierarchy of needs* in diagrammatic form. For clarity, each level is depicted as mutually exclusive; however, according to the theory, there is some overlap between each level, as no need is ever completely satisfied. For this reason, though all levels of need below the dominant level continue to motivate behavior to some extent, the *prime* motivator—the major driving force within the individual—is the lowest level of need that remains largely unsatisfied.

PHYSIOLOGICAL NEEDS. In the hierarchy of needs theory, the first and most basic level of needs is *physiological.* These needs, which are required to sustain biological life, include food, water, air, shelter, clothing, sex—all the biogenic needs, in fact, that were listed as primary needs earlier. According to Maslow,

**FIGURE 3-5 Maslow's Hierarchy of Human Needs**

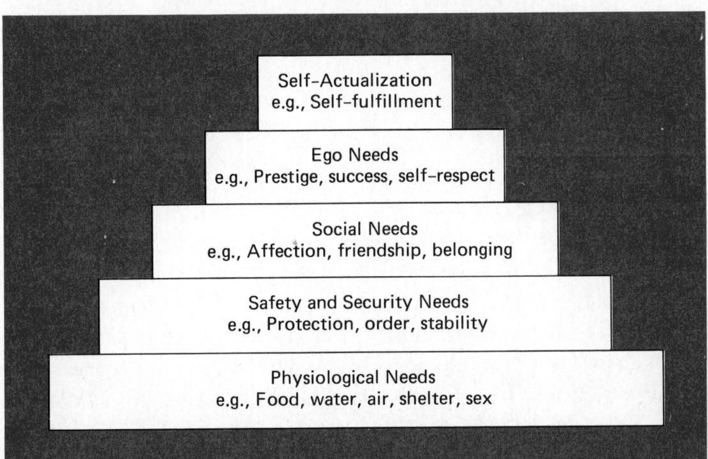

physiological needs are dominant when they are chronically unsatisfied: "For the man who is extremely and dangerously hungry, no other interest exists but food. He dreams food, he remembers food, he thinks about food, he emotes only about food, he perceives only food and he wants only food.[18] For most citizens in this country, the biogenic needs are generally satisfied; thus the higher-level needs are dominant. However, the lives of the unfortunate homeless who can be found in many of our major cities are focused almost entirely on biogenic needs: the need for food, for clothing, for shelter from the elements in freezing weather.

SAFETY NEEDS. After the first level of needs is satisfied, *safety* and *security* needs become the driving force behind an individual's behavior. These needs are concerned with much more than physical safety. They include order, stability, routine, familiarity, and certainty—the knowledge, for example, that the individual will eat dinner not only that day and the following day, but also far into the future.

The impetus for the growth of labor unions in the United States derives from the safety need, since unions provide members with the security of knowing that their employment does not depend on the day-to-day whims of their employers. The social welfare programs enacted by this country (e.g., social security, unemployment insurance, Medicare) have traditionally provided some degree of security to American citizens. Savings accounts, insurance policies, education, and vocational training are all means by which individuals satisfy the need for security.

Like the physiological need level, the safety level tends to be fairly well satisfied for many American citizens. However, in times of real or threatened cutbacks in federal spending for social programs, such as the threatened reduction of social security benefits, the security need becomes manifest among the poor and the elderly.

SOCIAL NEEDS. The third level of Maslow's hierarchy includes such needs as love, affection, belonging, and acceptance. People seek warm and satisfying human relationships with other people and are motivated by love for their families (see Figure 3-6). The importance of group acceptance and group influence on consumer behavior is examined more fully in Chapter 11. Because of the importance of *social motives* in our society, advertisers of personal care products often emphasize this appeal in their advertisements.

EGOISTIC NEEDS. When the social needs are more or less satisfied, the fourth level of Maslow's hierarchy becomes operative. This level is concerned with *egoistic needs*. These needs can take either an inward or an outward orientation, or both. Inwardly directed ego needs reflect an individual's need for self-acceptance, for self-esteem, for success, for independence, for personal satisfaction with a job well done. Outwardly directed ego needs include the need for prestige, for reputation, for status, for recognition from others. The desire to "keep up with the Joneses" is a reflection of an outwardly oriented ego need. Figure 3-7 presents an advertisement designed to appeal to the ego need.

FIGURE 3-6 Social Appeal

Courtesy of Canon USA, Inc.

NEED FOR SELF-ACTUALIZATION. According to Maslow, most people do not satisfy their ego needs sufficiently ever to move to the fifth level—the need for *self-actualization* or self-fulfillment. This need refers to an individual's desire to fulfill his or her own potential—to become everything he or she is capable of becoming. "What a man *can* be, he must be."[19] This need is expressed in different ways by different people. A young man may desire to be the best athlete he possibly can (e.g., Eric Heiden, who won more gold medals in speed skating in the 1980 Olympics than any individual in history, worked single-mindedly

FIGURE 3-7 Egoistic Appeal

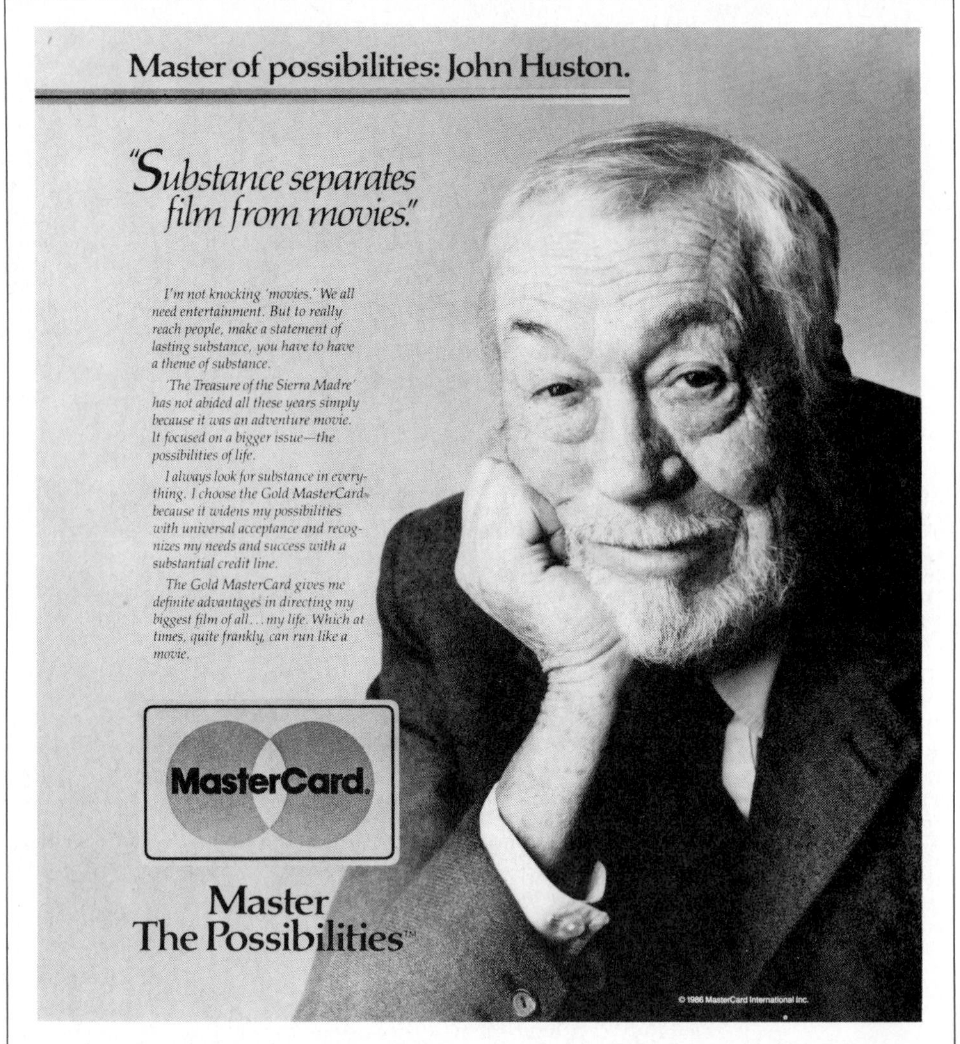


Courtesy of MasterCard International Inc.

for years to become the best in his sport). An artist may need to express herself on canvas; a business executive may try to build an empire. Maslow noted that the self-actualization need is not necessarily a creative urge, but that in people with some capacity for creativity, it is likely to take that form. Advertisements for art lessons, for banking services, and even for new graduate recruitment often try to appeal to the self-actualization need. Figure 3-8 presents an advertisement designed to appeal to this need.

In summary, the *hierarchy of needs* theory postulates a five-level hierarchy of prepotent human needs. Higher-order needs become the driving force behind human behavior as lower-level needs are satisfied. The theory says, in effect, that dissatisfaction, not satisfaction, motivates behavior.

FIGURE 3-8 Self-Actualization Appeal

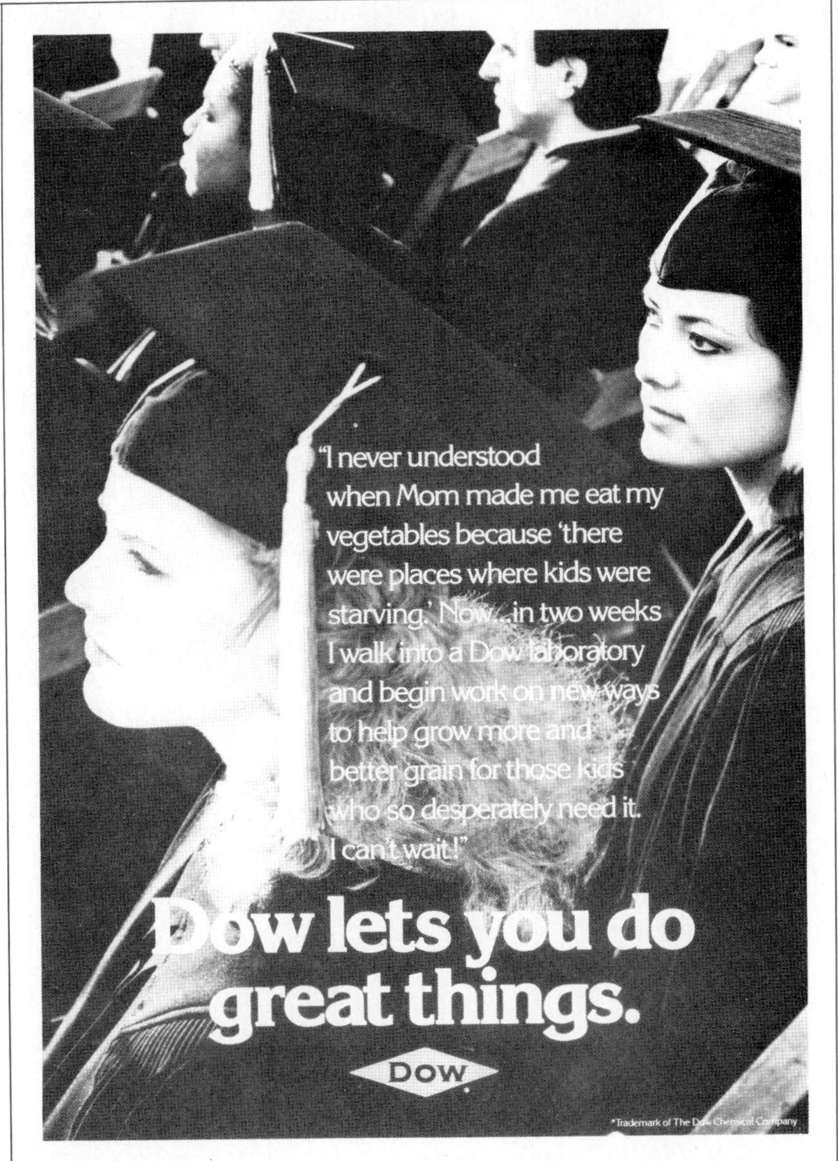


Courtesy of Dow Chemical USA

## AN EVALUATION OF THE NEED HIERARCHY

The need hierarchy has received wide acceptance in many social disciplines because it appears to reflect the assumed or inferred motivations of many people in our society. The five levels of need postulated by the hierarchy are generic enough to encompass most lists of individual needs. Some critics, however, maintain that Maslow's concepts are too general. To say that hunger and self-esteem are similar, in that both are needs, is to obscure the urgent, involuntary nature of the former and the largely conscious, voluntary nature of the latter. The major problem with the theory is that it cannot be tested empirically; there is no way to measure precisely how well satisfied one need is before the next higher need becomes operative. The need hierarchy also appears to be very closely bound to our contemporary American culture (i.e., it appears to be culture and time bound).

Despite these criticisms, Maslow's hierarchy is a useful tool for understanding consumer motivations and is readily adaptable to marketing strategy, primarily because consumer goods often serve to satisfy each of the need levels. For example, individuals buy houses, food, and clothing to satisfy physiological needs; they buy insurance and radial tires and vocational training to satisfy safety and security needs. Almost all personal care products (cosmetics, toothpaste, shaving cream) are bought to satisfy social needs. Luxury products such as furs or jewels or big cars are usually bought to fulfill ego needs, and college training and banking services are sold as ways to achieve self-fulfillment.

The hierarchy provides a useful, comprehensive framework for marketers trying to develop appropriate advertising appeals for their products. It is adaptable in two ways: first, it enables marketers to focus their advertising appeals on a need level that is likely to be shared by a large segment of the prospective audience; second, it facilitates product positioning.

SEGMENTATION APPLICATIONS. The need hierarchy is often used as the basis for market segmentation, as specific advertising appeals are directed to individuals on one or more need levels. For example, soft-drink ads directed to teenagers may stress a social appeal by showing a group of young people mutually sharing good times as well as the advertised product. Figure 3-9 presents an ad directed to would-be achievers in a variety of occupations.

POSITIONING APPLICATIONS. Another way to utilize the hierarchy is for positioning products—that is, deciding how the product is to be perceived by prospective consumers. The key to positioning is to find a niche that is not occupied by a competing brand. This application of the need hierarchy relies on the notion that no need is ever fully satisfied, that it always continues to be somewhat motivating. For example, most manufacturers of luxury cars use status appeals ("Impress your friends"), or self-actualizing appeals ("You deserve the very best"), or even social appeals ("The whole family can ride in luxurious comfort"). To find a unique position among its luxury competitors, Mercedes Benz has used a safety appeal in advertisements to well-to-do executives ("When your wife is driving the two children home on a dark and stormy night, you can relax if she's driving the Mercedes").

It is interesting, in light of the cigarette-cancer controversy, to recall that in the late 1940s, most cigarette commercials stressed medical endorsements ("Two out of three doctors interviewed smoke Camels"). Cigarette smoking was advertised as relaxing, soothing, and good for the nervous system; in effect, as a means of fulfilling physiological needs. Then a new competitive campaign broke upon the scene which **repositioned** the Old Golds brand by suggesting social fulfillment. The advertisement showed a young man surrounded by a bevy of beautiful girls with a headline that read: "For a treat instead of a treat-

**FIGURE 3-9** Appeal to Would-Be Achievers Source: Reprinted with permission of Dow Jones & Company, Inc. and Fallon McElligott Rice. © 1985.

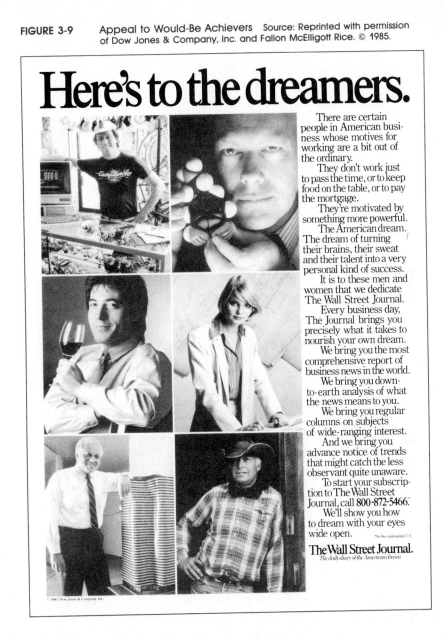


ment, smoke Old Golds." By repositioning its product to fulfill social needs, Old Golds captured a significant share of the market.

VERSATILITY OF THE NEED HIERARCHY. One way to illustrate the usefulness of the need hierarchy in designing promotional programs is to show how workable appeals for a single product can be developed from each level. Consider, for example, the following potential promotional appeals for a microwave oven. An appeal to *physiological* needs would show how quickly food can be prepared (i.e., satisfy hunger needs) in a microwave oven. A *safety* appeal would demonstrate how safe the microwave oven is in comparison with other cooking appliances (e.g., no burned fingers). *Social* appeals can be invoked by illustrations of party and holiday dinners prepared with a microwave oven. *Status* is easily demonstrated through a standard appeal such as "Every well-equipped kitchen must have a microwave oven." Finally, appeals to *self-actualization* may point out to career couples how easy it is to prepare last-minute dinners after a long and challenging work-day.

## A TRIO OF NEEDS

Some psychologists believe in the existence of a trio of basic needs: the needs for **power**, for **affiliation**, and for **achievement**.[20] These needs can each be subsumed in Maslow's need hierarchy; considered individually, however, they each have a unique relevance to consumer motivation.

POWER NEEDS. The power need relates to an individual's desire to control his or her environment. It includes the need to control other persons and various objects. This need appears to be closely related to the ego need, in that many individuals experience increased self-enhancement when they exercise power over objects or people. A number of products lend themselves to promises of power or superiority for users. An automobile advertisement might stress enormous speed capability, even though this capability can rarely be exercised because of legal or practical limits. This is consistent with a recent study showing that individuals with a high power need were less likely to consider factual information and more likely to consider a smaller number of alternatives than persons with a low power need.[21] The headline in Figure 3-10 could be viewed as an appeal to the power need.

AFFILIATION NEEDS. Affiliation is a well-known and well-researched social motive that has far-reaching influence on consumer behavior. The affiliation need suggests that behavior is highly influenced by the desire for friendship, for acceptance, for belonging (see Figure 3-11). People with high affiliation needs tend to have a strong social dependence on others. They often select goods they feel will meet with the approval of friends. People who go to crafts fairs or to garage sales, teenagers who hang out at malls on Saturdays, car buffs who congregate at automobile shows, often do so more for the satisfaction of being with others than for making a purchase. Such individuals appreciate the assistance and the opinions of friendly salespeople and may purchase clothing or even household goods to win the approval of an encouraging salesperson. People with high affiliation needs often adapt their purchase behavior to the norms and standards of their reference groups (see Chapter 11).

ACHIEVEMENT NEEDS. A number of research studies have focused on the achievement need.[22] Individuals with a strong need for achievement often regard personal accomplishment as an end in itself. The achievement need is closely related to the egoistic need, in that satisfaction with a job well done serves to enhance the individual's self-esteem. It is also related to the self-actualization need. People with a high need for achievement have certain traits that

FIGURE 3-10 Appeal to the Power Need

EMERGE FROM THE FREEWAY VICTORIOUS, NOT VICTIMIZED.
Highways extract a bitter toll from modern drivers. Not at the coin booths, but in the continual onslaught of noise, traffic jams and pollution.
For those forced to cope with such a demoralizing situation, BMW has engineered a most vivifying solution. The 528e.
A car whose high-torque, high-efficiency* Eta engine lets you power through traffic without endlessly shifting through the gears.
Whose orthopedically-designed seats and ergonomically-designed climate controls ensure you not only negotiate the highway nimbly, but navigate it in total comfort.
Whose ingenious ABS anti-lock braking system can actually mean the difference between emerging victorious from hazardous roads, and not emerging at all.
And whose parts and pieces mesh together so well that one automotive critic was moved to characterize the 528e as "sumptuous in a no-nonsense way and immaculately crafted" (Motor Trend).
Your local BMW dealer would be happy to arrange a thorough test drive of the BMW 528e. A triumph of technology in which every day you share in the victory.
BMW
THE ULTIMATE DRIVING MACHINE.
*EPA-estimated 20 mpg, 24 highway. Fuel efficiency figures are for comparison only. Your actual mileage may vary, depending on speed, weather and trip length. ©1985 BMW of North America, Inc. The BMW trademark and logo are registered.
LET YOUR METROPOLITAN AREA BMW DEALER ARRANGE A THOROUGH TEST DRIVE.


Courtesy of BMW of North America, Inc.

make them open to relevant appeals. They are more self-confident, enjoy taking calculated risks, research their environment actively, and are very much interested in feedback (see Figure 3-12). Their interest in money rewards or profits is primarily due to the feedback that money provides as to how they are doing. In an old movie called *The Wheeler Dealers,* James Garner explains that it's not the money that drives him and his friends to make deals, ". . . it's just the way we keep score." People with high achievement needs like situations in which they can take personal responsibility for finding solutions.[23] They prefer

**FIGURE 3-11** Advertisement Depicting the Affiliation Need

Kent Connection.
6034
6034
Chairman Harry Bruce and President Jim Martin were on the right track when they enrolled at Kent State University.
Today, as the driving forces of the Illinois Central Gulf Railroad, they still carry Kent State Alumni Cards to remind them of their strong ties with Kent State.
**Harry J. Bruce,** chairman and chief executive officer of ICG, holds a bachelor's degree in transportation and industrial management from Kent State and a master's degree from the University of Tennessee. For Bruce, transportation is truly his life, from his first job as a fireman in the Hoboken yards to his joining Illinois Central Gulf as senior vice president. In addition to his present position, Bruce serves on the ICG Board of Directors and is chairman of the board's executive committee.
Bruce reflects on his college days with pride: "I still remember the quality of my math and English faculty members at Kent. The people in English, especially in creative writing, helped bring out some latent talent in me." Bruce is currently writing his third book.
**James E. Martin,** president and chief operating officer of ICG, started "workin' on the railroad" as a yard clerk right out of high school. Later, Martin earned a bachelor of science degree in education.
"When I left Kent I had a degree in education and a desire to coach," he recalls. "A supervisor on the New York Central urged me to give railroading a year's try." The rest is history. Since then, Martin has demonstrated the value of a good education, hard work, and a willingness to try. His drive and determination have been an integral part of ICG's progress.
The successes of Harry Bruce and Jim Martin have been impressive right down the line — from their beginnings at KSU to their powerful positions with one of America's major railroads. When you want to start making tracks towards your future, make your connection with Kent State University — an experience in excellence.
KentState
University
Kent, OH 44242
— an experience in excellence
MEMBER
Kent State University
Alumni Association


Courtesy of Kent State University

activities that allow self-evaluation[24] and respond positively to feedback concerning their own competence.[25]

High-achievement people are often good prospects for cleverly presented innovative products, for do-it-yourself projects, for older houses, and even for moderately speculative stock issues. They are also likely to be receptive to appeals from advertisers in whom they recognize similar needs (i.e., with whom they can identify). For example, the Nissan slogan "We are driven" might strike a responsive note in individuals with high achievement needs.

**FIGURE 3-12** Appeal to High Need Achievers

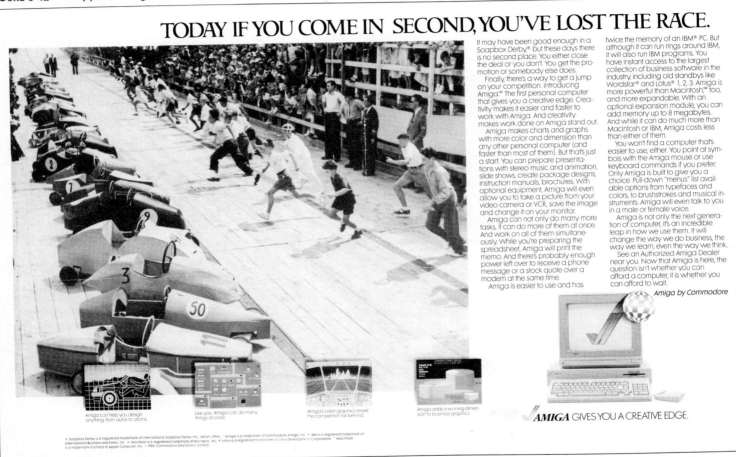

Courtesy of Commodore Business Machines

Several research studies indicate that individuals with a high need for achievement may constitute a special market segment for certain products. For example, one study found that men with a high need for achievement tend to favor products considered virile and masculine, such as boating equipment, straight razors, and skis. Men with low need for achievement scores preferred to buy products characterized as meticulous or fastidious, such as mouthwash, deodorants, and automatic dishwashers.[26] Another study suggested that many of the people who engage in active outdoor sports have a high need for achievement.[27] People with a high need for achievement are more likely to patronize stores that not only use appeals of excellence, but liberally use positive achievement words.[28]

A recent study showed that the dominant needs of people may be related to their career progress. The study showed that *achievement* was a dominant need for MBA students and Air Force officers, the need for *power* was dominant for partners in a "Big Eight" accounting firm, and the need for *affiliation* was dominant among high school seniors, freshman cadets at the Air Force Academy, and undergraduate accounting students. Such findings imply that different promotional approaches should be targeted at consumers according to their occupational progress.[29]

In summary, individuals with specific psychological needs tend to be receptive to advertising appeals directed to those needs. They also tend to be receptive to certain kinds of products. Thus, awareness of such needs provides marketers with additional bases on which to segment their markets.

## THE MEASUREMENT OF MOTIVES

How are motives identified? How are they measured? How do researchers know which motives are responsible for certain kinds of behavior? These are difficult questions to answer because motives are **hypothetical constructs;** that is, they cannot be seen or touched, handled, smelled, or otherwise tangibly observed. For this reason, no one measurement method can be considered a reliable index. Instead, researchers usually rely on a combination of methods used in tandem to try to establish the presence and/or the strength of various motives. These methods are complementary and include **observation and inference, self-reports,** and **projective techniques**.

### Observation and Inference

Motivations are often inferred from the actions and statements of individuals. If a person undertakes extensive search behavior for a specific kind of product and continues such activity until he or she makes a purchase selection, then inferences are often made as to the need that motivated the search behavior. For example, if, prior to buying a washing machine, a couple visits appliance stores to examine and to price washing machines, and if they study appliance advertisements and seek relevant information from *Consumer Reports,* the logical inference is that they have a need for an efficient, practical way to wash clothes. Of course, motive identification through inference can be somewhat circular in reasoning; that is, a motive may be attributed to observed behavior and then be used to explain the behavior from which it was inferred. Observers may assume that a man's purchase of a mink coat is motivated by his need for prestige, and then they "explain" his wearing of mink as a reflection of his need for prestige. Mink, however, is actually an extremely warm, durable, and lightweight fur. For someone who can afford it, a mink coat may simply be the most practical way to keep warm in the winter.

Although we may feel that we can plausibly infer a motive from certain kinds of behavior, we cannot validly claim to do so. For example, it may seem reasonable to assume that people who devote time and effort to school board activities do so out of esteem or self-actualization needs; in reality, they may find such activities a way of fulfilling social needs. Similarly, it may seem reasonable to assume that a person who works long hours in business has a strong achievement motive, but in reality he or she may simply have nothing of interest to do in the evenings.

In addition to observation, another source of inference about the motives of individuals is the nonstructured **depth interview**. In this type of interview, respondents are questioned individually for as long as several hours by an interviewer who is trained to establish rapport and not to guide the discussion excessively. Respondents are encouraged to talk freely about their activities or interests, or about a specific subject or brand under study. Verbatim accounts of interviews are then carefully studied, together with reports of respondents' moods and any gesture or body language they might have used to convey attitudes or motives. Such studies are very useful, especially for giving marketers a lead on appeals they might use.

A variation of the depth interview is the so-called **focus group**, in which eight to ten participants are encouraged to discuss their product usage, product reactions, interests, attitudes, lifestyles, and so on. Though similar in many respects to the depth interview, focus groups rely on the principles of *group dynamics* to yield richer insights than may be possible by interviewing the same people sequentially. Focus groups can be done in much less time and therefore are much less expensive to conduct than depth interviews. For example, a researcher can conduct two focus groups—with a total of twenty respondents—in one afternoon, while it could take that same researcher six or seven days to conduct twenty individual depth interviews.

Nevertheless, some marketers still prefer the individual in-depth interview, because they feel that the respondent is free of group pressure, is less likely to give socially desirable responses, is more likely to remain attentive the whole time and, because of the greater personal attention, is more likely to reveal new information.[30]

A criticism of the depth interview is that while it is often aimed at developing new products and advertising themes, it is frequently focused too narrowly on existing products. To overcome this problem, one market research agency uses "storytelling" as a vehicle to expand the insights that depth interviews typically provide. Consumers' anecdotes regarding the use of the product or service under study provide important insights into what the product means to them. For example, one marketer was interested in researching entertainment, media, and fitness preferences among college students. Students were asked a purposely broad question: "What are college students doing now that they weren't doing a year or two ago?" Areas of direct interest to the marketer were probed later. Many students expressed strong identification with their parents' preference for classic clothing (often previously worn by their parents), and nostalgia for past eras they have never known. Clearly, such findings have important implications for marketing to today's college students.[31]

Because focus group interviews are relatively inexpensive and can be completed in much less time than other research techniques, they are gaining in popularity. Obviously, analysis of responses elicited in either a depth interview or a focus group requires a great deal of skill on the part of the researcher, and critics warn that the techniques can be overused.[32]

To avoid errors of inference, a motivational analysis that is based on observation or depth interviews is often supplemented with other methods, such as subjective or self reports.

## Self-Reports

Some researchers claim that the best way to find out about the needs and goals of individuals is simply to ask them, either verbally or with a written questionnaire. A number of pencil-and-paper "tests" given to consumers inquire directly about their wants, desires, fears, goals, successes, failures. The information obtained is then quantified (assigned a numerical score) to yield a measure of the strength of a specific need or motive.

There are two potential problems with self-reports. First, individuals may not themselves be aware of the actual reasons or motives underlying their behavior and may unconsciously rationalize their actions; that is, they may assign reasons or motives that are acceptable to their personalities but are not, in fact, accurate. They do this with no awareness that they are rationalizing. A couple may justify a move to the suburbs by saying they want more room and fresh air for the children, when their actual motive is to escape the anonymity of big-city apartment life. Or they may send their children to summer camp because "the fresh air and organized activities are good for them," but may not consciously realize that they do so primarily to free themselves from oppressive child care responsibilities for two months.

Aside from unconsciously rationalizing their own motives, people may be unwilling to reveal their true motives and are inclined to give *socially desirable* (i.e., socially acceptable) responses. Thus they may deliberately falsify self-report inventories to impress the researcher, to please the researcher, or to avoid personal embarrassment. It is difficult for a researcher to distinguish among true reports, rationalized reports, or deliberately falsified reports. For this reason, psychologists and other researchers interested in motivation have developed techniques designed to combat rationalization of motives and falsification of self-reports. Some researchers report using *biobehavioral measures* to complement the respondent's verbal responses. Here biological evidence such as brain waves, blood volume, and heart activity are used to evaluate the reliability of the subject's responses concerning attitudes and feelings about the product or advertisement.[33]

Others report using *response latency*—that is, the speed at which the respondent gives the answer to the question—as an indicator of the degree of his or her motivation. One study showed that in a phone interview, faster responses to questions regarding preferences between two alternatives indicated a stronger preference.[34] In another study, the motivating strength of commercials was evaluated by the speed at which respondents answered preference questions regarding the advertised brands after viewing the commercials. Advertisements which evoked quicker responses to the preference questions were viewed as more motivating than commercials which generated slower responses.[35]

Researchers have also developed techniques designed to delve below the consumer's level of conscious awareness, to tap the underlying motives of individuals despite their unconscious rationalizations or conscious concealment. These methods are called **projective techniques.**

## Projective Techniques

Projective techniques are designed to reveal a person's true feelings and motivations. They consist of a variety of *disguised tests* that contain ambiguous stimuli, such as incomplete sentences, untitled pictures or cartoons, inkblots, word-association tests, and other-person characterizations. (See Figures 3-13 and

FIGURE 3-13 Example of Thematic Apperception Test

**FIGURE 3-14** Applications of Projective Techniques Used in Consumer Research

WORD ASSOCIATION

Respondents are presented with a series of words or phrases and are are asked to answer quickly with the first word that comes to mind after hearing each stimulus word.

*Application:* AT&T used this approach to choose the name for long distance direct dialing from among several alternatives. Respondents interpreted the name "Nationwide Dialing" as "worldwide" dialing. The name "Custom Toll Dialing" was associated with "money," "charges," and the cost of a long distance phone call. The name "Direct Distance Dialing" was chosen by AT&T because it communicated to respondents the notion of long distance dialing without operator assistance and had no unfavorable associations.[a]

SENTENCE COMPLETION

The beginning of a sentence is read to the respondent, who is asked to complete it with the first thought that comes to mind.

*Application:* In an effort to create more effective advertising, a study was conducted to probe the motivation for buying cars. The results indicated that men and women view automobiles differently. When women were asked to complete the sentence: "When you first get a car, . . . "their responses were in the direction of "you can't wait till you drive" and "you would go for a ride." Men's responses to the same sentence stem were in the direction of "you take good care of it," "check the engine," and "polish it." These results indicate that for women a car is something to use, while men view a car as something for which they should be protective and responsible.[b]

THE THIRD PERSON TECHNIQUE

Respondents are asked to describe a third person about whom they are given some information.

*Application:* When instant coffee was introduced in 1950, a study was conducted to identify the symbolic meaning of the new product. Two groups of homemaker respondents were each given a shopping list that was identical except for the type of coffee listed. The first group's shopping list included instant coffee; the other group's list included drip grind coffee. Respondents were asked to describe the woman whose shopping list they saw, and the differences in their descriptions were attributed to the only experimental variable: the type of coffee listed. Homemakers perceived women who used instant coffee as lazy housekeepers and poor wives, and users of regular grind coffee as thrifty and good wives. In 1950, this research suggested that convenience foods evoked a feeling of guilt and skepticism. However, a 1970 replication of this study indicated that the stigma associated with instant coffee had disappeared; this was attributed to the general acceptance of instant coffee and convenience foods which had taken place since the original study was conducted.[c]

THEMATIC APPERCEPTION TEST

Respondents are asked to interpret one or more pictures or cartoons relating to the product or topic under study.

*Application:* A study was designed to measure the price/quality perception of women regarding cosmetics. One-half of the respondents were shown a cartoon of a woman buying a 49-cent beauty cream; the other half were presented with the picture of a woman buying a $5 beauty cream. Both groups were asked to describe the beauty cream. The 49-cent product was perceived as "greasy and oily" and bought by someone who "falls for advertising claims and doesn't have too much money to spend on cosmetics". The $5 cream was viewed as leaving the skin "clear, refreshed and young-looking", "softening and cleansing the skin", and purchased by "someone who cares what she looks like—possibly a business woman". These results demonstrate that women consider more expensive cosmetics to be of higher quality.[d]

[a]Paul E. Green and Donald S. Tull, *Research for Marketing Decisions,* 3rd ed. (Englewood Cliffs, N.J.: Prentice-Hall, 1975), 141–43.

[b]J. W. Newman, *Motivation Research and Marketing Management* (Cambridge, Mass: Harvard University Graduate School of Business Administration, 1957), 227–28.

[c]Mason Haire, "Projective Techniques in Marketing Research," *Journal of Marketing,* 14 (April 1950), 649–50; and Frederick E. Webster, Jr., and Fredrick Von Pechmann, "A Replication of the 'Shopping List' Study," *Journal of Marketing,* 34 (April 1970), 61–63.

[d]Green and Tull, *Research for Marketing Decisions.*

3-14 for examples of projective tests.) The respondent is asked to complete, describe, or explain the meaning of various stimuli. The theory behind projective tests is that individuals' own needs and motives will influence how they perceive ambiguous stimuli. The stories they tell or the sentences they complete are actually projections of their own feelings, though they attribute their responses to something or someone else. In this way, respondents are expected to reveal their underlying needs, wants, fears, aspirations, and motives, whether or not they are fully aware of them. For example, if a subject looks at a picture of a man wearing a business suit and describes him as a "big-shot," one may infer that the subject is concerned with ego needs.

The basic assumption underlying projective techniques is that respondents are unaware that they are exposing their own feelings. This is sometimes illustrated by the old joke about a psychologist who shows a subject a series of geometric figures and asks him to describe what he sees. In each case, the subject reports seeing a lewd or lascivious scene. When the psychologist comments that the subject has an obvious sexual fixation, the latter retorts, "It's not *my* fixation; after all, it's *you* who are showing me the dirty pictures."

Obviously, the identification and measurement of human motives is still a very inexact process. Some psychologists are concerned that most measurement techniques do not meet the crucial test criteria of **validity** and **reliability.** *Validity* ensures that the test measures what it purports to measure; *reliability* refers to the consistency with which the test measures what it does measure.

The findings of projective research methods are highly dependent upon the analyst; they focus not on the data themselves, but on what the analyst *thinks* they imply. Therefore, by using a combination of assessments based on behavioral data (e.g., observation), subjective data (e.g., self-reports), and projective techniques, many consumer researchers feel confident that they gain more valuable insights into consumer motivations than they would by using any one technique alone. Though some marketers are concerned that such research does not produce hard numbers that objectively "prove" a point under investigation, others are convinced that qualitative studies can be just as revealing, and often less expensive, than quantitative studies. However, there is a clear need for improved methodological procedures for measuring human motives.

## MOTIVATIONAL RESEARCH

The term **motivational research,** which should include all types of research into human motives, is generally used to refer to qualitative research designed to uncover the consumer's *subconscious* or *hidden motivations.*[36] Operating on the premise that consumers are not always aware of the reasons for their actions, motivational research attempts to discover underlying feelings, attitudes, and emotions concerning product, service, or brand use. Table 3-3 describes the "personalities" consumers have attributed to selected products through motivational research studies.

**TABLE 3-3 Selective Product Personality Profiles**

| PRODUCT | DESCRIPTION OF PRODUCT PERSONALITY |
|---|---|
| prunes | Long identified with their laxative properties, prunes are a symbol of old age; they are like dried-out spinsters, and have none of the soft pleasurableness of plums. |
| rice | Rice is viewed as a feminine food. It typically suggests a strong, healthy, fertile female. Throwing rice at newly married couples symbolizes the wish that the marriage be blessed with children. |
| power tools | Power tools are a symbol of manliness. They represent masculine skill and competence, and are often bought more for their symbolic value than for active do-it-yourself applications. Ownership of a good power tool or circular saw provides a man with feelings of omnipotence. |
| ice cream | Ice cream is often associated with love and affection. It derives particular potency from childhood memories, when it was given to a child for being "good," and withheld as an instrument of punishment. People refer to ice cream as something they "love" to eat. |

Adapted from Handbook of Consumer Motivations, by Ernest Dichter. Copyright 1964. McGraw-Hill Book Company. Used with permission of McGraw-Hill Book Company.

## Methodology and Analysis

Because emotional feelings are not easily or accurately revealed by consumers on direct questioning, motivational researchers use clinical psychological methods such as the *nondirective* (depth) *interview* and *projective techniques* (word-association tests, sentence completion tests, inkblot and cartoon tests, other-person characterizations). Careful analysis of the data generated by these techniques provides varying degrees of insight into the underlying reasons why consumers buy or do not buy products or product categories under study.

Motivational research analyses often suggest new ways for marketers to present their products to the public. For example, a study prepared for a hair coloring manufacturer revealed that women regarded becoming blond as a way of changing their image and personality. Respondents considered blonds to be attractive and sexy women, leading "fun" and "swinging" lives. These and other findings provided the company with substantial material on which to base a new advertising campaign.

## Development of Motivational Research

Motivational research became popular in the early 1950s when Dr. Ernest Dichter, formerly a psychoanalyst in Vienna, adapted his psychoanalytic techniques to the study of consumer buying habits. Marketing research up to this time had focused on *what* consumers did (i.e., quantitative, descriptive studies) rather than on *why* they did it. Marketers were quickly fascinated by the glib, entertaining, and usually surprising explanations offered for consumer behavior, especially since many of these explanations were rooted in sex. (Most early motivational researchers were Freudian in their thinking and took the approach that all behavior is sexually motivated [see Chapter 4].) Thus marketers were told that cigarettes and lifesaver candies were bought because of their sexual symbolism, that men regarded convertible cars as surrogate mistresses, that women baked cakes to fulfill their reproductive yearnings.[37] Before long, almost every advertising agency on Madison Avenue had a psychologist on staff to conduct motivational research studies.

## Shortcomings of Motivational Research

By the early 1960s, marketers realized that motivational research had some drawbacks. Because of the intensive nature of qualitative research, samples were necessarily small; thus there was concern about generalizing findings to the total market. Also, marketers soon realized that the analysis of projective tests and depth interviews was highly subjective. The same data given to three different analysts could produce three different reports, each offering its own explanation of the consumer behavior examined. Critics noted that many of the projective tests that were used had originally been developed for clinical purposes, rather than for studies of marketing or consumer behavior. (One of the basic criteria for test development is that tests be developed and validated for the specific purpose and on the specific audience from which information is desired.)

Finally, too many motivational researchers imputed highly exotic reasons to rather prosaic consumer purchases. Marketers began to question their recommendations (e.g., Is it better to sell a man a pair of suspenders as a means of holding up his pants or as a "reaction to castration anxiety"? Is it easier to persuade a woman to buy a garden hose to water her lawn or as a symbol of the "futility of genital competition for the female?")[38] Motivational researchers often came up with sexual explanations for the most mundane activities. For example, an ad showing a hostess behind a beverage table filled with large bottles of soft drinks was commended by a leading motivational researcher for its "clever use of phallic symbolism."[39]

## Motivational Research Today

Despite these criticisms, motivational research is still being used by marketers who want to gain deeper insights into the whys of consumer behavior than conventional marketing research techniques can yield. There is new and compelling evidence that the unconscious is the site of a far larger portion of mental life than even Freud envisioned. Research studies show that the unconscious mind may understand and respond to meaning, form emotional responses, and guide most actions largely independent of conscious awareness. The findings imply that, despite the subjective belief of being in conscious control of their feelings, thoughts, decisions, and actions, people are directed far more than they realize by their subconscious mind.[40]

Since motivational research often reveals unsuspected consumer motivations concerning product or brand usage, its principal use is in the development of new ideas for promotional campaigns, ideas that can penetrate the consumer's conscious awareness by appealing to unrecognized needs. Thus manufacturers of house paint were able to convince Minnesota consumers to try more vivid colors on the exteriors of their homes after researchers discovered a latent "color hunger" among people living in that gray, wintry climate.[41] Motivational research also provides marketers with a basic orientation for new-product categories and enables them to explore consumer reactions to ideas and advertising copy at an early stage so that costly errors can be avoided. Furthermore, motivational research provides marketers with basic cues for more structured, quantitative marketing research studies—studies that can be conducted on larger, more representative samples of consumers.

Motivation research has also been used "profitably" by nonprofit organizations. For example, Dichter found that people subconsciously resist making charitable donations because they feel that once they have given, they will no longer be the objects of attention. Using that insight, the United Way and other fundraisers now spend almost as much time thanking people for their donations as soliciting new donations in order to generate goodwill for future campaigns.[42]

Motivational research continues to be a useful tool for many marketers who want to know the actual reasons underlying consumer behavior. However, it is no longer considered the *only* method for uncovering human motivation, but rather one of a variety of research techniques available to the consumer researcher.

## *summary*

Motivation is the driving force within individuals that impels them to action. This driving force is produced by a state of uncomfortable tension, which exists as the result of an unfilled need. All individuals have needs, wants, and desires. The individual's subconscious drive to reduce need-induced tension results in behavior that he or she anticipates will satisfy needs and thus bring about a more comfortable state.

All behavior is goal-oriented. Goals are the sought-after results of motivated behavior. The form or direction behavior takes—the goal that is selected—is a result of thinking processes (cognition) and previous learning. There are two types of goals: generic goals and product-specific goals. A generic goal is a general category of goal that may fulfill a certain need; a product-specific goal is a specifically branded or labeled product that the individual sees as a way to fulfill a need.

Innate needs—those an individual is born with—are primarily physiological (biogenic); they include all the factors required to sustain physical life (e.g., food, water, clothing, shelter, sex). Acquired needs—those an individual develops after birth—are primarily psychological (psychogenic); they include esteem, fear, love, and acceptance. For any given need, there are many different and appropriate goals. The specific goal selected depends on the individual's experiences, physical capacity, prevailing cultural norms and values, and the goal's accessibility in the physical and social environment.

Needs and goals are interdependent and change in response to the individual's physical condition, environment, interaction with other people, and experiences. As needs become satisfied, new, higher-order needs emerge which must be fulfilled.

Failure to achieve a goal often results in feelings of frustration. Individuals react to frustration in two ways: they may cope by finding a way around the obstacle that prohibits goal attainment or by finding a substitute goal, or they may adopt a defense mechanism that enables them to protect their self-esteem. Defense mechanisms include aggression, regression, rationalization, withdrawal, projection, autism, identification, and repression.

Motives cannot easily be inferred from consumer behavior. People with different needs may seek fulfillment through selection of the same goals; people with the same needs may seek fulfillment through different goals.

While some psychologists have suggested that individuals have different need priorities, others believe that most human beings experience the same basic needs, to which they assign a similar priority ranking. Maslow's hierarchy of needs theory proposes five levels of prepotent human needs: physiological needs, safety needs, social needs, egoistic needs, and self-actualization needs. A trio of other needs widely used in consumer appeals are the needs for power, affiliation, and achievement.

There are three commonly used methods for identifying and "measuring" human motives: observation and inference, subjective reports, and projective techniques. None of these methods is completely reliable by itself; therefore, researchers often use a combination of two or three techniques in tandem to assess the presence or strength of consumer motives.

Motivational research is qualitative research designed to delve below the consumer's level of conscious awareness. Despite some shortcomings, motivational research has proved to be of great value to marketers concerned with developing new ideas and new copy appeals.

## *discussion questions*

1. What is motivational research? What are its strengths and its weaknesses? How can it best be utilized in the development of marketing strategy?
2. How can a marketer design a promotional strategy to reduce consumer frustrations? Find an advertisement that illustrates this attempt.
3. Choose five magazine advertisements for different consumer goods. Carefully review Murray's list of human needs. Identify, through the advertising appeal used, which need(s) each product is presumed to satisfy.

4. Briefly explain how marketers can employ Maslow's need hierarachy in their marketing strategies. Give at least two examples.
5. Explain briefly the needs for power, affiliation, and achievement. Find three advertisements, each aimed at satisfying one of these needs through the purchase of the advertised product.
6. Suppose you are the vice-president of consumer research for a large U.S. liquor distributor. You are assigned to a new project which requires you to determine *why* people drink alcoholic beverages. Discuss the measurement techniques you would employ.
7. Develop five different advertising appeals—one for each level of Maslow's hierarchy—that the General Motors marketing staff might employ for a new line of automobiles.
8. Consumers have both innate and acquired needs. Give examples of each kind of need and show how the same purchase can serve to fulfill either or both kinds of needs.

## *endnotes*


1. "The Zinger of Silicon Valley," *Time*, February 6, 1984, 50.
2. Bill Saporito, "Hewlett-Packard Discovers Marketing," *Fortune*, October 1, 1984, 51.
3. Robert Sommer, "The Case for Farmers' Markets: Satisfying Unfulfilled Consumer Needs Breeds Success," *Marketing News*, March 1, 1985, 22.
4. Mary J. Rudie, "The CMA Revolution," *Marketing Review*, 40, 1 (September–October 1984), 19–21.
5. L. Wilkens and C. P. Richter, "A Great Craving for Salt by a Child with Cortico-Adrenal Insufficiency," *Journal of the American Medical Association*, 14 (1940), 866–68.
6. George Katona, "Rational Behavior and Economic Behavior," *Psychological Review*, 60 (September 1953), 307–18.
7. Peter Weinberg and Wolfgang Gottwald, "Impulsive Consumer Buying as a Result of Emotions," *Journal of Business Research*, 10 (1982), 43–57.
8. "Forget Wants, Needs, Listen to Consumers' Problems: Dillon," *Marketing News*, June 2, 1978, 6.
9. See Abraham H. Maslow, "A Theory of Human Motivation," *Psychological Review*, 50 (1943), 370–96; Abraham H. Maslow, *Motivation and Personality* (New York: Harper & Row, 1954); and Abraham H. Maslow, *Toward a Psychology of Being* (New York: Van Nostrand Reinhold, 1968), 189–215.
10. A number of studies have focused on human levels of aspiration. See, for example, Kurt Lewin et al., "Level of Aspiration," in J. McV. Hunt, *Personality and Behavior Disorders* (New York: Ronald Press, 1944); Howard Garland, "Goal Levels and Task Performance, a Compelling Replication of Some Compelling Results," *Journal of Applied Psychology*, 67 (1982), 245–48; Edwin A. Locke, Elizabeth Frederick, Cynthia Lee, and Philip Bobko, "Effect of Self Efficacy, Goals and Task Strategies on Task Performance," *Journal of Applied Psychology*, 69, 2 (1984), 241–51; and Edwin A. Locke, Elizabeth Frederick, Elizabeth Buckner, and Philip Bobko, "Effect of Previously Assigned Goals on Self-Set Goals and Performance," *Journal of Applied Psychology*, 69 (1984), 694–99.

11. Rolph E. Anderson, "Consumer Dissatisfaction: The Effect of Disconfirmed Expectancy on Perceived Product Performance," *Journal of Marketing Research,* 10 (February 1973), 38–44.
12. Richard H. Buskirk and James T. Rothe, "Consumerism—An Interpretation," *Journal of Marketing,* 34 (October 1970), 61–62, 65. See also George S. Day and David A. Aaker, "A Guide to Consumerism," *Journal of Marketing,* 34 (July 1970), 12–19.
13. Pat Sloan, "Klein's Sultry Avedon Ads for Obsession Hit TV," *Advertising Age,* March 25, 1985, 104; and Michael McWilliams, "Calvin Bests Fellini with Obsession Spots," *Advertising Age,* April 8, 1985, 81.
14. Weinberg and Gottwald, "Impulsive Consumer Buying," 43.
15. Ron J. Markin, "Motivation in Buyer Behavior Theory: From Mechanism to Cognition", in Arch Woodside, Jagdish N. Sheth, and Peter O. Bennett, eds., *Consumer and Industrial Buying Behavior* (New York: Elsevier–North Holland, 1977), 37–48.
16. James A. Bayton, "Motivation, Cognition, Learning—Basic Factors in Consumer Behavior," *Journal of Marketing,* 23 (January 1958), 282–89.
17. Maslow, "A Theory of Human Motivation," 380.
18. Ibid.
19. Ibid.
20. See, for example, Edward M. Tauber, "Why Do People Shop?" *Journal of Marketing,* 36 (October 1972), 46–59.
21. Eugene M. Fodor and Terry Smith, "The Power Motive as an Influence on Group Decision Making," *Journal of Personality and Social Psychology,* 42 (1982), 178–185.
22. See, for example, David C. McClelland, *Studies in Motivation* (New York: Appleton-Century-Crofts, 1955).
23. David C. McClelland, "Business Drive and National Achievement," *Harvard Business Review,* (July–August 1962), 99; "Achievement Motivation Can Be Developed," *Harvard Business Review,* (November–December 1965), 5–24, 178; and Abraham K. Korman, *The Psychology of Motivation* (Englewood Cliffs, N.J.: Prentice-Hall, 1974), 190.
24. A. G. Greenwald, "Ego Task Analysis: An Integration of Research on Ego-Involvement and Self Awareness," in A. H. Hastorf and A. M. Isen, eds., *Cognitive Social Psychology* (New York: Elsevier–North Holland, 1982), 109–47.
25. Judith M. Harackiewicz, Carol Sansone, and George Manderlink, "Competence, Achievement Orientation, and Intrinsic Motivation: A Process Analysis," *Journal of Personality and Social Psychology,* 48 (1985), 493–508.
26. E. Laird Landon, Jr., "A Sex Role Explanation of Purchase Intention Differences of Consumers Who Are High and Low in Need for Achievement," in M. Venkatesan, ed., *Proceedings of the Third Annual Conference* (Association for Consumer Research, 1972), 1–8.
27. David M. Gardner, "An Exploratory Investigation of Achievement Motivation Effects on Consumer Behavior," in Venkatesan, *Proceedings of the Third Annual Conference,* 20–33.
28. Charles D. Schewe, "Selected Social Psychological Models for Analyzing Buyers," *Journal of Marketing,* 37 (July 1973), 31–39; and David C. McClelland and Alvin M. Liberman, "The Effect of Need for Achievement on Recognition of Need-Related Words," *Journal of Personality,* 18 (December 1949), 236–51.
29. Michael J. Stahl and Adrian M. Harrell, "Evaluation and Validation of a Behavioral Decision Theory Management Approach to Achievement, Power, and Affiliation," *Journal of Applied Psychology,* 67 (1982), 744–51.
30. Hal Sokolow, "In-depth Interviews Increasing in Importance," *Marketing News,* September 13, 1985, 26.
31. Judith Langer, " 'Story Time' Is Alternative Research Technique," *Marketing News,* September 13, 1985, 19.

32. See George J. Szybillo and Robert Berger, "What Advertising Agencies Think of Focus Groups," *Journal of Advertising Research,* 19 (June 1979), 29–33; and Theodore J. Gage, "Theories Differ on Use of Focus Group," *Advertising Age,* February 4, 1980, 19–22.
33. "Biobehavioral System Can Enhance Verbal Responses," *Marketing News,* September 13, 1985, 57.
34. Priscilla LaBarbera and James MacLachlan, "Response Latency in Telephone Interviews," *Journal of Advertising Research,* 19 (1979), 49–56.
35. James MacLachlan and John G. Myers, "Using Response Latency to Identify Commercials That Motivate," *Journal of Advertising Research,* 23 (October–November 1983), 51–57.
36. Ernest Dichter, *A Strategy of Desire* (Garden City, N.Y.: Doubleday, 1960).
37. For additional reports of motivational research findings, see Dichter, *Strategy of Desire;* Vance Packard, *The Hidden Persuaders* (New York: Pocket Books, 1957); and Pierre Martineau, *Motivation in Advertising* (New York: McGraw-Hill, 1957).
38. R. Ferber and H. G. Wales, eds., *Motivation and Market Behavior* (Homewood, Ill.: Irwin, 1958), 20.
39. Leslie Kanuk, "Emotional Persuasion in Print Advertising" (Master's thesis, City College of New York, 1964).
40. Daniel Goleman, "New View of Mind Gives Unconscious an Expanded Role," *New York Times,* February 7, 1984, C1–2.
41. Dichter, "Interpretative versus Descriptive Research," 72.
42. Rena Bartos, "Ernest Dichter: Motive Interpreter," *Journal of Advertising Research,* 17 (June 1977), 8.

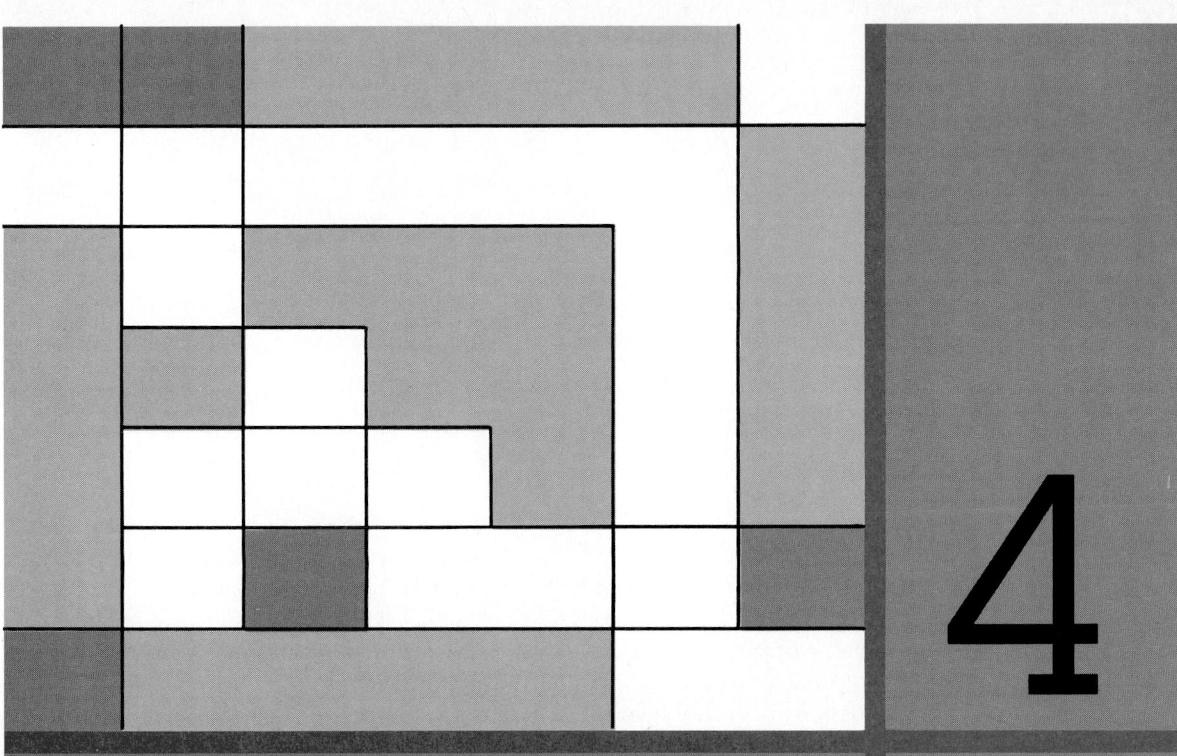

4

# Personality and Consumer Behavior

## *introduction*

FOR several decades, marketers have been seeking to identify specific market segments in terms of personality characteristics. Their purpose has been to isolate the personality traits of market segments they would like to reach so that they can develop strategies that will attract them as customers. Interest in segmenting consumers on the basis of personality is founded on the belief that consumers make purchase decisions that in part reflect their personalities. Possible personality-related questions that marketers might pose with regard to current or potential customers are these:

**AT&T** What type(s) of callers are most likely to remain loyal when forced to select a long distance company?

**Sony** What personality traits are associated with the very first purchasers of compact disc players?

**Revlon** What personality characteristics distinguish young men who will or will not adopt a routine skincare program?

This chapter is designed to help the reader understand the answers to such questions about the relationship between personality and specific market segments. To accomplish this, it examines what personality is, and how it interrelates with other consumer behavior concepts. It reviews several major personality theories and describes how they have stimulated marketers' interest in the study of consumer personality.

> *A man is like a bit of labrador spar, which has no lustre as you turn it in your hand, until you come to a particular angle; then it shows deep and beautiful colors.*
>
> EMERSON
> "Experience," Essays: Second Series (1844)

## WHAT IS PERSONALITY?

The examination of personality has been approached by theorists in a variety of ways. Some have emphasized the dual influence of heredity and early childhood experiences on personality development; others have stressed broader social and environmental influences and the fact that personalities develop continuously over time. Some theorists prefer to view personality as a unified whole; others focus on specific traits. The wide variation in viewpoints makes it difficult to arrive at a single definition. However, we propose that *personality* be defined as *those inner psychological characteristics that both determine and reflect how a person responds to his or her environment.*

The emphasis in this definition is on *inner characteristics*—those specific qualities, attributes, traits, factors, and mannerisms that distinguish one individual from other individuals. As discussed later in this chapter, the deeply ingrained characteristics that we call personality are likely to influence the individual's product and store choices; they also affect the way the consumer responds to a firm's communication efforts. Therefore the identification of specific personality characteristics associated with consumer behavior may be highly useful in the development of a firm's market segmentation strategies.

## THE NATURE OF PERSONALITY

In approaching the study of personality, three distinct properties are of central importance: (1) personality is the essence of *individual differences;* (2) personality is *consistent* and *enduring;* and (3) personality can *change.*

### Personality Reflects Individual Differences

Because the inner characteristics that constitute an individual's personality are a unique combination of factors, no two individuals are exactly alike. Nevertheless, many individuals tend to be similar in terms of a single personality characteristic. For instance, many people can be described as "high" in sociability (the degree of interest they display in social or group activities), while others can be described as "low" in sociability. Personality is a useful consumer behavior concept because it enables us to categorize people into different groups on the basis of a single **trait** or a few traits. If each person were different in *all* respects, it would be impossible to segment people into similar consuming groups; and there would be little reason to develop standardized products and promotional campaigns.

### Personality Is Consistent and Enduring

An individual's personality is commonly thought to be both consistent and enduring. Indeed, the mother who comments that her child "has been stubborn from the day he was born" is supporting the contention that personality has both consistency and endurance. Both of these qualities are essential if marketers are to explain or predict consumer behavior in terms of personality.

The stable nature of personality suggests that it is unreasonable for marketers to attempt to change consumers' personalities to conform to certain products. At best, they may learn which personality characteristics influence specific consumer responses, and attempt to appeal to relevant traits inherent in their target group of consumers.

Even though an individual's personality may be consistent, consumption behavior may vary considerably because of psychological, sociocultural, and environmental factors that affect behavior. For instance, while an individual's personality may be largely stable, specific needs or motives, attitudes, reaction to group pressures, and even responses to brands that are now available may cause a change in the person's behavior. Personality is only one of a combination of factors that influence how a consumer behaves.

### Personality Can Change

Although personality tends to be consistent and enduring, it may still change under various circumstances. For instance, an individual's personality may be altered because of major life events (the birth of a child, the death of a loved one, a divorce, a major career promotion). An individual's personality changes not only in response to abrupt events in life, but also as part of a gradual maturing process.

## THEORIES OF PERSONALITY

In this section we will briefly review three major theories of personality: (1) **Freudian** theory, (2) **neo-Freudian** theory, and (3) **trait** theory. These theories have been chosen for discussion from among many theories of personality because each has played a prominent role in the study of the relationship between consumer behavior and personality.

### Freudian Theory

Sigmund Freud's **psychoanalytic theory of personality** is the cornerstone of modern psychology. This theory was built on the premise that *unconscious needs* or *drives,* especially biological and sexual drives, are at the heart of human motivation and personality. Freud constructed his theory on the basis of patients' recollections of early childhood experiences, analysis of their dreams, and the specific nature of their mental and physical adjustment problems.

## ID, SUPEREGO, AND EGO

Based upon his analyses, Freud proposed that the human personality consists of three interacting systems—the **id,** the **superego,** and the **ego.** The *id* was conceptualized as a "warehouse" of primitive and impulsive drives—basic physiological needs such as thirst, hunger, and sex—for which the individual seeks immediate satisfaction without concern for the specific means of satisfaction.

In contrast, the *superego* is conceptualized as the individual's internal expression of society's moral and ethical codes of conduct. The superego's role is to see that the individual satisfies needs in a socially acceptable fashion. Thus the superego is a kind of "brake" that restrains or inhibits the impulsive forces of the id.

Finally, the *ego* is the individual's conscious control. It functions as an internal monitor that attempts to balance the impulsive demands of the id and the sociocultural constraints of the superego.

## STAGES OF PERSONALITY DEVELOPMENT

In addition to specifying a structure for personality, Freud emphasized that an individual's personality is formed as he or she passes through a number of distinct stages of infant and childhood development. Freud labeled these stages of development to conform to the area of the body on which he believed the child's sexual instincts are focused at the time. They include the **oral, anal, phallic, latent** and **genital** stages:

1. *Oral stage*—The infant first experiences social contact with the outside world through the mouth (e.g., eating, drinking, and sucking). A crisis develops at the end of this stage as the child is weaned from the mother's breast or from the bottle.
2. *Anal stage*—During this stage, the child's primary source of pleasure is the process of elimination. A second crisis develops at the end of this stage as parents try to toilet-train the child.
3. *Phallic stage*—The child experiences self-oriented sexual pleasure during this phase with discovery of the sexual organs. A third crisis occurs as the child experiences sexual desire for the parent of the opposite sex. How the child resolves this crisis affects later relationships with persons of the opposite sex and with authority figures.
4. *Latency stage*--Freud believed that the sexual instincts of the child lie dormant from about the age of five until the beginning of adolescence, and that no important personality changes occur during this dormant stage.
5. *Genital stage*—At the age of adolescence, the individual develops a sexual interest in persons of the opposite sex, beyond self-oriented love and love for parents. If this crisis is adequately resolved, the individual's personality enters into the genital stage.

According to Freud, an adult's personality is determined by how well an individual deals with the crises that are experienced as he or she passes through each of these stages (particularly the first three). For instance, if a child's *oral* needs are not adequately satisfied at the first stage of development, the person may become fixated at this stage and display an adult personality that includes such traits as ". . . dependence, passivity, greediness, and excessive tendencies toward oral activities, as in smoking, chewing, or garrulous speech."[1] If an individual is fixated at the *anal* stage, the adult personality may display traits of stinginess, obstinacy, excessive need for neatness, and problems in relating to others.[2]

## APPLICATIONS OF FREUDIAN THEORY TO CONSUMER BEHAVIOR

Motivational researchers have applied Freud's psychoanalytic theory to the study of consumer behavior by underscoring the belief that human drives are largely *unconscious,* and that consumers are not consciously aware of their true motives. Thus the emphasis in motivational research studies has been on discovering the **underlying motivations** for specific consumer behavior. To discover consumers' basic motivations, researchers use a variety of clinical or qualitative measurement procedures, such as *observation and inference, projective techniques, focus group* discussions, and *depth interviews* (discussed in Chapter 3). The same basic measurement procedures are used to study *motivations* and *personality* as unified or complementary psychological constructs.

In applying psychoanalytic personality theory, the motivational researcher tends to focus on the consumer's purchases, treating them as a reflection and an extension of the consumer's own personality. For example, a recent advertising campaign for the Renault automobile made the point that "You are what you drive." The motivational researcher, in essence, tries to determine the product's "personality" (or image) and then works backward to determine the consumer's personality. The following comment captures this viewpoint: "Indications of a person's personality can be gained not only from the type of food he eats, but also from the way in which he eats it. Food habits are among the first ones we acquire. Any mother of several children knows how early in life these habits are developed and how they vary with different children."[3]

This view of **product personality** is illustrated by both parts of Figure 4-1, where an ad for Napier jewelry characterizes the product and wearer as "nervier," suggesting that wearing such fashion jewelry is associated with being "bold" and "exciting"—traits that are reinforced by the model's facial expression.

**Brand personality** research undertaken by a major ad agency revealed that almost 40 percent of those interviewed saw Holiday Inn as "cheerful"; while only 6 percent saw Birds Eye as "cheerful." Similarly, almost 40 percent saw Oil of Olay as "gentle," whereas none saw Miller High Life beer as "gentle." Oil of Olay was also characterized as "sophisticated," "mature," "exotic," "mysterious," and "down to earth." It was, moreover, associated with the animal "mink," the country "France," the occupation "secretary," the fabric "silk," the activity "swimming," and the magazine *Vogue.* Constructing a composite picture of the brand's personality gives us:[4]

> . . . a secretary on the Riviera, by the swimming pool, in a silk bathing suit, reading *Vogue,* with her mink coat on the adjacent chair.

FIGURE 4-1 Advertisement Suggesting That a Product Has Its Own Personality

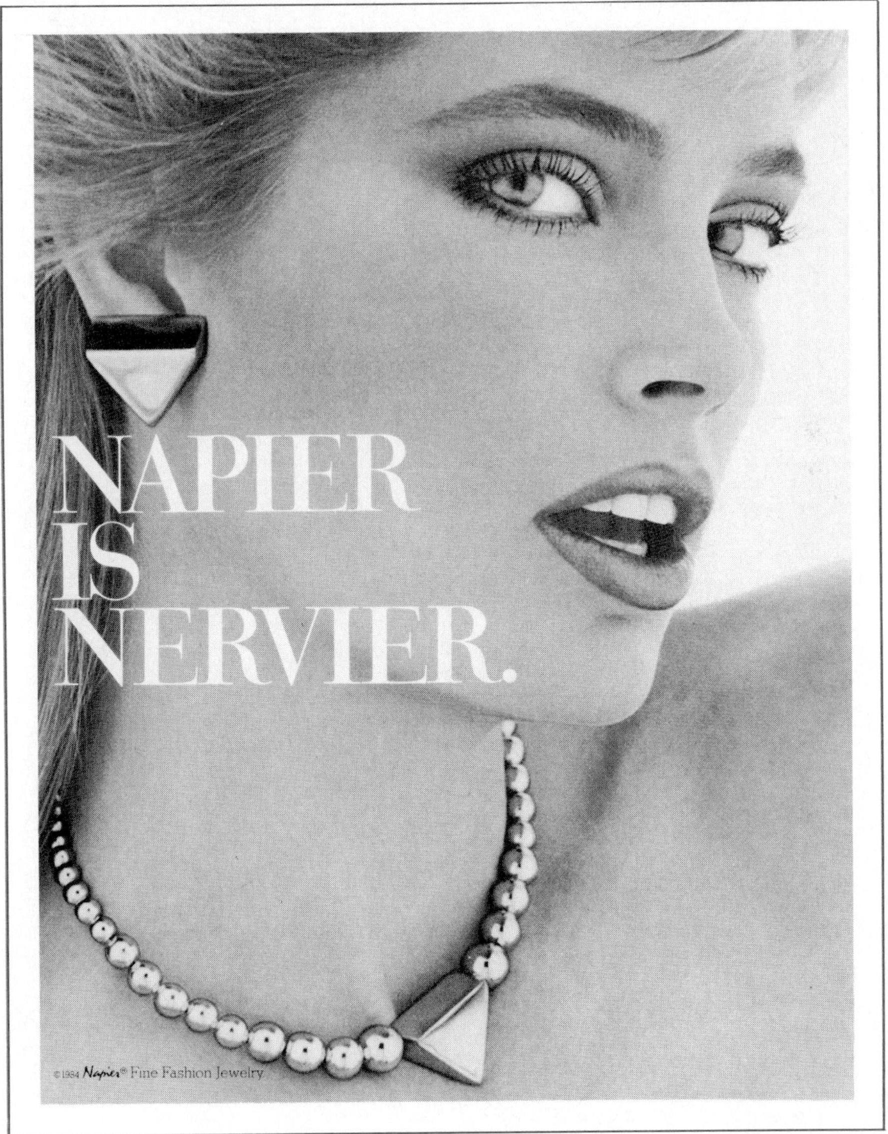


Courtesy of The Napier Company

This and other evidence shows that consumers are able to ascribe various descriptive traits or characteristics—the ingredients of brand personalities—to different brands in a wide variety of product categories.

A novel example of linking a brand (and its name) with a particular personality trait is provided by Procter & Gamble's effort to associate its Sure deodorant with a self-help magazine called *How to Be Sure About Yourself*. The magazine, a giveaway with the purchase of Sure, is designed to provide readers with useful insights in the form of articles on *self-confidence*—a major personality trait.[5]

FIGURE 4-1 (cont.)

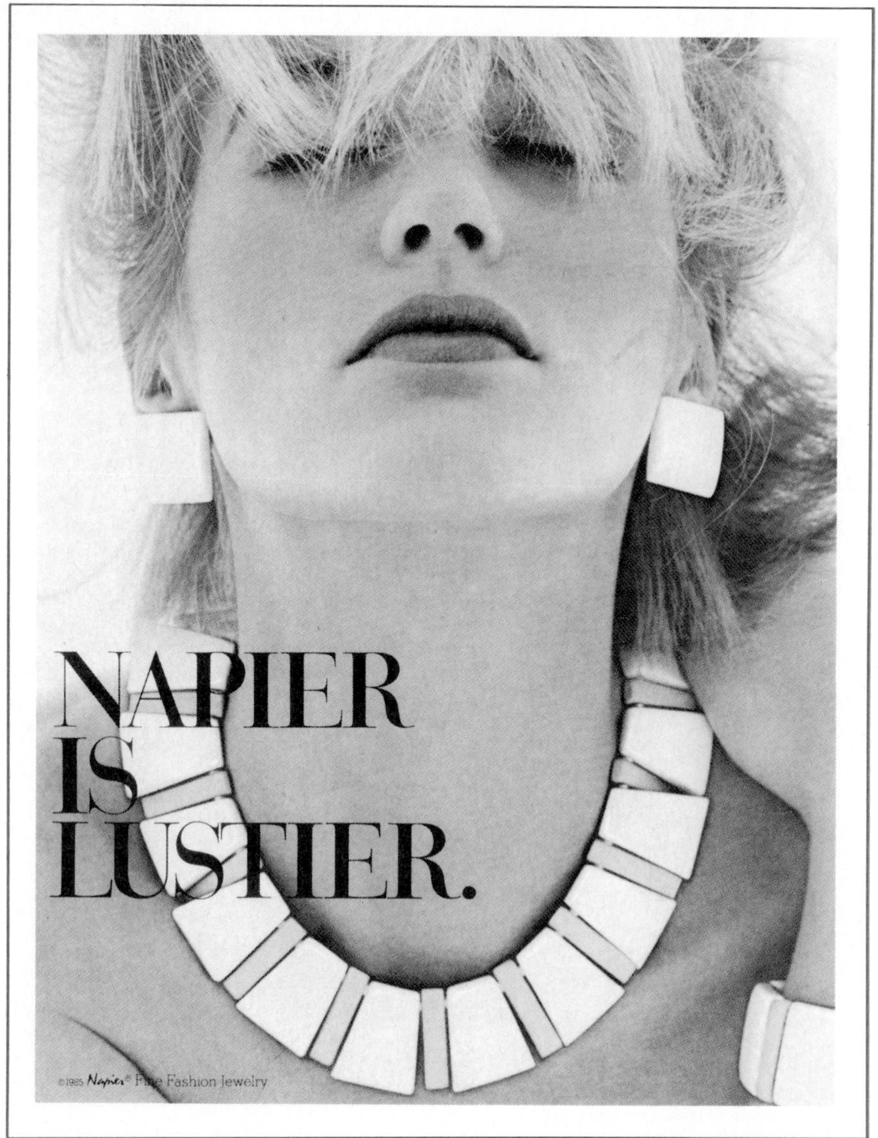


Courtesy of The Napier Company

## Neo-Freudian Personality Theory

Several of Freud's colleagues disagreed with his contention that personality is primarily instinctual and sexual in nature. Instead, these neo-Freudians believed that **social relationships** are fundamental to the formation and development of personality. For instance, Alfred Adler viewed human beings as seeking to attain various rational goals, which he called *style of life*. He also placed much emphasis on the individual's efforts to overcome feelings of *inferiority* (i.e., to strive for superiority).

Harry Stack Sullivan, another neo-Freudian, stressed that people continuously attempt to establish significant and rewarding relationships with others. He was particularly concerned with the individual's efforts to reduce tensions such as *anxiety*.

Like Sullivan, Karen Horney was also interested in anxiety. She focused on the impact of *child-parent* relationships, especially the individual's desire to conquer feelings of anxiety. Horney proposed that individuals be classified into three personality groups: **compliant, aggressive,** and **detached**.[6]

1. *Compliant* individuals are those who move *toward* others (they desire to be loved, wanted, and appreciated).
2. *Aggressive* individuals are those who move *against* others (they desire to excel and win admiration).
3. *Detached* individuals are those who move *away* from others (they desire independence, self-sufficiency, and freedom from obligations).

Neo-Freudian theories of personality have received surprisingly little attention from consumer researchers, despite their emphasis on the importance of the individual's sociocultural environment as a determinant of personality. However, several researchers have applied Horney's classification system to the study of consumer behavior. For example, one consumer researcher developed a personality test based on Horney's theory and found some tentative relationships between college students' responses and their product and brand usage patterns.[7] Highly *compliant* students were found to prefer name brand products, such as Bayer aspirin; students classified as *aggressive* showed a preference for Old Spice deodorant over other brands (seemingly because of its masculine appeal); and highly *detached* students proved to be heavy tea drinkers (possibly reflecting their desire not to conform). More recent studies employing the same personality test have found Horney's scheme to be useful in exploring selective aspects of consumer behavior.[8] However, additional work is necessary to refine and assess the appropriate conditions under which this personality measure can be fruitfully used.[9]

Although neo-Freudian theories of personality have not received wide attention, it is likely that marketers have employed some of these theories intuitively. For example, marketers who position their products as providing "unexcelled" craftsmanship or quality (as Rolls Royce Motors does) seem to be guided by Adler's theory that individuals constantly strive for *superiority*. Figure 4–2 is an example from the ad campaign that depicts owners of other fine cars as envious of owners of a Rolls Royce—"Simply the best motor car in the world."

## Trait Theory

Trait theory constitutes a major departure from the basically *qualitative* measures that typify the Freudian and neo-Freudian movements (personal observation, self-reported experiences, dream analysis, and projective techniques).

The orientation of trait theory is primarily *quantitative* or *empirical;* it focuses on the measurement of personality in terms of specific psychological

FIGURE 4-2 Advertisement That Appeals Innately to the Sense of Superiority

Courtesy of Rolls-Royce Motors, Inc.

characteristics of the individual called traits. **Trait** is defined as ". . . any distinguishing, relatively enduring way in which one individual differs from another."[10] Accordingly, trait theorists are concerned with the construction of personality tests or inventories that pinpoint individual differences in terms of specific traits.

Viewing personality as a set of enduring traits has a natural appeal because it conforms to many commonly held beliefs. For example, many individuals distinguish between friends as *reserved* or *outgoing*. In this way, they are intuitively evaluating and "labeling" them in terms of traits.

## Constructing a Personality Scale

To more fully understand what is meant by a personality trait, and why the trait approach is considered quantitative rather than qualitative, we will briefly consider how a **personality test** is developed.

A personality test usually consists of one or more scales, each of which measures a specific personality trait. A **scale** is a series of questions or items designed to measure a single personality *trait.* The scores achieved by an individual on each of the items in the scale are combined to produce a single *index,* which reflects the degree to which he or she possesses that trait. Some personality tests consist of a single scale; that is, they are designed to measure only one trait, such as *dogmatism* (how willing a person is to accept a different viewpoint).[11] Other personality tests include more than one scale, with each scale measuring a different trait. An example of a **multitrait personality test** is the 480-item California Psychological Inventory, which consists of eighteen scales, each measuring a specific trait (e.g., *dominance, sociability, self-acceptance, tolerance*).[12] Later in this chapter we will examine how single-trait and multitrait personality inventories have been used in the study of consumer behavior.

In constructing a scale to measure a specific trait, test developers start by observing the behavior of people they feel typify the personality trait they wish to measure. They then develop a large number of questions that seem to reflect the actual observed behavior, and administer these questions to samples of people who might reasonably be expected to score either high or low on the trait under study. For example, if the researchers were developing a scale to measure *achievement motivation,* they might administer their questions to a sample of "high-tech" entrepreneurs and a sample of assembly-line workers. If they have developed questions that do appropriately measure the trait, they should find that entrepreneurs, who might be expected to score high on *achievement motivation,* do in fact score high, and that assembly-line workers, who might be expected to score low on *achievement motivation,* do indeed score low. After repeated testing on different samples with similar results, the researchers can conclude that their series of questions constitutes a valid scale for the measurement of *achievement motivation.* They will then try to reduce the number of questions (through **factor analysis**) without impairing the scale's ability to measure the trait in question.

Because personality scales are easy to combine and administer in the form of a questionnaire, such *paper-and-pencil* personality tests have become the most popular approach for assessing consumer personality.

# PROBLEMS AND PROMISES OF PERSONALITY TRAITS AND CONSUMER BEHAVIOR

Although consumer personality research has been conducted for more than two decades, the results of this research have been very uneven.[13] Some studies have found that personality traits add little to our understanding of consumer behavior, while more recent studies have been more encouraging.

## Disappointing Consumer Personality Research

As a group, consumer studies that have *not* revealed a relationship between personality and consumer behavior have tended to possess one or more of the following limiting qualities: (1) they were based on convenient *multitrait* rather than selected *single-trait* personality tests; (2) they employed personality tests *designed for diagnosis of social adjustment problems* rather than for identifying the range of normal healthy behavior; (3) they had *no a priori hypotheses* that proposed a relationship between the traits under study and specific consumer behavior; (4) they *focused on single brand choices* rather than on more general product category usage patterns; (5) they focused on consumers' brand choice rather than on the dimensions of the decision process leading to the choice; and (6) they assumed that the personality-consumer behavior relationship is consistent across situations rather than influenced by the particular situation.

The earliest and most controversial application of a standard multitrait personality inventory examined two groups of consumers: those who owned 1955–58 Fords and those who owned comparable year Chevrolets.[14] The objective of the study was to determine the extent to which personality traits could distinguish between the owners of these two makes of cars. The study employed eleven of the fifteen traits measured by the Edwards Personal Preference Schedule (EPPS). Table 4-1 lists and briefly defines these traits and indicates the ones selected for the Ford-Chevrolet study.

Generally, the results revealed that the personality traits measured did not discriminate between the owners of the two types of cars. However, when the data were reanalyzed on the basis of specific *hypotheses* concerning the relationship of certain personality traits to ownership of one or the other make of car, the results revealed some improvement in the ability of the EPPS to differentiate between Ford and Chevrolet owners.[15] Most important, the reanalysis underscored the need to justify the measurement of specific personality traits by hypothesizing how each trait *relates* to the consumer behavior under investigation.

Other studies have used multitrait personality tests in attempts to explain such consumer-related activities as the ownership of different types of cars (convertibles, standards, and compacts), the purchase and use of various convenience goods, the purchase of store brands versus national brands, and usage of specific types of banking institutions.[16] Like the original Ford-Chevrolet study, the results of these studies have typically been disappointing.[17] In summary, it appears that the inability of much personality research to find significant relationships between personality and consumer behavior is due to the fact that researchers indiscriminately have used *all* the scales (traits) included in the standard multitrait personality test they employ, without specifying how each trait is expected to relate to the specific consumer behavior under study.

## Promising Studies in Consumer Personality Research

The persistent efforts of both marketing practitioners and consumer researchers to demonstrate that personality is an inherently useful tool for segmenting consumer markets have recently paid off in some encouraging refinements in consumer personality research.

**TABLE 4-1 A Summary of Personality Traits Measured by the Edwards Personal Preference Schedule**

*1. *Achievement:* To do one's best, accomplish tasks of great significance, do things better than others, be successful, be a recognized authority.

*2. *Deference:* To get suggestions, follow instructions, do what is expected, accept leadership of others, conform to custom, let others make decisions.

3. *Order:* To have work neat and organized, make plans before starting, keep files, have things arranged to run smoothly, have things organized.

*4. *Exhibition:* To say clever things, tell amusing jokes and stories, talk about personal achievements, have others notice and comment on one's appearance, be the center of attention.

*5. *Autonomy:* To be able to come and go as desired, say what one thinks, be independent in making decisions, feel free to do what one wants, avoid conformity, avoid responsibilities and obligations.

*6. *Affiliation:* To be loyal to friends, do things for friends, form new friendships, make many friends, form strong attachments, participate in friendly groups.

*7. *Intraception:* To analyze one's motives and feelings, observe and understand others, analyze the motives of others, predict their acts, put one's self in another's place.

8. *Succorance:* To be helped by others, seek encouragement, have others feel sorry when sick, have others be sympathetic about personal problems.

*9. *Dominance:* To be a leader, argue for one's point of view, make group decisions, settle arguments, persuade and influence others, supervise others.

*10. *Abasement:* To feel guilty when wrong, accept blame, feel need for punishment, feel timid in presence of superiors, feel inferior, feel depressed about inability to handle situations.

11. *Nurturance:* To help friends in trouble, treat others with kindness, forgive others, do small favors, be generous, show affection, receive confidence.

*12. *Change:* To do new and different things, travel, meet new people, try new things, eat in new places, live in different places, try new fads and fashions.

13. *Endurance:* To keep at a job until finished, work hard at a task, keep at a problem until solved, finish one job before starting others, stay up late working to get a job done.

*14. *Heterosexuality:* To go out with opposite sex, be in love, kiss, discuss sex, become sexually excited, read books about sex.

*15. *Aggression:* To tell others what one thinks of them, criticize others publicly, make fun of others, tell others off, get revenge, blame others.

*The eleven traits used in the Ford-Chevrolet study.



For instance, evidence suggests that other consumer behavior variables, such as *demographic* factors (age, sex, education, income) or the type or amount of *risk perceived,* can be used to help crystallize the relationship between personality and consumer behavior.[18] For example, researchers may find no significant relationship between the purchase of a new diet cola and selected personality traits. However, if they were to divide the sample of consumers by gender, and then separately examine for males and females the relationship between selected personality traits and the purchase of specific brands of diet cola, they might find that significantly different personality profiles emerge. In such instances, the additional consumer behavior variables would serve as *filters* to purify the relationship between personality and consumer behavior.

Another promising approach to consumer personality research involves the use of carefully selected **single-trait personality tests** (tests that measure just one trait, such as *self-confidence*) rather than **multitrait inventories.** In addition, there has recently been some effort to develop personality scales specifically designed for the study of consumer behavior. Examples of such tailor-made personality tests include a test that measures Horney's *compliant-aggressive-detached* personality types (see the discussion earlier in this chapter); a test that measures *self-actualization* (derived from Maslow's need hierarchy described in Chapter 3); a test that taps various aspects of *time* that might influence consumer behavior (i.e., focus, activity, structure, and tenacity); a test that measures consumer *estheticism* and *practicality* (how individuals differ in response to appeals of appearance versus performance of things and products); a test that measures consumer *use innovativeness* (variety seeking in product use); a test that measures *temporal variety* (variety-seeking behavior); and tests that measure consumer *innovativeness* (how receptive a person is to new experiences) and consumer *venturesomeness* (how attracted a person is to novel things and products).[19]

The more careful selection and application of available personality tests, and the development of new **consumer-specific** personality tests, are two promising steps designed to make personality a more useful consumer behavior variable. In addition, we have recently begun to appreciate that it is more realistic to expect personality to be linked to how consumers *make their choices,* or to the purchase or consumption of a *broad product category* (rather than a specific brand), especially if the particular purchase or consumption *situation* is taken into consideration. As an example, it may be more realistic to perceive a relationship between personality and whether or not an individual purchases a microwave oven, than to assume an association between personality and the brand of microwave oven purchased.[20]

## PERSONALITY AND MARKET SEGMENTATION

Marketers are interested in understanding how consumers' personalities influence consumption behavior because such knowledge enables them to segment markets and to select one or more target segments likely to respond favorably to their promotional strategies. This section examines a number of specific types of consumer behavior in which the influence of personality characteristics appears to be particularly promising for market segmentation.

### Personality and Brand Usage

Consumer researchers have had little success in using personality traits to predict consumers' brand choices. As already noted, it is somewhat unrealistic to expect personality traits that are designed to capture broad dimensions of individual behavior to account for the purchase or usage of a single brand (e.g., Crest toothpaste) or even a single product category (e.g., toothpaste in general). It would seem more reasonable to expect personality to reflect the usage of a *broad product category* (the use of oral care products in general), or better yet, to reflect still more general *dimensions of behavior*—such as personal care or grooming patterns.

However, several advertising agencies and consumer goods firms have reported successfully linking specific personality traits to consumer brand choice. For example, a leading advertising agency has reported the successful development of market segmentation strategies based on personality traits for specific brands in such product categories as women's cosmetic products, cigarettes, insurance, and liquor.[21] Table 4-2 lists personality traits that were found to be helpful in segmenting the women's cosmetic market. A clinical psychologist employed by the advertising agency makes the initial selection of personality traits that could plausibly influence brand choice decisions. Pilot studies are then undertaken to eliminate traits that do not appear to contribute to an understanding of consumer differences. In the final phase of the **personality segmentation research,** scales related to product and brand purchase behavior are used to develop **profiles** of specific brand usage segments.

**TABLE 4-2 Personality Scales Found Useful in the Segmentation of the Women's Cosmetic Market**

| SCALE | DESCRIPTION |
|---|---|
| Narcissism— | Tendency to be preoccupied with the details of one's personal appearance |
| Appearance Conscious— | Emphasis on the social importance of looking properly groomed |
| Exhibitionism— | Tendency toward self-display and attention seeking |
| Impulsive— | Tendency to act in a carefree, impetuous and unreflective manner |
| Order— | Tendency to be compulsively neat, and live by rules and schedules |
| Fantasied Achievement— | Measure of narcissistic aspiration for distinction and personal recognition |
| Capacity for Status— | Measure of the personal qualities and attributes that underline and lead to status |
| Dominant— | Need to be superior to others by being in control and in the forefront |
| Sociable— | Need for informal, friendly, agreeable relationship with others |
| Active— | Need to be on the go, doing things, achieving goals set out for oneself |
| Cheerful— | Tendency to feel bright, cheerful and optimistic about life |
| Deference— | Tendency to submit to opinions and preferences of others perceived as superior |
| Subjective— | Tendency toward naive, superstitious and generally immature thinking |

Source: Shirley Young "The Dynamics of Measuring Unchange," in Russell I. Haley, ed., Attitude Research in Transition (Chicago: American Marketing Association, 1972), 62.

## PERSONALITY AND BEER CONSUMPTION

Anheuser-Busch, a leading marketer of beer, has sponsored consumer behavior research designed to segment beer and other alcoholic beverage drinkers into specific drinker personality types.[22] This research effort represents a good case history of the successful application of personality theory to market segmentation.

An extensive amount of exploratory research identified four distinct types of alcoholic beverage drinkers with correspondingly unique personality types: *social drinkers, reparative drinkers, oceanic drinkers,* and *indulgent drinkers.* Table 4-3 presents a simplified summary of these four drinker personality types. With this classification scheme, researchers have been able to identify advertising messages and media exposure patterns that effectively reach the specific drinker personality types that constitute the prime market for Budweiser, Michelob, and Busch (three brands produced by Anheuser-Busch). Armed with information about the susceptibility of each drinker personality type to specific advertising messages, Anheuser-Busch has been able to boost the sales of Michelob beer by appealing successfully to the drinkers in a large drinker personality segment. (The Michelob ad in Figure 4-3 is directed to the *social drinker.*)

**TABLE 4-3 Drinker Personality Characteristics**

| TYPE OF DRINKER | PERSONALITY TYPE | DRINKING PATTERN |
|---|---|---|
| social drinker | Driven by his own needs, particularly to achieve, and attempts to manipulate others to get what he wants. Driven by a desire to get ahead. Usually a younger person. | Controlled drinker who may sometimes become high or drunk but is unlikely to be an alcoholic. Drinks primarily on the weekends, holidays, and vacations, usually in a social setting with friends. Drinking is seen as a way to gain social acceptance. |
| reparative drinker | Sensitive and responsive to the needs of others and adapts to their needs by sacrificing his own aspirations. Usually middle-aged. | Controlled drinker who infrequently becomes high or drunk. Drinks primarily at the end of the workday, usually with a few close friends. Views drinking as a reward for sacrifices made for others. |
| oceanic drinker | Sensitive to the needs of others. Often a failure who blames himself for his nonachievement. | Drinks heavily, especially when under pressure to achieve. At times shows a lack of control over his drinking and is likely to become high, drunk, and even alcoholic. Drinking is a form of escape. |
| indulgent drinker | Generally insensitive to others and places the blame for his failures on others' lack of sensitivity to him. | Like the oceanic drinker, he drinks heavily, often becomes high, drunk, or alcoholic. Drinks as a form of escape. |

Source: Adapted from Russell L. Ackoff and James R. Emshoff, "Advertising Research at Anheuser-Busch, Inc. (1968–74)," Sloan Management Review, 16, No. 3 (Spring 1975), 1–15.

**FIGURE 4-3** Advertisement That Appeals to the Social Drinker

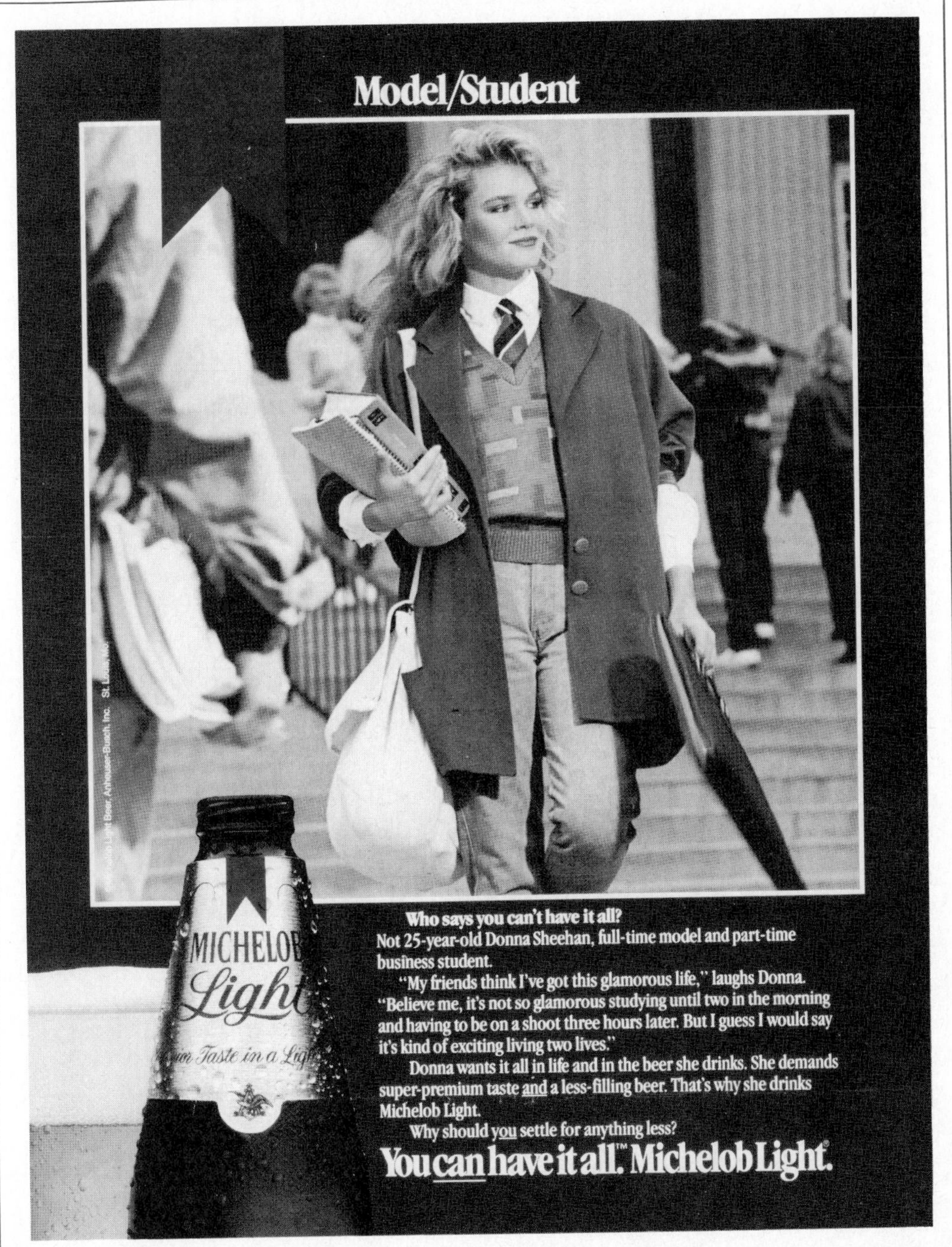


Courtesy of Anheuser Busch Inc.

Further research indicated which drinker personality types were most likely to be *brand switchers* and which were most likely to be *brand loyal.* Such insights are invaluable to marketers introducing a new brand, entering a new market, or combatting the advances of competitive brands.

This research project, which has been ongoing since 1968, exemplifies the fact that a marketer who is willing to expend the funds for creative personality research can reap handsome rewards.

## Consumer Innovators

Marketing practitioners must learn all they can about consumers who are willing to try new products or brands, for the market response of such innovators is often crucial to the ultimate success of a new product.

Personality traits that have proved useful in differentiating between **consumer innovators** and **non-innovators** include *dogmatism, social character, category width,* and *optimum stimulation level.* (Chapter 17 examines additional distinguishing characteristics between these two groups.)

### DOGMATISM

*Dogmatism* is a personality trait that measures the degree of rigidity an individual displays toward the unfamiliar and toward information that is contrary to his or her own established beliefs.[23] A person who is highly dogmatic approaches the unfamiliar defensively and with considerable discomfort and uncertainty. At the other end of the spectrum, a person who is low in dogmatism will readily consider unfamiliar or opposing beliefs.

In two closely parallel experiments, subjects who were low in dogmatism (open-minded) were found to be significantly more likely to prefer innovative products to established or traditional alternatives.[24] In contrast, highly dogmatic subjects (closed-minded) were more likely to choose established rather than innovative product alternatives. A third study found that early patrons of self-service gas stations (then highly innovative) were significantly less dogmatic than customers of traditional full-service stations.[25]

An interesting extension of this research found that the relationship between dogmatism and intended innovative behavior was influenced by **situational** factors.[26] Specifically, when thinking of a purchase for personal use, low dogmatic consumers were more willing to buy innovative products than highly dogmatic consumers. However, when the purchase was slated as a gift, the results were reversed; that is, highly dogmatic consumers were more willing to purchase an innovative product alternative than low dogmatic consumers.

It seems that when contemplating a gift, highly dogmatic consumers are more "anxious" than low dogmatic consumers to portray to gift recipients an image of more venturesomeness than when they purchase for their own consumption. As an example, think of the person who selects a pair of bright, multicolored argyle socks as a gift for a friend, but only wears solid colors himself.

If confirmed by future research, these findings suggest that marketers of novel new products, especially those that are likely to be gifts, should realize that purchasing for personal use or for gift giving may present very different consumer-related situations.

Research suggests that the promotional appeal employed to present information about a new or unfamiliar product is extremely relevant to how low and highly dogmatic consumers are likely to respond. For instance, it has been noted that highly dogmatic consumers may be more willing to accept new products if the products are presented in an *authoritative* manner (e.g., by an admired celebrity, by a recognized expert, or in the context of a reassuring and ego-boosting message).[27] In contrast, low dogmatic consumers seem to be more receptive to messages that stress factual differences and product benefits. For this reason, the marketer of a new computer might be wise to emphasize in a promotional campaign targeted at knowledgeable consumers the *reasons why* the computer is technically as good as or better than competitive products. To reach more resistant consumers, the company might alter the promotional approach and employ a celebrity, since resistant or highly dogmatic consumers are more likely to respond favorably to celebrity testimonial appeals. Consider the computer ad in Figure 4-4, where NCR features the well-know comedian Dom DeLuise, together with a reassuring headline. This type of ad not only provides information, but does it in a lighthearted way that is likely to be attractive to less knowledgeable and/or more resistant potential computer purchasers.

## SOCIAL CHARACTER

The personality trait known as *social character* has its origin in sociological research, which focuses on the identification and classification of societies into distinct sociocultural types. As it is used in consumer psychology, social character is a personality trait that ranges on a continuum from **inner-directedness,** to **other-directedness.** Available evidence indicates that *inner-directed* consumers tend to rely on their own "inner" values or standards in evaluating new products and are more likely to be consumer-innovators. Conversely, *other-directed* consumers tend to look to others for direction on what is right or wrong; thus they are less likely to be consumer innovators.[28]

Research on *innovativeness* and *social character* has found that when new food products were ranked in terms of how much they differed from more traditional alternatives, the more novel the product, the more likely it was to be purchased by inner-directed consumers, and the less likely it was to be purchased by other-directed consumers.[29]

A study that compared the first purchasers of the Ford Maverick (when it was introduced in April 1969) with later purchasers of the same car and concurrent purchasers of a firmly established small car, found that the consumer innovators who first purchased the Maverick were significantly more inner-directed than later purchasers of Mavericks and concurrent purchasers of the established car.[30] These findings strongly support the notion that innovators tend to have inner-directed personalities, while later adopters have other-directed personalities.

FIGURE 4-4 Advertisement That Is Reassuring to Resistant Consumers

IT'S SO FAST, YOU'LL FLY THROUGH YOUR WORK.

**Introducing the NCR PC6.**

Whoosh!

That's information coming up on the new NCR PC6.

The PC6 is NCR's most powerful personal computer yet. It's powered by the advanced Intel 8088-2 microprocessor. So you can process information nearly twice as fast as the PC XT.™

At that rate, you can load programs faster. Recall files in an instant. Calculate in a flash. And get home earlier.

The PC6 stores a lot, too—up to 40MB of hard disk space, or about 7,575 single-spaced typewritten pages.

Of course the PC6 is compatible—running over 10,000 business software programs. In fact, a special switch lets you operate at either 8 MHz or 4.77 MHz, allowing you to run software that some other high performance PCs, like the PC AT,™ can't run.

And, just in case, you can get a built-in streaming tape back-up system to guard against accidental erasures, disk damage, or coffee spills.

The NCR PC6. To see it, fly on down to your NCR dealer today. For your nearest NCR dealer, call toll free 1-800-544-3333.*

**A better personal computer. It's exactly what you'd expect from NCR.**

NCR

PC6

Courtesy of NCR Corporation

Available evidence also suggests that *inner-* and *other-directed* consumers are likely to have different preferences in terms of promotional messages.[31] Inner-directed people prefer ads that stress product features and personal benefits (enabling them to use their own values and standards in evaluating products), while other-directed people prefer ads that feature a social environment or social acceptance (in keeping with their tendency to look to others for direction).

Related research has focused directly on people's reactions to the product being advertised, rather than their preference for either objective or social promotional appeals.[32] These findings offer some confirmation that other-directed individuals are generally more easily influenced because of their natural inclination to go beyond the content of an ad and think in terms of likely social approval of a potential purchase.

For marketing practitioners, this research suggests that while consumers tend to respond favorably to promotional themes that are consistent with their personalities, *other-directed* consumers seem to be more easily persuaded by advertisements, regardless of their content appeal.

## CATEGORY WIDTH

Another personality trait that has been found to discriminate between innovative and noninnovative consumers is **category width.** This trait seems to tap an important dimension of a person's risk-handling strategy. Research has shown that people handle risky decisions differently.[33] Some people tend to have a tolerance for error; that is, they are willing to accept the possibility of poor or negative outcomes in order to maximize the number of satisfying or positive alternatives from which to choose. Other people handle risk in the opposite way; that is, they have a low tolerance for error and prefer to forgo potentially satisfying or positive alternatives in order to minimize the possibility of selecting poor or negative alternatives. As measured by the category-width scale, individuals who have a high tolerance for error are called **broad categorizers,** while individuals with a low tolerance for error are called **narrow categorizers.**

The first use of the *category-width scale* in consumer behavior research explored its relationship to individuals' perceived willingness to try new products.[34] The results found that student subjects who were *broad categorizers* were willing to try qualitatively different brands (innovations), while those who were *narrow categorizers* tended to choose established or familiar alternatives (noninnovations). These findings were substantiated in later research among actual consumers.[35]

Another study found that homemakers who were *broad categorizers* were more likely to have purchased genuinely new products (e.g., nonrefrigerated main dishes), while those who were *narrow categorizers* were more likely to have purchased superficially new products (e.g., lime-scented dishwashing detergent).[36] For the marketer, this study indicates that the degree of newness inherent in a product may influence consumers differently, depending upon their personalities. That is, broad categorizers may be more willing to purchase genuinely new or novel products, while narrow categorizers may be more receptive to superficially new products. Thus it would seem that marketing practitioners should carefully consider the *degree* of newness inherent in a new product when they design their marketing strategies.

## OPTIMUM STIMULATION LEVEL

Some people seem to prefer a simple, uncluttered, and calm existence, while others seem to prefer an environment crammed with novel, complex, and unusual experiences. Consumer researchers have begun to examine how such variations (called *optimum stimulation levels*) may be influenced by selected personality traits, and how in turn specific stimulation levels may be related to consumer behavior.[37] So far, this research has linked high *optimum stimulation levels* (OSLs) with being more open to risk taking, trying new products, being innovative, seeking purchase-related information, and accepting new retail facilities. A recent study also found that *OSL* is related to a person's desired level of lifestyle stimulation. For instance, if consumers' actual lifestyle stimulation is equal to their *OSL,* then they are likely to be quite satisfied. On the other hand, if their lifestyle is understimulated (i.e., their *OSL* is greater than current reality), they are likely to be bored; if their lifestyle is overstimulated (i.e., their *OSL* is less than current reality), they are likely to seek rest or relief.

This suggests that the relationship between consumers' lifestyles and their OSL is likely to influence their choices of alternative types of products or services, and how they manage their time. For instance, a person who feels bored (an understimulated consumer) is likely to be attracted to a vacation that offers much activity and an exciting time. In contrast, a person who feels overwhelmed (an overstimulated consumer) is likely to seek a quiet, isolated, relaxing, and rejuvenating vacation.[38]

In light of these findings, it might be useful for marketers to consider segmenting markets for selected products or services in terms of *OSL*. Consumers requiring higher levels of stimulation might be expected to respond favorably to products, service environments, and promotional campaigns that stress *more,* rather than *less* risk, novelty, or excitement; while the reverse would be true for consumers needing lower levels of stimulation.

The research reported on here indicates that the consumer innovator differs from the noninnovator in terms of personality orientation. A knowledge of these personality differences should help marketers segment the markets for new products and design distinct promotional strategies for both consumer innovators and later adopters.

## Cognitive Personality Factors

Consumer researchers have recently become interested in exploring how **cognitive personality** factors influence various aspects of consumer behavior.[39] One highly promising area of cognitive consumer personality research classifies consumers as *visualizers* and *verbalizers.* Findings suggest that consumers who are *visualizers* prefer visual information and products that stress the visual, while consumers who are *verbalizers* prefer written or verbal information and products that offer verbal-oriented experiences (e.g., a verbal-oriented game like Trivial Pursuit).

## The Acceptance of Foreign-Made Products

Several consumer studies suggest that personality characteristics may be useful in distinguishing between consumer segments that are likely to be receptive to foreign-made products and those that are not.

Specifically, evidence indicates that American consumers who have purchased foreign compact automobiles are less conservative and less dogmatic than those who have purchased American-made compact cars.[40] Supporting this conclusion, another personality study found that highly dogmatic consumers were significantly more likely to rate favorably products manufactured in countries perceived to be similar to the United States (e.g., England and West Germany) than those manufactured in countries rated dissimilar.[41] The opposite was also true: low dogmatic consumers were more accepting of products manufactured in countries judged dissimilar to the United States. This study also found that highly dogmatic consumers have a more favorable image of products manufactured in the United States than low dogmatic consumers.

Dogmatism has also been found to be associated with foreign visitors' general acceptance of American products. For example, a study found that Nigerian students who scored low on the dogmatism scale were more willing to accept unfamiliar American products prior to their arrival in the United States than those scoring high on dogmatism.[42]

These studies suggest that the low dogmatic consumer should be the prime market segment for marketers of foreign-made products. For American consumers, promotional appeals should stress the distinctive features and benefits of foreign-made products over American alternatives. On the other hand, domestic marketers wishing to impede inroads of foreign products should stress a nationalistic theme in their promotional appeals (e.g., "Made in America"), for such appeals are likely to attract the more dogmatic consumer. Taking advantage of the "Made in America" appeal, and the fact that blue-collar beer drinkers are especially likely to be responsive to such appeals, Miller Brewing has positioned its beer as "Made the American Way" (see Figure 4-5). Similarly, while appealing to a different socioeconomic group (the upscale consumer), clothing designer Perry Ellis introduced the Perry Ellis America Line as "a collection of sportswear for all America—looks you'll pledge allegiance to." Figure 4-6 shows one of the ads in this campaign.

## Personality and Store Choice

Personality also influences the choice of stores in which the consumer decides to shop. The consumer's *self-confidence* has been found to be associated with the type of retailer from which he or she purchases certain kinds of merchandise. For instance, female clothing shoppers who scored high in self-confidence were found to prefer discount stores as a place to buy their clothing, while shoppers with less self-confidence tended to favor the more traditional neighborhood retailer.[43] Another study reported that consumers who purchased expensive audio equipment (record players, tape players, tuners, and amplifiers) from an audio equipment specialty store were more self-confident than consumers who purchased from a traditional department store.[44]

The findings of these two studies show that the newer types of retailing establishments (e.g., the off-price and the audio equipment specialty store) tend to attract a more self-confident customer than the more traditional retailer.

FIGURE 4-5 Advertisement That Employs a "Made in America" Theme

Courtesy of Miller Brewing Co.

This suggests that new types of retailers should try to target a more self-confident market segment by appealing to the consumer's ability to recognize and properly evaluate unlabeled or specialty merchandise. More traditional retailers should attempt to reassure less-confident customers that they will stand behind their merchandise and assist them in their shopping tasks.

Evidence indicates that shoppers' personalities may even influence the kind of salesperson they prefer to have serve them. Specifically, *dependent* shoppers seem to prefer an aggressive salesperson who makes suggestions and

FIGURE 4-6 Advertisement That Stresses an American Look in Clothing

Courtesy of Perry Ellis America

takes the initiative, while *independent* shoppers prefer a less aggressive salesperson.[45]

*Color preferences* have also been linked to personality traits and shopping behavior. Specifically a consumer favoring red tends to be more fashion-conscious than a person who prefers gray. Those favoring brown or green seem to dislike using credit.[46] Table 4-4 presents various personality types that are associated with different color preferences.

**TABLE 4-4 Color-Related Personality Types and Shopper Profiles**

| COLOR | COLOR-RELATED PERSONALITY TYPES | SHOPPER TYPES | SAMPLE ITEM OF SHOPPER TYPE |
|---|---|---|---|
| green | stable, frank, loyal, intelligent, seeks success | (+) deliberate shopper<br>(−) credit user | I make good buying decisions.<br>I don't buy on credit. |
| yellow | innovative, idealistic, impatient with others, indulging | (−) deliberate Shopper<br>(+) credit user | I don't know what features I want.<br>I buy on credit. |
| red | aggressive, impulsive, quick to make judgments, variety seeking | (+) fashion and recreational shopper | I like to shop with friends. |
| gray | detached, not revealing, uninvolved | (−) fashion and recreational shopper | I don't like to shop with friends. |
| brown | steady, reliable, sense of belonging | (−) credit user | I don't buy on credit |

Source: Adapted from John C. Rogers, Mark Slama, and Terrell G. Williams, "An Exploratory Study of Luscher Color Test Predicted Personality Types and Psychographic Shopping Profiles," in Patrick E. Murphy et al., eds., *1983 AMA Educator's Proceedings* (Chicago: American Marketing Association, 1983), 30–34.

## *summary*

Personality can be described as the psychological characteristics that both determine and reflect how a person will respond to his or her environment. Although personality tends to be consistent and enduring, it has been known to change abruptly in response to major life events, as well as gradually over time.

Three theories of personality are prominent in the study of consumer behavior: psychoanalytic theory, neo-Freudian theory, and trait theory. Freud's psychoanalytic theory provides the foundation for the study of motivational research, which operates on the premise that human drives are largely unconscious in nature and serve to motivate many consumer actions. Neo-Freudian theory tends to emphasize the fundamental role of social relationships in the formation and development of personality. Alfred Adler viewed human beings as seeking to overcome feelings of inferiority. Harry Stack Sullivan believed that people attempt to establish significant and rewarding relationships with others. Karen Horney saw individuals as trying to overcome feelings of anxiety and categorized them as compliant, aggressive, or detached. Both Freudian theory and neo-Freudian theory use qualitative measures such as observation, self-report, and projective techniques to identify and measure personality characteristics.

Trait theory is a major departure from the qualitative or subjective approach to personality measurement. It postulates that individuals possess innate psychological traits (e.g., self-confidence, aggression, responsibility, curiosity) to a greater or lesser degree, and that these traits can be measured by specially designed scales or inventories. Because they are simple to use and to score and can be self-administered, personality inventories are the preferred method of many researchers for the assessment of consumer personality.

Results of consumer personality research have been somewhat uneven. Findings suggest that to improve matters, consumer researchers should (1) use single-trait tests based on prior hypotheses, (2) examine the relationship between personality and a broad product category (rather than a specific brand), and (3) consider the specific purchase or usage situation.

The identification of personality variables (e.g., dogmatism, social character, category width) that appear to be linked logically to product usage is likely to improve marketers' ability to segment markets on the basis of personality characteristics. They can design specific products that will appeal to certain personality types or design promotional strategies that will appeal to the personality characteristics of existing target audiences.

## *discussion questions*

1. Contrast the major characteristics of the following personality theories:
   a. Freudian theory
   b. Neo-Freudian theory
   c. Trait theory
2. How would you explain the fact that although no two individuals have identical personalities, personality is used in consumer research to identify distinct market segments—each consisting of many consumers?
3. What is the importance to an advertiser in knowing whether a product's target market consists primarily of inner-directed or other-directed consumers?
4. How does personality influence the choice of stores in which a consumer decides to shop?
5. Would a manufacturer of a new "high-tech" kitchen appliance be more interested in attracting the attention of broad or narrow categorizers? Why?
6. Find a print advertisement for one of Anheuser-Busch's beers (Budweiser, Busch, or Michelob). Compare the contents of the ad with the drinker personality profiles described in Table 4-3. Which drinker personality type(s) does the ad appeal to and why?

7. Describe the type of promotional message that would seem most suitable for individuals with the following personality characteristics:
   a. Low dogmatic consumers
   b. High dogmatic consumers
   c. Inner-directed consumers
   d. Other-directed consumers
8. What type of individual would most readily purchase foreign-made products?

## endnotes


1. David Krech, Richard S. Crutchfield, and Norman Livson, *Elements of Psychology*, 2nd ed. (New York: Knopf, 1969), 746.
2. William D. Wells and Arthur D. Beard, "Personality and Consumer Behavior," in Scott Ward and Thomas S. Robertson, eds., *Consumer Behavior: Theoretical Sources* (Englewood Cliffs, N.J.: Prentice-Hall, 1973), 146.
3. Ernest Dichter, *Handbook of Consumer Motivations* (New York: McGraw-Hill, 1964), 58.
4. Joseph T. Plummer, "How Personality Can Make a Difference," *Marketing News* (March–April, 1984), 17–20.
5. Maryann Mrowca, "Some Help for the Truly Anxious: A Magazine With Your Deodorant," *Wall Street Journal,* July 28, 1983, p. 21.
6. For example, see Karen Horney, *The Neurotic Personality of Our Time* (New York: Norton, 1937).
7. Joel B. Cohen, "An Interpersonal Orientation to the Study of Consumer Behavior," *Journal of Marketing Research,* 6 (August 1967), 270–78.
8. Arch G. Woodside and Ruth Andress, "CAD Eight Years Later," *Journal of the Academy of Marketing Science,* 3 (Summer–Fall 1975), 309–13.
9. Jon P. Noerager, "An Assessment of CAD—A Personality Instrument Developed Specifically for Marketing Research," *Journal of Marketing Research,* 16 (February 1979), 53–59; and Pradeep K. Tyagi, "Validation of the CAD Instrument: A Replication," in Richard P. Bagozzi and Alice M. Tybout, eds., *Advances in Consumer Research* (Ann Arbor: Association for Consumer Research, 1983), 112–14.
10. J. P. Guilford, *Personality* (New York: McGraw-Hill, 1959), 6.
11. Milton Rokeach, *The Open and Closed Mind* (New York: Basic Books, 1960).
12. H. G. Gough, *Manual for the California Psychological Inventory* (Palo Alto, Calif.: Consulting Psychological Press, 1964).
13. Harold H. Kassarjian, "Personality and Consumer Behavior: A Review," *Journal of Marketing Research,* 8 (November 1971), 409–18.
14. Franklin B. Evans, "Psychological and Objective Factors in the Prediction of Brand Choice: Ford versus Chevrolet," *Journal of Business,* 32 (October 1959), 340–69.
15. Jacob Jacoby, "Personality and Consumer Behavior: How *Not* to Find Relationships" (Purdue Papers in Consumer Psychology, Paper No. 102, 1969).

16. Ralph Westfall, "Psychological Factors in Predicting Product Choice," *Journal of Marketing,* 26 (April 1962), 34–40; Ronald E. Frank, "Market Segmentation Research: Findings and Implications," in F. M. Bass, C. W. King, and Edgar A. Pessemier, eds., *Applications of the Sciences in Marketing Management* (New York: Wiley, 1968), 49–61; John G. Myers, "Determination of Private Brand Attitudes," *Journal of Marketing Research,* 4 (February 1967), 73–81; and Henry J. Claycamp, "Characteristics of Owners of Thrift Deposits in Commercial Banks and Savings and Loan Associations," *Journal of Marketing Research,* 2 (May 1965) 163–70.

17. For a detailed review, see Wells and Beard, "Personality and Consumer Behavior," 178–90.

18. For example, see Robert P. Brody and Scott M. Cunningham, "Personality Variables and the Consumer Decision Process," *Journal of Marketing Research,* 5 (February 1968), 50–57; Joseph N. Fry, "Personality Variables and Cigarette Brand Choice," *Journal of Marketing Research,* 8 (August 1971), 298–304; and Robert A. Peterson, "Moderating the Personality—Product Usage Relationships," in Ronald C. Curhan, ed., *1974 Combined Proceedings* (Chicago: American Marketing Association, 1975), 109–12.

19. George Brooker, "An Instrument to Measure Consumer Self-Actualization," in Mary Jane Schlinger, ed., *Advances in Consumer Research* (Association for Consumer Research, 1975), II, 563–75; Cohen, "An Interpersonal Orientation"; Marvin E. Goldberg, "Identifying Relevant Psychographic Segments: How Specifying Product Functions Can Help," *Journal of Consumer Research,* 3 (December 1976), 163–69; Clark Leavitt and John Walton, "Development of a Scale for Innovativeness," in Schlinger, *Advances in Consumer Research,* II, 543–54; Robert B. Settle, Pamela L. Alreck, and John W. Glasheen, "Individual Time Orientation and Consumer Life Style," in H. Keith Hunt, ed., *Advances in Consumer Research* (Ann Arbor, Mich.: Association for Consumer Research, 1978), V, 315–19; Edgar Pessemier and Moshe Handelsman, "Temporal Variety in Consumer Behavior," *Journal of Marketing Research,* 21 (November 1984), 435–44; Linda L. Price and Nancy M. Ridgway, "Development of a Scale to Measure Innovativeness," in Richard P. Bagozzi and Alice M. Tybout, eds., *Advances in Consumer Research* (Ann Arbor: Association for Consumer Research, 1983), X, 679–84; and Russell W. Belk, "Three Scales to Measure Constructs Related to Materialism: Reliability, Validity, and Relationships to Measures of Happiness," in Thomas C. Kinnear, ed., *Advances in Consumer Research* (Ann Arbor: Mich.: Association for Consumer Research, 1984), XI, 291–97.

20. Lawrence A. Crosby and Sanford L. Grossbart, "A Blueprint for Consumer Behavior Research on Personality," in Kinnear, ed., *Advances in Consumer Research,* XI, 447–52.

21. For example, see Shirley Young, "The Dynamics of Measuring Unchange," in Russell I. Haley, ed., *Attitude Research in Transition* (Chicago: American Marketing Association, 1972), 63.

22. Russell L. Ackoff and James Emshoff, "Advertising Research at Anheuser-Busch, Inc. (1968–74)," *Sloan Management Review,* 16 (Spring 1975), 1–15.

23. Rokeach, *The Open and Closed Mind.*

24. Jacob Jacoby, "Personality and Innovation Proneness," *Journal of Marketing Research,* 8 (May 1971), 244–47; and Kenneth A. Coney, "Dogmatism and Innovation: A Replication," *Journal of Marketing Research,* 9 (November 1972), 453–55.

25. J. M. McClurg and I. R. Andrews, "A Consumer Profile Analysis of the Self-Service Gasoline Customer," *Journal of Applied Psychology,* 59 (February 1974), 119–21.

26. Kenneth A. Coney and Robert Harman, "Dogmatism and Innovation: A Situational Perspective," in William L. Wilkie, ed., *Advances in Consumer Research* (Ann Arbor, Mich.: Association for Consumer Research, 1979), VI, 118–21.

27. Brian Blake, Robert Perloff, and Richard Heslin, "Dogmatism and Acceptance of New Products," *Journal of Marketing Research,* 7 (November 1970), 483–86; and Michael B. Mazis and Timothy W. Sweeney, "Novelty and Personality with Risk as a Moderating Variable," in Boris W. Becker and Helmut Becker, eds., *1972 Combined Proceedings* (Chicago: American Marketing Association, 1973), 406–11.

28. James H. Donnelly, Jr., "Social Character and Acceptance of New Products," *Journal of Marketing Research,* 7 (February 1970), 111–13; James H. Donnelly, Jr., and John M. Ivancevich, "A Methodology for Identifying Innovator Characteristics of New Brand Purchasers," *Journal of Marketing Research,* 11 (August 1974), 331–34; and John Jay Painter and Max L. Pinegar, "Post-High Teens and Fashion Innovation," *Journal of Marketing Research,* 8 (August 1971), 368–69.

29. Donnelly, "Social Character," 112.

30. Donnelly and Ivancevich, "Methodology for Identifying Innovator Characteristics."

31. Harold H. Kassarjian, "Social Character and Differential Preference for Mass Communication," *Journal of Marketing Research,* 11 (May 1965), 146–53; and Robert B. Settle and Richard Mizerski, "Differential Response to Objective and Social Information in Advertisements," in Thomas V. Greer, ed., *1973 Combined Proceedings* (Chicago: American Marketing Association, 1974), 250–55.

32. Richard W. Mizerski and Robert B. Settle, "The Influence of Social Character on Preference for Social versus Objective Information in Advertising," *Journal of Marketing Research,* 16 (November 1979), 552–58.

33. Thomas F. Pettigrew, "The Measurement and Correlates of Category Width as a Cognitive Variable," *Journal of Personality,* 26 (December 1956), 532–44.

34. Donald I. Popielarz, "An Exploration of Perceived Risk and Willingness to Try New Products," *Journal of Marketing Research,* 4 (November 1967), 368–72.

35. James H. Donnelly, Jr., Michael J. Etzel, and Scott Roeth, "The Relationship between Consumers' Category Width and Trial of New Products," *Journal of Applied Psychology,* 57 (May 1973), 335–38; James H. Donnelly, Jr., and Michael J. Etzel, "Degree of Product Newness and Early Trial," *Journal of Marketing Research,* 10 (August 1973), 295–300; and Leon G. Schiffman, "Perceived Risk in New Product Trial by Elderly Consumers," *Journal of Marketing Research,* 9 (February 1972), 106–8.

36. Donnelly and Etzel, "Degree of Product Newness," 299.

37. P. S. Raju, "Optimum Stimulation Level: Its Relationship to Personality, Demographics, and Exploratory Behavior," *Journal of Consumer Research,* 7 (December 1980), 272–82; Leigh McAlister and Edgar Pessemier, "Variety Seeking Behavior: An Interdisciplinary Review," *Journal of Consumer Research,* 9 (December 1982), 311–22; Edgar Pessemier and Moshe Handelsman, "Temporal Variety in Consumer Behavior," *Journal of Marketing Research,* 21 (November 1984), 435–44; Erich A. Joachimsthaler and John L. Lastovicka, "Optimal Stimulation Level—Exploratory Behavior Models," *Journal of Consumer Research,* 11 (December 1984), 830–35; and Elizabeth C. Hirschman, "Experience Seeking: A Subjectivist Perspective of Consumption," *Journal of Business Research,* 12 (1984), 115–36.

38. Russell G. Wahlers and Michael J. Etzel, "A Consumer Response to Incongruity between Optimal Stimulation and Life Style Satisfaction," in Elizabeth C. Hirschman and Morris B. Holbrook, eds., *Advances in Consumer Research* (Provo, Utah: Association for Consumer Research, 1985), 97–101.

39. Morris B. Holbrook et. al., "Play as a Consumption Experience: The Roles of Emotions, Performance, and Personality in the Enjoyment of Games," *Journal of Consumer Research,* 11 (September 1984), 728–39.

40. William H. Cunningham and J. E. Crissy, "Market Segmentation by Motivation and Attitude," *Journal of Marketing Research,* 9 (February 1972), 100–2.

41. Richard C. Tongberg, "An Empirical Study of the Relationship between Dogmatism and Attitudes toward Foreign Products," in Greer, *1973 Combined Proceedings,* 87–91.

42. Leon G. Schiffman, William R. Dillon, and Festus E. Ngumah, "The Influence of Subcultural and Personality Factors on Consumer Acculturation," *Journal of International Business Studies,* 12 (Fall 1981), 137–43.

43. H. Lawrence Issacson, "Store Choice" (Doctoral dissertation, Graduate School of Business Administration, Harvard University 1964), 85–89.

44. Joseph F. Dash, Leon G. Schiffman, and Conrad Berenson, "Risk and Personality-Related Dimensions of Store Choice," *Journal of Marketing,* 40 (January 1976), 36.

45. James E. Stafford and Thomas V. Greer, "Consumer Preferences for Types of Salesmen: A Study of Independence-Dependence Characteristics," *Journal of Retailing,* 41 (Summer 1965), 27–33.

46. John C. Rogers, Mark Slama, and Terrell G. Williams, "An Exploratory Study of Luscher Color Test Predicted Personality Types and Psychographic Shopping Profiles," in Patrick E. Murphy et al., eds., *1983 AMA Educator's Proceedings* (Chicago: American Marketing Association, 1983), 30–34.

5

# Consumer Psychographics

## *introduction*

Psychographic research has captured the imagination of many marketers. During the period roughly corresponding to the first two editions of this book (i.e., since 1978), psychographics has matured to the point where it is now a common component of many firms' ongoing research efforts—especially where the goal is to isolate profitable market segments. The following partial roster of well-known products, brands, services, and publications that have benefited from psychographic studies is testimony to its popularity: Schlitz beer, Colgate-Palmolive's Irish Spring soap, Sony Betamax, Jack Daniel's whiskey, Peter Paul's Mounds, TUMS, *Holiday Magazine,* AT&T, *Los Angeles Times, Better Homes and Gardens,* Lava Soap, Union 76 gasoline, Kentucky Fried Chicken, Nescafé coffee, *People,* and Dewar's White Label Scotch. Figure 5-1 presents an example from the ongoing series of magazine ads for Dewar's White Label. The ads feature psychographic profiles of multifaceted, interesting, and sometimes well-known individuals. In much the same way as these ads depict, many marketers of goods and services conduct psychographic research to capture insights and create profiles of the consumers they wish to target.

In Chapter 2 we briefly discussed psychographics and its growing importance as a basis for segmentation. The present chapter identifies different forms of psychographics, considers how psychographic inventories are constructed, and presents a wide range of real-world illustrations and applications of this highly pragmatic segmentation tool.

> *Why is it that, in spite of all the mirrors in the world, no one really knows what he looks like?*
>
> *SCHOPENHAUER, Further Psychological Observations*

**FIGURE 5-1** Advertisement Portraying Interesting Consumers in the Form of a Psychographic Profile

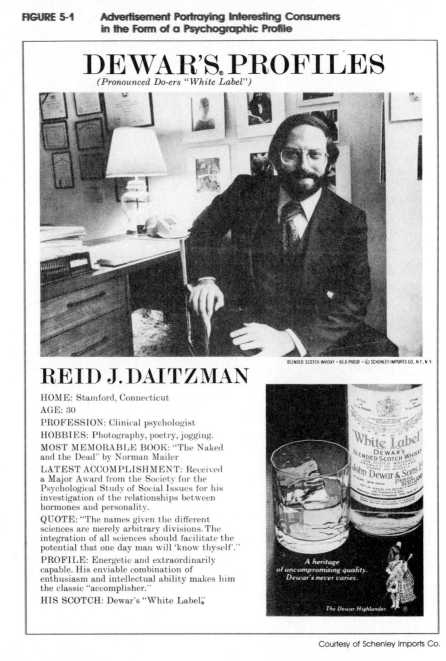

# DEWAR'S® PROFILES

*(Pronounced Do-ers "White Label")*

BLENDED SCOTCH WHISKY • 86.8 PROOF • © SCHENLEY IMPORTS CO., N.Y., N.Y.

## REID J. DAITZMAN

HOME: Stamford, Connecticut
AGE: 30
PROFESSION: Clinical psychologist
HOBBIES: Photography, poetry, jogging.
MOST MEMORABLE BOOK: "The Naked and the Dead" by Norman Mailer
LATEST ACCOMPLISHMENT: Received a Major Award from the Society for the Psychological Study of Social Issues for his investigation of the relationships between hormones and personality.
QUOTE: "The names given the different sciences are merely arbitrary divisions. The integration of all sciences should facilitate the potential that one day man will 'know thyself'."
PROFILE: Energetic and extraordinarily capable. His enviable combination of enthusiasm and intellectual ability makes him the classic "accomplisher."
HIS SCOTCH: Dewar's "White Label"®

Courtesy of Schenley Imports Co.

## WHAT IS PSYCHOGRAPHICS?

**Psychographics**, also commonly referred to as **lifestyle analysis** or **AIO research** (activities, interests, and opinions), is a form of consumer research that has been heartily embraced by both marketing practitioners and academic consumer researchers. The appeal of psychographics lies in the frequently vivid and practical profiles of consumer segments that it makes possible.

In its most common form, a psychographic study consists of a battery of statements designed to capture relevant aspects of a consumer's personality, buying motives, interests, attitudes, beliefs, and values. More product-specific forms of psychographic research have consumers respond to selective statements about products, services, brands, or specific consumption situations.[1]

In order to gain a sharper picture of psychographics, it is useful to compare it with consumer demographics and with motivational research, two aspects of consumer behavior that have a bearing on the development of psychographics.

## PSYCHOGRAPHICS VERSUS DEMOGRAPHICS

**Psychographic** and **demographic profiles** are often portrayed as competitive segmentation approaches, as if marketers could choose only one. They are, however, highly complementary approaches that work best together.[2]

As noted in Chapter 2, *demographics* consists of objective and measureable characteristics of a population, such as age, income, education, sex, and marital status. *Psychographics,* on the other hand, tends to include relatively intangible variables, such as motives, interests, attitudes, and values; these variables add vitality to consumer profiles that cannot easily be captured by demographics. Tables 5-1 and 5-2 provide a classic illustration of the very different types of information that marketers can gain from demographic and psychographic profiles of consumer segments.

Table 5-1 reveals that heavy shotgun shell buyers differ from nonbuyers in terms of demographic characteristics; they are younger, have lower incomes and less education, are typically drawn from blue-collar occupations, and are concentrated in rural areas, particularly in the southern sections of the United States.

Such insights are invaluable for targeting the most appropriate market segment for ammunition. Moreover, the demographic profile can be compared with the available demographics of various advertising media, enabling a firm selling ammunition to make reasonably good decisions as to where to spend its advertising budget.

However, the demographic profile does not indicate precisely what an ad directed to this market segment should say (or show), and what psychological characteristics best explain the buyer of ammunition. By scanning Table 5-2 we can see that hunters are usually outdoor types that are attracted to violence and adventure. They can also be characterized as risk avoiders and self-indulgent pleasure seekers.

While this additional information does not *locate* the target market, it does tell us more about it. By combining the knowledge gained from demographics and psychographics, the marketer is provided with powerful information about

TABLE 5-1 Demographic Profile of the Heavy User of Shotgun Ammunition

| | PERCENT WHO SPEND $11+ PER YEAR ON SHOTGUN AMMUNITION (141) | PERCENT WHO DON'T BUY (395) |
|---|---|---|
| **age** | | |
| Under 25 | 9 | 5 |
| 25–34 | 33 | 15 |
| 35–44 | 27 | 22 |
| 45–54 | 18 | 22 |
| 55+ | 13 | 36 |
| **occupation** | | |
| Professional | 6 | 15 |
| Managerial | 23 | 23 |
| Clerical-Sales | 9 | 17 |
| Craftsman | 50 | 35 |
| **income** | | |
| Under $6,000 | 26 | 19 |
| $6,000–$10,000 | 39 | 36 |
| $10,000–$15,000 | 24 | 27 |
| $15,000+ | 11 | 18 |
| **population density** | | |
| Rural | 34 | 12 |
| 2,500–50,000 | 11 | 11 |
| 50,000–500,000 | 16 | 15 |
| 500,000–2 million | 21 | 27 |
| 2 million+ | 13 | 19 |
| **geographic division** | | |
| New England–Mid-Atlantic | 21 | 33 |
| Central (N, W) | 22 | 30 |
| South Atlantic | 23 | 12 |
| E. South Central | 10 | 3 |
| W. South Central | 10 | 5 |
| Mountain | 6 | 3 |
| Pacific | 9 | 15 |

Source: William D. Wells, "Psychographics: A Critical Review," *Journal of Marketing Research*, 12 (May 1975), 197.

its target market. A well-known consumer researcher has noted that ". . . psychographic information can put flesh on demographic bones."[3]

## PSYCHOGRAPHICS VERSUS MOTIVATIONAL RESEARCH

Like motivational research, psychographic research provides the marketer with a comprehensive profile of the consumer. Unlike motivational research, with its typically *qualitative* portrayal of consumer characteristics, psychographic research produces *quantified* insights that are usually presented in tabular format. Psychographic measurement is similar to the measurement of personality traits, in that it requires the use of self-administered questionnaires or *inventories* con-

**TABLE 5-2 Psychographic Profile of the Heavy User of Shotgun Ammunition**

| BASE | PERCENT WHO SPEND $11+ PER YEAR ON SHOTGUN AMMUNITION (141) | PERCENT WHO DON'T BUY (395) |
|---|---|---|
| I like hunting | 88 | 7 |
| I like fishing | 68 | 26 |
| I like to go camping | 57 | 21 |
| I love the out-of-doors | 90 | 65 |
| A cabin by a quiet lake is a great place to spend the summer | 49 | 34 |
| I like to work outdoors | 67 | 40 |
| I am good at fixing mechanical things | 47 | 27 |
| I often do a lot of repair work on my own car | 36 | 12 |
| I like war stories | 50 | 32 |
| I would do better than average in a fist fight | 38 | 16 |
| I would like to be a professional football player | 28 | 18 |
| I would like to be a policeman | 22 | 8 |
| There is too much violence on television | 35 | 45 |
| There should be a gun in every home | 56 | 10 |
| I like danger | 19 | 8 |
| I would like to own my own airplane | 35 | 13 |
| I like to play poker | 50 | 26 |
| I smoke too much | 39 | 24 |
| I love to eat | 49 | 34 |
| I spend money on myself that I should spend on the family | 44 | 26 |
| If given a chance, most men would cheat on their wives | 33 | 14 |
| I read the newspaper every day | 51 | 72 |

Source: William D. Wells, "Psychographics: A Critical Review," *Journal of Marketing Research,* 12 (May 1975), 198.

sisting of statements or questions tapping consumer needs, perceptions, attitudes, beliefs, values, interests, activities, tastes, and problems. It is this blending of the desirable characteristics of both motivational research and standard paper-and-pencil personality tests that gives psychographic measurement a distinctive appeal as a consumer behavior research tool.

While psychographic research initially generates quantitative results, these results can easily be transformed from tabular form to verbal profiles similar to the qualitative profiles associated with motivational research.

For example, starting with an abundance of psychographic data, consumer researchers at a major advertising agency were able to convert their tables into descriptive verbal profiles of various market segments.[4] Table 5-3 describes (and assigns vivid names to) the profiles of the five major psychographic segments these researchers created from their mountains of data. To make

**TABLE 5-3 Five Major Psychographic Segments of the Female Population**

**thelma, the old-fashioned traditionalist (25%)**

This lady has lived a "good" life—she has been a devoted wife, a doting mother, and a conscientious housewife. She has lived her life by these traditional values and she cherishes them to this day. She does not condone contemporary sexual activities or political liberalism, nor can she sympathize with the women's libbers. Even today, when most of her children have left home, her life is centered around the kitchen. Her one abiding interest outside the household is the church which she attends every week. She lacks higher education and hence has little appreciation for the arts or cultural activities. Her spare time is spent watching TV, which is her prime source of entertainment and information.

**mildred, the militant mother (20%)**

Mildred married young and had children before she was quite ready to raise a family. Now she is unhappy. She is having trouble making ends meet on her blue-collar husband's income. She is frustrated and she vents her frustrations by rebelling against the system. She finds escape from her unhappy world in soap operas and movies. Television provides an ideal medium for her to live out her fantasies. She watches TV all through the day and into late night. She likes heavy rock and probably soul music, and she doesn't read much except escapist magazines such as True Story.

**candice, the chic suburbanite (20%)**

Candice is an urbane woman. She is well educated and genteel. She is a prime mover in her community, active in club affairs and working on community projects. Socializing is an important part of her life. She is a doer, interested in sports and the outdoors, politics and current affairs. Her life is hectic and lived at a fast clip. She is a voracious reader, and there are few magazines she doesn't read. However, TV does relatively poorly in competing for her attention—it is too inane for her.

**cathy, the contented housewife (18%)**

Cathy epitomizes simplicity. Her life is untangled. She is married to a worker in the middle of the socioeconomic scale, and they, along with their several preteen children, live in a small town. She is devoted to her family and faithfully serves them as mother, housewife, and cook. There is a certain tranquility in her life. She enjoys a relaxed pace and avoids anything that might disturb her equilibrium. She doesn't like news or news-type programs on TV but enjoys the wholesome family entertainment provided by Walt Disney, The Waltons, and Happy Days.

**eleanor, the elegant socialite (17%)**

Eleanor is a woman with style. She lives in the city because that is where she wants to be. She likes the economic and social aspects of big city living and takes advantage of the city in terms of her career and leisure time activities. She is a self-confident on-the-go woman, not a homebody. She is fashion-conscious and dresses well. She is a woman with panache. She is financially secure; as a result she is not a careful shopper. She shops for quality and style, not price. She is a cosmopolitan woman who has traveled abroad or wants to.

Source: Sunil Mehrota and William D. Wells, "Psychographics and Buyer Behavior: Theory and Recent Empirical Findings," in Arch G. Woodside et al., eds., *Consumer and Industrial Buying Behavior* (New York: North-Holland, 1977), 54.

these distilled profiles even more useful for segmenting female markets for specific products, the researchers then portrayed the five segments in terms of an index of product usage (see Table 5-4) and media habits (see Table 5-5).

Combining these various pieces of consumer insights, we can see, for example, that Thelma—a stereotype of the old-fashioned *traditionalist*—is most likely to color her hair, but least likely to use eye makeup. Moreover she is a country and western music fan and her magazine tastes lean toward the *Reader's Digest*. Such information would be quite useful to a firm like Clairol if it wished to reach the Thelmas of the world. In contrast, a marketer of a prestige line of cosmetics and fragrances, like Estée Lauder (see Figure 5-2), is likely to prefer to target women like Eleanor, *the elegant socialite*. Such women are predisposed to using cologne, lipstick, hair spray, nail polish, and various other forms of expensive makeup, and are devoted readers of *Cosmopolitan*, *Glamour* and *Vogue*—which is where Estée Lauder is likely to reach this consumer segment.

**TABLE 5-4** An Index of Cosmetic Product Usage for the Five Female Psychographic Segments

| | THELMA | ELEANOR | CANDICE | CATHY | MILDRED |
|---|---|---|---|---|---|
| I often wear very expensive cologne | 79 | 175 | 111 | 80 | 82 |
| Lipstick | 100 | 156 | 111 | 100 | 81 |
| Hair spray | 114 | 150 | 92 | 100 | 72 |
| Nail polish | 76 | 142 | 100 | 88 | 142 |
| Hair coloring | 200 | 142 | 150 | 65 | 15 |
| Eye makeup | 31 | 135 | 115 | 104 | 127 |
| Wig | 80 | 124 | 100 | 106 | 103 |
| Breath freshener | 132 | 139 | 86 | 82 | 93 |
| Medicated face makeup | 70 | 106 | 94 | 106 | 140 |
| Cleansing face cream or lotion | 96 | 129 | 107 | 82 | 121 |
| Suntan lotion | 35 | 126 | 126 | 118 | 140 |
| Hand lotion | 100 | 99 | 108 | 100 | 95 |
| Shampoo | 90 | 92 | 107 | 106 | 111 |

Source: Sunil Mehrota and William D. Wells, "Psychographics and Buyer Behavior: Theory and Recent Empirical Findings," in Arch G. Woodside et al., eds., *Consumer and Industrial Buying Behavior* (New York: North-Holland, 1977), 57.

**TABLE 5-5** An Index of Media Habits for the Five Female Psychographic Segments

| | THELMA | ELEANOR | CANDICE | CATHY | MILDRED |
|---|---|---|---|---|---|
| Heavy rock | 14 | 71 | 92 | 86 | 257 |
| Popular music | 65 | 92 | 98 | 112 | 143 |
| Middle-of-the-road music | 79 | 102 | 130 | 100 | 98 |
| Country and western | 112 | 89 | 81 | 115 | 102 |
| Classical/semiclassical | 90 | 97 | 162 | 67 | 79 |
| Time | 64 | 100 | 206 | 53 | 92 |
| Newsweek | 60 | 113 | 180 | 67 | 73 |
| US News and World Report | 90 | 100 | 172 | 73 | 45 |
| People | 46 | 115 | 154 | 85 | 115 |
| Cosmopolitan | 43 | 150 | 121 | 64 | 136 |
| Vogue | 50 | 167 | 167 | 33 | 83 |
| Glamour | 40 | 130 | 130 | 80 | 120 |
| Playboy | 21 | 129 | 121 | 100 | 171 |
| True Story | 83 | 50 | 33 | 133 | 233 |
| Redbook | 83 | 93 | 113 | 103 | 113 |
| TV Guide | 76 | 103 | 84 | 108 | 137 |
| Parents | 60 | 70 | 130 | 120 | 180 |
| Family Circle | 93 | 100 | 115 | 171 | 85 |
| Better Homes and Gardens | 92 | 106 | 129 | 90 | 86 |
| House and Garden | 83 | 117 | 133 | 78 | 100 |
| American Home | 86 | 114 | 124 | 81 | 100 |
| Good Housekeeping | 86 | 104 | 120 | 104 | 88 |
| Ladies' Home Journal | 95 | 115 | 117 | 102 | 80 |
| McCall's | 95 | 114 | 116 | 93 | 86 |
| Reader's Digest | 106 | 100 | 110 | 100 | 82 |
| Morning newspaper | 107 | 115 | 144 | 78 | 60 |
| Evening newspaper | 100 | 105 | 105 | 113 | 79 |
| Sunday newspaper | 100 | 112 | 118 | 100 | 76 |

Source: Sunil Mehrota and William D. Wells, "Psychographics and Buyer Behavior: Theory and Recent Empirical Findings," in Arch G. Woodside et al., eds., *Consumer and Industrial Buying Behavior* (New York: North-Holland, 1977), 58.

FIGURE 5-2 An Ad Appeal to the "Eleanors" of the World

Courtesy of Estee Lauder Inc.

## TYPES OF PSYCHOGRAPHIC VARIABLES

As previously noted, psychographic variables are often referred to as **AIOs,** for much psychographic research focuses on the measurement of **activities, interests,** and **opinions**:[5]

*Activities:* How a consumer (or a family) spends time.
*Interests:* A consumer's (or a family's) preferences and priorities.
*Opinions:* How a consumer feels about a wide variety of events and things.

Table 5-6 lists the general elements often included within each of these major dimensions of psychographic analysis.

### Personal and Family Psychographic Statements

**Psychographic (AIO) inventories** usually require consumers to evaluate their personal (individual) or their family's (household's) stand in relation to a wide variety of statements. To illustrate, if Polaroid decided to reassess the target

**TABLE 5-6** **AIO Studies Encompass a Wide Variety of Variables**

| ACTIVITIES | INTERESTS | OPINIONS |
|---|---|---|
| Work | Family | Themselves |
| Hobbies | Home | Social issues |
| Social events | Job | Politics |
| Vacation | Community | Business |
| Entertainment | Recreation | Economics |
| Club membership | Fashion | Education |
| Community | Food | Products |
| Shopping | Media | Future |
| Sports | Achievement | Culture |

Source: Joseph T. Plummer, "The Concept and Application of Life Style Segmentation," *Journal of Marketing*, 38 (January 1974), 34.

market for its instant-photo cameras in terms of psychographic characteristics, it might use the following psychographic statements to capture individual and family predispositions to picture-taking and instant photography:

*Personal Statements:*

I'm an emotional person.
When I do something, I want to know immediately how well I have done.
I probably think of my children more than my friends think of their children.
I spend a lot of time looking at old family pictures.
My parents took many pictures of me when I was a child.

*Family Statements:*

Compared to most, we are an especially good-looking family.
We tend to go on at least one vacation a year as a family.
We have family pictures on display all over the house.
We have lots of gadgets in our home.
We would do well living in an unfamiliar part of the world.

Respondents are asked to evaluate such statements in terms of degree of "agreement" or "importance." Sometimes psychographic research focuses on the amount of time spent by an individual (or family) on various activities and interests. Table 5-7 lists some of the lifestyle activities and interests this time-oriented approach is designed to capture.

## General and Product-Specific Statements

In addition to reflecting either personal or family activities, interests, and opinions, psychographic statements can be designed to be either **general** or **product-specific.**[6] In carrying out a psychographic study of a specific product category, consumer researchers are likely to include both general and product-specific statements.

For example, a study aimed at examining the practice of serving soup for lunch might include such *general* statements as these: "It is more important for

**TABLE 5-7 Time Spent on Specific Activities and Interests**

For each of the following activity or interest areas, please place an "X" in the box that best indicates how often you have engaged in the activity during the past 12 months.

| | 0 TIMES | 1–2 TIMES | 3–4 TIMES | 5 OR MORE TIMES |
|---|---|---|---|---|
| Went to a library | ☐ | ☐ | ☐ | ☐ |
| Went to a gym or health club | ☐ | ☐ | ☐ | ☐ |
| Had food sent in | ☐ | ☐ | ☐ | ☐ |
| Went to a basketball game | ☐ | ☐ | ☐ | ☐ |
| Wrote a letter to a friend | ☐ | ☐ | ☐ | ☐ |
| Attended a concert | ☐ | ☐ | ☐ | ☐ |
| Went on a vacation | ☐ | ☐ | ☐ | ☐ |
| Went shopping for clothing | ☐ | ☐ | ☐ | ☐ |
| Attended an art museum | ☐ | ☐ | ☐ | ☐ |
| Played bridge | ☐ | ☐ | ☐ | ☐ |

**FIGURE 5-3 A General/Product-Specific Psychographic Continuum** Source: Adapted from Michel A. Zins, "An Exploration of the Relationship between General and Specific Psychographic Profiles," in Kenneth Bernhardt, ed., *Marketing: 1776–1976 and Beyond* (Chicago: American Marketing Association, 1976). 508.

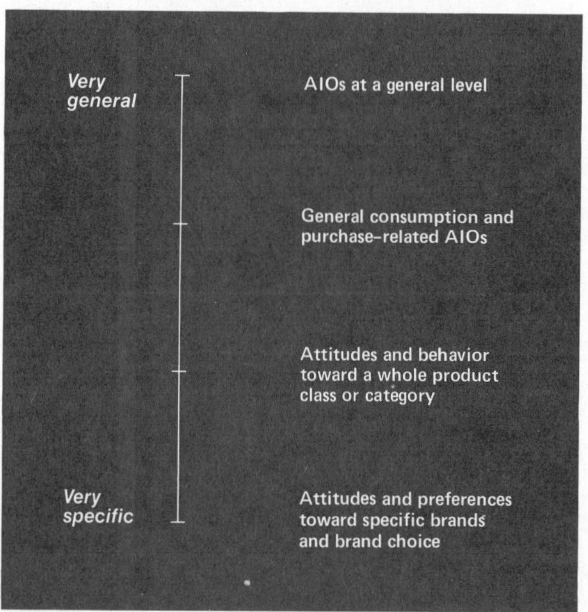

food to taste good than be nutritious;" "I always try to give my family what they like for lunch." It might also include such *product-specific* statements as "I really believe the claim that 'Soup is good food'; " "When I was a child, my mother regularly served soup at mealtime." Both types of statements supply valuable insights regarding consumers' attitudes; however, the product-specific statements pertain directly to the product and its use, while the general statements focus on broader perceptions, preferences, or *style of life*.

The range of psychographic statements can actually be thought of as a continuum with very general lifestyle statements at one end of the continuum and highly product- or brand-specific attitudinal and behavioral statements at the other end.[7] The simple schematic in Figure 5-3 characterizes the range of psychographic statements on a *general* to *specific* continuum.

In setting out to conduct a segmentation study for a particular brand or product category, a consumer researcher would probably be wise to consider constructing psychographic statements that span the full range of this continuum. Using travelers checks as an illustration, Table 5-8 provides examples of the interaction of the four major types of psychographic statements we have discussed in this section.

**TABLE 5-8 Classification of Different Types of Psychographic Statements for Travelers Checks**

| | INDIVIDUAL/PERSONAL | FAMILY/HOUSEHOLD |
|---|---|---|
| general | "I think about my safety and security when planning a trip." | "When on vacation our family is always shopping." |
| | "I use a seat belt even when going to the local store for milk." | "We use hotel safes to store our valuables when away on a family trip." |
| product-specific | "Travelers checks are for people who are inexperienced travelers." | "We wouldn't even go on an overnight trip without travelers checks." |
| | "I almost always keep some travelers checks in my wallet." | "We really appreciate the peace of mind that travelers checks provide." |

## CONSTRUCTING A PSYCHOGRAPHIC INVENTORY

In constructing an inventory of psychographic items (statements), researchers first review available market research studies that might be of help in isolating psychographic variables. Motivational research studies are a particularly good source, for they tend to include consumers' reflections on their experiences and needs. Based upon such a review, psychographic statements are prepared which reflect the range of activities, interests, and opinions that the researcher

**TABLE 5-9** **A Sample of AT&T Psychographic Categories and Statements**

| thriftiness | gadget-oriented |
|---|---|
| People who have stylish telephones are lucky because they can afford them.<br>Those who know me would consider me to be thrifty.<br>I usually look for the lowest possible prices when I shop.<br>I usually wait to learn how good a new product is before trying it. | A pushbutton phone is for people with more money than they know what to do with.<br>I find pushbutton telephones unattractive.<br>I prefer pushbutton phones even though they are more expensive.<br>A dial light on a telephone is an example of an unnecessary luxury.<br>The trimline phone is very stylish.<br>I prefer colored appliances.<br>I wouldn't pay extra for a decorator telephone. |
| **fashion innovator** | **keeping-in-touch** |
| If a new style of telephone were introduced, I would be more likely to get it than my friends.<br>We will probably move within the next three years.<br>I would enjoy moving to a different part of the country.<br>When I must choose between the two, I usually dress for fashion, not comfort.<br>I admit that I dress to please others.<br>I enjoy trying new products when they first come out. | I prefer to have several telephones in my home as a convenience.<br>My home is small so I don't need more than one telephone.<br>I need several telephones in my home because of my work/business.<br>I spend a lot of time talking on the telephone.<br>I probably make more long distance calls than most people I know.<br>We frequently have someone in the family away from home.<br>My home is an open house, with friends and neighbors always visiting. |

Source: John J. Veltri and Leon G. Schiffman, "Fifteen Years of Consumer Lifestyle and Value Research at AT&T," in Robert E. Pitts, Jr. and Arch G. Woodside, eds., *Personal Values and Consumer Psychology* (Lexington, MA: Heath, 1984), 277.

wishes to evaluate. Table 5-9 lists several psychographic categories and corresponding statements identified by AT&T while carrying out various segmentation studies designed to better understand the needs of its residential consumers.

In constructing a **psychographic inventory**, it is important to determine whether consumers will understand the meaning of each of the statements as the marketer intended them to be interpreted, or whether other interpretations are possible—which would produce invalid results. It is also important to avoid statements that lead consumers to make a *socially acceptable response* which really does not reflect their true feelings or likely actions. Actually, the same thing used in the construction of a reliable and valid personality scale (Does it provide consistent results? Do different scores reflect true differences between people?) is also used in the construction of a psychographic instrument.

In responding to a psychographic inventory, consumers are usually asked to rate the extent of their agreement or disagreement with each statement. Table 5-10 presents a portion of a psychographic inventory used by AT&T to study various aspects of consumers' telephone behavior.

**TABLE 5-10** **A Portion of an Actual Psychographic Inventory**

*Please read each statement and put an "X" in the box which best indicates how strongly you agree or disagree with the statement.*

| Statement | Agree Completely | Agree Somewhat | Agree a Little | Disagree a Little | Disagree Somewhat | Disagree Completely |
|---|---|---|---|---|---|---|
| I am the kind of person who carefully plans whatever I do | ☐1 | ☐2 | ☐3 | ☐4 | ☐5 | ☐6 |
| I try to set a limit in dollars for my monthly long distance calling | ☐1 | ☐2 | ☐3 | ☐4 | ☐5 | ☐6 |
| I will probably move within the next three years | ☐1 | ☐2 | ☐3 | ☐4 | ☐5 | ☐6 |
| I would like to use a home computer to send and receive messages and information over the telephone ... | ☐1 | ☐2 | ☐3 | ☐4 | ☐5 | ☐6 |
| Before trying a new product or service, I seldom seek the advice of others | ☐1 | ☐2 | ☐3 | ☐4 | ☐5 | ☐6 |
| I would be willing to pay a monthly fee for a plan that would save me money on each of my long distance calls | ☐1 | ☐2 | ☐3 | ☐4 | ☐5 | ☐6 |
| When it comes to enjoying myself, I prefer going out rather than staying at home | ☐1 | ☐2 | ☐3 | ☐4 | ☐5 | ☐6 |
| I would enjoy moving to a different part of the country | ☐1 | ☐2 | ☐3 | ☐4 | ☐5 | ☐6 |
| I would use any long distance telephone company that would save me a couple of dollars a month | ☐1 | ☐2 | ☐3 | ☐4 | ☐5 | ☐6 |
| My work keeps me away from home too much | ☐1 | ☐2 | ☐3 | ☐4 | ☐5 | ☐6 |
| It's important to keep in touch with close relatives by long distance | ☐1 | ☐2 | ☐3 | ☐4 | ☐5 | ☐6 |
| I think the cost of a long distance call is a good value for the money | ☐1 | ☐2 | ☐3 | ☐4 | ☐5 | ☐6 |
| When I am feeling low, a long distance call to the right person can pick me up | ☐1 | ☐2 | ☐3 | ☐4 | ☐5 | ☐6 |
| When I call someone long distance, it suggests that I care more than if I sent a letter | ☐1 | ☐2 | ☐3 | ☐4 | ☐5 | ☐6 |
| Many of my long distance calls are to get specific answers to specific questions | ☐1 | ☐2 | ☐3 | ☐4 | ☐5 | ☐6 |
| Close friends and relatives usually feel good after I call them long distance | ☐1 | ☐2 | ☐3 | ☐4 | ☐5 | ☐6 |
| I would really like to give some of my relatives a special card that would allow them to call only me, and I would be billed for the calls | ☐1 | ☐2 | ☐3 | ☐4 | ☐5 | ☐6 |

Courtesy of AT&T.

## APPLICATIONS OF PSYCHOGRAPHIC ANALYSIS

Psychographic analysis is particularly useful in three closely related areas of marketing strategy: (1) **segmenting markets**, (2) **positioning** and **repositioning** products, and (3) developing **specific promotional campaigns**.

### Market Segmentation

Psychographic research is an especially useful tool in segmenting markets. Before the divestiture of the Bell System, for example, AT&T was involved in segmenting its markets for various services—including Touch-Tone service. Table

5-11 presents a psychographic-demographic profile of customers with Touch-Tone telephone service. The evidence suggests that Touch-Tone was particularly attractive to young, upscale, mobile families; users of expensive, colorful gadgets; fashion innovators; heavy telephone users; risk takers and those not price conscious. Such a psychographic/demographic profile is useful in providing direction as to which segments to target, what to say to them, and even which advertising media might best be used to reach them.

Psychographic research is an efficient way of identifying psychological and sociocultural characteristics of specific target markets.[8] For example, the psychographic profile in Table 5-12 compares drivers who have had no automobile accidents during a five-year period with drivers who have had at least two accidents. The findings reveal that accident-prone drivers are risk takers and more pressured and impulsive than drivers who had no accidents. Also, though they seem to have more money problems, accident-prone drivers were found to be generally more optimistic about the future, more cosmopolitan in their interests, and more adventurous and less conservative in their lifestyles.[9] Armed with such a profile of the accident-prone driver, insurance companies and highway safety agencies are in a better position to develop public service campaigns to effectively motivate particular segments of the driving public to drive cautiously.

Psychographics has been applied successfully in a variety of retail settings. It has also proved useful in segmenting consumers into various retail shopper categories.[10] Table 5-13 shows the results of a study that compares *recreational* shoppers (consumers who enjoy shopping and consider it a leisure-time activity) with *economic* shoppers (consumers who are indifferent to or even dislike shopping and view it from a strictly time- or money-saving perspective). The results indicate that recreational shoppers tend to exhibit the following preferences and characteristics as compared with economic shoppers.[11]

**TABLE 5-11 A Psychographic-Demographic Profile of Touch-Tone Service Customers**

| | |
|---|---|
| **gadget-oriented** | **keeping-in-touch** |
| Prefer expensive features | Several phones |
| Mechanical interests | Talk a lot on phone |
| Colorful appliances | Family on the go |
| **fashion innovators** | **thriftiness** |
| More innovative | Not thrifty |
| New products | Risk-takers |
| Fashion conscious | |
| More mobile | |
| **demographics** | |
| Young head-of-household | |
| Early + life cycle | |
| Upscale | |
| Large dwelling | |
| More mobile | |

Source: John J. Veltri and Leon G. Schiffman, "Fifteen Years of Consumer Lifestyle and Value Research at AT&T," in Robert E. Pitts, Jr. and Arch G. Woodside, eds., *Personal Values and Consumer Psychology* (Lexington, MA: Heath, 1984), 278.

1. They spend more time shopping, and they prefer enclosed shopping malls and department stores.
2. They attach greater importance to stores featuring quality products, a wide selection of merchandise, and a pleasant decor.
3. They are more likely to be impulse shoppers.
4. They have greater exposure to retail-oriented mass media.
5. They enjoy outdoor activities and are more inclined to entertain guests at home.

These findings suggest that recreational shoppers are an especially profitable consumer segment that should be actively pursued by the operators of enclosed shopping malls and by department stores.

**TABLE 5-12 A Brief Psychographic Profile of the Accident-Prone Driver (in percentages)**

| | NUMBER OF ACCIDENTS IN PAST FIVE YEARS | |
|---|---|---|
| | two or more | none |
| risk taker | | |
| I don't like to take chances (disagree). | 42 | 31 |
| I am the kind of person who will try anything once. | 64 | 53 |
| restless | | |
| I would probably be content to live in the same town the rest of my life (disagree). | 40 | 28 |
| We will probably move at least once in the next five years. | 50 | 32 |
| pressured | | |
| I work under a great deal of pressure most of the time. | 69 | 57 |
| impulse buyer | | |
| I am an impulse buyer. | 47 | 35 |
| When I see a brand somewhat different from the usual, I investigate it. | 73 | 63 |
| money problems | | |
| Our family is too heavily in debt today. | 36 | 25 |
| Worrying about money. | 52 | 30 |
| optimistic | | |
| My greatest achievements are ahead of me. | 78 | 61 |
| Five years from now our family income will probably be a lot higher than it is now. | 81 | 60 |
| cosmopolitan | | |
| I like to think I am a bit of a swinger. | 46 | 28 |
| I would like to spend a year in London or Paris. | 41 | 30 |
| interested in movies | | |
| I like to watch disaster movies. | 47 | 32 |
| Attended an x-rated movie. | 19 | 9 |
| less conservative | | |
| Communism is the greatest peril in the world today. | 48 | 59 |
| U.S. would be better off if there were no hippies. | 46 | 60 |
| Unions have too much power in America today. | 67 | 77 |
| Most big companies are just out for themselves. | 77 | 67 |

Source: Sunil Mehrota and William D. Wells, "Psychographic and Buyer Behavior: Theory and Recent Empirical Findings," in Arch G. Woodside et al., eds., *Consumer and Industrial Buying Behavior* (New York, North-Holland, 1977), 60.

**TABLE 5-13** **A Psychographic Comparison of Recreational Shoppers and Economic Shoppers**

| VARIABLE | | PERCENTAGE OF RECREATIONAL SHOPPERS | PERCENTAGE OF ECONOMIC SHOPPERS |
|---|---|---|---|
| Spend at least one hour per shopping trip | | 97 | 76 |
| Usually shop at: | Closed shopping mall | 83 | 67 |
| | Open shopping center | 12 | 23 |
| | Downtown | 5 | 6 |
| Type of store shopped at: | Department | 72 | 52 |
| | Discount | 11 | 16 |
| | Specialty | 17 | 32 |
| Consider quality of merchandise to be important | | 68 | 60 |
| Consider variety of merchandise to be important | | 59 | 42 |
| Consider store decor to be important | | 35 | 19 |
| Usually have an idea of what I am going to buy | | 90 | 100 |
| Continue to shop after making a purchase | | 73 | 37 |
| Usually buy what I would like to have | | 45 | 23 |
| Usually buy products that I like but don't need immediately | | 20 | 6 |
| Enjoy watching TV | | 67 | 52 |
| Enjoy hiking | | 60 | 40 |
| Enjoy cooking | | 35 | 50 |
| Enjoy camping | | 65 | 35 |
| Enjoy sewing | | 11 | 31 |
| Enjoy attending sports events | | 84 | 70 |
| Enjoy entertaining guests at home | | 87 | 73 |
| Daily reading of local newspaper | | 70 | 30 |
| Three or more hours of TV viewing | | 12 | 4 |

Source: Adapted from Danny N. Bellenger and Pradeep K. Korgaonkar, Profiling the Recreational Shopper," *Journal of Retailing*, 56 (Fall 1980), 84–85.

## Product Positioning and Repositioning

If a company is not certain which segment should be the target for new product development, it can use psychographic analysis to identify those consumers who seem to be least satisfied with existing products, and thus more likely to respond favorably to a new product. On the basis of its findings, the company can design a product and marketing strategy that specifically appeals to this market.

An interesting new-product application of **psychographic positioning** relates to General Foods' line of Cycle canned dog foods. Originally General Foods, though a leading marketer of dog foods, did not market canned dog foods. To gain a foothold in this important submarket, it undertook an intensive research program that examined various sociocultural changes that might influence dog ownership and dog care.[12] An important part of this research focused on the identification of five major dog owner segments, each with a unique set of needs or motives concerning ownership or care. Table 5-14 (on pages 156–157) summarizes the main characteristics of these segments together with important information about their pet-feeding attitudes and behavior. Based upon this and other research, General Foods launched its Cycle canned dog foods. Figure 5-4 shows an early advertisement for the product line.

**FIGURE 5-4** **An Advertisement for a Product Line Developed as an Out-Growth of Psychographic Research** Source: Advertisement for CYCLE® dog food reproduced with permission of General Foods Corporation, White Plains, New York.

# Announcing Cycle.®

## The first line of dog foods formulated to meet your dog's changing nutritional needs.

**Read why your dog's needs change as he goes through life from puppyhood to old age. Discover how Cycle®– a new line of specially balanced meals– meets these changing needs as no single dog food can.**

Until today, most dog foods have been basically the same. In one important respect. They have been designed for the *average* needs of the *average* dog. But what is an "average" dog?

A dog, like a person changes. He grows up. He slows down. He grows old. He may be trim or fat. As he goes through these different stages, his teeth, bones, coat, digestion, kidney function—all these things and more—change.

But, canned, dry or soft-moist—there's never been a line of dog foods designed to meet all these changing needs.

**Nutrition dogs need – in flavors dogs love**

Cycle is not just one more dog food. It is a line of *four distinctly different foods, formulated for each important stage in your dog's life.*

Each Cycle meal is a complete, balanced dinner of meaty chunks—in delicious beef and chicken flavors. Your dog will love it. Even more importantly, he will thrive on it.

**Cycle® 1 – for puppies (up to 18 months)**

During this short time, your puppy should grow to his full adult size. Pound for pound, he burns up 100% more calories than he will as an adult. He needs extra protein, and about twice the vitamins and minerals to build muscle and bone. Cycle 1 concentrates all this extra nutrition in a formula specially balanced for puppy-sized stomachs. (And unlike dry puppy foods, Cycle 1 comes in tender, meaty broiled chunks.)

**Cycle® 2 – for young adult dogs (ages 1 to 7)**

Cycle 2 is specifically formulated for your dog's *peak years.* For the way his body burns up energy, and uses protein. With the correct balance of vitamins and minerals to help keep him trim and fit. (And the good, meaty taste it takes to keep him happy.)

**Cycle® 3 – for overweight dogs**

A few excess pounds can be unhealthy for your dog. So even though he may not *appear* overweight (decreased activity can often be the only visible sign), check with your veterinarian. If your dog *is* overweight, he should be fed Cycle 3. Its tasty formula contains *less fat and 20% fewer calories than the leading canned dog food.* With normal exercise, Cycle 3 can help an overweight dog return to his proper, healthy weight again.

**Cycle® 4 – for older dogs (over 7 years)**

Depending on the breed of your dog, the signs of age may appear slowly. A little grayness around the muzzle, slight changes in his coat or a decrease in his activity. But regardless of breed, by the time your dog is seven, his age begins to tell —*inside where it doesn't show.* Cycle 4 is formulated specifically for these later years. It is made especially easy for an older dog to chew and digest. It contains extra calcium to help strengthen his aging bones. And, to help reduce stress on his tired kidneys (perhaps the most common weakness in the older dog), Cycle 4 contains high-quality protein in an amount he can easily use.

**To take the best care of your dog, visit your veterinarian regularly. And feed nutritious Cycle.**

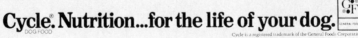

**Cycle.® Nutrition...for the life of your dog.**

DOG FOOD

Cycle is a registered trademark of the General Foods Corporation.

**TABLE 5-14** **A Profile of Five Key Psychographic Segments of the Dog Food Market**

| NAME | FUNCTIONALIST | FAMILY MUTT | BABY SUBSTITUTE | NUTRITIONALISTS | MIDDLE OF ROAD |
|---|---|---|---|---|---|
| size: | | | | | |
| % of Dog Owners | 40% | 25% | 10% | 13% | 12% |
| % of Commercial Dog Food Feedings | 55% | 20% | 5% | 10% | 10% |
| demography: (Note these are tendencies based upon a given group's profile relative to the other groups) | Multiple dog ownership; Children present; lower income/C, D counties | Own one dog; Average size; Children present; lower income/C, D counties | Own one very small, older dog; Kids not present; higher income, urban | Multiple dog ownership; largest dogs; low probability of kids; Eastern, urban, higher income | No distinctive characteristics |
| attitudes: (Note these are tendencies based upon a given group's profile relative to other groups) | Dogs outdoor/hearty; eat anything, no bother; Little attachment to dog; Interested in ownership benefits; Average interest in nutrition; Housewife not involved with dog. | Little interest in dog; Dog playful, no bother; Below average menu acceptance; Interest in owner-benefits; Least interest in nutrition; Housewife not involved, dog is for kids. | Dog fragile, indoor animal; above average attachment to dog; Heavily involved in choice of food; Dog finicky eater, great desire to prepare what dog wants. | Very personally attached to dog; Dog belongs to housewife; Most interested in nutrition; Least interested in cost, food flexibility; Virile dog. | |

| | | | | | |
|---|---|---|---|---|---|
| types used: | Basically meal feeders—very little use of other types. | Heavy meal usage but also atypically high use of low priced canned. | High degree of canned use, relatively little of meal; High relative use of soft-moist and biscuits. | Most feedings meal—relatively strong high priced canned and biscuit use. | Feed meal and canned to about same extent; High relative use of soft-moist. |
| % of total feedings given to each type | Soft-Moist 2.0%<br>Meal 88.2<br>*Canned* *8.9*<br>High 1.2<br>Parity 1.8<br>Economy 5.9<br>Biscuits 0.9 | Soft-Moist 6.4%<br>Meal 63.7<br>*Canned* *28.4*<br>High 3.2<br>Parity 8.2<br>Economy 17.0<br>Biscuits 1.5 | Soft-Moist 7.8%<br>Meal 59.0<br>*Canned* *27.1*<br>High 10.2<br>Parity 7.4<br>Economy 9.5<br>Biscuits 6.1 | Soft-Moist 25.4%<br>Meal 22.7<br>*Canned* *44.9*<br>High 14.9<br>Parity 16.9<br>Economy 13.1<br>Biscuits 7.0 | Soft-Moist 41.0%<br>Meal 43.7<br>*Canned* *37.7*<br>High 6.7<br>Parity 12.5<br>Economy 18.5<br>Biscuits 4.6 |
| location: post region | Stronger than average in Central & South; very weak in West. | Stronger than average in East; very weak in West. | Stronger than average in West; relatively weak in East. | Very strong in South & East; very weak in West. | Stronger than average in East and Central; Western South. |

Source: F. Stewart DeBruicker and Scott Ward, *Cases in Consumer Behavior* (Englewood Cliffs, N.J.: Prentice-Hall, 1980), 28.

As a further example of how AT&T uses psychographic research to position or reposition products, Table 5-15 presents side-by-side profiles of households that own the Mickey Mouse phone and households that own the Snoopy and Woodstock phones. Research indicated that the Mickey Mouse phone appealed to all ages within the $15,000–$25,000 family income range, while the Snoopy and Woodstock phones attracted a younger, more affluent group of consumers. In terms of psychographic differences, the findings suggest that households with the Mickey Mouse phone have a lifestyle that centers around the home as a place to entertain family and friends, and this phone was likely to be located in a family room where it was readily observable. On the other hand, Snoopy and Woodstock phone owners were more likely to be outdoorsy people who engage in a wide variety of physical and recreational activities. Consistent with their generally more informal outlook, they located their character phones in the child's room, where it was less likely to be observed by adult visitors. Also important to AT&T in terms of ultimate sales revenue was the finding that the Mickey Mouse phone was frequently a replacement for some other premium phone, while the Snoopy and Woodstock phones tended to be a "net" new phone for the household. Prior to this research, it was frequently assumed that all character phones had the same general appeal.

## Promotional Campaigns

Psychographic analysis has been widely used in the development of advertising campaigns to answer three questions: "*Whom* should we target?" "*What* should we say?" "*Where* should we say it?" To help advertisers answer the third question, most mass media vehicles sponsor psychographic and demographic research as the basis for carefully detailed *audience profiles*. Table 5-16 presents a brief comparison of heavy *Playboy* readers and heavy *Reader's Digest* readers. By offering media buyers psychographic studies of their audiences, in addition to

**TABLE 5-15 A Psychographic–Demographic Comparison of Two Character Model Telephones**

| DESCRIPTOR | THE MICKEY MOUSE PHONE | THE SNOOPY AND WOODSTOCK PHONES |
|---|---|---|
| Dominant psychographic traits | Eclectic in home decorating outlook | At ease/informal |
| Age | Broad age appeal | Under 35 years old |
| Family income | $15,000–$25,000 | Over $25,000 |
| Room placement | Family room | Child's room |
| Total phone impact | Replacement of "premium" set | Additional set |
| Mass media | Low TV and magazine readers | Low media |
| Lifestyle activities | Home and family/friends oriented | Physically and recreationally active |

Source: John J. Veltri and Leon G. Schiffman, "Fifteen Years of Consumer Lifestyle and Value Research at AT&T," in Robert E. Pitts, Jr. and Arch G. Woodside, eds., *Personal Values and Consumer Psychology* (Lexington, MA: Heath, 1984), 282.

TABLE 5-16 A Psychographic Comparison of *Playboy* and *Reader's Digest* Readers

| | PERCENT WHO DEFINITELY AGREED AMONG | |
|---|---|---|
| | heavy *Playboy* readers | heavy *Reader's Digest* readers |
| My greatest achievements are still ahead of me. | 50 | 26 |
| I go to church regularly. | 18 | 40 |
| Movies should be censored. | 14 | 40 |
| Most men would cheat on their wives if the right opportunity came along. | 27 | 12 |

Source: Douglas J. Tigert, "Life Style Analysis as a Basis for Media Selection," in William D. Wells, ed., *Life Style and Psychographics* (Chicago: American Marketing Association, 1974), 179.

traditional demographic profiles, mass media publishers and broadcasters make it possible for advertisers to select media that have audiences most closely resembling their target markets.

Numerous examples of company-sponsored psychographic research suggest that the outlook for such segmentation analysis is bright.

As an alternative to individually sponsored or customized psychographic research, a number of marketing research and social science research companies (e.g., Simmons Market Research Bureau, Mediamark Research, Inc. [MRI], and National Family Opinion panel) sell, on a subscription basis, the results of consumer psychographic research. One of the best known of these syndicated consumer research services is the SRI Values and Lifestyles (VALS) program.[13]

## SRI VALS: CONSUMER SEGMENTATION RESEARCH

Taking its roots from Maslow's need hierarchy and the concept of social character, researchers at SRI in the late 1970s developed a generalized segmentation scheme of the American population known as the **VALS** (Values and Lifestyles) typology.[14] In recent years, selected marketers have reported that they have successfully used the VALS typology to segment markets for their products and services, and to target their promotional efforts.

### The Nine VALS Lifestyles

The VALS typology classifies the American population into four general consumer groups, and then subdivides these categories into a total of nine distinctive subgroups or segments. The four major groupings are the *need-driven* (the

**FIGURE 5-5** **SRI's Values and Lifestyle Segments** Source: Thomas C. Thomas, "Values and Lifestyles—The New Psychographics?" (Paper presented at the Advertising Research Foundation Conference, New York, February 24, 1981), 6.

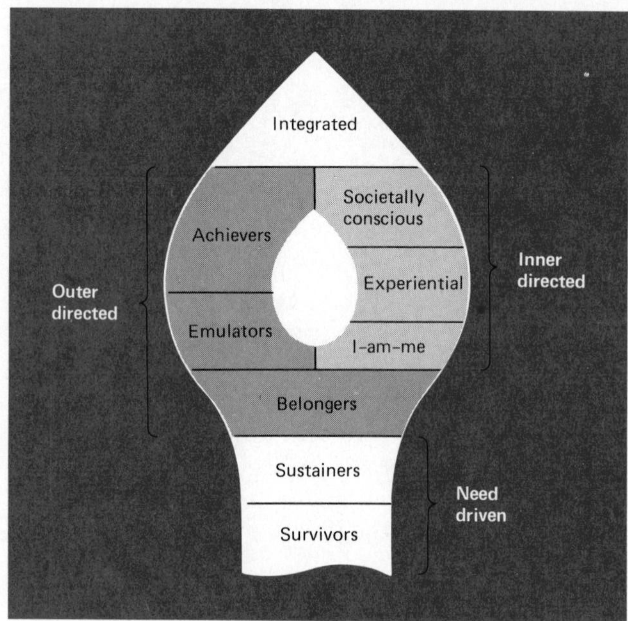


poor and uneducated—about 11 percent of the population), the *outer-directed* (middle- and upper-middle-class consumers whose lifestyles are directed by external criteria—about 67 percent of the population), and the *inner-directed* (people who often are more motivated by personal needs than by the expectations of others—about 20 percent of the population). The fourth segment, called *integrated* (2 percent of the population), represents individuals who have been able to combine the best of both outer-directed and inner-directed values.[15] The VALS model, shown in Figure 5-5, consists of the four major groupings. These groupings, in turn, are divided into nine specific VALS segments. A capsule description of each of these segments follows.[16]

## NEED DRIVEN (11 Percent of the Population)

**Survivors** are the most impoverished consumer segment, and represent about 4 percent of the adult American population. Most are poorly educated and elderly, and tend to be depressed, withdrawn, insecure, and mistrustful. Their desire for a comfortable old age has not been realized. Much of their time is spent at home—their refuge against what is perceived to be a generally hostile world.

**Sustainers** (7 percent of the population) are a group that has not yet given up hope. They are angry people, trying to climb out of poverty and join the middle class. Incomes of this group are slightly higher than for *Survivors,* and their median age is half that of *Survivors.* About half this group consists of particularly downscale "baby-boomers," who believe the system is currently working against them. *Sustainers* include the largest percentage of nonwhites.

### OUTER-DIRECTED (67 Percent of the Population)

**Belongers** constitute the largest VALS segment (35 percent of the population). Above all else, the members of this group want to "fit in." They make up what is commonly regarded as upper-lower and lower-middle-class America, and tend to be traditional, conservative, family-oriented, and moral. Most members are high school graduates, hold blue collar, craft, or service jobs, and have modest income levels. Although they may be characterized as "old fashioned," they are basically satisfied with their lifestyle.

**Emulators** (10 percent of the population) tend to be ambitious, competitive, hard-working, fairly successful, and demand a great deal of themselves as they try to climb the social class ladder. Members of this group tend to be young and to live in an urban environment. More than 20 percent are nonwhite. Generally, they are *not* especially happy, as they have yet to reach the goals they have set for themselves. *Emulators* try to be like *Achievers,* and often spend beyond their means. They constitute a middle ground between the lifestyle of the *Belongers* and the lifestyle of the *Achievers.*

**Achievers** are well educated and affluent—they have achieved success in their lives and have realized the American dream. Members of this segment (22 percent of the population) are hard-working and happy. They have a great deal of self-confidence (a trait *Emulators* lack) and view life as a challenge they can master.

### INNER-DIRECTED (20 Percent of the Population)

**I-Am-Me**'s is the youngest of the VALS groups and represents only 5 percent of the population. Members of this segment are in a transition stage, undergoing a transformation from the *outer-directed* way of life in which they were raised to the *inner-directed* life they seek. This is a relatively short-lived and turbulent life phase, with members simultaneously being conformers and innovators.

**Experientials** (7 percent of the population) are older than *I-Am-Me's,* and often join this category as they mature and marry out of the *I-Am-Me* lifestyle. They are interested in directly acquiring life experiences, and are generally happy with their lives. They obtain most of their gratification from nonwork activities. Although they are unambitious when compared to *Achievers,* they consider themselves to be liberated, impulsive, and willing to try almost anything once.

**Societally conscious** consumers (8 percent of the population) are a mature group concerned with societal issues. They are influential and successful,

**TABLE 5-17 Demographics of the VALS Groups**

| | NEED DRIVEN | | OUTER-DIRECTED | | | INNER-DIRECTED | | | |
|---|---|---|---|---|---|---|---|---|---|
| | survivors | sustainers | belongers | emulators | achievers | I-am-me | experiential | societally conscious | integrated |
| Population* | 4 | 7 | 35 | 10 | 22 | 5 | 7 | 8 | 2 |
| Median age | 66 | 33 | 52 | 27 | 43 | 21 | 27 | 39 | 40 |
| Sex—female | 77 | 55 | 68 | 47 | 40 | 36 | 55 | 52 | 54 |
| Married | 24 | 49 | 77 | 57 | 83 | 1 | 53 | 70 | 67 |
| Caucasian | 72 | 64 | 95 | 79 | 95 | 91 | 91 | 86 | 90 |
| College graduate | 9 | 3 | 7 | 6 | 33 | 8 | 38 | 58 | 21 |
| Social class | | | | | | | | | |
| Lower | 35 | 46 | 21 | 40 | 4 | 19 | 15 | 9 | 19 |
| Middle | 50 | 42 | 65 | 55 | 55 | 59 | 62 | 58 | 59 |
| Upper | 15 | 12 | 14 | 5 | 41 | 22 | 23 | 33 | 22 |
| Politics | | | | | | | | | |
| Conservative | 53 | 29 | 46 | 25 | 66 | 30 | 21 | 28 | 43 |
| Middle-of-road | 28 | 48 | 44 | 46 | 27 | 18 | 33 | 20 | 35 |
| Liberal | 19 | 23 | 10 | 29 | 8 | 52 | 46 | 53 | 23 |
| Work full-time | 11 | 39 | 34 | 85 | 70 | 38 | 53 | 73 | 54 |
| Professional or technical careers | 3 | 2 | 3 | 9 | 29 | 3 | 27 | 59 | 18 |
| Retired | 47 | 3 | 20 | 0 | 3 | 0 | 1 | 3 | 9 |
| Average income 1979 (000) | $ 5 | $11 | $17 | $18 | $31 | $ 9 | $24 | $27 | $18 |
| Place of residence | | | | | | | | | |
| Large or medium city | 48 | 47 | 25 | 50 | 30 | 47 | 46 | 42 | 35 |
| Suburb | 33 | 20 | 24 | 37 | 49 | 33 | 33 | 27 | 33 |
| Rural | 19 | 33 | 51 | 13 | 21 | 21 | 22 | 32 | 32 |

*All figures except age and income are percentages.

Source: Adapted from Arnold Mitchell, *The Nine American Lifestyles* (New York: Macmillan, 1983), 279–81.

and represent the inner-directed equivalent of *Achievers*. This group has the highest education level, highest percentage of professional occupations, and the most liberal point of view of all the VALS segments. They consider the nonmaterial aspects of life to be more important than the material ones, and many members of this group live in less densely populated areas.

### INTEGRATED (2 Percent of the Population)

This final VALS category-segment is the smallest of all the groups, and consists of individuals who have successfully put together the strengths of both the inner-directed and outer-directed lifestyles. Members of this group tend to be open, self-assured, and self-expressive. Because of this group's particularly small size, the segment is not as critical to most marketers as the other VALS segments.

The demographic characteristics of each of the nine VALS segments is summarized in Table 5-17; Table 5-18 provides an attitudinal profile of each group.

**TABLE 5-18 General Attitudes of Each VALS Type**

**survivors**

I tend to judge people in terms of their success in the world.
I often feel left out of things going on around me.
I don't have much to look forward to in life.
I prefer family get-togethers to activities with my friends.
You really can't trust strangers these days.
Science cannot replace human intuition.
Married couples ought to have children if they can.
I accept my own feelings as the surest guide to what is right.
Other people seem to get more breaks than I do.
I believe that people can *think* themselves from physical illness to health.
These days I don't know whom I can depend on.

**sustainers**

I keep my feelings mostly to myself.
I feel that I am driven by a desire for power.
I disregard the rules and regulations that hamper my freedom.
Arriving at a deep understanding of life is more important than being practical.

**belongers**

Over the years, my beliefs and values have not changed very much.
I feel uncomfortable disagreeing with somebody in authority.
Foreigners who criticize our nation should not be allowed to live here.
I like things to be certain and predictable.
There's little I can do to change my life.
I try not to show my emotions.
I certainly am more conventional than experimental.
Married couples ought to have children if they can.
It is wrong for an unmarried man or an unmarried woman to have sexual relations.
I prefer my relationships with people to be simple and uncomplicated.

**TABLE 5-18 General Attitudes of Each VALS Type (continued)**

**emulators**

Getting ahead in the world depends on whether you were born rich or poor.
I often don't get the credit I deserve for things I do well.
I tend to be interested in things like ESP, astrology, and Zen.
Money is power.

**achievers**

I usually influence others more than they influence me.
The American economic system has given me excellent opportunities to improve my position in life.
I adopt a common-sense attitude toward life.
I feel satisfied with my life.

**I-am-me's**

I often don't get the credit I deserve for things I do well.
I try to get my own way regardless of others.
My greatest achievements are ahead of me.
I have a number of ideas which some day I would like to put into a book.
I am quick to accept new ideas.
I often think about how I look and what impression I am making on others.
I am a competitive person.
I feel upset when I hear that people are criticizing or blaming me.
I'd like to be a celebrity.
I get a real thrill out of doing dangerous things.
I feel that almost nothing in life can substitute for great achievement.
It's important for me to be noticed.
I keep in close touch with my friends.
I spend a good deal of time trying to decide how I feel about things.
I often think I can feel my way into the innermost being of another person.

**experientials**

The Eastern religions are more appealing to me than Christianity.
I feel satisfied with my life.
I enjoy getting involved in new and unusual situations.
Overall, I'd say I'm happy.
I feel I understand where my life is going.
I like to think I'm different from other people.
I adopt a common-sense attitude toward life.

**societally conscious**

I feel that ideals are powerful motivating forces in me.
I think someone can be a good person without believing in God.

Note: Integrated segment not measured.

Source: Arnold Mitchell, *Inner Selves: Americans As They See Themselves* (Menlo Park, CA: SRI International, 1984), 74–84.

## Using the VALS Typology

In what has become the classic VALS success story, Merrill Lynch repositioned itself from being "Bullish on America" (depicted as a herd of bulls) to being "A breed apart" (depicted as a single bull). In applying the VALS segmentation scheme, the company discovered that its earlier promotional theme attracted *Belongers,* while heavy investors, whom Merrill Lynch was primarily interested in cultivating as customers, are predominantly *Achievers.* Achievers are less interested in America's growth, and more interested in how an investment firm might help them obtain a bigger share of that growth. Most important, Achievers don't want to "fit in"—they want to "stand out" (thus, a single bull—"A breed apart"). Figure 5-6 presents a recent Merrill Lynch ad with the headline "Local hero," and body copy that notes one of their executives is "a breed apart."[17]

Other marketers have successfully employed VALS research to more effectively market their products or services. For example, Midway Airlines determined that frequent business travelers typically fell within the *Achiever* cate-

**FIGURE 5-6 An Advertisement Appealing to Achievers**

# Local hero.

He heads the largest municipal finance organization in the world, but he's a local hero to hundreds of cities and towns across the country. He's Jean Rousseau, head of our municipal market professionals.

This year alone, Jean and his group have helped raise nearly $70 billion for schools, hospitals, highways and other local projects in every state, the District of Columbia and Puerto Rico.

Using the vast resources of Merrill Lynch, they have created more municipal investment opportunities than any other securities firm. And they did it with innovative financing that made these public projects cost less. Cost less? Now that's the stuff heroes are made of.

More resources, better solutions.
They make Merrill Lynch people a breed apart.

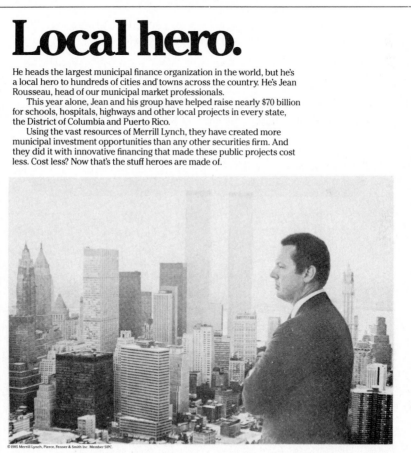

Courtesy of Merrill Lynch, Pierce, Fenner & Smith Inc.

gory. The airline created new advertisements to more closely correspond to this lifestyle.[18] In another example, the Medical Products Corporation, owned by Timex, ranked each VALS group according to its likelihood of purchasing or using Timex's Healthcheck products (e.g., electronic blood pressure monitors). This process allowed the company to eliminate certain reluctant VALS types, such as *Belongers*; and to focus on the especially promising *Achievers* and *Societally Conscious* consumers who would be responsive to such "high-tech" products.[19]

In yet another VALS application, this one an ad campaign developed for the Mercury Capri, the agency initially zeroed in on the car's European styling and American performance (i.e., Lincoln-Mercury quality with good gas mileage and a wide range of options). The campaign lasted less than a year because it failed to recognize that the *Emulator* and *I-Am-Me* VALS types were the vehicle's key prospects. Once the targeting problem had been diagnosed, new and more suitable commercials were developed.

## *summary*

During the past two decades psychographic (lifestyle, or AIO) research has become an important basis for market segmentation and related strategic marketing efforts. Its popularity with marketing practitioners and academic researchers is due to the vivid and actionable consumer profiles that are produced from psychographic instruments.

In its more general form, a psychographic inventory is a battery of statements designed to capture relevant aspects of a consumer's personality, buying motives, interests, attitudes, beliefs, and values. In contrast, product-specific inventories have consumers respond to selective statements about products, services, brands, or specific consumption situations. Both types of psychographic statements are useful because they tap different dimensions of a consumer's psychological and social nature.

Psychographics came into existence as an answer to marketers' search for a quantitative research method that could be computer-analyzed and that would provide the dramatic insights of motivational research and resemble personality measures in format. Psychographic profiles are complementary to traditional demographic profiles. While demographic variables help marketers "locate" their target markets, psychographic variables help them acquire a picture of the "inner consumer;" that is, they provide insights as to what consumers are feeling and what should be stressed in the firm's promotional campaign.

In constructing psychographic inventories, researchers strive to capture activities (how a consumer or a family spends time), interests (how a consumer's or family's preferences and priorities are determined), and opinions (how a consumer feels about a wide variety of events or things). In constructing psychographic inventories, it is important to (1) review existing market research studies that might aid in the identification of psychographic items; (2) prepare psychographic statements that reflect the full range of activities, interests, and opinions that the marketer wishes to assess; (3) select an appropriate rating scale (often an "agree-disagree" scale); (4) evaluate the instrument for clarity and socially desirable responses; and (5) test the instrument to determine its reliability and validity.

The strongest endorsement for the application of psychographic research has been its wide use by both practitioners and academic consumer researchers. As a real-world research tool, psychographics has proved useful in three closely related areas of marketing strategy: segmenting markets, positioning and repositioning products, and designing promotional campaigns.

## *discussion questions*

1. A media buyer for a local beverage distributor has relied entirely on demographic profiles to identify magazines and TV shows in which to place the company's advertising. Describe several benefits that the company might receive by using psychographic profiles to identify target audiences.
2. When is consumer demographic information likely to be more useful than psychographic information?
3. Describe why both reader demographics and reader psychographics are desirable types of consumer information for the publisher of a consumer magazine (such as *Newsweek* or *Sports Illustrated*).
4. In response to a request from a local hospital, you have been given the task of heading a committee of marketing executives who have volunteered their time to design and implement a campaign to increase blood donorship. From what you have learned about psychographics, make suggestions as to whom this campaign might be directed.
5. Consider both Eleanor and Thelma, two of the five psychographic segments profiled in Table 5-3. Both types of women surely reside in your town or city. Make a list of the local newspapers, radio stations, and major department stores, and then determine which ones would have each woman as a reader, listener, or shopper.
6. Find three advertisements in consumer magazines that you believe are targeted at a particular psychographic segment or lifestyle. Do you feel that each of these three ads is effective? Why or why not?
7. If you were the owner of a sporting goods store located in a large shopping mall, how might you use the comparison of recreational and economic shoppers in Table 5-13?
8. The president of a fast-food chain has asked you to prepare a psychographic profile of families living in a number of communities surrounding a new location he is considering. Construct a 10-question psychographic questionnaire appropriate for segmenting families in terms of dining-out preferences.

# *endnotes*

1. For a discussion of various alternative ways of conceptualizing "psychographics" and "lifestyle," see W. Thomas Anderson and Linda Golden, "Lifestyle and Psychographics: A Critical Review and Recommendations," in Thomas C. Kinnear, ed., *Advances in Consumer Research* (Ann Arbor: Association for Consumer Research, 1984), 11, 405–11.
2. A. Marvin Roscoe, Jr., Arthur Le Claire, Jr., and Leon G. Schiffman, "Theory and Management Applications of Demographics in Buyer Behavior," in Arch G. Woodside et al., eds. *Consumer and Industrial Buying Behavior* (New York: North-Holland, 1977), 70–71.
3. William D. Wells, "Psychographics: A Critical Review," *Journal of Marketing Research,* 2 (May 1975), 198.
4. Sunil Mehrota and William D. Wells, "Psychographics and Buyer Behavior: Theory and Recent Empirical Findings," in Woodside et al., *Consumer and Industrial Buying Behavior,* 52–57.
5. William D. Wells and Douglas J. Tigert, "Activities, Interests and Opinions," *Journal of Advertising Research,* 11 (August 1971), 27–35; and Joseph T. Plummer, "The Concept of Life Style Segmentation," *Journal of Marketing,* 38 (January 1974), 33–37.
6. Stuart Van Auken, "General versus Product-Specific Life Style Segmentation," *Journal of Advertising,* 7 (Fall 1978), 31–35; and Michel A. Zins, "An Exploration of the Relationship between General and Specific Psychographic Profiles," in Kenneth Bernhardt, ed., *Marketing: 1776–1976 and Beyond* (Chicago: American Marketing Association, 1976), 507–11.
7. Zins, "Relationship between General and Specific Psychographics," 508.
8. For example, see Ken Kono, "Psychographic Profile of Generics Buyers," in Patrick E. Murphy et al., eds., *1983 AMA Educator's Proceedings* (Chicago: American Marketing Association, 1983), 11–15; John J. Burnett, "Psychographic and Demographic Characteristics of Blood Donors," *Journal of Consumer Research,* 8 (June 1981), 62–66; and Alfred S. Boote, Interactions in Psychographics Segmentation: Implications for Advertising," *Journal of Advertising,* 13 (1984), 43–48.
9. Mehrota and Wells, "Psychographics and Buyer Behavior," 57.
10. William R. Darden and William D. Perreault, Jr., "Identifying Interurban Shoppers: Multiproduct Purchase Patterns and Segmentation Profiles," *Journal of Marketing Research,* 13 (February 1976), 51–60; William R. Darden and Dub Ashton, "Psychographic Profiles of Patronage Preference Groups," *Journal of Retailing,* 50 (Winter 1974–75), 99–112; and John M. Hawes and James R. Lumpkins, "Understanding Out-shopping," *Journal of the Academy of Marketing Science,* 12 (Fall 1984), 200–18.
11. Danny N. Bellenger and Pradeep K. Korgaonkar, "Profiling the Recreational Shopper," *Journal of Retailing,* 56 (Fall 1980), 83–92.
12. F. Stewart DeBruicker and Scott Ward, *Cases in Consumer Behavior* (Englewood Cliffs, N.J.: Prentice-Hall, 1980), 11–33.
13. For a comprehensive discussion of the VALS Program, see Arnold Mitchell, *The Nine American Lifestyles* (New York: Macmillan, 1983).
14. Rebecca H. Holman, "A Values and Lifestyles Perspective on Human Behavior," in Robert E. Pitts, Jr., and Arch G. Woodside, *Personal Values & Consumer Psychology* (Lexington, Mass.: Lexington Books, 1984), 35–54.
15. See Holman, "A Values and Lifestyles Perspective," 35–54; Ogilvy & Mather, *Listening Post,* No. 57, December 1983, 8.

16. Adapted from Arnold Mitchell, "Nine American Lifestyles," *The Futurist,* August 1984, 4–14; Holman, "A Values and Lifestyles Perspective," 40–52; Ogilvy & Mather, *Listening Post.*

17. "Emotions Important for Successful Advertising," *Marketing News,* April 12, 1985, 18.

18. Scott Hume, "Midway Campaign Built on 'Achiever,' " *Advertising Age,* February 7, 1985, 51.

19. "Timex and VALS Engineer a Psychographic Product Launch," *Ad Forum,* September 1984, 12–14.

20. See William D. Wells, ed., *Life Style and Psychographics* (Chicago: American Marketing Association, 1974); and Thomas C. Kinnear and James R. Taylor, "Psychographics: Some Additional Findings," *Journal of Marketing Research,* 13 (November 1976), 422–25.

# 6

# Consumer Perception

## *introduction*

As individuals, we tend to see the world in our own special ways. Four people can view the same event at the same time, and each will report in total honesty a story different from all the others. For example, the classic Japanese film *Rashomon*—shown frequently on late night television—tells the story of the abduction and rape of a woodcutter's wife and the murder of her husband, first from the point of view of the bandit, then the wife, then the husband, and finally a hidden bystander. Each story varied because each participant perceived the events that occurred in a different way. Hard to believe? Not really. For each individual, reality is a totally personal phenomenon, based on that person's needs, wants, values, and personal experiences.

Reality to an individual is merely that individual's **perception** of what is "out there"—of what has taken place. Individuals act and react on the basis of their perceptions, not on the basis of objective reality (i.e., reality as recorded by a camera). Thus, consumers' perceptions are much more important to the marketer than their knowledge of objective reality. For, if one thinks about it, it's not what actually *is* so, but what consumers *think* is so, that affects their actions, their buying habits, their leisure habits, and so forth. And because individuals make decisions and take actions based on what they *perceive* to be reality, it is important that marketers understand the whole notion of perception and its related concepts so they can more readily determine what influences consumers to buy.

This chapter examines the psychological and physiological bases of hu-

> *Every man takes the limits of his own field of vision for the limits of the world.*
>
> SCHOPENHAUER
> "Further Psychological Observation," *Parerga and Paralipomena* (1851)

man perception and discusses the principles that control our reception and interpretation of the world we see. Knowledge of these principles enables astute marketers to develop advertisements that have a good chance of being seen and remembered by their target consumers.

The double-spread ad depicted in Figure 6-1 demonstrates one marketer's recognition of the perception/reality dichotomy and how it can influence sales.

**FIGURE 6-1** Perception/Reality Dichotomy Can Influence Sales

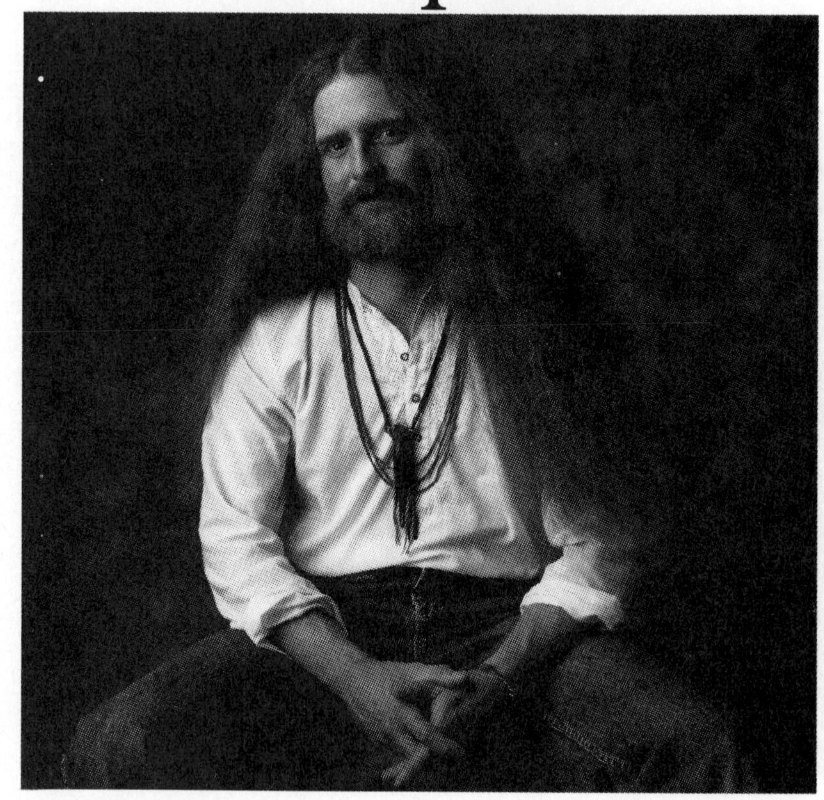

## WHAT IS PERCEPTION?

**Perception** can be described as "how we see the world around us." Two individuals may be subject to the same stimuli under apparently the same conditions, but how they recognize them, select them, organize them, and interpret them is a highly individual process based on each person's own needs, values,

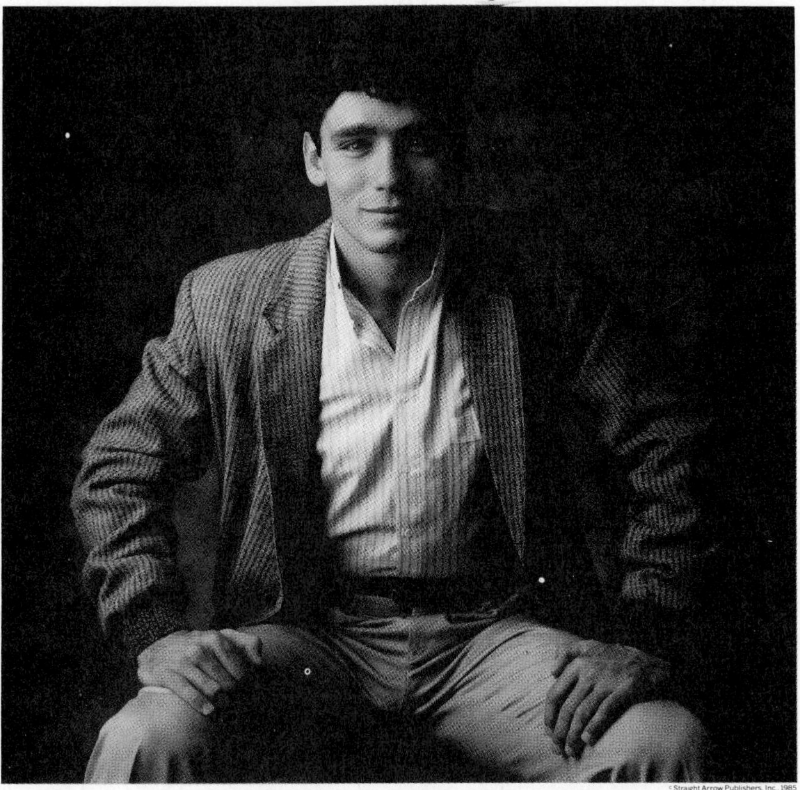

Reality.
© Straight Arrow Publishers, Inc. 1985
If your idea of a Rolling Stone reader looks like a holdout from the 60's, welcome to the 80's.
Rolling Stone ranks number one in reaching concentrations of 18-34 readers with household incomes exceeding $25,000. When you buy Rolling Stone, you buy an audience that sets the trends and shapes the buying patterns for the most affluent consumers in America. That's the kind of reality you can take to the bank.
Source: Simmons 1984

Courtesy of Rolling Stone Magazine

expectations, and the like. The influence that each of these variables has on the perceptual process, and its relevance to marketing, will be examined in some detail. First, however, we will examine some of the basic concepts that underlie the perceptual process. These will be discussed within the framework of consumer behavior.

*Perception* is defined as *the process by which an individual selects, organizes, and interprets stimuli into a meaningful and coherent picture of the world.* A **stimulus** is any unit of input to any of the senses. Examples of stimuli (i.e., *sensory inputs*) include products, packages, brand names, advertisements, and commercials. **Sensory receptors** are the human organs (the eyes, ears, nose, mouth, and skin) that receive sensory inputs. Their sensory functions are to see, hear, smell, taste, and feel. All of these functions are called into play—either singly or in combination—in the evaluation and use of most consumer products. The study of perception is largely the study of what we subconsciously add to or subtract from raw sensory inputs to produce a private picture of the world.

## Sensation

**Sensation** is the immediate and direct response of the sensory organs to simple stimuli (an advertisement, a package, a brand name). Human sensitivity refers to the experience of sensation. Sensitivity to stimuli varies with the quality of an individual's *sensory receptors* (e.g., eyesight or hearing) and the amount or intensity of the stimuli to which he or she is exposed. For example, a blind person may have a more highly developed sense of hearing than the average sighted person and may be able to hear sounds that the average person cannot.

Sensation itself depends on *energy change* or *differentiation of input.* A perfectly bland or unchanging environment—regardless of the strength of the sensory input—provides little or no sensation at all. Thus a person who lives on a busy street in midtown Manhattan would probably receive little or no sensation from the inputs of such noisy stimuli as horns honking, tires screeching, and fire engines clanging, since such sounds are so commonplace in New York City. One honking horn more or one less would never be noticed. In situations where there is a great deal of sensory input, the senses do not detect small intensities or differences in input.

As the sensory input *decreases,* however, our ability to detect changes in input or intensity *increases,* to the point where we attain maximum sensitivity under conditions of minimal stimulation. This accounts for the statement "It was so quiet I could hear a pin drop." It also accounts for the increased attention given to a commercial that appears alone during a program break, or the attention given to a black-and-white advertisement in a magazine full of four-color advertisements. This ability of the human organism to accommodate itself to varying levels of sensitivity as external conditions vary not only provides more sensitivity when it is needed, but also serves to protect us from damaging, disruptive, or irrelevant bombardment when the input level is high.

### THE ABSOLUTE THRESHOLD

The lowest level at which an individual can experience a sensation is called the **absolute threshold.** The point at which a person can detect a difference between "something" and "nothing" is that person's absolute threshold for that stimulus. To illustrate, the distance at which a driver can note a specific billboard on the highway is that individual's absolute threshold. Two people riding together may first spot the billboard at different times (i.e., at different distances); thus they appear to have different absolute thresholds.

Under conditions of constant stimulation, such as driving through a "corridor" of billboards, the absolute threshold *increases* (that is, the senses tend to become increasingly dulled). After an hour of driving through billboards, it is doubtful that any one billboard will make an impression. Hence we often speak of "getting used to" a hot bath, a cold shower, the bright sun, or even the odor in a college locker room. In the field of perception, the term **adaptation** refers specifically to "getting used to" certain sensations, becoming accommodated to a certain level of stimulation.

Sensory adaptation was a problem experienced by TV advertisers during the 1984 summer Olympics. Advertising research studies found that the brilliantly executed TV commercials shown during the Olympics were not cost effective, because of poor viewer recall relative to their excessively high costs. This is explained by the fact that they were all competing with one another as well as with the Olympic Games for viewer attention. Given the very high level of stimulation, no one commercial stood out among the rest.[1] It is because of *adaptation* that advertisers tend to change their advertising campaigns regularly. They are concerned that consumers will get so used to their current print ads and TV commercials that they will no longer "see" them; that is, the ads will no longer provide sufficient sensory input to be noted.

In an effort to cut through the advertising clutter and ensure that consumers note their ads, some marketers try to increase sensory input. For example, Apple Computer once bought all the advertising space in an issue of *Newsweek* magazine. Some marketers seek unusual media in which to place their advertisements in an effort to gain attention. Some have advertised their products on pedicabs (three-wheeled rickshaw-like cycles that transport people); others have used parking meters and shopping carts; still others pay to have their products appear in movies.[2]

Fragrance marketers have begun to include fragrance samples in their direct mail and in their magazine advertisements through sealed perfume inserts. Rémy Martin makes a direct appeal to sensual stimulation in its double-spread Cognac ads (see Figure 6-2).

Package designers try to determine consumers' absolute thresholds to make sure their new-product designs exceed this level, so that new products will stand out from the competition on retailers' shelves. Marketers are retaining packaging consultants and using marketing research to determine which colors and which shapes will be perceived more readily. A French winery developed an unusual bottle with a three-dimensional cluster of grapes embossed on its front in an effort to appeal to consumers' sense of touch.[3]

### THE DIFFERENTIAL THRESHOLD

The minimal difference that can be detected between two stimuli is called the **differential threshold,** or the **j.n.d.** (for *just noticeable difference*). A nineteenth-

FIGURE 6-2 Appeal to Sensual Stimulation

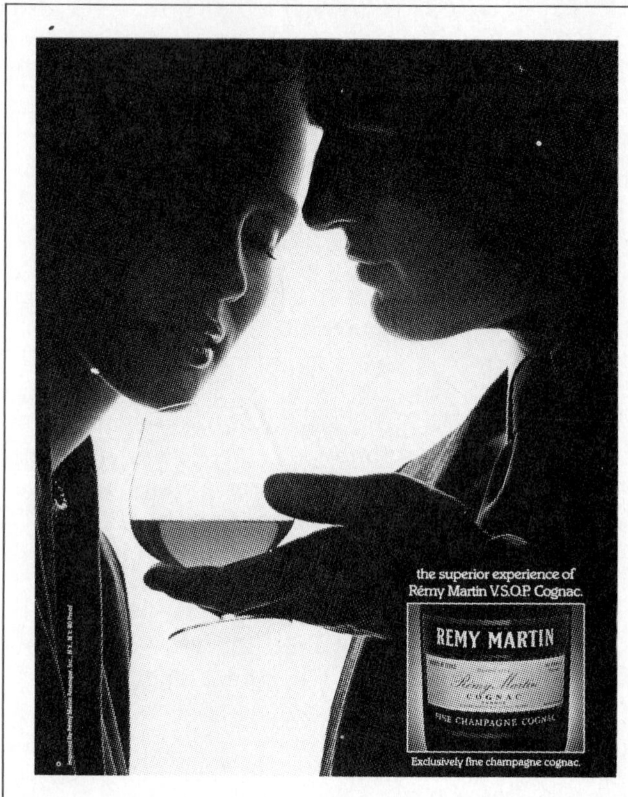
the superior experience of
Rémy Martin V.S.O.P. Cognac.
REMY MARTIN
COGNAC
FINE CHAMPAGNE COGNAC
Exclusively fine champagne cognac.

century German scientist named Ernst Weber discovered that the just noticeable difference between two stimuli was not an absolute amount, but an amount relative to the intensity of the first stimulus. *Weber's law,* as it has come to be known, states that the stronger the initial stimulus, the greater the additional intensity needed for the second stimulus to be perceived as different. For example, if the price of an automobile were increased by fifty dollars, it would probably not be noticed (that is, the increment would fall below the *j.n.d.*); it may take an increase of two hundred dollars or more before a differential in price would be noticed. However, a fifty-cent increase in the price of gasoline would be noticed very quickly by consumers because it is a significant percentage of the base cost of the gasoline.

According to Weber's law, an additional level of stimulus equivalent to the *j.n.d* must be added for the majority of people to perceive a difference between the resulting stimulus and the initial stimulus.

Let us say that a manufacturer of silver polish wishes to improve the product sufficiently to claim that it retards tarnish longer than the leading competitive brand. In a series of experiments, the company has determined that the *j.n.d.* for its present polish, which now gives a shine that lasts about twenty

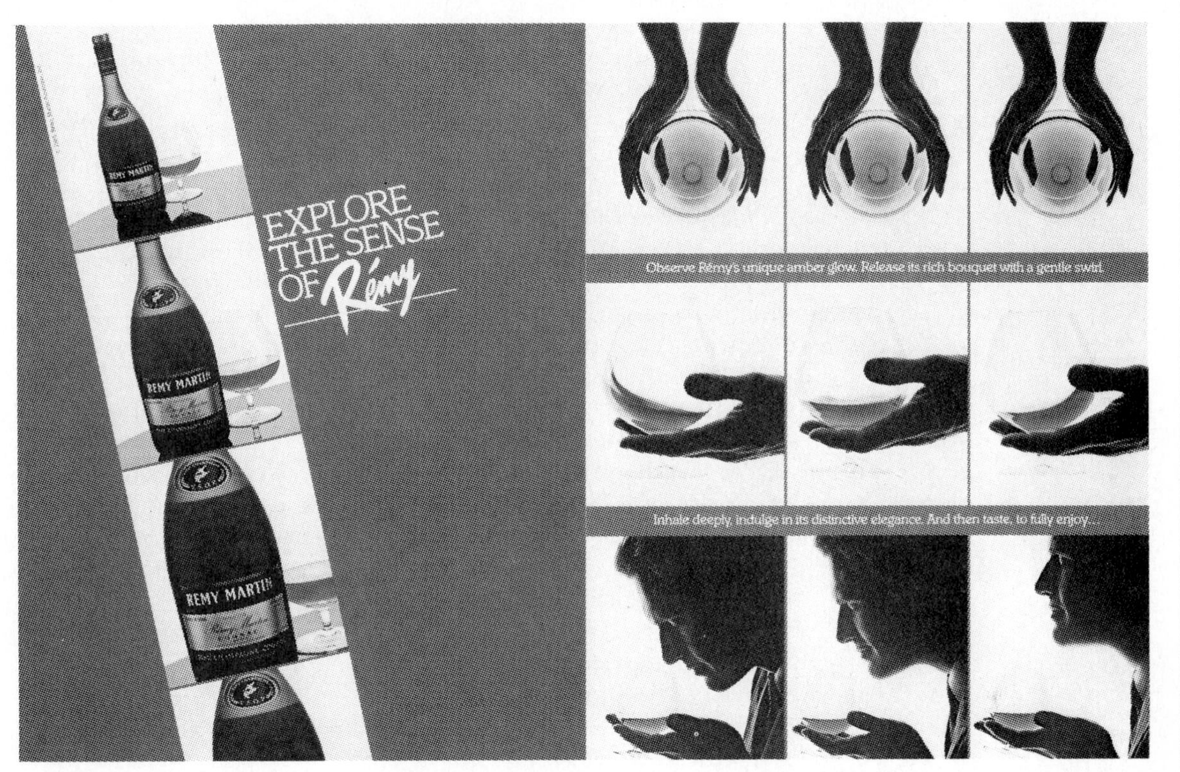
EXPLORE
THE SENSE
OF Rémy
REMY MARTIN
Observe Rémy's unique amber glow. Release its rich bouquet with a gentle swirl.
Inhale deeply, indulge in its distinctive elegance. And then taste, to fully enjoy...

Copyright Rémy Martin Amerique, Inc.

days, is five days, or one-fourth longer. That is, the shine given by the improved silver polish must last at least one-fourth longer than that of the present polish for it to be perceived by the majority of users as improved. By finding this *j.n.d.* of five days, the company has isolated the minimum amount of time necessary to make its claim of "lasts longer" believable to the majority of consumers.

If the company had decided to make the silver polish effective for forty days, it would have sacrificed a good deal of purchase frequency. If it had decided to make the polish effective for twenty-three days (just three extra days of product life), its claim of "lasts longer" would not be perceived as true by most consumers. Making the product improvement just equal to the *j.n.d.* thus becomes the most efficient decision management can make.

The *j.n.d.* has other uses as well. For example, retailers have long made use of a general rule of thumb that markdowns of merchandise must amount to at least 20 percent of the old price, since a smaller amount often goes unnoticed by consumers.[4] They recognize that the *just noticeable difference* is not an absolute amount, but rather a relative amount contingent upon the level of the initial price. For the same reason, the Federal Trade Commission monitors the size of the printed warnings in cigarette advertisements to ensure that they apear in a type size sufficiently large in relation to the size of the ad to be perceived and read.[5]

Weber's law is concerned with comparisons between two stimuli. It holds for all the senses and for almost all intensities. In cases involving vision and hearing, it is operable in more than 99.9 percent of the usable stimulus range (the broad normal range of intensities).[6]

MARKETING APPLICATIONS OF THE J.N.D. Weber's law has important applications for marketing. Manufacturers and marketers endeavor to determine the relevant *j.n.d.* for their products for two very different reasons: (1) so that reductions in product size, increases in product price, or changes in packaging *are not* readily discernible to the public; and (2) so that product improvements *are* readily discernible to the public without being wastefully extravagant. For example, because of rising costs, many manufacturers are faced with the choice of increasing prices or reducing the quantity (or quality) of the product offered at the existing price. Hershey has done both. Over the past twenty-five years, it has increased the price of its chocolate bar and altered its weight many times. Because a candy bar is so inexpensive to begin with, price increases are very noticeable, so decreasing the size of the bar to just under the *j.n.d.* has been the preferred strategy.

Manufacturers who choose to reduce the quality of their products also try to ensure that product changes remain just *under* the point of noticeable difference. For example, when the price of coffee beans goes up, coffee processors often downgrade quality by using inferior beans, up to but not including the *j.n.d.*—the point at which the consumer will notice a difference in taste.

Another type of problem faced by many marketers is the need to update existing packaging without losing the ready recognition of consumers who have been exposed to years of cumulative advertising impact. In such cases, marketers usually make a number of small changes, each one carefully designed to fall below the *j.n.d.* so that consumers will not perceive the difference. For example, the familiar Crackerjack package which we have all known as children has undergone some twenty changes in small increments over the years without alerting consumers that changes have been made.

Dundee Mills, Incorporated used four package changes over a five-year period to create a transition from the Chix brand of baby products (acquired when it bought Johnson & Johnson's Baby Products Division) to the Dundee name; with each package alteration, the new name became more prominent in order to create a smooth transition in the consumer's mind (see Figure 6-3).[7]

The Campbell Soup Company has been one of the most subtle of all marketers in changing its package. An alteration here, a slight typographic change there, refinement of its logotype, have all combined to keep the product looking up-to-date without losing any of the valuable Campbell image. Campbell is still one of the most widely recognized packages in the world today.

Another interesting example is Ivory soap, which was introduced in 1879. The subtle packaging changes Ivory experienced over the years were each small enough to avoid notice, but they managed to retain a contemporary look (see Figure 6-4). The latest Ivory package is considerably different from the original, but the changes made each step of the way were so skillfully designed that the transition has been hardly noticeable to the consumer.

Marketers also use the *j.n.d.* to determine the ideal level of distribution of goods or services, the optimum ratio of copy to headline in print ads, and the frequency with which ads must be repeated to have maximum effect.

The examples given here are concerned with changes that marketers do *not* want consumers to perceive. When it comes to product improvements, however, marketers very much want to meet or exceed the consumer's *differential threshold;* that is, they want consumers to perceive readily improvements made to the original product. Such marketers can use the *j.n.d.* to determine the amount of improvement they should make in their products. Less than the *j.n.d.* is wasted because it will not be perceived; more than the *j.n.d.* may be wasteful because it will reduce the level of repeat sales.

## Subliminal Perception

In Chapter 3 we spoke of people being motivated "below their level of conscious awareness." People are also *stimulated* below their level of conscious

**FIGURE 6-3** **Gradual Brand Name Change Below the J.N.D.**

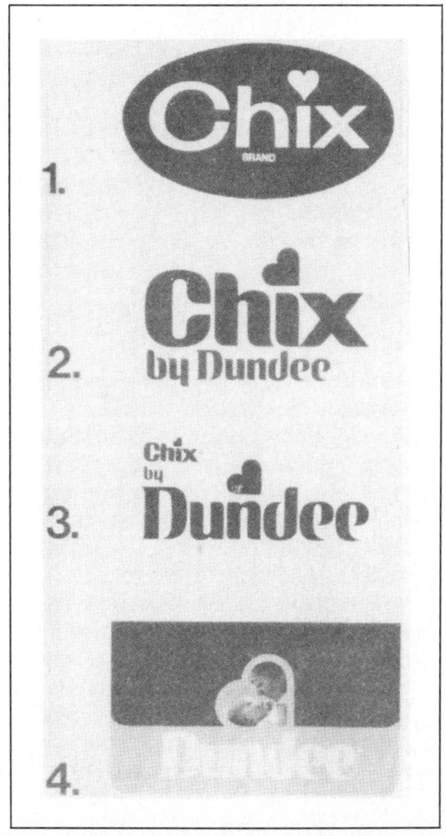


Courtesy of Dundee Mills, Incorporated

FIGURE 6-4 Sequential Changes in Packaging Below the J.N.D.

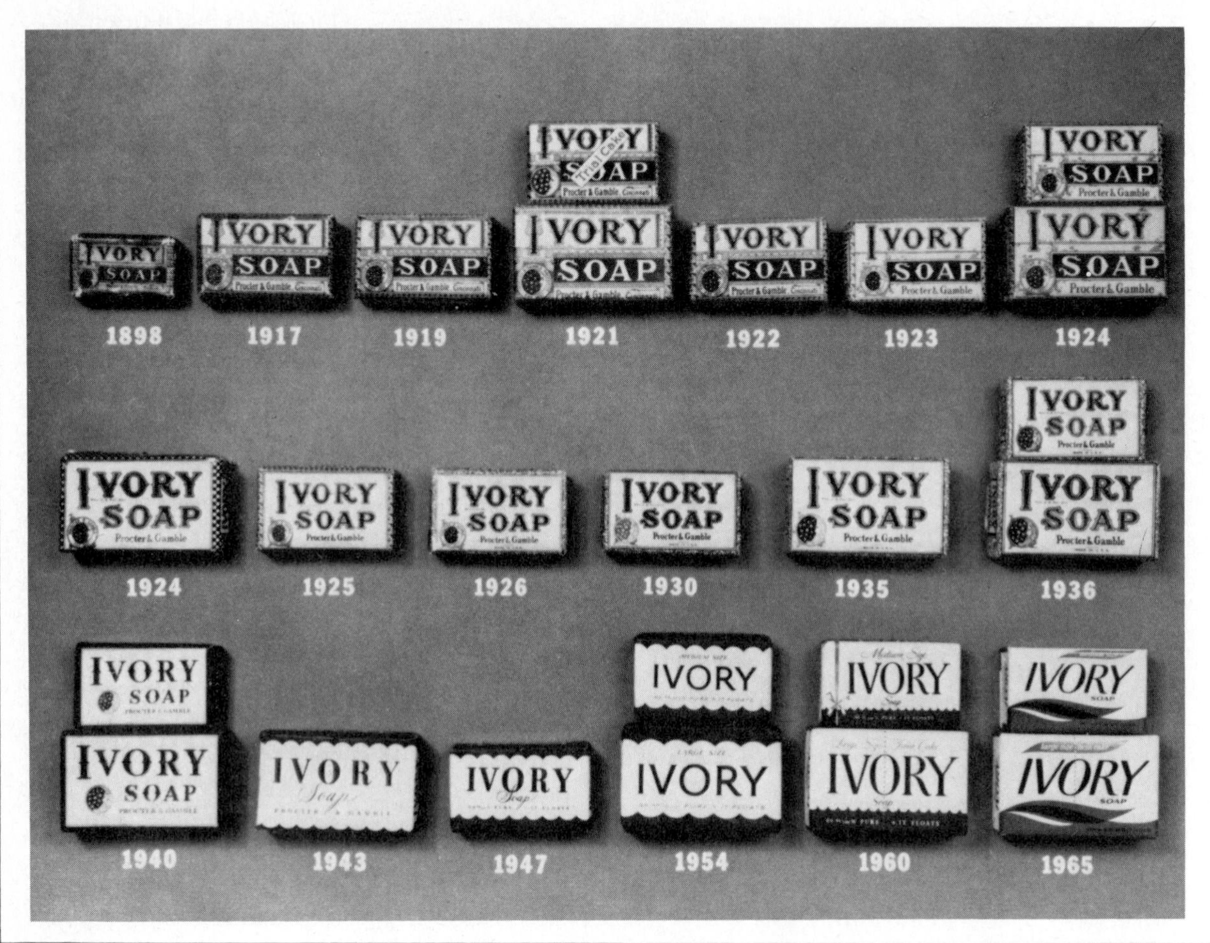




awareness; that is, they can perceive stimuli without being consciously aware of the stimuli in question. The threshold for conscious awareness or conscious recognition appears to be higher than the absolute threshold for effective perception. Stimuli that are too weak or too brief to be consciously seen or heard may nevertheless be strong enough to be perceived by one or more receptor cells. This process is called **subliminal perception** because the stimulus is *beneath* the threshold, or "limen," of awareness, though obviously not beneath the absolute thresholds of the receptors involved. (Perception of stimuli that are *above* the level of conscious awareness is called *supraliminal perception.*)

Subliminal perception created a great furor in the late 1950s when it was reported that advertisers could expose consumers to subliminal messages that they were not aware of receiving. These messages purportedly could persuade people to buy goods or act in ways that could benefit the advertiser without being aware of why they did so. The effectiveness of so-called *subliminal advertising* was reportedly tested in a drive-in movie in New Jersey, where the words "eat popcorn" and "drink Coca-Cola" were flashed on the screen during the movie. Exposure times were so short that viewers were unaware of seeing a message. It was reported that during the six-week test period, popcorn sales increased 58 percent and Coca-Cola sales increased 18 percent.[8] However, no scientific controls were used, and researchers were never able to replicate the results. Nevertheless, public indignation at the possibility of such manipulation was so widespread that both the Federal Communications Commission and the U.S. Congress conducted hearings to determine whether subliminal advertising should be outlawed. The resultant publicity reawakened academic interest in the subject of subliminal perception.

A series of highly imaginative laboratory experiments that followed gave some support to the notion that individuals could perceive below the level of their conscious awareness, but found no evidence that they could be persuaded to act in response to such subliminal stimulation.

For example, one researcher found that while the simple subliminal stimulus COKE served to arouse thirst in subjects, the subliminal command to DRINK COKE did not have a greater effect, not did it have any behavioral consequences.[9] In another experiment, the same researcher found that subliminal stimuli associating a brand name with a sexy girl did not significantly affect recall or choice of the product by either sex.[10] A recent study supported this conclusion and found that sexually suggestive copy or pictures does not increase purchase intentions.[11]

Although researchers have been unable to demonstrate that subliminal messages have any effect on consumer behavior, they have recently shown that subliminal messages can have some interesting psychological effects. For example, by playing a subliminal message ("I am honest; I won't steal; stealing is dishonest") just below the perceptible level on the Muzak sound track in six large department stores, a researcher reported that he was able to produce a 37.5 percent decline in shoplifting in a nine-month period.[12]

Interest in the topic of subliminal perception was reawakened again in the mid 1970s by the charge that even though subliminal messages may not work, *subliminal embeds* may have the desired effect. Embeds were defined as still pictures (not words) planted in print ads. It was alleged, for example, that liquor advertisers try to increase the subconscious appeal of their products by embedding sexually suggestive symbols in ice cubes floating in a pictured drink.[13] These claims have been dismissed by academic researchers and advertising executives for lack of scientific documentation. One investigator who tried to test the effectiveness of embeds found no significant influence on brand recall, but remarked that recall may be an invalid measure of whether an ad has had an impact.[14] He noted that advertisements may do their job by merely evoking recognition among consumers when they see a brand name or package after being exposed to it in an ad.[15]

Recent research studies have tried to document the existence or the effectiveness of subliminal advertising without success. One study pointed out that many studies of subliminal perception are flawed because the investigators assumed that some specific exposure duration or stimulus intensity automatically guaranteed that the stimulus would be sufficiently below threshold that its presence would be undetected by experimental subjects. However, since perceptual thresholds differ widely between individuals and even for the same individuals from day to day and minute to minute, there exists no absolute cutoff point for stimulus intensity below which stimulation is imperceptible and above which it is always detected.[16]

In summary, while there is some marginal evidence that subliminal stimuli may influence affective reactions, there is no evidence that subliminal stimulation could influence consumer-relevant motives or actions, or that advertisers engage in "subliminal advertising." As to sexual embeds, most researchers are of the opinion that "what you see is what you get"; i.e., that a vivid imagination can see whatever it wants to see in just about any situation, including any illustration.[17] And that pretty much sums up the whole notion of perception: Individuals see what they want to see, and what they expect to see. A 1983 survey of public perceptions about subliminal advertising found that many people—particularly more highly educated ones—believe there is such a phenomenon, that it is widely and frequently used, and that it is successful in selling products.[18] They also called it an unacceptable, unethical, and harmful advertising technique, and reported that knowledge that a particular advertiser was using subliminal techniques would affect their buying behavior.

These findings place advertisers in a peculiar dilemma. Since people act on the basis of their perceptions, rather than on the basis of hard reality, the belief that advertisers may be using subliminal advertising techniques may be a source of negative attitudes about advertising that, in turn, negatively affects purchase behavior, even though research indicates that subliminal advertising does not exist and would not be effective if it did. To correct such misperceptions, the advertising community might be well advised to sponsor more ads like the one depicted in Figure 6-5, which refutes the notion that subliminal techniques are effective or used in advertising applications.

## THE DYNAMICS OF PERCEPTION

The preceding section explained how the individual receives sensations from stimuli in the outside environment, and how the human organism adapts to the level and intensity of sensory input. We now come to one of the major principles of perception: *Raw sensory input by itself does not produce or explain the coherent picture of the world that most adults possess.*

The human being is constantly bombarded with stimuli during every minute and every hour of every day. The sensory world is made up of an almost infinite number of discrete sensations, which are constantly and minutely changing. According to the principles of sensation, such heavy intensity of stimulation should serve to "turn off" most individuals, as the body protects itself from the heavy bombardment to which it is subjected. Otherwise the billions of different stimuli to which we are constantly exposed might serve to totally confuse us and keep us perpetually disoriented in a constantly changing environ-

FIGURE 6-5 Subliminal Embeds: In the Eye of the Beholder

PEOPLE HAVE BEEN TRYING TO FIND THE BREASTS IN THESE ICE CUBES SINCE 1957.

The advertising industry is sometimes charged with sneaking seductive little pictures into ads.

Supposedly, these pictures can get you to buy a product without your even seeing them.

Consider the photograph above. According to some people, there's a pair of female breasts hidden in the patterns of light refracted by the ice cubes.

Well, if you really searched you probably *could* see the breasts. For that matter, you could also see Millard Fillmore, a stuffed pork chop and a 1946 Dodge.

The point is that so-called "subliminal advertising" simply doesn't exist. Overactive imaginations, however, most certainly do.

So if anyone claims to see breasts in that drink up there, they aren't in the ice cubes.

They're in the eye of the beholder.

**ADVERTISING**

**ANOTHER WORD FOR FREEDOM OF CHOICE.**

American Association of Advertising Agencies

Courtesy of American Association of Advertising Agencies

ment. However, neither of these consequences tends to occur, because perception is not a function of sensory input alone; rather, it is the result of two different kinds of inputs which interact to form the personal pictures—the perceptions—that each individual experiences.

One type of input is *physical stimuli* from the outside environment; the other type of input is provided by individuals themselves in the form of certain predispositions, such as *expectations, motives,* and *learning* based on previous experience. The combination of these two very different kinds of inputs produces for each of us a very private, very personal picture of the world. Because each individual is a unique entity, with unique experiences, wants, needs, wishes, and expectations, it follows that each individual's perceptions are also unique. This explains why no two people see the world in precisely the same way.

Individuals are very *selective* in terms of which stimuli they "recognize;" they *organize* the stimuli they do recognize subconsciously according to widely held psychological principles; and they give meaning to such stimuli (i.e., they *interpret* them) subjectively in accordance with their own needs, expectations, and experiences. Let us examine in more detail each of these three aspects of perception: **selection, organization,** and **interpretation** of stimuli.

## Perceptual Selection

Consumers subconsciously exercise a great deal of selectivity regarding which aspects of the environment—which stimuli—they perceive. An individual may look at some things, ignore others, and turn away from still others. In total, people actually receive—or perceive—only a small fraction of the stimuli to which they are exposed. Consider, for example, a woman in a supermarket. She is exposed to literally thousands of products of different colors, sizes, and shapes; to perhaps a hundred people (looking, walking, searching, talking); to smells (from fruit, from meat, from disinfectant, from people); to sounds within the store (cash registers ringing, shopping carts rolling, air conditioners humming, and clerks sweeping, mopping aisles, stocking shelves); and to sounds from outside the store (planes passing, cars honking, tires screeching, children shouting, car doors slamming). Yet she manages on a regular basis to visit her local supermarket, select the items she needs, pay for them, and leave, all within a relatively brief time, without losing her sanity or her personal orientation to the world around her. This is because she exercises *selectivity* in perception.

Which stimuli get selected depends on two major factors in addition to the nature of the stimulus itself: the consumer's *previous experience* as it affects her expectations (what she is prepared or "set" to see) and her *motives* at the time (her needs, desires, interests, and so on). Each of these factors can serve to increase or decrease the probability that the stimulus will be perceived, and each can affect the consumer's selective exposure to and selective awareness of the stimulus itself.

### NATURE OF THE STIMULUS

Marketing stimuli include an enormous number of variables, all of which affect the consumer's perception, such as the nature of the product, its physical attributes, the package design, the brand name, the advertisements and commercials (including copy claims, choice and sex of model, positioning of model, size of ad, and typography), the position of the ad or time of the commercial, and the editorial environment.

In general, **contrast** is one of the most attention-compelling attributes of a stimulus. Advertisers often use extreme attention-getting devices to achieve maximum contrast and thus penetrate the consumer's perceptual screen. However, advertising does not have to be "way out" to achieve a high degree of differentiation; it simply has to contrast with the environment in which it is run. The use of lots of white space in a print advertisement, the absence of sound in a commercial's opening scene, a sixty-second commercial among a string of twenty-second spots—all of these offer sufficient contrast from their environment to achieve differentiation and merit the consumer's attention. Figure 6-6 shows how Volkswagen has used white space in a print advertisement to attract attention.

In the same vein, an advertising agency attracted attention by running a classified ad on the front page of the *New York Times,* a page which is usually reserved for news.[19] The essence of Wendy's highly successful "Where's the beef?" commercial is the visual presentation of a very small beef patty on a huge bun, which further minimizes the small size of the burger attributed to a competitor.

An opposite tack, but one that has been used effectively in TV commercials, is to make the commercial seem so close to the story line of a program that viewers are unaware that they are watching an ad until they are well into it. During the television coverage of the marriage of Prince Charles to Lady Diana, for example, a commercial filmed in a great English mansion, complete with liveried footmen, led the unsuspecting viewer into a sales pitch for the "Royal" line of photocopiers. Similarly, some print ads are made to resemble editorial material; others match their design features with facing editorials.

In the case of children's programming, the Federal Trade Commission has severely limited the use of this technique. TV stars or cartoon characters are prohibited from promoting products during children's shows in which they appear. However, many toy manufacturers are creating children's television shows around an advertised product, such as a licensed cartoon character—a practice likely to result in loud consumer outcries.[20]

With respect to packaging, astute marketers usually try to differentiate their packaging sufficiently to ensure rapid consumer perception. Since the average package on the supermarket shelf has about one-tenth of a second to make an impression on the consumer, it is important that every aspect of the package—its name, shape, color, label, and copy—provide sufficient sensory stimulation to be noted and remembered. A survey designed to test whether consumers could recognize a number of well-known packages with brand names concealed found that many packages did not achieve the recognition their marketers assumed.[21] The packages which received low recognition scores obviously did not provide sufficient sensory input to the consumer to be readily perceived and remembered.

### EXPECTATIONS

People usually see what they expect to see, and what they expect to see is usually based on familiarity, on previous experience, or on preconditioned "set." A number of interesting experiments have supported this notion. For example,

FIGURE 6-6 **Contrast Attracts Attention**

Think small.
Our little car isn't so much of a novelty any more.
A couple of dozen college kids don't try to squeeze inside it.
The guy at the gas station doesn't ask where the gas goes.
Nobody even stares at our shape.
In fact, some people who drive our little flivver don't even think 32 miles to the gallon is going any great guns.
Or using five pints of oil instead of five quarts.
Or never needing anti-freeze.
Or racking up 40,000 miles on a set of tires.
That's because once you get used to some of our economies, you don't even think about them any more.
Except when you squeeze into a small parking spot. Or renew your small insurance. Or pay a small repair bill. Or trade in your old VW for a new one.
Think it over.

Courtesy of Volkswagen United States, Inc.

one researcher had a "guest speaker" give the same prepared lecture to two different college classes. He preconditioned the students in the first class by telling them in advance that the speaker was an expert in his field but "cold" in nature; the second class was told that the speaker was an expert and "warm" in nature. Questionnaires completed after each lecture showed that the students who were "set" to hear a cold lecturer did indeed find him cold; those who anticipated a warm lecturer found him to be warm. Furthermore, there was more interaction and participation in the classroom discussion from those students who expected the lecturer to be warm than from those who expected him to be cold.[22]

In a marketing context, people tend to perceive products and product attributes according to their own **expectations.** A man who has been told by his friends that a new brand of Scotch has a bitter taste will probably perceive the taste to be bitter; a teenager who attends a horror movie that has been billed as terrifying will probably find it so.

On the other hand, stimuli that conflict sharply with expectations often receive more attention than those that conform to expectations. In other words, novelty tends to promote perception. An advertisement for bathing suits by Cole of California showed a lineup of pretty girls on a beach wearing a variety of bathing suit styles. However, the girl on the end wore no suit at all. Research showed that many readers simply glanced at the advertisement and started to turn the page but then did a double take when they realized what they had seen, and turned back to look at the ad more closely. Thus the ad ended up receiving much more attention than it otherwise would have, simply because of the inclusion of an element that surprised readers. Similarly, the ad presented in Figure 6-7 was designed to startle the reader with the unexpected picture of a woman shaving.

For years certain advertisers have used blatant sexuality in advertisements for products to which sex was not relevant because they knew such advertisements attracted a high degree of attention; however, such ads often defeated their own purpose because readers tended to remember the sex (e.g., the girl), but not the product or brand.[23] Nevertheless, sexually suggestive ads for cognac seem to have increased sales, and advertisers continue to use erotic appeals in promoting exercise machines, perfume, underwear, and jeans. Certain of these products are appropriate candidates for suggestive advertising, as they deliberately appeal to a consumer's need for romance and for products designed to enhance sexual desirability (see Figure 6-8); too many other products are not. (The use of sex in advertising is discussed in greater detail in Chapter 10.)

## MOTIVES

People tend to perceive things they need or want; the stronger the need, the greater the tendency to ignore unrelated stimuli in the environment. A man who wants to replace his windows will carefully note every advertisement for windows in his local newspaper; one who has no need of new windows will rarely notice such advertisements. In general, there is a heightened awareness of stimuli that are relevant to one's needs and interests, and a decreased awareness of stimuli that are irrelevant to those needs (see Figure 6-9).

FIGURE 6-7 The Unexpected Attracts Attention

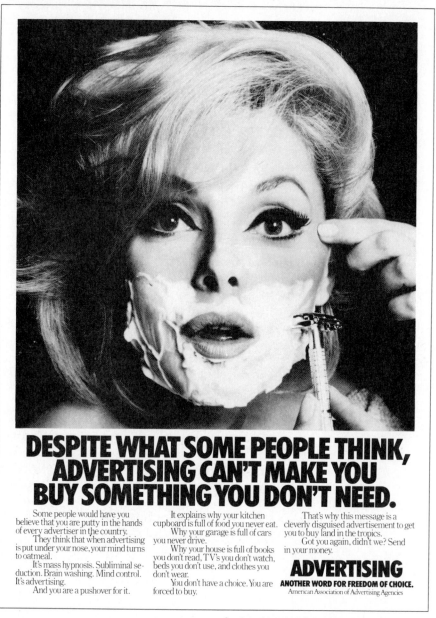

DESPITE WHAT SOME PEOPLE THINK, ADVERTISING CAN'T MAKE YOU BUY SOMETHING YOU DON'T NEED.
Some people would have you believe that you are putty in the hands of every advertiser in the country.
They think that when advertising is put under your nose, your mind turns to oatmeal.
It's mass hypnosis. Subliminal seduction. Brain washing. Mind control. It's advertising.
And you are a pushover for it.
It explains why your kitchen cupboard is full of food you never eat.
Why your garage is full of cars you never drive.
Why your house is full of books you don't read, TV's you don't watch, beds you don't use, and clothes you don't wear.
You don't have a choice. You are forced to buy.
That's why this message is a cleverly disguised advertisement to get you to buy land in the tropics.
Got you again, didn't we? Send in your money.
ADVERTISING
ANOTHER WORD FOR FREEDOM OF CHOICE.
American Association of Advertising Agencies


Courtesy of American Association of Advertising Agencies

An individual's perceptual process simply attunes itself more closely to those elements of the environment that are important to that person. Someone who is hungry looks for, and more readily perceives, restaurant signs; a sexually repressed person perceives sexual symbolism where none may exist.

Marketing managers recognize the efficiency of targeting their products to the perceived needs of consumers. In this way, they help to ensure that their

FIGURE 6-8 Sexually Suggestive Ads Attract Attention

wear it well into the night.
pierre cardin

Courtesy of Jacqueline Cochran

products will be perceived by potential prospects. The identification of perceived consumer needs has a number of different applications. For example, marketers can determine through marketing research what consumers consider to be the ideal attributes of the product category, or what consumers perceive their needs to be in relation to the product category. The marketer can then segment the market on the basis of these needs into a number of smaller market segments, each composed of individuals with similar perceived needs in

FIGURE 6-9 Selective Perception

Courtesy of American Association of Advertising Agencies

connection with the product category. The marketer is now able to develop different marketing strategies for each segment which stress how the product can fulfill the perceived needs of that segment. In this way, the marketer can vary the product advertising to specific market segments so that consumers in each segment will perceive the product as meeting their own specific needs, wants, and interests.

## RELATED CONCEPTS

As the preceding discussion illustrates, the consumer's "selection" of stimuli from the environment is based on the interaction of expectations and motives with the stimulus itself. These factors give rise to a number of important concepts concerning perception.

SELECTIVE EXPOSURE. Consumers actively seek out messages that are pleasant or with which they are sympathetic, and they actively avoid painful or threatening ones. Thus heavy smokers avoid articles that link cigarette smoking to cancer and note (and quote) the relatively few that deny the relationship. Consumers also selectively expose themselves to advertisements that reassure them of the wisdom of their purchase decisions.

SELECTIVE ATTENTION. Consumers have a heightened awareness of stimuli that meet their needs or interests and a decreased awareness of stimuli irrelevant to their needs. Thus they are likely to note ads for products that meet their needs or for stores with which they are familiar and disregard those in which they have no interest.[24] While estimates of the number of advertisements the average consumer is exposed to each day vary widely (from about three hundred to fifteen hundred exposures per day), daily exposure to magazines, newspapers, television, radio, billboards, direct mail, transit advertising and the like is undoubtedly far above the five hundred mark. *Exposure,* however, is not equivalent to *perception.*

People also vary in terms of the *kind of information* in which they are interested and in the *form of message* and *type of medium* they prefer. Some people are more interested in price, some in appearance, and some in social acceptability. Some people like complex, sophisticated messages; others like simple graphics. Consumers therefore exercise a great deal of **selectivity** in terms of the attention they give to commercial stimuli.

PERCEPTUAL DEFENSE. Consumers subconsciously screen out stimuli that for them are important *not* to see, even though exposure has already taken place. Thus, threatening or otherwise damaging stimuli are less likely to achieve awareness than neutral stimuli at the same level of exposure. Furthermore, individuals may distort information that is not consistent with their needs, values, and beliefs. For example, a consumer may "hear" that a set of dishes she loves is dishwasher safe (even though the salesclerk has clearly warned her it is not), because the dishes match her dining-room rug so perfectly. This is another example of people hearing what they want to hear rather than what has actually been said.

PERCEPTUAL BLOCKING. Consumers protect themselves from bombardment of stimuli by simply "tuning out"—blocking such stimuli from conscious awareness. Research shows that enormous amounts of advertising are screened out by consumers; this problem may be more severe for television than for print. Various hypotheses have been offered to explain why television advertising recall scores are falling, such as the greater amount of time allotted for commercials, the use of shorter commercials (and thus the increased number of advertising messages aired within the same period of time), the larger number of commercials that are strung together back-to-back, the increased number of advertisers, and the greater number of products being advertised. This problem is discussed in more detail in Chapter 10.

In addition to the sheer number of television ads, TV ads may have low recall because consumers tend to view the medium as less informative and truthful than print media.[25]

## Perceptual Organization

People do not experience the numerous stimuli they select from the environment as separate and discrete sensations; rather, they tend to *organize* them into groups and perceive them as unified wholes. Thus the perceived characteristics of even the simplest stimulus are viewed as a function of the whole to which the stimulus appears to belong. This method of organization simplifies life considerably for the individual.

The specific principles underlying perceptual organization are often referred to by the name given the school of psychologists who first developed and stressed **Gestalt psychology** (*Gestalt* in German means "pattern" or "configuration.") Three of the most basic principles of organization center on **figure and ground** relationships, **grouping,** and **closure.**

### FIGURE AND GROUND

We noted earlier that to be noticed, stimuli must *contrast* with their environment. A sound must be louder or softer, a color brighter or paler. The simplest visual illustration consists of a *figure* on a *ground* (i.e., background). The figure is usually perceived clearly because, in contrast to its ground, it appears to be well defined, solid, and in the forefront. The ground, however, is usually perceived as indefinite, hazy, and continuous. The common line that separates the figure and the ground is perceived as belonging to the figure rather than to the ground, which helps give the figure greater definition. Consider the stimulus of music. People can either "bathe" in music or listen to music. In the first case, music is simply *ground* to other activities; in the second, it is *figure.* Figure is more clearly perceived because it apears to be dominant; by contrast, ground appears to be subordinate and therefore less important.

People have a tendency to organize their perceptions into *figure and ground* relationships. However, learning affects which stimuli will be perceived as figure and which as ground. We are all familiar with reversible figure-ground patterns, such as the picture of the woman in Figure 6-10. How old would you say she was? Look again, very carefully. Depending on how you perceived figure and how you perceived ground, she can be either in her early twenties or her late seventies.

Like perceptual selection, perceptual organization is affected by *motives* and by *expectations* based on *experience*. For example, how a reversible figure-ground pattern is perceived can be influenced by prior pleasant or painful associations with one or the other element in isolation. The consumer's own physical state can also affect how he or she perceives reversible figure-ground illustrations. For example, after a particularly strenuous week, the thirty-five-year-old secretary of one of the authors happened to note with surprise the picture of the old woman shown in Figure 6-10. It took a great deal of concentrated effort for her to recognize it as the reversal of the picture of the smartly dressed young woman that she had been accustomed to seeing on the author's desk.

Advertisers have to plan their advertisements carefully to make sure that the stimulus they want noted is seen as figure and not as ground. The musical background must not overwhelm the jingle; the background of an advertisement must not detract from the product. Some print advertisers often silhouette their products against a white background to make sure that the features

**FIGURE 6-10** **Figure-Ground Reversal**

they want noted are clearly perceived. Others use reverse lettering (white letters on a black background) to achieve contrast; however, they must be careful to avoid the problem of figure-ground reversal.

Marketers sometimes make the mistake of running advertisements that confuse the consumer because there is no clear indication of which is figure and which is ground. A steel company that produces the steel for a variety of products, including bedsprings, once ran an ad that showed a sexy-looking girl bouncing up and down on a bed. Many critics wondered aloud just what it was the sponsor was selling—i.e., which was figure and which was ground.

We also tend to structure the social environment into figure and ground, much as we do the impersonal environment. We see the world clearly as "us" and "them," as "good guys" and "bad guys," as friends and enemies. Politicians and reporters often structure the world into the "free world" and the "Communist world," ignoring many of the other differences between nations and governments and people.

## GROUPING

Individuals tend to *group stimuli automatically* so that they form a unified picture or impression. Experiments have shown that the perception of stimuli as groups or "chunks" of information, rather than as discrete bits of information, facilitates their memory and recall.[26] For example, most of us can remember and repeat our social security numbers because we automatically group them into three *chunks* rather than nine separate numbers. When the telephone company introduced the idea of all-digit telephone numbers, consumers objected strenuously on the grounds that they would not be able to recall or repeat so many numbers. However, because we automatically group telephone numbers into two *chunks* (or three, with the area code), the problems that were anticipated never occurred. The same objection was raised to the notion of adding four more digits to the ZIP code, and the same experience will no doubt prevail.

**Grouping** can be used advantageously by marketers to imply certain desired meanings in connection with their products. For example, an advertisement for tea may show a young man and woman sipping tea in a well-furnished room before a blazing hearth. The grouping of stimuli by proximity leads the consumer to associate the drinking of tea with romance, fine living, and winter warmth.

## CLOSURE

Individuals have a need for **closure.** They express this need by organizing their perceptions so that they form a complete picture. If the pattern of stimuli to which they are exposed is incomplete, they tend to perceive it, nevertheless, as complete; that is, they consciously or subconsciously fill in the missing pieces. Thus a circle that has a section of its periphery missing will invariably be perceived as whole. The need for closure is also seen in the tension an individual experiences when a task is incomplete, and the satisfaction and relief that come upon its completion.

A classic study reported in 1972 found that incomplete tasks are better remembered than complete tasks.[27] One explanation for this phenomenon is that the person who begins a task develops a need to complete it. If he or she is prevented from doing so, a state of tension is created which manifests itself in improved memory for the uncompleted task. One researcher extended this theory to advertising messages and suggested that hearing the beginning of a message leads to the development of a need to hear the rest of it—"rather like waiting for the second shoe to drop."[28] The resulting tension leads to improvement in memory for that part of the message that has already been heard.

The need for closure has some interesting implications for marketers. The presentation of an incomplete advertising message "begs" for completion by consumers, and the very act of completion serves to involve them more deeply in the message itself. Figure 6-11 invites completion by the reader, thus enhancing interest in and memorability of the advertised product. Thus an incomplete ad tends to be perceived more readily than a complete one. Clever marketers have tried to exploit this phenomenon by constructing commercials that are deliberately "interrupted" before their expected finish. For example, Salem cigarettes very successfully ran a commercial that featured a catchy musical jingle that went: "You can take Salem out of the country, *but,* you can't take the country out of Salem." After repeating the jingle a number of times, the commercial ceased abruptly on a high note after the *"but."* Due to their need for closure, for completion, listeners invariably completed the jingle themselves, either aloud or silently: ". . . you can't take the country out of Salem." Such close involvement with the commercial served to increase its overall impact on the consumer.

In a related vein, advertisers have discovered that they can use the soundtrack of a frequently shown television commercial on radio with excellent results. Consumers who are familiar with the TV commercial perceive the audio part alone as incomplete; in their need for completion, they mentally play back the visual content as well.

In summary, it is clear that perceptions are not equivalent to the raw sensory input of discrete stimuli or the sum total of discrete stimuli. Rather, people tend to add to or subtract from stimuli to which they are exposed according to their own expectations and motives, using generalized principles of organization based on *Gestalt* theory.

## Perceptual Interpretation

The preceding discussion has emphasized that perception is a personal phenomenon. People exercise *selectivity* in terms of which stimuli they perceive, and they *organize* these stimuli on the basis of certain psychological principles. The *interpretation* of stimuli is also uniquely individual, since it is based upon what individuals expect to see in light of their previous experience, on the number of plausible explanations they can envision, and on their motives and interests at the time of perception.

FIGURE 6-11 Viewer Closure Enhances Memorability

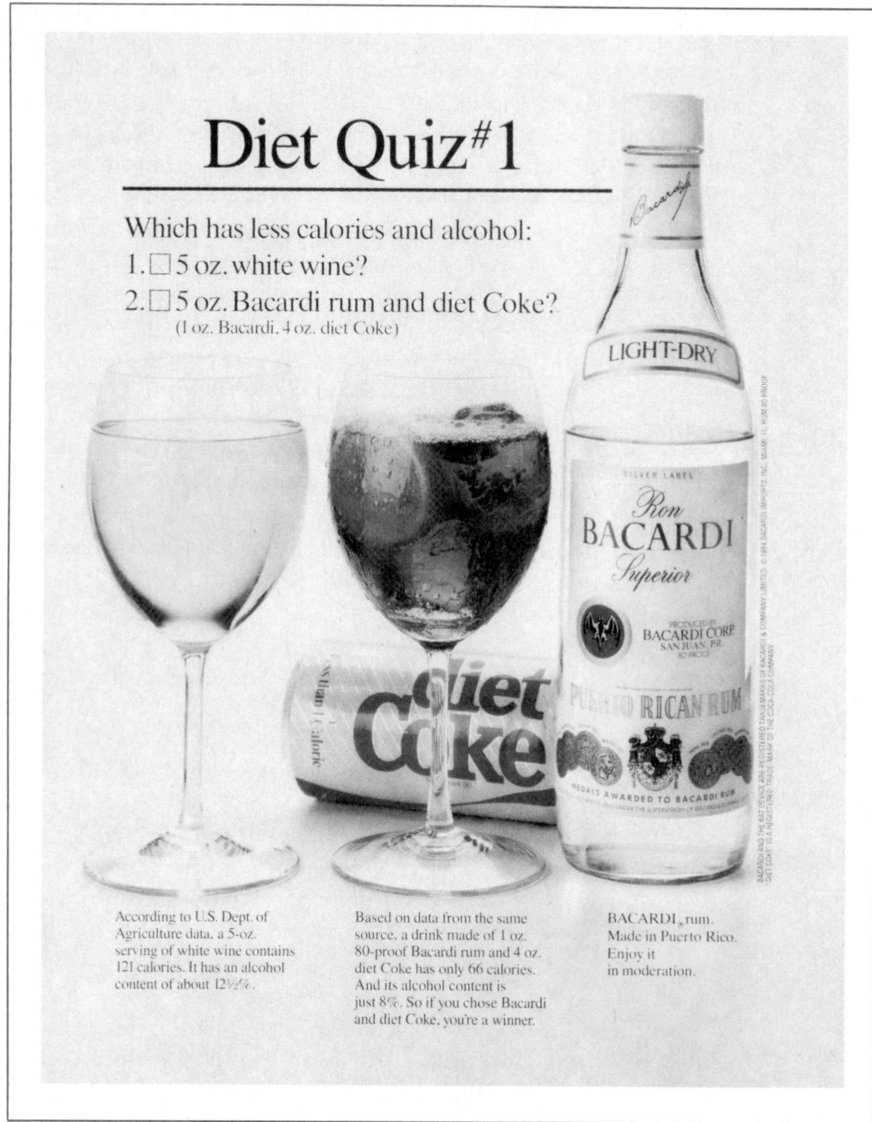


Courtesy of Bacardi Imports, Inc.

Stimuli are often highly ambiguous. Some stimuli are weak because of such factors as poor visibility, brief exposure, high noise level, and constant fluctuation. Even stimuli that are strong tend to fluctuate dramatically because of such factors as different angles of viewing, varying distances, and changing levels of illumination.

Consumers usually attribute the sensory input they receive to sources they consider most likely to have caused the specific pattern of stimuli. Past experiences and social interactions may help to form certain expectations which provide categories or alternatives that individuals use in interpreting stimuli. The narrower the individual's experience, the more limited is the access to alternative categories.

When stimuli are highly ambiguous, an individual will usually interpret them in such a way that they serve to fulfill personal needs, wishes, interests, and so on. It is this principle that provides the rationale for the projective tests discussed in Chapter 3. Such tests provide ambiguous stimuli (such as incomplete sentences, unclear pictures, untitled cartoons, and inkblots) to respondents who are asked to interpret them. How a person describes a vague illustration, what meaning the individual ascribes to an inkblot, is a reflection not of the stimulus itself, but of the subject's own needs, wants, and desires. Thus, through the interpretation of ambiguous stimuli, respondents reveal a great deal about themselves.

How close a person's interpretations are to reality, then, depends on the *clarity of the stimulus,* the *past experiences* of the perceiver, and his or her *motives and interests* at the time of perception.

## DISTORTING INFLUENCES

Individuals are subject to a number of influences that tend to distort their perceptions, some of which are discussed below.

PHYSICAL APPEARANCES. People tend to attribute the qualities they associate with certain people to others who may resemble them, whether or not they consciously recognize the similarity. For this reason, the selection of models for advertisements and for television commercials can be a key element in their ultimate persuasibility. That is why baking advice given by a woman who looks like somebody's kindly old grandmother is likely to be perceived as very helpful. Recent studies on physical appearance have found that attractive models are more persuasive and have a more positive influence on consumer attitudes and behavior than average-looking models.[29] One explanation for this phenomenon is that consumers may prefer to identify with an attractive model (e.g., as an aspect of their preferred self-image).

Studies have found that more attractive men are perceived as more successful businessmen than average-looking men; that more attractive women are perceived as less able in business; and that females wearing severely tailored clothing are more likely to be hired.[30]

STEREOTYPES. Individuals tend to carry "pictures" in their minds of the meaning of various kinds of stimuli. These *stereotypes* serve as expectations of what specific situations or people or events will be like, and are important determinants of how such stimuli are subsequently perceived. For example, a number of critics have claimed that in advertising, women have been underrepresented in working roles and overrepresented in decorative and sex-object roles. However, recent studies suggest that these stereotypes are changing as more men are cast in sex-object roles, while women are portrayed more positively in today's TV commercials.[31]

RESPECTED SOURCES. We tend to give added perceptual weight to advice coming from sources we respect. Marketers often use celebrities or known experts to give testimonials for their products or to act as company spokespersons to ensure that their products will be well perceived. Figure 6-12 is an example of using a respected source to endorse an unrelated service.

IRRELEVANT CUES. When required to form a difficult perceptual judgment, consumers often respond to irrelevant stimuli. For example, many high-priced automobiles are purchased because of their color, or a luxury option like retractable headlights or leather upholstery, rather than on the basis of mechanical or technical superiority.

FIRST IMPRESSIONS. First impressions tend to be lasting, yet in forming such impressions the perceiver does not yet know which stimuli are relevant, important, or predictive of later behavior. For example, researchers found that prior attitudes toward President Reagan significantly influenced the emotions of students who viewed videotapes of various presidential speeches.[32] Because first impressions are often lasting, introducing a new product before it has been perfected may prove fatal because subsequent information about its superiority, even if true, will often be negated by memory of its early failure.

JUMPING TO CONCLUSIONS. Many people tend to jump to conclusions before examining all the relevant evidence. For example, the consumer may perceive just the beginning of a commercial message and draw conclusions regarding the product or service being advertised on the basis of such limited information. For this reason, copywriters should be careful not to save their most persuasive arguments for last.

HALO EFFECT. A generalized impression that may be favorable or unfavorable is extended to the interpretation of nonrelevant stimuli. This effect tends to be more pronounced when the perceiver is interpreting stimuli with which he or she has had little experience. Historically, the *halo* effect has been used to describe situations where the evaluation of a single object or person on a multitude of dimensions is based upon the evaluation of just one or a few dimensions. (A man is trustworthy, fine, and noble because he looks you in the eye when he speaks.) Here we broaden the notion of the halo effect to include the evaluation of multiple objects (a product line) on the basis of the evaluation of just one dimension (a brand name or a spokesperson). Using this broader definition, marketers take advantage of the halo effect when they extend a brand name associated with one line of products to another. Bic, playing on the reputation it had gained in marketing inexpensive, reliable, disposable pens, introduced a line of disposable razors under the Bic name, with a great deal of success. Consumers bought the new Bic razor on the basis of their favorable evaluation of the Bic pen. (An extension of this phenomenon is known as **stimulus generalization,** which will be discussed in Chapter 7.)

Under our broadened definition, the mushrooming field of *licensing* also is based on the halo effect. Manufacturers and retailers hope to acquire instant

FIGURE 6-12 Endorsement by a Respected Source Enhances Credibility

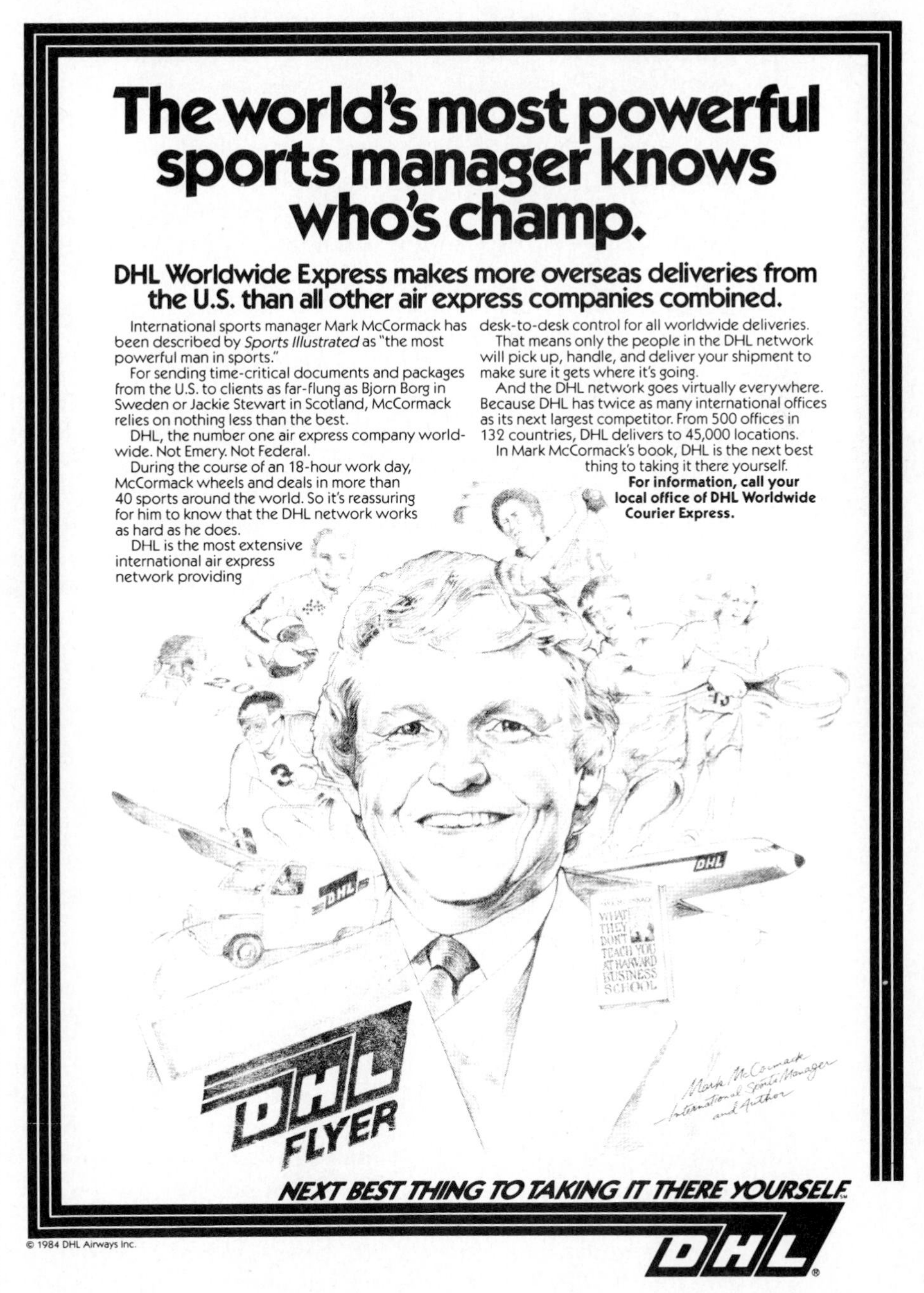


Courtesy of DHL Worldwide Express

recognition and status for their products by association with a favorably thought of celebrity or designer name. For example, some thirty-three firms are marketing licensed products, including jewelry, high-fashion clothing, and fragrances under the "Dynasty" or "Carrington" names, betting a large investment on the connection between their products and America's most popular and glamorous prime-time soap opera.

Joan Collins, the show's ruthless manipulator of men, is promoting Scoundrel Musk perfume as "Unmistakeably Female. Undeniably Provocative"—a clear reference to her role in the TV hit (see Figure 6-13). As part of a campaign sponsored by Cannon bed and bath products, she is also appearing in a highly provocative towel advertisement. As part of the same campaign, Larry Hagman, top villain in the TV show "Dallas," is promoting a line of bedsheets—a clear reference to his notorious and constant womanizing in his role as J. R. Ewing.

Marketers have begun to recognize the need to estimate the strength and direction of perceptual biases like the halo effect.[33] The reader may well ask how "realistic" perception can be, given the many subjective influences on perceptual interpretations. It is therefore somewhat reassuring to remember that previous experiences usually serve to resolve stimulus ambiguity in a realistic way and help in its interpretation. It is only in situations of unusual or changing stimuli conditions that expectations may lead to wrong interpretations.

## CONSUMER IMAGERY

Consumers have a number of enduring perceptions, or **images,** which are particularly relevant to the study of consumer behavior. These include the image they hold of themselves, and their perceived images of products and product categories, of retail stores, and of producers.

### Self-Image

Each individual has a perceived image of himself or herself as a certain kind of person, with certain traits, habits, possessions, relationships, and ways of behaving. As with other types of perceptions, the individual's **self-image** is unique, a product of that person's own background and experience. Individuals develop a perceived self-image through interactions with other people: initially their parents, then other individuals or groups with whom they relate over the years.

Products and other objects have *symbolic value* for individuals, who evaluate them on the basis of their consistency (i.e., congruence) with their personal pictures of themselves. Some products seem to agree with the individual's self-image; others seem totally alien. Consumers attempt to preserve or enhance their self-image by buying products they believe are congruent with that self-image and avoiding products that are not.[34] Figure 6-14 presents an ad designed to appeal to the self-image of successful women. Retail stores select man-

FIGURE 6-13 Celebrity "Halo" Extended to Perfume

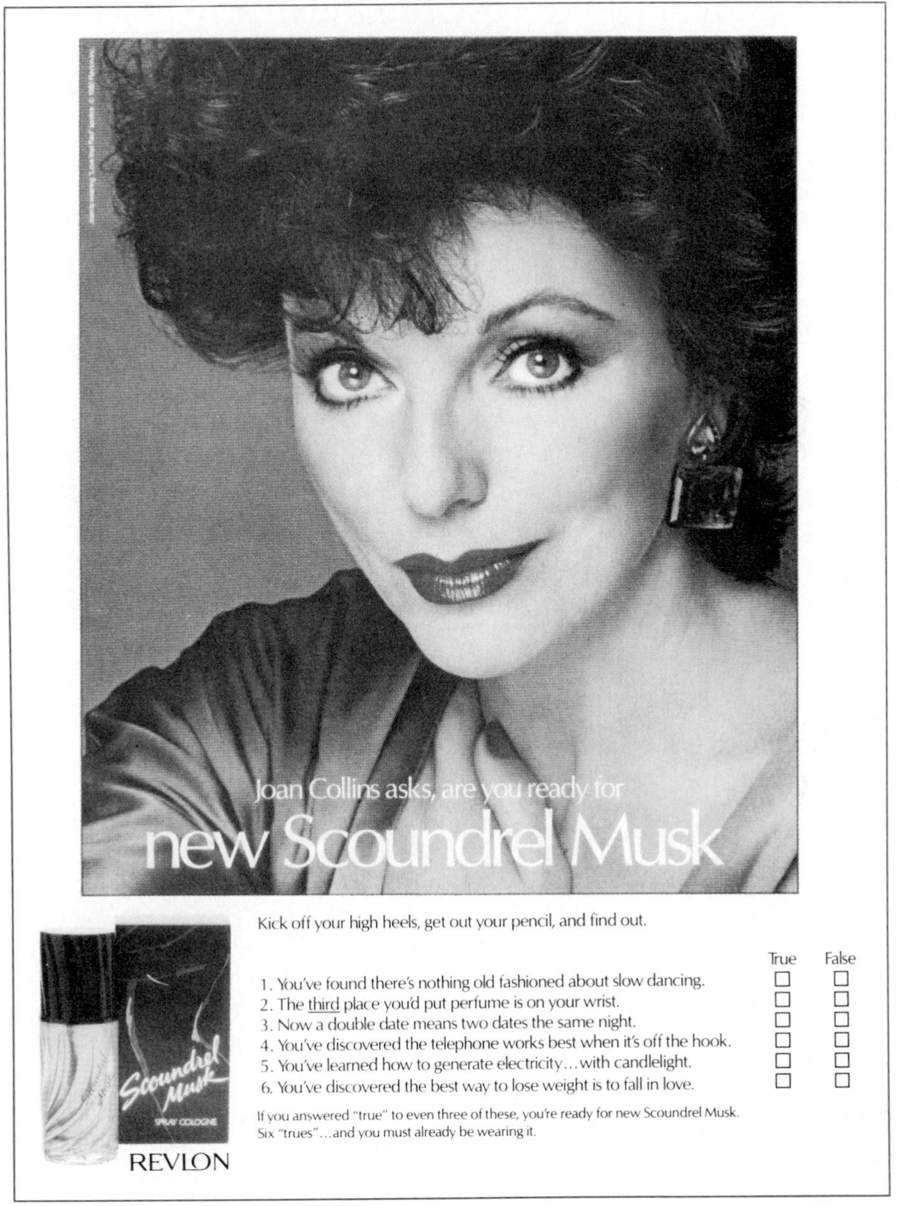

Joan Collins asks, are you ready for
new Scoundrel Musk
Kick off your high heels, get out your pencil, and find out.
True False
1. You've found there's nothing old fashioned about slow dancing.
2. The third place you'd put perfume is on your wrist.
3. Now a double date means two dates the same night.
4. You've discovered the telephone works best when it's off the hook.
5. You've learned how to generate electricity...with candlelight.
6. You've discovered the best way to lose weight is to fall in love.
If you answered "true" to even three of these, you're ready for new Scoundrel Musk.
Six "trues"...and you must already be wearing it.
Scoundrel Musk
SPRAY COLOGNE
REVLON

Courtesy of Revlon Inc.

nequins that they feel reflect the store's image as well as the consumer's self-image. In the 1970s, for example, some female mannequins were made in bold, upright stances with tightly clenched fists to reflect women's fight for equality; today they have a confident, outgoing but softer appearance. Some mannequins also have a more athletic look in response to the fitness craze that has swept the country, and are shown running, diving, and jumping in addition to

FIGURE 6-14 Appeal to Self-Image

Courtesy of Collagen Corporation

more traditional poses. The general belief is that if the customer identifies with the mannequin, he or she is more likely to purchase the product.

Research indicates that consumers tend to shop in stores that have an image consistent with their own self-image. Thus, in New York, upper-class shoppers have said they prefer Bloomingdale's because of its "modern, sophisticated, extravagant" aura.[35]

Several researchers explored the notion that individuals' **ideal self-concept** (that is, how they would *like* to perceive themselves) is more relevant to consumption behavior than **actual self-concept** (how they do in fact perceive themselves).[36] Now researchers have distinguished an intermediate concept, **expected self-concept** (how individuals expect to see themselves at some specified future time). They have concluded that as self-concept changes from *actual* self-image to some future or *expected* self-image, product preferences also change, and that *expected* self-concept may be more valuable than *ideal* self-concept as a guide for designing and promoting products.[37]

The concept of self-image has strategy implications for marketers. For example, marketers can segment their markets on the basis of relevant consumer self-images and position their products or stores as symbols of such self-images. Such a strategy is in complete agreement with the classical marketing concept, in that the marketer first determines the needs of a consumer (both in respect to the product category and in respect to an appropriate symbol of self-image) and then proceeds to develop and market a product that will meet both criteria.

## Product Positioning

The way the product is perceived—that is, how it is **positioned** in the mind of the consumer—is probably more important to its ultimate success than are its actual characteristics. Marketers try to position their brands so that they are perceived by the consumer to fit a distinctive niche in the marketplace—a niche occupied by no other product. They try to differentiate their products from competitive brands by telling the consumer that their products possess attributes which will fulfill the consumer's needs better than competing brands.[38] However, marketers must be careful not to stress too many attributes in their product promotion lest they confuse the consumer.[39] Apple Computer recently ran an advertisement which included a two-page list of the programs available for its computers, yet this two-page list really communicated only one major attribute—the range of software available to Apple users.[40]

Marketers must endeavor to find out which attributes are important to consumers and which they are willing to trade off for other features. For example, since the early 1970s, Americans have been willing to trade off bigger, flashier, and more comfortable cars for smaller, fuel-efficient automobiles. In the process, many luxury cars lost their distinctiveness. Indeed, a recent TV campaign for the Lincoln Town Car suggests that most contemporary luxury cars are similar in appearance and design, and that only the Lincoln stands above the crowd. A print ad for the Lincoln Continental (see Figure 6-15) tries to emphasize its luxury by showing it parked in front of one of the most exclusive retail stores in America. The ad also tries to appeal to both inner-directed and other-directed consumers (see Chapter 4).

**Positioning strategy** is the essence of the marketing mix; it complements the company's segmentation strategy and selection of target markets.[41] In our overcommunicated society, the marketer must create product distinctiveness in the mind of the consumer. Volkswagen did so with its classic advertising campaign for the Beetle, which sharply distinguished it from its competition. When Avis challenged Hertz by saying "We're number two. We try harder," it distinguished itself in the consumer's mind as the underdog—a clever marketing strategy, since many Americans tend to favor the underdog. When Seven-Up

FIGURE 6-15 Product Positioning

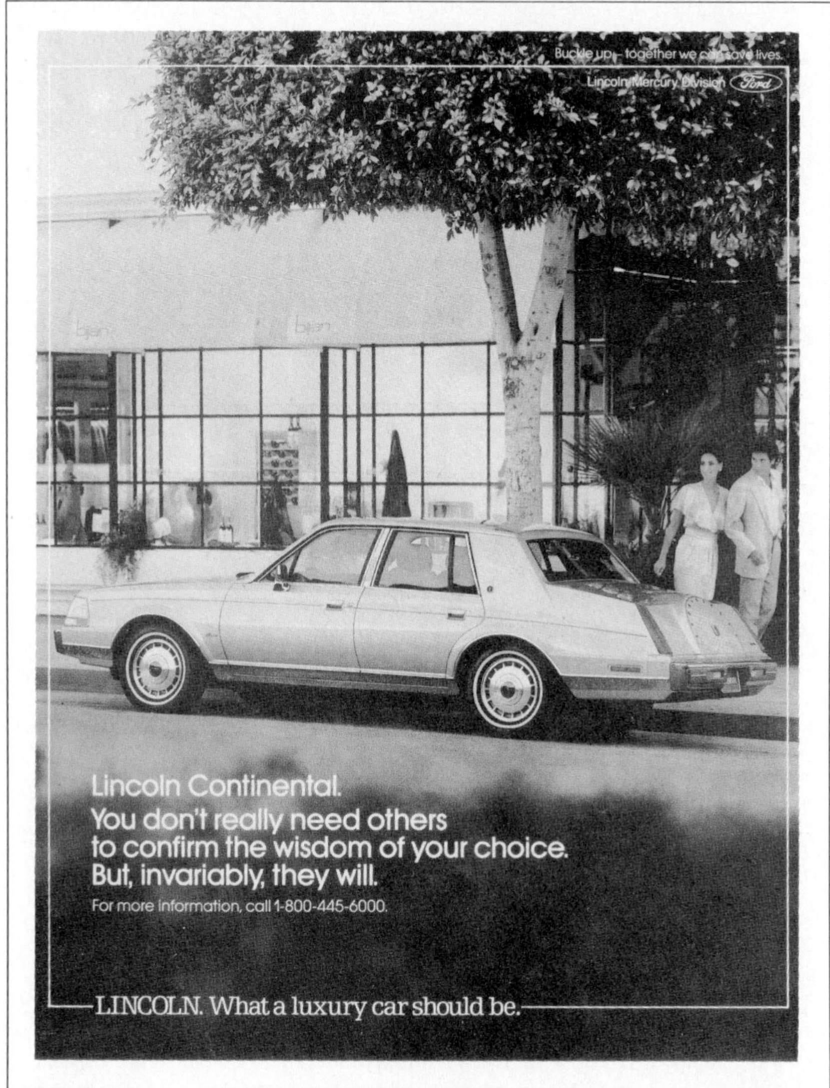


Courtesy of Lincoln-Mercury Division of the Ford Motor Company

advertised itself as the Uncola, it differentiated itself from the leading soft drinks.[42] In each of these cases, the advertising messages urged consumers to fulfill their needs through attributes which only their products possessed.

A successfully differentiated product gives the marketer pricing and distribution leverage. Thus, Bayer aspirin sells above the price of competing brands despite the identical chemical composition of aspirin. Similarly, Tide laundry detergent, Heinz Ketchup, and Kleenex tissues sell at higher prices, are carried by all supermarkets and grocery stores, and stand out on cluttered shelves because of their successful positioning.

## PRODUCT IMAGE

The result of successful positioning is a distinctive brand image, and every aspect of the product's design, price, promotion, and distribution should reflect that image. Thus Scope, positioned as a refreshing mouthwash, is green in color; Listerine, positioned as an antiseptic mouthwash, is yellow. Consumers rely on their perceptions of **brand images, product images,** and **people images** in making consumer choices. Politicians have begun to recognize the critical importance of image in winning elections, and are hiring marketing experts to develop appropriate marketing strategies that assure the creation and communication of a positive and desirable image (see Chapter 20).

By design or not, products often do communicate an image. For example, in a study of brand image where students were asked to match cars with occupations, they matched young executives to BMWs, senior executives to Mercedes and Cadillacs, and grandmothers to Dodge Darts and Buick Skylarks (see Table 6-1).[43]

Brand images should be clear and distinct in the minds of consumers. A postmortem analysis of Anheuser Busch's unsuccessful attempt to enter the adult soft drink market with Chelsea suggests that its failure was due to the fact that the product did not communicate a clear image. Its bottle resembled a beer bottle, it was foamy when poured, and it was advertised as a "not-so-soft" drink. The company was accused of trying to sell beer in disguise, and the product was dubbed "baby beer." Because of the public protest that resulted, the product was withdrawn from the market.[44]

In today's highly competitive environment, a distinctive product image is most important. Consumers tend to distinguish one brand from another on the basis of the promotional message and the use or ownership of the brand. As

**TABLE 6-1 Brand Images of Cars**

When 300 students at the University of Pennsylvania were asked which car was most appropriate for the following people, they made the following choices from a list of 30 cars.

| | |
|---|---|
| Young executive | BMW |
| Grandmother | Dodge Dart or Buick Skylark |
| College male | Mustang |
| Senior executive | Mercedes or Cadillac |
| Playboy | Corvette |
| Nurse | Toyota |
| College professor | Volvo |
| Teacher | VW Rabbit |
| Doctor | Mercedes |
| College female | Toyota or Datsun |

Source: Thomas S. Robertson, Joan Zielinski, and Scott Ward, *Consumer Behavior* (Glenview, Ill.: Scott, Foresman, 1984), p. 182.

products become more complex and the marketplace more crowded, consumers rely more on the product's image in making purchase decisions.[45]

### PERCEPTUAL MAPPING

The technique of **perceptual mapping** helps marketers to determine just how their products appear to consumers in relation to competitive brands on one or more product characteristics. It enables them to see gaps in the positioning of all brands in the product class, and to identify areas in which consumer needs are not being adequately met. A manufacturer of laundry detergent A (see Figure 6-16) may discover that consumers perceive its product to be very similar to products B and C; at the same time, it may note that consumers do not perceive any laundry detergents to have both good cleansing power and be gentle on fabrics. To carve out a new market segment consisting of consumers who want both features, the manufacturer may decide to **reposition** its product from point *A* to point *A′* (i.e., as a gentle but powerful laundry cleanser). This could be accomplished through a promotional campaign which stresses both cleansing power and gentle impact on clothes. Of course, such a campaign could not succeed unless the product actually had both features.

Figure 6-17 shows another perceptual map, this one designed to show perceived similarity among brands of headache remedies.

## Product Repositioning

Regardless of how well positioned a product appears to be, the marketer may be forced to **reposition** it in response to market events, such as a competitor

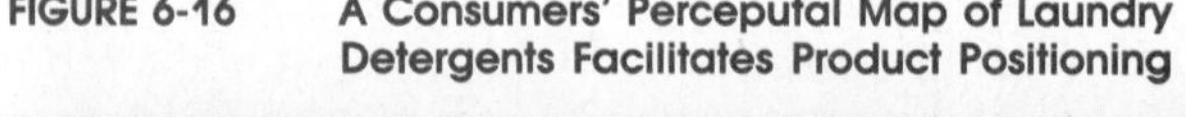
**FIGURE 6-16** A Consumers' Perceputal Map of Laundry Detergents Facilitates Product Positioning

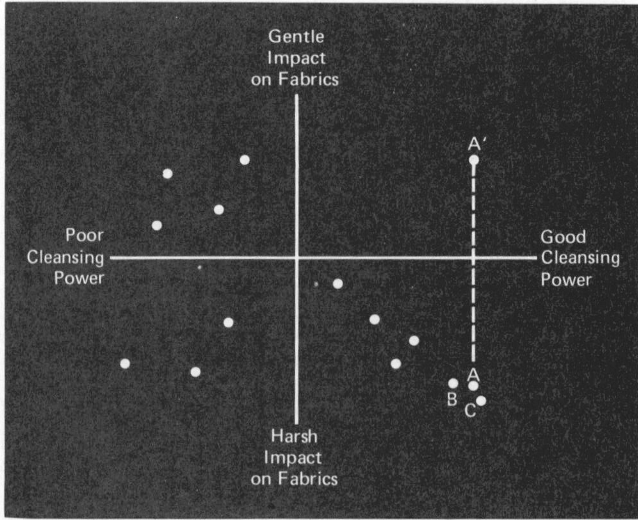

FIGURE 6-17 Perceptual Map Depicts Perceived Similarity Among Pain-Relievers

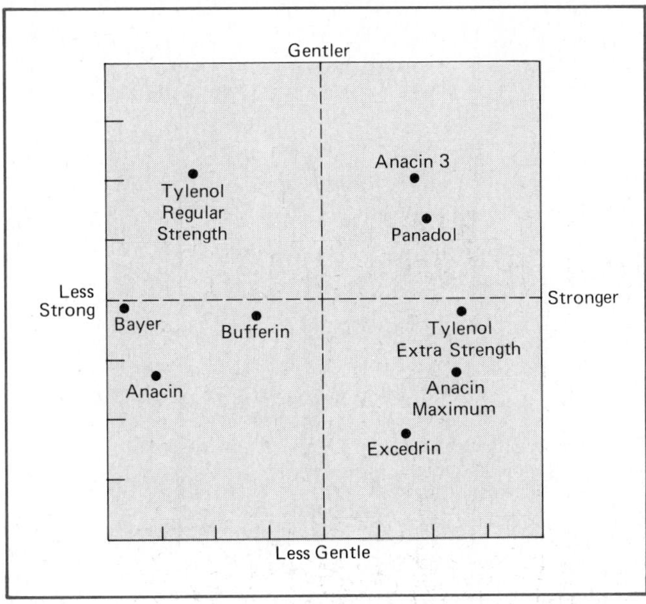


who is cutting into the brand's market share. For example, Baskin Robbins Ice Cream revised its advertising and is altering the child-oriented decor of its stores in an effort to appeal to young urban adults who switched to Haagen-Dazs.[46] Similarly, U.S. underwear manufacturers have repositioned underwear from a commodity to a glamorous and fashionable product, following the lead of European manufacturers who have dominated the upscale American underwear market.[47] Figure 6–18 illustrates Johnson & Johnson's strategy to reposition Johnson's Baby Lotion as an adult body lotion.

Another reason to reposition a product might be changing consumer preferences. Thus, as consumers became aware of the dangers of intense suntanning, alert cosmetic companies began to add sunscreens to lipsticks, moisturizers, and foundation creams and to promote this new benefit as a major attribute, thus repositioning specific product lines.[48] The emergence of new market segments might require product repositioning. Old Tyme Ginger Beer, which for twenty years had been sold in health food stores, was repositioned to appeal to young professionals and promoted as a beverage to have with exotic foods. In response to changing consumer preferences in soft drinks, Seven-up has repositioned itself from the Uncola to a caffeine-free soft drink with the message: "Caffeine. Never had it. Never will." This slogan distinguishes the drink from the new caffeine-free versions of the traditional colas.

**FIGURE 6-18 Product Repositioning**

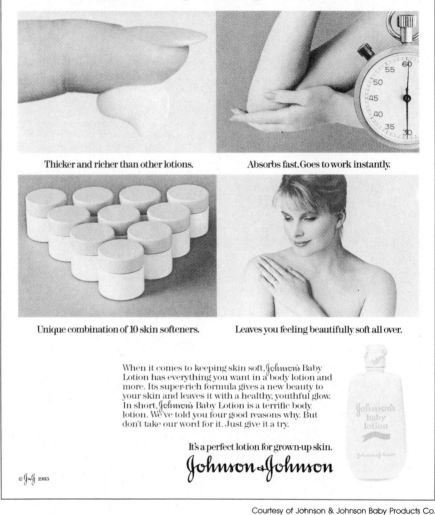

Four good reasons why Johnson's Baby Lotion is the perfect "grown-up" body lotion.

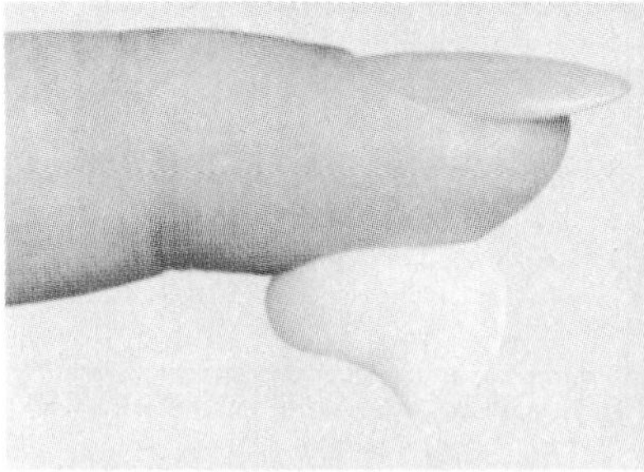

Thicker and richer than other lotions.

Absorbs fast. Goes to work instantly.

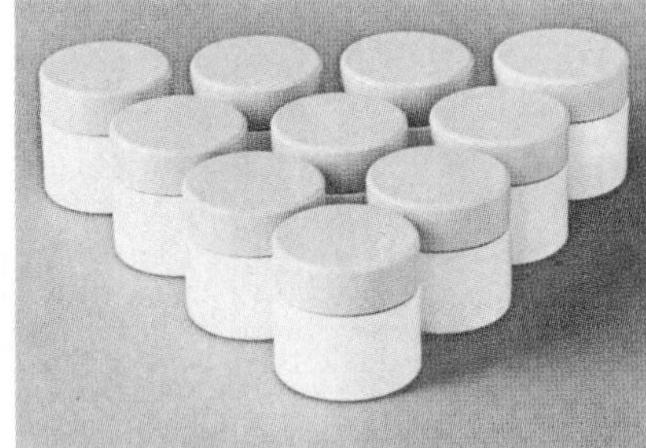

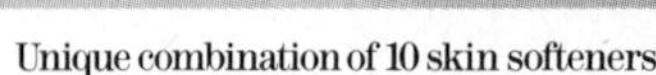


Leaves you feeling beautifully soft all over.

When it comes to keeping skin soft, Johnson's Baby Lotion has everything you want in a body lotion and more. Its super-rich formula gives a new beauty to your skin and leaves it with a healthy, youthful glow. In short, Johnson's Baby Lotion is a terrific body lotion. We've told you four good reasons why. But don't take our word for it. Just give it a try.

It's a perfect lotion for grown-up skin.

Johnson & Johnson

Courtesy of Johnson & Johnson Baby Products Co.

## Evoked Set

The specific brands a consumer will consider in making a purchase choice in a particular product category are known as the **evoked set;** the brands in the forefront of the evoked set tend to be the ones purchased and used most frequently.[49] A consumer's evoked set is distinguished from his or her *inept set,* consisting of brands the consumer excludes from purchase consideration, and the *inert set,* consisting of brands the consumer is indifferent toward because they are not perceived as having any particular advantages.[50] Regardless of the total number of brands in a product category, a consumer's evoked set tends to be quite small. A study concerning such large product categories as toothpaste and laundry detergent revealed an average evoked set of only three brands and five brands, respectively.[51] This is not surprising, since research indicates that most people have a span of recall limited to approximately seven items.[52]

Recent studies indicate that the size of the evoked set increases as the purchase nears.[53] In the case of cars, consumers who enlarged their evoked sets were those who spent more time on information searches; yet these same people were likely to purchase a car which was consistent with their initial evoked set.[54]

Among those brands with which the consumer is familiar, there are *acceptable* brands, *unacceptable* brands, and *overlooked* (or forgotten) brands. The evoked set consists of the small number of brands the consumer is familiar with, remembers, and finds acceptable. Figure 6-19 presents a simple model of the evoked set as a subset of all available brands in a product category. As the figure indicates, it is essential that a product be part of a consumer's evoked set if it is to be considered at all. The four terminal positions in the model which do *not* end in purchase (labeled 1, 2, 3, and 4) would appear to have perceptual problems. For example: (1) brands may be *unknown* because of consumers' selective exposure to advertising media and their selective perception of advertising stimuli; (2) brands may be *unacceptable* because of poor or inappropriate positioning in either advertising or product characteristics, or both; (3) brands

**FIGURE 6-19 The Evoked Set as a Subset of All Brands in a Product Class**

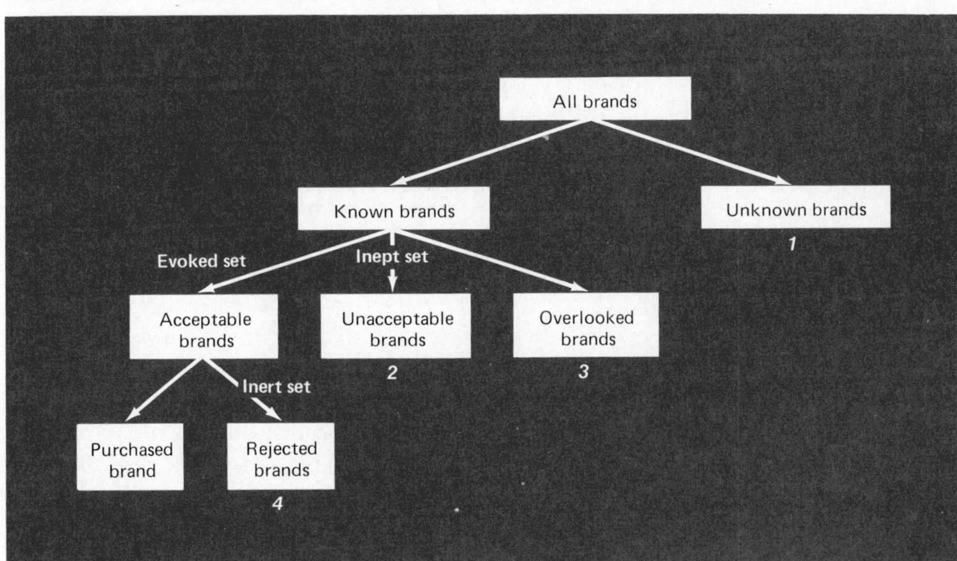

may be *overlooked* because they have not been clearly positioned or sharply targeted at the consumer market segment under study; and (4) brands may be *rejected* because they are perceived by consumers as unable to satisfy their perceived needs as thoroughly as the brand they select.

In each of these instances, the implication for marketers is that promotional techniques should be designed to impart a more favorable, perhaps more relevant, product image to the target consumer. This may sometimes require a change in product attributes as well.

## Perceived Quality

Consumers often judge the quality of a product on the basis of a variety of informational cues which they associate with the product. Some of these cues are *intrinsic* to (inherent in) the product, such as specific product characteristics; others are *extrinsic* to (external to) the product, such as price, store image, brand image, and promotional message.[55] Either singly or in composite, such cues provide the basis for perceptions concerning product quality.

### INTRINSIC CUES

Cues that are intrinsic concern physical characteristics of the product itself, such as size, color, flavor, or aroma. In some cases, consumers use physical characteristics to judge product quality. For example, research has found that consumers judge the flavor of ice cream, the mildness of dishwashing detergent, and the quality of shirts by color cues.[56] Even the perceived quality of laundry detergents has been affected by color cues. For example, sales of Proctor & Gamble's Cheer detergent skyrocketed when its color was changed to blue, undoubtedly because housewives associated the color with the "bluing" their mothers used to add to wash to whiten and brighten their laundry.[57]

Consumers like to believe they base their product quality evaluations on intrinsic cues, because they can justify resulting product decisions (either positive or negative) on the basis of "rational" or "objective" product choice. More often than not, however, the physical characteristic they select on which to judge quality has no intrinsic relation to the product's quality. Thus, though many consumers claim they buy a brand because of its superior taste, they are often unable to identify that brand in blind taste tests.

In one study, Budweiser-loyal beer drinkers were asked to sample two beers: first Budweiser, and then a second brand of beer which they had professed to dislike. The subjects could not bring themselves to finish the second beer because of its "skunky" and "terrible" taste. In actuality, both samples of beer were Budweiser. In this situation, perception of taste was clearly based on the product images, not on actual taste differences.[58] In another taste test, consumers claimed a preference for the taste of a national brand grape jelly to that of a generic brand, when actually both were the same product.[59] In still another study, housewives were asked to evaluate the tastes of two different beverages successively, identified as Coke and Diet Coke.[60] The housewives were enthusiastic about the Coke but complained about the bitter aftertaste of Diet Coke.

Both samples, however, actually contained the same beverage—regular Coke. Because some of the early diet beverages did have a bitter aftertaste, many consumers simply attributed that characteristic to all diet sodas and thus "tasted" (perceived) what they expected to taste. Other consumers may not have wished to identify with a product designed for overweight people because of its lack of congruence with their own self-images.

### EXTRINSIC CUES

In the absence of actual experience with a product, consumers often "evaluate" quality on the basis of factors quite external to the product itself, such as its price, the image of the store(s) that carries it, or the image (that is, the reputation) of the manufacturer that produces it.

PRICE-QUALITY RELATIONSHIP. A number of research studies support the view that consumers rely on price as an indicator of product quality. Several studies have shown that consumers attribute different qualities to identical products that carry different price labels. One study reported that subjects ranked the quality of three samples of unlabeled beer in direct relationship to their prices: The high-priced beer was ranked first in quality, the medium-priced beer second, and the low-priced beer as lowest in quality, despite the fact that all three samples were actually the same brand.[61] Another study found that housewives rated high-priced pantyhose as better in quality than medium-priced or low-priced pantyhose, even though the three samples were of identical quality.[62] Because price is so often considered an indicator of quality, some products deliberately emphasize a high price to underscore their claims of quality (see Figure 6-20).

How closely are price and quality actually related across product lines? One researcher found such a relationship for only 51 percent of the products he analyzed. For 14 percent of the products, the higher prices were actually associated with poorer-quality products.[63] Recent evidence on this issue is conflicting. For example, data collected by *Consumer Reports* suggests that the prices that some manufacturers charge for certain kitchen appliances are unrelated to the products' quality.[64] A study of electrical and electronic products in the Japanese market supports this conclusion.[65] However, another researcher argues that when marketers know that consumers use prices as an indicator of quality, they are encouraged to raise the quality of their products.[66] Unfortunately, it is a lot easier for them simply to raise their prices to *imply* quality.

Some marketers have successfully used the **price-quality relationship** to position their products as the top-quality offering in their product category. For example, Chock Full O'Nuts coffee was introduced as a high-priced coffee that was "worth the difference" in cost because of its allegedly "superior" flavor and taste.

If price and quality are so tenuously related, why do consumers continue to use price as a guide to product selection? The answer seems to be that they use price as a surrogate indicator if they have little other information to go by, or if they have little confidence in their own ability to make the choice on other grounds. When brand names are known or experience with a product is great,

**FIGURE 6-20** **Promotion Based on Perceived Price/Quality Relationship**
*Source:* © The Glenlivet Distilling Co., N.Y., N.Y.

# Just a word about the price of The Glenlivet. Preposterous.

Is the premium we place on The Glenlivet really so outlandish? No more so than the premium placed on great vintage wines and fine champagne cognacs. The reason? Taste. Just one sip and you'll know that The Glenlivet has a taste that's without equal.

The Glenlivet is Scotland's first and finest single malt Scotch, from Scotland's oldest licensed distillery. And, just as it always has been, this 100% Highland malt whisky is distilled from natural spring water and fine malt barley, then aged in oaken casks.

Only The Glenlivet's time-honored methods can achieve this unequaled taste. A taste that sets us apart. Its smoothness, body and bouquet are qualities found only in this unique Scotch.

Of course, some people may still insist that The Glenlivet is too expensive. We have just one word to say about that. Preposterous!

**The Glenlivet**
12-year-old unblended Scotch.
About $20 the bottle.

© 1985 THE GLENLIVET DISTILLING CO., N.Y.

price declines as a factor in product selection.[67] Recent evidence supports the notion that consumers who use price as an indicator of quality do so because they believe quality differences do exist. Not surprisingly, such consumers show greater preference for higher-priced brands than individuals who do not believe that quality varies among brands.[68]

STORE IMAGE. Retail stores have images of their own that serve to influence the perceived quality of products they carry, as well as the decisions of consumers as to where to shop. Retail stores may have a variety of images, such as a high-fashion image, a low-price image, a wide-selection image, or a good-service image.[69]

The type of product the consumer wishes to buy will influence his or her selection of retail outlet; conversely, the consumer's evaluation of a product will be influenced by the knowledge of where it was bought. A consumer wishing to buy an elegant dress for a special occasion may go to a store with an elegant, high-fashion image, such as Bergdorf Goodman in New York. Regardless of what she actually pays for the dress she selects (regular price or marked-down price), she will probably perceive its quality to be high. However, she may perceive the quality of the same dress to be much lower if she buys it in a discount store with a low-price image.

Most studies of the effects of extrinsic cues on perceived product quality have focused on just one variable—price or store image. However, where a second extrinsic cue is available, it is likely that perceived quality will be a function of the interaction of both cues on the consumer. To test this hypothesis, four identical samples of carpet—cut from the same bolt—were given to female subjects who were asked to rate their quality on a scale ranging from very low to very high.[70] Each carpet sample was labeled with a price and the name of a store, as follows: (1) high-image store, high price; (2) high-image store, low price; (3) low-image store, high price; and (4) low-image store, low price.

The researchers discovered that the samples with the high price were perceived to be of significantly better quality than the samples with the low price; similarly, the samples from the prestige store had a somewhat better perceived image than the samples from the low-prestige store. In addition, the researchers found that the interactive effects of both price and store image significantly altered the subjects' perceptions of product quality from the perceptions achieved by either cue alone.

A recent study found that when brand and retailer images become associated, the less favorable image becomes enhanced at the expense of the more favorable image. Thus when a low-priced store carries a brand with a high-priced image, the image of the store will improve, while the image of the brand will be negatively affected.[71]

MANUFACTURER'S IMAGE. Consumer imagery extends beyond perceived price and store image to the producers themselves. Manufacturers who enjoy a favorable image generally find that their new products are accepted more readily than those of manufacturers who have a less favorable or a "neutral" image. Obviously, consumers have greater confidence that they will not be disappointed in a major name-brand product. Advertising has an important role in estabishing a favorable brand image. Studies have shown, for example, that advertised brands of both peanut butter and cat food were perceived as higher in quality than nonadvertised brands, and that people expressed a greater willingness to buy the advertised than the unadvertised brands.[72]

Many companies have definite images in the consumer's mind. For many years IBM reigned as the most admired U.S. corporation on such attributes as quality of management, long-term investment value, and financial soundness. Kodak was most admired in terms of community and environmental responsibility, and Hewlett-Packard in terms of its ability to attract, develop, and keep talented people.[73] On the other hand, Union Carbide's image has taken a severe beating since the chemical accident in its plant near Bhopal, India, which killed thousands of people.[74]

Today, companies are using advertising, exhibits, and sponsorship of community events to enhance their image.[75] However, some marketers argue that product and service advertising would do more to boost their corporate image than **institutional** (i.e., image) **advertising.**[76] Others see both types of advertising—product and institutional—as integral and complementary components of a total corporate communications program.

## PERCEIVED RISK

Consumers must constantly make decisions regarding what products or services to buy and where to buy them. Because the outcomes (or consequences) of such decisions are often uncertain, the consumer faces some degree of "risk" in making a purchase decision. *Perceived risk* is defined as *the uncertainty that consumers face when they cannot foresee the consequences of their purchase decisions.* This definition highlights two relevant dimensions of **perceived risk:** *uncertainty* and *consequences.*

The degree of risk consumers perceive and their own tolerance for risk-taking serve to influence their purchase strategies. It should be stressed that consumers are influenced only by risk that they *perceive,* whether or not such risk actually exists. Risk that is not perceived—no matter how real or how dangerous—will not influence consumer behavior. Furthermore, the amount of money involved in the purchase is not directly related to the amount of risk perceived. Selecting the right mouthwash may present as great a risk to a consumer as selecting a new television set.

### Why Consumers Perceive Risk

In making product decisions, consumers perceive risk because they may have little or no experience with the product or product category they are considering—either because they have never used it or because it is new on the market. Or they may have had an unsatisfactory experience with other brands and are concerned about making a similar mistake. Their financial resources may be very limited, so their selection of one product may require them to forgo purchase of another. Finally, they may feel that they have very limited knowledge on which to base a decision, or may lack confidence in their ability to make the "right" decision.

The major types of risk consumers perceive in making product decisions include: **functional risk, physical risk, financial risk, social risk, psychological risk,** and **time risk.**

1. *Functional risk*—the risk that the product will not perform as expected. ("Will the dishwasher really clean my dishes *and* my pots?")

2. *Physical risk*—the risk to self and to others which the product may pose. ("Is a microwave oven really safe, or does it emit harmful radiation?")
3. *Financial risk*—the risk that the product will not be worth its cost. ("Will graduate school really help me get a better job?")
4. *Social risk*—the risk that a poor product choice may result in embarrassment before others. ("Will that new deodorant really suppress perspiration odor?")
5. *Psychological risk*—the risk that a poor product choice will bruise the consumer's ego. ("Will I really be proud of this house?")
6. *Time risk*—the risk that the time spent in product search may be wasted if the product does not perform as expected. ("Will I have to go through the shopping effort all over again?")

Table 6-2 lists the specific types of uncertainty that the consumer faces in making product choices, categorized by the types of perceived risk listed above.

### THE PERCEPTION OF RISK VARIES

Studies show that the perception of risk by the consumer varies, depending on the person, the product, the situation, and the culture.

RISK PERCEPTION VARIES BY CONSUMER. The *amount* of risk perceived depends on the consumer. Some consumers tend to perceive high degrees of risk in various consumption situations; others tend to perceive little risk.[77] **High-risk perceivers** have been described as *narrow categorizers,* since they limit their product choices to a few safe alternatives.[78] They would rather exclude some perfectly good alternatives than chance a poor selection. **Low-risk perceivers** have been described as *broad categorizers,* since they tend to make their choices

**TABLE 6-2 Types of Uncertainty Faced by Consumers Making Purchase Decisions**

| TYPE OF RISK | TYPE OF UNCERTAINTY |
|---|---|
| Functional | 1. Will it do what it's supposed to do?<br>2. Will it last?<br>3. Will it work as well as or better than competitive products? |
| Physical | 1. Is it safe to use?<br>2. Does it pose any physical threat to others?<br>3. Does it pose any danger to the environment? |
| Financial | 1. Is it the best use of my limited funds?<br>2. Is it worth the money (or time or effort) it costs?<br>3. Am I paying the best price for it? |
| Social | 1. Will my family and friends approve?<br>2. Will it please others whose opinions are important to me?<br>3. Is it similar to products used by groups with whom I identify? |
| Psychological | 1. Will I feel good using it?<br>2. Will it impress others?<br>3. Do I deserve it? |
| Time | 1. Will I have to return or exchange it?<br>2. Will I have to go through the shopping effort all over again? |

from a much wider range of alternatives. They would rather risk a poor selection than limit the number of alternatives from which they can choose.

Some consumer researchers suggest that there may be a difference in the type of perceived risk consumers associate with a specific alternative as opposed to the risk associated with the choice *between* alternatives.[79] The *kind* of risk perceived also depends on the consumer. For example, a study of the acceptance of a new product found that low-risk perceivers reported perceiving only one risk in buying the new product (inconvenience—a functional risk), while high-risk perceivers perceived two major risks (wasting money—a financial risk, and their spouses' disapproval—a social risk).[80] Along these lines, other consumer researchers have suggested that the importance of perceived negative consequences of a specific purchase decision may vary by individual and thus may be a relevant variable on which to segment markets.[81]

Generally, marketers use self-reports to measure perceived risk. To measure performance risk, for example, they might ask: "In your opinion, what is the likelihood that there will be something wrong with product X?" "If you bought product X, what are the chances that you would not be satisfied with the way it performed?" To measure social risk, they might ask: "If you bought product X, what are the chances that your friends would approve of your choice?" Each of these questions would have a response scale ranging from very great to very slight.

RISK PERCEPTION VARIES BY PRODUCT CATEGORY. An individual's perception of risk varies with *product categories.* For example, purchasers of headache remedies were found to perceive higher perceived risk than did purchasers of dry spaghetti.[82] Similarly, consumers were found to perceive a higher degree of risk in the purchase of color television sets than in the purchase of golf clubs.[83]

Some researchers have suggested that it is possible to classify products on the basis of *type* and *intensity* of risk. For example, color television sets would be classified as high-risk products because they engender more different types of perceived risk and potentially greater losses than products classified as medium-risk products, such as lawn furniture, or as low-risk products, such as personal stationery.[84]

RISK PERCEPTION VARIES WITH THE SHOPPING SITUATION. Researchers have found that the degree of risk perceived by the consumer is affected by the *shopping situation.* For example, consumers were found to perceive a higher degree of risk in ordering from nonstore retailers by mail or telephone, from catalogs or direct mail solicitations, or from door-to-door salespeople.[85] However, the sharp increase in mail-order catalog sales in recent years suggests that on the basis of positive experiences and word-of-mouth, consumers perceive less risk in mail-order shopping than they once did.

RISK PERCEPTION VARIES BY CULTURE. Not all people around the world exhibit the same level of risk perception. Research shows, for example, that risk is a less important determinant of consumer behavior in Mexico than in the United States.[86] However, marketers who do business in several countries should not generalize the results of consumer behavior studies done in one country to other countries without further research.

## How Consumers Handle Risk

Consumers characteristically develop their own unique strategies for reducing perceived risk. These risk-reduction strategies enable them to act with increased confidence in making product decisions, even though the consequences of such decisions are still somewhat uncertain. Some of the more common risk-reduction strategies are listed in Table 6-3 and discussed below.

### CONSUMERS SEEK INFORMATION

Consumers seek information about the product and the product class through *word-of-mouth communication* (from friends and family, from people whose opinions are valued, from stores and from salespeople) and from *mass media communications* (such as newspapers and magazines, consumer reports, testimonials and endorsements). A recent study shows that consumers spend more time thinking about their choice, and search for more information regarding the product choice, when they associate a high degree of risk with the purchase.[87] This strategy is straightforward and logical, since the more information the consumer has regarding the product and the product category, the more predictable the probable consequences, and thus the lower the perceived risk.

One researcher reported that high-risk perceivers were more likely than low-risk perceivers to have engaged in product-related conversations during the past six months for two out of three products studied.[88] Furthermore, high- and medium-risk perceivers were more likely than low-risk perceivers to seek information when they initiated a product-related conversation. High-risk perceivers are also more likely to act upon the advice they seek than are low-risk perceivers. Research has found, for example, that high-risk perceivers are more affected by both favorable and unfavorable information than low-risk perceivers.[89]

Since consumers tend to seek out information, especially from those who are already product users, astute marketers try to influence word-of-mouth communications in their ads. For example, ads showing group discussions of

**TABLE 6-3 Types of Risk-Reduction Strategies**

1. Information Seeking
   —Informal sources (friends, family, opinion leaders, etc.)
   —Formal sources (stores, salespeople, advertisements, endorsements, editorials, consumer reports, etc.)
2. Brand Loyalty
3. Major Brand Image
4. Store Image
5. Most Expensive Model
6. Reassurance
   —Money-back guarantees
   —Warranties
   —Government and private laboratory tests
   —Prepurchase trial (ten-day trial, free samples, etc.)

possible product risks and the overriding rewards, by people representing the target market, may reassure high-risk perceivers to buy the product. Zenith used this strategy in introducing color television. To allay doubts about the risks involved (relatively high price and uncertainty about quality), ads showed informal peer group discussions of the product in which the messages were "I've bought one," "Everyone's buying Zenith," and "It's handcrafted." The strategy proved successful.[90]

### CONSUMERS ARE BRAND LOYAL

Consumers can avoid risk by remaining loyal to a brand with which they have been satisfied instead of purchasing new or untried products. A study of the acceptance of a new food product revealed that high-risk perceivers were more likely to be loyal to their old brands and less likely to purchase the new product.[91] A study of consumers of headache remedies found that a significantly greater number of high-risk perceivers were brand loyal as compared with low-risk perceivers.[92]

### CONSUMERS SELECT BY BRAND IMAGE

If consumers have had no experience with a product, they tend to "trust" a favored or well-known brand name. Consumers often think well-known brands are better and are worth buying for the assurance offered of quality, dependability, performance, and service. Marketers' promotional efforts supplement the perceived quality of their products in helping to build and sustain a favorable brand image.

### CONSUMERS RELY ON STORE IMAGE

If consumers have no other information about a product, they will trust the judgment of the merchandise buyers of a reputable store and will depend on them to have made careful decisions in selecting products for resale. Store image also imparts the implication of product testing and the assurance of service, return privileges, and adjustment in case of dissatisfaction.

### CONSUMERS BUY THE MOST EXPENSIVE MODEL

When in doubt, consumers may feel that the most expensive model is probably the best in terms of quality; i.e., they equate price with quality. (The price-quality relationship was discussed earlier in this chapter.)

### CONSUMERS SEEK REASSURANCE

Consumers who are uncertain about the wisdom of a product choice seek reassurance through money-back guarantees, government and private laboratory test results, warranties, and prepurchase trial (through free samples or limited free trials). Figure 6-21 illustrates the reassurance Kodak provides to consumers of Kodak diskettes. Apple Computer provided dramatic reassurance to con-

FIGURE 6-21 Manufacturers Reduce Risk Perception Through Performance Guarantees

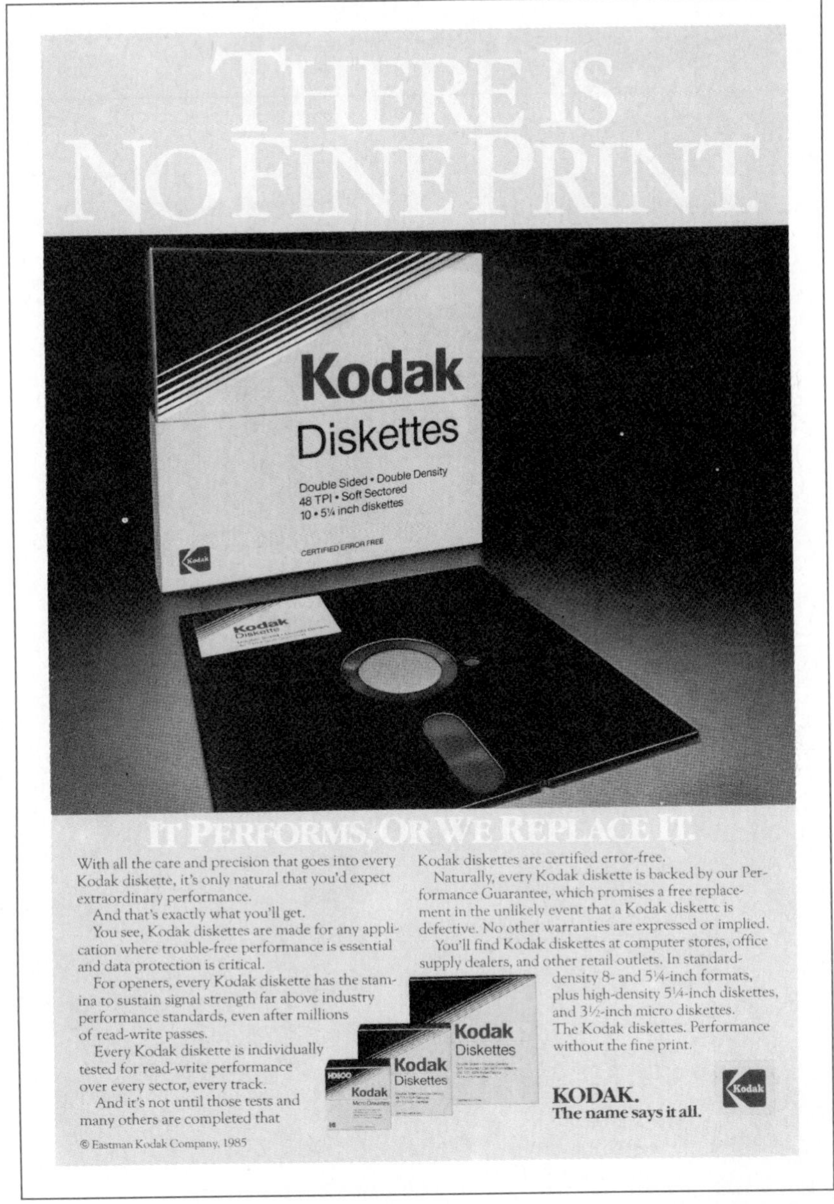


Courtesy of Eastman Kodak Company

sumers with its offer to take home a MacIntosh and "test drive" it free (see Fig. 6-22). Products that do not easily lend themselves to free trials present a challenge to the marketer. This challenge was successfully met by Teledyne Water Pik which received an award from the Point-of-Purchase Advertising Institute for a store display which enabled consumers to feel the pulsating effect of a shower head on their hands through a waterproof membrane.[93]

FIGURE 6-22 Free Home Trial Reduces Risk Perception

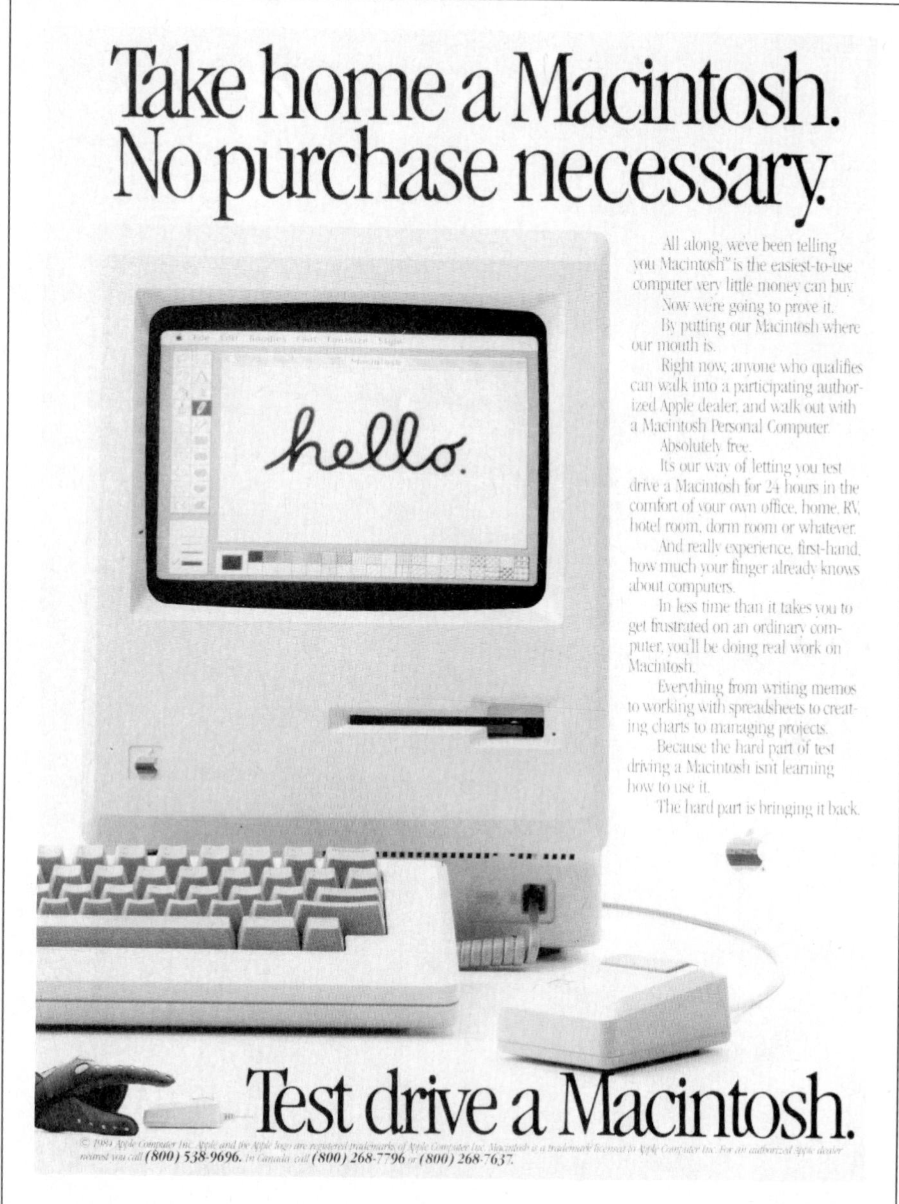


Courtesy of Apple Computer, Inc.

Of the risk-reduction strategies given above, the most favored strategies to reduce perceived risk tend to be the warranty's coverage, the product's perceived quality, and the manufacturer's perceived reputation, and the least-favored strategies buying the most expensive model, private laboratory tests, money-back guarantees, and endorsements.

A recent study found that the risk-reduction strategy employed by consumers varies among product classes. Brand loyalty was the best risk reducer for shampoos, detergents, and canned mushrooms; money-back guarantees and store image were the best strategies for reducing risk in the purchase of electric appliances; and comparison shopping was the risk-reduction strategy of choice for dresses and dishes.[94] These findings suggest that marketers should first determine the kinds of risks perceived by potential customers and then create a mix of "risk relievers" tailored to their target markets.

The concept of perceived risk has major implications for the introduction of new products. Since high-risk perceivers are less likely to purchase new products than low-risk perceivers, it is important to provide such consumers with acceptable risk-reduction strategies, such as distribution through reputable retail outlets, informative advertising, publicity stories in the media, impartial test results, free samples, and money-back guarantees. And, of course, as will be discussed in Chapter 16, it is most important to reach the influentials—the **opinion leaders**—from whom product advice and information are actively sought and acted upon by others.

## *summary*

Perception is the process by which individuals select, organize, and interpret stimuli into a meaningful and coherent picture of the world. It has strategy implications for marketers because consumers make decisions based upon what they perceive, rather than on the basis of objective reality.

The lowest level at which an individual can perceive a specific stimulus is called the absolute threshold. The minimal difference perceived between two stimuli is called the differential threshold, or just noticeable difference (j.n.d.).

Most stimuli are perceived above the level of the consumer's conscious awareness; however, weak stimuli can be perceived below the level of conscious awareness (i.e., subliminally). Research has not demonstrated that subliminal stimuli have an effect on consumer buying decisions.

Consumers' selection of stimuli from the environment is based on the interaction of their expectations and motives with the stimulus itself. The principle of selective perception includes the following concepts: selective exposure, selective attention, perceptual defense, and perceptual blocking. People usually perceive things they need or want, and block the perception of unfavorable or painful stimuli.

The interpretation of stimuli is highly subjective and is based on what the consumer expects to see in light of previous experience, on the number of plausible explanations he or she can envision, on motives and interests at the time of perception, and on the clarity of the stimulus itself. Influences that tend to distort objective interpretation include physical appearances, stereotypes, halo effects, respected sources, irrelevant cues, first impressions, and the tendency to jump to conclusions.

Each individual has a perceived self-image as a certain kind of person, with certain traits, habits, possessions, relationships, and ways of behaving. The consumer attempts to preserve or enhance that self-image by buying products or shopping at stores believed to be consistent with self-image and by avoiding products and stores that are not.

Products also have images (i.e., symbolic meanings) for the consumer. The way the product is perceived (i.e., positioned) is probably more important to its ultimate success than are its actual product characteristics. Products that are perceived favorably obviously have a better chance of being purchased. The brands that a consumer considers in making a purchase choice in a particular product category are known as the evoked set.

In the absence of direct experience, consumers often judge the quality of a product on the basis of cues that are intrinsic to the product (e.g., flavor) or extrinsic to the product (e.g., price, store image, or brand image).

Consumers often perceive risk in making product selections because of uncertainty as to the consequences of their product decisions. The most frequent types of risk that consumers perceive are functional risk, physical risk, financial risk, social risk, psychological risk, and time risk. Studies show that the perception of risk by the consumer varies with the individual, the product, the shopping situation, and the culture.

People characteristically develop their own strategies for reducing or handling risk. Some of these strategies include seeking added information through word-of-mouth and through the media, being loyal to brands with which they have previously been satisfied, buying products that carry major brand names, buying from stores that have a favorable image, buying the most expensive model, and seeking reassurance in the form of money-back guarantees, warranties, laboratory test results, and prepurchase trial.

The concept of perceived risk has important implications for marketers, who can facilitate the introduction and acceptance of new products by providing consumers with an optimal number of acceptable risk-reduction strategies.

## *discussion questions*

1. Give two examples of how marketers of consumer detergents can apply their knowledge of differential threshold in a period of rising prices and increasing competition.
2. An advertising consultant has submitted a proposed promotional campaign based on subliminal advertising to the marketer of an established line of male fragrances. As vice-president of marketing of the company, how would you evaluate the prospects for this new campaign?

3. As a market researcher for an automobile manufacturer, you are attempting to segment the market in terms of consumer self-image. Would you want to determine actual, ideal, or expected self-image? Discuss.
4. Find three different wine advertisements that you believe are directed to different market segments. In each case, has the marketer effectively positioned the product to communicate a specific image? Discuss.
5. Choose two product advertisements from different product categories. List the possible risks the consumer may perceive in purchasing these products. Have the marketers incorporated any risk-reduction strategies in their advertisements? Discuss.
6. Recently the management of a well-known quality cosmetic company decided to add shampoo to its product line. From your knowledge of perceived risk, outline a strategy to reduce consumers' perceived risk in the new shampoo introduction.
7. Discuss the relationship of (a) extrinsic cues and (b) intrinsic cues in the perception of product quality of a line of ready-made draperies.
8. Mrs. Brown spent the hour from 1:00 to 2:00 P.M. ironing while she watched her favorite soap operas. Yet when questioned by a television researcher two hours later, she could not recall even one commercial she had seen, though she could repeat the story line of both TV shows in detail. How can you explain her apparent forgetfulness?

## endnotes


1. Ronald Alsop, "Study of Olympics Ads Casts Doubts on Value of Campaigns," *Wall Street Journal,* December 6, 1984, 33.
2. "A *Newsweek* Full of Apples," *Business Week,* October 15, 1984, 88; "Pedal Power Equals Peddle Power," *Marketing News,* March 29, 1985, 15; and Kim Foltz, "Ads Popping Up All Over," *Newsweek,* August 12, 1985, 50–51.
3. Ronald Alsop, "Color Grows More Important in Catching Consumers' Eyes," *Wall Street Journal,* November 29, 1984, 37; and Janet Meyers, "French Winery Pours into U.S.—Skalli Touches on Tactile Tactic," *Advertising Age,* February 25, 1985, 65E.
4. Richard Lee Miller, "Dr. Weber and the Consumer," *Journal of Marketing,* 26 (January 1962), 57–61.
5. John Revett, "FTC Threatens Big Fines for Undersized Cigarette Warnings," *Advertising Age,* March 17, 1975, 1, 74.
6. Bernard Berelson and Gary A. Steiner, *Human Behavior: An Inventory of Scientific Findings* (New York: Harcourt, Brace & World, 1964), 87–130.
7. "Three Step Name Change lets Firm Retain Brand Loyalty," *Marketing News,* August 17, 1984, 3.
8. H. Brean, "What Hidden Sell Is All About," *Life,* March 31, 1958, 104–14.
9. Del Hawkins, "The Effects of Subliminal Stimulation on Drive Level and Brand Preference," *Journal of Marketing Research,* 7 (August 1970), 322–26.

10. Ibid.
11. John G. Caccavale, Thomas C. Wanty III, and Julie A. Edell, "Subliminal Implants in Advertisements: An Experiment," in Andrew A. Mitchell, ed., *Advances in Consumer Research* (Association for Consumer Research, 1981), IX, 418–23.
12. "Mind Benders," *Money,* 7 (September 1978), 24.
13. Wilson Bryan Key, *Subliminal Seduction* (New York: New American Library, 1973).
14. J. Steven Kelly, "Subliminal Embeds in Print Advertising: A Challenge to Advertising Ethics," *Journal of Advertising,* 8 (Summer 1979), 43–46.
15. For an extended discussion of the differences between recall and recognition and their importance for advertisers, see Herbert E. Krugman, "Memory without Recall, Exposure without Perception," *Journal of Advertising Research,* 17 (August 1977), 7–12.
16. Timothy E. Moore, "Subliminal Advertising: What You See Is What You Get," *Journal of Marketing,* 46 (Spring 1982), 38–47.
17. Ibid.
18. Eric J. Zanot, J. Davis Pincus, and E. Joseph Lampt, "Public Perceptions of Subliminal Advertising," *Journal of Advertising,* 12 (1983), 39–45.
19. Lisa Phillips, " 'Mike' Spurs Spate of Ads," *Advertising Age,* April 1, 1985, 38.
20. "Viewpoint: Editorial—A TV License to Steal, From Kids," *Advertising Age,* April 8, 1985, 18.
21. Walter P. Margulies, "How Many Brands Can You Spot with Names Off Packages?" *Advertising Age,* August 21, 1972, 37.
22. H. H. Kelley, "The Warm-Cold Variable in First Impressions of Persons," *Journal of Personality,* 18 (1950), 431–39.
23. Anne Anastasi, *Fields of Applied Psychology* (New York: McGraw-Hill, 1964); and M. Wayne Alexander and Bed Judd, Jr., "Do Nudes in Ads Enhance Brand Recall?" *Journal of Advertising Research,* 18 (February 1978), 47–50.
24. Jacob Hornik, "Quantitative Analysis of Visual Perception of Printed Advertisements," *Journal of Advertising Research,* 20 (December 1980), 41–48.
25. Ernest F. Larkin, "Consumer Perceptions of the Media and Their Advertising Content," *Journal of Advertising,* 8 (Spring 1979), 5–7.
26. George A. Miller, "The Magical Number Seven, Plus or Minus Two: Some Limits on Our Capacity for Processing Information," *Psychological Review,* 63 (March 1956), 81–97.
27. James T. Heimbach and Jacob Jacoby, "The Zeigarnik Effect in Advertising," in M. Venkatesan, ed., *Proceedings of the Third Annual Conference* (Association for Consumer Research, 1972), 746–58.
28. Ibid.
29. Kathleen Debevec and Jerome B. Kernan, "More Evidence on the Effects of a Presenter's Physical Attractiveness—Some Cognitive, Affective and Behavioral Consequences," in Thomas C. Kinnear, ed., *Advances in Consumer Research* (Association for Consumer Reserach, 1983), XI, 127–32; and Gordon L. Patzer, "An Experiment Investigating the Influence of Communicator Physical Attractiveness on Attitudes," in Patrick E. Murphy, O. C. Ferrell, Gene R. Laczniak, Robert F. Lurch, Paul F. Anderson, Terence A. Shimp, Russell W. Belk, and Charles B. Weinberg, eds. *1983 American Marketing Association Educators' Proceedings,* 49 (Chicago: American Marketing Association, 1983), 25–29.
30. Madeline E. Heilman and Melanie H. Stopeck, "Attractiveness and Corporate Success: Different Causal Attributions for Males and Females," *Journal of Applied Psychology,* 70 (1985), 379–88; and Sandra Forsythe, Mary Frances Drake, and Charles E. Cox, "Influence of Applicant's Dress on Interviewer's Selection Decisions," *Journal of Applied Psychology,* 70 (1985), 374–78.

31. Gordon L. Patzer, "Product Perception as a Function of Communicator's Sex," in Patrick E. Murphy et al., eds., *1983 American Marketing Association Educators' Proceedings,* 41–44; G. U. Skelly and W. J. Lundstrom, "Male Sex Roles in Magazine Advertising, 1959–1979," *Journal of Consumer Affairs,* 31 (1981), 52–57; and Dean Sharits and H. Bruce Lammers, "Perceived Attributes of Models in Prime-Time and Daytime Television Commercials: A Person Perception Approach," *Journal of Marketing Research,* 20 (February 1983), 64–73.
32. Gregory J. McHugo, John T. Lanzetta, Denis G. Sullivan, Roger D. Masters, and Basil G. Englis, "Emotional Reactions to a Political Leader's Expressive Displays," *Journal of Personality and Social Psychology,* 49 (1985), 1–17.
33. Morris B. Holbrook, "Using a Structural Model of Halo Effect to Assess Perceptual Distortion Due to Affective Overtones," *Journal of Consumer Research,* 10 (September 1983), 247–52.
34. Ishmael P. Akaah and Edward A. Riordan, "Self-Brand Image Congruency and the Effects of Trait Desirability," in Bruce J. Walker, William O. Bearden, William R. Darden, Patrick E. Murphy, John R. Nevin, Jerry C. Olson, and Barton A. Weitz, eds., *An Assessment of Marketing Thought and Practice—1982 Educators' Conference Proceedings,* 48 (Chicago: American Marketing Association, 1982), 16–20.
35. See Danny N. Bellinger, Earle Steinberg, and Wilbur W. Stanton, "The Congruence of Store Image and Self Image," *Journal of Retailing,* 52 (Spring 1976), 17–32; and Bruce L. Stern, Ronald F. Bush, and Joseph F. Hair, Jr., "The Self-Image/Store Image Matching Process: An Empirical Test," *Journal of Business,* 50 (January 1977), 63–69.
36. See, for example, E. Laird Landon, Jr., "Self-Concept, Ideal Self-Concept, and Consumer Purchase Intentions," *Journal of Consumer Research,* 1 (September 1974), 44–51.
37. Humberto S. Tapia, Terrence V. O'Brien, and George W. Summers, "Self-Concept in Consumer Motivation," *Proceedings of the American Marketing Association,* 37 (Chicago: American Marketing Association, 1975), 225–27; and Terrence V. O'Brien, Humberto S. Tapia, and Thomas L. Brown, "The Self-Concept in Buyer Behavior," *Business Horizons,* 20 (October 1977), 65–71.
38. William Knobler, "Marketing Positioning: How to Gain Unfair Advantage over Competition," *Marketing Review,* 40 (December–January 1985), 13–17; and Thomas J. Reynolds and Jonathan Gutman, "Advertising Is Image Management," *Journal of Advertising Research,* 24 (February–March 1984), 27–37.
39. For example, Raymond L. Horton, "An Experimental Study of the Effects of Number of Available Brands and Attributes on Consumer Information Acquisition," in Patrick E. Murphy et al., 102–7.
40. "Apple—Displaying What's Required," *Advertising Age,* December 31, 1984, 10.
41. Philip Kotler, *Marketing Management,* 5th ed. (Englewood Cliffs, N.J.: Prentice-Hall, 1984), 252–75.
42. Al Ries and Jack Trout, *Positioning: The Battle for your Mind* (New York: Warner Books, 1982).
43. Thomas S. Robertson, Joan Zielinski, and Scott Ward, *Consumer Behavior* (Glenview, Ill.: Scott, Foresman, 1984), 181–82.
44. Ibid., 171–72.
45. Teresa A. Swartz, "Brand Symbols and Message Differentiation," *Journal of Advertising Research,* 23 (October–November 1983), 59–64; Ernest Dichter, "What's in an Image?" *The Journal of Consumer Marketing,* 2 (Winter 1985), 75–81.
46. Ruth Stroud, "Baskin Robbins Wants to Scoop up Adults," *Advertising Age,* February 11, 1985, 88.
47. Francine C. Brevetti, "Underwear Moves to Trade's Top Drawer," *Journal of Commerce,* March 28, 1985, 3A.

48. Pat Sloan, "Sunscreens Shine in Cosmetics," *Advertising Age,* May 6, 1985, 70.

49. James V. McNeal, Stephen W. McDaniel, and Denise T. Smart, "The Brand Repertoire: Its Content and Organization," in Patrick E. Murphy et al., 92–96.

50. Chem L. Narayana and Rom J. Markin, "Consumer Behavior and Product Performance: An Alternative Conceptualization," *Journal of Marketing,* 39 (October 1975), 2.

51. Lance P. Jarvis and James B. Wilcox, "Evoked Set Size—Some Theoretical Foundations and Empirical Evidence," in Thomas V. Greer, ed., 1973 *Combined Proceedings* (Chicago: American Marketing Association, 1974), 326–40.

52. Miller, "Magical Number Seven," 82.

53. Sevgin A. Eroglu, Glenn S. Omura, and Karen A. Machleit, "Evoked Set Size and Temporal Proximity to Purchase," in Patrick E. Murphy et al., 97–101.

54. David W. Stewart and Girish Punj, "Factors Associated with Changes in Evoked Set Among Purchasers of New Automobiles," in Bruce J. Walker et al., 61–65.

55. George J. Szybillo and Jacob Jacoby, "Intrinsic versus Extrinsic Cues as Determinants of Perceived Product Quality," *Journal of Applied Psychology,* 59 (February 1974), 74–77.

56. Donald F. Cox, "The Measurement of Information Value: A Study in Consumer Decision Making," in *Emerging Concepts in Marketing* (Chicago: American Marketing Association, 1962), 414–17; and David M. Gardner, "An Experimental Investigation on the Price-Quality Relationship," *Journal of Retailing,* 46 (Fall 1970), 39–40.

57. Pierre Martineau, *Motivation in Advertising* (New York: McGraw-Hill, 1957), 114.

58. David M. Stander, "Testing New Product Ideas in an 'Archie Bunker' World," *Marketing News,* November 15, 1973, 1, 4, 5, and 10.

59. Joseph A. Bellizzi and Warren S. Martin, "The Influence of National Versus Generic Branding on Taste Perceptions," *Journal of Business Research,* 10 (1982) 385–96.

60. Stander, "Testing New Products," 10.

61. J. Douglas McConnell, "Effect of Pricing on Perception of Product Quality," *Journal of Applied Psychology,* 52 (1968), 331–34.

62. Barry Berman, "The Influence of Socioeconomic and Attitudinal Variables on the Price-Quality Relationship" (Doctoral dissertation, City University of New York, 1973).

63. George B. Sproles, "New Evidence on Price and Product Quality," *Journal of Consumer Affairs,* 11 (Summer 1977), 63–67.

64. David J. Faulds, "Measuring Price and Quality Competition in the Kitchen Appliance Product Category: Preliminary Results," in Patrick E. Murphy et al., 217–21.

65. Yoshiko Yamada and Norleen Ackerman, "Price-Quality Correlations in the Japanese Market," *Journal of Consumer Affairs,* 18 (Winter 1984), 251–65.

66. Steven M. Shugan, "Price Quality Relationships," in Thomas C. Kinnear, ed., *Advances in Consumer Research* (Association for Consumer Research, 1983), XI, 627–32.

67. Robert A. Peterson, "Consumer Perceptions as a Function of Product Color, Price and Nutrition Labeling," in William D. Perreault, Jr., ed., *Advances in Consumer Research* (Atlanta: Association for Consumer Research, 1977), 61–63.

68. Carl Obermiller and John J. Wheatley, "Price Effects on Choice and Perception under Varying Conditions of Experience, Information and Beliefs in Quality Differences," in Thomas C. Kinnear, ed., *Advances in Consumer Research,* 453–58.

69. C. Jerome Greenberg, Elaine Sherman, and Leon G. Schiffman, "The Measurement of Fashion Image as a Determinant of Store Patronage," in William R. Darken and Robert F. Lusch, eds., *Patronage Behavior and Retail Management* (New York: North Holland, 1983), 151–63.

70. Ben M. Enis and James E. Stafford, "Consumer's Perception of Product Quality as a Function of Various Informational Inputs," in Phillip R. McDonald, ed., *Marketing Involvement in Society and the Economy* (Chicago: American Marketing Association, 1969), 340–44.

71. Jacob Jacoby and David Mazursky, "Linking Brand and Retailer Images—Do the Potential Risks Outweigh the Potential Benefits?" *Journal of Retailing,* 60 (Summer 1984), 105–22.

72. Arch G. Woodside and James L. Taylor, "Consumer Purchase Intentions and Perceptions of Product Quality and National Advertising," *Journal of Advertising,* 7 (Winter 1978), 48–51; and Leonard N. Reid and Lauranne Buchanan, "A Shopping List Experiment of the Impact of Advertising on Brand Images," *Journal of Advertising,* 8 (September 1979), 26–28.

73. Patricia Sellers, "America's Most Admired Corporations," *Fortune,* January 7, 1985, 18–30.

74. Stuart Jackson, "Union Carbide's Good Name Takes a Beating," *Business Week,* December 31, 1984, 40.

75. Scott Hume, "Honeywell Pops for $1 million Ad," *Advertising Age,* May 6, 1985, 6; and E. Jane Lorimer, "Create a Positive Image with Corporate Exhibits," *Marketing News* (student edition, November 1984), 8.

76. "Brand Ads Can Do More to Boost Corporate Image Than Image Ads Do in Most Cases," *Marketing News,* August 17, 1984, 1.

77. Imran S. Currim and Rakesh K. Sarin, "A Procedure for Measuring and Estimating Consumer Preferences under Uncertainty," *Journal of Marketing Research,* 20 (August 1983), 249–56; and Gordon G. Bechtel and Jaime Ribera, "Risk Acceptability in Segments with Distinct Value Orientations," in Richard P. Bagozzi and Alice M. Tybout, eds., *Advances in Consumer Research,* 590–95.

78. Thomas F. Pettigrew, "The Measurement and Correlates of Category Width as a Cognitive Variable," *Journal of Personality,* 26 (December 1968), 532.

79. John W. Vann, "A Multi-Distributional Conceptual Framework for the Study of Perceived Risk," in Thomas C. Kinnear, ed., *Advances in Consumer Research,* 442–46.

80. Johan Arndt, "Perceived Risk, Sociometric Integration and Word of Mouth in the Adoption of a New Food Product," in Donald F. Cox, ed., *Risk Taking and Information Handling in Consumer Behavior* (Boston: Division of Research, Graduate School of Business, Harvard University, 1967), 303.

81. J. Paul Peter and Michael J. Ryan, "An Investigation of Perceived Risk at the Brand Level," *Journal of Marketing Research,* 13 (May 1976), 184–88.

82. Scott Cunningham, "Major Dimensions of Perceived Risk," in Cox, *Risk Taking and Information Handling,* 87.

83. Michael Perry and B. Curtis Hamm, "Canonical Analysis of Relations between Socioeconomic Risk and Personal Influence in Purchase Decisions," *Journal of Marketing Research,* 6 (August 1969), 352.

84. "Investigation of the Role of Product Characteristics in Risk Perception," *Review of Business and Economic Research,* 13 (Fall 1977), 19–34.

85. Pradeep K. Korgaonkar, "Non-Store Retailing and Perceived Product Risk," in Bruce J. Walker et al., *An Assessment of Marketing Thought and Practice—1982 Educators' Conference Proceedings,* 204–7.

86. Robert J. Hoover, Robert T. Green, and Joel Saegert, "A Cross National Study of Perceived Risk," *Journal of Marketing,* 42 (July 1978), 102–8.

87. Rohit Deshpande and Wayne D. Hoyer, "Consumer Decision Making: Strategies, Cognitive Effort and Perceived Risk," in Patrick E. Murphy et al. *1983 American Marketing Association Educators' Proceedings,* 88–91.

88. Scott M. Cunningham, "Perceived Risk as a Factor in Informal Consumer Communication," in Cox, *Risk Taking and Information Handling,* 274.

89. Arndt, "Perceived Risk, Sociometric Integration," 315.
90. Arch G. Woodside and M. Wayne DeLozier, "Effects of Word-of-Mouth Advertising on Consumer Risk-Taking," *Journal of Advertising,* 5 (Fall 1976), 12–16.
91. Arndt, "Role of Product-Related Conversations," 294.
92. Scott M. Cunningham, "Perceived Risk and Brand Loyalty," in Cox, *Risk Taking and Information Handling,* 513.
93. Julie Franz, "Computers Pop Up in Stores," *Advertising Age,* February 11, 1985, 58.
94. C. Derbaix, "Perceived Risk and Risk Relievers: An Empirical Investigation," *Journal of Economic Psychology,* 3 (1983), 19–38.

# 7

# Learning and Consumer Involvement

## introduction

LEARNING is a human activity that is as natural as breathing. Studies show that learning begins even before we leave our mother's womb. Before we die, we will have collected enough information through learning to fill an average-sized library.

Despite the fact that learning is all-pervasive in our lives, psychologists do not agree on how learning takes place. At the present time, learning theorists are divided into two camps: the behaviorists, who believe that all learning is a result of stimulus and response, and the cognitive scientists, who view learning as a function of purely mental processes that operate like computers in processing information.

How individuals learn is a subject of immense importance to marketers, who want consumers to learn about goods and services and new ways of behaving that will satisfy not only the consumer's needs, but the marketer's objectives. In this chapter we will examine the two general categories of learning theory—behavioral theory and cognitive theory. Though these theories differ markedly in a number of essentials, each theory offers insights to marketers on how to shape their messages to consumers to bring about desired purchase behavior. At the end of the chapter, we will show how each theory lends itself to understanding an important type of learned consumer behavior—brand loyalty.

## WHAT IS LEARNING?

Since psychologists disagree on how individuals learn, it is difficult to come up with a generally acceptable definition. From a marketing perspective, however,

"

*I am always ready to learn, although I do not always like being taught.*

WINSTON CHURCHILL

*consumer learning* is *the process by which individuals acquire the purchase and consumption knowledge and experience they apply to future related behavior.* Several points in this definition are worth noting.

First, consumer learning is a *process;* that is, it continually evolves and changes as a result of newly acquired knowledge (which may be gained from reading or observation or thinking) or from actual experience. Both newly acquired *knowledge* and *experience* serve as feedback to the individual and are the basis upon which he or she acts, sustains, or modifies behavior in similar situations in the future. The definition makes clear that learning results from acquired knowledge or experience. This qualification distinguishes learning from instinctive behavior, such as sucking in infants.

The role of experience in learning does not mean that all learning is deliberately sought. Some learning may be *intentional*—that is, it may be acquired as the result of a careful search for information. But much learning is *incidental,* secured without much effort. Ads often induce learning in consumers (of brand names, for example), even though the consumer's attention is elsewhere (on a magazine article instead of the advertisement on the facing page).

## Basic Principles of Learning

The term *learning* encompasses the total range of learning, from simple conditioned responses to the learning of concepts and complex problem solving. Some psychologists would deny that "higher learning" is different from simple learned responses. But most learning theorists recognize the existence of different types of learning and explain the differences among them through the use of distinctive models of learning.

Despite their disagreements, learning theorists in general agree that in order for learning to occur, certain basic elements must be present. The elements included in most learning theories are **motivation, cues, response,** and **reinforcement.** Some theorists would deny that all of these are equally important. Some would add other elements, and others would subtract one or more of those listed. These concepts are discussed here because they will recur in the theories discussed later in this chapter.

### MOTIVATION

The concept of *motivation* discussed in Chapter 3 is an important one in learning theory. Remember, motivation is based on needs and goals. Motivation thus acts as a spur to learning, with needs and goals serving as stimuli. For example, men and women who want to become good tennis players are motivated to learn all they can about tennis and to practice whenever they can. They may seek information concerning the prices and quality and characteristics of tennis racquets if they "learn" that a good racquet is instrumental to playing a good game. Conversely, individuals who are not interested in tennis are likely to ignore all information related to the game. The goal object (proficiency in tennis) simply has no relevance. Uncovering consumer motives is one of the prime tasks of marketers, who then set about teaching "motivated" consumer segments why their product will best fulfill the consumer's needs.

## CUES

If motives serve to stimulate learning, *cues* are the stimuli that give direction to those motives. An advertisement for a tennis camp may serve as a cue for tennis buffs who may suddenly "recognize" that attending a tennis camp is a concentrated way to improve their game while taking a vacation. The ad is the cue, or stimulus, that suggests a specific way to satisfy a salient motive. In the marketplace, price, styling, packaging, advertising, and displays all serve as cues to help consumers fulfill their needs in product-specific ways.

Cues serve to direct consumer drives when they are consistent with consumer *expectations.* Marketers must be careful to provide cues that do not upset those expectations. For example, consumers expect high-fashion stores to carry designer clothes at high prices. Thus a high-fashion designer should distribute his or her clothes only through exclusive stores and advertise only in quality fashion magazines. Each aspect of the marketing mix must reinforce the others if cues are to serve as the stimuli that guide consumer actions in the direction desired by the marketer.

## RESPONSE

How an individual reacts to a drive or cue constitutes his or her *response.* Learning can occur even if responses are not overt. The carpet manufacturer who provides consistent cues to a consumer may not always succeed in stimulating a purchase, even if that individual is motivated to buy. Instead, the manufacturer may succeed only in forming a favorable image of the carpet in the consumer's mind—that is, evoking a *tendency* to respond by buying.

A response is not tied to a need in a one-to-one fashion. Indeed, as Chapter 3 pointed out, a need or motive may evoke a whole variety of responses. For example, there are many ways to respond to the need for physical exercise besides tennis playing. Cues provide some direction, but there are many cues competing for the consumer's attention. Which response he or she will make depends heavily on previous learning. That, in turn, may depend on which responses were reinforced in the past.

## REINFORCEMENT

Reinforcement increases the likelihood that a specific response will occur in the future as the result of particular cues or stimuli. If a college student finds that he is able to ward off the beginnings of a cold by taking vitamin C tablets, he is more likely to take the advertised brand of vitamin C tablets at the next sign of a cold. Clearly, through reinforcement, learning has taken place, since the vitamin C tablets lived up to expectations in the past. On the other hand, if the vitamin C tablets did not help the first time, the student would be less likely to use them again, despite extensive advertising or store display cues for the product.

Reinforcement is a controversial concept in learning theory. Some theorists believe that an explicit reward is not necessary for a response to become part of learned behavior. But many marketers intuitively find that reinforcement serves to teach their customers a desired behavior. For example, telephone companies that give cash discounts to customers who pay their bills promptly are acting to ensure prompt payment in the future.

With these basic principles, we can now discuss some well-known theories or models of how learning occurs.

## BEHAVIORAL LEARNING THEORIES

Behavioral learning theories are sometimes referred to as *stimulus-response* theories because they are based on the premise that learning takes place as the result of observable responses to external stimuli. If a person acts (i.e., responds) in a predictable way to a known stimulus, he or she is said to have "learned." Two behavioral theories with great relevance to marketing are **classical conditioning** and **instrumental conditioning.**

### Classical Conditioning

In everyday speech, the word *conditioned* has come to mean a kind of "knee-jerk" or automatic response to a situation built up through repeated exposure. If you get a headache every time you think of taking an exam, your reaction may be conditioned from years of "all-nighters" when long hours of study for an exam resulted in headaches caused by lack of sleep. Ivan Pavlov, a Russian physiologist, was the first to describe conditioning and to propose it as a general model of how learning occurs. According to Pavlovian theory, *conditioned learning* results when a stimulus that is paired with another stimulus that elicits a known response serves to produce the same response by itself.

Pavlov demonstrated what he meant by conditioned learning in his studies with dogs. The dogs were hungry and highly motivated. In his experiments, Pavlov sounded a tone and immediately followed it by applying a meat paste to the dogs' tongues, which caused salivation. Learning (i.e., conditioning) occurred when, after a sufficient number of repetitions of the tone, followed almost immediately by the food, the tone alone caused salivation. The tone had been "learned" to be an indicator of the reward of meat paste. In Pavlov's terms, the dogs learned to make the response of salivating by associating an **unconditioned stimulus** (known to cause the response) with a **conditioned stimulus,** which acquired the capacity to elicit the response because of repeated pairing.

An analogous situation would be one where the smells of dinner cooking would cause your mouth to water. If you usually listen to the six o'clock news while waiting for dinner to be served, you would tend to associate the six o'clock news with dinner; so that eventually the sounds of the six o'clock news alone would cause your mouth to water, even if dinner was not being prepared and even if you were not hungry. Figure 7-1 diagrams this basic relationship.

A great deal of advertising fits the model of conditioned learning. For example, commercials for Nestea, which invite viewers to "take the Nestea plunge," try to condition the audience to associate a plunge into a pool with the sipping of iced tea. The ads imply that the response—cool refreshment—is the same for both.

Three basic concepts derive from conditioned learning: **repetition, stimulus generalization,** and **stimulus discrimination.** Each of these concepts is important to an understanding of consumer behavior.

## REPETITION

Just as dogs may learn to salivate at the sound of a bell after repeated trials, so too consumers may learn a message that a marketer wants to impart by repeated exposure to the same message through advertising. Evidence of the efficiency of sheer repetition to impart a message is plentiful. One experiment tested the effects of various levels of exposure to magazine ads on consumers' familiarity with the brand name, willingness to buy, and belief in the brand claim. Copies of a magazine were sent to participants on two separate days. Some of the participants received copies with no ads for the brands being tested, others received copies containing the relevant ads on only one day, and still others saw the ads on both days. For those who were exposed to the ads on both days, brand familiarity and willingness to buy doubled, and belief in the brand claim tripled.[1]

**FIGURE 7-1 Classical Conditioning**

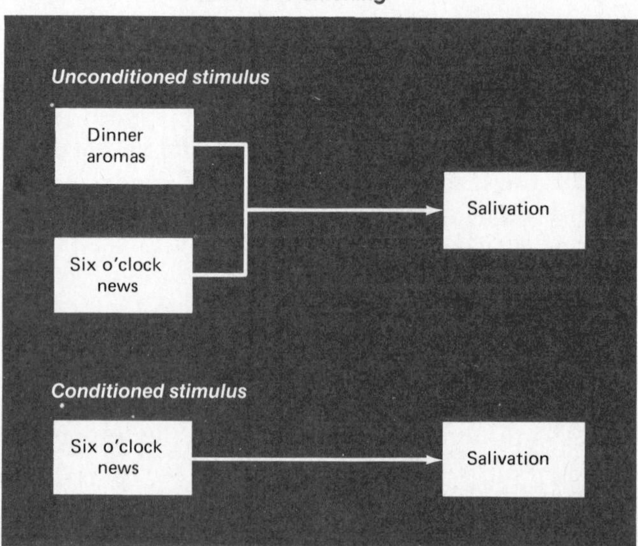

Some researchers believe that repetition works by increasing the strength of the association and by slowing the process of forgetting, which is seen as a process of *decay.* Apparently there is a limit to the amount of repetition that will aid retention. The evidence suggests that some **overlearning,** or repetition beyond what is necessary to learn, aids retention.[2] But with exposure beyond a certain point, an individual can become satiated, and attention and retention can decline.

Three researchers demonstrated this phenomenon by inducing in subjects 100 percent learning (after seven exposures to an ad), an estimated 200 percent learning (i.e., fourteen exposures), and an estimated 300 percent learning (twenty-one exposures). They found that more retention resulted from fourteen exposures to the ad than from twenty-one exposures, as measured after a lapse of twenty-eight days. Apparently, at the higher number of exposures boredom set in, leading to inattention and negative reactions. It has been suggested that this effect, known as *advertising wearout,* can be decreased by varying the advertising message.[3] For example, Jello Pudding has varied advertising messages that associate the dessert with fun for children by showing comedian Bill Cosby as the object of different jokes children play while eating the dessert. Other techniques to achieve variety in an advertising campaign include stressing different benefits or using a number of different advertising spokespersons. However, one researcher found that repeated exposure to a series of slightly varied TV commercials for a single product resulted in increased negative consumer evaluation of these messages; in addition, this wearout occurred in spite of advertising strategies designed to enhance attention.[4]

Though the principle of repetition is well established in advertising circles, not everyone agrees on the effectiveness of massive doses. In fact, one researcher maintains that the optimum number of exposures to an advertisement is just three—one to make consumers aware of the product, a second to show consumers the relevance of the product, and a third to remind them of its benefits. According to this *three-hit theory,* all other ad repetitions are wasted effort.[5] However, some researchers suggest that an average frequency of eleven to twelve exposures is needed to increase the probability that consumers will actually receive three exposures.[6]

If the three-hit theory is correct, repetition may be important, not so much to maintain the association in the consumer's mind, as to ensure that the proper association is made when the consumer is motivated to see the connection. Generally, classical conditioning theorists tend to deny the importance of inner processes such as motivation and to stress the automatic nature of paired associations. Controversy over the role of repetition continues today because of this basic disagreement.

## STIMULUS GENERALIZATION

According to classical conditioning theorists, learning depends not only on repetition, but also on the ability of individuals to generalize. Pavlov noted, for example, that a dog could learn to salivate not only to the tone of a bell, but also to the somewhat similar sound of jangling keys. If we were not capable of **stimulus generalization**—that is, of making the same response to slightly different stimuli—not much learning would occur.

Stimulus generalization explains why imitative "me too" products usually crowd onto the market immediately after the introduction of an innovative product.[7] It also explains why manufacturers of private brands try to make their packaging resemble the national brand leaders.

Another marketing strategy that works on the principle of stimulus generalization is *product line extension*—the practice of adding related products to an already established brand. Clairol, which originally specialized in hair dyes, has extended its line to all kinds of hair care products—from hair dryers to shampoos. The key to the success of this type of strategy is to remain within the limits of the consumer's ability to generalize. Kool-Aid failed with a line of party cups, as did Arm & Hammer with a deodorant, because they exceeded those limits.[8]

Increasingly, brand-name extension is the name of the game in packaged goods marketing. Consider these examples: Beatrice/Hunt-Wesson foods has introduced a corn oil under its Wesson brand; Pepperidge Farm introduced a premium ice-cream under the Pepperidge Farm label; Coca-Cola USA is extending its Minute Maid brand to an orange soda; Lever Bros. is manufacturing a powdered version of its Wisk detergent. Figure 7-2 lists a number of brand-extension entries by some well-known marketers.

**Family branding,** the practice of marketing a whole line of company products under the same brand name, is another strategy that capitalizes on the consumer's ability to generalize favorable brand associations from one product to the next. The Campbell Soup Company continues to add new soup entrees to its product line under the Campbell brand name, achieving ready acceptance for the new products from satisfied consumers of other Campbell soup products.

**Licensing** is another type of marketing strategy that operates on the principle of family branding. Designers, celebrities, and even cartoon characters lend their names for a fee to a variety of products, enabling the manufacturers and marketers of such products to achieve instant recognition and implied quality for the licensed products. Figure 7-3 shows the variety of products that are licensed by Jordache, originally known for its line of jeans. Other successful licensors include Pierre Cardin, Bill Blass, Calvin Klein, and Christian Dior, whose names appear on an exceptionally wide variety of products from sheets to shoes and from luggage to perfume. The highly successful Haagen Dazs Ice Cream Company licensed its name to Hiram Walker, Inc., which hoped that adult ice cream aficionados would generalize the taste of the ice cream to its new Haagen Dazs Cream Liqueur. The licensing of cartoon characters has also become big business. For example, Mickey Mouse and other Disney characters can be seen on a multitude of products from school bags to tee shirts to beach towels. The recent nostalgia trend has also brought back the old cartoon characters of Betty Boop and Grumby, whose names can now be found on clothing, posters, exercise books and some three hundred other product categories.[9] The increase in licensing has made *counterfeiting* a booming business, as counterfeit-

**FIGURE 7-2** **Examples of Brand-Extension Strategies by National Package Goods Marketers**
Source: Adapted from "Label This Game 'Brand Extension,'" *Advertising Age,* May 6, 1985, 90.

BIC CORPORATION
Bic 2000, a downsize version of the Bic disposable lighter

CAMPBELL SOUP COMPANY'S Pepperidge Farm Division
Pepperidge Farm premium ice cream

CHURCH & DWIGHT
Arm & Hammer all-fabric bleach

COCA-COLA COMPANY USA
Minute Maid orange soda

HELENE CURTIS INDUSTRIES
Finesse Mousse and Suave Soft Highlights shampoo and conditioner

DOW CHEMICAL
Pine Magic spray cleaner

ECONOMICS LABORATORIES
Scrub-Free heavy-duty toilet bowl cleaner and kitchen cleanser

R. T. FRENCH COMPANY
French's Spice Your Rice seasonings

GENERAL BISCUIT OF AMERICA/BURRY-LU
Chips Chocolat chocolate chip pecan cookies

GENERAL FOODS CORPORATION
Maxwell House decaffeinated instant coffee
Maxwell House Master Collection premium brews

KEEBLER COMPANY
Soft Batch fudge-covered cookies in caramel, graham, mint, and walnut flavors

LAND O'LAKES
Land O'Lakes Sweet Cream margarine

LOEW'S CORPORATION'S Lorillard Division
Old Gold Lights 100s cigarettes

PHILIP MORRIS INC.'s Seven-Up Co.
Sugar-Free Like cola

NABISCO BRANDS' Life Savers
Two new Bubble Yum Gum flavors, banana-strawberry and lemon-lime

SCHERING-PLOUGH CORP.
St. Joseph aspirin-free tablets for older children

**FIGURE 7-3** Licensing Is Based on Stimulus Generalization

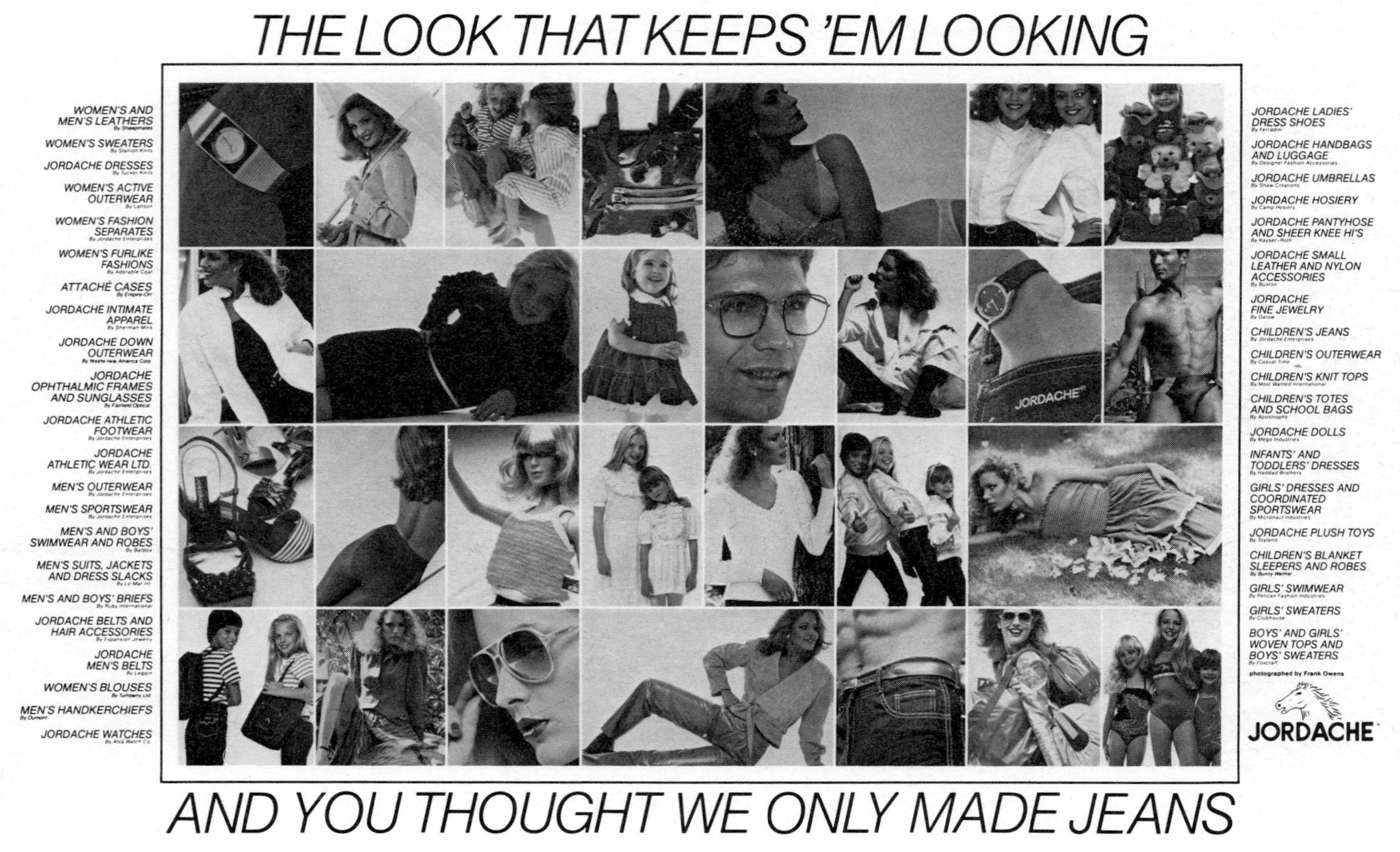

THE LOOK THAT KEEPS 'EM LOOKING

WOMEN'S AND MEN'S LEATHERS
WOMEN'S SWEATERS
JORDACHE DRESSES
WOMEN'S ACTIVE OUTERWEAR
WOMEN'S FASHION SEPARATES
WOMEN'S FURLIKE FASHIONS
ATTACHÉ CASES
JORDACHE INTIMATE APPAREL
JORDACHE DOWN OUTERWEAR
JORDACHE OPHTHALMIC FRAMES AND SUNGLASSES
JORDACHE ATHLETIC FOOTWEAR
JORDACHE ATHLETIC WEAR LTD.
MEN'S OUTERWEAR
MEN'S SPORTSWEAR
MEN'S AND BOYS' SWIMWEAR AND ROBES
MEN'S SUITS, JACKETS AND DRESS SLACKS
MEN'S AND BOYS' BRIEFS
JORDACHE BELTS AND HAIR ACCESSORIES
JORDACHE MEN'S BELTS
WOMEN'S BLOUSES
MEN'S HANDKERCHIEFS
JORDACHE WATCHES

JORDACHE LADIES' DRESS SHOES
JORDACHE HANDBAGS AND LUGGAGE
JORDACHE UMBRELLAS
JORDACHE HOSIERY
JORDACHE PANTYHOSE AND SHEER KNEE HI'S
JORDACHE SMALL LEATHER AND NYLON ACCESSORIES
JORDACHE FINE JEWELRY
CHILDREN'S JEANS
CHILDREN'S OUTERWEAR
CHILDREN'S KNIT TOPS
CHILDREN'S TOTES AND SCHOOL BAGS
JORDACHE DOLLS
INFANTS' AND TODDLERS' DRESSES
GIRLS' DRESSES AND COORDINATED SPORTSWEAR
JORDACHE PLUSH TOYS
CHILDREN'S BLANKET SLEEPERS AND ROBES
GIRLS' SWIMWEAR
GIRLS' SWEATERS
BOYS' AND GIRLS' WOVEN TOPS AND BOYS' SWEATERS

photographed by Frank Owens

JORDACHE

AND YOU THOUGHT WE ONLY MADE JEANS

Courtesy of Jordache Enterprises, Inc.

ers add well-known licensor names to a variety of products without benefit of contract or quality control, and sell them as licensed goods. Counterfeiting has spread to many product categories, and a lot of counterfeit merchandise is virtually identical to the original.[10]

Columbia Pictures' *Ghostbusters,* one of the hottest movies of 1984, was the target of low-quality counterfeit tee shirts and other merchandise bearing the movie's logo, resulting in complaints and lawsuits for shoddy merchandise against Columbia Pictures. High-quality clothing companies such as Levi's and Lacoste have also been hurt by counterfeiting. New tough federal and state laws have been enacted to control this growing problem.[11]

## STIMULUS DISCRIMINATION

*Stimulus discrimination* is the opposite of stimulus generalization, and results in the selection of a specific stimulus from among similar stimuli. The consumer's ability to discriminate among stimuli is the basis of positioning strategy, which seeks to establish a unique image for a brand in the consumer's mind.

Imitators want consumers to *generalize* their experience, but market leaders want to retain the top spot by convincing consumers to *discriminate.* The Adolph Coors Company, a brewery located in Colorado, sued Robert Corr, a soft drink company based in Chicago, for infringing on its trademark in an apparent effort to trade on the Coors reputation (through stimulus generalization). The soft drink firm agreed to change the name on its products from *Corr's* to *Robert Corr* (see Figure 7-4).[12]

It is often quite difficult to unseat a brand leader once stimulus discrimination has occurred. For example, when National Cash Register challenged IBM with a heavy media campaign that stressed the slogan "NCR Means Computers," it failed, presumably because consumers simply did not believe the claim. One explanation is that the leader is usually first in the market and has had a longer period to teach consumers (through advertising and selling) to associate the brand name with the product. Because of its strong association in the consumer's mind with computers, IBM was able to capture the personal computer market despite its relatively late entry into the PC field. In general, the longer the period of learning—of associating a brand name with a product—the more likely the consumer is to discriminate, and the less likely to generalize the stimulus.

For marketers who do enter the field late, the best strategy is to capture a unique position in the consumer's mind by highlighting some special product feature or by offering a unique price, distribution, or promotional strategy. Hewlett-Packard has survived in the highly competitive pocket calculator market by offering models that have more functions than those of competing brands. American Express has retained a significant share of the credit card market with an innovative ad campaign that features celebrities whose names are better known than their faces. In both cases, success resulted from the unique pairing of a brand-name cue with an already established stimulus-response condition.

FIGURE 7-4 A Competitor's Attempt at Stimulus Generalization. Coors was afraid that Corr's would trade on its brand name through consumer stimulus generalization.

Coors and Corr's resolved their brand name dispute when Corr agreed to change its brand name to "Robert Corr."

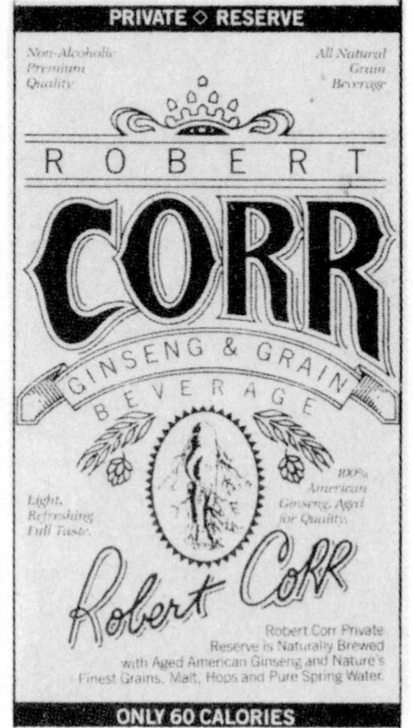


## EVALUATION OF CLASSICAL CONDITIONING

The principles of classical conditioning provide the theoretical underpinnings for many marketing applications. Repetition, stimulus generalization, and stimulus discrimination are useful concepts in explaining how consumers learn to behave in the marketplace. However, they do not explain all the activities classified as consumer learning. Classical conditioning assumes that consumers are passive beings who react with predictable responses to stimuli after a number of trials. While some of our purchase behavior—for example, the purchase of branded convenience goods—tends to be spontaneous and may have been shaped to some extent by repeated advertising messages, other purchase behavior results from a more active search for and evaluation of product information. Our judgment of which product is best often rests on the rewards we experience as a result of making specific purchases—in other words, from **instrumental conditioning.**

# Instrumental Conditioning

The name most closely associated with instrumental conditioning is that of an American psychologist, B. F. Skinner. According to Skinner, most learning takes place in an effort to control the environment (that is, to obtain favorable outcomes). Control is gained by means of a *trial-and-error* process during which one behavior of the individual results in a more favorable response than other behaviors. The reward reinforces the behavior associated with the favorable response; that is, it is *instrumental* in teaching the individual a specific behavior that gives him or her more control over the outcome.

Like Pavlov, Skinner developed his model of learning by working with animals. Such animals as rats or pigeons were placed in his "Skinner Box"; if they made appropriate movements and depressed levers or pecked keys, they received food reinforcement. Skinner and his many followers have been able to do amazing things with this simple apparatus, including teaching pigeons to play Ping-Pong, to dance, and even to act as the guidance system in a missile. In a marketing context, the consumer who tries several brands and styles of jeans before finding a style that fits her figure may be said to have engaged in instrumental learning. Presumably, the brand that fits best is the one she will continue to buy. This model of instrumental conditioning is presented in Figure 7-5.

Note the differences between classical and instrumental conditioning, as summarized in Table 7-1. Although the experimenter controls the reward in instrumental conditioning, it is the subject's action that causes the reward to happen. This situation differs from classical conditioning, where the subject's response (e.g., salivation) is involuntary. Another difference is that the "learned" response in instrumental conditioning is the result of trial and error among several behaviors, rather than a paired response to a specific stimulus. The subject tries a number of stimuli, and the one that yields the most rewarding response is the one that is "learned." Finally, while classical conditioning is useful in explaining how we learn very simple kinds of behaviors or feelings, instrumental conditioning is more helpful in explaining complex, goal-directed activities.

Marketers are interested in instrumental learning theory because it seems to describe better than classical conditioning how consumers learn about goods that involve a great deal of prepurchase search for information. The purchase

**FIGURE 7-5 A Model of Instrumental Conditioning**

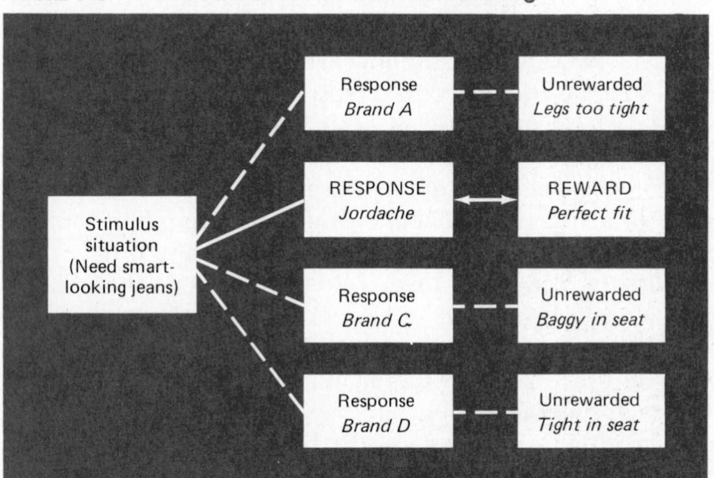

**TABLE 7-1 Classical and Instrumental Conditioning Compared**

| | CLASSICAL | INSTRUMENTAL |
|---|---|---|
| 1. Cause of response | Association of a conditioned with an unconditioned stimulus | Association of a reward with a specific response |
| 2. Type of response | Automatic, involuntary | Deliberate, to obtain reward |
| 3. Type of learning | Simple behaviors, attitudes, and feelings | Relatively complex, goal-directed behavior |

of a car, for example, involves more than learning a simple association of brand name with the need for transportation. Marketers have to convince consumers that ownership of a particular automobile will give them specific rewards. In accomplishing this, *repetition* and *discrimination* are important, but even more so may be the form, amount, and timing of *reinforcement* provided.

### POSITIVE AND NEGATIVE REINFORCEMENT

Skinner distinguished two types of reinforcement or reward that influence the chances that a response will be repeated. The first type, **positive reinforcement,** consists of events that strengthen the likelihood of a specific response. Giving food to pigeons that depress a bar is an example of positive reinforcement and is likely to result in a repetition of the behavior in order to get more food.

**Negative reinforcement** is an unpleasant or negative outcome that serves to discourage a specific response. For example, an animal will learn to avoid pressing a bar that results in an electric shock. Parents sometimes use negative reinforcement to stop a child from thumb-sucking by applying an unpleasant-tasting substance to the thumb. Instead of giving solace or comfort to the child, thumb-sucking then becomes a distasteful experience to be avoided.

Marketers make use of both positive and negative reinforcement to encourage consumers to buy their products. The most effective way for a marketer to encourage consumers to repeat specific buying behavior is to maintain high product quality over time. But there are other, more overt, ways of using positive reinforcement. For example, many hotels have their night staffs leave chocolates or flowers on turned-down beds as a reminder to guests that the service has been rendered; conference sponsors give participants such items as notebooks or paperweights to remind them of the conference. Similarly, airlines mail their frequent fliers tangible reminders of their services in the form of mileage statements, luggage tags, and so forth. Figure 7-6 is an example of an advertising campaign sponsored by the Helmsley Hotels to reinforce the notion of personal service.

**FIGURE 7-6 Positive Reinforcement**

Courtesy of The Helmsley Park Lane Hotel

Marketers also sometimes use negative reinforcement. Fear appeals in ad messages are an example (see Chapter 10). Life insurance commercials which warn husbands that in the event of sudden death they can leave their wives penniless widows rely on negative reinforcement. The purchase of a policy is shown as the way to avoid the threatened consequences. Marketers of headache remedies use negative reinforcement when they illustrate the unpleasant symptoms of an unrelieved headache; marketers of mouthwash when they show the loneliness suffered by someone with bad breath.

Either positive or negative reinforcement can be used to elicit a desired response. When a learned response is no longer reinforced, it diminishes to the point of *extinction;* that is, to the point where it no longer occurs. Individuals may not totally forget a behavior once it is learned, but they may engage in the behavior less and less frequently.

## MASSED OR DISTRIBUTED LEARNING

Another important influence on consumer learning is *timing*. Should a learning schedule be spread out over a period of time **(distributed)**, or should it be "bunched up" all at once **(massed)**? The question is an important one for advertisers planning a media schedule.

Research seems to indicate that massed advertising produces more initial learning than does distributed advertising. However, learning usually persists longer with a more spread-out schedule.[13]

*Unaided recall* is the research technique used to measure the influence of timing on learning schedules. The researcher asks consumers (who acknowledge that they have read a certain periodical) to describe any ads they remember seeing in the magazine. Their ability to recall the ads, and the accuracy with which they do so, serves to measure the efficiency of the learning schedule. In unaided recall tests, respondents are given no clues as to the type of advertisements they are asked to recall. In contrast, there are *aided recall* tests, in which consumers may be told the product class of the advertisement to be recalled, and *recognition* tests, in which the consumer is shown a specific advertisement and asked whether he or she has seen it. Each of the aided or unaided recall tests can vary a great deal in terms of the criteria used to evaluate responses. Chapter 10 discusses these advertising research techniques in greater detail.

One study examined unaided recall for five different schedules and intensities of television advertising: 13 weeks, 100 rating points; 26 weeks, 50 rating points; 52 weeks, 25 rating points; 6–7 weeks, 100 rating points; every 4 weeks for one year, 100 rating points. (*Rating points* refer to the intensity of advertising during the period.) The highest level of recall (24 percent) was achieved with the thirteen-week schedule. (See Figure 7-7.) But after a year's time, the schedule that produced the most recall (8 percent) was the one every 4 weeks stretched out over fifty-two weeks.[14] The conclusion seems to be that if advertisers want an immediate impact (e.g., to introduce a new product or to counter a competitor's blitz campaign), they should use a massed schedule. However, when the goal is long-lasting repeat buying on a regular basis, a distributed schedule is preferable. Automobile manufacturers use a combination of the

FIGURE 7-7 **Advertising Effects of Massed and Distributed Reinforcement** Source: Herbert A. Zielske and Walter A. Henry, "Remembering and Forgetting Television Ads," *Journal of Advertising Research*, 20 (April 1980), 9.

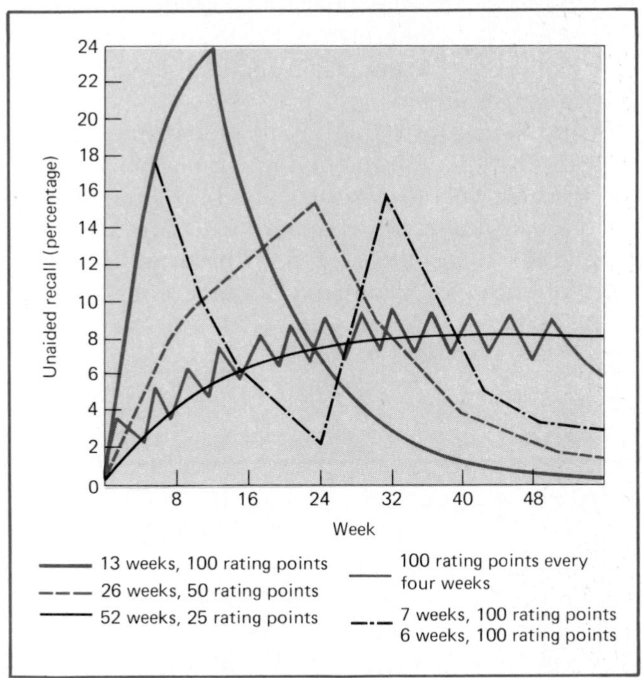


two: they use concentrated advertising during the first few weeks of a new style introduction, and then distributed advertising over the rest of the product year.

## EVALUATION OF INSTRUMENTAL CONDITIONING

Instrumental learning theorists believe that learning occurs through a trial-and-error process, with habits formed as a result of rewards given for certain responses or behaviors. This model of learning applies to many situations in which consumers learn about products, services, and stores. For example, we learn which stores have the clothing we want by shopping in a number of stores, looking for the colors, sizes, and styles we prefer at the prices we can afford. When we find a store that carries clothing which meets our requirements, we tend to frequent that store to the exclusion of others. Every time we purchase a suit or a dress we like at a price we want to pay, our store loyalty is rewarded (*reinforced*) and is more likely to be repeated.

Critics of instrumental learning theory point out, however, that a considerable amount of learning takes place in the absence of direct rewards, either positive or negative. We do not have to be burned to know that fire will hurt us. Children, in fact, learn a great deal through a process psychologists call *modeling*. They observe the behavior of others, remember it, and imitate it.[15] Instrumental theorists argue that children learn in this way because they can see the reward and therefore imitate the behavior that leads to it. But critics maintain that instrumentalists confuse learning and performance (behavior). Children, and adults too, for that matter, learn a great deal that they do not act upon. Moreover, they may learn merely for the sake of learning, not for the sake of rewards. The belief that learning is a function of thinking, of mental processes, is known as **cognitive theory.**

Some researchers argue that because instrumental learning theory views behavior as a result of environmental manipulation rather than cognitive processes, it is applicable only to products that have little personal relevance or importance to the consumer. Other marketers claim that instrumental learning theory is applicable to products of both high and low relevance to the consumer.[16] The question of product relevance will be discussed later in this chapter.

## COGNITIVE LEARNING THEORY

Not all learning takes place as a result of repeated trials. A considerable amount of learning takes place as the result of consumer thinking and problem solving. Sudden learning is also a reality. When confronted with a problem, we sometimes see the solution instantly. More often, however, we are likely to search for information on which to base a decision, and carefully evaluate what we learn in order to make the best decision possible for our purposes. Learning based on mental activity is called **cognitive learning**.

Cognitive learning theory holds that the kind of learning most characteristic of human beings is *problem solving,* which enables individuals to gain some control over their environment. Unlike behavioral learning theory, cognitive theory holds that learning involves complex mental processing of information. Instead of stressing the importance of repetition or the association of rewards with a specific response, cognitive theorists emphasize the role of motivation and mental processes in producing a desired response.

### Information Processing

Like the computer, the human mind is engaged in the processing of information it receives as input. Of central importance to the processing of information is the human **memory.** A basic research concern of most cognitive scientists is discovering how information gets stored in memory, and how it is retrieved.

#### THE STRUCTURE OF MEMORY

Information processing occurs in stages. Consequently, according to one widely accepted view, there must be separate "storehouses" where information can be kept temporarily while waiting to be processed further. In this model, there are actually three separate storage units: a *sensory store,* a *short-term store,* and a *long-term store.*[17]

SENSORY STORE. All data come to us through our senses; however, the image of a sensory input lasts for just a second or less in the mind's sensory store. For example, after staring at a TV image for a few seconds and then looking away, we retain an after-image. That after-image, though very short-lived, is packed with more information than we tend to use or process further. As noted in Chapter 6, we subconsciously block out a great deal of information. For marketers, this means that although it is relatively easy to get information into the consumer's sensory store, it is difficult to make a lasting impression.

SHORT-TERM STORE. The store-term store is the stage of real memory in which information is processed and held for just a brief period. Anyone who has ever looked up a number in a telephone book, only to forget it right before dialing, knows how briefly information lasts in this storage unit. Information in the short-term store which undergoes the process known as *rehearsal* is then transferred into the long-term store. The transfer process takes from two to ten seconds. If information is not rehearsed and transferred, it is lost within about thirty seconds or less. The amount of information that can be held in short-term storage is also limited. Originally it was thought that this store could hold about seven items, or *chunks,* of information (such as numbers),[18] but more recent research indicates that four or five items is more likely.

LONG-TERM STORE. In contrast to the short-term store, where information lasts only a few seconds, the long-term store retains information for relatively extended periods of time. Although it is possible to forget something within a few minutes after the information has reached long-term storage, it is more common for data in that bank to last for days, weeks, and even years. Almost all of us, for example, can remember the name of our first-grade teacher.

It is somewhat misleading to refer to the long-term store as a bank, because information does not just sit there waiting to be retrieved. In the long-term store, information is constantly being organized and reorganized as new links between chunks of information are forged. In fact, many information-processing theorists consider the long-term store to be like a network consisting of *nodes,* (i.e., concepts), with links between the nodes.[19] Consider the concept we have of a single product—wine. We know that various wines share certain attributes (red or white, sweet or dry, expensive or inexpensive). We link the wines we have experienced by means of these attributes (e.g., Blue Nun is more expensive than Ripple and less expensive than French champagne). As we gain more knowledge of wines, we expand our network of relationships, and sometimes our search for additional information. In fact, research studies have found that previous experiences and stored beliefs about the marketplace significantly influence the consumer's external search for information.[20] They have also found that product information stored in memory is brand-based, and that consumers interpret new information in a manner consistent with the existing organization.[21] Because of the importance of the long-term store as the basis for consumer learning and behavior, marketers are most interested in discovering the processes by which information enters into long-term storage.

## MEMORY PROCESSES

Four processes are key to understanding memory: **rehearsal, encoding, storage,** and **retrieval.**

REHEARSAL. How much information is available for delivery from the short-term store to the long-term store depends on the amount of rehearsal an individual gives to it. Rehearsal has been defined as the *silent, mental repetition of material.*[22] In this view, we need rehearsal to amplify the weak signal that comes from the sensory store. Another view of rehearsal is that it involves relating new data to old to make the material meaningful. For example, we may remember the price of a product not by repetition, but by relating it to the price of a similar product.[23]

Failure to rehearse an input, either by repeating it or by relating it to other data, can cause fading and eventual loss of the information. Information can also be lost because of competition for attention. For example, if the short-term store receives a number of inputs from the sensory store simultaneously, its capacity may be reduced to only two or three pieces of information.[24]

Since short-term memory is so limited in capacity, marketers must be certain that the information they convey to consumers is simple enough to be absorbed without much loss. This is particularly important if the time available to convey a message is limited. One researcher has suggested that only two or three bits of information can be conveyed in a fifteen-second commercial if the marketer's goal is later recall.[25] Others suggest that only one point can be made effectively in a fifteen-second commercial.

ENCODING. The purpose of rehearsal is to hold information in the short-term storage unit long enough for encoding to take place. Encoding is *the process by which we select and assign a word or visual image to represent a perceived object.* Marketers, for example, help consumers encode brands by using brand *symbols.* Borden revived the symbol of Elsie the Cow for its dairy products because it was shown that the image generated high consumer recognition.[26] A memorable brand name, such as Smucker's, can also aid in the consumer's encoding process.

Some studies show that learning a picture takes less time than learning verbal information, but that both types of presentation are important in forming an overall mental image.[27] A recent study found that an illustration within a print ad which is accompanied by verbal information is more likely to be encoded and stored than an illustration without verbal cues.[28] Another study found that verbal labeling of pictures containing products or characters was an effective encoding mechanism in establishing a short-term memory of the product/character among children.[29]

Besides being able to code information with the aid of words and symbols, we are able to recode what we have already encoded to include larger amounts of information. This purely human ability to group objects or events together into categories is called *chunking* (see Chapter 6). Those individuals new to a typewriter keyboard must type letter by letter. Those with more experience type in chunks of whole words or phrases. It is important for marketers to discover the groupings or chunks of information that consumers can handle. Recall may be hampered if the chunks offered in an advertisement do not match those in the consumer's frame of reference. The degree of prior knowledge is an important consideration.[30] The amount and type of information given in an automobile ad in a specialty magazine such as *Road and Track* can be much more detailed than that in a general interest magazine such as *Time.* The experts can take in more complex chunks of information.

When consumers are presented with too much information (*information overload*), they may encounter difficulty in encoding and storing it all. It has been argued that consumers can become cognitively overloaded if they are given a lot of information in a limited time. The result of this overload is confusion, resulting in poor purchase decisions.[31] However, one of the pioneers of research in this area has concluded that, contrary to his earlier findings, consumers can handle large amounts of information without experiencing overload.[32] The apparent contradiction between these findings is probably due to the lack of precise definition as to what constitutes information overload. One experiment which concluded that consumers are confused and make poor choices as a result of information overload provided consumers with ten to twenty-five choice alternatives, and with information concerning fifteen to twenty-five product attributes.[33] Research is needed to determine at what point information overload sets in for various subsets of consumers.

STORAGE. Storage is *the process by which we organize and reorganize the information in long-term memory received from the short-term store.* One theory of storage is that it actually consists of two processes. In one process, information is organized *episodically*—that is, by the order in which it was acquired in the past. In the other process, information is stored *semantically,* according to significant concepts.[34] Thus we may remember having gone to a movie last Saturday because of our ability to store data episodically, and we may remember the plot, the stars, and director because of our ability to store data semantically.

In the past, most research in consumer behavior concentrated on episodic memory. For example, recall is used by advertisers as a measure of episodic storage. More recently, however, researchers have explored the way semantic storage operates. Many theorists now believe that memories stored semantically are organized into frameworks by which we integrate new data with previous experience. For information about a new brand of toothpaste to enter our memory, we would have to relate it to our previous experience with toothpaste in terms of taste, cavity prevention, whitening, and breath-freshening qualities.

*Information processing* is related to both the consumer's cognitive ability and the complexity of the information to be processed.[35] Studies have found that consumers process information by attributes, brands, comparisons between pairs of brands, or a combination of these factors.[36] While the number of alternatives and number of attributes included in the brand's message influence the intensity of information processing, studies have found that consumers with higher cognitive ability acquired more product information and were more capable of integrating information on several product attributes.[37] Thus, marketers can expect variations in information processing patterns among consumers.

One related finding is that the more experience a consumer has with a product category, the greater his or her ability to make use of product information.[38] For auto repair services, prior experiences are a major determinant of search behavior. For example, one study found that consumers who were dissatisfied with the service they received in the past were most likely to engage in additional information search on auto repair choices, while satisfied consumers knew exactly where they intended to have their cars repaired the next time they needed to do so.[39] This demonstrates the importance of previously stored information.

It has been shown that greater familiarity with the product category increased cognitive activity and learning during a new car purchase decision, particularly in relation to technical information.[40] This suggests that advertising of technical features and technical evaluations of products (e.g., by *Consumer Reports*) will have greater impact on the purchase decisions of consumers who are already knowledgeable about the product category.

Researchers have sought to distinguish less knowledgeable consumers from more knowledgeable ones by differentiating the product comparisons and judgments they are able to make. Table 7-2 summarizes the levels of knowledge consumers display, as inferred from their statements about products and brands. The not-so-knowledgeable consumer at level 5 can only make simple statements about a product's attributes (e.g., "I like the appearance of the car."). The highly knowledgeable consumer at level 1 is able to compare several brands and many different attributes and come up with a statement of brand preference. To make this judgment, he or she would have to pass through the other levels of knowledge summarized in the table. People at the intermediate levels are most likely to seek out product information and to use

**TABLE 7-2 Consumers Display Different Levels of Product Knowledge**

| DESCRIPTION | SAMPLE STATEMENT |
|---|---|
| 1. Best brand | "Of all the turbo-engined cars available, Saab is the best." |
| 2. Whole brand or attribute rankings or comparisons | "I like Saabs better than BMWs." |
| 3. Whole brand or attribute evaluations | "I have always preferred Saabs." |
| 4. Single pair comparisons or rankings | "Saabs are engineered better than BMWs." |
| 5. Single brand-attribute evaluation | "I like the appearance of the Saab." |

Source: Adapted from J. Edward Russo and Eric J. Johnson, "What Do Consumers Know about Familiar Products?" in Jerry C. Olson, ed., *Advances in Consumer Research* (Ann Arbor, Mich.: Association for Consumer Research, 1980), VII, 418.

it because they have a framework of knowledge within which to place new information.[41]

Just as advertisers must try to judge the complexity of the frameworks of knowledge possessed by their target audiences, so too must public policy makers. In the past, they have not always done so. For example, legislation has been passed requiring marketers to include certain nutritional information on packages. In enacting such laws, however, no studies were made of the level of information consumers already possessed concerning nutrition. As a result, researchers have found that most consumers neither use nor comprehend nutritional labels since they lack the proper framework of knowledge.[42] (Chapter 20 discusses the issue of nutritional labeling.)

RETRIEVAL. Retrieval is *the process by which we recover information from long-term storage.* Most people have had the experience of not being able to recollect something with which they are quite familiar. Information processing theorists look upon such forgetting as a failure of the retrieval system. There is research evidence that retrieval from memory is a rather simple process. For example, it is widely believed that consumers remember the product's *benefits* rather than its *attributes.* However, it has been shown that consumers are *not* more likely to recognize, recall, or retrieve benefits than attributes. Also, they do not automatically form a mental link between attributes and benefits. Furthermore, they retrieve different numbers of attributes under various conditions.[43] The marketing implications of these findings suggest that advertising messages will be most effective if they combine the product's attributes with the benefits that consumers seek in the product, and clearly provide the linkage between the two. Of course, marketers must first find out precisely what benefits consumers are looking for in that product category. (Attitude models discussed in Chapters 8 and 9 can be used to help determine desired benefits.) Reassuring to most marketers are findings that show that when people retrieve information, they rarely search for negative information, though they sometimes do search for disconfirming information.[44]

One reason for a failure to retrieve information is **interference.** There are actually two kinds of interference. *New learning* may interfere with the retrieval of already stored material. There are times when a marketer would prefer that retrieval did not take place. In a laboratory simulation of the rumor that there were worms in McDonald's hamburgers, a refutational message that did *not* specifically mention the rumor was found to be more effective than a message which did; the refutational comment which specifically denied the existence of worms actually triggered the retrieval of the original rumor.[45] *Old learning* may also interfere with the recall (retrieval) of recently learned material. This kind of interference probably accounted for the failure of National Cash Register to gain a foothold in the computer market against IBM. The latter was already too well established in the consumer's mind.

Advertisers who anticipate the effects of interference on retrieval can prevent it. With both kinds of interference, the problem is the similarity of old and new information. Advertising that creates a distinctive brand image can help consumers better retain the message. Figure 7-8 depicts the relationships of the

FIGURE 7-8 Information-Processing Stores and Processes

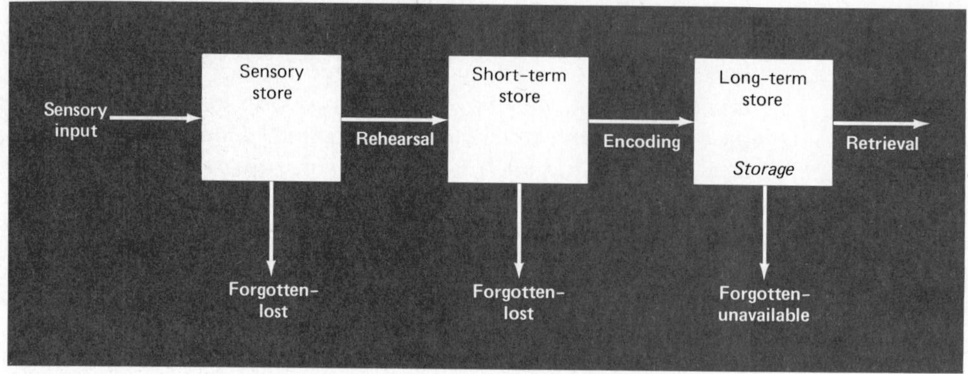


memory stores and processes described in this model of consumer information processing.

## Limited and Extensive Information Processing

The discussion above examined the structure and operation of memory in the processing of information. For a long time, consumer researchers believed that all consumers passed through a complex series of mental and behavioral stages in arriving at a purchase decision. These stages ranged from *awareness* (exposure to information) to *evaluation* (preference, attitude formation) to *behavior* (purchase) to *final evaluation* (adoption or rejection). This same series of stages is often presented as the consumer adoption process (see Chapter 17). This approach is also compatible with the tricomponent attitude model (discussed in Chapter 8), which views the composition of an attitude as consisting of *cognition* (thinking), *affect* (feeling or evaluation), and *conation* (behavior).

A number of models have been developed over the years to express the same notion of sequential processing of information by consumers (see Figure 7-9). Initially, marketing theorists maintained that such sequential, extensive, and complex processing of information by consumers was applicable to all purchase decisions. However, on the basis of their own subjective experiences as consumers, some theorists began to realize that there were some purchase situations that simply did not call for extensive information processing and evaluation, that sometimes consumers simply went from awareness of a need to a routine purchase without a whole lot of information search, mental evaluation, and attitude formation. Such purchases were considered of minimal personal relevance (i.e., of *low involvement*), as opposed to more complex, search-oriented purchases (i.e., *high involvement*).

**Involvement theory,** as it has come to be known, originally focused on the notions of high and low involvement media; it then evolved into the notion of high and low consumer involvement with products and purchases. The following section describes the evolution of involvement theory and discusses its strengths, its weaknesses, and its application to marketing strategy.

## INVOLVEMENT THEORY

Involvement theory developed from a stream of research called *hemispheral lateralization* or *split-brain theory*. The basic premise of the split-brain theory is that the right and left hemispheres of the brain "specialize" in the kinds of information they process. The left hemisphere is primarily responsible for cognitive activities such as reading and speaking. Individuals who are exposed to verbal information cognitively analyze the information through left-brain processing and form mental images. Unlike the left hemisphere, the right hemisphere of the brain is concerned with nonverbal, timeless, and pictorial information.[46] Put another way, the left side of the brain is supposed to be rational, active, realistic; the right side is emotional, metaphoric, impulsive, and intuitive.

### High- and Low-Involvement Media

Building on the notion of hemispheral lateralization, a pioneer consumer researcher theorized that when individuals are engaged in right-brain processing of information, it is possible for them to process and store such information *passively* (that is, without active involvement).[47] Since TV viewing is a right-brain activity (it entails the passive perception of images through the focused eye), TV is a *low-involvement* medium. Passive learning occurs through repeated exposures to a specific TV commercial, and produces changes in consumer behavior (such as a product purchase) prior to any change in the consumer's attitude toward the product.

Print advertisements trigger the left side of the brain, which is in charge of reading, speaking, and translating information into mental images; thus newspapers and magazines are *high-involvement* media. Under this theory, print advertising causes the complex, sequential series of cognitive stages depicted in the classic models of information processing shown in Figure 7-9.[48]

#### PASSIVE LEARNING RESULTS FROM RIGHT-BRAIN PROCESSING OF LOW INVOLVEMENT MEDIA

The right-brain/passive processing of information theory is consistent with the classical conditioning approach. Through repetition, the product is paired with a favorable visual image to produce the desired response: purchase behavior. According to this theory, in situations of passive learning (generated by low-involvement media), repetition is all that is needed to produce the desired response: purchase behavior. The behavior itself, in turn, is likely to lead to a favorable attitude change.[49] In marketing terms, the theory suggests that televi-

FIGURE 7-9 **Cognitive Learning Models**

| Tricomponent Model | Promotional Model | Decision-Making Model | Innovation Adoption Model | Innovation Decision Process |
|---|---|---|---|---|
| Cognitive | Attention | Awareness<br>Knowledge | Awareness | Knowledge |
| Affective | Interest<br>Desire | Evaluation | Interest<br>Evaluation | Persuasion |
| Conative | Action | Purchase<br>Postpurchase Evaluation | Trial<br>Adoption | Decision<br>Confirmation |

sion advertising is likely to be most effective when it is of short duration and frequently repeated. This strategy is consistent with the passive learning generated by TV; it ensures brand familiarity but is not designed to produce detailed evaluation of the message content.[50]

The passive learning model is supported by the growing use of fifteen-second TV commercials. Research has shown that such brief commercial messages are more efficient in terms of cost than longer commercials. A study found that time-compressed commercials are no less effective (in terms of producing intention to buy) than non-time-compressed commercials.[51] (*Time compression* of commercials can be achieved through the use of an electronic device that compresses audio and visual channels some 20 percent while retaining normal voice pitch and appropriate balance between pauses and speech.)

The passive learning model also stresses the importance of the visual component of advertising, including the creative use of symbols. Thus highly visual (rather than informational) TV commercials, in-store displays, and packaging have been found to generate familiarity with the brand and induce purchase behavior.[52] One example of this strategy is Procter & Gamble's format for TV advertising of detergents; its commercials have high repetition, are of short duration, and include a number of visual symbols. P&G's large TV advertising budget commands significant shelf space at the retail level. Consumers instantly recognize the product packaging they have passively learned through TV advertising; this familiarity promotes purchase behavior. Other examples of products that use a similar TV advertising strategy of high-repetition, short-duration commercials that are rich in visual symbolism include Bounty paper towels, Miller Beer, and Kleenex tissues.

Recent evidence confirms the fact that pictorial cues (which activate right-brain processing) are more effective for generating recall and familiarity with the product, while verbal cues (which trigger left-brain processing) generate cognitive activity that encourages consumers to evaluate the advantages and disadvantages of the product.[53]

There are limitations to the application of the split-brain theory to marketing strategy.[54] Research suggests that the right and left hemispheres of the brain do not operate independently of each other, but work together to process information. Furthermore, *activation research*—the methodology for measuring brain activity—is highly complex, and the findings are difficult to interpret.

## High and Low Consumer Involvement

The preceding section discussed the active processing of information produced by high involvement media (such as magazines) and the passive processing of information produced by low-involvement media (such as TV) and pictorial rather than verbal cues. In this section, we will discuss the degree of information processing produced by high and low consumer involvement with the product or purchase situation.

In this context, involvement is defined as *the degree of personal relevance which the product holds for the consumer.* High-involvement purchases are those which are very important to the consumer in terms of perceived risk (see Chapter 6) and which prompt the consumer to engage in extensive problem solving. Low-involvement purchases are purchases which are not very important to the consumer, hold little relevance and little perceived risk, and thus lead the consumer to engage in very limited information processing. Two theories that illustrate the concepts of extensive and limited problem-solving for high- and low-involvement purchase situations are the *Central and Peripheral Routes to Persuasion* theory and the *Social Judgment* theory.

### CENTRAL AND PERIPHERAL ROUTES TO PERSUASION

The major premise of the Central and Peripheral Routes to Persuasion theory is that individuals are more likely to carefully weigh information concerning a product and to devote considerable cognitive effort to evaluating it when they are highly involved with the product category.[55] The theory suggests that there is a very strong likelihood that consumers will carefully evaluate the merits and/or weaknesses of a product when the purchase is of high relevance to them. Conversely, the likelihood is great that consumers will engage in very limited information search and evaluation when the purchase holds little relevance or importance for them. Thus, for *high-involvement* purchases, the *central* route to persuasion—the instigation of considered thought about the product—is likely to be a highly effective marketing strategy. For *low-involvement* purchases, the *peripheral* route to persuasion is likely to be more effective. In this instance, because the consumer is less motivated to exert cognitive effort, learning is more likely to occur through repetition and the passive processing of visual cues.

There is a great deal of research support for the high-relevance/high-involvement—low-relevance/low-involvement theory of consumer information processing. For example, a number of studies indicate that high involvement with an issue produces more extensive processing of information about the issue, and that in such situations, the quality of the argument presented in the persuasive message is very influential in the decision outcome.[56] Consumer research supports this evidence. It was demonstrated that highly involved consumers use more attributes to evaluate brands than less involved consumers.[57] Consumers tend to apply very simple choice rules (that is, they make a quick and effortless decision) when the purchase is not important and when the product is purchased frequently (and thus presents very little perceived risk.)[58]

The marketing implications of the two-routes-to-persuasion theory is that for high-involvement purchases, marketers should use arguments stressing the strong, solid, high-quality attributes of their products—thus utilizing the *central* (that is, highly cognitive) route. For low-involvement purchases, marketers should use the *peripheral* route to persuasion, focusing on the method of presentation rather than the content of the message (e.g., through the use of celebrity spokespersons or highly visual and symbolic advertisements).

### SOCIAL JUDGMENT THEORY

The central premise of the Social Judgment theory is that an individual's processing of information about an issue is determined by his or her own involvement with the issue.[59] Individuals who are highly involved with an issue and have a strong or definite opinion about it will accept very few alternative opinions (that is, they will have a *narrow latitude of acceptance* and a *wide latitude of rejection*). Highly involved individuals will interpret a message which is congruent with their positions as more positive than it actually is (this is known as the *assimilation effect*), and one that is not congruent as more negative than it actually is (the *contrast effect*). Persons who are uninvolved with an issue will be more receptive to arguments for and against (they will have a *wide latitude of acceptance*) or take no position at all (have a *wide latitude of noncommitment.*)

The marketing implications of the Social Judgment theory suggest that highly involved consumers would find fewer brands acceptable (they would be narrow categorizers) and would interpret messages about these brands in a manner congruent with their previous experiences and opinions about the product.[60] The uninvolved consumer will be receptive to a greater number of messages regarding the purchase (will consider more brands and be a wide categorizer).[61] This type of person is less likely to be brand loyal and is a likely target for brand switching.

## Evaluation of Involvement Theory for Marketing Applications

While the theories on involvement presented above appear to be straightforward, it has been difficult to operationalize them for marketing strategy applications. This is quite likely due to the fact that they have been developed by information theorists, rather than by marketing theorists, and deal with the processing and learning of information about issues, rather than about products. In accordance with these theories, many consumer researchers now believe that involvement is consumer-related rather than product-related or media-related. That is, it is a function of the consumer's mental state regarding the product, rather than a function of the product itself. Thus, though some consumer researchers have considered high-priced products to be high-involvement products, they are only high involvement in relation to the consumer's state of mind. For example, if the purchase of an automobile presents high perceived financial risk to a consumer, to such a consumer an automobile may be a high-involvement purchase. By the same token, an inexpensive toiletry product like shampoo might be a high-involvement purchase to a consumer with perceived social risk.

A major problem in operationalizing consumer involvement theory is the great variation in the conceptualization and measurement of the consumer's mental state regarding a purchase. For example, a recent review of consumer involvement research revealed more than thirty conceptual and empirical attempts to operationalize involvement.[62] Many psychological and social theories have also been used to explain consumer "involvement."[63] Most consumer researchers agree that there is no single, widely accepted understanding of involvement, because the term has been neither carefully defined nor well conceptualized.[64] One widely quoted study identified familiarity, commitment, and importance of the product as the components of involvement.[65] Another review specified ego involvement, commitment, communication involvement, purchase importance, and extent of information search as the five types of involvement.[66] Some researchers have identified the person, product, and situation as the major components of involvement.[67] Others view low involvement as applicable to purchases where there is little information search and no attitude formation regarding the product prior to the purchase.[68]

In addition to problems of *definition,* there are also problems of *measurement.* The measurement of involvement has varied greatly. Researchers who regard involvement as a cognitive state are concerned with the measurement of ego involvement, risk perception, and importance of the purchase; researchers who focus on the behavioral aspects of involvement measure such factors as the search for and evaluation of product information.[69] Some researchers consider decision time an effective measure of involvement.[70] Others argue that involvement should be measured by the degree of importance the product has to the buyer.[71] A recent study has concluded that since there really are so many kinds of consumer involvement, efforts should be made to measure an involvement *profile* rather than a single involvement level.[72] This recommendation is consistent with previous studies which argue that involvement should be measured on a *continuum* rather than as a dichotomy consisting of two mutually exclusive categories of "high" and "low" involvement.[73]

One study views long-term involvement with a product as leisure behavior; under this theory, long-term products are considered high-involvement products. Thus durable products which deliver pleasure on a continuing basis (such as cars, stereo equipment, and home computers) are viewed as high-involvement products.[74] However, if high-involvement products are defined as continuous pleasure-giving products, it is just as reasonable to extend the term to nondurables such as cigarettes or chewing gum, since it is obvious that some consumers derive continuous pleasure from these products, as evidenced by their repeat purchases.

At the present time, involvement research is clearly at a crossroads. The thrust of such research thus far seems to have been an attempt to distinguish *limited* information processing from the classical view of *extensive* information processing. Indeed, one researcher has concluded that the low-involvement notion is an incomplete learning theory which should be put to rest.[75] However, the view of right-brain/passive information processing does seem to have strong implications for the length, duration, and content of TV advertising.

The issue of personal relevance of the product to the consumer appears to be more complicated. Before the degree of relevance can be measured, the researcher must define exactly what it is that should be measured—ego, motivation, task involvement, situational variables, or what. It is clear that solid and widely accepted measures of product relevance need to be developed. Of course, too many variables may make it extremely difficult to operationalize the consumer involvement issue in a way that can be realistically integrated into marketing strategy.

### Evaluation of Behavioral Theory Versus Cognitive Theory

The new emphasis in marketing circles on the consumer as an information processor revives the long standing dispute among learning theorists about the relative importance of behavioral versus mental processes—the old "nature versus nurture" argument about whether the mind comes equipped with innate ideas or inherited tendencies to think and behave in specific ways, or whether the mind is a blank slate at birth and comes to think only in ways that have been "written" upon it by experience and training. The movie *Trading Places,* with Eddie Murphy and Dan Ackroyd, depicts this age-old question in an entertaining format, and supports the view suggested by recent research that learning is the product of an interaction between nature and nurture; each is essential, but neither is wholly controlling.

## BRAND LOYALTY

A major goal of marketers concerned with understanding how consumers learn is to encourage **brand loyalty**. As straightforward as it may seem, however, brand loyalty is not a simple concept. Just as there are different approaches to the definition and measurement of information processing, so too there are different views as to the definition and measurement of brand loyalty. A basic issue among researchers is whether to define the concept in terms of consumer *behavior* or consumer *attitudes*. One behavioral researcher proposed that a consumer be considered brand loyal if he or she has made three successive purchases of the same brand.[76] Another suggested that brand loyalty be measured by the proportion of total product purchases a household devotes to the brand most frequently purchased.[77]

From the viewpoint of cognitive learning theorists, such behavioral definitions lack precision, since they do not distinguish between the "real" brand-loyal buyer who is intentionally faithful, and the spurious brand-loyal buyer who repeats a brand purchase because it is the only one available at the store or because it is displayed more prominently than others, or who flies a specific airline because its telephone number comes most easily to mind. Such theorists say that loyalty must be measured by attitudes toward a brand rather than by purchase consistency. Other theorists suggest that brand loyalty be measured by degree of *involvement* (i.e., high involvement leads to extensive information search, to attitude change, to purchase behavior, and ultimately to brand loyalty; while low involvement lends itself to exposure and brand awareness, to purchase behavior, possibly to attitude change, and then to brand habit.) If brand loyalty is defined as *commitment,* clearly the low-involvement consumer could not be considered brand-loyal.

*Spurious brand awareness* occurs in situations where consumers "think" they have heard of a product with a plausible-sounding name. Such situations suggest low involvement, and the influence of visual cues on consumer awareness and ultimate purchase. Thus low involvement may in fact promote a kind of brand loyalty, suggesting that for some products, heavy exposure of the product name and package may be more persuasive than quality arguments in building repeat purchase behavior.

## Developing Brand Loyalty

Not only do definitions of brand loyalty differ, but so too do views on how brand loyalty is established. Behavioral scientists who favor the theory of instrumental conditioning believe that brand loyalty results from an initial product trial that is reinforced through satisfaction, leading to repeat purchase. Cognitive researchers, on the other hand, emphasize the role of mental processes in building brand loyalty. They believe that consumers engage in extensive problem-solving behavior involving brand and attribute comparisons, leading to a strong brand preference and repeat purchase behavior. Involvement theory suggests that frequent exposure to TV commercials that are rich in visual cues and symbolism and short in duration, buttressed by strong in-store displays, creates a type of brand loyalty for low-involvement purchases.

Marketers are interested not only in *how* brand loyalty develops, but in *when* it develops. Research evidence suggests that a great deal of brand loyalty develops quite early in life, within the context of family life.[78] One study comparing middle-school children with high-school students found that both groups scored high on the ability to express brand preferences, but that the older group had significantly more brand preferences.[79] What children learn is apparently quite lasting. A long-term study among children in grades 3 through 11 found, twenty years later, that about a quarter of the subjects who responded preferred and still used the same brands they did in the earlier study.[80]

## Brand Switching

Not all consumers are brand-loyal. Some engage in *brand switching* because they become dissatisfied or bored with a product, others because they are more concerned with price than with brand name. Nevertheless, a recent study using data from the Target Group Index (TGI) on consumer purchase habits reported that brands with larger market shares have proportionately larger groups of loyal buyers.[81] Another study reported that, contrary to many marketers' beliefs, brand loyalty is *not* declining significantly. The slight decline that has been measured appears to be due to an increase by marketers in sales promotion (e.g., special price deals, coupons, sweepstakes, free samples) at the expense of advertising, and to greater consumer awareness of price, more comparative advertising, and more targeting toward specialty niches.[82] Research evidence has found that special price deals do induce consumers to switch brands. However, after the special offer ends and another deal comes along, the same consumers are just as likely to switch again. Thus, while sales promotion deals do increase market share, they do not necessarily create brand loyalty, whether defined as *commitment* or *habit*.

One researcher reported that brand-loyal consumers tend to increase their purchases of the brand when advertising is increased, but that this strategy has little impact on less loyal consumers. The same researcher advocates refining the measures of advertising effectiveness to distinguish between the campaign's ability to attract *new* customers and its ability to reinforce *current* buyers.[83]

Because services are intangible, many marketers believe it is more difficult to establish service brand loyalty than product brand loyalty. Some service organizations have started to promote consistency of operation and convenience in an effort to combat shifting loyalties.[84] Frequent-flier plans are a recent example of efforts to increase brand loyalty for services. Hotel chains have begun to offer "frequent guest" plans. There is some evidence that such plans have generated more repeat usage by consumers, but it remains to be seen whether such "brand loyalty" will continue after these sales promotion deals are withdrawn.

Despite the diversity of viewpoints among learning theorists, most marketers are interested in all measures of brand loyalty. They are concerned with actual consumer purchasing patterns, with consumer beliefs and opinions concerning their brand and competing brands, and with knowing how important the product is to the consumer. Developing a highly consistent market share of brand-loyal consumers is the ultimate goal of marketing strategy. Discovering how consumers learn about brands and become attached to certain brands assists marketers in achieving this goal.

## summary

Consumer learning is the process by which individuals acquire the purchase and consumption knowledge and experience they apply to future related behavior. While some learning is intentional, much learning appears to be incidental. Basic elements that contribute to an understanding of learning are motivation, cues, response, and reinforcement. Motivation acts as a stimulus to learning. Cues give direction to motives and help consumers fulfill their needs in product-specific ways. An individual's response to a drive or stimulus (cue) often depends on previous learning, which in turn is often the result of the type and degree of reinforcement received. Reinforcement increases the likelihood that a specific response will occur in the future as the result of particular cues.

There are two widely divergent theories of how individuals learn: behavioral theories and cognitive theories. Both contribute to an understanding of consumer behavior. Traditional behavioral theories include classical conditioning and instrumental conditioning. Three principles of classical conditioning provide the theoretical underpinnings for many marketing applications: repetition, stimulus generalization, and stimulus discrimination. Instrumental learning theorists believe that learning occurs through a trial-and-error process that associates a reward with a certain behavior. Both positive and negative reinforcement can be used to affect the likelihood of eliciting the desired response (behavior). The timing of learning schedules influences how long the learned material is retained. Massed learning produces more initial learning than distributed learning; however, learning usually persists longer with distributed (that is, spread-out) schedules.

Cognitive learning theory holds that the kind of learning most characteristic of humans is problem solving, which involves mental processes rather than the purely behavioral components of learning stressed by the classical or instrumental conditioning theorists. Cognitive theorists are chiefly concerned with how information is processed by the human mind, and they draw an analogy with information processing by computers. A very simple model of the structure and operation of memory suggests the existence of three separate storage units: a sensory store, a short-term store, and a long-term store. The processes of memory include rehearsal, encoding, storage, and retrieval.

Involvement theory suggests that people engage in limited information processing in purchasing situations of low importance or relevance to them, and in extensive information processing in situations of high relevance or involvement. It also suggests that TV is a low-involvement medium which entails information processing by the right side of the brain, and print is a high-involvement medium which requires left-brain processing.

A basic issue among researchers is whether to define brand loyalty in terms of consumers' behavior or consumers' attitudes toward the brand. For marketers, the purpose of understanding how consumers learn is to teach them that their brand is best, and to develop brand loyalty.

## discussion questions

1. Which of the following consumer behaviors demonstrate real learning as opposed to mere behavior? Why or why not?
   a. Buying the "store brand" of canned peas when it is the only one available.
   b. Recommending a brand you have used for years.
   c. Telling a friend about a funny television commercial but forgetting the brand name.
2. When a person is in a supermarket, his or her ultimate actions are affected by the types of learning discussed in this chapter. Give an example of how each may have affected your shopping behavior during your last trip to a supermarket.
3. How might classical conditioning affect our responses to certain kinds of food?
4. In what ways can brand purchasing behavior be affected by *both* stimulus generalization and stimulus discrimination?
5. Kraft Foods uses family branding, but Procter & Gamble (Crest, Duncan Hines, Charmin, Tide) does not. Yet both companies are successful. Describe in "learning terms" the conditions under which family branding is a good policy and those under which it is not. What do you think are the reasons for the difference in family-branding policy between Kraft and P&G?
6. How does involvement theory distinguish between extensive and limited information processing?
7. Assume that you are advising the brand manager of Royal Crown Cola. Using your knowledge of brand loyalty, outline the strategies he or she might use for capturing a greater market share from the leaders, Pepsi and Coke.
8. Discuss the basic differences between behavioral theories of learning and cognitive theories of learning. Which of these learning theories do you think is more applicable to consumer behavior? Why?

## endnotes


1. Politz Media Studies, *The Rochester Study* (New York: Saturday Evening Post, 1960). For subsequent similar studies, see also D. B. Lucas and S. H. Britt, *Measuring Advertising Effectiveness* (New York: McGraw-Hill, 1963); and A. W. Hubbard, *A Study of Advertising Effects in "Modern Medicine"* (New York: Modern Medicine, 1970).
2. W. L. Kruger, "The Effects of Overlearning on Retention," *Journal of Experimental Psychology,* 12 (1929), 71–78; and "Further Studies in Overlearning," *Journal of Experimental Psychology,* 13 (1930), 152–63. See also L. Postman, "Retention as a Function of Overlearning," *Science,* 135 (1962), 656–67.

3. C. S. Craig, B. Sternthal, and K. Olshan, "The Effect of Overlearning on Retention," *Journal of General Psychology,* 87 (1972), 85–94; and C. S. Craig, B. Sternthal, and C. Leavitt, "Advertising Wearout: An Experimental Analysis," *Journal of Advertising Research,* 16 (November 1976), 365–72.

4. Bobby J. Calder and Brian Sternthal, "Television Commercial Wearout: An Information Processing View," *Journal of Marketing Research,* 17 (May 1980), 173–86.

5. Herbert Krugman, "What Makes Advertising Effective?" *Harvard Business Review,* 53 (March–April 1975), 96–103.

6. Howard Kamin, "Advertising Reach and Frequency," *Journal of Advertising Research,* 18 (February 1978), 21–25.

7. George Miaoulis and Nancy D'Amato, "Consumer Confusion and Trademark Infringement," *Journal of Marketing,* 42 (April 1978), 48–55.

8. Bernice Kanner, "DFS Develops System to Find New Extension," *Advertising Age,* November 19, 1979, 20. See also Herbert Zeltner, "Product Line Extensions Can Spur Profitable New Volume," *Advertising Age,* April 26, 1976, 60, 62.

9. Kevin T. Higgins, "Old Characters Refuse to Fade," *Marketing News,* October 25, 1985, 1.

10. Kevin T. Higgins, "Licensing Industry Combating Counterfeiters," *Marketing News,* October 25, 1985, 6.

11. William M. Borchard, "Law Gets Tough on Counterfeit Goods," *Advertising Age,* January 7, 1985, 26.

12. Scott Hume, "Of Corr's There's a Happy Ending," *Advertising Age,* June 11, 1984, 12.

13. See H. A. Zielske, "The Remembering and Forgetting of Advertising," *Journal of Marketing,* 23 (January 1959), 231–43; and E. C. Strong, "The Effects of Repetition of Advertising: A Field Study" (Ph.D. dissertation, Stanford University, 1972).

14. H. A. Zielske and Walter A. Henry, "Remembering and Forgetting Television Ads," *Journal of Advertising Research,* 20 (April 1980), 7–13.

15. The chief advocate of modeling, or social learning theory, is Albert Bandura. See his *Social Learning Theory* (Englewood Cliffs, N.J.: Prentice-Hall, 1977). Social learning theory has become particularly important in explaining how children learn from television, including TV advertising. See Elzora Dalrymple, "Learning Theory: Children and Television," in Barbara J. Redman, *Consumer Behavior: Theory and Applications* (Westport, Conn.: AVI Publishing Co., 1979), 164–76.

16. J. Paul Peter and Walter R. Nord, "A Classification and Extension of Operant Conditioning Principles in Marketing," *Journal of Marketing,* 46 (Summer 1982), 102–7.

17. R. C. Atkinson and R. M. Shiffrin, "Human Memory: A Proposed System and Its Central Processes," in E. W. Spence and J. T. Spence, eds., *The Psychology of Learning and Motivation* (New York: Academic Press, 1968), Vol. II.

18. See George A. Miller, "The Magical Number Seven, Plus or Minus Two: Some Limits on Our Capacity for Processing Information," *Psychological Review,* 63 (1956), 81–97; and Herbert A. Simon, "How Big Is a Chunk?" *Science,* 183 (February 1974), 482–88.

19. See, for example, Nicoll Frijda, "Simulation of Human Long-Term Memory," *Psychological Bulletin,* 77 (January 1972), 1–31.

20. Noel Capon and Roger Davis, "Basic Cognitive Ability Measures as Predictors of Consumer Information Processing Strategies," *Journal of Consumer Research,* 11 (June 1984), 551–63.

21. Walter A. Henry, "The Effect of Information-Processing Ability on Processing Accuracy," *Journal of Consumer Research,* 7 (June 1980), 42–48.

22. Peter H. Lindsay and Donald A. Norman, *Human Information Processing: An Introduction to Psychology* (New York: Academic Press, 1972), 340.

23. For a review of the literature on rehearsal and some of the other processes discussed here, see James R. Bettman, "Memory Factors in Consumer Choice: A Review," *Journal of Marketing,* 43 (Spring 1979), esp. 39–42.

24. Nancy C. Waugh and Donald A. Norman, "Primary Memory," *Psychological Review,* 72 (1965), 89–104.

25. Bettman, "Memory Factors in Consumer Choice," 50.

26. Sam Harper, "Elsie Moo-ves Back into Ad Limelight," *Marketing News,* November 19, 1979, 1.

27. Thomas Hofacker, "Identifying Consumer Information Processing Strategies: New Methods of Analyzing Information Display Board Data," in Thomas C. Kinnear, ed., *Advances in Consumer Research,* 11 (Provo, Ut.: Association for Consumer Research 1983), 579–84.

28. Klaus P. Kaas, "Factors Influencing Consumer Strategies in Information Processing," in Thomas C. Kinnear, ed., *Advances in Consumer Research,* 585–90.

29. M. Carole Macklin, "Verbal Labeling Effects in Short-Term Memory for Character/Product Pairing," in Thomas C. Kinnear, ed., *Advances in Consumer Research,* 343–47.

30. Bettman, "Memory Factors in Consumer Choice," 50.

31. Naresh K. Malhotra, "Reflections on the Information Overload Paradigm in Consumer Decision Making," *Journal of Consumer Research,* 10 (March 1984), 436–40; and "Information Load and Consumer Decision Making," *Journal of Consumer Research,* 8 (March 1982), 419–30.

32. Jacob Jacoby, "Perspectives on Information Overload," *Journal of Consumer Research,* 10 (March 1984), 432–35.

33. Thomas E. Muller, "Buyer Response to Variations in Product Information Load," *Journal of Applied Psychology,* 69 (1984), 300–6.

34. Endel Tulvig, "Episodic and Semantic Memory," in Endel Tulvig and W. Donaldson, eds., *Organization of Memory* (New York: Academic Press, 1972), 381–403.

35. Calvin P. Duncan and Richard W. Olshavsky, "External Search: The Role of Consumer Beliefs," *Journal of Marketing Research,* 19 (February 1982), 32–43.

36. Gabriel Biehal and Dipankar Chakravarti, "Information-Presentation Format and Learning Goals as Determinants of Consumers' Memory Retrieval and Choice Processes," *Journal of Consumer Research,* 8 (March 1982), 431–41.

37. See, for example, Terry L. Childers and Michael J. Houston, "Imagery Paradigms for Consumer Research: Alternative Perspectives from Cognitive Psychology," in Richard P. Bagozzi and Alice M. Tybout, eds., *Advances in Consumer Research,* 10 (Chicago: Association for Consumer Research, 1982), 59–64 and Julie A. Edell and Richard Staelin, "The Information Processing of Pictures in Print Advertisements," *Journal of Consumer Research,* 10 (June 1983), 45–61.

38. Eric J. Johnson and J. Edward Russo, "Product Familiarity and Learning New Information."

39. Gabriel J. Biehal, "Consumers' Prior Experiences and Perceptions in Auto Repair Choice," *Journal of Marketing,* 47 (Summer 1983), 82–91.

40. Eric J. Johnson and J. Edward Russo, "Product Familiarity and Learning New Information," *Journal of Consumer Research* (June 1984), 542–50.

41. J. Edward Russo and Eric J. Johnson, "What Do Consumers Know about Familiar Products?" in Jerry C. Olson, ed., *Advances in Consumer Research* (Ann Arbor, Mich.: Association for Consumer Research, 1980), VII, 418.

42. Jacob Jacoby, Robert W. Chestmist, and William Silberman, "Consumer Uses and Comprehension of Nutrition Information," *Journal of Consumer Research,* 4 (September 1977), 119–28.

43. Lorne Bozinoff and Victor J. Roth, "Recall and Recognition Memory for Product Attributes and Benefits," in Thomas C. Kinnear, ed. *Advances in Consumer Research,* 348–52; and Biehal and Chakravarti, "Information Presentation Format."

44. John H. Lingle, Janet M. Dukerich, and Thomas M. Ostrom, "Accessing Information in Memory-Based Impression Judgments: Incongruity versus Negativity in Retrieval Selectivity," *Journal of Personality and Social Psychology,* 44 (1983) 262–72.

45. Alice M. Tybout, Bobby J. Calder, and Brian Sternthal, "Using Information Processing Theory to Design Marketing Strategies," *Journal of Marketing Research,* 18 (February 1981), 73–79.

46. Flemming Hansen, "Hemispheral Lateralization: Implications for Understanding Consumer Behavior," *Journal of Consumer Research,* 8 (June 1981), 23–36; Peter H. Lindzay and Donald Norman, *Human Information Processing* (New York: Academic Press, 1977); and Merlin C. Wittrock, *The Human Brain* (Englewood Cliffs, N.J.: Prentice-Hall, 1977).

47. Herbert E. Krugman, "The Impact of Television Advertising: Learning without Involvement," *Public Opinion Quarterly,* 29 (Fall 1965) 349–56; "Brain Wave Measures of Media Involvement," *Journal of Advertising Research,* 11 (February 1971), 3–10; and "Memory without Recall, Exposure without Perception," *Journal of Advertising Research, Classics,* 1 (September 1982), 80–85.

48. Ibid.

49. Ray Arora, "Consumer Involvement and Advertising Strategy," *International Journal of Advertising,* 4 (1985), 119–30.

50. Herbert E. Krugman, "Why Three Exposures May be Enough," *Journal of Advertising Research,* 12 (December 1972), 11–14; and Michael L. Rothschild, "Advertising Strategies for High and Low Involvement Situations," in John C. Maloney and Bernard Silverman, eds., *Attitude Research Plays for High Stakes* (Chicago: American Marketing Association, 1979), 74–93.

51. Mary Jane Rawlins Schlinger, Linda F. Alwitt, Kathleen E. McCarthy, and Leila Green, "Effects of Time Compression on Attitudes and Information Processing," *Journal of Marketing,* 47 (Winter 1983), 79–85; Mark N. Vamos, "The Coming Avalanche of 15-second TV Ads," *Business Week,* February 11, 1985, 80; and Robert Parcher, "Fifteen-Second TV Commercials Appear to Work 'Quite Well,' " *Marketing News,* January 3, 1986, 1.

52. Michael L. Rothschild in Maloney and Silverman, *Attitude Research,* 74–93.

53. See, for example, Terry L. Childers and Michael J. Houston, "Conditions for a Picture-Superiority Effect on Consumer Memory," *Journal of Consumer Research,* 11 (September 1984) 643–54; Morris B. Holbrook and William L. Moore, "Feature Interactions in Consumer Judgments of Verbal Versus Pictorial Presentations," *Journal of Consumer Research,* 8 (June 1981), 103–13; and Ruth Ann Smith, Michael J. Houston and Terry L. Childers, "Verbal versus Visual Processing Modes: An Empirical Test of the Cyclical Processing Hypothesis," in Thomas C. Kinnear, ed., *Advances in Consumer Research,* 75–80.

54. William A. Katz, "Point of View: A Critique of Split-Brain Theory," *Journal of Advertising Research,* 23 (April–May 1983), 63–66.

55. Richard E. Petty, John T. Cacioppo, and David Schumann, "Central and Peripheral Routes to Advertising Effectiveness: The Moderating Role of Involvement," *Journal of Consumer Research,* 10 (1983), 135–46.

56. See, for example, Richard E. Petty and John T. Cacioppo, "Issue Involvement Can Increase or Decrease Persuasion by Enhancing Message-Relevant Cognitive Responses," *Journal of Personality and Social Psychology,* 37 (1979) 1915–26; Cacioppo and Petty, "The Need for Cognition," *Journal of Personality and Social Psychology,* 42 (1982), 116–31; and Cacioppo, Petty, and Katherine J. Morris, "Effects of Need for Cognition on Message Evaluation, Recall and Persuasion," *Journal of Personality and Social Psychology,* 45 (1983), 805–18.

57. Michael L. Rothschild and Michael J. Houston, "The Consumer Involvement Matrix: Some Preliminary Findings," in Barnett A. Greenberg and Danny N. Bellenger, eds., *Proceedings of the American Marketing Association Educators' Conference,* 41 (Chicago: American Marketing Association, 1977), 95–98.

**58.** Wayne D. Hoyer, "An Examination of Consumer Decision Making for a Common Repeat Purchase Product," *Journal of Consumer Research,* 11 (December, 1984), 822–29.

**59.** Muzafer Sherif and Carl I. Hovland, *Social Judgment Assimilation and Contrast Effects in Communication and Attitude Change* (New Haven, Conn.: Yale University Press, 1961); and Carolyn E. Sherif, Muzafer Sherif, and R. W. Nebergall, *Attitude and Attitude Change: The Social Judgment-Involvement Approach,* (Philadelphia: Saunders, 1965).

**60.** Rothschild and Houston, "The Consumer Involvement Matrix."

**61.** Mark B. Traylor, "Product Involvement and Brand Commitment," *Journal of Advertising Research,* 21 (December 1981), 51–56.

**62.** Ravi Parameswaran and Teri Spinelli, "Involvement: A Revisitation and Confirmation" in Russell W. Belk, Robert Peterson, Gerald S. Albaum, Morris H. Holbrook, Roger A. Kerin, Naresh K. Malhotra, and Peter Wright, eds., *Proceedings of the American Marketing Association Educators' Conference,* 50 (Chicago: American Marketing Association, 1984), 57–61.

**63.** Anthony G. Greenwald and Clark Leavitt, "Audience Involvement in Advertising: Four Levels," *Journal of Consumer Research,* 11 (June 1984), 581–92.

**64.** For example, see the following articles in Thomas C. Kinnear, ed., *Advances in Consumer Research (1983):* James A. Muncy and Shelby D. Hunt, "Consumer Involvement: Definitional Issues and Research Directions," 193–96; John H. Antil, "Conceptualization and Operationalization of Involvement," 203–09; and Michael L. Rothschild, "Perspectives on Involvement: Current Problems and Future Directions," 216–17.

**65.** J. L. Lastovicka and David M. Gardner, "Components of Involvement," in Maloney and Silverman, *Attitude Research Plays, 53–73.*

**66.** Muncy and Hunt in Thomas C. Kinnear, ed., *Advances in Consumer Research.*

**67.** Antil in Thomas C. Kinnear, ed., *Advances in Consumer Research.*

**68.** David W. Finn, "The Integrated Information Response Model," *Journal of Advertising,* 13 (1984), 24–33.

**69.** Robert N. Stone, "The Marketing Characteristics of Involvement," in Thomas C. Kinnear, ed., *Advances in Consumer Research,* 210–15.

**70.** Daniel L. Sherrell and Terence A. Shimp, "Consumer Involvement in a Laboratory Setting," in Bruce J. Walker, et al., eds., *An Assessment of Marketing Thought and Practice—Proceedings of the American Marketing Association Educators' Conference,* 48 (Chicago: American Marketing Association, 1982), 104–08.

**71.** Finn, "The Integrated Information Response Model."

**72.** Gilles Laurent and Jean-Noel Kapferer, "Measuring Consumer Involvement Profiles," *Journal of Marketing Research,* 22 (February 1985), 41–53.

**73.** Antil, in Thomas C. Kinnear, ed., *Advances in Consumer Research,* 203–09.

**74.** Peter H. Block and Grady D. Bruce, "Product Involvement as Leisure Experience," in Thomas C. Kinnear, ed., *Advances in Consumer Research,* 197–202.

**75.** David W. Finn, "It Is Time to Lay the Low Involvement Hierarchy to Rest," in Bruce J. Walker et al. 99–103.

**76.** W. T. Tucker, "The Development of Brand Loyalty," *Journal of Marketing Research,* 1 (August 1964), 33.

**77.** Ross Cunningham, "Brand Loyalty—What, Where, How Much," *Harvard Business Review,* 34 (January–February 1956), 116.

**78.** George P. Moschis, Roy L. Moore, and Thomas J. Stanley, "An Exploratory Study of Brand Loyalty Development," in Thomas C. Kinnear, ed., *Advances in Consumer Research,* 412–17.

**79.** Roy L. Moore and Lowndes F. Stephens, "Some Communication and Demographic Determinants of Adolescent Consumer Learning," *Journal of Consumer Research,* 2 (September 1975), 85.

80. Lester Guest, "Brand Loyalty Revisited: A Twenty-Year Report," *Journal of Applied Psychology,* 48 (1964), 97.
81. S. P. Raj, "Striking a Balance Between Brand 'Popularity' and Brand Loyalty," *Journal of Marketing,* 49 (Winter 1985), 53–59.
82. "Declining Brand Loyalty: More Fiction than Fact," *Marketing News,* January 6, 1984, 4.
83. S. P. Raj, "The Effects of Advertising on High and Low Loyalty Consumer Segments," *Journal of Consumer Research,* 9 (June 1982), 77–89; and "Attractive and Retentive Effects of Advertising," *Journal of Advertising Research,* 22 (April–May 1982), 53–59.
84. "Attracting Customers, Promoting 'Brand' Loyalty Challenge Services Businesses," *Marketing News,* December 6, 1985, 12.

# 8

# The Nature of Consumer Attitudes

## *introduction*

EVERY time consumers are asked whether they *like* or *dislike* a product (e.g., Classic Coke), a service (e.g., Lawn King), an advertising theme (e.g., AT&T's "Reach Out and Touch Someone"), or a particular retailer (e.g., Banana Republic), they are being asked to express their **attitudes**. Within the realm of consumer behavior, attitude research has been employed to study a wide range of critical marketing strategy questions. For example, attitude research is commonly undertaken to ascertain the likelihood that consumers will accept a proposed new-product idea, to gauge why a firm's target audience has not reacted more favorably to its revised promotional theme, or to learn how target customers are likely to react to a proposed change in the firm's packaging and label.

In fact, it is difficult to imagine any consumer research project that does not measure some aspect of consumer attitudes. As an outgrowth of this pervasive interest in consumer attitudes, it is not surprising that attitudes have received so much attention in the consumer behavior literature.

In this chapter we will discuss the reasons why attitude research has had such a pervasive impact on consumer behavior. We will also discuss the properties that have made attitudes so attractive to consumer researchers, as well as some of the common frustrations encountered in conducting attitude research. Particular attention will be given to a number of important models relating to the structure and composition of attitudes. Finally, we will review the approaches frequently employed to measure consumer attitudes. In Chapter 9 we will continue our discussion of attitudes by focusing on the central topics of attitude formation and attitude change, and on a number of related issues.

> *In your heart you know he's right.*
>
> POLITICAL BILLBOARD (1964)

## WHAT ARE ATTITUDES?

As the opening sentence of this chapter implies, attitudes are an expression of inner feelings that reflect whether a person is favorably or unfavorably predisposed to some "object" (e.g., a brand, a service, a retail establishment). As an outcome of some psychological processes, attitudes are not directly observable, but must be inferred from what people say or from their behavior. Consumer researchers therefore tend to assess attitudes by asking questions or making inferences from behavior. For example, if a researcher determined from questioning a consumer that the individual has consistently bought Panasonic products and recommends them to friends, the researcher would be likely to infer a positive attitude toward Panasonic products.

This illustration suggests that a whole universe of consumer behaviors—consistent purchase, recommendations to others, top rankings, beliefs, evaluations, and intentions—are related to attitudes. What, then, are attitudes? According to one popular definition, an *attitude* is *a learned predisposition to respond in a consistently favorable or unfavorable manner with respect to a given object.*[1] Each part of this definition is an important property of an attitude and is critical to understanding the role that attitudes play in the examination of consumer behavior.

### The Attitude "Object"

The word *object* in our adopted definition of attitude is designed to be interpreted broadly. Any one of many more specific concepts might be substituted in its place—issues, actions, behavior, practices, persons, or events. In examining consumer behavior, we would be inclined to substitute consumer- or marketing-related concepts, such as product category, brand, service, advertisement, price, or retailer.

In conducting attitude research, we might even be more specific. For example, if we were interested in ascertaining shoppers' attitudes toward a number of major mass merchandisers, our "object" might include Sears, J.C. Penney, and K mart; if we were examining consumer attitudes toward a number of major brands of soap, our "object" might include Dial, Ivory, Irish Spring, and Palmolive.

### Attitudes Are a Learned Predisposition

There is general agreement that attitudes are *learned.* This means that attitudes relevant to purchase behavior are formed as an outgrowth of direct experience with the product, information acquired from others, and exposure to mass media (e.g., advertising). Closely related to the idea that attitudes are learned is the realization that attitudes are not synonymous with behavior, but reflect either a favorable or an unfavorable evaluation of the attitude object. As a predisposition, attitudes might have a motivational quality; that is, they might propel the consumer *toward* a particular behavior.

## Attitudes Have Consistency

Another characteristic of an attitude is that it is relatively *consistent* with the behavior that it reflects. However, we should avoid confusing *consistency* with *permanence*. Attitudes are not necessarily permanent; they do change. We will explore attitude change in the next chapter.

It is important to illustrate what we mean by consistency. Normally we expect consumer attitudes to correspond with behavior; that is, if a segment of consumers report that they especially like Kodak film, we expect that they will buy Kodak film. Similarly, if these consumers are not particularly fond of Fuji film, we do *not* expect them to buy this brand of film. Thus, when consumers are free to act as they wish, we anticipate that their actions will be consistent with their attitudes. However, circumstances are not always uniform. Therefore we must consider the influence of the *situation* on consumer attitudes and behavior.

## Attitudes Occur Within a Situation

It is not immediately evident from our definition that attitudes occur within and are affected by the situation. *Situations* are events or circumstances that, at a point in time, influence the relationship between attitudes and behavior. A situation can cause consumers to behave in a manner seemingly inconsistent with their attitudes. For instance, let us assume that a consumer purchases a different brand of coffee each time his inventory runs low. Although his brand switching may seem to reflect a negative attitude or dissatisfaction, it actually may have been influenced by a specific situation—the need to economize. Although the consumer may have a strong preference for Maxwell House coffee, a tight budget may influence him to purchase whatever brand is on "special" at the supermarket.

The opposite is also true. If a consumer purchases a can of Brim each time her supply runs low, we may erroneously infer that she has a favorable attitude toward Brim. On the contrary, the consumer may dislike the taste of Brim but may be following doctor's orders to reduce the amount of caffeine in her diet. She therefore regards Brim favorably as a means of accomplishing this goal.

In a similar vein, individuals can have different attitudes toward a particular behavior, each corresponding to a particular situation. A man may feel it is suitable to eat lunch at McDonald's but may not consider it appropriate for dinner. In this case, McDonald's has its "time and place," which functions as a boundary indicating those situations when McDonald's is acceptable. However, if the individual is coming home late one night, feels exhausted and hungry, and spots a McDonald's, he may just decide to have "dinner" there. Why? Because it is late, he is tired and hungry, and McDonald's is convenient. Has he changed his attitude? Probably not.

In recent years, attention has been given to how consumer attitudes vary from situation to situation. For instance, one study examined whether consumer preferences for different fast-food chains operating in a midwestern city (e.g., Arby's, Burger King, McDonald's, and Wendy's) varied in terms of four eating situations (i.e., lunch on a weekday, snack during a shopping trip, evening meal when rushed for time, and evening meal with family when not rushed for time).[2] The results revealed some distinct differences in consumer preferences for the various fast-food restaurants, depending upon the anticipated eating situation. McDonald's, for example, was the frontrunner across all four eating situations, whereas Wendy's was found to be strongest with consumers who were seeking a place to have evening dinner with the family when not in a rush. The findings suggest that Wendy's might emphasize increasing consumer acceptance as a nice place to take the family for a leisurely (and inexpensive) dinner.

The lesson to be gained from each of these instances is that we must consider the situation in which the behavior takes place when measuring attitudes, or we can misinterpret the relationship between attitudes and behavior. Table 8-1 presents some additional examples of how specific situations might influence consumer attitudes toward specific brands of products or services.

## STRUCTURAL MODELS OF ATTITUDES

Now that we have defined what attitudes are and elaborated on their basic properties, it is appropriate that we examine several important attitude models: the **tricomponent attitude model**, **single-component attitude models**, and **multi-attribute attitude models**. Each of the models provides a somewhat different

**TABLE 8-1 Examples of How Situations Might Influence Attitudes**

| PRODUCT OR SERVICE | SITUATION | ATTITUDE |
|---|---|---|
| Swatch watch | Gift | "A great gift—ideal for my teenage daughter." |
| Hertz Rent-a-Car | Business trip | "They are really dependable." |
| AT&T International | Emergency call to a relative in Rome | "Easy to make a call anywhere, anytime." |
| Four Seasons Restaurant (New York City) | A special occasion | "It's your birthday, let's go to the very best in the city." |
| John Hancock Life Insurance | Birth of first child | "It's time to buy more life insurance." |
| *The Wall Street Journal* | Every weekday | "I feel bad if I miss even one day." |
| "Miami Vice" | Every Friday night | "I wouldn't miss this show." |
| White Castle hamburgers | Breakfast | "I love them, but I wouldn't eat them for breakfast." |

perspective as to the number of component parts of an attitude, and how those parts are arranged or interrelated.

## Tricomponent Attitude Model

Motivated by a desire to understand the attitude-behavior relationship, behavioral scientists, especially social psychologists, have endeavored to construct models that capture the underlying dimensions of an attitude.[3] To this end, the focus has been on specifying more precisely the composition of an attitude in order to better explain or predict behavior.

Attitudes are frequently portrayed as consisting of three major components: a cognitive component, an affective component, and a conative component (see Figure 8-1).

### THE COGNITIVE COMPONENT

The first component of the tricomponent attitude model consists of a person's knowledge *(cognitions)* and perceptions that are acquired by a combination of direct experience with the attitude-object, and related information secured from various sources. This knowledge and resulting perceptions frequently take the form of *beliefs;* that is, the consumer believes that the attitude-object possesses various attributes and that specific behavior will lead to specific outcomes.

**FIGURE 8-1** A Simple Representation of the Tricomponent Attitude Model

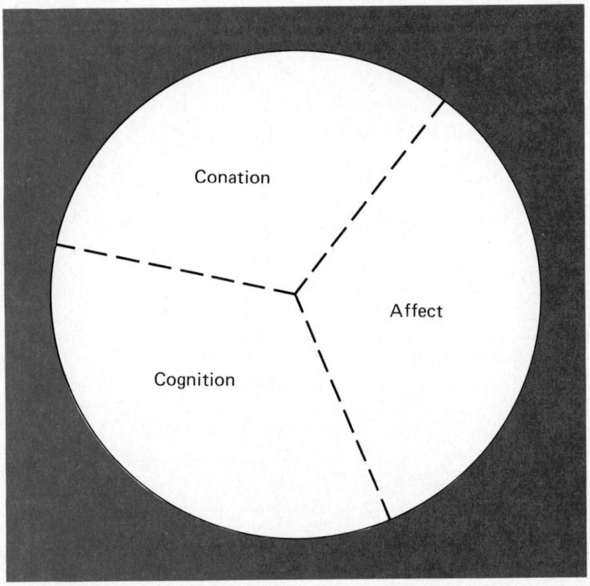

While capturing only a portion of a consumer's belief system toward two brands of mouthwash, Figure 8-2 illustrates just how complex a consumer's belief system can be. It is interesting that, with the exception of the attribute "dentist," the same basic attributes for both brands are included in the consumer's belief system. However, the beliefs about several of the attributes are different. For instance, the consumer sees Scope as tasting "sweet like a soft drink," whereas Listerine is perceived as tasting "like medicine." Also, the consumer does not necessarily evaluate the same basic belief similarly for each brand. For example, with regard to *long-lasting quality,* Scope is evaluated positively, while Listerine is evaluated negatively.

Such insights are useful in positioning a particular brand against competing brands (see the discussion of *perceptual mapping* in Chapter 6 for more detail on this topic).

## THE AFFECTIVE COMPONENT

A consumer's emotions or feelings with respect to a particular product or brand constitute the *affective* component of an attitude. These emotions and feelings are primarily *evaluative* in nature. They capture an individual's *overall*

**FIGURE 8-2** **A Consumer's Belief System for Two Different Brands of Mouthwash**

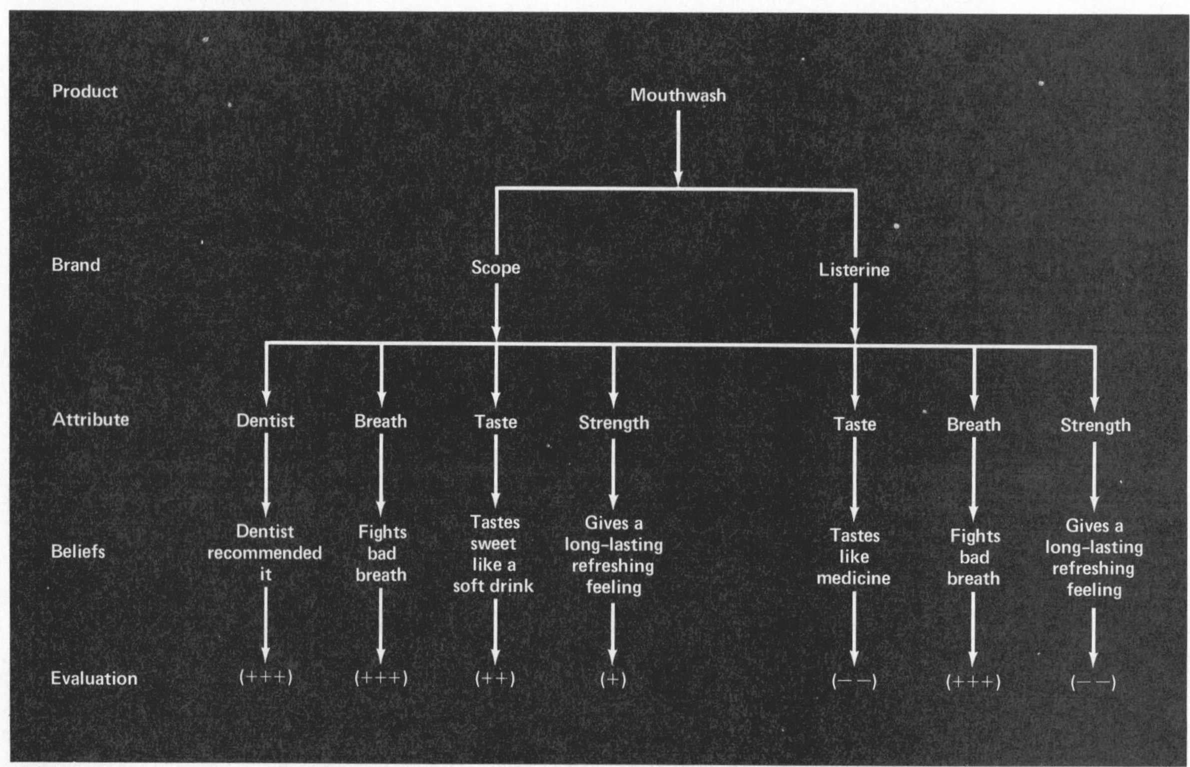

assessment of the attitude-object; that is, the extent to which the individual rates the attitude-object as favorable or unfavorable.

Since the affective component assesses overall feelings about the attitude-object, it is frequently considered the essential aspect of an attitude. Indeed, as we will discuss later, some researchers treat the affective component as being the attitude itself, and the two other components as serving some related or supportive functions.

### THE CONATIVE COMPONENT

Conation, the final component of the tricomponent attitude model, is concerned with the *likelihood* or *tendency* that an individual will undertake a specific action or behave in a particular way with regard to the attitude-object. According to some interpretations, the conative component may include the actual behavior itself.

In marketing and consumer research, the conative component is frequently treated as an expression of the consumer's *intention to buy*. Buyer intention scales are employed to assess the likelihood of purchasing a product or behaving in a certain way. Table 8-2 provides examples of a number of common intention-to-buy scales.

## Single-Component Attitude Models

In contrast to the tricomponent perspective, researchers subscribing to a single-component attitude model treat the *affective,* or feeling, component as the attitude itself.

Following this viewpoint, a consumer's attitude toward various brands of 35mm cameras would be equal to the individual's overall evaluation of the comparative merit (e.g., *good* versus *bad, positive* versus *negative, favorable* versus *unfavorable*) of the brands being considered (i.e., the consumer's **evoked set).**

**TABLE 8-2 Two Examples of Intention-to-Buy Scales**

Which of the following statements best describes the chance that you will buy a Sony compact disc player during the next 12 months?

_____ I *definitely* will buy one.
_____ I *probably* will buy one.
_____ I am *uncertain* if I will buy one.
_____ I *probably will not* buy one.
_____ I *definitely will not* buy one.

How likely are you to buy a Sony compact disc player during the next 12 months?

_____ Very likely
_____ Likely
_____ Unlikely
_____ Very unlikely

The single-component attitude model is especially popular with marketing researchers who want to save time and space by including a single evaluative scale on a questionnaire.[4] However, although it is uncomplicated, the single-component model fails to provide useful insights as to what influences or explains a consumer's evaluative rating. To illustrate, two consumers may possess the same positive attitude (i.e., the same level of affect) toward Dial soap, with quite different salient beliefs. One may like it because of its deodorant protection, while the other may like it because of its pleasant fragrance. Unless the researcher measured each consumer's beliefs and evaluations about each attribute of Dial, all that would be known is that both possess the same basic attitude or level of affect toward Dial soap. Thus we would be left in the dark as to the underlying knowledge and beliefs the consumers bring to bear in arriving at their overall assessment. Moreover, we would not be provided with any relevant insights about the relationship between their evaluations and the consumers' intention to buy.

To overcome the shortcomings of the single-component attitude model, attitude researchers have suggested a compromise between the broadly conceived tricomponent attitude model and the narrowly focused single-component model. The resulting **modified single-component attitude model** still considers *affect* to be the attitude, but includes *cognition* and *conation* as interrelated and important factors that influence the affective component (see Figure 8-3). In a sense, the modified model is a *rearrangement* of the tricomponent model—with the affect component treated as the attitude, and the two other components downgraded to supporting roles.

Modified single-component attitude models are also called **multi-attribute attitude models**.

## Multi-Attribute Attitude Models

Multi-attribute attitude models are particularly appealing to both consumer researchers and marketing practitioners because they examine attitudes in terms of selected product attributes or beliefs.[5] While there are many variations of

**FIGURE 8-3** **A Modified Single-Component Attitude Model** Source: Adapted from Richard J. Lutz, "The Role of Attitude Theory in Marketing," in Harold H. Kassarjian and Thomas S. Robertson, eds., *Perspectives in Consumer Behavior,* 3rd ed. (Glenview, Ill.: Scott, Foresman, 1981), 235.

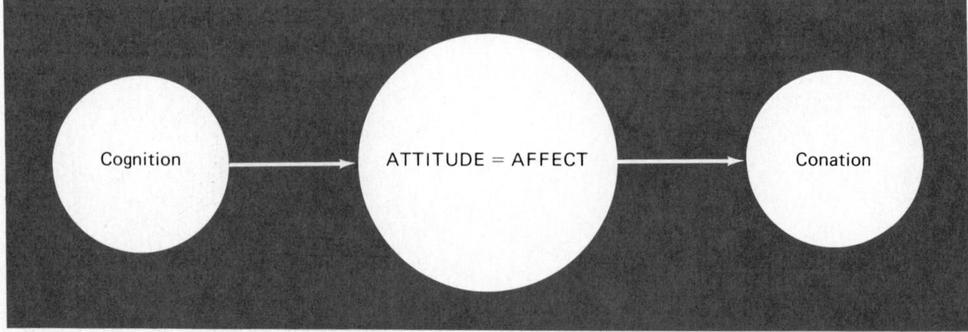

this type of attitude model, those proposed by Fishbein and his associates have stimulated the greatest amount of research interest.[6] We have selected three Fishbein models to consider here because of their potential merit in applied consumer behavior research: the **attitude-toward-object** model, the **attitude-toward-behavior** model, and the **theory of reasoned action** model.

### THE ATTITUDE-TOWARD-OBJECT MODEL

The attitude-toward-object model is especially suitable for measuring attitudes toward a *product* or specific *brands* (i.e., the object).[7] In accordance with this model, a consumer's attitude is defined as a function of the presence (or absence) *and* evaluation of a number of product-specific beliefs or product attributes possibly possessed by a product or specific brands of a product. Following from this, consumers will generally have favorable attitudes toward those brands they assess as having an adequate level of positive attributes, and unfavorable attitudes toward those brands they feel have an inadequate level of desired attributes or too many negative attributes. Table 8-3 lists two different belief systems (one favorable and the other unfavorable) for two different consumers.

The Fishbein *attitude-toward-object* model is usually depicted in the form of the following equation:[8]

$$\text{Attitude}_0 = \sum_{i=1}^{n} b_i e_i$$

where $\text{Attitude}_0$ is a separately assessed overall measure of *affect* for or against the attitude-object (e.g., a product, brand, service, retail establishment); $b_i$ is the *strength* of the belief that the attitude-object contains the $i$th attribute (e.g., the likelihood that Duncan Hines cake mix tastes "homemade"); $e_i$ is the evaluative dimension associated with the $i$th attribute (e.g., how good or bad is the quality of being "homemade"); and $\Sigma$ indicates that there are $n$ salient attributes over which the $b_i$ and $e_i$ combinations are summated.

**TABLE 8-3 Two Hypothetical Belief Systems Concerning IBM Personal Computers**

Consumer 1 (mainly negative)

IBM PCs are expensive.
IBM PCs are too complex.
IBM PCs are used by businesses.
IBM PCs are high quality.

Consumer 2 (mainly positive)

IBM PCs are high quality.
IBM PCs are dependable.
IBM PCs are used by businesses.
IBM PCs are worth the investment.

Source: Inspired by Icek Ajzen and Martin Fishbein, *Understanding Attitudes and Predicting Social Behavior* (Englewood Cliffs, N.J.: Prentice Hall, 1980), 63.

Before moving on to the next model proposed by Fishbein and his colleagues, it should be pointed out that numerous modified versions of the Fishbein attitude-toward-object model have been suggested in the consumer behavior and marketing literature.[9] These models, which have been referred to as "ad hoc" or "intuitive," frequently examine the relationship between some overall evaluation of a brand (e.g., preference, affect, intention, or brand choice) and a combination of consumer beliefs as to the brand's possession of specific product attributes and the importance attached to these attributes. As a group, these intuitive models can be criticized for not faithfully testing the attitude models that were borrowed from social psychology.

## THE ATTITUDE-TOWARD-BEHAVIOR MODEL

The focus of Fishbein's attitude-toward-behavior model is the individual's *attitude toward behaving or acting with respect to an object,* rather than the attitude toward the object itself.

The appeal of the attitude-toward-behavior model is that it seems to correspond more closely with actual behavior than does the attitude-toward-object model. For instance, knowing a consumer's attitude about the act of *purchasing* a $40,000 BMW car (i.e., attitude toward the behavior) is more revealing about the potential act of purchasing than simply knowing the consumer's attitude toward the car (i.e., attitude toward the object). This seems logical, for a consumer might have a positive attitude toward the $40,000 car, but a negative attitude as to the prospects of purchasing such an expensive automobile.

The attitude-toward-behavior model is depicted by the following equation:[10]

$$\text{Attitude}_{(\text{beh})} = \sum_{i=1}^{n} b_i e_i$$

where Attitude $_{(\text{beh})}$ is a separately assessed overall measure of affect for or against carrying out a specific action or behavior (e.g., buying, preparing, or serving a Duncan Hines cake); $b_i$ is the *strength* of the belief that an *i*th specific action will lead to a specific outcome (e.g., that the preparation of a Duncan Hines cake will indeed taste "homemade"); $e_i$ is an evaluation of the *i*th outcome (e.g., the "favorableness" of a cake tasting homemade); and $\Sigma$ indicates that there are *n* salient outcomes over which the $b_i$ and $e_i$ combinations are summated.[11]

## THEORY OF REASONED ACTION MODEL

The *theory of reasoned action* builds on the earlier research conducted by Fishbein and his associates. It represents a comprehensive arrangement of attitude components integrated into a structure that is designed to lead to both better prediction and better explanations of behavior. Like the basic tricomponent attitude model, the theory of reasoned action incorporates a *cognitive* component, an *affective* component, and a *conative* component; however, these are arranged in a pattern different from that of the tricomponent model.

Figure 8-4 is a model of the theory of reasoned action. Examine it carefully. Working backward from *behavior* (e.g., the act of purchasing a particular product or brand), the model suggests that the best predictor of behavior is *intention to act*. Thus if consumer researchers were solely interested in predicting behavior, they would directly measure intention (i.e., use an intention-to-act scale). However, if they were also interested in understanding the underlying factors that contribute to intention to act in a particular consumer situation, they would look behind intention and consider the factors that lead to intention; that is, the consumer's *attitude-toward-behavior* and the *subjective norm*.

Continuing with the same basic logic, attitude-toward-behavior can be directly measured as *affect* (i.e., a measure of overall favorability toward the act of purchasing a product or brand). Further, as with intention, we can get behind the attitude to its underlying dimensions (see the discussion of the attitude-toward-behavior model).

**FIGURE 8-4** **A Simplified Version of the Theory of Reasoned Action**
Source: Adapted from Icek Ajzen and Martin Fishbein, *Understanding Attitudes and Predicting Social Behavior* (Englewood Cliffs, N.J.: Prentice-Hall, 1980), 84.

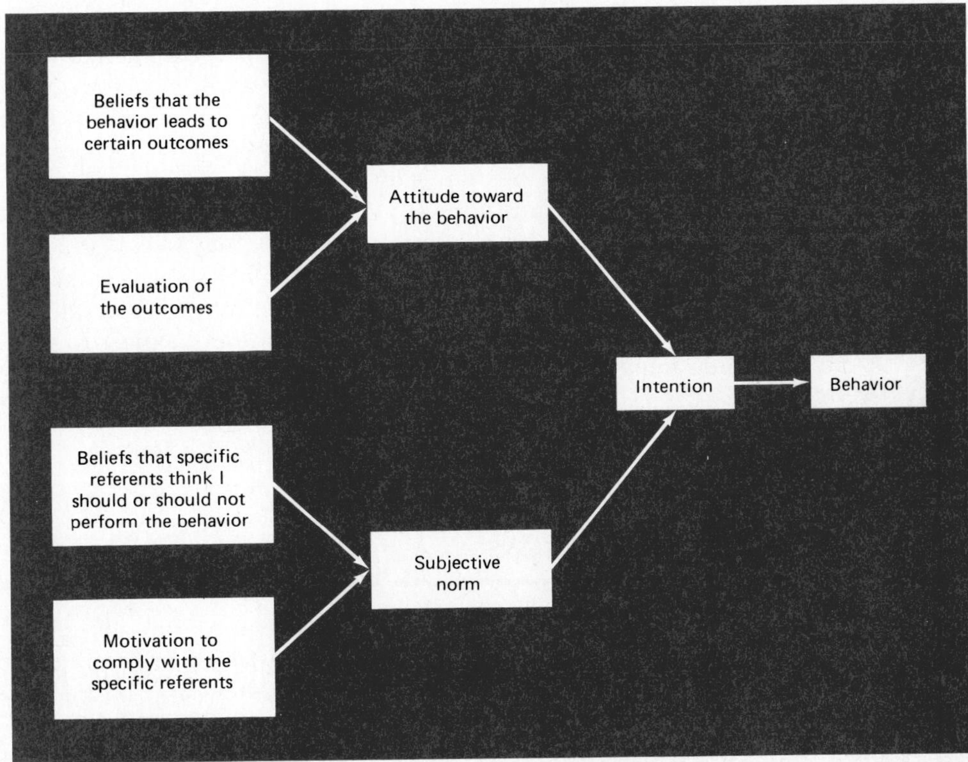

In accordance with this expanded model, to understand intention we must also measure the *subjective norm* that influences an individual's intention to act. A subjective norm can be measured directly by assessing a consumer's feelings as to what relevant others (family, friends, roommates, co-workers) would think of the action being contemplated; that is, would they look favorably or unfavorably on the anticipated action? Within a consumer behavior context, if a college student were considering purchasing micro-stereo equipment for his dormitory room and stopped to ask himself what his parents or roommate would think of such behavior (i.e., approve or disapprove), such a reflection would constitute his subjective norm.

As with an attitude, consumer researchers can get behind the subjective norm to the underlying factors that are likely to produce it. They accomplish this by assessing the *normative beliefs* that the individual attributes to relevant others, as well as the individual's *motivation to comply* with each of the relevant others. For instance, consider the student who is contemplating the purchase of micro-stereo equipment. To understand his subjective norm about the anticipated purchase, we would have to identify his relevant others (parents and roommate); his beliefs as to how each would respond to his purchase of the equipment (e.g., "Mom and Dad would consider the purchase extravagant, but my roommate would love it"); and finally, his motivation to comply with his parents and/or roommate.

The above discussion and examples suggest that the theory of reasoned action is a series of interrelated attitude components (i.e., beliefs precede attitude and normative beliefs precede subjective norms; attitudes and subjective norms precede intention; and intention precedes actual behavior).[12]

Consistent with the theory of reasoned action, an attitude is not as strongly or as directly linked to behavior as intention is linked to behavior. In part, this flows from the observation that intention is usually more highly associated with behavior than is attitude.

Why study attitudes at all, if intention is ultimately a better predictor of behavior? The answer is simple: *Intention* may be a better predictor, but it does not provide an adequate explanation of behavior. If marketers want to understand *why* consumers act as they do, they require something more than a basically mechanical measure of what consumers expect to do (e.g., their buying intentions). Similarly, a measure of *affect* may predict an attitude; however, marketers usually want to know the underlying or salient attributes or beliefs that produce the specific attitude.

## THE MEASUREMENT OF ATTITUDES

Now that we have explored the structure of various attitude models, let us briefly examine several attitude measurement approaches frequently employed to determine consumer attitudes: **observation and inference, qualitative research methods,** and **self-report attitude scales.**

## Observation of Behavior

Since we cannot get inside consumers' heads to observe their attitudes directly, we must rely on *indirect* measures of attitudes. One such measurement approach is to observe consumers' behavior and to infer their attitudes from their behavior. (Chapter 3 discussed observation and inference in connection with the measurement of motives.)

The practice of inferring attitudes from behavior is done constantly, not only by professional researchers, but by each of us in the course of our daily lives. For instance, if you were to observe that the person ahead of you on the supermarket checkout line was buying five cans of Bumble Bee tuna, you might conclude that several members of the shopper's family liked the brand.

In much the same way as you might informally observe and draw conclusions from another's behavior, so do professional researchers observe behavior. The difference is that they are *trained observers* and they scrutinize consumer behavior in order to draw conclusions that will become part of a research report.

Although observational research is quite useful, drawing conclusions about consumers' attitudes from their behavior is often quite difficult and very likely to be subjective. For instance, the shopper who was observed purchasing five cans of tuna fish might have done so to take advantage of the store's special low price, rather than because family members particularly liked the brand.

It is difficult for an observer, even a highly trained one, to be confident about inferring attitudes from a single action, in a single situation. However, if the researcher were to observe the same behavior at different points in time (e.g., see the same shopper purchase the same brand of tuna fish on subsequent trips to the supermarket), or see the shopper purchase the tuna fish under different circumstances (e.g., when the brand was *not* on store special), then the researcher might be more confident that the behavior reflected a positive attitude. Since researchers seldom have the opportunity to observe the same consumers repeatedly, it is common practice to employ observations as a supplement to other research approaches, rather than as the primary research method.

## Qualitative Research Methods

Attitude researchers have found qualitative research methods, especially *depth interviews* and *focus group* sessions, to be very useful in understanding the nature of consumers' attitudes.

While these two research methods differ in composition (see Chapter 3), both are closely associated with motivational research and have their roots in the psychoanalytic and clinical aspects of psychology. In particular, both stress open-ended and free-response types of questioning that stimulate respondents to reveal their inner thoughts and beliefs.

These two popular qualitative research methods are regularly employed in the early stages of attitude research to pinpoint relevant product-related beliefs or attributes. To illustrate, let us assume that as a result of several focus group sessions, a leading marketer of erasable ballpoint pens notices that users are more interested in the ease of erasing errors than in the longevity of the pen. This finding suggests that the pen company, in advertising its pen, should stress the ease of erasing errors, rather than the long life of the pen.

As the illustration implies, depth interviews and focus groups are frequently conducted to determine which product or brand attributes potential product users are likely to use in judging alternative brands. Table 8-4 lists a sample of product attributes associated with four different product categories. Such lists of attributes are often developed from depth interviews, focus group sessions, and related forms of qualitative research.

To provide a still better understanding of how qualitative research methods are used to develop an initial picture of consumer attitudes (especially the beliefs and attributes they associate with particular products and services), Figure 8-5 presents a portion of a discussion guide. Such a guide might be employed in a focus group session to gain insights into the attitudes of brokerage customers toward various brokerage firms and their services, and their attitudes about a proposed new financial service (one not shown in Figure 8-5).

## Self-Report Attitude Scales

The most common way of assessing consumer attitudes is through the administration of a questionnaire containing *attitude scales.* While a great many attitude-scaling procedures have been proposed, the three most popular are **Likert scales, semantic differential scales,** and **rank-order scales.**[13]

### LIKERT SCALES

The *Likert* scale is by far the most popular form of attitude scaling because it is easy for researchers to prepare and uncomplicated for consumers to respond. Likert scales can be recognized by their characteristic "agreement" scale, which provides respondents with the opportunity to indicate their degree of agreement or disagreement with a series of statements that fully describe the attitude-object under investigation. Figure 8-6 presents a sample of Likert scales as they were employed in a consumer attitude survey of flea market shopping experiences.

A principal attraction of Likert scales is that they give researchers the option of treating the response to each attitude statement as a separate scale, or combining the responses of items that pertain to the same basic attitude dimension into a composite or weighted attitude score. It is because of this feature that Likert scales are frequently referred to as *summated scales.*

### SEMANTIC DIFFERENTIAL SCALES

Similar to the Likert scale, the *semantic differential* scale is relatively easy to construct and administer. The scale typically consists of a series of bipolar antonyms (adjectives or phrases, such as good-bad, liberal-conservative, like-dis-

**TABLE 8-4 Examples of Product Attributes Associated with Four Different Product Categories**

mouthwash:

- effective against colds and sore throats
- gives long-lasting protection
- effective for killing germs
- recommended by dentists
- effective against bad breath
- leaves mouth feeling refreshed
- not too strong tasting
- effective for relief of gum trouble
- leaves no unpleasant after-taste
- pleasant flavor

juice drinks:

- convenient
- children can drink as much as they like
- excellent source of Vitamin C
- great wake-up taste
- cost-per-serving
- nutritional
- high fresh-fruit content
- appealing taste
- uniquely suitable for children
- significant contribution to diet

household disinfectant:

- kills flu virus
- prevents spread of colds
- eliminates significant number of germs and viruses
- medically beneficial in reducing spread of colds
- kills germs on environmental surfaces
- reduces incidence of colds
- eliminates odor
- kills germs that cause illnesses
- protects your family
- kills viruses and germs in the air

washing machines:

- variable wash and spin speeds
- wash water temperature control
- frequency of repair record
- variable fill levels
- rinse-water temperature control
- detergent requirements
- availability of repair service
- guarantee
- price
- maximum load capacity

Source: Winifred A. Adams, "Evaluation of an Expectancy Screening Model for Federal Trade Commission Reviews of Advertising Deception," in John C. Maloney and Bernard Silverman, eds., *Attitude Research Plays for High Stakes* (Chicago: American Marketing Association, 1979), 357.

like, sweet-sour, high priced-low priced) which, when anchored at the ends of a 5-point or 7-point scale, provide respondents with an opportunity to evaluate a concept (e.g., United Airlines, 7-Eleven stores, All-Temperature Cheer). The major feature of the semantic differential is that it lends itself to the creation of profiles of consumer attitudes that can be depicted in graphic form.

FIGURE 8-5 Selected Portions of a Discussion Guide

PERSONAL FINANCIAL SERVICES STUDY

I. INTRODUCTION

A. What do you like ( and dislike) about the various financial services that you have accounts with? Which is your primary brokerage house? Why?
B. What would it take to get you to change brokers?
C. List the services and accounts that a "perfect" or "ideal'" brokerage house would provide you.

.
.
.

V. REACTIONS TO THE PROPOSED BROKERAGE SERVICE

(Read aloud with group following along; and probe each area of exploration)

A. Does anything need clarification?
B. Overall reaction
C. Specific likes/dislikes
D. Possible improvements/modifications (make better)
E. Occasion and frequency of use
F. Which brokerage houses in this area would be most likely to be first to offer this service/account? Why?
G. Would it encourage you to switch brokerage houses? Why/why not?)

VI. OTHER SECTIONS OF THE GUIDE

.
.
.

A popular application of the semantic differential scaling procedure is in the examination of shoppers' attitudes toward competitive retail establishments. Such studies are frequently referred to as *store image studies.* Figure 8-7 presents a semantic differential instrument used in an actual store image study. The findings superimposed on the instrument in graphic form have been partitioned into two groups ("shoppers" and "buyers") for each of the two types of stores compared (retailer A—a traditional full-line department store, and retailer B—a promotional furniture and appliance store.)

## RANK-ORDER SCALES

As its name implies, a *rank-order scale* has subjects rank a set of attitude-objects (e.g., brands of peanut butter) in terms of some criterion (e.g., fresh taste). Rank-order scaling procedures are especially suitable in attitude measurement because they allow consumers to evaluate alternative brands, and thus they are an important way of assessing brand preference or brand choice. Figure 8-8 shows how the rank-order scale is utilized in consumer attitude research.

**FIGURE 8-6** **An Application of Likert Scales to Assess Consumer Attitudes Toward Shopping at Flea Markets** Source: Elaine Sherman, Kevin McCrohan, and James D. Smith, "Informal Retailing: An Analysis of Products, Attitudes and Expectations," in Elizabeth C. Hirschman and Morris B. Holbrook, eds., *Advances in Consumer Research* (Provo, UT: Association for Consumer Research, 1985), 12, 206.

Instruction:

Please place an "X" in the space which best indicates how strongly you agree or disagree with each of the following statements about your experiences in shopping at flea markets.

| | Agree Strongly | Agree | Neither Agree nor Disagree | Disagree | Disagree Strongly |
|---|---|---|---|---|---|
| It is fun to shop at a flea market | ______ | ______ | ______ | ______ | ______ |
| Products often cost more than they are worth | ______ | ______ | ______ | ______ | ______ |
| It is a good place to meet my friends and neighbors | ______ | ______ | ______ | ______ | ______ |
| Many of the sellers are rude and aggressive | ______ | ______ | ______ | ______ | ______ |
| There is no waiting for delivery | ______ | ______ | ______ | ______ | ______ |
| Most flea markets are difficult to reach | ______ | ______ | ______ | ______ | ______ |
| There are no taxes to be paid | ______ | ______ | ______ | ______ | ______ |

**FIGURE 8-7** **An Example of Image Profiles That Can Be Constructed with Semantic Differential Scales** Source: G.H.G. McDougall and J.N. Fry, "Combining Two Methods of Image Measurement," *Journal of Retailing*, 50 (Winter 1974-75), 60.

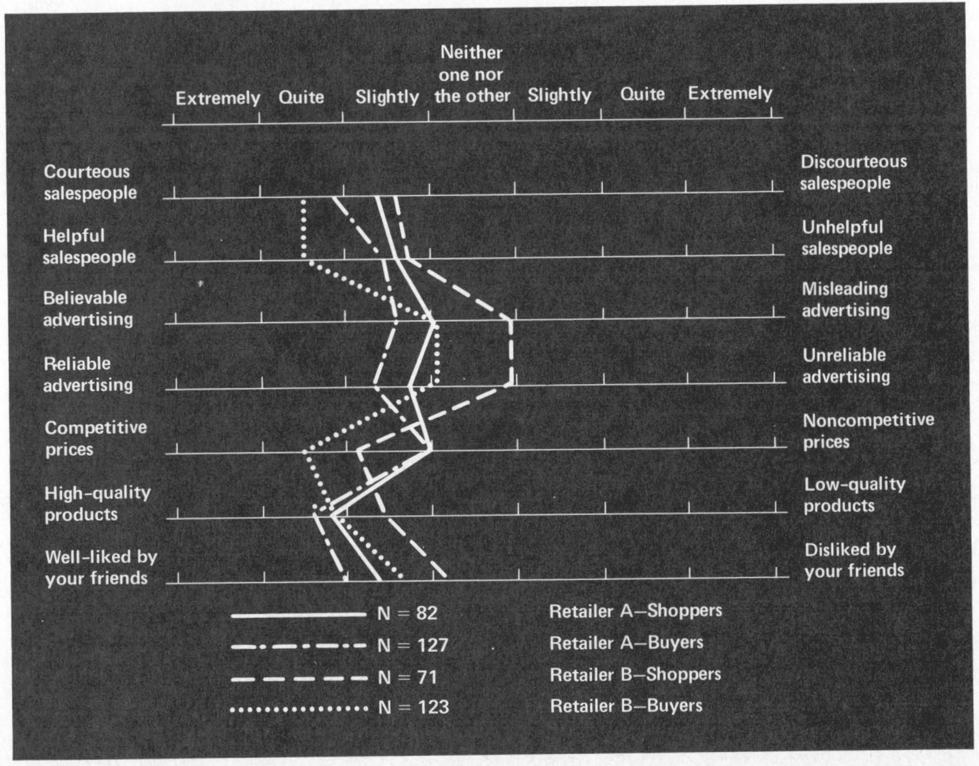

FIGURE 8-8 Examples of Rank-Order Scales Used in Attitude Research

A. The following are six brands of candy bars. We are interested in learning your preference for each of these brands. Place a 1 alongside the brand that you would be most likely to buy, a 2 alongside the brand that you would be next most likely to buy. Continue doing this until you have ranked all six brands.

_____ Hershey chocolate bar

_____ Snickers

_____ Three Musketeers

_____ M&Ms

_____ Mounds

_____ Twix

B. Rank the following electric razors from 1 to 6 in terms of closeness of shave.

_____ Remington

_____ Norelco

_____ Shick

_____ Braun

_____ Panasonic

_____ Ronson

C. We're interested in knowing how much you enjoy each of the following four types of TV professional sports programs. Please rank them from 1 to 4, where a 1 means that you enjoy it the most and 4 means that you enjoy it least.

_____ Baseball

_____ Football

_____ Basketball

_____ Hockey

## *summary*

An attitude is a learned predisposition to respond in a consistently favorable or unfavorable manner with respect to a given object (e.g., a product category, a brand, a service, an advertisement, or a retail establishment). Each property of this definition is critical for understanding why and how attitudes are relevant in consumer behavior and marketing.

Of considerable importance in understanding the role of attitudes in consumer behavior is an appreciation of the structure and composition of an attitude. Three broad categories of attitude models have received attention: the tricomponent attitude model, single-component attitude models, and multi-attribute attitude models.

The tricomponent model of attitudes consists of three parts: a cognitive component, an affective component, and a conative component. The cognitive component captures a consumer's knowledge and perceptions (frequently in the form of beliefs) about products and services. In contrast, the affective component focuses on a consumer's emotions or feelings with respect to a particular product or service. Evaluative in nature, the affective component ascertains an individual's overall assessment of the attitude-object in terms of some kind of rating of favorableness. Finally, the conative component is concerned with the likelihood or tendency that a consumer will act in a specific fashion with respect to the attitude-object. In marketing and consumer behavior, the conative component is frequently measured in terms of a consumer's intention to buy.

Single-component attitude models depict an attitude as consisting of just one overall affective (feeling) component. In this case, the cognitive and conative components either are ignored or play a more supportive secondary role. As popular extensions of single-component attitude models, multi-attribute attitude models have received much attention from consumer researchers. As a group, these models examine consumer beliefs about specific product attributes (e.g., product or brand features or benefits). In particular, three multi-attribute models (i.e., attitude-toward-object, attitude-toward-behavior, and the theory of reasoned action), each proposed by Fishbein and his associates, tend to represent the present "state of the art" in applying attitude models to consumer behavior problems.

The measurement of attitudes is accomplished by observation and inference, qualitative research methods (especially focus group sessions and depth interviews), and a variety of self-report attitude scales (notably Likert scales, semantic differential scales, and rank-order scales).

## *discussion questions*

1. Explain how situational factors are likely to influence the degree of consistency between attitudes and behavior.
2. Considering the examples presented in Table 8-4, what attributes do you associate with college textbooks?
3. Since attitudes are learned predispositions to respond, why don't marketers and consumer researchers just measure purchasing behavior and forget attitudes?

4. Develop a 10-item semantic differential scale that would be appropriate for the assessment of attitudes toward Chevrolet's Corvette automobile.
5. Explain a person's possible attitude toward eating at a fast-food establishment in terms of the tricomponent attitude model.
6. Why might the attitude-toward-object model discussed in this chapter be appropriate for Sears to use in assessing attitudes toward their models of 19-inch color televisions?
7. Under what conditions might a researcher employ focus group sessions rather than Likert or semantic differential scales?
8. What are the potential limitations of attempting to ascertain consumer attitudes from observing behavior?

## endnotes

1. Martin Fishbein and Icek Ajzen, *Belief, Attitude, Intention, and Behavior* (Reading, Mass.: Addison-Wesley, 1975), 6.
2. Kenneth E. Miller and James L. Ginter, "An Investigation of Situational Variations in Brand Choice Behavior and Attitude," *Journal of Marketing Research,*16 (February 1979), 111–23.
3. George S. Day, "Theories of Attitude Structure and Change," in Scott Ward and Thomas S. Robertson, eds., *Consumer Behavior: Theoretical Sources* (Englewood Cliffs, N.J.: Prentice-Hall, 1973), 303–53; and Richard J. Lutz, "The Role of Attitude Theory in Marketing," in Harold H. Kassarjian and Thomas S. Robertson, eds., *Perspectives in Consumer Behavior,* 3rd ed. (Glenview, Ill.: Scott Foresman, 1981), 233–50.
4. Russell I. Haley and Peter B. Case, "Testing Thirteen Attitude Scales for Agreement and Brand Discrimination," *Journal of Marketing,* 43 (Fall 1979), 21–30.
5. Richard J. Lutz and James R. Bettman, "Multi-Attribute Models in Marketing: A Bicentennial Review," in Arch G. Woodside et al., eds., *Consumer and Industrial Buying Behavior* (New York: North-Holland, 1977), 137-49.
6. Icek Ajzen and Martin Fishbein, *Understanding Attitudes and Predicting Social Behavior* (Englewood Cliffs, N.J.: Prentice-Hall, 1980); and Fishbein and Ajzen, *Belief, Attitude, Intention, and Behavior.*
7. Martin Fishbein, "An Investigation of the Relationships between Beliefs about an Object and the Attitude toward the Object," *Human Relations,* 16 (1963), 233–40; and Martin Fishbein, "A Behavioral Theory Approach to the Relations between Beliefs about an Object and the Attitude toward the Object," in Martin Fisbein, ed., *Readings in Attitude Theory and Measurement* (New York: Wiley, 1967), 389–400.
8. Fishbein and Ajzen, *Belief, Attitude, Intention, and Behavior,* 223.
9. For excellent reviews, see William L. Wilkie and Edgar A. Pessemier, "Issues in Marketing's Use of Multi-Attribute Attitude Models," *Journal of Marketing Research,* 10 (November 1973), 428–41; and Lutz and Bettman, "Multi-Attribute Models in Marketing," 137–49.
10. Ajzen and Fishbein, *Understanding Attitudes,* 62–73.
11. For marketing applications, see Michael J. Ryan and Michael J. Etzel, "The Nature of Salient Outcomes and Referents in the Extended Model," in Beverlee B. Anderson, ed., *Advances in Consumer Research* (Atlanta: Association for Consumer Re-

search, 1976), III, 485–90; Michael J. Ryan and E. H. Bonfield, "Fishbein's Intentions Model: A Twist of External and Pragmatic Validity, *Journal of Marketing,* 44 (Spring 1980), 82–95; and Paul R. Warshaw, "A New Model for Predicting Behavioral Intentions: An Alternative to Fishbein," *Journal of Marketing Research,* 17 (May 1980), 153–72.

12. Terence A. Shimp and Alican Kavas, "The Theory of Reasoned Action Applied to Coupon Usage," *Journal of Consumer Research,* 11 (December 1984), 795–809; Barbara Loken, "The Theory of Reasoned Action: Examination of the Sufficiency Assumption for a Television Viewing Behavior," in Richard P. Bagozzi and Alice M. Tybout, eds., *Advances in Consumer Research* (Ann Arbor: Association for consumer Research, 1983), X, 100–5; and Uday Tate and Terry Ball, "Attitude-Intention-Behavior Relations: An Examination of the Theory of Reasoned Action," in Patrick E. Murphy et al., eds., *1983 AMA Educator's Proceedings* (Chicago: American Marketing Association, 1983), 83–87.

13. E. H. Bonfield, "A Comment on the State of Attitude Measurement in Consumer Research: A Polemic," in William L. Wilkie, ed., *Advances in Consumer Research* (Ann Arbor, Mich.: Association for Consumer Research, 1979), VI, 238–44.

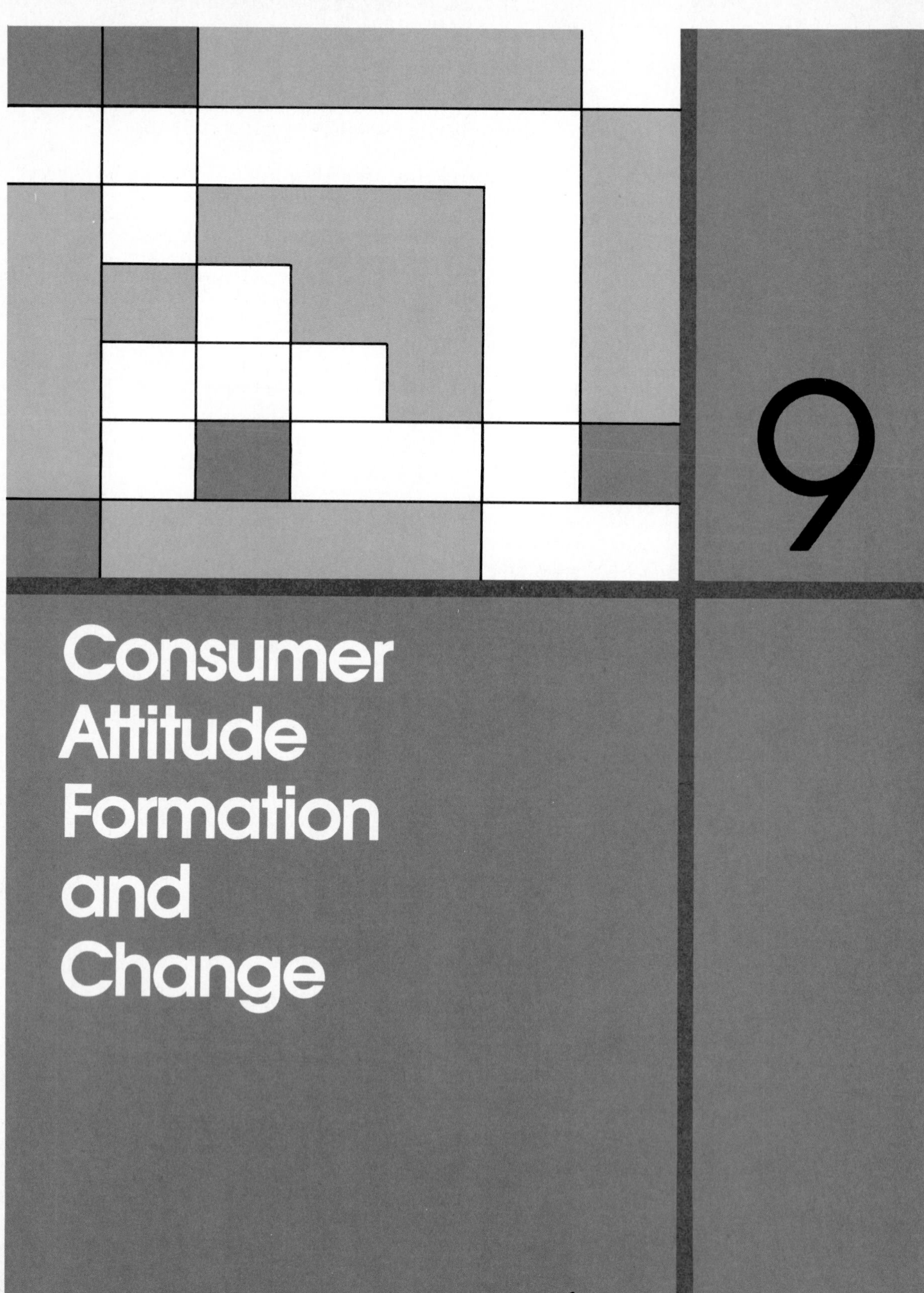

# 9

# Consumer Attitude Formation and Change

## *introduction*

THIS chapter continues the discussion of attitudes begun in Chapter 8. While the preceding chapter defined what we mean by an attitude and explored its various properties—including an examination of several attitude models and attitude measurement techniques—this chapter focuses on the important topics of **attitude formation** and **attitude change.** Moreover, as an outgrowth of our exploration of attitude change, we will consider **cognitive dissonance** theory and **attribution** theory, two different perspectives on how attitude change follows behavior. The chapter concludes with a brief discussion of consumer involvement theory as a framework for understanding when attitudes are likely to precede or follow behavior.

## ATTITUDE FORMATION

How do young people form their initial attitudes toward using computers in general, and Apple, AT&T, or IBM computers in particular? How do family members and friends, admired celebrities, and mass media advertising influence the establishment of attitudes about owning and using personal computers? Why do some attitudes seem to be maintained indefinitely (e.g., a positive attitude toward a particular political party)? The answers to such questions are important to marketers, for unless they have some idea of *how* attitudes are formed, they are unlikely to be able to understand or affect consumer attitudes or behavior.

> *A man bears beliefs as a tree bears apples.*
>
> EMERSON
> *Worship*

Our examination of attitude formation is divided into three areas: the *learning* of attitudes, the *sources of influence* on attitude formation, and the *impact of personality* on attitude formation.

## Learning of Attitudes

When we speak of the formation of an attitude, we are referring to the shift from *no* attitude toward a given object (e.g., a banana) to *some* attitude toward it (e.g., a banana is a fruit to put in breakfast cereal). To understand this shift *(attitude formation)* requires an appreciation of the basic learning processes involved. We will briefly focus on how attitudes are learned by considering how the learning theories discussed in Chapter 6 relate to attitude formation.

### CLASSICAL CONDITIONING

An originally neutral stimulus, such as the brand name for a new product, can produce a favorable or unfavorable attitude if it is repeatedly followed by or associated with a reward or punishment. The idea of family branding is based on this form of attitude learning; by giving a new brand of perfume, Coco, the benefit of a well-known and respected family name—Chanel perfume—the marketers are counting on an extension of the favorable attitude already associated with the Chanel brand name to the new product.

Similarly, marketers who associate their new products with well-known and respected celebrities are trying to create a positive bond between the celebrity who already enjoys a positive attitude and the "neutral" new product. They hope to transfer recognition and goodwill from the celebrity to their product so that potential consumers will more quickly acquire a positive attitude toward the new product. This is the theory on which licensing (discussed in Chapter 7) is based.

### INSTRUMENTAL CONDITIONING

Consumers can purchase a brand *without* having an attitude toward it. They may buy a brand, for instance, because it is the only product of its kind left on a store shelf; or they may make a trial purchase of a new brand from a product category they feel does not warrant more information than an awareness of its existence. If they find the brand satisfactory, they may eventually develop a favorable attitude toward the brand.

### COGNITIVE LEARNING THEORY

In situations where consumers are quite involved in a purchase decision, cognitions (knowledge and beliefs) are likely to be a major input in the formation of attitudes. If a shopper who is interested in a new video camera learns that automatic focusing and low light level capability are two essential attributes of a fine-quality video camera, and that certain of Panasonic's video cameras possess these two features, then the shopper could be expected to form a positive attitude toward Panasonic video cameras. Generally speaking, the more information (up to a point) an individual has about a product or service, the more likely he or she is to have an attitude toward it—either positive or negative.

### INFORMATION PROCESSING

As an outgrowth of cognitive learning theory, the focus of the information-processing framework centers on the *limits* of consumers' abilities or interests to process purchase-related information. Consumers often use only a relatively small amount of the information available to them. Experimental research suggests that the summation of the three most important beliefs about a product dominates when it comes to the formation of attitudes, and that less important beliefs provide little additional input.[1]

## Sources of Influence in Attitude Formation

Although learning theories tell us how attitudes may be established, identification of the sources from which consumers obtain information, advice, and influence is also important. The principal sources that affect the formation of consumer attitudes include *experience, personal influence,* and *mass media.*

### DIRECT AND PAST EXPERIENCE

The primary means by which attitudes are formed toward goods and services are through the direct experience of trying and evaluating them. Recognizing the importance of direct experience, marketers frequently attempt to stimulate trial of new products by offering cents-off coupons or even free-trial samples. Their objective is to get consumers to experience the new product and then to evaluate it. If a product proves satisfactory, it is likely that consumers will form positive attitudes and possibly purchase the product when they again have need of it.

### PERSONAL INFLUENCE

As we come in contact with others, especially family, close friends, and admired individuals (e.g., a respected teacher), we acquire attitudes that influence our lives. The family is an extremely important source of influence when it comes to the establishment of attitudes, for it is the family that provides us with many of our basic values and a wide range of less central beliefs. For instance, children growing up in France might initially dislike wine as a beverage; but by observing other family members, they generally learn to enjoy it with most of their meals.[2] In a similar manner, young American children who are exposed to sweet foods and candy as part of their daily diet often retain a taste for (and positive attitude toward) sweets as adults.

#### EXPOSURE TO MASS MEDIA

It seems inevitable that in a country where people have easy access to newspapers and an almost infinite variety of general and special-interest magazines and television and cable channels, mass media advertising would be an important source of information to influence our attitudes.

### Personality Factors

In addition to recognizing the critical role that learning theory plays in the understanding of attitude formation and the contribution that various sources of information make in influencing consumer attitudes, it is also important to realize that personality plays an important role in attitude formation. Introverted individuals, for instance, are likely to express their introversion in negative attitudes toward flashy cars, dancing classes, group tours, and public activities. Similarly, consumer attitudes toward new products and new consumption situations are strongly influenced by their own personality characteristics.

## ATTITUDE CHANGE

As we begin our discussion of attitude change, it is important to recognize that what we have said about attitude formation is also basically true of attitude change. That is, attitude changes are *learned,* they are influenced by *personal experience* and other *sources of information,* and *personality* affects both the receptivity and the speed with which attitudes are likely to be altered.

### Strategies of Attitude Change

Altering consumer attitudes is a key strategy consideration for most marketers. If a marketer is in the fortunate position of having its brand possess the lion's share of the market, the overriding goal is likely to be to *fortify* the existing positive attitudes of its customers so that they will not succumb to the blandishments of competitors and defect. For instance, in product categories like yogurt, where the Dannon brand has dominated for years, or mustard, where Gulden's has dominated, most competitors take aim at the market leaders when developing their own marketing strategies.

To understand the dynamics of attitude change, we will examine a number of attitude change strategies that can be classified under the following categories: (1) changing the basic motivational function, (2) associating the product with a specific group or event, (3) relating to conflicting attitudes, (4) altering components of the multi-attribute model, and (5) changing beliefs about competitors' brands.

## CHANGING THE BASIC MOTIVATIONAL FUNCTION

One way of changing attitudes toward a product or brand is to make new needs prominent. One attitude change theory that demonstrates how changing basic motivations can change attitudes is known as the **functional approach.**[3] With this approach, we classify attitudes in terms of four functions: the *utilitarian* function, the *ego-defensive* function, the *value-expressive* function, and the *knowledge* function.

THE UTILITARIAN FUNCTION. We hold certain brand attitudes partly because of the brand's utility. If a product has helped us in the past, even in a small way, our attitude toward it tends to be favorable. One way of changing attitudes in favor of a product is by showing people that it can solve a utilitarian goal they may not have considered. To illustrate, while clothing ads normally stress fashion, the advertisement for Bion II fabric coating (see Figure 9-1) stresses its utilitarian benefits (i.e., it allows body heat and vapor to escape).

THE EGO-DEFENSIVE FUNCTION. We want to protect our self-concept from inner feelings of doubt. Cosmetics and personal hygiene products, by acknowledging this need, increase their relevancy to the consumer and heighten the possibility of a favorable attitude by offering reassurance to the consumer's self-concept. Dry Idea, an aerosol anti-perspirant and deodorant, applies the ego-defensive function in a magazine ad that states: "Gain Control: Never Let Them See You Sweat" (see Figure 9-2).

THE VALUE-EXPRESSIVE FUNCTION. Attitudes are one expression of general values, lifestyle, and outlook. If a consumer segment generally holds a high evaluation (i.e., a positive attitude) towards being "in fashion," and high-fashion clothing and accessories are treated as symbols of that lifestyle, then attitudes toward fashion and fashionable clothing will reflect these positive attitudes. If a consumer segment holds a low evaluation of the "fashionable life," however, this segment will have negative attitudes toward the lifestyle that faddish fashion symbolizes. The General Motors ad in Figure 9-3 on page 298 encourages the reader to consider the possibility of leasing a GM car. The ad is a wholehearted appeal to an admired American lifestyle that values living in the present, as well as the rational management of one's financial affairs.

THE KNOWLEDGE FUNCTION. Individuals have a strong need to know and understand the people and things with whom they come in contact, especially if they think they might influence behavior. The "need to know," a cognitive need, is important to marketers concerned with product positioning. Indeed, most product and brand positionings are attempts to satisfy consumers' needs

**FIGURE 9-1** Advertisement Appealing to the Utilitarian Function

**FROM A BOSTON HOSPITAL TO THE BOSTON MARATHON.**

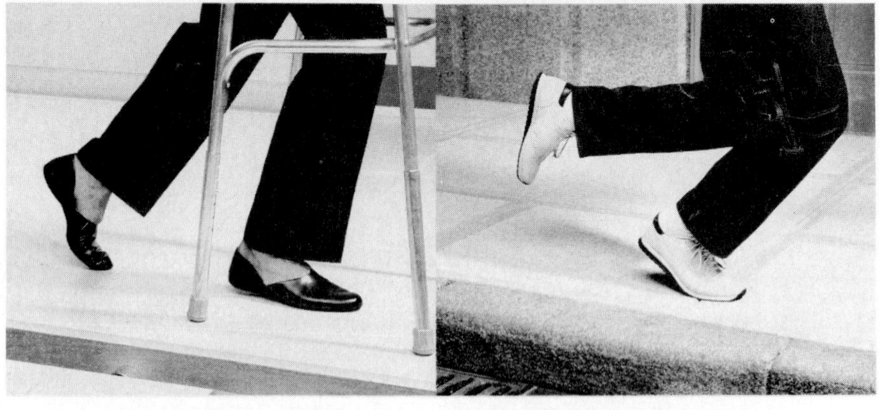

This year, the best dressed patients are wearing hospital surgical dressings with incredible skin-like characteristics. Surgical dressings that are absolutely waterproof, yet elastic and breathable so the healing process can occur naturally.

These dressings are in fact a duplication of the skin's own protective and breathable properties.

And now we've successfully adapted this technology to fabrics. Which means now exists a fabric coating with all these same skin-like characteristics. A fabric coating that, when bonded to a material, makes that material the most waterproof, and the most comfortable you can wear.

This fabric coating is called BION II.™ And it truly is a 'second skin' for fabrics.

Runningwear coated with BION II will stand out in any weather. You'll even stay absolutely dry running in the heaviest downpours. We're so sure of this, in fact, we'll guarantee the waterproofness of BION II for a full three years.

And because the BION II coating allows body heat and vapor to escape while you're running, you'll be far more comfortable than you've ever been before.

The BION II coating also makes runningwear far more durable. So your runningwear investment will keep you drier mile after mile after mile.

In fact, Outward Bound USA, the adventure-based education organization recently conducted extensive field testing of BION II coated products and chose to nationally endorse BION II as the most waterproof breathable fabric coating you can buy.

Runningwear with this incredible BION II coating will soon be available in your area. Look for it. You'll find our tag attached.

Spend your money on anything else and you'll just be getting soaked.

BION·II™

**THE ULTIMATE IN WATERPROOF, BREATHABLE COMFORT.**

BION II is a trademark of Biotex Industries, Inc., Westport, CT, a subsidiary of Thoratec Laboratories, Inc.

Courtesy of Biotex Industries, Inc.

to know and increase their positive attitudes toward the brand by clarifying its advantages over competitive brands. For instance, ads for Secret, a deodorant targeted to women, point out that a woman's pH level can be higher than a man's (see Figure 9-4 on page 299). The inclusion of color photographs showing differences in male and female pH levels appeals to the knowledge function and is designed to positively influence female attitudes toward Secret deodorant.

One consumer-oriented study that applied the four-function framework

FIGURE 9-2 Advertisement Appealing to the Ego-Defensive Function

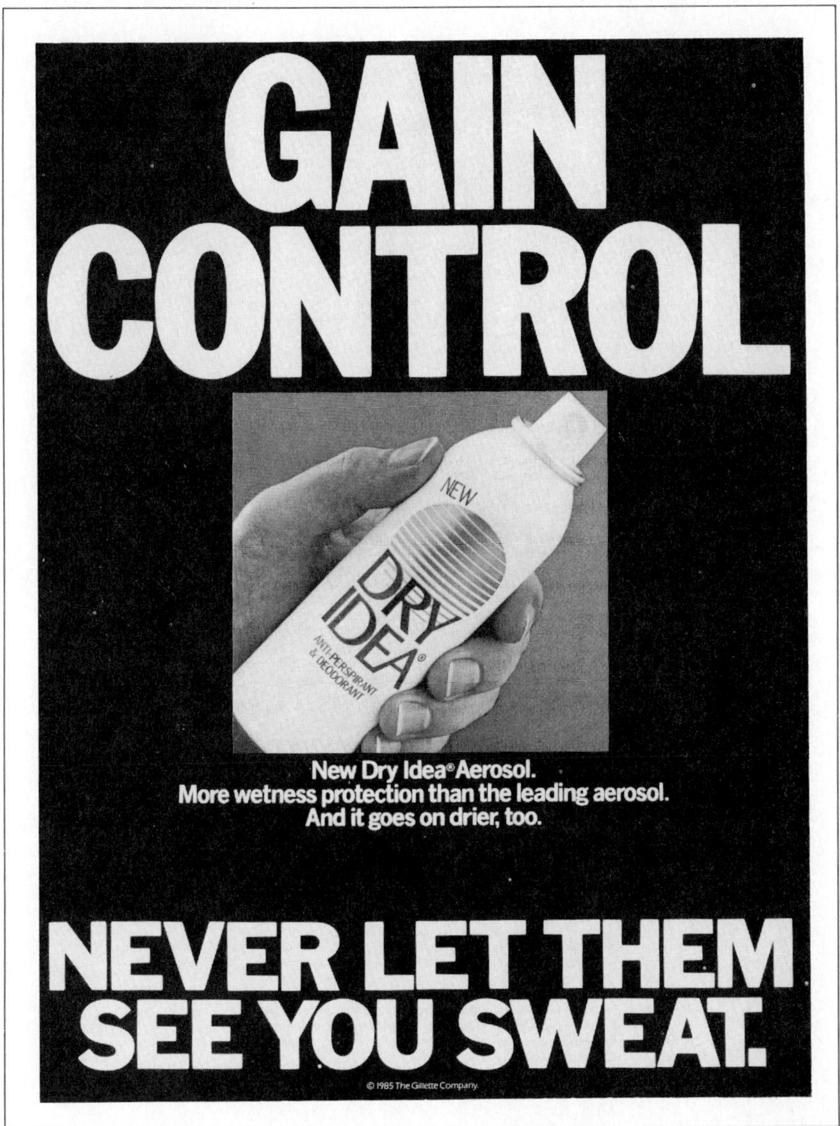


Reprinted with the permission of The Gillette Company

to an examination of attitudes toward playing tennis found it to be useful, and suggests that different consumers may like or dislike the same product or service for different reasons.[4] For instance, although two consumers might both have very positive attitudes toward a Head tennis racquet, one may be responding to the fact that the racquet provides greater control (a utilitarian function), while the other may be reacting to the masculine image of the sports celebrities used in Head's advertising (an ego-defensive function).

**FIGURE 9-3** **Advertisement Appealing to a Value-Expressive Function**

"I own a PC, a VCR, a condo on the beach and my own company.

But I don't own a car.

I lease with GMAC.

For my life-style, leasing makes more sense than buying. I wanted a new GM car, but didn't want to tie up my money in a major down payment.

So I asked my GM Dealer about leasing. We worked together to determine if leasing offered me more advantages than buying.

Then we worked out the terms of my lease. In addition to saving me a major down payment, GMAC helped lower my monthly payments—because I helped decide the amount I pay, the options I want and how long the lease will run.

And it was easy. I handled everything with just *one* stop at my participating GM Dealer.

Now I can take the money I've saved by *not* owning a car—and use it to enjoy some of the *other* good things in life.

Ask your GM Dealer for a copy of 'LEASING. Easy for Everyone.' It'll give you an idea if leasing's as right for you...as it was for me."

***Leasing is as easy as...***

GMAC
The Financial Services People
from General Motors


CHEVROLET · PONTIAC · OLDSMOBILE · BUICK · CADILLAC · GMC TRUCKS

Courtesy of General Motors Acceptance Corp.

## ASSOCIATING THE PRODUCT WITH A GROUP OR EVENT

Attitudes are related, at least in part, to certain groups or social events. It is possible to alter attitudes toward products, services, and brands by pointing out their relationships to particular social groups and events. For instance, the Manufacturers Hanover Westchester Classic golf tournament advertisement in

FIGURE 9-4 Advertisement Appealing to the Knowledge Function

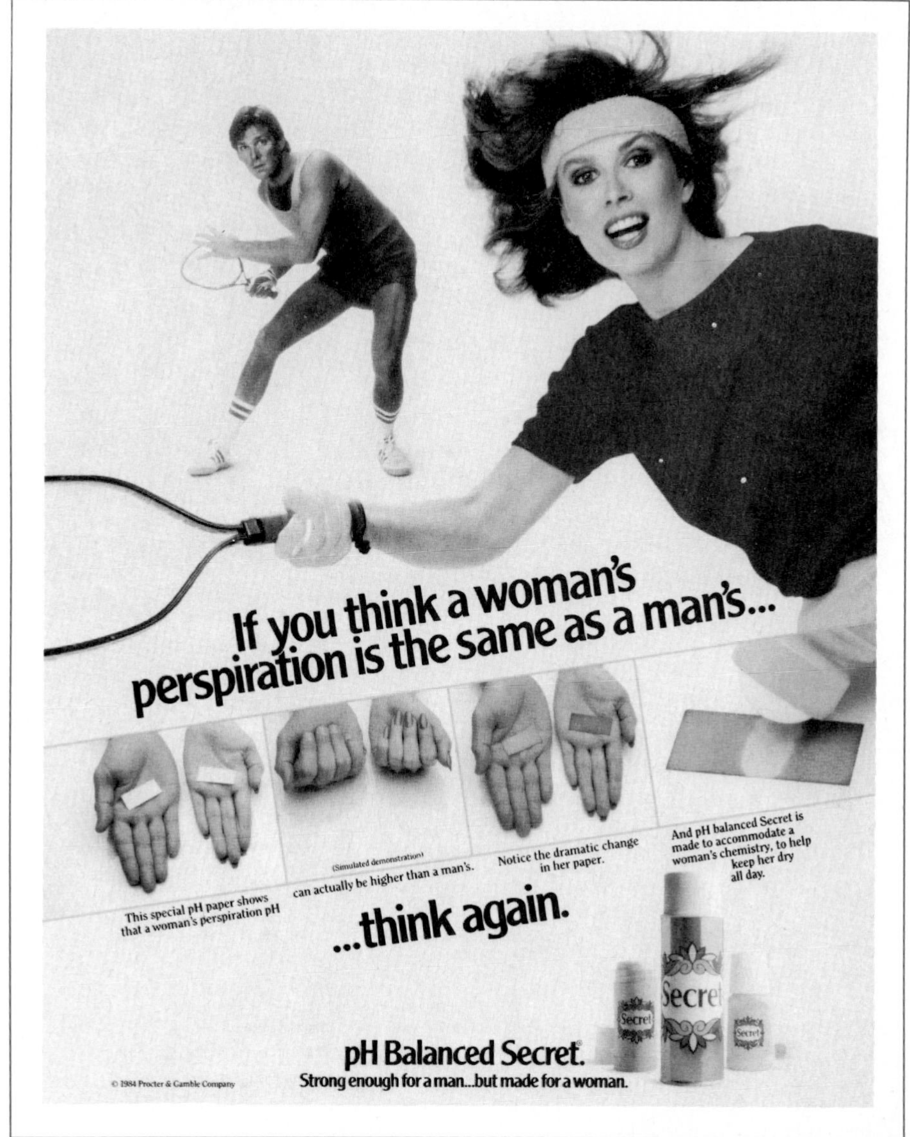


Courtesy of The Procter & Gamble Company

Figure 9-5 indicates that proceeds from this bank-sponsored event help support a number of area hospitals.

## RELATING TO CONFLICTING ATTITUDES

Attitude change strategies can also be designed to take advantage of actual or potential conflict between attitudes. Specifically, if consumers can be made to see that their brand attitude is in conflict with another more basic attitude, they

FIGURE 9-5 Advertisement Linking the Product to a Special Event

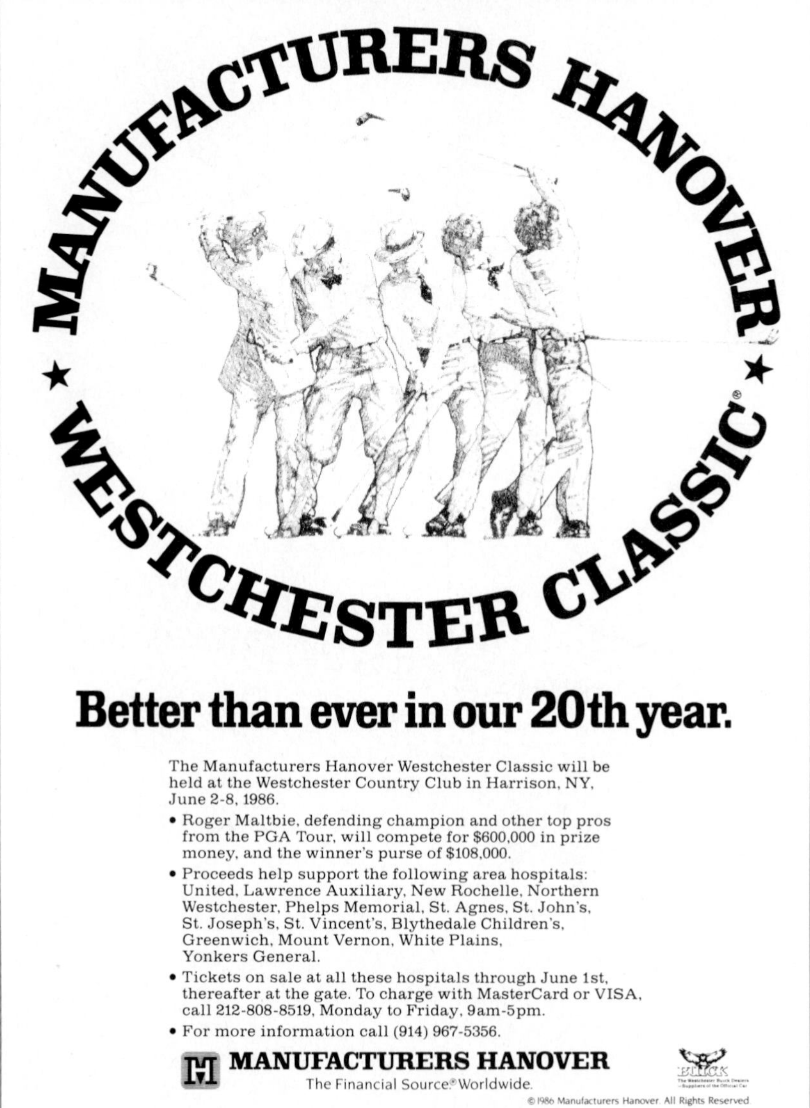


Courtesy of Manufacturers Hanover Trust Co.

may be "forced" to change their evaluation of the brand.

A simple theoretical notion—**balance theory**—shows how this attitude change mechanism works.[5] It assumes that individuals attempt to avoid inconsistency and instead seek consistency, balance, or harmony. Specifically, balance theory proposes that consumers subconsciously alter their attitudes in such a way as to place their attitudes in balance. In general terms, the theory can be thought of as a *triangular* relationship between an individual and two attitudes that are initially in conflict. To illustrate how balance theory works, let us consider two friends, Peter and John, their attitudes toward a brand of toothpaste, and one friend's attitude toward the other. The key attitudinal relationships are: (1) Peter's attitude toward Colgate toothpaste, (2) Peter's attitude toward his friend John, and (3) John's attitude toward Colgate toothpaste.

There are several instances where Peter's attitude might change in direction:

1. Peter initially has a *negative* attitude toward Colgate, and John, an admired dentist friend, recommends Colgate. This personal/professional endorsement is likely to represent a strong case for Peter to change his preliminary negative attitude to a positive attitude toward Colgate (Figure 9-6a).
2. Peter initially has a *positive* attitude toward Colgate, and his friend John, who happens to be a dentist, recommends Crest. This situation also represents a strong case for attitude change. Here Peter's initially positive attitude toward Colgate may be replaced by a favorable attitude toward Crest (Figure 9-6b).

The key to changing attitudes by relating them to other attitudes is to choose object-attitudes that are very strong and clearly conflicting with the one the marketer wishes to change. For instance, if consumers really respect a particular medium (e.g., *The Wall Street Journal*), they may reevaluate their negative attitude toward a particular product that advertises in the medium. Similarly, if a product endorsement by an admired person is both strong and in conflict with a consumer's preexisting views, it may effect an attitude change.

## ALTERING COMPONENTS OF THE MULTI-ATTRIBUTE MODEL

In Chapter 8 we discussed a number of multi-attribute attitude models. These models have important implications for attitude-change strategies. Using the popular Fishbein *attitude-toward-object* model, we will consider the following strategies for carrying out programs of attitude change: (1) changing the *rela-*

**FIGURE 9-6** **Changing the Direction of Attitudes According to Balance Theory**

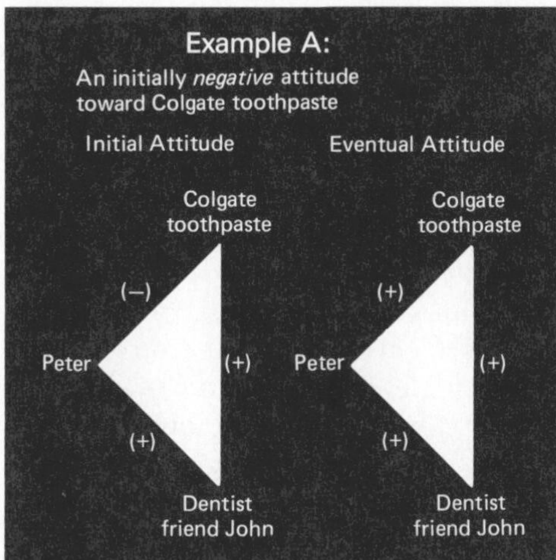


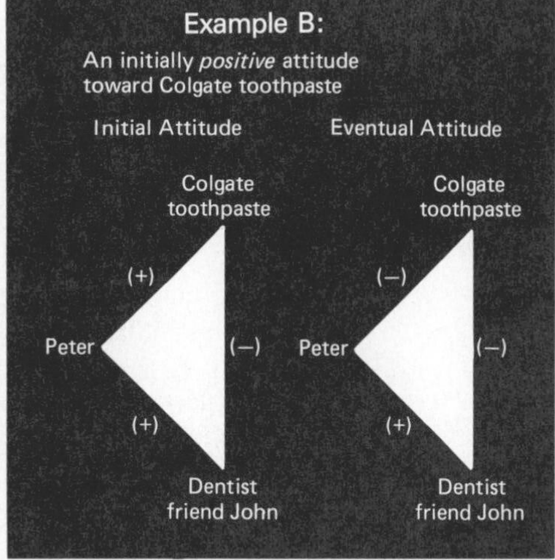

*tive evaluation of attributes* ($e_i$), (2) changing *brand beliefs* ($b_i$), (3) *adding an attribute* (combined $b_ie_i$), and (4) changing the *overall brand rating* ($A_0$).[6]

CHANGING THE RELATIVE EVALUATION OF ATTRIBUTES. The market for many product categories is structured so that different consumer segments are attracted to brands that offer different features or beliefs. For instance, within a product category such as headache remedies, there are brands like Extra-Strength Anacin that stress potency, and brands like Tylenol that stress gentleness (i.e., contain no aspirin). These two brands of headache remedy have historically appealed to different segments of the overall headache remedy market. Similarly, when it comes to chewing gum, the market may be divided between regular gum and sugar-free gum, or between regular gum and bubble gum.

In general terms, when a product category is naturally divided with respect to distinct product features or promised benefits that appeal to a particular segment of consumers, there is usually an opportunity for the marketer to attempt a "cross over"; that is, to convince consumers who prefer one version of the product (e.g., regular chewing gum) to shift their attitudes toward another version of the product (e.g., sugar-free gum), and vice versa.

Such a strategy is tantamount to *altering the relative evaluation of conflicting product attributes.* Stated somewhat differently, it serves to upgrade consumer beliefs about one product attribute, and either downgrade some other attribute or convince consumers that it is *not* in conflict with the upgraded attribute. Since the attributes slated for change are usually important and distinctive, if consumers' evaluation of one attribute can be upgraded, it is likely that there may be a shift in overall attitude or even intention to buy.

CHANGING BRAND BELIEFS. A second cognitive-oriented strategy for changing attitudes concentrates on changing beliefs or perceptions about the brand itself. This is by far the most common form of advertising appeal. Advertisers are constantly reminding us that their product has "more" or is "better" or "best" in terms of some important product attribute. For example, Colgate toothpaste might improve its brand rating by changing beliefs about the extent to which the brand "has a pleasant taste" and "is fun to brush with." If advertising could improve perceptions on these two attributes, consumers not presently using Colgate might develop a more favorable brand attitude.

Two cautions are necessary here. First, in the long run a brand-attribute perception change will not work if the brand does not actually have the attribute in question. Second, changes in the relative evaluations of both the attributes and the brand-attribute beliefs must not be too drastic, because too extreme an advertising position would probably result in rejection of the whole message. This caution is based on the **assimilation-contrast** theory.[7] This theory warns that marketers trying to change attitudes by altering the relative evaluations of either attributes or brand-attribute beliefs must be careful to avoid "overkill" or overselling their case. According to the theory, a target segment will *assimilate* (or accept) only *moderate* changes. If the change suggested by a message is too extreme, the *contrast* will likely result in distortion of the whole message and result in the message being rejected as too extreme.

FIGURE 9-7 Advertisement Designed to Address Brand Beliefs

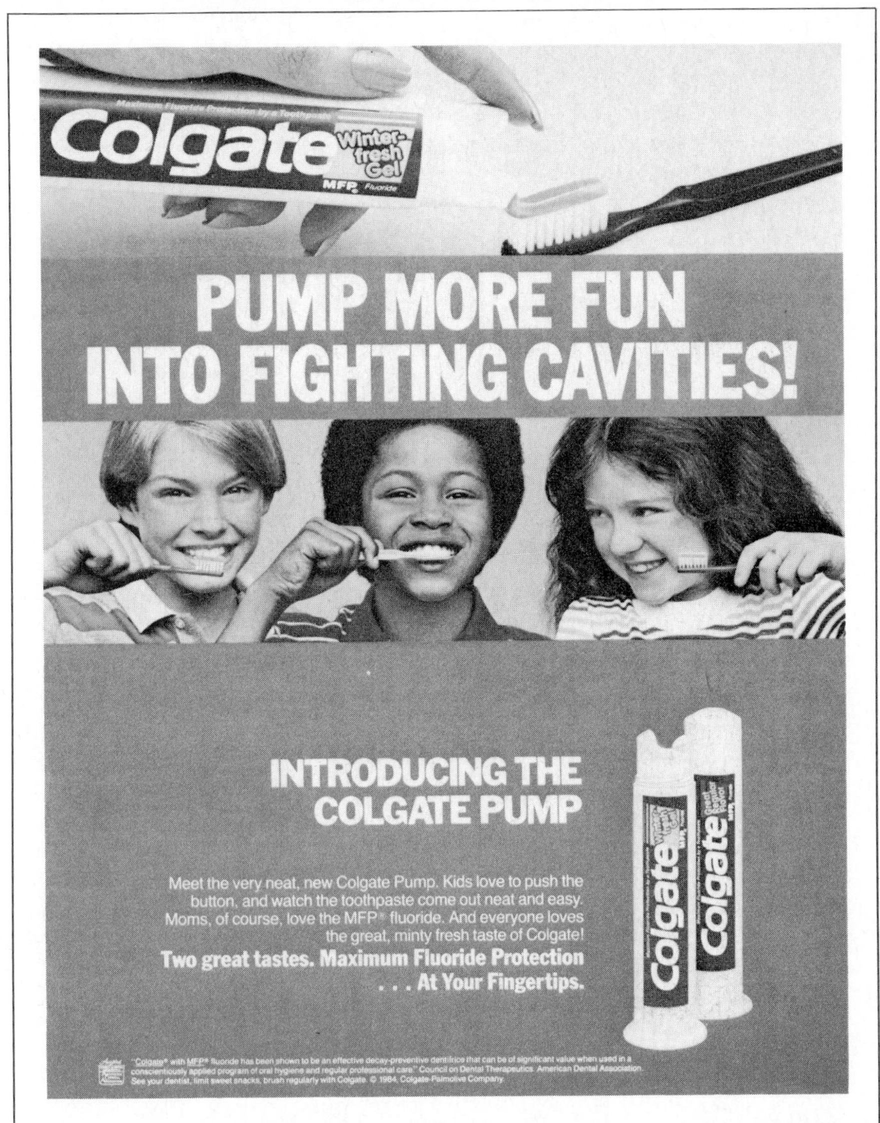


Courtesy of Colgate Palmolive Corp. Photography by Mark Kozlowski.

ADDING AN ATTRIBUTE. Another cognitive strategy consists of *adding an attribute*. This can be accomplished by either adding an attribute that has previously been ignored or adding an attribute that represents a technological improvement or innovation.

The first route—adding a previously ignored attribute—may be difficult to accomplish because, for most product classes, most existing attributes have been considered by consumers at one time or another. For this reason, the second route—adding an attribute based on an actual product change or technological innovation—is preferable. Thus Colgate seems to have been on the right track in its decisions to introduce a gel version of its toothpaste and to offer both regular and gel versions in pump containers (see Figure 9-7).

CHANGING THE OVERALL BRAND RATING. Still another cognitive-oriented strategy consists of attempting to alter consumers' *overall assessment of the brand* directly without attempting to improve or change their evaluation of any single brand attribute. Such a strategy frequently relies on providing some form of significant global statement that the brand is the largest selling brand, or that it is the brand all others try to imitate, or a similar claim that sets the brand apart from all its competitors.

### CHANGING BELIEFS ABOUT COMPETITORS' BRANDS

A final strategy involves changing consumer beliefs about the *attributes of competitive brands* or product categories. This has become a more heavily utilized strategy as the popularity of **comparative advertising** has grown. For instance, Hormel has undertaken a comparative campaign that contrasts its Light & Lean Ham with other foods. In the advertisement, Hormel claims that six ounces of its Light & Lean Ham has the same number of calories as substantially smaller weight portions of fish, beef, and chicken.

However, this strategy must be used with caution. Some evidence suggests that comparative advertising can boomerang by giving visibility to competitive brands and claims.[8] Further evidence indicates that if the audience is sophisticated and involved, its attitudes may be quite difficult to change with any kind of message.[9] (Chapter 10 discusses comparative advertising in greater depth.)

## BEHAVIOR PRECEDING ATTITUDES

Our discussion of attitude formation and attitude change has stressed the traditional "rational" view that consumers develop their attitudes prior to actions (e.g., "Know what you are doing before you do it"). There are alternatives to this attitude-precedes-behavior perspective, which upon careful analysis are likely to be just as logical and rational. We will consider two alternatives, **cognitive dissonance** theory and **attribution** theory, each of which provides a different explanation as to why behavior might be expected to *precede* attitudes.

### Cognitive Dissonance Theory

According to *cognitive dissonance* theory, discomfort or dissonance occurs when a consumer receives new information concerning a belief or an attitude that is in conflict with the original belief or attitude.[10] For instance, when consumers have made a commitment to buy a product, particularly an expensive one such as an automobile, the unique positive qualities of the brands *not* selected remind the consumers that they may not have made the wisest choice. Because purchase decisions often require some amount of compromise, such feelings of cognitive dissonance—especially when occurring *after* a purchase (i.e., postpurchase dissonance)—are quite normal; nevertheless, they are likely to leave consumers with an uneasy feeling about their prior beliefs or actions.

**Postpurchase dissonance** is discussed here within the context of *changes in behavior leading to changes in attitudes* because the conflicting thoughts or dissonant information that follow a purchase are seen as prime factors that induce consumers to change attitudes so that they will be consonant with the actual purchase behavior. Thus attitude change is seen as an *outcome* of behavior.

To illustrate how attitude change occurs within the context of postpurchase dissonance, let us return to the toothpaste example.[11] The thought (i.e., the belief) that "All fluoride toothpastes taste bad" is *dissonant* with the behavior of using Colgate Toothpaste daily. To reduce the dissonance arising out of this conflict, the consumer can elect one or both of the following basic strategies: (1) introduce new cognitive beliefs supporting the original attitude or behavior, or (2) reevaluate the conflicting beliefs to create *consonance.* To make the daily use of Colgate consonant with the negative belief of unpleasant taste, the consumer can introduce a new supportive belief—e.g., "The reason why I had no cavities on my last visit to the dentist was because I have been using a toothpaste with fluoride." Alternatively, the consumer may reevaluate the dissonant belief and reject it—e.g., "I don't mind the taste of fluoride toothpaste."

What makes postpurchase dissonance relevant to marketing strategists is the premise that dissonance propels consumers to take steps to reduce the unpleasant feelings created by the rival thoughts.

A variety of tactics are open to consumers to reduce postpurchase dissonance. The consumer could rationalize the decision as being wise, seek out advertisements that support the choice (while avoiding those of dissonance-creating competitive brands), try "selling" friends on the positive features of the brand, or look to satisfied owners for their reassurance.

In addition to such consumer-initiated tactics to reduce postpurchase uncertainty, a marketer can relieve consumer dissonance by including messages in its advertising specifically aimed at reinforcing consumer decisions, offering a stronger guarantee or warranty, increasing the number and effectiveness of its services, or providing detailed brochures on how to use its products correctly.

## Attribution Theory

As a group of loosely interrelated social psychological principles, *attribution theory* attempts to explain how people assign causality to events in terms of either their own behavior or the behavior of others.[12] In other words, a person might say "I contributed to Cancer Care, because it really helps people in need," or "He tried to persuade me to buy that unknown washing machine because he makes a bigger commission." In attribution theory, the underlying question is why: "Why did I do this?" "Why did he try to get me to switch brands?" This process of making inferences about one's own or another's behavior is a major component of attitude formation and change.

Attribution theory portrays attitude formation and change as an outgrowth of people's interpretations of their own behavior and experiences.

## SELF-PERCEPTION THEORY

Of the various perspectives on attribution theory that have been proposed, individuals' inferences or judgments as to the causes of their own behavior, known as **self-perception theory,** are a good beginning point for a discussion of attribution.

In terms of consumer behavior, self-perception theory suggests that attitudes develop as consumers *look at and make judgments about their own behavior.* Simply stated, if a woman observes that she routinely purchases *The Wall Street Journal* on her way to work, she is apt to conclude from such behavior that she likes *The Wall Street Journal* (i.e., she has a positive attitude toward this newspaper).[13]

INTERNAL AND EXTERNAL ATTRIBUTIONS. Drawing inferences from one's own behavior is not always as simple or clear-cut as the newspaper example might suggest. To appreciate the complexity of self-perception theory, it is useful to distinguish between **internal** and **external attributions.** Let us assume that you have just finished baking your first apple pie and that it is delicious. If upon tasting this "masterpiece" you think to yourself, "I'm really a naturally good baker," this statement would be an example of an *internal attribution.* It is an internal attribution because you are giving yourself credit for the outcome (e.g., your ability, your skill, or your effort). That is, you are saying, "This pie is good because of me." On the other hand, if you were to conclude that the successful apple pie was due to factors beyond your control (e.g., ingredients, the assistance of a friend, or just "luck"), this would be an example of an *external attribution.* Here you might be saying, "This pie is good because of beginner's luck."

This distinction between internal and external attributions may be of strategic marketing importance. For instance, it would generally be in the best interests of a firm such as Pillsbury if bakers, especially inexperienced ones, internalized their successful baking experiences. If they internalize such positive experiences, it seems more likely they will repeat the behavior and perhaps start baking on a regular basis. Alternatively, however, if they were to externalize their success, it would be preferable that they attribute it to Pillsbury ingredients, rather than to an incidental environmental factor such as "beginner's luck," or a friend's "foolproof" recipe.

According to the principle of **defensive attribution,** consumers are likely to accept credit personally for success (internal attribution), and to credit failure to others or to outside events (external attribution). For this reason, it is crucial that marketers offer uniformly high-quality products that allow consumers to perceive themselves as the reason for the success—i.e., "I'm competent." Moreover, a company's advertising should serve to reassure consumers, particularly inexperienced ones, that its products will not let them down but will make them "heroes" instead.

FOOT-IN-THE-DOOR TECHNIQUE. Self-perception theorists have explored situations where consumer compliance with a small or simple request affects subsequent attempts to gain compliance with a more substantial request.[14] This strategy, which is commonly referred to as the **foot-in-the-door** technique, is based on the premise that individuals look at their prior behavior (compliance with the minor request) and come to the conclusion that they are the kind of person who says yes to such requests (i.e., an internal attribution). If effective, such self-attribution serves to increase the likelihood that they will say yes to the more substantial request. Someone who donates $5 to Cancer Research may be persuaded to donate a much larger amount if properly approached. The initial donation is, in effect, the *foot-in-the-door.*

Applications of the foot-in-the-door technique have concentrated on how specific incentives (e.g., cents-off coupons of varying amounts) ultimately influence consumer attitudes and subsequent purchase behavior. The research has generally found that different-size incentives tend to create different degrees of internal attribution, which in turn lead to different amounts of attitude change.[15] For instance, individuals who try a brand without any inducements, or individuals who repeatedly buy the brand, are progressively more likely to infer increasingly positive attitudes toward the brand from their respective behaviors (e.g., "I buy this brand because I like it"). In contrast, individuals who try a free sample are least committed to changing their attitudes toward the brand ("I tried this brand because it was free").

Thus, contrary to what might be expected, it is not the biggest incentive that is most likely to lead to positive attitude change. If an incentive is too big, marketers run the risk that consumers might externalize the cause of their behavior to the incentive and be *less* likely to change their attitudes and *less* likely to make future purchases of the brand. Instead, what seems most effective is a *moderate* incentive, one that is just big enough to stimulate initial purchase of the brand, but still small enough to encourage consumers to internalize their own positive usage experience and allow a positive attitude change to occur.

## ATTRIBUTIONS TOWARD OTHERS

Although consumer researchers usually focus most of their attention on self-perception theory, they are also interested in understanding attributions toward *others.*[16]

Attributions toward others would seem to have a wide variety of potential applications within the realm of consumer behavior and marketing. As suggested earlier in this section, every time a person asks "Why?" about a statement or action of another person—a family member, a friend, a salesperson—attribution theory is relevant. For example, if a husband and wife were in an audio store contemplating the purchase of a new compact stereo system, the salesperson's recommendation that they purchase a Pioneer system which cost $300 more than the one they were initially considering would logically lead to the question "Why?" If the couple conclude that the salesperson has suggested it because of its superior features, then they are likely to judge the salesperson's motives as "sincere" and will possibly purchase the more expensive model. However, if they conclude that the salesperson is interested only in the greater commission from selling the more expensive model, then they might judge the salesperson as "insincere" and be unlikely to buy the more expensive model. Indeed, they might leave and go elsewhere because they no longer trust the salesperson or the store. The consumer is really asking, "Is the salesperson trying to sell me the more expensive model because of the superiority of the model or because of the increased commission?"

This illustration suggests that in evaluating the words or deeds of others, the consumer tries to determine if the other person's motives or skills are consistent with the consumer's best interests. If these motives or skills are judged congruent, the consumer is likely to respond favorably. Otherwise the consumer is likely to reject the other person's words, and make the purchase elsewhere.

### ATTRIBUTIONS TOWARD THINGS

Attributions toward *things* also have considerable appeal for consumer researchers, especially since a product or service can be thought of as a "thing."[17] It is in the area of judging product performance that consumers are most likely to form product attributions. Specifically, they want to find out why a product meets or does not meet their expectations. In this regard, they could attribute the product's success (or failure) to themselves, to the product itself, to other people or situations, or to some combination of these factors.[18]

### HOW WE TEST OUR ATTRIBUTIONS

After making initial attributions of a product's performance or a person's words or actions, we often attempt to determine if the inference we made is correct. According to a leading attribution theorist, individuals acquire conviction about particular observations by acting like "naive scientists"; that is, by collecting additional information in an attempt to confirm (or disconfirm) prior inferences. In collecting such information, they often employ the following criteria:[19]

1. *Distinctiveness*—The consumer attributes an action to a particular person or product if the action occurs when the person or product is present, and does not occur in its absence.
2. *Consistency over time*—Each time the person or product is present, the consumer's reaction must be the same, or nearly so.
3. *Consistency over modality*—The reaction must be the same even though the situation in which it occurs varies.
4. *Consensus*—The action is perceived the same way by other consumers.

A consumer behavior example illustrates how each of these criteria are used to assess inferences about product performance and people's actions. If a homeowner (let us call him Jim) who prides himself on his lawn observes that his grass seems to be more evenly cut with his new Lawn-Boy mower than with his former lawnmower, he is likely to credit the new Lawn-Boy for the improved appearance of his lawn (i.e., *distinctiveness*). Furthermore, if Jim finds that his new Lawn-Boy produces the same high-quality results each time he uses it, he tends to be more confident about his initial observation (i.e., the inference has *consistency over time*). Similarly, he will also be more confident if he finds that his satisfaction with the Lawn-Boy extends across a wide range of other related tasks, such as mulching grass and picking up leaves (i.e., *consistency over modality*). Finally, Jim will have still more confidence in his inferences to the extent that his friends who own Lawn-Boys have also had similar experiences (i.e., *consensus*).

Much like Jim, we go about gathering additional information from our experiences with people and things, which we use to *test* our initial inferences.

Clearly, attributions are quite relevant to consumers' satisfaction with a product, a salesperson, or even a retail establishment.[20] Moreover, since attributions are closely associated with consumer satisfaction, we can expect that an attribution perspective is likely to become more popular as we increasingly look at the public policy effects of advertising substantiation, packaging legislation, sales cooling-off laws, and product liability practices.[21]

## CONSUMER INVOLVEMENT AND ATTITUDE DYNAMICS

A brief examination of how consumer involvement influences the informational needs of consumer decision makers is an appropriate way to conclude our examination of attitude formation and change, because it serves to tie together a number of loose ends about the direction of the attitude-behavior relationship (i.e., whether attitudes precede or follow from behavior).

At its simplest, consumer involvement theory is concerned with limited versus extensive information search. When consumers believe a purchase decision is highly relevant and important and are willing to exert effort to acquire information, we consider such concern to be indicative of *high involvement.* On the other hand, when consumers believe a purchase is unimportant (i.e., lacks relevance) and see little reason to acquire product information, we consider such concern to be indicative of *low involvement.*

As Chapter 7 has indicated, *high involvement* was until quite recently, the only perspective considered when describing consumer decision making.[22] However, we are now beginning to appreciate the importance of *low involvement*—particularly given the likelihood that a significant portion, if not the majority, of all consumer decisions are probably of the low-involvement (i.e., low relevance) variety.[23]

A useful portrayal of the differences in information search between high involvement and low involvement purchases is given in Figure 9-8. The four models, two high-involvement models and two low-involvement models, are based on the relevance of the product to the consumer (i.e., high or low involvement) and the degree to which the consumer *perceives* differences among brands (i.e., "little" or "great" with respect to product features or promised benefits).[24]

## Active Learning Model

The *active learning* model, as depicted in the upper-left-hand cell of Figure 9-8, is based on traditional cognitive learning theory (see Chapter 7). Within the context of this model, consumers are *active* learners and engage in extensive problem solving. They are highly involved with the potential purchase and see the brand alternatives as quite different in their benefits and ability to provide satisfaction. Consumers are likely to perceive decisions involving high relevance and high brand differences as quite risky; therefore the acquisition of information about each alternative is likely to be seen as a necessary prerequisite to making a choice.

Since decisions in this category are especially important, it is not surprising that the model portrays consumers as progressing through a three-stage hi-

**FIGURE 9-8** **Four Consumer Involvement/Brand Differentiation Decision-Making Models** Source: Adapted from F. Stewart DeBruicker, "An Appraisal of Low-Involvement Consumer Information Processing," in John C. Maloney and Bernard Silverman, eds., *Attitude Research Plays for High Stakes* (Chicago: American Marketing Association, 1979), 124; which in part is based on Michael Ray, "Marketing Communication and the Hierarchy of Effects," in F.G. Kline and P. Clark, eds., *Sage Annual Reviews in Communication Research* (Beverly Hills, Calif.: 1973).

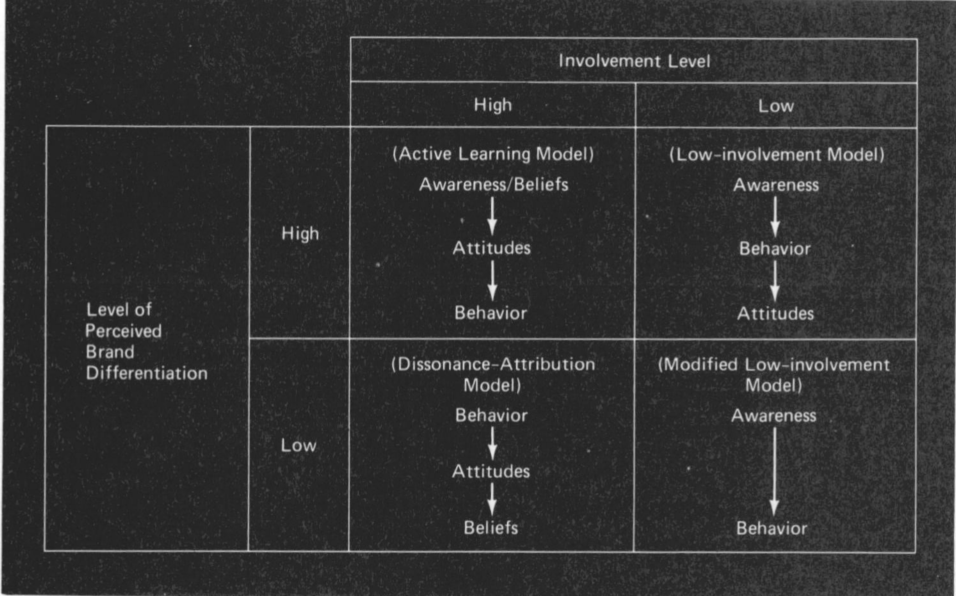

erarchy—from awareness and knowledge to the formation of attitudes, and then to behavior. Thus the model is a classical example of "Think before you act."

## Dissonance-Attribution Model

The *dissonance attribution* model (lower-left-hand cell of Figure 9-8) represents a decision situation that couples high relevance to the consumer with little or no perceived differences among brands. In this model, behavior *precedes* attitudes, and attitudes precede beliefs and knowledge. The three stages of this model correspond to the *behavior-before-attitude* that characterizes postpurchase dissonance theory and attribution theory.

## Original Low-Involvement Model

The third model (upper-right-hand cell of Figure 9-8) couples low-involvement in the purchase decision with the perception of distinct brand differences.

In this case, the three-stage hierarchy begins with a progression from awareness to behavior, and then from behavior to attitudes. In essence, the model suggests that awareness of alternatives is likely to be sufficient information for consumers to make a purchase decision under conditions of low product relevance. Following from this, attitudes are depicted as an *outcome* of consumers' experiences with the brand; that is, attitudes are formed as consumers establish preferences for the brand that provides them with the greatest amount of satisfaction. This model is consistent with instrumental conditioning theory and depicts the low-involvement process as a relatively *passive* learning experience.

## Modified Low-Involvement Model

The fourth and final model (lower-right-hand cell of Figure 9-8), portrays a situation where consumers have little involvement and perceive little difference between the various brands. In this case, the model consists of only two stages—*brand awareness* and *behavior.* In essence, no brand-specific attitude need ever develop. The consumer perceives the various brands to be so uniform that preexisting attitudes toward the overall product category are sufficient for all brands, and there is no additional need to establish brand-specific attitudes. This fourth model can be considered a *highly passive* learning process, with little brand-level learning actually taking place.

Although some of the assumptions of the four models have been questioned by various researchers, the models provide a useful framework for distinguishing those situations where attitudes precede or follow from behavior. Furthermore, the models provide beginning support for the idea that the degree and nature of consumer involvement in a particular purchase decision, as well as the perceived degree of brand differentiation, are likely to influence which comes first: attitudes or behavior. Knowledge of which comes first indicates important alternative approaches for marketers, since the effort to influence *behavior* directly is very different from influencing *attitudes.*

## *summary*

How consumer attitudes are formed and how they are changed are two closely related issues of considerable concern to marketing practitioners.

When it comes to attitude formation, it is useful to remember that attitudes are learned, and that different learning theories provide unique insights as to how attitudes may initially be formed. Attitude generation is facilitated by direct personal experience, and influenced by the ideas and experiences of friends and family members, and the impressions acquired by exposure to mass media. In addition, it is likely that an individual's personality plays a major role in attitude formation.

These same factors also have an impact on attitude change; that is, attitude changes are learned, they are influenced by personal experiences and information gained from various personal and impersonal sources, and one's own personality affects both the acceptance and the speed with which attitudes are likely to be altered.

Strategies of attitude change can be classified into five distinct categories: (1) changing the basic motivational function, (2) associating the product with a specific group or event, (3) relating to conflicting attitudes, (4) altering components of the multi-attribute model, and (5) changing beliefs about competitors' brands. Each of these strategies provides the marketing practitioner with alternative ways of carrying out a program to alter consumers' existing attitudes.

Most discussions of both attitude formation and attitude change stress the traditional view that consumers develop attitudes before they act. However, this may not always, or even usually, be true. Both cognitive dissonance theory and attribution theory provide alternative explanations for attitude formation and change which suggest that behavior might precede attitudes. Cognitive dissonance theory suggests that conflicting thoughts or dissonant information that follow a purchase decision might propel consumers to change their attitudes to make them consonant with their actions. Attribution theory focuses on how people assign causality to events and how they form or alter attitudes as an outcome of assessing their own behavior, or the behavior of other people or things.

The level of consumer involvement influences the extent of consumer information processing and may therefore affect the direction of the attitude-behavior relationship (i.e., whether attitudes precede or follow behavior). Additional research is needed to expand and test notions about the sequence in which attitude and behavior occur.

## *discussion questions*

1. Explain a recently formed attitude toward a product or service in terms of both instrumental conditioning and cognitive learning theory.
2. Describe a situation in which you felt you acquired an attitude toward a new product through exposure to an advertisement for that product.
3. Find advertisements that illustrate each of the four motivational functions of attitudes.
4. Explain how a marketer of breakfast cereal might change consumer attitudes toward the brand by changing beliefs about competing brands.
5. Why would marketers generally prefer consumers to make internal rather than external attributions?
6. How can the following attitude theories help to change attitudes: (a) the functional approach, (b) the assimilation-contrast theory, (c) cognitive dissonance, and (d) the self-perception theory?
7. Consider the case of a college student who has just purchased a new Apple IIe computer. What might cause this individual to experience postpurchase dissonance? How might the student overcome it? How can the computer's manufacturer help?
8. To an advertiser, what is the important difference between the active learning model and the passive learning model presented in the chapter?

## *endnotes*


1. Morris B. Holbrook, "Beyond Attitude Structure: Toward the Informational Determinants of Attitude," *Journal of Marketing Research,* 15 (November 1978), 550–51; also see Morris B. Holbrook, David A. Velez, and Gerard J. Tabouret, "Attitude Structure and Search: An Integrative Model of Importance-Directed Information Processing," in Kent B. Monroe, ed., *Advances in Consumer Research* (Ann Arbor, Mich.: Association for Consumer Research, 1981), VIII, 35–41; and Jerry C. Olson, "Ideas on Integrating Attitude Theory with Information Processing Theory," in Richard W. Olshavsky, ed., *Attitude Research Enters the 80's* (Chicago: American Marketing Association, 1980), 1–13.
2. Robert B. Zajonc and Hazel Markus, "Affective and Cognitive Factors in Preferences," *Journal of Consumer Research,* 9 (September 1982), 123–31.
3. Daniel Katz, "The Functional Approach to the Study of Attitudes," *Public Opinion Quarterly,* 24 (Summer 1960), 163–91; Richard J. Lutz, "A Functional Approach to Consumer Attitude Research," in H. Keith Hunt, ed., *Advances in Consumer Research* (Ann Arbor, Mich.: Association for Consumer Research, 1978), V, 360–69; and Richard J. Lutz, "A Functional Theory Framework for Designing and Pretesting Advertising Themes," in John C. Maloney and Bernard Silverman, eds., *Attitude Research Plays for High Stakes* (Chicago: American Marketing Association, 1979), 37–49.
4. William B. Locander and W. Austin Spivey, "A Functional Approach to Attitude Measurement," *Journal of Marketing Research,* 15 (November 1978), 576–87.

5. George S. Day, "Theories of Attitude Structure and Change," in Scott Ward and Thomas Robertson, eds., *Consumer Behavior: Theoretical Sources* (Englewood Cliffs, N.J.: Prentice-Hall, 1973), 303–53, esp. 331–33; Martin Fishbein and Icek Ajzen, *Belief, Attitude, Intention and Behavior* (Reading, Mass.: Addison-Wesley, 1975), esp. chap. 2; and Bobby J. Calder, "Cognitive Consistency and Consumer Behavior," in Harold H. Kassarjian and Thomas S. Robertson, eds., *Perspectives in Consumer Behavior,* 3rd ed. (Glenview, Ill.: Scott, Foresman, 1981), 258–70.

6. Richard J. Lutz, "Changing Brand Attitudes through Modification of Cognitive Structure," *Journal of Consumer Research,* 1 (March 1975), 49–59; Richard J. Lutz, "An Experimental Investigation of Causal Relations among Cognitions, Affect, and Behavioral Intention," *Journal of Consumer Research,* 3 (March 1977), 197–208; and Andrew A. Mitchell and Jerry C. Olson, "Are Product Attribute Beliefs the Only Mediator of Advertising Effects on Brand Attitude?" *Journal of Marketing Research,* 18 (August 1981), 318–32.

7. Carl I. Hovland, O. J. Harvey, and Muzafer Sherif, "Assimilation and Contrast Effects in Reactions to Communication and Attitude Change," *Journal of Abnormal and Social Psychology,* 55 (July 1957), 244–52; and Rolph E. Anderson, "Consumer Dissatisfaction: The Effect of Disconfirmed Expectancy on Perceived Product Performance," *Journal of Marketing Research,* 10 (February 1973), 38–44.

8. Alan G. Sawyer, "The Effects of Repetition of Refutational and Supportive Advertising Appeals," *Journal of Marketing Research,* 10 (February 1973), 23–33; and William L. Wilkie and Paul Farris, "Comparison Advertising: Problems and Potential," *Journal of Marketing,* 39 (October 1975), 7–15.

9. Sawyer, "Effects of Repetition of Refutational and Supportive Advertising Appeals"; and Wilkie and Farris, "Comparison Advertising."

10. Leon Festinger, A Theory of Cognitive Dissonance (Stanford, Calif.: Stanford University Press, 1957).

11. William H. Cummings and M. Venkatesan, "Cognitive Dissonance and Consumer Behavior: A Review of the Evidence," *Journal of Marketing Research,* 13 (August 1976), 303–8. Also see, for example, Shelby D. Hunt, "Post-Transaction Communication and Dissonance Reduction," *Journal of Marketing,* 34 (July 1970), 46–51; S. Oshikawa, "The Measurement of Cognitive Dissonance: Some Experimental Findings," *Journal of Marketing,* 36 (January 1972), 64–67; S. Oshikawa, "Dissonance Reduction or Artifact?" *Journal of Marketing Research,* 8 (November 1971), 514–15; and Jagdish N. Sheth, "Dissonance Reduction or Artifact? A Reply," *Journal of Marketing Research,* 8 (November 1971), 516–17.

12. Edward E. Jones et al., *Attribution: Perceiving the Causes of Behavior* (Morristown, N.J.: General Learning Press, 1972).

13. Chris T. Allen and William R. Dillon, "Self-Perception Development and Consumer Choice Criteria: Is There a Linkage?" in Richard P. Bagozzi and Alice M. Tybout, eds., *Advances in Consumer Research* (Ann Arbor, Mich.: Association for Consumer Research, 1983), X, 45–50.

14. Carol A. Scott, "Self-Perception Processes in Consumer Behavior: Interpreting One's Own Experiences," in Hunt, *Advances in Consumer Research,* V, 714–20; and Carol A. Scott; "Forming Beliefs from Experience: Evidence from Self-Perception Theory," in Harold H. Kassarjian and Thomas S. Robertson, eds., *Perspectives in Consumer Behavior,* 3rd ed. (Glenview, Ill.: Scott, Foresman, 1981), 296–306.

15. Carol A. Scott, "Modifying Socially-Conscious Behavior: The Foot-in-the-Door Technique," *Journal of Consumer Research,* 4 (December 1977), 156–64; Carol A. Scott, "The Effects of Trial and Incentives on Repeat Purchase Behavior," *Journal of Marketing Research,* 13 (August 1976), 263–69; Joe A. Dodson, Alice M. Tybout, and Brian Sternthal, "Impact of Deals and Deal Retraction on Brand Switching," *Journal of Marketing Research,* 15 (February 1978), 72–81; and Joel Brockner et al., "Organizational Fundraising: Further Evidence on the Effect of Legitimizing Small Donations," *Journal of Consumer Research,* 11 (June 1984), 611–14.

16. Richard W. Mizerski, Linda L. Golden, and Jerome B. Kernan, "The Attribution Process in Consumer Decision Making," *Journal of Consumer Research,* 6 (September 1979), 123–40.

17. Mizerski, Golden, and Kernan, "The Attribution Process," 126–27; and Robert E. Burnkrant, "Cue Utilization in Product Perception," in Hunt, *Advances in Consumer Research,* V, 724–29.

18. Alain Jolibert and Robert A. Peterson, "Causal Attributions of Product Failure: An Exploratory Investigation," *Journal of the Academy of Marketing Science,* 4 (Winter 1976), 446–55; and Valerie S. Folkes, "Consumer Reactions to Product Failure: An Attributional Approach," *Journal of Consumer Research,* 10 (March 1984), 398–409.

19. Harold H. Kelley, "Attribution Theory in Social Psychology," in David Levine, ed., *Nebraska Symposium on Motivation* (Lincoln: University of Nebraska Press, 1967), XV, 197.

20. S. Krishnan and Valerie A. Valle, "Dissatisfaction Attributions and Consumer Complaint Behavior," in William L. Wilkie, ed., *Advances in Consumer Research* (Ann Arbor, Mich.: Association for Consumer Research, 1979), VI, 445–49; and Valerie Valle and Melanie Wallendorf, "Consumers' Attributions of the Cause of Their Product Satisfaction and Dissatisfaction," in Ray L. Day, ed., *Consumer Satisfaction, Dissatisfaction and Complaining Behavior* (Bloomington: Department of Marketing, School of Business, Indiana University, 1977), 26–30.

21. Linda Golden, "Attribution Theory Implications for Advertising Claim Credibility," *Journal of Marketing Research,* 14 (February 1977), 115–17; Robert B. Settle and Linda L. Golden, "Attribution Theory and Advertiser Credibility," *Journal of Marketing Research,* 11 (May 1974), 181–85; and Robert E. Smith and Shelby D. Hunt, "Attributional Processes and Effects in Promotional Situations," *Journal of Consumer Research,* 5 (December 1978), 149–58.

22. Harold H. Kassarjian and Waltraud M. Kassarjian, "Attitudes under Low Commitment Conditions," in John C. Maloney and Bernard Silverman, eds., *Attitude Research Plays for High Stakes* (Chicago: American Marketing Association, 1979), 3–13.

23. Herbert E. Krugman, "The Impact of Television Advertising: Learning without Involvement," *Public Opinion Quarterly,* 29 (Fall 1965), 349–56; "Brain Wave Measures of Media Involvement," *Journal of Advertising Research,* 11 (February 1971), 3–10; and "Low Involvement Theory in the Light of New Brain Research," in John C. Maloney and Bernard Silverman, eds., *Attitude Research Plays for High Stakes* (Chicago: American Marketing Association, 1979), 16–24.

24. F. Stewart DeBruicker, "An Appraisal of Low-Involvement Consumer Information Processing," in Maloney and Silverman, *Attitude Research Plays for High Stakes,* 112–30; Michael Ray, "Marketing Communication and the Hierarchy of Effects," in F. G. Kline and P. Clark, eds., *Sage Annual Reviews in Communication Research* (Beverly Hills, Calif.: Sage Press, 1973); Bobby J. Calder, "When Attitudes Follow Behavior—A Self-Perception/Dissonance Interpretation of Low Involvement," in Maloney and Silverman, *Attitude Research Plays for High Stakes,* 25–36; Michael L. Rothschild, "Advertising Strategies for High and Low Involvement Situations," in Maloney and Silverman, *Attitude Research Plays for High Stakes,* 74–94; and Robert E. Smith and William R. Swinyard, "Involvement and the Hierarchy of Effects: An Integrated Framework," in George B. Hafer, ed., *A Look Back, A Look Ahead* (Chicago: American Marketing Association, 1980), 86–98.

# 10

# Communication and Consumer Behavior

## *introduction*

THE preceding chapters focused on individual consumers: what motivates them, how they perceive and learn, how their personality and attitudes influence their buying choices, and how these attitudes can sometimes be modified by persuasive marketing information. This chapter, which concludes Part II, explores the ways in which the consumer receives and is influenced by such marketing information. It discusses the structure and process of communication, the effects of communication sources on consumer buying decisions, and the types of marketing messages that tend to be most persuasive.

Part III discusses consumers not as individuals, but in the context of their sociocultural involvement with others: family, friends, and other groups to which they may belong or aspire to belong. Because communications with and from such outside influences tend to have a major impact on each individual's consumption behavior, it is important to understand how communication operates to influence and persuade consumers to make buying choices. In effect, communication is the bridge between individual consumers and their sociocultural world.

## WHAT IS COMMUNICATION?

Everyone "knows" what communication is, yet textbooks often vary in their definitions. At a basic level, most writers agree that *communication* is *the transmission of a message from a sender to a receiver by means of a signal of some sort sent*

> *Good communication is stimulating as black coffee, and just as hard to sleep after.*
>
> ANNE MORROW LINDBERGH
> *"Argonauta," Gift from the Sea (1955)*

*through a channel of some sort.* Figure 10-1 depicts this basic communication model.

However, the model leaves us with too many unknowns. What type of message does the sender wish to convey? Has he or she put it into a format that conveys its precise meaning? Through what medium (or what channel) is the message transmitted? Does the intended audience have access to this channel? Can the message surmount the psychological barriers that invariably surround all human receivers? Will the audience understand the message in the same way as the sender intended? And finally, how does the sender know if communication has taken place? Let us defer the answers to these questions until after we have examined the structure and process of communication. In so doing, we will explore many of the questions posed above concerning the basic communications process.

## THE STRUCTURE AND PROCESS OF COMMUNICATION

There are four basic components of all communication: a **source,** a **destination,** a **medium,** and a **message.** The source, as the initiator of the message, may wish to impart a feeling, an attitude, a belief, or a fact to another person or persons. To do so, the source must first find some way to *encode* this message so that it will accurately convey the message to the intended destination. He or she may use words, or pictures, or a facial expression, or some other kind of signal or code, that is familiar to the receiver, for the receiver to understand the intended meaning.

The source must then find an appropriate *channel* through which to transmit the message. To facilitate its delivery, the channel must have direct access to the receiver and be relatively free of distortion and static. The receiver must be willing and ready to accept the message. After receiving it, he *decodes* the message within the realm of his own experience. His acknowledgment of the message, in whatever form it may take, provides **feedback** to the sender that the message was received. In communications between two people, acknowledgment may consist of a nod, a smile, a frown, or a signed contract. In an impersonal communication (e.g., an advertisement), acknowledgment may consist of a purchase, a vote, or a redeemed coupon. The basic communication model, then, should be somewhat modified, as depicted in Figure 10-2.

**FIGURE 10-1 Basic Communication Model**

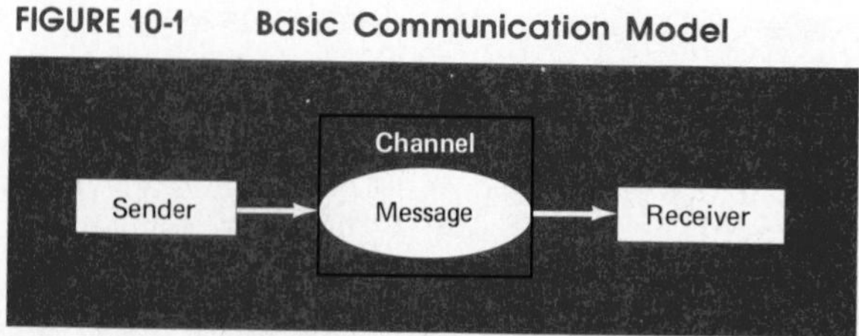

**FIGURE 10-2** Modified Communication Model

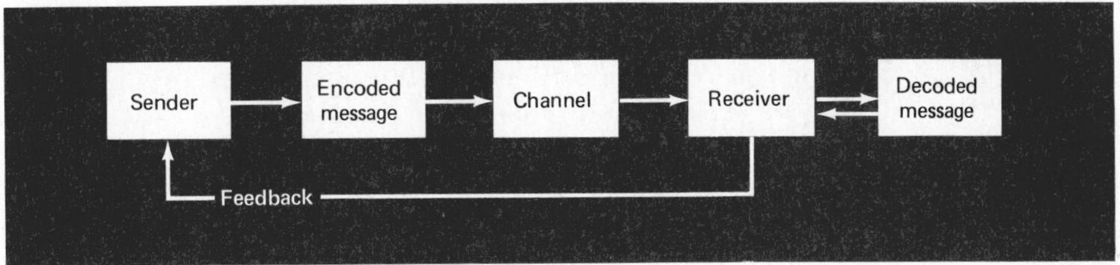


## Types of Communication

There are basically two types of communication to which a consumer is exposed: **interpersonal communication** and **impersonal** (or **mass**) **communication.** Their impact and influence differ markedly.

### INTERPERSONAL COMMUNICATION

Communication that occurs on a personal level between two or more people is called interpersonal communication. Such communication may take place between two people who meet on a face-to-face basis, who speak with each other on the telephone, or who correspond by mail. Interpersonal communication may be either **formal** or **informal.**

*Informal communication* concerning products or services differs from formal communication in that the sender does not speak in the capacity of a professional or commercial communicator (e.g., a sales representative), but more likely as one friend to another. Such *word-of-mouth* communication tends to be highly persuasive because the sender apparently has nothing to gain from the receiver's subsequent actions. (This is discussed later in the chapter as a function of source credibility.) For that reason, positive word-of-mouth can be very beneficial to a marketer; conversely, negative word-of-mouth can be disastrous, particularly because it is so difficult to control.[1] For example, malicious rumors spread across the country several years ago to the effect that the Procter & Gamble man-in-the-moon logotype represented Satan worship; not surprisingly, this nonsensical rumor had a very negative impact on sales. After first ignoring the rumor, the company tried without success to refute it, and finally—in order to eliminate it once and for all—removed the 103-year-old symbol from all its packages.[2] Needless to say, this was a very costly decision that underscores the power of informal communication.

Word-of-mouth has a positive side as well. The young entrepreneurs who developed the California Cooler (a wine and fruit juice bottled drink) relied mainly on word-of-mouth from satisfied customers to introduce the product. It was not until the product caught on that they hired an advertising agency.[3]

The problem with word-of-mouth as a deliberate marketing strategy is that it is generally uncontrollable; rumors spread like wildfire and it is difficult to predict if and when they will turn negative.

Recent studies suggest that *interpersonal informal communication* is an important consumer decision strategy, particularly for services, such as banks. This may be due to the fact that services are intangible and cannot be physically examined or returned for credit; thus consumers are more likely to seek informal product information from other consumers.[4]

*Formal interpersonal communication* is the kind of communication that takes place between a salesperson and a prospect, in which the salesperson serves as the sender and the prospect the receiver of product information.

Interpersonal communication tends to be effective because it enables the sender to detect almost at once the receiver's reaction to his or her message. This is particularly true of face-to-face communication, and to a lesser extent of telephone communication. Mail correspondence also permits feedback, but it is obviously slower. It depends on the receiver's willingness and ability to answer, and the time required for mail transmission and delivery.

Face-to-face communication may be both *verbal* and *nonverbal.* A mother may express displeasure with her child through a frown; a customer may express his indifference to a sales pitch through a yawn. Other types of nonverbal communication include smiles, fear, quizzical expressions, finger drumming, fist clenching, and applause.[5] Table 10-1 lists other examples of nonverbal communication; Figure 10-3 illustrates an appeal based on nonverbal communication.

INTERPERSONAL FEEDBACK. Both verbal and nonverbal *feedback* give the sender some indication of how the receiver has accepted the message and enable the sender to modify, repeat, or explain the message in greater detail. An experienced communicator is very attentive to feedback and constantly modifies messages in light of what he or she sees or hears from the audience.

Immediate feedback is the factor that makes personal selling so effective. It enables the salesperson to tailor the sales pitch to the expressed needs and observed reactions of each prospect. Similarly, it enables a political candidate to selectively stress specific aspects of his or her platform in response to questions posed by prospective voters in face-to-face meetings. Immediate feedback in terms of inattention serves to alert the college professor to the need to awaken the interest of a dozing class; thus the professor may make a deliberately provocative statement, such as "This material will probably appear on your final exam."

Only through feedback can the sender know if and how well the message has been received. That is why, in our model of the communication process, feedback is shown to be an integral link.

## IMPERSONAL COMMUNICATION

Communication directed to a large and diffuse audience is called *impersonal* or *mass communication.* It operates in much the same way as interpersonal communication, even though there is no direct contact between source and receiver. The sources of mass communication are usually organizations that develop and transmit appropriate messages through specific departments or spokespersons.

**TABLE 10-1 A Listing of Nonverbal Behaviors**

mouth region

1. Simple smile
2. Upper smile
3. Broad smile
4. Compressed smile
5. Wry smile
6. Oblong smile
7. Lip-in smile
8. Play face
9. Grin
10. Open grin
11. Mouth corners tremble
12. Mouth corners back
13. Squared mouth
14. Mouth corners out
15. Oblong mouth
16. Intention bite
17. Lip up
18. Sneer
19. Bite lips
20. Tight lips
21. Lips in
22. Lower lip out
23. Point
24. Purse
25. Small mouth
26. Twist mouth
27. Lips forward
28. Open mouth
29. Spit
30. Kiss
31. Intention speak
32. Chew
33. Tongue between lips
34. Tongue out
35. Lick
36. Mouth corners down
37. Scowl
38. Lower lip tremble
39. Yawn
40. Basic mouth

eyebrows

41. Raise
42. Flash
43. Angry frown
44. Sad frown
45. Sad raise
46. Low frown

eyelids and eyes

47. Shut
48. Blink
49. Narrow eyes
50. Droop
51. Wink
52. Stare
53. Widen
54. Pouch
55. Tears
56. Open

gaze direction

57. Look at
58. Look away
59. Look down
60. Look up
61. Look around

additional facial

62. Grimace
63. Screwface
64. Flare
65. Twitch
66. Sweat
67. Facial reddening
68. Blanch
69. Smooth face
70. Normal face

head movement

71. Threat
72. Head forward
73. Chin out
74. Head to side
75. Head movement
76. Jerk
77. Nod
78. Shake
79. Bob
80. Chin in
81. Hang
82. Head rock
83. Evade
84. Level

hands and arms

85. Shrug
86. Sit on hands
87. Scratch
88. Caress
89. Rub
90. Pick
91. Adjust
92. Fumble
93. Tap
94. Hand flutter
95. Digit suck
96. Mouth
97. Cup
98. Teeth
99. Cover eyes
100. Face
101. Finger face
102. Offensive beating posture
103. Defensive beating posture
104. Beat
105. Incomplete beat
106. Hand on neck
107. Arm over face
108. Clap
109. Pound
110. Push gesture
111. Demonstrate
112. Show
113. Gesture
114. Flat gesture
115. Palms up
116. Akimbo
117. Fold
118. Fist
119. Link
120. Grasp
121. Hands behind back
122. Hold
123. Punch
124. Touch
125. Single

lower limb

126. Cross legs
127. Shuffle
128. Tap floor
129. Leg tremor
130. Foot
131. Foot rock
132. Circle
133. Swing

trunk

134. Slope
135. Crouch
136. Hunch

Source: Christopher R. Branigan and David A. Humphries, "Nonverbal Behavior," in N. Burton Jones, ed., *Ethological Studies of Child Behavior* (Cambridge: Cambridge University Press, 1972).

The destinations, or *receivers,* for such messages are usually a specific audience or several audiences that the organization is trying to inform, influence, or persuade. For example, the American Cancer Society may wish to persuade teenagers not to smoke, or a bank may wish to convince businesspeople to use its services, or a detergent company may wish to persuade homemakers to use its soap powder.

FIGURE 10-3 The Appeal of Nonverbal Communication

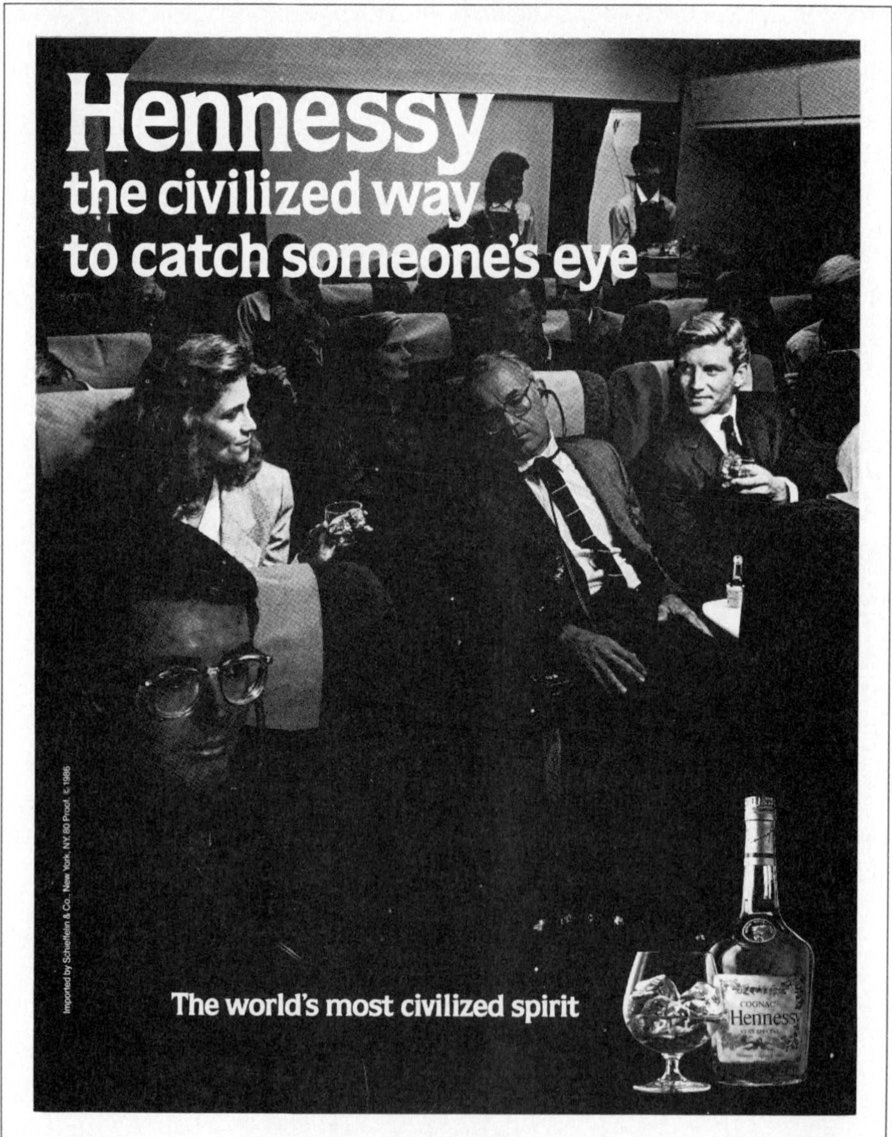


Courtesy of Schieffelin & Co.

In general, a company's marketing communications are designed to induce purchase, to foster the development of a positive attitude toward the product, to give the product a symbolic meaning, and/or to show that it can solve the consumer's problem better than the competition.

Impersonal communication is carried by such mass-media channels as television, radio, newspapers, magazines, and billboards. Because mass communications sources are organizations, their messages are considered formal. When such organizations are marketing organizations, their mass communications usually have commercial objectives (e.g., to persuade consumers to buy their products). Obviously, however, not all mass communications have commercial objectives. A school board may wish to persuade townspeople to support the new school budget, or the government may wish to persuade taxpayers to file their tax returns early.

IMPERSONAL FEEDBACK. *Feedback* is just as important a concept in mass communications as it is in interpersonal communications. Indeed, because of the large sums of money required for mass communication, many people consider such feedback even more essential than interpersonal feedback.

The organization that initiates the communication must develop some method for determining whether its mass communications are, in fact, received by its intended audience, understood in the intended way, and successful in achieving its intended objectives. Unlike interpersonal communication feedback, mass communication feedback is rarely direct; indeed, it is usually inferential. Receivers buy (or do not buy) the advertised product, renew (or do not renew) their magazine subscriptions, vote (or do not vote) for the candidate. The sender infers how persuasive its message is from the resulting action (or inaction) taken by the audience.

New modes of *interactive communication* that permit the audiences of mass media to provide direct feedback have made the distinction between interpersonal and impersonal communication less obvious. For example, TV news programs sometimes conduct opinion polls among viewers asking them to telephone a special number to register their agreement or disagreement with a burning issue of the day.

Mass communication feedback does not have the timeliness of interpersonal feedback; instead, it is usually somewhat delayed. Marketers rarely have the opportunity to find out immediately how effective their consumer advertising is. Since the pipeline from factory to consumer is fairly long, they must usually wait some time for reorders to occur in order to judge the effects of a national campaign. For this reason, they often buy information from research services like the Market Research Corporation of America, which collects data (based on purchase diaries of a panel of 7500 households scattered throughout the country) on weekly movements of brand shares, sizes, prices and deals. Retail executives, on the other hand, can usually assess the effectiveness of newspaper advertisements by midday on the basis of sales activity for the advertised product.

Mass communication sources often try to gauge the effectiveness of their messages by conducting audience research to find out which media are read, which television programs are watched, and which advertisements are remembered by their target audience. If negative feedback can be obtained fairly promptly, the source has the opportunity to modify or revise the message so that the intended communication does, in fact, take place. (Media feedback is discussed in more detail later in the chapter.)

Another type of feedback that companies seek from mass audiences is the degree of customer satisfaction or dissatisfaction with a product purchase. Smart marketers know that it is in their company's best interests to discover and correct any problems that occur as swiftly as possible in order to retain the brand's image of reliability. Procter & Gamble has a toll-free number for consumer comments on the package of each one of its products. Many utility companies now provide residential customers with written feedback (included in the monthly bill) on their energy consumption levels, accompanied by information on conservation practices.[6]

## THE AUDIENCE

While marketers are primarily concerned with directing mass communications to multiple, or mass, audiences, such audiences must not be thought of as large, undifferentiated masses, but rather as hundreds or thousands or even millions of individual consumers. Since messages are received *by* individuals; they must be written and directed *to* individuals, albeit many of them. To do so successfully, the marketer must understand those personal characteristics of individuals that operate to help or hinder the acceptance of persuasive communications.

### Barriers to Communication

There are many barriers to communication: some are physical, others are psychological. Among the psychological barriers that serve to impede receipt of mass communications are **selective exposure** and **selective perception.** Both of these selectivity "filters" are part of a larger body of theory known as **consistency** or **balance theory,** which postulates that individuals seek information that is consistent with their needs, interests, and attitudes, and avoid information that is not.[7]

As Chapter 6 indicated, most individuals are bombarded daily with more messages (i.e., stimuli) than any one person could possibly comprehend; to preserve their sanity, they subconsciously confine their attention to those messages that are in their realm of interest or experience, and ignore those that are not. In a marketing context, people selectively perceive information about products or services in which they are interested or which relate to their way of life, and they ignore information concerning products in which they have no interest. It is because of selective perception that *market segmentation* is such an effective marketing strategy. Marketers segment their markets on the basis of a relevant product interest or need. Prospects who are homogeneous in relation to that product interest are likely to perceive advertisements which address that interest, while those who are not interested in the product category simply ignore them.

For example, a young married couple looking for a new car will see and hear and read advertisements for all cars within their relevant price range; however, they may not even notice an ad for a Rolls Royce. A similar couple, exposed to the same media but not interested in purchasing a car, would probably notice no automobile ads at all. However, if the couple had just bought a new car, they would be likely to continue to note and read selected automobile advertisements in an attempt to reassure themselves that they had made the right choice—i.e., they would try to alleviate their **postpurchase dissonance.**[8]

In general, people tend to avoid dissonant or opposing information. They seek information that agrees with their beliefs, and they avoid information that does not. Thus Democrats tend to read Democratic campaign literature, listen to Democratic political speeches, and attend Democratic political rallies. Conversely, Republicans read Republican campaign literature, listen to Republican political speeches, and attend Republican political rallies. Each side carefully avoids information furnished by the opposing party. Political campaign efforts to recruit votes through mass-communication efforts are often pointless, since such political messages are "received" only by those who intend to vote for the party anyway. The only campaign efforts that are truly worthwhile are those directed at new voters and voters who have not yet made up their minds.

Even though people tend to avoid viewpoints opposite to their own, there are times when it makes sense to advertise to hostile audiences. Though it may not change the beliefs of those fully persuaded, an ad can prevent others from being infected with the same degree of hostility. This was the experience of the oil companies during the oil shortage situations of the middle and late 1970s. Chevron, Exxon, and Mobil did a great deal of advertising to explain their positions and boost their sagging company images. According to one researcher, such campaigns did indeed stop a further downward slide in public opinion.[9]

**Psychological noise** is another barrier to communication. Just as static on a telephone can impair reception of a message, so too can such factors as competing advertising messages or distracting thoughts. A viewer faced with the clutter of nine successive commercial messages during a program break may actually receive and retain almost nothing of what he has seen. Similarly, a woman planning her dinner menu while driving to work may be too engrossed in her thoughts to hear a radio commercial. On a more familiar level, a student daydreaming about his Saturday night date may simply not "hear" a question directed to him by his professor. He is just as much a victim of *noise*—albeit psychological noise—as the student who literally cannot hear a question because of hammering in the next room.

In all the instances mentioned, the best way for a sender to overcome noise is simply to repeat the message several times, much as the sailor does when sending an SOS over and over again to make sure it is received. (The effects of repetition on learning were discussed in Chapter 7.) *Redundancy* is constantly practiced by marketers who repeat the same advertisements over and over in the same medium and in supplementary media. For example, an advertising campaign usually consists of several different commercials and/or advertisements that feature the same advertising appeals presented in different contexts.

The principle of redundancy is also seen in advertisements that use both illustrations and copy to emphasize the same points. A major advantage of television is that it enables the advertiser to repeat the same message both verbally and visually. Redundancy frequently occurs in interpersonal communication; not only can the sender give examples and analogies to clarify the message, but he or she can also reinforce them with facial expressions and body movements.

Repeated exposure to an advertising message (redundancy of the advertising appeal) helps surmount a very real barrier to message reception and thus facilitates communication.

## The Mass Audience as Individual Receivers

We stressed earlier that all communications, whether interpersonal or impersonal, are ultimately received by individuals. A mass audience is simply a great number of individual receivers, each with his or her own interests, experiences, needs, wants, desires. It is unlikely that a marketer could develop a single communications campaign that would simultaneously appeal to the specific interests of great numbers of individuals in words they all understand via media they all see. For this reason, marketers who do try to reach their total audience with a single communications effort (i.e., those who do not segment their markets) often are unsuccessful. Efforts to use "universal" appeals phrased in simple language that all can understand invariably result in advertisements to which few people will closely relate.

Clearly, all individuals are *not* unique; they have specific traits or interests or needs that are shared by many others. A market segmentation strategy enables experienced marketers to exploit this fact by dividing their total audience into a number of smaller audiences, each of which is *homogeneous* in relation to some characteristic pertinent to the product. The marketer can then design a specific advertising message for each market segment which will appeal directly to the common interests of all the people in the segment, and run it in a specific medium that appeals to that segment. As a result, each individual in each market segment may feel that the advertising message received is specifically addressed to him or her in that it focuses directly on that individual's special interests or needs.

Since individuals with similar interests and attitudes frequently expose themselves to the same media, the marketer can place such messages in the specific media each market segment prefers.

For example, fashion-oriented consumers have reported that magazine ads are a more important source of information than either television or radio.[10] To reach such consumers, marketers should obviously use magazines. Because it enables marketers to tailor their appeals to the specific needs of like groups of people, market segmentation overcomes some of the problems inherent in trying to communicate with mass audiences.

## Multiple Audiences

All organizations—and certainly marketing organizations—recognize that their ultimate success depends on their ability to persuade many different kinds of audiences of the worthwhile nature of their products or other endeavors. Such audiences include *selling intermediaries* (distributors, wholesalers, and retailers), as well as other publics that are important to the organization's ultimate well-being.

Some companies with many diverse audiences have found it useful to develop a communications strategy that consists of an overall or "umbrella" communications message to all their audiences, from which they spin off a series of related messages targeted directly at the specific interests of each individual audience (e.g., customers, distributors, employees, stockholders).[11]

## SELLING INTERMEDIARIES

Most national manufacturers concern themselves primarily with transmitting persuasive communications to their ultimate consumers, but they must at the same time persuade the people through whom they sell their products—their *channels of distribution*—to buy and stock their products. It would be pointless to persuade final consumers to buy their products if consumers could not find such products at their local stores. Thus, in addition to advertising to the ultimate consumer (called *national advertising*), manufacturers usually direct advertising messages to each functional level of their distribution channels, utilizing appeals and media that are unique to that function (see Table 10-2).

For example, *trade advertising* is transmitted to product resellers (distributors, wholesalers, and retailers) through the relevant trade media by using appeals that are of specific interest to them, such as high profit, fast turnover, and

**TABLE 10-2 Types of Mass-Communication Efforts Initiated by Manufacturers and Selling Intermediaries**

| SOURCE | AUDIENCE | TYPE OF ADVERTISING | TYPICAL APPEALS | TYPICAL MESSAGE |
|---|---|---|---|---|
| Manufacturer | Wholesalers Retailers | Trade | Assortment, profit, turnover, store traffic, etc. | "Stock and display my product." |
| Manufacturer | Consumers | National | Convenience, personal benefits | "Buy my product anywhere." |
| Manufacturer | Other manufacturers | Industrial | Product improvement, cost savings, profits, etc. | "Use my product to make your product." |
| Manufacturer | Professionals | Professional | Satisfied clients, relieved patients | "Recommend or prescribe my product." |
| Wholesaler | Retailers | Trade | Large assortment, delivery, service | "Buy your stock from me." |
| Retailer | Consumers | Local or retail | Convenience, service, price | "Shop and buy all your needs at my store." |

increased store traffic. *Industrial advertising* is directed from one manufacturer to other manufacturers to persuade them to use the advertised product to make their own products (e.g., a thread manufacturer may advertise to clothing manufacturers). The type of appeal used in industrial advertising stresses the fact that the advertised product will enhance the second manufacturer's product (or decrease costs). Where appropriate, manufacturers also advertise to professionals in the field in order to persuade them to recommend or prescribe or otherwise specify the advertised product to patients or clients. An example of such *professional advertising* is a drug manufacturer who advertises a new product to physicians, hoping that they in turn will prescribe the product for their patients.

Retailers monopolize the nation's newspapers with *retail advertising* directed to the ultimate consumer. Such ads often feature products, sale prices, store services, and facilities; their prime purpose is to bring consumers into the store to shop. Whether they actually buy the products or brands advertised is of little importance to the retailer, so long as they make their purchases at the retailer's store.

The marketer also tries to reach other intermediaries (designers, salespeople, manufacturers) in the hope that each of these receivers will favorably affect the ultimate reception of the product by the end user.

## OTHER AUDIENCES

Wise managers are very much aware of the influence that many outside publics have on the ultimate success of their organizations. Table 10-3 lists some of these publics and the reasons why their good favor is important. For example, suppliers who think well of a firm will advance it credit and give prompt delivery of materials in short supply. Stockholders who are impressed with a company and its prospects will buy and retain its stocks. Employees who are con-

**TABLE 10-3 Audiences Outside the Channel of Distribution with Which Favorable Communications Must Be Maintained**

| AUDIENCE | COMMUNICATIONS OBJECTIVES |
|---|---|
| Suppliers | Obtain credit, prompt delivery |
| Customers | Encourage sales, profits |
| Government | Discourage unfavorable or restrictive legislation; encourage favorable legislation |
| Stockholders | Encourage stock purchases and reduce trading of company's stock |
| Community | Receive local support for building programs; attract labor pool; etc. |
| Employees | Motivate workers; improve product quality and production |
| Financial community | Raise short- and long-term capital at favorable rates when needed |

vinced they are working for a fine organization will be loyal, hardworking, and highly motivated. The financial community will readily advance short- and long-term funds for operations and expansions.

To maintain favorable communications with all their publics, most large organizations employ public relations counselors or establish their own public relations departments to provide favorable information about the company and to suppress unfavorable information. A good public relations person will develop a close working relationship with editors and program directors of all the relevant media in order to facilitate editorial placement of desired messages. Publicity campaigns designed to promote the image of the company are becoming increasingly popular, and marketers have developed methods to monitor and increase their effectiveness.[12] The greater credibility of editorial vehicles as compared with paid messages (advertisements) is discussed in greater detail in the next section.

## THE SOURCE

The *source* of a communication—the initiator of the message—is not only an integral component of the communications process itself, but also a vital influence on the impact of the message. A recent study reported that consumers acquire product information from both internal sources (their own experiences) and from external sources (e.g., sellers, the government, various organizations that provide consumption data, and personal friends and family).[13]

### Classification of Sources of Consumer Communications

We have already noted that there are basically two types of communication: interpersonal and mass communication. Sources of *interpersonal* communication may be either formal or informal. *Informal sources* include friends, family, neighbors, fellow employees, and the like, who speak with the receiver regularly or irregularly and may, in the course of conversation, impart product or service information. (Chapter 11 discusses the effects of such informal interpersonal influences.) *Formal interpersonal sources* include representatives of formal organizations, such as salespeople, company spokespersons, or political candidates, who are compensated in one form or another for influencing or persuading consumers to act in a prescribed way.

*Impersonal* sources of consumer communications are usually organizations—either commercial or noncommercial (nonprofit)—such as manufacturers, service companies, institutions, charities, government and political groups, who want to promote an idea, a product, a service, or an organizational image to the consumer. Such organizations generally appoint a specific department or person to create and transmit approved messages to desired audiences. These communications are usually *encoded* in paid advertising messages and transmitted via impersonal or mass media such as television, radio, newspapers, magazines, and billboards. In addition, they sometimes use such personal media as direct mail or sales promotion techniques (e.g., coupon or sample distribution) to transmit intended messages.

Sometimes a medium itself will be the source or initiator of product-related messages. This is particularly true of media with independent editorial departments, which can take specific stands on issues, ideas, and products and impart their views to their audiences. Included among such media are specialized rating publications, such as *Consumer Reports*. To avoid jeopardizing their reputation for impartial evaluations, these publications do not accept advertising.

Very often an organization's public relations department will encode a desired message within a newsworthy story format and transmit it via the editorial sections of mass media. The ensuing story is called *publicity* and differs from advertising only in that it appears in space or time that has not been bought by the sender. Since creation of the story events and subtle placement of the message may cost the sender considerably more in terms of money and trouble than a paid advertisement, cost savings are obviously not the basic motivation for publicity stories. The prime reason why companies prefer publicity is the increased **credibility** with which receivers regard editorial sources as compared with commercial sources of product communications.

Figure 10-4 depicts the various kinds of communications sources for consumer messages and the vehicles they use to transmit these messages. Among the most effective vehicles used by impersonal sources are *formal interpersonal communication,* such as face-to-face meetings with sales representatives or other company spokespeople.

In an effort to determine the relative importance of various communications sources in the purchase decision process, women respondents were asked the following questions concerning purchases of small appliances, clothing, and food items: (1) Could you tell me how this product came to your attention for *the very first time?* (2) How *else* did you hear about this product before you bought it? (3) Which one of these ways was your *most important* source of infor-

**FIGURE 10-4** **Sources of Consumer Communications and Related Message Vehicles**

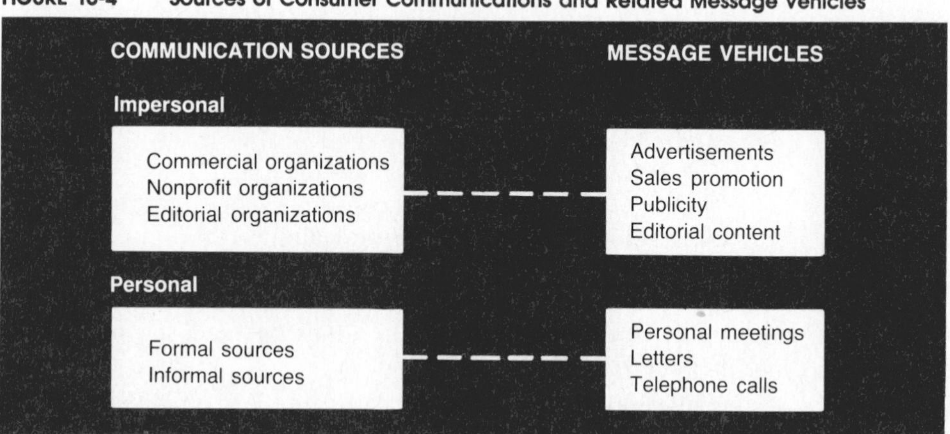

mation on your decision to buy this product?[14] They reported that informal interpersonal sources were most influential in the purchase decision process for each of the product categories under study. In the case of clothing purchases, sales promotion (such as displays) also played a very important part. For small appliances and food, neutral sources such as editorials and consumer rating services had surprisingly little influence.

In another study, women were asked to name the sources of information that influenced them to purchase (1) a man's shirt and (2) a television set in a specific retail store.[15] In this case previous experience with the store ranked first and second, respectively, while information from *Consumer Reports* or other neutral rating sources ranked sixth. Impersonal sources such as advertisements were clearly more influential for a high-priced technical product like a television set, while interpersonal sources such as friends were more influential for an inexpensive utilitarian item like a shirt.

Research suggests that it may even be possible to segment markets on the basis of the sources of information used in making purchase decisions. A study of major appliance buyers distinguished four segments of buyers on the basis of the number of stores visited and the types of information sources used: *objective shoppers,* who rely mainly on neutral sources of information; *personal advice seekers,* who rely mainly on personal sources; *store intense shoppers,* who rely heavily on physical visits to stores as well as on personal advice; and *moderate shoppers,* who seek more neutral sources of information and who rely less on store visits.[16] A different marketing strategy would be necessary to reach each segment. For example, ads stressing objective information would be most appropriate for objective shoppers, whereas advice from trained sales personnel would be most effective with personal advice seekers.

## The Credibility of Communication Sources

The source of the communication—his or her perceived honesty and objectivity—has an enormous influence on whether or not the communication is accepted by the receiver. If the source is well respected and highly thought of by the intended audience, the message is much more likely to be believed. Conversely, messages from a source considered unreliable or untrustworthy will be received with skepticism and ultimately rejected.

The *credibility* of the source is a vital element in the ultimate persuasibility of the message. Credibility is built upon a number of factors, the most important of which is the perceived intentions of the source. Receivers ask themselves: "Just what does he (or she) stand to gain if I do what is suggested?" If the receiver perceives any type of personal gain for the sender as a result of the proposed action or advice, the message may become suspect: "He wants me to buy that product just to earn a commission."

One of the major reasons why informal sources such as friends, neighbors, and relatives have such a strong influence on a receiver's behavior is simply that they are perceived as having no "ax to grind." Since they apparently have nothing to gain from a product transaction they recommend, their advice is considered totally objective, and their intentions are perceived to be in the best interests of the receiver.

Interestingly enough, such informal sources, called **opinion leaders,** often do profit—psychologically if not tangibly—by providing product information to others. A person may obtain a great deal of ego satisfaction by providing solicited as well as unsolicited information and advice to friends. As Chapter 16 points out, this ego gratification may actually improve the quality of the information provided, since the opinion leader will deliberately seek out impartial information in order to enhance his or her own position as "expert" on a particular product category. The fact that the opinion leader does not receive material gain from the action recommended improves the likelihood that the advice will be seriously considered. Experienced marketers try to utilize the phenomenon of opinion leadership by targeting their mass communications to opinion leaders, hoping that they, in turn, will pass these communications on to the rest of the population.

Even with informal sources, intentions are not always what they appear to be. Individuals who experience *postpurchase dissonance* often try to alleviate their uncertainty by convincing others to make a similar purchase choice. Each time they persuade a friend or an acquaintance to make the same brand selection, they are somewhat reassured that their own product choice was a wise one. The receiver, on the other hand, regards product advice from "the man who owns one" as totally objective, since the source had obviously conducted his own information search and is also able to speak from actual experience. Thus the increased credibility accorded the informal source may not really be warranted, despite the aura of perceived objectivity.

Such formal sources as neutral rating services or editorial sources have greater credibility than commercial sources because of the likelihood that they are more objective in their product assessments. That is why publicity is so valuable to a manufacturer; citations of a product in an editorial context, rather than in a paid advertisement, give the reader much more confidence in the message.

## MULTIPLICITY OF PERCEIVED SOURCES

Where the intentions of the source are clearly profit making, then reputation, expertise, and knowledge become important factors in message credibility. The credibility of commercial messages is often based on the composite evaluation of the reputations of the *initiator* (the organization that approves and pays for the advertising message), the *retail outlet* that carries the product, the *medium* that carries the message, and the *company spokesperson* (the actor or sales representative who delivers the message).

THE MESSAGE INITIATOR. Initiators of commercial messages include manufacturers, service companies, commercial institutions, and retailers. Since their intentions are clearly to make a profit, their credibility is based on such factors as past performance, the kind and quality of service they are known to render, the quality and image of other products they manufacture, the type of retail outlets through which they sell, and their position in the community (e.g., their stand on such issues as social responsibility or equal employment).

Firms with well-established reputations generally have an easier time selling their products than do firms with less well established reputations. This was demonstrated in an experiment in which the researcher showed a group of subjects two films of sales presentations. One film showed a poor sales presentation by a representative from a well-known company; the other showed a good sales presentation by a representative from an unknown company. The group preferred the products of the well-known company, even though they found the sales presentation less convincing.[17]

The ability of a quality image to invoke credibility is one of the reasons for the growth of **family brands.** Manufacturers with favorable brand images prefer to give their new products the existing brand name in order to obtain ready acceptance from consumers (i.e., *stimulus generalization*). A study conducted among housewives in four cities across the nation concluded that a new product has a much better chance for acceptance if it comes in under an existing brand name.[18]

Besides allowing a company to market new products with less risk, a quality image permits a company to experiment more freely in many areas of marketing than would otherwise be considered prudent. The long-established manufacturer can open new retail outlets, try new price levels, or experiment with innovative promotional techniques with confidence that the company's good image will carry over. Because a manufacturer with a good reputation generally has high credibility among consumers, many companies spend a sizable part of their advertising budget on *institutional advertising,* which is designed to promote a favorable company image rather than to promote specific products.

THE RETAILER AS A PERCEIVED SOURCE. The reputation of the *retailer* who sells the product also has a major influence on credibility. Products sold by well-known quality stores seem to carry the added endorsement (and implicit guarantee) of the store itself: "If Bloomingdale's carries it, it must be good." The aura of credibility generated by reputable retail advertising reinforces the manufacturer's message as well. A product carried in a quality store such as Saks Fifth Avenue is usually perceived as being of better quality than one carried by a mass merchandiser; therefore a message concerning its attributes is more readily believed. That is why so many national advertisements (i.e., manufacturer-initiated ads) carry the line "Sold at better stores everywhere."

THE MEDIUM AS A PERCEIVED SOURCE. The reputation of the *medium* that carries the advertisement affects the credibility of the message. Marshall McLuhan underscored this fact in his book *The Medium Is the Message.*[19] The image of a prestige magazine like the *New Yorker* confers added status on the products whose advertisements it carries. The reputation of the medium in terms of honesty or objectivity also affects the credibility of the advertising. Consumers often think that a medium they respect would not accept advertising for products it did not "know" were good. For example, the *Good Housekeeping* Seal of Approval carries a lot of weight with some consumers. For this reason, manufacturers are often happy to avail themselves of the merchandising services offered by some media, and purchase and distribute supplementary promotional material, such as counter cards and product hangtags that say, for example, "As Advertised in *Vogue* Magazine."

In recent years there has been a large increase in the number of men's and women's fashion magazines, and their revenues have significantly and steadily risen. This indicates growing interest in fashion and high perceived credibility of fashion publications. On the other hand, studies have shown that people perceive various news media as exploitative—as more interested in sensationalism and invasion of privacy than in accuracy. Because of this credibility problem, marketers may reevaluate placing their messages in such media.[20]

THE SPOKESPERSON AS A PERCEIVED SOURCE. People sometimes regard the person who gives the product message as the source (or initiator) of the message. Thus the "pitchman"—whether he or she appears personally or in an advertisement—has a major influence on message credibility. In interpersonal communication, a salesperson who engenders confidence, and who gives the impression of honesty and integrity, is generally more successful in persuading a prospect than one who does not have these characteristics. Such confidence or credibility is created in diverse ways. A salesperson who "looks you in the eye" may appear more honest than one who evades direct eye contact. For many products, a sales representative who dresses well and drives an expensive, late-model car may have more credibility than one without such outward signs of success (and inferred representation of a best-selling product). For some products, however, a salesperson may achieve more credibility by dressing in the role of expert. For example, a man selling home improvements may achieve more credibility by looking like someone who has just climbed off a roof or out of a basement than by looking like a stockbroker.

Interaction between the spokesperson and the medium affects the overall credibility of the presentation. Thus, in two experiments, a "likable" communicator's message was more persuasive in videotaped and audiotaped form, while the "unlikable" communicator was more persuasive in written format.[21] Along these lines, during the 1960 Kennedy-Nixon presidential campaign debates, Kennedy achieved greater impact on TV than Nixon did, but radio listeners found Nixon more persuasive.

In impersonal communication, the reputation or expertise of the advertising spokesperson may strongly influence the credibility of the message. That accounts for the popularity and effectiveness of testimonials as a promotional technique. In general, four types of individuals are used as advertising spokespersons: the *celebrity,* the professional (or recognized) *expert,* a top *corporate officer* (CEO), and the *typical consumer.*

Experts are particularly sought after for testimonials. If a known or reputed expert in a specific field endorses a related product, consumers are usually ready to follow his or her advice, even though the endorsement is clearly profit-motivated. This is true of testimonials given by recognized experts as well as testimonials given by unknown but stereotypical actors with inferred or implied expertise. White-coated actors who look like doctors have been able to persuade viewers to buy over-the-counter drugs, despite the fact that the audience was warned that the commercial was a staged presentation.

Karl Malden, well known for his roles as a police officer in films and on TV, has lent some of that air to his role as a spokesperson for American Express traveler's checks. His warning "Don't leave home without them" has an air of believability about it because viewers associate him with crime prevention.

Marketers who use a *testimonial* strategy should recognize that the potential success of their advertising rests on the credibility of the spokespeople they use. If celebrities are used, they should have some obvious knowledge about the product or recognized expertise in the product category. Guidelines issued by the Federal Trade Commission require endorsers to have the experience, special competence, or expertise to form the judgment expressed by their endorsement. Persuasive endorsements by nonusers are considered deceptive advertising.

Advertisers who use testimonials must be sure that the specific wording of the endorsement lies within the recognized competence of the spokesperson. A movie actress can believably endorse a face cream with comments about its overall skin coverage or smoothing effects; however, a recitation of its chemical properties is beyond her expected knowledge and expertise and thus reduces rather than enhances, message credibility. A radio campaign that featured actress Joan Fontaine endorsing Pepperidge Farm's heat-and-bake dinner rolls lacked credibility because few listeners could envision the glamorous Joan in a kitchen preparing dinner. (Chapter 11 explores the credibility of various types of spokespersons in greater detail.)

## AUDIENCE ATTITUDES AFFECT CREDIBILITY

The initial opinion that an audience holds prior to receiving the message can affect the persuasiveness of both high- and low-credibility sources. When the audience is favorably predisposed to the message *prior* to its presentation, moderately credible sources produce more attitude change than highly credible sources. However, when the audience is opposed to the communicator's position, the high-credibility source is more effective than the less-credible source.[22]

This was demonstrated in a study where a highly credible source was more effective than a moderately effective source in advocating a consumption pattern (i.e., buy rather than lease) that the respondents viewed unfavorably; conversely, the moderately credible source was more persuasive when advocating a practice (lease rather than buy) that the respondents favored.[23] If an audience perceives a message to be incompatible with its source, a high-credibility source will be no more believable than a low-credibility source.[24] If the arguments used are unfamiliar to the audience, the high-credibility source induces about the same amount of opinion change as the low-credibility source.[25]

The consumer's own experience with the product or the retail channel also acts to affirm or deny the credibility of the message. A product or a store that lives up to its advertised claims increases the credibility with which future claims are received. Research suggests that fulfilled product expectations tend to increase the credibility accorded future messages by the same advertiser, while unfulfilled product claims or disappointing products tend to reduce the credibility of future messages.[26] The significant increase in mail order sales has been attributed to the fact that reputable catalog houses have lived up to their advertised claims of providing full and prompt refunds on all merchandise returns.

### THE EFFECTS OF TIME ON SOURCE CREDIBILITY

The persuasive effect of high-credibility sources does not endure over time. Though a high-credibility source is initially more influential than a low-credibility source, research has found that both the positive and negative credibility effects of communications sources tend to disappear after several weeks. This phenomenon has been termed the **sleeper effect.**[27] Recent studies support the fact that over time, people dissociate the message from its source.[28] However, reintroduction of the message serves to jog the audience's memory and the original effect remanifests itself—that is, the high-credibility source remains more persuasive than the low-credibility source.[29] The implication for marketers who utilize high-credibility sources is that they must repeat the message by the source frequently in order to maintain its persuasiveness.

## THE MEDIUM

To receive a message, an individual must, at the very least, be exposed to the medium through which it is transmitted. But just as individuals expose themselves *selectively* to advertisements, so too do they expose themselves selectively to media. There are so many different categories of media available today and so many media alternatives available within each category, that individuals tend to develop their own special preferences. Consumers cannot avail themselves of all media options—there are simply too many. And since an individual can reasonably watch only one TV channel or listen to only one radio station at a time, he or she can be exposed to only one of the numerous advertising messages that are broadcast simultaneously.

In general, media are undergoing *demassification*—that is, they are moving from large, general interest audiences to small, special interest audiences. What was once a mass (undifferentiated) audience has broken down into smaller, more specialized groups. In response to their special interests, there is more programming available on cable TV, magazines continue to proliferate, and new radio networks have developed, while newspapers, a more general medium, are experiencing declines in circulation.

Changes in lifestyle have affected media habits. For example, daytime television was once considered the best way to reach women. Now, however, with so many women working, advertisers have had to rethink their media strategies. Today much of the daytime viewing audience consists of other demographic groups—such as elderly people and youth. These, in turn, have attracted a different type of advertiser to daytime television.[30] Since consumers have more media to choose from, their viewing and reading habits are more likely to be based on individual interests. It is this factor that makes market segmentation such a viable marketing strategy.

## Media Strategy

**Media strategy** is an essential component of a market segmentation strategy. (Remember, *accessibility* to the audience is one of the five criteria for a successful market segmentation strategy.) It calls for the placement of ads in the specific media read, viewed, or heard by selected target markets. To accomplish this, advertisers develop, through research, a **consumer profile** of their target customers that includes the specific media they read or watch. The media also research their own audiences in order to develop descriptive **audience profiles** (see Figure 10-5). A cost-effective media choice is one that closely matches the advertiser's *consumer profile* to a medium's *audience profile.*

Another aspect of media strategy focuses on the product and the intended message. Advertisers must select a general media category that will enhance the message they wish to convey. Some media categories are more appropriate vehicles for certain products or messages than others. For example, a retailer who wants to advertise a clearance sale should advertise in local newspapers, since that is where consumers are accustomed to looking for sale announcements. A manufacturer who wants to present a detailed argument in favor of its sewing machines should advertise in household magazines, where readers are accustomed to reading detailed articles and stories. A marketer who wants to promote a power mower with unique cutting features would be wise to use a medium like television, where the mower can be demonstrated in action. Once marketers have identified the appropriate media *category,* they can then choose the specific medium in that category that reaches their intended audiences.

Some evidence indicates that the same advertisement will generate different communications effects when run in different media. A study of the interaction of two types of magazine vehicles (a prestige magazine like the *New Yorker* and an "expert" or special interest magazine like *Tennis World*) and two types of copy approaches (*reason-why* and *image* copy) found that, for nonusers of the product in question, prestige magazines were more persuasive in communicating product quality and image than expert magazines. Conversely, expert magazines were more effective in delivering factual information.[31] These results give support to the notion that a media vehicle induces a "mood" of receptivity that affects the impact of a persuasive communication.

## Print Versus Broadcast Media

The two major media categories are **print** (magazines, newspapers, direct mail, outdoor) and **broadcast** (television, cable, radio). Which category the marketer selects depends on the product or service to be advertised, the market segments to be reached, and the advertising objectives. Rather than select one media category to the exclusion of the other, many advertisers use a *multimedia* campaign

**FIGURE 10-5** A Media Advertisement Targeted at Advertisers

# Does he get angry when you say dumbbell?

## Or does he know you know more about muscles than he does?

She's not just smart about dumbbells. Right now she's lifting weights. Working her way through the October Vogue Spot/Toning Plan.

October Vogue also tells her woman does not live by exercise alone. To feel better, look great, she has to 'Let Go!' "Not only," assures Vogue, "is relaxation not self-indulgent, it's as essential as exercise to survival."

Vogue heralds the return of the spa. And maybe even the siesta.

**"Never trust those who don't like to eat."**

Vogue talks healthy food. Introduces "Le Hamburger," perfectly balanced for nutrition, it's an exclusive Vogue recipe from Michael Guerard.

The care and feeding of Bordeaux wines is in October Vogue.

So is help on avoiding hidden sugar. Secret salt.

**Takes the Paris Pulse.**

Sixteen Paris couture pages proclaim the genius of St. Laurent. The daring of Ungaro. All photographed on Brooke Shields by Avedon.

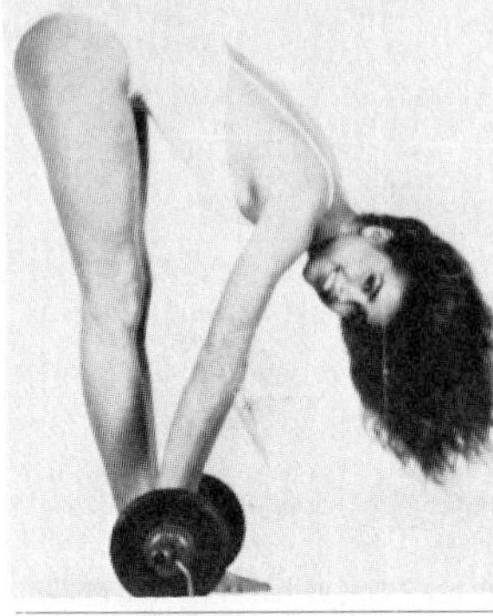

**The book women live better by.**

Nothing important to women escapes Vogue. Nothing in Vogue escapes women.

Vogue prescribes. 5.2 million Vogue readers subscribe. To everything Vogue suggests. Thanks to Vogue they know what to eat. And what not. How and how much to exercise.

**Healthy climate for advertisers.**

75% of Vogue readers say they buy Vogue to read the ads. That means almost 4 million of the most educated, affluent, intelligent, influential women in America are eager to know what's on your mind. Got a swimming new idea for pools?

20% of Vogue families are pool owners. Ready to plunge right into your message.

How about bicycles? Tennis or golf equipment? Skis? Weights? Water skis? Fishing or boating gear? More than one hundred thousand Vogue families are hitting the water in their own boats.

**Healthy incomes, too.**

Vogue's 5.2 million have the millions to get what they want and go where they want. 73% of subscribers own stock. 49% own real estate, in addition to their own homes. A

whopping 94% have department store charge accounts. And last year alone 90% spent an average of $3500 on pure pleasure travel. It's a rich market that can afford the things that make it look good. And feel good. And travel far. And entertain well. And decorate to the teeth.

And live gloriously.

**Vogue says.**

Next to Bartlett's, no book is quoted more. In the office. On the plane. At the bar. And now, even in the examining room.

# VOGUE

## The book women live by.

Courtesy Vogue. Copyright © 1980 by the Condé Nast Publications Inc.

strategy, with one primary category carrying the major burden of the campaign, and the second category providing supplemental support.

Numerous research studies have compared the effectiveness of one medium over the other for various products, audiences, and advertising objectives. In general, the findings have been inconclusive. Each media category has certain advantages and disadvantages which the marketer must consider in developing a media strategy for a specific campaign. The following sections summarize the pertinent characteristics of each category and discuss some feedback mechanisms available for evaluating advertising effectiveness.

## PRINT MEDIA—MAGAZINES AND NEWSPAPERS

**Magazines** are an important medium for advertisers to consider when they want to describe the features and resulting benefits of their products, when they have a persuasive argument to present, and when they want high-quality reproduction. In addition, magazines have broad geographic coverage as well as geographic flexibility (through regional editions). They provide credibility, prestige, long life, multiple readership, and pass-along readership. Not only do magazines engender cognitive processing of information that improves memorability and recall, but they are generally targeted to specific demographic, geographic, and lifestyle (e.g., special interest) market segments.

A disadvantage of magazines is the long lead time needed to submit advertisements; this often prohibits timely reaction to topical events. For example, advertisements for the Ford Aerostar, featuring visual references to the Challenger space shuttle, appeared in magazines ten days after the Challenger exploded upon takeoff in January 1986. Similarly, advertisements for Tylenol capsules appeared in *Time* magazine the day after a Tylenol-related death was reported in newspapers and on TV. These ads could not be "pulled" in time to avoid embarrassment for their companies. Despite generally high audience selectivity, in some cases magazine advertisers pay for waste circulation that was lured more by premiums earned for subscribing than by reader interest.[32]

**Newspapers** are a timely, widely read, geographically flexible medium that reaches a local audience on a regular (usually daily) basis. They thus provide an ideal medium for local retailers. Lead time for advertising submissions is usually short. Newspapers have broad acceptance and high believability from a relatively heterogeneous audience. On the down side, newspapers have a short life, poor reproduction quality, limited alternatives for color and presentation format, and little *pass-along* readership. As the competition with TV news programs intensifies, newspapers are losing circulation. However, they are still the place where consumers look for retail announcements and sales.

The major issues that marketers must consider when selecting specific newspapers and magazines to carry their ads are the characteristics of the audience, overlapping audiences, and determining the effectiveness of their print advertisements. Each of these issues will be examined in turn.

AUDIENCE CHARACTERISTICS. Marketers use various syndicated marketing research services to obtain data on magazine audiences—their demographics, product purchases, brand preferences. In order to be successful in this era of magazine proliferation, most magazines try to carve a niche for themselves in the marketplace by catering to the needs and interests of a specific target segment. The failure to identify its target market precisely can spell disaster. For example, Time, Inc., which publishes such successful magazines as *Time, Money, People,* and *Sports Illustrated,* lost $47 million on its *TV Cable Week* venture. This loss has been attributed to the publisher's failure to delineate carefully its intended audience: cable operators. In contrast, *Cable Guide,* published by two independent businessmen, became an overnight success. Its success was attributed to the publishers' understanding of the needs of cable operators as well as TV viewers.[33] Perhaps in response to its *TV Cable Week* failure, Time, Inc., conducted an extensive market test of its proposed new magazine, *Picture Week,* targeted at the young, 9 to 5 working woman who wants a magazine below (yes, below) the intellectual level of *People,* but above that of supermarket tabloids. Time, Inc. tested various cover story approaches and two price levels in an effort to get a firmer grip on the characteristics of *Picture Week*'s intended audience.[34]

Newspaper audiences are more diversified than magazine audiences because newspapers tend to target a geographic (i.e., local) audience, rather than specific demographic or lifestyle characteristics. To some extent, they try to target the entire local community, though some newspapers do develop *positioning* strategies designed to enhance a desired image among specific target audiences.[35] Thus newspapers vary in the audiences they attract. For example, the demographic and lifestyle characteristics of *The Wall Street Journal* or the *New York Times* readers vary considerably from those of the *New York Post* or the *Daily News.*

OVERLAPPING AUDIENCES. Since many media—especially those with similar editorial features and formats—have *overlapping audiences,* advertisers usually place their advertising messages simultaneously or sequentially in a number of media with similar audience profiles. This enables them to achieve both **reach** and **frequency.** The term *reach* refers to the number of different people or households that are exposed to the advertisement (either because they hear or watch the program or read the newspaper or magazine); *frequency* refers to how often they are exposed to it during a specified period of time. Most advertisers want to reach their audiences more than once; by using similar media, they can reach a wider audience with the same relevant market characteristics and reach the same individuals in several media in order to give them repeated exposure to the same advertising message. For example, many women read one or more fashion magazines. A perfume manufacturer who wishes to reach fashion-conscious women may run an ad simultaneously in *Vogue* and *Harper's Bazaar.* Each advertisement will reach a unique part of the desired market segment that reads only that magazine; in addition, each ad will reach women who read both magazines and thus see the ad twice. As Figure 10-6 illustrates, a *Vogue* ad will reach women in the desired market segment who read *Vogue* but not *Harper's Bazaar* (subset *A*); a *Harper's Bazaar* ad will reach women who read *Harper's Bazaar* but not *Vogue* (subset *B*); the overlapping area (subset *C*) reaches women who read both magazines and therefore see the advertisement twice. By using both media, the advertiser increases the size of the market segment exposed

**FIGURE 10-6** **Unique and Overlapping Readership of Magazines with Similar Audience Profiles**

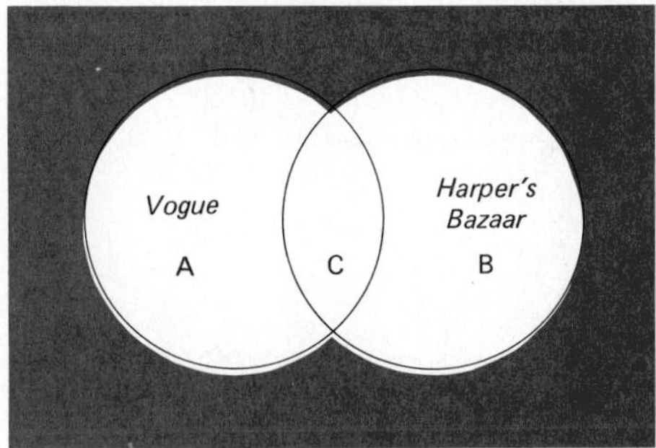


to the advertisement and, in instances of overlapping readership, increases the frequency (and impact) of the advertising message.

MEASURING FEEDBACK OF PRINT COMMUNICATIONS. Earlier we noted the importance of **feedback** in the communications process. Feedback enables the communicator to know if, and to what extent, a message has been received by the intended audience. Obtaining feedback in interpersonal communications is relatively easy. It is more difficult with impersonal communications, such as print and broadcast advertisements. Nevertheless, it is important for advertisers to obtain feedback in order to assess and, where necessary, improve the effectiveness of their messages.

Advertising effectiveness research—often called **copy testing**—can be done before the advertising is actually run in media *(pretesting)* or after it appears *(posttesting)*. Pretests are used to determine which, if any, elements of an advertising message should be revised before major media expenses are incurred; posttests are used to evaluate the effectiveness of an ad to see which elements should be changed to improve the impact of future ads.

One popular method for evaluating the effectiveness of magazine advertisements is through a syndicated service called the Starch Readership Service. Readers of a given issue of a magazine are asked to point out which ads they "noted," which they "associated" with the sponsor, and which they "read most." The resulting readership score is meaningful when compared to similar ads (in terms of size), to competitive ads, and to the marketer's own prior ads. Figure 10-7 presents Starch Readership scores for a TRW ad in *Business Week*.

In a recent study using the Starch readership scores, male readers were found more likely to "note" ads that had female models; less likely to note ads that showed a male and female model together, and least likely to note ads that showed a male model alone. Readership of an ad (Starch's "read most" category) was found to be more influenced by product type than by the model shown. For example, automobile ads were found to have a higher readership score than liquor and cigarette ads, and liquor ads had higher readership than cigarette ads.[36]

**FIGURE 10-7** **Starch Readership Scores Provide Communication Feedback for Print Advertisements**

Courtesy of Starch Inra Hooper, Inc.

Among other recognition and recall copy tests, it is interesting to note a newly proposed method based on the reader's ability to form *closure* (guess the missing words in an ad) and enjoy the message. Research has demonstrated that closure and enjoyment are good indications of message recall.[37]

A number of studies have tried to manipulate the proportions of illustrations and body copy used in print ads to determine the impact on recall and persuasion, but the findings have been fragmented and inconclusive. For example, a recent study showed that in some instances body copy alone induced more favorable consumer evaluations than body copy used in conjunction with a picture; in other instances the reverse was true. Verbal or visual cues designed to cause the consumer to retrieve information from memory were not always related to persuasion.[38] One researcher found that all-copy print ads were rated as more utilitarian/rational, and all-visual print ads were rated as more familiar.[39] Other researchers found that the attractiveness of the picture in the print ad influenced brand attitudes.[40] While the evidence is somewhat inconclusive as to what makes a print ad memorable or persuasive, it is generally agreed that *creativity* and successful *positioning* are essential components in creating persuasive print communications.

## OTHER FORMS OF PRINT MEDIA—OUTDOOR AND DIRECT MAIL

**Outdoor media** (billboards, transit cards) are geographically flexible and provide repeated exposures at a relatively low cost. While billboards and transit cards can be bought in specific "markets" to reach desired audiences, there is still a great deal of waste coverage in terms of the audience reached. Nevertheless, outdoor media tend to provide good visual support to print and TV campaigns.

The growth of **direct mail** advertising has been enormous during the past several years. Since direct mail is *advertising that is sent directly to the mail address of a target customer,* it is highly selective in terms of the audience it reaches. Furthermore, direct mail is personalized, geographically flexible, and rarely experiences direct competition within the same medium. However, it is high in cost and tends to have a "junk mail" image because of the high degree of mailbox clutter.

*Direct marketing,* sometimes confused with *direct mail,* is not a medium but a marketing technique that uses one or more media (direct mail, print, broadcast, telephone) for the purpose of soliciting a direct response from a consumer by mail, telephone, or other access (e.g., interactive cable). Its objective is to make a sale or obtain a sales lead or inquiry. A major reason for the explosive growth in direct marketing is its ability to generate measurable responses. This capability enables direct marketers to measure the profitability of their efforts directly through such variables as cost-per-inquiry, cost-per-sale, and income-per-advertisement, and to evaluate the timing and frequency of campaigns. Computers are an indispensable tool in direct marketing; they are used to generate profitability figures for market segmentation and for personalized direct mail solicitations.

## BROADCAST MEDIA—RADIO AND TELEVISION

The advantages of **radio** are its widespread use (particularly during "drive time" to and from work and during the summer season), its geographic flexibility, and its low cost. Radio is a very local medium, yet it is useful in reaching highly selective target segments. Its major disadvantage is that, as an aural medium only, it is less an attention-getter than TV. Radio has long been ignored because marketers prefer the glamour of TV. Now, however, several advertisers have begun to use the sound tracks of television commercials on radio to achieve greater frequency and impact for their commercials at a lower-than-TV cost. Based on the principle of **closure** (see Chapter 6), listeners who have seen a TV commercial mentally "play back" the video track as they listen to the audio portion on radio, thus closing the gap between the two media through *audience participation.*

**Television** held great promise as an advertising medium when it was first introduced precisely because it most closely simulated interpersonal communication. It was the closest thing, advertisers said, to having a salesperson in the consumer's living room. There is no question that TV is an exciting medium; it stimulates two senses—both sight and sound. It has a capacity for dramatization, it serves as an attention-getter through the use of sophisticated visual images and special effects, it is highly popular, and it reaches vast audiences.

Television also has disadvantages as an advertising medium. Because of the very high costs of television time, commercials are getting shorter and shorter, resulting in a long string of back-to-back commercials for different products, called advertising *clutter.* Clutter tends to reduce memorability. Furthermore, according to involvement theory (see Chapter 7), television viewing is a right-brained, passive information-processing activity that is less likely to change attitudes than the left-brained cognitive activity invoked by print media. Because of the vast reach of television, most programs reach a more diversified audience than advertisers using a segmentation strategy might wish.

MEASURING TELEVISION ADVERTISING EFFECTIVENESS. Syndicated services such as the A. C. Nielsen Company and Arbitron collect data on the size and characteristics of the viewing audience through electronic means, supplemented by diaries kept by a national sample of viewers. *Recall* and *recognition studies* are also conducted to determine whether consumers remember seeing a commercial and whether they can recall its content, and to assess the commercial's influence on attitudes toward the product and on buying intentions.

Television has been a highly successful advertising medium since its commercial inception in the late 1940s; however, some recent developments have important implications for television advertisers. These are the issues of **clutter, "zapping"** and **"flicking,"** and **audience miscomprehension.**

TV CLUTTER. *Clutter,* or a high "noise" condition, occurs when viewers are exposed to a number of commercials within a short period of time. Studies show that as the amount of clutter increases, consumers are less likely to recall the brands advertised or recognize commercials they have seen, particularly when exposed to several competing ads in a brief period of time. This suggests that, when buying advertising time, advertisers should insist on exclusive or restrictive placement.[41] Commercials have also been found to be intrusive (and therefore objectionable) to viewers, particularly when they are perceived as "interrupting" interesting programs.[42] To add to the clutter problem, many advertisers make use of new technologies to *time compress* their commercials.

Thus, more information can be squeezed into a single commercial, and more commercials can be run in the same time slot. This adds to the clutter problem.

ZAPPING AND FLICKING. New technologies enable TV viewers to be considerably more selective in what they watch. Thus, most VCR owners eliminate commercials from their viewing of previously recorded programs by either pressing the fast-forward button ("zapping"), or using the pause button while recording. Many viewers with remote control (or cable boxes) "flick" channels during commercials and/or programs; this activity is particularly prevalent at end-of-program breaks.[43] Among the reasons given for these activities are: to see what else is on, to avoid commercials, boredom, for variety, and—in just a few cases—to watch several shows simultaneously.[44] Advertisers concerned with flicking sometimes "roadblock" their commercials on all three networks. *Roadblocking* entails scheduling the same commercial on all three networks for the same time period. This way, if viewers switch from show to show in order to avoid commercials, they will still be exposed to the commercial as long as they don't switch to an independent or cable station. McNeil Laboratories recently used the "roadblock" tactic to announce to its consumers that it was removing all its Extra Strength Tylenol Capsules from the shelves as a result of the February, 1986 Tylenol tampering. A recent study of the "flickers" and "zappers" found that males are more likely to do so than females; younger persons are more likely to do so than older individuals, and children are more likely to do so than their parents.[45] Figure 10-8 presents an ad placed by *TV Guide* which hopes to capitalize on this problem.

In response to the problems of clutter, flicking and zapping, advertisers are reaching out for new forms of audiovisual presentation of their product. There is some consideration to putting commercials on videocassette movies and even on blank cassettes in the hopes that consumers will watch them before recording over them. Also, more companies are paying for product "plugs" in TV shows and movies. For example, in *The Goonies,* a recent Steven Spielberg film, one of the characters appears with several containers of Swensen's ice cream, and in another scene refers to the product by name. Similarly, a Michelin tire was prominently displayed in a recent James Bond movie, and the company built several promotions based on this placement.[46]

VIEWER MISCOMPREHENSION. Recent studies show that a large portion of TV viewers (approximately 30 percent) miscomprehend the information communicated to them.[47] Both *message* characteristics and *receiver* characteristics appear to contribute to this phenomenon. Miscomprehension appears to be more widespread among older and lower-income viewers. Somewhat surprisingly, viewer familiarity with the message was unrelated to miscomprehension.[48] Frequent scene changes and the employment of both video and audio simultaneously to convey the same message (e.g., a brand name) was found to increase the level of miscomprehension, although the complexity of information was not.[49]

One implication of these findings is that marketers should reduce distraction in their commercials and give viewers less stimuli to process at the same time. Despite some questions regarding projection of laboratory findings to the

FIGURE 10-8 A Magazine Advertisement Highlights an Acute Television Problem

# THE VCR BLUES.

A lot of advertisers are singing them. As video shops spring up like mushrooms. As VCR penetration climbs toward one out of four households.* As zapping becomes an everyday term.

If you've got a feeling your TV schedule is being jilted by a lot of VCR owners, TV Guide can help.

We'll give you the national impact you need in spite of VCR's, cable, discs, video games and computers. TV Guide is big enough all by itself to add important GRPs to your schedule. And your message will get to the biggest audience of VCR owners of any magazine. Plus reach more light viewers than any other weekly—over 23% of all adults in the two lightest viewing quintiles.

Add TV Guide to your schedule, and our more than 39 million adult readers will help chase those blues away.

SOURCES: SMRB 1984 Special Tabulation. SMRB 1985. *Industry Estimate    TV Guide® and the TV Guide logo are trademarks of Triangle Publications, Inc.

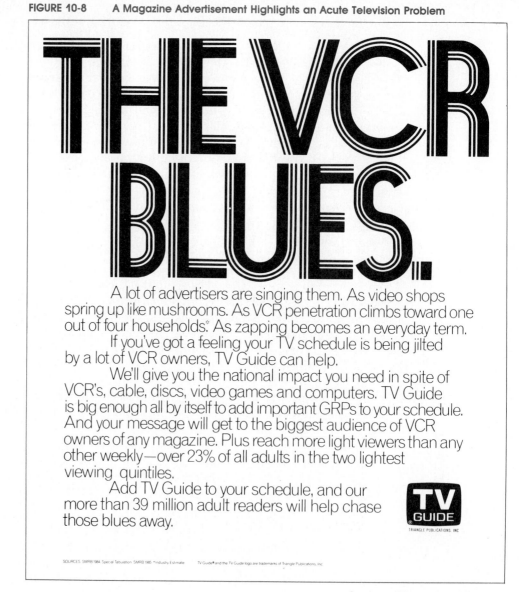

Courtesy of Triangle Publications Inc.

total population, prominent researchers in this field maintain that the findings are applicable to most TV audiences in the United States.[50]

Clearly, marketers must be familiar with the characteristics of their audiences and the characteristics of media if they are to make wise media choices. To implement the most effective media strategies, however, they must also be familiar with the characteristics of their products. That is a prime requisite for preparing a persuasive message.

The **message** is often considered the most vital component of all in the communications process. The message is the *thought, idea, attitude, image or other information that the sender wishes to convey to the intended audience.* In trying to encode the message in a form that will enable the audience to understand its precise meaning, the sender must clearly recognize exactly what it is that he or she is trying to say and why (what the objectives are and what the message is supposed to accomplish).

The marketer's objectives tend to vary with the audience. Objectives in communicating with consumers, for example, may be one or all of the following: (1) informing them what is for sale, (2) creating brand awareness, (3) getting them to buy the product, (4) reducing their uneasiness after the purchase is made. The marketer's objective with intermediary customers is to get them to stock the product; with other manufacturers, to get them to buy the product and use it to make their own.

Senders must also know their audiences' characteristics in terms of education, interests, needs, and realms of experience. They must then endeavor to encode or phrase their messages in such a way that they will fall within the consumers' zones of understanding and familiarity.

To attract the attention and interest of their target audiences, marketers should start their advertisements with an appeal to the needs and interests of the audience, and end with an appeal relevant to their own needs (with an effective sales closing). Marketers have found that the most effective ads conclude by telling the audience exactly what it is they want them to do: "Visit your Chevrolet showroom today"; "Ask for it at your favorite cosmetic counter"; Send us your order by return mail." Advertisements that do not conclude with an "action" closing tend to provoke much *less* action on the part of the consumer than those that do. Table 10-4 lists twelve techniques summarized from

**TABLE 10-4 Communication Techniques to Make a Message Memorable**

1. Get the audience aroused.
2. Give the audience a reason for listening.
3. Use questions to generate involvement.
4. Cast the message in terms familiar to your audience and build on points of interest.
5. Use thematic organization—tie material together by a theme and present in a logical, irreversible sequence.
6. Use subordinate category words; i.e., more concrete, specific terms. (Example: *duck* rather than *bird, duck* being a subordinate word to *bird.*)
7. Repeat key points.
8. Use rhythm and rhyme.
9. Use concrete rather than abstract terms.
10. Use the *Zeigarnik* effect—leave the audience with an incomplete message, something to ponder so that they have to make an effort to achieve *closure.*
11. Ask your audience for a conclusion.
12. Tell the audience the implications of their conclusion.

Source: James MacLachlan, "Making a Message Memorable and Persuasive," *Journal of Advertising Research,* 23 (December 1983–January 1984), 51–59.

the literature on communications to make a message more memorable and persuasive.[51]

## Method of Presentation

We have already demonstrated that to be effective, a message must (1) be directed to the appropriate audience, (2) use appeals that are relevant to the interests and experience of the audience, and (3) be transmitted via media to which the audience is exposed. In addition, the *manner* in which a message is presented strongly influences its impact. The method of presentation affects the readiness with which the message is received, accepted, and acted upon. The following discussion examines some well-known principles concerning message presentation.

### TWO ROUTES TO COMMUNICATION PERSUASION

Researchers have identified two routes—the central and peripheral routes—to persuasion.[52] The implications of this approach for consumer *information processing* have been reviewed in Chapter 7. Here we will discuss their implications for *message presentation.*

According to the theory, messages with strong, issue-relevant arguments are a **direct** or **central route to persuasion.** Thus a well-documented advertisement concerning the pros (and/or cons) of the product encourages active, cognitive information processing that may induce the consumer to buy the product. Favorable *noncontent message cues,* on the other hand—such as the background scenery in a commercial or the personality of the spokesperson—provide the consumer with pleasant indirect associations with the product and provoke favorable inferences about its merits; thus this **peripheral route** also leads to persuasion.

Researchers have also demonstrated that the presentation to individuals of messages that are consistent with their self-images triggers cognitive, *central* route processing of information.[53] Other researchers report that the inclusion of quantitative information in the message stimulates people to rely on a *peripheral* cue, such as the spokesperson, while nonquantitative information stimulates individuals to process the content of the message cognitively *(centrally).*[54]

Some marketers tend to oversimplify the two-route approach by differentiating between emotional (i.e., peripheral route) and rational (central route) message appeals. The distinction between these two approaches is readily seen in advertisements that make heavy use of emotional, symbolic cues in their formats as opposed to straightforward, factual presentations. However, researchers argue that it is impossible to deliver either a completely rational or a completely emotional message.[55] Therefore, marketers should consider a combination of both routes when designing a message. When the product message directly and factually addresses unfulfilled needs, it will trigger cognitive evaluation by the consumer, and thus central processing. The use of highly visual, symbolic cues in the advertisement to support the product claim (i.e., the peripheral route) is likely to enhance the persuasiveness of the message; thus the two routes in combination are likely to be more persuasive than either would be alone.

## ONE-SIDED VERSUS TWO-SIDED MESSAGES

Should marketers tell their audiences only the good points about their products or should they also tell them the bad (or the commonplace)? Should they pretend theirs is the only product of its kind, or should they acknowledge competing products? These are very real strategy questions marketers face every day, and the answers depend on the nature of the audience and the nature of the competition.

If the audience is friendly (e.g., if it uses the advertiser's products), if it initially favors the communicator's position, or if it is not likely to hear an opposing argument, then a **one-sided** *(supportive)* communication that stresses only favorable information is most effective. However, if the audience is critical or unfriendly (e.g., if it uses competitive products), if it is well educated, or if it is likely to hear opposing claims, then a **two-sided** *(refutational)* message is most effective.[56]

These findings are especially relevant in today's marketing environment, in which many competing products claim superiority over others. Less sophisticated marketers continue to stress only positive factors about their products and pretend that competition does not exist. However, when competition does exist, and when it is likely to be vocal, such advertisers tend to lose credibility with the consumer. Some recent research suggests that claim credibility can be enhanced by actually *disclaiming* superiority in some product features in relation to a competing brand.[57]

Communication researchers not only have explored the problem of persuading audiences to take some prescribed action (e.g., to buy a product), but also have investigated ways to keep existing customers safe from outside persuasion.[58] Their findings suggest that two-sided appeals containing both pro and con arguments about the brand serve to **inoculate** consumers against arguments that may be raised by competitors. In effect, this strategy provides consumers with **counterarguments** with which to rationalize against future attacks by competing brands.

A practical illustration of two-sided advertising is seen in **comparative advertising,** a marketing strategy used by increasing numbers of marketers. Comparative advertising has been defined as *advertising that explicitly names or identifies one or more competitors of the advertised brand for the purpose of claiming superiority,* either on an overall basis or in selected product attributes (see Figure 10-9). It can be useful for product positioning, for target market selection, and for brand differentiation strategies (which stress the differential advantage of the "underdog" product over leading brands). To reinforce credibility, marketers usually cite an independent research organization as the supplier of data used for the comparison (see Figure 10-10).

FIGURE 10-9 An Example of Comparative Advertising

# A message to consumers from the Pepsi-Cola Company.

We have believed for a long time that we produce a better-tasting product than our leading competitor. But we wanted to be sure of that fact. We did not want to advertise it until we had it documented by careful, objective, independent research. We now have that documentation.

**Truth in advertising is very important to us. And the truth is:**

**NATIONWIDE, MORE COCA-COLA DRINKERS PREFER PEPSI THAN COKE.**

The better taste we always thought we had has now been confirmed by blind taste tests conducted among thousands of people in over a hundred cities and towns throughout this country. This concrete fact may explain some of the strange advertising sponsored by the Coca-Cola Company lately. Advertising like the silly blindfold commercials comparing Fresca (a sugar-free, citrus flavored drink) with Pepsi. These commercials announce that one third of the participants chose Fresca. They fail to point out that what this actually means is that *two thirds* preferred Pepsi.

Now they've come out with a series of comparative commercials in which both Pepsi and Coke are tasted side-by-side. In these, they claim that New Yorkers prefer Coke to Pepsi 2 to 1. But each product in these commercial tests is clearly identified. How can the results be valid when the only fair test must be a *blind* test, eliminating the bias of habit, which may have nothing to do with taste.

All this is Coca-Cola's attempt to answer what we call, "The Pepsi Challenge." The fact that none of these efforts constitute a real answer is not surprising. After all, how can there be a real answer when there is no real question, no question whatsoever that NATIONWIDE, MORE COCA-COLA DRINKERS PREFER PEPSI THAN COKE. (And, of course, Pepsi-Cola drinkers overwhelmingly prefer Pepsi.)

But don't take our word for it. Don't take anybody's word for it—

**Let your taste decide. Take the Pepsi Challenge.**

For a summary of these research findings, please write to P.O. Box 102, Purchase, New York 10577

Reprinted with permission of PepsiCo, Inc.

Although comparative advertising is widely used, it is not without critics. Researchers dispute its effectiveness in aiding message recall. Some maintain the message-recall effectiveness of comparative ads is somewhat higher than that of ads which do not explicitly name the competition.[59] Others maintain that though recall is better immediately afterward, it is not better twenty-four hours later, and that comparative advertising may aid recall of the competitor's

FIGURE 10-10 Comparative Advertising Cites Research Data

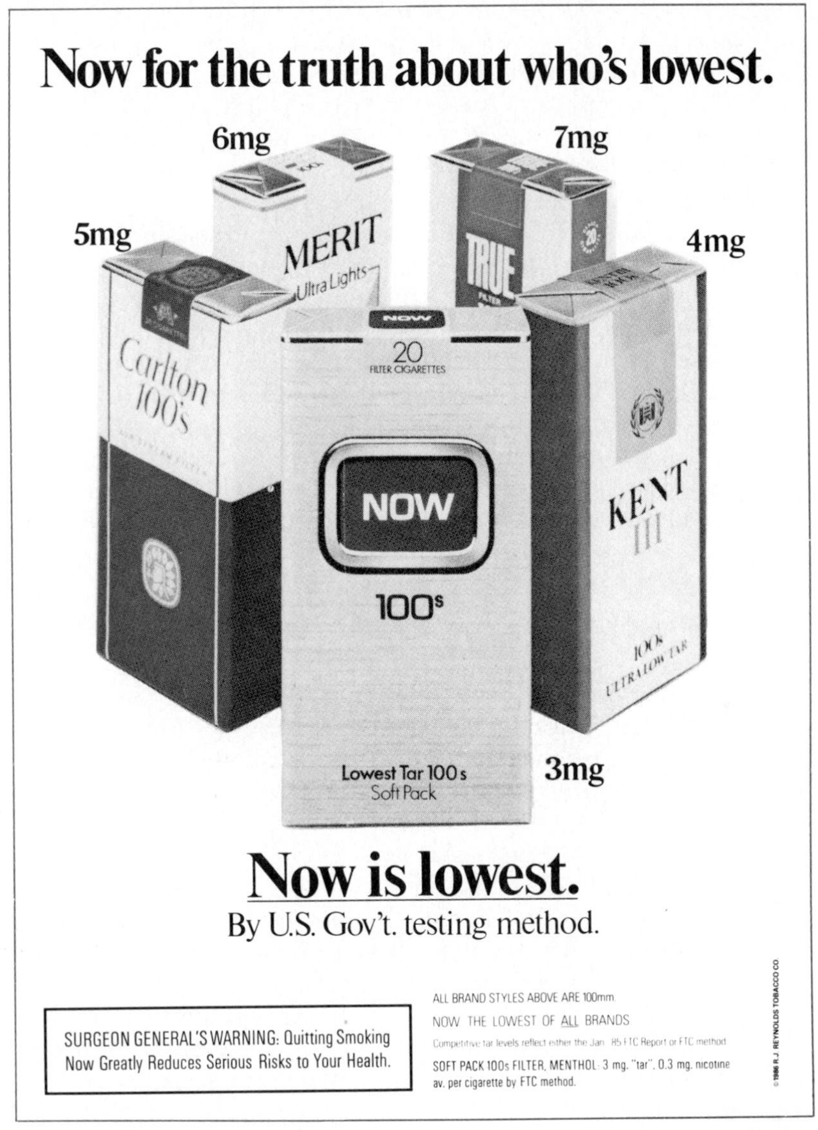


Courtesy of R.J. Reynolds

brand as much as that of the advertised brand.[60] There is evidence that incorporating two-sided claims into the comparative message (i.e., where the marketer disclaims superiority on minor product attributes) increases the acceptance of the ad.[61] Such an approach was found to generate better initial attitudes toward a new brand as well.[62] It is not clear whether comparative advertising holds more promise for market *leaders* or for market *challengers*. One study showed that non-comparative messages were more effective than comparative appeals for new brands competing with a dominant brand.[63] However, another study showed that comparative advertising by a brand challenging the leader increased consumers' perceived similarity between the two brands.[64] When Avis ran its now legendary campaign against Hertz ("We're number two; we try harder"), it was, in fact, way behind Hertz in terms of market share. However, the campaign helped to place it on fairly equal footing in consumers' perceptions.

Findings are also mixed regarding consumers' reactions to comparative advertising. One advertising agency found that audiences perceived comparative commercials as more confusing and less believable than non-comparative commercials.[65] The reason appeared to be that the points of comparison seemed arbitrarily selected. Other more recent studies have found no major differences between comparative and non-comparative ads in increasing awareness of product features.[66]

In defense of comparison ads, research has found that consumers think them more interesting but generally less informative than non-comparative ads.[67] Research also indicates that they are more effective for branded convenience and specialty goods than for shopping goods.[68]

## ORDER EFFECTS

Is it best to present your commercial first or last? Should you give the bad news first or last? Communication researchers have found that the order in which a message is presented affects audience receptivity.[69] For this reason, politicians and other professional communicators often jockey for position when they address an audience sequentially; they are aware that the *first* and *last* speeches are more likely to be retained in the audience's memory than those in between. The media recognize the impact of **order effects** by according "preferred position" placement to front, back, and inside covers of magazines, which means they charge more for these positions than for inside magazine pages because of their greater visibility and recall.

Order is also important in arranging points within a message. Should the most important point be first or last? If audience interest is low, the most important point should probably be made first to get attention. However, if interest is already high, it is not necessary to pique curiosity, and so points can be arranged in order until the most important point is made at the end.

When just two competing messages are presented, one after the other, the evidence is somewhat conflicting as to which position is more effective. Some researchers have found that the material presented first produces a greater effect (the *primacy* effect), while others have found that the material presented last is more effective (the *recency* effect).[70]

On TV, the position of a commercial in a commercial break was shown to be critical. The commercials shown first were recalled best, those in the middle the least, and the ones at the end slightly better than those in the middle.[71] When both favorable information and unfavorable information are to be presented (for example, in an annual stockholders' report), placing the favorable material first often produces greater tolerance for the unfavorable news. It also produces greater acceptance and better understanding of the total message.[72]

## Copy Approach

As the discussion on the two routes to persuasion theory pointed out, sometimes rational or *factual* appeals are more effective; sometimes nonrational or *emotional* ones are. It depends on the kind of audience to be reached and the product itself. In general, logical, reason-why appeals are more effective in persuading high-IQ audiences, who tend to be "turned off" by unsupported generalities, irrelevant arguments, or emotional appeals. Conversely, emotional appeals have been found to be more effective in persuading people of lower intellectual achievement.[73]

### FEAR APPEALS

Fear is often used as an appeal in marketing communication. Research findings report a negative relationship between the intensity of fear appeals and their ability to persuade. That is, strong fear appeals were found to be *less* effective than mild fear appeals.[74] For example, after a brief decline in cigarette smoking following the *Attorney General's Report* in 1964 linking cigarette smoking to lung cancer, cigarette consumption actually increased. A number of explanations have been offered for this phenomenon. Strong fear appeals concerning a highly relevant topic (e.g., a cigarette habit) cause the individual to experience cognitive dissonance, which he or she resolves either by rejecting the habit or by rejecting the unwelcome information. Since giving up a cherished habit is difficult, consumers more readily reject the threat. This they do by a variety of techniques, including denial of the validity of the fear claims ("There still is no real proof"), the belief that they are immune to personal disaster ("It can't happen to me"), and a diffusing process that robs the claim of its true significance and thereby renders it impotent ("I play it safe by smoking only filter cigarettes").[75]

There is some indication that mention of possible harmful effects of a product category, in the context of showing the safety of the advertised product, causes negative attitudes toward the product itself. Thus, ads for tampons which illustrated the benefits and safety of the advertised feminine sanitary product against toxic shock syndrome were not as effective as those that did not include a direct reference to toxic shock.[76] Findings on the relationship between the intensity of fear appeals and persuasion suggest that strong fear appeals are more persuasive than mild fear appeals when source credibility is high.[77] A recent study showed that moviegoers who were given prior knowledge of the upcoming frightening events in the movie were more intensely frightened and upset by the movie than people who were not forewarned.[78] Thus, forewarning may not be an effective strategy to reduce emotional upsets;

not mentioning the frightening events may be a better strategy. Conversely, if the movie producer wants people to be scared, he or she should mention the anticipated horrors in advertisements for the movie.

Fear appeals are more effective when they pose a threat to the audience's loved ones or deal with unfamiliar topics.[79] Characteristics of the audience may also influence the persuasive effects of fear appeals. For example, individuals who can cope well and who are high in self-esteem or low in perceived vulnerability appear to be most easily persuaded by fear.[80] So are older individuals, especially blue-collar blacks or those who are more liberal politically.[81] Recent research suggests that future studies on fear appeals should differentiate between physical and psychological fear approaches (e.g., health versus social disapproval), and should develop better measures of fear levels.[82] For example, it would be useful to measure the difference in impact of a fear appeal that portrays the product as a preventative against a crippling bone disease and one that portrays the product as a preventative against slipping dentures.

## HUMOR IN ADVERTISING

Many advertisers use humor in their advertising in the implicit belief that humor will increase the acceptance and the persuasibility of their communications. Other advertisers avoid the use of humor because they fear their product will become an object of ridicule, that consumers will laugh *at* them rather than *with* them. The use of humor in advertising has increased considerably during the 1980s. Several recent studies have outlined the advantages and limitations of humorous commercials:[83]

1. Humor aids awareness of and brings attention to the commercial.
2. Humor, in general, does not aid persuasion or source credibility. People may like the ad, but that does not mean they will switch brands.
3. Humor may impair comprehension of the ad. It may distract the viewer from the ad copy.
4. Humorous commercials have a short life span. (How many times can a person laugh at the same joke?)
5. Humor should be related to the product and should not be used with sensitive goods and services. For example, such topics as money (e.g., bank advertising) and safety (insurance advertising) are not laughing matters to most people.
6. Radio and TV are the best media in which to use humor. Radio humor, in particular, tends to "humanize" an ad and helps it stand out when a listener is bombarded with messages.

There is evidence that audience characteristics may confound the effects of humor. For example, blacks and whites in the United States do not always perceive the same things to be humorous.[84] Younger, better-educated, upscale and professional persons are best suited for humorous messages. The program or editorial matter that surrounds a humorous message also influences its effectiveness. Humorous commercials have been found to work best when presented in an action-adventure environment, rather than in a situation-comedy environment.[85] This is an illustration of the Gestalt principle of *contrast* (see Chapter 6.) With so many qualifying conditions on its effectiveness, perhaps the wisest policy for marketers to follow is to use humor very selectively for products and audiences that seem to lend themselves strongly to this approach.

### "AGONY" ADVERTISING

All of us have at one time or another been repelled by the so-called agony commercials which depict in diagrammatic detail the internal and intestinal effects of heartburn, indigestion, clogged sinus cavities, and hammer-induced headaches. Nevertheless, pharmaceutical companies continue to run such commercials with great success because they appeal to a certain segment of the population that suffers from ailments that are not visible, and which therefore evoke little sympathy from family and friends. Their complaints are legitimized by commercials with which they immediately identify. With the sponsor's credibility established ("They really understand the misery I'm going through"), the message itself is often highly persuasive in getting consumers to buy the advertised product.

### ABRASIVE ADVERTISING

How effective can unpleasant or annoying ads be? Studies of the *sleeper effect,* discussed earlier, suggest that an individual's agreement with a persuasive communication from a low-credibility source is stronger a long time after exposure rather than immediately thereafter.[86] This has interesting implications for marketing—and helps explain the old public relations dictum: "It matters not whether they think well of you or ill of you so long as they remember your name." It suggests that the memory of an unpleasant commercial that saturates the media and antagonizes listeners or viewers may in the end dissipate, leaving only the brand name and the persuasive message in the minds of consumers.

### SEX IN ADVERTISING

The combination of ever-increasing competition from new products and the traditional worry that consumers are being inundated by too many advertising claims has convinced many advertising people that **emotional persuasion** (i.e., sex appeal) is a necessary ingredient in advertising. Sex in advertising ranges from the blatancy of nudes and obvious double entendre to devices so subtle it takes a trained observer to recognize them. There are many instances where advertisers who have used sex as a thematic appeal have been most successful. In other instances, such advertising has proved either damaging or highly ineffectual. Consumer reaction to advertisements with sexual appeals is difficult to predict. There is evidence, for example, that women who tell researchers that a sensuous girl or a nude in an ad is "disgusting" are among the first to run out and buy the product.

If effects are so unpredictable, why do advertisers continue to use sex in their advertising? The answer is simple. There are few appeals in advertising that equal its attention-getting value. Sex is one of the most basic of all human motives (see Chapter 3.) Many psychologists believe that the skillful manipulation of sexual appeals—in visual images, in copy, or in both—may arouse subconscious desires that manifest themselves in the purchase of goods or services. For this reason, many advertisers use sex in their thematic appeals, hoping to catch the consumer's attention and persuade him or her beneath the level of conscious awareness. Readership studies show that sex is one element that arouses the immediate interest of both men and women.

Nevertheless, many people believe that the use of sexual appeals in advertising is simply not good marketing. While sexual themes may attract a reader's attention, they rarely encourage curiosity about the product. There are strong indications that the type of interest sex evokes often stops exactly where it started—with sex. If a "sexy" illustration is not relevant to the product advertised, it makes no selling impression on the reader. For example, a study of the effectiveness of several "sexy" commercials for jeans found that, in terms of "stopping power," the commercials scored *higher* than the norm for clothing commercials. In terms of achieving a "favorable buying attitude," however, they scored *below* the average for clothing.[87] This highlights the potential risk of sexually oriented advertising: the advertiser may be trading persuasiveness for stopping power.

One study of sexually oriented ads compared the recall scores of ads that used sexual elements (1) as an attention-getting device, (2) to display the function of a product, (3) as fantasy images, or (4) symbolically.[88] It found that ads which used sexual themes and sexual elements solely as *attention-getting devices* proved to have the lowest brand recall scores. (These findings have been confirmed by other studies.) Ads in which sexual themes were presented as part of a *fantasy fulfillment* enjoyed good recall scores. Still better recall scores were obtained by ads that used sexual elements in a *functional* fashion, such as ads for bras or lingerie (see Figure 10-11). The ads that received the highest recall scores were those that used sexual elements in a highly *symbolic* manner, such as an ad for Eve cigarettes, which featured the picture of a lit cigarette lying horizontally across the top of an apple.

Researchers have found that men and women respond differently to sex in advertising.[89] For one thing, perceptions among males of an ad's sexiness correlated highly with the extent of nudity portrayed. For females, romantic content was the primary determinant of whether an ad was considered sexy. Even more interesting are gender differences regarding brand recall. Though extremely sexy ads provoked dropoffs in brand recall for females as well as males, findings showed that females could tolerate ads that produced a high level of sexual arousal and still recall the product names, while males who saw ads with high sexual arousal couldn't remember anything about the product.[90] Given such findings, it is not surprising that there are far more ads with nudes

FIGURE 10-11 Sex Used in a Functional Manner to Sell Lingerie

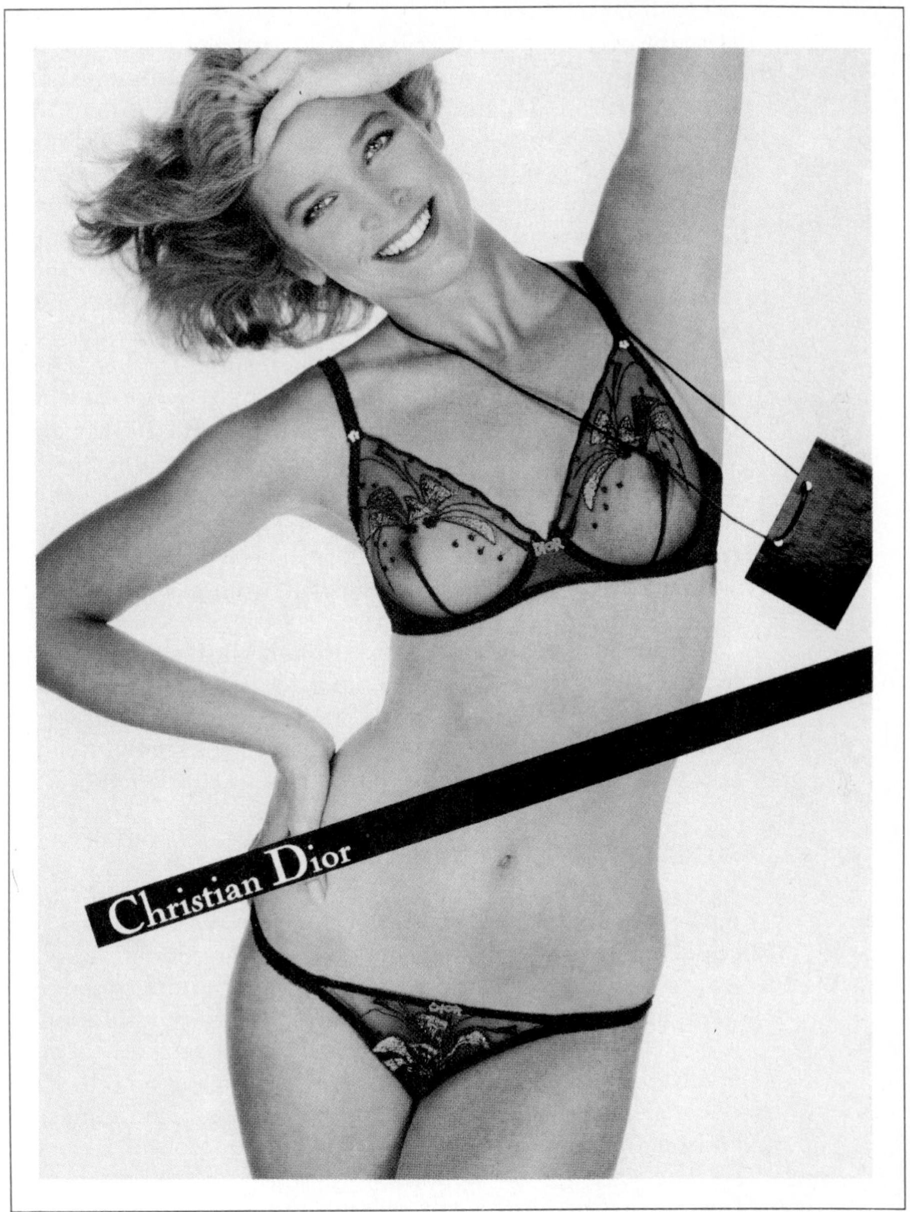


Courtesy of Christian Dior–New York, Inc.

and sexy themes in female magazines like *Vogue* and *Cosmopolitan* than in male magazines like *Playboy*. The remarkable ability of erotic ads to distract rather than inform, especially when the audience is predominantly male, suggests that the many industrial marketers who use sex to sell industrial equipment may be wasting their advertising budgets.

Researchers have also examined qualitative responses to sexy ads. In one study, housewife subjects were organized into six focus groups based on social class (blue collar versus white collar) and age (18 to 25, 30 to 40, and 55+).[91] Each group was shown a series of television commercials for Underalls pantyhose, Muriel cigars, and Aviance perfume. The women reacted *positively* to an Underalls ad which focused on female derrières when it stressed the primary benefit of the product (the elimination of panty lines), and *negatively* to another version which suggested that Underalls look like "you're wearing nothing at all." The reactions to the Muriel cigar ads split along age lines, with young women objecting to the demeaning, subservient role of the scantily clad woman in the commercial (who sits on the late-working husband's lap to light up his cigar), and reported feeling threatened by the ad, while older women liked the commercials. There was also a split response on female fantasy ads, as evidenced by reactions to a commercial for Aviance perfume. The commercial opens with a young wife, dressed in apron and rubber gloves ready for housework, who suddenly breaks into a striptease, immerses herself in an Aviance bubblebath, sprays Aviance perfume down her low-cut blouse, and greets her handsome husband at the door—"ready for an Aviance night." Young blue-collar women hated the commercials, and found them threatening and offensive. On the other hand, white-collar women reported that the Aviance commercial was one of their favorites.

One thread seems to run through all the research findings regarding sex in advertising: The advertiser must be sure that the product, the ad, the target audience, and the use of sexual themes and elements all match up. When sex is relevant to the product, the results can be striking. Evidence shows that when sex does fit, it can be an extremely potent copy theme.

### AUDIENCE PARTICIPATION

Earlier we spoke about the importance of *feedback* in the communications process. The provision of feedback changes the communications process from one-way to two-way communication. This is important to senders, because it enables them to determine whether and how well communication has taken place. But it is also important to receivers, because it enables them to participate, to be involved, to experience in some way the message itself. Participation by the receiver *reinforces* the message. An experienced communicator will ask questions and opinions of an audience to draw them into the discussion. Many professors use the participative approach in classrooms rather than the more sterile lecture format because they recognize that student participation tends to facilitate internalization of the information discussed.

Although participation is easily accomplished in interpersonal situations, it takes a great deal of ingenuity in impersonal situations. Thus it is a challenge for imaginative marketers to get consumers involved in their advertising. The counter-argumentation provoked by two-sided messages may be one feasible way to do so. Incomplete messages, requiring closure, may be another (see Figure 10-12). Interactive or two-way television (also known as videotex) is a prom-

FIGURE 10-12 Advertisement Designed to Encourage Audience Participation

*At THE RUG WAREHOUSE whether you have $100 or $10,000 to spend on a fine oriental or oriental design rug we have New York's largest selection to show you.*

**For $0**

- Our knowledge and experience to guide you in choosing the finest quality rug to suit your needs and decor.
- Our free 7 day home trial.
- Our unconditional money back guarantee that our prices are the lowest anywhere.
- Our thanks and appreciation even if you only come into browse.

**$100 - $250**

- All 4x6 and 6x9 Dhurrie rugs.
- Over 150 2x2 to 4x6 handmade new, semi-antique and antique rugs.
- All 4x6 and 6x9 oriental design and Berber rugs.
- Over 30 4x6 handmade Turkish Kilms.
- Excellent selection of 8x11 all wool oriental design rugs.
- Good selection of runners 2⁶x6 to 2⁶x10.

**$250 - $500**

- Over 100 8x10 and 9x12 Dhurrie rugs.
- All 4x6 90L 5/8" super Chinese.
- Over 50 8x10 and 9x12 top quality oriental design rugs.
- All 4x6 super fine silky Bokharas.
- All 4x6 new Tribal Turkish, Afghan, Caucasian, rugs.
- Over 50 pcs 4x6 handmade Persian design rugs from India, Pakistan, China, etc.

**$500 - $1500**

- Over 100 new Indian, Pakistan, Rumanian, Caucasian, Turkish rugs in 5x7 and 6x9 sizes.
- Large selection of Persian and Turkish Kilims.
- All 6x9 and 8x10 90L 5/8" super Chinese.
- Over 50 8x10 new Indian, Pakistan, Rumanian, Caucasian, Turkish rugs.
- Large selection of new 9x12 handmade India, Pakistan, and Rumanian rugs.

**$1500 - $3000**

- Over 30 9x12 to 12x18 semi-antique and antique Persian rugs.
- All 9x12 90L 5/8" super Chinese rugs.
- Our finest quality 6x9 Pakistan Kashans.
- Over 50 9x12 new rugs from India, Pakistan, Turkey, Persia, Rumania, etc.
- Over 20 10x14 new and used handmade rugs.
- Large selection of antique and semi-antique Kazaks, Shirvans, Soumaks, Sarouks, Kashans, etc., in 4x6 to 6x9 sizes.
- All our beautiful Portuguese needlepoint rugs.

**$3,000 - $10,000**

- Over 40 7x10 to 9x12 antique and semi-antique rugs.
- Our finest quality Pakistan Kashan rugs.
- More than 30 oversize rugs from 10x14 to 13x25 new semi-antique and antique.
- A collection of extremely fine and collectible antique Caucasian and Persian rugs.

**The Rug Warehouse, Inc.**

2222 Broadway (79th St.) N.Y. Telephone: 787-6665
Hours: Monday-Saturday, 10-6, Sunday 11-5
Master Charge and Visa Accepted

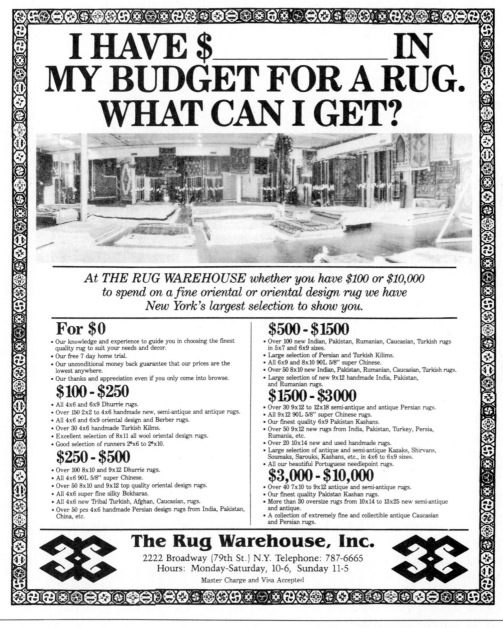

Courtesy of The Rug Warehouse, Inc.

ising new technology that should enhance audience participation in TV advertising communication.

## summary

This chapter has described how the consumer receives and is influenced by marketing communications. Communication is defined as the transmission of a message from a sender to a receiver by a signal of some sort sent through a channel of some sort.

There are four basic components of all communication: a source, a destination, a medium, and a message. The source is the initiator of the message; the destination is the audience. The audience can be a single individual or many individuals—collectively called a mass audience.

There are two types of communication: interpersonal and impersonal (or mass) communication. Interpersonal communication occurs on a personal level between two or more people and may be verbal or nonverbal. In mass communication, there is no direct communication between source and receiver. Interpersonal communication takes place in person, by telephone, or by mail; mass communication uses such impersonal media as television, radio, newspapers, and magazines. In both types of communication, feedback is an essential step because it provides the sender with some notion as to if and how well the message has been received.

Barriers to communication include selective exposure and selective perception. Repetition or redundancy of the message is used to surmount the barrier of psychological noise. Informal sources of interpersonal communication include friends, family, neighbors, and co-workers. Formal interpersonal sources include organizational representatives, such as salespeople or company spokespersons. Impersonal sources of consumer communications are organizations (both commercial and noncommercial) and the media (including neutral rating publications).

The credibility of the source, a vital element in the ultimate persuasibility of a message, is often based upon his or her perceived intentions. Informal sources and neutral or editorial sources are generally considered highly objective and, therefore, highly credible. The credibility of a commercial source is usually more problematic and is based on a composite evaluation of reputation, expertise, and knowledge, and that of the medium, the retail channel, and the company spokespeople it uses.

Media selection depends on the product, the audience, and the advertising objectives of the campaign. The two major media categories are print and broadcast; each has specific strengths and weaknesses. Marketers cannot communicate effectively with large, heterogeneous audiences by using general appeals. Instead, they usually segment their markets on the basis of some relevant product or market characteristic and transmit individually tailored messages to these segments via media to which they are exposed. In addition to ultimate consumers, a marketer's audiences include selling intermediaries and other publics that are relevant to the organization's success.

The manner in which a message is presented influences its impact. For example, one-sided messages are more effective in some situations and with some audiences; two-sided messages are more effective with others. Comparative advertising can be an effective strategy for brand challengers. Various copy approaches, such as fear and humor, are effective with certain products and certain audiences. When sexual themes are relevant to the product, they can be very effective; when used solely as an attention-getter, they rarely achieve brand recall.

Hopefully, future research will identify the many product, audience, and situational variables that mediate the effects of message order and presentation in persuading consumers to buy.

## *discussion questions*

1. List and discuss the effects of psychological barriers on the communications process. How can a marketer overcome the communications barrier known as "noise"?
2. How may a consumer use an informal communications situation to reduce postpurchase dissonance?
3. Select two advertisements with different advertising messages: one supportive and the other refutational. Explain why you believe each marketer chose that specific message strategy.
4. List and discuss the factors that influence the credibility of impersonal sources of product information.
5. Explain the differences between feedback from interpersonal communications and feedback from impersonal communications. How does the marketer obtain and use each kind of feedback?
6. You are the marketing manager for a headache remedy. Your advertising agency has just presented two different promotional strategies, one using a humorous approach and one taking an "agony" approach. Which approach would you suggest they adopt? Why?
7. Why are publicity stories often more effective than advertisements for the same product?
8. What are the advantages and disadvantages of (a) interpersonal communication and (b) impersonal communication for the marketing of consumer products?

9. For what kind of audiences would you consider using comparative advertising? Why?

## endnotes


1. See Barry L. Bayus, "Word of Mouth: The Indirect Effects on Marketing Efforts," *Journal of Advertising Research* 25 (June–July 1985), 31–9, and Marsha L. Richins, "Negative Word-of-Mouth by Dissatisfied Consumers: A Pilot Study," *Journal of Marketing,* 47 (Winter 1983), 68–78.
2. "The Man in the Moon Disappears," *Time,* May 6, 1985, 63.
3. "The Concoction That's Raising Spirits in the Wine Industry," *Business Week,* October 8, 1984, 182.
4. Joseph L. Orsini, "Differences between Goods and Services: An Empirical Analysis of Information Source Importance," in Bruce J. Walker, et al., eds., *An Assessment of Marketing Thought and Practice—1982 Educators' Conference Proceedings,* 48 (Chicago: American Marketing Association, 1982), 208–11, and W. Thomas Anderson, Jr., and Linda L. Golden, "Bank Promotion Strategy," *Journal of Advertising Research,* 24 (April–May 1984), 53–65.
5. For a review of research on nonverbal communication and its implications for marketers, see Thomas V. Bonoma and Leonard C. Felder, "Nonverbal Communication in Marketing: Toward a Communicational Analysis," *Journal of Marketing Research,* 14 (May 1977), 169–80.
6. Richard A. Winett and John H. Kagel, "Effects of Information Presentation Format on Resource Use in Field Studies," *Journal of Consumer Research,* 11 (September 1984), 655–67.
7. Lawrence C. Soley and Gary Kurzbard, "Selective Exposure Reexamined," in Donald R. Glover, ed., *Proceedings of the 1984 Convention of the American Academy of Advertising* (Nebraska: American Academy of Advertising, 1984), 92–7.
8. Shelby D. Hunt, "Post Transaction Communication and Dissonance Reduction," *Journal of Marketing,* 34 (July 1970), 46–51; and Eldon M. Wirtz and Kenneth E. Miller, "The Effect of Post-purchase Communication on Consumer Satisfaction and on Consumer Recommendation of the Retailer," *Journal of Retailing,* 53 (Summer 1977), 39–46.
9. Lewis C. Winters, "Should You Advertise to Hostile Audiences?" *Journal of Advertising Research,* 17 (June 1977), 7–15.
10. Jonathan Gutman and Michael K. Mills, "Fashion Lifestyle and Consumer Information Usage: Formulating Effective Marketing Communications," in Bruce J. Walker et al., *An Assessment of Marketing Thought and Practice—1982 Educators' Conference Proceedings,* 199–203.
11. "Communicating 'Differential Advantage' is Essential," *Marketing News,* October 25, 1985, 26.
12. "Computer-based Publicity 'Tracking Model' Evaluates Performance of Campaign," *Marketing News (Student Edition),* March 1984, 1.
13. Howard Beales, Michael B. Mazis, Steven C. Salop, and Richard Staelin, "Consumer Search and Public Policy," *Journal of Consumer Research,* 8 (June 1981), 11–22.
14. Thomas S. Robertson, "The Effect of the Informal Group upon Member Innovative Behavior," in Robert L. King, ed., *Marketing and the New Science of Planning* (Chicago: American Marketing Association, 1968), 334–40.

15. Ben M. Enis and Gordon W. Paul, "Store Loyalty as a Basis for Market Segmentation," *Journal of Retailing,* 46 (Fall 1970), 46.

16. Robert A. Westbrook and Claes Fornell, "Patterns of Information Source Usage among Durable Goods Buyers," *Journal of Marketing Research,* 16 (August 1979), 303–12.

17. Theodore Leavitt, "Communications and Industrial Selling," *Journal of Marketing,* 31 (April 1967), 15–21.

18. Leo Bogart and Charles Lehmann, "What Makes a Brand Name Familiar?" *Journal of Marketing Research,* 10 (February 1973), 17–22.

19. Marshall McLuhan, *The Medium Is the Message* (New York: Random House, 1967).

20. "News Media Credibility a Problem for Marketers," *Marketing News,* January 3, 1986, 58.

21. Shelly Chaiken and Alice H. Eagly, "Communication Modality as a Determinant of Persuasion: The Role of Communicator Salience," *Journal of Personality and Social Psychology,* 45 (1983), 241–56.

22. Brian Sternthal, Ruby Dholakia, and Clark Leavitt, "The Persuasive Effect of Source Credibility: Tests of Cognitive Response, *Journal of Consumer Research,* 4 (March 1978), 252–60.

23. Robert R. Harmon and Kenneth A. Coney, "The Persuasive Effects of Source Credibility in Buy and Lease Situations," *Journal of Marketing Research,* 19 (May 1982), 255–60.

24. A. Eagly and J. Chaiken, "An Attribution Analysis of the Effect of Communicator Characteristics on Opinion Change: The Case of Consumer Attractiveness," *Journal of Personality and Social Psychology,* 32 (1975), 136–44.

25. James McCroskey, "A Summary of Experimental Research on the Effects of Evidence in Persuasive Communication," *Quarterly Journal of Speech,* 55 (1969), 169–76.

26. Sternthal, Dholakia, and Leavitt, "The Persuasive Effect of Source Credibility: Tests of Cognitive Response.

27. Carl I. Hovland, Arthur A. Lumsdaine, and Fred D. Sheffield, *Experiments on Mass Communication* (New York: Wiley, 1949), 182–200.

28. Darlene B. Hannah and Brian Sternthal, "Detecting and Explaining the Sleeper Effect," *Journal of Consumer Research,* 11 (September 1984), 632–42.

29. Herbert C. Kelman and Carl I. Hovland, "Reinstatement of the Communication in Delayed Measurement of Opinion Change," *Journal of Abnormal and Social Psychology,* 48 (1953), 327–35.

30. "TV: Networks Fighting Changes in Viewership," *Advertising Age,* November 29, 1984, 14.

31. David A. Aaker and Phillip K. Brown, "Evaluating Vehicle Source Effects," *Journal of Advertising Research,* 12 (August 1972), 11–16; and Gert Assmus, "An Empirical Investigation into the Perception of Vehicle Source Effects," *Journal of Advertising,* 7 (Winter 1978), 4–10.

32. Susan Spillman, "Magazines Escalate Freebies for Subscribers," *USA Today,* January 21, 1986, B1.

33. Edwin Diamond, "*Time*'s Own Edsel: The *TV-Cable Week* Fiasco," *New York,* January 20, 1986, 15–17; and "*Cable Guide* Shows Savvy and Success," *New York Times,* October 15, 1984, D1.

34. Edwin Diamond, "People Lite? Tough Test for *Picture Week,*" *New York,* January 6, 1986, 8–9.

35. "In Search of That Elusive Thing Called Image," *Advertising Age,* January 30, 1984, M9.

36. Leonard N. Reid and Lawrence Soley, "Decorative Models and the Readership of Magazine Ads," *Journal of Advertising Research,* 23 (April–May 1983), 27–32.

37. George M. Zinkhan, Betsy D. Gelb, and Claude R. Martin, "The Cloze Procedure," *Journal of Advertising Research,* 23 (June–July 1983), 15–20.

38. Jolita Kisielius and Brian Sternthal, "Detecting and Explaining Vividness Effects in Attitudinal Judgments," *Journal of Marketing Research,* 21 (February 1984), 54–64.

39. Elizabeth C. Hirschman and Michael R. Solomon, "Utilitarian, Aesthetic, and Familiarity Responses to Verbal versus Visual Advertisements," in Thomas C. Kinnear, ed., *Advances in Consumer Research,* 11 (Provo, UT.: Association for Consumer Research, 1983), 426–31.

40. Yehoshua Tsal, "Effects of Verbal and Visual Information on Brand Attitudes," in Elizabeth C. Hirschman and Morris B. Holbrook, eds., *Advances in Consumer Research,* 12 (Provo, UT.: Association for Consumer Research, 1984), 265–67.

41. See, for example, Arch G. Woodside and Gail B. Glenesk, "Thought Processing of Advertisements in Low versus High Noise Conditions," *Journal of Advertising,* 13 (No. 2, 1984), 4–11.

42. Herbert E. Krugman, "Television Program Interest and Commercial Interruption," *Journal of Advertising Research,* 23 (February–March 1983), 21–23.

43. David A. Yorke and Philip J. Kitchen, "Channel Flickers and Video Speeders," *Journal of Advertising Research,* 25 (April–May 1985), 21–25.

44. Carrie Heeter and Bradley S. Greenberg, "Profiling the Zappers," *Journal of Advertising Research,* 25 (April–May 1985), 15–19.

45. "We'll Return to the Movie After This Message," *Marketing News,* January 3, 1986, 54.

46. Kevin T. Higgins, "There's Gold in Silver Screen Product Plugs," *Marketing News,* October 11, 1985, 6.

47. Jacob Jacoby and Wayne D. Hoyer, "Viewer Miscomprehension of Televised Communication: Selected Findings," *Journal of Marketing,* 46 (Fall 1982), 12–26.

48. Gary T. Ford and Richard Yalch, "Viewer Miscomprehension of Televised Communication—A Comment," 27–31; Richard W. Mizerski, "Viewer Miscomprehension Findings are Measurement Bound," 32–34; and Jacob Jacoby and Wayne D. Hoyer, "On Miscomprehending Televised Communication: A Rejoinder," 35–43; all in *Journal of Marketing,* 46 (Fall 1982).

49. Ibid.

50. Ibid.

51. James MacLachlan, "Making a Message Memorable and Persuasive," *Journal of Advertising Research,* 23 (December 1983–January 1984), 51–59.

52. John T. Cacioppo, Richard E. Petty, and Joseph A. Sidera, "The Effects of a Salient Self-Schema on the Evaluation of Pro-attitudinal Editorials: Top-Down versus Bottom-Up Message Processing," *Journal of Experimental Social Psychology,* 18 (1982), 324–38.

53. Ibid.

54. Richard F. Yalch and Rebecca Elmore-Yalch, "The Effect of Numbers on the Route to Persuasion," *Journal of Consumer Research,* 11 (June 1984), 522–27.

55. Russell I. Haley, Jack Richardson, and Beth M. Baldwin, "The Effects of Nonverbal Communications in Television Advertising," *Journal of Advertising Research,* 24 (August–September 1984), 11–18.

56. Hovland, Lumsdaine, and Sheffield, *Experiments on Mass Communication.*

57. William J. McGuire, "Inducing Resistance to Persuasion: Some Contemporary Approaches," in Leonard Berkowitz, ed., *Advances in Experimental Social Psychology* (New York: Academic Press, 1964), I, 191–229; Peter L. Wright, "The Cognitive Processes Mediating Acceptance of Advertising," *Journal of Marketing Research,* 10 (February 1973), 53–62; Alan G. Sawyer, "The Effects of Repetition of Refutational and Supportive Advertising Appeals," *Journal of Marketing Research,* 10 (Feb-

ruary 1973), 23–33; and George J. Szybillo and Richard Heslin, "Resistance to Persuasion: Innoculation Theory in a Marketing Concept," *Journal of Marketing Research,* 10 (November 1973), 396–403.

58. Ibid.

59. Kanti V. Prasad, "Communications Effectiveness of Comparative Advertising: A Laboratory Analysis," *Journal of Marketing Research,* 13 (May 1976), 128–37.

60. Subhash C. Jain and Edwin C. Hackleman, "How Effective Is Comparative Advertising for Stimulating Brand Recall?" *Journal of Advertising,* 7 (Summer 1978), 24.

61. Mark I. Alpert and Linda L. Golden, "The Impact of Education on the Relative Effectiveness of One-Sided and Two-Sided Communications," in Bruce J. Walker, et al., *An Assessment of Marketing Thought and Practice—1982 Educators' Conference Proceedings,* 30–33.

62. William R. Swinyard, "The Interaction Between Comparative Advertising and Copy Claim Variation," *Journal of Marketing Research,* 18 (May 1981), 175–86; and Michael Etgar and Stephen A. Goodwin, "One-Sided versus Two-Sided Comparative Message Appeals for New Brand Introductions," *Journal of Consumer Research,* 8 (March 1982), 460–65.

63. John H. Murphy II and Mary S. Amundsen, "The Communications Effectiveness of Comparative Advertising for a New Brand on Users of the Dominant Brand," *Journal of Advertising,* 10 (1981), 14–20.

64. Gerald J. Gorn and Charles B. Weinberg, "The Impact of Comparative Advertising on Perception and Attitude: Some Positive Findings," *Journal of Consumer Research,* 11 (September 1984), 719–27.

65. "Comparative Ads Ineffective: O&M Study," *Advertising Age,* October 13, 1975, 16.

66. See Linda L. Golden, "Consumer Reaction to Comparative Advertising," in Beverlee B. Anderson, ed., *Advances in Consumer Research* (Atlanta: Association for Consumer Research, 1976), III, 63–67; and William Pride, Charles W. Lamb, and Barbara A. Pletcher, "The Informativeness of Comparative Advertisements: An Empirical Investigation," *Journal of Advertising,* 8 (Spring 1979) 29–35.

67. Terrence A. Shimp and D. C. Dyer, "The Effects of Comparative Advertising Mediated by Market Position of Sponsoring Brand," *Journal of Advertising,* 7 (Summer 1979), 13–19.

68. Jain and Hackleman, "How Effective Is Comparative Advertising?" 24–25.

69. For basic readings in this area, see Carl I. Hovland, ed., *The Order of Presentation in Persuasion* (New Haven, Conn.: Yale University Press, 1957).

70. Frederick E. Webster, Jr., *Marketing Communication* (New York: Ronald Press, 1971).

71. Peter H. Webb and Michael L. Ray, "Effects of TV Clutter," *Journal of Advertising Research,* Classics, Volume II (September 1984), 19–24.

72. Scott M. Cutlip and Allen H. Center, *Effective Public Relations,* 4th ed. (Englewood Cliffs, N.J.: Prentice-Hall, 1971), 151.

73. Donald F. Cox, "Clues for Advertising Strategists: Part I," *Harvard Business Review,* September–October 1961, 160–76.

74. Irving L. Janis and Seymour Feshbach, "Effects of Fear-Arousing Communications," *Journal of Abnormal and Social Psychology,* 48 (January 1953), 78–92.

75. John R. Stuteville, "Psychic Defenses against High Fear Appeals: A Key Marketing Variable," *Journal of Marketing,* 34 (April 1970), 39–45.

76. Meryl P. Gardner and Rosalyn S. Levin, "Truth and Consequences: The Effects of Disclosing Possibly Harmful Results of Product Use," in Bruce J. Walker et al., *An Assessment of Marketing Thought and Practice—1982 Educators' Conference Proceedings,* 39–42.

77. Gerald R. Miller and M. A. Hewgill, "Some Recent Research on Fear Arousing Message Appeals," *Speech Monographs,* 33 (1966), 377–91.

78. Joanne Cantor, Dean Ziemke, and Glenn G. Sparks, "Effects of Forewarning on Emotional Responses to a Horror Film," *Journal of Broadcasting,* 28 (Winter 1984), 21–31.

79. M. Karlins and H. I. Abelson, *Persuasion,* 2nd ed. (New York: Springer Publishing, 1970), 9–10.

80. Michael Ray and William Wilkie, "Fear: The Potential of an Appeal Neglected by Marketing," *Journal of Marketing,* 34 (January 1970), 54–62.

81. John J. Burnett and Richard L. Oliver, "Fear Appeal Effects in the Field: A Segmentation Approach," *Journal of Marketing Research,* 16 (May 1979), 190–91.

82. Lynette S. Unger and James M. Stearns, "The Use of Fear and Guilt Messages in Television Advertising: Issues and Evidence," in Patrick E. Murphy et al., *1983 American Marketing Association Educators' Proceedings,* 16–20.

83. See Thomas J. Madden and Marc G. Weinberger, "Humor in Advertising: A Practitioner's View," *Journal of Advertising Research,* 24 (August–September 1984), 23–29; John Koten, "After Serious 70s Advertisers are Going For Laughs Again," *The Wall Street Journal,* February 23, 1984, B1; "Humor Needs to Hit Home, But Not Too Hard," *Advertising Age,* April 14, 1985, 36; Kevin Higgins, "Humor Takes the 'Ho-Hum' Out of Radio Ads," *Marketing News,* June 7, 1985, 23; and Betsy D. Gelb and Charles M. Pickett, "Attitude-Toward-the-Ad: Links to Humor and to Advertising Effectiveness," *Journal of Advertising,* 12 (No. 2, 1983), 34–42.

84. Avraham Shama and Maureen Coughlin, "An Experimental Study of the Effectiveness of Humor in Advertising," in *1979 Educators Conference Proceedings* (Chicago: American Marketing Association, 1979), 249–52.

85. John H. Murphy, Isabella C. M. Cunningham, and Gary B. Wilcox, "The Impact of Program Environment on Recall of Humorous Television Commercials," *Journal of Advertising,* 8 (Spring 1979), 17–21.

86. For a critical review of the sleeper effect, see Noel Capon and James Hulbert, "The 'Sleeper Effect'—An Awakening," *Public Opinion Quarterly,* 37 (Fall 1973), 322–58.

87. Reported in B. G. Yovovich, "Sex in Advertising—The Power and the Perils," *Advertising Age,* May 2, 1983, M4–5.

88. Ibid.

89. Ibid.

90. Ibid.

91. Ibid.

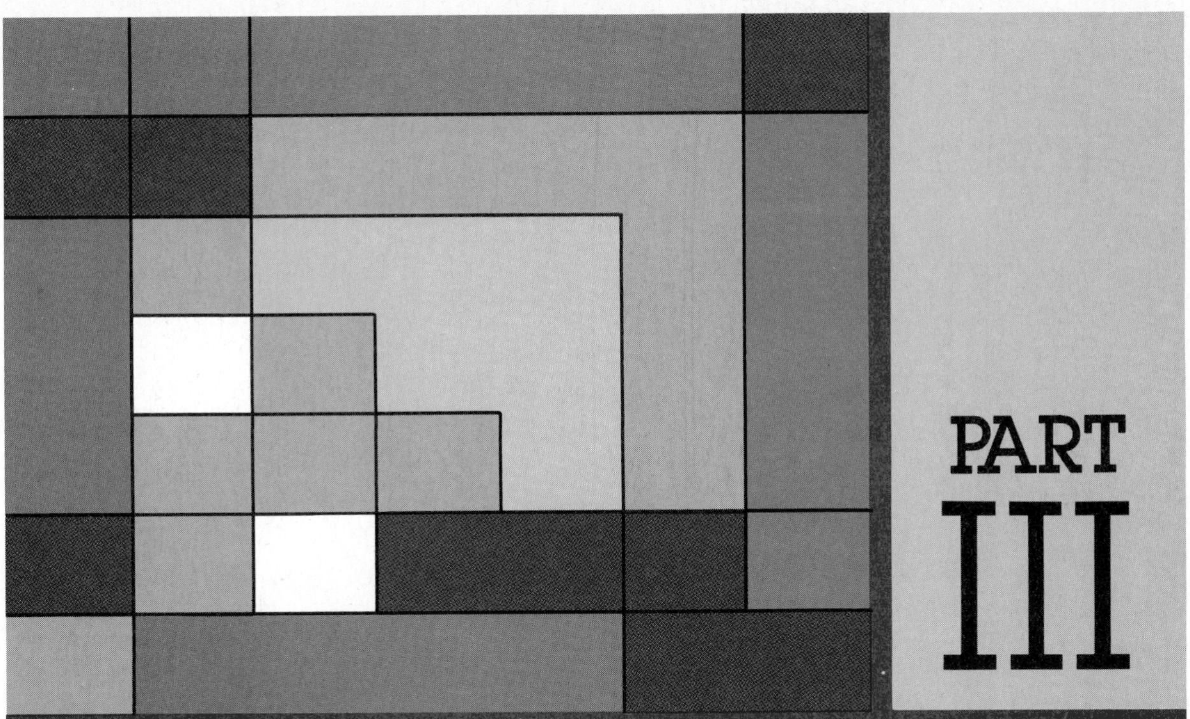

# PART III

# CONSUMERS IN THEIR SOCIAL AND CULTURAL SETTINGS

The five chapters that follow are designed to provide the reader with a detailed picture of the social and cultural dimensions of consumer behavior. The objectives of Part III are to (1) explain how social and cultural concepts affect the attitudes and behavior of individuals, and (2) show how these concepts can be employed by marketing practitioners to achieve their marketing objectives.

# 11

# Group Dynamics and Consumer Reference Groups

## introduction

WITH the exception of those very few people who can be classified as hermits, people tend to be involved with others on a rather constant basis. Like almost all behavior, an individual's social relationships are often motivated by the expectation that they will help in the satisfaction of specific needs. For example, a person might become a volunteer ambulance driver to satisfy a need for community recognition. Another person might join a computer club in an effort to find compatible friends to satisfy social needs. A third person might join a health food cooperative to obtain the benefits of group buying power. These are just a few of the almost infinite number of reasons why people involve themselves with others.

This chapter discusses the basic concepts of social involvement and group dynamics. It gives particular emphasis to the role that reference groups play in both directly and indirectly influencing consumer behavior. The four chapters that follow discuss other social and societal groupings that influence consumer buying processes: the family, socioeconomic classes, culture, and subculture.

## WHAT IS A GROUP?

A **group** may be defined as *two or more people who interact to accomplish either individual or mutual goals.* Within the broad scope of this definition are both an intimate "group" of two neighbors who informally attend a department store fashion show together and a larger, more formal group, such as a Neighborhood

> *Every man with an idea has at least two or three followers*
>
> *BROOKS ATKINSON*
> *"January 2,"* Once Around the Sun *(1951)*

Watch Association, whose members are mutually concerned with reducing crime in their neighborhood. Included in this definition, too, are more remote, one-sided, social relationships where an individual consumer looks to others for direction as to which products or services to buy, even though these others are largely unaware that they are serving as consumption-related *models.*

## TYPES OF GROUPS

To simplify our discussion, we will consider four different types of group classification: *primary* versus *secondary* groups, *formal* versus *informal* groups, *large* versus *small* groups, and *membership* versus *symbolic* groups.

### Primary versus Secondary Groups

If a person interacts on a regular basis with other individuals (with members of his or her family, with neighbors, or with co-workers whose opinions are valued), then these individuals can be considered a *primary group* for that person. On the other hand, if a person interacts only occasionally with such others, or does not consider their opinions to be important, then these others constitute a *secondary group* for that person. From this definition, it can be seen that the critical distinctions between primary and secondary groups are the *importance* of the groups to the individual and the *frequency* or *consistency* with which the individual interacts with them.

### Formal versus Informal Groups

Another useful way to classify groups is by the extent of their formality; that is, the extent to which the group structure, the members' roles, and the group's purpose are clearly defined. If a group has a highly defined structure (e.g., a formal membership list), specific roles and authority levels (a president, treasurer, and secretary), and specific goals (to support a political candidate, improve their children's education, increase the knowledge or skills of members), then it would be classified as a *formal group*. The local chapter of the American Red Cross, with elected officers and members who meet regularly to discuss topics of civic interest, would be classified as a formal group. On the other hand, if a group is more loosely defined—if it consists, say, of four women who were in the same college sorority and who meet for dinner once a month, or three co-workers who, with their spouses, see each other frequently—then it is considered an *informal group*.

From the standpoint of consumer behavior, informal social or friendship groups are generally more important to the marketer, since their less clearly defined structures provide a more conducive environment for the exchange of information and influence about consumption-related topics.

## Large versus Small Groups

It is often desirable to distinguish between groups in terms of their size or complexity. However, it is difficult to offer a precise breaking point as to when a group is considered large or small. A *large group* might be thought of as one in which a single member is not likely to know more than a few of the group's members personally or be fully aware of the specific roles or activities of more than a limited number of other group members. Examples of large groups include such complex organizations as General Motors, with its numerous subordinate divisions, and the American Bar Association, with its many state, county, and city chapters.

In contrast, members of a *small group* are likely to know every member personally and to be aware of every member's specific role or activities in the group. For example, each staff member of a college newspaper is likely to know all the other members and be aware of their duties and interests within the group.

In the realm of consumer behavior, we are principally concerned with the study of small groups, since such groups are more likely to influence the consumption behavior of group members.

## Membership versus Symbolic Groups

Another useful way to classify groups is by membership versus symbolic groups. A *membership group* is a group to which a person either belongs or would qualify for membership. For example, the group of women with whom a young homemaker plays golf weekly or with whom she hopes to play golf when an opening occurs would be considered, for her, a membership group.

In contrast, a group in which an individual is not likely to receive membership, despite acting like a member by adopting the group's values, attitudes, and behavior, is considered a *symbolic group*. For example, professional baseball players may constitute a symbolic group for an amateur baseball player who identifies with certain players by imitating their behavior whenever possible (e.g., in the purchase of a specific brand of baseball glove or bat); however, the amateur does not and probably never will qualify for membership as a professional baseball player because the skill or opportunity to compete professionally is lacking. Clearly, actual membership groups offer a more direct, and thus a more compelling, influence on consumer behavior.

In summary, we can say that small, informal, primary membership groups are of the greatest interest to marketers because they exert the greatest potential influence on consumer purchase decisions.

# CONSUMER-RELEVANT GROUPS

To more fully comprehend the kind of impact that specific groups have on individuals, we will examine six basic consumer-relevant groups: the family, friendship groups, formal social groups, shopping groups, consumer action groups, and work groups.

## The Family

An individual's *family* is often in the best position to influence his or her consumer decisions. The family's importance in this regard is based upon the frequency of contact that the individual has with other family members and the extent of influence that the family has on the establishment of a wide range of values, attitudes, and behavior. (Chapter 12 examines the family's influence on purchase and consumption behavior.)

## Friendship Groups

*Friendship groups* are typically classified as informal groups because they are usually unstructured and lack specific authority levels. In terms of relative influence, after an individual's family, it is friends who are most likely to influence the individual's purchase decisions.

Seeking and maintaining friendships is a basic drive of most people. Friends fulfill a wide range of needs: they provide companionship, security, and opportunities to discuss problems that an individual may be reluctant to discuss with members of his or her own family. Friendships are also a sign of maturity and independence, for they represent a breaking away from the family and the forming of social ties with the outside world.

The views and opinions of friends can be an important force in influencing the products or brands a consumer ultimately selects. Recognizing the power of peer group influence, especially when it comes to teenagers, R. J. Reynolds Tobacco Company is offering young nonsmokers advice on how to resist pressures to smoke until they are adults and can make up their own minds (see Figure 11-1).

Consumers are more likely to seek information from those friends they feel have values or outlooks similar to their own; the greater the similarity, the more they are likely to trust them and be influenced by their judgment in arriving at a purchase decision.

## Formal Social Groups

In contrast to the relative intimacy of friendship groups, *formal social groups* are more remote and serve a different function for the individual. A person joins a formal social group to fulfill such specific goals as making new friends, meeting "important" people (e.g., for career advancement), broadening perspectives, pursuing a special interest, or promoting a specific cause. Because members of a formal social group often consume certain products together, such groups are of interest to marketers. For example, the membership of a scuba diving club would be of particular interest to tour operators, travel agents, sporting goods retailers, scuba magazine publishers, and the manufacturers of scuba equipment. The membership list of a men's club would be of interest to local men's clothing stores, insurance agents, automobile dealers, tax accountants, and special interest publications.

FIGURE 11-1 Advertisement Recognizing the Power of Peer Pressure

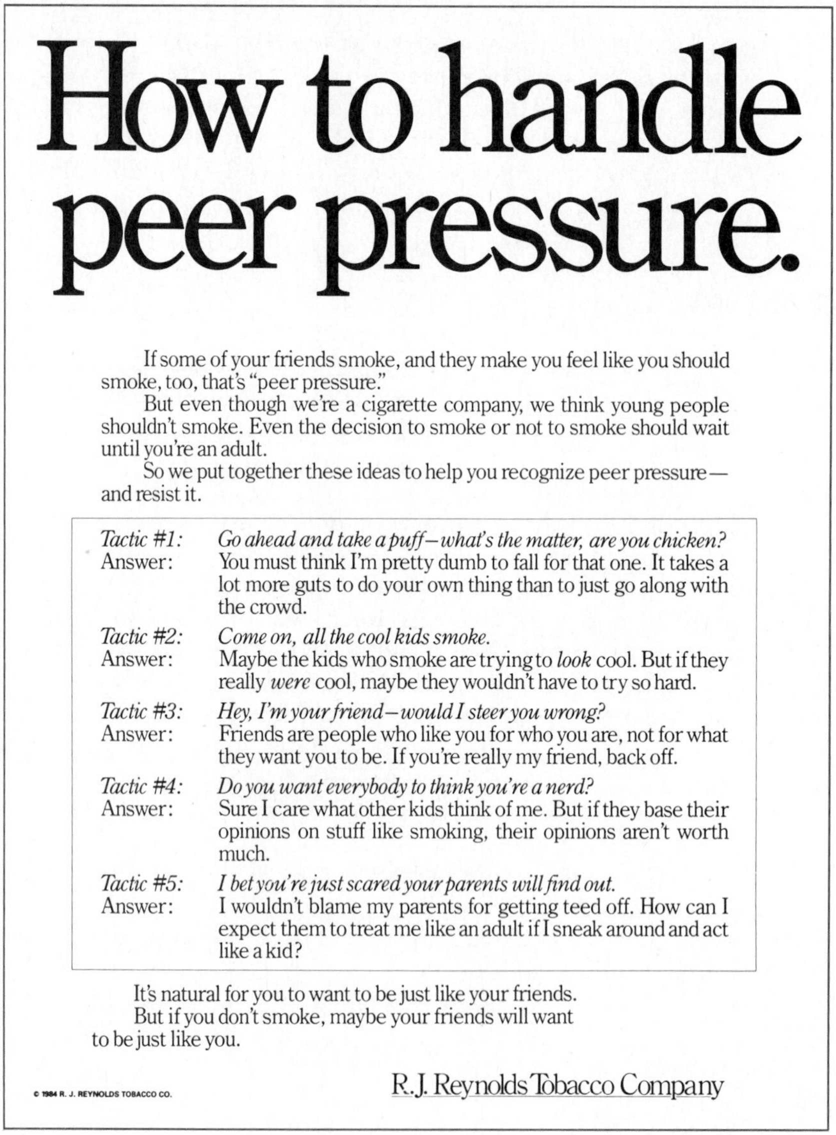

# How to handle peer pressure.

If some of your friends smoke, and they make you feel like you should smoke, too, that's "peer pressure."

But even though we're a cigarette company, we think young people shouldn't smoke. Even the decision to smoke or not to smoke should wait until you're an adult.

So we put together these ideas to help you recognize peer pressure—and resist it.

*Tactic #1:* *Go ahead and take a puff—what's the matter, are you chicken?*
Answer: You must think I'm pretty dumb to fall for that one. It takes a lot more guts to do your own thing than to just go along with the crowd.

*Tactic #2:* *Come on, all the cool kids smoke.*
Answer: Maybe the kids who smoke are trying to *look* cool. But if they really *were* cool, maybe they wouldn't have to try so hard.

*Tactic #3:* *Hey, I'm your friend—would I steer you wrong?*
Answer: Friends are people who like you for who you are, not for what they want you to be. If you're really my friend, back off.

*Tactic #4:* *Do you want everybody to think you're a nerd?*
Answer: Sure I care what other kids think of me. But if they base their opinions on stuff like smoking, their opinions aren't worth much.

*Tactic #5:* *I bet you're just scared your parents will find out.*
Answer: I wouldn't blame my parents for getting teed off. How can I expect them to treat me like an adult if I sneak around and act like a kid?

It's natural for you to want to be just like your friends.

But if you don't smoke, maybe your friends will want to be just like you.



R.J. Reynolds Tobacco Company

Courtesy of R.J. Reynolds Tobacco Company

Membership in a formal social group may influence a consumer's behavior in several ways. For example, members of such groups have frequent opportunity to informally discuss products, services, or stores. Some members may copy the consumption behavior of other members whom they admire.

Because Americans are active in so many different kinds of formal social groups, this country has been called a "nation of joiners." Research that examined membership in formal social organizations (e.g., veterans, civic, political, fraternal, church, economic, cultural, and social associations) found that active formal social group participants tend to be married, better educated, earn higher incomes, and have higher-status occupations than inactive members or nonmembers.[1] Such information can be helpful to marketing managers concerned with segmenting markets for new or existing products.

## Shopping Groups

Two or more people who shop together—whether for food, for clothing, or simply to pass the time—can be called a *shopping group.* Such groups are often offshoots of family or friendship groups. People like to shop with others who are pleasant company or who they feel have more experience with or knowledge about a desired product or service. Shopping with others also provides an element of social fun to an often boring but necessary task. In addition, it reduces the risk that a purchase decision will be socially unacceptable. In instances where none of the members have knowledge about the product being sought, a shopping group may form for defensive reasons; members may feel more confident with a collective decision.

Relatively few marketing or consumer behavior studies have examined the nature of shopping groups. However, one study of the in-store behavior of shoppers revealed some differences between group and individual shopping.[2] The research found that shopping parties of at least three persons deviated more from their original purchase plans (they bought either more or less than originally planned) than did either single shoppers or two-party groups. Furthermore, two or more people shopping together were almost twice as likely to buy more than planned than if they had shopped alone. The study also found that shopping groups tended to cover more territory in the store than individuals shopping alone, and thus had more opportunity to see and examine merchandise and to make unplanned purchases.

A special type of shopping group is the *in-home shopping group,* which typically consists of a group of women who gather together in the home of a friend to attend a "party" devoted to the marketing of a specific line of products. The in-home party approach provides marketers with an opportunity to demonstrate the features of their products simultaneously to a group of potential customers. Early purchasers tend to create a bandwagon effect in that undecided guests often overcome a reluctance to buy when they see their friends make positive purchase decisions. Furthermore, some of the guests may feel obliged to buy because they are guests in the home of the sponsoring hostess.

## Consumer Action Groups

A particular kind of consumer group—a *consumer action group*— has emerged in response to the consumerist movement. This type of consumer group has become increasingly visible since the 1960s and has been able to influence product design and marketing practices of both manufacturers and retailers.

Consumer action groups can be divided into two broad categories: those that organize to correct a specific consumer abuse and then disband, and those that organize to address broader, more pervasive, problem areas and operate over an extended or indefinite period of time. A group of tenants who band together to dramatize their dissatisfaction with the quality of service provided by their landlord, or a group of irate community members who unite to block the entrance of a fast-food outlet into their middle-class neighborhood, are examples of temporary, *cause-specific* consumer action groups. An example of a more enduring consumer action group is Action for Children's Television (A.C.T.), which was organized in the 1960s by a group of Boston mothers who were distressed by the quality of children's television programs. Today, A.C.T. is involved in a wide range of related problem areas, including the content and timing of commercials concerned with toys, breakfast cereals, and other product categories directed primarily at children.

The overriding objective of many consumer interest groups is to bring sufficient pressure to bear on selected members of the business community to make them correct perceived consumer abuses. Through their collective action, a number of consumer interest groups have influenced the actions of the business community to a degree not possible by an individual consumer acting on his or her own behalf.

### Work Groups

The sheer amount of time that people spend at their jobs—frequently more than thirty-five hours per week—provides ample opportunity for *work groups* to serve as a major influence on the consumption behavior of members.

Both the formal work group and the informal friendship/work group have the potential for influencing consumer behavior. The formal work group consists of those individuals who work together as a team. Their direct and sustained work relationship offers substantial opportunity for one or more members to influence the consumer-related attitudes and activities of other team members. Informal friendship/work groups consist of people who have become friends as a result of working for the same firm, regardless of whether or not they work together as a team. Members of informal work groups may influence the consumption behavior of other members during coffee or lunch breaks or after-hours meetings.

## REFERENCE GROUPS

**Reference groups** are groups that serve as a frame of reference for individuals in their purchase decisions. This basic concept provides a valuable perspective for understanding the impact of other people on an individual's consumption beliefs, attitudes, and behavior. It also provides some insight into methods that can be used to effect desired changes in consumer behavior.

## What Is a Reference Group?

A *reference group* is *any person or group that serves as a point of comparison (or reference) for an individual in the formation of either general or specific values, attitudes, or behavior.* The usefulness of this concept is enhanced by the fact that it places no restrictions on group size or membership, nor does it require that consumers identify with a tangible group (i.e., the group can be *symbolic:* prosperous business people, rock stars, sports heroes).

Reference groups that influence general values or behavior are called *normative reference groups.* An example of a child's normative reference group is the immediate family, which is likely to play an important role in molding the child's general consumer values and behavior (e.g., which foods to select for good nutrition, appropriate ways to dress for specific occasions, how and where to shop, what constitutes "good" value).

Reference groups that serve as benchmarks for specific or narrowly defined attitudes or behavior are called *comparative reference groups.* A comparative reference group might be a neighboring family whose lifestyle appears to be admirable and worthy of imitation (the way they maintain their home, their choice of home furnishings and cars, the number and types of vacations they take).

Both normative and comparative reference groups are important. Normative reference groups influence the development of a basic code of behavior; comparative reference groups influence the expression of specific consumer attitudes and behavior. It is likely that the specific influences of comparative reference groups are to some measure dependent upon the basic values and behavior patterns established early in a person's development by normative reference groups.

### BROADENING THE REFERENCE GROUP CONCEPT

Like many other concepts borrowed from the behavioral sciences, the meaning of *reference group* has changed over the years. As originally employed, reference groups were narrowly defined to include only those groups with which a person interacted on a direct basis (e.g., family and close friends). However, the concept has gradually broadened to include both direct and indirect individual or group influences. *Indirect reference groups* consist of those individuals or groups with whom a person does *not* have direct face-to-face contact, such as movie stars, sports heroes, political leaders, or TV personalities.

*Referents* that a person might use in evaluating his or her own general or specific attitudes or behavior vary from an individual to several family members to a broader kinship, from a voluntary association to a social class, a profession, an ethnic group, a community, or even a nation. As Figure 11-2 indicates, the major societal groupings that influence an individual's consumer behavior are, in order: family, friends, social class, and culture. (These important consumer reference groups are discussed more fully in Chapters 12 to 15).

FIGURE 11-2 Major Consumer Reference Groups

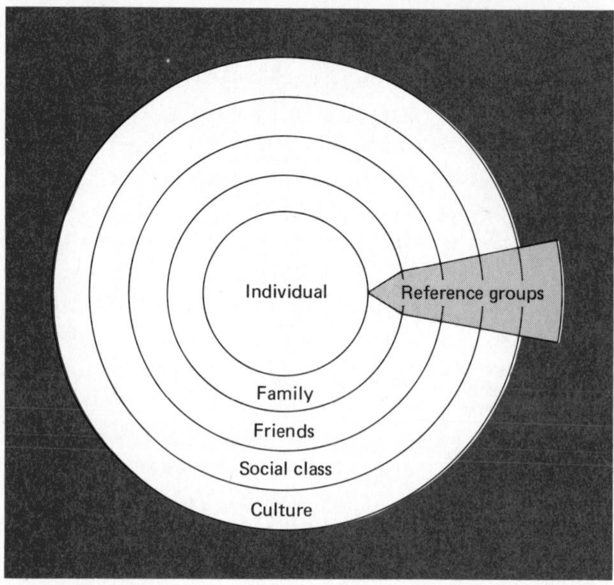


## TYPES OF REFERENCE GROUPS

Reference groups can be classified in terms of a person's membership or degree of involvement with the group and in terms of the positive or negative influences they have on his or her values, attitudes, and behavior. Table 11-1 depicts four types of reference groups that emerge from a cross-classification of these factors: contactual groups, aspirational groups, disclaimant groups, and avoidance groups.

A **contactual group** is a group in which a person holds membership or has regular face-to-face contact and of whose values, attitudes, and standards he or she approves. Thus a contactual group has a positive influence on an individual's attitudes or behavior.

TABLE 11-1 Types of Reference Groups

| | MEMBERSHIP GROUP | NONMEMBERSHIP GROUP |
|---|---|---|
| POSITIVE INFLUENCE | Contactual group | Aspirational group |
| NEGATIVE INFLUENCE | Disclaimant group | Avoidance group |

An **aspirational group** is a group in which a person does not hold membership and does not have face-to-face contact, but wants to be a member. Thus it serves as a positive influence on that person's attitudes or behavior.

A **disclaimant group** is a group in which a person holds membership or has face-to-face contact but disapproves of the group's values, attitudes, and behavior. Thus the person tends to adopt attitudes and behavior that are in opposition to the norms of the group.

An **avoidance group** is a group in which a person does not hold membership and does not have face-to-face contact and disapproves of the group's values, attitudes, and behavior. Thus the person tends to adopt attitudes and behavior that are in opposition to those of the group.

Consider Sue Blake, a senior majoring in advertising at a large state university in the southwestern United States. The school's Advertising Club, of which she is vice-president, serves as one of Sue's *contactual* groups. Sue believes that continuing her education to obtain an MBA will enhance her career opportunities. It is clear that individuals who hold the MBA degree serve as an *aspirational* group for her. Still further, although she enjoys her position as a reporter on the university's newspaper, the recent editorials (endorsed by most of the staff) urging students to adopt a more conservative political philosophy run counter to her own views; thus the newspaper staff is currently a *disclaimant* group. Finally, Sue personally knows a number of students who have quit college during their final year; these former students serve as an *avoidance* group.

## Factors That Affect Reference Group Influence

The degree of influence that a reference group exerts on an individual's behavior usually depends on the nature of the individual and the product and on specific social factors. This section discusses how and why some of these factors operate to influence consumer behavior.

### INFORMATION AND EXPERIENCE

An individual who has firsthand experience with a product or service, or can easily obtain full information about it, is less likely to be influenced by the advice or example of others. On the other hand, a person who has little or no firsthand experience with a product or service, and does not expect to have access to objective information about it (e.g., a person who believes that relevant advertising may be misleading or deceptive), is more likely to seek out the advice or example of others. Research on imitative behavior provides some interesting insights on how insufficient experience or information concerning a product makes consumers more susceptible to the influence—either positive or negative—of others.[3]

For example, if a medical school student wants to impress his new girlfriend, he may take her to a restaurant that he knows from experience to be good or to one that has been highly recommended by the local newspaper's Dining-Out Guide. If he has neither personal experience nor information he regards as valid, he may seek the advice of friends or imitate the behavior of others by taking her to a restaurant he knows is frequented by physicians whom he admires.

### CREDIBILITY, ATTRACTIVENESS, AND POWER OF THE REFERENCE GROUP

A reference group that is perceived as credible, attractive, or powerful can induce consumer attitude and behavior change. For example, when consumers are concerned with obtaining accurate information about the performance or quality of a product or service, they are likely to be persuaded by those they consider to be trustworthy and knowledgeable. That is, they are more likely to be persuaded by sources with *high credibility.* When consumers are primarily concerned with the acceptance or approval of others they like, with whom they identify, or who offer them status or other benefits, they are likely to adopt their product, brand, or other behavioral characteristics.

When consumers are primarily concerned with the power that a person or group can exert over them, they might choose products or services that conform to the norms of that person or group in order to avoid ridicule or punishment. However, unlike other reference groups that consumers follow either because they are credible or because they are attractive, *power groups* are not likely to cause attitude change. Individuals may conform to the behavior of a powerful person or group but are not likely to experience a change in their own attitudes.

Different reference groups may influence the beliefs, attitudes, and behavior of an individual at different points in time or under different circumstances. For example, the dress habits of a young female attorney may vary, depending on her place and role. She may conform to the dress code of her office by wearing conservative business suits by day and drastically alter her mode of dress after work by wearing more conspicuous, flamboyant styles.

### CONSPICUOUSNESS OF THE PRODUCT

The potential influence of a reference group varies according to how visually or verbally conspicuous a product is to others. A visually conspicuous product is one that can be seen and identified by others, and that will stand out and be noticed (e.g., a luxury item or novelty product). Even if a product is not visually conspicuous, it may be verbally conspicuous—it may be highly interesting or it may be easily described to others. Products that are especially conspicuous and status-revealing (a new automobile, fashion clothing, home furniture) are most likely to be purchased with an eye to the reactions of relevant others. Products that are less conspicuous (canned fruits, laundry soaps) are less likely to be purchased with a reference group in mind.[4]

The success of a brand of status running shoes like Reebok (see Figure 11-3) is aided by the fact that it is relatively easy to spot a person wearing them—given the distinctive flag symbol on the side of each shoe.

FIGURE 11-3 Advertisement Incorporating the Conspicuousness of the Product



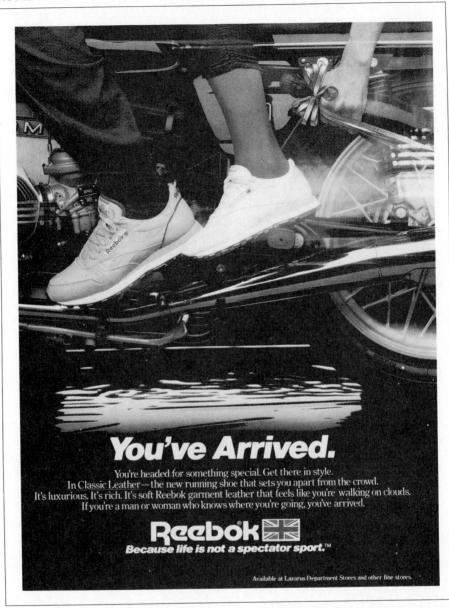

Reprinted by permission from Reebok International Ltd.

## REFERENCE GROUP IMPACT ON PRODUCT AND BRAND CHOICE

In some cases, and for some products, reference groups may influence both a person's product category and brand (or type) choices. Such products are called *product-plus, brand-plus* items. In other cases, reference groups influence only the product category decision. Such products are called *product-plus, brand-minus* items. In still other cases, reference groups influence the brand (or type) decision. These products are called *product-minus, brand-plus* items. Finally, in some cases, reference groups influence neither the product category nor the brand decision; these products are called *product-minus, brand-minus* items. The idea of classifying products and brands into four groups in terms of the suitability of a reference group appeal was first suggested in the mid-1950s, along with an initial classification of a small number of product categories.[5] Table 11-2 lists the results of a recent reexamination and extension of this earlier research.[6]

## Reference Groups and Consumer Conformity

Marketers are particularly interested in the ability of reference groups to change consumer attitudes and behavior (i.e., to encourage *conformity*). To be capable of such influence, a reference group must

1. Inform or make the individual aware of a specific product or brand;
2. Provide the individual with the opportunity to compare his or her own thinking with the attitudes and behavior of the group;
3. Influence the individual to adopt attitudes and behavior that are consistent with the norms of the group;
4. Legitimize an individual's decision to use the same products as the group.

The ability of reference groups to influence consumer conformity is demonstrated by the results of a classic experiment designed to compare the effects

**TABLE 11-2** **Reference Group Influence on Product and Brand Choices**

| REFERENCE GROUP INFLUENCE ON *BRAND OR TYPE* | REFERENCE GROUP INFLUENCE ON PRODUCT CATEGORY: weak (−) | REFERENCE GROUP INFLUENCE ON PRODUCT CATEGORY: strong (+) |
|---|---|---|
| strong (+) | *Cell 1*<br>Magazines<br>Furniture<br>Clothing<br>Instant coffee<br>Aspirin<br>Air conditioners<br>Stereos<br>Laundry detergent<br>Microwave ovens | *Cell 2*<br>Automobiles<br>Color TV |
| weak (−) | *Cell 3*<br>Canned peaches<br>Toilet soap<br>Beer<br>Cigarettes<br>Small cigars | *Cell 4* |

Source: Donald W. Hendon, "A New and Empirical Look at the Influence of Reference Groups on Generic Product Category and Brand Choice: Evidence from Two Nations," in *Proceedings of the Academy of International Business: Asia-Pacific Dimensions of International Business* (Honolulu: College of Business Administration, University of Hawaii, 1979), 757.

of lectures versus group discussions on family food consumption habits.[7] The purpose of the study was to find the most effective method for inducing homemakers to serve such culturally undesirable cuts of meat as beef hearts, sweetbreads, and kidneys to their families during World War II. Findings indicated that group discussions were far more effective in inducing conformity than lectures in which group opinions were not aired (32 percent versus 3 percent).

A study of male college students' responses to group pressure provides some insights on consumer conformity.[8] Three men's suits—labeled, respectively, *A*, *B* and *C*—were described to groups of students as being of different quality and manufacture, though they were actually of identical quality and color and manufactured by the same firm. The experiment compared the evaluations of *control groups* (in which naive subjects selected a preferred suit in private) with the evaluations of *conformity groups* (in which naive subjects made their evaluations and choices publicly after three cooperating confederates in each group all chose the same suit). The results of the experiment indicated that the naive subjects in each of the conformity groups tended to conform to the product choices of the cooperating confederates, while the naive members of the control groups, who made their choices in private, made random choices. The marketing implication of this study is that, in the absence of objective quality standards, individual consumers tend to conform to group norms—that is, to the choices of the majority.

A study of male college friendship groups offers some additional evidence on the relationship between group cohesiveness and brand choice conformity.[9] In this study, four low-cost consumer packaged goods (beer, after-shave lotion, deodorant, and cigarettes) were studied in an attempt to determine to what extent the purchase of different brands depends on group influence. The results of the study indicated that for two of the products—beer and after-shave lotion—the more cohesive the group, the greater the brand choice conformity. No significant relationship between the extent of group cohesiveness and brand choice conformity was found in the initial analysis for either deodorants or cigarettes. However, when market share for each brand was considered, a significant relationship was found between group cohesiveness and brand choice conformity in the case of cigarettes, but not deodorants.[10] Note that for the three products where conformity was found to influence purchase choice (beer, after-shave lotion, cigarettes), the product categories tended to be more socially conspicuous than for the fourth category—deodorants. This study supports the proposition that consumer conformity is likely to vary, depending on the product category.

Recent research provides additional support that the social dynamics of group membership affects brand choice. Most significant, this study indicates that group influence is likely to be a complex affair that is regulated by a mix of (1) the specific product (e.g., pizza versus toothpaste), (2) the type of social relationship (roommates, friends, dates), and (3) the social structure of the group (extent of personal ties between group members). The research, conducted among members of a college sorority, also found that members of close-knit groups were more likely to reveal a preference for the same brands. In contrast to previous research, however, these results suggest that product conspicuousness is unnecessary for similarity of brand choice to occur. Specifically, the evidence indicates that even for relatively "private" products (e.g., shampoo and toothpaste), there may be strong brand congruence when the particular social setting provides an opportunity for such products to be observed—for example, when sorority sisters happen to share the same bathroom.[11]

The research evidence underscores the fact that a consumer's selection of a product category, brand, style, or type of product may be influenced by the preferences and actions of others.

## PROMOTIONAL APPLICATIONS OF THE REFERENCE GROUP CONCEPT

Reference group appeals are used very effectively by some advertisers to segment their markets. Group situations or people with whom a segment of the audience can identify are used to promote goods and services by subtly inducing the prospective consumer to identify with the pictured user of the product. This identification may be based on admiration (e.g., of an athlete), on aspiration (of a celebrity or way of life), on empathy (with a person or situation), or on recognition (of a person—real or stereotypical—or a situation). In some cases, the prospective consumer thinks, "If she uses it, it must be good. If I use it, I'll be like her." In other cases, the prospective consumer says to himself, "He's got problems I've got. What worked for him will work for me."

There are three major types of reference group appeals in common marketing usage: **celebrities, experts,** and the **common man**. These appeals, as well as less frequently employed appeals, are often operationalized in the guise of testimonials or endorsements. In the case of the *common man,* they may be presented as "slice of life" commercials.

### Celebrities

Celebrities, particularly movie stars, TV personalities, and sports heroes, provide a popular type of reference group appeal. To their loyal followers and to much of the general public, celebrities represent an idealization of life that most people would love to live. Advertisers spend enormous sums of money to have celebrities promote their products in the expectation that the reading or viewing audience will react positively to the celebrity's association with their product. In fact, it has been estimated that one of every three TV commercials uses a famous person to endorse a consumer product or service.[12]

America seems to have a fascination with celebrities. Eleven-year-old *People* magazine has a circulation of more than 2.8 million people (actual public exposure is much higher, due to pass-along readership), and the TV show "Entertainment Tonight" is carried by 150 stations. People appear to be very interested in other people, and the media have discovered that "Names make news—Big names make bigger news."[13]

A recent study compared the impact of advertisements with and advertisements without celebrity endorsers, and found that those with celebrities were rated more positively. This was especially true for teenagers, where the celebrity's credibility was particularly likely to be extended to the advertising message and the endorsed product.[14]

In Figure 11-4 Alan Alda offers a testimonial for AtariWriter word processing software, and, indirectly, Atari computers. Not only is Alan Alda a highly recognized celebrity who is well liked, but his devotion to a number of

**FIGURE 11-4** Advertisement Employing a Well-Known Celebrity

Courtesy of Atari Corp.

social issues (such as the women's movement) gives him a great deal of credibility with the American public. Few people would think that he would endorse a product in which he did not believe.

### HOW CELEBRITIES ARE USED

A firm that decides to employ a celebrity to promote its product has a choice of using the celebrity to give a **testimonial,** to give an **endorsement,** as an **actor** in a commercial, or as a company **spokesperson**. These promotional roles differ as follows:[15]

1. *Testimonial.* If the celebrity has personally used the product or service and is in a position to attest to its quality, he or she may give a testimonial citing its benefits. An example would be a testimonial for a specific brand of baseball glove given by a professional ballplayer such as Pete Rose.
2. *Endorsement.* A celebrity who may or may not be expert with regard to a product or service may be asked to lend his or her name and physical appearance to an advertisement. John Newcombe's appearance in ads for Rolex is an example of an endorsement.
3. *Actor.* A celebrity may be asked to present the product or service as part of a character enactment, rather than as a personal testimonial or endorsement. An example of celebrities used in this way is Jerry Stiller and Anne Meara for the Amalgamated Bank of New York.
4. *Spokesperson.* A celebrity who represents a brand or company over an extended period of time, often in print, television, and in personal appearances, can be called a company spokesperson. Eventually, the celebrity's appearance becomes closely associated with the brand or company. Cliff Robertson is a spokesperson for AT&T Communications, and is closely identified with most of its advertising to the consumer market.

Table 11-3 presents examples of these somewhat distinct uses of celebrities as reference group appeals.

### CREDIBILITY OF THE CELEBRITY

Of all the positive characteristics that a celebrity might contribute to a firm's advertising program (fame, talent, charisma), credibility with the consumer audience is the most important. By *credibility* we mean the audience's perception of both the celebrity's *expertise* (how much the celebrity knows about the product area) and *trustworthiness* (how honest the celebrity is about what he or she knows about the product). To increase this credibility, recent evidence suggests that using a celebrity on an exclusive basis (the celebrity does not endorse any other products) has some very positive benefits.[16] Specifically, the research reveals that when a celebrity endorses only one product, consumers are likely to perceive the product in a more favorable light and to indicate a greater intention to purchase it. Endorsement of a variety of products apparently underscores the commercial nature of the celebrity's efforts.

Other research efforts have shed additional light on the issue of celebrity-endorser credibility. For instance, the *age* of the audience seems important.

**TABLE 11-3 How Celebrities Are Used in Reference Group Appeals**

| TYPES OF USE | CELEBRITY | BRAND OR COMPANY |
|---|---|---|
| 1. Testimonial | John McEnroe | Bic Shavers |
| | Loretta Lynn | Crisco Oil |
| | Mary Lou Retton | Pony Sneakers |
| | Rachel McLish | Jack LaLanne Health Spas |
| 2. Endorsement | Joan Collins | Scoundrel Perfume |
| | Cheryl Tiegs | Sears Clothing |
| | Dinah Shore | Holly Farm Chicken |
| | Merlin Olsen | FTD Florists |
| | Linda Evans | Forever Krystle Perfume |
| | Lynda Carter | Maybelline |
| | Jack Klugman | Canon Copiers |
| 3. Actor | Dom DeLuise | NCR Computers |
| | Larry Hagman | BVD |
| 4. Spokesperson | O. J. Simpson and Arnold Palmer | Hertz |
| | James Garner | Mazda |
| | Cliff Robertson | AT&T |
| | John Houseman | Smith Barney |
| | Bob Hope | Texaco |

Teenagers were found to be more impressed and more likely to respond positively to products endorsed by a celebrity than those endorsed by an unknown person.[17] The *physical attractiveness* of the endorser has also been examined. One study found that the more attractive the endorser, the more likely was he or she perceived as trustworthy, expert and a person to be liked.[18] Research also suggests that celebrity endorsers aid recall of the products they advertise.[19]

## The Expert

A second type of reference group appeal used by marketers is the expert—a person who, because of his or her occupation, special training, or experience, is in a unique position to help the prospective consumer evaluate the product or service the advertisement promotes. For example, an advertisement for Sharp office-quality typewriters features the endorsements of secretaries; an ad for Nikon cameras contains the endorsements of several professional photographers. Still another example is the Whistler radar detector ad depicted in Figure 11-5. As the ad states, no one knows more about life on the road than America's professional truckers. Similarly, Figure 11-6 depicts the well known jazz/pop musician, George Benson, in an ad for Sony digital audio equipment. The ad describes how Benson thought enough of Sony digital recording equipment to invest in it, and then goes on to suggest that it would be a good idea to play him back on a Sony portable compact disc player. This ad is particularly impressive because it combines the celebrity and expert into a single message.

FIGURE 11-5 Advertisement Employing the Concept of Experts

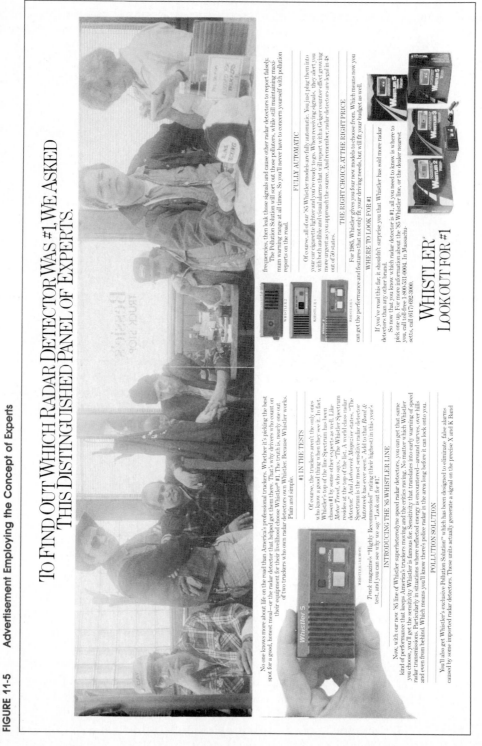

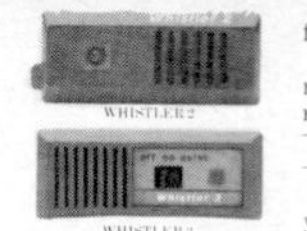


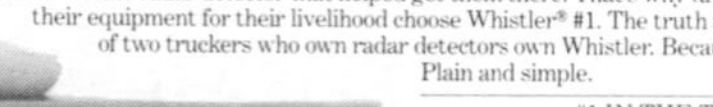

Courtesy of Controlonics Corp.

FIGURE 11-6 Advertisement Combining the Celebrity and Expert

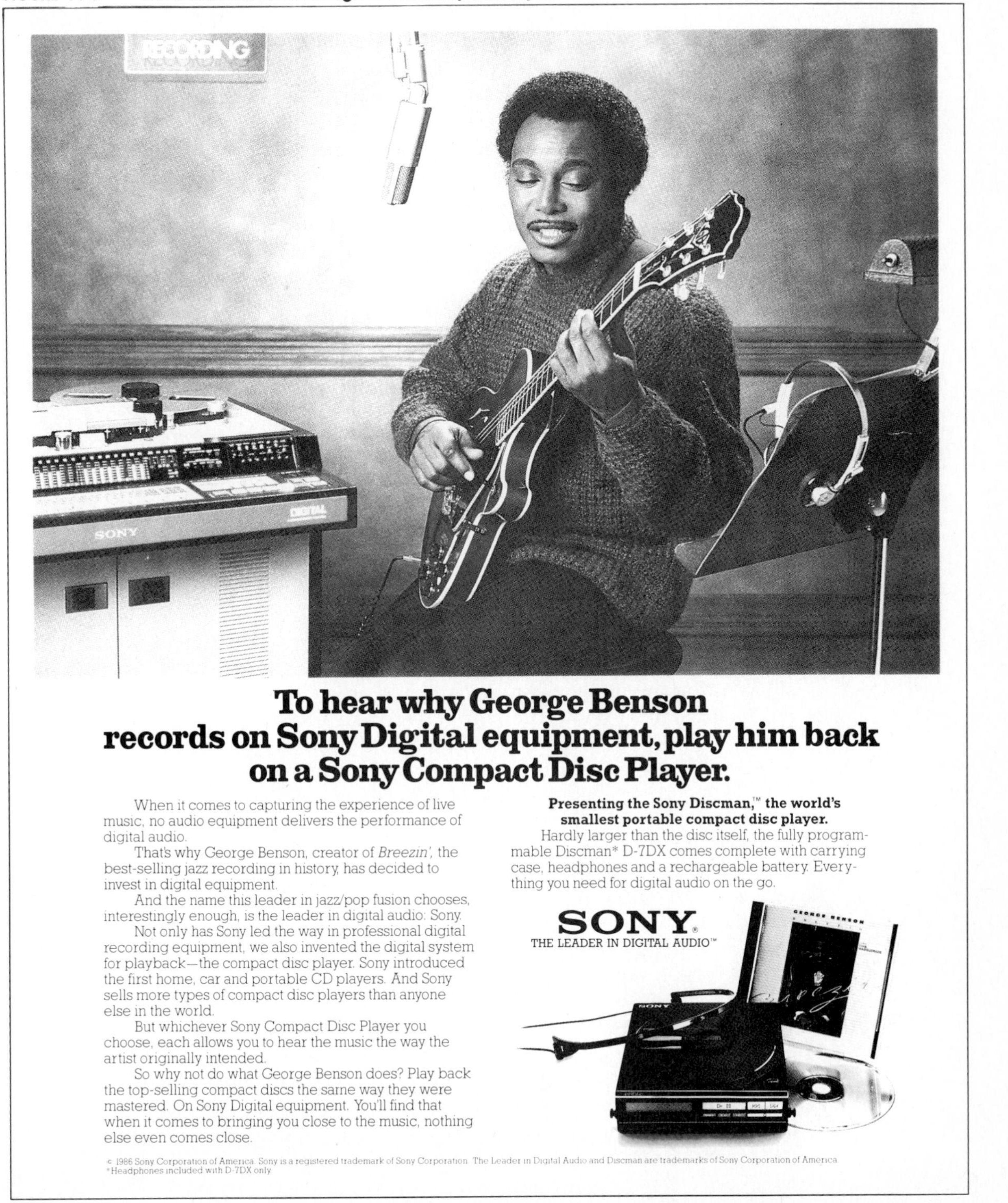

# To hear why George Benson records on Sony Digital equipment, play him back on a Sony Compact Disc Player.

When it comes to capturing the experience of live music, no audio equipment delivers the performance of digital audio.

That's why George Benson, creator of *Breezin'*, the best-selling jazz recording in history, has decided to invest in digital equipment.

And the name this leader in jazz/pop fusion chooses, interestingly enough, is the leader in digital audio: Sony.

Not only has Sony led the way in professional digital recording equipment, we also invented the digital system for playback—the compact disc player. Sony introduced the first home, car and portable CD players. And Sony sells more types of compact disc players than anyone else in the world.

But whichever Sony Compact Disc Player you choose, each allows you to hear the music the way the artist originally intended.

So why not do what George Benson does? Play back the top-selling compact discs the same way they were mastered. On Sony Digital equipment. You'll find that when it comes to bringing you close to the music, nothing else even comes close.

**Presenting the Sony Discman,™ the world's smallest portable compact disc player.**

Hardly larger than the disc itself, the fully programmable Discman* D-7DX comes complete with carrying case, headphones and a rechargeable battery. Everything you need for digital audio on the go.

*Headphones included with D-7DX only.

Courtesy of Sony Corporation of America

## The "Common Man"

A third type of reference group appeal employs the testimonials of satisfied customers. The advantage of this *common man* appeal is that it demonstrates to the prospective customer that someone just like him uses and is satisfied with the product or service advertised. The common man appeal is especially effective in public health announcements (e.g., antismoking or high-blood-pressure messages), for most people seem to identify with people like themselves when it comes to such messages.[20]

An ad for an electric shaver that depicts four stereotypical male shavers, each giving their specific reasons for satisfaction with the product, is an example of a common man appeal. For the potential buyer, such an ad presents various reasons for this particular brand's superiority. For those who have already bought the brand, it reassures them that they made the correct brand choice.

A promotional campaign that includes the common man appeal has been used by Maytag to emphasize the dependability of its appliances. Since washing machines and dishwashers perform functional rather than glamorous tasks, the common man appeal seems to be ideally suited. In a similar approach, Revere Ware uses the common man appeal to promote its pots and pans. Figure 11-7 portrays a homemaker offering a host of reasons why she is glad she purchased Revere Ware cookware.

Many television commercials depict widely prevalent problem situations and show how a typical family or person has solved the problem by using the advertised product. These commercials are known as *slice of life* commercials because they depict situations "out of real life" with which the viewer can identify. For example, one commercial shows a teenage boy refusing to take out the garbage because the last time he tried to do so the garbage bag broke; another shows a working mother coming home too tired to prepare dinner for her family, so she walks over to her refrigerator and takes several "gourmet" frozen dinners out of the freezer. If viewers identify with the situation, they are likely to adopt the solution that worked in the TV commercial.

In recent years, a number of advertisers have adopted the approach of "listening in" or showing a group interview (not unlike a focus group session) in which, for example, women are asked to discuss their present cold remedies and evaluate the benefits of a new 12-hour cold pill. If the prospective consumer can identify with the medication needs or other needs discussed by consumer-actors who are apparently just like her, she is likely to follow the product wisdom expressed and buy the advertised product.

## Other Reference Group Appeals

A variety of other promotional strategies can creatively function as a frame of reference for consumers. During the past ten years, an increasing number of firms have used their top executives as spokespersons in consumer ads. The popularity of this type of advertising is probably due to the success and publicity received by a number of innovative executive spokespersons. For instance, Lee Iacocca has been highly effective in persuading consumers that Chrysler

FIGURE 11-7 Advertisement Depicting a "Common Man" Endorsement

Courtesy of Revere Ware

automobiles are worthy of their purchase consideration. Similarly, Frank Perdue talks about the superiority of his Perdue chickens; Victor Kiam, the president of Remington Products, frequently tells consumers about the benefits of his made-in-America shavers.

Like the celebrity spokesperson, executive spokespersons seem to be admired by the general population because of their achievements and the status implicitly conferred upon business leaders in the United States. "When the man at the top says that he stands behind his product," the American consumer

**FIGURE 11-8** Advertisement Employing a Corporate Executive as a Spokesperson

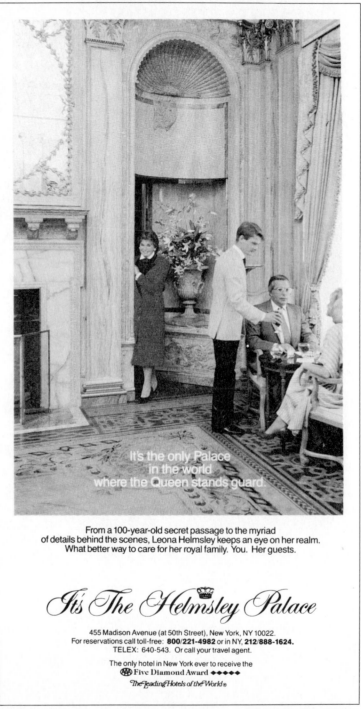

From a 100-year-old secret passage to the myriad of details behind the scenes, Leona Helmsley keeps an eye on her realm. What better way to care for her royal family. You. Her guests.

455 Madison Avenue (at 50th Street), New York, NY 10022.
For reservations call toll-free: **800/221-4982** or in NY, **212/888-1624.**
TELEX: 640-543. Or call your travel agent.

The only hotel in New York ever to receive the
AAA Five Diamond Award ◆◆◆◆◆
The Leading Hotels of the World®

Courtesy of The Helmsley Palace

tends to believe him.[21] Consider, for example, Leona Helmsley, the president of the Helmsley hotel chain. For the past several years, she has appeared in advertisements for Helmsley-owned hotels in New York City. Her recurring theme, as Figure 11-8 shows, is that a guest in one of her hotels should not have to settle for less than she would herself.

Table 11-4 presents a partial list of corporate heads who have appeared in advertising for the firms over which they preside.

Respected retailers and the editorial content of selected special interest magazines can also function as frames of reference that influence consumer attitudes and behavior. For instance, a customer might feel that if a leading fashion specialty store like Saks Fifth Avenue features or depicts a particular fashion as suitable for a certain occasion, then it must be acceptable or in good taste.[22] Similarly, a regular reader of *Vogue* might judge a particular fashion featured in the magazine as being in good taste just because it appears in its pages. In these two instances, the retailer and the magazine are functioning as frames of reference that influence consumer behavior.

It is interesting to note that trade characters (e.g., Betty Crocker, Smokey the Bear, Tony the Tiger) as well as familiar cartoon characters (Mickey Mouse, Snoopy, Superman, Smurf) also serve as kind of quasi-celebrity endorsers. In a recent *People* magazine poll, it was discovered that Mr. Clean, a character that has not been seen on TV in 10 years, who was associated with the cleaning product was better known than the vice-president of the United States.[23]

Finally, *seals of approval* and even objective *product ratings* can serve as positive endorsements that encourage consumers to act favorably toward selected products. For instance, *Good Housekeeping* magazine's seal of approval is well regarded by many consumers as an indication that a particular brand is likely to function as promised. Similarly, many parents of young children look for the American Dental Association's seal of approval before selecting a brand of toothpaste. A high rating by an objective rating magazine such as *Consumer Reports* can serve as an endorsement for a brand.

**TABLE 11-4 Corporate Heads Who Have Appeared in Their Firm's Advertisements**

| NAME | COMPANY |
|---|---|
| Bill Blass | Bill Blass Clothing |
| Tom Carvel | Carvel Ice Cream |
| Jimmy Dean | Jimmy Dean Sausage |
| Leona Helmsley | Helmsley Hotels |
| Russell Hogg | MasterCard International |
| Lee Iacocca | Chrysler Corporation |
| Victor Kiam | Remington Products |
| David Mahoney | Avis Rent-A-Car |
| Bill Marriott | Marriott Hotels |
| Frank Perdue | Perdue Farms |
| L. S. Shoen | U-Haul International |
| John Sweet | U.S. News and World Report |

Source: Drawn from Joseph Poindexter, "Voices of Authority," *Psychology Today,* August 1983, 53–61.

## Benefits of the Reference Group Appeal

Reference group appeals have two principal benefits for the advertiser: they increase brand awareness and they serve to reduce perceived risk.

### INCREASED BRAND AWARENESS

Reference group appeals provide the advertiser with the opportunity to gain and retain the attention of prospective consumers with greater ease and effectiveness than is possible with many other types of promotional campaigns. This is particularly true of the *celebrity* form of reference group appeal, where the personality employed is generally well known to the relevant target segment. Celebrities tend to draw attention to the product through their own popularity. This gives the advertiser a competitive advantage in gaining audience attention, particularly on television where there are so many brief and similar commercial announcements.

### REDUCED PERCEIVED RISK

The use of one or more reference group appeals may also serve to lower the consumer's perceived risk in purchasing a specific product. The example set by the endorser or testimonial-giver may demonstrate to the consumer that uncertainty about the product purchase is unwarranted. Following are examples of how reference group appeals serve to lower the consumer's perceived risk.

CELEBRITY. Consumers who admire a particular celebrity often have the following reactions to the celebrity's endorsement or testimonial:

"She wouldn't do a commercial for that product if she didn't believe it was really good."

"An important person like him doesn't need the money, so he must be plugging the product because he really believes in it."

"If it's good enough for him, it's good enough for me."

EXPERT. When consumers are concerned about the technical aspects of a product, they welcome the comments of an acknowledged or apparent expert:

"If he says it works, then it really must work."

"If an expert uses the product, it has to be good."

COMMON MAN. When consumers are worried about how a product will affect them personally, they are likely to be influenced by a common man endorsement or testimonial:

"People just like me are using that product."

"If it can help her, it's just as likely to help me."

"She has the same problem that I have; I wonder if it will help me also?"

On the basis of very positive experiences in the marketplace, advertisers continue to use celebrities, experts, and common man appeals as well as other reference group appeals to promote and to differentiate their products.

## *summary*

Almost all individuals regularly interact with other people who directly or indirectly influence their purchase decisions. Thus the study of groups and their impact on the individual is of great importance to marketers concerned with influencing consumer behavior. Groups may be classified according to regularity of contact (primary or secondary groups), by structure and hierarchy (formal or informal groups), by size or complexity (large or small groups), and by membership or aspiration (membership or symbolic groups).

Six basic types of consumer-relevant groups influence the consumption behavior of individuals: family, friendship groups, formal social groups, shopping groups, consumer action groups, and work groups.

Consumer reference groups are groups that serve as a frame of reference for individuals in their purchase decisions. Any or all of the groups listed above can serve as reference groups. Reference groups that influence general values or behavior are called normative reference groups; those that influence specific attitudes are called comparative reference groups. The concept of consumer reference groups has been broadened to include groups with which consumers have no direct face-to-face contact, such as celebrities, political figures, social classes, and cultures.

Reference groups that are classified in terms of a person's membership and the positive or negative influences they exert include contactual groups, aspirational groups, disclaimant groups, and avoidance groups.

The credibility, attractiveness, and power of the reference group affect the degree of influence it has. In some cases, and for some products, reference groups may influence either the product category or brand choice purchase decisions, or both. Reference group appeals are used very effectively by some advertisers in promoting their goods and services because they subtly induce the prospective consumer to identify with the pictured user of the product.

The three types of reference groups most commonly used in marketing are celebrities, experts, and the common man. Celebrities are used to give testimonials or endorsements, as actors, and as company spokespersons. Experts may be recognized experts in the product category or actors playing the part of experts (e.g., an automobile mechanic). The common man approach is designed to show that individuals "just like" the prospect are satisfied with the advertised product.

Reference group appeals are effective promotional strategies because they serve to increase brand awareness and reduce perceived risk among prospective consumers.

## *discussion questions*

1. Prepare a list of the formal and informal groups to which you belong. How many groups are on each list?
2. Name and briefly describe three different types of groups that might influence an individual's consumer behavior. What is the importance of each of these groups for marketers in planning their marketing strategy?
3. As a marketing consultant for a large retail chain, you have been asked to evaluate a new promotional campaign. The campaign strategy is aimed at increasing group shopping. What recommendations would you make?
4. Given the relationship between group discussion and perceived risk, what advertising advice do you have for the manufacturer of Right Guard deodorant?
5. With a paper and pencil, spend one hour watching prime-time network television. Record the total number of commercials that aired. For each commercial using a celebrity endorser, record the celebrity's name, the product or service advertised, and whether the celebrity was used in a testimonial, as an endorser, actor, or spokesperson.
6. Does the appearance of singer Michael Jackson in a Pepsi TV commercial convince people to switch to Pepsi?
7. Imagine that you are the vice-president of advertising for a large furniture manufacturer. Your advertising agency is in the process of negotiating a contract to employ this year's most valuable baseball player to promote your products. Discuss.
8. Find a magazine advertisement for a consumer product that uses the *expert* as a reference group appeal. What impact do you feel this appeal has on consumers? Explain.

## *endnotes*


1. Murray Hausknecht, *The Joiners* (New York: Bedminister Press, 1962).
2. Donald H. Granbois, "Improving the Study of Customer In-Store Behavior," *Journal of Marketing,* 32 (October 1968), 28–32.
3. Solomon E. Asch, *Social Psychology* (Englewood Cliffs, N.J.: Prentice-Hall, 1952).
4. V. Parker Lessig and C. Whan Park, "Promotional Perspectives of Reference Group Influence: Advertising Implications," *Journal of Advertising,* 7 (Spring 1978), 41–47.
5. Foundation for Research on Human Behavior, *Group Influence in Marketing and Public Relations* (Ann Arbor, Mich.: The Foundation, 1956), 8–9.
6. Donald W. Hendon, "A New and Empirical Look at the Influence of Reference Groups on Generic Product Category and Brand Choice: Evidence from Two Nations," in *Proceedings of the Academy of International Business: Asia-Pacific Dimen-*

*sions of International Business* (Honolulu: College of Business Administration, University of Hawaii, 1979), 752–61.

7. Kurt Lewin, "Group Decision and Social Change," in Theodore M. Newcomb and Eugene L. Hartley, eds., *Readings in Social Psychology* (New York: Henry Holt, 1947), 330–44.
8. M. Venkatesan, "Experimental Study of Consumer Behavior Conformity and Independence," *Journal of Marketing Research,* 3 (November 1966), 384–87.
9. Robert E. Witt, "Informal Social Group Influence on Consumer Brand Choice," *Journal of Marketing Research,* 6 (November 1969), 473–76.
10. Robert E. Witt and Grady D. Bruce, "Purchase Decisions and Group Influence," *Journal of Marketing Research,* 7 (November 1970), 533–35.
11. Peter H. Reingen, Biran L. Foster, Jacqueline Johnson Brown, and Stephen B. Seidman, "Brand Congruence in Interpersonal Relations: A Social Network Analysis," *Journal of Consumer Research,* 11 (December 1984), 771–83.
12. Jon B. Freiden, "Advertising Spokesperson Effects: An Examination of Endorser Type and Gender on Two Audiences," *Journal of Advertising Research,* 24 (October–November 1984), 33.
13. Edwin Diamond, "Celebrating Celebrity," *New York Magazine,* May 13, 1985, 22 and 27.
14. Charles Atkin and Martin Block, "Effectiveness of Celebrity Endorsers," *Journal of Advertising Research,* 23 (February–March 1983), 57–61.
15. Joseph M. Kamen, Abdul C. Azhari, and Judith R. Kragh, "What a Spokesman Does for a Sponsor," *Journal of Advertising Research,* 15 (April 1975), 17.
16. John C. Mowen and Stephen W. Brown, "On Explaining and Predicting the Effectiveness of Celebrity Endorsers," in Kent Monroe, ed., *Advances in Consumer Research* (Ann Arbor, Mich.: Association for Consumer Research, 1981), VIII, 437–41.
17. Charles Atkin and Martin Block, "Effectiveness of Celebrity Endorsers," *Journal of Advertising Research,* 23 (February–March 1983), 57–61. Also see Jon B. Freiden, "Advertising Spokesperson Effects: An Examination of Endorser Type and Gender on Two Audiences," *Journal of Advertising Research,* 24 (October–November 1984), 33–41.
18. Gordon L. Patzer, "Source Credibility as a Function of Communicator Physical Attractiveness," *Journal of Business Research,* 11 (1983), 229–241.
19. Hershey H. Friedman, "Endorser Effectiveness as a Function of Product Type," *Journal of Advertising Research,* 19 (October 1979), 63–74; also see Hershey H. Friedman and Linda W. Friedman, "Does the Celebrity Endorser's Image Spill Over to the Product?" *Mid-Atlantic Journal of Business,* 18 (May 1980), 31–36.
20. "Study Identifies Qualities of Effective Public Health Service Announcements," *Marketing News,* April 3, 1981, 7.
21. "Consumers Believe in the Man at the Top," *Advertising Age,* August 8, 1983, 12.
22. Elizabeth C. Hirschman and Ronald W. Stampfl, "Roles of Retailing the Diffusion of Popular Culture: Microperspectives," *Journal of Retailing,* 56 (Spring 1980), 31–32.
23. "New Life for Madison Avenue's Old-Time Stars," *Business Week,* April 1, 1985, 94.

12

# The Family

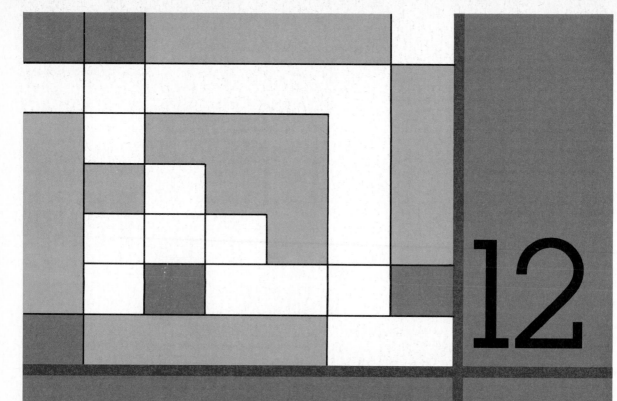

## *introduction*

THE family is a major influence in the consumer behavior process. As the basic group to which an individual belongs, the family provides early childhood learning about products and product categories, provides the opportunity for product exposure and repetition, and sets the consumption norms for family members. As a major consumption unit, the family is a prime target for most products and product categories.

To understand how the family makes its purchase decisions and affects the future purchase behavior of its young, it is useful to understand the functions provided and roles enacted by family members to fulfill their consumption needs. By way of background, we will first examine some basic family terminology; then we will discuss family consumer decision making and the marketing implications of the family life cycle.

## WHAT IS A FAMILY?

Although the term **family** is a very basic concept, it is not easy to define because family structure and the roles fulfilled by family members vary considerably from society to society. Traditionally, however, *family* is defined as *two or more persons related by blood, marriage, or adoption who reside together.* In a more dynamic sense, the individuals who constitute a family might be described as members

> *The family is the association established by nature for the supply of man's everyday wants.*
>
> *ARISTOTLE*
> Politics *(4th cent. B.C.)*

of the most basic social group who live together and interact to satisfy their personal and mutual needs.

Though families are sometimes referred to as *households,* not all households are families. For example, a household might also include individuals who are not related by blood, marriage, or adoption, such as unmarried couples, family friends, roommates, or boarders. However, households and families are usually treated as synonymous within the context of consumer behavior, and we will continue this tradition.

In the United States, as in most Western societies, three types of families dominate: the married couple, the nuclear family, and the extended family. The simplest type of family, in terms of numbers, is the *married couple*—a husband and wife. As a basic household unit, the married couple is generally representative of new marrieds who have not yet started a family and older couples who have already raised their children. A husband and wife and at least one child constitute a *nuclear family.* This type of family is the cornerstone of family life as it now exists in the United States. The nuclear family, together with at least one grandparent living within the household, is called an *extended family.* This three-generation family, which at one time was most representative of the American family, has declined in recent years as increased mobility often separates parents and their adult offspring.

## Functions of the Family

Four basic functions provided by the family are particularly relevant to a discussion of consumer behavior. These include **economic well-being, emotional support, suitable lifestyles,** and **childhood socialization**.

### ECONOMIC WELL-BEING

Although the family in an affluent nation like the United States is no longer formed primarily for economic security, the provision of financial means to its dependents is unquestionably a basic family function. How the family divides its responsibilities for the provision of economic well-being has changed considerably during the past twenty years. No longer are the traditional roles of husband as economic provider and wife as homemaker and child rearer still valid; the majority of wives in this country are employed outside the home and their husbands share household responsibilities. The economic role of children also has changed. Today, despite the fact that many teenage children work, they rarely assist the family financially. Instead, they are expected to complete their formal educational training and prepare themselves to be financially independent.

### EMOTIONAL SUPPORT

The provision of emotional and therapeutic support to its members is an important basic function of the contemporary family. In fulfilling this function, the family attempts to assist its members in coping with personal or social problems. If the family cannot provide adequate assistance when it is needed, it may turn to a professional counselor or psychologist as an alternative. In general terms, the selection of such professional services is similar to other types of consumption decisions made by the family.

## SUITABLE LIFESTYLES

Another important family function in terms of consumer behavior is the establishment of a suitable *lifestyle* for the family. Upbringing, experience, and the personal and jointly determined goals of the spouses determine the importance placed on education or career, on reading, on television viewing, on the frequency and quality of dining out, and the selection of other entertainment and recreational activities. Family lifestyle commitments, including the allocation of time, greatly influence consumption patterns. For example, the increase in married women working has reduced the time they have available for household chores and created a market for convenience products and fast-food restaurants.

## CHILDHOOD SOCIALIZATION

The socialization of young children is a central family function. In large part, this process consists of imparting to children the basic values and modes of behavior consistent with the culture, which may include personality development, interpersonal competence, dress and grooming habits, appropriate manners and speech, and the selection of a suitable occupation or career. Socialization factors are imparted to the child directly through instruction, and indirectly through the behavior of parents and older siblings.

The aspect of childhood socialization that is most relevant to the study of consumer behavior is **consumer socialization,** which is defined as *the process by which children acquire the skills, knowledge, and attitudes necessary to function as consumers.* Several studies have focused on how children develop consumption skills. One researcher demonstrated that children's consumer behavior norms are acquired through observation of their parents, who function as role models.[1] While preadolescent children tend to rely on their parents and older siblings as the major source of cues for basic consumption learning, adolescents and teenagers are likely to look to outside friends for models of acceptable behavior.[2]

Consumer socialization fulfills a unique function as a tool by which parents influence other aspects of the socialization process. For instance, parents frequently use the promise or reward of material goods as a device to modify or control a child's behavior. A mother may reward her child with a gift when the child does something to please her, or withhold or remove it if the child disobeys. One study showed that children's consumer knowledge structure becomes more sophisticated as they grow older. Thus younger children (ages 4 to 6) describe grocery shopping with their mothers in highly specific *(episodic)* terms ("Get a shopping cart . . . go get some pop, milk, fruit for my dad's lunch, pizza, spaghetti"). Older children (ages 7 to 10), on the other hand, tend to give very general *(categorical)* descriptions ("We go in the store, look around, find all the stuff you need . . . come up to the counter and pay for it and then you can go home").[3] One study found that parents can teach children to apply economic reasoning. Children who were taught that they cannot have everything and must choose among realistic alternatives were found to be more satisfied with their choices.[4] These findings were supported by a study which found that although children are generally satisfied with the presents they receive from their parents, children with high parent interaction experience somewhat more satisfaction.[5] A study of black and white consumers suggests that observed differences in consumer behavior are attributable to different socialization patterns in each subculture.[6]

Consumer socialization has two distinct components: those directly related to consumption, such as the acquisition of skills, knowledge, and attitudes concerned with budgeting, pricing, and brand attitudes; and those indirectly related to consumption, such as the underlying motivations that spur a young man to purchase his first razor or a young girl to want her first bra. While both are significant, the indirect component of consumer socialization is of most interest to marketing executives, who want to understand *why* people buy their products.

The socialization process is not confined to childhood; it is an ongoing process. For example, when a newly married couple establishes a household, their adjustment to living and consuming together is part of that continuing process.

## FAMILY DECISION MAKING

While many marketers acknowledge the family as the basic decision-making unit, they usually examine consumer behavior concerning their own products in terms of the one family member they believe to be the major decision maker. Although such a research approach can be justified in terms of simplicity and cost, it may provide a distorted picture of the specific contributions of various family members to a purchase decision.[7] For instance, men's formal wear might logically be thought of as a male-dominated decision, but the wife strongly influences the purchase decision. Similarly, men's underwear is more often purchased by women who independently select such items for their husbands or unmarried sons. Because the user is not always the sole decision maker or even the buyer, marketers should try to identify the family member who makes the decision for their own product categories and target a substantial portion of their promotional efforts to that member who affects or selects the product purchase.

### Family Role Structure

For a family to function as a cohesive unit, roles or tasks—such as setting the dinner table, taking out the garbage, or walking the dog—must be carried out by one or more family members. Family-related roles are constantly changing in the highly dynamic society in which we live. A 1980 research study found that husbands had assumed a host of nontraditional family roles: 32 percent shopped for food; 74 percent took out the garbage; 47 percent cooked for the family; 53 percent washed the dishes; 29 percent did the laundry; 28 percent cleaned the bathroom; 39 percent vacuumed the house; and 80 percent took care of the children (in households with children under twelve years of age.)[8] Given the greater number of married women working today, and the greater acceptability of household tasks by men, those percentages are likely to have increased substantially. Marketers need to be alert to how shifting family roles may be affecting the composition of their target markets in order to make timely adjustments to their marketing strategies.

In the context of consumer purchase decisions, family members play a variety of roles. A family's purchase of a motorboat might be subject to the following role influences: The teenage son generates initial family interest, the husband collects relevant information from friends and from specialized media, both spouses jointly agree on the amount to be spent, all family members agree on the product features to be sought, the husband selects the dealer from which to buy the boat, and the entire family goes along when the purchase is actually made. Each member of the family thus participates in the purchase decision.

Since family roles tend to vary by product category, and since different families are apt to establish somewhat different family roles for the same product decision, it is difficult to develop a marketing strategy that reflects the specific roles of each family member. Through carefully conceived consumer research, however, marketers can usually uncover a pattern of decision making that describes the majority of families who are potential consumers of their products.

## KEY FAMILY CONSUMPTION ROLES

There are eight distinct roles involved in the family decision-making process. They provide further insight into how family members interact in their various consumption-related roles:

*Influencers.* Family member(s) who provide information to other members about a product or service

*Gatekeepers.* Family member(s) who control the flow of information about a product or service into the family

*Deciders.* Family member(s) with the power to unilaterally or jointly determine whether or not to purchase a specific product or service

*Buyers.* Family member(s) who make the actual purchase of a particular product or service

*Preparers.* Family member(s) who transform the product into a form suitable for consumption by other family members

*Users.* Family member(s) who use or consume a particular product or service

*Maintainers.* Family member(s) who service or repair the product so that it will provide continued satisfaction

*Disposers.* Family member(s) who initiate or carry out the disposal or discontinuation of a particular product or service

The number and identity of the family members who fill these roles varies from family to family and product to product. In some cases, a single family member will independently assume a number of roles; in other cases, a single role will be performed jointly by two or more family members. In still other cases, one or more of these basic roles may not be required. For example, a husband browsing through a supermarket may pick up a jar of Dijon mustard; his decision to purchase it does not directly involve the influence of other family members. He is the *decider,* the *buyer,* and in a sense the *gatekeeper;* however, he may or may not be the *preparer,* and is likely not to be the sole *user.*

In considering family consumption behavior, it is often useful to distinguish between the *decision making* that leads to the purchase and the *consumption* (or use) of the product. Products may be consumed by a single family member (beer, lipstick), consumed or used directly by two or more family members (frozen vegetables, shampoo), or consumed indirectly by the entire family (draperies, paintings).

## Dynamics of Husband/Wife Decision Making

Because a married couple is the basic decision-making unit, the relative strengths of husband and wife influence on family consumption decisions is of great interest to consumer researchers. Most husband/wife influence studies classify family consumption decisions as *husband-dominated, wife-dominated, joint* (or syncratic), and *autonomic* (or unilateral).

Studies that have examined both the extent and nature of husband/wife influence in family decisions have found that such influence is fluid and likely to shift, depending on the specific product or service, the specific stage in the decision-making process, and the specific product features under consideration. All these factors are also mediated by changing lifestyles, particularly the increase in the number of working wives. A recent study found that families with modern sex-role norms showed less wife influence and greater joint and husband influence in areas traditionally assigned to the wife; conversely, there was less husband influence and greater joint and wife influence in areas traditionally handled by the husband.[9]

### PRODUCT OR SERVICE VARIATIONS

Research on husband/wife decision making has consistently found that the relative influence of a spouse depends in part on the product or service category. For instance, studies in the mid-1950s revealed that the purchase of an automobile was strongly husband-dominated, while food and some financial decisions were wife-dominated. For other products or services studied, husbands and wives tended to contribute equally (e.g., the selection of a house or apartment, vacations, savings).[10] Some twenty years later, research designed to replicate the earlier study found that life insurance had become a husband-dominated decision, and food and groceries even more wife-dominated. The selection of family housing and vacations were increasingly joint decisions, intensifying earlier findings.

Significant changes in the area of automobile decision making were reported. Husbands continued to dominate the purchase decision, though less so (52 percent versus 70 percent in the earlier study), and there was a substantial shift toward joint decision making (45 percent versus 25 percent).[11] This study suggests a generalized shift in the locus of family decision making. A study of 2,500 married men and women found that husbands continued to dominate in some consumption areas (automobiles and television sets) and wives in other areas (the selection of movies and television programs).[12]

Additional insights into the dynamics of husband and wife decision making are provided by a study that focused on a single decision area: family financial management.[13] The research was specifically designed to identify which spouse in newly married couples undertook the principal responsibility for family money management (payment of bills and the use of extra funds). An initial interview during the first year of marriage revealed that most couples shared equally in money management. Follow-up interviews during the second year of marriage showed a decline in joint financial decision making and a shift to wife-dominated money management. The findings indicate that financially inexperienced newlyweds are likely to start out sharing the burdens of financial decision making; however, in a relatively short time, wives take the lead in this area. This suggests that newly married women may be an important target market for banking and other financial services.

A recent study found that husbands had more influence in the selection of insurance and legal professionals, and that wives had more influence in selecting a pharmacist. The choice of a family physician was not so clear-cut: in some families, the decision was husband-dominated; in others it was wife-dominated.[14]

## VARIATIONS BY FAMILY ROLE STRUCTURE ORIENTATION

Several studies show that the family's orientation regarding sex roles plays a key factor in family consumption decisions. In families with a modern sex-role orientation, decisions were equally distributed between the two spouses. Such families also engaged in increased interaction among family members regarding decisions; in more contemporary couples, less disagreement among husband and wife was likely to occur.[15] Another study indicated that family role structure in financial management is a function of sex-role attitudes and educational level. It found that women who perceive financial need as the reason for working tend to make autonomic decisions on various aspects of their families' finances ("If I can make the money, then I have the right to decide how to spend it").[16]

Role structure and decision making within the family appear to be related to *culture*. One study showed that Mexican-American families tend to be more husband-dominant than Anglo families, and that Anglo families engage in more joint purchase decisions.[17] Another cross-cultural study reported that husbands in less developed nations made significantly more unilateral decisions than husbands in developed nations, and that significantly more joint decisions took place in developed nations than in less developed nations. Comparisons between family decision making in the United States and France revealed no significant differences. Dutch wives were found to make fewer decisions, and Dutch husbands more decisions, than their American counterparts.[18]

### VARIATIONS BY STAGE IN THE DECISION-MAKING PROCESS

The roles of husbands and wives often differ during the decision-making process. A study of Belgian households, for example, found that the roles of husbands and wives varied for a number of products in terms of a simple three-stage decision-making model: *problem recognition, search for information,* and *final decision.*[19] Following the same basic research design, another study explored shifts among American consumers in husband/wife decision making for some twenty consumer products. Figure 12-1 plots the shifts in husband/wife decisions from stage 1 (problem recognition) to stage 2 (search for information), and from stage 2 to stage 3 (final decision). The results show that for the majority of items, the initial decision-making pattern established in stage 1 continues during the two remaining stages; however, for a few items, there are stage-to-stage shifts. For instance: recognition of the need for a new washing machine is wife-dominant, the search for information concerning the potential purchase is largely autonomic (usually by the wife), and the final decision is made jointly by both spouses.

A recent study showed that husband and wife decision criteria change over time in the purchase of a new home. Specifically, preference and tradeoff dimensions change during the decision period, while rejection criteria remain the same—an apparent effort to avoid conflict with one's spouse.[20]

### VARIATIONS BY PRODUCT FEATURES

An exploratory study sponsored by *Time* magazine suggests that marketers should examine husband/wife decision making in terms of specific purchase factors.[21] For example, the study found that in the determination of brand, the husband dominated for automobiles and television sets, the wife dominated for washing machines, and the brand of dress shirts was jointly determined. Table 12-1 presents these results and evidence pertinent to seven other purchase factors. For the marketer, this study suggests that it is unwise to generalize the relative influence of spouses from one product to another, but to determine it separately for each product category. Second, it would appear that a global measure of husband/wife influence is less helpful than an examination of each spouse's impact at specific stages of the decision-making process or in terms of specific purchase factors.

## Reliability of Husband/Wife Influence Studies

Studies of family decision making indicate that there can be substantial disagreement between spouses as to their relative influence on consumer purchases.[22] That is, each spouse, when interviewed alone, reports his or her influence as dominant in the purchase decision. For that reason, studies of family

**FIGURE 12-1** **Changes in Marital Roles Over the Decision-Making Process** Source: E.H. Bonfield, "Perception of Marital Roles in Decision Processes: Replication and Extension," in H. Keith Hunt, ed., *Advances in Consumer Research* (Ann Arbor, Mich.: Association for Consumer Research, 1978), V. 302.

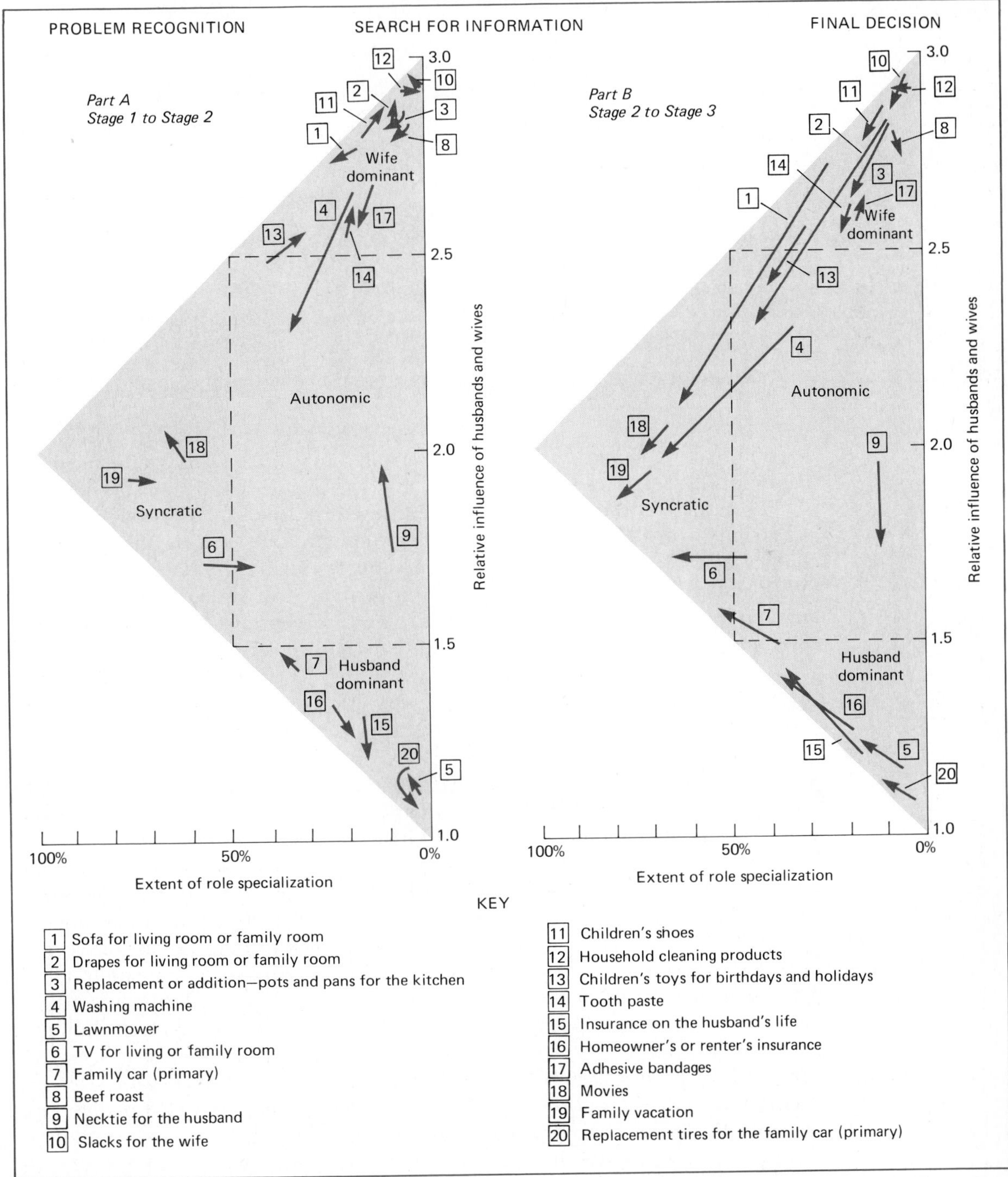

**TABLE 12-1 Relative Influence of Husband and Wife on Selected Purchase Factors**

| PURCHASE FACTORS | AUTOMOBILES | DRESS SHIRTS | TELEVISION SETS | WASHERS |
|---|---|---|---|---|
| Brand (make) | H | = | H | W |
| Performance features | H | W | H | W |
| Style | W | H | W | W |
| Size | H | H | H | W |
| Warranty (guarantee) | = | × | H | H |
| Price | H | W | H | H |
| Store (dealer) | H | = | W | H |
| Service | H | × | H | H |

Key: H—Husband more influential than wife.
W—Wife more influential than husband.
=—Husband and wife equally influential.
×—Not applicable to product category.

Source: Adapted from *Family Decision Making* (New York: Time Magazine, Time Marketing Information Research Report 1428, 1967).

decision making should be carefully controlled to ensure validity and reliability of findings.

Several researchers have proposed new directions for improving the research on husband/wife influence. One study presents a scale that measures conflict arousal and resolution between spouses during the decision process.[23] Other researchers point out the need to investigate the tradeoff between power and interest of the two decision makers and perceptions of each other's sex roles, in the context of longitudinal studies where possible.[24]

## Children

Children play an important role in family decision making. They not only are influenced *by* their families in terms of consumer socialization, they also exert influence *on* their families in terms of family purchase decisions[25]

Young children attempt to influence family decisions as soon as they possess the basic communication skills needed to interact with other family members. ("Buy me a cookie." "I want Sugar Loops." "Let's eat at McDonald's.") Older children are likely to participate more directly in family consumption activities. Table 12-2 reports findings concerning participation by family members in the decision to eat at a fast-food restaurant.[26] The study confirms the fact that children significantly influence family decisions. For each of the three major decision *stages,* there was a significant amount of child input into the decision. Children also played an influential role in the major *dimensions* of the decision, with the exception of how much to spend, which largely remained the province of the parents. Related research indicates that the age of a child and the type of restaurant being considered affects the extent of influence a child will have. Specifically, children over five are more likely to share in the family's decision to eat out, and parents tend to allow children more say when the

**TABLE 12-2** **Family Member Participation in the Decision to Eat Out at a Fast-Food Restaurant**

| | HUSBAND OR WIFE ALONE | HUSBAND AND WIFE TOGETHER | CHILD/ CHILDREN | A PARENT AND CHILD | BOTH PARENTS AND CHILD | TOTAL |
|---|---|---|---|---|---|---|
| part a. major decision stages | | | | | | |
| Initiate purchase | 1% | 6 | 11 | 27 | 55 | 100% |
| Provide information | 3% | 4 | 10 | 22 | 61 | 100% |
| Final decision | 2% | 10 | 4 | 13 | 71 | 100% |
| part b. dimensions of the decision | | | | | | |
| When to go | 4% | 23 | 1 | 12 | 60 | 100% |
| What type of food | 1% | 9 | 2 | 13 | 75 | 100% |
| Which competing establishment | 2% | 7 | 2 | 12 | 77 | 100% |
| How much to spend | 19% | 60 | — | 2 | 19 | 100% |

Source: Adapted from George J. Szybillo and Arlene Sosanie, "Family Decision Making: Husband, Wife and Children," in William D. Perreault, Jr., ed., *Advances in Consumer Research* (Atlanta: Association for Consumer Research, 1977), IV, 47 and 48.

choice is to be made among fast-food restaurants rather than conventional restaurants.[27]

The parent-child relationship as it relates to consumer behavior can be viewed as an **influence versus yield** situation. Specifically, children attempt to *influence* their parents to make a purchase (to *yield*). In-store observations of purchase behavior in supermarkets indicate that children not only attempt to influence their parents in areas of special interest to them (cereal, candy), but also with products of remote interest (laundry detergents).[28] Several consumer behavior studies report conflicting results on the nature of influence and yielding. One study that focused exclusively on breakfast cereals found that the more involved the mother was with her child, the more likely she was *not* to yield to the child's preference for sugar-coated breakfast cereals, presumably because she considered such cereals to be nutritionally unsound.[29]

Another study, which examined child-parent interaction across a number of products (including cereals), found a significant positive relationship between the number of children's influence attempts and the yielding of their mothers.[30] The study also found that children's attempts to influence tended to *decrease* somewhat with age, and mothers' yielding tended to *increase* with the child's age. These results seem to indicate that children become more discriminating in their requests as they get older, and that parents acknowledge their children's increased judgment by acceding more readily to their purchase requests.

## CHILDREN AND TELEVISION

A number of studies have investigated the impact of television viewing and advertising on children. One study found that older children and those with more media exposure tend to recall more advertising slogans.[31] Another study showed that as children get older and acquire more education, they watch less television. However, a younger child in the family tends to expand the older child's TV use. Another provocative finding was that TV use tends to increase by some 15 minutes a day for each $10,000 of parental income.[32]

Parents have expressed concern regarding the impact of TV advertising on their children. One study showed that parents with high socioeconomic status were concerned with the nutrition and quality (especially the high sugar content) of foods advertised to children, while parents lower on the socioeconomic scale were more concerned that such advertising would lead to family conflict with the child, and less concerned that it would promote bad eating habits.[33]

The impact of TV advertising varies among children in different age groups. One study showed that preschoolers respond to perceptual cues and do not truly understand the difference between programs and commercials.[34] It was found that commercials targeted to adults have great influence on children. For example, TV commercials for lipstick favorably influenced nine- and ten-year-old girls' perceptions of the product and brand, because they associated the product with being an adult.[35] A recent study showed that older children recognize more *symbolism* in advertising than younger children. Those who had experience with the product held strong consumption-based stereotypes, suggesting that personal experience is more important than media exposure.[36]

There is some indication that children of parents who more strictly control their children's viewing behavior (and who generally were found to be of a higher socioeconomic level) exhibit a better understanding of the purpose and nature of advertising and make fewer purchase requests of their parents.[37] Several studies point out the need to develop better measures of children's understanding of TV commercials. One study showed that traditional verbal measures usually underestimate the child's ability to understand TV ads, while nonverbal measures, such as asking the child to point at something, indicate that young children are capable of understanding TV commercials.[38]

### TEENAGE CHILDREN

A number of researchers have examined the influence of teenage children on family decision making. There is some evidence that girls with working mothers are somewhat more involved in homemaking activities than girls with nonworking mothers. An ongoing survey sponsored by *Co-ed* (a magazine for teenage girls) indicates that an impressive number of high school girls plan or participate in the planning of family meals and shop for their family's food needs.[39]

Although teenagers constitute a shrinking percentage of the American population, a significant number work, and most of their income is discretionary. Estimates of teen spending power range from $30 billion to over $40 billion a year.[40] High school students in grades 7 through 12 are most interested in sports and fitness. Boys aged sixteen to nineteen spend most of their money on movies, dating, entertainment, car expenses, and clothing, while girls of that age spend most of their money on clothing, cosmetics, and fragrances. The income of both groups is about the same, and some 60 percent of it is earned. Another study found that adolescents with earned income are more likely to save money than those who receive the money as a gift, but dual-income teenagers (allowance and earnings) are more inclined to spend the money on themselves.[41] Teenagers are an important market segment not only because they influence family consumption decisions, but because the teenage years are formative ones in terms of later consumption patterns.[42]

College students have also been shown to exert influence over the purchase decisions of their families. In one study, college students reported that they often attempted to influence family decisions concerning the purchase of television sets and automobiles, and they perceived that they often did in fact influence these decisions.[43]

Despite the numbers of studies that have addressed the role children play in influencing family consumption decisions, the extent and specific nature of their influence (the range of products and the extent of their influence over such decisions) is still largely undocumented. Nevertheless, evidence makes it very clear that children wield important influence in family purchase decisions and thus constitute an important market segment.

## THE FAMILY LIFE CYCLE

Behavioral scientists, particularly family sociologists, have utilized the concept of a **family life cycle (FLC)** to classify family units into significant groupings. These groupings have particular relevance to marketing strategy.

### Stages of the FLC

The family life cycle is conceptualized as a *progression of stages through which most families pass,* starting with bachelorhood, moving on to marriage (and creation of the basic family unit), to family growth (with the birth of children), to family contraction (as grown children leave the household), and ending with the dissolution of the basic family unit (due to the death of one spouse.)

FLC analysis is an important strategic tool for marketers because it enables them to segment families into meaningful target markets. The FLC is a composite variable created by systematically combining such commonly used demographic variables as *marital status, size of family, age of family members* (usually oldest or youngest child), and *employment status* of the head of household. Age of the parents and the relative amount of disposable income are usually inferred from the stage in the family life cycle.

By classifying families on the basis of stage in the family life cycle, a richer picture of the family is obtained than would be possible using any single variable alone. Table 12-3 presents, in schematic fashion, several alternative FLC models. The models differ primarily in terms of the number of stages (or substages) utilized; these in turn reflect how finely the researcher cares to examine

**TABLE 12-3 Alternative Family Life-Cycle Models**

| BROAD CATEGORIES | LANSING AND KISH (1957)* | BLOOD AND WOLFE (1958)† | FARBER (1964)‡ | WELLS AND GUBAR (1966)§ |
|---|---|---|---|---|
| Stage I: Bachelorhood | Young single | | Premarital stage | Bachelor stage, not living at home |
| Stage II: Honeymooners | Young married couple, no children | Honeymoon stage, childless and married less than four years | Couple stage | Newly married couple, young with no children |
| Stage III: Parenthood | Young married couple, with youngest child under 6 | Preschool stage, oldest child under 6 | Preschool phase | Full nest I, youngest child under 6 |
| | Young married couple, with youngest child 6 or over | Preadolescent stage, oldest child 6 to 12 | Elementary school phase | Full nest II, youngest child 6 or over |
| | | Adolescent stage, oldest child 13 to 18 | High school phase | Full nest III, older married couples with dependent children |
| | | Unlaunched stage, oldest child 19 or older and still living at home | College phase | |
| | | | Postschool phase | |
| Stage IV: Postparenthood | Older married couple, no children | Postparental stage | In-law phase | Empty nest I, no children at home, head in labor force |
| | | | Grandparent phase | Empty nest II, head retired |
| Stage V: Dissolution | Older single | Retired stage, nonemployed husband 60 or over | Widowhood and remarriage | Solitary survivor, in labor force |
| | | | End of cycle | Solitary survivor, retired |

Sources: *John B. Lansing and Leslie Kish, "Family Life Cycle as an Independent Variable," *American Sociological Review*, 22 (October 1957), 512–19.

†Robert O. Blood, Jr., and Donald M. Wolfe, *Husbands and Wives* (Glencoe, Ill.: Free Press, 1960).

‡Bernard Farber, *Family: Organization and Interaction* (San Francisco: Chandler, 1964).

§William D. Wells and George Gubar, "Life Cycle Concept in Marketing Research," *Journal of Marketing Research*, (November 1966), 355–63.

family development. The various FLC models depicted in the table can be synthesized into just five stages, as listed below.

Stage I: **Bachelorhood**—a young single adult living apart from parents
Stage II: **Honeymooners**—a young married couple
Stage III: **Parenthood**—a married couple with at least one child living at home

Stage IV: **Postparenthood**—an older married couple with no children living at home
Stage V: **Dissolution**—only one of the original spouses living

The following discussion examines the five stages in detail, and shows how they lend themselves to market segmentation strategies.

## STAGE I: BACHELORHOOD

The first FLC stage consists of young single men and women who have established households apart from their parents. Although most members of this FLC stage are fully employed, many are college students who have left their parents' home. Young single adults are apt to spend their income on rent, basic home furnishings, the purchase and maintenance of automobiles, travel and entertainment, and clothing and accessories. Members of the *bachelorhood* stage frequently have sufficient disposable income to indulge in a kind of hedonistic lifestyle. Marketers target singles for a wide variety of products and services (see Figure 12-2). In most large cities, one can find travel agents, housing developments, health clubs, sports clubs, and so forth, that find this FLC stage a lucrative target market for products and services. It is relatively easy to reach this segment, since many special interest publications cater to singles. For example, *Oui* and *Penthouse* are directed to a young, sophisticated single male audience, while *Cosmopolitan* and *Glamour* are directed to young single females.

After the fling of bachelorhood wears off, singles often turn to the serious business of finding a mate. Here again, the individual is likely to be offered numerous services (e.g., travel and dating services) designed to provide the opportunity to meet the "perfect" mate. When the right individual is found, there is usually a period of courtship, sometimes including a period of living together, and sometimes followed by a formal engagement. In our society, engagement announcements often trigger an onslaught of marketing efforts from specialized services eager to provide the betrothed couple and their parents with a full-scale wedding—a catered affair complete with music, photographs, bridal gown, men's formal wear, wedding rings, flowers, and honeymoon. Other marketers bombard the couple with communications concerning the products they are likely to need in setting up a household. This market is so fertile and so eager for information that the two leading bridal magazines, *Bride's* and *Modern Bride,* have little difficulty in filling their pages with product and service advertisements.

## STAGE II: HONEYMOONERS

The *honeymoon* stage starts immediately after the marriage vows are taken and generally continues up to the arrival of the couple's first child. This FLC stage serves as a period of adjustment to married life. Since many young husbands and wives both work, they have available a combined income that often permits a pleasure-seeking lifestyle similar to that enjoyed by many singles. The difference is that they are now spending together. Today's honeymooners tend to be part of the baby boom population, and to some extent because they seek mate-

FIGURE 12-2 The Bachelorhood Stage Is a Ripe Target Market

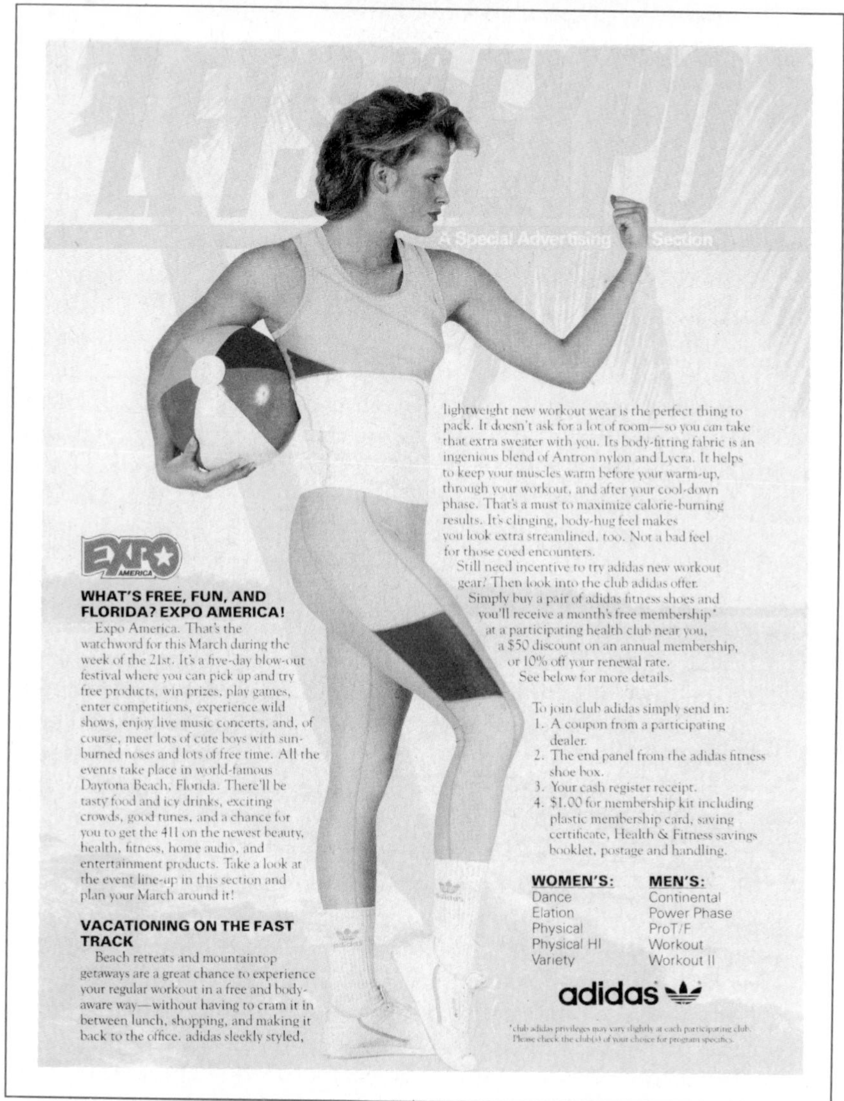


Courtesy of Women's Marketing, Inc. and Adidas USA, Inc. Photo by David Herrenbruck

rialistic pleasures, they represent an opportunity for marketers who can identify and satisfy the needs of this market.

In addition to joint pleasure seeking, honeymooners have considerable startup expenses in establishing a new home (major and minor appliances, bedroom and living room furniture, carpeting, drapes, dishes, and a host of utensils and accessory items). During this stage, the advice and experience of other married couples are likely to be important to the newlyweds. Also important as sources of new product information are the so-called shelter magazines, such as *Better Homes and Gardens, Apartment Ideas,* and *House Beautiful.*

## STAGE III: PARENTHOOD

When a married couple has its first child, the honeymoon is considered over. The *parenthood* stage usually extends over more than a twenty-year period. Because of its long duration, it is useful to divide this stage into shorter phases: the preschool phase, the elementary school phase, the high school phase, and the college phase. Throughout these parenthood phases, the interrelationships of family members and the structure of the family gradually changes. Furthermore, the financial resources of the family change significantly, as one (or both) parents progress in a career, and as childrearing and educational responsibilities gradually increase and finally decrease when the child becomes self-supporting.

The responsibilities of parenthood invariably cause changes in the young couple's lifestyle. Time and money previously spent on home furnishings, dining out, and vacations tend to be redirected to baby sitters, baby furniture, diapers, and toys. Entertainment and social activities are likely to center more on the home and the local community.

An increase in the number of births among post-World War II baby boomers has resulted in what some writers call the "baby boomlet." The new parents are older—twenty-eight to thirty-five—better educated, more affluent ($35,000+ annual household income), and more socially aware. The child often becomes the focus of their lives, and they spend money accordingly. These young parents have become an important target for companies that serve the baby market. Sales of juvenile furniture and accessories alone (not including food, clothing, or toys) reached an estimated $1.5 billion in 1984. This represents a 20 percent increase over 1983 sales and almost doubles 1980 sales of $800 million.[44]

This new generation of parents are more demanding regarding the quality and nutritional value of baby food and the educational value of toys. Figure 12-3 depicts an ad for a child's toy which is based upon the fitness craze of young adults. Parents buy clothes for their babies and young children that follow the latest fashions. Financial marketers are selling them on the idea of financing their children's education right from the start. There is no question that the parenthood stage today represents a very lucrative market for a variety of traditional as well as innovative products and services. Kimberly Clarke, for example, has introduced a new "motherhood" product—a medically treated facial tissue that kills common cold and flu viruses—to stop colds from spreading within the family.

Many magazines cater to the information and entertainment needs of parents and children. Table 12-4 lists various media directed to parents, and shows the percentage of readers who are either expecting a baby or have children under two years of age. Figure 12-4 on page 216 shows an ad for AT&T based on a parenthood appeal. For children, there are many special interest publications, such as *Humpty Dumpty,* designed for the young child just learning to read; *Scholastic Magazine,* for the elementary school pupil; *Boy's Life,* which is targeted to youths; and *American Girl, Seventeen, Glamour,* and *Mademoiselle,* for teen and post-teen girls interested in fashion.

FIGURE 12-3 Parenthood Stage

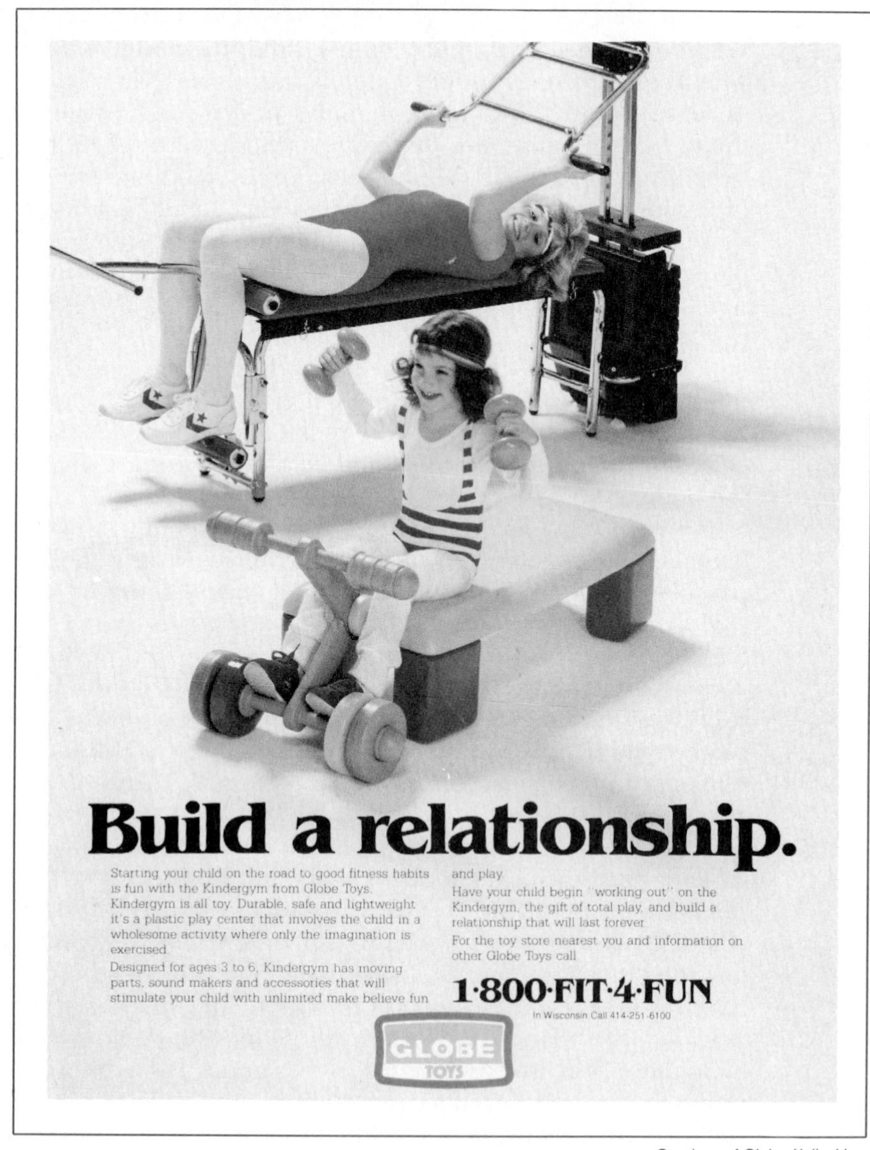


Courtesy of Globe United Inc.

## STAGE IV: POSTPARENTHOOD

Since parenthood extends over many years, it is only natural to find that *post-parenthood*—when all the children have left home—is traumatic for some parents, and liberating for others. This so-called *empty nest* stage signifies for many

**TABLE 12-4** Media for Childrearing

| | PERCENT OF EXPECTANT READERS OR THOSE WITH CHILDREN AGE 2 AND UNDER |
|---|---|
| American Baby | 100% |
| Baby Talk | 100 |
| Childbirth '85 | 100 |
| Expecting | 100 |
| First Year of Life | 100 |
| Mothers Today | 46 |
| Parents | 30 |
| Redbook's Young Mother | 100 |
| Working Mother | 17.3 |
| Working Parents | 35 |

parents almost a "rebirth"—a time for doing all the things they could not do while the children were at home and they had to worry about soaring educational expenses. For the wife, it is a time to further her education, to enter or reenter the job market, to seek new interests. For the husband, it is a time to indulge in new hobbies. For both, it is the time to travel, to entertain, perhaps to refurnish their home or to sell it in favor of a luxury condominium.

It is during this stage that married couples tend to be best off financially. Today's empty nesters have more leisure time. They travel more frequently, take extended vacations, and are likely to purchase a second home in a warmer climate. They have higher disposable income because of savings and investments, and fewer expenses (no mortgage or college tuition bills). For this reason, families in the postparenthood stage are an important market for luxury goods, for new automobiles, expensive furniture, and vacations to faraway places.

Many empty nesters retire early, while they are still in good health. Retirement provides the opportunity to seek new interests, to travel, and to fulfill unsatisfied needs. Hotels, airlines, and car leasing companies have responded to this market with discounts to consumers over sixty; some airlines have established senior citizen travel clubs with unlimited mileage for a flat fee; adult communities have sprung up in many parts of the nation. Of course, for older retired couples who do not have adequate savings or income, retirement is often far different and very restrictive.

Older consumers tend to use television as an important source of information and entertainment. They favor programs that provide the opportunity to "keep up with things," especially news and public affairs programs. In addition, there are a number of special interest magazines that cater exclusively to this market, such as *Modern Maturity* and *50 Plus.*

**FIGURE 12-4 Parenthood Appeal**

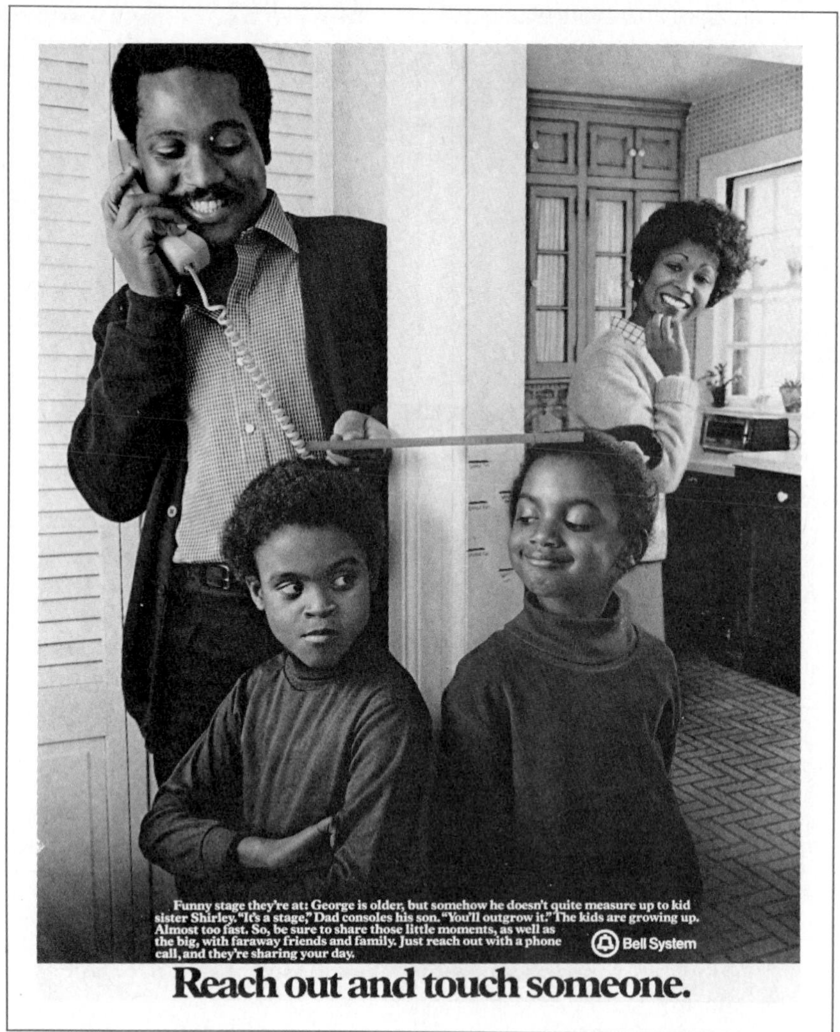

Funny stage they're at: George is older, but somehow he doesn't quite measure up to kid sister Shirley. "It's a stage," Dad consoles his son. "You'll outgrow it." The kids are growing up. Almost too fast. So, be sure to share those little moments, as well as the big, with faraway friends and family. Just reach out with a phone call, and they're sharing your day.
Bell System
Reach out and touch someone.

Courtesy of AT&T Communications

## STAGE V: DISSOLUTION

*Dissolution* of the basic family unit occurs with the death of one spouse. If the surviving spouse is in good health, is working or has adequate savings, and has supportive family and friends, the adjustment is easier. The surviving spouse tends to seek a simpler, often more economical lifestyle (Chapter 15 contains an in-depth discussion of the elderly consumer as a subcultural market segment). Many surviving spouses seek each other out for companionship; others enter into second (or even third and fourth) marriages.

As the number of elderly people in this country continues to grow, astute marketers are finding a rewarding segment at which to target such products and services as retirement communities, trips, tours, insurance, and social activities. Figure 12-5 illustrates a social service ad that promises intergenerational interaction for the elderly.

**FIGURE 12-5** **Social Service Advertisement Promises Intergenerational Interaction for the Elderly**

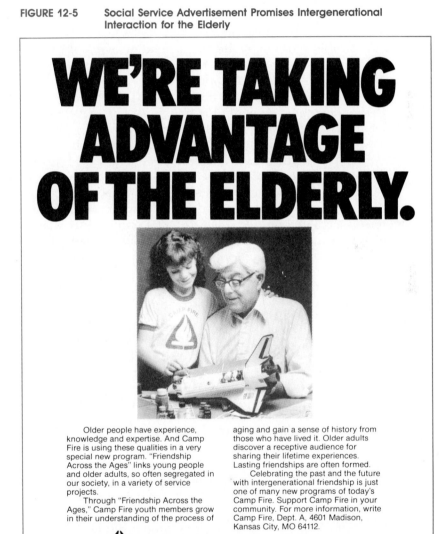

# WE'RE TAKING ADVANTAGE OF THE ELDERLY.

Older people have experience, knowledge and expertise. And Camp Fire is using these qualities in a very special new program. "Friendship Across the Ages" links young people and older adults, so often segregated in our society, in a variety of service projects.

Through "Friendship Across the Ages," Camp Fire youth members grow in their understanding of the process of aging and gain a sense of history from those who have lived it. Older adults discover a receptive audience for sharing their lifetime experiences. Lasting friendships are often formed.

Celebrating the past and the future with intergenerational friendship is just one of many new programs of today's Camp Fire. Support Camp Fire in your community. For more information, write Camp Fire, Dept. A, 4601 Madison, Kansas City, MO 64112.

Courtesy of Camp Fire Inc.

## Limitations of the FLC

Conventional FLC models (see Table 12-3) generally do not include all possible life-cycle factors. This can create a classification problem for the consumer researcher. Family factors that usually are not considered in traditional FLC models include childless couples, single parents (either mother or father), divorced parents, young widowed parents, middle-aged couples who marry late in life, couples who have their first child in their late thirties, unmarried couples, homosexual couples, and extended families (grandparents living with married children, or newly married couples living with in-laws). Working wives, and a subset working mothers, also tend to muddy the lifestyle assumptions implicit in the traditional FLC. For example, Figure 12-6 focuses on a family segment not addressed in traditional FLC analyses.

FLC researchers have not developed a systematic method for dealing with respondents who do not fit the traditional FLC stages. Some researchers simply eliminate such respondents if they consider them to be few in number; others add them to the traditional life cycle stages to which they most closely conform. Several researchers have established separate FLC categories to accommodate these respondents. Given the large number of atypical family groupings in American society today, consumer researchers are increasingly likely to adopt this latter stategy and create additional stages to account for emerging FLC segments.[45] Table 12-5 (see pages 420-421) compares a traditional FLC model with one that includes alternative family lifestyle stages. (The table indicates that some 11.8 million people would go unaccounted for in the traditional model).

Several recent studies have focused on life-cycle situations that are not included in the traditional FLC. One study showed that when households undergo status changes (e.g., divorce, temporary retirement, new person moving into the household, death of a spouse) they often undergo spontaneous changes in brand preferences and thus become attractive targets for many marketers.[46] One study found that female single parents are better shopping planners than male single parents, who require more learning and startup time regarding purchase behavior when their marital status changes.[47] Another study showed that children in single-parent families are more likely to apply economic reasoning in requests to their parents.[48] This might be attributed to the fact that children in single-parent homes are likely to be better informed about the household's financial limitations, and more likely to be consulted about expenditures.

Several studies have examined the influence of the wife's employment on the household's consumption patterns. As expected, one study found that the wife's employment influenced family expenditures on time-saving services such as child care, domestic services (cleaning), clothing care (dry cleaning and repair), personal care (beauty salons), and take-out food.[49] Another study found that the wife's employment status was *not* significantly related to the household's expenditures on time-saving durables (e.g., a dishwasher).[50] Some researchers argue that marketers need to develop a better understanding of the working and the nonworking wife. Wives can be segmented into at least four categories: the *stay-at-home* housewife; the *plan-to-work* housewife, the *just-a-job* working wife, and the *career-oriented* working wife. Each segment realistically

FIGURE 12-6 Nontraditional Families Don't Fit Within Traditional FLC Stages

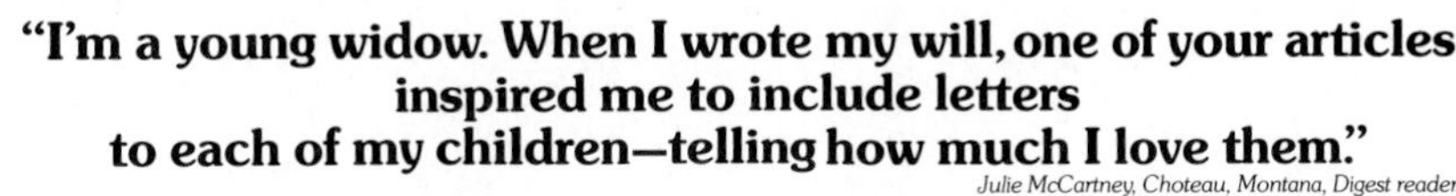

"I'm a young widow. When I wrote my will, one of your articles inspired me to include letters to each of my children—telling how much I love them."
Julie McCartney, Choteau, Montana, Digest reader.

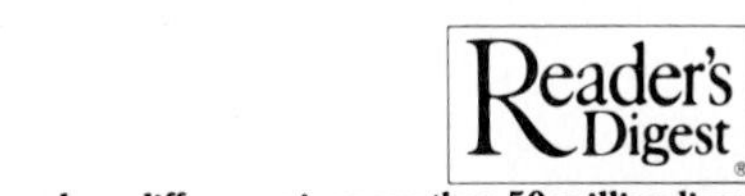

Reader's Digest
We make a difference in more than 50 million lives.

Courtesy of Readers Digest Association Inc.

represents a separate market for many goods and services. One study suggests the development of a "role overload" concept to be used along with the wife's occupational status when segmenting this market.[51]

## Marketing Applications of FLC Analysis

Even with its limitations, the traditional FLC model has demonstrated its value for market segmentation. It has provided insights into specific consumption activities that could not be obtained by using a single demographic variable. For

**TABLE 12-5 Comparison of Population Distributions Across the Stages of Two Family Life Cycles, 1970***

| MURPHY AND STAPLES | | | WELLS AND GUBAR | | |
|---|---|---|---|---|---|
| stage | no. individuals or families (000's) | % total U.S. population† | stage | no. individuals or families (000's) | % total U.S. population† |
| 1. Young single | 16,626 | 8.2 | 1. Bachelor | 16,626 | 8.2 |
| 2. Young married without children | 2,958 | 2.9 | 2. Newly married couples | 2,958 | 2.9 |
| 3. Other young | | | | | |
| a. Young divorced without children | 277 | 0.1 | | | |
| b. Young married with children | 8,082 | 17.1 | 3. Full nest I | 11,433 | 24.2 |
| Infant‡ | | | | | |
| Young (4-12 years old)‡ | | | | | |
| Adolescent‡ | | | | | |
| c. Young divorced with children | 1,144 | 1.9 | 4. Full nest II | 6,547 | 13.2 |
| Infant | | | | | |
| Young (4-12 years old) | | | | | |
| Adolescent | | | | | |
| 4. Middle-aged | | | | | |
| a. Middle-aged married without children | 4,815 | 4.7 | | | |
| b. Middle-aged divorced without children | 593 | 0.3 | | | |
| c. Middle-aged married with children | 15,574 | 33.0 | 5. Full nest III | 6,955 | 14.7 |
| Young | | | | | |
| Adolescent | | | | | |

| | | | | | |
|---|---|---|---|---|---|
| d. Middle-aged divorced with children | 1,080 | 1.8 | | | |
| Young | | | | | |
| Adolescent | | | | | |
| e. Middle-aged married without dependent children | 5,627 | 5.5 | 6. Empty nest I | 5,627 | 5.5 |
| f. Middle-aged divorced without dependent children | 284 | 0.1 | | | |
| 5. Older | | | | | |
| a. Older married | 5,318 | 5.2 | 7. Empty nest II | 5,318 | 5.2 |
| b. Older unmarried | 3,510 | 2.0 | 8. Solitary survivor—in labor force | 428 | 0.2 |
| Divorced | | | | | |
| Widowed | | | 9. Solitary survivor—retired | 3,510 | 2.0 |
| All other§ | 34,952 | 17.2 | All other§ | 46,738 | 23.3 |
| | 203,210‖ | | | 203,210‖ | |

†As there are single and divorced individuals in some of the stages, the numbers were calculated as a percentage of the entire population, not just the number of families. Also, the percentages of the total for families were determined by multiplying the number of families by 2.3 (average number of children per family in 1970) and adding the parents (or parent, in divorced instances) to the number. For example, the 17.1 percent in the young married with children was computed as follows:

$$\frac{8{,}082\ (2.3\ \text{children}) + 16{,}164\ (\text{parents})}{203{,}210} = 17.1\%$$

‡As many families have children at more than one of these age levels, it is not meaningful to compute the numbers for each of these ages independently.

§Includes all adults and children not accounted for by the family life cycle stages.

‖Source: U.S. Bureau of the Census 1970. The numbers do not add to this total because of the calculations explained in Footnote†.

Source: Patrick E. Murphy and William A. Staples, "A Modernized Family Life Cycle," *Journal of Consumer Research*, 6 (June 1979), 16.
*Figures for this table were taken or derived from U.S. Bureau of the Census 1973. Tables 2 and 9.

example, evidence indicates a substantially greater decline in the proportion of home ownership for consumers in the *dissolution* stage (solitary survivors) than would be revealed by a census of consumers in the over sixty-five age category. The reason for this difference between FLC analysis and age categorization is that age does not distinguish between households in which both the elderly husband and wife are living and those in which only one of the partners is alive. Because of this, a firm renting or selling retirement housing might find that information gleaned from FLC analyses offers a more sensitive profile of its target market than could be derived from age data alone.

### FLC ANALYSES BY PRODUCT CATEGORY

Marketers and researchers have found that FLC analysis can provide an in-depth understanding of family consumption behavior for a variety of product categories.

RESIDENTIAL TELEPHONE USAGE. AT&T has employed FLC variables in its efforts to better serve household telephone customers. Table 12-6 presents the FLC model that AT&T researchers have found most clearly accounts for family telephone usage. An examination of this model indicates that AT&T had rede-

**TABLE 12-6 AT&T Family Life-Cycle Status Categories**

| FLC STAGE | VARIABLES EMPLOYED | DESCRIPTION OF STAGE |
|---|---|---|
| Younger No children | —Age of head-of-household | —Under 55 years of age |
| | —Size of family | —a. Single person<br>b. Couple |
| Younger Young children | —Age of head-of-household | —Under 55 years of age |
| | —Size of family | —Three or more persons |
| | —Age of children | —Under 12 years of age |
| Younger Older children | —Age of head-of-household | —Under 55 years of age |
| | —Size of family | —Three or more persons |
| | —Age of children | —a. One child 12 years or older<br>b. Two or more children 12 years or older |
| Older | —Age of head-of-household | —55 years or older |
| | —Employment status | —a. Employed<br>b. Unemployed (Retired) |

Source: Adapted from Richard B. Ellis, "Composite Population Descriptors: The Socio-Economic Life Cycle Grid," in Mary Jane Schlinger, ed., *Advances in Consumer Research* (Association for Consumer Research, 1974), Vol. II. Also, courtesy of the American Telephone and Telegraph Company.

FIGURE 12-7 **Average Monthly Long-Distance Telephone Expenditures by Family Life-Cycle Stages** Source: A. Marvin Roscoe, Jr., and Jagdish N. Sheth, "Demographic Segmentation of Long Distance Behavior: Data Analysis and Inductive Model Building," in M. Venkatesan, ed., *Third Annual Conference of the Association for Consumer Research 1972,* 262. Also, courtesy of AT&T.

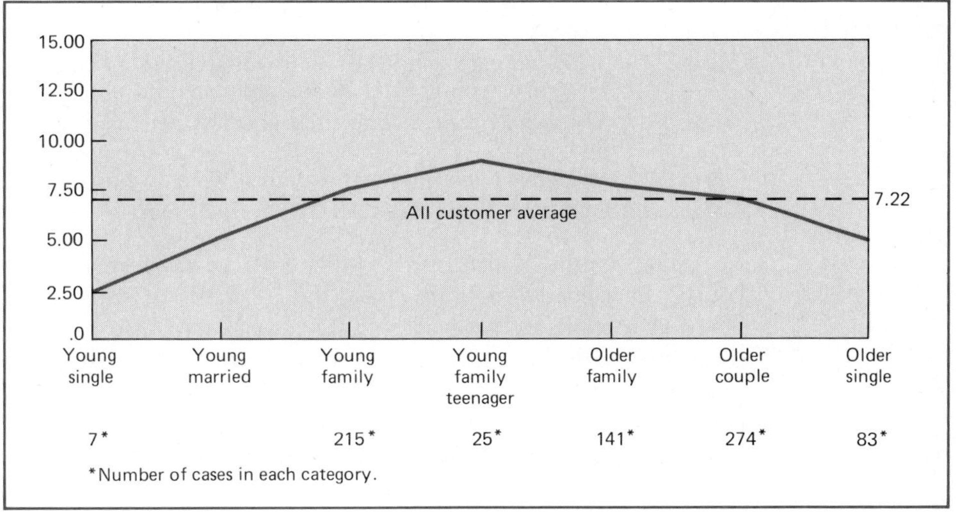


fined some of the FLC stages listed in the prototype models shown in Table 12-3. Most notable among the differences are the division of *age of head of household* into younger or older than fifty-five years, and *families* into those whose youngest child is over or under twelve years of age. These refinements reflect the nature of residential telephone usage.

Figure 12-7 shows the average monthly expenditures on long-distance calls for each FLC stage. Note that young marrieds spend more than singles on long-distance calls, while both groups spend less than the average of all households studied. On the other hand, young families with and without teenage children spend more than the average, while those with teenagers spend more than those at any other stage. Finally, older couples spend about the average, while older singles spend less than the overall average. Although these results are limited to a sample of telephone users in the northeastern states, similar analyses are available for other geographic areas.[52] AT&T uses these life-cycle analyses to better understand fluctuations in family telephone expenditure patterns and equipment usage in order to plan future products and services.

FAMILY FOOD CONSUMPTION. FLC analysis has been used in a study of food purchases and other consumption activities of over four thousand urban homemakers in seven southern states.[53] One of the dimensions of food consumption explored was the "goal satisfaction" of the homemaker. Goal satisfaction was measured by asking each homemaker to evaluate such food-related activities as time spent in meal preparation, foods served, and attention given his or her own food preferences. On the basis of each homemaker's responses, an overall food-consumption satisfaction score was determined. Respondents were then categorized into one of the following FLC stages based upon the age of youngest and oldest children.[54]

Stage I: *Childless young married* (married less than ten years with no children)

Stage II: *Expanding* (youngest child less than six years old and no child sixteen or older)

Stage III: *Stable* (youngest child six years or older and no child at home older than age fifteen; or youngest child less than six and oldest child older than fifteen)

Stage IV: *Contracting* (at least one child aged sixteen years or older and no child less than six)

Stage V: *Postparental* (couples with children living at home)

Stage VI: *Childless older married* (childless couples married more than ten years)

The results of this study indicated that homemakers in Stage I (childless young married) were highly satisfied in terms of food consumption, those in Stage II (expanding) were less satisfied, while those in Stage V (postparental) were most satisfied with their food consumption activities. The high degree of satisfaction expressed by the young married and postparental homemaker groups is most likely related to their more leisurely lifestyles and relatively fewer financial pressures. This is supported by evidence that respondents' satisfaction with food consumption is closely related to the amount of per capita income available, which was greatest for those in Stages I and V.[55] Another factor that may contribute to satisfaction may be that fewer compromises are required to satisfy the needs and desires of multiple family members.

ENTERTAINMENT ACTIVITIES. An exploratory study of family choice of leisure-time activities provided another opportunity to utilize the FLC concept.[56] Employing a rather simplified FLC model, families were placed into one of the following FLC stages: (1) under forty years of age without children, (2) under forty years of age with children, (3) forty years of age or older with children, and (4) forty years of age or older without children. The study found that bowling and expensive dining out were more frequently engaged in by those in later life-cycle stages, while attending movies, nightclubs, and school-related athletic events were activities more frequently engaged in by those in earlier FLC stages.

Table 12-7 summarizes the findings of a study that examined recreational involvement by stage in the FLC for some eighteen different activities. The study found that those in the *bachelorhood* and *honeymoon* stages were heavily involved in many of the activities explored. Families in the *full nest Ia* stage maintained an average level of involvement for many of the activities, reflecting the demands of parenthood. This was supported by the fact that families with older children *(full nest Ib)* reported greater involvement than families with younger children. While certain activities remained relatively high, there was a distinct tendency for involvement levels to drop in the last four stages of the FLC.[57] Knowledge of fluctuations in recreational activity over the FLC provides important insights to marketers of recreational products and services in the development of market strategies.

**TABLE 12-7 Participation in Selected Recreational Activities by Family Life-Cycle Stage**

| FLC STAGE | DEFINITION | ACTIVITIES WITH ABOVE-AVERAGE PARTICIPATION |
|---|---|---|
| Bachelor | Single, under 40, no children | Tennis, handball, swimming, baseball, soccer, volley ball, picnicking, horse riding, hiking, water skiing, biking, camping, running, and dancing |
| Newly Married | Young, married, no children | Tennis, handball, lake swimming, baseball, volley ball, skeet trapping, picnicking, hiking, water skiing, biking, camping, hunting, fishing, and running |
| Full Nest Ia | Young, married, youngest child less than 6 | Tennis, handball, swimming, soccer, volley ball, horse riding, camping, hunting, and running |
| Full Nest Ib | Young, married, youngest child 6 to 13 | Above average in all activities but running |
| Full Nest II | Older, married, dependent children 14 or older | Tennis, handball, pool swimming, baseball, soccer, skeet trapping, horse riding, hiking, water skiing, biking, camping, hunting, fishing |
| Empty Nest Ia | Older, married, no children at home, head working | Pool swimming |
| Empty Nest Ib | Older, married, no children at home, head retired | Below average on all activities |
| Solitary Survivor | Older, single | Below average on all activities |

Source: Adapted from E. Laird Landon, Jr., and William B. Locander, "Family Life Cycle and Leisure Behavior Research," in William L. Wilkie, ed., *Advances in Consumer Research* (Ann Arbor, Mich.: Association for Consumer Research, 1979), VI, 136.

A study of energy consumption by stage in the FLC found that singles consume the least energy; middle-aged married-with-children households consume the most total energy; young and middle-aged singles with children generally consume little energy; and segments that have greater amounts of discretionary income (young and middle-aged marrieds without children) consume more vacation-related energy.[58]

Two studies of media exposure by stage in the FLC explored the media habits of working and nonworking wives, and married and unmarried men and women. They found that housewives who plan to work and those who do not plan to work are both heavy viewers of daytime TV. Just-a-job working wives and career women are both just under the norm in viewing prime-time TV shows, and are more likely to listen to the radio than nonworking housewives. Career-oriented women are the heaviest readers of magazines, read more magazines than men, and read many categories of magazines. Plan-to-work housewives are also heavy magazine readers. Career women are heavy readers of newspapers, while stay-at-home women are not. Among married couples, TV viewing was considered as a shared activity that did not disrupt interaction with spouse or friends, though wives watched more TV than their husbands. Married couples tend to hover at the norm for radio listening, while unmarried men and women are particularly responsive to radio. Husbands are more likely than their wives to be heavy newspaper readers and to see outdoor advertising. Unmarried career women are the heaviest readers of magazines, while unmarried men are just over the norm in terms of magazine readership. Both unmarried career women and unmarried men are heavy newspaper readers. Unmarried men and women spend more time in their cars and are exposed to more outdoor advertising.[59]

## FLC APPLICATIONS TO STRATEGIC MARKET PLANNING

Table 12-8 presents an overview of an FLC model that lists characteristic consumption activities for various stages of the family life cycle. Examination of the model reveals the potential usefulness of FLC analyses for strategic market planning.

FLC analysis permits marketers to segment the total universe of families into distinct, mutually exclusive markets composed of family units that are relatively homogeneous in terms of age, interests, needs, time availability, relative disposable income, and so forth. Segmentation by stage in the FLC enables marketers to develop products and services to meet the very specific needs of

**TABLE 12-8 An Overview of the Family Life Cycle**

| BACHELOR STAGE; YOUNG SINGLE PEOPLE NOT LIVING AT HOME | NEWLY MARRIED COUPLES; YOUNG, NO CHILDREN | FULL NEST I; YOUNGEST CHILD UNDER SIX | FULL NEST II; YOUNGEST CHILD SIX OR OVER |
|---|---|---|---|
| Few financial burdens.<br>Fashion opinion leaders.<br>Recreation oriented.<br>Buy: Basic kitchen equipment, basic furniture, cars, equipment for the mating game, vacations. | Better off financially than they will be in near future.<br>Highest purchase rate and highest average purchase of durables.<br>Buy: Cars, refrigerators, stoves, sensible and durable furniture, vacations. | Home purchasing at peak.<br>Liquid assets low.<br>Dissatisfied with financial position and amount of money saved.<br>Interested in new products.<br>Like advertised products.<br>Buy: Washers, dryers, TV, baby food, chest rubs and cough medicine, vitamins, dolls, wagons, sleds, skates. | Financial position better.<br>Some wives work.<br>Less influenced by advertising.<br>Buy larger sized packages, multiple-unit deals.<br>Buy: Many foods, cleaning materials, bicycles, music lessons, pianos. |

families at each stage in their lives, and to design and implement promotional strategies with which their target audiences will identify.

## THE FUTURE OF THE FAMILY

Despite spiraling divorce rates and the emergence of unconventional alternatives to the traditional nuclear family, the survival of the family seems assured because of its capacity to fulfill such basic functions as the provision of economic and emotional well-being to its members, childrearing, and child socialization. Moreover, as a dynamic institution, the family may become even more influential in the future as it serves to fortify its members against the strains of continued technological and social change.

Crystal ball gazing into the future of the family is not without risks. However, consumer researchers must delve into the horizons; they must be able to predict change in order to predict how consumers will react to such change. In this spirit, Table 12-9 identifies a number of social-environmental trends that seem likely to influence the future of the family.

| FULL NEST III; OLDER MARRIED COUPLES, WITH DEPENDENT CHILDREN | EMPTY NEST I; OLDER MARRIED COUPLES, NO CHILDREN LIVING WITH THEM, HEAD IN LABOR FORCE | EMPTY NEST II; OLDER MARRIED COUPLES, NO CHILDREN LIVING AT HOME, HEAD RETIRED | SOLITARY SURVIVOR, IN LABOR FORCE | SOLITARY SURVIVOR, RETIRED |
|---|---|---|---|---|
| Financial position still better.<br>More wives work.<br>Some children get jobs.<br>Hard to influence with advertising.<br>High average purchase of durables.<br>Buy: New, more tasteful furniture, auto travel, nonnecessary appliances, boats, dental services, magazines. | Home ownership at peak.<br>Most satisfied with financial position and money saved.<br>Interested in travel, recreation, self-education.<br>Make gifts and contributions.<br>Not interested in new products.<br>Buy: Vacations, luxuries, home improvements. | Drastic cut in income.<br>Keep home.<br>Buy: Medical appliances, medical care, products which aid health, sleep, and digestion. | Income still good but likely to sell home. | Same medical and product needs as other retired group, drastic cut in income.<br>Special need for attention, affection, and security. |

Source: William D. Wells and George Gubar, "Life Cycle Concept in Marketing Research," *Journal of Marketing Research,* 3 (November 1966), 362.

**TABLE 12-9 Factors Affecting the Future of the Family**

| TREND | IMPACT |
|---|---|
| More leisure time | A shorter workweek will mean increased emphasis on family recreation and entertainment. There should also be a greater demand for products that make the use of time more rewarding and enjoyable. |
| More formal education | Better education will mean a more aware consumer, which should increase the demand for more reliable products. There should also be increased interest in products and services that satisfy the need for individualism. |
| More working married women | A higher total family income should mean less economic pressure and more money available for the purchase of products previously out of reach for the family. There should also be increased joint husband-wife decision making, a greater sharing of domestic responsibilities, and a continued preference for smaller families. |
| Increased life expectancy | As people live longer, the demand for products and services designed to cater to the health, recreation, and entertainment needs of an older population will increase. There should also be a greater emphasis placed on proper nutrition and diet. |
| Smaller-size families | Fewer children (zero population growth) will mean that parents will be able to spend more time and money on the development of each child's skills and capabilities. There will also be more discretionary income available for parents to spend on their own development, to pursue their own interests, and to improve the general standard of the family's lifestyle. |
| Women's movement | Husbands and wives will increasingly share household responsibilities, including joint decision making. Moreover, as an outgrowth of the women's movement, traditional sex-linked roles will continue to decline, and products that have generally been aimed at either males or females will increasingly be targeted to members of both sexes. |

## *summary*

The family is a major influence on the consumption behavior of its members; in addition, it is the prime target market for most products and product categories. As the most basic membership group, families are defined as two or more persons related by blood, marriage, or adoption who reside together. There are three types of families: married couples, nuclear families, and extended families. The basic functions of the family are the provision of economic and emotional support, childhood socialization, and a suitable lifestyle for its members.

The members of a family assume specific roles and tasks in their everyday functioning; such roles or tasks extend to the realm of consumer purchase decisions. Key consumer-related roles of family members include influencers, gatekeepers, deciders, buyers, preparers, users, maintainers, and disposers. A family's decision-making style is often influenced by its social class, lifestyle, role orientation, and stage in the family life cycle, and by the product importance, perceived risk, and time constraints of the purchase itself.

The majority of consumer studies classify family consumption decisions as husband-dominated, wife-dominated, joint, or autonomic decisions. The extent and nature of husband/wife influence in family decisions is dependent on the specific product or service, the stage in the decision-making process (problem recognition, information search, and final decision), and the specific product features under consideration.

Consumer socialization is an important component of the socialization process of children. It is the vehicle through which the family imparts consumer-relevant knowledge, attitudes, and skills. Children are not only influenced *by* their families; they also influence their family consumption decisions.

Classification of families by stage in the family life cycle provides valuable insights into family consumption behavior. These stages, which generally include bachelorhood, honeymooners, parenthood (children under six), parenthood (children over six), postparenthood, and dissolution, are an important segmentation basis for many products and services. Segmentation by stage in the family life cycle enables marketers to develop products and services to meet the specific needs of families at each stage in their lives, and to design and implement relevant promotional strategies.

Marketers must be alert to changing family lifestyles (unmarried couples, late marriages, single parents, divorced parents, childless couples) that may affect traditional consumption patterns.

## *discussion questions*

1. How does the family influence the consumer socialization of children?
2. Think of a recent major purchase your family has made. Analyze the roles performed by the various family members in terms of the following consumption roles: influencers, gatekeepers, deciders, buyers, preparers, users, maintainers, disposers.
3. Develop an FLC market segmentation strategy for each of the following product categories:
   a. Cosmetics
   b. Food
   c. Vacations
   d. Housing

4. In purchasing a new television set, how would you expect the following factors to influence the locus of family decision making:
   a. Social class
   b. Perceived risk
   c. Sex-role orientation
   d. Time pressure
5. If you were the marketing manager for Lean Line frozen dinners, how would you use FLC analyses to segment your market? Which family member(s) would you target? Why?
6. How would you revise the traditional family life cycle so that it better accounts for changes in the structure and composition of families in the late 1980s?

## *endnotes*


1. George P. Moschis, Roy L. Moore, and Ruth B. Smith, "The Impact of Family Communication on Adolescent Consumer Socialization," in Thomas C. Kinnear, ed., *Advances in Consumer Research,* 11 (Provo. Ut.: Association for Consumer Research, 1983), 314–19.
2. Scott Ward, "Consumer Socialization," *Journal of Consumer Research,* 1 (September 1974) 9; Roy Moore and George P. Moschis, "Social Interaction and Social Structural Determinants in Adolescent Consumer Socialization," in Jerry Olson, ed., *Advances in Consumer Research,* (Ann Arbor, Mich.: Association for Consumer Research, 1980) VII, 757–59; and George P. Moschis and Roy L. Moore, "Decision Making among the Young: A Socialization Perspective," *Journal of Consumer Research,* 6 (September 1979), 101–12.
3. Deborah Roedder John, "The Development of Knowledge Structures in Children," in Elizabeth C. Hirschman and Morris B. Holbrook, eds., *Advances in Consumer Research,* 12 (Chicago: Association for Consumer Research, 1984), 329–33.
4. Marilyn Kourilsky and Trudy Murray, "The Use of Economic Reasoning to Increase Satisfaction with Family Decision Making," *Journal of Consumer Research,* 8 (September 1981), 183–88.
5. Thomas S. Robertson, John R. Rossiter, and Scott Ward, "Consumer Satisfaction among Children," in Hirschman and Holbrook, eds., *Advances in Consumer Research,* 279–84.
6. George P. Moschis and Roy L. Moore, "Racial and Socioeconomic Influences on the Development of Consumer Behavior," in Hirschman and Holbrook, eds., *Advances in Consumer Research,* 525–31.
7. John F. Grashof and Donald F. Dixon, "The Household: The 'Proper' Model for Research into Purchasing and Consumption Behavior," in Jerry Olson, ed., *Advances in Consumer Research,* 486–91.
8. Theodore Dunn, "Large Numbers of Husbands Buy Household Products, Do Housework," *Marketing News,* October 13, 1980, 1 and 3.
9. Charles M. Schaninger, W. Christian Buss, and Rajiv Grover, "The Effect of Sex Roles on Family Finance Handling and Decision Influence," in Bruce J. Walker, et al., eds., *As Assessment of Marketing Thought and Practice—1982 Educators' Conference Proceedings,* 48 (Chicago: American Marketing Association, 1982), 43–47.

10. Elizabeth H. Wolgast, "Do Husbands or Wives Make the Purchase Decisions?" *Journal of Marketing,* 23 (October 1958), 151–58; and Harry Sharp and Paul Mott, "Consumer Decisions in the Metropolitan Family," *Journal of Marketing,* 21 (October 1956), 149–56.

11. Isabella C. M. Cunningham and Robert T. Green, "Purchasing Roles in U.S. Family, 1955 and 1973," *Journal of Marketing,* 30 (October 1974), 61–64.

12. "Who Really Makes the Decisions?" *The Bruskin Report:* A Market Research Newsletter (New Brunswick, N.J.: R. H. Bruskin Associates, September 1974), 1.

13. Robert Ferber and Lucy Chao Lee, "Husband-Wife Influence in Family Purchasing Behavior," *Journal of Consumer Research,* 1 (June 1974), 43–50.

14. Jack J. Kasulis and Marie Adele Hughes, "Husband-Wife Influence in Selecting a Family Professional," *Journal of the Academy of Marketing Science,* 12 (Spring 1984), 115–27.

15. William J. Qualls, "Changing Sex Roles: Its Impact upon Family Decision Making," in Andrew A. Mitchell, ed., *Advances in Consumer Research,* 9 (Chicago: Association for Consumer Research, 1981), 267–70; William J. Qualls, "Sex Roles, Husband-Wife Influence, and Family Decision Behavior," in Kinnear, ed., *Advances in Consumer Research,* 270–75; and David Brinberg and Nancy Schwenk, "Husband-Wife Decision Making: An Exploratory Study of the Interaction Process," in Hirschman and Holbrook, eds., *Advances in Consumer Research,* 487–91.

16. Dennis L. Rosen and Donald H. Granbois, "Determinants of Role Structure in Family Financial Management," *Journal of Consumer Research,* 10 (September 1983), 253–58.

17. Giovanna Imperia, Thomas C. O'Guinn, and Elizabeth A. MacAdams, "Family Decision Making Role Perceptions among Mexican-American and Anglo Wives: A Cross Cultural Comparison," in Hirschman and Holbrook, eds., 71–74.

18. Robert T. Green, Jean-Paul Leonardi, Jean-Louis Chandon, Isabella C. M. Cunningham, Bronis Verhage, and Alain Strazzieri, "Societal Development and Family Purchasing Roles: A Cross-National Study," *Journal of Consumer Research,* 9 (March 1983), 436–42.

19. Harry L. Davis and Benny P. Rigaux, "Perception of Marital Roles in Decision Processes," *Journal of Consumer Research,* 1 (June 1974), 51–62.

20. C. Whan Park and Richard J. Lutz, "Decision Plans and Consumer Choice Dynamics," *Journal of Marketing Research,* 19 (February 1982), 108–15; and C. Whan Park, "Joint Decisions in Home Purchasing: A Muddling-Through Process," *Journal of Consumer Research,* 9 (September 1982), 151–62.

21. *Family Decision Making* (New York: Time Magazine, Time Marketing Information Research Report 1428, 1967).

22. Rosann L. Spiro, "Persuasion in Family Decision Making," *Journal of Consumer Research,* 9 (March 1983), 393–402; and Arch G. Woodside and William H. Motes, "Husband and Wife Perceptions of Marital Roles in Consumer Decision Processes for Six Products," in Neil Beckwith et al., eds., *1979 Educators' Conference Proceedings* (Chicago: American Marketing Association, 1979), 214–19.

23. Daniel Seymour and Greg Lessne, "Spousal Conflict Arousal: Scale Development," *Journal of Consumer Research,* 11 (December 1984), 810–21.

24. W. Christian Buss and Charles M. Schaninger, "The Influence of Sex Roles on Family Decision Processes and Outcomes," in Richard P. Bagozzi and Alice M. Tybout, *Advances in Consumer Research,* 10 (Chicago: Association for Consumer Research, 1982), 439–44; and Sunil Gupta, Michael R. Hagerty, and John G. Myers, "New Directions in Family Decision Making Research," in Bagozzi and Tybout, eds., 445–50.

25. Pierre Filiatrault and J. R. Brent Ritchie, "Joint Purchasing Decisions: A Comparison of Influence Structure in Family and Couple Decision-Making Units," *Journal of Consumer Research,* 7 (September 1980), 131–40.

26. George J. Szybillo and Arlene Sosanie, "Family Decision Making: Husband, Wife, and Children," in William D. Perreault, Jr., ed., *Advances in Consumer Research* (Atlanta: Association for Consumer Research, 1977), IV, 46–49.

27. James E. Nelson, "Children as Information Sources in the Family Decision to Eat Out," in William L. Wilkie, ed., *Advances in Consumer Research* (Ann Arbor, Mich.: Association for Consumer Research, 1979), VI, 419–23; and George J. Szybillo, Arlene K. Sosanie, and Aaron Tenebein, "Should Children Be Seen But Not Heard?" *Journal of Advertising Research,* 17 (December 1977), 7–12.

28. William D. Wells and Lenard A. LoSciuto, "Direct Observation of Purchase Behavior," *Journal of Marketing Research,* 3 (August 1966), 227–33; and Charles K. Atkin, "Observation of Parent-Child Interaction in Supermarket Decision-Making," *Journal of Marketing,* 42 (October 1978), 41–45.

29. Lewis A. Berey and Richard W. Pollay, "The Influencing Role of the Child in Family Decision Making," *Journal of Marketing Research,* 5 (February 1968), 70–72.

30. Scott Ward and Daniel Wackman, "Purchase Influence Attempts and Parental Yielding," *Journal of Marketing Research,* 9 (August 1972), 316–19.

31. Bonnie B. Reece, "Children's Ability to Identify Retail Stores from Advertising Slogans," in Kinnear, ed., 320–23.

32. W. Keith Bryant and Jennifer L. Gerner, "Television Use by Adults and Children: A Multivariate Analysis," *Journal of Consumer Research,* 8 (September 1981), 154–61.

33. Sanford L. Grossbart and Lawrence A. Crosby, "Understanding the Bases of Parental Concern and Reaction to Children's Food Advertising," *Journal of Marketing,* 48 (Summer 1984), 79–92.

34. Nancy Stephens and Mary Ann Stutts, "Preschoolers' Ability to Distinguish Between Television Programming and Commercials," *Journal of Advertising,* 11 (1982), 16–26.

35. Gerald J. Gorn and Renee Florsheim, "The Effects of Commercials for Adult Products on Children," *Journal of Consumer Research,* 11 (March 1985), 962–67.

36. Russell Belk, Robert Mayer, and Amy Driscoll, "Children's Recognition of Consumption Symbolism in Children's Products," *Journal of Consumer Research,* 10 (March 1984), 386–97.

37. Alan R. Wiman, "Parental Influence and Children's Responses to Television Advertising," *Journal of Advertising,* 12 (1983), 12–18.

38. M. Carole Macklin, "Do Children Understand TV Ads?" *Journal of Advertising Research,* 23 (February–March, 1983), 63–70.

39. *Grocery Store Shopping Habits of the Young Consumer . . . for Her Family,* Research Report No. 2 (New York: Co-ed Magazine, published by Scholastic Magazines, Inc., 1974).

40. Doris L. Walsh, "Targeting Teens," *American Demographics,* 7 (February 1985) 21–25.

41. Russell W. Belk, Clifford Rice, and Randall Harvey, "Adolescents' Reported Saving, Giving and Spending as a Function of Sources of Income," in Hirschman and Holbrook, eds., 42–46.

42. George P. Moschis and Roy L. Moore, "A Longitudinal Study of the Development of Purchasing Patterns," in Patrick E. Murphy, O. C. Ferrell, Gene R. Laczniak, Robert F. Lurch, Paul F. Anderson, Terence A. Shimp, Russell W. Belk, and Charles B. Weinberg, eds., *1983 American Marketing Association Educators' Proceedings,* 49 (Chicago: American Marketing Association, 1983), 114–17.

43. William D. Perreault, Jr., and Frederick A. Russ, "Student Influence on Family Purchase Decision," in Fred C. Allvine, ed., *1971 Combined Proceedings* (Chicago: American Marketing Association, 1971); 386–89.

44. Ed Fitch, "Special Report: Youth Marketing," *Advertising Age,* February 14, 1985, 15–34.

45. Mary C. Gilly and Ben M. Enis, "Recycling the Family Life Cycle: A Proposal for Redefinition," in Andrew A. Mitchell, ed., *Advances in Consumer Research,* 271–76; Frederick W. Derrick and Alane K. Lehfeld, "The Family Life Cycle: An Alternative Approach," *Journal of Consumer Research,* 7 (September 1980), 214–17; and Patrick E. Murphy and William A. Staples, "A Modernized Family Life Cycle," *Journal of Consumer Research,* 6 (June 1979), 12–22.

46. Alan R. Andreason, "Life Status Changes and Changes in Consumer Preferences and Satisfaction," *Journal of Consumer Research,* 11 (December 1984), 784–94.

47. James M. Sinkula, "A Look at Some Shopping Orientations in Single Parent Households," in Russell W. Belk et al., eds., *1984 American Marketing Association Educators' Proceedings,* 50 (Chicago: American Marketing Association), 22–25.

48. M. Kourilsky and T. Murray, "The Use of Economic Reasoning," 187.

49. Don Bellante and Ann C. Foster, "Working Wives and Expenditure on Services," *Journal of Consumer Research,* 11 (September 1984), 700–707.

50. Charles B. Weinberg and Russell S. Winer, "Working Wives and Major Family Expenditures: Replication and Extension," *Journal of Consumer Research,* 10 (September 1983), 259–63.

51. Shreekant G. Joag, James W. Gentry, and JoAnne Hopper, "Explaining Differences in Consumption by Working and Non-Working Wives;" in Hirschman and Holbrook, eds., 582–85.

52. A. Marvin Roscoe, Jr., and Jagdish N. Sheth, "Demographic Segmentation of Long Distance Behavior: Data Analysis and Inductive Model Building," in M. Venkatesan, ed., *Third Annual Conference of the Association for Consumer Research,* 1972, 258–78.

53. C. Milton Coughenour, "Functional Aspects of Food Consumption Activity and Family Life Cycle Stages," *Journal of Marriage and the Family,* 34 (November 1972), 656–64.

54. Ibid., 660.

55. Ibid., 662.

56. Robert D. Hisrich and Michael P. Peters, "Selecting the Superior Segmentation Correlate," *Journal of Marketing,* 38 (July 1974), 60–63.

57. E. Laird Landon, Jr., and William B. Locander, "Family Life Cycle and Leisure Behavior Research," 133–38; and Johan Arndt, "Family Life Cycle as a Determinant of Size and Composition of Household Expenditures," in Wilkie, *Advances in Consumer Research,* 128–32.

58. David J. Fritzsche, "An Analysis of Energy Consumption Patterns by Stage of Family Life Cycle," *Journal of Marketing Research,* 18 (May 1981), 227–32.

59. Rena Bartos, "Beyond the Cookie Cutter," *Marketing Review,* 38 (November–December 1982), 31–35; and Walter Gantz, "Exploring the Role of Television in Married Life," *Journal of Broadcasting and Electronic Media,* 29 (Winter 1985), 65–78.

# 13

# Social Class and Consumer Behavior

## introduction

SOME form of class structure or social stratification has existed in all societies throughout the history of human existence. Therefore it is not surprising that even in America, the "land of equal opportunity," there is much evidence of social class groupings. As an indication of the presence of social classes in America, the people who are better educated or have more prestigious occupations generally have higher status than people with little education or less prestigious occupations. For example, the occupations of physician and lawyer are often more highly valued than those of truck driver and farmhand.[1] All four occupations, however, are necessary for our society's well-being. Moreover, as will be discussed later, a wide range of differences in values, attitudes, and behavior has been shown to exist between members of different social classes.

The major questions we will explore in this chapter are these: What is social class? What are its determinants? How is it measured? How do members of specific social class groups behave? How do social class-linked attitudes and behavior influence consumer behavior?

## WHAT IS SOCIAL CLASS?

While **social class** can be thought of as a continuum—a range of social positions—on which each member of society can be placed, researchers have preferred to divide the continuum into a small number of specific social classes, or

> *All the people like us are We, and every one else is They.*
>
> RUDYARD KIPLING
> "We and They" (1926)

**strata.** Within this framework, the concept of social class is used to assign individuals or families to a social class category. Consistent with this practice, *social class* is defined as *the division of members of a society into a hierarchy of distinct status classes, so that members of each class have relatively the same status and members of all other classes have either more or less status.*

To appreciate more fully the complexity of social class, we will briefly consider several underlying concepts pertinent to our definition.

## Social Class and Social Status

Researchers often measure social class in terms of social status; that is, they define each social class by the amount of status the members of that class have in comparison with members of other social classes. In the behavioral sciences, **status** is frequently conceptualized as the relative rankings of members of each social class in terms of specific status factors. For example, relative *wealth* (amount of economic assets), *power* (the degree of personal choice or influence over others), and *prestige* (the degree of recognition received from others) are three popular factors frequently employed in the estimation of social class.[2] When it comes to consumer behavior and marketing research, status is most often defined in terms of one or more of the following convenient demographic **(socioeconomic)** variables: *family income, occupational status,* and *educational attainment.* These socioeconomic variables, as expressions of status, are used by marketing practitioners on a daily basis to measure social class.

### SOCIAL CLASS IS HIERARCHICAL

Social class categories are usually ranked in a hierarchy ranging from low to high status. Thus members of a specific social class perceive members of other social classes as having either more or less status than they do. To many people, therefore, social class categories suggest that others are either equal to them (about the same social class), superior to them (higher social class), or inferior to them (lower social class).

This hierarchical aspect of social class is important to marketers. Consumers may purchase certain products because they are favored by members of their own or a higher social class, and they may avoid other products because they perceive them to be "lower class" products.

### SOCIAL CLASS AND MARKET SEGMENTATION

The various social class strata provide a natural basis for market segmentation for many products and services. In many instances, consumer researchers have been able to relate product usage to social class membership. Thus marketers can effectively tailor products, channels of distribution, and promotional messages to the needs and the interests of a specific social stratum.

### SOCIAL CLASS AND BEHAVIORAL FACTORS

The classification of society's members into a small number of social classes has enabled researchers to note the existence of shared values, attitudes, and behavioral patterns among members *within* each social class, and differing values, attitudes, and behavior *between* social classes. Consumer researchers have been able to relate social class standing to consumer attitudes concerning specific products, and to examine social class influences on the actual consumption of products.

### SOCIAL CLASS AS A FRAME OF REFERENCE

Social class membership serves as a frame of reference (i.e., a **reference group**) for the development of consumer attitudes and behavior. In the context of reference groups, we might expect members of a specific social class to turn most often to other members of the *same* class for cues (or clues) as to appropriate behavior.

## SOCIAL CLASS CATEGORIES

There is little agreement among sociologists on how many distinct class divisions are necessary to describe adequately the class structure of the United States.[3] For example, most early studies divided the social class organizations of specific communities into five-class or six-class social structures. However, other researchers have found nine-class, four-class, three-class, and even two-class schemes to be suitable for their purposes. The choice of how many separate classes to use depends on the amount of detail the researcher believes is necessary to explain adequately the attitudes or behavior under study. Marketers are interested in the social class structures of communities that offer potential markets for their products and in the specific social class level of their potential customers. Tables 13-1 and 13-2 illustrate the number and diversity of social class schemes, and show the distribution of the United States population in terms of several different subdivisions (five-category, six-category, and seven-category subdivisions).

As Table 13-2 reveals, the percentage of the population accounted for in each social class appears to fluctuate depending upon the number of categories employed and the classification of each category. It also shows the reason that most *mass marketers* simply ignore the *upper-upper* class. On the other hand, its small size and highly cultivated tastes make the upper-upper class a particularly desirable target market for specialty firms that have a particular expertise and the ability to cater to the very small number of super-affluent consumers.

**TABLE 13-1 Variations in the Number and Types of Social Class Categories**

two-category social class schemes

blue-collar, white-collar
Lower, upper
Lower, middle

three-category social class schemes

Blue-collar, gray-collar, white-collar
Lower, middle, upper

four-category social class scheme

Lower, lower-middle, upper-middle, upper

five-category social class schemes

Lower, working-class, lower-middle, upper-middle, upper
Lower, lower-middle, middle, upper-middle, upper

six-category social class scheme

Lower-lower, upper-lower, lower-middle, upper-middle, lower-upper, upper-upper

seven-category social class scheme

Real lower-lower, a lower group of people but not the lowest, working class, middle class, upper-middle, lower- upper, upper-upper

nine-category social class scheme

Lower-lower, middle-lower, upper-lower, lower-middle, middle-middle, upper-middle, lower-upper, middle-upper, upper-upper

**TABLE 13-2 Selected Social Class Distribution in Population**

| NUMBER OF CLASSES | PERCENT OF POPULATION |
|---|---|
| Five-category* | |
| Upper | 11.4% |
| Upper-middle | 12.7 |
| Middle | 20.6 |
| Lower-middle | 16.6 |
| Lower | 28.0 |
| Six-category† | |
| Upper-Upper }<br>Lower-Upper } | 0.9 |
| Upper-Middle | 7.2 |
| Lower-Middle | 28.4 |
| Upper-Lower | 44.0 |
| Lower-Lower | 19.5 |
| Seven-category‡ | |
| Upper-upper | 0.3 |
| Lower-upper | 1.2 |
| Upper-middle | 12.5 |
| Middle | 32.0 |
| Working | 38.0 |
| A lower group but not the lowest | 9.0 |
| Real lower-lower | 7.0 |

Sources:
*Adapted from McKinley L. Blackburn and David E. Bloom, "What's Happening to the Middle Class?" *American Demographics,* January 1985, 21.
†Adapted from *Motivation in Advertising,* by Pierre Martineau. Copyright 1957, McGraw-Hill Book Company. Used with permission of McGraw-Hill Book Company.
‡Adapted from Richard P. Coleman, "The Continuing Significance of Social Class to Marketing," *Journal of Consumer Research,* 11 (December 1983), 267.

**TABLE 13-3 Methods Used in the Measurement of Social Class**

| MEASUREMENT TECHNIQUE | METHOD EMPLOYED |
|---|---|
| Subjective | Self-perception |
| Reputational | Perception of others |
| Objective | Single- or composite-variable index based on: Occupation; Education; Income (source, amount); Quality of neighborhood; Quality of dwelling; Inventory of possessions |

## THE MEASUREMENT OF SOCIAL CLASS

Although most behavioral scientists tend to agree that social class is a valid and useful concept, there is no general agreement as to how to measure it. To a great extent, researchers are uncertain as to what constitutes the underlying dimensions of social class structure. To attempt to resolve this dilemma, researchers have employed a wide range of measurement techniques that they feel capture the spirit, if not the essence, of social class. Of course, no one can be certain that a particular approach does, in fact, fully measure the various complexities of social class. In many cases, however, social class measures are believed to give a "fair" approximation.

Systematic approaches for measuring social class fall into the following broad categories: **subjective measures, reputational measures,** and **objective measures.** These measures are described below and summarized in Table 13-3.

### Subjective Measures

In the subjective approach to measuring social class, individuals are asked to estimate their own social-class positions. Typical of this approach is the following question:[4]

> If you were asked to use one of these four names for your social class, which would you say you belong in: the middle class, the lower class, the working class, or the upper class?

The resulting classification of social class membership is based on the participants' self-perceptions or self-images. Social class is treated as a "personal" phenomenon, one that reflects an individual's sense of belonging or identification with others. This feeling of social group membership is often referred to as *class consciousness.*

Subjective measures of social class membership have been criticized because they tend to produce an overabundance of people who classify themselves as *middle class* (thereby understating the number of people—the "fringe" people—who would, perhaps, be more correctly classified as either *lower* or *upper* class), and because very few people elect to say "don't know," thereby avoiding classification altogether.[5]

To date, subjective procedures have not been employed in consumer behavior studies. It is likely, however, that subjective perception of social class membership, as a reflection of self-image, is related to product usage (see Chapter 6). Unfortunately, there is no available research that attempts to support this hypothesis.

## Reputational Measures

The *reputational* approach for measuring social class requires participants to make judgments concerning the social class membership of *others* within the community, rather than themselves.

Perhaps the best known of all reputational procedures is the **evaluated participation** approach, which uses the evaluations of selected community informants concerning the social class membership of others in the community to determine the class structure of the community.[6] While this method requires informants to evaluate other community members, the final task of assigning community members to social class positions belongs to the trained researcher.

Sociologists have employed the reputational approach to obtain a better understanding of the specific class structures of the communities under study. However, consumer researchers are concerned with the measurement of social class in order to obtain a better understanding of markets and marketing behavior, not of social structure. In keeping with this more focused goal, the reputational approach has proved to be impractical.

## Objective Measures

In contrast to the subjective and reputational methods, which require people to evaluate their own class standing or that of other community members, *objective measures* consist of selected demographic or socioeconomic variables concerning the individual(s) under study. These variables are measured through questionnaires which ask respondents to answer several factual questions about themselves, their families, or their places of residence. In selecting objective measures of social class, most researchers favor one or more of the following variables: *occupation, amount of income,* and *education.* To these socioeconomic factors they sometimes add *geodemographic* market data in the form of zip code and residence-neighborhood information. These socioeconomic indicators are especially important as a means of locating concentrations of consumers with specific social class membership.

Socioeconomic measures of social class are of considerable value to marketers concerned with segmenting markets. The criteria for effective market segmentation, remember, are *identification, responsiveness, adequate market potential, accessibility,* and *stability* (or growth). Marketing managers who have developed socioeconomic profiles of their target markets can locate these markets (i.e., identify and measure them) by studying the socioeconomic data periodically issued by the U.S. Bureau of the Census and numerous commercial geodemographic data services. In order to reach a desired target market, marketers match the *socioeconomic profiles* of their markets to the *audience profiles* of selected advertising media (see Chapter 10). Socioeconomic audience profiles are regularly developed and routinely made available to potential advertisers by most of the mass media (see Table 13-4). Reader median income data for a variety of print media are presented in Table 13-5.

Objective measures of social class fall into two basic categories: **single-variable indexes** and **composite-variable indexes.**

## SINGLE-VARIABLE INDEXES

A single-variable index uses just one socioeconomic variable to evaluate social class membership. Some of the variables that are used for this purpose are discussed below.

OCCUPATION. Occupation is a widely accepted and probably the best documented measure of social class because it infers occupational status. The importance of occupation as a social class indicator is dramatized by the frequency with which people ask others they meet for the first time, "What do you do for a living?" The response to this question serves as a guide in "sizing up" (i.e., evaluating and forming opinions of) others.

Table 13-6 presents the results of a study that estimated the relative prestige that people assign to many basic occupational titles.[7] The findings of this study and similar studies are used by researchers to assign relative status scores to occupations included in the research.

**TABLE 13-4 Socioeconomic Profile of *Architectural Digest* Subscribers**

| | |
|---|---|
| income | |
| Median household income | $98,600* |
| Percent of income over $70,000 | 64% |
| Percent of income over $100,000 | 49% |
| net worth | |
| Median net worth | $729,200 |
| education | |
| College degree | 69% |
| Attended college | 49% |
| occupation | |
| Professional/managerial | 50% |
| home ownership | |
| Median home value | $223,400 |

*Based on the 1985 Mendelsohn Media Research (MMR) Survey of Adults and Markets of Affluence, which consists of households with $50,000 or more income.
Source: *Architectural Digest,* New York City.

**TABLE 13-5 Readers' Median Household Income for Selected Publications**

| MAGAZINE | MEDIAN HOUSEHOLD INCOME |
|---|---|
| Forbes | $47,891 |
| Wall Street Journal | 47,365 |
| PC World | 46,765 |
| Barron's | 44,605 |
| Architectual Digest | 44,596 |
| The New Yorker | 40,799 |
| Money | 39,820 |
| Smithsonian | 38,065 |
| Town & Country | 36,913 |
| Atlantic Monthly | 36,752 |
| Car & Driver | 35,213 |
| Newsweek | 34,713 |
| Time | 34,094 |
| National Geographic | 33,983 |
| Cosmopolitan | 32,212 |
| People | 31,903 |
| Playboy | 31,624 |
| Family Circle | 29,468 |
| Outdoor Life | 29,075 |
| Field & Stream | 29,036 |
| Hunting | 27,652 |
| Health | 27,212 |
| Ebony | 21,350 |
| True Story | 17,672 |

Source: *Magazine Audience Estimates Fall 1985* (New York: Mediamark Research, Inc.).

Most observers will agree that the occupations listed at the top of Table 13-6 tend to earn the greatest incomes and require the most formal education. As we move down the list of occupational rankings, the amount of income and required formal education tend to decrease. This suggests that there is a rather close association between occupational status, income, and education.

INCOME. Individual or family income is another socioeconomic variable frequently used to approximate social class standing. Researchers who favor income as a measure of social class use either *amount* or *source* of income.[8] Table 13-7 illustrates the types of categories used for each of these income variables.

While income is a popular estimate of social class standing, not all consumer researchers agree that it is an appropriate index of social class.[9] Some argue that a blue-collar automobile assembly-line worker and a white-collar high school teacher may both earn $22,000 a year, yet because of (or as a reflection of) social class differences, each will spend that income in a different way. How they decide to spend their incomes reflects different values. Some researchers believe it is the difference in *values* that is an important discriminant of social class between people, not the amount of *income* they earn. Table 13-8 vividly illustrates how two groups of consumers (labeled *passive* and *creative*) with the same basic income can have quite different activities, interests, and opinions. Moreover, such differences are very likely to be reflected in consumption-related tastes and patterns.

**TABLE 13-6 Prestige Ratings of Occupational Titles in the United States**

| OCCUPATION | SCORE |
|---|---|
| College administrator | 86 |
| Business professor | 78 |
| Physician | 78 |
| Lawyer | 72 |
| Civil engineer | 70 |
| Biological scientist | 68 |
| Bank officer | 67 |
| Airplane pilot | 66 |
| Psychologist | 66 |
| Chiropractor | 62 |
| Clergyman | 60 |
| Accountant | 59 |
| Photographer | 56 |
| Stockbroker | 56 |
| Draftsman | 55 |
| Librarian | 54 |
| Legal secretary | 53 |
| Dietician | 52 |
| Computer programmer | 51 |
| Dancer | 45 |
| Key punch operator | 45 |
| Musician | 45 |
| Dental hygienist | 44 |
| Typist | 42 |
| Police officer | 40 |
| Receptionist | 38 |
| Carpenter | 37 |
| Restaurant manager | 37 |
| Hairdresser | 35 |
| Retail sales clerk | 34 |
| Mail carrier | 33 |
| Bus driver | 32 |
| Cashier | 31 |
| Shoe repairman | 28 |
| Parking attendant | 24 |
| Peddler | 22 |
| Waiter | 23 |
| Maid | 17 |
| Garbage collector | 13 |

Source: Donald J. Treiman, *Occupational Prestige in Comparative Perspective* (New York: Academic Press, 1977), 306–15.

**TABLE 13-7 Typical Categories Used for Assessing Amount or Source of Income**

| AMOUNT OF INCOME | SOURCE OF INCOME |
|---|---|
| Under $5,000 per year | Public welfare |
| $5,000–$11,999 | Private financial assistance |
| $12,000–$19,999 | Wages (hourly) |
| $20,000–$39,999 | Salary (yearly) |
| $40,000–$74,999 | Profits or fees |
| $75,000–$124,999 | Earned wealth |
| $125,000 and over | Inherited wealth |
| | Interest, dividends, royalties |

**TABLE 13-8** **Comparative Differences in Activities, Interests, and Opinions of Passive and Creative Consumers with the Same Income Level**

| | $10,000-15,000 | |
|---|---|---|
| | passive | creative |
| Visited museum during past 6 months | 18.5% | 52.8% |
| Attended classical music concert, past 12 months | 5.4 | 25.8 |
| Member, or use, Book Rental or Book Club and/or Record Club | 21.2 | 46.0 |
| Read 5 or more non-fiction books in past 12 months | 13.8 | 57.6 |
| Ever taken Adult Education Courses | 43.1 | 70.6 |
| Are Negroes right about job opportunities being unequal | 21.5 | 51.5 |
| Chances of moving up in company in next 12 months (very good and excellent chance) | 30.9 | 49.1 |
| Had alcoholic beverage—other than beer or wine—outside home during past week | 41.0 | 67.5 |

Source: Emanuel Demby, "Psychographics and from Whence It Came," in William D. Wells, ed., *Life Style and Psychographics* (Chicago: American Marketing Association, 1974), 16.

OTHER VARIABLES. Level of education, quality of neighborhood and dollar value of residence are rarely used as sole measures of social class; however, they are frequently used informally to support or verify social class membership assigned on the basis of occupational status or income.

Finally, *possessions* have been used by sociologists as an index of social class. The best known and most elaborate rating scheme for evaluating possessions is Chapin's Social Status Scale, which focuses on the presence of certain items of furniture and accessories in the living room (types of floor or floor covering, drapes, fireplace, library table, telephone, bookcases) and the condition of the room (cleanliness, organization, general atmosphere).[10] Conclusions are drawn about a family's social class on the basis of such observations. Since the scale was developed over 50 years ago, a contemporary update is very much needed.

## COMPOSITE-VARIABLE INDEXES

Composite indexes systematically combine a number of socioeconomic factors to form *one* overall measure of social class standing. Such indexes are of interest to consumer researchers because they may better reflect the complexity of social class than single-variable indexes. We will now briefly review several of the more important composite indexes.

INDEX OF STATUS CHARACTERISTICS. A classic composite measure of social class is Warner's Index of Status Characteristics (ISC).[11] The ISC is a weighted measure of the following socioeconomic variables: occupation, source of income (*not* amount of income), house type, and dwelling area (quality of neighborhood). Table 13-9 presents the specific seven-point rating scale used for each of the four variables and the weights by which they are adjusted.

SOCIOECONOMIC STATUS SCORES. The U.S. Bureau of the Census Socioeconomic Status Score (SES) was developed for the 1960 census.[12] The SES combines three basic socioeconomic variables: occupation, family income, and educational attainment.

**TABLE 13-9 Scores and Weights for Warner's Index of Status Characteristics**

| OCCUPATION (weight of 4) | SOURCE OF INCOME (weight of 3) | HOUSE TYPE (weight of 3) | DWELLING AREA (weight of 2) |
|---|---|---|---|
| 1. Professionals and proprietors of large businesses | 1. Inherited wealth | 1. Excellent houses | 1. Very high: Gold Coast, North Shore, etc. |
| 2. Semi-professionals and officials of large businesses | 2. Earned wealth | 2. Very good houses | 2. High: the better suburbs and apartment house areas, houses with spacious yards, etc. |
| 3. Clerks and kindred workers | 3. Profits and fees | 3. Good houses | 3. Above average: areas all residential, larger than average space around houses; apartment areas in good condition, etc. |
| 4. Skilled workers | 4. Salary | 4. Average houses | 4. Average: residential neighborhoods, no deterioration in the area |
| 5. Proprietors of small businesses | 5. Wages | 5. Fair houses | 5. Below average: area not quite holding its own, beginning to deteriorate, business entering, etc. |
| 6. Semi-skilled workers | 6. Private relief | 6. Poor houses | 6. Low: considerably deteriorated, rundown and semi-slum |
| 7. Unskilled workers | 7. Public relief and non-respectable income | 7. Very poor houses | 7. Very low: slum |

Source: W. Lloyd Warner, Marchia Meeker, and Kenneth Eells, *Social Class in America: A Manual of Procedure for the Measurement of Social Status* (New York: Harper & Row, 1960), 123. Copyright © 1960 by Harper & Row, Publishers, Incorporated, Reprinted by permission.

**TABLE 13-10 Popular Composite Measures of Social Class**

| COMPOSITE INDEX | VARIABLES |
|---|---|
| Two-Factor Index of Social Position* | Occupation<br>Education |
| Index of Urban Status (revised)† | Occupation (husband and wife)<br>Education (husband and wife)<br>Neighborhood of residence<br>Quality of housing<br>Church affiliation<br>Community associations |
| Index of Cultural Classes‡ | Occupation<br>Education<br>Home value (or amount of rent) |

Sources: *Marie Haug, "Social-Class Measurement: A Methodological Critique," in Gerald W. Thielbar and Saul D. Feldman, eds., *Issues in Social Inequality* (Boston: Little, Brown, 1972), 433-38.

†Richard P. Coleman and Bernice L. Neugarten, *Social Status in the City* (San Francisco: Jossey-Bass, 1971).

‡James M. Carman, *The Application of Social Class in Market Segmentation* (Berkeley: Institute of Business and Economic Research, University of California Graduate School of business Administration, 1965).

OTHER COMPOSITE-VARIABLE INDEXES. Many other composite social-class measures are available to the consumer researcher. Table 13-10 identifies three of these indexes and the variables employed to establish their overall status scores.

## An Applied Comparison of Single and Composite Indexes of Social Class

AT&T has utilized a variety of single and composite indexes of social class in its efforts to understand customer needs more fully. The results obtained from a study of the penetration of Touch-Tone (push-button) service are presented graphically in Figure 13-1. Three single-variable indexes—*family income, education of head of household,* and *occupation of head of household*—are compared with a composite **Socioeconomic Status Score** index modeled after the SES index developed by the Bureau of the Census.

The single-variable analyses found that families with incomes in excess of $10,000 and those whose heads of household have generally higher occupational status scores (primarily managerial, professional, and technical people) have a higher than average level of subscription to the Touch-Tone service. Families classified by the composite SES index as lower class (composite scores between 10 and 39) and lower-middle class (scores between 40 and 69) tend to have lower than average levels of subscription, while families classified as upper-middle class (scores between 70 and 89) and upper class (scores between 90 and 99) have higher than average subscription levels. These results demonstrate that the insights gained from several single-variable indexes and from a composite index can reinforce each other in terms of the information they provide concerning customer behavior.

**FIGURE 13-1** **Touch-Tone Service Penetration by Socioeconomic Variables** Source: John J. Veltri and Leon G. Schiffman, "Fifteen Years of Consumer Lifestyle and Value Research at AT&T," in Robert E. Pitts, Jr., and Arch G. Woodside, eds., *Personal Values and Consumer Psychology* (Lexington, Mass.: Lexington Books, 1984), 274.

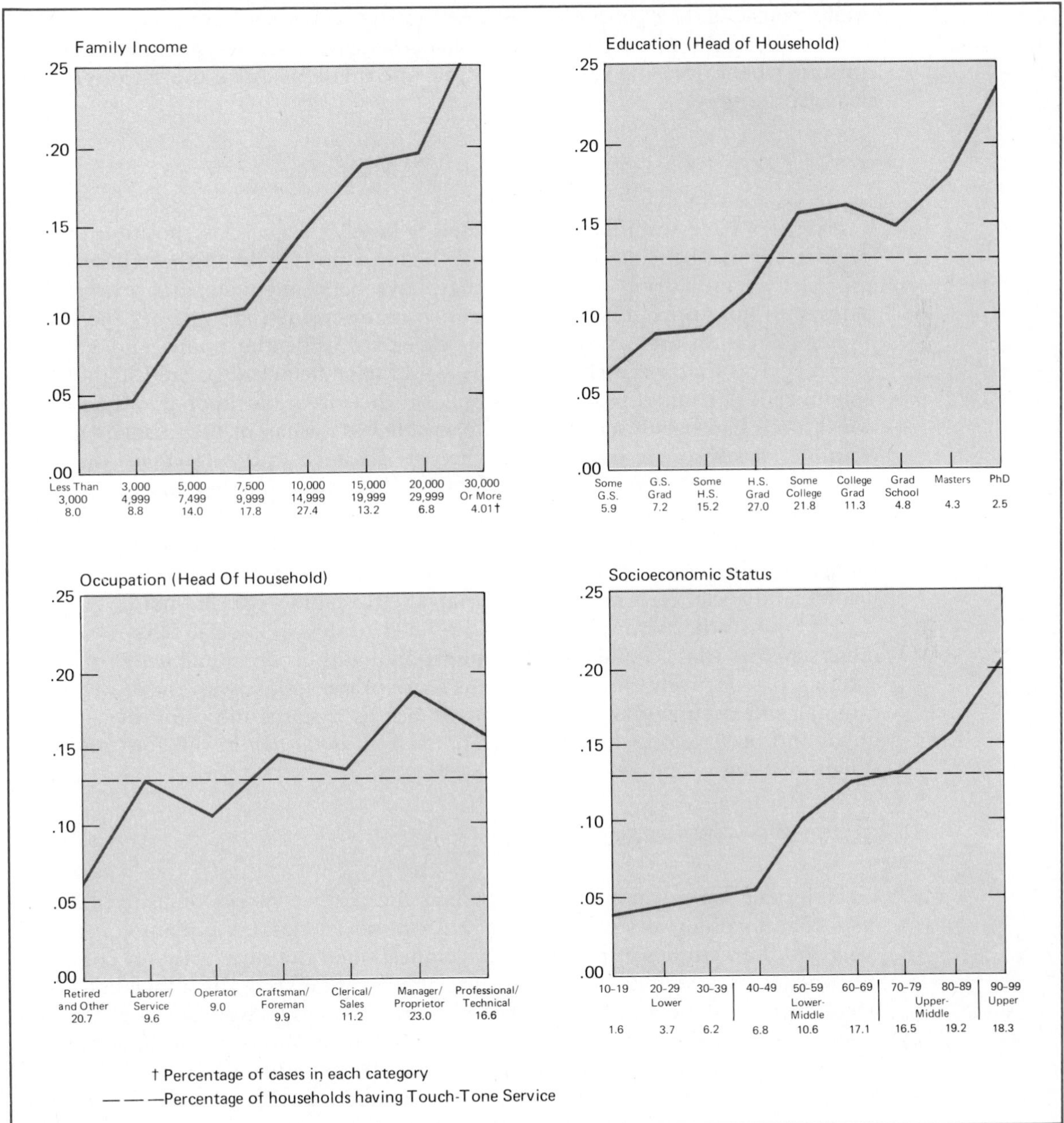

## Issues in the Measurement of Social Class

Before concluding our discussion of the measurement of social class, we will briefly consider three important issues: the role of *women* in the measurement of social class, the relative usefulness of social class versus income in explaining consumer behavior, and the impact of income divisions *within* the various social class groupings.

### SOCIAL CLASS: THE MISSING IMPACT OF WOMEN

Researchers have traditionally evaluated a family's social class position exclusively in terms of the status of the *male* head of household. Although such an approach to measuring social class may have been adequate in previous decades, it is not appropriate today when so many women are actively pursuing higher education and are engaged in careers outside the home. Indeed, research reveals that social class position would have been categorized higher for a significant portion of blue-collar families if the wife's educational and occupational levels had been used to calculate social class instead of the husband's. For example, based on a composite index of *education* and *occupation,* one researcher reported: "Around a third of all dual-work families include a wife who has a higher social class level than her husband. . . ."[13] A study concerned with the social class structure of a large urban metropolitan area (Kansas City) found that the wife's educational level was more closely related to the family's income and social class membership than the husband's educational level.[14]

These studies strongly suggest the need to develop social class measurement schemes that account for the educational and occupational levels of both spouses, or selectively employ the status score of the spouse with the *higher* educational and occupational attainment, or use as a status indicator the educational and occupational score of the spouse *most influential* in the consumption situation being examined.[15]

### COMPOSITE VERSUS SINGLE INDEXES

Considerable controversy exists regarding the relative merits of using a *single index* (like income) versus a *composite index* of social class to explain consumer behavior. Two studies in particular have questioned the superiority of composite indexes as a determinant. The first study compared the efficiency with which income alone and a composite measure of social class accounted for the presence (or absence) of a relatively large number of common household products (toiletries, detergents, soft drinks, liquor, frozen and canned food).[16] With few exceptions, the evidence revealed that income was as good as or better than the composite measure of social class as a predictor of whether a family would have a specific product on hand. A follow-up study focused on the purchase of durable goods (furniture, appliances, family clothing) and selected consumer services (travel) during the previous year.[17] Again, for the overwhelming majority of products, income was found to be equal to or better than the composite measure as a determinant of whether a specific purchase was made during the preceding year.

This research raises the question as to the conditions under which a composite index would be a better determinant of consumer behavior than income alone. In general, it appears that income is a superior predictor of *use* or *nonuse,* while a composite measure of social class is a better predictor of *frequency of use.* For example, income rather than social class was found to be positively related to whether a family did or did not "dine at expensive restaurants," while the composite measure of social class rather than income was positively related to the frequency of such dining out.[18] This study suggests that the research designs of the earlier studies were deficient in examining only one variable ("having" or "not having" a product on hand) and that a composite measure of social class may have been a more effective predictor of the frequency of such purchases.

Another study examined the relationship between *income, social class,* and numerous *lifestyle* (psychographic) items (see Chapter 5).[19] The objective of this study was to determine whether lifestyle characteristics (which are generally assumed to reflect social class) are in fact more closely associated with a composite social class index than with income alone. The findings support this hypothesis. Table 13-11 presents a sample of lifestyle items that were found to be strongly associated with social class.

While a debate about the relative merits of composite social class measures or income as a predictor of consumer behavior may seem to be academic, it has served to provoke a careful evaluation of the relationships between consumer behavior and social class. Out of such an assessment has come a better understanding of consumer behavior. Although more research is needed on this issue, it appears that which variable is the better predictor may be a function of

**TABLE 13-11 Selected Lifestyle Items That Were Found to Better Explain Social Class Than Income**

| LIFESTYLE ITEMS THAT ARE POSITIVELY ASSOCIATED WITH SOCIAL CLASS | LIFESTYLE ITEMS THAT ARE NEGATIVELY ASSOCIATED WITH SOCIAL CLASS |
|---|---|
| I enjoy going to concerts. | Somebody should stop all the protests that are going on. |
| I attend a bridge club regularly. | Long hair on boys should be banned. |
| I enjoy going through an art gallery. | I am a homebody. |
| I am usually an active member of more than one service organization. | If it was good enough for my mother, it is good enough for me. |
| I like ballet. | Any housewife who doesn't have a spring housecleaning is slovenly. |
| I think I'm a pretty nice looking person. | When I must choose between the two, I usually dress for comfort, not for fashion. |

Source: Adapted from James H. Myers and Jonathan Gutman, "Life Styles: The Essence of Social Class," in William D. Wells, ed., *Life Style and Psychographics* (Chicago: American Marketing Association, 1974), 250-51.

how consumption behavior (as a dependent variable) is defined. Income may be a more suitable predictor of consumer behavior for *acquisitive* types of behavior—"having" or "not having." Composite social class indexes may be more predictive of *expressive* types of consumer behavior, such as which brands are purchased, the price paid, in what type of store the product is purchased, and how the product is used.[20] It is also likely that composite social class indexes better reflect broad values such as the "inventory" or "bundle" of products a family possesses, whereas income may better reflect the ownership of certain specific products.

### INCOME WITHIN SOCIAL CLASS

Notwithstanding the correlation between *income* and *social class* (defined in terms of occupation and education), there is still a surprisingly wide range of incomes within any one social class. This has encouraged researchers to recommend that the members of each social class be divided into subgroups on the basis of relative incomes. The resulting **social class/relative income** variable embodies the notion that within any social class some members are clearly better off than others. More specifically, consumers who have incomes *above* the average of all members of their social class can be considered "overprivileged," while those who have incomes *below* the average can be considered "underprivileged."

Consider, for example, the marketplace behavior of "underprivileged" upper-class and "overprivileged" middle-class American families *with the same basic annual incomes.* Overprivileged middle-class consumers can be differentiated from underprivileged upper-class consumers by their more likely ownership of such products as campers, motorboats, pickup trucks, tractor lawnmowers, and backyard swimming pools. In contrast, underprivileged upper-class consumers with the same income spend relatively greater amounts on private club memberships, special educational experiences for their children, and cultural objects and events.[21] Studies that examined automobile preferences and the prices consumers were willing to pay for coffee confirm the usefulness of the social class/relative income variable.[22]

## LIFESTYLE PROFILES OF THE SOCIAL CLASSES

Consumer research has found evidence that within each of the social classes, there is a constellation of specific **lifestyle** factors (shared beliefs, attitudes, activities, and behaviors) that tend to distinguish the members of each class from the members of all other social classes.

To capture the lifestyle composition of the various social class groupings, we have pieced together from numerous sources a consolidated portrait of the members of each of the following six social classes: *upper-upper* class, *lower-upper* class, *upper-middle* class, *lower-middle* class, *upper-lower* class, and *lower-lower* class (Table 13-12).[23] Each of these profiles is only a generalized picture of the class. There may be people in any class who possess values, attitudes, and behavioral patterns that are a hybrid of two or more classes.

These lifestyle differences should be considered when choosing appropriate marketing-mix appeals to communicate with the core members of these social class groupings.

**TABLE 13-12 Social Class Characteristics**

the upper-upper class—country club establishment

-small number of well-established families
-belong to best country clubs and sponsor major charity events
-serve as trustees for local colleges and hospitals
-prominent physicians and lawyers
-may be heads of major financial institutions, owners of major long-established firms
-accustomed to wealth, so do not spend money conspicuously

the lower-upper class—new wealth

-not quite accepted by the upper crust of society
-represent "new money"
-successful business executives
-conspicuous users of their new wealth

the upper-middle class—achieving professional

-have neither family status nor unusual wealth
-career-oriented
-young successful professionals, corporate managers, and business owners
-most are college graduates, many with advanced degrees
-active in professional, community, and social activities
-have a keen interest in obtaining the "better things in life"
-their homes serve as symbols of their achievements
-consumption is often conspicuous
-very child-oriented

the lower-middle class—faithful followers

-composed of primarily nonmanagerial white-collar workers and highly paid blue-collar workers
-want to achieve "respectability" and be accepted as good citizens
-want their children to be well-behaved
-tend to be churchgoers and are often involved in church-sponsored activities
-prefer a neat and clean appearance, and tend to avoid faddish or highly styled clothing
-constitute a major market for do-it-yourself products

the upper-lower class—security-minded majority

-the largest social class segment
-solidly blue-collar
-strive for security (sometimes gained from union membership)
-view work as a means to "buy" enjoyment
-want children to behave properly
-high wage earners in this group may spend impulsively
-interested in items that enhance their leisure time (e.g., TV sets, hunting equipment)
-husbands typically have a strong "macho" self-image
-males are sports fans, heavy smokers, beer drinkers

the lower-lower class—rock bottom

-poorly educated, unskilled laborers
-often out of work
-children often are poorly treated
-tend to live a day-to-day existence

## SOCIAL CLASS MOBILITY

Social-class membership in this country is not as hard and fixed as it is in some other countries and cultures. While individuals can move either up or down in social class standing from the class position held by their parents, we primarily think in terms of upward mobility in this country because of the availability of free education and opportunities for self-development and self-advancement. Indeed, the classic Horatio Alger tale of a penniless young man who managed to achieve great success in business and in life is depicted over and over again in popular novels, movies, and television shows. Because upward mobility is possible in our society, the higher social classes often become reference groups for ambitious men and women of lower social status. The junior executive tries to dress like his boss; the middle manager aspires to belong to the president's country club; the graduate of a municipal college wants to send his daughter to Brown. The advertisement for Lucia women's fashions in Figure 13-2 is consistent with this upwardly-directed view of life.

Recognizing that individuals often aspire to membership in higher social classes, marketers often incorporate the symbols of higher-class membership (both as products and props) in advertisements targeted to lower social class audiences. For example, they might advertise a Buick to lower middle class consumers, or golf clubs to lower management ranks.

## GEODEMOGRAPHIC CLUSTERING

In recent years, traditional social class measures have been enhanced by the linking of geographic and socioeconomic consumer data to create more powerful **geodemographic** clusters. The underlying principle of geodemographic clusters is that "birds of a feather flock together."

Two of the most popular competing clustering services are *PRIZM* and *ClusterPlus*. Each of these services identifies a host of socioeconomic and demographic factors (education, income, occupation, family life cycle, ethnicity, housing, urbanization) drawn from U.S. Census data. They then locate concentrations of consumers with similar socioeconomic factors in the more than 36,000 residential zip code neighborhoods or over 250,000 block groups and enumeration districts.[24] This vast amount of geographic and socioeconomic/demographic data is combined initially to form about 40 clusters containing relatively homogeneous consumer segments. To make them simpler to deal with, these clusters can be collapsed into twelve PRIZM clusters or ten ClusterPlus clusters (see Table 13-13). Marketers can superimpose these geodemographic clusters onto a host of product and service usage data, media exposure data, and lifestyle data (such as VALS) to create a refined picture of their target markets.

To illustrate, Table 13-14 lists a sample of the useful market segmentation insights that emerge from the ClusterPlus scheme when it is coupled with spe-

FIGURE 13-2 Advertisement Suggesting Social Class Mobility

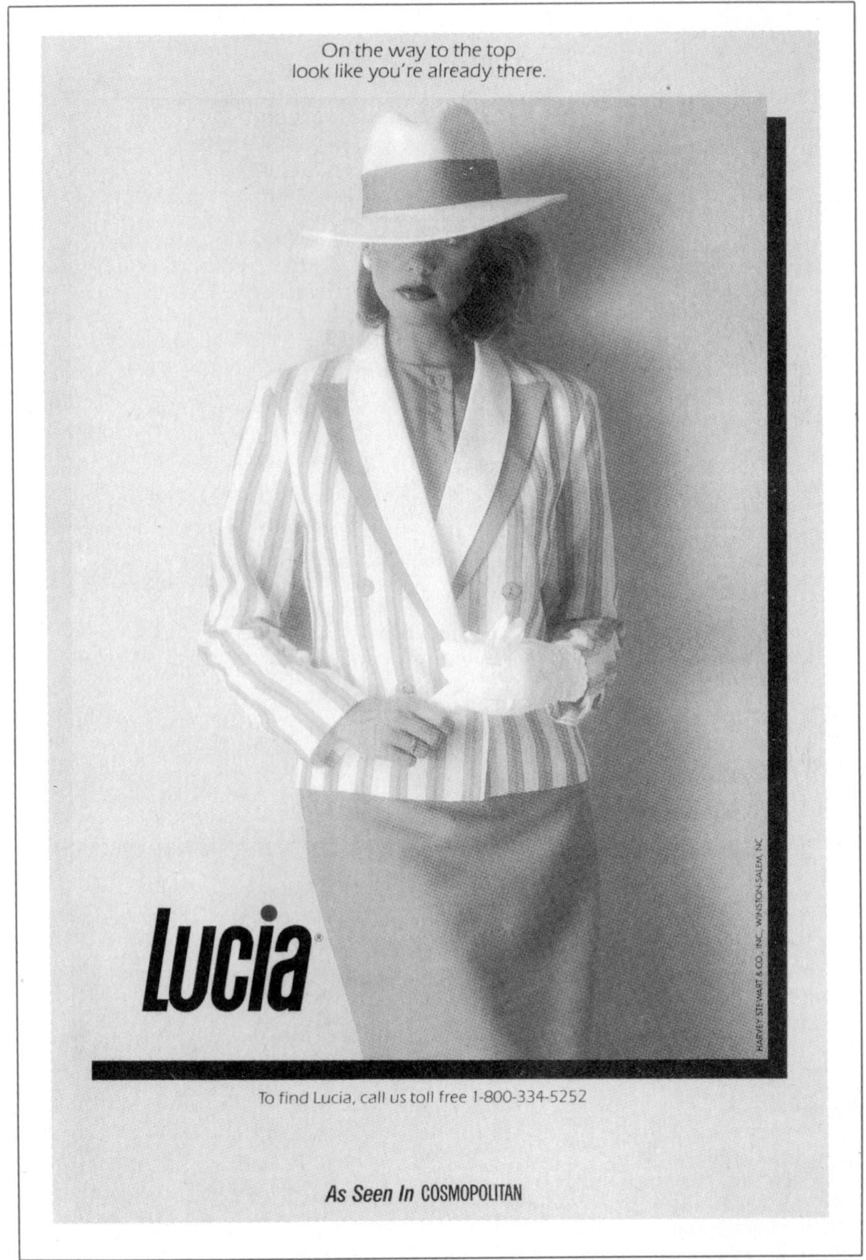

On the way to the top
look like you're already there.
Lucia
HARVEY STEWART & CO., INC., WINSTON-SALEM, NC
To find Lucia, call us toll free 1-800-334-5252
As Seen In COSMOPOLITAN


Courtesy of Lucia.

cific consumer-relevant information. In particular, it indicates that ClusterPlus *Cluster Group 1* (an upscale consumer segment) purchased new imported cars in the past year at better than twice the rate of the U.S. population as a whole. In contrast, *Cluster Group 9* (a downscale consumer segment) purchased such cars at a rate substantially less than the national average. Most important, the

**TABLE 13-13 PRIZM and ClusterPlus Clusters**

| PRIZM CODE | DESCRIPTION |
|---|---|
| S1 | Educated, affluent executives and professionals in elite metro suburbs |
| S2 | Pre- and post-child families and singles in upscale, white-collar suburbs |
| S3 | Upper-middle, childraising families in outlying owner-occupied suburbs |
| U1 | Educated, white-collar singles and couples in upscale, urban areas |
| T1 | Educated, young, mobile families in exurban satellites and boom towns |
| S4 | Middle-class, post-child families in aging suburbs and retirement areas |
| T2 | Mid-scale, child-raising, blue-collar families in remote suburbs and towns |
| U2 | Mid-scale families, singles, and elders in dense, urban row, and hi-rise areas |
| R1 | Rural towns and villages amid farms and ranches across agrarian mid-America |
| T3 | Mixed gentry and blue-collar labor in low-mid rustic, mill, and factory towns |
| R2 | Landowners, migrants, and rustics in poor rural towns, farms, and uplands |
| U3 | Mixed, unskilled service and labor in aging urban row and hi-rise areas |

| ClusterPlus CODE | DESCRIPTION |
|---|---|
| 1 | Well-educated, affluent, suburban professionals |
| 2 | Urban, mobile professionals, few children |
| 3 | Above-average income homeowners, families with children |
| 4 | Above-average income, older, white-collar workers, few children, old homes |
| 5 | Younger, mobile, above-average income families with children, new homes |
| 6 | Younger, mobile, below-average income singles, few children |
| 7 | Average income, blue-collar families, rural areas |
| 8 | Below-average income, older, few children |
| 9 | Less educated, downscale, rural families with children |
| 10 | Downscale, ethnic, urban apartment areas, old housing |

Source: Based on *PRIZM: 1985: A Review of Five Micro-Geographic Systems,* Claritas Corporation, 1985; "Segmenting Markets and Media with ClusterPlus," *Magazine Newsletter of Research* (New York: Magazine Publishers Association, December 1984), 1.

**TABLE 13-14 Comparision of ClusterPlus Cluster Segments 1 and 9**

| | AFFLUENT PROFESSIONAL CLUSTER 1 INDEX | URBAN DOWNSCALE CLUSTER 9 INDEX |
|---|---|---|
| Heavy domestic air travel | 298* | 34 |
| Car rental (past year) | 236 | 37 |
| AMEX card | 295 | 34 |
| Heavy domestic table wine usage | 208 | 32 |
| Index of TV exposure | 83 | 108 |
| Index of newspaper exposure | 125 | 81 |
| Index of magazine exposure | 130 | 80 |
| Bought new domestic car in the past year | 181 | 90 |
| Bought new imported car in the past year | 236 | 69 |
| $50,000 or more life insurance | 185 | 62 |

*An index of 100 is the average in each category for the U.S. population
Source: "Segmenting Markets and Media with ClusterPlus," *Magazine Newsletter of Research* (New York: Magazine Publishers Association, December 1984), 2 and 3.

**TABLE 13-15 An Overview Comparison of the Older Adults and Young Adults Cluster Segments**

older adults cluster segment

Primarily retired
Most are middle class
Couples and widows
Live in condos and suburban homes
Seek dependability, convenience, full service
Price-value concerned
Long distance a vital link to children and others

young adults cluster segment

Primarily first jobs or still in college
Just starting out and future-oriented
Mainly singles
Share apartments in urban areas or college towns
Seek "hassle-free" calling, value operator assistance
Shop and compare long distance prices
Particularly cost conscious
Long distance provides contact with parents

Courtesy of AT&T Communications.

geographic locations of the various consumer clusters (and subclusters) are pinpointed. This enables marketers to locate and directly target consumers with the desired social class and lifestyle mix.

As an example of geodemographic targeting, AT&T has developed a 12-category typology of residential long distance customers. This segmentation scheme provided the basis for the design of direct-mail pieces that pointed up distinctive benefits likely to be sought by the members of specific geodemographic customer segments. The purpose of the mailings was to encourage customers to select AT&T as their primary long distance company.

Table 13-15 presents a portion of the profiles of two of these clusters: *Older Adults* consists primarily of retired middle-class consumers; *Young Adults* is composed of young singles who are just starting out. Figure 13-3 presents parts of two promotional pieces targeted to these geodemographic segments. An examination of the two messages reveal how each is targeted to the specific interests of these two audiences.

## THE AFFLUENT

Affluent U.S. households constitute an especially attractive target segment because its members have incomes that provide them with a disproportionately larger share of all discretionary income—the "extras" that allow the purchase of luxury cruises, foreign sports cars, time-sharing ski-resort condos, and fine jewelry.[25]

FIGURE 13-3 AT&T Long Distance Equal-Access Direct Mail Campaign: (a) Targeted to Older Adult Cluster Segment

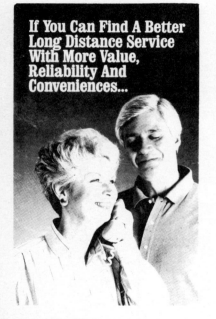

**If You Can Find A Better Long Distance Service With More Value, Reliability And Conveniences...**

# AT&T Challenges You To Compare

## Compare Before You Choose!

Because all long distance companies can now choose to have equal access to the same local telephone lines as AT&T, your local telephone company is asking you to choose the easy access long distance company you prefer. But remember, equal access does not mean equal service. The only way to be sure you get the best buy for your long distance dollar is to compare the companies before you choose.

So take a moment and compare the differences now. See for yourself why AT&T is the right choice for you.

## Compare Services

There's no comparison. AT&T delivers real advantages. Only AT&T assures you of all these services.

## You Compare The Difference

| Valuable Extra Service | AT&T | Others |
|---|---|---|
| Long distance operators to assist you 24 hours a day, 365 days a year. | YES | |
| Immediate credit for wrong numbers or disconnected calls. | YES | |
| Collect and Person-to-Person calling. | YES | |
| AT&T Cards offer speed, economy, and convenience when calling while away from home. | YES | |
| International calling to more than 250 countries and locations throughout the world. | YES | |

## Compare Value

**There's no comparison. AT&T delivers real savings.** Since early 1984, AT&T dropped its prices more than 11% on most out-of-state, direct dialed calls. And you can count on discounts off our daytime prices over 70% of the time. That's real savings when you need and want them, and when you have the time to enjoy them.

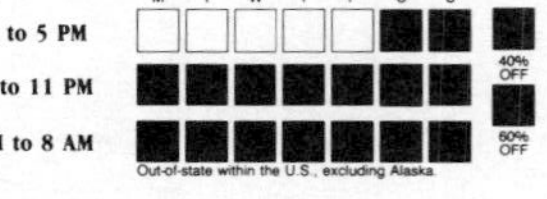


**There's no comparison. AT&T delivers valuable extras. Only AT&T offers both of these additional benefits:**

- **AT&T Opportunity Calling℠ Program**
  - You can earn a dollar of credit for every dollar you use of AT&T Long Distance whenever your monthly calls total $15 or more — up to $300 in Opportunity Credits every month!
  - Credits you can turn into extra buying power — money-saving discounts you can use in addition to most sales, discounts, and other promotions.
  - A great way to save on name brand products and services for your family and home!

- **Reach Out℠ America**
  - A different way to buy long distance during our weekend/night rate periods.
  - Buy an hour's worth of direct dialed, out-of-state AT&T Long Distance calls for just $9.45 a month!
  - Get additional hours of long distance for even less — only $8.25!
  - Plus a 15% discount off our already reduced evening rates for just $1.40 more a month.

## Make The Right Choice...Now!

Now that you've seen the real difference for yourself, take advantage of your opportunity to make the right choice. Your local telephone company is asking you to choose which long distance company you want. The only way to assure you get AT&T is to pick AT&T. So return the attached authorization card today.

Remember! If you don't choose, your local telephone company will randomly assign you to a long distance company . . . without regard for your needs. And it may not be AT&T!

To be sure of the right choice, simply complete and mail the attached authorization card now. That's all. We'll notify your local telephone company and send you a confirmation of your long distance choice.

If you need more information, call us toll free, Monday through Friday, 8AM to 7PM, **1 800 222-0300.**

(b) Targated to Young Adult Cluster Segment

# Before You Choose A Long Distance Company...

## Compare The Facts On These 20 Minute Calls.

| | AT&T | MCI | SPRINT |
|---|---|---|---|
| Los Angeles, CA to Houston, TX (Weekend / Night) | $3.18 | $3.14 | $3.12 |
| Denver, CO to Philadelphia, PA (Evening) | $4.78 | $4.72 | $4.62 |
| Louisville, KY to Cincinnati, OH (Evening) | $4.06 | $3.94 | $4.00 |
| Minneapolis, MN to Oklahoma City, OK (Weekend / Night) | $3.10 | $3.05 | $3.06 |
| Augusta, GA to Columbia, SC (Day) | $6.78 | $6.56 | $6.51 |

Based on tariffs on file with the FCC and effective as of September 15, 1985
Rates subject to change.
Prices do not include any additional discounts

# It's simple... You get what you pay for. Here are the Facts:

### Fact 1. AT&T Doesn't Cost As Much As You Think.

Since early 1984, AT&T prices have dropped more than 11% on most out-of-state long distance calls. And you can count on discounts off our daytime prices over 70% of the time. That's real savings when you need and want them, and when you have the time to enjoy them.

**AT&T LONG DISTANCE DISCOUNT CHART**

| | M | T | W | T | F | S | S |
|---|---|---|---|---|---|---|---|
| 8 AM to 5 PM | | | | | | | |
| 5 PM to 11 PM | | | | | | | |
| 11 PM to 8 AM | | | | | | | |

40% OFF
60% OFF

Out-of-state within the U.S., excluding Alaska.

Carefully consider your calling needs: price isn't everything. Compare all the factors before you choose your long distance company. Make sure you get everything you need and want. The chart below was developed to help you make an easy comparison. You will see for yourself how AT&T delivers the value and services you want and expect.

### Fact 2. AT&T Delivers Real Value.

With AT&T Long Distance you get many extras — a combination of conveniences, benefits and exclusive services you can't buy from other companies at any price.

**You Compare The Difference**

| Valuable Extra Savings & Service | AT&T | Others |
|---|---|---|
| Discounts off our daytime prices over 70% of the time | YES | |
| Collect and Person-to-Person calling | YES | |
| The ability to buy long distance by the hour, not the mile, as you can with AT&T Reach Out℠ America. | YES | |
| Two AT&T Cards offer speed, economy, and convenience when calling away from home. The versatile, all-purpose AT&T Card and the specialized, one number AT&T Call Me Card. | YES | |
| Immediate credit for wrong numbers or disconnected calls. | YES | |
| Long distance operators to assist you 24 hours a day, 365 days a year. | YES | |
| The ability to turn your long distance dollars into savings on brand name products and services with the AT&T Opportunity Calling℠ program. | YES | |
| International calling — to more than 250 countries and locations throughout the world. | YES | |
| Customer service representatives to answer your questions and recommend the services that best fit your needs. | YES | |

## Act Now! Make The Right Choice!

### Fact 3. Equal Access Does Not Mean Equal Service or Quality.

All long distance companies may now choose to have equal access to the same local connections as AT&T. Your local company is asking you to pick the easy access company you want. But the only way to be sure of getting high quality service, savings, and extra value is to make the right choice . . . AT&T. Do it today.

### Choose or They'll Choose For You.

If you don't choose in time, your local telephone company will randomly assign you to a long distance company without taking your calling needs into account. And it might not be AT&T. In fact, it may be a company you have never heard of.

All you have to do is complete and return the attached authorization card to us. We'll notify your local telephone company and send you a confirmation of your choice. But remember, we need your signed card. So mail it today. For more information, just call us toll free between 8:00 a.m. and 7:00 p.m., Monday through Friday . . . **1 800 222-0300.**

**Sign & Mail The Authorization Card Today!**

Courtesy of AT&T Communications.

TABLE 13-16 A Comparison of Affluent and Typical U.S. Households

| CATEGORY | AFFLUENT ($50,000-PLUS) HOUSEHOLD | U.S. AVERAGE HOUSEHOLD |
|---|---|---|
| Average income | $91,300 | $27,500 |
| Average number of automobiles | 2.6 | 1.7 |
| Average stereo component expenditure in the past year | $105 | $20 |
| Average personal computer expenditure in past year | $356 | $60 |
| Average VCR expenditure in past year | $205 | $40 |
| Average number of glasses of wine per adult per week | 4.0 | 1.2 |
| Average total entertainment & appliance expenditures in past year | $719 | $229 |

Source: *Affluence 1985–1986: 1985 Survey of Adults in Markets of Affluence* (New York: Mendelsohn Media Research, Inc., 1985), 14–17.

For over a decade, Mendelsohn Media Research (MMR) has conducted an annual study of the *affluent* market (currently defined as $50,000+ in household income). While presently consisting of only 13 percent of all households, this high-end market segment purchases 29 percent of all color TVs, 59 percent of all VCRs, 59 percent of all stereo components, and 68 percent of all personal computers.[26] Table 13-16 presents a number of additional consumer-relevant comparisons between the affluent household and the average U.S. household. The evidence points up why marketers eagerly seek out affluent consumers.

As might be expected, the media habits of the affluent also differ from those of the general population. For example, those earning more than $50,000 a year view an average of 190 minutes of TV a day, compared to the 241 minutes watched by those with an income between $15,000 and $25,000. Each year an increasingly larger number of magazines are targeted to the affluent reader. For instance, *Private Clubs,* a new magazine published by American Airlines, claims that its readers have an average household income in excess of $140,000.[27] Other thriving magazines that cater to the tastes and interests of the affluent include *Architectural Digest, Avenue, Connoisseur, Gourmet, Southern Accents,* and *Town & Country.* Figure 13-4 presents an ad for *Nation's Business,* targeted to potential advertisers, that claims its audience has an average income of $114,000 and a net worth of $737,000. The ad depicts an executive wearing a sure sign of success—a Rolex watch.

Because not all affluent consumers share the same lifestyles (i.e., activities, interests, and opinions), various marketers have tried to isolate meaningful segments of the affluent market. For instance, the Cadillac division of GM identified three segments of the affluent market and plans to offer specific Cadillac cars to each of these submarkets (see Table 13-17).

To assist the many marketers interested in reaching subsegments of the affluent market, Mediamark Research, Inc. (MRI) has developed the following

FIGURE 13-4 An Advertisement Revealing the Affluence of a Magazine's Audience

Courtesy of *Nation's Business* magazine.

**TABLE 13-17 How Cadillac Thinks of the Luxury Car Market**

| SEGMENT NAME | INCOME LEVEL | TYPE OF CAR |
|---|---|---|
| Ultraluxury performance | $100,000+ | Rolls-Royce, top-of-line Mercedes-Benz, Jaguar, some BMWs, Ferrari, Maserati, and Aston Martin |
| Traditional luxury | $50,000+ | Cadillac, Lincoln, Chrysler Fifth Avenue, and other selected domestic cars |
| Near luxury | $30,000+ | Alfa Romeo, Audi, Peugeot, Saab, Volvo, Cadillac Cimarron |

Source: Created from Raymond Serafin, "Awailing Allante," *Advertising Age*, March 13, 1986, 4–5.

affluent market segmentation scheme (defined as the top 10 percent of households in terms of income):[28]

1. *Well-feathered nests.* Those households that have at least one high-income earner, and children present.
2. *No strings attached.* Those households that have at least one high-income earner, and no children.
3. *Nanny's in charge.* Those households that have two or more earners, neither high income, and children present.
4. *Two careers.* Those households that have two or more earners, neither high income, and no children present.
5. *The good life.* Those households that have a high degree of affluence with no person employed, or with the head-of-household not employed.

Armed with these various *affluent lifestyle* segments, MRI provides subscribing firms with profiles of users of a variety of goods and services frequently targeted to the more affluent consumer (e.g., domestic and foreign travel, leisure clothing, lawn care services, rental cars, and various types of recreational activities). For instance, in seeking recreation, *well-feathered nesters* can be found on the tennis court, the *good lifers* may be playing golf, while the *two careers* couples may be off sailing.[29]

## ADDITIONAL CONSUMER BEHAVIOR APPLICATIONS OF SOCIAL CLASS

Social class profiles provide a broad picture of the values, attitudes, and behavior that distinguish the members of various social classes. This section focuses on specific consumer research that relates social class to the development of marketing strategy.

## Clothing and Fashion

A Greek philosopher once said, "Know, first, who you are; and then adorn yourself accordingly."[30] This bit of wisdom is relevant to clothing marketers today, since most people dress to fit their self-images, which include their perceptions of their own social class membership. A study that examined the fashion interests of women found that all women respondents, regardless of social class, considered fashionable clothing to be important; however, *upper-* and *middle-class* women were found to be somewhat more involved in fashion than their *lower-class* counterparts. This was demonstrated by such factors as more active readership of fashion magazines, more frequent attendance at fashion shows, and more frequent discussions of fashion with others, particularly their friends and husbands.[31] Members of specific social classes also differ in terms of what they consider to be fashionable or in good taste. For instance, lower-middle-class consumers have a strong preference for T-shirts, caps, and other clothing that offer an external point of identification, such as the name of an admired person or group, a respected company or brand name (Heineken), or a valued trademark (Adidas).[32] These consumers are prime targets for licensed goods. In contrast, upper-class consumers are likely to buy clothing that is free from such "supporting" associations. Bottega Veneta, a high priced leather goods manufacturer, advertises "When your own initials are enough." Upper class consumers seek clothing with a more subtle look, such as the kind of sportswear found in an L. L. Bean catalog, rather than status designer jeans.

Further evidence that there are social class differences regarding fashion is found in the use of cosmetics. Research has revealed, for example, that middle-class women are more likely to be heavy users of cosmetics than lower-class women.[33] More research is needed to examine the relationship between various appearance-related purchase behaviors and social class membership.

## Home Decoration

To the extent that a family's home is its castle, the decor of the home should provide clues to the family's social class position. Of all the rooms in the home, the living room seems to best express how a family wants to be seen by those it entertains. Therefore, living-room furnishings are likely to be particularly sensitive to class influences. As noted earlier, Chapin's **Social Status Scale** uses the presence and condition of living-room furnishings to measure a family's social class standing. The appropriateness of using living room furnishings as a barometer of social class standing is underscored by a leading consumer researcher who noted: "The living-room of a home is essentially the face you present the world of your friends and acquaintances, and the average housewife is consciously or unconsciously concerned with the impression it makes."[34]

Figure 13-5 presents a typology of social class status based on the owner-

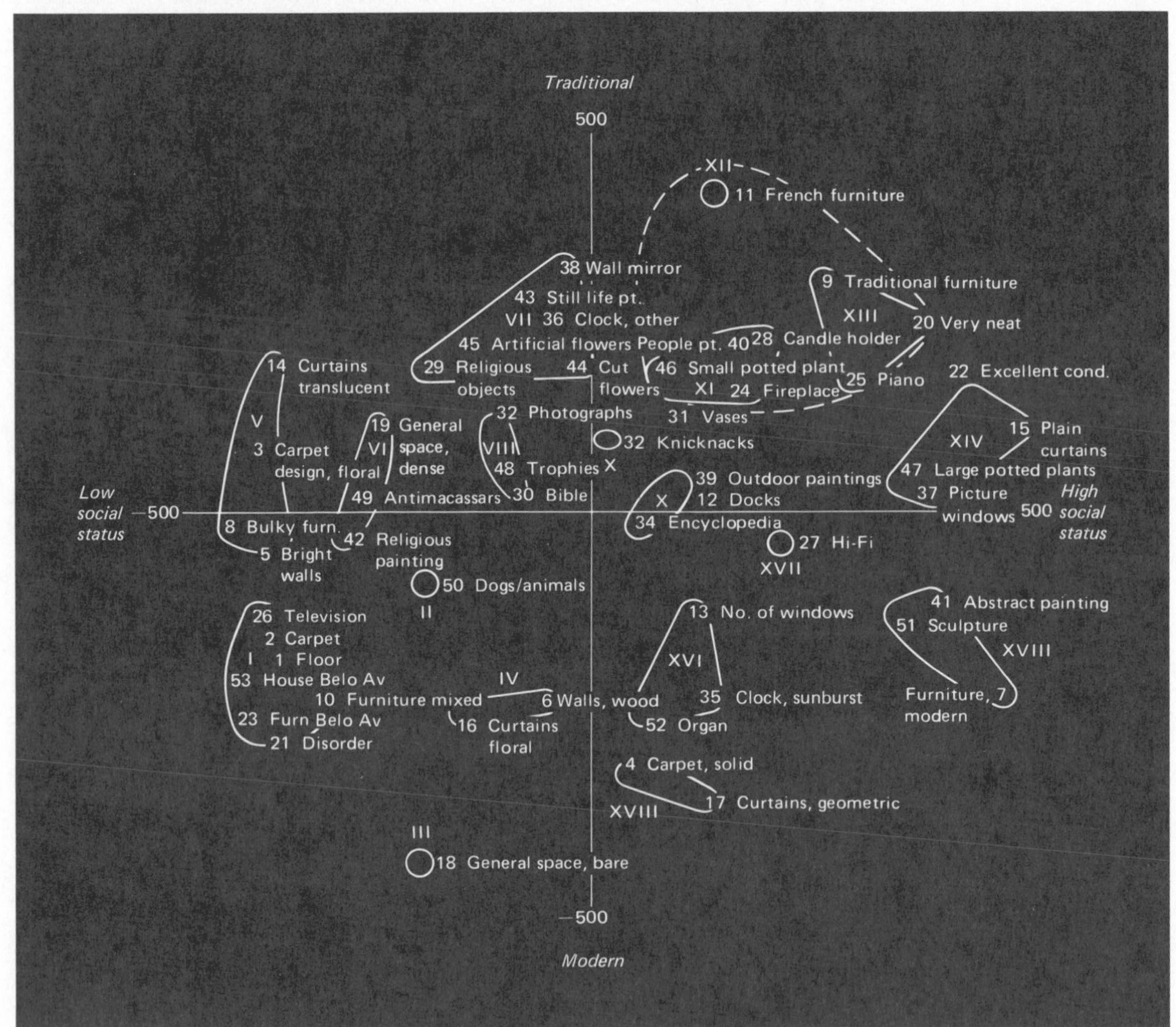


**FIGURE 13–5** **A Typology of Social-Class Status Based on Ownership of Living-Room Objects** Sources: Edward O. Laumann and James S. House, "Living Room Styles and Social Attributes: The Patterning of Material Artifacts in a Modern Urban Community," *Sociology and Social Research,* 54 (April 1970), 326. Reprinted by permission of the University of Southern California.

ship of specific types of living-room furniture and accessories. It classifies fifty-three living-room items or characteristics in terms of high or low social-class status and modern or traditional decor. This classification scheme results in four distinct groupings: (1) low-status traditional (upper left quadrant), (2) high-status traditional (upper right quadrant), (3) high-status modern (lower right quadrant), and (4) low-status modern (lower left quadrant).

This type of classification scheme is useful to marketers of home-furnishings concerned with developing products or promotional campaigns for specific target segments. For example, the location of television sets in the lower left quadrant indicates that a television set in the living room is more likely to occur in lower-class households. Indeed, further analysis reveals that lower-class families are likely to place their television sets in the living room, while middle- and upper-class families usually place their television sets in the bedroom or family room.[35] The marketing implications of these findings suggest that advertisements for television sets targeted at the lower-class consumer should show the set in a living-room, while advertisements directed to middle- or upper-class consumers should show the set in either a bedroom or a family room.

A study undertaken by AT&T provides some additional insights into the relationship between style consciousness in home furnishings and social class.[36] Table 13-18 reveals a significant difference in attitude among the four social classes studied concerning telephone design and basic style in home furnishings. An examination of the product-specific statements suggests that *lower middle class* consumers feel that telephones should improve the style of a room and be available in a variety of patterns and designs. In contrast, *lower class* consum-

**TABLE 13-18 A Psychographic Profile of Style Consciousness in Home Furnishings by Socioeconomic Status**

| SELECTED STYLE CONSCIOUSNESS STATEMENTS | LOWER-CLASS AGREEMENT | LOWER-MIDDLE-CLASS AGREEMENT | UPPER-MIDDLE-CLASS AGREEMENT | UPPER-CLASS AGREEMENT |
|---|---|---|---|---|
| *product-specific statements* | | | | |
| Phones should come in patterns and designs as well as colors. | 60% | 80% | 63% | 58% |
| A telephone should improve the decorative style of a room. | 47 | 82 | 73 | 77% |
| Telephones should be modern in design. | 58 | 85 | 83 | 89% |
| A home should have a variety of telephone styles. | 8 | 46 | 39 | 51% |
| You can keep all those special phones, all I want is a phone that works. | 83 | 67 | 68 | 56% |
| The style of a telephone is unimportant to me. | 86 | 54 | 58 | 51% |
| *general-lifestyle statements* | | | | |
| Our home is furnished for comfort not style. | 96 | 87 | 79 | 79% |
| I have more modern appliances in my home than most people. | 17 | 23 | 41 | 48% |
| I prefer colored appliances. | 57 | 73 | 87 | 92% |

Source: Adapted from A. Marvin Roscoe, Jr., Arthur LeClaire, Jr., and Leon G. Schiffman, "Theory and Management Applications of Demographics in Buyer Behavior," in Arch G. Woodside, Jagdish N. Sheth, and Peter D. Bennett, eds., *Foundations of Consumer and Industrial Buying Behavior* (New York: American Elsevier, 1977), 74-75.

ers simply express a desire for a telephone that works. Thus lower middle class consumers might be an important market for new, stylish telephones. The table also suggests that *upper class* consumers would be the best market for a variety of telephone styles, particularly those that are modern in design. The three general lifestyle statements tapped a broader aspect of home decorating interests; findings suggest that *upper middle class* consumers have a greater preference for style than comfort in home decorations and that they are also more likely to buy colored appliances.

## The Pursuit of Leisure

For many products and services, social class membership is closely related to the choice of recreational and leisure-time activities. Research suggests that upper class consumers are likely to attend the theater and concerts, to play bridge, and to attend college football games. Lower-class consumers tend to be avid television watchers and fishing enthusiasts and enjoy attending drive-in movies and baseball games.[37] Furthermore, the lower-class consumer spends more time on commercial types of activities (bowling, playing pool or billiards, visiting taverns) and craft activities (model building, painting, woodworking projects).[38] Table 13-19 presents some additional evidence as to how the members of specific social classes differ in terms of their leisure-time activities.

## Saving, Spending, and Credit

Saving, spending, and credit-card usage all seem to be related to social class standing. Research suggests that upper-class consumers are future-oriented and confident of their financial acumen, to the extent that they are more willing to invest in insurance, stocks, and real estate. In comparison, lower-class consumers are more concerned with immediate gratification; when they do save, they are primarily interested in safety and security. A study which focused on bank credit-card usage found that members of the lower social classes tend to use their bank credit cards for installment purchases, while members of the upper social classes pay their credit card bills in full each month.[39] In other words, lower-class purchasers tend to use their credit cards to "buy now and pay later" for things they might not otherwise be able to afford, while upper-class purchasers use their credit cards as a convenient substitute for cash.

## Social Class and Communication

Social class groupings differ in terms of how they transmit and receive communications, and in their *media* habits. Knowledge of these differences is invaluable to marketers who segment markets on the basis of social class. It enables them to develop promotional strategies specifically designed to "penetrate" their prospects' perceptual screens.

**TABLE 13-19** Rank Order of Leisure Activities According to Social Class

| ACTIVITY | SOCIAL CLASS | |
|---|---|---|
| | middle | lower |
| Reading | 1 | 4 |
| Participation in sports | 2 | 3 |
| Television/radio | 3.5* | 1 |
| Outdoor recreation | 3.5 | 6 |
| Socializing/partying | 5 | 2 |
| Listening to music | 6 | 7 |
| Sewing/needlework | 7 | 8 |
| Resting/relaxing | 8.5 | 5 |
| Yardwork/gardening | 8.5 | 10 |
| Exercise | 10.5 | 13.5 |
| Traveling | 10.5 | 17 |
| Hobbies (painting, photography, models) | 12 | 11 |
| Games (cards, bingo, chess) | 13 | 9 |
| Cooking | 14 | 15 |
| Cultural activities | 15.5 | 22 |
| Volunteer activities | 15.5 | 16 |
| Auto/motorcycle repairs | 18.5 | 19 |
| Eating out/movies | 18.5 | 18 |
| Shopping | 18.5 | 13.5 |
| Watching sports | 18.5 | 21 |
| Household activities | 21 | 11 |
| Church | 22 | 20 |

*A number with .5 signifies two- or more-way tie.
Source: Spurgeon M. Stamps, Jr., and Miriam B. Stamps, "Race, Class and Leisure Activities of Urban Residents," *Journal of Leisure Research,* 17, 1 (1985), 46.

## COMMUNICATION PATTERNS

In describing their world, lower-class members tend to portray it in rather personal and concrete terms, while middle-class members are able to describe their experiences from a number of different perspectives. A simple example illustrates that members of different social classes tend to see the world differently. Following are the responses to a question asking where the respondent usually purchases chewing gum:[40]

> Upper-Middle-Class answer: "At a cashier's counter or in a grocery store."
> Lower-Middle-Class answer: "At the National or the corner drugstore."
> Lower-Class answer: "From Tony."

These variations in response indicate that middle-class consumers have a broader or more general view of the world, while lower-class consumers tend to see the world through their own immediate experience.

There also seem to be important social class differences in the *choice* of words used to describe things, people, and events. For example, one sociologist noted the following differences in word usage between lower- and upper-class members:[41]

| LOWER-CLASS USAGE | UPPER-CLASS EQUIVALENT |
|---|---|
| evening | afternoon |
| dinner | lunch |
| supper | dinner |

An awareness of such differences in language enables marketers to appeal more directly to their target markets with their advertising copy, their packaging, and their labeling.

Regional differences in terminology, choice of words and phrases, and patterns of usage also tend to increase as we move down the social class ladder.[42] Therefore, in targeting appeals to the lower classes, marketers should try to word advertisements to reflect any regional differences that exist.

### MEDIA EXPOSURE

There is evidence that *selective exposure* to various types of mass media differs by social class. Higher-class consumers tend to have greater exposure to magazines and newspapers than do their lower-class counterparts.[43] Lower-class consumers are likely to have greater exposure to publications that dramatize romance and the lifestyles of movie and television celebrities. For example, magazines such as *True Story* appeal heavily to blue-collar or working-class women, who enjoy reading about the problems, fame, and fortunes of others. Notice that in Table 13-5, *True Story* has the lowest median household income of all the publications listed. In the selection of specific television programs and program types, higher social class members tend to prefer current events and drama, while lower-class individuals tend to prefer soap operas, quiz shows, and situation comedies.[44]

## Retail Shopping

Consumers' shopping values, attitudes, and behavior are also influenced by social class. For example, although most women tend to enjoy shopping, their reasons vary by social class. A study of the shopping behavior of Cleveland women found that the *acquisition* of new clothing and household products was the principal enjoyment received by lower-class shoppers. In contrast, upper-middle-class and upper-class shoppers tended to enjoy the *act* of shopping itself (store atmosphere and displays) and tended to shop more frequently than lower-class women.[45]

Furthermore, while department stores attract a large portion of shoppers from all social classes, there is a definite tendency for higher-class women to favor traditional department stores, and lower-class women to patronize mass merchandisers. An analysis of the type of department store preferred by women from different social classes indicates that *price appeal stores* draw lower-class shoppers, *broad appeal stores* attract middle-class shoppers, and stores that feature a *high-fashion image* are preferred by upper-class shoppers.[46]

A study that investigated the retail preferences of different social classes found that upper-class consumers prefer department and specialty stores for items they perceive to be *socially risky,* but are willing to use discount stores for other items.[47] On the other hand, lower-class consumers are willing to patronize discounters for products of both high and low social risk. The study indicates that discounters have successfully developed acceptance across class boundaries for a wide range of products with low social risk. However, they have not attracted large numbers of upper-class consumers for products that can be classified as socially risky (such as clothing or conspicuous home furnishings).

Finally, there is evidence that in-home consumers—those who purchase from a catalog, by mail, or by telephone—are socioeconomically different from those who rely solely on retail stores.[48] The results indicate that in-home consumers tend to have high family incomes, white-collar occupations, and more formal education than consumers who do not shop at home. These findings suggest that middle- and upper-class consumers are a fertile market for direct mail and telephone marketing.

## *summary*

Social stratification—the division of members of a society into a hierarchy of distinct social classes—exists in all societies and cultures. *Social class* is usually defined by the amount of status that members of a specific class possess in relation to members of other classes. Social class membership often serves as a frame of reference (a reference group) for the development of consumer attitudes and behavior.

The measurement of social class is concerned with classifying individuals into social class groupings. These groupings are of particular value to marketers, who use social classification as an effective means to identify and segment target markets.

There are three basic methods for measuring social class: subjective measurement, reputational measurement, and objective measurement. Subjective measures rely on an individual's self-perception, reputational measures rely on an individual's perceptions of others, and objective measures use specific socioeconomic measures, either alone (as a single-variable index) or in combination with others (as a composite-variable index). Composite-variable indexes combine a number of socioeconomic factors to form one overall measure of social class standing.

Class structures range from two-class to nine-class systems. A frequently used classification system consists of six classes: upper-upper, lower-upper, upper-middle, lower-middle, upper-lower, and lower-lower. Profiles of each of these classes indicate that the socioeconomic differences between classes are reflected in differences in attitudes, in leisure activities, and in consumption habits. That is why segmentation by social class is of special interest to marketers.

In recent years some marketers have turned to geodemographic clustering as an alternative to a strict social class typology. Geodemographic clustering is a technique that combines geography and socioeconomic factors to locate concentrations of consumers with particular characteristics. Particular attention is currently being directed to affluent consumers, who represent the fastest-growing segment in our population.

Research has revealed social class differences in clothing habits, home decoration, telephone usage, leisure activities, retail patronage, and saving, spending, and credit habits. Thus the astute marketer will differentiate product and promotional strategies for each social class target segment.

## *discussion questions*

1. Think of the weekly or monthly magazine you most enjoy reading. In approximately 50 words, describe the audience to whom this publication is targeted. Then determine whether this publication's appeal is to a social class, an income class, or a geodemographic cluster.
2. Marketing researchers have generally used the objective method to measure social class, rather than the subjective or reputational methods. Why has the objective method been preferred by researchers?
3. What is the principal drawback of evaluating a family's social class position exclusively in terms of the male head of household?
4. Under what circumstances would you expect income to be a better predictor of consumer behavior than a composite measure of social class (based on income, education, and occupation)? On the other hand, when would you expect the composite social class measure to be superior?
5. Consider the Rolex watch, which has a retail price of about a thousand dollars for a stainless steel model to thousands of dollars for a solid gold model. How might the Rolex company make use of geodemographic clustering in its marketing efforts?

6. If you were invited to a family's home for the first time, what factors might you consider in making an estimate of their social class standing? Explain.
7. Everybody (or almost everybody) has a telephone, and most people periodically make long distance calls. Why is it necessary, therefore, for AT&T to develop different promotional materials for different socioeconomic groups?
8. What information contained in this chapter might help Apple sell its computers to individuals for household (nonbusiness) use?

## *endnotes*


1. Robert W. Hodges, Paul M. Siegel, and Peter H. Rossi, "Occupational Prestige in the United States, 1925–1963," *American Journal of Sociology,* 70 (November 1964), 286–302.
2. David Popenoe, *Sociology,* 2nd ed. (Englewood Cliffs, N.J.: Prentice-Hall, 1974), 251–58.
3. Marcus Felson, "A Modern Sociological Approach to the Stratification of Material Life Styles," in Mary Jane Schlinger, ed., *Advances in Consumer Research* (Association for Consumer Research, 1975), II, 34.
4. Richard Centers, *The Psychology of Social Class* (New York: Russell and Russell, 1961), 233.
5. Hadley Cantril, "Identification with Social and Economic Class," *Journal of Abnormal and Social Psychology,* 38 (January 1943), 75–79.
6. W. Lloyd Warner, Marchia Meeker, and Kenneth Eells, *Social Class in America: Manual of Procedure for the Measurement of Social Status* (New York: Harper & Brothers, 1960).
7. Donald J. Treiman, *Occupational Prestige in Comparative Perspective* (New York: Academic Press, 1977), 306–15.
8. Stephen J. Miller, "Source of Income as a Market Descriptor," *Journal of Marketing Research,* 15 (February 1978), 129–31.
9. Chester R. Wasson, "Is It Time to Quit Thinking of Income Classes?" *Journal of Marketing,* 33 (April 1969), 54–57.
10. F. Stuart Chapin, *Contemporary American Institutions* (New York: Harper, 1935), 373–97.
11. Warner, Meeker, and Eells, *Social Class in America.*
12. *Methodology and Scores of Socioeconomic Status,* Working Paper No. 15 (Washington, D.C.: U.S. Bureau of the Census, 1963).
13. Marie R. Haug, "Social Class Measurement and Women's Occupational Role," *Social Forces,* 52 (September 1973), 92.
14. Richard P. Coleman and Bernice L. Neugarten, *Social Status in the City* (San Francisco: Jossey Bass, 1971), IX; and William W. Philliber and Dana V. Hiller, "A Research Note: Occupational Attainments and Perceptions of Status among Working Wives," *Journal of Marriage and the Family,* 41 (February 1979), 59–62.

15. See Arun K. Jain, "A Method for Investigating and Representing Implicit Social Class Theory," *Journal of Consumer Research,* 2 (June 1975), 53–59; Peter H. Rossi, William A. Sampson, Christine E. Bose, Guillermina Jasso, and Jeff Passel, "Measuring Household Social Standing," *Social Science Research,* 3 (1974), 169–90; and Terence A. Shimp and J. Thomas Yokum, "Extensions of the Basic Social Class Model Employed in Consumer Behavior," in Kent Monroe, ed., *Advances in Consumer Research* (Ann Arbor, Mich.: Association for Consumer Research, 1981), VIII, 702–07.

16. James H. Myers, Roger R. Stanton, and Arne F. Haug, "Correlates of Buying Behavior: Social Class vs. Income," *Journal of Marketing,* 35 (October 1971), 8–15.

17. James H. Myers and John F. Mount, "More on Social Class vs. Income as Correlates of Buying Behavior," *Journal of Marketing,* 37 (April 1973), 71–73.

18. Robert D. Hisrich and Michael P. Peters, "Selecting the Superior Segmentation Correlate," *Journal of Marketing,* 38 (July 1974), 60–63.

19. James H. Myers and Jonathan Gutman, "Life Style: The Essence of Social Class," in William D. Wells, ed., *Life Style and Psychographics* (Chicago: American Marketing Association, 1974), 235–56.

20. J. Michael Munson and V. Austin Spivey, "Product and Brand User Stereotypes among Social Classes," in Monroe, *Advances in Consumer Research,* VIII, 696–701.

21. Richard P. Coleman, "The Continuing Significance of Social Class to Marketing," *Journal of Consumer Research,* 10 (December 1983), 274.

22. Richard P. Coleman "The Significance of Social Stratification in Selling," in Martin L. Bell, ed., *Marketing: A Mature Discipline* (Chicago: American Marketing Association, 1961), 171–84. William H. Peters, "Relative Occupational Class Income: A Significant Variable in the Marketing of Automobiles," *Journal of Marketing,* 34 (April 1970), 74–77, and R. Eugene Klippel and John F. Monoky, Jr., "A Potential Segmentation Variable for Marketers: Relative Occupation Class Income," *Journal of the Academy of Marketing Science,* 2 (Spring 1974), 351–56.

23. The social class profiles in this section are drawn from a variety of sources, including Coleman and Neugarten, *Social Status*; Harold M. Hodges, Jr., "Peninsula People: Social Stratification in a Metropolitan Complex," in Clayton Lane, ed., *Permanence and Change* (Cambridge, Mass.: Schenkman, 1969), 5–36; Saxon Graham, "Class and Conservatism in the Adoption of Innovations," *Human Relations,* 9 (February 1956), 91–100, and *A Study of Working-Class Women in a Changing World* (prepared for Macfadden-Bartell Corporation by Social Science Research, Inc., May 1973).

24. *Prism Creditrend* (brochure), Claritas Corporation, 1984; and *Magazine Newsletter of Research,* Number 48 (New York: Magazine Publishers Association, December 1984), 1.

25. "The Gold Plated Consumer," *Marketing Communications,* December 1984, 23–27.

26. *Affluence 1985–1986* (1985 Survey of Adults and Markets of Affluence, Mendelsohn Media Research, Inc., 1985), 1, 2, 17.

27. Ronald Alsop, "Wealth of Affluent Magazines Vie for Advertisers' Attention," *The Wall Street Journal,* January 9, 1986, 23.

28. *How to Get to the Rich Quick* (brochure), Mediamark Research, Inc., 1985.

29. Ibid.

30. Epictetus, *Discourses* (second century), 31, trans. Thomas Higginson.

31. Stuart U. Rich and Subhash C. Jain, "Social Class and Life Cycle as Predictors of Shopping Behavior," *Journal of Marketing Research,* 5 (February 1968), 43–44.

32. Paul Fussell, *Class* (New York: Ballantine Books, 1983), 52–74.

33. William D. Wells, "Seven Questions about Life Style and Psychographics," in Boris W. Bunker and Helmut Becker, eds., *1972 Combined Proceedings* (Chicago: American Marketing Association, 1973), 464.

34. Burleigh B. Gardner, "Social Status and Consumer Behavior," in Lincoln H. Clark, ed., *The Life Cycle and Consumer Behavior* (New York: New York University Press, 1955), 58.

35. Edward O. Laumann and James S. House, "Living Room Styles and Social Attributes: The Patterning of Material Artifacts in a Modern Urban Community," *Sociology and Social Research,* 54 (April 1970), 324–27; and Joan Kron, *Home-Psych* (New York: Potter, 1983), 90–102.

36. A. Marvin Roscoe, Jr., Arthur LeClaire, Jr., and Leon G. Schiffman, "Theory and Management Applications of Demographics in Buyer Behavior," in Arch. G. Woodside, Jagdish N. Sheth, and Peter D. Bennett, eds., *Foundations of Consumer and Industrial Buying Behavior* (New York: American Elsevier, 1977), 67–76.

37. William R. Cotton, Jr., "Leisure and Social Stratification," in Gerald W. Thielbar and Saul D. Feldman, eds., *Issues in Social Inequality* (Boston: Little, Brown, 1972), 520–38.

38. Alfred C. Clarke, "Leisure and Occupational Prestige," *American Sociological Review,* 21 (June 1956), 305–6; and Robert B. Settle, Pamela L. Alreck, and Michael A. Belch, "Social Class Determinants of Leisure Activity," in William L. Wilkie, ed., *Advances in Consumer Research* (Ann Arbor, Mich.: Association for Consumer Research, 1979), VI, 139–45.

39. H. Lee Mathews and John W. Slocum, Jr., "Social Class and Commercial Bank Credit Usage," *Journal of Marketing,* 33 (January 1969), 71–78.

40. Leonard Schatzman and Anselm Strauss, "Social Class and Modes of Communication," *American Journal of Sociology,* 60 (January 1955), 329–38.

41. John Kenneth Morland, *Millways of Kent* (Chapel Hill: University of North Carolina Press, 1958), 192, 277.

42. Thomas E. Lasswell, *Class and Stratum* (Boston: Houghton Mifflin, 1965), 231.

43. Leah Rozen, "Coveted Consumers Rate Magazines over TV: MPA," *Advertising Age,* August 20, 1979, 64.

44. Sidney J. Levy, "Social Class and Consumer Behavior," in Joseph W. Newman, ed., *On Knowing the Consumer* (New York: Wiley, 1966), 155.

45. Rich and Jain, "Social Class," 44.

46. Ibid., 46.

47. V. Kanti Prasad, "Socioeconomic Product Risk and Patronage Preferences of Retail Shoppers," *Journal of Marketing,* 39 (July 1975), 42–47.

48. Peter L. Gillett, "A Profile of Urban In-Home Shoppers," *Journal of Marketing,* 34 (July 1970), 40–45.

14

# The Influence of Culture on Consumer Behavior

## *introduction*

THE study of **culture** is a challenging undertaking because its primary focus is on the broadest component of social behavior—an entire society. In contrast to the psychologist, who is principally concerned with the study of individual behavior, or the sociologist, who is concerned with the study of groups, the **anthropologist** is primarily interested in identifying the very fabric of society itself.

This chapter explores the basic concepts of culture, with particular emphasis on the role culture plays in influencing consumer behavior in American society. We will first consider the specific dimensions of culture that make it a powerful force in regulating human behavior. After reviewing several measurement approaches that researchers employ in their efforts to understand the impact of culture on consumption behavior, we will show how a variety of core American cultural values influence consumer behavior.

This chapter is concerned with the more general aspects of culture; the following chapter focuses on **subcultures** and on foreign cultures, and will show how marketers can use such knowledge to shape and modify their marketing strategies.

## WHAT IS CULTURE?

Given the broad and pervasive nature of culture, its study generally requires a global examination of the character of the total society, including such factors

> *Culture is not an exotic notion studied by a select group of anthropologists in the South Seas. It is a mold in which we are all cast, and it controls our daily lives in many unsuspected ways.*
>
> EDWARD T. HALL
> *The Silent Language* (1959)

as language, knowledge, laws, religions, food customs, music, art, technology, work patterns, products, and other artifacts which give the society its distinctive flavor. In a sense, culture is a society's *personality*. For this reason, it is not easy to define its boundaries.

Since our specific objective is to understand the influence of culture on consumer behavior, we will define *culture* as the *sum total of learned beliefs, values and customs which serve to regulate the consumer behavior of members of a particular society.*

The *belief* and *value* components of our definition refer to the accumulated feelings and priorities that individuals have about "things." More precisely, **beliefs** consist of the very large number of mental or verbal statements (i.e., "I believe that . . . ") which reflect a person's particular knowledge and assessment of *something* (another person, a store, perhaps a product, a brand). **Values** are also beliefs. However, values differ from other beliefs in that they meet the following criteria: (1) They are *relatively few* in number; (2) they serve as a guide for *culturally appropriate* behavior; (3) they are *enduring* or difficult to change; (4) they are *not tied to specific objects* or situations; and (5) they are *widely accepted* by the members of a society.[1]

Therefore, in a broad sense, both beliefs and values are *mental images* that affect a wide range of specific attitudes, which in turn influence the way a person is likely to respond in a specific situation. For example, the criteria a person employs in evaluating alternative brands (e.g., a Bulova versus a Seiko watch) and his or her eventual conclusions concerning these brands, are influenced by that person's specific beliefs and more general values (mental images related to quality, workmanship, status, accuracy, and design and esthetics).

Figure 14-1 presents a simple conceptualization of a consumer value sys-

**FIGURE 14-1** **A Model of Consumers' Value-Belief Systems** Source: Donald E. Vinson, Jerome E. Scott, and Lawrence M. Lamont, "The Role of Personal Values in Marketing and Consumer Behavior," *Journal of Marketing,* 41 (April 1977), 46.

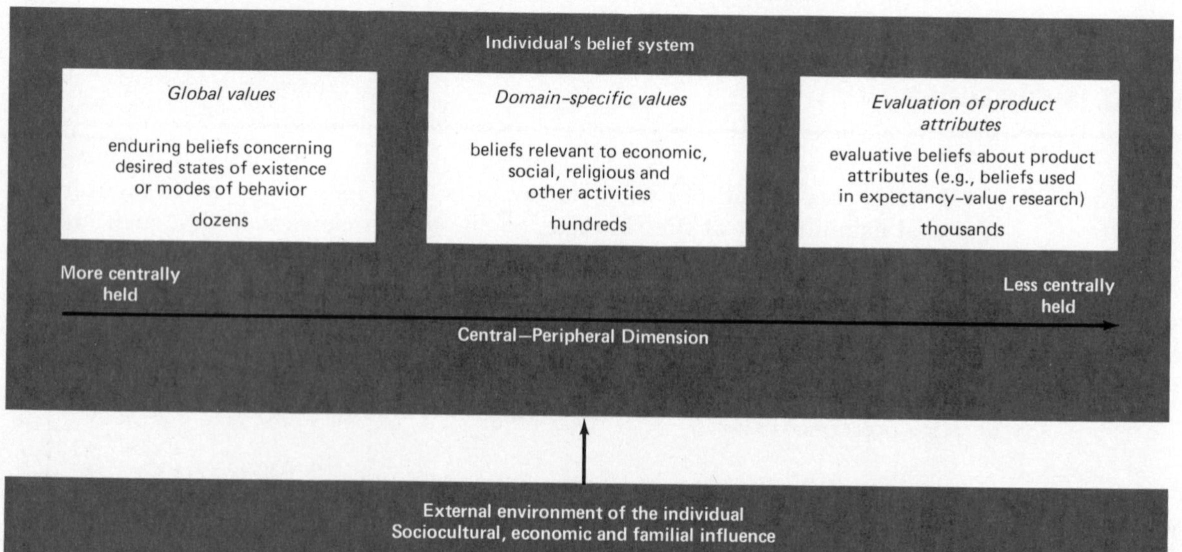

tem that consists of three interrelated belief components: a very small number of *global values* that guide behavior across a wide range of situations (e.g., "It is better to give than to receive"); a small number of *domain-specific values* people acquire as part of their experience in specific situations, such as aspects of economic, social, and religious life ("It's important to save money"); and a large number of *evaluative beliefs* about product categories and brands that are important components of consumer attitudes ("Epson printers last forever"). The figure also indicates that a consumer's belief system is produced and altered through exposure to the external environment.[2]

In comparison with beliefs and values, **customs** are *overt modes of behavior that constitute culturally approved or acceptable ways of behaving in specific situations.* Customs have been called ". . . behavior at its most commonplace."[3] For example, a consumer's routine behavior, such as serving lemon with diet colas or going to the bank on Fridays, involves customs. Thus, while beliefs and values are *guides* for behavior, customs are *usual and acceptable ways of behaving.*

Within the context of our definition, it is easy to see how an understanding of the beliefs, values, and customs of a society enables marketers to accurately anticipate consumer acceptance of their products.

## CHARACTERISTICS OF CULTURE

To more fully comprehend the scope and complexity of culture, it is useful to examine a number of its underlying characteristics.

### The Invisible Hand of Culture

The impact of culture is so natural and so automatic that its influence on behavior is usually taken for granted. For example, when consumer researchers ask people why they do certain things, they frequently answer, "Because it's the right thing to do." This seemingly superficial response partially reflects the ingrained influence of culture on our behavior. Frequently, it is only when we are exposed to people with different cultural values or customs (e.g., when visiting a different region or a different country) that we become aware of how culture has molded our own behavior. The following statement dramatically illustrates the invisible nature of culture and the difficulties of objectively studying its impact on human behavior:

> It has been said that the last thing which a dweller in the deep sea would be likely to discover would be water. He would become conscious of its existence only if some accident brought him to the surface and introduced him to air. Man, throughout most of his history, has been only vaguely conscious of the existence of culture and has owed even this consciousness to contrasts between the customs of his own society and those of some other with which he happened to be brought into contact.[4]

Thus a true appreciation of the influence culture has on our daily life requires some knowledge of at least one other society with different cultural characteristics. For example, to understand that brushing our teeth twice a day with flavored toothpaste is a cultural phenomenon requires some awareness that members of another society either do not brush their teeth at all or do so in a manner distinctly different from our own.

## Culture Satisfies Needs

Culture exists to satisfy the needs of the people within a society. It offers *order, direction,* and *guidance* in all phases of human problem solving by providing "tried and true" methods of satisfying physiological, personal, and social needs. For example, culture provides standards and "rules" regarding when to eat, where to eat, and what is appropriate to eat for breakfast, lunch, dinner, and snacks, and what to serve to guests at a dinner party, a picnic, or a wedding. The White Castle fast-food chain, as part of a marketing strategy centered on its famous hamburgers, has hoped to influence its loyal customers by a display sign which states: "Why not have White Castles for breakfast!" Because most Americans do not consider hamburgers as suitable breakfast food, White Castle's real challenge is to overcome culture, not competition.

Cultural beliefs, values, and customs continue to be followed so long as they yield satisfaction. However, when a specific standard no longer satisfies the members of a society, it is modified or replaced, so that the resulting standard is more in line with current needs and desires. Thus culture gradually but continually *evolves* to meet the needs of society.

Within a cultural context, a firm's products and services can be viewed as offering appropriate or acceptable solutions for individual or societal needs. If a product is no longer acceptable because a value or custom that is related to its use does not adequately satisfy human needs, then the firm producing it must be ready to adjust or revise its product offerings. Marketers must also be alert to newly embraced customs and values. For example, as Americans have become more health- and fitness-conscious, there has been an increase in the number of walkers, joggers, and runners crowding the nation's streets and roads. Astute shoe manufacturers who responded by offering an increased variety of appropriate footwear have been able to improve their market positions. In contrast, marketers who were not perceptive enough to note the opportunities created by changing values and lifestyles lost market share and, in some cases, were squeezed out of the market.

## Culture Is Learned

Unlike innate biological characteristics (e.g., sex, skin, hair color, intelligence), culture is *learned.* At an early age we begin to acquire from our social environment a set of beliefs, values, and customs that constitute our culture.

## HOW IS CULTURE LEARNED?

Anthropologists have identified three distinct forms of cultural learning: **formal learning**, in which adults and older siblings teach a young family member "how to behave"; **informal learning**, in which a child learns primarily by imitating the behavior of selected others (family, friends, TV heroes); and **technical learning**, in which teachers instruct the child in an educational environment as to *what* should be done, *how* it should be done, and *why* it should be done.[5]

A little boy who is told by his mother to stop playing house because "Boys don't do that" is *formally* learning a value his mother feels is right. If he "dresses up" by copying his father or older brother, he is *informally* learning certain dress habits (see Figure 14-2). Finally, if he is given karate lessons, he is experiencing *technical* learning.

Although a firm's advertising can influence all three types of cultural learning, it is likely that many product advertisements enhance informal cultural learning by providing the audience with a model of behavior to imitate. For instance, in Figure 14-3, the Soloflex advertisement is attempting to communicate the muscular or fitness benefit that may result from the use of its exercise machines. Inclusion in the advertisement of the especially fit and well-respected boxer Ken Norton enhances the notion that the exercise machine is a serious fitness product. Most important, the ad provides a "model" for the target audience to imitate.

The repetition of advertising messages creates and/or reinforces cultural beliefs and values. For example, many advertisers continually stress the same selected benefits as integral features of their products or brands. To illustrate, ads for computer floppy disks often stress one or more of the following benefits: superior internal construction, better quality materials, lifetime warranty, reliability. After several years of cumulative exposure to such potent advertising appeals, it is difficult to say with any degree of certainty whether computer owners *inherently* desire these benefits from floppy disks or whether they have been *taught* by marketers to desire them. In a sense, while specific product advertising may reinforce the benefits consumers want from the product (as determined by consumer behavior research), such advertising also "teaches" future generations of consumers to expect the same benefits from the product category.

## ENCULTURATION AND ACCULTURATION

In discussing the acquisition of culture, anthropologists often distinguish between the learning of one's own or *native* culture and the learning of some other culture. The learning of one's own culture is known as **enculturation**. The learning of a new or foreign culture is known as **acculturation**. In the next chapter we will see that acculturation is an important concept for marketers who plan to sell their products in foreign or multinational markets. In such cases, marketers must study the specific culture(s) of their potential target markets in order to determine whether their products will be acceptable to its mem-

FIGURE 14-2 Advertisement That Illustrates Informal Cultural Learning

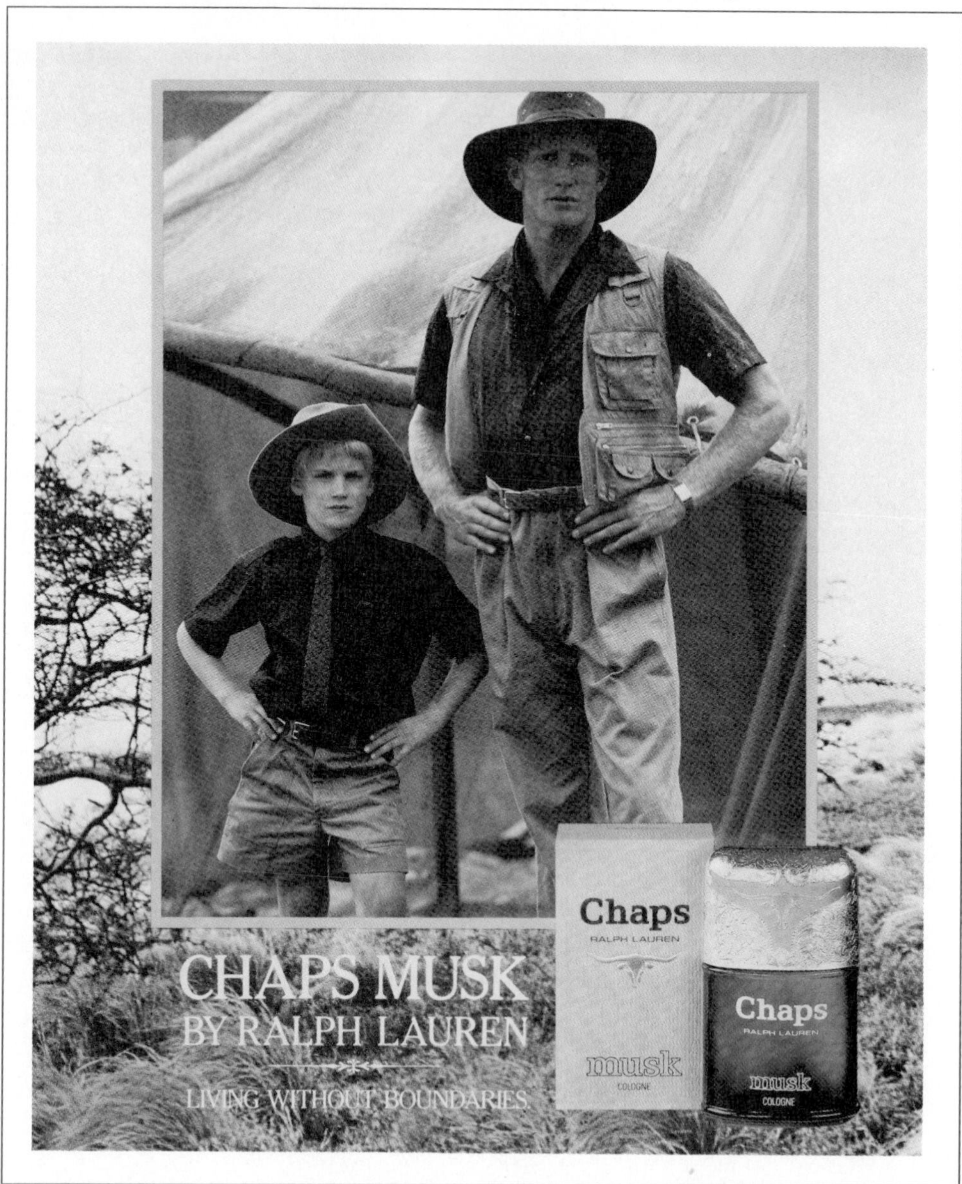


Courtesy of Cosmair, Inc. Photograph courtesy of Bruce Weber

bers, and if so, how they can best communicate the characteristics of their products to persuade the target market to buy.

## LANGUAGE AND SYMBOLS

To acquire a common culture, the members of a society must be able to communicate with each other through a common language. Without a common

FIGURE 14-3 Advertisement That Reinforces Informal Cultural Learning

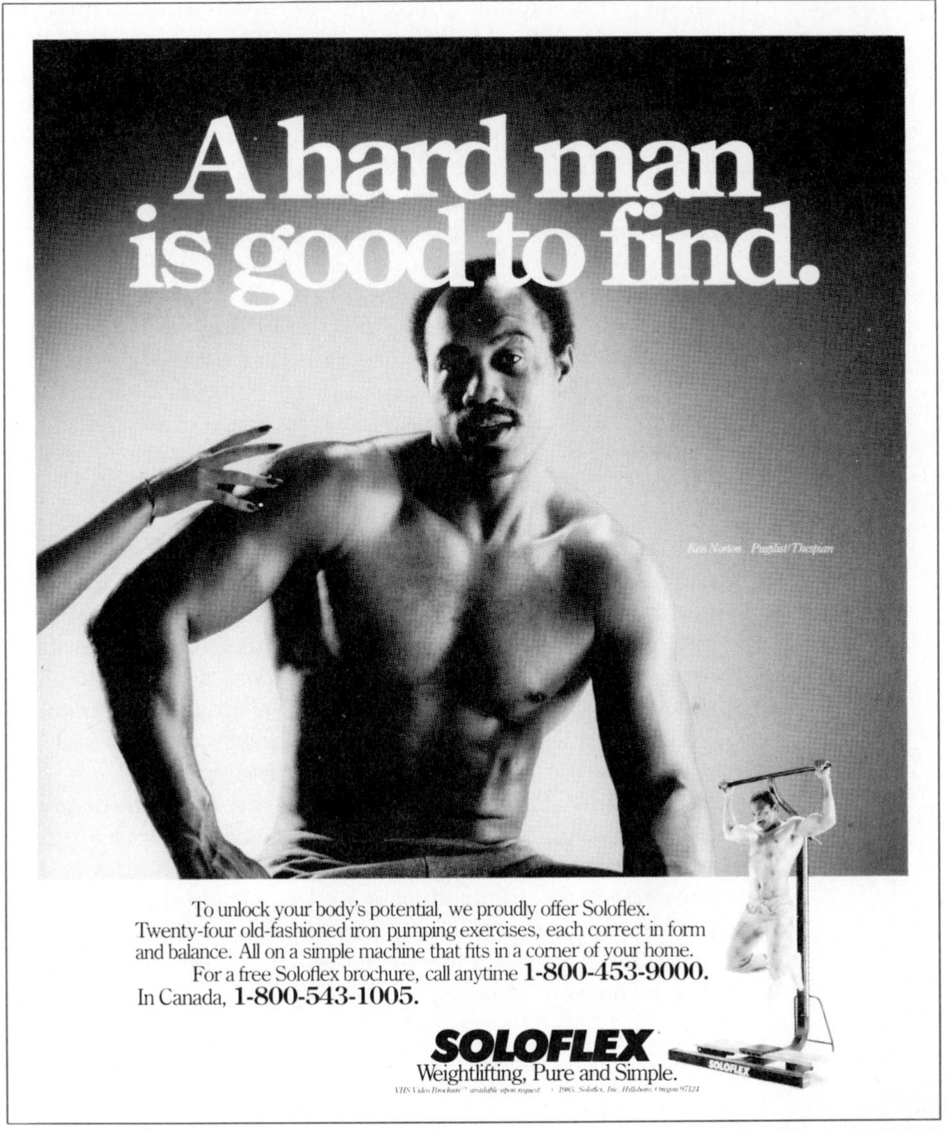


Courtesy of Soloflex Inc.

language, shared meaning could not exist and true communication would not take place (see Chapter 10).

To communicate effectively with their audiences, marketers must use appropriate **symbols** to convey desired product images or characteristics. These symbols can be *verbal* or *nonverbal*. Verbal symbols may include a television announcement or an advertisement in a magazine. Nonverbal communication includes the use of such symbols as figures, colors, shapes, and even textures to provide additional meaning to print or broadcast advertisements, to trademarks, and to packaging or product designs.

Basically, it is the symbolic nature of human language that sets it apart from all other animal communication. A *symbol* is anything that stands for something else.[6] Any word is a symbol. The word *razor* calls forth a specific image related to an individual's own knowledge and experience. The word *hurricane* not only calls forth the notion of wind and rain, but also has the power to stir us emotionally, arousing feelings of danger and the need for protection and safety. Similarly, the word *jaguar* has symbolic meaning; to some it suggests a fine luxury automobile, to others it implies wealth and status, to still others it suggests an animal to be seen at the zoo.

Because the human mind can process symbols, it is possible for a person to experience an advertisement for a product such as Michelin tires (see Figure 14-4) and understand that the placing of the baby in close proximity to the tire is a visual reinforcement of the point that choosing the right tires is a very important decision. The capacity to learn symbolically is primarily a human phenomenon; most other animals learn by direct experience. Clearly, the ability of humans to understand symbolically how a product or an idea may satisfy their needs makes it easier for marketers to "sell" the features and benefits of their products.

Inasmuch as a symbol may have several meanings, even contradictory ones, it is important that the advertiser ascertain exactly what the symbols are communicating to an intended audience. For example, the advertiser who uses a trademark depicting an old craftsman to symbolize careful workmanship may instead be communicating an image of old age, outmoded methods, and lack of style. The marketer who uses slang in an advertisement to attract a teenage audience must do so with great care. Slang that is misused or outdated will symbolically date the marketer's firm and product.

Price and channels of distribution are also significant symbols of the marketer and the marketer's product. For example, price often implies quality to potential buyers (see Chapter 6). For certain products (e.g., clothing), the type of store in which the product is sold is also an important symbol of quality. In fact, all the elements of the marketing mix—the product, its promotion, price, and the stores at which it is available—are symbols that communicate ranges of quality to potential buyers.

## RITUAL

In addition to language and symbols, culture includes various ritualized experiences and behaviors that until recently have been neglected by consumer researchers. A **ritual** is a type of symbolic activity consisting of a series of steps (*multiple behaviors*) occurring in a fixed sequence and repeated over time.[7]

In practice, rituals extend over the human life cycle—from birth to death, including a host of intermediate events (e.g., confirmation, graduations, marriage). They can be very public, elaborate religious or civil ceremonies, or they can be as mundane as an individual's grooming behavior.[8] Ritualized behavior is typically rather formal, and is often scripted behavior (e.g., a religious service requiring a prayerbook, or the code of proper conduct in a court of law). It is also likely to occur repeatedly over time (e.g., singing the national anthem before a baseball game).

FIGURE 14-4 Advertisement Incorporating Symbolic Learning

Courtesy of Michelin Tire Corporation

Most important from the standpoint of marketers, rituals tend to be replete with ritual *artifacts* (products) that are associated with or somehow enhance performance of the ritual. For instance, a tree, stockings, and various food items are linked to the ritual of Christmas celebration; other rituals (such as a graduation, a wedding, the Thursday night card game, or the Saturday afternoon visit to the beauty parlor) have their own specific artifacts associated with them (see Table 14-1). Even the two-piece business suit worn by many women executives has been deemed a ritual artifact of our present society.[9] To

**TABLE 14-1 Selected Rituals and Associated Artifacts**

| SELECTED RITUALS | TYPICAL ARTIFACTS |
|---|---|
| Graduation | Pen, U.S. savings bond, car, typewriter |
| Birth of child | Bank account, silver baby spoon |
| Sunday football | Beer, potato chips, pretzels |
| First wedding | Wedding ring, white gown, honeymoon |
| Retirement | Company party, watch, plaque |
| Grooming | Various personal care products (for hair, face, skin, eyes, beard, nails) |
| Fishing trip | New fishing equipment, rental of a cabin, fun foods |

illustrate how relatively mundane a ritual can be, Table 14-2 presents a brief description of the weekly nail care ritual (part of the overall grooming ritual) of a teenage girl.

## Culture Is Shared

To be considered a cultural characteristic, a particular belief, value, or practice must be shared by a significant portion of the society. Accordingly, culture is frequently viewed as *group customs* that link together the members of a society. Of course, common language is the critical cultural component that makes it possible for people to share values, experience, and customs.

Various social institutions within a society transmit the elements of culture and make the sharing of culture a reality. Chief among such institutions is the *family*, which serves as the primary agent for enculturation—the passing along of basic cultural beliefs, values, and customs to society's newest members. A vital part of the enculturation role of the family is the consumer socialization of the young (see Chapter 12). This includes the teaching of such basic consumer-related values and skills as the meaning of money, the relationship between price and quality, the establishment of product tastes, preferences, and habits, and appropriate methods of response to various promotional messages.

In addition to the family, two other institutions traditionally share much of the responsibility for the transfer of selected aspects of culture—the *school* and the *church*. Educational institutions are specifically charged with imparting basic learning skills, history, patriotism, citizenship, and the technical training needed to prepare people for significant roles within society. Religious institutions provide and perpetuate religious consciousness, spiritual guidance, and moral training. Although it is in the family environment that the young receive much of their consumer training, the educational and religious systems reinforce such training through the teaching of economic and ethical concepts.

A fourth, frequently overlooked, social institution that plays a major role in the transfer of culture throughout society is the *mass media*. Given the extensive exposure of the American population to both print and broadcast media, and the easily ingested, entertaining format in which the contents of such media are usually presented, it is not surprising that the mass media are a powerful vehicle for imparting a wide range of cultural values.

**TABLE 14-2 Steps in a Teenage Girl's Weekly Nail Care Ritual**

1. I remove my old polish with Cutex nail polish remover.
2. Then I take an emery board and file my nails till they are all round and I push my cuticles back with the file.
3. Next, I wash my hands in burning hot water with soap; and while I let the water run on them I continue to push back the cuticles.
4. Then I take Oil of Olay cream and put it all over my hands, still pushing back my cuticles with the file.
5. Then I coat my nails with Develop 10, which is my base coat. It helps strengthen my nails to prevent peeling and breaking.
6. Next, I use two coats of color polish. I usually use Revlon because I prefer it.
7. Then I finish it all off with a top coat of Develop 10 to seal all of it.
8. Finally, every night I put one top coat of Develop 10 on, and at the end of the week I start all over again.

Advertising is an important component of most mass media to which we are exposed daily. It not only underwrites or makes economically feasible the editorial or programming contents of the media, but also transmits much about our culture. Without advertising, it would be almost impossible to disseminate information about products, ideas, and causes. A leading historian noted: ". . . advertising now compares with such long-standing institutions as the schools and the church in the magnitude of its social influence."[10]

Consumers receive important cultural information from advertising. For example, it has been hypothesized that one of the roles of advertising in sophisticated magazines such as the *New Yorker* is to instruct readers how to dress, how to decorate their homes, and what foods and wines to serve guests—in other words, what types of behavior are most appropriate to their particular social class.[11]

Thus, while the scope of advertising is often considered to be limited to influencing the demand for specific products or services, in a cultural context advertising has the expanded mission of reinforcing established cultural values and aiding in the dissemination of new tastes, habits, and customs. In planning their advertising, marketers should recognize that advertising is an important agent of social change in our society.

## Culture Is Dynamic

To fulfill its need-gratifying role, culture must continually evolve if it is to function in the best interests of a society. For this reason, the marketer must carefully monitor the socio-cultural environment in order to market an existing product more effectively, or to develop promising new products.

This is not an easy task, since many factors are likely to produce cultural changes within a given society (new technology, population shifts, resource shortages, wars, changing values, customs borrowed from other cultures). For example, a major cultural change in our society is the expanding role choices of American females. In the 1980s, it is expected that most women will work outside the home, frequently in careers that once were considered exclusively male (see Figure 14-5). Also, women are increasingly active in social and ath-

FIGURE 14-5 Advertisement Illustrating the Blurring of Traditional Sex Roles

letic activities outside the home. All this adds up to a blurring of traditional male-female sex roles. These changes mean that marketers must reconsider *who* are the purchasers and the users of their products (males only, females only, or both), *when* they do their shopping, *how* and *where* they can be reached by the media, and *what* new product and service needs are emerging.

FIGURE 14-6 Advertisement Pointing Up the Changing Nature of Culture

The American Express Card.
It's part of a lot of interesting lives.

Courtesy of American Express Co.

Marketers who monitor cultural changes often find new opportunities to increase corporate profitability. For example, American Express has been targeting a portion of its advertising budget to women for more than ten years (see Figure 14–6). Not too long ago, credit card advertising was almost exclusively directed to male heads-of-household. But the cultural changes implicit in the increased number of working women and the increased number of executive and professional women have justified such marketing efforts. Marketers of life insurance, leisure wear, toy electric trains, and small cigars, among others, have attempted to take advantage of the dramatically shifting definition of what is "feminine." This sex-role shift has also had an impact on traditional male roles. For instance, as Chapter 1 pointed out, today cosmetic firms are successfully marketing skincare and other cosmetic products to men. Other aspects of the impact of changing sex roles on consumer behavior will be examined in Chapter 15 as part of the discussion of **subculture**.

## THE MEASUREMENT OF CULTURE

A wide range of measurement techniques are employed in the study of culture. Some of these techniques have already been described in earlier chapters. For example, the *projective tests* used by psychologists to study motivation and personality (discussed in Chapters 3 and 4), and the *attitude measurement techniques* used by social psychologists and sociologists (Chapter 8), are relatively popular tools in the study of culture.

In addition, **observational fieldwork, content analysis,** and **value measurement instruments** are three data collection techniques that are frequently associated with the examination of culture.

### Observational Fieldwork

In examining a specific society, anthropologists frequently immerse themselves in the environment under study. As trained observers, they are likely to select a small sample of people from a particular society and carefully observe their behavior. Based upon their observations, they draw conclusions about the values, beliefs, and customs of the society under investigation. To illustrate, if researchers were interested in how people select a videocassette to rent, they might position trained observers in video-movie rental stores and note how specific types of cassettes are selected ("hit" movies versus classics, action versus horror films, cartoons versus porno flicks). The researchers might also be interested in the degree of indecision that accompanies the choice; that is, how frequently consumers tend to hesitate (take a cassette off the shelf, read the description, place it back again) before selecting the cassette they finally rent.

The distinct characteristics of **field observation** are (1) it takes place within a natural environment, (2) it is sometimes performed without the subjects' awareness, and (3) it focuses on observation of behavior. Since the emphasis is on a natural environment and observable behavior, field observation concerned with consumer behavior is usually limited to in-store behavior, and only rarely to in-home preparation and consumption. In some cases, instead of just observing behavior, researchers become **participant-observers** (that is, they become an active member of the environment they are studying). For example, if a researcher were interested in examining how women select new clothes, the researcher might take a sales position in a women's clothing store in order to observe directly and even interact with customers in the transaction process.

Both field observation and participant-observer research require highly skilled researchers who can separate their own emotions from what they actually observe in their roles as researchers. Both techniques provide valuable insights that might not easily be obtained through survey research that simply asks consumers questions about their behavior.

## Content Analysis

Conclusions about a society, or specific aspects of a society, can sometimes be drawn from an examination of the content of its messages. *Content analysis*, as its name implies, focuses on the content of verbal and pictorial communications (e.g., the copy and art components of an ad).[12]

Content analysis can be used as an objective means for determining whether social and cultural changes have occurred within a specific society. For instance, the next chapter discusses the results of several content analysis studies designed to determine how the roles of blacks and females, as depicted in magazine ads, have changed with the passage of time. Content analysis is useful to both marketers and public policy makers interested in comparing the advertising claims of competitors within a specific industry, and for evaluating the nature of the advertising claims targeted to specific audiences (e.g., women, children).

## Value Measurement Survey Instruments

Anthropologists have traditionally observed the behavior of members of a specific society and *inferred* from such behavior the dominant or underlying values of the society. In recent years, however, there has been a gradual shift to measuring values *directly* by means of survey (questionnaire) research. Researchers use data collection instruments called **value instruments** to ask people how they feel about such basic personal and social concepts as freedom, comfort, national security, and peace.

Research involving the relationship between people's values and their actions as consumers is still in its infancy. However, it is an area that is destined to receive increased attention, for it taps a broad dimension of human behavior that could not be explored effectively before the availability of standardized value instruments.

A popular value instrument that has been employed in consumer behavior studies is the *Rokeach Value Survey*.[13] This self-administered value inventory is divided into two parts, with each part measuring different but complementary types of personal values (see Table 14-3). The first part consists of eighteen *terminal value* items, which are designed to measure the relative importance of *end-states of existence* (i.e., personal goals). The second part consists of eighteen *instrumental value* items, which measure basic *approaches* an individual might follow to reach end-state values. Thus the first half of the measurement instrument deals with *ends*, while the second half considers *means*.

**TABLE 14-3** **The Rokeach Value Survey Instrument**

| TERMINAL VALUES | INSTRUMENTAL VALUES |
|---|---|
| A comfortable life (a prosperous life) | Ambitious (hard-working, aspiring) |
| An exciting life (a stimulating, active life) | Broadminded (open-minded) |
| A world at peace (free of war and conflict) | Capable (competent, effective) |
| Equality (brotherhood, equal opportunity for all) | Cheerful (lighthearted, joyful) |
| Freedom (independence, free choice) | Clean (neat, tidy) |
| Happiness (contentedness) | Courageous (standing up for your belief) |
| National security (protection from attack) | Forgiving (willing to pardon others) |
| Pleasure (an enjoyable life) | Helpful (working for the welfare of others) |
| Salvation (saved, eternal life) | Honest (sincere, truthful) |
| Social recognition (respect, admiration) | Imaginative (daring, creative) |
| True friendship (close companionship) | Independent (self-reliant, self-sufficient) |
| Wisdom (a mature understanding of life) | Intellectual (intelligent, reflective) |
| A world of beauty (beauty of nature and the arts) | Logical (consistent, rational) |
| Family security (taking care of loved ones) | Loving (affectionate, tender) |
| Mature love (sexual and spiritual intimacy) | Obedient (dutiful, respectful) |
| Self-respect (self-esteem) | Polite (courteous, well-mannered) |
| A sense of accomplishment (lasting contribution) | Responsible (dependable, reliable) |
| Inner harmony (freedom from inner conflict) | Self-controlled (restrained, self-disciplined) |

Source: Milton Rokeach, *The Nature of Human Values* (New York: Free Press, 1973), 28.

One of the first consumer studies to employ the Rokeach Value Survey examined the relationship between the thirty-six values and subjects' evaluations of automobile attributes (style, amount of service required, amount of pollution produced, economy of operation, and quality of warranty).[14] The findings revealed that specific values were associated with specific automobile attributes. For instance, the attribute *style* was found to be related to such terminal values as "a comfortable life," "an exciting life," and "pleasure." The attribute *amount of pollution produced* was found to be related to the terminal value "a world at peace" and the instrumental values "helpful" and "loving."

In a more recent study that explored the impact of personal values on attitudes and store choice behavior, the Rokeach Value Survey was administered to customers who had purchased household furniture items from one of two different types of retailers (a traditional full-line furniture store versus a discount furniture store).[15] Results found that personal values influence price sensitivity (an *attitude*) and consequently the type of store from which the furniture was purchased (a *behavior*). Specifically, consumers who were price sensitive ranked significantly *higher* the instrumental value "obedient" and *lower* the instrumental value "broad-minded." Price-sensitive consumers were also more concerned with traditional religious values than price-insensitive consumers. With respect to the two stores whose patrons participated in this research, over 80 percent of the price-sensitive consumers chose to purchase from a discount furniture store, while approximately two-thirds of the price-insensitive group bought their furniture from a traditional full-line furniture store. Thus, personal values, as reflected by the Rokeach Value Survey, seem to be related to both price sensitivity and store choice behavior.

The results of these and other studies suggest that the Rokeach Value Survey can be used by marketers to segment markets by specific values and by perceptions of specific product attributes.[16] Such information is useful in developing new products for specific market segments.

## The Yankelovich Monitor

The *Yankelovich Monitor* is a commercial research service (conducted by Yankelovich, Skelly, and White) which systematically tracks social trends designed to reflect a variety of cultural values. The Yankelovich Monitor was first conducted in 1970 and has been updated annually since then. The Monitor currently tracks over fifty social trends (for examples see Table 14-4) and provides detailed information about potential shifts in the size, direction, and implications of these trends to consumer marketing.[17]

By carefully interpreting social trends and determining which demographic segments are most affected by a particular group of trends, the Monitor service is capable of providing advanced warnings to likely shifts in demand for various product categories. For instance, researchers working with the Monitor were able to forecast the shift away from "brown" whiskey (e.g., rye blends and Scotch) to "white" liquor (vodka and gin).[18] They based their prediction on the observation that young adults were seeking instant gratification (it takes time to develop a taste for Scotch), were concerned with health and fitness, were searching for novelty, and were generally less preoccupied with doing the "standard" or "correct" thing. All this added up to the forecast that vodka and gin would become increasingly popular.

More recently, the Monitor detected a shift in public attitudes with respect to spending on children. The 1970s parental attitude of "Let's spend more on ourselves; the children will have their turn later" has been replaced by a greater concern for and increased spending on children.[19] Such a pattern might influence the frequency and size of parental purchases of various products and services designed to enrich children's experiences. For instance, one could speculate that many parents who have purchased home computers for their children

**TABLE 14-4 A Sample of Social Trends Examined by the Yankelovich Monitor Service**

**Trend No. 1—Personalization**

Monitor's measurement of the size of a group committed to **Personalization** comprises a series of scaled items including: (1) the emphasis placed on buying "products that reveal their style and personality"; (2) the need to add "one's own personal touch" to products; (3) the acceptance of nonconformity in appearance and life-style, even with some social and economic penalties; (4) the degree of desirability ascribed to being different from other people and showing it, rather than the value assigned to "fitting in."

**Trend No. 3—Physical Fitness and Well-Being**

Monitor's measurement of **Physical Fitness and Well-Being** is based on a series of scaled items including: (1) the importance attributed to preventive (rather than therapeutic) health measures; (2) the concern about being in "top shape"; (3) the belief that without taking active measures, people tend to get "soft"; (4) the commitment to "taking care of oneself."

**Trend No. 20—Living for Today**

Monitor's measurement of **Living for Today** is based on a series of scaled items including: (1) belief that one should focus on optimizing one's life "today" and "let the future take care of itself"; (2) acceptance of the principle that at least some portion of current earnings should be put aside against the future even if it means being deprived of something one "thinks is needed now"; (3) the choice of a future-oriented versus a present-oriented course of action in the spending of an unexpected windfall (e.g., banking or investing the money versus using it for a vacation or for the purchase of a luxury); (4) extent of commitment to planning ahead; (5) belief in the idea that the future of one's children is more important than one's own current well-being.

**Trend No. 33—Concern about Privacy**

Monitor's measurement of **Concern about Privacy** is based on a series of scaled items including: (1) concern about maintaining one's right to privacy; (2) perceived violations of privacy by certain government agencies; (3) attitudes toward wiretapping under specified conditions; (4) attitudes toward legislation designed to protect the consumer from perceived invasions of privacy by business.

**Trend No. 47—Responsiveness to Fantasy**

Monitor's measurement of **Responsiveness to Fantasy** is based on a series of scaled items including: (1) the need to remove oneself from one's daily experience—by imagination and/or the pursuit of "unusual," out-of-the-ordinary activities; (2) the preference for participatory entertainment experiences.

**Trend No. 52—Accommodation to Technology**

The **Accommodation to Technology** is measured via several scaled items, including: (1) the pressing need to feel more comfortable with the new technologies; (2) agreement that people will be at a disadvantage in the future if they are "turned off" by the new technologies; and (3) sentiments regarding the need to adapt to technological change.

Source: The Yankelovich Monitor, *Technical description/Appendix/Index to Trend Reference Book* (New York: Yankelovich, Skelly and White, 1985), 47–56.

may have done so in order to ensure that they will not be at a disadvantage in the future.

From these examples, it appears that *standardized value* and *social trend measurement instruments* are promising avenues for continued consumer behavior research, especially segmentation analysis. When combined with other behavioral variables examined in this book, values can be employed to predict shifts in consumption patterns. Such insights are particularly useful in developing new product concepts, repositioning existing products, and adjusting the firm's general marketing efforts.

## AMERICAN CORE VALUES

What is the American culture? In this section we will identify a number of **core values** that both affect and reflect the character of American society. This is a difficult undertaking for several reasons. First, the United States is a diverse country, consisting of a variety of *subcultures* (religious, ethnic, regional, racial, and economic groups), each of which interprets and responds to society's basic beliefs and values in its own specific way. Second, America is a dynamic society, one that has undergone almost constant change in response to its leadership role in the development of new technology. This element of rapid change makes it especially difficult to monitor changes in cultural values. Finally, the existence of contradictory values in American society is often somewhat confusing. For instance, Americans traditionally embrace *freedom of choice* and *individualism*, yet simultaneously they show great tendencies to *conform* (in dress, in furnishings, in fads) to the rest of society. In the context of consumer behavior, Americans like to have a wide choice of products and prefer those that uniquely express their personal lifestyles. Yet there is often a considerable amount of implicit pressure to conform to the values of family members, friends, and other socially important groups. It is difficult to reconcile such seemingly inconsistent values; however, their existence demonstrates that America is a complex society with numerous paradoxes and contradictions.

In selecting the specific core values to be examined here, we were guided by three criteria:

1. The value must be *pervasive*. A significant portion of the American people must accept the value and employ it as a guide for their attitudes and actions.
2. The value must be *enduring*. The specific value must have influenced the actions of the American people over an extended period of time (as distinguished from a short-run trend).
3. The value must be *consumer-related*. The specific value must provide insights that help us understand the consumption actions of the American people.

Meeting these criteria are a number of basic values that expert observers of the American scene consider the "building blocks" of that rather elusive concept called the **American Character**.[20]

### Achievement and Success

Chapter 3 pointed out that the *need for achievement* is often a propellant for individual behavior. In a broader cultural context, **achievement** is a major American value, with historical roots that can be traced to the traditional religious belief—the Protestant work ethic—that hard work is wholesome, spiritually rewarding, and an appropriate end in itself. Indeed, substantial research evidence shows that the *achievement* orientation is closely associated with the technical development and general economic growth of American society.[21]

**Success** is a closely related American cultural theme. However, achievement and success do differ. Specifically, achievement is its own direct reward (it is implicitly satisfying to the achiever), while success implies an extrinsic reward (such as financial or status improvements).

Both achievement and success influence consumption. They often serve as social and moral justification for the acquisition of goods and services. For example, "You owe it to yourself," "You worked for it," and "You deserve it" are popular achievement themes used by advertisers to coax consumers into purchasing their products. When it comes to personal development and preparation for future careers, the themes of achievement and success are also especially appropriate. Figure 14-7 depicts one in a series of ads for Hofstra University that stresses success—"We Teach Success."

## Activity

Americans attach an extraordinary amount of importance to being *active* or *involved*. Keeping busy is widely accepted as a healthy and even necessary part of the American lifestyle. The hectic nature of American life is attested to by foreign visitors who frequently comment that they cannot understand why Americans are always "on the run" and seemingly unable to relax.

The premium placed on **activity** has had both a positive and a negative effect on the popularity of various products. For example, the main reason for the enormous growth of fast-food chains, such as McDonald's and Kentucky Fried Chicken, is that so many people want quick, prepared meals when they are away from the house. In contrast, one of the reasons for the decline in the consumption of eggs for breakfast is that Americans are usually too rushed in the morning to prepare and eat a traditional breakfast. According to an egg industry executive, "There's nothing that could make most people sit down and eat a 25-minute breakfast ever again."[22] Along similar lines, Figure 14-8 presents an ad for Avis that acknowledges Americans' great distaste for waiting or wasting time.

## Efficiency and Practicality

With a basic philosophy of down-to-earth pragmatism, Americans pride themselves on being efficient and practical. When it comes to **efficiency**, they admire anything that saves time and effort. In terms of **practicality**, they are generally receptive to any new product that can make tasks easier and can help solve problems. For example, Americans wholeheartedly accepted such a labor-saving institution as the sawmill, which was outlawed in England (where it was developed) for fear that it would create unemployment.[23]

Here in America, where mass production has been so ingeniously refined, it is now possible for a manufacturer of almost any product category to offer the public a wide range of interchangeable components. For example, a consumer can design his or her own "customized" sofa from such standard components as compatible bases, cushions, arm styles, and fabrics at a cost not much greater than a completely standardized unit. The capacity of American manu-

**FIGURE 14-7** Advertisement Incorporating Achievement and Success Appeals

What does it take to be the best?

It takes brainwork. But it also takes hard work.

Qualities which place Hofstra University in the top 10 percent of American colleges and universities in almost all academic criteria and resources.

Professionally accredited programs in such areas as business, engineering, law, psychology and education.

Outstanding educators on a full-time faculty of over 400 professionals. Over 80 percent hold the highest degree in their fields.

One of only 242 colleges and universities, among almost 4,000 nationwide, honored with a chapter of Phi Beta Kappa.

An accounting program ranked 7th in the nation in a survey of the top 25 accounting firms.

A library with over 1.1 million volumes *on campus*–a collection larger than that of 95 percent of American universities.

At Hofstra, determination, inspiration and hard work are qualities our faculty demands in itself and instills in our students.

These qualities are what it takes to be the best. In anything.

HOFSTRA UNIVERSITY

WE TEACH SUCCESS.

50th Anniversary
Hempstead, L.I., New York 11550

THE NEW YORK TIMES MAGAZINE / JUNE 1, 1986 51

Courtesy of Hofstra University

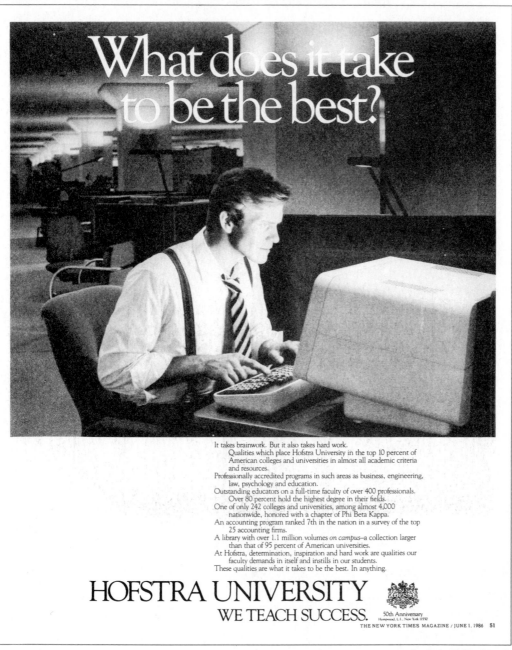

FIGURE 14-8 **Advertisement Depicting Americans' Dislike of Waiting**

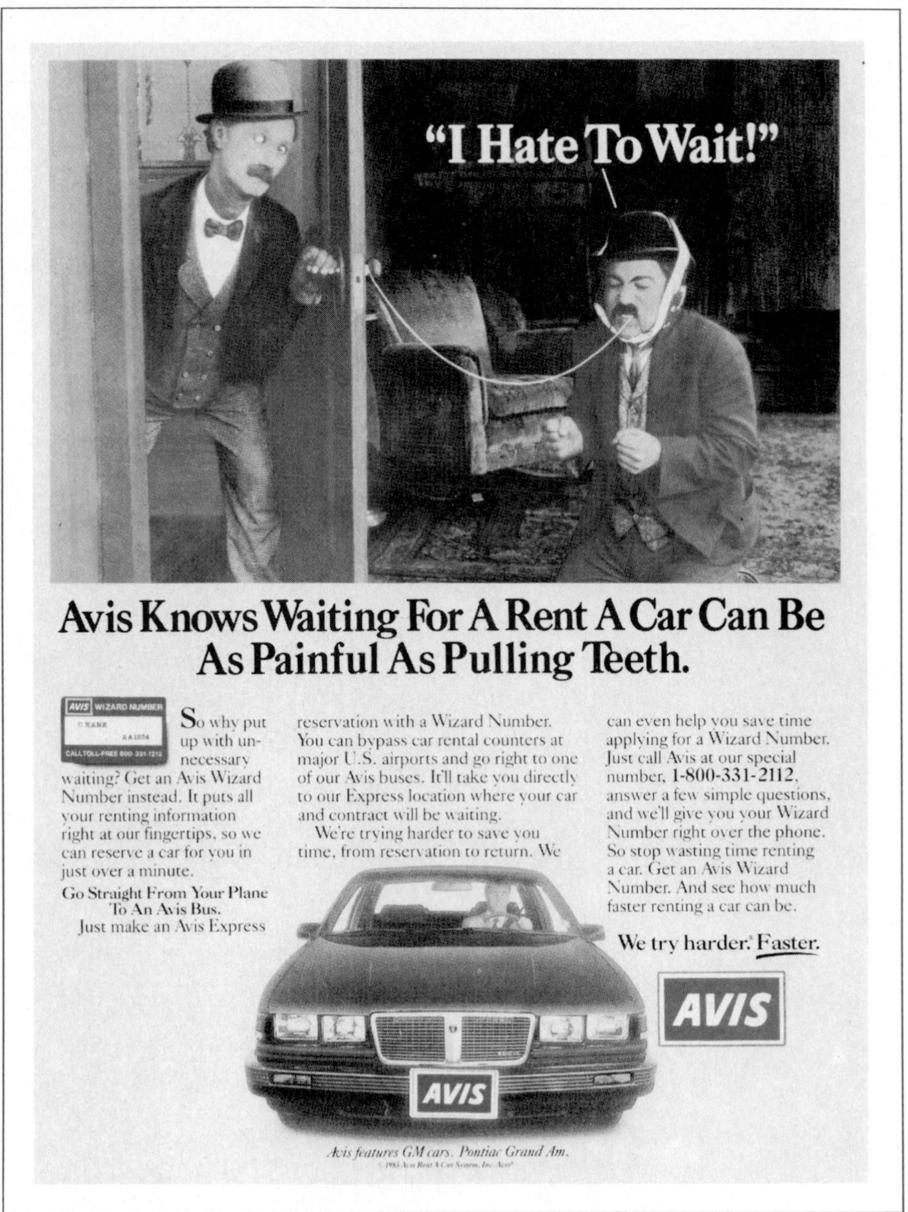


Courtesy of Avis Rent A Car System, Inc.

facturers to create mass-produced components that offer the consumer a customized product has in some instances blurred the differences between two basically contradictory concepts, *mass produced* and *customized*.

Another illustration of Americans' attentiveness to efficiency and practicality is the extreme importance attached to *time*. Americans seem to be convinced that "time waits for no man," which is reflected in their habitual attention to being prompt. The frequency with which Americans look at their watches, and the importance attached to having an accurate timepiece, tend to support the American value of **punctuality**. The very rapid consumer acceptance of the food processor as a kitchen appliance is still another example of Americans' love affair with products that save time and effort in providing efficiency and practicality. Specifically, in promoting its food processor, Cuisinart has emphasized the benefits of ease, accuracy, and timesaving (see Figure 14-9). Similarly, in positioning its briefcase-sized computer, NEC has stressed the time efficiency of owning this computer and taking it with you.

## Progress

**Progress** is another watchword of American society. Indeed, America has been labeled a "cult of progress."[24] Its receptivity to progress appears to be closely linked to other core values already examined (*achievement* and *success, efficiency* and *practicality*) and to the central belief that people can always improve themselves, that tomorrow should be better than today.

In a consumption-oriented society such as the United States, progress often means the acceptance of change—new products or services designed to fulfill previously undersatisfied or unsatisfied needs. In the name of progress, Americans appear to be receptive to product claims that stress "new," "improved," "longer-lasting," "speedier," "quicker," "smoother and closer," and "increased strength." Figure 14-10 depicts an advertisement for the newly improved Duracell alkaline battery that offers progress in the form of extended battery life.

## Material Comfort

For most Americans, **material comfort** signifies the attainment of "the good life"—a life that may include a self-defrosting refrigerator, a microwave oven, an air conditioner, a hot tub, and an almost infinite variety of other convenience-oriented and pleasure-providing goods and services.

General acceptance of products that save time and labor is a rather new phenomenon for most Americans. In fact, for many Americans, the acceptance of convenience products has not been an emotionally easy task. People tend to have mixed feelings about the benefits of convenience products. On the one hand, these products provide material comfort, which is symbolic of achievement and success. On the other hand, they produce anxiety and guilt, for they run counter to the notion of "hard work" as a symbol of self-worth.

A landmark consumer behavior study supports the contention that convenience products initially produce feelings of uncertainty and guilt. This study, reported in 1950 when instant coffee was still in its infancy, found that homemakers perceived women who used instant coffee as lazy housekeepers and poor wives. In contrast, users of regular coffee were perceived as thrifty and good wives.[25] This research suggested that convenience foods are some-

FIGURE 14-9 Advertisement Appealing to Efficiency and Practicality

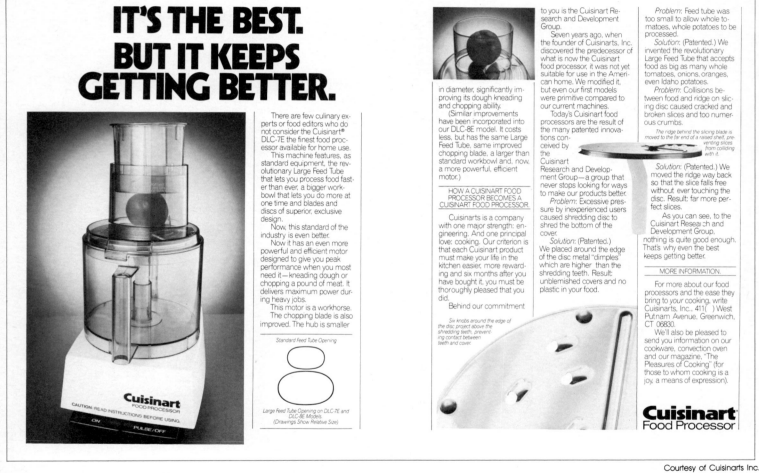

# IT'S THE BEST. BUT IT KEEPS GETTING BETTER.

There are few culinary experts or food editors who do not consider the Cuisinart® DLC-7E the finest food processor available for home use.

This machine features, as standard equipment, the revolutionary Large Feed Tube that lets you process food faster than ever, a bigger workbowl that lets you do more at one time and blades and discs of superior, exclusive design.

Now, this standard of the industry is even better.

Now it has an even more powerful and efficient motor designed to give you peak performance when you most need it—kneading dough or chopping a pound of meat. It delivers maximum power during heavy jobs.

This motor is a workhorse.

The chopping blade is also improved. The hub is smaller

*Standard Feed Tube Opening*

*Large Feed Tube Opening on DLC-7E and DLC-8E Models. (Drawings Show Relative Size)*

in diameter, significantly improving its dough kneading and chopping ability.

(Similar improvements have been incorporated into our DLC-8E model. It costs less, but has the same Large Feed Tube, same improved chopping blade, a larger than standard workbowl and, now, a more powerful, efficient motor.)

HOW A CUISINART FOOD PROCESSOR BECOMES A CUISINART FOOD PROCESSOR.

Cuisinarts is a company with one major strength: engineering. And one principal love: cooking. Our criterion is that each Cuisinart product must make your life in the kitchen easier, more rewarding and six months after you have bought it, you must be thoroughly pleased that you did.

Behind our commitment to you is the Cuisinart Research and Development Group.

Seven years ago, when the founder of Cuisinarts, Inc. discovered the predecessor of what is now the Cuisinart food processor, it was not yet suitable for use in the American home. We modified it, but even our first models were primitive compared to our current machines.

Today's Cuisinart food processors are the result of the many patented innovations conceived by the Cuisinart Research and Development Group—a group that never stops looking for ways to make our products better.

*Problem*: Excessive pressure by inexperienced users caused shredding disc to shred the bottom of the cover.

*Solution*: (Patented.) We placed around the edge of the disc metal "dimples" which are higher than the shredding teeth. Result: unblemished covers and no plastic in your food.

*Six knobs around the edge of the disc project above the shredding teeth, preventing contact between teeth and cover.*

*Problem*: Feed tube was too small to allow whole tomatoes, whole potatoes to be processed.

*Solution*: (Patented.) We invented the revolutionary Large Feed Tube that accepts food as big as many whole tomatoes, onions, oranges, even Idaho potatoes.

*Problem*: Collisions between food and ridge on slicing disc caused cracked and broken slices and too numerous crumbs.

*The ridge behind the slicing blade is moved to the far end of a raised shelf, preventing slices from colliding with it.*

*Solution*: (Patented.) We moved the ridge way back so that the slice falls free without ever touching the disc. Result: far more perfect slices.

As you can see, to the Cuisinart Research and Development Group, nothing is quite good enough. That's why even the best keeps getting better.

MORE INFORMATION.

For more about our food processors and the ease they bring to *your* cooking, write Cuisinarts, Inc., 411( ) West Putnam Avenue, Greenwich, CT 06830.

We'll also be pleased to send you information on our cookware, convection oven and our magazine, "The Pleasures of Cooking" (for those to whom cooking is a joy, a means of expression).

**Cuisinart** Food Processor

Courtesy of Cuisinarts Inc.

FIGURE 14-10 Advertisement Incorporating a Progress Appeal

Courtesy of Duracell, Inc.

times viewed with skepticism, and that people tend to judge others by the cultural acceptability of the products they own or use. In response to our dynamic culture, American values with regard to convenience products, particularly instant coffee, have shifted toward general acceptance during the past thirty years. Indeed, a replication of the original study indicated that the stigma attached to the use of instant coffee had disappeared.[26]

Although the use of convenience products by American households is now almost entirely culturally acceptable, many marketers are still reluctant to stress convenience in promoting some products. For example, in promoting Pampers disposable baby diapers, Procter & Gamble makes no reference to how easy or convenient the product is for mothers. Instead, it stresses how much softer, drier, and more comfortable the product is for baby. This copy approach avoids possible guilt feelings of the mother that she is selfishly using the product to satisfy her own needs rather than those of her baby.

## Individualism

Americans place a strong value on "being themselves." Self-reliance, self-interest, self-confidence, self-esteem, and self-fulfillment are all exceedingly popular expressions of **individualism**. The striving for individualism seems to be linked to the rejection of dependency.[27] That is, it is better to rely on one's self than on others.

In terms of consumer behavior, an appeal to individualism frequently takes the form of reinforcing the consumer's own sense of identity with products or services that both reflect and emphasize that identity (including products like Perrier water and fashion items that offer status designer labels).

Marketers with effective segmentation strategies often design their entire marketing mix—product, price, promotion, and retail channels—with the view of enhancing the feeling of individuality among selected audience segments. For example, advertisements for high-styled clothing and cosmetics usually promise the reader that their products will emphasize the consumer's exclusive or distinctive character and set him or her apart from others. An advertisement for Prudential life insurance shown in Figure 14-11 explicitly appeals to individualism; the headline states: "Finally, life insurance as individual as you are."

## Freedom

**Freedom** is another very strong American value, one that has historical roots in such democratic ideals as "freedom of speech," "freedom of the press," and "freedom of worship." As an outgrowth of these democratic beliefs in freedom, Americans have a strong preference for *freedom of expression*—the desire to be oneself and to feel responsible solely to oneself. The advertisement for a camera in Figure 14-12 appeals to the reader's desire for "the freedom to capture the moment" and "the freedom to be your best."

Americans also demonstrate a strong need for *freedom of choice*—the opportunity to choose from a wide range of alternatives. This preference is reflected in the large number of competitive brands and product variations that can be found on the shelves of the modern supermarket or department store. For many products, consumers can select from a wide variety of sizes, colors,

FIGURE 14-11 Advertisement Stressing Individualism

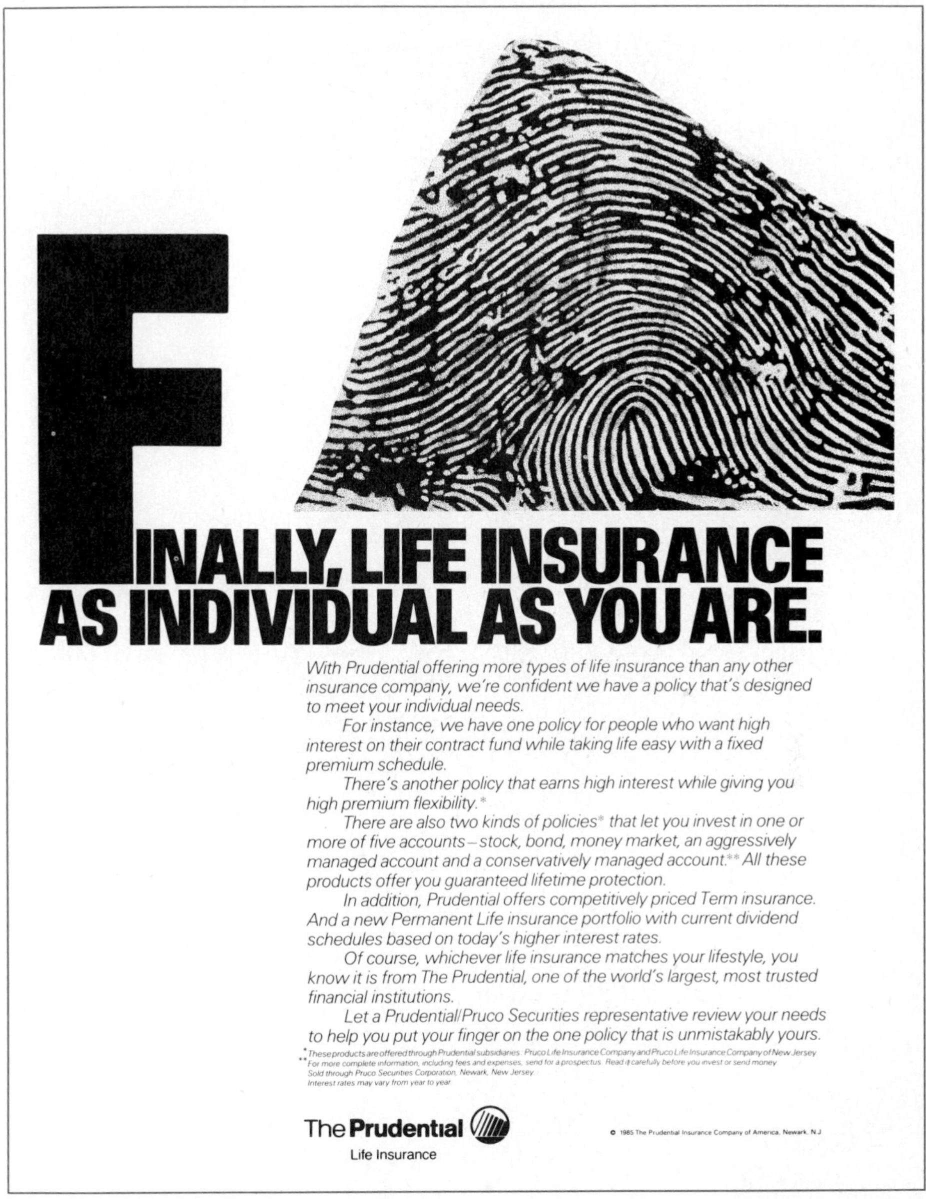


Courtesy of The Prudential Insurance Company of America

flavors, features, styles, and even special ingredients (e.g., toothpaste with stannous fluoride, or toothpaste designed to prevent tartar).

Given all this choice, it may just be possible that American consumers are beginning to feel they have too much choice; making a selection from many competing brands can often be difficult. One study found consumers believed that *overchoice* existed for such product categories as facial tissue, margarine, breakfast cereal, cake mix, and laundry detergent.[28]

FIGURE 14-12 Advertisement Appealing to Freedom of Expression

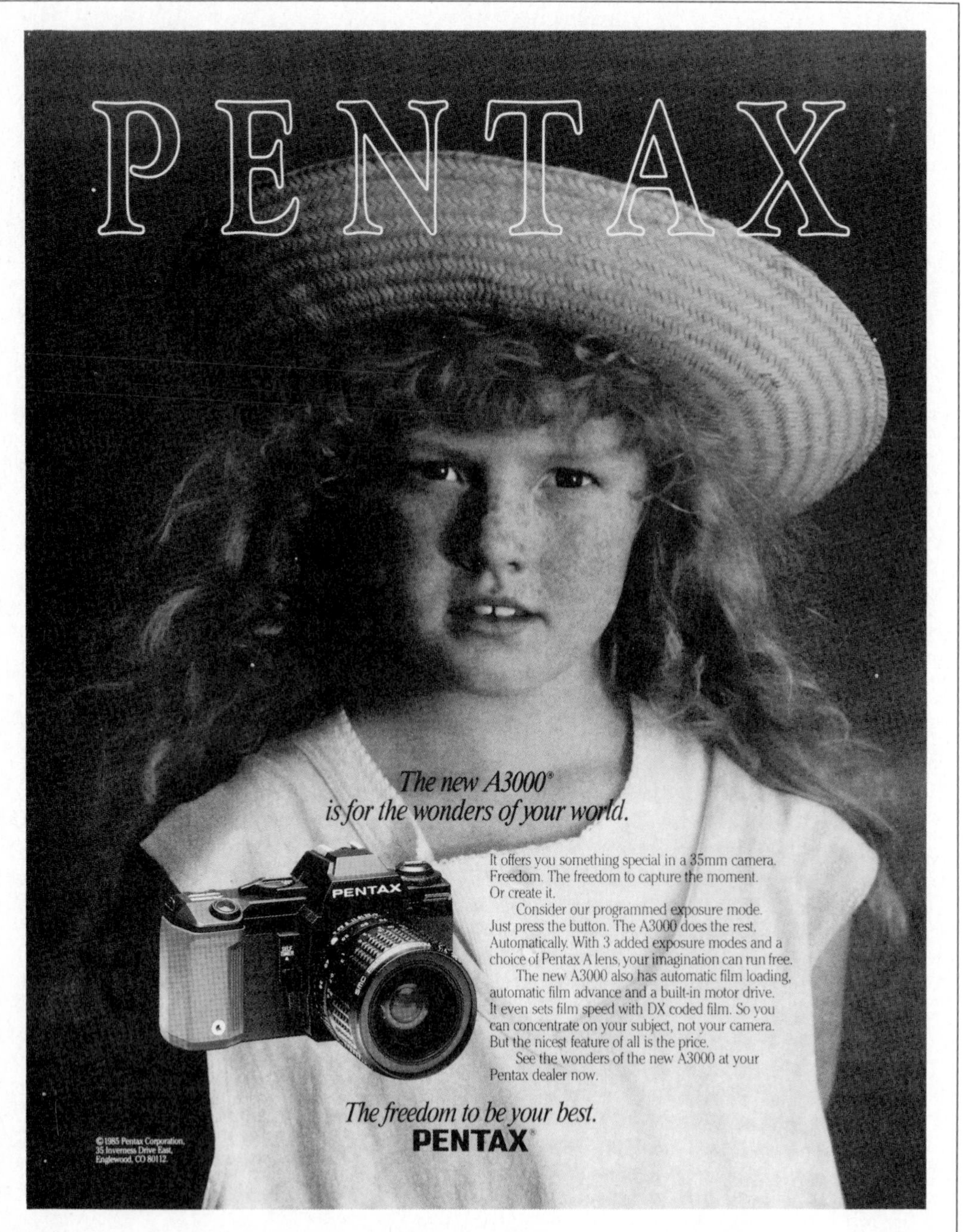


Courtesy of the Pentax Corporation

## External Conformity

Although Americans deeply embrace *freedom of choice* and *individualism*, they nevertheless accept the reality of **conformity**. External conformity is a necessary process by which the individual adapts to society. It has been said that "no social organization, no culture, no form of institutionalized relationship whatever could exist without the process of interaction we call conformity."[29]

In the realm of consumer behavior, conformity (or uniformity) takes the form of standardized goods and services. Standardized products have been made possible by mass production. The availability of a wide choice of standardized products places the consumer in the unique position of being *individualistic* (by selecting specific products that close friends do not have) or *conforming* (by purchasing a similar product). It is within this context that individualism and conformity exist side by side as choices for the American consumer.

Consumer dress behavior would seem to be a particularly potent and observable area of external conformity. A study that explored the relationship between male college students' dress patterns and their socio-cultural attitudes found that students categorized as "radical" dressers (e.g., unkempt hair, unpressed or dirty clothing) were politically more liberal, had more permissive sexual attitudes, were more conscious of youth as a distinct social grouping, and were more likely to play down conventional male-female sex role differences than were members of the "traditionally" dressed student group.[30] This research suggests that dress behavior functions as a visible symbol of attitudes, which in turn may foster external conformity among those who wish to be associated with a specific point of view.

## Humanitarianism

Americans are a generous people when it comes to those in need. They support with a passion many humane and charitable causes, and they sympathize with the "underdog" who must overcome adversity or get ahead by working hard.[31] They also tend to be charitable, and willing to come to the aid of people less fortunate than they are.

This **humanitarian** spirit seems to extend to decisions concerning products and services. A classic illustration is the Avis promotional campaign which stressed that because the company was only "number two" (i.e., an underdog) in the automobile rental business (behind Hertz), it had to "try harder" to satisfy its customers. A more recent example is GoldStar (see Figure 14-13), a Korean consumer electronics corporation (e.g., color TVs) competing in the United States against well established Japanese firms. Within this context, GoldStar is the underdog, and without explicitly saying so is suggesting that as the underdog, they have to "try harder."

## Youthfulness

Americans tend to place an almost sacred value on **youthfulness**. This emphasis is a reflection of America's rapid technological development. In an atmo-

FIGURE 14-13 Advertisement Appealing for Support for the Underdog

Courtesy of GoldStar Electronics Int'l. Inc.

sphere where "new" is so constantly stressed, being "old" is often equated with being "outdated." This is in contrast to traditional European, African, and Asian societies, where the elderly are revered for possessing the wisdom of experience which comes with age.

*Youthfulness* should not be confused with *youth*, which describes an age grouping. Americans are preoccupied with *looking* and *acting* young, regardless of their actual age. For Americans, youthfulness is a state of mind and a state of being, sometimes expressed as being "young at heart," "young in spirit," or "young in appearance."

A great deal of advertising is directed to people's sense of urgency about retaining their youth and to their fear of aging. Hand cream ads talk about "young hands," skin treatment ads state "I dreaded turning 30 . . . ," fragrance and cosmetic ads stress looking "sexy and young," and detergent ads ask the reader "Can you match their hands with their ages?" Such advertising themes reflect the American premium placed on youthfulness as they promise the consumer the benefits of youth.

Figure 14-14 shows an advertisement for Ultima II—an anti-aging complex for face and throat. The product claims to offer "opportunity and hope for skin of any age."

## Fitness and Health

Americans' preoccupation with **fitness** and **health** is emerging as a core value. This value has manifested itself in a number of alternative fashions, including the tennis, raquetball, and jogging fads, as well as new consciousness on the part of Americans that "You are what you eat [or drink]."

According to some, the fitness trend is an outgrowth of the "Me decade." Today nearly half the population engages in one or more athletic activities daily, in contrast to only 25 percent of the population exercising on a regular basis a generation ago. Also, today over twenty different magazines are devoted exclusively to some phase of fitness, and consumers are spending over $30 billion yearly at health clubs.[32] The home exercise equipment market has exploded, with growth running generally at 20 percent a year, though some manufacturers report almost doubling sales each year.[33] Traditional food manufacturers have begun catering to the health-conscious consumer. Campbell has reduced the sodium content in many of its soups; and other companies—catering especially to the demand for health and diet foods—are finding specific niches in the marketplace. For instance, Slim-Fast, whose major product is a 190-calorie substitute for meals, had $215 million in sales in 1984, compared to $50 million in 1979.[34]

Some of the biggest changes have occurred with respect to what people drink. Diet beverages are the supergrowth segment of the soft drink industry; they not only account for 32 percent of sales, but are growing at a 20 percent annual rate. Coffee sales have experienced a 2 percent yearly decrease in per capita consumption, while sales of decaffeinated coffee have risen 30 percent since 1980.[35] Americans are also abstaining from hard liquor, as more states enact tougher drunk driving laws, raise the drinking age, and increase liquor taxes. Wine and wine cooler sales are increasing, and light beers now represent 36 percent of the total beer market. Finally, the consumption of bottled water (see Figure 14-15) nearly doubled between 1980 and 1984.[36]

All these specific consumer trends speak to the emergence of the fitness and health core value.

FIGURE 14-14 Advertisement Appealing to America's Emphasis on Youthfulness

ULTIMA II INTRODUCES PROCOLLAGEN,
in an unprecedented anti-aging complex that offers opportunity and hope for skin of any age.
AGE 20 Even skin in the bloom of youth isn't exempt from the effects of aging. New ProCollagen Anti-aging Complex is unprecedented. Its preventive skin care capacity is surprising. This super active formula, ProCollagen Complex, has a special affinity for skin, thus giving it unusual skin caring properties. It also helps conserve internal collagen. ProCollagen Complex has ultraviolet absorbers that protect skin against the sun's harsh realities. Start now. It's not a moment too soon.
AGE 40 Ah, forty. The age, of enlightenment. New ProCollagen Anti-aging Complex offers basic truth for forty-year-old skin. Procollagen is the support system for collagen, the ingredient of firm, young skin. In this exclusive complex there is the capacity to help stop age breakdown on areas like your throat, your forehead, the corners of your mouth. It even firms skin tissue. The sooner you start the sooner you will witness its benefits.
AGE 60 Sixty isn't what it used to be. In this new age of alternatives, if you've chosen aging well over just aging, ProCollagen Anti-aging Complex will be important to you. It is the first skin care complex of its kind. Because of its exclusive composition, ProCollagen Complex has remarkable moisture reparative capacities. It will actually diminish the length and depth of dry wrinkles. It works deeply as a moisturizer, and clings long and lovingly. All in all, this is skin care like you've never known before.
ProCollagen
ULTIMA II
CHR ProCollagen Anti-aging Complex
L. to r.
Kim Alexis
Barbara Alexis
'Aunt' Nancy
© 1985 Charles Revson, Inc.


Courtesy of Ultima II; Charles Revson, Inc.

## Core Values Not an American Phenomenon

The cultural values just examined are not all uniquely or originally American. Some of these values have been borrowed, particularly from European society, as people emigrated to the United States. Some values that originated in America are now part of the fabric of other societies. Furthermore, all Americans do

**FIGURE 14-15** **Advertisement Extolling the Virtues of Drinking Water**

EARTH'S FIRST SOFT DRINK.

Back in the Ice Age, a fortunate homme des cavernes (French caveman) came upon a marvelously refreshing spring, gurgling among the icy pebbles.

And so, the very first Perrier-on-the-rocks was born.

We can only surmise that some clever descendant of his discovered that among the other gifts of nature were the lemon, orange and lime. And that a bit of the peel added a delicate allure to this delicious drink.

WITH A TWIST.

That's why, today, we bring you Perrier With A Twist. A twist of lemon. A twist of lime. Or a twist of orange. No sugar, no salt, no calories. Nothing artificial at all. Just the natural taste you would get with a twist.

And it's still the same primeval Perrier from the same sparkling mineral spring. Created by the earth when it was new.

© 1985 Perrier

BOTTLED ONLY AT THE MINERAL SPRING OF PERRIER, VERGEZE, FRANCE.

Courtesy of Perrier

not necessarily accept each of these values. However, these values, taken as a whole, do account for much of the American character. Table 14-5 summarizes a number of American core values, and indicates their relevance to consumer behavior.

**TABLE 14-5 Summary of American Core Values**

| VALUE | GENERAL FEATURES | RELEVANCE TO CONSUMER BEHAVIOR |
|---|---|---|
| Achievement and success | Hard work is good; success flows from hard work | Acts as a justification for acquisition of goods ("You deserve it") |
| Activity | Keeping busy is healthy and natural | Stimulates interest in products that are time-savers and enhance leisure-time activities |
| Efficiency and practicality | Admiration of things that solve problems (e.g., save time and effort) | Stimulates purchase of products that function well and save time |
| Progress | People can improve themselves; tomorrow should be better | Stimulates desire for new products that fulfill unsatisfied needs; acceptance of products that claim to be "new" or "improved" |
| Material comfort | "The good life" | Fosters acceptance of convenience and luxury products that make life more enjoyable |
| Individualism | Being one's self (e.g., self-reliance, self-interest, and self-esteem) | Stimulates acceptance of customized or unique products that enable a person to "express his or her own personality" |
| Freedom | Freedom of choice | Fosters interest in wide product lines and differentiated products |
| External conformity | Uniformity of observable behavior; desire to be accepted | Stimulates interest in products that are used or owned by others in the same social group |
| Humanitarianism | Caring for others, particularly the underdog | Stimulates patronage of firms that compete with market leaders |
| Youthfulness | A state of mind that stresses being young at heart or appearing young | Stimulates acceptance of products that provide the illusion of maintaining or fostering youth |
| Fitness and health | Caring about one's body, including the desire to be physically fit and healthy | Stimulates acceptance of food products, activities, and equipment perceived to maintain or increase physical fitness |

## *summary*

The study of culture is the study of all aspects of a society—its language, knowledge, laws, customs—which give that society its distinctive character and personality. In the context of consumer behavior, culture is defined as the sum total of learned beliefs, values, and customs which serve to regulate the consumer behavior of members of a particular society. Beliefs and values are guides for consumer behavior; customs are usual and accepted ways of behaving.

The impact of culture on society is so natural and so ingrained that its influence on behavior is rarely noted. Yet culture offers order, direction, and guidance to members of society in all phases of human problem solving. Culture is dynamic, and gradually and continually evolves to meet the needs of society.

Culture is learned as part of social experience. Children acquire from their environments a set of beliefs, values, and customs which constitute culture (i.e., they are "encultured"). These are acquired through formal learning, informal learning, and technical learning. Advertising enhances formal learning by reinforcing desired modes of behavior and expectations; it enhances informal learning by providing models for behavior.

Culture is communicated to members of the society through a common language and through commonly shared symbols. Because the human mind has the ability to absorb and to process symbolic communication, marketers can successfully promote both tangible and intangible products and product concepts to consumers through mass media.

All the elements in the marketing mix serve to communicate symbolically with the audience. Products project images of their own; so does promotion; price and retail outlets symbolically convey images concerning the quality of the product.

The elements of culture are transmitted by three pervasive social institutions: the family, the church, and the school. A fourth social institution that plays a major role in the transmission of culture is the mass media—both through editorial content and through advertising.

A wide range of measurement techniques are employed to study culture. These include projective techniques, attitude measurement methods, field observation, participant observation, content analysis, and value measurement survey techniques.

A small number of core values of the American people appear to be relevant to the study of consumer behavior. These include achievement and success, activity, efficiency and practicality, progress, material comfort, individualism, freedom, conformity, humanitarianism, youthfulness, and fitness and health.

Since each of these values varies in importance to the members of our society, they provide an effective basis for segmenting consumer markets.

## *discussion questions*

1. Distinguish between beliefs, values, and customs. Illustrate how the clothing a person wears, at different times or for different occasions, is influenced by custom.

2. Give a consumer behavior example from your own experience of each of the following types of cultural learning:
   a. Formal learning
   b. Informal learning
   c. Technical learning
3. Describe how "The Tonight Show," starring Johnny Carson, participates in the transmission of cultural beliefs, values, and customs.
4. As the media planner for a large advertising agency, you have been asked by top management to identify recent cultural changes that affect your selection of the media in which to place clients' advertising. List five cultural changes you believe have bearing on the selection of television shows for different types of products.
5. Consider the faculty of a typical university. What ritual artifacts are usually associated with college professors?
6. Find two advertisements for the same product category (e.g., perfume, deodorant, automobiles, televisions) that appeal to different core values (as summarized in Table 14-5). Describe your choices.
7. Consider the Nissan 300ZX automobile. Which basic American cultural values would you expect to influence the purchase of this car?

## endnotes


1. Milton Rokeach, *The Nature of Human Values* (New York: Free Press, 1973), 5; and Francesco M. Nicosia and Robert N. Myer, "Toward a Sociology of Consumption," *Journal of Consumer Research*, 3 (September 1976), 67.
2. Donald E. Vinson, Jerome E. Scott, and Lawrence M. Lamont, "The Role of Personal Values in Marketing and Consumer Behavior," *Journal of Marketing*, 41 (April 1977), 44–50.
3. Ruth Benedict, "The Science of Custom," *Century Magazine*, 117 (1929), 641.
4. Ralph Linton, *The Cultural Background of Personality* (New York: Appleton-Century-Crofts, 1945), 125.
5. Edwart T. Hall, *The Silent Language* (Greenwich, Conn.: Fawcett, 1959), 69–72.
6. Raymond Firth, *Symbols: Public and Private* (Ithaca, N.Y.: Cornell University Press, 1973), 47.
7. Dennis W. Rook, "The Ritual Dimension of Consumer Behavior," *Journal of Consumer Research*, 12 (December 1985), 251–64.
8. Dennis W. Rook, "Ritual Behavior and Consumer Symbolism," in Thomas C. Kinnear, ed., *Advances in Consumer Research* (Ann Arbor, Mich.: Association for Consumer Research, 1984), 11, 279–84.
9. Michael R. Solomon and Punam Anand, "Ritual Costumes and Status Transition: The Female Business Suit as Totemic Emblem," in Elizabeth C. Hirschman and Morris B. Holbrook, eds., *Advances in Consumer Research* (Provo, Ut.: Association for Consumer Research, 1985), 12, 315–18.
10. David M. Potter, *People of Plenty* (Chicago: University of Chicago Press, 1954), 167.

11. Russell W. Belk and Richard W. Pollay, "Images of Ourselves: The Good Life in Twentieth Century Advertising, *Journal of Consumer Research*, 11 (March 1985), 888.

12. For a comprehensive discussion of content analysis, see Harold H. Kassarjian, "Content Analysis in Consumer Research," *Journal of Consumer Research*, 4 (June 1977), 8–18; Fred N. Kerlinger, *Foundations of Behavioral Research*, 2nd ed. (New York: Holt, Rinehart & Winston, 1973), 525–34; and Morris B. Holbrook, "More on Content Analysis in Consumer Behavior," *Journal of Consumer Research*, 4 (December 1977), 176–77.

13. Rokeach, *Nature of Human Values*; and Milton Rokeach, "Change and Stability in American Value Systems, 1968–1971," *Public Opinion Quarterly*, 38 (Summer 1974), 222–38.

14. Jerome E. Scott and Lawrence M. Lamont, "Relating Consumer Values to Consumer Behavior: A Model and Method for Investigation," in Thomas V. Greer, ed., *1973 Combined Proceedings* (Chicago: American Marketing Association, 1974), 283–88.

15. Boris W. Becker and Patrick E. Connor, "The Influence of Personal Values on Attitudes and Store Choice Behavior," in Bruce J. Walker et al., eds., *An Assessment of Marketing Thought and Practice* (Chicago: American Marketing Association, 1982), 21–24.

16. Michael Munson and Shelby H. McIntyre, "Personal Values: A Cross Cultural Assessment of Self Values and Values Attributed to a Distant Cultural Stereotype," in H. Keith Hunt, ed., *Advances in Consumer Research* (Ann Arbor, Mich.: Association for Consumer Research, 1978), 5, 160–66; J. Michael Munson and Shelby H. McIntyre, "Developing Practical Procedures for the Measurement of Personal Values in Cross-Cultural Marketing," *Journal of Marketing Research*, 16 (February 1979), 48–52; and Thomas J. Reynolds and James P. Jolly, "Measuring Personal Values: An Evaluation of Alternative Methods," *Journal of Marketing Research*, 17 (November 1980), 531–36.

17. The Yankelovich Monitor, *Technical description/Appendix/Index to Trend Reference Book* (New York: Yankelovich, Skelly and White, 1985), 47–56.

18. Olivia Schieffelin Nordberg, "Lifestyle's Monitor," *American Demographics*, 3 (May 1981), 22; and B. G. Yovovich, "Finding the Answers," *Advertising Age*, July 20, 1981, 41–42 and 44.

19. B. G. Yovovich, "It's 1982—Do You Know What Your Values Are?" *Advertising Age*, October 18, 1982, M-28.

20. Many of the ideas for the value concepts examined in this section were inspired by the comprehensive treatment in "Major Value Orientations in America," appearing in Robin M. Williams, Jr., *American Society: A Sociological Interpretation* (New York: Knopf, 1970), 438–504.

21. David C. McClelland, *The Achieving Society* (New York: Free Press, 1961), 150–51.

22. Steve Lohr, "Hens Are Willing But People Aren't," *New York Times*, July 11, 1976, Sec. 3,1.

23. Henry Fairlie, *The Spoiled Child of the Western World* (Garden City, N.Y.: Doubleday, 1976), 79.

24. Williams, *American Society*, 468.

25. Mason Haire, "Projective Techniques in Marketing Research," *Journal of Marketing*, 14 (April 1950), 649–56.

26. Frederick E. Webster, Jr., and Frederick Von Pechmann, "A Replication of the 'Shopping List' Study," *Journal of Marketing*, 34 (April 1970), 61–63. Also see Johan Arndt, "Haire's Shopping List Revisited," *Journal of Advertising Research*, 13 (October 1973), 57–61.

27. Lowell D. Holmes, *Anthropology* (New York: Ronald Press, 1965), 121.

**28.** Robert B. Settle and Linda L. Golden, "Consumer Perceptions: Overchoice in the Market Place," in Scott Ward and Peter Wright, eds., *Advances in Consumer Behavior* (Association for Consumer Research, 1974), I, 29–37.

**29.** Robert A. Nisbet, *The Social Bond* (New York: Knopf, 1970), 69.

**30.** L. Eugene Thomas, "Clothing and Counterculture: An Empirical Study," *Adolescence*, 8 (Spring 1973), 93–112.

**31.** Williams, *American Society*, 462.

**32.** "A Long Race for Fitness Marketers," *Marketing and Media Decisions* (March 1984), 60–61, 138.

**33.** "Home Exercise Gear: Another Industry Gets Fat On Fitness," *Business Week*, January 28, 1985, 118; and "Soloflex Puts More Muscle in Its Hard Sell," *Business Week*, January 28, 1985, 122.

**34.** "A Long Race," 138.

**35.** "A Company That's Getting Fat Because America Wants to Be Thin," *Business Week*, November 19, 1984, 70.

**36.** Stratford P. Sherman, "American's New Abstinence," *Fortune*, March 18, 1985, 20–23.

15

# Subcultural and Cross-Cultural Aspects of Consumer Behavior

## *introduction*

CULTURE has a potent influence on all consumer behavior. Individuals are brought up to follow the beliefs, values, and customs of their society and to avoid behavior that is frowned upon or considered taboo. Marketers who incorporate an understanding of culture into their marketing strategies are likely to satisfy consumers more fully by providing them with added, though intangible, product benefits. However, culture, as a concept, has a very broad beamed focus in that it embraces total societies. To even better satisfy consumers, marketers have learned to segment society into smaller subgroups or **subcultures** that are homogeneous in relation to certain customs and ways of behaving. These subcultures provide important marketing opportunities for astute marketing strategists.

Our discussion of subcultures, therefore, will have a *narrower* focus than the discussion of culture. Instead of examining the dominant beliefs, values, and customs that exist within an entire society, we will explore the marketing opportunities created by the existence of certain beliefs, values, and customs among specific subcultural groups *within* a society. Subcultural divisions based on nationality, religion, geographic locality, race, age, and sex often enable marketers to segment a market in terms of the specific beliefs, values, and customs shared by members of a specific subcultural group.

In the second section of this chapter we will broaden our scope of analysis and consider the marketing implications of cultural differences and similarities that exist between the people of two or more nations. Recognition of cross-cultural differences can provide expanded sales and profit opportunities for multinational marketers, who can tailor their marketing mix to the specific customs of each target nation.

"

*Different men seek after happiness in different ways and by different means . . .*

*ARISTOTLE*
*Politics (4th cent. B.C.)*

"

In the world of primitive tribal society, the same set of cultural values and customs prevails throughout the group; there are few subgroups with distinctive cultural traits. A society with such a highly unified culture is ruled by "commonness." All its people worship the same god, all have a common racial background, all eat the same kinds of food. Social organizations and institutions are extremely simple. In contrast, in a complex society like the United States, there is considerable diversity in religious beliefs, racial backgrounds, food customs, and other social practices and institutions. Indeed, the members of a complex society belong to many different kinds of subcultural groups. It is such diversity that makes subculture a useful segmentation variable.

## What Is Subculture?

A **subculture** can be thought of as *a distinct cultural group which exists as an identifiable segment within a larger, more complex society.*[1] The members of a specific subculture tend to possess beliefs, values, and customs that set them apart from other members of the same society. In addition, they adhere to most of the *dominant* cultural beliefs, values, and behavioral patterns of the overall society.

Thus the cultural profile of a society or nation can be viewed as a composite of two distinct elements: (1) the unique beliefs, values, and customs subscribed to by members of specific subcultures; and (2) the central core cultural themes that are shared by most of the population, regardless of specific subcultural memberships. Figure 15-1 presents a model of the relationship between two subcultural groups (easterners and westerners) and the larger culture. As the figure depicts, each subculture has its own unique traits, yet both groups share the dominant traits of the overall American culture.

Let us look at it another way: Each American is in large part a product of the "American way of life." However, each American is at the same time a

FIGURE 15-1 Relationship between Culture and Subculture

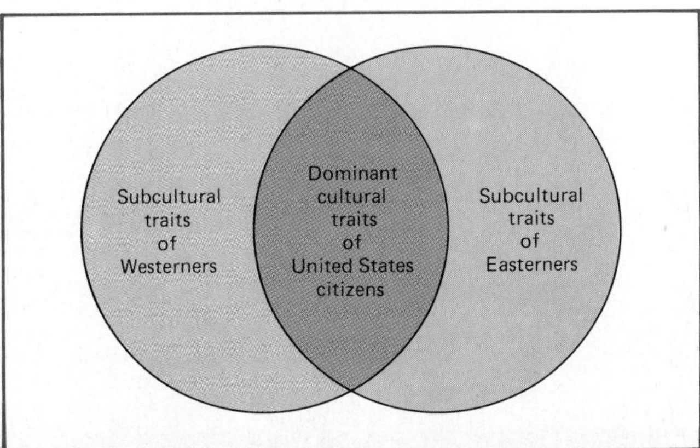

member of various subcultures. For example, a fourteen-year-old girl may simultaneously be black, Baptist, a teenager, and a midwesterner. We would expect that membership in each different subculture would provide its own set of specific beliefs, values, attitudes, and customs. Table 15-1 lists typical subcultural categories and corresponding examples of specific subcultural groups. This list is by no means exhaustive. For example, college graduates, feminists, Girl Scouts, and single parents—in fact, any group that shares common beliefs and customs—may be classified as a subculture.

## SUBCULTURES AS MARKET SEGMENTS

Subcultural analysis enables the marketing manager to focus on rather large and "natural" market segments. In carrying out such analyses, the marketer must determine whether the beliefs, values, and customs shared by members of a specific subgroup make them desirable candidates for special marketing attention. According to one marketing expert, "Subcultures are the relevant units of analysis for market research. *They represent definable target groups for specific products and logical units for segmenting of larger markets.*"[2]

The following section examines the marketing implications of the following subcultural categories: nationality, religion, geographic location, race, age, and sex. (Occupational and social class subgroups are discussed in detail in Chapter 13.)

### Nationality Subcultures

While most United States citizens, especially those born in the United States, see themselves as "Americans," they frequently retain a sense of identification and pride in the language and customs of their ancestors.

When it comes to consumption behavior, this ancestral pride is manifested most strongly in the consumption of ethnic foods, in travel to the "homeland" country, and in the purchase of numerous cultural artifacts (ethnic clothing,

**TABLE 15-1 Subcultural Categories**

| SUBCULTURAL CATEGORY | TYPES OF SUBCULTURES |
|---|---|
| Nationality (i.e., birthplace of ancestors) | Italian, Puerto Rican, Hispanic |
| Religion | Mormon, Protestant, Jew |
| Region | Midwestern, Northern, Southern |
| Race | Black, White, Oriental |
| Age | Elderly, Teenage, Middle-age |
| Sex | Female, Male |
| Occupation | Carpenter, Lawyer, Schoolteacher |
| Social class | Lower, Middle, Upper |

art, music, foreign-language newspapers). Interest in such goods and services has expanded rapidly as younger Americans attempt to better understand and more closely associate themselves with their ethnic roots.

Unfortunately, with the exception of the Hispanic subculture, there is little information available about the consumption behavior of the many nationality subgroups found in the United States.

### HISPANIC SUBCULTURES

Hispanic Americans represent slightly less than 10 percent of the U.S. population (about 20 million people). With a 65 percent population increase during the 1970–1980 decade, Hispanic-Americans are projected to supplant blacks within twenty years as this nation's largest minority group. Indeed, Hispanics have already become the dominant minority in New York, Los Angeles, San Diego, Phoenix, San Francisco, and Denver, and represent the majority in San Antonio, Texas.

This subcultural group is not a single market, but rather a number of subcultural markets that correspond to their country of origin. The three largest Hispanic subcultural groups consist of Mexican-Americans, Puerto Ricans, and Cubans. These subcultures are heavily concentrated geographically, with about 70 percent of their members residing in California, Texas, New York, and Florida.[3]

### UNDERSTANDING HISPANIC CONSUMER BEHAVIOR

According to available evidence, Hispanic and Anglo consumers differ in terms of a variety of important buyer behavior variables. For instance, Hispanic consumers are highly brand-loyal and prefer well-established brands. Table 15-2

**TABLE 15-2 Characteristics of the Hispanic-American Market**

Exhibit high brand loyalty
Trust well-known or familiar brands
Likely to buy what their parents bought
Buy brands perceived to be more prestigious
Prefer fresh to frozen or prepared items
Buy brands advertised by their ethnic group stores
Prefer to shop at smaller stores
Dislike impersonal stores
Tend not to be impulse buyers
New product adoption inhibited by difficulty with English
Are less confident shoppers
Are price-oriented, careful shoppers
Are more negative about marketing practices and government intervention in business

Adapted from: Wayne D. Hoyer and Rohit Deshpande, "Cross-Cultural Influences on Buyer Behavior: The Impact of Hispanic Ethnicity," *AMA 1982*, pp. 89–92; Robert E. Wilkes and Humberto Valencia, "Shopping Orientation of Mexican-Americans," *AMA 1984*, pp. 26–31; Danny N. Bellenger and Humberto Valencia, "Understanding the Hispanic Market, *Business Horizons*, May–June 1982, pp. 47–50; and Peter L. Benzinger, "Hispanics: A Profitable Consumer Segment," *Marketing Review*, 41 (December 1985–January 1986), 19–20.

presents in list form these and other key distinctive characteristics of the overall Hispanic market. Table 15-3 indicates considerable differences in brand preferences (as reflected in brand share) between Hispanic and non–Hispanic consumers for common supermarket-type products.

Not only do Hispanic and non-Hispanic consumers differ, but specific Hispanic communities located in different sections of the United States (such as the Puerto Rican communities of New York and the Mexican-American communities in California) also differ from one another. For example, one study found that while Hispanics in general exhibit high brand loyalty, Mexican-Americans tend to exhibit low brand loyalty.[4]

## REACHING THE HISPANIC CONSUMER

Some marketers feel it is worthwhile to cater separately to each of the Hispanic-American markets. Anheuser-Busch, for example, recently produced ads for four separate Hispanic groups: Puerto Ricans, Latin Americans, Mexicans, and Cubans. Ads aimed at Mexicans contained mariachi music, whereas salsa rhythms were featured in advertisements directed at Puerto Rican consumers.[5]

**TABLE 15-3 Brand Shares: Hispanics Versus Non-Hispanics**

| | SHARE OF USERS | | |
|---|---|---|---|
| | non-hispanics | hispanics | total market |
| Canned fruit | | | |
| Libby's | 8% | 40% | 14% |
| Chocolate milk flavoring | | | |
| Nestle's Quik | 44 | 89 | 55 |
| Cooking/salad oil | | | |
| Mazola | 19 | 67 | 25 |
| Fruit-flavored drink | | | |
| Hawaiian Punch | 22 | 72 | 32 |
| Hot dogs | | | |
| Oscar Mayer | 14 | 42 | 19 |
| Ice cream | | | |
| Breyers | 29 | 57 | 32 |
| Margarine | | | |
| Parkay | 23 | 60 | 28 |
| Packaged cookies | | | |
| Almost Home | 8 | 32 | 12 |
| Powdered drink | | | |
| Tang | 4 | 33 | 11 |
| Rice | | | |
| Vitarroz | 1 | 33 | 5 |
| Spaghetti sauce | | | |
| Ragu | 39 | 53 | 41 |
| Vegetable: frozen | | | |
| Green Giant | 11 | 66 | 15 |
| Cold remedies | | | |
| CoTylenol | 16 | 28 | 18 |

Source: Elisa Soriano and Dale Dauten, "Hispanic 'Dollar Votes' Can Impact Market Shares," *Marketing News*, published by the American Marketing Association, September 13, 1984, 45.

**TABLE 15-4 Segmenting the Hispanic Market by Degree of Acculturation**

group i: least acculturated
Most comfortable with things closely associated with the Hispanic culture and the Spanish language
Generally in the United States for only a short period of time
Tend to cluster in close-knit family groups and Hispanic neighborhoods
Uncertain as to how to "make it" in America
Low-income and blue-collar workers
Focused on providing for family's basic needs (food, clothing and shelter)
Eat at home
Heavy supermarket shoppers
Overwhelmingly "tuned-in" to Spanish-language media

group ii: moderately acculturated
Bicultural and bilingual
Combine the characteristics of Group I (above) and Group III (below)

group iii: most acculturated
Very comfortable with the English language
Americanized in their lifestyles
Lived in United States for three or more generations
May understand some Spanish, but speak little or none at all
Achieved higher educational levels
Many are professionals and community leaders
Overwhelmingly "tuned-in" to English-language media
Have strong pride in their Hispanic roots

Source: Madhav N. Segal and Lionel Sosa, "Marketing to the Hispanic Community," *California Management Review*, 26, 1 (Fall 1983), 130–31.

Many national advertisers, including Pepsi-Cola, Gillette, Kraft, McDonald's, Chrysler, Procter & Gamble, Bristol-Myers, AT&T, American Airlines, Colgate-Palmolive, and Campbell Soup have made efforts to penetrate Hispanic markets using Spanish-language mass media.[6]

The Spanish language is the bridge that links the various Hispanic subcultures. However, though they share a common language, each of the major Hispanic subcultural groups do have some distinct beliefs, values, and customs. It has been suggested that ". . . what may be popular in New York [i.e., among Puerto Ricans] might fail in Miami [i.e., among Cubans]. . . ."[7] Thus a marketer may wish to segment the Hispanic market by appealing to the distinct cultural values of a specific nationality.

Still another way of segmenting the Hispanic market may be in terms of their degree of *acculturation* to the dominant American cultural values, customs, artifacts, and rituals. Table 15-4 presents a potentially useful three-category segmentation scheme that focuses on the degree to which Hispanic consumers are acculturated to the American way of life.

## Religious Subcultures

Over 220 different organized religious groups reportedly flourish in the United States. Of this number, the major Protestant denominations, Roman Catholicism, and Judaism are the principal organized religious faiths. The members of all these religious groups are at times likely to make purchase decisions that are influenced by their religious identity. However, as American life has become increasingly secularized (i.e., as religion plays less of a central role in determining basic beliefs and values), adherence to traditional religious rules tends to diminish. Therefore it is likely that consumer behavior is most directly affected by religion in terms of products that are *symbolically* and *ritualistically* associated with the celebration of various religious holidays. For example, as the major gift-purchasing season of the year, Christmas is important to many marketers of consumer goods.

Although members of most major religions can be reached through religious publications, marketers are often reluctant to reach religious subcultures this way because they feel uncomfortable about mixing religion and business. However, it has been shown that advertising in religious media can be rewarding. Specifically, research concerned with measuring the impact of special interest media aimed at Jewish households provides some striking insights about brand purchase behavior. Research contrasting brand penetration in Jewish and non-Jewish households revealed that in the New York market, Maxwell House coffee is used in 61 percent of Jewish homes (versus 33 percent of non-Jewish homes); My-T-Fine puddings are used in 73 percent of Jewish homes (versus 29 percent non-Jewish); and Star-Kist tuna is used in 35 percent of Jewish homes (versus 16 percent non-Jewish).[8] Another example of the potential usefulness of religion-oriented media is the discovery made by J&B Scotch. Its consumer research revealed that a significant segment of J&B Scotch drinkers are both single and Jewish.[9] To take advantage of this information, the company placed ads in the personal classified columns of national Jewish publications read by single Jewish people.

Notwithstanding these examples, very little consumer research has been devoted to examining how religious affiliation influences consumer preferences and loyalties. One stream of research that has examined leisure activity preferences of individuals with different religious backgrounds found a number of interesting distinctions. For example, Protestant and Catholic consumers were found to have a stronger orientation toward solitary leisure pursuits, whereas Jewish consumers preferred activities that provided companionship and/or sensory stimulation.[10] Related research indicates that New York Jewish consumers seem to be particularly innovative and may serve as generalized **opinion leaders.**[11] (Opinion leadership is discussed in Chapter 16.)

## Geographic or Regional Subcultures

The United States is a large country, one that enjoys a wide range of climatic and geographic conditions. Given the country's size and physical diversity, it is only natural that the American people have a sense of regional identification and use this identification as a way of describing others (e.g., "He's a big Texan"). Such labels often assist us in developing a mental picture—a *stereotype*—of the person in question.

Anyone who has traveled across the United States has probably noted many regional differences in consumption behavior. For example, coffee preferences differ in different sections of the country (a *mug* of black coffee typifies the West, while a *cup* of coffee with milk and sugar is especially popular in the East). There are also geographic differences in the consumption of a staple food like bread. Specifically, in the South and Midwest, soft bread (white bread) is preferred, while on the East and West coasts firmer breads (rye, whole wheat, and French and Italian breads) are favored.

Fashion tastes and preferences also seem to have a regional identity. Indeed, two major cities in the same state may have quite different fashion orientations. For example, according to the chief executive officer of a leading Texas-based fashion specialty chain, Dallas has historically been more sophisticated and upbeat, while Houston has been more fundamental or practical in outlook. Therefore, he concludes: "In Dallas, you could sell the sizzle. In Houston, you had to sell the steak."[12]

There are few research studies available to document such differences in consumption patterns. Most academic consumer research focuses on single geographic areas (usually the locale of the researcher's university). However, the findings of a large-scale study of consumer lifestyles and buying preferences suggest that commercially sponsored studies can provide rich insights into regional variations of consumer behavior. This study, which questioned two thousand male and two thousand female consumers, reported the following specific geographic differences:[13]

1. Southern men were more likely to use mouthwash or deodorants than Eastern men.
2. Southern men were more likely to listen to western music than any other regional group, and least likely to read a Sunday newspaper. Also, a Southern household was more likely to own a freezer than other regional households.
3. Western men tend to consume more cottage cheese, vitamins, and regular coffee than either Easterners or Southerners. A Western family is also more likely to own a garbage-disposal unit.

The results of a study that sought to determine the percentage of households in each region that had made at least one wine purchase during the preceding twelve-month period found a considerable amount of interregional variation. Only 20 percent of those residing in the East and South Central States had purchased wine, whereas over 50 percent of those residing in the Pacific States had purchased wine. Overall, 38 percent of those participating in the study had purchased wine.[14] To further illustrate the importance of regional differences, Table 15-5 presents the number-one market for selected products. These regional variations provide additional support for marketers who argue that it is important to take geographic consumption patterns into account when planning marketing and promotional efforts.

Such regional differences tend to dispel the myth sometimes held that American consumers represent one big *mass market,* and reinforce the need for *market segmentation* for a variety of goods and services.

**TABLE 15-5 Number-One Markets for Selected Products**

| MARKET AREA | PRODUCT |
|---|---|
| Atlanta | Antacids and aspirin |
| Dallas/Fort Worth | Popcorn |
| Denver | Vitamins |
| Grand Rapids | Rat poison |
| Indianapolis | Shoe polish |
| Miami | Prune juice |
| New York | Laundry soaps |
| New Orleans | Ketchup |
| Oklahoma | Motor oil additives |
| Philadelphia | Ice tea |
| Pittsburgh | Coffee |
| Portland (Oregon) | Dry cat food |
| Salt Lake City | Candy bars and marshmallows |
| Savannah | MSG and meat tenderizers |
| Seattle | Toothbrushes |

Source: "Different Folks, Different Strokes," *Fortune,* September 16, 1985, 65.

## Racial Subcultures

The major racial subcultures in the United States are white, black, Oriental, and American Indian. Although there are differences in lifestyles and consumer spending patterns among all these groups, the vast majority of racially oriented consumer research has focused on black-white consumer differences.

### THE BLACK CONSUMER

Black consumers currently constitute the largest racial minority of the U.S. population (approximately 12 percent). This group of over 27 million consumers, spending more than $150 billion annually, has too frequently been portrayed as a single, undifferentiated "black market" consisting of economically deprived consumers who have a uniform set of consumer needs. In reality, while a substantial portion of the black population is economically less well off than the white majority, there does exist an important and growing black middle class. Moreover, research indicates that the difference among better-educated and more affluent black consumers and their poorer, less-educated counterparts is greater than the differences between both whites and blacks of the middle class.[15] Therefore, just as the white majority has been divided into a variety of submarket segments, each with its own distinctive needs and tastes, so too can the black market be segmented. Unfortunately, there is not sufficient research data available concerning market segments within the total black market to examine them in detail. For this reason, the following sections deal with more general consumer dimensions of the black subculture.

PURCHASE MOTIVES AND BEHAVIOR. As consumers, blacks have been characterized in terms of their motivation to strive (or not to strive) for middle-class values, as such values are reflected in the consumption of material goods. According to this *striving* framework, the black consumer faces the dilemma of ". . . whether to strive against odds for middle-class values as reflected in material goods, or to give in and live more for the moment."[16] *Strivers* have been identified as those black consumers who perceive that it is possible for them, in terms of present or expected incomes, to attain a middle-class lifestyle. *Nonstrivers* are described as those black consumers who feel financially blocked from such goals and who therefore do not seek the material goods associated with being "middle class."

A comparison of two groups of black students—one that strongly subscribed to basic American values and one that did not—found that those black students who identified strongly with basic American values were more likely to be *strivers* (i.e., aspire to attain higher social-class status) than those who did not.[17]

Segmentation of the black market on the basis of motivation suggests that strivers and nonstrivers may constitute distinct market segments. If this is true, then it is likely that they have to be reached through different copy appeals (see Figure 15-2). The striver-nonstriver framework also suggests that as more blacks acquire middle-class economic status, the striver segment of the black market increases.

Other research studies that have explored the product preferences and brand purchase patterns of black consumers have found they are: (1) usually predisposed to popular or leading brands, (2) brand loyal, and (3) unlikely to purchase private-label and generic products. Table 15-6 outlines the possible motives for these consumer-related traits.

Supporting these consumer traits of the black consumer, Table 15-7 presents the results of a study that explored toothpaste brand preferences for blacks, whites, and Hispanics. The evidence reveals that the leading brand among both blacks and whites is Colgate, and among Hispanics is Crest, which is the overall market share leader.[18] For marketers, the findings confirm the payoff to be gained by appealing to national and racial market groups.

DO BLACKS PAY MORE? Most of the evidence on this question has focused on poor blacks living in central-city communities. A review of the topic indicates that supermarket chain stores charge the same prices in stores located in black communities as they do in stores located in predominantly white urban or suburban communities.[19] However, the research also indicates that small independent groceries located in black communities do charge more than the major supermarket chains, and therefore blacks who shop at these stores are likely to pay more. Since almost all these studies examined the "price asked" (displayed price) by retailers located inside and outside of black communities rather than the "price paid," it is difficult to determine whether black consumers actually do pay more. One study found that blacks tend to avoid the higher prices charged by small independent stores in their communities by shopping outside their immediate community.[20]

REACHING THE BLACK AUDIENCE. A question of central importance to marketers is: What is the best way to reach the black consumer? Traditionally, mar-

FIGURE 15-2 Advertisement Appealing to the Striver Segment of the Black Market

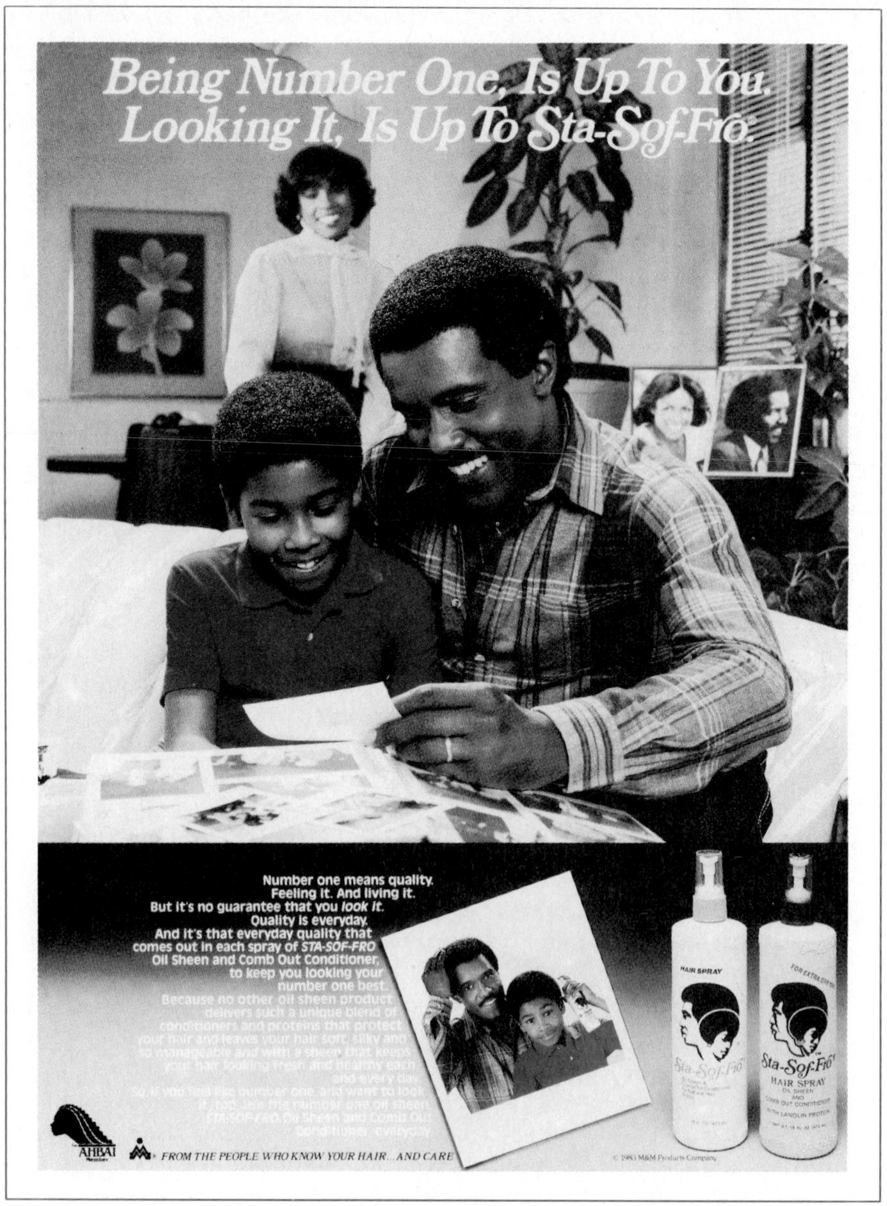


Courtesy of M&M Products Co.

keters have subscribed to one of two distinct marketing strategies. Some have followed the policy of running all their advertising in general mass media in the belief that blacks have the same media habits as whites; others have followed the policy of running additional advertising in selected media directed exclusively to blacks.

Both strategies may be appropriate in specific situations and for specific

**TABLE 15-6 Understanding Black Consumers' Brand Preferences**

| CONSUMER TRAITS | POSSIBLE MOTIVATIONS |
|---|---|
| Purchase popular or leading brands | A strong desire to impress others<br>Buy the "best" to reduce perceived risk<br>Feel better about one's self |
| Brand loyal | Avoid perceived risk<br>Reduce the time spent searching for product information |
| Less likely to buy private-label or generic products | Reduce perceived risk<br>Avoid feeling that they have "settled" for second best |

Source: Kelvin A. Wall, "Positioning Your Brand in the Black Market," *Advertising Age,* June 18, 1973, 71; Robert B. Settle, John H. Faricy, and Richard W. Mizerski, "Racial Differences in Consumer Locus of Control," in Fred C. Allvine, ed., *1971 Combined Proceedings* (Chicago: American Marketing Association, 1972), 629–33; Raymond A. Bauer, Scott M. Cunningham, and Lawrence H. Wortzel, "The Marketing Dilemma of Negroes," *Journal of Marketing,* 29 (July 1965), 4; and Alphonzia Wellington, "Traditional Brand Loyalty," *Advertising Age,* May 18, 1981, S-2.

**TABLE 15-7 Toothpaste Brand Shares Among Blacks, Whites, and Hispanics**

| BRAND | BLACKS | HISPANICS | WHITES |
|---|---|---|---|
| Crest | 25.6% | 37.8% | 20.1% |
| Colgate | 29.6 | 23.1 | 39.0 |
| Close-up | 16.5 | 13.2 | 13.4 |
| Aim | 11.5 | 11.7 | 9.6 |
| Aqua Fresh (2 Stripes) | 11.5 | 9.4 | 13.8 |
| Ultra-Brite | 5.2 | 4.8 | 4.1 |

Source: Alphonzia Wellington, "Blacks and Hispanics: Power in Numbers and Market Concentration," *Marketing Review,* 38 (January–February 1983), 26.

product categories. For products of very broad appeal (e.g., aspirin, toothpaste), it is quite possible that the mass media (primarily television) may effectively reach all relevant consumers, black and white. However, for other products (e.g., personal grooming products, food products), an advertiser may find that the general mass media do *not* communicate effectively with the relevant black market. Instead, black-oriented media may be more effective.

Media exposure habits of black consumers have been shown to differ from those of the general population. As one black advertising executive remarked: "Black people are not dark-skinned white people—there are cultural values which cause us to be subtly different from the majority population."[21] In recent years, there has been an increase in the number of new black advertising agencies and in the number of companies that wish to target promotional messages to black consumers.

It would seem appropriate for a marketer who feels that a product is not realizing its potential among black consumers to supplement general advertising with black-targeted advertisements in magazines, newspapers, and other media directed specifically to blacks. If marketers are offering a product exclusively for the black market (e.g., a line of shampoos for black consumers), they should probably spend the major part of their advertising budget in black media, where it will most effectively reach the target audience. In fact, in an attempt to woo customers away from giant competitors such as Revlon and Alberto-Culver, several black-owned hair-care companies have initiated a program under which a special logotype is attached to their products which identifies the item as the product of a black-owned company.

Several studies have compared the responses of black and white consumers to advertising and point-of-purchase promotions that feature all black models, all white models, or both black and white models ("integrated" promotions).[22] Not surprisingly, the majority of these studies indicate that black consumers tend to favor more strongly ads that feature black models. White consumers tend to respond either neutrally or positively to ads that feature black models. This research suggests that, while black consumers prefer ads that include black models, white consumers are unlikely to respond adversely to such ads.

## Age Subcultures

All major age subgroupings of the population might broadly be thought of as separate subcultures. Within the context of the family life cycle, Chapter 12 examined the major age segments of the adult population. Each stage of the life cycle (bachelorhood, honeymooners, parenthood, postparenthood, and dissolution) could be considered a separate subculture, since important shifts occur in the demand for specific types of products and services.

In this section we will limit our examination of age subcultures to just two groups: the *baby boomers* and the *elderly*. These two age groups have been singled out because they are on opposite ends of the age spectrum of the adult population, and because their distinctive lifestyles qualify them for consideration as subcultural groups.

### THE BABY BOOMER MARKET

In recent years, marketers have found baby boomers to be a particularly desirable target audience because (1) they are the single largest distinctive age category alive today, (2) they frequently make important consumer purchase decisions, and (3) they contain a small subsegment of trendsetting consumers known as *Yuppies* (young upwardly mobile professionals), who sometimes influence the tastes of consumers in other age segments of society.

WHO ARE THE BABY BOOMERS? When we speak of baby boomers, we are referring to the age segment of the population that was born between 1946 and 1964. Thus baby boomers are in the broad age category that extends from the early twenties to the early forties. This age range corresponds to a period of time when birth rates were quite high (see Figure 15-3).

**FIGURE 15-3** **Baby Boomers Are the Biggest Age Category Market** Source: *The Baby Boom Generation: Its Attitudes, Values and Lifestyle,* (New York: Research Presentation, Market Research Department of *People* Magazine, undated).

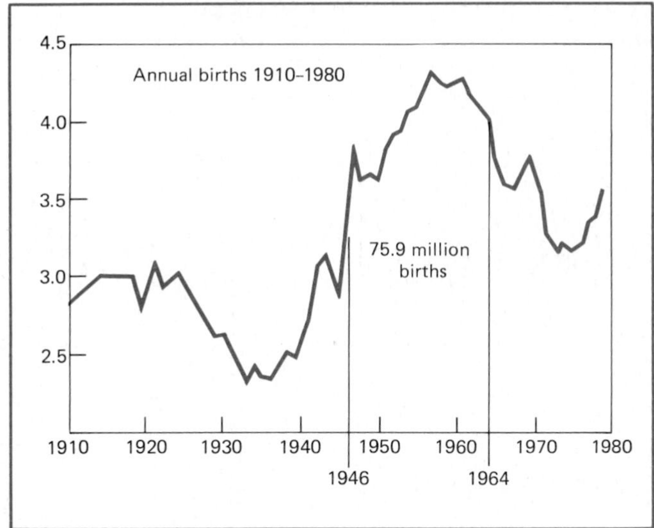


The baby boomers constitute approximately 45 percent of the adult population (some 76 million individuals). The magnitude of this statistic alone would make them a much-sought-after age segment. However, they are also prized because they currently comprise about 50 percent of all those in professional and managerial occupations, 57 percent of those with at least a college degree, and 54 percent of those households with a dual income (38 percent have $30,000-plus household incomes).[23]

CONSUMER CHARACTERISTICS OF BABY BOOMERS. Baby boomers are consumers. They enjoy buying for themselves, for their homes or apartments, and for others. Table 15-8 demonstrates just how consumer-oriented the baby boomer market is. The index numbers reveal that these baby boomers exceed forty-plus adult consumers in all areas of usage/purchase expenditures on the list.

Baby boomers are also more active physically and more involved in a host of leisure-time pursuits than individuals over forty. Demonstrating this point, Table 15-9 contrasts baby boomers and non-boomers in terms of various physical and leisure activities. From these results it is easy to see why marketers of active/action-oriented goods and services fight over the baby boomer market.

SEGMENTING THE BABY BOOMER MARKET. Though an age segment by itself, baby boomers can be further subdivided into two subsegments: (1) *younger boomers,* those age twenty-one to twenty-nine; and (2) *older boomers,* those thirty to forty. As might be expected, this age split influences living arrangements and lifestyles; that is, younger boomers are more likely to be single and living at home with their parents; older boomers are more likely to be married and/or

**TABLE 15-8 Baby Boomers Are a Consuming Generation†**

| AREAS OF USAGE/PURCHASE | INDEX OF BOOMERS 20–39 VS. ADULTS 40+ |
|---|---|
| Stereo equipment | 148† |
| Portable/walkabout stereo | 142 |
| VCR | 156 |
| Electronic games | 187 |
| Home/personal computer | 142 |
| Computer software | 133 |
| Paperback books | 149 |
| Hardcover books | 143 |
| Blank tapes | 206 |
| Pre-recorded records or tapes | 180 |
| Telephone | 134 |
| 35 mm camera | 140 |
| Imported car | 158 |
| Sport/utility vehicle | 124 |
| Active in sports | 160 |
| Sporting goods | 254 |
| Backpacking/camping equipment | 225 |
| Health club membership | 206 |
| Active sportswear | 174 |
| Jeans | 212 |
| Disposable shavers | 128 |
| Suntan products | 170 |
| Cologne | 117 |
| Deodorants* | 132 |
| Shampoo* | 235 |
| Fast food restaurants | 155 |
| Diet soda* | 112 |
| Frozen dinners* | 120 |
| Yogurt | 137 |
| Candy bars* | 129 |
| Wines | 123 |
| Aperitif & specialty wines | 123 |
| Cordials & liqueurs | 123 |
| Food processor | 113 |
| Bedroom furniture | 152 |
| Sofabed | 117 |
| Carry $50,000+ life insurance | 139 |
| Movie attendance* | 280 |
| European travel | 118 |
| Domestic business air travel | 128 |
| Theme park visit | 130 |
| Credit card usage | 115 |

*Heavy usage.

†The index for adults 40+(non-boomers) = 100 percent. So, for example, boomers are 48 percent more likely to purchase stereo equipment, 58 percent more inclined to purchase imported cars; 135 percent more likely to be heavy users of shampoo than non-boomers.

Source: 1984 SMRB.

Source: *The Experts' Guide to the Baby Boomers* (New York: People Magazine, 1985), 40–41.

**TABLE 15-9 Physical and Leisure-Time Interests of Baby Boomers**

physical activities

Baby boomers are more likely than other adults to belong to a health club, to participate in exercise classes, and to engage in a variety of sports.

| | | | BABY BOOMERS | | | | |
|---|---|---|---|---|---|---|---|
| | | | ACTIVES | | SEDENTARIES/INACTIVES | | |
| | BABY BOOMERS | NON-BABY BOOMERS | all-around actives | exercisers | cable tv viewers | readers | inactives |
| Total respondents answering | (1262) | (812) | (385) | (208) | (115) | (72) | (481) |
| Belong to a health club | 17% | 8% | 6% | 72% | 14% | 15% | 2% |
| Currently participate in exercise classes | 18% | 9% | 6% | 72% | 19% | 17% | 4% |
| Engage in on a regular basis: | | | | | | | |
| Walking (or climbing stairs) | 56% | 56% | 58% | 52% | 57% | 54% | 54% |
| Swimming | 46 | 23 | 55 | 58 | 55 | 36 | 36 |
| Dancing (e.g., aerobic, disco, ballroom) | 39 | 18 | 52 | 58 | 25 | 26 | 27 |
| Baseball/softball | 30 | 7 | 47 | 30 | 32 | 14 | 17 |
| Camping | 31 | 20 | 46 | 28 | 38 | 31 | 18 |
| Fishing | 29 | 26 | 42 | 24 | 33 | 32 | 19 |
| Regular bicycling | 29 | 11 | 39 | 37 | 26 | 25 | 19 |
| Boating | 19 | 13 | 34 | 17 | 13 | 22 | 9 |
| Jogging (running) | 26 | 10 | 33 | 37 | 23 | 24 | 17 |
| Football | 18 | 4 | 31 | 18 | 25 | 11 | 7 |
| Hiking | 17 | 10 | 27 | 17 | 14 | 24 | 9 |
| Basketball | 18 | 3 | 26 | 21 | 20 | 18 | 8 |
| Calisthenics (home or gym) | 23 | 13 | 26 | 48 | 17 | 31 | 12 |
| Hunting | 14 | 10 | 24 | 6 | 17 | 21 | 8 |
| Tennis | 19 | 5 | 24 | 30 | 17 | 19 | 9 |
| Racquetball | 12 | 3 | 20 | 23 | 10 | 11 | 2 |
| Skiing | 14 | 3 | 19 | 26 | 11 | 11 | 4 |
| Stationary bicycling | 9 | 5 | 9 | 16 | 13 | 7 | 6 |
| Mean (number of activities) | (4.5) | (2.4) | (6.1) | (5.5) | (4.5) | (4.2) | (2.8) |

leisure activities

Baby boomers are far more likely than any other adults to attend movies, but less likely to do volunteer work.

| | BABY BOOMERS | NON-BABY BOOMERS | all-around actives | exercisers | cable tv viewers | readers | inactives |
|---|---|---|---|---|---|---|---|
| Total respondents answering | (1262) | (812) | (385) | (208) | (115) | (72) | (481) |
| ATTENDING EVENTS: | | | | | | | |
| Movies | 66% | 35% | 84% | 74% | 49% | 63% | 52% |
| Sporting events | 36 | 29 | 56 | 50 | 39 | 25 | 16 |
| Concerts | 33 | 16 | 54 | 41 | 30 | 26 | 15 |
| Plays | 18 | 19 | 31 | 34 | 10 | 19 | 2 |

**TABLE 15-9 Physical and Leisure-Time Interests of Baby Boomers (continued)**

| | BABY BOOMERS | NON-BABY BOOMERS | BABY BOOMERS | | | | |
|---|---|---|---|---|---|---|---|
| | | | ACTIVES | | SEDENTARIES/INACTIVES | | |
| | | | all-around actives | exercisers | cable tv viewers | readers | inactives |
| OTHER ACTIVITIES: | | | | | | | |
| Attending parties/ social gatherings | 66% | 49% | 91% | 82% | 43% | 69% | 45% |
| Eating out | 68 | 67 | 80 | 83 | 57 | 58 | 55 |
| Hobbies (outside of home) | 30 | 17 | 38 | 32 | 43 | 35 | 19 |
| Work-related education | 22 | 14 | 28 | 33 | 17 | 26 | 14 |
| Non-work-related education | 16 | 9 | 23 | 30 | 7 | 17 | 7 |
| Gambling | 11 | 9 | 16 | 13 | 10 | 13 | 5 |
| Volunteer work | 12 | 19 | 15 | 15 | 13 | 8 | 9 |
| AT HOME: | | | | | | | |
| Listening to radio | 78% | 66% | 84% | 76% | 78% | 75% | 74% |
| Playing stereo/ records | 71 | 46 | 80 | 77 | 65 | 57 | 65 |
| Watching television | 80 | 85 | 77 | 78 | 97 | 67 | 83 |
| Entertaining friends | 59 | 56 | 69 | 63 | 62 | 61 | 48 |
| Reading | 63 | 65 | 64 | 75 | 60 | 82 | 55 |
| Garden and lawn work | 49 | 61 | 51 | 50 | 60 | 56 | 44 |
| Home improvements | 46 | 48 | 51 | 50 | 47 | 53 | 39 |
| Repair/work on automobile | 33 | 25 | 44 | 29 | 39 | 38 | 24 |
| Entertaining relatives | 44 | 55 | 44 | 49 | 45 | 53 | 41 |
| Hobbies (at home) | 36 | 32 | 41 | 43 | 31 | 50 | 28 |
| Playing video games | 25 | 8 | 29 | 28 | 37 | 25 | 17 |
| Caring/babysitting for children | 25 | 19 | 19 | 23 | 36 | 29 | 27 |
| Using a home computer | 4 | 4 | 7 | 4 | 1 | 1 | 1 |

Source: Barbara I. Brown, "How the Baby Boomer Lives," *American Demographics*, 6 (May 1984), 36-37.

living in households separate from their parents. These factors are likely to affect consumption needs and behavior. For instance, older boomers have enjoyed a number of advantages that younger boomers are unlikely to be able to duplicate in the near future. More precisely, older boomers came of age in a period when it was much easier to get a career started and to afford to purchase a home. Thus, although many younger boomers are well educated and aspire to "the good life," it has been much more difficult for them to attain their dreams. The increased competition for a smaller number of desired career opportunities has made it more difficult for them to fulfill their expectations. Political marketers (see Chapter 20) divide the baby boomer market by

**TABLE 15-10 Demographic/Psychographic Traits That Describe the Affluent Baby Boomers**

Males and females
25 to 40 years of age
Reside in major metropolitan areas
Single's income of $30,000+; couple's/family income $40,000+
Professional/managerial positions or self-employed
Four-year college education at minimum
Personality/psychographic traits:
- Achievement-oriented
- High-fashion involvement
- Recreational shoppers
- Credit card users
- Status-brand purchasers
- Physical-fitness concerns

income into *yuppies* and *new collars*—a subgroup consisting of fast food managers, truck drivers, mechanics, etc.

AFFLUENT BABY BOOMERS. "Yuppies" are by far the most sought-after subgroup of baby boomers. While consisting of only 5 percent of the population, they are generally well off financially, well educated, and on "the way up" in envious professional or managerial careers. Table 15-10 presents a list of traits and characteristics that identify this desired group of consumers.

When it comes to purchases, yuppies have often been associated with many status brand names, such as: BMWs, Volvo station wagons, Rado watches, cable TVs, and Cuisinart food processors (see Figure 15-4).[24]

## THE ELDERLY CONSUMER

Unlike the baby boomers, who are often glorified as a market segment, the elderly are frequently misunderstood and avoided. The distorted image some marketers have of the elderly has been aptly summed up as follows: "The tendency of marketers is either to treat the elderly, over sixty-five, consumers as a more or less homogeneous group, or to pay virtually no attention to them at all."[25]

WHO IS THE ELDERLY CONSUMER? In the United States, "old age" is officially assumed to begin with a person's sixty-fifth birthday (i.e., when the individual qualifies for full social security insurance and Medicare). However, research suggests that Americans who are seventy years old still tend to view themselves as "middle aged," and that it is only when they reach their seventy-fifth birthday that they begin to consider themselves "elderly."[26]

This and other research suggest that people's *perceptions* of their ages may be more important in determining behavior than their chronological ages (i.e., the number of years lived). In fact, people may at the same time have a number of different subjective or **perceived ages.** Table 15-11 shows the percentage of

FIGURE 15-4 Advertisement Appealing to Young Sophisticated Consumers

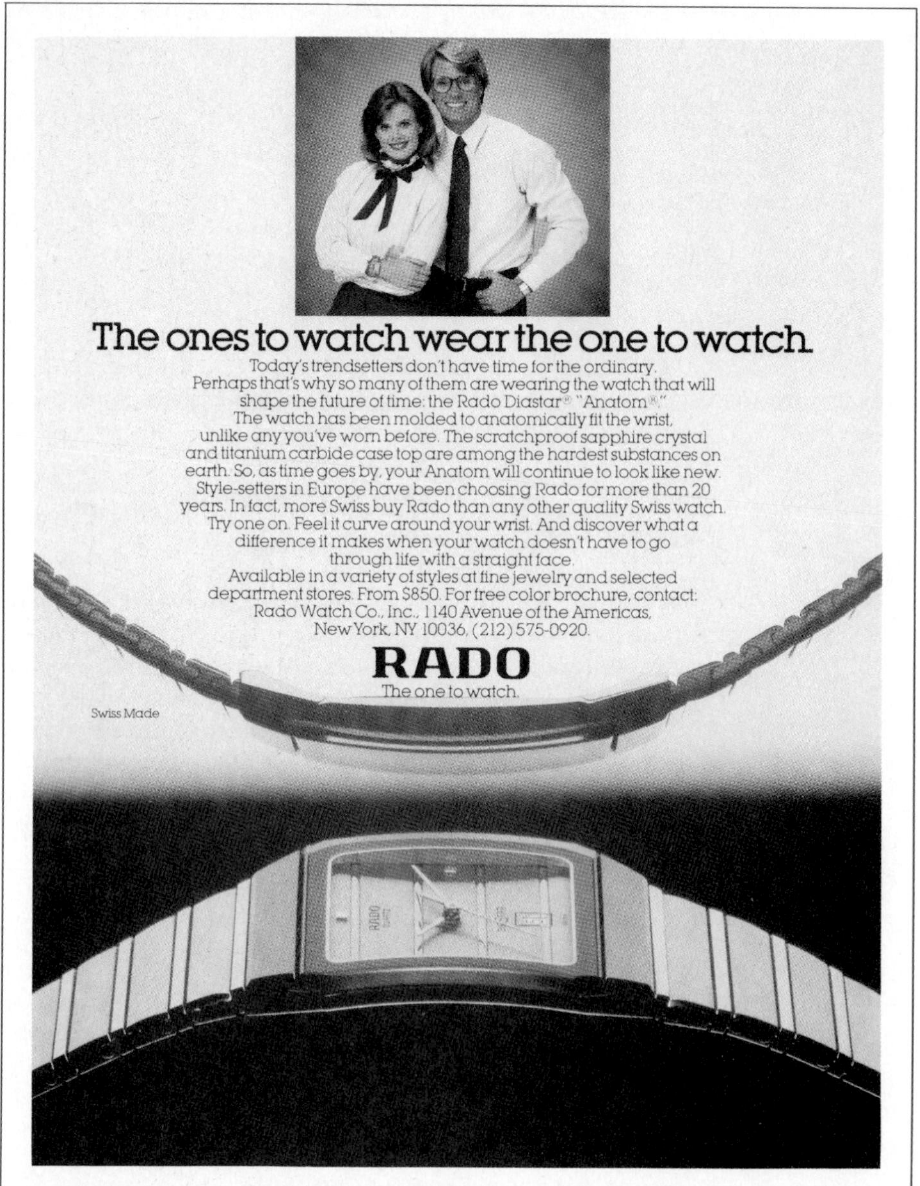


Courtesy of Rado Watch Co.

elderly consumers who perceived themselves to be younger than their chronological age on four perceived age dimensions: *feel-age,* how old a person feels; *look-age,* how old a person looks; *do-age,* how involved a person is in activities favored by members of a certain age group; and *interest-age,* how similar a person's interests are to those of members of a certain age group.[27] The results support other research which indicates that elderly consumers are more likely to consider themselves *younger* than their chronological age. The mean percentages in the last column of the table show that as their chronological age in-

**TABLE 15-11 Percentage of Elderly Expressing a Perceived Age That Is Younger Than Their Chronological Age**

| DECADE | FEEL-AGE | LOOK-AGE | DO-AGE | INTEREST-AGE | MEAN % |
|---|---|---|---|---|---|
| 50's | 54% | 52% | 69% | 66% | 60% |
| 60's | 67 | 63 | 77 | 71 | 70 |
| 70's | 63 | 66 | 80 | 77 | 72 |
| 80's | 74 | 68 | 79 | 84 | 76 |

Source: Benny Barak and Leon G. Schiffman, "Cognitive Age: A Nonchronological Age Variable," in Kent B. Monroe, ed., *Advances in Consumer Research* (Ann Arbor, Mich.: Association for Consumer Research, 1981), VIII, 604.

creases, elderly consumers are more likely to identify with a younger perceived age grouping. For marketers, these findings underscore the importance of looking beyond chronological age to consumers' perceived ages when attempting to segment markets. An advertising executive who specializes in the elderly market noted: "Some people are into looking young and others don't care—they just want to look good. Both attitudes are fine, but both require [different] creative responses. . . ."[28]

THE APPEAL OF ELDERLY CONSUMERS. As a sign that America is aging rather quickly, the number of elderly consumers is growing twice as fast as the overall United States population. There are over 27 million Americans within this sixty-five-plus age category, representing close to 12 percent of the country's population. This number is expected to more than double in the next fifty years, with the elderly segment eventually accounting for about 20 percent of the American population. This expected growth in the elderly population can be explained by the declining birth rate, improved medical diagnoses and treatment, and the resultant increase in general life expectancy.

A STILL LARGELY MISUNDERSTOOD MARKET. While more and more marketers are coming to recognize the consumer potential of the elderly, some still have an extremely narrow and inaccurate picture of the elderly consumer. For example, marketers too frequently are reluctant to target the elderly market because they mistakenly believe that, in general, the elderly cannot afford to buy new products and services. This stereotypical view of the elderly fails to consider that today many older people have sufficient funds available for products that could improve the quality of their lives. In reality, less than 20 percent of the elderly live below the poverty line; 76 percent own their own homes, and many have already paid off their mortgages.[29]

Indeed, as more and more elderly consumers receive the benefits of private pension funds in addition to social security and Medicare, and with an increasing percentage working longer, this age segment is even more likely to afford new products and services in the future. Furthermore, available evidence suggests that the elderly are very willing to try new products, especially those designed to promote or maintain good health.[30] Table 15-12 presents a summary of the major myths and related realities about the elderly as consumers.

**TABLE 15-12 Five Myths About Older Consumers**

*Myth 1: The Elderly Are Not a Separate Market*
*Reality: Elderly Have Distinguishing Traits:*
- They are price-value conscious
- They are deal-prone
- They like to shop—it has special meaning
- They are tuned-in to the mass media
- They read direct mail, package labels, and package inserts

*Myth 2: The Elderly Are One Homogeneous Group*
*Reality: The Elderly Market Can Be Segmented:*
- Psychographic Segments: Isolationists, traditionalists, outgoers (Towle & Martin, 1976)

*Myth 3: The Elderly Are Not a Substantial Market*
*Reality: America Is Aging Rapidly:*
- There are approximately 18 million households headed by a person 65+
- Median age rose quickly during the 1970s and early 1980s
- Rapid growth is expected through the year 2,000+
- This implies more older women

*Myth 4: The Elderly Lack Buying Power*
*Reality: They Have the Money:*
- 7 out of 10 over-65s own their home
- 85% of homeowners have *no* mortgages
- Empty nests mean more discretionary income
- More older-working women mean more two-income households (again, more discretionary income)

*Myth 5: The Elderly Are Not Innovative Consumers*
*Reality: Under the Right Circumstances, They Are Innovative.*

Source: Elaine Sherman and Leon G. Schiffman, presentation before various academic and professional groups, 1985.

THE NEEDS AND MOTIVATIONS OF ELDERLY CONSUMERS. The elderly are by no means a homogeneous subcultural group; they can be segmented by following a number of useful guidelines. It will be recalled that as part of the discussion of market segmentation in Chapter 2, we explored the merits of dividing the elderly into three chronological age categories: the *young-old* (those sixty-five to seventy-four years of age); the *old* (those seventy-five to eighty-four); and the *old-old* (those eighty-five years of age and older). This simplistic market segmentation scheme provides some useful consumer-relevant insights. For instance, the members of the *young-old* subsegment tend to have both health and money, and therefore comprise a profitable market for all types of travel programs. In contrast, members of the fast-growing *old-old* subsegment are in an age-category that is likely to require various specialized housing and medical services.[31]

The elderly can also be segmented in terms of *motivations* and *adjustment orientation.* One such segmentation scheme first divided the elderly into three major segments (*healthy adjustment, fair adjustment,* and *poor adjustment*). With three further subsegments in each of these major categories, the segmentation consists of a total of nine subsegments.[32] Table 15-13 presents a brief description of each of these nine groups and their chosen lifestyles. For example, according to experts, the *reorganizer* group (estimated to be about 20 percent of the elderly population) are likely to be particularly innovative, enjoy the physical pleasures of life and be especially outgoing when it comes to socializing with friends and relatives (see Figure 15-5).

**TABLE 15-13** **Adjustment Patterns for Senior Citizens**

healthy adjustment

The *reorganizers* have had success integrating themselves into retirement living. They attempt to stay active by reorganizing their lives, substituting new activities for those that were abandoned after retirement. They enjoy life by seeking new experiences and social interaction. (21.1%)

The *focused* group shows a mature approach to old age. Life has been and continues to be satisfying for them. The focused people have chosen a rather small number of activities to which they devote time and energy. (19%)

The *disengaged* are self-directed, calm, and contented. They have accepted old age by reducing their activities to a relatively low level. Although interested in the goings-on of the world, they prefer to withdraw from most of their past personal associations and activities. (9.2%)

fair adjustment

The *constricted* people are preoccupied with their physical well-being. They have lived a satisfying life but view old age, new experiences, and social interaction as threatening that satisfaction. To avoid these threats, they structure a narrow set of activities for themselves which they pursue in a habitual pattern. (10.8%)

The *holding-on* group contains achievement-oriented people who drive themselves hard. They are defensive about their age, fear the rocking chair image, and are reluctant to admit that they are indeed old. In keeping with this defensive posture, they try to hold on to life by keeping busy. (9.5%)

The *succorance seekers,* although moderately active, prefer a passive life. They have strong dependency needs and lean on others for emotional support and responsiveness. Retirement for them is a refuge, a safe port after the turbulent working years. (13.2%)

poor adjustment

The *angry* group consists of aggressive, rigid, and highly suspicious people who see themselves as victims of circumstance. They desire little pleasure from life and look back on the past as a series of disappointments. They view life as a failure, but project the blame for that failure onto others rather than onto themselves. (5.4%)

The *apathetic* group contains elderly people who have truly retreated to their rocking chairs. They feel that life is hard and there is not much they can do about it. They limit social interaction and make little effort to keep up with things outside their immediate surroundings. (7.1%)

The *self-blamers* look back on life as a series of unattained goals. These perceived failures have caused them to be highly critical and contemptuous of themselves. They sit in depression, showing little sign of ambition or initiative. (4.7%)

Source: Warren A. French and Richard Fox, "Segmenting the Senior Citizen Market," *The Journal of Consumer Marketing,* 2 (Winter 1985), 62.

To develop special products and special promotional programs to meet the needs of these market segments, marketers must not only recognize their different approaches to life, but also conduct research into their specific needs. The elderly seem to derive most satisfaction from meaningful social involvement and purposeful activity; on the other hand, they are most fearful of financial and physical dependency and of loneliness. This suggests that the elderly need products and services that help them feel their lives are useful and socially enjoyable, and which reduce their fears of dependency. Builders of retirement communities for the elderly have successfully recognized these needs by promoting the organized activities and the security measures these communities offer.

In aiming products at the elderly, marketers must not only take into consideration their needs and motivations, but must also be careful not to embarrass them, or make them feel uneasy about their age. In a classic marketing blunder, Heinz once made the mistake of introducing a line of "senior foods" after observing that many elderly people were buying its baby foods. The new product failed because elderly consumers were ashamed to admit that they required strained foods; instead, they continued to buy baby food which they

**FIGURE 15-5 Advertisement That Might Appeal to the Reorganized/Focused Older Segments**

Courtesy of AT&T Communications

could always pretend they were buying for a grandchild. Table 15-14 presents a number of mistakes marketers have made in attempting to market to elderly consumers.

SHOPPING EXPERIENCES OF THE OLDER CONSUMER. Service organizations (retailers, financial institutions, and hotel and travel companies), rather than manufacturers, have been most attuned to the needs of the elderly and quickest to

TABLE 15-14 Mistakes Marketers Make When Considering Mature/Elderly Consumers

| |
|---|
| They ignore them. |
| They do not treat them with respect. |
| They treat them as undifferentiated consumers. |
| They place too much emphasis on chronological age. |
| They rely on traditional age categories. |
| They perceive older consumers as having little money to spend. |
| They perceive older consumers as set in their ways and noninnovative. |
| They employ complex messages in their advertisements. |

realize their value as consumers (see Figure 15-6). Large retail food chains have been particularly sensitive to the needs of older consumers. For instance, Kroger, the large midwestern supermarket chain, has promoted a Senior Citizens Club which offers anyone who is over fifty-nine years of age and on a fixed income a special shopping program designed to cut food costs. Many of the major fast-food chains have also sponsored various promotional programs designed to attract the business of older consumers. Along similar lines, Sears, the nation's largest retailer, now operates a "club" for individuals aged fifty-five and older. Club members receive discounts on goods and services (including Allstate insurance), and a quarterly magazine, *Mature Outlook,* all for a $7.50 membership fee.[33]

In terms of shopping behavior, research has generally suggested that older consumers are more apt to pay cash for their purchases, use cents-off coupons, avoid using credit cards for installment payments, prepare shopping lists, and be comparison shoppers.[34]

REACHING THE ELDERLY CONSUMER. Studies indicate that the elderly often perceive that they are negatively portrayed in advertisements.[35] Therefore, marketers should be careful that their advertisements do not contain negative stereotypes of the elderly, but do in fact cater to their preferences. Research has consistently shown that the elderly spend more time watching TV or reading newspapers than do younger individuals, and that they prefer information over entertainment. Newspapers are their most important medium, in contrast to younger consumers, for whom television is most important.[36] Despite this, TV viewing does seem to increase with age.[37]

The number of publications targeted directly at the elderly or mature market has proliferated in recent years. *Modern Maturity* reaches the 20 million members of the American Association of Retired Persons; newer periodicals, such as *50 Plus,* aim at the upscale subsegment of the elderly market. *Mature Outlook,* another new magazine, has grown rapidly.[38]

## Sex as a Subculture

It may seem surprising to see sex (gender) included in a discussion of subcultures. Sex-related characteristics have not usually been treated as subcultural differences. However, as one marketing expert pointed out, this is a "notable

**FIGURE 15-6** Service Advertisement Aimed at Elderly Consumers

RAMADA®

YOUR SENIORITY IS WORTH 20% OFF

If you're 55 or over, clip this coupon and cash in on your seniority at Ramada.

Participating Ramadas throughout New England will give you a big 20% off the regular room rate.

You'll enjoy all the good things when you stay at Ramada . . . superb guest rooms, fine restaurants and lounges, recreational facilities and much more.

Call for reservations and cash in on your seniority now at these participating New England Ramadas.

RAMADA

RAMADA

RAMADA

**CONNECTICUT**

Hartford/Wethersfield
1330 Silas Deane Hwy.
(203) 563-2311

Hartford/Metro
100 E. River Dr.
(203) 528-9703

Hartford/E. Windsor
161 Bridge St.
(203) 623-9411

Hartford/Bradley
Int'l Airport
5 Turnpike Rd.
(203) 623-9494

Hartford/Bradley
Int'l Airport
3316 Airport Rd.
(203) 623-2441

Danbury
I-84 at Exit 8
(203) 792-3800

Mystic
I-95 & Rte. 27
(203) 536-4281

Stamford/Greenwich
19 Clarks Hill Rd.
(203) 327-4300

**MAINE**

Bangor
357 Odlin Rd.
(207) 947-6961

Lewiston
490 Pleasant St.
(207) 784-2331

Portland
1230 Congress St.
(207) 774-5611

**MASSACHUSETTS**

Boston/Brighton
1234 Soldiers Field Rd.
(617) 254-1234

Boston/Woburn
15 Middlesex Canal Pk. Rd.
(617) 935-8760

**NEW HAMPSHIRE**

Concord
172 N. Main St.
(603) 224-9534

Keene
401 Winchester St.
(603) 357-3038

**VERMONT**

Bennington
Rt. 7 & Kocher Dr.
(802) 442-8145

S. Burlington
1117 Williston Rd.
(802) 658-0250

**For reservations call toll-free 800-228-2828**

Guest's Signature ______________________

This coupon must be presented at a participating New England area Ramada upon check-in. Offer applies to minimum one person/one bed or two person/two bed room rate. Rollaway beds are available at a slight extra charge; offer subject to availability. One coupon per entire stay. Not valid in combination with other discounts, promotions or during special events listed in the current issue of the Ramada Worldwide Directory. Coupon has no cash value. Void where prohibited by law. Coupon good through 12/31/83.

MONEY SAVING COUPON

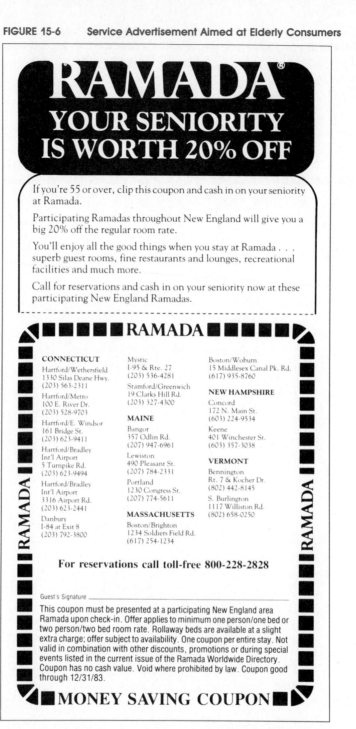

Courtesy of Ramada Hotels Inc.

omission."[39] Indeed, since sex roles are largely culturally determined, it is quite fitting to examine gender as a subcultural category. Moreover, given the extensive amount of attention that changing sex roles and sex discrimination have received in recent years, this is a timely issue.

## SEX ROLES AND CONSUMER BEHAVIOR

All known societies assign certain traits and roles to males and others to females. In American society, for instance, aggressiveness, competitiveness, independence, and self-confidence are considered to be traditional *masculine* traits; neatness, tactfulness, gentleness, and talkativeness are considered to be traditional *feminine* traits.[40] In terms of role differences, women have historically been cast as homemakers with responsibility for child care, and men as the providers or breadwinners. While such traits and roles are no longer strongly associated with members of a specific sex, they are nevertheless still prevalent. Many advertisers still appeal to such sex-linked roles, and consumer tastes are frequently influenced by sex-role factors.

CONSUMER PRODUCTS AND SEX ROLES. Within every society, it is quite common to find products that are either exclusively or strongly associated with the members of one sex. In the United States, for example, shaving equipment, cigars, pants, ties, and work clothing were historically male products; bracelets, hair spray, hair driers, and sweet-smelling colognes were generally considered to be feminine products. For most of these products, the sex link has either diminished or disappeared; for others, the prohibition still lingers.

Despite the fact that the line between "male only" and "female only" products has become blurred in recent years, research indicates that males and females tend to impute a sex, or gender, to products. Table 15-15 lists the results of a study that explored the gender that male and female respondents attributed to twenty-four products. These findings suggest that advertising executives should consider not only the sex of their target market, but also the *perceived* sex of the product category in the development of advertising campaigns.

MASS MEDIA AND SEX ROLES. In the twenty-year period between 1958 and 1978, a series of investigations have employed *content analysis* to examine the portrayal of women in mass-media advertising.[41] These studies have generally indicated that women have been depicted inaccurately in terms of the range of their current roles. For instance, general audience magazine advertisements tended to stereotype women into four restrictive feminine roles: (1) a woman's place is in the home; (2) women do not make important decisions or do important things; (3) women are dependent and need men's protection; and (4) men regard women primarily as sexual objects. From the late 1970s through the present, there appears to have been some real improvement in the proportion of magazine ads that portray women in a working environment, or in some other nontraditional yet realistic setting.

**TABLE 15-15** **Gender Ascribed to 24 Products**

| masculine-image products | feminine-image products | indeterminate products |
|---|---|---|
| Pocket knife | Umbrella | Key ring |
| Tool kit | Mouthwash | |
| Shaving cream | Fountain pen | |
| Cuff links | Sun glasses | |
| Poker chips | Sandals | |
| Brief case | Gloves | |
| Mechanical pencil | Bedroom slippers | |
| Blue jeans | Silk shirt | |
| Tennis shoes | Hair spray | |
| Nail clippers | Hand lotion | |
| | Baby oil | |
| | Nylon underwear | |
| | Scarf | |

Source: Neil K. Allison, Linda L. Golden, Gary M. Mullet, and Donna Coogan, "Sex-Typed Product Images: The Effects of Sex, Sex Role Self-Image and Measurement Implications," in Jerry C. Olson, ed., *Advances in Consumer Research* (Ann Arbor, Mich.: Association for Consumer Research, 1980), VII, 606.

Supporting this conclusion, it is acknowledged today that advertisers who appeal creatively to the expanded role of contemporary women are likely to have their efforts rewarded. The people at *Ms.* magazine, for example, believe that advertising to women should be more realistic and diverse, including the use of older female models.[42] To illustrate, Figure 15-7 proclaims: "Now there's no age limit to beautiful hair!"

### THE WORKING WOMAN

Marketers and consumer researchers have been increasingly interested in the working woman, especially the *married* working woman. They recognize that working wives are a large and growing market segment whose needs differ from those of women who do not work outside the home. It is the size of the working woman market that makes it so attractive. According to government statistics, 52 percent of all American women are employed; they constitute over 40 percent of the workforce, up from only 28 percent in 1950. It has been estimated that today only 37 percent of all women are full-time homemakers.[43] Young women, with young children, have been the fastest-growing segment in the female workforce. The number of working wives with children under the age of six has risen by over 400 percent since 1948, and among those with children six to seventeen, the increase has been over 200 percent.[44]

WHY DO MARRIED WOMEN WORK? Many sociocultural forces are responsible for why so many married women now work. Some of the chief factors are (1) the increased level of female educational attainment, (2) the need to supplement the husband's income, (3) the high divorce rate, (4) the growing conviction that women can simultaneously be mothers and have careers, (5) the

FIGURE 15-7 Advertisement Targeted at the Mature Woman

Courtesy of Johnson & Johnson Baby Products Co.

growth in the number of service jobs that appeal to women, (6) the trend toward fewer children, and (7) the availability of products that make homemaking easier and less time consuming.

SEGMENTING THE WORKING WOMEN MARKET. To better account for the various factors that contribute to why women work and to provide a richer market segmentation framework, it is useful to develop segmentation categories that explain the motivations of working and nonworking women. For instance, a number of studies have divided the female population into four segments: (1) *stay-at-home* housewives (28 percent of the female population); (2) *plan-to-work* housewives (13 percent); (3) *just-a-job* working women (37 percent); and (4) *career-oriented* working women (22 percent).[45]

SHOPPING PATTERNS OF WORKING WOMEN. Working women spend less time shopping than nonworking women. They accomplish this "time economy" by shopping less often and by being brand and store loyal. Not surprisingly, working women are also likely to shop during evening hours or on the weekend. They are also more likely to report *role overload.* Wives reporting role overload are more likely to serve convenience foods and to own time-saving kitchen and household products.[46]

REACHING THE WORKING WOMAN. With respect to the appropriate message necessary to reach women, one study found that homemaker advertisements appealed more to the little-desire-to-work group and career ads were better received by the high-desire-to-work group.[47] Consistent with this research, a number of firms, particularly marketers of automobiles, financial services, and life insurance, have begun producing commercials specifically targeted to career-oriented women.

### Subcultural Interaction

It should be remembered that all consumers are simultaneously members of more than one subcultural segment (for example, a consumer may be a young, Hispanic, Catholic, working wife living in the northeastern section of the country). For this reason, marketers should strive to understand how multiple subcultural memberships *interact* to influence target consumers' relevant consumption behavior. Promotional strategy should not be limited to a single subcultural membership.

## CROSS-CULTURAL CONSUMER ANALYSIS

In our examination of psychological, social, and cultural concepts, we have continuously pointed out how various segments of the American consuming public differ. If such diversity exists among segments of a *single* society, then even more diversity should exist among the members of two or more societies. International marketers must understand the differences inherent among different societies (i.e., cross-culturally) so that they can develop appropriate marketing strategies to penetrate effectively each foreign market of interest.

## What Is Cross-Cultural Consumer Analysis?

To determine whether and how to enter a foreign market, the marketer should conduct **cross-cultural consumer analyses.** Within the scope of this discussion, *cross-cultural consumer analysis* is defined as the effort to determine *to what extent the consumers of two or more nations are similar or different.* Such an analysis will provide the marketer with an understanding of the differences in psychological, social, cultural, and environmental characteristics to permit the design of effective marketing strategies for each of the specific countries involved.

### SIMILARITIES AND DIFFERENCES AMONG PEOPLE

A major objective of cross-cultural consumer analysis is the determination of how consumers in two or more societies are similar, and how they are different. An understanding of the similarities and differences that exist between nations is critical to the multinational marketer, who must devise appropriate strategies to reach consumers in specific foreign markets. The greater the similarity between nations, the more feasible it is to employ relatively similar strategies in each nation. On the other hand, if the cultural beliefs, values, and customs of specific target countries are found to differ widely, then a highly *individualized* marketing strategy is indicated for each country.

How successful a firm is likely to be in introducing an established product in a number of foreign countries is likely to be influenced by how similar the beliefs, values, and customs are that govern the use of the product. For example, the seven-country comparison in Figure 15-8 shows the percentage of consumers who agreed with the statement "A house should be dusted and polished three times a week." While much additional information is likely to be required, if a multinational firm like Unilever was planning to market a new line of furniture polishes, it would be quite interested in such research for its potential usefulness in establishing the firm's marketing priorities.

## Global Marketing

Some marketers have argued that world markets are becoming more and more similar and that standardized marketing strategies are therefore becoming more and more feasible. An increasing number of firms have created *world brands*—products that are manufactured, packaged, and positioned the same way regardless of which country they are sold in.[48] Philip Morris, for example, has successfully used the Marlboro cowboy all over the world (see Figure 15-9). Playtex has also been converting from a strategy of nation-by-nation advertising to a global advertising strategy.[49] Other multinational companies, such as Colgate-Palmolive, Unilever, Kodak, Parker Pen, Fiat, and Gillette, are also exploring global advertising for various products.

Other marketers, however, feel that the world brand concept may be go-

FIGURE 15-8 **Cross-National Comparison of the Value Placed on Housecleaning** Source: Joseph T. Plummer, "Consumer Focus in Cross-National Research," *Journal of Advertising*, 6 (Spring 1977), 10.

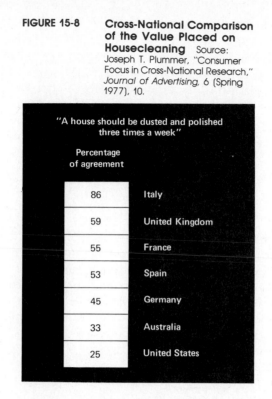

"A house should be dusted and polished three times a week"

| Percentage of agreement | |
|---|---|
| 86 | Italy |
| 59 | United Kingdom |
| 55 | France |
| 53 | Spain |
| 45 | Germany |
| 33 | Australia |
| 25 | United States |

ing too far. Procter & Gamble has four brands that are marketed under the same name worldwide (Camay soap, Crest toothpaste, Head & Shoulders shampoo, and Pampers diapers), but the flavor and smell are likely to vary from country to country. The company believes that globally standardized products may not be desirable. Another major consumer products manufacturer, Gillette, has found the development of world brands difficult, and presently sells 800 products in over 200 countries, most of them under different names.[50] These marketers argue that differences between countries are sufficiently glaring to make *localized* marketing a more effective approach. Hoover Ltd., the British subsidiary of the United States company, decided to sell clothes washers to other European nations. When research indicated that consumers in other countries wanted a host of different features, the company decided to drop its expansion plans.

The controversy over world brands is very real, with some firms attempting to establish such brands and other firms designing individual marketing mixes for each individual nation. One marketing authority has aptly summed up the arguments as follows: "The only ultimate truth possible is that humans are both deeply the same and obviously different. . . ."[51]

This book is based upon the very same thesis. Earlier chapters have described the underlying similarities that exist between people, and the external influences that, at the same time, serve to differentiate them into distinct market segments. If we believe in tailoring marketing strategies to specific segments in the American market, it follows that we also believe in tailoring marketing

FIGURE 15-9 A Popular Advertising Theme Used Worldwide

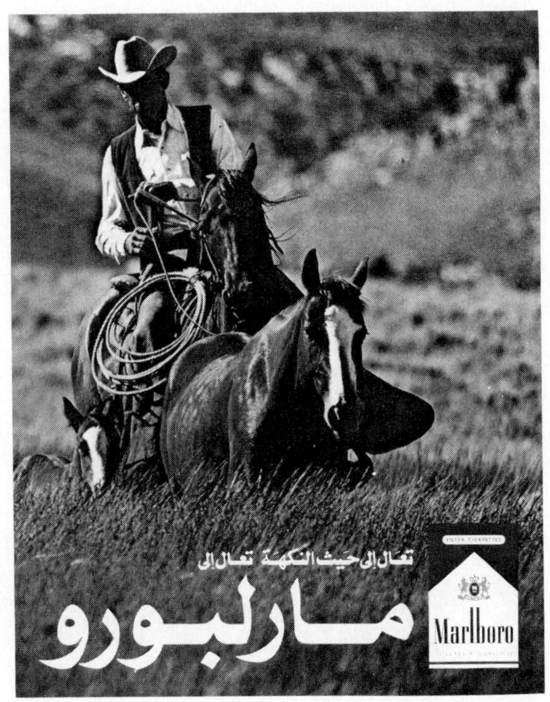


Courtesy of Philip Morris International

strategies to the needs—psychological, social, cultural, and functional—of specific foreign segments. Table 15-16 presents an interesting extension of the VALS classification of the American population (see the detailed discussion in Chapter 5) to some five European countries. While the research basically indicates that the VALS segmentation typology can be extended to these European countries, it also reveals some important differences that should be taken into consideration when planning marketing strategy. The specific VALs segmentation information might be useful to marketers developing country-by-country marketing strategies for their products; it also might suggest whether or not global advertising is a viable option.

## ACCULTURATION IS A NEEDED MARKETING VIEWPOINT

Many United States marketers make the strategic error of believing that "if Americans like it, then everyone will." Such a biased viewpoint increases the likelihood of marketing failures abroad. It reflects a complete lack of understanding of the unique psychological, social, cultural, and environmental characteristics of distinctly different cultures. To overcome such a narrow and culturally myopic view, marketers must become *acculturated;* that is, they must learn everything that is relevant to their product usage in the foreign countries in which they plan to operate.

**TABLE 15-16 A Values and Lifestyle (VALS) Comparison of the United States and Five European Countries**

| COMPARISON OF EUROPEAN AND U.S. LIFE STYLE TYPES | SURVIVOR | SUSTAINER | BELONGER | EMULATOR |
|---|---|---|---|---|
| United States | Old; intensely poor; fearful; depressed; despairing; far removed from the cultural mainstream; misfits. | Living on the edge of poverty; angry and resentful; streetwise; involved in the underground economy. | Aging; traditional and conventional; contented; intensely patriotic; sentimental; deeply stable. | Youthful and ambitious; macho; show-off; trying to break into the system, to make it big. |
| France | Negligible number, but attributes as in U.S.; some older. Belongers and Sustainers share same characteristics. | Old peasant women and retireds; poor; little education; fearful; live by habit; unable to cope with change. | Aging; need family and community; concerned about financial security, appearance, surroundings, health; able to cope with change, but avoid it. | Youthful, but older and quieter than in the U.S.; better educated; entertain at home rather than outside; consider ideologies to be dangerous; concerned about health. |
| Italy | Similar to U.S. survivors; live in northern urban slums. | Aging; uneducated; uprooted from agrarian society; dependent; concerned with health and appearance; escapist. | Aging; poorly educated; strongly authoritarian; self-sacrificing for family or church; fearful of change; fatalistic; save rather than spend; reject industrial society and its problems. | Youthful; mostly male; highly educated; reject family ties; highly materialistic; insensitive to nature; read more than average. |
| Sweden | Two categories: an older group similar to U.S.; a very young group of unemployed school dropouts who are alienated, apathetic. | Wealthier than others; fearful of children's economic future; concerned with own economic security and pensions; afraid of big government and big business. | As in the U.S., but more suspicious of government and big business. | Slightly older than others; concerned with prestige; want beautiful homes; prefer quieter life styles. |
| United Kingdom | Two groups similar to those in Sweden: older group is very similar to that in the U.S. The younger, unemployed, are more aggressive than those in Sweden—form cliques. | Working-class values; concerned about economic security; family-centered; afraid of government and big business; mainly women; the youngest group is 35 years and over. | Two groups: one as in the U.S., with addition of wanting more satisfying work; the other traditional but more active, complaining: more concerned about education, creativity, emotions. | Older than others: mostly female; more interested in social status than job status; sacrifice comfort and practicality for fashion. |
| West Germany | Survivors in a psychological rather than economic or demographic sense; fearful, envious, and alienated; concerned about social position, physical appearance; antibusiness; many are women. | Sustainers in a psychological sense only; negative feelings toward all aspects of life; resigned and apathetic; avoid risks; high level of hypochondria. | As in the U.S., although wealthier and better educated; more concerned about prestige and social standing. | Fairly young; well educated; mostly male; conscious about job status and social standing; concerned about physical safety. |

Source: Arnold Mitchell, "Nine American Lifestyles: Values and Societal Change," *The Futurist,* published by the World Future Society, 4916 St. Elmo Ave., Bethesda, MD 20814, 18 (August 1984), 4–13.

| ACHIEVER | I-AM-ME | EXPERIENTIAL | SOCIETALLY CONSCIOUS | INTEGRATED |
|---|---|---|---|---|
| Middle-aged and prosperous; able leaders; self-assured; materialistic; builders of the "American dream." | Transition state; exhibitionistic and narcissistic; young; impulsive; dramatic; experimental; active; inventive. | Youthful; seek direct experience; person-centered; artistic; intensely oriented toward inner growth. | Mission-oriented; leaders of single-issue groups; mature; successful; some live lives of voluntary simplicity. | Psychologically mature; large field of vision; tolerant and understanding; sense of fittingness. |
| Two groups: older, more mature are similar to U.S.; younger are more intuitive; both groups less materialistic than U.S. Achievers; both concerned about ecology, environment, etc. | Older (20-30); well educated; contemplative; little concern for financial security; social success, or materialism; enjoy their work. | Young; predominantly male; highly educated; not fulfilled by work but by leisure; enjoy the present; hedonistic. | Too few to be statistically significant, although most people have stronger Societally Conscious tendencies than in the U.S. | Same as in U.S. |
| Middle-aged; predominantly female; links to family and religion; indifferent to self-fulfillment from work; want success and prestige, but otherwise escapist. | Highly educated; middle- to upper-class; 25-35 age; reject both traditional and consumer/industrial societies; political extremists; live now; bored; take light drugs. | Too few to be statistically significant; athough some I-Am-Mes exhibit Experiential characteristics. | Well-educated; generally fairly young; led by protagonists of 1968 protests; satisfied; want more education; socially committed. | Same as in U.S. |
| As interested in status as in money; save more than U.S. Achievers; buy valuables for their children to inherit; this group is the most middle-class of all. | Older than in the U.S.; entrepreneurial; self-expressive; concerned about self-improvement; reject drugs and alcohol; seek rich inner and emotional life, warm relationships. | Hedonists; risk-takers; crave experience and excitement; enjoy dangerous pursuits. | Want simpler, more basic ways of life; active in communities; questioning and critical; concerned about physical environment and impersonality of large organizations. | Same as in U.S. |
| Too few to be statistically significant; status geared to social position; wealthy become more inner-directed; older people are unwilling to change. | Too few to be statistically significant; exhibit self-expressive characteristics, but are more Societally Conscious. | Highly educated; want excitement and adventure; risk-takers; creative and self-expressive; want meaningful work; want to demonstrate abilities. | Family-oriented, young; well educated; creative; want personal growth and meaningful, satisfying work; question authority and technology. | Same as in U.S. |
| As in the U.S., although more are politically active; more concerned about the environment. | Older than in the U.S.; find work meaningful and self-fulfilling; want to have an impact on society; have a high level of anxiety; emotional vacuum, looking for ideologies. | Too few to be statistically significant. | Too few to be statistically significant. | Same as in U.S. |

In a sense, acculturation is a dual process for marketers who are entering a foreign market with which they are not familiar. First, they must thoroughly orient themselves to the values, beliefs, and customs of the new society if they hope to be successful in marketing their products. Second, to gain acceptance of a culturally new product in a foreign society, they must persuade the members of that society to break with their own traditions. For example, a social marketing effort designed to encourage consumers in developing nations to use birth control devices would require a dual acculturation process. First, the marketer must acquire an in-depth picture of the society's present attitudes and customs with regard to birth control; then the marketer must devise promotional strategies that will persuade the target market to adopt the new practice in place of its traditional customs.

It stands to reason that the more similar the target society is to our own, the easier the process of acculturation. A study that focused on consumer acculturation found that foreign students who came from *developed* countries, with cultural heritages similar to the United States, were most likely to become acculturated; those who came from *developing* nations were significantly less likely to adopt American consumption values and behavior.[52] Related evidence indicates that the interaction of personality factors and religious affiliation is useful in understanding consumer acculturation.[53]

## DISTINCTIVE CHARACTERISTICS OF CROSS-CULTURAL ANALYSIS

The same research techniques used to study the American consumer are used to study consumers in foreign lands. In cross-cultural analysis, however, there is the additional burden that language and word usage often differ from nation to nation.

To illustrate how important proper wording is in cross-cultural analysis, and the necessity of designing questionnaires that reflect a country's specific beliefs, values, and customs, consider the following:[54]

1. A six-nation study indicated that consumption of spaghetti and macaroni was substantially greater in France and West Germany than in Italy. Upon further consideration, however, the researchers realized that their question had asked about the purchase of "packaged and branded spaghetti" rather than about level of consumption. Since many Italians purchase their spaghetti loose, their responses in no way reflected their actual purchase or consumption of spaghetti. Thus the finding that Italians were lighter spaghetti consumers than the French and West Germans had no basis in fact.
2. A pretest of a seven-country study designed to discover whether married or engaged women had received an engagement ring identified the following problems with the wording of the original questionnaire: (a) the word "engaged" did not mean the same thing in all nations (e.g., for a young Italian or Spanish woman, it refers to a relationship with any man who has taken her out more than once); (b) the question "Do you own an engagement ring?" is not appropriate for all countries (e.g., in Germany it is common practice for a young woman to receive a gold wedding band upon her engagement). These and other aspects of the questionnaire were modified to meet the specific cultural traits of each country studied.

To avoid such research design problems, marketers and consumer researchers must familiarize themselves with the availability of research facilities in the countries that are being evaluated as potential markets. Table 15-17 lists eight basic factors multinational marketers must consider in planning cross-cultural consumer research.

## Marketing Mistakes: A Failure to Understand Differences

In most cases, the gamble for American marketers in international marketing is not knowing if the product, the promotional appeal, the pricing policy, or the retail channels that are effective in this country will also work in other countries, and what specific changes should be made to ensure acceptance in each foreign market. The following examples of some international marketing blunders illustrate that failure to tailor marketing strategy to the target market's distinctive cultural traits can lead to costly mistakes.

### PRODUCT PROBLEMS

International marketers frequently neglect to modify their products to meet local customs and tastes. One American marketer learned the hard way (through poor sales performance) that English homemakers were not interested in American-style cake mixes, but preferred instead ". . . a tough, rather spongy

**TABLE 15-17 Eight Basic Factors Influencing Cross-Cultural Analysis**

| FACTORS | EXAMPLES |
|---|---|
| Language differences | The words or concepts of a promotional theme may not translate adequately, and the meaning might be lost. |
| Differences in consumption patterns | Two countries may differ substantially in the level of consumption of a product. |
| Differences in potential market segments | The income or social class, age, and sex of consumers may differ dramatically in different countries. |
| Differences in the way that products or services are used | Two nations may use the same product or service in very different ways. |
| Differences in the criteria for evaluating products and services | The benefits that consumers seek from a product or service may differ from country to country. |
| Differences in economic and social conditions | The locus of family decision making may vary significantly from country to country. |
| Differences in marketing conditions | The types and quality of retail outlets may vary greatly between countries. |
| Differences in marketing research opportunities | High illiteracy rates or lack of telephones may inhibit data collection in certain countries. |

Source: Adapted from Paul Howard Berent, "International Research is Different," in Edward M. Mazze, ed., *1975 Combined Proceedings* (Chicago: American Marketing Association, 1975), 295.

item which was traditional for tea."[55] To avoid such problems, marketers must ascertain whether the physical characteristics of their products are acceptable to the new market. For instance, Nestlé learned that it was necessary to market more than sixty different formulations of Nescafé in order to meet local foreign coffee preferences in their target markets.[56]

Color is an extremely critical variable in international marketing because the same color frequently has different meanings in different cultures. To illustrate, a yellow cologne failed to sell in Africa because consumers believed it was animal urine; it sold successfully when its color was changed to green. General Foods, which markets its Instant Maxwell House coffee worldwide in a red can, found that red was inappropriate in Japan where it means "fire sale."[57]

### PROMOTIONAL PROBLEMS

When communicating with consumers in different parts of the world, it is imperative that the promotional message be consistent with the language and customs of the specific society. International marketers have faced various problems in communicating with widely different customer groups. For example, the Seven-Up Company's highly successful Uncola theme, developed for the United States market, was considered inappropriate for many foreign markets because it did not translate well into other languages.[58] In its place, Seven-Up used a theme that featured a pair of white-gloved hands coming out of a green box. It was determined that this theme could easily be translated into the respective languages of some eighty countries.

In Japan, Seiko employed the headline "Like a Wind, I am the Color of a Bird" to introduce a new line of colored dial watches. To a Japanese consumer, this headline might mean "This watch is light and delicate. It perhaps floats on your hand like a seedpod on the wind. Or a bird. A hummingbird with its jewel-like colors, the colors of the watch itself."[59] Yet to most Americans, the headline would be meaningless.

Product names also cause considerable problems for international marketers. The Chevrolet Nova did not sell well in Latin America because *Nova,* when spoken as two words in Spanish, translates to "It doesn't go." Similarly, Colgate-Palmolive experienced a name problem when it attempted to sell Cue toothpaste in France. The company learned too late that "Cue" is the name of a popular pornographic magazine.[60] To avoid product name difficulties, marketers must often use different names in different countries. For example, General Foods' Dream Whip is called Dream Topping in England and Copo Imperial in Venezuela.[61]

### PRICING AND DISTRIBUTION PROBLEMS

International marketers must also adjust their pricing and distribution policies to meet local economic conditions and customs. For instance, in many developing nations where the average income is quite low, small-sized product packages are often a necessity because consumers cannot afford the cash outlay required for the larger sizes popular in the United States and other affluent countries. Even in developed nations, there are important differences. To illustrate, supermarkets are very popular in Switzerland, but in France, which is just across the border, consumers prefer smaller and more intimate stores for grocery shopping.[62] Thus marketers must vary their distribution channels by nation.

The price of an imported brand relative to local brands can also be an inhibiting factor in international sales. Anheuser-Busch's Budweiser beer experienced encouraging sales when it was introduced into the Swedish marketplace. But a strong United States dollar caused the brand's price to rise steadily, until it was selling for 20 percent more than comparable European imports. This caused the original importer to drop the product.[63]

## *summary*

Subcultural analysis enables marketers to segment their markets to meet the specific needs, motivations, perceptions, and attitudes that are shared by members of a specific subcultural group. A subculture is a distinct cultural group which exists as an identifiable segment within a larger, more complex society. Its members possess beliefs, values, and customs that set them apart from other members of the same society; at the same time, they hold to the dominant beliefs of the overall society. Major subcultural categories in this country include nationality, religion, geographic location, race, age, sex, and occupation. Each of these can be broken down into smaller segments which can be reached through special copy appeals and selective media choices. In some cases (e.g., the elderly consumer), product characteristics can be tailored to the specialized needs of the market segment. Since all consumers are simultaneously members of several subcultural groups, the marketer should try to determine how specific subcultural memberships interact to influence the consumer's overall purchase decisions.

With such diversity among the members of just one nation, it is easy to understand that numerous larger differences exist between citizens of different nations. If international marketers are to penetrate selected foreign markets effectively, they must understand the relevant similarities and differences that exist among the peoples of these countries. Cross-cultural analyses are needed to provide marketers with sufficient understanding of the psychological, social, cultural, and environmental characteristics of foreign markets to develop appropriate marketing strategies.

For some international marketers, acculturation may be a dual process: first, they must learn everything that is relevant to the society in which they plan to market; then they must persuade the members of that society to break with their own traditional ways of doing things to adopt the new product. The more similar the target society is to our own, the easier the process of acculturation. Conversely, the more different the target society, the more difficult the process of acculturation.

Some of the problems involved in cross-cultural analysis include differences in language, consumption patterns, needs, product usage, economic and social conditions, marketing conditions, and market research opportunities. There is an urgent need for more systematic and conceptual cross-cultural analyses concerning the consumption habits of foreign consumers. Such analyses would serve to identify increased marketing opportunities that would benefit both international marketers and the consumers they seek to serve.

## *discussion questions*

1. Discuss the importance of subcultures in segmenting the market for food products.
2. What specific recommendations would you offer the management of a firm that produces household detergents on how they might more effectively reach (a) the Hispanic market and (b) the black market?
3. What factors should a manufacturer like Johnson & Johnson consider if it wishes to introduce and promote a new arthritis remedy targeted to the elderly market?
4. Consider Table 15-15, "Gender Ascribed to 24 Products." Do you believe that any of the products listed as "masculine" or "feminine" should no longer be classified this way?
5. As the owner of a Buick automobile dealership, what changes or programs would you wish to institute as a result of the tremendous increase in the number of working women?
6. How can a multinational company use cross-cultural consumer analysis to design each factor in its marketing mix? Discuss.
7. If you wanted to name a new product so that it would be acceptable throughout the world, what cultural factors would you consider?
8. What factors might inhibit an attempt by Smith-Corona to make its electronic portable typewriters a "world brand?"

## *endnotes*

1. Robin M. Williams, Jr., *American Society: A Sociological Interpretation,* 3rd ed. (New York: Knopf, 1970), 415.
2. Gerald Zaltman, *Marketing: Contributions from the Behavioral Sciences* (New York: Harcourt, Brace & World, 1965), 8.
3. U.S. Department of Commerce, "More than Three-Fifths of U.S. Hispanic Popu-

lation in California, Texas and New York, 1980 Census Shows," *Commerce News,* July 17, 1981; "Marketing to Hispanics," *Advertising Age,* March 21, 1985, 13; Craig Endicott, "Marketing to Hispanics," *Advertising Age,* March 19, 1984, M-9; Madhav N. Segal and Lionel Sosa, "Marketing to the Hispanic Community," *California Management Review,* 26 (Fall 1983), 121.

4. Robert E. Wilkes and Humberto Valencia, "Shopping Orientations of Mexican-Americans," in Russell W. Belk et al., eds., *1984 AMA Educators' Proceedings* (Chicago: American Marketing Association, 1984), 30.
5. "Marketing to Hispanics," *Advertising Age,* March 21, 1985, 18.
6. Segal and Sosa, "Marketing to the Hispanic Community"; and David Astor, "The Hispanic Market: An In-Depth Profile," *Marketing Communication,* July 1981, 15–19; Kitty Dawson, "Advertising's Missed Opportunity: The Hispanic Market," *Marketing and Media Decisions,* January 1981, 68–69 and 132–36.
7. Chuck Wingis, "Spanish TV Net Grows, Looks to East," *Advertising Age,* August 18, 1975, 214. See also Thomas G. Exter, "Focusing on Hispanics," *American Demographics,* 7 (August 1985), 28–33.
8. Richard A. Jacobs, "Jewish Media Provide What Others Don't," *Advertising Age,* April 16, 1979, S-28.
9. "Marketing Briefs," *Marketing News,* January 17, 1986, 14.
10. Elizabeth C. Hirschman, "Ethnic Variation in Leisure Activities and Motives," in Bruce J. Walker et al., eds., *An Assessment of Marketing Thought and Practice* (Chicago: American Marketing Association, 1982), 93–98.
11. Elizabeth C. Hirschman, "American Jewish Ethnicity: Its Relationship to Some Selected Aspects of Consumer Behavior," *Journal of Marketing,* 45 (Summer 1981), 102–10.
12. William K. Stevens, "Neiman-Marcus's Challenger," *New York Times,* August 6, 1981, D4.
13. Philip H. Dougherty, "Matching Products to Lifestyle," *New York Times,* April 21, 1976, 58. Also see William D. Wells and Fred D. Reynolds, "Psychological Geography," in Jagdish Sheth, ed., *Research in Marketing* (Greenwich, Conn.: JAI Press, 1979), II, 345–57.
14. Raymond J. Folwell, "Marketing to the Wine Consumer—An Overview," in Jerry C. Olson, ed., *Advances in Consumer Behavior* (Ann Arbor, Mich.: Association for Consumer Research, 1980), 7, 92.
15. Milton Rokeach and Seymour Parker, "Values as Social Indicators of Poverty and Race Relations in America," *Annals of the American Academy of Political and Social Science,* 388 (March 1970), 97–111; and B. G. Yovovich, "The Debate Rages On," *Advertising Age,* November 29, 1982, M-9.
16. Raymond A. Bauer, Scott M. Cunningham, and Lawrence H. Wortzel, "The Marketing Dilemma of Negroes," *Journal of Marketing,* 29 (July 1965), 3.
17. Joseph F. Hair, Jr., Ronald F. Bush, and Paul S. Busch, "Acculturation and Black Buyer Behavior," in Edward M. Mazze, ed., *1975 Combined Proceedings* (Chicago: American Marketing Association, 1975), 253–56.
18. Alphonzia Wellington, "Blacks and Hispanics: Power in Numbers and Market Concentration," *Marketing Review,* 38 (January–February 1983), 26.
19. Donald E. Sexton, Jr., "Comparing the Cost of Food to Blacks and Whites: A Survey," *Journal of Marketing,* 35 (July 1971), 40–46.
20. Charles S. Goodman, "Do the Poor Pay More?" *Journal of Marketing,* 32 (January 1968), 18–24.
21. Marie Spadoni, "Marketing to Blacks—How Media Segment the Target Audience," *Advertising Age,* November 19, 1984, 43.
22. Mary Jane Schlinger and Joseph T. Plummer, "Advertising in Black and White," *Journal of Marketing Research,* 9 (May 1972), 149–53; John W. Gould, Norman B. Sigband, and Cyril E. Zoerner, Jr., "Black Consumer Reactions to 'Integrated' Ad-

vertising: An Exploratory Study," *Journal of Marketing,* 34 (July 1970), 20–26; Leah Rozen, "Black Presenter Makes a Difference," *Advertising Age,* October 13, 1980, 20; and Ronald F. Bush, Joseph F. Hair, Jr., and Paul J. Solomon, "Consumers' Level of Prejudice and Response to Black Models in Advertising," *Journal of Marketing Research,* 16 (August 1979), 341–45.

23. "The Big Chill (Revisited) or Whatever Happened to the Baby Boom?" *American Demographics,* 7 (September 1985), 23–29.
24. Stevie Pierson, "Are You a Yuppie?" *Metropolitan Homes,* April 1985, 60–78.
25. Jeffrey G. Towle and Claude R. Martin, Jr., "The Elderly Consumer: One Segment or Many?" in Beverlee B. Anderson, ed., *Advances in Consumer Research* (Association for Consumer Research, 1976), III, 463.
26. Ethel Shanas, "What's New in Old Age?" *American Behavioral Scientist,* 14 (September–October 1970), 5.
27. Benny Barak and Leon G. Schiffman, "Cognitive Age: A Nonchronological Age Variable," in Kent B. Monroe ed., *Advances in Consumer Research* (Ann Arbor, Mich.: Association for Consumer Research, 1981), VIII, 602–6.
28. Theodore J. Gage, "Ads Targeted at Mature in Need of Creative Hoist" *Advertising Age,* August 25, 1980, S-5.
29. Maria B. Dwight and Harold N. Urman, "Affluent Elderly Is a Unique Segment," *Marketing News,* August 16, 1985, 8.
30. Leon G. Schiffman, "Perceived Risk in New Product Trial by Elderly Consumers," *Journal of Marketing Research,* 9 (February 1972), 106–8.
31. Martha Farnsworth Riche, "Retirement's Lifestyle Pioneers," *American Demographics,* 8 (January 1986), 42–56.
32. Warren A. French and Richard Fox, "Segmenting the Senior Citizen Market," *The Journal of Consumer Marketing,* 2, (Winter 1985), 62.
33. Lynn Folse, "They're Not Getting Older; They're Getting Bigger," *Advertising Age,* October 3, 1985, 44.
34. Ivan Ross, "Information Processing and the Older Consumer: Marketing and Public Policy Implications," in Andrew Mitchell, ed., *Advances in Consumer Research* (Ann Arbor, Mich.: Association for Consumer Research, 1982), 9, 31–39.
35. "Ads Promote a Negative Image of the Elderly," *Marketing News,* September 28, 1984, 10–11.
36. Ganesan Visvabharathy and David R. Rink, "The Elderly: Neglected Business Opportunities," *Journal of Consumer Marketing,* 1 (1984), 35, 42.
37. Alan M. Rubin, "Directions in Television and Aging Research," *Journal of Broadcasting,* 26 (Spring 1982), 537–51.
38. Folse, "They're Not Getting Older."
39. Frederick D. Sturdivant, "Subculture Theory: Poverty, Minorities and Marketing," in Scott Ward and Thomas S. Robertson, eds., *Consumer Behavior: Theoretical Sources* (Englewood Cliffs, N.J.: Prentice-Hall, 1973), 476.
40. Inge K. Broverman, Susan Raymond Vogel, Donald M. Broverman, Frank E. Clarkson, and Paul S. Rosenkrantz, "Sex Role Stereotypes: A Current Appraisal," *Journal of Social Issues,* 28 (1972), 63.
41. Alice E. Courtney and Sarah Wernick Lockeretz, "A Woman's Place: An Analysis of the Roles Portrayed by Women in Magazine Advertisements," *Journal of Marketing Research,* 8 (February 1971), 92–95; Louis C. Wagner and Janis B. Banos,"A Woman's Place: A Follow-up Analysis of the Roles Portrayed by Women in Magazine Advertisements," *Journal of Marketing Research,* 10 (May 1973), 213–14; and Ahmed Belkaoui and Janice M. Belkaoui, "A Comparative Analysis of the Roles Portrayed by Women in Print Advertisements: 1958, 1970, 1972," *Journal of Marketing Research,* 13 (May 1976), 168–72. Also see Marc G. Weinberger, Susan M. Petroshius, and Stuart A. Westin, "Twenty Years of Women in Magazine Advertis-

ing: An Update," in Neil Beckwith et al., eds., *1979 Educators' Conference Proceedings* (Chicago: American Marketing Association, 1979), 373–77.

42. Mary McCabe English, "Marketing to Women: A Cut above the 'Slice-of-Life' Ads," *Advertising Age,* October 3, 1983, M-9.

43. Lori Kesler, "Behind the Wheel of a Quiet Revolution," *Advertising Age,* July 26, 1982, M11–13.

44. Ibid.

45. Thomas Barry, Mary Gilly, and Lindley Doran, "Advertising to Women with Different Career Orientations," *Journal of Advertising Research,* 25 (April–May 1985), 26–35.

46. Michael D. Reilly, "Working Wives and Convenience Consumption," *Journal of Consumer Research,* 8 (March 1982), 407–18.

47. Ibid.

48. Dennis Chase, "Global Marketing: The New Wave," *Advertising Age,* June 25, 1984, 49.

49. "Playtex Kicks Off a One-Ad-Fits-All Campaign," *Business Week,* December 16, 1985, 48–49.

50. "P&G Moving Fast on World Market Entry," *Advertising Age,* June 25, 1984, 50, and "Gillette Finds World-Brand Image Elusive," *Advertising Age,* June 25, 1984, 50, 72.

51. Sidney J. Levy, "Myth and Meaning in Marketing," in Ronald C. Curhan, ed., *1974 Combined Proceedings* (Chicago: American Marketing Association, 1975), 555–56. Also see Saul Sands, "Can You Standardize International Marketing Strategy?" *Journal of the Academy of Marketing Science,* 7 (Spring 1979), 117–28.

52. Joseph Franklin Hair, Jr., and Rolph E. Anderson, "Culture, Acculturation and Consumer Behavior: An Empirical Study," in Boris W. Becker and Helmut Becker, eds., *1972 Combined Proceedings,* (Chicago: American Marketing Association, 1973), 426.

53. Leon G. Schiffman, William R. Dillon, and Festus E. Ngumah, "The Influence of Subcultural and Personality Factors on Consumer Acculturation," *Journal of International Business Studies,* 12 (Fall 1981), 137–43.

54. Paul Howard Berent, "International Research Is Different," in Edward M. Mazze, ed., *1975 Combined Proceedings* (Chicago: American Marketing Association, 1975), 294.

55. Albert Stridberg, "U.S. Advertisers Win Some, Lose Some in Foreign Market," *Advertising Age,* May 6, 1974, 18.

56. J. Douglas McConnell, "The Economics of Behavioral Factors on the Multi-National Corporation," in Fred C. Allvine, ed., *1971 Combined Proceedings* (Chicago: American Marketing Association, 1972), 263; and H. T. Parker, "International Markets Look Bright," *Advertising Age,* May 13, 1974, 53.

57. Eliyahu Tal, "Advertising in Developing Countries," *Journal of Advertising,* 3 (Spring 1974), 21; and "GF International Moves to Centralized Policies," *Advertising Age,* February 25, 1974, 148.

58. Ramona Bechtos, "Man in the Green Box Sells 7UP in World Markets," *Advertising Age,* May 19, 1975, 25, 43, and 45.

59. Larry O'Neill, "How to Cope with 'Tokyo Trauma,'" *Advertising Age,* May 28, 1974, 32.

60. Kathleen Wisniewski, "Corporations Prepare Future Generation of Cross-Cultural Employees," *Marketing News,* September 14, 1984, 43.

61. "GF International Moves to Centralized Policies," 148.

62. Walter Weir, "What Americans Can Learn from Europe—Market Segmentation," *Advertising Age,* February 16, 1976, 41.

63. Dennis Chase, "A-B Beer Goes Flat in Europe, But Scores in Canada, Japan," *Advertising Age,* February 14, 1983, 12, 57.

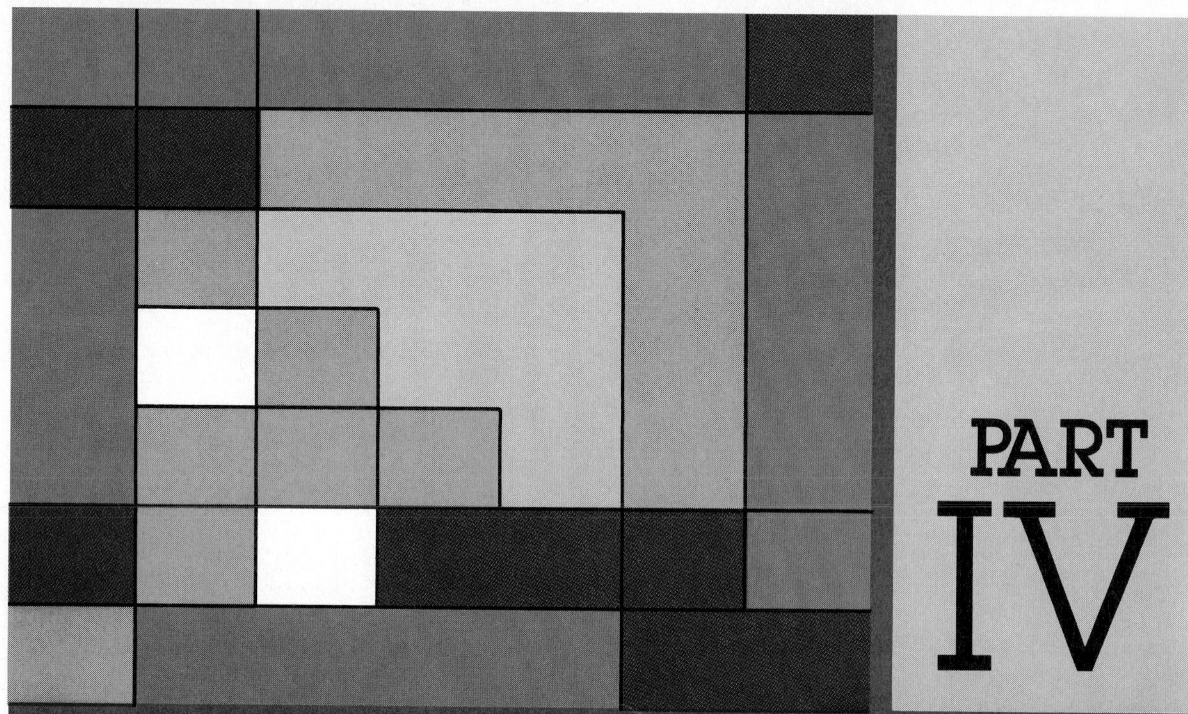

# PART IV

# THE CONSUMER'S DECISION-MAKING PROCESS

Part IV focuses on various facets of consumer decision making. The first two chapters are concerned with (1) the influence of informal social communication on consumer decision making, and (2) how consumers make decisions about new products and services. The next chapter takes a broader perspective and demonstrates, by means of a simple model, how the contributions of psychological, sociological, and cultural theory influence the consumer's consumption-related decisions. The final chapter in this section briefly reviews several comprehensive models of consumer decision making.

# 16

# Personal Influence and the Opinion Leadership Process

## introduction

CONSUMERS are often influenced by advice they receive from other people, especially in choosing products to buy and services to use. Just how powerful and important personal influence can be is pointed up by the following comment by an ad agency executive: "Today, 80 percent of all buying decisions are influenced by someone's direct recommendations."[1]

This influence from others includes what movie to see next Friday night, to what running shoes to buy, to what word processing package is most compatible with a new computer user's needs.

This chapter describes the influence friends, neighbors, acquaintances, coworkers, and others have on the individual's consumption behavior. It examines the nature and dynamics of this influence, called the **opinion leadership** process, and the personality and motivations of those who influence *(opinion leaders)* and those who are influenced *(opinion receivers).*

## WHAT IS OPINION LEADERSHIP?

*Opinion leadership* is *the process by which one person (the opinion leader) informally influences the actions or attitudes of others, who may be opinion seekers or merely opinion recipients.* This influence is informal and verbal, but it may be supported by observing the actions of others. The informal flow of consumer-related influence between two people is sometimes referred to as product-related conversation, or *word-of-mouth* communication.

> *The art of conversation is the art of hearing as well as of being heard*
>
> *WILLIAM HAZLITT*
> *"On The Conversation of Authors," The Plain Speaker*
> *(1826)*

The key characteristic of such communication is that it is interpersonal and informal and takes place between two or more people, none of whom represents a commercial selling source. Word-of-mouth implies personal, or face-to-face, communication, although it may also take place by telephone.

One of the parties in an informal communications encounter usually offers advice or information about a specific product or product category, such as which of several brands is best, or how a particular product may be used. That person, the **opinion leader,** may become an *opinion receiver* when another product or product category is discussed.

Individuals who actively seek information and advice about products are sometimes called *opinion seekers*. For purposes of simplicity, the term *opinion receiver* will be used in the following discussion to identify both those who actively seek product information from others and those who receive unsolicited information.

Simple examples of opinion leadership at work include the following:

1. When his car needs repair, a resident new to the area calls his neighbor for the name of "a good mechanic."
2. When two friends are looking over photographs of a just completed joint vacation, one suggests to the other that she try a different brand of film.
3. While two friends watch Sunday's football game, one suggests to the other that a new type of TV antenna might bring the set into sharper focus.

Most studies of opinion leadership are concerned with the identification and measurement of the behavioral impact that opinion leaders have on the consumption habits of others.

## DYNAMICS OF THE OPINION LEADERSHIP PROCESS

The opinion leadership process is very dynamic. This section discusses the specific dimensions of opinion leadership that make it such a powerful consumer force.

### Credibility

Opinion leaders are highly credible sources of product-related information because they are usually perceived as neutral (and thus objective) concerning the information or advice they dispense. Their intentions are perceived as being in the best interests of the opinion recipients, since they receive no compensation for the advice and apparently have no "ax to grind." Because opinion leaders often base their product advice on firsthand experience, the advice reduces the perceived risk or anxiety inherent in new product trial for opinion receivers. Since opinion leaders are often unaware that they are influencing others, their product-related advice can be considered "soft sell."

## Positive and Negative Product Information

Information provided by marketers is invariably favorable to the product; thus the very fact that opinion leaders provide both favorable and unfavorable information adds to their credibility. An example of an unfavorable or negative product comment is this: "The problem with daisywheel computer printers is that they are relatively slow."

In comparison to positive or even neutral comments, negative comments are relatively less common. For this reason, consumers are especially likely to note such information and generally avoid products or brands receiving negative evaluations. In this way, negative comments about a product or service tend to focus consumer attention on a select few brands that receive *positive* commentary from others.

## Information and Advice

Opinion leaders are the source of both information and advice. They may simply talk about their experiences with a product, relate what they know about a product, or more aggressively, advise others to buy or to avoid a product. Some examples of the kinds of product-related information that opinion leaders are likely to transmit during a conversation include the following:

1. *Which of several brands is best:* "Sony microcassette recorders have excellent fidelity."
2. *How a person might best use a specific product:* "Staplers work best with the slightly-more expensive round wire staples."
3. *Where is the best place to shop:* "When Neiman-Marcus has a sale, the values are exceptional."
4. *Who provides the best product-related service:* "Chemlawn has a system of lawn care that can't be beat."

## Opinion Leadership Is a Two-Way Street

A person who is an opinion receiver in one product category may become an opinion leader in another. Consider the following example: A college student contemplating the purchase of a new color TV set may seek information and advice from other people to reduce her indecision about which brand to select. Once the TV has been bought, however, she may experience **postpurchase dissonance** and have a compelling need to talk favorably about the purchase to other people to confirm the correctness of her own choice.

An opinion leader may also be influenced by an opinion receiver as the result of a product-related conversation. For example, a person may tell a friend about a favorite gambling casino in Puerto Rico and, in response to questions from the opinion receiver, come to realize that the casino is too large, too noisy, and does not offer its customers as many amenities as do other casinos.

## Opinion Leadership Is Category-Specific

Opinion leadership tends to be **category-specific;** that is, opinion leaders often "specialize" in certain product categories about which they offer information and advice. When other product categories are discussed, they may reverse their roles and become opinion receivers. A person who is considered particularly knowledgeable about stocks and bonds may be an opinion leader in terms of this subject, yet when it comes to the purchase of a telephone answering machine, the same person may seek advice from others—perhaps even from someone who has sought his investment advice.

## The Motivations Behind Opinion Leadership

To understand opinion leadership, it is necessary to appreciate the motivations of those who participate in informal product-related conversations. To this end, we will review the underlying motivations of those who provide and those who receive product-related information and advice.

### THE NEEDS OF OPINION RECEIVERS

Opinion leaders fulfill a number of needs for opinion receivers. First, they provide new product or new-usage information. Second, they often reduce the perceived risk of opinion seekers by relating firsthand knowledge about a specific product or brand. Third, they reduce the search time entailed in the identification of a needed product or service. Moreover, opinion receivers can be certain of receiving the approval of a person whose opinion they obviously respect when they follow that person's advice or product endorsement. For all these reasons, consumers often look to friends, neighbors, and other acquaintances for product information.

Not only do opinion receivers satisfy a variety of needs by engaging in product-related conversations, but there is evidence that the type of person from whom opinion receivers tend to seek their information varies, depending on cultural background.[2] Some researchers found that white American and British subjects tended to select close friends of similar age as sources of advice, whereas Chinese subjects preferred an opinion leader who had acquired authority and respect as a group standard bearer or as a male head of family. In contrast, black Americans were drawn to individuals who had achieved a degree of notoriety or who were typecast by the press as charismatic. Finally, Indian subjects were likely to select individuals recognized as possessing a strong philosophical outlook. These findings suggest that subcultural and cross-cultural factors (see Chapter 15) are likely to influence the traits judged desirable in an opinion leader.

### THE NEEDS OF OPINION LEADERS

What motivates a person to talk about a product or service? Motivation theory suggests that people may provide information or advice to others in order to satisfy some basic need of their own (see Chapter 3). This notion is supported by a study which reported that "nobody will speak about products or services unless the talking itself, or the expected action of the listener, promises satisfaction of some kind—popularly speaking, unless he gets something out of it."[3]

However, opinion leaders may be unaware of their own underlying motives. As suggested earlier, opinion leaders may simply be trying to reduce their own postpurchase dissonance. If a man buys a new snowblower and then is uncertain as to the wisdom of his choice, he may try to reassure himself by "talking up" the snowblower's virtues to others. In this way, he relieves his own psychological discomfort; furthermore, if he can influence a friend or neighbor to also buy that brand, he confirms his own good judgment in selecting the product first. Thus the opinion leader's motivation may really be one of self-confirmation or self-involvement. Furthermore, the information or advice that opinion leaders dispense may serve to gain them attention, help them to achieve status, assert their superiority, demonstrate their awareness and expertise, enable them to feel innovative, and give them the feeling of having inside information and of "converting" less adventurous souls.

In addition to *self*-involvement, the opinion leader may also be motivated by *product* involvement, *other* involvement, and *message* involvement.[4] Opinion leaders who are motivated by *product* involvement may find themselves so pleased or so disappointed with a product that they simply must tell others about it. Those who are motivated by involvement with *others* have a need to share product-related experiences. In this type of situation, opinion leaders use their product-related conversations as an expression of friendship, neighborliness, and love.

The pervasiveness of advertising in our society encourages *message* involvement, in that individuals who are bombarded with advertising messages and slogans tend to discuss them and the products they are designed to sell. Such word-of-mouth conversation is typified by the line "Where's the beef?" promoted by Wendy's and widely repeated by consumers.

Table 16-1 compares the motivations of opinion receivers with those of opinion leaders.

## MEASUREMENT OF OPINION LEADERSHIP

Consumer researchers are interested in identifying and measuring the impact of the opinion leadership process on consumption behavior. In measuring opinion leadership, the researcher has a choice of four basic measurement techniques: (1) the **self-designating** method, (2) the **sociometric** method, (3) the **key informant** method, and (4) the **objective** method. We will briefly review each of these measurement methods in terms of strengths, weaknesses, and applications to consumer research.

### Self-Designating Method

In the *self-designating* method, respondents are asked to evaluate the extent to which they have provided others with information about a product category or

**TABLE 16-1 A Comparison of the Motivations of Opinion Leaders and Opinion Receivers**

| OPINION LEADERS | OPINION RECEIVERS |
|---|---|
| 1. *Self-Involvement Motivations:*<br>a. To reduce postpurchase uncertainty or dissonance<br>b. To gain attention or status<br>c. To assert superiority and expertise<br>d. To feel like an adventurer<br>e. To experience the power of "converting" others | 1. *Self-Involvement Motivations:*<br>a. To reduce the risk or uncertainty of making a purchase commitment<br>b. To reduce search time (e.g., to avoid the necessity of shopping around) |
| 2. *Product-Involvement Motivations:*<br>To express satisfaction or dissatisfaction with a product or service | 2. *Product-Involvement Motivations:*<br>a. To learn how to use or consume a product<br>b. To learn what products are new in the marketplace |
| 3. *Other-Involvement Motivations:*<br>To express neighborliness and friendship by discussing products or services that may be useful to others | 3. *Other-Involvement Motivations:*<br>To buy products that have the approval of others, thereby ensuring acceptance |
| 4. *Message-Involvement Motivations:*<br>To express one's reaction to a stimulating advertisement by telling others about it | |

specific brand or have otherwise influenced the purchase decisions of others.

Figure 16-1 shows three types of self-designating question formats that can be used to determine a respondent's opinion leadership activity. The first consists of a single question, while the other two consist of series of questions. The use of multiple questions enables the researcher to determine a respondent's opinion leadership more reliably on the basis of several supporting statements.

In most cases where researchers use the self-designating method, they divide consumer respondents into two categories: those who influence others (opinion leaders), and those who do not (non-opinion leaders). While this two-category classification scheme is simple and easy to use, it does not realistically reflect the extent to which an individual might function as an opinion leader. Some people classified as nonleaders may truly have no influence on others, while others so classified may actually influence the consumption decisions of other people to some degree. Therefore, it would be more realistic to employ a classification scheme consisting of three or more categories—one that explicitly considers a *range* of opinion-leading activity: those who *never* or *infrequently* influence others, those who *frequently* influence others, and those who are *highly influential* opinion leaders.

The self-designating technique is used more frequently than other methods for measuring opinion leadership because consumer researchers find it easy to include in market research questionnaires. However, because this method relies on consumers' self-evaluation of their opinion leadership activity, it may be open to bias should respondents perceive "opinion leadership" (even though the term is not used) to be a desirable characteristic and thus overestimate their own roles as opinion leaders.

**FIGURE 16-1** **Self-Designating Method of Measuring Opinion Leadership** Sources: [a]Alvin J. Silk, "Overlap Among Self-designated Opinion Leaders: A Study of Selected Dental Products and Services," *Journal of Marketing Research*, 3 (August 1968), 255–59. [b]John O. Summers, "The Identity of Women's Clothing Fashion Opinion Leaders," *Journal of Marketing Research*, 7 (May 1970), 178–85. [c]Fred D. Reynolds and William R. Darden, "Mutually Adaptive Effects of Interpersonal Communication," *Journal of Marketing Research*, 8 (November 1971), 449–54.

**Single-Question Approach**

a. Have you recently been asked your advice or opinion about __*__?[a]
   Yes ________ No ________
   Respondents answering "yes" are classified as opinion leaders.

In one survey using this single question approach, opinion leadership for the following dental products and services were determined: electric toothbrushes, toothpastes, mouthwashes, and dentists.

**Multiple-Question Approaches**

a. In general do you like to talk about __*__ with your friends?[b]
   Yes ____ 1    No ____ 2
b. Would you say you give very little information, an average amount of information, or a great deal of information about __*__ to your friends?
   You give very little information 1
   You give an average amount of information 2
   You give a great deal of information 3
c. During the past six months, have you told anyone about __*__ ?
   Yes ____ 1    No ____ 2
d. Compared with your circle of friends, are you less likely, about as likely, or more likely to be asked for advice about __*__ ?
   Less likely to be asked ______ 1
   About as likely to be asked ______ 2
   More likely to be asked ______ 3
e. If you and your friends were to discuss __*__ , what part would you be most likely to play? Would you mainly listen to your friends' ideas or would you try to convince them of your ideas?
   You mainly listen to your friends' ideas ______ 1
   You try to convince them of your ideas ______ 2
f. Which of these happens more often? Do you tell your friends about __*__ , or do they tell you about __*__ ?
   You tell them about __*__ ______ 1
   They tell you about __*__ ______ 2
g. Do you have the feeling that you are generally regarded by your friends and neighbors as a good source of advice about __*__ ?
   Yes ____ 1    No ____ 2

Please read the following sentences and place the number that most closely responds to the correct answer in the space following. The range of answers is 1 through 5, as follows:
   1—strongly agree
   2—agree
   3—neither agree nor disagree
   4—disagree
   5—strongly disagree

a. My friends and neighbors often ask my advice about clothing fashions. ______[c]
b. I sometimes influence the types of clothes my friends buy. ______
c. My friends come to me more often than I go to them about clothes. ______
d. I feel that I am generally regarded by my friends as a good source of advice about clothing fashions: ______
e. I can think of at least two people whom I have told about some clothing fashion in the last six months. ______

*Insert relevant product or product category.

## Sociometric Method

The *sociometric* method measures the person-to-person informal communication of consumers concerning products or product categories. In this method, respondents are asked to identify (a) the specific individuals (if any) to whom they provided advice or information about the product or brand under study, and (b) the specific individuals (if any) who provided *them* with advice or information about the product or brand under study. In the first instance, if respondents identify one or more individuals to whom they have provided some form of product information, they are tentatively classified as opinion leaders. The researcher then seeks to validate this determination by interviewing the individuals named by the primary respondents and then asking them to recall whether or not they did, in fact, receive such product information.

In the second instance, respondents are asked to identify individuals who provided them with information about a product under investigation. Individuals so designated by the primary respondent are tentatively classified as opinion leaders. Again, the researcher attempts to validate this determination by asking the individuals so named whether or not they did in fact provide the relevant product information.

Thus, if consumer A reports that information or advice concerning a specific product was received from consumer B, consumer B must confirm that such information or advice was given to consumer A. In this way the sociometric method validly identifies the opinion leaders and opinion receivers in product-related conversations.

### SOCIOMETRIC RESEARCH DESIGNS

In using the *sociometric* method, researchers have two options in terms of research design: They can study a self-contained community, or they can study a more widespread respondent sample. If they study a specific community that has definite physical boundaries (such as all the residents in a particular housing project), they will find it relatively simple to verify product-related conversations. If they choose a more widespread respondent sample, they must be prepared to trace the web of word-of-mouth contacts by seeking out all individuals named by the primary respondent group, regardless of where they are located. Most sociometric consumer studies have focused on "intact" or self-contained communities because such research is so much less costly and easier to manage.[5]

### CONSUMER BEHAVIOR APPLICATIONS

An early application of the sociometric approach to the study of consumer behavior examined opinion leadership among wives of graduate students living in university-sponsored housing.[6] The intact community provided the opportunity to measure the flow of word-of-mouth conversation concerning a new brand of coffee and the subsequent impact of such conversation on the trial of the new product. The researcher found that wives who received favorable comment or information concerning the product were more likely to try it than those who either received no information or negative information. This pioneering study concluded that positive informal communication promotes the acceptance of new products among members of a given community.

Figure 16-2 illustrates the type of questioning employed in the sociometric research approach. It presents a series of questions used in a study of opinion leadership among elderly consumers residing in a retirement community. The

**FIGURE 16-2** Sociometric Questioning Approach to Assess Informal Communication about a New Product

A. *Providing Information to Others*

1. Did you tell anyone, living here at Kissena I, about the "Brand X" salt substitute?

   yes ______ no ______

2. If "yes"
   Which person did you first tell about the salt substitute?

   First Name ______ Family Name ______ Apt. or Floor ______

3. Which other people, living here at Kissena I, did you tell about the "Brand X" salt substitute?

   (Space for three other names and locations)

4. Did you suggest that they try or not try the "Brand X" salt substitute?

   Try ______ Not Try ______ Other ______

B. *Receiving Information from Others*

1. What was the first thing you remember hearing about the "Brand X" salt substitute?
2. Do you remember who made this first comment about "Brand X" salt substitute?

   yes ______ no ______

3. If "yes," what was her name?

   First Name ______ Family Name ______ Apt. or Floor ______

4. Does she live here at Kissena I?

   yes ______ no ______

5. Did this person recommend that you *try* or *not try* the "Brand X" salt substitute?

   Try ______ Not Try ______ Other ______

6. If the respondent bought "Brand X" salt substitute, then ask:

   "Did this conversation occur before or after you bought the "Brand X" salt substitute?

   Before ______ After ______ Do not remember ______

7. Can you name any other persons, living at Kissena I, who have mentioned the "Brand X" salt substitute to you?

   (Space for three other names and locations)

objective of the study was to determine the impact of product-related informal communication on community members' subsequent decisions to purchase or not to purchase a new salt substitute. The results of this study indicated that individuals who provided others with information or advice concerning the new product (the opinion leaders) and those who received positive information or advice from others concerning the new product (the opinion receivers) were both more likely to have purchased it than those who did not engage in an exchange of informal information about the product.[7]

## Key Informant Method

A third way to measure opinion leadership is through the use of a *key informant*—a person who is keenly aware or knowledgeable about the nature of social communication among members of a specific consumer group. This person, the key informant, is asked to identify those individuals in the group who are most likely to be opinion leaders.

The key informant does not have to be a member of the group under study (for example, a professor may serve as the key informant for a college class). This research method is relatively inexpensive, since it requires that only one individual—or at most several individuals—be intensively interviewed, while the self-designating and sociometric methods require that an entire consumer sample or community be interviewed. However, the key informant method is generally not used by marketers because of the difficulties inherent in identifying an individual who can *objectively* identify opinion leaders in a relevant consumer group.

This method would seem to be of greatest potential use in the study of industrial or institutional opinion leadership. For example, a firm's salespeople might serve as key informants in the identification of specific customers who are most likely to influence the purchase decisions of other firms in their industry. Similarly, the purchasing agent of a specific firm might serve as a key informant by providing an outside salesperson with the names of those persons in his or her organization who are most likely to influence the purchase decision. In the study of consumers, possible key informants include influential community members such as the mayor, the president of a local club, the head of the PTA, or a prominent local retailer.

## Objective Method

The *objective* method of determining opinion leadership is much like a controlled experiment. It involves the deliberate placement of new products or new product information with selected individuals and then tracing the resultant web of interpersonal communication concerning the relevant product(s).

An intriguing study designed to measure the influence of opinion leaders on household matters provides a unique example of the objective method.[8] Fifteen friendship groups of women living in a self-contained community were individually interviewed via the sociometric method to assess their levels of opinion leadership with regard to household management matters. The women who scored *highest* as opinion leaders in each of nine groups were chosen to serve as opinion leader confederates (i.e., to cooperate with the researcher). In each of the other six groups, the women who scored *lowest* in opinion leadership were also chosen to serve as opinion leader confederates. This research design enabled the researcher to compare the influence exerted by those identified as opinion leaders with the influence exerted by those identified as nonleaders when all were placed in a "controlled" situation to serve as opinion leaders.

All fifteen participants selected by the researcher to function as opinion leaders were provided with new freeze-dried food items and asked to serve them to their families. They were also asked to give samples of the new food products to all other members of their friendship groups and to suggest that they, in turn, serve the items to their families.[9]

The results indicated that those individuals who received the new food items from "natural" opinion leaders tended to echo the leaders' opinions concerning the new product. Conversely, those individuals who received samples of the new food items from artificially created opinion leaders shifted away from the opinion leaders' sentiments. These findings suggest that true opinion leaders are capable of altering group members' opinions in the direction of their own opinions, whereas nonleaders (those who score low in opinion leadership studies) may adversely influence those they attempt to influence.

Table 16-2 presents an overview of each of the four methods of measuring opinion leadership.

## A PROFILE OF THE OPINION LEADER

Just who are opinion leaders? Can they be recognized by any distinctive characteristics? Can they be reached through specific media? Marketers have long sought answers to these questions, for if they are able to identify the relevant opinion leaders for their products, they can direct their promotional efforts to these leaders, confident that they in turn will influence the consumption behavior of others. For this reason, consumer researchers have attempted to develop a realistic profile of the opinion leader. This has not been easy to do. It was pointed out earlier that opinion leadership tends to be category-specific; that is, an individual who is an opinion *leader* in one product category may be an opinion *receiver* in another product category. Thus the generalized profile of opinion leaders is likely to be influenced by the context of specific product categories.

### Knowledge and Interest

It has been suggested that shared interest is the foundation upon which most informal communication is based.[10] However, some studies indicate that opinion leaders possess a keener level of interest in the product category than do

**TABLE 16-2 Methods of Measuring Opinion Leadership—Advantages and Limitations**

| OPINION LEADERSHIP MEASUREMENT METHOD | DESCRIPTION OF METHOD | SAMPLE QUESTIONS ASKED | ADVANTAGES | LIMITATIONS |
|---|---|---|---|---|
| 1. Self-designating method | Each respondent is asked a series of questions to determine the degree to which he perceives himself to be an opinion leader. | Do you influence other people in their selection of products? | Measures the individual's own perceptions of his or her opinion leadership. | Dependent upon the objectivity with which respondents can identify and report their personal influence. |
| 2. Sociometric method | Members of a social system are asked to whom they go for advice and information about a product category. | Whom do you ask? Who asks you for information about that product category? | Sociometric questions have the greatest degree of validity and are easy to administer. | Very costly and analysis is often very complex. Requires a large number of respondents. Not suitable for sample designs where only a portion of the social system is interviewed. |
| 3. Key informant method | Carefully selected key informants in a social system are asked to designate opinion leaders. | Who are the most influential people in the group? | Relatively inexpensive and less time-consuming than the sociometric method. | Informants who are not thoroughly familiar with the system would provide invalid information. |
| 4. Objective method | Artificially places individuals in a position to act as opinion leaders and measures results of their efforts. | Have you tried the product? | Measures individual's ability to influence others under controlled circumstances. | Requires the establishment of an experimental design and the tracking of the resulting impact on the participants. |

Source: Based in part on Everett M. Rogers, *Diffusion of Innovations*, 3rd ed. (New York: Free Press, 1983), 278.

opinion receivers.[11] Because of their interest, opinion leaders are likely to be better informed; and because of their knowledge, others may turn to them for their expertise. Chief among the characteristics that distinguish opinion leaders from nonleaders is their unique *involvement* with the subject of interest.[12] Compared with nonleaders in a particular product category, opinion leaders read more about related consumer issues, are more knowledgeable about related new product developments, participate more often in related consumer activities, and derive greater satisfaction from these product-related activities.

## Consumer Innovators

Consistent with their greater interest in a product category, consumer opinion leaders are more likely to try new products.[13] Thus opinion leaders tend to speak with some authority when providing advice to others who have not yet tried the new product.

Studies of consumer innovators for a variety of products and services (e.g., stereo equipment, solar energy devices, car care services, telephone equipment) have found that individuals identified as innovators tend to function as opinion leaders by recommending specific products or services based on their own experiences, or by showing or displaying products to others. Innovative consumers often feel that those receiving their remarks have bought the specific products or services because of them.

Research conducted on behalf of the film industry confirms the close link between innovators and their influence on others' consumption actions.[14] For example, frequent moviegoers who attend a movie within its first two weeks of release have been found to influence the attendance of their friends. Similarly, a study of subscribers to a community cable television service found that individuals who were the first to sign up were more likely to be TV opinion leaders.[15] These studies indicate that consumer innovators are likely to be opinion leaders in their area of innovation.

## Personality Traits

Very few studies have explored the relationship between personality and opinion leadership. Of those that have, several personality characteristics of opinion leaders appear to bridge specific product-related contexts. Among these are *self-confidence* and *gregariousness* (i.e., sociability). It may be that, to advise others, individuals must first have confidence in themselves and their ideas. Several studies have reported that opinion leaders scored higher in terms of local friendships than did nonleaders.[16] This is not surprising, when one considers that opinion leaders must be involved in social interaction in order to function.

## Attitudes and Intention

Little attention has been given to the role that *attitudes* play in the likelihood that consumers will (or will not) serve as opinion leaders. One study found that consumers who liked a new brand of coffee they were asked to sample were more inclined to talk about it than those who did not like it (i.e., who held unfavorable attitudes).[17] The study also revealed that consumers who proclaimed a willingness or intention to buy the product when it became available were more likely to have talked to others about the brand than those who did not. Finally, heavy coffee users were found to be more likely to initiate word-of-mouth conversations about the new brand than light or infrequent users.

If this link between *attitude–intention* behavior and *opinion leadership* is correct, it provides further support for the commonsense notion that creating and maintaining strong favorable attitudes for a product, especially a new brand, should be a critical marketing goal. Marketers frequently "buy" consumer experience (and ultimately market share) by providing consumers with free samples or cents-off coupons to induce trial. The hope is that trial will create a *positive* attitude, which will in turn foster continued use and positive word-of-mouth, and ultimately widespread consumer adoption.

## Media Habits

A number of interdisciplinary studies concerned with opinion leadership and the diffusion of information have concluded that opinion leaders make greater use of mass media—they tend to use "more impersonal and technically accurate" and more "cosmopolitan" (i.e., widespread) sources of information than nonleaders.[18] Few studies within the marketing or consumer behavior literature have been able to confirm these findings. Rather, opinion leaders have been found to have much greater readership of special publications devoted to the specific product category in which they "lead." For example, automotive opinion leaders read publications like *Car and Driver, Motor Trend,* and *Road and Track.* Such special interest magazines not only serve to inform car buffs about new models and accessories that may be of personal interest, but also place them in a better position to make recommendations to the relatives, friends, and neighbors who turn to them for advice. Thus the opinion leader would appear to have greater exposure to media specifically relevant to his or her area of interest than would nonleaders, but not necessarily greater exposure to mass media in general.

## Social Status Characteristics

As with other characteristics of the opinion leader, social status characteristics appear to depend upon the topic of interest. In most marketing studies, the opinion leader has been found to belong to the same socioeconomic group (social class) as the opinion receiver. This is not surprising; it would seem reasonable to expect an individual to turn to a person with whom he or she feels comfortable—someone within the same social class grouping. Similarly, opinion leaders are most likely to give information or advice to those people with whom they regularly engage in informal communication, the people within their own social stratum.

**TABLE 16-3 Profile of Opinion Leaders**

| GENERALIZED ATTRIBUTES ACROSS PRODUCT CATEGORIES | CATEGORY-SPECIFIC ATTRIBUTES |
|---|---|
| Innovativeness | Interest |
| Willingness to talk | Knowledge |
| Self-confidence | Special-interest media exposure |
| Gregariousness | Same age |
| | Same social status |
| | Social exposure outside group |

### Demographic Characteristics

A number of studies indicate that informal communication generally flows between people of similar age. This characteristic is again category-specific. For example, one research study concerned with moviegoing found that the majority of all informal communication concerning movies occurred among people of the same age category.[19] However, a study of women's clothing fashions showed that opinion leaders tended to be younger and have more education, higher incomes, and higher occupational status than fashion opinion receivers.[20]

These and other studies suggest that for specific areas of interest, people may seek information and advice from people whom they perceive to be highly qualified informants. In the context of physician selection, older people may be perceived as having more information and experience. In the context of women's fashions, younger people, those with higher incomes, and/or those with higher occupational status may be perceived as being more qualified informants.

In summary, it is difficult to construct a generalized profile of the opinion leader outside the context of a specific category of interest. However, on the basis of the limited evidence available (as shown in Table 16-3), opinion leaders, across all product categories, tend to exhibit the following attributes: innovativeness, greater willingness to talk, self-confidence, and gregariousness. Within the context of specific subject areas, opinion leaders tend to have greater interest in and knowledge of the product category and more exposure to relevant special-interest media. They also tend to belong to the same socioeconomic and age groups as the opinion receivers.

## FREQUENCY AND OVERLAP OF OPINION LEADERSHIP

Opinion leadership is not a rare phenomenon. Often more than one-third of the people studied in a consumer research project are classified as opinion leaders.[21] One researcher reported that almost half (47.5 percent) of his respondents identified themselves as opinion leaders in one or more of the product categories investigated.[22] In another study, 69 percent of the 976 respondents qualified as opinion leaders in at least one of six product areas examined.[23] The frequency of consumer opinion leadership tends to suggest that people are sufficiently interested in at least one product or product category to talk about it and give advice concerning it to others.

This leads to two interesting questions: Is opinion leadership generalized? Do opinion leaders in one product category tend to be opinion leaders in other product categories? Consumer researchers have concerned themselves with these questions in their search for a generalized profile of the opinion leader.

### Overlap of Opinion Leadership

A number of studies have investigated the overlap of opinion leadership across several product categories. The research findings suggest that opinion leadership tends to overlap across certain combinations of *interest areas*. For instance, one study found that opinion leadership overlap was highest among product categories that involved similar interests (large and small appliances; women's clothing fashions and cosmetics; personal grooming aids; household cleansers and detergents; and packaged food products).[24] Similarly, when the members of a national consumer panel were questioned about sixteen categories of consumer spending, the findings indicated that opinion leadership overlaps product areas in which the opinion leaders' interests overlap (for example, buying and preparing food, or new clothing styles and furnishing a home).[25]

The above evidence indicates that opinion leaders in one product area are often opinion leaders in related areas in which they are also interested.

## THE OPINION LEADERSHIP SITUATIONAL ENVIRONMENT

Product-related discussions between two people do not take place in a vacuum. Two people are not likely to meet and spontaneously break into a discussion in which product-related information is sought or offered. Rather, product discussions generally occur *within relevant situational contexts*—e.g., when a specific product or a similar product is being used or served, or as an outgrowth of a more general discussion which in some way touches upon the product category. Thus, if two co-workers are discussing the forthcoming annual company picnic and one asks, "What are you going to wear?" their discussion might eventually lead to one asking the other for advice on the appropriateness of a new style or fashion. In this situation, the opinion leader will provide information to the opinion receiver as an outgrowth of a conversation concerning the company picnic both plan to attend.

A study of homemakers' awareness of a new General Foods brand of coffee revealed that discussions concerning the new coffee were most likely to come up in a food-related context.[26] Specifically, over three-quarters of the consumers who *provided* information about the new coffee to others reported doing so in a food-related context, while three-quarters of the consumers who reported *receiving* such information did so in a food-related context.

## Opinion Leaders Are Friends or Neighbors

It is not surprising that opinion leaders and opinion receivers are often friends, neighbors, or work associates, since existing friendships provide numerous opportunities for conversation concerning product-related topics. *Physical proximity* is likely to increase the occurrences of product-related conversations.[27] A community center, for example, increases the opportunities for neighbors to meet and engage in informal communication concerning product-related topics.

The importance of physical proximity in the opinion leadership process is supported by a study concerning interpersonal influence in physician selection.[28] Analysis revealed that 11 percent of the participants in two-person discussions (dyads) were members of the same club, 15 percent belonged to the same church, 15 percent were employed by the same company, 27 percent lived within one block of each other, and 67 percent had visited the other person's home.

Additional support for the importance of physical proximity in informal product-related conversations comes from a study of word-of-mouth influence among elderly residents in a high-rise retirement community. The study found that 81 percent of the exchange of information and advice occurred between persons who lived on the same floor; the remaining 19 percent occurred between residents living just one floor apart.[29]

These studies demonstrate that product-related conversations generally occur between friends, neighbors, or work associates who have some physical proximity in a situational context relevant to the product under discussion. Opinion leadership based on physical proximity is important to marketers when it comes to door-to-door selling (Avon), party selling (Tupperware), and direct marketing efforts based on geodemographic clusters (see the discussion in Chapter 13).

# THE INTERPERSONAL FLOW OF COMMUNICATION

How does information provided by the mass media reach and influence the total population? Several theories suggest that the opinion leader is a vital link in the transmission of information and influence.

## Two-Step Flow of Communication Theory

A study of voting behavior some fifty years ago concluded that ideas often flow from radio and print to opinion leaders and from them to the general public.[30] This so-called **two-step flow of communication** theory portrayed opinion lead-

FIGURE 16-3 **Two-Step Flow of Communication Theory**

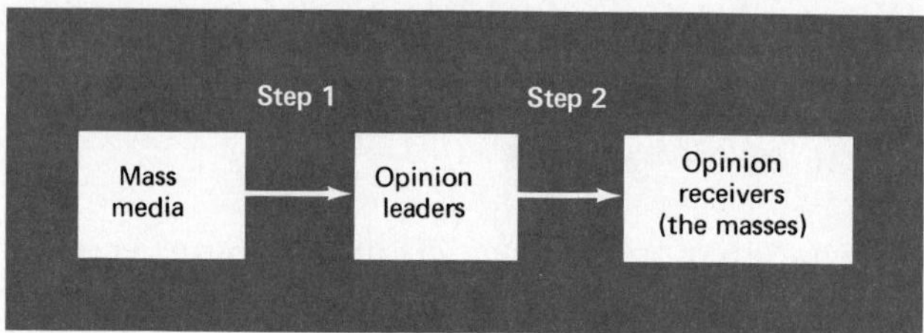


ers as direct receivers of information from impersonal mass-media sources, who in turn transmitted (and interpreted) this information to the masses. This theory views the opinion leader as a *middleman* between the impersonal mass media and the majority of society.

The major contribution of the two-step flow of communication theory was that it demonstrated that social interaction between people serves as the principal means by which information is transmitted, attitudes developed, and behavior stimulated. The theory rejected the notion that mass media alone influenced the sale of products, political candidates, and ideas to a mass audience.

Figure 16-3 presents a model of the two-step flow of communication theory. Information is depicted as flowing in a single direction (i.e., one way) from the mass media to the opinion leaders (Step 1), and then from the opinion leaders (who interpret, legitimize, and transmit the information) to friends, neighbors, and acquaintances, who constitute the "masses" (Step 2).

The two-step flow of communication theory is insightful in that it illustrates how people acquire information about issues of interest. However, it no longer seems to be an accurate portrayal of the flow of information and influence. The need for modification of this theory is in large part based on advances in communication technology, and research evidence which suggests that:[31]

1. Mass media may *inform* both opinion leaders and opinion receivers; however, the opinion receiver is more likely to be *influenced* by the opinion leader than by the media.
2. Not all interpersonal communication is initiated by opinion leaders and directed to opinion receivers. Very often those who are receivers may initiate the interpersonal communication by requesting information or advice from the opinion leaders.
3. Those who receive information and advice *from* others (i.e., opinion receivers) are more likely to offer advice *to* others (including opinion leaders) than those who do not receive advice from others.
4. Opinion leaders are more likely than those who are nonleaders to both receive and seek advice from others.

## Multistep Flow of Communication Theory

It is apparent that the two-step flow of communication theory does not fully account for the complexity of interpersonal communications. A more recent

FIGURE 16-4 Multistep Flow of Communication Theory

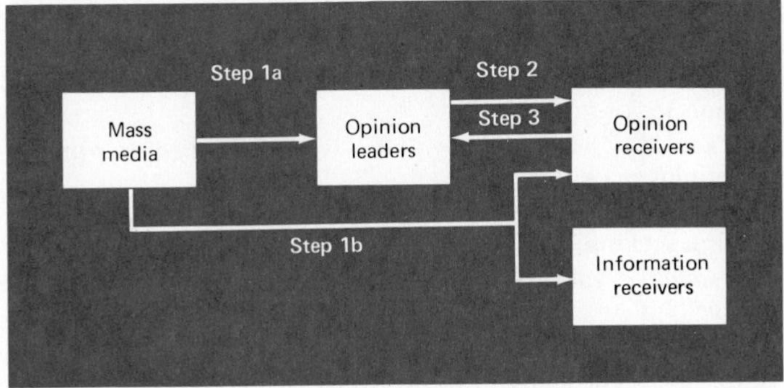


model depicts the transmission of information from the media as a **multistep flow of communication.** The revised model takes into account the fact that information and influence are often two-way processes in which opinion leaders both influence and are influenced by opinion receivers.

Figure 16-4 presents a model of the *multistep flow of communication* theory. Steps 1a and 1b depict the flow of information from the mass media simultaneously to opinion leaders, opinion receivers, and information receivers (who neither influence nor are influenced by others). Step 2 shows the transmission of information and influence from opinion leaders to opinion receivers. Step 3 reflects the transfer of information and influence from opinion receivers to opinion leaders.

### MARKETING IMPLICATIONS OF THE MULTISTEP THEORY

Research evidence provides support for the multistep theory of communication.[32] It suggests that interpersonal communication cannot be neatly dichotomized into dominant, all-powerful opinion leaders and passive opinion receivers. For the marketing practitioner, the multistep flow of communication theory suggests that it is important to identify and reach opinion leaders because of the critical roles they play in transmitting information and influence about products to opinion receivers. However, the theory also suggests that it is equally important to identify and reach individuals who are the receivers or seekers of product advice, for these individuals are likely to function eventually as opinion leaders themselves. As one astute observer remarked: ". . . it appears that rather than distinguishing among opinion leaders and followers, one should distinguish among consumers engaging in more or [in] less personal communication about the product."[33]

## A Broader Approach to Interpersonal Communication

Several consumer studies have combined measures of opinion leadership and opinion seeking to form a richer picture of the interpersonal communication process than is possible by examining opinion leadership alone. These studies have used the following four-way categorization of interpersonal communication:[34]

1. The **socially integrated:** Those who score *high* on both opinion leadership and opinion seeking;
2. The **socially independent:** Those who score *high* on opinion leadership and *low* on opinion seeking;
3. The **socially dependent:** Those who score *low* on opinion leadership and *high* on opinion seeking;
4. The **socially isolated:** Those who score *low* on both opinion leadership and opinion seeking.

This typology is basically consistent with the multistep flow of communication theory. The four interpersonal communication groups are formed by cross-classifying consumers in terms of their responses to questions designed to establish the extent to which they are opinion leaders and/or opinion seekers (see Table 16-4). The advantage of this four-way classification over the traditional two-way classification (i.e., opinion leaders versus nonleaders) is that it distinguishes those consumers who transmit and/or seek information and advice from those who neither transmit nor seek advice and information.

To illustrate how the four-way classification scheme can be employed to compare interpersonal communication patterns for different products, Table 16-5 lists the results of seven consumer behavior studies in terms of the interpersonal communication scheme. It reveals that most consumers are involved in some form of product-related conversation, and that the percentage of respondents in each of the four groups tends to vary by product category.

Most important, the four-way classification scheme enables us to see patterns that would otherwise be masked if we simply contrasted opinion leaders with nonleaders. For example, Table 16-5 indicates that with the exception of audio-equipment buyers (the only really big-ticket item in the study), consumers of historical romance novels are the most socially integrated; that is, more of them engage in interpersonal communication than do consumers of the other product categories studied. Futhermore, very few of the historical romance readers are socially isolated. Both findings provide support for the frequent contention that despite the absence of substantial advertising budgets,

**TABLE 16-4 Four-Way Categorization of Interpersonal Communication**

| | | OPINION SEEKING SCORES | |
|---|---|---|---|
| | | high | low |
| OPINION LEADERSHIP SCORES | high | Socially Integrated | Socially Independent |
| | low | Socially Dependent | Socially Isolated |

**TABLE 16-5 Representative Results of the Four-Way Categorization of Interpersonal Communication**

| | STAINLESS STEEL BLADES* | HOUSEHOLD CLEANSERS AND DETERGENTS† | COSMETICS AND PERSONAL GROOMING AIDS† | DIET FOOD PRODUCTS‡ | WOMEN'S CLOTHING FASHIONS§ | HISTORICAL ROMANCE NOVELS‖ | AUDIO EQUIPMENT# |
|---|---|---|---|---|---|---|---|
| Socially integrated | 14% | 21% | 22% | 28% | 32% | 38% | 51% |
| Socially independent | 4 | 6 | 4 | 16 | 18 | 24 | 14 |
| Socially dependent | 35 | 35 | 40 | 21 | 18 | 8 | 25 |
| Socially isolated | 47 | 38 | 34 | 35 | 32 | 30 | 10 |
| Total | 100% | 100% | 100% | 100% | 100% | 100% | 100% |

Sources: Adapted from the following:

*Jagdish N. Sheth, "Word-of-Mouth in Low Risk Innovations," *Journal of Advertising Research*, 11 (June 1971), 17.

†John O. Summers and Charles W. King, "Interpersonal Communication and New Product Attitudes," *Proceedings* (Chicago: Fall Conference, American Marketing Association, 1969), 295.

‡Leon G. Schiffman, "Social Interaction Patterns of the Elderly Consumer," *Proceedings* (Chicago: Fall Conference, American Marketing Association, 1972), 446.

§Fred D. Reynolds and William R. Darden, "Mutually Adaptive Effects of Interpersonal Communication," *Journal of Marketing Research*, 8 (November 1971), 451.

‖Leon G. Schiffman and Steven P. Schnaars, "The Consumption of Historical Romance Novels: Consumer Aesthetics in Popular Literature," in Elizabeth C. Hirschman and Morris Holbrook, eds., *Symbolic Consumer Behavior* (Ann Arbor, Mich.: Association for Consumer Research, 1980), 50.

#Leon G. Schiffman et al., "Interpersonal Communication: An Opinion Leadership/Opinion Seeking Composite Approach," *1975 Combined Proceedings* (Chicago: American Marketing Association, 1975), 230.

historical romances attain widespread consumer acceptance due to word-of-mouth communication.

Cross-tabulating the four interpersonal communication groups with other consumer-relevant factors (demographics, personality traits, attitudes, and psychographics) offers additional insights into the dynamics of interpersonal communication. To illustrate this, Table 16-6 presents a cross-tabulation of the four interpersonal communication groups and a variety of popular consumer behavior variables. The outcome is a profile of each of the four types of communicators. For example, socially integrated consumers exhibit the following characteristics:

They are younger and less educated.
They eat out more frequently.
They tend to view themselves as "swingers."
TV is less likely to be their primary form of entertainment.
They like romantic movies.
They tend to seek out the advice of others regarding various products and brands.
They are likely to have others come to them for advice concerning various products and brands.

**TABLE 16-6 Relationships between Interpersonal Communication Typology and Significant Consumer Behavior Variables**

| | SOCIALLY INTEGRATED | SOCIALLY INDEPENDENT | SOCIALLY DEPENDENT | SOCIALLY ISOLATED |
|---|---|---|---|---|
| I went to a club meeting | 38% | 21% | 67% | 37% |
| I went out to dinner at a restaurant | 96 | 88 | 83 | 76 |
| I like to think I am a bit of a swinger | 56 | 35 | 50 | 17 |
| TV is my primary form form of entertainment | 29 | 49 | 25 | 52 |
| I like romantic movies | 94 | 64 | 83 | 83 |
| I often seek out the advice of my friends regarding brands and products | 57 | 29 | 42 | 29 |
| My friends and neighbors often come to me for advice about products and brands | 68 | 56 | 50 | 34 |
| Age (% under 30) | 55 | 32 | 25 | 21 |
| Education (% with schooling beyond H.S.) | 57 | 50 | 92 | 67 |

Source: Leon G. Schiffman and Steven P. Schnaars, "The Consumption of Historical Romance Novels: Consumer Aesthetics in Popular Literature," in Elizabeth C. Hirschman and Morris Holbrook, eds., *Symbolic Consumer Behavior* (Ann Arbor, Mich.: Association for Consumer Research, 1980), 50.

This single example indicates that the four-way interpersonal communication typology is capable of providing additional insights into the dynamics of word-of-mouth communication.

## OPINION LEADERSHIP AND THE FIRM'S PROMOTIONAL STRATEGY

Marketers have long been aware of the powerful influence that opinion leadership exerts on consumer behavior. They try to encourage word-of-mouth communication and other favorable informal conversations concerning their products because they recognize that consumers place more credibility in informal communication sources than in paid advertising. The seeking of product information and advice tends to be the most widely used consumer strategy for reducing perceived risk.

One marketing strategist suggested that new-product designers exploit the effectiveness of word-of-mouth communication by deliberately designing products to have word-of-mouth potential. He said that new products "should give customers something to talk about, and to talk with—a powerful advantage idea that can be expressed in words."[35] Examples of products that had such word-of-mouth potential include the Polaroid camera, the Sylvania flashcube, the Water Pik, Cabbage Patch dolls, Crest toothpaste with tartar control, Trivial Pursuit, the Swatch watch, and the Minolta 7000 camera. These revolutionary products "sold themselves" as consumers sold them to each other by word-of-mouth.

In some instances where informal word-of-mouth did not spontaneously emerge from the uniqueness of the product or its marketing strategy, marketers have deliberately attempted to stimulate or to simulate opinion leadership.

### Advertisements That Stimulate Opinion Leadership

Advertisements designed to get consumers to "tell your friends how much you like our product" are one way in which marketers have used advertising to increase product-related discussions. The objective of a promotional strategy of *stimulation* is to run advertisements that are sufficiently interesting and informative to provoke consumers into discussing the virtues of the product with others. For example, the pioneer of heart transplants, Dr. Christiaan Barnard, affiliated himself with a new line of skin care products that promised to "make older skin behave and look like younger skin." The ad for these products, presented in Figure 16-5, provides consumers with sufficient information to enable them to talk about the merits of these skin care products with others.

To stimulate recognition, interest, and discussion about a new "designer personality," Murjani (a major sportswear manufacturer) has run ads featuring its young clothing designer Tommy Hilfiger. The ads liken "Tommy" to such American designer greats as Geoffrey Beene, Bill Blass, Stanley Blacker, Calvin Klein, Perry Ellis, and Ralph Lauren (see Figure 16-6).

FIGURE 16-5 Advertisement Designed to Stimulate Informal Communication

Courtesy of Alfin Fragrances Inc.

## Advertisements That Simulate Opinion Leadership

A firm's advertisements can also be designed to *simulate* product discussions by portraying people in the act of informal communication. Such a promotional tactic has the characteristic of suggesting that it is appropriate to discuss a particular subject or product. For example, a simulated informal communication encounter between two or more women has often been employed in TV advertising for a variety of personal-care products to persuade women to discuss their use or contemplated use. Such simulations reduce the need for consumers to actually seek product advice from others—by functioning as a convenient substitute.

A specific example of advertising designed to simulate informal communication is shown in Figure 16-7. This diet Coke advertisement depicts Martin Mull, the actor, "passing along" the information that diet Coke beat Diet Pepsi in a taste test for the second year in a row. Furthermore, the ad includes a cents-off coupon to encourage trial and usage.

FIGURE 16-6 Advertisement Designed to Stimulate Informal Communication

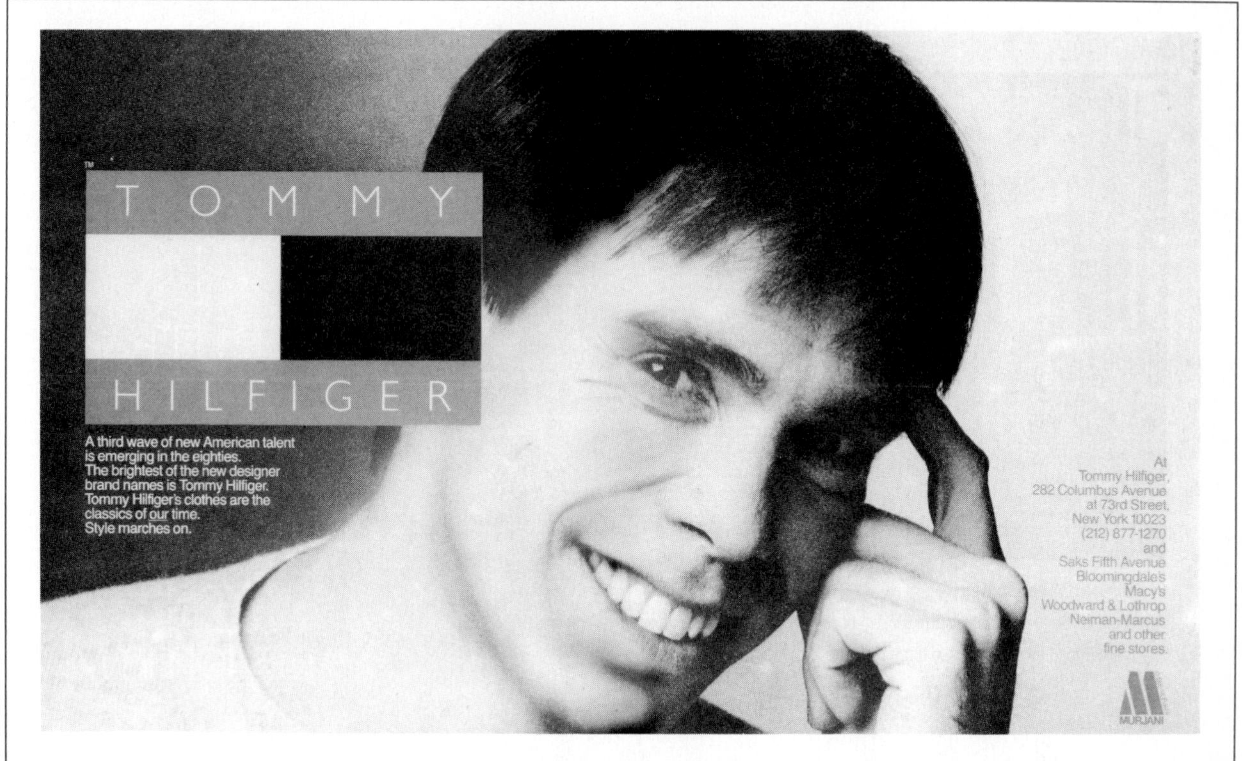


Courtesy of Murjani for Tommy Hilfiger

## Word-of-Mouth May Be Uncontrollable

Although most marketing managers believe that word-of-mouth communication is extremely effective, one problem they sometimes overlook is the fact that such informal communication is not easy to control.[36] Negative comments—frequently in the form of rumors that are untrue—can sometimes sweep through a population to the detriment of the product in question.

Following are some of the more common rumor themes that have beset firms, and in certain cases have unfavorably influenced sales: (1) the product was produced under unsanitary conditions; (2) the product contained an unwholesome or culturally unacceptable ingredient; (3) the product functioned as an undesirable depressant or stimulant; (4) the product included some cancer-causing element or agent; and (5) the firm was owned or influenced by an unfriendly or misguided foreign country, governmental agency, or religious cult.

Combatting unfounded rumors is a difficult task. Chapter 10 discussed the rumor that plagued Procter & Gamble for years concerning its man-in-the-moon corporate logo. In the past several years, other companies that have had to deal with damaging rumors include General Foods, Life Savers, McDonald's,

FIGURE 16-7 Advertisement Depicting Word-of-Mouth Communication

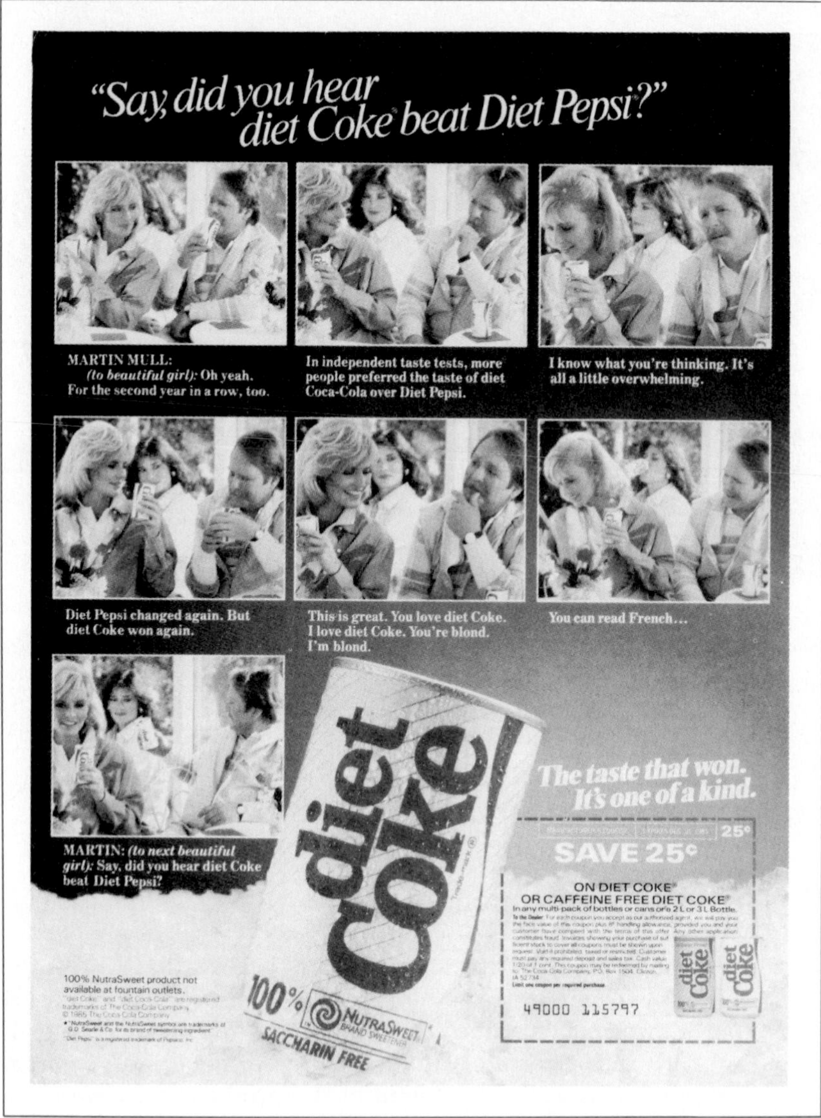


Courtesy of The Coca-Cola Company

and Squibb.[37] Most of these firms found that negative rumors cannot be ignored. Instead, they must be responded to quickly before they spread out of control. Sometimes ads have been employed to refute rumors and to demonstrate that they are unfounded.

## Creation of Opinion Leaders

**Personal Influence and the Opinion Leadership Process**

Marketing strategists agree that promotional efforts would be significantly improved if they could segment their markets into opinion leaders and opinion receivers relevant to their product category. Then they could direct their promotional messages directly to the people most likely to "carry the word" to the masses. However, because of the difficulties inherent in identifying appropriate opinion leaders, some researchers have suggested that it might be more fruitful to "create" product-specific opinion leaders.

In one study, a group of socially influential high-school students (class presidents, sports captains) were asked to become members of a panel that would rate new rock-and-roll phonograph records. As part of their responsibilities, panel participants were encouraged to discuss their record choices with friends. Preliminary examination suggested that these influentials would not qualify as opinion leaders for records because of their relatively meager ownership of the product category.[38] However, by *encouraging their interest,* some of the records the group evaluated made the top-ten charts in the cities where they lived; these same records did *not* make the top-ten charts in any other city. This study suggests that product-specific opinion leaders can be created by taking socially involved or influential people and deliberately increasing their enthusiasm for a product category.

## summary

Opinion leadership is the process by which one person (the opinion leader) informally influences the actions or attitudes of others, who may be opinion seekers or merely opinion recipients. Opinion receivers perceive the opinion leader to be a highly credible objective source of product information who can help reduce their search time and perceived risk. Opinion leaders, in turn, are motivated to give information or advice to others in part because doing so enhances their own status and self-image, and because such advice tends to reduce their own postpurchase dissonance. Other motives include product involvement, other involvement, and message involvement.

Market researchers identify opinion leaders by the self-designated method, the key-informant method, the sociometric method, and the objective method. Studies of opinion leadership indicate that the phenomenon tends to be product-specific; that is, individuals "specialize" in a product or product category in which they are highly interested and involved. An opinion leader for one product category may be an opinion receiver for another.

Generally, opinion leaders are gregarious, self-confident, innovative people who like to talk. They acquire information about their areas of interest through avid readership of special interest magazines and by new product trial. Their interests often overlap adjacent product areas; thus their opinion leadership may extend into related areas.

The opinion leadership process usually takes place among friends, neighbors, and work associates who have frequent physical proximity and thus ample opportunity to hold informal product-related conversations. Such conversations usually occur naturally in the context of the product-category usage.

The two-step flow of communication theory, developed some fifty years ago, highlighted the role of interpersonal influence in the transmission of information from the mass media to the population at large. This theory provides the foundation for a revised multistep flow of communication model, which takes into account the fact that information and influence are often two-way processes, and that opinion leaders both influence and are influenced by opinion receivers.

Marketers recognize the strategic value of segmenting their audiences into opinion leaders and opinion receivers for their product categories. If they can direct their promotional efforts to the more influential segments of their markets, these individuals will in turn transmit this information to those who seek product advice. Marketers have found that they can also "create" opinion leaders for their products by taking socially involved or influential people and deliberately increasing their enthusiasm for a product category.

## *discussion questions*

1. Why is the opinion leader a more credible source of product information than a product advertisement?
2. As a marketing research consultant, you have been asked by a manufacturer of a new brand of instant coffee to identify the opinion leaders for this product category. Which one of the following measurement techniques would you recommend: self-designating method, sociometric method, key-informant method, or objective method? Explain your selection.
3. Why would a consumer who has just gone out and purchased a Mercury Sable automobile attempt to influence the purchase behavior of others?
4. Is an opinion leader for stereo equipment likely to be an opinion leader for fashion clothing? Discuss.
5. In the mid-1980s, Minolta introduced an autofocusing 35mm single-lens reflex camera named the Minolta Maxxum. Using Table 16-3 as a guide, identify and discuss those category-specific attributes of an opinion leader that you feel would be particularly useful in planning a marketing strategy.
6. The two-step flow of communication theory has been modified to portray more accurately the flow of information. Briefly describe this modification and explain its relevance to the marketing decision maker.
7. Examine the following list of products and services. For each, indicate who you would go to for information and advice on that topic and what that person's relationship is to you. If you feel you are an opinion leader

in any of these areas, then think of a person who has recently come to you to ask a question on that subject matter and note the relationship. *Subjects:* fashion, banking, computers, air travel, vacation destinations, compact disk players.

8. You have been asked by Sony to develop a print advertisement that would simulate word-of-mouth conversation. What type of promotional story line might you recommend? Explain why you think it would be effective.

## *endnotes*

1. Philip Voss, Jr., "Status shifts to peer influence," *Advertising Age,* May 17, 1984, M-10.
2. Stephen C. Cosmas and Jagdish N. Sheth, "Identification of Opinion Leaders across Cultures: An Exploratory Assessment" (Urbana-Champaign: University of Illinois, May 1978), Working Paper No. 123; and Lawrence F. Feick, Linda L. Price, and Robin A. Higie, "People Who Use People: The Other Side of Opinion Leadership," in Richard J. Lutz, ed., *Advances in Consumer Research* (Provo, Utah: Association for Consumer Research, 1986), 13, 301–05.
3. Ernest Dichter, "How Word-of-Mouth Advertising Works," *Harvard Business Review,* 44 (November–December 1966), 148.
4. Ibid., 149–52.
5. Dorothy Leonard-Barton, "Experts as Negative Opinion Leaders in the Diffusion of a Technological Innovation," *Journal of Consumer Research,* 11 (March 1985), 914–26.
6. Johan Arndt, "Role of Product-Related Conversations in the Diffusion of a New Product," *Journal of Marketing Research,* 4 (August 1967), 292–94.
7. Leon G. Schiffman, "Sources of Information for the Elderly," *Journal of Advertising Research,* 11 (October 1971), 33–37.
8. John G. Myers, "Patterns of Interpersonal Influence in the Adoption of New Products," in Raymond M. Haas, ed., *Proceedings* (Chicago: American Marketing Association, 1966), 750–57.
9. Ibid., 756–57.
10. Elihu Katz and Paul F. Lazarsfeld, *Personal Influence* (New York: Free Press, 1955), 32.
11. For example, see David B. Montgomery and Alvin J. Silk, "Patterns of Overlap in Opinion Leadership and Interest for Categories of Purchase Activity," in Phillip R. McDonald, ed., *Proceedings* (Chicago: American Marketing Association, 1969), 377–86; and James H. Myers and Thomas S. Robertson, "Dimensions of Opinion Leadership," *Journal of Marketing Research,* 9 (February 1972), 41–46.
12. Lawrence G. Corey, "People Who Claim to Be Opinion Leaders: Identifying Their Characteristics by Self-Report," *Journal of Marketing,* 35 (October 1971), 48–53.
13. For example, see John O. Summers, "The Identity of Women's Clothing Fashion Opinion Leaders," *Journal of Marketing Research,* 7 (May 1970), 178–85; Steven A. Baumgarten, "The Innovative Communicator in the Diffusion Process," *Journal of Marketing Research,* 12 (February 1975), 12–18; Jacob Jacoby, "Opinion Leadership and Innovativeness: Overlap and Validity," in M. Venkatesan, ed., *Proceedings, Third Annual Conference* (Baltimore: Association for Consumer Research, 1972), 642–49; and Duane L. Davis and Ronald S. Rubin, "Identifying the Energy Con-

scious Consumer: The Case of the Opinion Leader," *Journal of the Academy of Marketing Science,* 11 (Spring 1983), 169–90.

14. Aljean Harmetz, "For Films, Word of Mouth Means Success," *New York Times,* November 27, 1978, C13.

15. John H. Holmes, "Communication Patterns and the Diffusion of a Consumer Innovation: Preliminary Findings," *Proceedings of the Second Annual Meeting* (Baltimore: Association for Consumer Research, 1971), 459–63.

16. For example, see Summers, "Identity of Women's Clothing," 181–83; Fred D. Reynolds and William R. Darden, "Mutually Adaptive Effects of Interpersonal Communication," *Journal of Marketing Research,* 8 (November 1971), 449–54; Thomas S. Robertson and James H. Myers, "Personality Correlates of Opinion Leadership and Innovative Buyer Behavior," *Journal of Marketing Research,* 6 (May 1969), 164–68; and Leon G. Schiffman and Vincent Gaccione, "Opinion Leaders in Institutional Markets," *Journal of Marketing,* 38 (April 1974), 51.

17. John H. Holmes and John D. Lett, Jr., "Product Sampling and Word of Mouth," *Journal of Advertising Research,* 17 (October 1977), 35–40; and Davis and Rubin, "Identifying the Energy Conscious Consumer," 188–90.

18. For example, see Bruce Ryan and Neal C. Gross, "The Diffusion of Hybrid Seed Corn in Two Iowa Communities," *Rural Sociology,* 8 (March 1943), 15–24; and Verling C. Troldahl and Robert Van Dam, "Face-to-Face Communication about Major Topics in the News," *Public Opinion Quarterly,* 29 (Winter 1965), 626–32.

19. Katz and Lazarsfeld, *Personal Influence,* 305–6.

20. Summers, "Identity of Women's Clothing," 179.

21. For example, see Corey, "People Who Claim to Be Opinion Leaders"; Charles W. King and John O. Summers, "Overlap of Opinion Leadership across Consumer Product Categories," *Journal of Marketing Research,* 7 (February 1970), 43–50; and Alvin J. Silk, "Overlap across Self-designated Opinion Leaders: A Study of Selected Dental Products and Services," *Journal of Marketing Research,* 3 (August 1966), 253–59.

22. Silk, "Overlap across Self-designated Opinion Leaders," 257.

23. King and Summers, "Overlap of Opinion Leadership," 46.

24. Ibid., 48–50.

25. David B. Montgomery and Alvin J. Silk, "Clusters of Consumer Interests and Opinion Leaders' Spheres of Influence," *Journal of Marketing Research,* 8 (August 1971), 317–21.

26. Russell W. Belk, "Occurrence of Word-of-Mouth Buyer Behavior as a Function of Situation and Advertising Stimuli," in Fred C. Allvine, ed., *Proceedings* (Chicago: American Marketing Association, 1971), 419–22.

27. For example, see William H. White, "The Web of Word of Mouth," *Fortune,* November 1954, 140–43; and Linda L. Price and Lawrence F. Feick, "The Role of Interpersonal Sources in External Search: An Informational Perspective," in Thomas C. Kinnear, ed., *Advances in Consumer Research* (Ann Arbor, Mich.: Association for Consumer Research, 1984), IX, 250–55.

28. For example, see Sidney P. Feldman, "Some Dyadic Relationships Associated with Consumer Choice," in Haas, *Proceedings,* 768–71.

29. Leon G. Schiffman, "Social Interaction Patterns of the Elderly Consumer," in Boris W. Becker and Helmut Becker, eds., *Combined Proceedings* (Chicago: American Marketing Association, 1972), 451.

30. Paul F. Lazarsfeld, Bernard Berelson, and Hazel Gaudet, *The People's Choice,* 2nd ed. (New York: Columbia University Press, 1948), 151.

31. For example, see Thomas S. Robertson, "Purchase Sequence Response: Innovators vs Non-Innovators," *Journal of Advertising Research,* 8 (February 1968), 47–52; John O. Summers, "New Product Interpersonal Communication," in Fred C. Allvine, ed., *Combined Proceedings* (Chicago: American Marketing Association, 1971),

429–30; Reynolds and Darden, "Mutually Adaptive Effects," 451; Jagdish N. Sheth, "Word-of-Mouth in Low Risk Innovations," *Journal of Advertising Research,* 11 (June 1971), 15–18; and Schiffman and Gaccione, "Opinion Leaders," 51–52.

32. Robertson, "Purchase Sequence Response," 47–52; Summers, "New Product Interpersonal Communication," 429–30; Reynolds and Darden, "Mutually Adaptive Effects," 451; Sheth, "Word-of-Mouth in Low Risk Innovations, 15–18; and Schiffman and Gaccione, "Opinion Leaders," 51–52.

33. Flemming Hansen, "Backwards Segmentation Using Hierarchical Clustering and Q Factor Analysis," in Venkatesan, *Proceedings 3rd Annual Conference,* 226.

34. Reynolds and Darden, "Mutually Adaptive Effects," 450; Schiffman, "Social Interaction Patterns," 447; Leon G. Schiffman, Joseph F. Dash, and William R. Dillon, "Interpersonal Communication: An Opinion Leadership/Opinion Seeking Composite Approach," in Edward M. Mazze, ed., *Combined Proceedings* (Chicago: American Marketing Association, 1975), 228–32; and Leon G. Schiffman and Steven P. Schnaars, "The Consumption of Historical Romance Novels: Consumer Aesthetics in Popular Literature," in Elizabeth C. Hirschman and Morris Holbrook, eds., *Symbolic Consumer Behavior* (Ann Arbor, Mich.: Association for Consumer Research, 1980), 46–51.

35. James J. Sheeran, " 'Me-Too' Marketing Mania," *New York Times,* March 11, 1973, 17.

36. Mark B. Traylor and Alicia M. Mathias, "The Impact of TV Advertising Versus Word of Mouth on the Image of Lawyers: A Projective Experiment," *Journal of Advertising,* 12 (1983), 42–49; and Barry L. Bayus, "Word of Mouth: The Indirect Effects of Marketing Efforts," *Journal of Advertising Research,* 25 (June–July 1985), 31–38.

37. Robert Levy, "Tilting at the Rumor Mill," *Dun's Review,* July 1981, 52–54.

38. Joseph R. Mancuso, "Why Not Create Opinion Leaders for New Product Introduction?" *Journal of Marketing,* 33 (July 1969), 20–25.

# 17

# Diffusion of Innovations

## *introduction*

THIS chapter examines a major aspect of consumer behavior—the acceptance of *new* products and services. The introduction of new products is vital to both the consumer and the marketer. For the consumer, new products represent an increased opportunity for better satisfaction of personal, social, and environmental needs. For the marketer, new products provide an important mechanism for keeping the firm competitive and profitable.

The framework for exploring consumer acceptance of new products is drawn from the area of research known as the **diffusion of innovations**. The study of the diffusion of innovations is interdisciplinary in scope and has its earliest roots in anthropology and rural sociology. Other disciplines, such as communications, education, medical sociology, and marketing, have more recently investigated selected aspects of diffusion. Table 17-1 lists topics and units of analyses examined by these various behavioral disciplines.

The central interests of consumer researchers who have specialized in the diffusion of innovations have been to better understand (a) how the acceptance of a new product spreads within a market, and (b) the individual consumer decision-making process that led to the acceptance or rejection of a new product.

Within the scope of our discussion on the diffusion of innovations, we will concentrate on two closely related processes: the **diffusion** process and the **adoption** process. In the broadest sense, *diffusion* is a *macro* process concerned with the spread of a new product (an innovation) from its source to the con-

*We have learned so well how to absorb novelty that receptivity itself has turned into a kind of tradition—"the tradition of the new."*

*RICHARD HOFSTADTER*
*Anti-Intellectualism in American Life (1963)*

TABLE 17-1 Types of Diffusion of Innovation Studies by Discipline

| DISCIPLINE | TYPICAL INNOVATIONS STUDIED | MAIN UNIT OF ANALYSIS |
|---|---|---|
| Anthropology | Technological ideas (steel ax) | Tribes or peasant villages |
| Early sociology | City manager government, postage stamps, ham radios | Communities or individuals |
| Rural sociology | Mainly agricultural ideas (weed sprays, hybrid seed, fertilizers) | Individual farmers in rural communities |
| Education | Teaching/learning innovations (kindergartens, modern math, programmed instruction, team teaching) | School systems, teachers, or administrators |
| Public health and medical sociology | Medical and health ideas (drugs, vaccinations, family planning methods, CAT scanner) | Individuals or organizations like hospitals |
| Communication | News events, technological innovations | Individuals or organizations |
| Marketing | New products (a coffee brand, the touch-tone telephone, clothing fashions) | Individual consumers |
| Geography | Technological innovations | Individuals and organizations |

Source: Adapted with permission of The Free Press, a Division of Macmillan, Inc. from *Diffusion of Innovations,* Third Edition, by Everett M. Rogers. Copyright © 1983 by The Free Press, pp. 44–45.

suming public. In contrast, *adoption* is a *micro* process which focuses on the stages through which an individual consumer passes in making a decision to accept or reject a new product. In addition to these two interrelated processes, we will present a profile of **consumer innovators**—those who are the first to purchase a new product. The ability to identify and reach this important group of consumers plays a major role in the success or failure of new product marketing efforts.

## THE DIFFUSION PROCESS

The diffusion process is concerned with the general dimension of how innovations spread—how they are assimilated—within a market. More precisely, the *diffusion process* is the process by which the *acceptance of an innovation* (a new product, new service, new idea, new practice) *is spread by communication* (mass media, salespeople, informal conversations) *to members of a social system* (a target market) *over a period of time.* This definition includes the four basic elements of the diffusion process: (1) the innovation, (2) the channels of communication, (3) the social system, and (4) time.

### The Innovation

Defining what is meant by a "product innovation" or a "new product" is not an easy task. The various approaches that have been used to define a *new product* can be classified as **firm-oriented**, **product-oriented**, **market-oriented**, and **consumer-oriented** definitions.

A *firm-oriented* approach treats newness of a product from the perspective of the company producing or marketing the product; that is, if it is "new" to the company, it is considered *new*. This definition ignores whether or not the product is actually new to the marketplace (i.e., to competitors or consumers). Consistent with this view, copies or modifications of a competitor's product would qualify as new. While this definition has considerable merit if the objective is to examine the impact that a "new" product has on the firm, it is not especially useful if the goal is to understand consumer acceptance of a new product.

In contrast, a *product-oriented* approach focuses on the features inherent in the product itself, and the effects these features are likely to have on consumers' established usage patterns. One product-oriented framework considers the extent to which a new product is likely to disrupt established behavior patterns. It defines three types of product innovations: **continuous**, **dynamically continuous**, and **discontinuous**.

1. A *continuous* innovation has the least disruptive influence on established patterns. It involves the introduction of a *modified* product, rather than a totally new product. Examples: gel toothpaste, new automobile models, wine-fruit juice combinations.
2. A *dynamically continuous* innovation is somewhat more disruptive than a continuous innovation, but it still does not alter established behavior patterns. It may involve the creation of a new product or the modification of an existing product. Examples: compact disc players, erasable-ink pens, disposable diapers.
3. A *discontinuous* innovation requires the establishment of new behavior patterns. Examples: home computers, videocassette recorders, medical self-test kits.[1]

Table 17-2 shows how television, a discontinuous innovation of major magnitude, has produced over its life a variety of dynamically continuous and continuous innovations, and has even stimulated the development of other discontinuous innovations. The Seiko pocket color TV in Figure 17-1 is an illustration of a dynamically continuous innovation that couples extremely small size and color.

In another product-oriented approach, the extent of "newness" of a product is defined in terms of how much impact its physical features or attributes are likely to have on user satisfaction.[2] Thus the more satisfaction a consumer derives from a new product, the higher it ranks on the scale of "newness." This concept leads to the classification of products as *artificially new, marginally new,* or *genuinely new*. A genuinely new product would have features that satisfy the user in a manner that differs significantly from that of an older product. New products that have been judged to possess enough "newness" to qualify as genuinely new include nonrefrigerated prepared salad spreads, frozen breakfasts, canned puddings, and instant omelet mixes. The advertisement in Figure 17-2 is designed to create awareness and educate potential consumers as to the benefits of using an innovative self-test kit that will reveal if blood is present in the stool (a symptom of a number of potential illnesses, including colon-rectal cancer). This kit is one of an increasing number of in-home tests designed to make

TABLE 17-2 How Television Has Led to Related Innovations

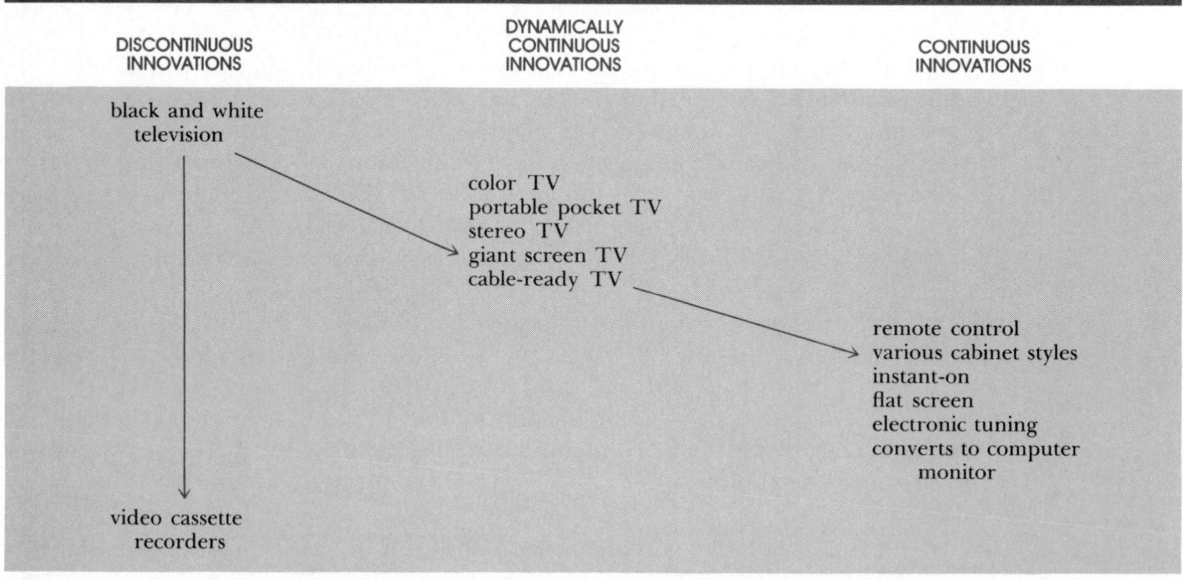


it easier and more convenient for consumers to identify the early stages of a particular medical condition or possible illness.

A *market-oriented* approach judges the newness of a product in terms of how much exposure consumers have to the new product. Two market-oriented definitions of product innovation have been used extensively in consumer studies:

1. A product is considered new if it has not been purchased by more than a relatively small (fixed) percentage of the potential market.
2. A product is considered new if it has been available on the market for a relatively short (specified) period of time.

Both of these market-oriented definitions are basically subjective because they leave to the researcher the task of establishing the degree of sales penetration within which it is appropriate to call the product an innovation (such as the first 5 percent to use the new product) or how long a product can be on the market and still be considered "new" (such as the first three months the product is available).

These approaches have been useful to consumer researchers in their attempts to study the diffusion of innovations. But some researchers have suggested that a *consumer-oriented* approach is the most appropriate way to define an innovation.[3] Within this context, a "new" product is any product that a potential consumer judges to be new. In other words, newness is based on the consumer's *perception* of the product, rather than on physical features or market

**FIGURE 17-1** **Advertisement for a Dynamically Continuous Innovation**

Anywhere you go, Seiko.

You're looking at the finest color television set that ever went out in the noonday sun. Because it's the only set specifically created to work perfectly in outdoor light.

Ordinary portables still use "picture tube" technology that fades outdoors. Seiko® uses "thin film transistor" technology (52,800 transistors to be exact!) that gives you a brilliant 2 inch diagonal picture outdoors. The brighter the light, the better the picture.

It's why we smugly say, "Seiko is the best TV under the sun." And the most portable. No matter which Seiko you choose–black and white or color–it fits in your hand. Your pocket. Your purse. Indoors and outdoors. Daytime or nighttime. There's no comparison. And no comparable gift you could give this Christmas.

SEIKO
"The best TV under the sun."

Simulated TV Pictures

For a store near you: 1-800-453-6413. In CA (213) 603-9550 between 9AM-5PM

©1985 Hattori Corporation of America

Courtesy of Hattori Corporation of America

FIGURE 17-2 Advertisement Stressing the Benefits of a New Product

# Answer these 4 questions and see if you're a colorectal cancer risk

If you answer these questions honestly, you will be able to tell whether or not you're at risk for colorectal cancer, the No. 2 cancer killer of men and women today.

There is growing evidence that age, diet and genetic factors play an important part in determining the incidence of colorectal cancer. It is also a medical fact that if this disease could be detected and treated in its earliest stages, it would be virtually wiped out as a cause of death.

**The hidden early symptom**

It is ironic that when colorectal cancer is most curable, in its earliest stages, there are no visible symptoms, no perceptible warning signals to alert you to its presence. The American Cancer Society estimates that 75% of the people who will die this year of colorectal cancer could have been saved through early detection and prompt treatment.

**Early Detector® detects what you can't see**

Early Detector is a very simple test for hidden blood in the stool—an early symptom of colorectal cancer as well as other disorders such as colitis, diverticulosis, polyps, ulcers and hemorrhoids. You can do the Early Detector test comfortably and quickly in the privacy of your own home and read the results immediately. And, unlike other home tests, Early Detector is as easy to use as bathroom tissue.

## 1. Age

(Most colorectal cancer patients are over 40, and men and women are affected in about equal numbers.)

Are you over 40? YES ☐ NO ☐

## 2. Diet

Is your diet high in fats?

Fried Foods YES ☐ NO ☐
Whole milk/cheese YES ☐ NO ☐
Fatty meats, beef, pork, lamb YES ☐ NO ☐

## 3. Family History

Have you or any close relatives (mother, father, siblings, grandparents) had:

Colorectal cancer YES ☐ NO ☐
Gardner's Syndrome YES ☐ NO ☐
Ulcerative colitis YES ☐ NO ☐
Polyps YES ☐ NO ☐
Crohn's Disease YES ☐ NO ☐

## 4. Medical Check-ups

Has it been more than one year since you have had one of these tests? YES ☐ NO ☐

Digital Rectal Examination
Guaiac Test for Hidden Blood
Proctosigmoidoscopy
Fiberoptic Colonoscopy
Barium Enema with Air Contrast Examination

SCORE: If you have answered yes to two or more of these questions, you may be at potential risk of colorectal cancer. If you are at risk, Early Detector could help save your life.

**No sticks, no mess**

Unlike other tests for hidden blood in the stool which require sticks and slides for sample collection, with Early Detector, you simply use specially prepared tissue as you would toilet tissue to obtain the sample. You then spray the Developer solution on the stool sample on the tissue. You read the results within one minute and flush the tissue away. If the results show a color change on the tissue, indicating a potential disorder, you should consult your doctor.

**Test results have been proven reliable**

You can have confidence in Early Detector test results. They have been clinically proven to be as reliable as the leading test doctors and hospitals use. Research has proven that consumers can perform the test and read the results as well as medical professionals. If you have any questions about Early Detector or want additional information, consult your doctor or pharmacist, or call the convenient 800 number 1-800-E.D.-HELPS (1-800-334-3577). In New Jersey call collect 1-201-540-2458.

**Physicians advise this kind of test**

Doctors recommend this kind of test be taken annually if you're over forty, and more frequently if you are at a higher than average risk of developing cancer of the colon or rectum. Remember, early detection of any disease is important, but early detection and prompt treatment of cancer of the colon and rectum is vital.

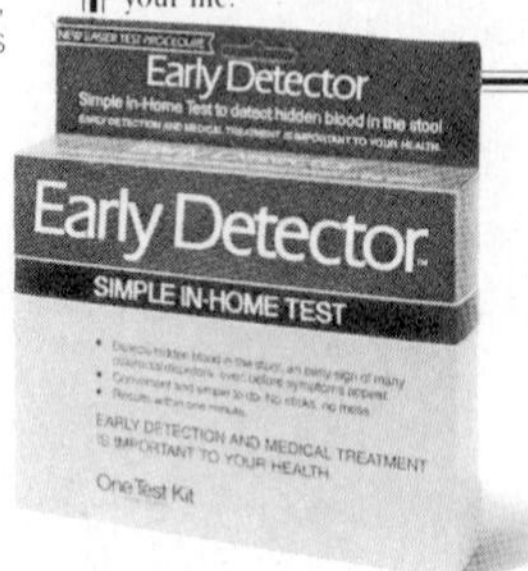

Early Detector
Early Detector
SIMPLE IN-HOME TEST
EARLY DETECTION AND MEDICAL TREATMENT IS IMPORTANT TO YOUR HEALTH
One Test Kit


**This test could save your life**



Courtesy of Warner-Lambert Co.

realities. Although the consumer-oriented approach has been endorsed by some advertising practitioners and marketing strategists, it has received little systematic attention from consumer researchers.

## Product Characteristics That Influence Diffusion

All products that are "new" do not have equal potential for consumer acceptance. Some products seem to catch on almost overnight (e.g., erasable pens), while others take a very long time to gain acceptance (e.g., organ donor programs). Some new products never seem to achieve widespread consumer acceptance (e.g., four-channel sound systems).

It would reduce the uncertainties of product marketing if marketers could anticipate how consumers will react to their products. For example, if a marketer knew that a product contained features that were likely to inhibit its acceptance, the marketer could develop a marketing strategy that would compensate for these features or decide not to market the product at all. While there are no precise formulas by which marketers can evaluate a new product's likely acceptance, diffusion researchers have identified five product characteristics that seem to influence consumer acceptance of new products: (1) **relative advantage**, (2) **compatibility**, (3) **complexity**, (4) **trialability**, and (5) **observability**.[4]

*Relative advantage* is the degree to which potential customers *perceive* a new product as superior to existing substitutes. For example, in the mid-1980s Crest began marketing a version of its fluoride toothpaste called Tartar Control Formula. Rather than appealing to youngsters, as it did with its original 1960s fluoride formula, Crest designed this product to help control the tartar buildup in adult mouths that can lead to serious dental problems. As another example, the advertisement in Figure 17-3 illustrates the relative advantage of a new cough product—a "whip" formulation that never spills. The ad also provides a cents-off coupon to make it easier to try the new product.

In addition to unique product features, a promotional program that includes cents-off coupons, two-for-one sales, a seal of approval, and a variety of special services also has the potential of being perceived as offering a relative advantage and may lead to increased acceptance. To illustrate, Figure 17-4 presents an ad for *Good Housekeeping's* Seal and suggests that its use will aid marketers in gaining consumer acceptance for new products.

*Compatibility* is the degree to which potential consumers feel a new product is consistent with their present needs, values, and practices. To illustrate, it is not too difficult to imagine men making the transition from permanent razors—where only the blade is disposed of—to completely disposable razors, where everything is thrown away after the blade becomes dull. Such a change is fully compatible with adult males' established wet-shaving rituals. However, it is difficult to imagine male shavers shifting to a new depilatory cream designed to remove facial hair. While potentially simpler to use, a cream would be basically incompatible with most males' current values with regard to daily shaving practices.

*Complexity* is the degree to which a new product is difficult to understand

**FIGURE 17-3** Advertisement Depicting a Product's Relative Advantage

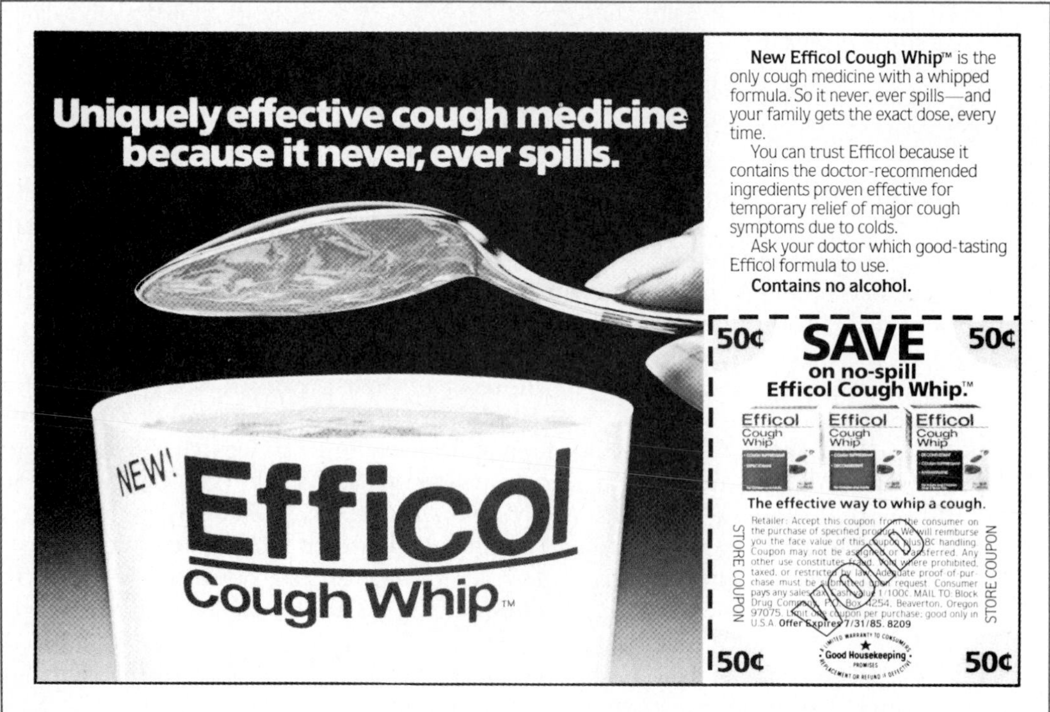


Courtesy of Block Drug Company

or use. Clearly, the easier it is to understand and use a new product, the greater the likelihood that it will be accepted. For example, the acceptance of such convenience foods as frozen pizza, instant oatmeal, and powdered iced tea packets is generally due to their appeal to consumer desires for ease of preparation and use. Similarly, a couple spending a weekend in Atlantic City or Las Vegas might prefer playing blackjack or the slot machines because they are easier to understand (less complex) than craps or roulette.

*Trialability* is the degree to which a new product is capable of being tried on a limited basis. The greater the opportunity to try a new product, the easier it will be for consumers to evaluate it. In the case of NEW TRAIL (a new granola bar), the inherent quality of the product ("100% natural") and its no-risk offer (the free trial coupon) make it relatively easy to try (see Figure 17-5). On the other hand, durable items such as refrigerators or ovens are difficult to try without making a major commitment. This may explain why publications like *Consumer Reports* are so widely used for their ratings of infrequently purchased durable goods.

**FIGURE 17-4** **Advertisement Suggesting the Power of a Seal in Helping Diffuse a New Product**

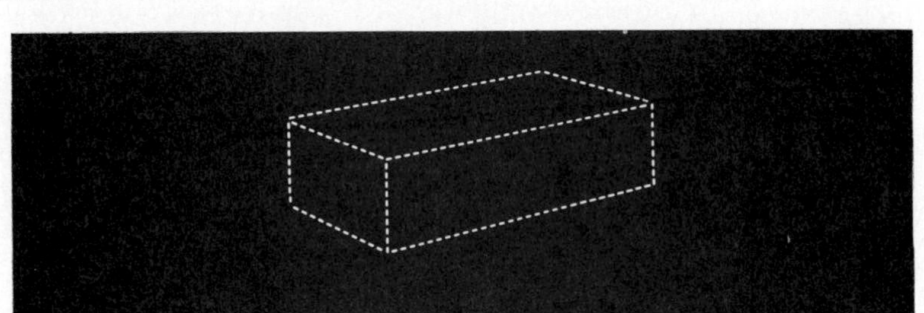

How to give your new product
an instantly-recognizable, well-respected name.

Each year, untold millions are spent on new product research and development, on test markets and product sampling.

The result of all this sophisticated effort?

Most new products fail, dismally.

Which means every new product needs all the help it can get.

And perhaps nothing can help your new product's introduction better than the name that needs no introduction, the Good Housekeeping Seal, one of the most respected buying guides in America.

When they see the Seal on your product, millions of American women will be seeing something they know and respect. In fact, 8 out of 10 women say the Seal positively influences their purchasing decisions.

They aren't alone, either. Over 77% of retailers surveyed say the Good Housekeeping Seal helps to increase sales. So they're more likely to stock your product. And stock it prominently.

Once it's on the shelves, the Seal will get your new product on trial. Because every product eligible to wear the Seal carries a money-back, limited warranty, courtesy of Good Housekeeping.

So, in today's competitive climate, associating your new product with a name that's been respected for generations isn't merely great.

It's Good Housekeeping.

Our pages do more.

Source: Crossley Surveys, Inc.

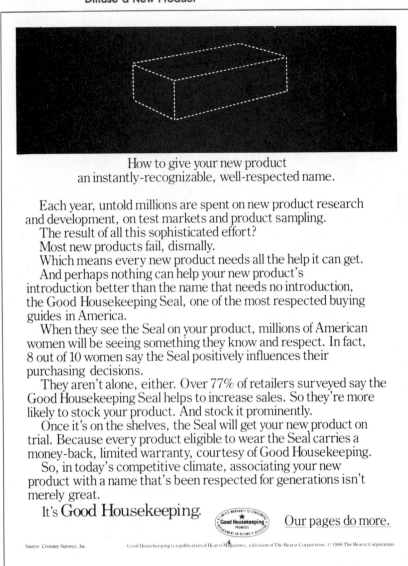

Good Housekeeping is a publication of Hearst Magazines, a division of The Hearst Corporation. © 1986 The Hearst Corporation.



As a general rule, it would seem that frequently purchased household products tend to have qualities that make trial relatively easy. Figure 17-6 indicates that 63 percent of the consumers studied made a trial purchase of a new brand in a smaller quantity than they usually purchased (33 percent bought a smaller package and 18 percent purchased both a smaller size and fewer units). For the marketer of selected household products, these findings suggest that it

**FIGURE 17-5** **A New Product Advertisement That Stresses Trial** Source: THE NEW TRAIL granola snack bar advertisement is reprinted by permission of the copyright owner, Hershey Foods Corporation, Hershey, Pennsylvania, U.S.A. HERSHEY'S and NEW TRAIL are registered trademarks of Hershey Foods Corporation and used with permission.

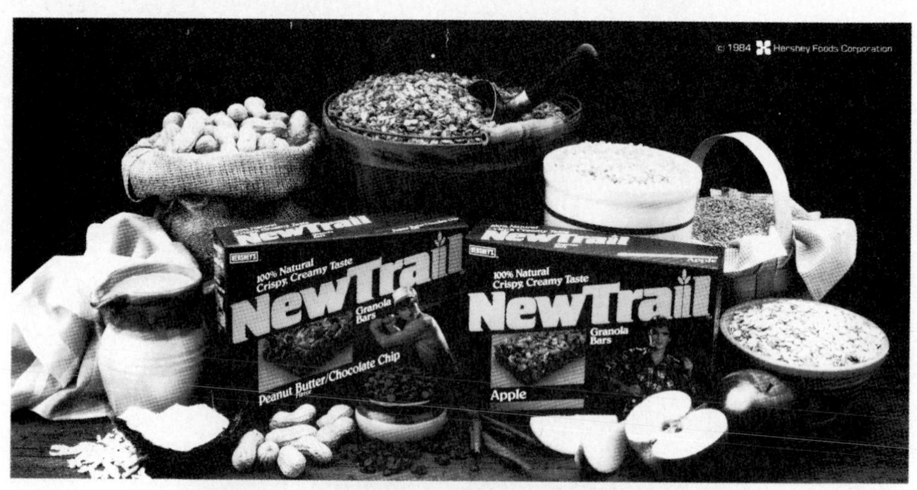


# NEW TRAIL INTRODUCES TWO NEW NATURALLY GOOD TASTES.

BRAND

**NEW PEANUT BUTTER FLAVOR/CHOCOLATE CHIP AND NEW APPLE GRANOLA BARS. TRY ONE FREE FROM HERSHEY.**

Discover what great-tasting snacks New Trail™ Granola Bars are! You'll love every crispy, creamy bite.

Our new Apple is tangy. Our new Peanut Butter flavor/Chocolate Chip combines Hershey's real chocolate chips and a natural and nutty peanut butter flavor.

How did we do what we did to them? You'll have to taste them to find out. Taste all six flavors! Cinnamon, Chocolate Chip, Honey Graham, Peanut Butter, and now new Apple and new Peanut Butter flavor/Chocolate Chip. Every crispy, creamy bite of every New Trail Granola Bar is 100% natural.

35¢ TRY A BAR FREE 35¢
OR TAKE 35¢ OFF ANY FLAVOR 6-PACK OF NEW TRAIL GRANOLA BARS.
STORE COUPON
TO THE RETAILER: Hershey Chocolate Company will redeem this coupon for the full purchase price of one bar or 35¢ off the six-pack size, plus 8¢ handling if you receive and handle it strictly in accordance with the terms of this offer and if upon request, you submit evidence thereof satisfactory to Hershey Chocolate Company. Coupon may not be assigned or transferred. Customer must pay any sales tax. Void where prohibited, taxed, or restricted by law. Good only in U.S.A. Cash value 1/20¢. For redemption of properly received and handled coupon, mail to Hershey Chocolate Company, P.O. Box 1757, Clinton, Iowa 52734. LIMIT ONE COUPON PER PURCHASE. OFFER EXPIRES OCTOBER 31, 1985.
VOID
STORE COUPON
34000 105147

Appearing in **BLAIR INSERTS** on Sunday Oct. 14, 1984

Remember, Sunday inserts are a fast redeeming coupon vehicle. So don't be caught short . . . stock and display extra cases during this promotion.

FIGURE 17-6 **Classification of Households by Type of Change in Trial Purchase** Source: Robert W. Shoemaker and F. Robert Shoaf, "Behavioral Changes in the Trial of New Products," *Journal of Consumer Research*, 2 (September 1975), 107.

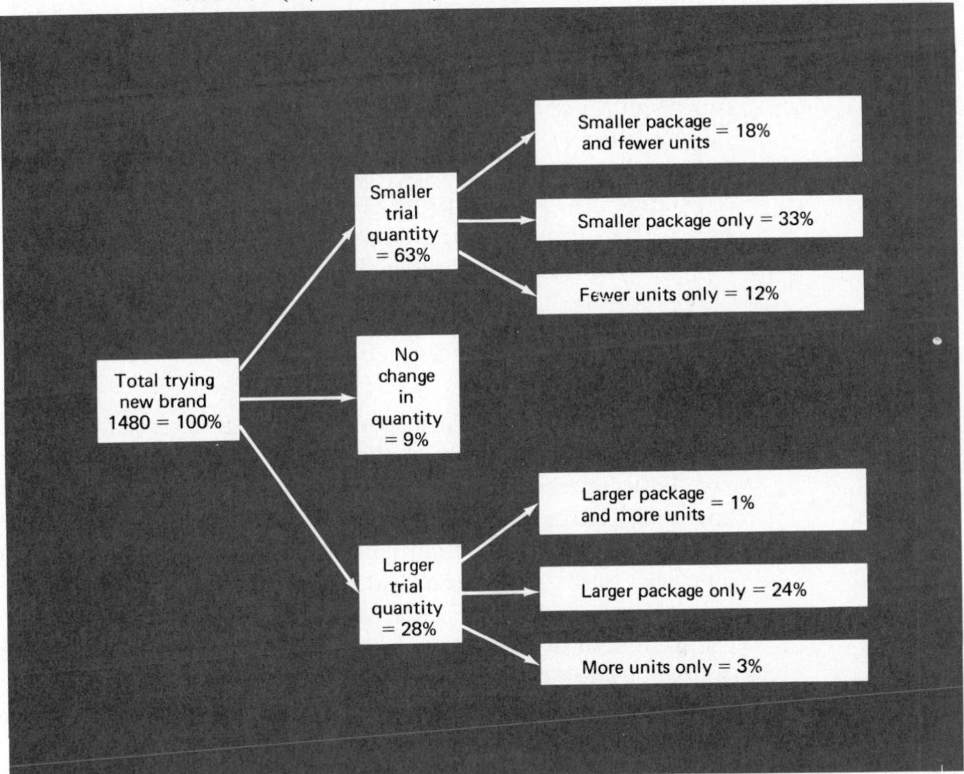


may be wise to offer a new product initially in smaller than typical sizes in order to stimulate trial.

Because it recognized the importance of trialability, Gillette undertook a massive promotional campaign to introduce the Trac II razor blade. It mailed a free razor handle and single Trac II blade to a large segment of the adult male population. By supplying the free, reusable razor handle, Gillette was able to establish an almost instantaneous replacement market for its new Trac II blades. Beecham launched its Aqua-fresh toothpaste in the United States by mailing a free sample to some 45 million homes. This mammoth program to gain large-scale trial, coupled with a massive introductory advertising campaign, rocketed the brand to second place in sales. Test drives for automobiles and money-back guarantees and free samples for packaged goods enhance the acceptance of these products by making consumer trial easy.

*Observability* (or communicability) is the ease with which a product's benefits or attributes can be observed, imagined, or described to potential consumers. Products that have a high degree of social visibility, such as fashion items, are more easily diffused than products that are used in private, such as a new brand of toothpaste. Similarly, a tangible product is more easily promoted than an intangible product (i.e., a service).

To date, only a few studies have examined the influence of these five innovation characteristics on consumers' trial of new products. The first consumer study to examine these five characteristics found that *relative advantage*, *compatibility*, *trialability*, and *observability* were positively associated with consumer *intentions to buy* a variety of new product concepts.[5] This study did not examine actual purchase behavior; however, its findings were supported by subsequent studies that used actual purchase data.[6]

It must be recognized that each of these product attributes is dependent on consumer perception. A product that is *perceived* as having a strong relative advantage, as fulfilling present needs and values, as easy to try on a limited basis, and as simple to understand and to see (and/or examine), is more likely to be purchased than a product that is not so perceived.

## The Channels of Communication

How quickly an innovation spreads through a market depends to a great extent on communication between the marketer and the consumer, and communication between consumers. For this reason, researchers interested in diffusion have paid particular attention to the transmission of product-related information through various channels of communication, and to the impact of the messages and the channels on the adoption or rejection of new products. Of central concern has been the influence of both impersonal sources (e.g., advertising and editorial matter) and interpersonal sources (salespeople and informal opinion leaders). In fact, most of our discussion of personal influence and the opinion leadership process (see Chapter 16) was based on evidence that is part of the general tradition of diffusion research.

One major stream of communication research has focused on the relative importance of certain *types* of information sources on early versus later adoption of new products. Specifically, the following generalizations gleaned from the general diffusion literature are important to marketers:[7]

1. Early adopters have more *change-agent-contact* (e.g., with salespeople) than later adopters.
2. Early adopters have *greater exposure to mass-media* communication channels than later adopters.
3. Early adopters *seek information about innovations* more frequently than later adopters.
4. Early adopters have *greater knowledge of innovations* than later adopters.
5. Early adopters have a *higher degree of opinion leadership* than later adopters.

We will discuss these generalizations in greater detail in our examination of the consumer innovator.

## The Social System

The diffusion of a new product usually takes place in a social setting—frequently referred to as a **social system**. Within the framework of consumer behavior, the terms *market segment* or *target market* are equivalent to the term *social* *system* used in diffusion research. Regardless of what it is called, however, a social system is a *physical, social, or cultural environment to which people belong and within which they function.* For example, for a new hybrid seed corn, the social system might consist of all farmers in a number of local communities; for a new drug, the social system might consist of all physicians within several specified cities; for a new special-diet product, the social system might include all residents of a geriatric community. As these examples indicate, the social system serves as the boundary within which the diffusion of a new product is examined.

The orientation of a social system, with its own special *values* or *norms*, is likely to influence the acceptance or rejection of new products. If the social system is *modern* in orientation, the acceptance of innovations is likely to be high. In contrast, if a social system is *traditional* in orientation, innovations that are perceived as radical or as infringements on established custom are likely to be avoided. According to one authority, the following characteristics typify a modern social system:[8]

- A positive attitude toward change.
- An advanced technology and skilled labor force.
- A general respect for education and science.
- An emphasis on rational and ordered social relationships rather than on emotional ones.
- An outreach perspective, in which members of the system frequently interact with outsiders, thus facilitating the entrance of new ideas into the social system.
- The system's members can readily see themselves in quite different roles.

The orientations of a social system (either modern or traditional) may be national in scope and influence members of an entire society, or they may exist at the local level and influence only those who live in a specific community. The critical issue is that a social system's orientation is the *climate* in which marketers have to operate in attempting to gain acceptance for their new products. For example, the United States has in recent years experienced a decline in the demand for beef because the growing interest in health and fitness across the nation has created a climate where beef is considered too high in fats and caloric content. At the same time, the consumption of chicken has increased because chicken satisfies the prevailing nutritional values of a great number of consumers.

## Time

**Time** is the backbone of the diffusion process. It pervades the study of diffusion in three distinct but interrelated ways: (1) **purchase time**, (2) the identification of **adopter categories**, and (3) the **rate of adoption**.

### PURCHASE TIME

Purchase time is concerned with the amount of time that elapses between the consumer's initial awareness of a new product and the point at which he or she purchases it or rejects it. Figure 17-7 shows an average purchase time frame

**FIGURE 17-7** **Time Frame for First-Time Purchasers of Expensive Cameras**
Reprinted by permission of *Popular Photography*. Copyright © 1974 by Ziff-Davis Publishing Co. All rights reserved.

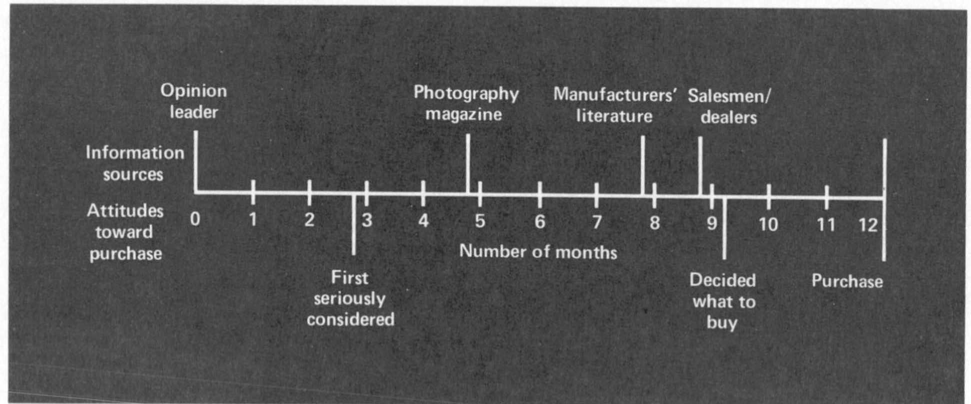


for an expensive camera and pinpoints the influence of various communications sources on the first-time purchaser. An examination of the overall time frame reveals that it takes about 12 months from contact with an opinion leader (a friend or relative who is perceived to be knowledgeable about photography and who introduces the idea of purchasing an expensive camera) to the actual purchase.

The figure illustrates how long and complex a process consumer decision making can be, and how different information sources become important at successive stages in the process. Purchase time is an important concept because the average time a consumer takes to adopt a new product is a predictor of the overall length of time that will be required for the new product to achieve widespread adoption. For example, when the individual purchase time is short, a marketer has reason to expect that the overall rate of diffusion will be faster than when the individual purchase time is long, as in the purchase of a new camera.

## ADOPTER CATEGORIES

The concept of *adopter categories* involves the determination of a classification scheme that indicates where a consumer stands in relation to other consumers in terms of when he or she adopts a new product. Five adopter categories are frequently cited in the diffusion literature: **innovators**, **early adopters**, **early majority**, **late majority**, and **laggards**. Table 17-3 describes each of these adopter categories and estimates their relative proportions within the total population that eventually adopts the new product.

As Figure 17-8 indicates, the adopter categories are generally depicted as taking on the characteristics of a normal distribution (a bell-shaped curve) which describes the total population that ultimately adopts a product. Some argue that the bell curve is an erroneous depiction, because it is based on the assumption that 100 percent of the members of the social system under study

**TABLE 17-3 Adopter Categories**

| ADOPTER CATEGORY | DESCRIPTION | RELATIVE PERCENTAGE WITHIN THE POPULATION WHICH EVENTUALLY ADOPTS |
|---|---|---|
| Innovators | *Venturesome*—very eager to try new ideas—acceptable if risk is daring—more cosmopolite social relationships—communicate with other innovators | 2.5 |
| Early adopters | *Respectable*—more integrated into the local social system—category contains greatest number of opinion leaders—are role models—the person to check with before using a new idea | 13.5 |
| Early majority | *Deliberate*—adopt new ideas just prior to the average time—seldom hold leadership positions—deliberate for some time before adopting | 34.0 |
| Late majority | *Skeptical*—adopt new ideas just after the average time—adopting may be both an economic necessity and a reaction to network pressures—innovations approached cautiously | 34.0 |
| Laggards | *Traditional*—the last members to adopt an innovation—most "localite" in outlook—oriented to the past—suspicious of anything new | 16.0 |
| | | 100.0 |

Source: Adapted with permission of The Free Press, a Division of Macmillan, Inc. from *Diffusion of Innovations*, Third Edition, by Everett M. Rogers, Copyright © 1983 by The Free Press. Pp. 248–50.

(the target market) will eventually accept the product innovation. This assumption is not in keeping with marketers' experiences, since very few, if any, products fit the needs of all potential consumers. For example, theoretically all American women could be expected to use a relatively new hair-care product—styling mousse—after washing their hair. In reality, however, a relatively small proportion of adult females use this product, and it would be unrealistic for

**FIGURE 17-8** **The Sequence and Proportion of Adopter Categories Among the Population That Eventually Adopts** Source: Adapted with permission of The Free Press, a Division of Macmillan, Inc. from *Diffusion of Innovations*, Third Edition, by Everett M. Rogers. Copyright © 1983 by The Free Press. P. 247.

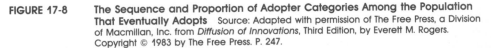

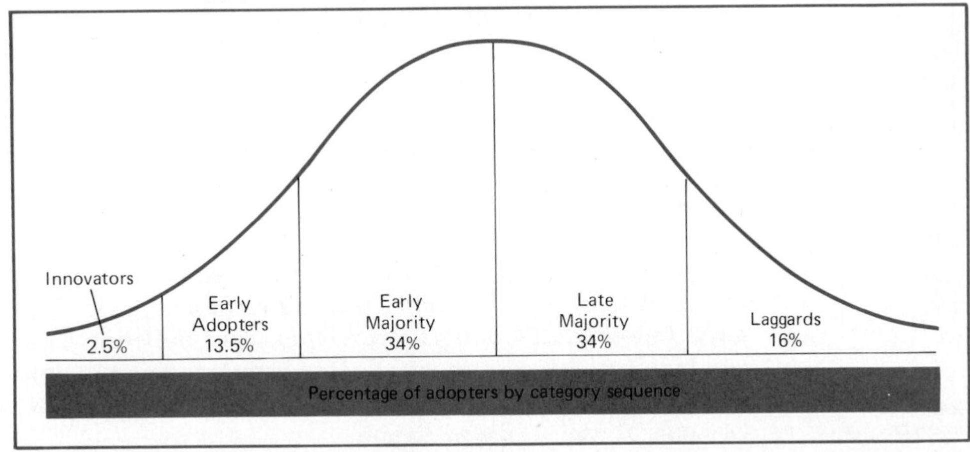

the hair-care industry to expect that all or even most women eventually will. For this reason, some researchers suggest an additional category, that of *nonadopters*. They argue that a "nonconsumer" category is in accord with marketplace reality, in that not all potential consumers do adopt a product innovation.

Consumer behavior studies usually avoid using the classic five-category adopter scheme. However, there is not as yet any generally accepted alternative procedure for defining adopter categories.[9] Instead, consumer researchers have employed a variety of schemes, most of which consist of two or three categories that compare *innovators* or *early triers* with *later triers* or *nontriers*. For example, recent research efforts have examined the characteristics of purchasers and nonpurchasers of home computers.[10]

As we will see, this focus on the innovator or early trier has produced some important generalizations that have practical significance for marketers planning the introduction of new products.

## RATE OF ADOPTION

The *rate of adoption* is concerned with *how long it takes for a new product to be adopted by members of a social system*; that is, how quickly a new product is accepted by those who will adopt it. Recent research has shown that the speed of adoption for new products has generally been increasing (i.e., getting shorter).[11]

The diffusion of television sets provides an illustration of this concept. Figure 17-9 compares the growth in the total number of United States households with the growth in television-owning households for the thirty-five year period 1950–85. Note the very rapid rate of adoption of television sets between 1950 and 1958, and the emergence of multiset homes as an important market segment since 1958. The ownership of color television sets is shown as having a very low rate of adoption within the ten-year period 1955–64, probably due to their high sales price, lack of color programming, and consumers' perceived functional risk (see Chapter 6). Since 1965, however, there has been a dramatic acceleration in the acceptance of color television sets.

In the marketing of new products, the objective is usually to gain wide acceptance of the product as quickly as possible. Marketers desire a rapid rate of product adoption in order to penetrate the market and establish market leadership (obtain the largest share of market) before competition takes hold. A **penetration policy** is usually accompanied by a relatively low introductory price designed to discourage competition from entering the market. Rapid product adoption also demonstrates to the channels of distribution (wholesalers and retailers) that the product is worthy of their full and continued support.

Under certain circumstances, marketers might prefer to avoid a rapid rate of adoption for a new product. For example, marketers who wish to employ a pricing strategy that will enable them to recoup their development costs quickly might follow a **skimming policy**—they first make the product available at a very high price to consumers who are willing to pay top dollar, and then gradually lower the price in a series of steps designed to attract additional market segments at each price reduction.

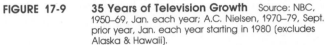

**FIGURE 17-9** **35 Years of Television Growth** Source: NBC, 1950–69, Jan. each year; A.C. Nielsen, 1970–79, Sept. prior year, Jan. each year starting in 1980 (excludes Alaska & Hawaii).

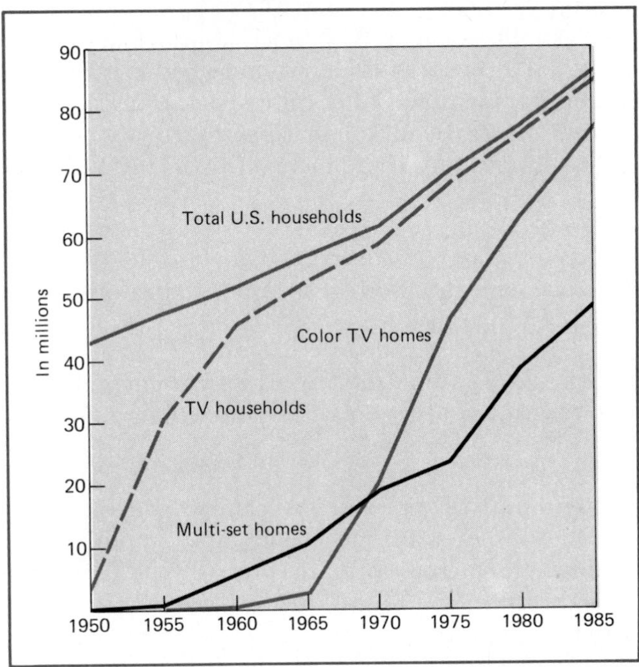


## THE ADOPTION PROCESS

The second major process within the overall scope of the diffusion of innovations is *adoption*. The focus of this process is the stages through which an individual consumer passes in arriving at a decision *to try* or *not to try, to continue using* or *to discontinue using* a new product. (The adoption process should not be confused with adopter categories.)

### Stages in the Adoption Process

It is often assumed that the consumer moves through five stages in arriving at a decision to purchase or reject a new product: (1) awareness, (2) interest, (3) evaluation, (4) trial, and (5) adoption (or rejection). The implicit assumption underlying the adoption process is that consumers engage in extensive information search (see Chapter 7). Consumer involvement theory suggests that for some products, limited information search is more likely.

AWARENESS. During the first stage of the adoption process, consumers are exposed to the product innovation. This exposure is somewhat neutral, since they are not yet sufficiently interested to search for additional product information.

INTEREST. When consumers develop an interest in the product or product category, they search for information about how the innovation can benefit them.

EVALUATION. Based upon their stock of information, consumers draw conclusions about the innovation or determine whether further information is necessary. The evaluation stage thus represents a kind of "mental trial" of the product innovation. If the evaluation is satisfactory, the consumer will actually try the product innovation; if the mental trial is unsatisfactory, the product will be rejected.

TRIAL. At this stage, consumers actually use the product on a limited basis. Their experience with the product provides them with the critical information they need to adopt or reject.

ADOPTION. Based upon their trials and/or favorable evaluation, consumers decide to use the product on a full rather than limited basis or they decide to reject it.

The adoption process provides a framework for determining which types of information sources consumers find most important at specific decision stages. For example, a study of early users of the first automobile diagnostic center in a midwestern city found that *mass-media sources* (magazines and radio publicity) were most important for disseminating general knowledge about such services and awareness of the specific service offered in the city. However, early users' final pretrial information was drawn primarily from informal discussions with *personal sources*.[12]

A study concerned with the acceptance of stainless steel blades among university students found that mass media were the principal sources of initial product awareness, while informal sources (friends and relatives) were influential in the final decision to try the new type of blade.[13] A study designed to examine the influence of various information sources on the *rejection* of a new clothing style found that mass media served as the main source of awareness for women concerning the style, while informal sources were most influential at the evaluation stage.[14]

These and other studies support the notion that impersonal mass media sources tend to be most valuable for creating initial product awareness; however, as the purchase decision progresses, the relative importance of these sources declines while the relative importance of interpersonal sources (friends, salespeople, and others) increases. Figure 17-10 depicts this relationship.

## Limitations of the Adoption Process

Although the traditional adoption process model has been instructive for consumer researchers, it has been criticized because of the following limitations:

- It does not adequately acknowledge that a need or problem recognition stage may precede the awareness stage.

**FIGURE 17-10** **The Relative Importance of Different Types of Information Sources, by Adoption Process Stages**

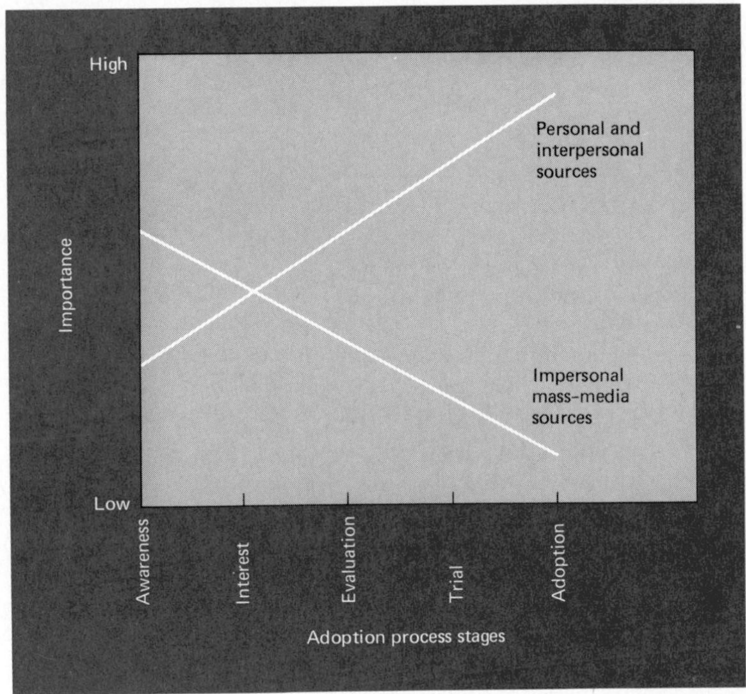


- It does not adequately provide for the rejection of a product after its trial (i.e., a consumer may never advance from the trial stage to the adoption stage but may reject the product after trial or never use the product on a continuous basis).
- It does not adequately recognize that evaluation occurs throughout the decision-making process and not solely at the "evaluation" stage.
- It does not adequately account for the possibility that the five stages may not always occur in the specific order suggested (e.g., trial may occur before evaluation); nor does it consider that some of the stages may, in fact, be skipped (e.g., in the case of consumer durables, such as a refrigerator, there may be no opportunity for trial).
- Finally, it does not explicitly include *postpurchase evaluation.* This evaluation may lead to a strengthened commitment, or it may lead to a decision to discontinue use of the product.[15]

Recent diffusion research has attempted to address itself to these concerns. One researcher has suggested that rather than merely studying adoption and diffusion, it may be just as important to examine *product discontinuance* and its impact on future adoptions.[16] Other investigators have agreed that studying the adoption process by itself is insufficient. They recommend that the focus be expanded to explore consumers' *current use* behavior, *expectations for future use,* and *level of satisfaction.*[17] It is likely that future diffusion studies will address these additional facets of the diffusion process.

## The Innovation Decision Process

In an effort to overcome the limitations discussed above, the traditional adoption process model has been updated into a more general decision-making model—the **innovation decision process**.[18] The five stages of the revised adoption process model are:

1. **Knowledge**. Consumers are exposed to the innovation's existence and gain some understanding of how it functions.
2. **Persuasion** (attitude formation). Consumers form favorable or unfavorable attitudes toward the innovation.
3. **Decision**. Consumers engage in activities that lead to a choice to adopt or reject the innovation.
4. **Implementation**. Consumers put an innovation into use.
5. **Confirmation**. Consumers seek reinforcement for their innovation decision, but may reverse this decision if exposed to conflicting messages about the product.[19]

Figure 17-11 depicts in diagrammatic form the operation of the innovation decision process. Very briefly, the model suggests that a number of prior conditions (e.g., *felt needs* and *social system norms*) and characteristics of the decision-making unit (e.g., *socioeconomic status* and *personality factors*) influence the reception of information about the product innovation during the *knowledge* stage. At the *persuasion* (attitude formation) stage, the consumer is further influenced by communications channels (sources) and by perceptions of the characteristics of the innovation (its relative advantage, compatibility, complexity, trialability, and observability). Additional information received during the *decision* stage enables the consumer to assess the innovation and decide whether to adopt or reject it. During the *implementation* stage, further communication is received as the consumer puts the innovation to use. The final stage, *confirmation,* is also influenced by communication sources; it is at this stage that consumers evaluate their purchase experiences, look for support for their behavior, and decide to continue or discontinue using the product.

The innovation decision process model is more comprehensive than the earlier adoption process model and eliminates many of its basic limitations. It is also much more attuned to the realities faced by the marketer launching a new product.

# A PROFILE OF THE CONSUMER INNOVATOR

Who is the consumer innovator? What characteristics set the innovator apart from later adopters and from those who never purchase? How can the marketer reach and influence the innovator? These are key questions to the marketing practitioner about to introduce a new product or service.

FIGURE 17-11 **The Innovation Decision Process** Source: Adapted with permission of The Free Press, a Division of Macmillan, Inc. from *Diffusion of Innovations*, Third Edition, by Everett M. Rogers. Copyright © 1983 by The Free Press. P. 165.

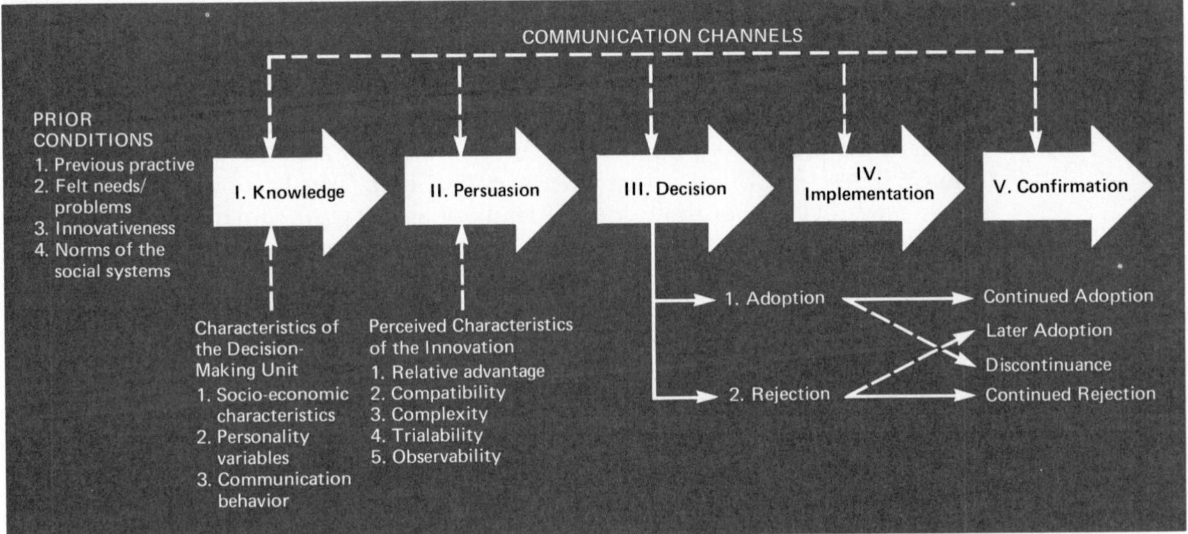


## Defining the Consumer Innovator

**Consumer innovators** can be defined as *the relatively small group of consumers who are the earliest purchasers of a new product.* The problem with the definition, however, centers on the concept "earliest," which is, after all, a relative term. Sociologists have treated this issue by sometimes defining *innovators* as the first 2.5 percent of the social system to adopt an innovation. In a good number of marketing diffusion studies, however, consumer researchers have *derived* the definition of the consumer innovator from the status of the new product under investigation. For example, if the researcher assesses the new product as an innovation for the first three months of its availability, then he or she defines the consumers who purchase it during this period as innovators.

Other researchers have defined innovators in terms of their *innovativeness*—that is, their purchase of some minimum number of new products from a selected group of new products. In a study of the adoption of new fashion items, innovators were defined as those consumers who purchased more than one fashion product from a group of ten new fashion products; noninnovators were defined as those who purchased only one or none of the new fashion products.[20] In other instances, researchers have defined innovators as those falling within an arbitrary proportion of the total market (e.g., the first 10 percent of the population in a specified geographic area to buy the new product).

## Interest in the Product Category

Not surprisingly, researchers have found that consumer innovators are much more interested than either later adopters or nonadopters in the product category that they are among the first to purchase. For example, the earliest purchasers of the rotary-engined Mazda automobile were found to have substantially greater interest in automobiles (they enjoyed looking at auto magazines and were interested in the performance and functioning of automobiles) than those who purchased different small cars during the same period, or those who purchased the Mazda during a later period.[21]

Similarly, male fashion innovators (who constitute approximately 8 percent of the men's clothing market) also demonstrate a sustained interest in fashion.[22] These individuals wore the "preppie" look long before it became popular; now that the preppie look is traditional, they are buying "advanced" or "fashion-forward" clothing that includes exaggerated silhouettes, unusual colors or fabrics, or unusual tailoring details (see Figure 17-12). While sales to these innovators may account for less than 10 percent of men's fashion sales at a store like Bloomingdale's, they account for half of all sales at the Charivari chain in New York.

Consumer innovators are more likely than noninnovators to seek information concerning their specific interests from a variety of informal and mass media sources.[23] Contrary to what might be expected, consumer innovators are not impulsive purchasers; rather, they seem to give greater deliberation to the purchase of new products than noninnovators.[24]

## The Innovator Is an Opinion Leader

In discussing the characteristics of the opinion leader (see Chapter 16), we indicated a strong tendency for consumer opinion leaders to be innovators. Within our present context, it is worthwhile to note that an impressive number of studies on the diffusion of innovations have found that consumer innovators are likely to provide other potential consumers with information and advice about new products, and that those who receive such advice frequently follow it. Thus, in the role of opinion leader, the consumer innovator often influences the acceptance or rejection of new products.

If innovators are enthusiastic about a new product and encourage others to try it, the product is likely to receive broader and quicker acceptance. If consumer innovators are dissatisfied with a new product and discourage others from trying it, its acceptance will be severely handicapped and it may die a quick death. With products that do not generate much excitement (either positive or negative), consumer innovators may not be sufficiently motivated to provide advice; in such cases, the marketer not only has to rely almost entirely on mass media and personal selling to influence future purchasers, but the absence of *informal* influence is likely to result in a somewhat slower rate of acceptance (or rejection) for the new product. Since motivated consumer innovators can speed up acceptance or rejection of a new product, they influence its eventual success or failure.

In an effort to attract innovators who will then transmit positive word-of-mouth to friends, Murjani International has undertaken the task of creating a new name (and a new trend) in women's fashion—designer Tommy Hilfiger (see Chapter 16). Mr. Hilfiger, who was a freelance designer, is being backed

FIGURE 17-12 Advertisement Depicting Fashion Forward in Men's Clothing

Courtesy of Jeff Hamilton Inc.

with up to $20 million in advertising. With his "The New American Classics" line, he offers a look that falls somewhere between Ralph Lauren and The Gap.[25]

## Personality Traits

In Chapter 4 we examined the *personality traits* that distinguish the consumer innovator from the noninnovator. In this section we will briefly highlight what researchers have learned about the personality of the consumer innovator.

First, consumer innovators have been found to be *less dogmatic* than noninnovators. They tend to approach new or unfamiliar products with considerable openness and little anxiety. In contrast, noninnovators seem to find new products threatening, to the point where they prefer to delay purchase until the product's success has been clearly established.

Consistent with their open-mindedness, consumer innovators are also *inner-directed*; that is, they rely on their own values or standards in making a decision about a new product. In comparison, noninnovators are *other-directed*, tending to rely on others for guidance on how to respond, rather than trusting their own personal values or standards. There is some research evidence that the initial purchasers of a new model automobile were inner-directed, and that later purchasers of the same model tended to be other-directed. This suggests that as acceptance of a product progresses from early to later adopters, there is a gradual shift in the personality type of adopters from inner- to other-directedness.

In terms of *category width*, which purports to measure an individual's risk-handling orientation (see Chapter 4), the consumer innovator has been found to be a broad categorizer, while the noninnovator tends to be a narrow categorizer. Broad categorizers tend to try many new products, even though by doing so they subject themselves to the risk of acquiring unsatisfactory products. On the other hand, narrow categorizers are so afraid of making poor product choices that they limit their trial of new products, even though they may forgo the benefits of desirable new products. However, for trivial or "artificially" new products (such as a new-flavored dessert), it appears that the narrow categorizer may adopt more quickly than the broad categorizer. This suggests that the true consumer innovator does not respond to superficially different products, but tends to single out substantially different products.

Researchers have also isolated a link between *variety seeking* and various personality traits and purchase behaviors that give insights into consumer innovators. Variety-seeking consumers have been found to be brand switchers and purchasers of innovative products and services. They have also been found to possess the following innovator-related personality traits: open mindedness (or low in dogmatism), to be extroverts, to be liberal, to be low in authoritarianism, to be able to deal with complex or ambiguous stimuli, and to be creative.[26]

To sum up, consumer innovators seem to be more receptive to the unfamiliar; they are more willing to rely on their own values or standards than on the judgments of others. They are also willing to run the risk of a poor product choice in order to increase their exposure to new products. For the marketer, the personality traits that distinguish innovators from noninnovators suggest the need for separate promotional campaigns for innovators and for later adopters.

Consumer innovators are more likely to react favorably to informative or fact-oriented advertising that appeals to their strong interest in the product category, and to readily evaluate the merits of a new product on the basis of their own personal standards. To reach noninnovators, it would seem appropriate to feature reference group settings and to use a recognized and trusted expert or celebrity to appeal to their other-directed responsiveness to authority figures.

## Venturesomeness

*Venturesomeness*—a personality-like variable—is a broad-based measure of a consumer's willingness to accept the risk of purchasing new products. Measures of venturesomeness have been used to evaluate a person's general values or attitudes toward trying new products. Typical questions include:

- I prefer to (try a new food product when it first comes out) (wait and learn how good it is before trying it).
- When I am shopping and see a brand of heavy-duty detergent I know about but have never used, I am (very anxious or willing to try it), (hesitant about trying it), (very unwilling to try it).
- I like to be among the first people to buy and use new products that are on the market (measured on a 5-point "agreement" scale).[27]

Research that has examined venturesomeness has generally found that consumers who indicate a willingness to try new products tend to be consumer innovators (as measured by their actual purchase of new products). On the other hand, consumers who express a reluctance to try new products are in fact less likely to purchase new products. Therefore venturesomeness seems to be an effective barometer of actual innovative behavior.

## Perceived Risk

*Perceived risk,* discussed in detail in Chapter 6, is another measure of a consumer's tendency to try new brands or products. Perceived risk can be thought of as the degree of uncertainty or fear as to the consequences of a purchase that a consumer feels when considering the purchase of a new product. For example, consumers experience uncertainty when they are concerned that a new product will not work properly or will not be as good as other alternatives. Research on perceived risk and the trial of new products overwhelmingly indicates that the consumer innovator is a low-risk perceiver.[28] Consumers who perceive little or no risk associated with the purchase of a new product are much more likely to purchase it than consumers who perceive a great deal of risk. In other words, high-risk perception limits innovativeness.

Consistent with their greater venturesomeness and lowered risk perception, consumer innovators are also likely to believe that they learn about innovations earlier than others. They also tend to be more intrigued with the prospect of "newness" than are noninnovators.[29]

## Purchase and Consumption Characteristics

Consumer innovators have purchase and usage traits that set them apart from noninnovators. Studies have shown that consumer innovators are *less* brand loyal—that is, more apt to switch brands. For example, with regard to a new brand of coffee as well as other grocery products, researchers have found consumer innovators to be less loyal to established brands than noninnovators or later adopters.[30] It is not surprising that innovators tend to be less brand loyal, for brand loyalty would seriously impede their willingness to try new products.

Consumer innovators are also more likely to be *deal-prone* (to take advantage of special promotional offers such as free samples and cents-off coupons). Not surprisingly, consumers who are deal-prone have generally been found to be less brand loyal.[31] Consumer innovators are also likely to be heavy users of the product category in which they innovate. For example, two different studies of the diffusion of new brands of coffee found that consumer innovators purchase larger quantities of coffee and consume more cups of coffee daily than noninnovators.[32]

These studies indicate a positive relationship between innovative behavior and heavy usage. They suggest that consumer innovators not only are an important market segment from the standpoint of being the first to use a new product, but also represent a substantial market in terms of quantity of the product used. However, their propensity to switch brands and to respond positively to promotional deals also suggests that they will continue to use a specific brand only so long as they do not perceive that a new and potentially better alternative is available.

## Are There Generalized Consumer Innovators?

Do consumer innovators in one product category tend to be consumer innovators in other product categories? The answer to this strategically important question is a guarded "no." The few studies that have specifically attempted to measure the overlap of innovativeness across product categories have noted some degree of overlap, particularly between product categories that seem to be related to the same basic interest area. The overlap, however, does not seem to be sufficiently strong to warrant a marketing strategy that would treat innovators in widely different product categories as members of the same basic target market.[33]

There is somewhat stronger evidence that consumers who are innovators in regard to one new food product or one new appliance are more likely to be innovators for other new products within the same general product category.[34] In other words, although no single or generalized consumer-innovativeness trait seems to operate *across* broadly different product categories, evidence suggests that consumers who innovate *within* a specific product category will innovate again within the same product category. For the marketer, these findings indicate that it may be good marketing strategy to target a new product to consumers who were the first to try other products in the same basic product category.

While there is little evidence to support the notion of a "universal" consumer innovator, there is evidence that indicates the existence of a relatively small number of consumers (about 12 percent of the United States population) who respond to new offerings across a variety of loosely related product and service categories. These consumers, who have been labeled **super innovators**, were among the first to purchase a new product or service in three or more of the five following areas: food and the kitchen environment, the home environment, electronics, leisure activities, and financial products and services.[35] (This special group of consumer innovators will be discussed in greater detail later in this chapter.)

Finally, other recent research suggests that purchasers of home computers are also adopters of other technology-related innovative products and services (telephone answering services, computer-prepared income tax statements, automatic bill payment programs, automated teller machines, microwave ovens, pocket calculators, cable television services, video recorders).[36]

## Media Habits

In launching a new product, it is desirable that the marketer be able to identify specific mass media that reach the consumer innovator. To accomplish this task, the marketer has to determine whether consumer innovators selectively expose themselves to any specific types of media that could be used to reach them more effectively.

Research studies that have compared the media habits of innovators and noninnovators across such widely diverse areas of consumption as fashion clothing and new automotive services suggest that innovators have somewhat greater total exposure to magazines than noninnovators.[37] Certain evidence also indicates that consumer innovators are likely to have greater exposure to *special interest magazines* devoted to the product category in which they innovate. For example, female fashion innovators have been found to have greater exposure to magazines such as *Glamour* and *Vogue* than noninnovators; male fashion innovators have been found to have greater exposure to male special interest publications such as *Playboy* and *Penthouse*.[38]

Studies outside the realm of fashion have also found that innovators are more likely to read special interest magazines. For example, women who were early adopters of household cleansers and detergents had greater exposure to magazines devoted to the home (e.g., *Better Homes and Gardens* and *Good Housekeeping*).[39] Though innovators tend to have greater *total* magazine exposure than noninnovators, it would be more efficient for the marketer to attempt to reach them through appropriate *special interest* magazines relevant to their specific product category rather than through general interest magazines. Special

**FIGURE 17-13** **Advertisement for a Magazine That Stresses the Innovative Characteristics of Its Readers** Source: The Condé Nast Package. Copyright © 1986 by The Condé Nast Publications Inc.

THE FIRST PEOPLE.
Someone was first to tango, again.
The First People take the first steps. They're first to step out to a new idea. First to step foot in a foreign place. First to take the first sip. The first bite. The first flight. They're the 20 million readers who lead the way, and who read their way through the pages of the Condé Nast Ltd. Package magazines, Vogue, Vanity Fair, House & Garden, GQ and Gourmet. To reach the 20 million readers who will be The First People to buy and try, contact Neil Jacobs a. 212/880-8329 for details on The Condé Nast Ltd.
THE CONDÉ NAST LTD.
THE FIRST PEOPLE. VOGUE VANITY FAIR HOUSE&GARDEN GQ GOURMET.

interest magazines frequently point to the fact that they reach innovative consumers in their own ads aimed at prospective advertisers (see Figure 17-13).

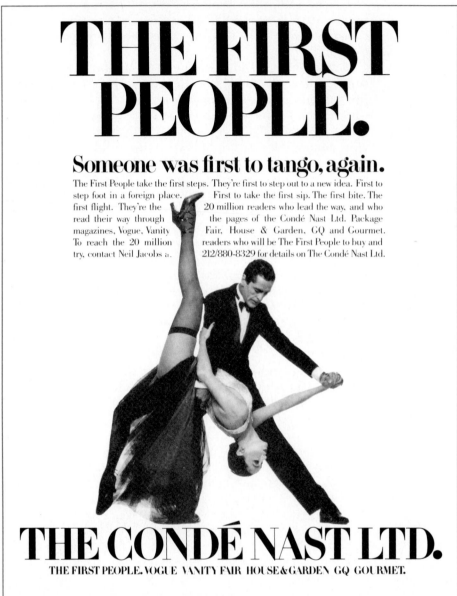

A number of studies reveal that consumer innovators are likely to have *less* exposure to television than noninnovators.[40] Table 17-4 presents the magazine and TV exposure levels from an ongoing survey of innovators in five product/service categories. A rating of 100 equals the average for the U.S. adult population. Notice how these results confirm the higher-than-average maga-

**TABLE 17-4 Media Exposure of Innovators**

| PRODUCT/SERVICE CATEGORY | MAGAZINE READERSHIP* | TV VIEWERSHIP* |
|---|---|---|
| Food and the kitchen environment | 150 | 80 |
| Home environment | 133 | 77 |
| Electronics | 143 | 93 |
| Leisure | 147 | 68 |
| Financial products | 135 | 69 |

*Note: The above represent top quintile scores for each product/service category, with a score of 100 equaling the average for all adults.
Source: *Mediamark Research Strategic Marketing Studies Number One: Consumer Innovators* (New York: Mediamark Research, Inc., 1984).

zine exposure and the lower-than-average TV exposure. This small body of evidence suggests that the mass appeal of TV does not make it a particularly effective medium for reaching consumer innovators.

Studies concerning the relationship between innovative behavior and exposure to other mass media, such as radio and newspapers, have been too few in number and too varied in results to draw any useful conclusions. Definitive research in this area is needed to provide marketers with more comprehensive guidelines as to where to reach the consumer innovator.

## Social Characteristics

Available evidence indicates that consumer innovators are more socially accepted and socially involved than noninnovators. For example, a number of studies reveal that consumer innovators are more socially integrated within the community than noninnovators. Specifically, innovators were found to be better accepted by others and to have more social involvement with other members of the community than noninnovators.[41]

Evidence also indicates that consumer innovators are more socially involved—that is, they are likely to belong to more social groups and organizations than noninnovators. For example, innovators in two such diverse areas as female fashions and cable TV were found to belong to more formal organizations than later adopters or noninnovators.[42] This greater social acceptance and involvement of consumer innovators may in part explain why they function as effective opinion leaders.

## Demographic Characteristics

It is reasonable to assume that the age of the consumer innovator is related to the specific product category in which he or she innovates; however, many studies have found consumer innovators to be younger than either later adopt-

**TABLE 17-5 Demographic Characteristics of Adopters and Nonadopters of Home Computers**

| DEMOGRAPHIC FACTORS | ADOPTERS | NONADOPTERS |
|---|---|---|
| Technical school graduate | 7.0% | 4.5% |
| Professional/graduate education | 52.2 | 36.3 |
| Professional/technical occupation | 73.2 | 54.8 |
| $40,000 plus income | 35.9 | 18.9 |
| Married | 72.2 | 48.7 |
| 36 to 55 years of age | 51.7 | 35.0 |
| Own a home | 82.8 | 58.6 |
| Reside in central/western states | 67.6 | 51.6 |

Source: Adapted from Mary Dee Dickerson and James W. Gentry, "Characteristics of Adopters and Nonadopters of Home Computers," *Journal of Consumer Research*, 10 (September 1983), p. 231.

ers or noninnovators.[43] The inconsistency between our expectations and available evidence is no doubt a function of the fact that many of the products selected for examination (fashion, convenience grocery products, new automobiles) are particularly attractive to younger consumers.

Research indicates that the consumer innovator has more formal education, higher personal or family income, and is more likely to have higher occupational status (to be a member of a profession or have a managerial position) than later adopters or noninnovators.[44] In other words, innovators tend to be more upscale than other consumer segments.

Table 17-5 presents a profile of some of the demographic characteristics that distinguish home computer adopters from nonadopters. Among other things, the profile reveals that owners of home computers have higher income and educational levels than nonadopters, and that almost three-quarters of all home computer adopters work at professional or technical jobs. These occupations suggest not only a natural affinity for computers, but also that many home computer adopters are likely to have cultivated their interest in computers through on-the-job experiences.

## Super Innovators

As part of the discussion of innovative overlap earlier in this chapter, we identified the so-called **super innovators**—defined as consumers who were among the first to buy products or services in three or more of the five areas examined. This select group of consumer innovators has a marketing "value" of from three to five times its size. For example, given a purchase index value of 100 for *all* financial products innovators in this study, these super innovators have a purchase index of 488.[45]

**TABLE 17-6 Selected Characteristics of Super Innovators**

| CHARACTERISTIC | RATING* |
|---|---|
| **Age** | |
| 18–24 | 87 |
| 25–34 | 127 |
| 35–44 | 150 |
| 45–54 | 117 |
| 55–64 | 77 |
| 65+ | 24 |
| **Education** | |
| Attended college | 149 |
| Graduated college | 195 |
| Post college | 210 |
| **Median household income** | |
| $50,000–$74,999 | 248 |
| $75,000+ | 284 |
| **Occupation** | |
| Professional/technical | 199 |
| Managerial/administrative | 191 |
| **Life Style** | |
| Membership in business clubs | 232 |
| Have been published | 197 |
| Addressed public meeting | 197 |
| Actively work for political party | 193 |
| **Media Exposure†** | |
| Newspapers | 128 |
| Magazines | 166 |
| Television | 65 |
| Radio | 109 |
| Outdoor | 147 |
| **Marketing Value** | |
| Have cash management account | 429 |
| Own home security system | 404 |
| Own hot tub | 356 |
| Own exercise equipment | 379 |
| Own VCR | 343 |

*Index of all adults = 100.
† Represents top quintile index.
Source: *Mediamark Research* Strategic Marketing Studies Number One: Consumer Innovators (New York: Mediamark Research, Inc., 1984).

Some of the major demographic and lifestyle characteristics of super innovators are presented in Table 17-6. Like innovators in general, these super innovators exhibit high income and education levels, have high occupational status, watch less TV, and read more magazines than the general population.

## Consumer Innovators Versus Later Adopters and Noninnovators

Table 17-7 summarizes the major differences between consumer innovators and later adopters or noninnovators. The major distinctions presented throughout this chapter are included.

**TABLE 17-7 Comparative Profiles of the Consumer Innovator and the Noninnovator or Later Adopter**

| CHARACTERISTIC | INNOVATOR | NONINNOVATOR (OR LATER ADOPTER) |
|---|---|---|
| Product interest | More | Less |
| Opinion Leadership | More | Less |
| Personality: | | |
| Dogmatism | Open-minded | Closed-minded |
| Social character | Inner-directed | Other-directed |
| Category width | Broad categorizer | Narrow categorizer |
| Venturesomeness | More | Less |
| Perceived Risk | Less | More |
| Purchase and Consumption Traits: | | |
| Brand loyalty | Less | More |
| Deal proneness | More | Less |
| Usage | More | Less |
| Media Habits: | | |
| Total magazine exposure | More | Less |
| Special-interest magazines | More | Less |
| Television | Less | More |
| Social Characteristics: | | |
| Social integration | More | Less |
| Social striving (e.g., social, physical, and occupational mobility) | More | Less |
| Group memberships | More | Less |
| Demographic Characteristics: | | |
| Age | Younger | Older |
| Income | More | Less |
| Education | More | Less |
| Occupational status | More | Less |

## *summary*

The diffusion process and the adoption process are two closely related concepts concerned with the acceptance of new products by consumers. The diffusion process is a macro process which focuses on the spread of an innovation (a new product, service, or idea) from its source to the consuming public. The adoption process is a micro process which examines the stages through which an individual consumer passes in making a decision to accept or reject a new product.

The term innovation can be defined in a firm-oriented sense (new to the marketing firm), in a product-oriented sense (as a continuous innovation, a dynamically continuous innovation, or a discontinuous innovation), in a market-oriented sense (by how long the product has been on the market or by the percentage of the potential target market that has purchased it), and in a consumer-oriented sense. Market-oriented definitions of innovation are most useful to the study of the diffusion and adoption of new products.

Five product characteristics influence the consumer's acceptance of a new product: relative advantage, compatibility, complexity, trialability, and observability (or communicability).

Diffusion researchers are concerned with two aspects of communication: the channels through which word of a new product is spread to the consuming public, and the types of messages that influence the adoption or rejection of new products. Diffusion is always examined within the context of a specific social system, such as a target market, a community, a region, or even a nation.

Time is an integral consideration in the diffusion process. Researchers are concerned with the amount of purchase time required for an individual consumer to adopt or reject a new product, with the rate of adoption, and with the identification of sequential adopter categories. The five adopter categories are innovators, early adopters, early majority, late majority, and laggards.

Marketing strategists try to control the rate of adoption in accordance with their new product pricing policies. Marketers who wish to penetrate the market in order to achieve market leadership try to achieve wide adoption in as short a period as possible with low prices; those who choose a skimming pricing policy deliberately plan a longer adoption process.

The traditional adoption process model describes five stages through which an individual consumer passes in arriving at the decision to adopt or reject a new product: awareness, interest, evaluation, trial, and adoption. The newer innovation decision process model is a more general decision-making model which focuses on five stages of adoption: knowledge, persuasion, decision, implementation, and confirmation. Both models offer a framework for determining the importance of various information sources to consumers at the various decision stages.

Marketers are vitally concerned with identifying the consumer innovator so that they may direct new product promotional campaigns to the people who are most likely to try new products, to adopt them, and to influence others. Consumer research has identified a number of consumer-related characteristics and personality traits that distinguish consumer innovators from later adopters. These serve as useful variables for the segmentation of markets for new product introductions.

## *discussion questions*

1. What are the essential differences between "product," "market," and "consumer" oriented definitions of a *new* product? Which definition do you feel is most suitable for the marketer? Why?

2. Describe how JVC might use knowledge of the following five product characteristics to speed up the acceptance of its new compact disk player:
   a. relative advantage
   b. compatibility
   c. complexity
   d. trialability
   e. observability
3. An appliance manufacturer is considering the introduction of a new microwave oven that cooks food three times as fast as competitive ovens while selling at about the same price. Identify those product characteristics that will influence the new oven's rate of acceptance.
4. Would you classify each of the following as a continuous innovation, a dynamically continuous innovation, or a discontinuous innovation? Explain your answer:
   a. the Sony Walkman
   b. the Sony Beta VCR system
   c. the Broxident electric toothbrush
   d. Bold 3 laundry detergent with fabric softener
5. How might Apple Computer Corporation alter its promotional appeal to reach members of each of the following adopter categories:
   a. Innovators
   b. Early adopters
   c. Early majority
   d. Late majority
   e. Laggards
6. Compare and contrast the *adoption* and *diffusion* processes. How are these two processes interrelated?
7. Suppose AT&T has developed a new type of telephone that can be preprogrammed to dial 24 different numbers upon hearing the user speak the name of the person he or she wishes to call. Considering what the chapter indicated to be the characteristics of innovators, what recommendation can you make to AT&T regarding the target market?
8. Select three characteristics of the consumer innovator summarized in Table 17-7. For each of these consumer characteristics, indicate how a marketer might effectively use the profile information to positively influence the adoption process.

## endnotes


1. Thomas S. Robertson, "The Process of Innovation and the Diffusion of Innovation," *Journal of Marketing*, 31 (January 1967), 14–19.
2. James H. Donnelly, Jr., and Michael J. Etzel, "Degrees of Product Newness and Early Trial," *Journal of Marketing Research*, 10 (August 1973), 295–300.

3. Everett M. Rogers, *Diffusion of Innovations*, 3rd ed. (New York: The Free Press, 1983); and Gerald Zaltman and Ronald Stiff, "Theories of Diffusion," in Scott Ward and Thomas S. Robertson, eds., *Consumer Behavior: Theoretical Sources* (Englewood Cliffs, N.J.: Prentice-Hall, 1973), 416–68.
4. Rogers, *Diffusion of Innovations*, 15–16.
5. Lyman E. Ostlund, "The Role of Product Perceptions in Innovative Behavior," in Philip R. McDonald, ed., *Marketing Involvement in Society and the Economy* (Chicago: American Marketing Association, 1969), 259–66.
6. Lyman E. Ostlund, "Perceived Innovation Attributes as Predictors of Innovativeness," *Journal of Consumer Research*, 1 (September 1974), 23–29; and Duncan G. LaBay and Thomas C. Kinnear, "Exploring the Consumer Decision Process in the Adoption of Solar Energy Systems," in *Consumer Behavior and Energy Use* (Banff, Alberta, Canada: Banff Centre, 1980), U1–U21.
7. Rogers, *Diffusion of Innovations*, 259.
8. Everett M. Rogers and F. Floyd Shoemaker, *Communication of Innovations*, 2nd ed. (New York: Free Press, 1971), 32–33; also see Elizabeth C. Hirschman, "Consumer Modernity, Cognitive Complexity, Creativity and Innovativeness," in Richard P. Bagozzi et al., eds., *Marketing in the 80's: Changes and Challenges* (Chicago: American Marketing Association, 1980), 135–39.
9. Robert A. Peterson, "A Note on Optional Adopter Category Determination," *Journal of Marketing Research*, 10, No. 3 (August 1973), 325–29.
10. See William D. Dando and James M. MacLachlan, "Research to Accelerate the Diffusion of a New Invention," *Journal of Advertising Research*, 23 (June–July 1983), 39–43, and Mary Dee Dickerson and James W. Gentry, "Characteristics of Adopters and Non-Adopters of Home Computers," *Journal of Consumer Research*, 10 (September 1983), 225–35.
11. Richard W. Olshavsky, "Time and the Rate of Adoption of Innovations," *Journal of Consumer Research*, 6 (March 1980), 425–28.
12. James F. Engel, Roger D. Blackwell, and Robert J. Kegerreis, "Consumer Use of Information in the Adoption of an Innovation," *Journal of Advertising Research*, 9 (December 1969), 3–8.
13. Jagdish N. Sheth, "Perceived Risk and Diffusion of Innovation," in Johan Arndt, ed., *Insights into Consumer Behavior* (Boston: Allyn & Bacon, 1968), 185; and Jagdish N. Sheth, "Word-of-Mouth in Low Risk Innovations," *Journal of Advertising Research*, 11 (June 1971), 15–18.
14. Fred D. Reynolds and William R. Darden, "Why the Midi Failed," *Journal of Advertising Research*, 12 (August 1972), 39–44.
15. Rogers and Shoemaker, *Communication of Innovations*, 104–5.
16. William Black, "Discontinuance and Diffusion: Examination of the Post Adoption Decision Process," in Richard P. Bagozzi and Alice M. Tybout, eds., *Advances in Consumer Research*, (Ann Arbor: Association for Consumer Research, 1983), X, 356–61.
17. Nancy M. Ridgway and Linda L. Price, "Use Innovativeness and Technology Integration: An Exploration of Personal Computers," in Russell W. Belk et al., eds., *1984 AMA Educators' Proceedings* (Chicago: American Marketing Association, 1984), 83–87.
18. Hubert Gatignon and Thomas S. Robertson, "A Propositional Inventory of New Diffusion Research," *Journal of Consumer Research,* 11 (March 1985), 849–67.
19. Rogers, *Diffusion of Innovations*, 164.
20. John Jay Painter and Max L. Pinegar, "Post-High Teens and Fashion Innovation," *Journal of Marketing Research*, 8 (August 1971), 368–69.
21. Lawrence P. Feldman and Gary M. Armstrong, "Identifying Buyers of a Major Automotive Innovation," *Journal of Marketing*, 39 (January 1975), 47–53.

22. Joan Kron, "A Few Daring Dressers Risk Sneers to Push Menswear into the Future," *The Wall Street Journal*, March 11, 1986, 1.

23. James F. Engel, Robert J. Kegerreis, and Roger D. Blackwell, "Word-of-Mouth Communication by Innovators," *Journal of Marketing*, 3 (July 1969), 15–19; and Thomas S. Robertson, "Purchase Sequence Responses: Innovators vs. Non-Innovators," *Journal of Advertising Research*, 8 (March 1968), 47–52.

24. Engel, Blackwell, and Kegerreis, "Consumer Use of Information," 5.

25. Lisa Belkin, "The Making of a Designer: Big Campaign for Hilfiger," *New York Times*, March 18, 1986, D1, D5.

26. Wayne D. Hoyer and Nancy M. Ridgway, "Variety Seeking as an Explanation for Exploratory Purchase Behavior: A Theoretical Model," in Thomas C. Kinnear, ed., *Advances in Consumer Research* (Provo, Utah: Association for Consumer Research, 1984), XI, 114–19.

27. Leon G. Schiffman, "Perceived Risk in New Product Trial by Elderly Consumers," *Journal of Marketing Research*, 9 (February 1972), 107; Thomas S. Robertson, "Consumer Innovators: The Key to New Product Success," *California Management Review*, 10 (Winter 1967), 28; Edgar A. Pessemier, Philip C. Burger, and Douglas J. Tigert, "Can New Product Buyers Be Identified?" *Journal of Marketing Research*, 4 (November 1967), 352; and William D. Dando and James M. MacLachlan, "Research to Accelerate the Diffusion of a New Invention," *Journal of Advertising Research*, 23 (June–July 1983), 40.

28. For example, see Johan Arndt, "Role of Product-Related Conversations in the Diffusion of a New Product," *Journal of Marketing Research*, 4 (August 1967), 291–95; and Schiffman, "Perceived Risk," 107–8.

29. J. M. McClurg and I. R. Andrews, "A Consumer Profile Analysis of the Self-Service Gasoline Customer," *Journal of Applied Psychology*, 59 (February 1974), 119–21; and Engel, Blackwell, and Kegerreis, "Consumer Use of Information," 5.

30. Johan Arndt, "Profiling Consumer Innovators," in Johan Arndt, ed., *Insights into Consumer Behavior* (Boston: Allyn & Bacon, 1968), 79; and Kenneth Uhl, Roman Andrus, and Lance Poulsen, "How Are Laggards Different? An Empirical Inquiry," *Journal of Marketing Research*, 7 (February 1970), 52.

31. Arndt, "Profiling Consumer Innovations," 79; David B. Montgomerey, "Consumer Characteristics Associated with Dealing: An Empirical Example," *Journal of Marketing Research*, 8 (February 1971), 118–20; and Leon G. Schiffman and Clifford J. Neiverth, "Measuring the Impact of Promotional Offers: An Analytic Approach," in Thomas V. Greer, ed., 1973 *Combined Proceedings* (Chicago: American Marketing Association, 1974), 256–60.

32. James W. Taylor, "A Striking Characteristic of Innovators," *Journal of Marketing Research*, 14 (February 1977), 104–7; Ronald E. Frank and William F. Massy, "Innovation and Brand Choice: The Folger's Invasion," in Stephen A. Greyser, ed., *Toward Scientific Marketing* (Chicago: American Marketing Association, 1964), 106; and Arndt, "Profiling Consumer Innovators," 79.

33. John O. Summers, "Generalized Change Agents and Innovativeness," *Journal of Marketing Research*, 8 (August 1971), 313–16; and Thomas S. Robertson and James H. Myers, "Personality Correlates of Opinion Leadership and Innovative Buying Behavior," *Journal of Marketing Research*, 6 (May 1969), 164–68.

34. Schiffman, "Perceived Risk," 107; and Robertson, "Consumer Innovators," 28.

35. *MRI Strategic Marketing Studies Number One: Consumer Innovators*, (New York: Mediamark Research, Inc., 1984), 143.

36. Mary Dee Dickerson and James W. Gentry, "Characteristics of Adopters," 232.

37. Engel, Blackwell, and Kegerreis, "Consumer Use of Information," 4; and Charles W. King, "Communicating with the Innovator in the Fashion Adoption Process," in Peter D. Bennett, ed., *Marketing and Economic Development* (Chicago: American Marketing Association, 1965), 429.

38. John O. Summers, "Media Exposure Patterns of Consumer Innovators," *Journal of Marketing*, 36 (January 1972), 43–49; John J. Painter and Kent L. Granzin, "Profiling the Male Fashion Innovator—Another Step," in Beverlee B. Anderson, *Advances in Consumer Research* (Association for Consumer Research, 1976), III, 43; and William R. Darden and Fred D. Reynolds, "Backward Profiling of Male Innovators," *Journal of Marketing Research*, 9 (February 1974), 79–85.

39. Summers, "Media Exposure Patterns," 47–48.

40. King, "Communicating with the Innovator," 428; Painter and Granzin, "Profiling the Male Fashion Innovator," 43; and Painter and Pinegar, "Post-High Teens," 369.

41. Robertson, "Purchase Sequence Responses," 49; and Arndt, "Role of Product-Related Conversations," 293.

42. King, "Communicating with the Innovator," 430; Painter and Pinegar, "Post-High Teens," 369; and Louis E. Boone, "The Search for the Consumer Innovator," *Journal of Business*, 43 (April 1970), 138.

43. For example, see Feldman and Armstrong, "Identifying Buyers," 50; McClurg and Andrews, "Consumer Profile Analysis," 120; William E. Bell, "Consumer Innovators: A Unique Market for Newness," in Stephen A. Greyser, ed., *Toward Scientific Marketing* (Chicago: American Marketing Association, 1963), 90–93; and Mary C. Gilly and Valarie A. Zeithaml, "The Elderly Consumer and Adoption of Technologies," *Journal of Consumer Research*, 12 (December 1985), 353–57.

44. For example, see Robert J. Kegerreis and James F. Engel, "The Innovative Consumer: Characteristics of the Earliest Adopters of a New Automotive Service," in McDonald, *Marketing Involvement in Society and the Economy*, 357–61; Feldman and Armstrong, "Identifying Buyers," 50; Bell, "Consumer Innovators," 90–93; and Boone, "Search for the Consumer Innovator," 138.

45. *MRI Strategic Marketing Studies Number One: Consumer Innovators* (New York: Mediamark Research, Inc., 1984).

# 18

# Consumer Decision Making

## introduction

THIS chapter ties many of the relevant psychological, social, and cultural concepts developed throughout the book into a simple framework for understanding how consumers make decisions. Unlike Chapter 17, which examined the dynamics of *new* product adoption, this chapter takes a broader perspective and examines consumer decision making within the context of *all* types of purchase choices, ranging from the purchase of new products to the selection of old and established products.

## WHAT IS A DECISION?

Each of us makes numerous decisions every day concerning every aspect of our everyday lives. However, we generally make these decisions without stopping to think about *how* we make them, about what is involved in the decision making itself. In the most general terms, a *decision* is *the selection of an action from two or more alternative choices.*[1] In other words, in order for a person to make a decision, there must be a choice of alternatives available. If a person has a choice between making a purchase and *not* making a purchase, or a choice between brand X and brand Y, we can say that this person is in a position to make a decision. On the other hand, if the consumer has no alternatives from which to choose, but rather is literally *forced* to make a particular purchase (e.g., purchase brand X), then this single "no-choice" action does not constitute a decision. A "no-choice" decision is often popularly referred to as a "Hobson's choice."

> *Nothing is more difficult, and therefore more precious, than to be able to decide.*
>
> *NAPOLEON I*
> *Maxims (1804–15)*

In actuality, a no-choice purchase or consumption situation is very rare in American society. It will be recalled from our discussion of core American cultural values (Chapter 14) that for consumers, *freedom* is often expressed in terms of a wide range of product choices. Thus, if there is almost always a choice, then there is almost always an opportunity for consumers to make decisions.

Table 18-1 summarizes various types of purchase-related decisions. While this list is not exhaustive, it does serve to demonstrate that the scope of consumer decision making is much broader than the mere selection of one brand from a number of brands.

## FOUR VIEWS OF CONSUMER DECISION MAKING

Before presenting a simple model of how consumers make decisions, we will consider several models of man that depict consumer decision making in distinctly different ways. The term *model of man* refers to a general perspective held by a significant number of people concerning how (and why) individuals behave as they do. Specifically, we will examine the following consumer-related models of man: (1) **economic man**, (2) **passive man**, (3) **cognitive man**, and (4) **emotional man**.

### Economic Man

In the field of theoretical economics which portrays a world of perfect competition, the consumer is often characterized as an *economic man*—that is, one who makes *rational decisions*. This model has been attacked by consumer researchers for a number of reasons. To behave rationally in the economic sense, a consumer would have to be aware of all available product alternatives, would have to be capable of correctly ranking each alternative in terms of its benefits and its disadvantages, and would have to be able to identify the one best alternative. However, consumers rarely have enough information, or sufficiently accurate information, or even an adequate degree of involvement or motivation, to make perfect decisions.

According to a leading social scientist, the *economic man* model is unrealistic for the following reasons: (a) man is limited by his existing skills, habits, and reflexes, (b) man is limited by his existing values and goals, and (c) man is limited by the extent of his knowledge.[2] Consumers operate in an imperfect world, one in which they do not maximize their decisions in terms of such economic considerations as price-quantity relationships, marginal utility, or indifference curves. Indeed, the consumer is often unwilling to engage in extensive decision-making activities and will instead settle for a "satisfactory" decision, one that is "good enough."[3] For this reason, the economic model is often rejected as too idealistic and simplistic.

**TABLE 18-1 Types of Purchase Decisions**

| DECISION CATEGORY | ALTERNATIVE A | ALTERNATIVE B |
|---|---|---|
| Basic purchase decision | To purchase a product (or service) | Not to purchase a product (or service) |
| Brand purchase decisions | To purchase a specific brand | To purchase another brand |
| | To purchase one's usual brand | To purchase another established brand (possibly with special features) |
| | To purchase a basic model | To purchase a luxury or status model |
| | To purchase a new brand | To purchase one's usual brand or some other established brand |
| | To purchase a standard quantity | To purchase more or less than a standard quantity |
| | To purchase an on-sale brand | To purchase a non-sale brand |
| | To buy a national brand | To buy a store brand |
| Channel purchase decisions | To purchase from a specific type of store (e.g., a department store) | To purchase from some other type of store (e.g., a discount store) |
| | To purchase from one's usual store | To purchase from some other store |
| | To purchase in-home (by phone or catalog) | To purchase in-store |
| | To purchase from a local store | To purchase from a store requiring some travel (out-shopping) |
| Payment-purchase decision | To pay for the purchase with cash | To pay for the purchase with a credit card |
| | To pay the bill in full when it arrives | To pay for the purchase in installments |

## Passive Man

Quite opposite to the economic man model is the *passive man* model, which depicts the consumer as basically submissive to the self-serving interests and promotional efforts of marketers. The following statement captures the flavor of the passive model:

> The image of man implied in advertising and in modern sales methods is one of a passive person, open and vulnerable to external and internal stimuli leading to spending. The unconscious becomes a vehicle for directing economic behavior. The prototype is the dissatisfied, restless housewife who, after husband and children have left for the day, visits the department store, lets herself be titillated by the exhibited goods, and spontaneously, without clear-cut wants and purpose, succumbs to the lure of salesmanship and buys something she does not "really" need and will later regret having bought.[4]

As this quotation implies, consumers are sometimes perceived as impulsive and irrational purchasers, ready to yield to the arms and aims of marketers. At least to some degree, the passive model of the consumer was subscribed to by the hard-driving supersalesman of old, who was trained to regard the consumer as an object to be manipulated. The following excerpt from a 1917 salesmanship text dramatically illustrates the long-held belief in the dominance of the salesman over the unresisting, somewhat passive consumer:

> In the development of the selling process, there are four distinct stages. First, the salesman must secure the prospect's undivided attention. Secondly, this attention must be sustained and developed into interest. Thirdly, this interest must be ripened into desire. And fourthly, all lingering doubts must be removed from the prospect's mind, and there must be implanted there a firm resolution to buy; in other words, the sale must be closed.[5]

Interestingly enough, this same formula is still being taught to salesmen today, with the acronym AIDA (attention, interest, desire, action).

The principal limitation of the passive model is that it fails to recognize that the consumer plays an equal, if not dominant, role in many buying situations by seeking information about product alternatives and selecting the product that appears to offer the greatest satisfaction. All that we know about motivation (Chapter 3), selective perception (Chapter 6), learning (Chapter 7), attitudes (Chapters 8 and 9), communication (Chapter 10), and opinion leadership (Chapter 16) serves to support the proposition that consumers are rarely objects of manipulation. Therefore, this simple and single-minded view should be rejected as unrealistic.

## Cognitive Man

The third model portrays the consumer as *cognitive man* or a *problem solver*. Within this framework, consumers are frequently pictured as either receptive to or actively seeking out products and services that fulfill their needs and enrich their lives. This model of man focuses on the *processes* by which consumers seek and evaluate information about selected brands and retail outlets.

Because *choice* is an inherent factor in consumer behavior, *risk* is frequently a component of the cognitive or problem-solving model. Chapter 6 discusses several types of consumer-perceived risk (functional risk, economic risk, physical risk, social risk, psychological risk, and time risk) and the strategies consumers adopt for handling risk (collecting information about alternatives, patronizing specific retailers, brand loyalty). Such strategies depict the consumer as a problem solver, attempting to effectively dispel the risk perceived in making choices.[6]

Within the context of this model, consumers may be viewed as *information-processing systems*. Such information processing leads to the formation of preferences and ultimately to purchase intentions. Consumers may also use a *preference formation strategy* that is "other-based," in which they allow another person—a trusted friend or an expert retail salesperson—to establish preferences for them.[7]

In contrast to the economic man model, the cognitive model more realistically portrays the consumer as unlikely to even attempt to obtain all available information about every choice alternative. Instead, the consumer's information-seeking efforts are likely to cease when what is perceived to be a sufficient amount of information is obtained concerning some of the alternatives—enough information to enable an "adequate" decision to be made. Information-processing research reveals that consumers frequently develop short-cut decision rules (called heuristics) to ease the decision-making process.[8] Some consumer researchers have even suggested that consumers can suffer from too much information—**information overload**.[9]

In a sense, the cognitive or problem-solving model depicts a consumer who is somewhere between the extremes of the economic and passive man models—a consumer who does not possess complete knowledge and therefore cannot make *perfect* decisions, but one who nevertheless actively seeks information and attempts to make *satisfactory* decisions.

The cognitive model seems to capture the essence of a well-educated and involved consumer who seeks information on which to base consumption decisions. Our discussions of specific aspects of consumer decision making throughout the book have generally depicted a consumer who is consistent with the cognitive or problem-solving model.

## Emotional Man

While long aware of the existence of an *emotional or impulsive* model of man, marketers have frequently preferred to think of consumers in terms of either economic or passive models. However, in reality, each of us is likely to associate deep feelings or emotions—fun, fear, love, prestige, hope, sexiness, fantasy, and even a little "magic"—with certain of our purchases or possessions.[10] Such feelings or emotions are likely to be highly involving. For instance, a person who misplaces a favorite pen might go to considerable lengths to find it in his apartment, despite the fact that he has six others at hand. Similarly, a teenage girl might be almost obsessive about getting the "right" shade of lipstick, feeling that her entire attraction to others is dependent upon the color of her lips. During World War II, there were many stories of how American GIs attributed protective powers to their Zippo lighters. Some even credited the lighter with saving their lives.

If any of us were to give considered thought to the nature of our recent purchases, we might be surprised to realize just how impulsive some of them were. Rather than carefully searching, deliberating, and evaluating alternatives before buying, we are just as likely to have made many of these purchases on impulse—on a whim—or because we were emotionally driven. As recent research suggests, and every consumer knows, one consequence of consumption is often the "fun" or "thrill" that consumers derive from a product—the feeling of pleasure that comes with product use.[11]

When a consumer makes a basically *emotional* purchase decision, less emphasis tends to be placed on searching for prepurchase information. Rather, more emphasis is placed on current mood and feelings—"go for it!" This is not to say that *emotional man* makes decisions that are not rational. As Chapter 3 points out, buying products that afford emotional satisfaction is a perfectly rational consumer decision. Furthermore, in the case of a good number of products, the choice of one brand over another has little to do with rationality. For instance, many consumers buy designer-label clothing not because they *look* any better in them, but because status labels make them *feel* better. Choosing a dress that makes one *feel* better than the alternative is a perfectly rational decision. Of course, if a woman with a husband and three children purchases a two-seater Porsche for herself, the neighbors might wonder about her level of rationality (though some might think it was deviously high). No such question would arise if the same woman selected Grey Poupon mustard instead of Heinz, though each might be an impulsive, emotional purchase decision. Advertisers are recognizing the renewed importance of emotional or *feeling-oriented* advertising.[12]

To illustrate the power of emotion in advertising, Figure 18-1 creates a strong sense of fun and adventure for Wings sunglasses—"The legend lives on!" Figure 18-2 presents a Spiegel Catalog ad that portrays a variation on a popular fairy tale—"I'm one Cinderella who didn't need a fairy godmother." Purina pet foods suggests: "When you make friends with a kitten you've made a friend for life." The American Greetings Corporation produces a line of cards designed to make it easier for people to express feelings of anger, passion, or loneliness. The cards have front cover messages like "Any time, any place, But Only You." Figure 18-3 shows how American Greetings "In Touch" cards address specific emotions. Of all product categories, *emotional* ads are especially common for perfumes or colognes. A Chanel No. 5 perfume ad reminds us: "Live the fantasy"; English Leather Musk Cologne appeals to consumers' diverse emotional states or feelings—"When you're bold. When you're shy."

This trend toward emotional ads represents a sharp departure from the more rational or economics-oriented ads of the mid- and late-1970s that reflected the constraints of high gasoline prices and high mortgage rates.

## A MODEL OF CONSUMER DECISION MAKING

This section presents a simple model of consumer decision making that reflects the notion of the *cognitive* or *problem-solving* consumer. The model is designed to tie together many of the ideas on consumer decision making discussed throughout the book. It does not presume to provide an exhaustive picture of the complexities of consumer decision making; rather, it is designed to synthesize and coordinate relevant concepts into a significant whole. The model (see Figure 18-4) has three major components: **input**, **process**, and **output**.

### Input

The *input* component of our consumer decision-making model draws upon external influences that serve as sources of information about a particular product and influence a consumer's product-related values, attitudes, and behavior. Chief among these input factors are the **marketing-mix activities** of organizations that are trying to communicate the benefits of their products to potential

FIGURE 18-1 Emotional Advertisement Appealing to a Sense of Adventure

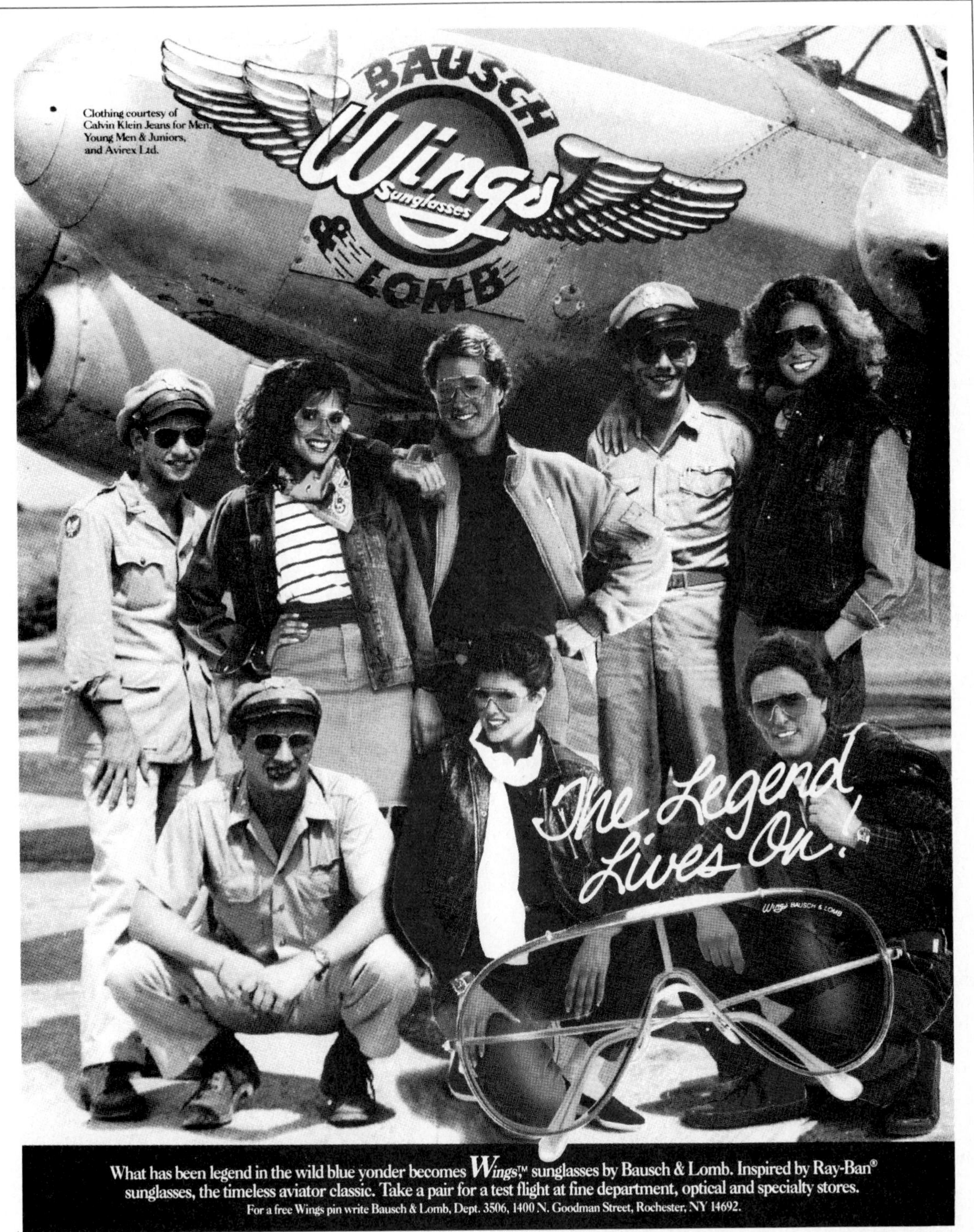


Courtesy of Bausch & Lomb

FIGURE 18-2 Emotional Advertisement Appealing to a Fairy Tale

"I'm one Cinderella who didn't need a fairy godmother."
"Glass slippers? No thanks, I have a hard enough time with pumps. But I decided that this year I'd finally go to the Spring Singles Ball, and I thought I'd dress the part.
Now, I knew enough about fashion to realize no one was going to tap me on the nose with a magic wand. So, as always, I just reached for the Spiegel Catalog.
What a great way to shop. Toll free calling day or night. Fast delivery. Even free UPS pick-ups for returns.
So I treated myself to this Eklektic dress and Calvin Klein shoes.
Who knows? Maybe I'll meet someone at the ball. He doesn't have to be a prince. Just charming."
To get your Spiegel Spring Catalog for $3, call toll free, 1 800 345-4500, ask for catalog 295 and charge it.
Spiegel®
Dress by Eklektic.
Shoes by Calvin Klein.


Courtesy of Spiegel, Inc.

FIGURE 18-3 Emotional Advertisement Appealing to Specific Feelings

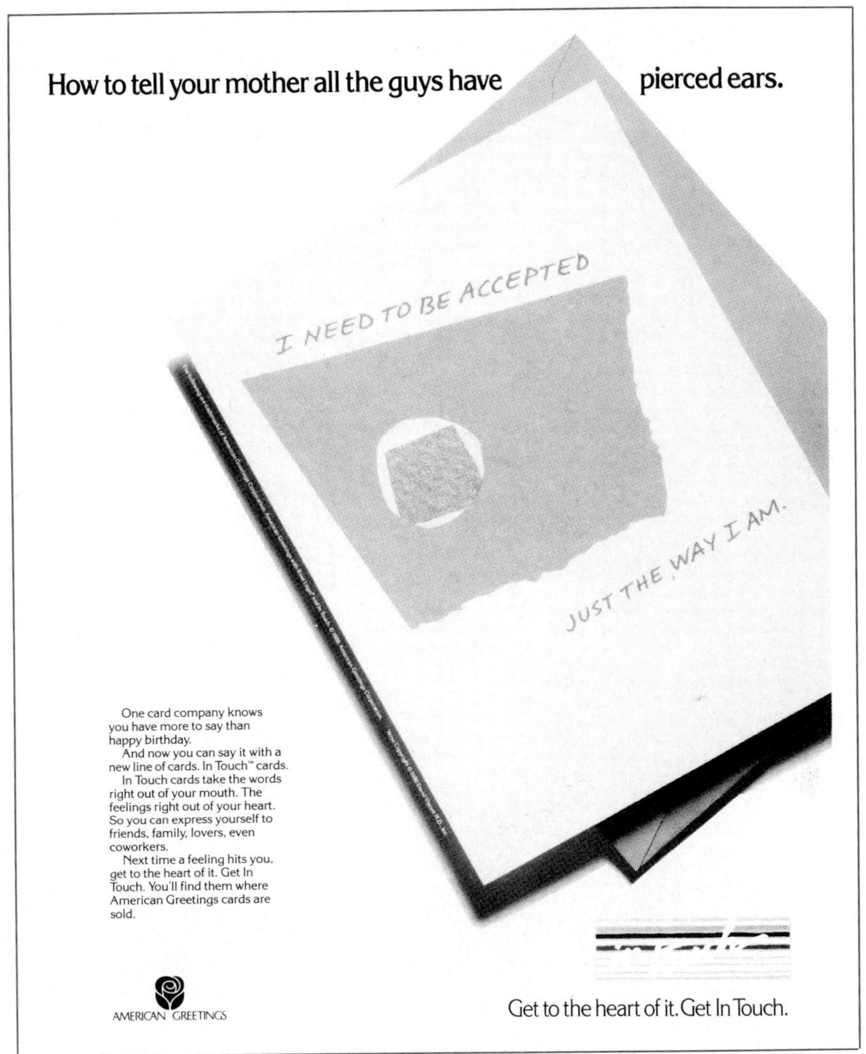


Courtesy of American Greetings

consumers, and nonmarketing **sociocultural influences** which, when internalized, affect the consumer's purchase decisions.

## MARKETING INPUTS

The firm's marketing activities constitute a direct attempt to reach, inform, and persuade consumers to buy and use its products. These inputs to the consumer's decision-making process take the form of specific marketing-mix strategies which consist of the product itself (including its package, size, and guarantees); mass media advertising, personal selling, and other promotional efforts;

FIGURE 18-4 A Simple Model of Consumer Decision Making

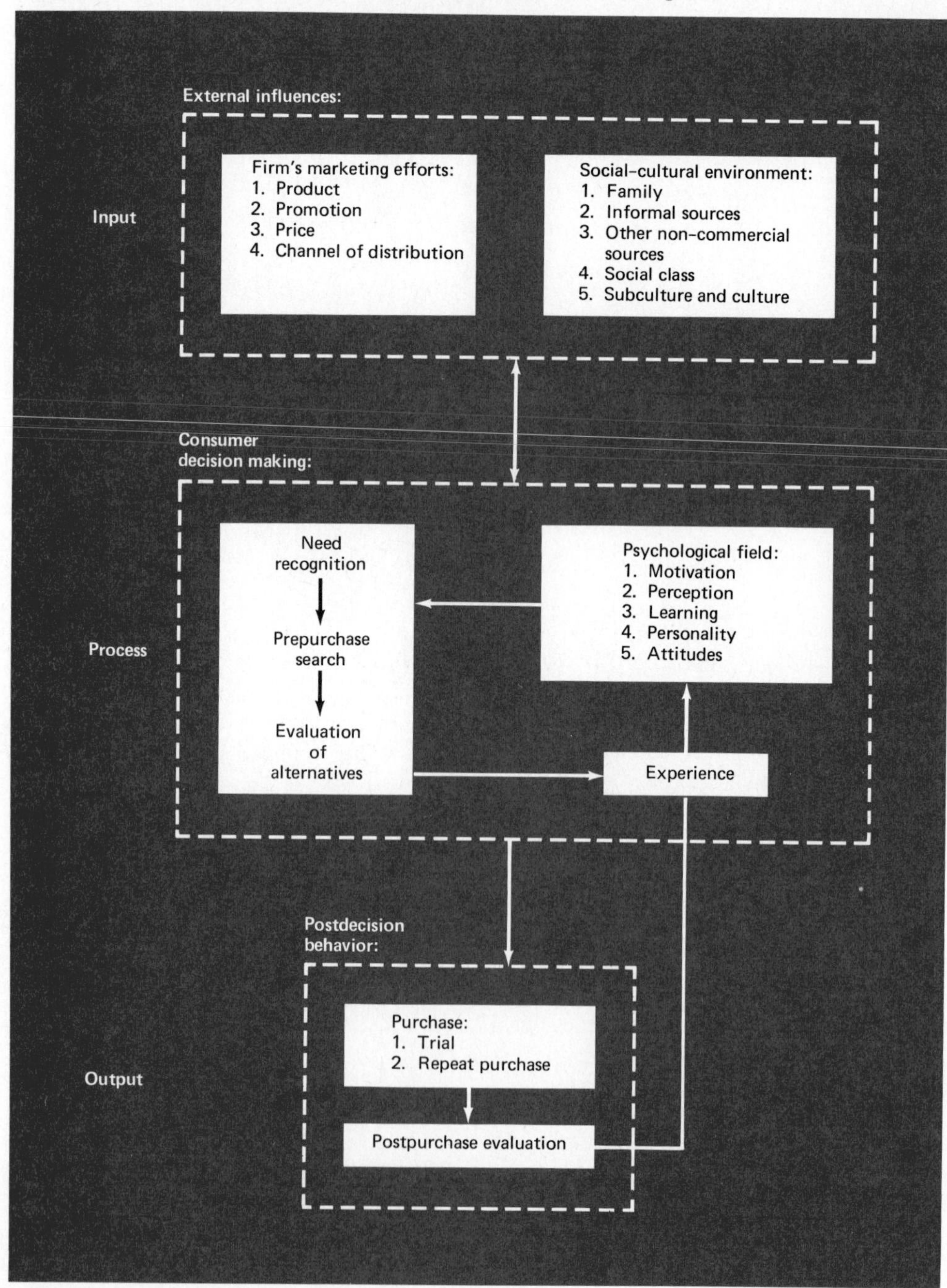

pricing policy; and the selection of distribution channels to move the product from the manufacturer to the consumer.

Ultimately, the impact of a firm's marketing efforts is in large measure governed by the consumer's perception of these efforts. This should serve to remind marketers that they must be diligently alert to consumer perceptions and must not rely on the *intended* impact of their marketing messages.

### SOCIOCULTURAL INPUTS

The second type of input, the *sociocultural environment,* also exerts a major influence on the consumer. Sociocultural inputs (examined in Part III) consist of a wide range of noncommercial influences. For example, the comments of a friend, an editorial in the paper, usage by a family member, or an article in *Consumer Reports* are all specific and direct noncommercial sources of information. The influences of social class, culture, and subculture, though less tangible, are important input factors that are internalized and affect how consumers evaluate and ultimately adopt (or reject) products.

The unwritten codes of conduct communicated by culture subtly indicate which purchases should be considered "right" or "wrong" at a particular point in time. For example, until the 1970s, most men would not have considered using a hair blower (or dryer), or a spray to keep their hair in place. Now these products are fairly commonplace among men.

Unlike the firm's marketing efforts, sociocultural inputs do not necessarily *support* the purchase of a specific product, but may influence consumers to *avoid* the product. For example, when fashion designers tried to introduce a longer hemline style some years ago, they were unable to do so because of widespread informal negative discussions among women.[13]

The cumulative impact of each firm's marketing efforts, the influence of family, friends, and neighbors, and society's existing code of behavior are all inputs that are likely to affect what consumers purchase and how they use what they buy. Since these influences may be directed *to* the individual or actively sought *by* the individual, a two-headed arrow is used to link the *input* and *process* segments of the model (Figure 18-4).

## Process

The *process* component of the model is concerned with how consumers make decisions. To understand this process, we must consider the influence of many of the psychological concepts examined in Part II. The *psychological field* represents the internal influences that affect the consumer's decision-making process (what they need or want, their awareness of various product choices, their information-gathering activities, and their evaluation of alternatives). As pictured in the process component, the act of making a consumer decision consists of three stages: (1) **need recognition**, (2) **prepurchase search**, and (3) **evaluation of alternatives**.

Before we examine these three stages in detail, it is important to remember that not all consumer decision situations receive (or require) the same degree of information search (see Chapter 7).

## LEVELS OF CONSUMER DECISION MAKING

If all purchase decisions required extensive effort, consumer decision making would be an exhausting process that left little time for anything else. On the other hand, if all purchases were routine, they would tend to be monotonous and would provide little pleasure or novelty. On a continuum of effort ranging from very high to very low, we can distinguish three specific levels of consumer decision making: *extensive problem solving, limited problem solving,* and *routinized response behavior.*[14]

EXTENSIVE PROBLEM SOLVING. When consumers have no established criteria for evaluating a product category or specific brands within the category, or have not narrowed down the number of brands they will consider to some small manageable subset (the *evoked set*), their decision-making efforts can be classified as *extensive problem solving.* At this level, the consumer needs a great deal of information in order to establish a set of criteria on which to judge specific brands, and a correspondingly large amount of information concerning each of the brands to be considered.

LIMITED PROBLEM SOLVING. At this level of problem solving, consumers have already established the basic criteria for evaluating the product category and the various brands within the category. However, they have no fully established preferences concerning a select group of brands. Their search for additional information is more like "fine tuning;" they have to gather additional brand information in order to discriminate among the various brands.

ROUTINIZED RESPONSE BEHAVIOR. At this level, consumers have had some experience with the product category and a well-established set of criteria with which to evaluate the brands in their evoked sets. In some situations, they may search for a small amount of additional information; in others, they simply review what they already know.

Just how extensive a consumer's problem-solving task is depends on how well established his or her criteria for selection are, how much information he or she has about each brand being considered, and how narrow the set of brands (the evoked set) is from which the choice will be made. Clearly, extensive problem solving implies that the consumer must seek a greater amount of information in order to make a choice, while routinized response behavior implies little need for additional information.

Let us now turn to the three stages of the *process* component of the decision-making model.

## NEED RECOGNITION

The *recognition of a need* is likely to occur when a consumer is faced with a problem. For example, consider the case of a consumer—let's call him David—who happens to operate a direct mail poster business from his home. After only nine months in business, David decides that the mountain of paperwork which he faces daily would be largely reduced with the use of a personal computer (PC). He envisions that a PC would help keep track of inventories, sales, payments, and business expenses, and that the printer could be used to prepare shipping labels and invoices. He has heard that with the addition of a modem (which allows a computer to communicate with other computers over telephone lines), he would be able to access lists of potential customers. The computer could then print labels for envelopes filled with promotional literature.

Although several of his friends suggested that David purchase a PC before he started the business, he was not then ready for one. However, with the company still in its infancy, he now realizes that a PC could help him with almost every facet of his firm's operation. David has *recognized the need* for a PC.

## PREPURCHASE SEARCH

The *prepurchase search* state begins when a consumer perceives a need that might be satisfied by the purchase and consumption of a product. A consumer is in this stage if he or she senses a need for information upon which to base a choice. The recollection of past experiences (drawn from long-term memory storage) might provide the consumer with adequate information for the present choice. On the other hand, if the consumer has had no prior experience, he or she may have to engage in extensive search of the outside environment for useful information upon which to base a choice.

The consumer usually searches his or her memory (the *psychological field* depicted in the model) before seeking out external sources of information regarding a given consumption-related need. Past experience is considered an *internal* source of information. The greater his or her relevant past experience, the less external information the consumer is likely to need in order to reach a decision. Many consumer decisions are based on a combination of past experience (internal sources) and marketing and noncommercial information (external sources). The degree of perceived risk may also influence this stage in the decision process. In high-risk situations, consumers are likely to engage in complex information search and evaluation; in low-risk situations, they are likely to use very simple search and evaluation tactics.[15]

Consider the case of David, the businessman in need of a computer. He has no experience with computers, but feels that a PC will save him a great deal of time in the running of his direct mail business. According to the categories listed in Table 18-2, David would fit into the *Appliance User* segment of the business user market—not especially concerned with how the computer operates, but seeing it as a means of reducing the tedious aspects of his business. At the other end of the experience spectrum, according to this segmentation scheme, is the *Professional Computer Expert/Engineer,* who holds advanced degrees in computer science or a related field, and sees computers as a way of life.

How much information a consumer will gather also depends on various *situational* factors. For example, David might feel he should make an immediate decision on the specific brand of PC to buy, and may go to the nearest Computerland or Sears Business Center store to make his selection. At the retail outlet, he might explain his business needs to the salesperson and purchase whatever

**TABLE 18-2 Segmenting the Business Computer User Market**

**the appliance user**

Approaches a computer like an appliance (a car or a microwave oven)
No concern with the inner-workings of computers
A single or limited-function user, with narrow software experience
An expert in a "profession" who uses the computer to make tedious aspects of the job less time-consuming

**the informed consumer**

More interested in the computer than the appliance user
Aware of different types of computers and software
A multifunction user, seeking multipurpose software
Reads computer magazines, and knows about industry "current events" and price changes

**the adaptive user**

Attends one or two computer conferences a year
Approaches the computer as fun and a challenge
Interested in programming
Heavy reader of selected computer and software magazines
Likely to have a home computer and experience in writing programs
Knows how to modify programs and customize printouts for specific needs

**the hacker**

Lives and breathes for the computer
Feels that the world's problems can be solved by the correct computer or program
While home-taught, has several years of experience with computers
Very interested in programming and modifying programs
Likes to know the computer inside and out
Called on by co-workers to fix business computer equipment
Likely to have fully outfitted home computers and related equipment
Attends computer shows and conferences

**professional computer expert/engineer**

Computers are a way of life and nothing especially astonishing
Frequently wonders why people make such a big deal about computers
Likely to have college degrees in computers or related areas
Frequently expert in hardware and/or software

Source: Adapted from Deborrah Willis, "Computers," *Working Women*, March 1984, 49–50, which in turn was adapted from Jerry Willis and Merl Miller, *Computers for Everybody* (Beaverton, Ore.: Dilithium Press, 1984).

is recommended to him. On the other hand, this type of rapid decision making style does not fit everyone. Many consumers prefer to approach an expensive and complex decision with much more deliberation.

Besides heading for the nearest computer dealer, a myriad of search alternatives exist. For example, David might examine some of the numerous publications that deal with computers during a lengthy prepurchase search period. As Table 18-3 indicates, the number of factors that are likely to increase prepurchase search in this specific situation include the fact that David has no past experience with computers. Furthermore, a computer is a relatively long-lasting product with a high price.

Let's consider several of the prepurchase search alternatives open to a prospective computer system buyer. At the most fundamental level, search alternatives may be classified as either personal or impersonal. *Personal* sources include more than a consumer's past experience with the product or product

TABLE 18-3 **Factors That Are Likely to Increase Prepurchase Search**

| |
|---|
| **product factors** |
| Long interpurchase time (a long-lasting or infrequently used product) |
| Frequent changes in product styling |
| Frequent price changes |
| Volume purchasing (large number of units) |
| High price |
| Many alternative brands |
| Much variation in features |
| **situational factors** |
| Experience: |
| First time purchase |
| No past experience because the product is new |
| Unsatisfactory past experience within the product category |
| Social Acceptability: |
| The purchase is for a gift |
| The product is socially visible |
| Value-related Considerations: |
| Purchase is discretionary rather than necessary |
| All alternatives have both desirable and undesirable consequences |
| Family members disagree on product requirements or evaluation of alternatives |
| Product usage deviates from important reference group |
| The purchase involves ecological considerations |
| Many sources of conflicting information |
| **personal factors** |
| Demographic Characteristics of Consumer: |
| Well educated |
| High income |
| White-collar occupation |
| Under 35 years of age |
| Personality: |
| Low dogmatic (open-minded) |
| Low risk perceiver (broad categorizer) |
| Other Personal Factors: |
| High product involvement |
| Enjoyment of shopping and search |

Source: Inspired by Donald H. Granbois, "The Role of Communication in the Family Decision Making Process," in Stephen A. Greyser, ed., *Toward Scientific Marketing* (Chicago: American Marketing Association, 1964), 50–56; and Girish N. Punj and David W. Stewart, "An Interaction Framework of Consumer Decision Making," *Journal of Consumer Research*, 10 (September 1983), 181–96.

category; they also include asking for information and advice from friends (possibly an *Adaptive User* or *Hacker* as listed in Table 18-2), other small business owners, and store sales personnel. David might turn to the Yellow Pages to make a list of local computer stores to visit. After a few such trips and after speaking with several computer-literate friends, he may visit a library and look through books and magazines to find articles evaluating different computers. For example, from time to time *Consumer Reports* has rated a number of IBM-compatible personal computers.

Table 18-4 presents some of the sources of information that David might use as part of his prepurchase search. Any or all of these sources might be employed as part of a typical search process.

**TABLE 18-4 Alternative Prepurchase Information Sources for the Purchase of a Computer**

| PERSONAL | IMPERSONAL |
|---|---|
| Friends | Articles in computer magazines |
| Business consultants | *Consumer Reports* |
| Neighbors | Promotional brochures from manufacturers |
| Relatives | Government data |
| Co-workers | Trade association data |
| Store salesmen | Newspaper articles |
| Seminars | Insights from computer advertisements |
| College computer classes | Computer books |

## EVALUATION OF ALTERNATIVES

When evaluating potential alternatives, consumers tend to employ two types of information: (a) a "list" of brands from which they plan to make their selection (the evoked set), and (b) the criteria they will use to evaluate each brand. The evoked set is generally only a part—a subset—of all the brands of which the consumer is aware; these brands in turn are frequently only a segment of all the brands in the market.[16] Making a selection from a *sample* of all possible brands is a human characteristic that helps simplify the decision-making process.

The criteria that consumers employ in evaluating the brands that constitute their evoked sets are usually expressed in terms of product attributes that are important to them. Examples of product attributes that consumers might employ as criteria in evaluating nine product categories are listed in Table 18-5.

Let's for a moment return to David, the small businessman in the market for a PC. After several weeks of reading computer brochures and magazine articles, visiting computer retailers, and talking to knowledgeable friends, his evoked set might consist of the AT&T 6300, the IBM PC, and the Compaq Deskpro. A portion of his newly acquired computer knowledge may have been derived directly from exposure to advertisements by the various computer manufacturers. For example, the AT&T ad presented in Figure 18-5 informs the reader of a number of attributes of the AT&T 6300 computer.

On the basis of his recently secured information about PCs, David has decided that the computer he purchases should be configured with 512K of memory, two floppy disk drives, and a monochrome display. To help him evaluate alternatives, David might mentally construct a table which compares the three brands of PCs in his evoked set in terms of a number of relevant features (see Table 18-6).

As part of his search process, David has also discovered information about other relevant points (or attributes) that may influence his final choice. For example, both the AT&T and Compaq computers cost less than the IBM computer. When it comes to processing speed, one review of the AT&T 6300 indicated that in a simple comparison, the IBM PC took 24 seconds to do what the AT&T 6300 accomplished in 8 seconds. However, not all the expansion

**TABLE 18-5 Product Attributes Used as Purchase Criteria for Product Categories**

| BRASSIERES | LIPSTICK | MOUTHWASH |
|---|---|---|
| Comfort | Color | Color |
| Fit | Container | Effectiveness |
| Life | Creaminess | Kills germs |
| Price | Prestige factor | Price |
| Style | Taste/flavor | Taste/flavor |
| **ORANGE JUICE (FROZEN)** | **TOILET TISSUE** | **TOOTHPASTE** |
| Nutritional value | Color | Decay prevention |
| Packaging | Package size | Freshens mouth |
| Price | Price | Price |
| Taste/flavor | Strength | Taste/flavor |
| Texture | Texture | Whitens teeth |
| **TIRES** | **AUTOMOBILES** | **SHOES** |
| Safety | Durability | Fit |
| Service policy | Safety | Care |
| Durability | Appearance | Durability |
| Ride | Ride | Style |
| Traction | Repairs | Comfort |

Source: Derived from Frank M. Bass and William L. Wilkie, "A Comparative Analysis of Attitudinal Predictions of Brand Preference," *Journal of Marketing Research*, 10 (August 1973), 263; and Andrew A. Mitchell, J. Edward Russo, and Meryl Gardner, "Strategy-Induced Low Involvement Perception of Advertising" (Working paper, Carnegie-Mellon University, August 1979).

slots (allowing hookups to accessories) in the AT&T computer are fully compatible with the hundreds of products made for the IBM PC, the industry standard.[17] Table 18-7 lists a number of PC attributes and indicates David's assessment of each attribute for each of the three brands in his evoked set. For instance, when it comes to processing speed, the AT&T 6300 is rated "best," followed by Compaq and then IBM. David might then weigh each attribute in terms of which is more important to him. If software and hardware compatibility are most important, he might choose the IBM over the AT&T model.

CONSUMER DECISION RULES, OR HEURISTICS. Consumer decision rules (often referred to as *heuristics*, *decision strategies*, and *consumer information-processing strategies*) are procedures employed by consumers to facilitate brand (or other) choices. Such rules serve to reduce the burden of making complex decisions by providing guidelines or routines that make the process less taxing.

Consumer decision rules have been broadly classified into two major categories: **compensatory** and **noncompensatory decision rules**.[18] In following a *compensatory decision rule*, a consumer evaluates each brand option in terms of each relevant attribute and computes a weighted or summated score for each brand. The computed score reflects each brand's relative merit as a potential purchase choice. There is an assumption that the consumer will generally select the brand that scores highest among the alternatives evaluated.

A unique feature of a compensatory decision rule is that it allows a positive evaluation of a brand on one attribute to balance out a negative evaluation

FIGURE 18-5 Advertisement Informing Consumers of the Characteristics of the AT&T 6300 Computer

Courtesy of AT&T

on some other attribute. For example, a positive assessment of a particular brand of automobile in terms of performance may offset an unacceptable assessment in terms of gasoline mileage.

In comparison, *noncompensatory decision rules* do not allow consumers to balance a positive evaluation of a brand on one attribute against a negative eval-

**TABLE 18-6 Comparison of Computer Features**

| FEATURE | AT&T | IBM | COMPAQ |
|---|---|---|---|
| Processing speed | 8 MHz* | 4.77 MHz | 7.14 or 4.77 MHz |
| Maximum memory on system board | 640K† | 256K | 640K |
| Number of expansion slots | 7 | 5 | 6 |
| Screen graphics with standard display | Yes | No | Yes |
| Includes serial port for modem | Yes | No | Yes |

*MHz stands for megahertz, the rate at which a computer's central processing unit performs its operations.
†K stands for 1,024 bytes. A byte is one unit of computer storage capacity.

**TABLE 18-7 Hypothetical Computer Brand-Attribute Ratings**

| CRITERIA | AT&T | IBM | COMPAQ |
|---|---|---|---|
| Price | 8* | 4 | 8 |
| Standard features† | 9 | 5 | 8 |
| Processing speed | 10 | 5 | 8 |
| Software compatibility | 8 | 10 | 9 |
| Hardware compatibility | 7 | 10 | 9 |

*The businessman's evaluations are on a 10-point scale; a higher number indicates a higher rating.
†Such as modem ports or number of expansion slots.

uation of the same brand on some other attribute. For instance, in the case of an automobile, a negative (unacceptable) rating on the vehicle's gasoline mileage would *not* be offset by a positive evaluation of performance. Instead, this particular car model would be disqualified from any further consideration.

A number of noncompensatory rules are described in the consumer behavior literature. We will briefly consider three of these rules here: the **conjunctive** rule, the **disjunctive** rule, and the **lexicographic** rule.[19]

CONJUNCTIVE RULE. In employing a *conjunctive* decision rule, the consumer establishes a separate minimally acceptable level as a cutoff point for each attribute. If any particular brand falls below the cutoff point on any one attribute, the brand is eliminated from further consideration.

Since the conjunctive rule can result in several acceptable alternatives, it becomes necessary in such cases for the consumer to apply an additional decision rule in order to arrive at a final selection—for example, to accept the first satisfactory brand. The conjunctive rule is particularly useful in quickly reducing the number of alternatives to be considered; the consumer can then apply another, more refined decision rule to arrive at a final choice.

DISJUNCTIVE RULE. The *disjunctive* rule has been called the "mirror image" of the conjunctive rule.[20] In employing this decision rule, the consumer also establishes a separate minimally acceptable level as the cutoff point for each attribute (which may be higher than the one normally established for a conjunctive rule).[21] In this case, if a brand alternative meets or surpasses the cutoff established for any *one* attribute, it is accepted. Here again, a number of brands might surpass the cutoff point, producing a situation where another decision rule is required. If this occurs, the consumer may accept the first satisfactory brand as the final choice or employ some other, perhaps more suitable, decision rule.

LEXICOGRAPHIC RULE. In employing a *lexicographic* decision rule, the consumer first ranks the attributes in terms of perceived relevance or importance. The consumer then compares the various brand alternatives in terms of the single attribute that is considered most important. If one brand scores sufficiently high on this top-ranked attribute (regardless of the score on any of the other attributes), it is selected and the process comes to a halt. If there are two or more surviving brand alternatives, the process is repeated with the second-highest-ranked attribute (and so on) until a point is reached where one of the brands is selected because it exceeds the others on a particular attribute.

In employing the lexicographic rule, the highest-ranked attribute (the one employed first) may reveal something about the individual's basic consumer or shopping orientation. For instance, a "buy the best" rule might indicate that a consumer is *quality oriented*; a "buy the most prestigious brand" rule might indicate that a consumer is *status oriented*; a "buy the least expensive" rule might reveal that the consumer is *economy-minded*.

We have considered only the most basic of an almost infinite number of possible consumer decision rules. Most of the decision rules described here can be combined to form new variations—e.g., conjunctive-compensatory, conjunctive-disjunctive, or disjunctive-conjunctive. It is likely that for many purchase decisions, consumers maintain in long-term memory overall evaluations of the brands in their evoked sets. This would make assessment by individual attributes unnecessary. Instead, the consumer would simply select the brand with the highest perceived overall rating. This type of synthesized decision rule has been labeled the **affect referral** rule and may represent the simplest of all rules.[22]

Table 18-8 captures the essence of each of the decision rules described in this section by revealing the kind of mental statement that David, the small business owner, might make in selecting a PC.

In discussing consumer decision rules, we have assumed that a choice is made among the brands evaluated. Of course, a consumer may also conclude that none of the alternatives offer sufficient benefits to warrant purchase. If this were to occur with a necessity like a refrigerator, the consumer would probably either lower his or her expectations and settle for the best of the available alternatives, or seek information about additional brands, hoping to find one that more closely meets his or her criteria. On the other hand, if the purchase is more discretionary (e.g., purchasing a second or third wristwatch), the consumer would probably postpone the purchase. In such a case, information gained from the search experience up to that point would be transferred to

**TABLE 18-8 Hypothetical Usage of Popular Decision Rules in Making a Purchase Decision**

| DECISION RULE | MENTAL STATEMENT |
|---|---|
| Compensatory rule | "I selected the brand of computer that came out best when I balanced the good ratings with the bad ratings." |
| Conjunctive rule | "I picked the computer that didn't have any bad features." |
| Disjunctive rule | "I selected the brand of computer that excelled in at least one attribute." |
| Lexicographic rule | "I looked at the feature that was the most important to me and chose the brand of computer that was best on that attribute." |
| Affect referral rule | "Everything that they do is outstanding, so I'll buy their computer." |

Source: Inspired by Michael Reilly and Rebecca H. Holman, "Does Task Complexity or Cue Intercorrelation Affect Choice of an Information Processing Strategy? An Empirical Investigation," in William D. Perreault, Jr., ed., *Advances in Consumer Research* (Atlanta: Association for Consumer Research, 1977), V, 187.

long-term storage (in the psychological field) and retrieved and reintroduced as input when and if the consumer regains interest in making such an acquisition.

In applying decision rules, it should be noted that consumers may at times attempt to compare dissimilar (noncomparable) alternatives. For example, rather than comparing the attributes of several brands of stereo cassette tape decks, a consumer may try to compare a tape deck and a hand-held TV set. This type of comparison occurs because, as alternative ways of allocating available funds become more and more dissimilar, consumers abstract the products to a level where comparisons are possible.[23] To illustrate, a consumer might weigh a tape deck and a hand-held TV set in terms of which will offer the greater amount of pleasure—or which, if either, is a necessity.

DECISION RULES AND MARKETING STRATEGY. An understanding of which decision rules consumers apply in selecting a particular product or service is useful to marketers concerned with formulating a promotional program.[24] A marketer familiar with the prevailing decision rule can prepare a promotional message in a format that would facilitate consumer information processing; the promotional message might even suggest how potential consumers should make a decision. The advertisement in Figure 18-6 provides information for readers on "five important things to know before you buy a home appliance." Whirlpool is suggesting which attributes consumers should use in selecting an appliance (or appliance manufacturer). In effect, Whirlpool is providing potential consumers with a basis for evaluating alternatives.

## Output

The *output* portion of the model is concerned with two closely associated kinds of postdecision activity: **purchase behavior** and **postpurchase evaluation**. The objective of both activities is to increase the consumer's satisfaction with his or her purchase.

FIGURE 18-6 Advertisement Suggesting Criteria for Decision Making

# Five important things to know before you buy a home appliance.

At Whirlpool, we know that buying a new appliance is a major decision. And that there is more to it than just the selection of color, size and features. So to us, what we can do *in other ways* to make your world a little easier is just as important as what our appliances can do.

**Whirlpool promise of quality.**

With every Whirlpool® appliance, you get our promise of good, honest quality. It's a promise we're proud of, and one we stand behind by offering a variety of helpful programs like these:

**Whirlpool toll-free, 24-hour Cool-Line service.**

It's important for you to have someone to talk to whenever you have questions about any of our appliances. Our Cool-Line® service* is an easy way to get information about appliance installation, proper operation, or even hints on saving energy. Plus, it's a great way to get help should you ever have a problem with a Whirlpool appliance.

**Whirlpool Do-It-Yourself Repair Manuals.**

We now offer manuals that can make do-it-yourself work easier. You can obtain them through Whirlpool dealers, parts distributors or Tech-Care® service companies. We have them for our automatic washers, dryers, dishwashers and trash compactors. And soon to come, manuals for our ranges and refrigerators.

**Whirlpool Tech-Care service.**

If you need service on any of our appliances, our independently owned Tech-Care service franchises make sure you get it. They have the right equipment, and highly trained personnel ready to answer your call. Just look in the Yellow Pages.

**Whirlpool Instant Service Parts.**

Our WISP® parts service is designed to reduce your waiting time for a special-order part. It's processed within 24 hours, then given special handling and shipping at *our* expense.

So *before* you buy your next appliance, think about these five important things that you can count on *later*. Like our appliances, they're designed to make your world a little easier.

*Call 800-253-1301.
In Alaska and Hawaii, 800-253-1121.
In Michigan, 800-632-2243.

Making your world a little easier.

Courtesy of Whirlpool Corporation

## PURCHASE BEHAVIOR

Consumers make two types of purchases: *trial purchases* and *repeat purchases*. If a consumer purchases a product (or brand) for the first time, and buys a smaller quantity than usual, such a purchase would be considered a trial. Thus a trial is the exploratory phase of purchase behavior in which consumers attempt to evaluate a product through direct use. Research evidence indicates that when consumers purchase a new brand about which they may be uncertain, they tend to purchase smaller quantities than they would if it were a familiar brand.[25]

If a new brand in an established product category (toothpaste, chewing gum, catsup) is found by trial to be more satisfactory or better than other brands, consumers are likely to repeat the purchase. Repeat purchase behavior is closely related to the concept of *brand loyalty*, which most firms try to encourage because it ensures them of stability in the marketplace. Unlike trial, in which the consumer uses the product on a small scale, a repeat purchase usually signifies that the product meets with the consumer's approval and that the consumer is willing to use it again and in larger quantities.

To encourage initial trial and ultimately repeat purchasing, Atlanta-based Food World has developed a frequent-buyer savings plan. Whenever consumers buy from a participating merchant, they receive coupons representing the dollar value of that purchase. By attaching $40 worth of these coupons to a "Save-A-Chek," a consumer receives a minimum of a $1 discount at a participating retailer. Some merchants offer patrons a much more generous discount of $5 or $15 for using the Save-A-Chek in their store.[26] Such a program fosters repeat purchasing and may lead to store loyalty.

Trial, of course, is not always feasible. For example, with most durable goods (clothes dryers, freezers, microwave ovens), a consumer usually moves directly from evaluation to a long-term commitment (through purchase), without the opportunity for an actual trial.

## POSTPURCHASE EVALUATION

As consumers use a product, particularly during a trial purchase, they evaluate its performance in light of their own expectations. For this reason, it is difficult to separate the trial of a product from its *postpurchase evaluation*. The two go hand in hand.

An important component of postpurchase evaluation is the reduction of uncertainty or doubt that the consumer might have about the selection. Consumers, as part of their postpurchase analysis, try to reassure themselves that their choice was a wise one; that is, they attempt to reduce *postpurchase cognitive dissonance* (see Chapter 9) by adopting one of the following strategies: they may rationalize the decision as being wise; they may seek advertisements that support their choice and avoid those of competitive brands; they may attempt to persuade friends or neighbors to buy the same brand (and thereby confirm their own choice); or they may turn to other satisfied owners for reassurance.

The degree of postpurchase analysis that consumers undertake is likely to depend on the importance of the product decision and the experience acquired in using the product. If the product lives up to expectations, they will probably buy it again.[27] However, if the product's performance is disappointing or does not meet expectations, they will search for more suitable alternatives. Thus the consumer's postpurchase evaluation "feeds back" as *experience* to the consumer's psychological field and serves to influence future related decisions.

## summary

The consumer's decision to purchase or reject a product is the moment of final truth for the marketer. It signifies whether the marketing strategy has been wise, insightful, and effective, or whether it was poorly planned and missed the mark. Thus marketers are particularly interested in the consumer decision-making process. In order for a consumer to make a decision, there must be more than one alternative available. (The decision not to buy is also an alternative.)

Theories of consumer decision making vary, depending on the researcher's own assumptions about the nature of humankind. The various "models of man" (economic man, passive man, cognitive man, and emotional man) depict consumers and their decision-making processes in distinctly different ways.

A simple consumer decision-making model ties together the psychological, social, and cultural concepts examined in Parts II and III into an easily understood framework. This decision model has three distinct sets of variables: input variables, process variables, and output variables.

Input variables that affect the decision-making process include commercial marketing efforts as well as noncommercial influences from the consumer's sociocultural environment. The decision process variables are influenced by consumers' own psychological fields, which affect their recognition of a need, their prepurchase search for information, and their evaluation of alternatives. The output phase of the model includes the actual purchase (either trial or repeat purchase) and postpurchase evaluation. Both prepurchase and postpurchase evaluation feed back in the form of experience into the consumer's psychological field and serve to influence future decision processing.

## discussion questions

1. Briefly compare and contrast the distinctions between the economic and emotional models of man.
2. Consider the Montblanc fountain pen, a writing instrument often used by Presidents, Heads of State, celebrities, and CEOs. The pen comes in a variety of sizes starting at a list price of $150, and its most deluxe version is covered in 18-carat gold. What kinds of marketing inputs would influence the purchase of this product?
3. Identify three different products that you believe require reasonably intensive prepurchase search by a consumer. Then, using Table 18-5 as a guide, identify the characteristics of these products that make intensive prepurchase search likely.

4. Select one of the following product categories: (a) compact disk players, (b) long-distance telephone companies, (c) typewriters, (d) shampoo. (1) Write down the brands that constitute your evoked set; (2) make a list of other brands that are not part of your evoked set, and indicate why. On what important attributes do the brands in your evoked set differ from the others?
5. Describe a recent purchase you have made in terms of the model of consumer behavior presented in Figure 18-1.
6. Describe the general characteristics of extensive, limited, and routinized decision making.
7. Let's assume that this coming summer you are planning to spend a month touring Europe and are therefore in need of a good 35mm camera. Distinguish the differences that would occur in your decision process if you were to employ compensatory versus noncompensatory decision rules.
8. Select a newspaper or magazine advertisement that attempts to provide the consumer with a decision strategy to be followed in making a purchase decision. Explain the decision strategy.

## *endnotes*


1. This definition is similar to the one suggested in Irwin D. J. Bross, *Design for Decision* (New York: Free Press, 1953), 1.
2. Herbert A. Simon, *Administrative Behavior*, 2nd ed. (New York, Free Press, 1965), 40.
3. James G. March and Herbert A. Simon, *Organizations* (New York: John Wiley, 1958), 140–41.
4. Walter A. Weisskopf, "The Image of Man in Economics," *Social Research*, 40 (Autumn 1973), 560.
5. John G. Jones, *Salesmanship and Sales Management* (New York: Alexander Hamilton Institute, 1917), 29.
6. For interesting ideas on consumer decision strategies, see Lawrence X. Tarpey, Sr., and J. Paul Peter, "A Comparative Analysis of Three Consumer Decision Strategies," *Journal of Consumer Research*, 2 (July 1975), 29–37.
7. Richard W. Olshavsky, "Towards a More Comprehensive Theory of Choice," in Elizabeth C. Hirschman and Morris B. Holbrook, eds., *Advances in Consumer Research* (Provo, Utah: Association for Consumer Research, 1985), XII 465–70.
8. James R. Bettman, *An Information Processing Theory of Consumer Choice* (Reading, Mass.: Addison-Wesley, 1979).
9. Jacob Jacoby, Donald E. Speller, and Carol A. Kohn, "Brand Choice Behavior as a Function of Information Load, *Journal of Marketing Research*, 11 (February 1974), 63–69; "Brand Choice Behavior as a Function of Information Load: Replication and Extension, *Journal of Consumer Research*, 1 (June 1974), 33–42.
10. Elizabeth C. Hirschman, "Primitive Aspects of Consumption in Modern American Society," *Journal of Consumer Research*, 12 (September 1985), 142–54; Meryl P. Gardner, "Mood States and Consumer Behavior: A Critical Review," *Journal of Consumer Research*, 12 (December 1985), 281–300. Also see Harold H. Kassarjian,

"Consumer Research: Some Recollections and a Commentary," in Richard J. Lutz, ed., *Advances in Consumer Research*, XIII (Provo, Utah: Association for Consumer Research, 1986), 6–8.

11. Morris B. Holbrook and Elizabeth C. Hirshman, "The Experiential Aspects of Consumption: Consumer Fantasies, Feelings, and Fun," *Journal of Consumer Research*, 9 (September 1982), 132–37.

12. For a recent example of research that focuses on emotional advertising, see Marian Friestad and Esther Thorson, "Emotional-Eliciting Advertising: Effects on Long Term Memory and Judgment," in Richard J. Lutz, ed., *Advances in Consumer Research*, XIII (Provo, Utah: Association for Consumer Research, 1986), 111–15.

13. Fred D. Reynolds and William R. Darden, "Why the Midi Failed," *Journal of Advertising Research*, 12 (August 1972), 39–44.

14. John A. Howard and Jagdish N. Sheth, *The Theory of Buyer Behavior* (New York: Wiley, 1969), 46–47.

15. Rohit Deshpande and Wayne D. Hoyer, "Consumer Decision Making: Strategies, Cognitive Effort and Perceived Risk," in Patrick E. Murphy et al., eds., *1983 AMA Educators' Proceedings* (Chicago: American Marketing Association, 1983), 88–91. Also see Wayne D. Hoyer, "An Examination of Consumer Decision Making for a Common Repeat Purchase Product, *Journal of Consumer Research*, 11 (December 1984), 822–29.

16. Howard and Sheth, *Theory of Buyer Behavior*, 26.

17. Russ Lockwood, "AT&T 6300/Clash of the Titans: Round One," *Creative Computing*, June 1985, 32–34.

18. Peter Wright, "Consumer Choice Strategies: Simplifying vs. Optimizing," *Journal of Marketing Research*, 12 (February 1975), 60–67; and Bettman, *Information Processing Theory*, 176–85.

19. Ibid.

20. Wright, "Consumer Choice Strategies," 61.

21. Bettman, *Information Processing Theory*, 181.

22. Wright, "Consumer Choice Strategies," 66; Bettman, *Information Processing Theory*, 179.

23. Michael D. Johnson, "Consumer Choice Strategies for Comparing Noncomparable Alternatives," *Journal of Consumer Research*, 11 (December 1984), 741–50.

24. Peter L. Wright, "Use of Consumer Judgment Models in Promotional Planning," *Journal of Marketing*, 37 (October 1973), 32.

25. Robert W. Shoemaker and F. Robert Shoaf, "Behavioral Changes in the Trial of New Products," *Journal of Consumer Research*, 2 (September 1975), 104–9.

26. "Global, Second-Generation, and Frequent-Buyer Set New Trends," *Marketing News*, June 7, 1985, 18.

27. For example, see Ralph L. Day, "Extending the Concept of Consumer Satisfaction," in W.D. Perreault, ed., *Advances in Consumer Research* (Atlanta: Association for Consumer Research, 1977), IV, 149–54; Richard L. Oliver, "A Cognitive Model of the Antecedents and Consequences of Satisfaction Decisions," *Journal of Marketing Research*, 17 (November 1980), 460–69; John E. Swan and Lind Combs, "Product Performance and Consumer Satisfaction: A New Concept," *Journal of Marketing*, 40 (April 1976), 26–33; Robert A. Westbrook, "A Rating Scale for Measuring Product/Service Satisfaction," *Journal of Marketing*, 44 (Fall 1980), 68–72; Robert B. Woodruff, Ernest R. Cadotte, and Roger L. Jenkins, "Modeling Consumer Satisfaction Processing Using Experience-Based Norms," *Journal of Marketing Research*, 20 (August 1983), 296–304; and Priscilla A. LaBarbera and David Mazursky, "A Longitudinal Assessment of Consumer Satisfaction/Dissatisfaction: The Dynamic Aspect of the Cognitive Process," *Journal of Marketing Research*, 22 (November 1985), 394–404.

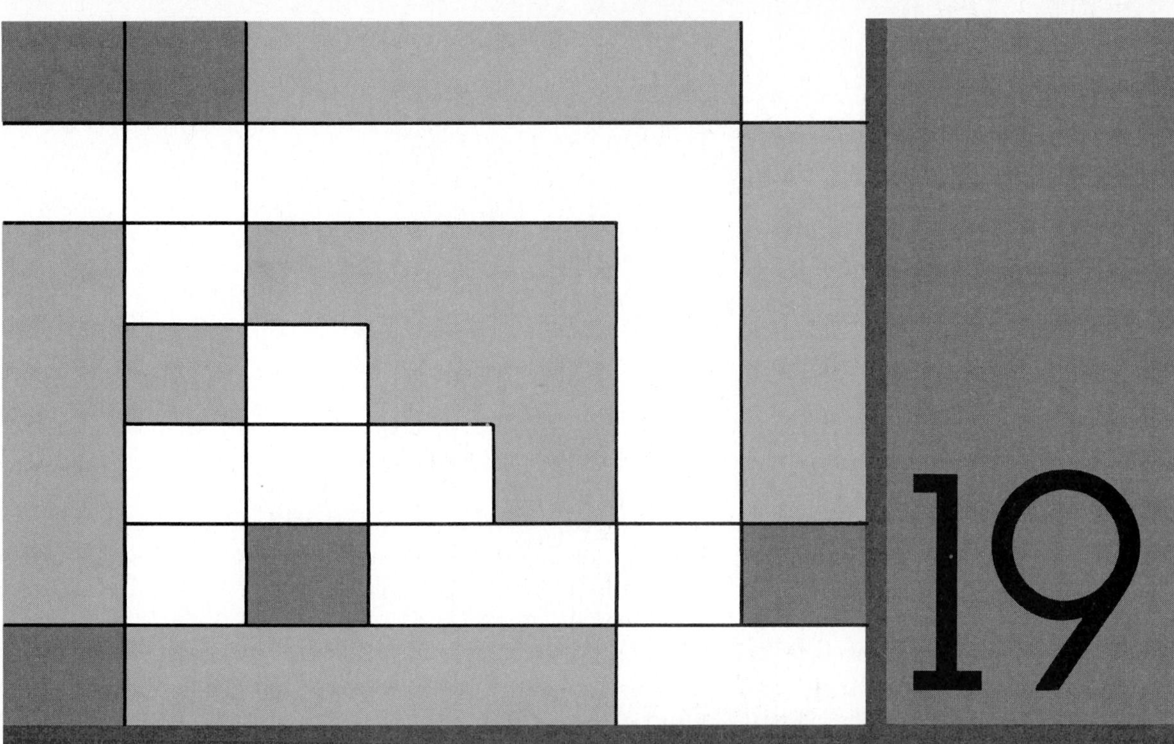

19

# Comprehensive Models of Consumer Decision Making

## *introduction*

THIS chapter will set out and briefly examine five comprehensive models of consumer behavior. These models reflect an effort to order and integrate the huge number of bits and pieces of knowledge that are now known about consumer behavior.[1]

The first three models focus on consumer decision making, especially on how individual consumers arrive at brand choices. The fourth model deals with family decision making. Particular attention is given to factors that influence the extent and nature of family members' contributions to a purchase decision. The final model takes a consumer information-processing perspective. It focuses on the cognitive aspects of information search and processing and indicates how consumers employ information to arrive at various types of buying decisions.

Some of the more complex consumer behavior models were designed primarily to tie together the contents of a specific consumer behavior book. Others were conceived to capture the dynamics of consumer decision making and to provide a framework for consumer researchers to test various dimensions of the models. Taken together, the models provide insights for the design of future research to increase understanding of consumer behavior.

We have attempted to keep our discussion of the components, variables, and interrelationships of the various parts of each model as simple as possible, even at the risk of understating the uniqueness or richness of a specific model. The reader who desires a complete description of any of these models is encouraged to consult the original sources.

> *The whole of science is nothing more than a refinement of everyday thinking.*
>
> *EINSTEIN*
> *Out of My Later Years, 1950*

The Nicosia model focuses on the relationship between the firm and its potential consumers.[2] In the broadest terms, the firm communicates with consumers through its marketing messages (advertising), and consumers communicate with the firm by their purchase responses. Thus the Nicosia model is *interactive* in design: The firm tries to influence consumers, and the consumers—by their actions (or inaction)—influence the firm.

In its full-blown form, the Nicosia model is an elaborate computer flowchart of the consumer decision making process. For our purposes, it is sufficient to examine a summary flowchart that highlights the full model. As depicted in Figure 19-1, the Nicosia model is divided into four major fields: (1) the span between the source of a message and the consumer's attitude, (2) search and evaluation, (3) the act of purchase, and (4) feedback.

FIELD 1: THE CONSUMER'S ATTITUDE BASED ON THE FIRM'S MESSAGES. The first field of the Nicosia model is divided into two subfields. Subfield *One* includes aspects of the firm's marketing environment and communications efforts that affect consumer attitudes, such as product attributes, the competitive environment, characteristics of relevant mass media, the choice of a copy appeal, and

**FIGURE 19-1 Summary Flowchart of the Nicosia Model of Consumer Decision Processes** Source: Francesco M. Nicosia, *Consumer Decision Processes* (Englewood Cliffs, N.J.: Prentice-Hall, 1966), 156.

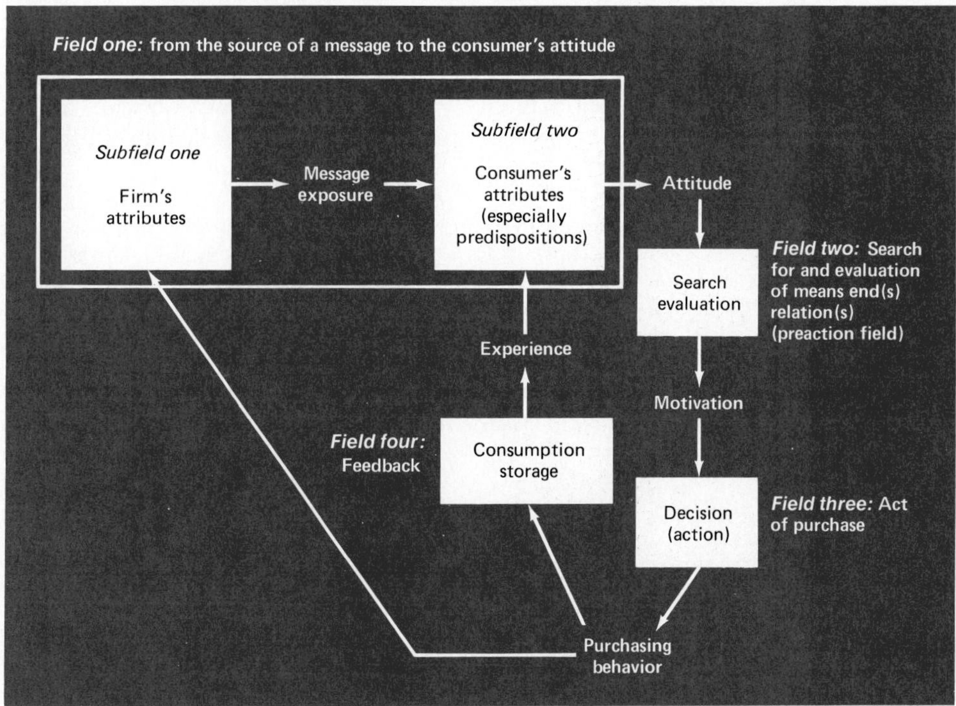

characteristics of the target market. Subfield *Two* specifies various consumer characteristics (e.g., personality, experience) that mediate reception of the firm's promotional messages.

The output of field 1 is an *attitude* toward the product based on the consumer's interpretation of the message.

FIELD 2: SEARCH AND EVALUATION. The second field of the Nicosia model deals with the search for relevant information and evaluation of the firm's brand in comparison with alternative brands. The output of this stage is *motivation to purchase* the firm's brand. (Of course, evaluation could also lead to rejection of the firm's brand; however, the model illustrates a positive response.)

FIELD 3: THE ACT OF PURCHASE. In the third field, the consumer's motivation toward the firm's brand results in actual *purchase* of the brand from a specific retailer.

FIELD 4: FEEDBACK. The final field consists of two important types of feedback from the purchase experience: one to the firm in the form of *sales data*, and the other to the consumer in the form of *experience* (satisfaction or dissatisfaction). The consumer's experience with the product affects the individual's attitudes and predispositions concerning future messages from the firm.

## HOWARD-SHETH MODEL

The Howard-Sheth model is a major revision of an earlier systematic effort to develop a comprehensive theory of consumer decision making.[3] This model explicitly distinguishes among three levels of learning (stages of decision making):

1. *Extensive problem solving*. The consumer's knowledge and beliefs about brands are very limited or nonexistent. At this initial point, the buyer has no brand preference, and therefore actively seeks information about a number of alternative brands.
2. *Limited problem solving*. Knowledge and beliefs about the brands are only partially established, which means that the consumer is not fully able to assess brand differences in order to arrive at a preference. Some comparative brand information is sought, although the choice criteria are likely to be fairly well defined.
3. *Routinized response behavior*. The consumer's knowledge and beliefs about brands are well established, and there is enough experience and information to avoid confusion about the various brands. The consumer is predisposed to the purchase of one particular brand.

Table 19-1 summarizes the main characteristics of each of the three stages of decision making. A simplified version of the basic Howard-Sheth model is shown in Figure 19-2. The model consists of four major sets of variables: (1) inputs, (2) perceptual and learning constructs, (3) outputs, and (4) exogenous (external) variables (not depicted in Figure 19-2).

**TABLE 19-1 Characteristics of the Three Stages of Decision Making**

| STAGE | AMOUNT OF INFORMATION NEEDED PRIOR TO PURCHASE | SPEED OF DECISION |
|---|---|---|
| Extensive Problem Solving | Great | Slow |
| Limited Problem Solving | Moderate | Moderate |
| Routinized Response Behavior | Little | Fast |

Source: John A. Howard, *Consumer Behavior: Application of Theory* (New York: McGraw-Hill, 1977), 10.

INPUTS. The input variables consist of three distinct types of stimuli (information sources) in the consumer's environment. Physical brand characteristics (*significative* stimuli) and verbal or visual product characteristics (*symbolic* stimuli) are furnished by the marketer in the form of product or brand information. The third type of stimulus is provided by the consumer's social environment (family, reference groups, social class). All three types of stimuli provide inputs concerning the product class or specific brands to the prospective consumer.

PERCEPTUAL AND LEARNING CONSTRUCTS. The central component of the Howard-Sheth model consists of psychological variables that are assumed to operate when the consumer is contemplating a decision. While these constructs are the heart of the model, Howard and Sheth treat them as abstractions that are not operationally defined or directly measured. Some of the variables are perceptual in nature; these *perceptual constructs* are concerned with the function of information processing—how the consumer receives and processes information acquired from the input stimuli and other parts of the model. For example, *stimulus ambiguity* occurs if a consumer is unclear about the meaning of information received from the environment; *perceptual bias* occurs if the consumer distorts the information received so that it fits his or her established needs or experiences.

There are also *learning constructs*, which serve the function of concept formation. Included in this category are the consumer's goals, information about brands in the evoked set, criteria for evaluating alternatives, preferences, and buying intentions. The proposed interaction (linkages) between the various perceptual and learning variables and the variables in other segments of the model give the Howard-Sheth model its distinctive character.

OUTPUTS. The model indicates a series of outputs that correspond in name to some of the perceptual and learning construct variables (attention, brand comprehension, attitudes, intention) in addition to the actual purchase.

EXOGENOUS VARIABLES. Exogenous variables are not directly part of the decision-making process and are not shown in the model presented here. However, because external variables influence the consumer, they should affect the marketer's segmentation efforts. Relevant exogenous variables include the importance of the purchase, consumer personality traits, time pressure, and financial status.

**FIGURE 19-2** **Simplified Version of the Howard-Sheth Model of Buyer Behavior** Source: John A. Howard and Jagdish N. Sheth, *The Theory of Buyer Behavior* (New York: John Wiley, 1969), 30.

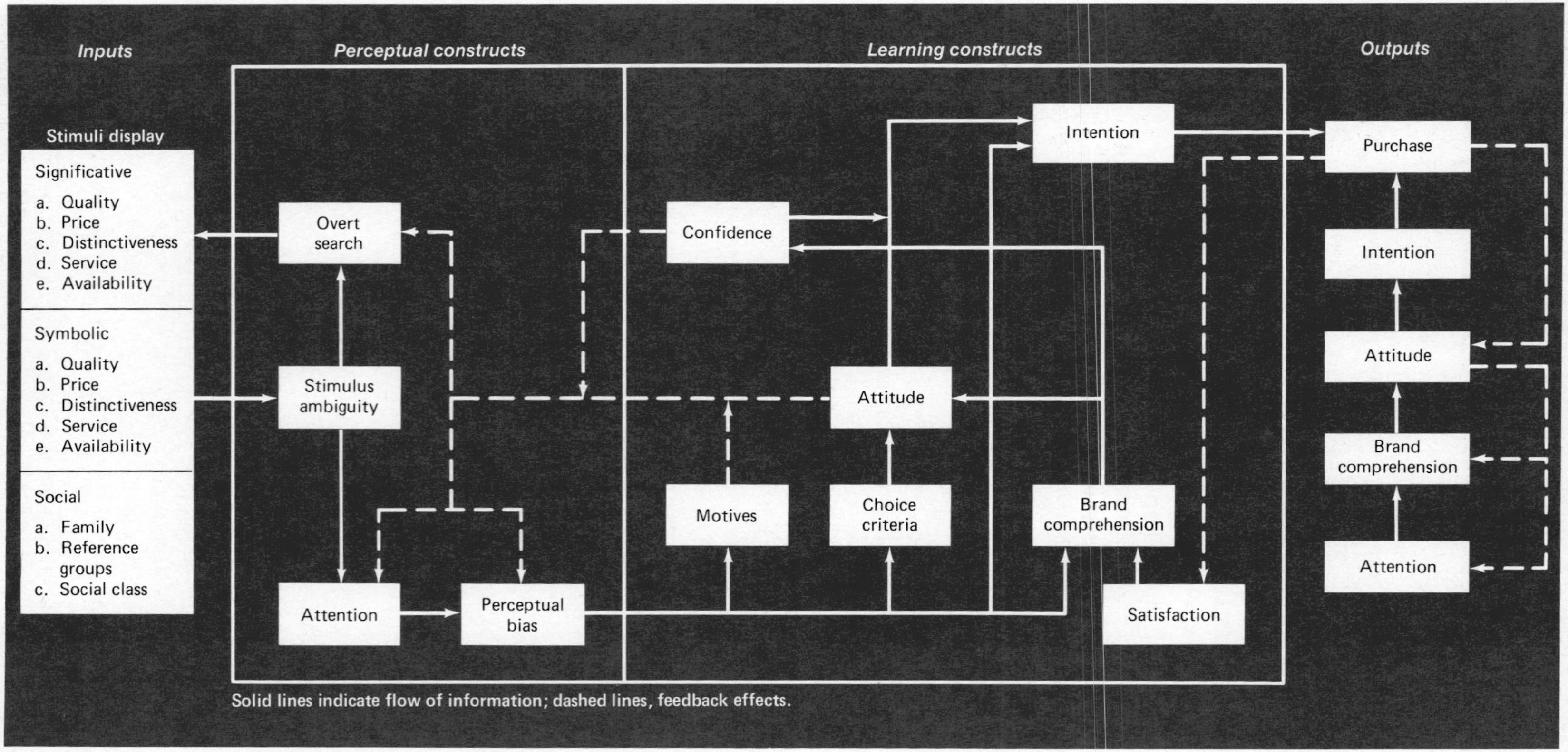

*Inputs*

Stimuli display

Significative
a. Quality
b. Price
c. Distinctiveness
d. Service
e. Availability

Symbolic
a. Quality
b. Price
c. Distinctiveness
d. Service
e. Availability

Social
a. Family
b. Reference groups
c. Social class

*Perceptual constructs*

Overt search
Stimulus ambiguity
Attention
Perceptual bias

*Learning constructs*

Confidence
Intention
Attitude
Motives
Choice criteria
Brand comprehension
Satisfaction

*Outputs*

Purchase
Intention
Attitude
Brand comprehension
Attention

Solid lines indicate flow of information; dashed lines, feedback effects.

In an effort to understand the underlying relationships among the variables, Howard and Sheth have promoted testing of the model with actual data on consumer decision making.[4] The first test focused on the instant breakfast market.[5] It found that consumers are quite systematic in their use of information and in their establishment of attitudes about brands. Another test of the model examined consumers' decisions to purchase an automobile.[6] From their analysis of the data, the researchers concluded that informal influence (particularly information acquired from friends) was more critical than information supplied by advertisements. Although advertising was found to be a relatively ineffective information source, exposure to advertising did have limited impact on comprehension of the car's features and on the intention to purchase.

## ENGEL-KOLLAT-BLACKWELL MODEL

The Engel-Kollat-Blackwell model of consumer behavior (Engel-Blackwell-Miniard model in its current revision) was originally designed to serve as a framework for organizing the fast-growing body of knowledge concerning consumer behavior.[7] Like the Howard-Sheth model, it has gone through a number of revisions aimed at improving its descriptive ability and clarifying basic relationships between components and subcomponents. Figure 19-3 presents the latest version of this comprehensive model, which consists of four sections: (1) decision process stages, (2) information input, (3) information processing, and (4) variables influencing the decision process.[8]

DECISION PROCESS STAGES. The central focus of the model is on five basic decision process stages: problem recognition, search, alternative evaluation (during which beliefs may lead to the formation of attitudes, which in turn may result in a purchase intention), purchase, and outcomes. How many of these stages actually figure in a specific purchase decision, and the relative amount of attention given to each stage, is a function of how extensive the problem-solving task is felt to be. For example, in "extended problem-solving behavior," the consumer is assumed to pass through all five stages; in "routine problem-solving behavior," the consumer is assumed not to require external search and alternative evaluation—for example, "She knows she wants Charlie perfume."

INFORMATION INPUT. Feeding into the information-processing section of the model is information from marketing and nonmarketing sources. After passing through the consumer's memory, which serves as a filter, the information is depicted as having its initial influence at the *problem recognition* stage of the decision-making process. Search for external information is activated if additional information is required in order to arrive at a choice or if the consumer experiences dissonance because the chosen alternative is assessed to be less satisfactory than was originally expected.

INFORMATION PROCESSING. The information processing section of the model consists of the consumer's exposure, attention, comprehension/percep-

FIGURE 19-3 **The Engel-Kollat-Blackwell (Engel-Blackwell-Miniard) Model of Consumer Behavior** Source: James F. Engel, Roger D. Blackwell, and Paul W. Miniard, *Consumer Behavior*, 5th ed. Copyright© 1986 by CBS College Publishing. Reprinted by permission.

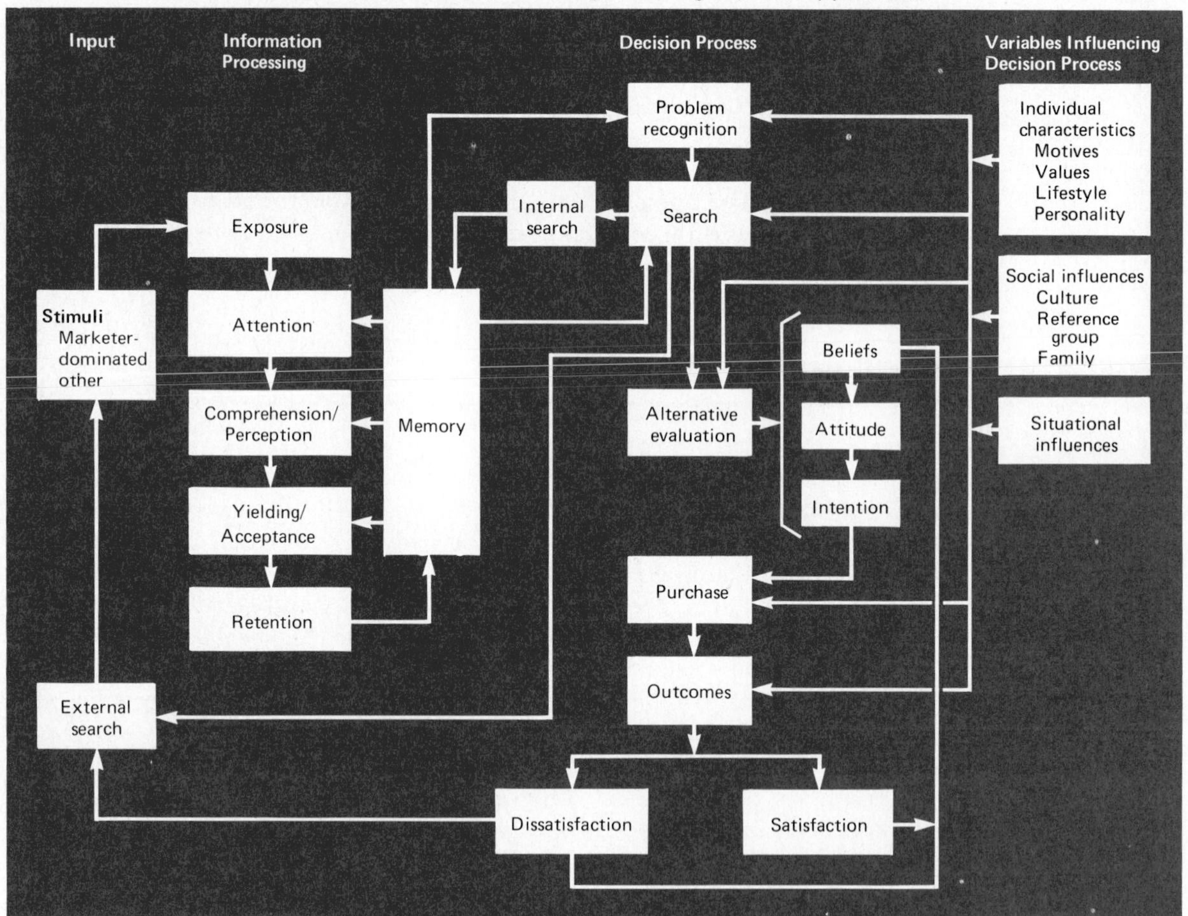


tion, yielding/acceptance, and retention of incoming marketer-dominated and nonmarketing information. As indicated in the model, before a message can be utilized, the consumer must: (1) be exposed to it, (2) allocate information-processing capacity to the incoming message, (3) interpret the stimulus, (4) be persuaded by it, and (5) retain the message by transferring the input to long-term memory. In order to be retained in long-term memory as information and experience, a stimulus must first pass through sensory memory, which analyzes the input in terms of its physical properties, and short-term memory, where the message (stimulus) is analyzed for meaning.

VARIABLES INFLUENCING THE DECISION PROCESS. The last section of the model consists of individual and environmental influences that affect all five stages of the decision process. Individual characteristics include motives, values, lifestyle, and personality; the social influences are culture, reference groups, and family. Situational influences, such as a consumer's financial condition, also influence the decision process.

## SHETH FAMILY DECISION-MAKING MODEL

The three comprehensive models presented thus far all focus on *individual* consumer decision making. An alternative perspective considers the *family* as the appropriate consumer decision-making unit. The Sheth family decision-making model is depicted in Figure 19-4.[9] The left side of the model shows separate psychological systems representing the distinct predispositions of the father, mother, and other family members. These separate predispositions lead into *family buying decisions*, which may be either individually or jointly determined.

The right side of the model lists seven factors that influence whether a specific purchase decision will be autonomous or joint: social class, lifestyle, role orientation, family life-cycle stage, perceived risk, product importance, and time pressure. The model suggests that joint decision making tends to prevail in families that are middle class, newly married, and close-knit, with few prescribed family roles. In terms of product-specific factors, it suggests that joint decision making is more prevalent when there is a great deal of perceived risk or uncertainty, when the purchase decision is considered to be important, and when there is ample time to make a decision.

## BETTMAN'S INFORMATION-PROCESSING MODEL OF CONSUMER CHOICE

Bettman's model of consumer choice subscribes to a distinctly cognitive and information-processing point of view.[10] Consistent with this perspective, the consumer is portrayed as possessing a *limited* capacity for processing information. When faced with a choice, the consumer rarely (if ever) undertakes very complex analyses of available alternatives. Instead, as suggested by the model, the consumer typically employs simple decision strategies or heuristics. These simplifying decision rules assist the consumer in arriving at a choice by providing a means for sidestepping the overly burdensome task of assessing all the information available about all the alternatives.

In its complete form, the Bettman model consists of a number of interrelated flowcharts that depict the various dimensions of the consumer choice process. The overview of the Bettman model in Figure 19-5 contains its seven basic components: (1) processing capacity, (2) motivation, (3) attention and perceptual encoding, (4) information acquisition and evaluation, (5) memory, (6) decision processes, and (7) consumption and learning processes.[11] In addition, the model includes, at appropriate points, mechanisms that continually scan the environment and receive and respond to interruptions.

PROCESSING CAPACITY. The processing capacity component of the Bettman model is founded on the notion that individuals have only a limited capacity for processing information. Thus, in making choices, consumers are likely to find complex computations and extensive information processing particularly difficult or burdensome. To deal with these demands, consumers are likely to

**FIGURE 19-4** **Sheth Family Decision-Making Model** Source: Figure 2.1 "A Theory of Family Buying Decisions," (pp. 22–23) from *Models of Buyer Behavior* by Jagdish N. Sheth (Harper & Row, 1974).

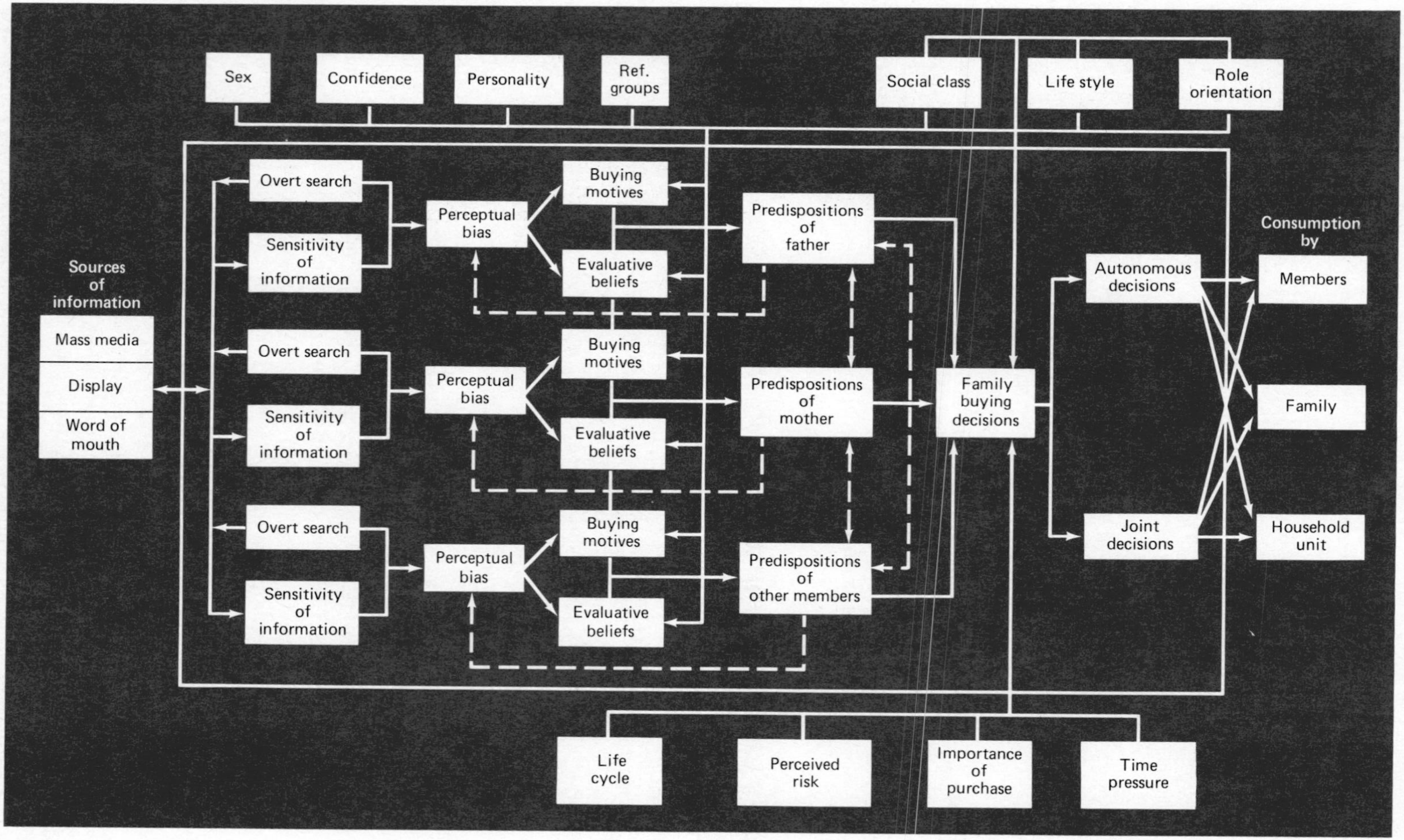

FIGURE 19-5 **The Bettman Information-Processing Model of Consumer Choice** Source: James R. Bettman, *An Information Processing Theory of Consumer Choice* (Reading, Mass.: Addison-Wesley, 1979), 17.

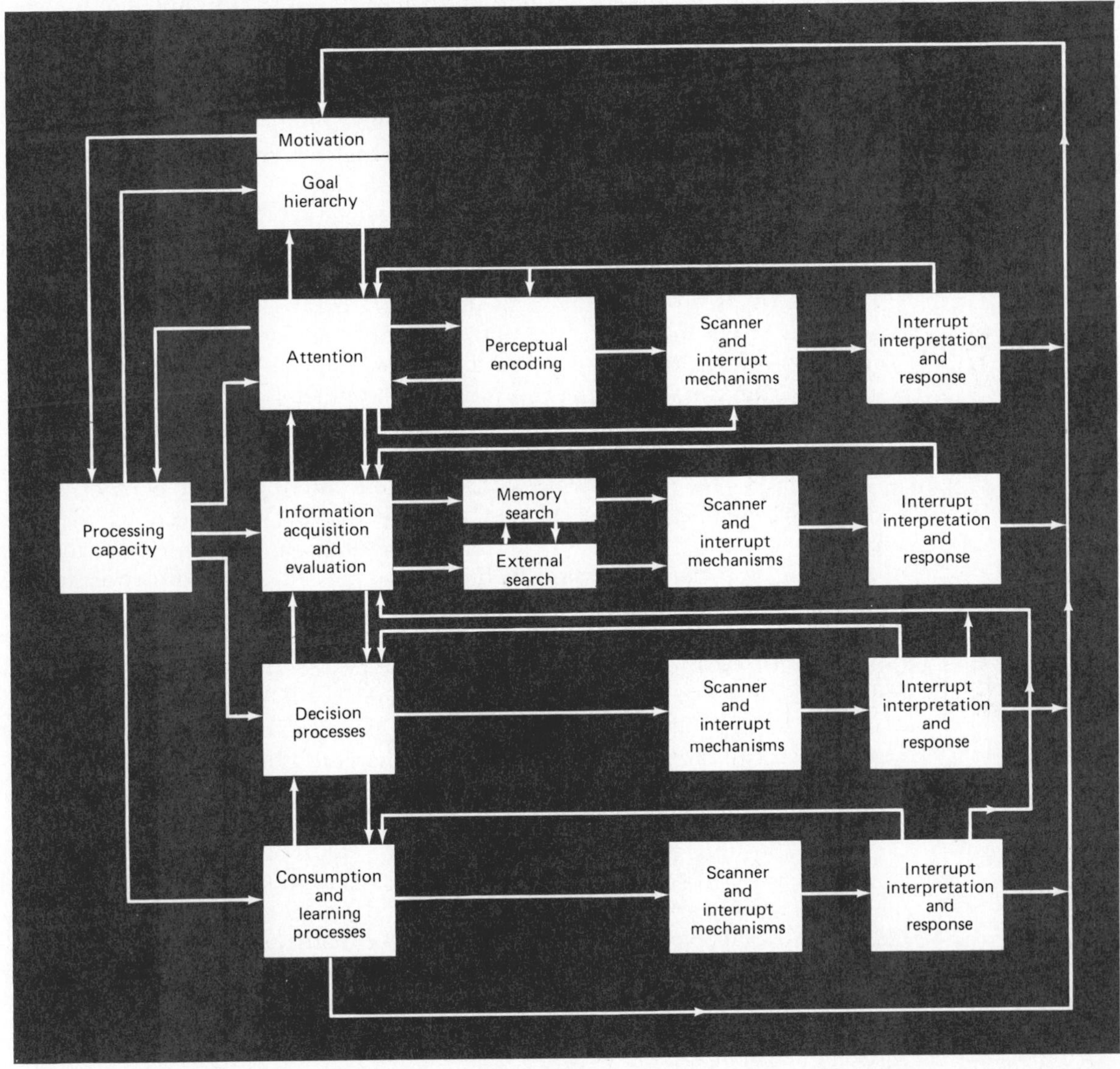


select choice strategies or rules of thumb that make product selection an easier and less taxing process.

As depicted in Figure 19-5, the process capacity component influences the other major components of the model. This has important implications for the kinds and scope of choice strategies consumers are likely to employ in evaluating and choosing among alternatives. More precisely, it affects the allocation of the limited processing capacity and sets the stage for the selection of simple choice rules as an effective way of adjusting to these constraints.

MOTIVATION. Since consumer choice in the Bettman model is conceived as being purposeful (i.e., designed to achieve one or more goals), motivation is a central component. Motivation influences both the direction and the intensity of consumer choice and stimulates the consumer to seek information required to evaluate alternatives and to make a choice (e.g., a purchase).

Motivation provides momentum by means of two basic mechanisms: (1) the *hierarchy of goals* and (2) an *interrupting and scanner mechanism*. The hierarchy-of-goals mechanism is a dynamic force in the form of a series of intermediate subgoals that lead to a desired end state—a choice. This mechanism is consistent with the notion of limited capacity: it suggests that as a consumer gains experience in a particular choice area, he or she will no longer have to employ an elaborate hierarchy of goals to arrive at a decision. Instead, acquired experiences eventually provide the consumer with the basis for employing less-demanding decision rules. Thus the goal-hierarchy mechanism channels the consumer's efforts in making a choice. Because the companion scanner and interrupt mechanisms are linked to all the components of the Bettman model, they will be discussed after we have considered the other components.

ATTENTION AND PERCEPTUAL ENCODING. The attention and perceptual encoding components are closely tied and are heavily influenced by the consumer's goal hierarchy. As conceived in the Bettman model, there are two types of attention: *voluntary attention*, which is a conscious allocation of processing capacity to current goals, and *involuntary attention*, which is more of an automatic response to disruptive events (e.g., conflicting views or newly acquired complex information). Each of these quite different types of attention influences how individuals progress in reaching goals and making choices.

The perceptual encoding element is an extension of the attention component. It accounts for the process by which the consumer organizes and interprets those stimuli that have been attended to, and it may provide insights as to the need for additional information.

INFORMATION ACQUISITION AND EVALUATION. Within the context of the Bettman model, the consumer undertakes external search to the extent that information now available in memory is judged to be inadequate. Acquired information is evaluated and its suitability or usefulness is assessed. The consumer continues to acquire additional information until all relevant information has been secured, or until the consumer perceives any additional effort to be too costly in terms of time or effort.

MEMORY. Memory is the component of the Bettman model through which all information flows. More precisely, memory is where a consumer first begins the search (internal search) for information on which to base a choice. If the internal information is insufficient, then the consumer undertakes external search.

As part of the dynamics of memory, information is stored either in short-term storage (which is limited in capacity and where information is processed) or in long-term storage.

DECISION PROCESSES. The Bettman model stresses that different types of choices are normally made in conjunction with the fulfillment of specific components of the model (e.g., choice of goals and choice of information to be acquired). Thus the choices made during the *decision processes* component are a particular form of choice, rather than *the* choice. Specifically, this component deals with the application of heuristics or rules of thumb in the evaluation of and selection among alternatives (e.g., selecting a specific brand).

This portion of the model emphasizes that the specific heuristics a consumer employs are influenced by both *individual* factors (e.g., personality differences) and *situational* factors (urgency of the decision). Therefore it is unreasonable to assume that a particular decision rule will consistently be employed by the same consumer in different situations, or by different consumers in the same situation.

CONSUMPTION AND LEARNING PROCESSES. The consumption and learning component of the Bettman model is concerned with the future utilization of experience acquired after the purchase choice has been made and the selected alternative has been consumed. Such consumption experiences not only serve the consumer as information to be applied to future choice situations, but also provide the basis for developing or refining heuristics. Thus, as an outgrowth of this component, a consumer's postpurchase and postconsumption evaluations are stored for repeat or related future use.

SCANNER AND INTERRUPT MECHANISMS. Throughout the Bettman model there are scanning and interrupting mechanisms that receive all kinds of messages from the environment. The scanner is continuously open to relevant information from the environment, whereas the interrupt mechanism is a device designed to deal with messages that tend to interfere with the progress of making a particular choice.

Cast in this light, the scanner is receptive to information, whereas the interrupt mechanism deals with messages that are more or less "forced" on the consumer. However, both mechanisms are capable of delaying the achievement of goals associated with a particular choice process and of diverting attention to a completely different area of choice (e.g., a more pressing problem).

Of all the consumer behavior models presented here, only the Howard-Sheth model has been subjected to more than a minimum of systematic testing. To the best of our knowledge at the time of this writing, the Engel-Kollat-Blackwell (Engel-Blackwell-Miniard) model has received only modest small-scale testing, while the Nicosia model, the Sheth family decision-making model, and the Bettman information-processing model have not been tested at all.[12]

Comprehensive models of consumer behavior are likely to receive periodic attention because they serve to tie together what is known about consumers and their choice processes, and because they provide a framework or starting point for more modest consumer research projects.

## summary

Consumer behavior models describe the decision-making or choice processes of consumers. Comprehensive models of consumer behavior include the Nicosia model, the Howard-Sheth model, the Engel-Kollat-Blackwell (Engel-Blackwell-Miniard) model, the Sheth family decision-making model, and the Bettman information-processing model.

As the study of consumer behavior progresses, it is likely that some consumer researchers will find the development and testing of these and other comprehensive models of consumer behavior a useful synthesizing device. Knowledge of how individuals and family units make consumption decisions is important to students of human behavior, to students of marketing behavior, and to the public policy planners who shape the environment in which we all must function.

## discussion questions

1. Describe a recent purchase that you have made in terms of the Nicosia model of consumer decision processes presented in Figure 19-1.
2. Describe the purchase of a new Tina Turner or Lionel Richie record album in terms of the Howard-Sheth model of buyer behavior presented in Figure 19-2.
3. Describe a recent purchase of a Sony portable compact disk player in terms of the Engel-Kollat-Blackwell (Engel-Blackwell-Miniard) model of consumer behavior presented in Figure 19-3.
4. Describe your last purchase of a candy bar or chewing gum in terms of the Engel-Kollat-Blackwell (Engel-Blackwell-Miniard) model of consumer behavior.
5. Describe a recent purchase you have made in terms of the Sheth family decision-making model presented in Figure 19-4.
6. How would you describe to a retailer of Apple personal computers the major implications of the Bettman model assumption that consumers have only a limited capacity for processing information?
7. Taken as a group, describe three strengths and three weaknesses of comprehensive models of consumer decision making.
8. How would you expect marketing executives to react to the comprehensive models of consumer decision making described in this chapter?

## endnotes

1. Several other noteworthy comprehensive models are not reviewed here: Alan R. Andreason, "Attitudes and Customer Behavior: A Decision Model," in Lee Preston, ed., *New Research in Marketing* (Berkeley: Institute of Business and Economic Research, University of California, 1965), 1–16; Flemming Hansen, *Consumer Choice Behavior* (New York: Free Press, 1972); and Frederick E. Webster, Jr., and Yoram Wind, "A General Model for Understanding Organizational Buying Behavior," *Journal of Marketing*, 36 (April 1972), 12–19.
2. Francesco M. Nicosia, *Consumer Decision Processes* (Englewood Cliffs, N.J.: Prentice-Hall, 1966), esp. 156–88.
3. John A. Howard and Jagdish N. Sheth, *The Theory of Buyer Behavior* (New York: Wiley, 1969), esp. 24–49.
4. For example, see John U. Farley, John A. Howard, and L. Winston Ring, *Consumer Behavior: Theory and Applications* (Boston: Allyn & Bacon, 1974); Donald R. Lehmann et al., "Some Empirical Contributions to Buyer Behavior Theory," *Journal of Consumer Research*, 1 (December 1974), 43–55; John A. Howard, *Consumer Behavior: Application of Theory* (New York: McGraw-Hill, 1977); John U. Farley and Donald R. Lehmann, "An Overview of Empirical Applications of Buyer Behavior System Models," in William D. Perreault, Jr., ed., *Advances in Consumer Research* (Atlanta: Association for Consumer Research, 1977), IV, 337–41; and Michel Larsche and John A. Howard, "Nonlinear Relations in a Complex Model of Buyer Behavior," *Journal of Consumer Research*, 6 (March 1980), 377–88.
5. Stanley E. Cohen, "Ads a 'Weak Signal' in Most Buying Decisions: Howard," *Advertising Age*, June 12, 1972, 3 and 78.
6. Ibid., 78.
7. James F. Engel, David T. Kollat, and Roger D. Blackwell, *Consumer Behavior* (New York: Holt, Rinehart & Winston, 1968), 40.
8. James F. Engel, Roger D. Blackwell, and Paul W. Miniard, *Consumer Behavior*, 5th ed. (Hinsdale, Ill.: Dryden Press, 1986), p. 35.
9. Jagdish N. Sheth, "A Theory of Family Buying Decisions," in Jagdish N. Sheth, ed., *Models of Buying Behavior* (New York: Harper & Row, 1974), 17–33.
10. James R. Bettman, *An Information Processing Theory of Consumer Choice* (Reading, Mass.: Addison-Wesley, 1979).
11. For a detailed flowchart, see ibid., 38–39.
12. For a discussion of the problems of testing consumer behavior models, see Gerald Zaltman, Christian R. A. Pinson, and Reinhard Angelman, *Metatheory and Consumer Behavior* (New York: Holt, Rinehart & Winston, 1973); and Shelby D. Hunt, *Marketing Theory* (Columbus, Ohio: Grid, 1976).

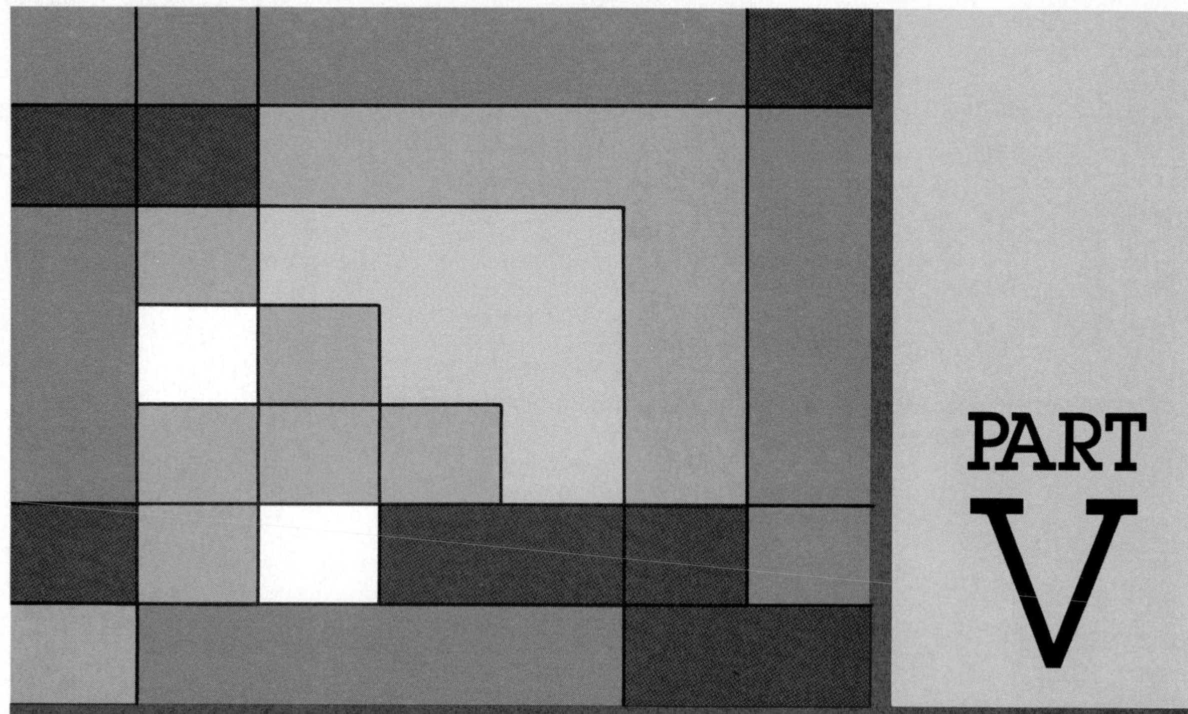

# PART V

# BROADENING THE CONCEPT OF CONSUMER BEHAVIOR

Part V describes the application of consumer behavior research findings to public policy issues. The extension of consumer behavior research techniques to the nonprofit sector has enabled the government and such organizations as hospitals, museums, and political parties to better serve the needs of clients, voters, and the general public.

# 20

# Consumer Behavior Applications for Profit and Not-for-Profit Service Organizations: Public Policy Considerations

## *introduction*

IN addition to the impetus given to the study of consumer behavior by developments in marketing philosophy and practice, the field has grown in response to the extension of marketing concepts to profit and not-for-profit service organizations and public policy needs. This chapter will discuss consumer behavior applications to the marketing of services by profit and not-for-profit organizations, including health care marketing and political marketing. It will examine the role of consumer research in the marketing of social causes, and conclude with a discussion of consumer protection and other public policy considerations.

## MARKETING OF SERVICES

The service sector is rapidly becoming the dominant factor in the United States economy. It presently accounts for 68 percent of the gross national product. About three-quarters of the non-farm labor force is employed in the provision of services, and almost half of every consumer dollar is spent on services.[1] Services are provided by individuals and businesses wishing to earn a profit (e.g., lawyers, car washes, restaurants), by not-for-profit organizations (hospitals, museums, charities), and by governmental agencies (consumer affairs departments, motor vehicle bureaus, post offices). Services are consumed by individuals for their personal use (haircuts, medical examinations, accounting services) and to benefit their assets or possessions (laundry, insurance); services are also

"*Public sentiment is to public officers what water is to the wheel of the mill.*

*HENRY WARD BEECHER*
*Proverbs from Plymouth Pulpit, 1887*"

consumed by organizations (employment agencies, syndicated information services, office cleaning services).

Clearly, services have become a pervasive and significant part of the national economy. The providers of services are faced with similar marketing problems as the producers of physical goods: they must identify and target appropriate market segments with services that fulfill the segment's needs; they must position themselves in relation to the competition; and they must promote their services effectively. While strategic market planning for services is not significantly different than that for manufactured goods, services do have a number of consumer-relevant characteristics that should be given special consideration.[2]

## Service Versus Product Characteristics

Services are *intangible*. Unlike physical goods, services cannot be touched, seen, or smelled. For this reason, services are usually closely associated in the consumer's mind with the company that provides them, whereas products are usually associated with a brand name. For example, consumers may not know which company manufactures Tide detergent, but they immediately link American Airlines and McDonald's to the services these companies provide.

Because services are *simultaneously produced and consumed*, service companies tend to have a production orientation rather than a consumer orientation. They are more likely than manufacturers to introduce new offerings without first determining their acceptability among consumers. For example, automatic price scanning was introduced into supermarkets without prior consideration of consumer reactions. Before consumers would accept them, however, the scanners had to be supplemented with an electronic voice readout or cash register readout.

Services are *less standardized* than products, and because they are usually labor-dependent, their *quality is inconsistent* over time. A hairdresser may differ in the quality of the service he provides the same consumer from one occasion to the next; a restaurant may differ in the quality of food presentation, depending on which chef is on duty at a particular time.

Services are *perishable and cannot be stored*. A service that is available at a particular time but not consumed is lost forever. An unused television commercial slot cannot be stored; its value is lost when the allotted time has passed. Similarly, common carriers (such as railroads) must adhere to their published schedules regardless of how many seats are left unfilled. Once a train leaves the station, the potential revenue from unoccupied seats is lost.

Despite these differences between product and service offerings, the same marketing rationale and marketing principles apply. However, service firms have generally lagged behind manufacturers in adopting a marketing orientation and in developing marketing strategies. Many service companies were started on the basis of a technical product or skill (airplanes, mainframe computers), and their founders focused more on technological improvements than on customer satisfactions. Some service providers were highly regulated by the government (e.g., banks) or governed by associations that prohibited or strongly discouraged advertising (doctors, lawyers). Because of strong competition in every sector of the service economy, many service providers are now recognizing the importance of strategic marketing. The adoption of such strategies is particularly visible in newly deregulated industries (railroads, banking) and in those where professional standards have been eased (law, accounting, medicine). In many cases, marketing is viewed as the key not only to profitability, but in some cases to survival.[3] As in product marketing, consumer research provides the basis for strategic service marketing.

## Consumer Research and New Service Development

The marketing concept is as relevant in the marketing of services as it is in the marketing of physical goods, particularly *because* services are intangible. Not only must the service meet consumer needs, but it must do so better than the competition. Recent innovations in financial services were designed to meet the needs of small investors (cash management accounts, discount brokerage services, zero coupon bonds). Hospitals are taking patient surveys to determine their needs; several New York teaching hospitals established the post of ombudsman to determine patient needs, satisfactions, and dissatisfactions. Physicians are researching both their patients and their competitors, and attending seminars in an effort to learn how to market their practices effectively.[4] In recent years, computerized information services have developed to answer the needs of many businesses for hard-to-find information delivered quickly and efficiently.[5] With the increased competition in the telecommunications field, AT&T developed new long distance services for its business customers to enable them to customize and manage private telephone networks quickly and cost-effectively.[6]

The growth in marketing orientation is also evident among public services and utilities. Houston's public transit system has undertaken major changes to improve its service and image; the California Department of Parks and Recreation has recruited corporate sponsors to promote state parks; and New York's public utilities have embarked on highly competitive advertising campaigns to lure residential customers away from each other.[7]

Consumer research findings have been used in the development of new services and the improvement of existing services. One study showed that price and friendliness of personnel were highly significant in the selection of some services (beauty salons and fast food outlets) and less important in others (banking and auto repair services).[8] A recent study focused on gaps between consumer expectations and management perceptions as the key to improving service quality.[9] The research revealed that, regardless of type of service, consumers use basically similar criteria in evaluating service quality. These criteria fall into 10 key categories, which are called *service quality determinants* and are described in Table 20-1. The table also provides examples of service-specific criteria.

It is important for a company to understand the diversity of consumer demand when it varies its service offerings to appeal to different segments. The Marriott Corporation walked potential customers through prototype hotel

**TABLE 20-1 Determinants of Service Quality**

**reliability** involves consistency of performance and dependability. It means that the firm performs the service right the first time. It also means that the firm honors its promises. Specifically, it involves:

- accuracy in billing;
- keeping records correctly;
- performing the service at the designated time.

**responsiveness** concerns the willingness or readiness of employees to provide service. It involves timeliness of service:

- mailing a transaction slip immediately;
- calling the customer back quickly;
- giving prompt service (e.g., setting up appointments quickly).

**competence** means possession of the required skills and knowledge to perform the service. It involves:

- knowledge and skill of the contact personnel;
- knowledge and skill of operational support personnel;
- research capability of the organization, e.g., securities brokerage firm.

**access** involves approachability and ease of contact. It means:

- the service is easily accessible by telephone (lines are not busy and they don't put you on hold);
- waiting time to receive service (e.g., at a bank) is not extensive;
- convenient hours of operation;
- convenient location of service facility.

**courtesy** involves politeness, respect, consideration, and friendliness of contact personnel (including receptionists, telephone operators, etc.). It includes:

- consideration for the consumer's property (e.g., no muddy shoes on the carpet);
- clean and neat appearance of public contact personnel.

**communication** means keeping customers informed in language they can understand and listening to them. It may mean that the company has to adjust its language for different consumers—increasing the level of sophistication with a well-educated customer and speaking simply and plainly with a novice. It involves:

- explaining the service itself;
- explaining how much the service will cost;
- explaining the trade-offs between service and cost;
- assuring the consumer that a problem will be handled.

**credibility** involves trustworthiness, believability, honesty. It involves having the customer's best interests at heart. Contributing to credibility are:

- company name;
- company reputation;
- personal characteristics of the contact personnel;
- the degree of hard sell involved in interactions with the customer.

**security** is the freedom from danger, risk, or doubt. It involves:

- physical safety (Will I get mugged at the automatic teller machine?);
- financial security (Does the company know where my stock certificate is?);
- confidentiality (Are my dealings with the company private?).

**understanding/knowing the customer** involves making the effort to understand the customer's needs. It involves:

- learning the customer's specific requirements;
- providing individualized attention;
- recognizing the regular customer.

**TABLE 20-1** (continued)

tangibles include the physical evidence of the service:

- physical facilities;
- appearance of personnel;
- tools or equipment used to provide the service;
- physical representations of the service, such as a plastic credit card or a bank statement;
- other customers in the service facility.

Source: A Parasuraman, Valarie A. Zeithaml, and Leonard L. Berry, "A Conceptual Model of Service Quality and Its Implications for Future Research," *Journal of Marketing*, 49 (Fall 1985), 47.

rooms with movable walls to test their reactions to different room widths and lengths. The research helped the company design its new entry into the mid-priced hotel market, the Courtyard.[10] Several other major hotel chains have begun to segment their markets. In 1981 the Quality Inn chain was split into three separate lodging chains: Comfort Inns for the low-budget traveler, Quality Inns at the mid-price level, and Quality Royale for the luxury hotel segment.[11] The Holiday Corporation, owner of Holiday Inns, the nation's largest hotel chain, has recently developed three new lodging chains to appeal to special segments: Embassy Suites for the affluent traveler, Hampton Inns for the budget-conscious traveler, and Residence Inns, a chain of apartment units for the "extended stay" market. Another subsidiary, Harrah's (acquired in 1980), has 3,500 rooms in hotel casinos in Las Vegas, Reno, Lake Tahoe, and Atlantic City, appealing to still another specialized segment.[12]

## The Positioning and Promotion of Services

Compared with manufacturing firms, service marketers face several unique problems in positioning and promoting their offerings. First, because services are *intangible,* it is more difficult to create a service image; perceived risk is likely to be higher, and further increased by the likelihood of variability in service delivery from one occasion to the next. Second, because services are *perishable,* promotion becomes particularly important. Third, because services are *simultaneously produced* and *consumed,* consumers tend to identify the service with the service providers. Therefore, it is critical that the service organization maximize employee understanding and consumer orientation at every stage of the service delivery to ensure customer satisfaction. A company that delivers outstanding service is probably one that markets itself effectively not only to its customers, but also to its employees.[13]

Because services are intangible, *image* becomes a key factor in differentiating the service from its competition. Here, the marketing objective is to enable the consumer to link a specific image with a specific brand name. Merrill Lynch conveyed a prestige image by its slogan "a breed apart"; E. F. Hutton a credibility image with the campaign "When E. F. Hutton speaks, people listen." United Airlines has positioned itself with "the friendly skies," American Airlines tells us they are doing what they do best, and Pan Am tries to differentiate itself from its competition by stressing its greater experience and more direct flights to international destinations.

Many service marketers have developed strategies to provide consumers with visual images and tangible reminders of their service offerings. These include painted delivery vehicles, restaurant matches, packaged hotel soaps and shampoos, and a variety of other specialty items.[14] Some financial companies try to associate their services with tangible objects. Prudential Insurance Company invites consumers to "get a piece of the rock"; Travelers Insurance Company advises consumers to get "under the Travelers umbrella" (see Figure 20-1); and Equitable offers the "key to financial opportunity."[15]

Because services are variable, companies are in a position to offer several versions to different market segments. However, they must be careful to avoid perceptual confusion among their customers. The American Express Company offers its regular card to consumers as a short-term credit instrument, but has also introduced its more prestigious gold and platinum cards, each with increased services available to the cardholder. Similarly, private banks that target affluent consumers focus on estate planning, investments, and trust funds to maintain an exclusive image; commercial banks offer cash machines and overdraft privileges to consumers with more modest financial means.[16]

The recent increase in sales promotion activities by packaged goods marketers has been matched to some extent by the service sector. Some credit card companies offer free one-month trials to consumers interested in credit card protection programs, banks offer a variety of premiums and gifts for initial deposits, and radio stations offer instant cash prizes to callers during broadcasts. One bank went to great lengths to boost the consumer usage rate of its automatic teller machines by randomly dispensing a cash giveaway to consumers using the machine.[17] The use of promotion as well as highly competitive pricing is evident in the deregulated airline industry. Airlines are offering long-term air passes and Frequent Flyer programs which offer discounts and free tickets for various levels of accumulated mileage (see Figure 20-2). Some airlines have offered significant discounts to lure back passengers lost during employee strikes. Sea Goddess Cruises, Ltd., a cruise company which has positioned itself as the ultimate in luxury cruising, sends tickets and boarding passes to passengers in a leather passport case enclosed in a red velvet box, holds reunion cocktail parties for passengers at elegant country clubs around the country, and sends them chatty newsletters implying membership in its small, exclusive Sea Goddess "Yacht Club."

## Importance of the Service Environment

The design of the *service environment* is an important aspect of service marketing strategy and sharply influences consumer impressions and behavior. The physical environment is particularly important in creating a favorable impression for such services as banks, retail stores, and professional offices, because consumers do not usually have objective criteria by which to judge the quality of the services they receive.[18] The service environment conveys the image of the service

FIGURE 20-1 A Tangible Object Is Used to Symbolize a Service

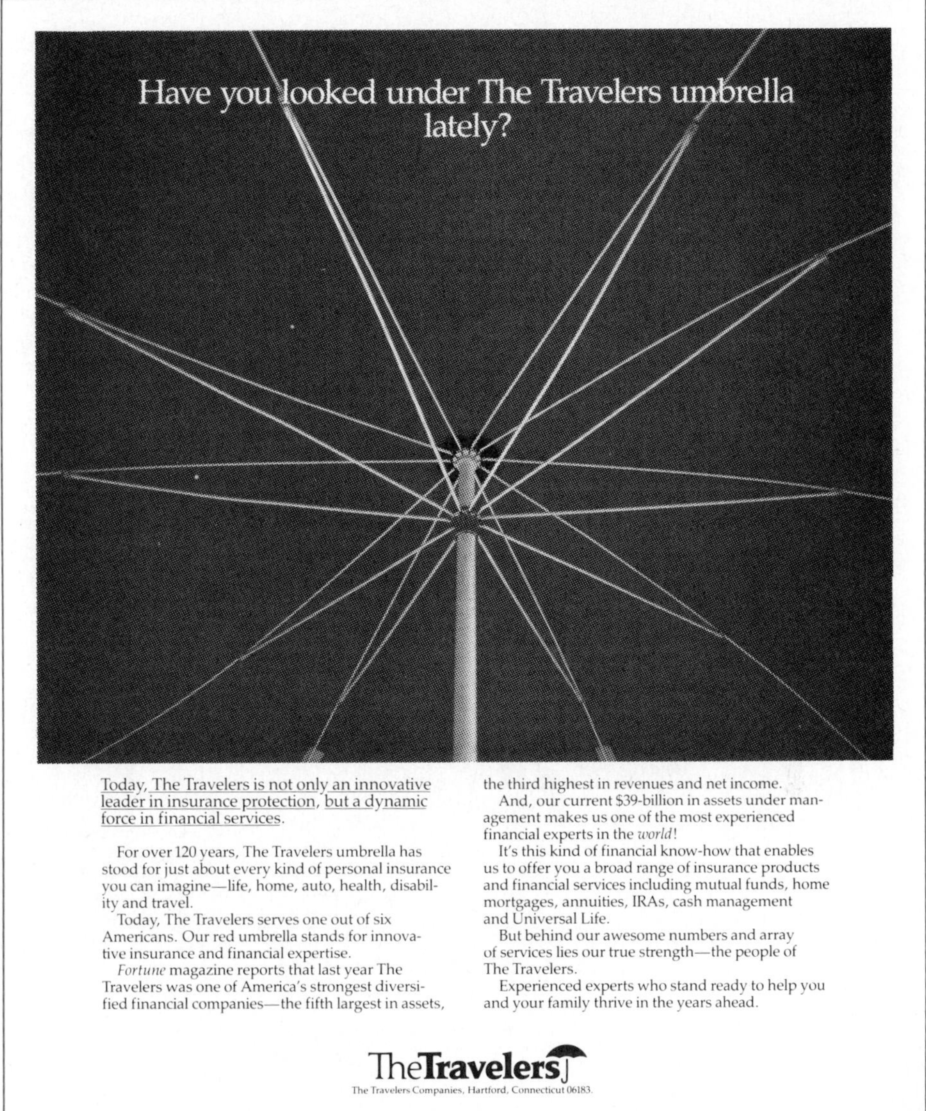
Have you looked under The Travelers umbrella lately?
Today, The Travelers is not only an innovative leader in insurance protection, but a dynamic force in financial services.
For over 120 years, The Travelers umbrella has stood for just about every kind of personal insurance you can imagine—life, home, auto, health, disability and travel.
Today, The Travelers serves one out of six Americans. Our red umbrella stands for innovative insurance and financial expertise.
Fortune magazine reports that last year The Travelers was one of America's strongest diversified financial companies—the fifth largest in assets, the third highest in revenues and net income.
And, our current $39-billion in assets under management makes us one of the most experienced financial experts in the world!
It's this kind of financial know-how that enables us to offer you a broad range of insurance products and financial services including mutual funds, home mortgages, annuities, IRAs, cash management and Universal Life.
But behind our awesome numbers and array of services lies our true strength—the people of The Travelers.
Experienced experts who stand ready to help you and your family thrive in the years ahead.
TheTravelers
The Travelers Companies, Hartford, Connecticut 06183.

Courtesy of the Travelers Companies

provider with whom the service is so closely linked. Thus, at Morgan Guaranty, expensive mahogany desks, leather chairs, and silk draperies project stability, solidity, wealth, and power. The New York Public Library stresses the environment it offers well-known writers and others who use its services (see Figure 20-3).

The new Polo/Ralph Lauren store in the renovated 1895 Rhinelander mansion in New York is the embodiment of the image Lauren tries to create for his clothes: traditionalism and Old World values. All the trappings of what

FIGURE 20-2 Airline Companies Use Sales Promotion to Sell Services

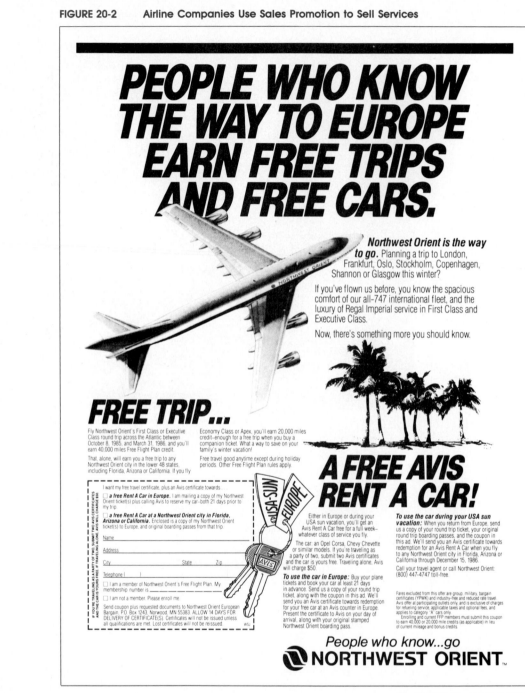


Courtesy of Northwest Orient Airlines

**FIGURE 20-3** **The Service Environment Is a Key Factor in Service Marketing**

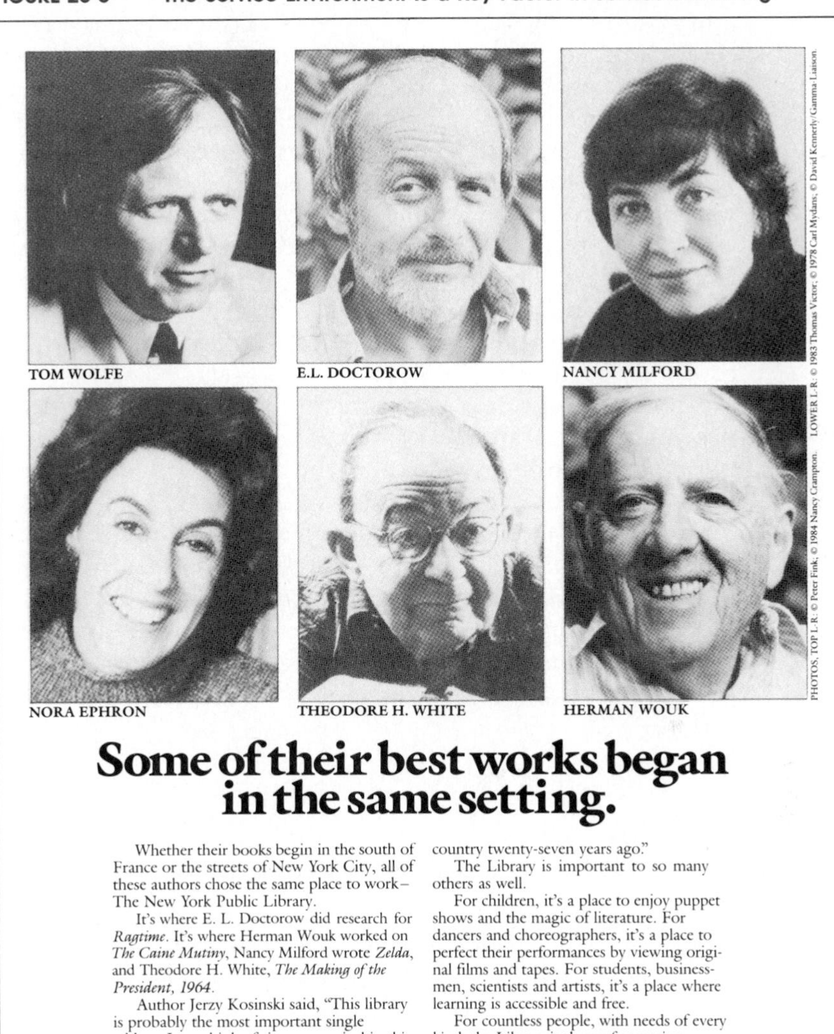


Courtesy of Jameson Advertising Inc. and The New York Public Library

one imagines to be the high-class and well-heeled ways of the very, very rich are here—from the baronial hand-carved staircase lined with family portraits to the plush sitting rooms focused on working fireplaces. Lauren said of the store: "It's not about clothes, but about elegance and classicism. The idea was to bring back an Old World quality of living and shopping that doesn't exist today."[19]

The service environment can be used to reposition a service. When Skipper's seafood chain changed from fast-food outlets to family-oriented restaurants, the physical environment was completely altered; interior partitions, more comfortable seats, natural wood textures, photographs, plants and subtle colors were added to communicate the new image. The environment can also be used to establish and reinforce an image. For example, at Speedi-Lube, a car oil change and lubricating service in the West, the environment projects an image of speed, efficiency, and competence. While their cars are serviced by workers wearing clean, neat uniforms, customers are served coffee in a clean waiting room, where graphic displays of the lubrication process hang on the walls. Work is completed within 10 minutes and, as a final touch, the car's door locks are oiled. The customer receives a brochure at the end of the visit, and a mail reminder three months later, both reinforcing the experience.[20] All these strategic uses of the physical environment are based on an understanding of consumer behavior.

Service providers have long recognized that the face-to-face contact between customers and service employees blurs the "boundaries" between employee and customer. A recent study showed that customer perceptions, attitudes, and future consumption intentions were significantly related to the employees' experiences and perception of the organization.[21] A dissatisfied employee results in a dissatisfied customer; a satisfied employee is most likely to result in a satisfied customer. Thus, one key to achieving customer satisfaction might be to achieve employee satisfaction. In order to achieve satisfied consumers, service companies would be wise to listen to their employees, motivate them, and convey to them the importance of a *service ethic* and consumer orientation.

## NONPROFIT MARKETING

Consumer behavior research is very effectively used in the marketing of not-for-profit services. The notion that nonprofit organizations, like commercial organizations, have clients with varying needs that require differentiated marketing efforts is still relatively new. Nevertheless, in the decade or so since the idea was introduced, all sorts of organizations—from political parties and government bodies to colleges, welfare agencies, hospitals, and museums—have adopted a consumer behavior approach. The State of New Jersey has used Governor Tom Kean and comedian Bill Cosby to advertise "New Jersey and You—Perfect Together." The State of Maine used advertising to dispel perceptions that it is too cold or too distant for a vacation.[22] The "I love New York" campaign that has been running for years is targeted at both tourists and New Yorkers. Advertising by states to lure vacationers has been particularly active in recent years to combat the trend to international travel. Such advertising is expected to increase as states vie for the consumer's vacation dollars.

Most colleges and universities are responding to the decline in enrollments with marketing plans and sophisticated promotional programs. Carnegie-Mellon University adopted a strategic plan focused on the needs of the school's customers—its students.[23] Its new consumer orientation resulted in a

15 percent growth in its applicant pool despite the national decline in the number of college applicants.

The marketing of nonprofit organizations is complicated by several factors.[24] Nonprofit organizations usually pursue several important objectives simultaneously, and it is difficult to formulate strategies that will satisfy all the objectives. For example, nonprofit organizations typically have two major publics: their supporters—from whom they must *attract* resources—and their clients, to whom they must *allocate* resources. These two publics require different marketing strategies. Furthermore, nonprofit organizations are usually under close public scrutiny because they provide public services that are often subsidized and tax-exempt. Excessive advertising expenditures are likely to arouse public criticism.

In the future, consumer behavior studies are expected to play a much stronger role in the design of marketing programs for the nonprofit sector. Nonprofit organizations chronically face financial difficulties, and cutbacks in government support will make the need to develop additional funding sources more pressing than ever. Several nonprofit organizations that no longer can depend on public funds to survive have turned to their own resources. A major portion of the expenses of the Children's Television Workshop were covered by licensing and other commercial ventures tied to *Sesame Street*'s popular cast of characters. Similarly, the Red Cross started selling first-aid kits.[25] It is likely that the managers of nonprofit organizations will recognize the necessity to focus more on the needs and wants of their publics (i.e., to adopt the marketing concept) than on the products or services they offer (their traditional product orientation).[26] A Pittsburgh hospital opened a downtown clothing store specializing in chic maternity clothes for expectant executives. The store is the only hospital-owned franchise of Mothers Work, a chain of upscale women's stores.

In the "salad" days of strong government support, many administrators of nonprofit organizations held themselves aloof from all notions of marketing, and consequently learned neither the jargon nor the concepts implicit in marketing strategy (such as segmentation, target marketing, marketing planning and control). To help such administrators make the transition necessary to even consider the adoption of a marketing orientation, several researchers have developed a self-study tool for organizations to facilitate their communications with marketing professionals. The 20-item questionnaire, entitled "Nonprofit Marketing Analysis for Organizational Self Study," is presented in Figure 20-4.[27]

Examples of consumer behavior research in the nonprofit sector can be found in the marketing of **social causes, health services,** and **political ideas.**

## Social Responsibility and the Marketing of Social Causes

In recent years, some have proposed that the marketing concept may not be appropriate in an era of environmental deterioration, resource shortages, and explosive population growth. They have suggested that the marketing concept should be restated so that the company's satisfaction of the needs and wants of its target markets be accomplished in ways that preserve and enhance the well-

**FIGURE 20-4** **Nonprofit Marketing Analysis for Organizational Self Study** Source: Doris C. Van Doren and Louise W. Smith, "Self-Analysis Can Gauge Marketing Orientation," *Marketing News*, December 5, 1985,14

# Nonprofit marketing analysis for organizational self-study

Rank the organization from 5 (high) to 1 (low).

## Orientation

The organization:

1. Is aware of client needs, problems, and opportunities. ______
2. Is aware of contributor needs, problems, and opportunities. ______
3. Uses rational and emotional appeals to present benefits to clients and contributors. ______
4. Has product/service knowledge so facts can be used to support promised benefits. ______
5. Knows its competition for clients and contributors. ______
6. Has developed a unique approach or distinguishing benefit compared to the competition. ______
7. Targets or directs marketing efforts to a defined group of clients or contributors. ______

## Research

The organization:

8. Plans and conducts research to learn about clients' and contributors' needs, problems, and opportunities. ______
9. Analyzes and uses research to adjust offerings to clients and contributors—their needs, problems, and opportunities. ______
10. Has designated individual(s) responsible for on-going research. ______

## Marketing Planning

The organization:

11. Concentrates on long-term planning vs. detailed how-to lists. ______
12. Develops a three-year marketing plan for the organization. ______
13. Has several strategies for marketing products/services to each target market of clients and contributors. ______
14. Includes product/service, price, place, and promotion in planning its marketing efforts. ______
15. Fully markets, rather than simply promotes, its products. ______
16. Has designated individual(s) responsible for implementing major marketing strategies. ______
17. Has fixed a time line for major marketing strategies. ______

## Marketing Control

The organization:

18. Uses evaluation measures to assess implementation of the plan. ______
19. Uses the feedback to redirect the orientation, research, and marketing planning of the group. ______
20. Has a person designated as the head marketer. ______

---

THE SELF-STUDY is divided into four sections designed to gauge the organization's orientation, research, marketing planning, and marketing control. A five-point rating system is used.

The first seven questions deal with orientation, and a low score here indicates the organization is unclear about the markets (client or contributor) it's trying to reach and the benefits it offers those markets. If so, a review of the products and services offered may be in order to assess why they are important.

**FIGURE 20-4 (Continued)**

The administrator and a business-oriented board member should be able to answer what is special about the group's products/services and who needs them. If another agency provides similar services, there should be a unique and distinguishing aspect to the group's approach to serving its client or contributor market.

Low scores on the three research questions indicate a seat-of-the-pants approach. All parties—the marketing professional, nonprofit administrator, and businessperson/board member—should be able to answer the question. "What are our information needs and what resources can assist in obtaining this information?"

Low scores on the seven marketing planning questions indicate a project-by-project approach. The business professional can help the staff develop a three-year strategy to set the organization's goals and ways to achieve them.

Low scores on questions 18 and 19 suggest a lack of control or feedback systems on marketing plan effectiveness. The staff needs to focus on areas such as slippage and large expenditures in order to develop definitions and measures of success. The question posed to the organization is, "Does our marketing planning expend its human and financial resources wisely?"

A low score on the final question gets to the heart of the problem: no one is responsible for marketing. Any organization, whether it's profit or nonprofit, suffers without a marketer. Someone with the appropriate attitude and skills needs to be hired to direct the organization's efforts to satisfy the needs, solve the problems, and respond to opportunities of the markets, both client and contributor.

A SCORE OF 80-100 on the self-study indicates an organization which is very "marketing smart." A score of 60-79 suggests a good organization, while a score of 40-59 indicates a weak organization. Any lower score calls into question the organization's ability to survive.

being of consumers and society as a whole. This revised concept was termed the **societal marketing concept.**[28]

The societal marketing concept can be implemented in two ways: first, by marketers adhering to principles of **social responsibility** in the marketing of their goods and services; and second, by the use of marketing concepts and techniques to win adoption of **socially beneficial causes.** Let us first consider the notion of social responsibility. Under the *societal marketing concept,* marketers should not sell cigarettes or drugs, or any other harmful substance, despite the fact that such products satisfy the needs of certain target segments, because these products are harmful to the consumer and ultimately to society as a whole.

Under the societal marketing concept, fast food restaurants would not sell hamburgers or fries or pies that are high in fat and starch and low in nutrients, despite apparent consumer acceptance (need) for these products. Similarly, marketers would not sell detergents which, though they answer consumer needs to make clothes whiter or brighter, at the same time pollute rivers and streams. Nor would marketers advertise alcoholic beverages to young people, or use young people in liquor commercials. Studies show that young people who have seen more television and magazine ads for beer, wine, and liquor generally drink more than those who have not.[29] Furthermore, they tend to be more favorably inclined toward alcoholic products that feature other young people in their promotion.[30]

Recognizing this issue, the Reagan administration, generally opposed to the regulation of business, required beer and wine advertisers to revise their marketing practices.[31] Specifically, they were required to drop athlete spokespersons (who serve as youth emulation models) from their advertising, eliminate on-campus promotions, and drop the "responsible use" notion that under-age kids are going to drink anyway. Some television networks have demonstrated social responsibility by refusing to broadcast various commercials that they deemed to be offensive. Interestingly enough, this included an antismoking public service message from the American Cancer Society which both NBC and CBS rejected as too graphic and offensive. The commercial showed a fetus smoking a cigarette to warn pregnant women of the dangers of smoking.[32] The networks have also rejected an ad which points out that standard-sized drinks of beer, wine, and liquor all have the same alcohol content, on the basis that they do not accept advertising for distilled spirits (see Figure 20-5).

In many cases, marketing concepts and techniques are used to advance *social causes*. The purpose may be merely to change attitudes among a given target market or, more ambitiously, to alter behavior. There are numerous examples of marketers advancing social causes. For example, TV stations today allocate considerable time for public service messages. Even though the Federal Communications Commission relaxed its regulation of TV stations, the time allotted to these messages has not declined.[33] Various American utilities agreed to include photos of missing children as inserts with their monthly bills, and pictures of missing youngsters are now printed on milk cartons and grocery bags as well.

Many marketers have volunteered their services to promote social causes. An advertising agency created and managed a multimedia campaign to combat illiteracy, a film company created TV spots to battle sexual abuse of children, and the American Marketing Association donated its marketing expertise to the Illinois Department of Alcoholism and Substance Abuse. Similarly, several personal managers of Hollywood stars donated their services to keep the *USA for Africa* campaign alive after the decline of the "We Are the World" hit song.[34]

Some assert that it might be difficult to apply marketing principles to social causes because marketing is generally designed to sell a solution to a need, while the objective of social marketing is to educate and to change attitudes.[35] However, marketers agree that consumer research holds the key to effective marketing of social causes.[36] Several studies have examined the effectiveness of advertising campaigns designed to promote socially desirable behavior. For example, consumer behavior studies have been conducted to determine the kinds of messages that are most effective in conveying the dangers of drug taking, and advertising research has been conducted to assess the effects of specific ads on changing attitudes about drugs.[37]

One study of high-school students tested the effects of three variations of a commercial: (1) the threat of serious versus minimal harm (death versus parental disapproval); (2) the drawing of an explicit conclusion versus no summary statement at the end; and (3) the presentation of the message in a monologue versus a dialogue format. The study concluded somewhat surprisingly that the threat of serious harm was no more effective than that of lesser harm, and that a dialogue format had no more effect than a monologue format. It did find, however, that explicit conclusions must be drawn in order for the ads

FIGURE 20-5 Rejected Commercial Designed to Correct Consumer Misperceptions of Comparative Alcoholic Beverages

# IT'S TIME AMERICA KNEW THE FACTS ABOUT DRINKING.

12 oz. of beer, 5 oz. of wine and 1¼ oz. of liquor all have the same alcohol content.

## It's time ABC, CBS and NBC let the facts be heard.

We submitted TV commercials to the networks which simply stated the facts of alcohol equivalency, and they have refused to put them on the air. Network policy bars advertising for distilled spirits. But these announcements are not commercials for products...ours or anyone else's. The message here is the fact of equivalence. A fact people have a right to know. A fact we want to tell.

**It's Time All Of Us Were Heard.**

We share the concern of other public spirited groups who believe that the popular misconceptions about beverage alcohol can be dangerous. The National Institute on Alcohol Abuse and Alcoholism urges every American to know the facts of equivalency.

The American Automobile Association incorporates the facts of equivalence in its driver safety and alcohol education programs.

The Motor Vehicle Departments of California and New Jersey explain the facts of equivalence in their drivers' manuals. And the Insurance Information Institute and Citizens for Highway Safety, to name others, are also publicizing the facts.

This message is *that* important.

The facts are, there is the same amount of alcohol in a 12 ounce can of beer, a 5 ounce glass of wine, and a 1¼ ounce serving of 80 proof whiskey, vodka, gin or rum. To be exact, the typical serving of beer contains 0.54 ounces of alcohol. The typical serving of wine contains 0.55 ounces of alcohol. The typical serving of spirits contains 0.50 ounces of alcohol.

**THE HOUSE OF SEAGRAM**

© 1985, THE HOUSE OF SEAGRAM, N.Y.

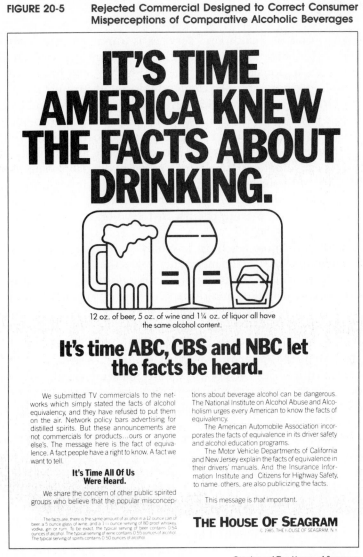

Courtesy of The House of Seagram

to have any influence. Another unexpected finding was that although the initial effect of the ads was to engender negative attitudes toward drugs, repeated exposure to the commercials usually weakened rather than strengthened such attitudes. Thus some drug abuse information programs may unintentionally defeat their own purpose by overkill—a finding that only careful research was able to uncover.

## Health Care Marketing

The provision of health care services is a major component of the nonprofit sector, with expenditures for health care amounting to a significant percentage of the gross national product. The health care field has become more competitive as supply has exceeded demand. Hospitals around the country are experiencing more empty beds than ever before, as government cost-cutting rules produce a sharp decline in hospitalization. Many hospitals have abandoned tradition and adopted marketing strategies to compete for fewer and fewer patients. Some hospitals offer free blood-pressure and cholesteral tests, others offer prospective patients free trips to Hawaii or cash rebates. One hospital hired the former director of the "I Love New York" campaign to market the hospital. Another hospital reported that when it advertised its alcohol and drug treatment services for private clients on television, it doubled the number of patients.[38]

Although most teaching hospitals emphasize sophisticated specialty care, many now find that maternity patients are the most profitable, and there is aggressive competition to attract them. One hospital, for example, is offering free T-shirts, baby blankets, and dinners of shrimp cocktail and filet mignon to parents who have their babies delivered there. The new vice president for marketing of a major hospital was quoted as saying: "Big hospitals don't talk about open hearts or transplants, it's market shares and babies."[39] St. Vincent's Hospital and Medical Center in New York is using institutional advertising to attract patients. In a series of newspaper advertisements, the hospital tells of cancer patients at St. Vincent's whose medical conditions improved against all hope, and of tiny, premature babies who were saved by medical technology and large doses of loving care (see Figure 20-6).

Hospitals and other health care providers are rapidly becoming oriented toward strategic planning and marketing. The New Jersey Hospital Association is devising new advertising and marketing strategies for its member hospitals in an effort to change the minds of some 10,000 New Jersey patients who go to New York City or Philadelphia every year for hospital care. In this competitive environment, health care providers are becoming more sophisticated in their use of consumer research. They are more responsive to the markets they serve and more concerned with the consistency of quality in the services they deliver. They are segmenting their markets, targeting, and advertising to attract more patients. They are using marketing research to identify opportunities and to test the effectiveness of their advertisements.[40]

### HEALTH CARE SEGMENTATION, TARGETING, AND PRODUCT PLANNING

Some health care providers target their services to older individuals because this group, on average, is responsible for more patient days than younger people. One hospital developed a health education radio program targeted at this segment.[41] Another hospital reaches this segment by targeting those who play a key role in the health care provided to older people: their families, and corporations that provide medical benefits to older workers and their spouses.[42]

**FIGURE 20-6** **Institutional Advertising by a Hospital**

# Jennifer Fernandez

Jennifer Fernandez was so tiny a nurse could hold her in the palm of one hand. Being twelve weeks premature and weighing less than a pound and a half, Jenny looked more like a miniature old woman than a baby. Her skin was wrinkled and transparent. Beneath matchstick ribs her tiny heart beat rapidly.

For a baby born as prematurely as Jenny, the complications are many. And without special care, her chances for survival were slim.

Just staying alive was a lot of hard work. Enclosed in the warm envelope of the incubator, her tiny body was obscured by tubes and tape. Sensors attached to her little belly monitored her heart rate and temperature. A tube fed her intravenously through her tiny hand. Through portholes in the side of her incubator, nurses could check the placement of a tube or change a diaper.

But none of these machines, nor any of the doctors or nurses, could make Jenny well. They could only help to keep her alive. The rest was up to her.

She seemed to want to live. Certainly every hour she was alive she defied the odds. "Our Jenny," said one of the nurses, "she's a fighter."

Maybe it was the attentive doctors. Or the nurses who talked to her and stroked her back. Or perhaps it was her mother's vigil that gave her a reason to live.

Whatever it was, fourteen weeks after she was admitted to St. Vincent's Neonatal Intensive Care Unit, Jennifer Fernandez went home a healthy five pounds, two ounces. And during those weeks, she taught all who knew her a powerful lesson about life and death—without ever uttering a single word.

*The art of medicine, the love of humanity.*

© 1986 St. Vincent's Hospital and Medical Center of New York City

Courtesy of St. Vincent's Hospital and Medical Center of New York



Another hospital uses demographic and lifestyle segmentation to target women, with different advertising appeals for stay-at-home housewives, just-a-job working women, and career-oriented working women.[43]

Many hospitals are targeting referral professionals as an important source for patients. One hospital identified all the referral professionals in its area (physicians, dentists, chiropractors, podiatrists and optometrists), studied their needs and preferences, and established contact and a follow-up system. As a result, the hospital significantly increased the number of patients referred to it by these doctors.[44] Increasingly, health care providers are using marketing research to identify the needs of their patients and then, in true marketing concept tradition, they translate these needs into delivery benefits. One hospital identified women aged 18 to 40 as a key target market, and redesigned its "product line" to fit the expressed needs of these consumers: personalized care, availability of high technology backup, and a fixed price for obstetric services.[45]

Today, health care providers also recognize that providing the service is not the end of the marketing process. More and more institutions in the field monitor the perceptions of their patients regarding the quality and delivery of services and their overall satisfaction; they use this feedback to improve the quality of the services they provide.[46]

## HEALTH CARE POSITIONING AND PROMOTION

Some health care providers use positioning as a strategic tool to distinguish their organizations from competitors and to provide a framework for communications with their publics.[47] Other hospitals have updated their visual symbols to reflect the image they want to convey.[48] Figure 20-7 presents a series of logo changes adopted by several hospitals to improve their perceived identity.

Health care providers use a variety of promotional approaches. ARA centers, a large nursing home chain, developed a highly effective advertising campaign targeted at the offspring of elderly individuals. Various versions of a print ad based on the theme "Is this someone you know?" were produced as part of a total advertising campaign. The strategy also included radio spots, the establishment of an 800 number for customer information, and the offer of a free book entitled *When Love Gets Tough* written by a Baptist minister, discussing the emotional issues of nursing center placement.[49]

One hospital used a new building as the focus of a promotional campaign.[50] On the basis of marketing research, two objectives were developed for the campaign: (1) to generate enthusiasm about the new building and create positive word-of-mouth; and (2) to establish the image of the new building as a more attractive facility than a competing hospital in the area. Promotional events were held for various groups, including physicians, physicians' office staffs, emergency service providers, older adults, the general public, and the hospital's employees and volunteer workers. The events were consistent with the lifestyles and habits of each group, and generated tremendous publicity and word-of-mouth for the hospital. Another hospital significantly boosted the number of patients using the facility by targeting two highly different segments with separate advertising campaigns: one featured sports medicine and was targeted at coaches, parents and amateur athletes; the other featured geriatric medicine, targeted at older individuals with need for a Medicare assignment program.[51]

One factor that is likely to have a significant influence on the marketing of health care services is the growth of hospital chains. These "supermeds" are expected to reshape the health care market and make it difficult for unaffilia-

**FIGURE 20-7** **Hospitals Change Their Logos to Create an Identity** Source: Elinor Selame, "The Symptoms, Cures and Relief of Health Care's Identity Crisis" in A. Terry Paul, ed., *Building Marketing Effectiveness in Health Care*, Proceedings Series (Chicago: Academy for Health Services Marketing, American Marketing Association, 1985).

**Identity Problem:** A name change associated with a substantial corporate gift necessitated the creation of a new signature and symbol. It also provided the opportunity to update and reorganize all the organization's visual communications materials.

**Selame Solution:** The initials "D" and "F" in a "Flame of Hope" format project the professional and progressive nature of this internationally renowned organization. A corporate design system for implementing the new identity has resulted in consistent, planned usage and an organization for substantial ongoing cost savings.

UNION H+SPITAL

**Identity Problem:** Two Massachusetts hospitals, Lynn and Union, merged and planned to expand into other healthcare fields. The new organizations sought a corporate name and visual identity that would help communicate their new stature as well as their continued commitment to professionalism and personal care.

**Selame Solution:** The contemporary Atlanticare name is used for the parent organization and for new ventures. An "umbrella" symbol visually unites all divisions while allowing the hospitals to retain the familiarity of their traditional names.

McLEAN
HOSPITAL

**Identity Problem:** McLean Hospital is one of the country's most respected mental care facilities. But its visual identity did not reflect its preeminence in the field. McLean wanted an upgraded look that would help attract the most qualified personnel as well as appear warm and welcoming to patients and their families.

**Selame Solution:** A modern yet warm and friendly symbol—the "M" and "C" representing the sun shining through the trees—was suggested by McLean's park-like suburban setting.

Healthcare
Corporation

**Identity Problem:** The company wanted to facilitate better consumer relations, increase investor interest and attract high-quality employees in an increasingly competitive field.

**Selame Solution:** A new corporate identity design system provides visual cohesiveness and a modern appearance. With the company now identified by a more memorable, shortened name, an "umbrella" symbol and a specific typestyle for all divisions, the overall advertising and public relations budget becomes far more effective.

INTERCOMMUNITY
FOUNDATION, INC.

FOXBORO AREA
HEALTH CENTER

Neponset Valley
Health System

Norwood Hospital

Foxboro Area
Health Center

Southwood
Community Hospital

Neponset Valley
Health System

**Identity Problem:** The newly named company had become a multi-institutional system for the efficient delivery of health services. However, because of growth, its visual methods of communication to its various publics were neither efficient nor economical.

**Selame Solution:** A comprehensive design system was developed that could serve as an umbrella. The parent corporation's initials, NVHS, over a graphic "valley," serve as the overall identifying mark.

**Selame Design**
2330 Washington Street
Newton Lower Falls
Massachusetts 02162
617 969-3150

Corporate, Retail and Product Identity

Courtesy of ARA Living Centers

ted hospitals to survive. Humana, Inc., a Louisville-based hospital chain, has attracted enormous publicity through artificial heart transplants performed in its facilities, and has received high praise from the industry for its innovative marketing efforts.[52] Humana is one of the major TV advertisers in the health care field.

It is clear that marketing is becoming an increasingly important tool for health care providers. Many have already discovered the benefits of segmentation, targeting, and positioning. They recognize the differential use of promotional campaigns to reach different market segments. And some sophisticated health care administrators use consumer research findings to help fill beds in a time of sharp competition due to severe cutbacks in government support.

## Political Marketing

Today political parties and political candidates recognize the need for strategic marketing planning based on careful consumer (voter) research. Campaign marketing consultants use voter research for segmentation studies, target voters who have specific interests and needs, position their candidates as the means to fulfill these needs, and promote candidates through the same media that carry packaged goods ads. Political organizations have become as sophisticated as the major catalog houses in the use of direct mail. In 1984, political candidates spent about $180 million on television, $90 million on radio advertising, $40 million on newspaper advertising, and bombarded American homes with several hundred million pieces of direct mail.[53]

In preparation for the 1988 presidential election, Democratic and Republican campaign consultants conducted demographic and psychographic research to help their candidates go after the single biggest bloc of voters in American history—the baby boomers. These 76 million men and women, born between 1946 and 1964, account for some 60 percent of the 1988 electorate. This group is particularly attractive to politicians because of their lack of allegiance to either party. As Chapter 10 points out, the only campaign efforts that are truly worthwhile are those directed to uncommitted voters. Loyal voters of either side are rarely swayed by campaign rhetoric or campaign literature.

As Chapter 15 points out, the term *baby boomer* refers to age alone. The baby boomer segment can be broadly divided by income into two popularized subgroups: the affluent *yuppies,* and the *new collars*—a numerous and therefore significant subgroup consisting of fast food managers, truck drivers, mechanics, and so forth. To better understand this population, political researchers conduct polls and surveys, attend concerts, study television commercials and the lyrics to rock music, and consult academic researchers. They have found that members of the baby boom generation—shaped by the assassination of President Kennedy, the civil rights and antiwar movements, and Watergate—are often anti-Establishment and frequently disdain traditional politicians. They are concerned with the environment, health care, child care, tax code revision, and civil rights. Political experts have called them economically conservative and socially liberal. As the 1984 election results suggest, whichever candidate captures their vote—assuming that it is not split—can win by a landslide. This group is targeted between presidential elections, with subtle direct mail pieces discussing the problems of new families and mortgages, rather than party loyalty.[54]

## IMAGERY IN POLITICS

Politicians are beginning to recognize the importance of imagery in positioning their candidates. The differential use of imagery was most evident in the 1984 presidential contest. Ronald Reagan's television messages showed sunsets, parades of flags, high school bands, picturesque landscapes, and pretty girls; Walter Mondale's commercials painted images of nuclear destruction, starvation and poverty. Reagan's theme was nostalgia, patriotism, and the opportunities America offers its young citizens; Mondale talked of raising taxes at home. Reagan, a former actor and professional communicator, projected a warm, likable, sincere manner on television; Mondale appeared tired, lifeless, and uncomfortable. Reagan's verbal imagery included words like prosperity, opportunity, respect, and growth; Mondale used words like debt, unfairness, and fear. After the political frustrations of the 1960s and 1970s, voters welcomed a candidate who reflected a current emphasis on nostalgia, love of country, self-improvement, hope, and pride. Reagan's campaign advisors demonstrated a solid understanding of demographic and psychographic trends in the nation.[55]

There is no question that consumer (voter) research will become increasingly important in the years ahead, not only for political parties and their candidates, but also for lobbyists and other organizations that promote the passage of legislation favorable to their causes and discourage legislation which is not.[56] For example, organized labor in Missouri used consumer research techniques to defeat a proposal outlawing union shops. Labor leaders were afraid that a massive voter turnout, which might be generated by a TV advertising campaign on the issue, would bring out enough unfriendly votes to pass the anti-union-shop amendment. Their strategy was to identify and target union sympathizers among the general public and promote the importance of voting to that segment alone.

Research revealed likely classes of voters who could be identified by income, education, and various sociological traits. To find out where such voters lived, researchers divided the state into block groups and assembled demographic data (available from census records) on the residents in each group. This information was then matched with the data already collected on pro-union sympathizers. The block groups with the best match were encouraged to "get out and vote" through a targeted direct mail campaign. The election resulted in a clear victory for organized labor.[57]

Several studies have investigated the impact of advertising on election outcomes. One study reported that as promotional spending increases, a House or Senate candidate's chance of receiving votes increases. However, the effects of promotional spending varied by candidate type and party affiliation. Spending had a more positive effect for independent and third party candidates, compared with Republican or Democratic candidates, and for challengers as opposed to incumbents.[58] Another study showed that recall was highly related to attitude towards the candidate. It found that people recall more information from a preferred candidate's commercials than from his or her opponent's.[59]

This finding is an example of *selective perception* (discussed in Chapters 3 and 10), and underscores the fact that people seek information that agrees with their beliefs and avoid dissonant or opposing information.

Political marketing is by far the most controversial area in which behavioral research is conducted. The potential for manipulation of the voter by politicians or special interest groups is undeniable. On the other hand, like other areas of consumer behavior research, voter behavior studies offer the promise of a deeper understanding of voter needs and the development of improved voter communication programs.

## CONSUMER PROTECTION: PUBLIC POLICY CONSIDERATIONS

Research into consumer behavior developed, in part, in response to the adoption by marketers of the marketing concept—which postulates that products and services developed to meet predetermined consumer needs achieve ready acceptance in the marketplace. The marketing concept, as noted in Chapter 1, followed a *production orientation*, where marketers could sell whatever they made to a consumer goods starved post-World War II populace; and a *selling orientation*, where marketers imposed a hard-sell approach on consumers in order to move the goods that they unilaterally decided to make. There is no doubt that the latter orientation fed the notion in some quarters that consumers could be manipulated into buying shoddy and unneeded merchandise, and this in turn led to widespread abuses in the marketplace.

The consumer movement that emerged in the late 1960s endeavored to correct the imbalance that had developed between buyers and sellers. Consumers complained of shoddy and hazardous products. They claimed that products were being sold by misrepresentation—through deceptive advertising and packaging, high-pressure salesmanship, and inadequate warranties—on credit terms that disguised their true costs. In response to these complaints, Congress enacted several major pieces of legislation designed to protect consumers, and state and local governments enacted dozens more.

Although the need for consumer legislation is widely documented and strongly supported, the effectiveness of resulting legislation in safeguarding consumer rights has proved to be somewhat uneven—probably because it was so rarely based on knowledge or insights into consumer behavior. The truth-in-lending law, for example, was enacted to ensure that consumers are aware of the true rates of interest they are charged for buying on credit. The law was intended to aid low-income consumers in particular, who most often rely on credit purchases. However, subsequent research found that only 34 percent of those who had made a credit purchase after passage of the law could report the true interest charges they agreed to pay; moreover, low-income shoppers were among those who were least aware of finance charges.[60] Many policymakers now concede that legislation like truth-in-lending, while well intentioned, was passed with little consideration of actual consumer behavior. They agree that research into consumers' attitudes and habits concerning their purchase behavior should have been a necessary precondition to the enactment of consumer legislation, and should be the requisite basis for remedying faults in current laws.[61]

Several government agencies that have used consumer behavior studies to aid in policymaking decisions are the Federal Trade Commission (FTC), the Food and Drug Administration (FDA), and the Consumer Products Safety Commission (CPSC). The FTC and the FDA have concerned themselves in recent years with the regulation of advertising—an area in which consumer abuse has frequently been charged. Sometimes misleading advertising is very difficult to detect—even by educated consumers. For example, researchers found that ads judged by the FDA to be misleading often were not perceived as such by physicians.[62] Another study found that variations in the content and format of the cigarette warning messages required in all cigarette advertising minimized the fear appeal intended by the warning.[63]

## Deceptive Advertising and Consumer Research

Both the FTC and the FDA have the power to halt any advertising they consider to be deceptive; yet over the years, no single definition of what constitutes deception in advertising has evolved. Cases brought before either regulatory agency are decided on an *ad hoc* basis—that is, on their own merits—so that advertisers have had difficulty in discerning broad regulatory guidelines as to what is considered improper or deceptive advertising. To remedy this situation, consumer behavior studies have been conducted to clarify the meaning of deceptive advertising. One study distinguished three categories of deception: (1) *unconscionable lies*, in which completely false claims are made and intended; (2) *claim/fact discrepancies*, in which some relevant qualifications of a claim are omitted, resulting in misrepresentation; and (3) *claim/belief discrepancies*, in which no deceptive claim is explicitly made, but a deceptive belief is created.[64]

Of the three categories, the one that is probably the most insidious is the last—claim/belief discrepancies. Industry watchdog agencies frequently guard against outright lies and insufficiently documented claims, but the clever manipulation of words to foster a misleading belief is more difficult to police. For example, a candy bar that is portrayed in its advertising as "wholesome" implies that it meets basic FDA requirements for vitamins and other nutrients, whether or not it does in fact do so. The FTC found that although no clinical tests had been conducted to support the claim that Anacin was superior to other analgesic medications, consumers assumed the advertised claim was based on research evidence, despite the absence of an explicit claim that such superiority had been proved. As a result, the Commission ruled that comparative advertising claims for over-the-counter pain relievers which do not refer to specific medical proof must be supported by test evidence, or must be qualified by a disclosure that the claim has not been proved or that there are "substantial questions" about its validity.[65] Another example of claim/belief discrepancies can be found in soup labeling. The phrase "no preservatives, no artificial ingredients" obscures the fact that onion soup may contain caramel powder as a coloring agent to make it look darker and richer.[66]

There has been a significant increase in licensed toys based on TV cartoon characters. (Sometimes the licensed toy is introduced simultaneously with the

TV character so that each bolsters the promotion of the other.) Parents and consumer advocates claim that such programs are deceptive because children do not distinguish between the commercials for the toys and the programs.[67] It has also been found that some third party certification marks are misleading. A recent study showed that consumers misperceived the purpose and meaning of the Good Housekeeping Seal, despite changes in its presentation implemented during the 1970s in response to government regulations. It was found that while college-educated consumers used the mark less frequently than high-school-educated consumers, their perception of the mark was no more accurate than that of less educated consumers.[68]

How can the FTC or the FDA determine whether a false belief has been created among consumers? Consumer behavior research offers some promising answers, but requires some creativity in design. In one study, subjects were exposed to product claims that might lead to the formation of false beliefs; they then were exposed to corrected claims for the same products. After some experimentation, the researchers developed a technique that reportedly enabled them to spot the existence of false beliefs, trace those beliefs to specific ads (not just generalized misimpressions that consumers might have held prior to seeing the ads in question), and measure the specific level of false belief created by the ads. Adoption of a similar technique would enable advertisers to pretest their advertising prior to widespread media release, and to revise any ads that research indicated might be misleading. The same technique would permit the FTC and the FDA to predetermine the strength of a misleading advertising case before deciding whether or not to prosecute.[69]

## Corrective Advertising and Consumer Research

In situations where the FTC has determined that an advertisement is deceptive, it has ordered the advertiser to cancel the ad and to run a series of *corrective ads* in an effort to eliminate any residual effects of the misleading claims on consumers. For example, the Warner-Lambert Company was ordered to run corrective advertising for a period of 17 months to correct its claims for Listerine as a cold remedy. The corrective ads stated that Listerine does not help to prevent colds or sore throats or lessen their severity (see Figure 20-8). The main purpose of corrective advertising is to dispel mistaken impressions created by misleading advertising and to help consumers make more informed product decisions. (An implicit purpose is to impose sanctions designed to discourage marketers from deliberately or thoughtlessly sponsoring such ads.)

Consumer behavior research into the effectiveness of corrective advertising in achieving its primary purpose has come up with some mixed results. For example, research has found that although deceptive claims are less widely believed after corrective advertising has been implemented, loyal brand users tend to ignore such ads and remain loyal, instead of changing their beliefs or their buying practices.[70] In a follow-up study of Listerine's corrective advertising, the FTC reported that although the ads had had some impact, many people continued to use the product as a remedy for sore throats and colds.

It appears that corrective advertising has the potential for being overly effective as well as ineffective. Research has revealed that some consumers tend to overgeneralize the corrective message, so that they disbelieve all subsequent advertising claims for the brand and for the product category.[71] Another study showed that consumers often decode corrective messages incorrectly, so that remedial advertising statements turn out to be as confusing and misleading as the messages they are supposed to correct.[72]

Research is needed to determine consumer responses to proposed corrective ads *before* the fact to ensure that the corrective ads fulfill their stated purpose. A recent comprehensive review of corrective advertising noted several barriers to the achievement of the prime objective, which is to correct misperceptions caused by the advertiser's prior promotional messages.[73] Communicating with consumers is inherently complex; thus it is difficult to create a corrective message that will capture the attention of consumers, sustain their interest, alter previous beliefs, and form new cognitions which they will retain. This is particularly difficult given the fact that corrective messages are usually buried within the context of regularly scheduled advertising.

Advertisers are legally required to carry out corrective advertising when so ordered, but, understandably, they do so with some reluctance. Their chief objective is to maintain and enhance their brand's sales, not necessarily to achieve the intent of the order. For example, examination of the storyboard for the Listerine corrective commercial shows the corrective message buried in the middle of the commercial. It is used neither in the opening frame of the commercial nor in its close; either position would have heightened consumer awareness of the corrective information (see the discussion of order effects in Chapter 10).

## Consumer Information

Laws and regulatory agencies are needed to protect basic consumer rights. Beyond protection, however, consumers need information and education to enable them to make wise buying decisions. Increasingly, government policymakers and consumer advocates are recognizing that they cannot protect consumers against every possible marketing abuse, and that the consumer's best defense is better product knowledge.

Today more than 30 federal agencies, as well as state and local agencies, are designing consumer education programs and disseminating consumer information. For example, the New York City Department of Consumer Affairs publishes a monthly Market Basket Survey of average prices of food items compared with the previous month, an Energy Report that compares average home energy costs for the previous month and the same month the previous year, and average gasoline prices. It also monitors and publishes reports of deceptive advertising, and other information deemed useful to the consumer.

FIGURE 20-8 A Corrective Advertisement for Listerine

# LISTERINE®

## "BRIDE"

ANNCR: Where will you be . . . when your mouthwash stops working?

FATHER: Here come the guests. (SFX: CLOUD)

BRIDE: Dad . . . bad breath.
FATHER: But I used . . .
BRIDE: Should have used Listerine.

ANNCR: Listerine works hours longer than the number two mouthwash.

LISTERINE
Listerine will not help prevent colds or sore throats or lessen their severity.

While Listerine will not help prevent colds or sore throats or lessen their severity - -

Listerine's strong formula keeps your breath clean for hours.

Hours later

It kills the germs that can cause bad breath.

(MUSIC UP & UNDER)
FATHER: What a day!
BRIDE: What a Dad!

You can bet your breath on it.
LISTERINE

ANNCR: Listerine Antiseptic. You can bet your breath on it.

Courtesy of Warner-Lambert Company

Consumer behavior research has been used in the evaluation of various consumer information programs, including **unit pricing** and **nutritional labeling.**

## UNIT PRICING

Supermarket shoppers often confront the difficult task of determining which is the best buy among the various brands and package sizes available. Is a 12-ounce house brand of peeled tomatoes at 60 cents a wiser purchase than a 1-pound national brand at 79 cents? To aid consumers to answer such questions, several states have instituted *unit pricing*, which requires the storekeeper to list the price per unit (e.g., per ounce) for each brand and size carried. Consumer behavior researchers have conducted a number of studies to determine the degree to which consumers use unit pricing and how useful it is to them. Early surveys reported that the system was not extensively used, particularly by the shoppers it was supposed to help most—the poor and the elderly.[74] However, a later study of a program that had been in operation for six years showed extensive use by all types of shoppers.[75]

Besides documenting its use, studies have been devoted to discovering the best way to display unit price information. Findings suggest that posted price lists near displays are more effective than individual shelf tags for every brand and size.[76] Research has found that both methods produce savings for consumers, since they encourage switching to cheaper store brands. The listing format produces more savings, however, apparently because it makes comparisons easier.[77]

## NUTRITIONAL LABELING

The concept of nutritional labeling covers a broad spectrum of programs and proposals for telling consumers about the nutritional value of the foods they buy. The FDA requires marketers to list on their labels the vitamin, protein, carbohydrate, and fat content of all processed foods for which nutritional claims are made. It has been proposed that fast-food restaurants be required to post nutritional content as well.

The growth in consumer health and fitness orientation has led to the establishment of salad bars in supermarkets, produce stores, and restaurants. To keep the cut-up fruits and vegetables from wilting and discoloration, retailers often sprayed them with sulfite solutions which they believed to be safe. In recent years these preservatives have been linked to several deaths and to many allergic reactions among consumers. Because salad bar produce is not labeled, the FDA has banned the use of several preservatives on fresh produce.[78]

The FDA prohibits health claims on food labels. However, enforcement of this prohibition can sometimes be difficult. For example, Kellogg notes on the package of its All-Bran cereal that eating high-fiber foods (such as bran cereals) could reduce the incidence of several types of cancer. The company maintains that this message is not a health claim, and that it is merely reporting information provided by the National Cancer Institute. The implication to the consumer that All-Bran cereal prevents cancer is obvious; however, Kellogg seems to have sidestepped the FDA ban on health claim labels.[79]

Many consumers lack the background to understand the meaning of the nutritional content of foods, and without more education they may not benefit from nutritional labeling requirements.

In line with the current emphasis on fitness, many processed food producers are listing caloric content per serving on their labels. This is another area that consumers must interpret with care. By reducing the recommended size of a serving, a food producer may imply that the caloric content of his product is lower than the competitor's brand. For example, brand X salad dressing may list the recommended serving as one teaspoon, with a caloric content per serving of 17 calories, while the competitive brand uses a tablespoon as the standard measure, with a caloric content of 25 calories per serving. The diet-conscious consumer is likely to choose brand X for its apparently lower caloric content, and end up with greater calorie consumption, rather than less.

## Consumer Education

In order for consumer information programs to have the greatest impact on their intended audiences, more extensive consumer education is needed. Without such education, further protective legislation may prove to be a wasted effort. How best to carry out consumer education has been the subject of a number of research studies. Several suggestions are particularly noteworthy.[80] The first involves a labeling program for all goods to certify *quality*. A cooperative effort by government officials, business people, consumer spokespersons, and academic researchers would be needed to establish the standards to be summarized on labels.

*Uniform labeling* would give consumers a basis for making product comparisons while shopping. Another suggestion that has been proposed to advance consumer education involves the development of computerized data banks containing product information (e.g., local prices, availability, and product test results) and general educational information (e.g., the meaning of nutritional information). Consumers could tap into such information banks by means of home computers or cable television.

It is important for parents to acquire as much product information as possible, since research shows that parents play an important role in the diffusion of consumer information among children.[81] It has also been suggested that consumer education programs be made mandatory in the public school system. At present, only a few states have such programs, and the content varies widely. Consumer behavior researchers could make a substantive contribution to the field of consumer education by designing appropriate curricula for such programs.[82]

Some researchers have proposed that consumer information be looked upon as a product. They suggest that the goal of public policy should be to market consumer information programs and make sure that appropriate product information is collected and readily available.[83] Such an approach implies decreased regulation of marketers because it assumes that, with adequate information available, consumers will make wise purchase decisions. Others argue that not only is actual usage of consumer information difficult to measure, but that such figures are largely irrelevant. These researchers believe that the prime benefit of consumer information programs is indirect; that widespread availability of such information, rather than consumer usage, will force marketers to offer better and cheaper products in the long run. They maintain that the goal of public policy should be to make consumer information available to the consumer, and that it should not concern itself with persuading the consumer to use this information.[84]

## The Future of the Consumer Movement

There are indications that present public attitudes toward consumerism are favorable and should remain strong for the next several years. Many consumers are willing to be active consumerists (i.e., join consumer groups), but actual participation appears to be limited, often because consumers feel that leaders of the consumer movement are out of touch with their needs. Furthermore, it is felt that federal policymakers do not accurately assess public attitudes and are not sensitive to consumer needs.[85]

There is also increased awareness among politicians regarding the conflicting goals of consumers and business, and the recognition that increased costs resulting from tighter regulation are passed through to the public. Legislators are aware of the need to weigh costs and benefits in implementing consumer legislation. In the advertising area, for example, such awareness has resulted in considerable deregulation in the past several years.[86]

Recognizing the need to keep in touch with the changing consumer environment, many firms provide mechanisms for voluntary consumer input (complaints, compliments, information) in addition to soliciting input through marketing research.[87] However, there are indications that such input is highly skewed because it is the educated consumer who takes advantage of company outreach programs and who participates in federal rule-making procedures; minority and less educated consumers are unlikely to involve themselves in such activities.[88]

It has been suggested that business has three available strategies to cope with consumerism during the 1980s. (1) Reduce the demand for consumerism by *improving product quality*, *expanding services*, *lowering prices*, *toning down advertising claims*, and *reducing the causes of consumer dissatisfaction* (all congruent with the marketing concept); (2) compete in the consumerism "industry" by having an *active consumer education program*; and (3) cooperate with nonbusiness competitors by *helping government agencies, nonprofit organizations, and consumer groups to educate consumers.*[89] This last approach can improve relations with these bodies and generate favorable publicity among consumers.

For most businesses, the best approach is to become and remain sensitive to public attitudes through consumer behavior research and to mount a strategy that includes all of the elements cited in the options above.

## *summary*

Consumer behavior research has grown in response to the extension of marketing concepts to profit and not-for-profit service organizations and public policy needs. Services have become a pervasive and significant part of the national economy. Service providers are faced with the same marketing problems as the producers of physical goods, and have the same marketing tools at their disposal, including segmentation, targeting, positioning, and planning based on consumer research. Consumer behavior research has proved to be an effective tool in marketing all types of nonprofit organizations—from government agencies to colleges, and from hospitals to museums. Consumer research is also used by health care providers and political organizations, and in the marketing of social causes.

Legislators and other public policy decision makers have recognized the need for consumer research studies to serve as the basis for consumer protection legislation. Consumer research has been used in studies of deceptive advertising and corrective advertising, and has revealed weaknesses in previous public policy programs directed at consumers. In order to cope with consumerism during the coming decade, businesses must become and remain sensitive to public attitudes through continued consumer behavior research.

## *discussion questions*

1. Explain the need for regulations and laws designed to protect the consumer. Have these laws been effective? Why or why not?
2. Consumers need to be informed about products and services so that they can make better product decisions. Explain this statement in relation to (1) unit pricing, (2) nutritional labeling, and (3) energy conservation.
3. Discuss three ways to improve consumer education. Which do you think would be the most effective? Why?
4. List and discuss at least three social marketing campaigns that have been run in the last year. Do you think they were effective?
5. Is political advertising beneficial to society or does it gloss over the essential issues? Explain your answer.
6. Is nonprofit marketing a useful tool in terms of social and health issues? Support your answer with examples.
7. Develop a campaign strategy to promote a drug rehabilitation center in your neighborhood, taking into consideration the fact that you might have local opposition.
8. Give three examples of what you think may be deceptive advertising. Do you think corrective advertising campaigns would be useful in counteracting their impact on consumers?

# endnotes


1. Leonard L. Berry, G. Lynn Shostack, and Gregory D. Upah, "Preface" in L.L. Berry et al., eds. *Emerging Perspectives on Services Marketing* (Chicago: American Marketing Association, 1983), 1.
2. For a detailed discussion of these distinctions, see Philip Kotler and Paul N. Bloom, *Marketing Professional Services*, (Englewood Cliffs, N.J.: Prentice-Hall, 1984), chaps. 1, 2, 3; and Philip Kotler, *Marketing for Nonprofit Organizations*, 2nd ed. (Englewood Cliffs, N.J.: Prentice-Hall, 1982), chap. 21.
3. See, for example, G. Lynn Shostack, "Breaking Free from Product Marketing," *Journal of Marketing*, April 1977, 73–80; A. Parasuraman, Leonard L. Berry, and Valarie A. Zeithaml, "Service Firms Need Marketing Skills," *Business Horizons*, November–December 1983, 28–31; Christopher H. Lovelock, "The Evolution of Services Marketing," a paper presented at the American Marketing Association Faculty Consortium on Services Marketing, Texas A&M University, July 7–11, 1985; and "Business Planning in the Eighties: A Call to Marketing," Coopers & Lybrand and Yankelovich, Skelly and White, Inc., 1985.
4. "Physicians Must Know Their Patients, Competitors, Service Areas to Effectively Market Their Practices," *Marketing News*, January 17, 1986, 15; and "Physician Marketing Series Scheduled for Three Cities," *Marketing News*, September 27, 1985, 6.
5. "Brokers Filling Businesses' Information Gaps," *Marketing News*, October 11, 1985, 3.
6. "AT&T Offers New Services to Business," *Marketing News*, December 6, 1985, 7.
7. "Corporate Sponsors Join California Parks Promotion," *Marketing News*, August 30, 1985, 8; and Kevin Higgins, "New York Fuel Marketers Get Nasty in Fight for Residential Heating Customers," *Marketing News*, collegiate ed., January 1985, 6.
8. Alan J. Dubinsky and Michael Levy, "A Study of Selected Behaviors in the Purchasing of Consumer Services: Implications for Marketers," in Kenneth Bernhardt et al., eds., *1981 Educators' Conference Proceedings* (Chicago: American Marketing Association, 1981), 58–61.
9. A. Parasuraman, Valarie A. Zeithaml, and Leonard L. Berry, "A Conceptual Model of Service Quality and Its Implications for Future Research," *Journal of Marketing*, 49 (Fall 1985), 41–50.
10. John Reilly, "Checking into Today's Hotels," *The Star-Ledger*, November 4, 1985, 51.
11. Ibid.
12. Leslie Wayne, "New Inns for New Markets," *New York Times*, April 22, 1986, D1.
13. Sidney H. Firestone, "Creating an Image for Service Companies," *Services Marketing Newsletter* (Chicago: American Marketing Association), Summer 1985, 1–2.
14. LuAnne Feik, "Tangibles, Intangibles Forge Promotional Tools," *Marketing News*, September 27, 1985, 19; and Robert C. Lewis, "Tangiblizing the Intangible in Hotel Advertising," in *Services Marketing Newsletter*, 3.
15. James H. Donnelly, Jr., "Intangibility and Marketing Strategy for Retail Bank Services," *Journal of Retail Banking*, June 1980, 39–43.
16. G. L. Shostack, "Market Positioning a Service," and Jim Shanahan, "Consumer Services," papers presented at the AMA Faculty Consortium on Services Marketing, 1985.
17. Christopher H. Lovelock and John A. Quelch, "Consumer Promotions in Service Marketing," *Business Horizons*, May–June 1983, 66–75; and "Bank Going All Out in Effort to Boost Customer ATM Use," *Marketing News*, student edition, November 1984, 1.
18. Mary J. Bitner, "Consumer Responses to the Physical Environment in Service Settings," paper presented at the AMA Faculty Consortium on Services Marketing, 1985.

19. Suzanne Slesin, "Ralph Lauren's Store: Part Palazzo, Part Club," *New York Times*, April 22, 1986, A22.

20. Bernard H. Booms and Mary J. Bitner, "Marketing Services by Managing the Environment," *The Cornell H.R.A. Quarterly*, May 1982, 35–40.

21. Benjamin Schneider and David E. Bowen, "Employee and Customer Perceptions of Service in Banks: Replication and Extension," *Journal of Applied Psychology*, 70 (1985), 423–33; and Benjamin Schneider, "Employee Issues in Service Delivery," paper presented at the AMA Faculty Consortium, 1985.

22. "Maine Sheds Cold Image," *Advertising Age*, November 12, 1984, 94.

23. "How Academia Is Taking a Lesson from Business," *Business Week*, August 27, 1984, 58–60.

24. Christopher Lovelock and Charles B. Weinberg, "Public and Nonprofit Marketing Comes of Age," in Gerald Zaltman and Thomas V. Bonoma, eds., *Review of Marketing 1978* (Chicago: American Marketing Association, 1978), 415–22.

25. William Meyers, "The Nonprofits Drop the 'Non,' " *New York Times*, November 24, 1985, 1E, 8E.

26. Alan R. Andreasen, "Nonprofits: Check Your Attention to Customers," *Harvard Business Review*, May–June 1982, 105–10.

27. Doris C. Van Doren and Louise W. Smith, "Self-Analysis Can Gauge Marketing Orientation," *Marketing News*, December 6, 1985, 14.

28. See, for example, Philip Kotler, *Marketing Management—Analysis, Planning and Control*, 5th ed. (Englewood Cliffs, N.J.: Prentice-Hall, 1984), 28–30.

29. Charles Atkin, John Hocking, and Martin Block, "Teenage Drinking: Does Advertising Make a Difference?" *Journal of Communication*, Spring 1984, 157–67.

30. Charles Atkin and Martin Block, "The Effects of Alcohol Advertising," in Thomas C. Kinnear, ed., *Advances in Consumer Research* (Chicago: Association for Consumer Research, 1983), XI, 688–93.

31. Steven W. Colford, "White House Offers Rx for Alcohol Ads," *Advertising Age*, March 25, 1985, 10.

32. William F. Gloede, "Antismoking Ads Ill-Conceived?" *Advertising Age*, December 17, 1984, 1; and "Networks Abort Antismoking Ad," *Advertising Age*, December 24, 1984, 6.

33. "Free TV Time Abounds for Public Service Messages," *Marketing News*, August 16, 1985, 7.

34. Laurel A. Hudson and Paul N. Bloom, "Potential Consumer Research Contributions to Combating Drinking and Driving Problems," 676–81; and Lawrence Wallack, "Social Marketing as Prevention: Uncovering Some Critical Assumptions," 682–87, in Kinnear, ed., *Advances in Consumer Research*.

35. Jeffrey A. Barach, "Applying Marketing Principles to Social Causes," *Business Horizons*, July–August 1984, 65–69.

36. Hudson and Bloom, "Potential Consumer Research Contributions to Combating Drinking and Driving Problems," and Wallack, "Social Marketing as Prevention."

37. Paul C. Feingold and Mark L. Knapp, "Anti-Drug Abuse Commercials," *Journal of Communication*, 27 (Winter 1977), 20–28.

38. "Hospitals, Competing for Scarce Patients, Turn to Advertising," *New York Times*, April 20, 1986, 47.

39. Ibid.

40. Robert N. Joffe, "Research is 'Insurance' for Hospitals," *Marketing News*, January 3, 1986, 49.

41. Michael M. Costello, "Hospital Airs Message Via Radio Infomercials," *Marketing News*, April 12, 1985, 10.

42. Jeffrey M. Ostroff, "Accessing Mature (Age 55+) Health Care Consumers Through Caregivers and Corporations," in Philip D. Cooper, ed., *Responding to the*

*Challenge: Health Care Marketing Comes of Age*, Proceedings Series (Chicago: Academy for Health Services Marketing, American Marketing Association, 1986), 48–50.

43. Barbara Bellman Alpern, "The Woman as Health Care Consumer: Successful Marketing Concepts," in Cooper, *Responding to the Challenge*, 83–86.

44. Adrian L. Roberg, "How to Develop a Successful Marketing Program to Increase Referrals from Physicians and Other Practitioners," in Cooper, *Responding to the Challenge*, 62–64.

45. Jan Elsesser, "Marketing Research Ideas Health Care Marketers Can Steal from the Consumer Packaged Goods Industry," in Cooper, *Responding to the Challenge*, 30–32.

46. Jukka M. Laitamaki and Jarmo R. Leftinen, "Applications of Service Quality and Services Marketing in Health Care Organizations," 45–48; and Robert C. Greene, Jr., C. P. Rao, and Ann Marie Thompson, "Perceived Quality of Health Care Delivery: A Case of a Small Rural Hospital," 106–9; in A. Terry Paul, ed., *Building Marketing Effectiveness in Health Care*, Proceedings Series (Chicago: Academy for Health Services Marketing, American Marketing Association, 1985).

47. Ellen Goldman, "The Power of Positioning," in Cooper, *Responding to the Challenge*, 109–11.

48. Elinor Selame, "The Symptoms, Cures and Relief of Health Care's Identity Crisis," in Paul, *Building Marketing Effectiveness*, 84–87.

49. Harley King, "Creating Successful Customer-Oriented Advertising," in Paul, *Building Marketing Effectiveness*, 59–62.

50. Arthur E. Gross, "Product Introduction: Promoting a New Building," in Paul, *Building Marketing Effectiveness*, 63–64.

51. L. Ivan Hilton, "Using a Total Marketing Approach to Boost Patient Usage of Your Hospital," in Paul, *Building Marketing Effectiveness*, 72–75.

52. "Lowe Receives 1986 Health Award for Initiating Humana Marketing," *Marketing News*, March 28, 1986, 1, 19.

53. "The New Politechs," *Grey Matter–Thoughts and Ideas on Advertising and Marketing*, 55 (New York: Grey Advertising, Inc., 1984); and Edwin Diamond and Stephen Bates, "30-Second Elections," *New York*, October 1, 1984, 46–51.

54. Sara Rimer, "Experts Study the Habits of Genus Baby Boomer," *New York Times*, April 21, 1986, B6.

55. Marshall Blonsky, "4 More Years: The Marketing Implications," *Marketing News*, January 4, 1985, 1, 50, 52.

56. Michael D. Hutt, Michael P. Mokwa, and Stanley J. Shapiro, "The Politics of Marketing: Analyzing the Parallel Political Marketplace," *Journal of Marketing*, 50 (January 1986), 40–51.

57. Warren Weaver, Jr., "A Pinpoint System Is Developed for Finding Voters for an Issue," *New York Times*, February 3, 1979, 16.

58. Leonard N. Reid and Lawrence C. Soley, "Promotional Spending Effects in High Involvement Elections: An Examination of the Voter Involvement Explanation," *Journal of Advertising*, 12 (1983), 43–50.

59. Ronald J. Faber and M. Claire Storey, "Recall of Information from Political Advertising," *Journal of Advertising*, 13 (1984), 39–44.

60. George S. Day, "Assessing the Effects of Information Disclosure Requirements," *Journal of Marketing*, 40 (April 1976), 46; and Homer Kripke, "Gesture and Reality in Consumer Credit Reform," in David A. Aaker and George S. Day, eds., *Consumerism: Search for the Consumer Interest*, 2nd ed. (New York: Free Press, 1974), 218–24.

61. Debra L. Scammon and Mary Jane Sheffet, "Regulation in the 80's: What Is the Role of Consumer Researchers," in Kinnear, *Advances in Consumer Research*, 463–65.

62. Richard L. Oliver, R. Hoyt Walbridge, and Peter H. Rheinstein, "A Study of Physicians' Perceptions of Advertising Judged Deceptive by the FDA," in Kinnear, *Advances in Consumer Research*, XI, 224–28.

63. Gaurav Bhalla and John L. Lastovicka, "The Impact of Changing Cigarette Warning Message Content and Format," in Kinnear, *Advances in Consumer Research*, 305–10.

64. David M. Gardner, "Deception in Advertising: A Conceptual Approach," *Journal of Marketing*, 39 (January 1975), 42.

65. Debra L. Scammon and Richard J. Semenik, "The FTC's 'Reasonable Basis' for Substantiation of Advertising: Expanded Standards and Implications," *Journal of Advertising*, 12 (1983), 4–11.

66. Marian Burros, "Labels on Soups: Read with Care," *New York Times*, February 22, 1986, 48.

67. John Wilke, Lois Therrien, Amy Dunkin, and Mark N. Vamos, "Are the Programs Your Kids Watch Simply Commercials?" *Business Week*, March 25, 1985, 53–54.

68. Michael V. Laric and Dan Sarel, "Consumer (Mis)perceptions and Usage of Third Party Certification Marks, 1972 and 1980: Did Public Policy have an Impact?" *Journal of Marketing*, 45 (Summer 1981), 132–42.

69. J. Edward Russo, Barbara L. Metcalf, and Debra Stephens, "Toward an Empirical Technology for Identifying Misleading Advertising," in Richard J. Harris, ed., *Information Processing Research in Advertising* (Hillsdale, N.J.: Lawrence Erlbaum Associates, 1982).

70. James R. Taylor and Thomas C. Kinnear, "Corrective Advertising: An Empirical Tracking of Residual Effects," in Richard P. Bagozzi et al., eds., *Marketing in the 80's: Changes and Challenges* (Chicago: American Marketing Association, 1980), 416–18.

71. Michael B. Mazis and Janice E. Adkinson, "An Experimental Evaluation of a Proposed Corrective Advertising Remedy," *Journal of Marketing Research*, 13 (May 1976), 178–83.

72. Jacob Jacoby, Margaret C. Nelson, Wayne D. Hoyer, and Hal G. Gueutal, "Probing the Locus of Causation in the Miscomprehension of Remedial Advertising Statements," in Kinnear, *Advances in Consumer Research*, 379–86.

73. William L. Wilkie, Dennis L. McNeill, and Michael B. Mazis, "Marketing's 'Scarlet Letter': The Theory and Practice of Corrective Advertising," *Journal of Marketing*, 48 (Spring 1984), 11–31.

74. See James M. Carman, "A Summary of Empirical Research on Unit Pricing in Supermarkets," *Journal of Retailing*, 48 (Winter 1972–73), 63–71; Hans R. Isakson and Alex R. Maurizi, "The Consumer Economics of Unit Pricing," *Journal of Marketing Research*, 10 (August 1973), 277–85; and John S. Coulson, "New Consumerists' Breed Will Fade Away," *Marketing News*, mid-June 1971, 5.

75. Bruce F. McElroy and David Asker, "Unit Pricing Six Years After Introduction," *Journal of Retailing*, 55 (Fall 1979), 44–57.

76. J. Edward Russo, Gene Krieser, and Sally Miyashita, "An Effective Display of Unit Price Information," *Journal of Marketing*, 39 (April 1975), 11–19.

77. J. Edward Russo, "The Value of Unit Price Information," *Journal of Marketing Research*, 14 (May 1977), 193–201.

78. Anastasia Toufexis, "Tossing Sulfites Out Of Salads," *Time*, October 14, 1985, 94.

79. Marian Burros, "Health Claims on Food Put FDA in a Corner," *New York Times*, February 19, 1986, C1.

80. These suggestions can be found in Hans B. Thorelli and Jack L. Engledow, "Information Seekers and Information Systems: A Policy Perspective," *Journal of Marketing*, 44 (Spring 1980), 19–21.

81. Sanford Grossbart, Lawrence A. Crosby, and Joyce Robb, "Parental Diffusion Roles and Children's Responses to Nutrition Education," in Bruce J. Walker, Wil-

liam O. Bearden, William R. Darden, Patrick E. Murphy, John R. Nevin, Jerry C. Olson, Barton A. Weitz, eds., *An Assessment of Marketing Thought and Practice—1982 Educators' Conference Proceedings*, 48 (Chicago: American Marketing Association, 1982), 355–58.

**82.** Some guidelines for establishing such a curriculum can be found in George P. Moschis, "Formal Consumer Education: An Empirical Assessment," in William L. Wilkie, ed., *Advances in Consumer Research* (Ann Arbor, Mich.: Association for Consumer Research, 1979), VI, 456–59.

**83.** Noel Capon and Richard J. Lutz, "A Model and Methodology for the Development of Consumer Information Programs," *Journal of Marketing*, 43 (January 1979), 58–67; and Noel Capon and Richard J. Lutz, "The Marketing of Consumer Information," *Journal of Marketing*, 47 (Summer 1983), 108–12.

**84.** Michael B. Mazis, Richard Staelin, Howard Beales, and Steven Salop, "A Framework for Evaluating Consumer Information Regulation," *Journal of Marketing*, 45 (Winter 1981), 11–21; and Dan Sarel, "A Comment on Capon and Lutz's Model and Methodology for the Development of Consumer Information Programs," *Journal of Marketing*, 47 (Summer 1983), 103–7.

**85.** Darlene Brannigan Smith and Paul N. Bloom, "Is Consumerism Dead or Alive? Some New Evidence," in Kinnear, *Advances in Consumer Research*, 369–73.

**86.** Paul N. Bloom, "Deregulation's Challenges for Marketers," 337–40, and Debra L. Scammon and Kenneth D. Bahn, "Government Regulation of Advertising: A Question of Balance," 346–49, in Walker et al., *An Assessment of Marketing Thought.*

**87.** Ivan Ross and Richard L. Oliver, "The Accuracy of Unsolicited Consumer Communication as Indicators of 'True' Consumer Satisfaction/Dissatisfaction," in Kinnear, *Advances in Consumer Research*, 504–8.

**88.** Priscilla A. LaBarbera and William Lazer, "Characteristics of Consumer Participants in Federal Trade Commission Rule Making," *Journal of Consumer Affairs*, 14 (Winter 1980), 405–17.

**89.** Paul N. Bloom and Stephen A. Greyser, "The Maturing of Consumerism," *Harvard Business Review*, November–December 1981, 130–39.

# Glossary

**Absolute Threshold.** The lowest level at which an individual can experience a sensation.

**Acculturation.** The learning of a new or "foreign" culture.

**Achieved Role.** A role expected of an individual as the result of some factor concerned with his or her personal attainment, such as level of education, income, occupational status, or marital status.

**Achievement Need.** The need for personal accomplishment as an end in itself.

**Acquired Needs.** Needs that are learned in response to one's culture or environment (such as the need for esteem, prestige, affection, or power). Also known as *psychogenic* or *secondary needs.*

**Actual Self Concept.** The image that an individual has of himself or herself as a certain kind of person, with certain characteristic traits, habits, possessions, relationships, and behavior.

**Adaptation.** In the field of perception, the term refers specifically to "getting used to" certain sensations or a certain level of stimulation, such as a hot bath.

**Adopter Categories.** A sequence of categories which describes now early (or late) a consumer adopts a new product in relation to other adopters. The five typical adopter categories are: innovators, early adopters, early majority, late majority, and laggards.

**Adoption Process.** The stages through which an individual consumer passes in arriving at a decision to try (or not to try), to continue using (or discontinue using) a new product. The five stages of the traditional adoption process are: awareness, interest, evaluation, trial, and adoption.

**Affective Component.** The part of the tricomponent attitude model that reflects a consumer's emotions or feelings (favorable or unfavorable) with respect to an idea or object.

**Affect Referral Rule.** A simplified decision rule whereby consumers make a product choice on the basis of their previously established overall ratings of the brands considered, rather than on specific attributes.

**Affiliation Need.** The need for friendship, for acceptance, and for belonging.

**Aggressive Individual.** One of three personality types identified by Karen Horney. The aggressive person is one who moves *against* others (e.g., competes with others).

**Aided Recall Measurement.** A technique used to measure advertising awareness in which a respondent is asked if he or she remembers seeing an advertisement for a specific product category.

**AIOs.** Psychographic variables that focus on activities, interests, and opinions.

**Ascribed Role.** A role expected of an individual as the result of factors over which he or she has no control, such as age, sex, family, race, or religion.

**Aspirational Group.** A group to which a nonmember would like to belong.

**Assimilation-Contrast Theory.** A theory of attitude change which suggests that consumers are likely to accept only moderate attitude changes. If the change suggested is too extreme, the contrast with presently held attitudes will cause rejection of the entire message.

**Attitude.** A learned predisposition to respond in a consistently favorable or unfavorable manner with respect to a given object.

**Attitude-Toward-Behavior Model.** A model that proposes that a consumer's attitude toward a specific behavior is a function of how strongly he or she believes that the action will lead to a specific outcome (either favorable or unfavorable).

**Attitude-Toward-Object Model.** A model that proposes that a consumer's attitude toward a product or brand is a function of the presence of certain attributes and the consumer's evaluation of those attributes.

**Attribution Theory.** A theory concerned with how people assign causality to events and form or alter their attitudes as an outcome of assessing their own or other people's behavior.

**Autonomic Decisions.** Family purchase decisions in which *either* the husband or the wife makes the final decision.

**Avoidance Group.** A group with which a nonmember does not identify and does not wish to be identified.

**Awareness.** The first stage of the traditional adoption process.

**Bachelorhood.** The first stage of the family life cycle, in which young single adults set up their own residence apart from their parents.

**Balance Theory.** An attitude-change theory that postulates that individuals avoid inconsistency and seek harmony (consistency) by changing the weaker conflicting attitude to agree with the stronger attitude.

**Behavioral Learning Theories.** Theories based on the premise that learning takes place as the result of observable responses to external stimuli. Also known as *stimulus-response theory*. (See Conditioned Learning and Instrumental Conditioning.)

**Beliefs.** Mental or verbal statements that reflect a person's particular knowledge and assessment about some idea or thing.

**Benefits Segmentation.** A form of psychological segmentation based on the kinds of benefits consumers seek in a product.

**Bettman's Information-Processing Model.** One of several comprehensive models of consumer behavior.

**Brand Loyalty.** Consistent preference and/or purchase of one brand in a specific product or service category.

**Category Width.** A cognitive personality scale that appears to be associated with the number of choices a person tends to consider when making product decisions. Broad categorizers are more likely to risk a poor product choice in order to maximize their product options; narrow categorizers prefer to limit their purchase decisions to known and safe choices.

**Classical Conditioning.** See Conditioned Learning.

**Closure.** A principle of Gestalt psychology that stresses the individual's need for completion. This need is reflected in the individual's subconscious reorganization and perception of incomplete stimuli as complete or whole pictures.

**Cognitive Component.** A part of the tricomponent attitude model that represents the knowledge, perception, and beliefs that a consumer has with respect to an idea or object.

**Cognitive Dissonance.** An attitude-change theory that postulates that consumers act to relieve the discomfort or dissonance that occurs as a result of conflicting information. (See Balance Theory.)

**Cognitive Learning Theory.** A theory that holds that the kind of learning most characteristic of human beings is problem solving, based on mental information processing.

**Cognitive Man Model.** A model of man that portrays consumers as active seekers of information that will enable them to make satisfactory purchase decisions.

**Communication.** The transmission of a message from a sender to a receiver by means of a signal of some sort sent through a channel of some sort.

**Comparative Advertising.** Advertising that explicitly names or identifies one or more competitors of the advertised brand for the purpose of claiming superiority, either on an overall basis or in selected product attributes.

**Comparative Reference Group.** A group whose norms serve as a benchmark for highly specific or narrowly defined types of behavior. (See also Normative Reference Group.)

**Compatibility.** The degree to which potential consumers feel that a new product is consistent with their present needs, values, and practices.

**Compensatory Decision Rule.** A type of decision rule whereby consumers evaluate each brand option in terms of each relevant attribute and then select the brand with the highest weighted score.

**Complexity.** The degree to which a new product is difficult to comprehend and/or use.

**Compliant Individual.** One of three personality types identified by Karen Horney. The compliant person is one who moves *toward* others (e.g., one who desires to be loved, wanted, and appreciated by others).

**Composite Variable Index.** An index that combines a number of socioeconomic variables (such as education, income, occupation) to form one overall measure of social class standing. (See also Single Variable Index.)

**Conative Component.** A part of the tricomponent attitude model that reflects a consumer's likelihood or tendency to behave in a particular way with regard to an attitude-object. Also referred to as "intention to buy."

**Concentrated Marketing.** Targeting a product or service to a single market segment with a unique marketing mix (price, product, promotion, method of distribution).

**Concept.** A mental image of an intangible trait, characteristic or idea.

**Conditioned Learning.** According to Pavlovian theory, conditioned learning results when a stimulus paired with another stimulus that elicits a known response serves to produce the same response by itself.

**Conformity.** The extent to which an individual adopts attitudes and/or behavior that are consistent with the norms of a group to which he or she belongs or would like to belong.

**Conjunctive Rule.** A noncompensatory decision rule in which consumers establish a minimally acceptable cutoff point for each attribute evaluated. Brands that fall below the cutoff point on any one attribute are eliminated from further consideration.

**Construct.** A term that represents or symbolizes an abstract trait or characteristic, such as *motivation* or *aggression.*

**Consumer Behavior.** The behavior that consumers display in searching for, purchasing, using, evaluating, and disposing of products, services, and ideas.

**Consumer Decision Rules.** Procedures adopted by consumers to reduce the complexity of making product and brand decisions.

**Consumer Education.** Programs designed to help consumers make better buying decisions.

**Consumer Heuristics.** See Consumer Decision Rules.

**Consumer Involvement.** The extent to which consumers are concerned with a particular purchase decision and consider it to be important to them.

**Consumer Learning.** The process by which individuals acquire the purchase and consumption knowledge and experience they apply to future related behavior.

**Consumer Protection Legislation.** Consumer-oriented laws that attempt to correct any power imbalance that exists between buyers and sellers.

**Consumer Socialization.** The process by which an individual first learns the skills and attitudes relevant to consumer purchase behavior.

**Consumers.** A term used to describe two different kinds of consuming entities: *personal consumers* (who buy goods and services for their own use or for household use), and *organizational consumers* (who buy products, equipment, and services in order to run their organizations).

**Contactual Group.** A formal or informal group with which a person has regular face-to-face contact and with whose values, attitudes, and standards he or she tends to agree.

**Content Analysis.** A method for systematically and quantitatively analyzing the content of verbal and/or pictorial communication. The method is frequently used to determine prevailing social values of a society.

**Continuous Innovation.** A new product entry that is an improved or modified version of an existing product rather than a totally new product. A continuous innovation has the least disruptive influence on established consumption patterns.

**Corrective Advertising.** Advertising designed to eliminate any residual effects of misleading advertising claims made by marketers.

**Cross-Cultural Consumer Analysis.** Research to determine the extent to which consumers of two or more nations are similar in relation to specific consumption behavior.

**Cues.** Stimuli that give direction to consumer motives; i.e., that suggest a specific way to satisfy a salient motive.

**Cultural Anthropology.** The study of human beings that traces the development of core beliefs, values, and customs passed down to individuals from their parents and grandparents.

**Culture.** The sum total of learned beliefs, values, and customs that serve to regulate the consumer behavior of members of a particular society.

**Customs.** Overt modes of behavior that constitute culturally acceptable ways of behaving in specific situations.

**Deceptive Advertising.** Advertising that presents or implies false or misleading information to the consumer.

**Decision.** A choice made from two or more alternatives.

**Decision Time.** Within the context of the diffusion process, the amount of time required for an individual to adopt (or reject) a specific new product.

**Defensive Attribution.** A principle that suggests consumers are likely to accept credit for success (internal attribution), and to blame others or outside events for failure (external attribution).

**Demarketing.** The marketing task of discouraging consumers or consumer segments from purchasing specific goods.

**Demographic Segmentation.** The division of a total market into smaller subgroups on the basis of such objective characteristics as age, sex, marital status, income, occupation, or education.

**Dependent Variable.** A variable whose value changes as a result of a change in another (i.e., independent) variable. For example, consumer purchases are a dependent variable subject to level and quality of advertising (independent variables).

**Depth Interview.** A research technique in which consumers are interviewed one at a time. It is designed to uncover a consumer's underlying attitudes and/or motivations through a lengthy and relatively unstructured interview.

**Detached Individual.** One of three personality types identified by Karen Horney. The detached person is one who *moves away* from others (e.g., who desires independence, self-sufficiency, and freedom from obligations).

**Differential Threshold.** The minimal difference that can be detected between two stimuli. Also known as the *j.n.d.* (*just noticeable difference*). See also Weber's Law.

**Differentiated Marketing.** Targeting a product or service to several segments, using a specifically tailored product, promotional appeal, price, and/or method of distribution for each.

**Diffusion Process.** The process by which the acceptance of an innovation is spread by communication to members of a social system over a period of time.

**Disclaimant Group.** A group in which a person holds membership, but of whose values, attitudes, and behavior he or she disapproves.

**Discontinuous Innovation.** A dramatically new product entry that requires the establishment of new consumption patterns.

**Disjunctive Rule.** A noncompensatory decision rule in which consumers establish a minimally acceptable cutoff point for each relevant product attribute so that any brand meeting or surpassing the cutoff point for any one attribute is considered an acceptable choice.

**Dissolution.** The final stage of the family life cycle with only one surviving spouse.

**Distributed Learning.** Learning spaced over a period of

time to increase consumer retention. (See Massed Learning.)

**Dogmatism.** A personality trait that reflects the degree of rigidity a person displays toward the unfamiliar and toward information that is contrary to his or her own established beliefs.

**Drive.** An internal force that impels a person to engage in an action designed to satisfy a specific need.

**Dynamically Continuous Innovation.** A new product entry that is sufficiently innovative to have some disruptive effects on established consumption patterns.

**Economic Man Model.** A model of man that depicts the consumer as a perfectly rational being who objectively evaluates and ranks each product alternative and selects the alternative that gives the best value.

**Ego.** In Freudian theory, the part of the personality that serves as the individual's conscious control. It functions as an internal monitor that balances the impulsive demands of the *id* and the sociocultural constraints of the *superego*.

**Ego-Defensive Function.** A component of the functional approach to attitude-change that suggests that consumers want to protect their self-concepts from inner feelings of doubt.

**Emotional Man Model.** A model of man that suggests consumers make decisions based on subjective criteria, such as love, pride, fear, affection, or self-esteem, rather than objective evaluation.

**Encoding.** The process by which individuals select and assign a word or visual image to represent a perceived object.

**Enculturation.** The learning of the culture of one's own society.

**Engel-Kollat-Blackwell (Engel-Blackwell-Miniard) Model.** One of several comprehensive models of consumer behavior.

**Evaluation.** The third stage of the traditional *adoption process*, in which the consumer either draws conclusions about a product innovation or determines if further information is needed.

**Evaluation of Alternatives.** A stage in the consumer *decision-making process* in which the consumer appraises the benefits to be derived from each of the product alternatives being considered.

**Evoked Set.** The specific brands a consumer considers in making a purchase choice in a particular product category.

**Expected Self Concept.** How individuals expect to see themselves at some specified future time.

**Exploratory Qualitative Phase.** The phase of an indepth segmentation study in which usage patterns, buying habits, benefits sought, and consumer attitudes about a product class are examined.

**Exploratory Quantitative Phase.** The phase of an indepth segmentation study in which brand similarities, consumer attitudes, perceptions of brand images, and preferences are measured.

**Extended Family.** A household consisting of a husband, wife, offspring, and at least one other blood relative.

**Extensive Problem Solving.** A search by the consumer to establish the necessary product criteria to evaluate knowledgeably the most suitable product to fulfill a need.

**Extinction.** The point at which a learned response ceases to occur because of lack of reinforcement.

**Extrinsic Cues.** Cues external to the product, such as price, store image, or brand image, that serve to influence the consumer's perception of a product's quality.

**Family.** Two or more persons related by blood, marriage, or adoption who reside together.

**Family Branding.** The practice of marketing several company products under the same brand name.

**Family Gatekeeper.** A family member who controls the flow of information to the family about products or services, thereby regulating the related consumption decisions of other family members.

**Family Influencer.** A family member who provides product-related information and advice to other members of the family, thereby influencing related consumption decisions.

**Family Life Cycle (FLC).** A progression of stages through which most families pass, including such traditional stages as bachelorhood, honeymooners, parenthood, post-parenthood, and dissolution.

**Focus Group.** A qualitative research method in which about eight to ten persons participate in an unstructured group interview about a product or service concept.

**Foot-in-the-Door Technique.** A theory of attitude change that suggests individuals form attitudes that are consistent with their own prior behavior.

**Formal Group.** A group that has a clearly defined structure, specific roles and authority levels, and specific goals (e.g., a political party).

**Formal Interpersonal Communication.** Direct communication between a person representing a profit or nonprofit organization and one or more others (e.g., a discussion between a salesman and a prospect).

**Freudian Theory.** A theory of personality and motivation developed by the psychoanalyst Sigmund Freud. (See Psychoanalytic Theory.)

**Functional Approach.** An attitude-change theory that classifies attitudes in terms of four functions: the utilitarian function, the ego-defensive function, the value-expressive function, and the knowledge function.

**Generic Goals.** The general classes or categories of goals that individuals select to fulfill their needs. (See Product-Specific Goals.)

**Geodemographic Clusters.** A composite segmentation strategy that uses both geographic variables (zip codes, neighborhoods, or blocks) and demographic variables (e.g., income, occupation, value of residence) to identify target markets.

**Geographic Segmentation.** The division of a total potential market into smaller subgroups on the basis of geographic variables (e.g., region, state, or city).

**Gestalt.** A German term meaning "pattern" or "configuration" which has come to represent various principles of perceptual organization. (See also Perceptual Organization.)

**Goals.** The sought-after results of motivated behavior. A person fulfills a need through achievement of a goal.

**Group.** Two or more people who interact either on a regular or irregular basis in their pursuit of individual or common goals.

**Group Cohesiveness.** The extent to which group members tend to "stick together" and follow group norms.

**Group Norms.** The implicit rules of conduct or standards of behavior which members of a group are expected to observe.

**Habit.** A consistent pattern of behavior performed without considered thought. Consistent repetition is the hallmark of habit.

**Habituation.** The mechanism by which an individual systematically ignores those stimuli (e.g., products or advertising messages) that are predictable or readily recognizable because of excessive repetition. (See also Wear-Out.)

**Hierarchy of Needs.** See Maslow's Need Hierarchy.

**High Involvement.** A situation where consumers judge a purchase decision to be important enough to engage in extensive information search prior to making a decision.

**Honeymooners.** The stage in the family life cycle after marriage but before the young married couple has a child.

**Howard-Sheth Model.** One of several comprehensive models of consumer behavior.

**Hypothesis.** A tentative statement of a relationship between two or more variables.

**Hypothetical Construct.** See Construct.

**Id.** In Freudian theory, the part of the personality that consists of primitive and impulsive drives that the individual strives to satisfy.

**Ideal Self Concept.** How individuals would *like* to perceive themselves (as opposed to Actual Self Concept—the way they *do* perceive themselves).

**Impersonal Communication.** Communication directed to a large and diffuse audience, with no direct communication between source and receiver. Also known as *mass communication*.

**Independent Variable.** A variable that can be manipulated to effect a change in the value of a second (i.e, dependent) variable. For example, price is an independent variable that often affects sales (the dependent variable).

**Index of Status Characteristics (ISC).** A measure of social class that combines occupation, source of income (not amount), house type, and dwelling area into a single weighted index of social class standing. Also known as *Warner's ISC*.

**Inept Set.** Brands that a consumer excludes from purchase consideration.

**Inert Set.** Brands that a consumer is indifferent towards because they are perceived as having no particular advantage.

**Informal Group.** A group of people who see each other frequently on an informal basis, such as weekly poker players or social acquaintances.

**Informal Interpersonal Communication.** Direct communication between two or more persons who are friends, neighbors, relatives, or co-workers.

**Information Overload.** A dysfunctional situation in which the consumer is presented with too much product- or brand-related information.

**Information Processing.** A cognitive theory of human learning patterned after computer information processing which focuses on how information is stored in human memory and how it is retrieved.

**Innate Needs.** Physiological needs for food, water, air, clothing, shelter, and sex. Also known as *biogenic* or *primary* needs.

**Innovation-Decision Process.** An update of the traditional *adoption process* model consisting of the following four stages: knowledge, persuasion, decision, and confirmation.

**Innovativeness.** A measure of a consumer's willingness to try new products.

**Innovator.** An individual who is among the earliest purchasers of a new product.

**Institutional Advertising.** Advertising designed to promote a favorable company image rather than to promote specific products.

**Instrumental Conditioning.** A form of learning based on a trial-and-error process, with habits formed as the result of positive experiences resulting from certain responses or behaviors. (See also Conditioned Learning.)

**Interest.** The stage of the traditional adoption process in which the consumer actively seeks out information concerning a new product innovation.

**Interpersonal Communication.** Communication that occurs directly between two or more people by mail, by telephone or in person.

**Intrinsic Cues.** Physical characteristics of the product (such as size, color, flavor, or aroma) that serve to influence the consumer's perceptions of product quality.

**Involvement Theory.** A theory of consumer learning which postulates that consumers engage in a range of information processing activity from extensive to limited problem solving, depending on the relevance of the purchase.

**Joint Decisions.** Family purchase decisions in which the

husband and wife are equally influential. Also known as *Syncratic Decisions*.

**Just Noticeable Difference (j.n.d.).** The minimal difference that can be detected between two stimuli. (See also Differential Threshold and Weber's Law.)

**Key Informant Method.** A method of measuring various aspects of consumer behavior (such as opinion leadership or social class) whereby a knowledgeable person is asked to classify individuals with whom he or she is familiar into specific categories.

**Knowledge Function.** A component of the functional approach to attitude-change theory that suggests consumers have a strong need to know and understand the people and things with which they come into contact.

**Learning.** The process by which individuals acquire the knowledge and experience they apply to future purchase and consumption behavior.

**Lexicographic Rule.** A noncompensatory decision rule in which consumers first rank product attributes in terms of their importance, then compare brands in terms of the attribute considered most important. If one brand scores sufficiently high, it is selected; if not, the process is continued with the second ranked attribute, and so on.

**Lifestyle.** See Psychographic Characteristics.

**Limited Problem Solving.** A limited search by a consumer for a product that will satisfy his or her basic criteria from among a selected group of brands.

**Long-Term Store.** In information-processing theory, the stage of real memory where information is organized, reorganized and retained for relatively extended periods of time.

**Low Involvement.** A situation where consumers judge a purchase decision to be so unimportant or routine that they engage in little information search prior to making a decision.

**Manufacturer's Image.** The way in which consumers view (i.e., perceive) the "personality" of the firm that produces a specific product.

**Marketing.** Activities designed to enhance the flow of goods, services, and ideas from producers to consumers in order to satisfy consumer needs and wants.

**Marketing Concept.** A consumer-oriented philosophy that suggests that satisfaction of consumer needs provide the focus for product development and marketing strategy to enable the firm to meet its own organizational goals.

**Marketing Mix.** The unique configuration of the four basic marketing variables (product, promotion, price, and channels of distribution) a marketing organization controls.

**Market Segmentation.** The process of dividing a potential market into distinct subsets of consumers and selecting one or more segments as a target market to be reached with a distinct marketing mix.

**Maslow's Need Hierarchy.** A theory of motivation that postulates that individuals strive to satisfy their needs according to a basic hierarchical structure, starting with physiological needs, then moving to safety needs, social needs, egoistic needs, and finally self-actualization needs.

**Mass Communication.** See Impersonal Communication.

**Massed Learning.** Compressing the learning schedule into a short time span to accelerate consumer learning. (See also Distributed Learning.)

**Mass Marketing.** The practice of offering a single product and marketing mix to the whole potential market.

**Medium.** A channel through which a message is transmitted (e.g., a television commercial, a newspaper advertisement, or a personal letter).

**Membership Group.** A group to which a person either belongs or qualifies for membership.

**Message.** The thought, idea, attitude, image, or other information that a sender conveys to an intended audience.

**Model.** A simplified representation of reality designed to show the relationships between the various elements of a system or process under investigation.

**Motivation.** The driving force within individuals that impels them to action.

**Motivational Research.** Qualitative research designed to uncover consumers' subconscious or hidden motivations. The basic premise of motivational research is that consumers are not always aware of, or may not wish to reveal, the basic reasons underlying their actions.

**Multiattribute Attitude Models.** Attitude models that examine the composition of consumer attitudes in terms of selected product attributes or beliefs.

**Need Recognition.** The realization by the consumer that there is a difference between "what is" and "what should be."

**Negative Reinforcement.** An unpleasant or negative outcome that serves to discourage repetition of a specific behavior.

**Neo-Freudian Personality Theory.** A school of psychology that stresses the fundamental role of social relationships in the formation and development of personality.

**Nicosia Model.** One of several comprehensive models of consumer behavior.

**Noncompensatory Decision Rule.** A type of consumer decision rule whereby positive evaluation of a brand attribute does not compensate for (i.e., is not balanced against) a negative evaluation of the same brand on some other attribute.

**Nonprofit Marketing.** The use of marketing concepts and techniques by not-for-profit organizations (such as museums or government agencies) to impart information, ideas, or attitudes to various segments of the public.

**Normative Reference Group.** A group that influences the general values or behavior of an individual. (See Comparative Reference Group.)

**Nuclear Family.** A household consisting of a husband and wife and at least one offspring.

**Objective Measurement of Social Class.** A method of measuring social class whereby individuals are asked specific socioeconomic questions concerning themselves or their families. On the basis of their answers, people are placed within specific social class groupings.

**Observability.** The ease with which a product's benefits or attributes can be observed, visualized, or described to potential customers.

**Observational Research.** A research procedure which examines the actual behavior of consumers in the marketplace.

**Opinion Leader.** A person who informally influences the attitudes or behavior of others.

**Opinion Leadership.** The process by which one person (the opinion leader) informally influences the actions or attitudes of others, who may be opinion seekers or opinion recipients.

**Opinion Leadership Overlap.** The degree to which people who are opinion leaders in one product category are also opinion leaders in one or more other categories.

**Opinion Receivers.** Individuals who either actively seek product information from others or receive unsolicited information.

**Optimizing Decision Strategy.** A strategy whereby a consumer evaluates each brand in terms of significant product criteria. (See also Simplifying Decision Strategy.)

**Optimum Stimulation Level (OSL).** The level or amount of novelty or complexity that individuals seek in their personal experiences. High OSL consumers tend to accept risky and novel products more readily than low OSL consumers.

**Organizational Consumer.** A purchasing agent (or group) employed by a business, government agency, or other institution, profit or nonprofit, that buys the goods, services, or equipment necessary for the organization to function.

**Parenthood.** The stage in the family life cycle where a married couple has at least one child living at home.

**Participant Observer.** A researcher who becomes an active member of the environment he or she is studying.

**Passive Man Model.** A theory of man that depicts the consumer as a submissive recipient of the promotional efforts of marketers.

**Perceived Quality.** The quality attributed to a product by the consumer on the basis of various informational cues associated with the product, such as price. (See Intrinsic Cues and Extrinsic Cues.)

**Perceived Risk.** The degree of uncertainty perceived by the consumer as to the consequences (outcome) of a specific purchase decision.

**Perception.** The process by which an individual selects, organizes, and interprets stimuli into a meaningful and coherent picture of the world.

**Perceptual Blocking.** The subconscious "screening out" of stimuli that are threatening or inconsistent with one's needs, values, beliefs, or attitudes.

**Perceptual Defense.** The process of subconsciously distorting stimuli to render them less threatening or inconsistent with one's needs, values, beliefs, or attitudes.

**Perceptual Mapping.** A research technique that enables marketers to plot graphically consumers' perceptions concerning product attributes of specific brands.

**Perceptual Organization.** The subconscious ordering and perception of stimuli into groups or configurations according to certain principles of Gestalt psychology.

**Personal Consumer.** The individual who buys goods and services for his or her own use, for household use, for the use of a family member, or for a friend. (Sometimes referred to as the *ultimate consumer* or *end user*.)

**Personality.** The inner psychological characteristics that both determine and reflect how a person responds to his or her environment.

**Personality Scale.** A series of questions or statements designed to measure a single personality trait.

**Personality Test.** A pencil-and-paper test designed to measure an individual's personality in terms of one or more traits or inner characteristics.

**Political Marketing.** The use of marketing concepts and techniques by candidates for political office and by those interested in promoting political causes.

**Positioning.** Establishing a specific image for a brand in relation to competing brands. (See also Product Positioning.)

**Positive Reinforcement.** A favorable outcome to a specific behavior that strengthens the likelihood that the behavior will be repeated.

**Postparenthood.** The stage in the family life cycle when a married couple has all children living permanently apart from them.

**Postpurchase Dissonance.** Cognitive dissonance that occurs after a consumer has made a purchase commitment. Consumers resolve this dissonance through a variety of strategies designed to confirm the wisdom of their choice. (See Cognitive Dissonance.)

**Postpurchase Evaluation.** An assessment of a product based on actual trial after purchase.

**Power Need.** The need to exercise control over one's environment, including other persons.

**Prepotent Need.** An overriding need, from among several needs, that serves to initiate goal-directed behavior.

**Prepurchase Search.** A stage in the consumer decision making process in which the consumer perceives a need and actively seeks out information concerning products that will help satisfy that need.

**Price-Quality Relationship.** The perception of price as an indicator of product quality (e.g., the higher the price, the higher the perceived quality of the product).

**Primacy Effect.** A theory that proposes that the first (i.e., the earliest) message presented in a sequential series of messages tends to produce the greatest impact on the receiver. (See also Recency Effect.)

**Primary Data.** Information that is collected through surveys, interviews, questionnaires, observation, or experimentation for a specific research project.

**Primary Group.** A group of people who interact (e.g., meet and talk) on a regular basis, such as members of a family, neighbors, or co-workers.

**Primary Needs.** See Innate Needs.

**PRIZM (Potential Rating Index by Zip Market).** A composite index of geographic and socioeconomic factors expressed in residential zip code neighborhoods from which consumer segments are formed.

**Product Image.** The "personality" that consumers attribute to a product or brand.

**Product Line Extension.** A marketing strategy of adding related products to an already established brand (based on the Stimulus Generalization Theory).

**Product Positioning.** A marketing strategy designed to project a specific image for a product.

**Product-Specific Goals.** The specifically branded or labeled products that consumers select to fulfill their needs. (See also Generic Goals.)

**Projective Techniques.** Research procedures designed to identify consumers' subconscious feelings and motivations. These tests often require consumers to interpret ambiguous stimuli such as incomplete sentences, cartoons, or inkblots.

**Psychoanalytic Theory.** A theory of motivation and personality which postulates that unconscious needs and drives, particularly sexual and other biological drives, are the basis of human motivation and personality.

**Psychographic Characteristics.** Intrinsic psychological, sociocultural and behavioral characteristics that reflect how an individual is likely to act in relation to consumption decisions. Also referred to as *lifestyle* or *activities, interests, and opinion* (AIO) *characteristics*.

**Psychographic Instrument.** A series of written statements designed to capture relevant aspects of a consumer's personality, buying motives, interests, attitudes, beliefs, and values.

**Psychological Segmentation.** The division of a total potential market into smaller subgroups on the basis of intrinsic characteristics of the individual, such as personality, buying motives, lifestyle, attitudes, or interests.

**Psychology.** The study of the intrinsic qualities of individuals, such as their motivations, perception, personality, and learning patterns.

**Quantitative Probability Phase.** The phase of an in-depth segmentation study that identifies the prime segments to be pursued in such terms as members' behavior, attitudes, demographic characteristics, or media habits.

**Rate of Adoption.** The percentage of potential adopters within a specific social system who have adopted a new product within a given period of time.

**Rate of Usage.** The frequency of use and repurchase of a particular product.

**Rational Motives.** Motives or goals based on economic or objective criteria, such as price, size, weight, or miles-per-gallon.

**Recency Effect.** A theory that proposes that the last (i.e., most recent) message presented in a sequential series of messages tends to be remembered longest. (See also Primacy Effect.)

**Recognition Measure.** A research technique in which the consumer is shown a specific advertisement and is asked whether he or she remembers having seen it.

**Reference Group.** A person or group that serves as a point of comparison (or reference) for an individual in the formation of either general or specific values, attitudes, or behavior.

**Rehearsal.** The silent, mental repetition of material. Also, the relating of new data to old data to make the former more meaningful.

**Reinforcement.** A positive or negative outcome that influences the likelihood that a specific behavior will be repeated in the future in response to a particular cue or stimulus.

**Relative Advantage.** The degree to which potential customers perceive a new product to be superior to existing alternatives.

**Reliability.** The degree to which a measurement instrument is consistent in what it measures.

**Repeat Purchase.** The act of repurchasing the same product or brand purchased earlier.

**Repositioning.** Changing the way a product is perceived by consumers in relation to other brands or product uses.

**Reputational Measurement of Social Class.** A method of measuring social class whereby knowledgeable community members are asked to judge the social class position of other members of their community. (See Key Informant Method.)

**Response.** The reaction of an individual to a specific stimulus or cue.

**Retrieval.** The stage of information processing in which individuals recover information from long-term storage.

**Rokeach Value Survey.** A self-administered inventory consisting of eighteen "terminal" values (i.e., personal goals) and eighteen "instrumental" values (i.e., ways of reaching personal goals).

**Role.** A pattern of behavior expected of an individual in a specific social position, such as the role of a mother, daughter, teacher, or lawyer. One person may have a number of different roles, each of which is relevant in the context of a specific social situation.

**Routinized Response Behavior.** A habitual purchase response based on predetermined criteria.

**Secondary Data.** Data that has been collected for reasons other than the specific research project at hand.

**Secondary Group.** A group of people who interact infrequently or irregularly, such as two women who meet occasionally in the supermarket.

**Secondary Needs.** See Acquired Needs.

**Selective Attention.** A heightened awareness of stimuli relevant to one's needs or interests. Also called Selective Perception.

**Selective Exposure.** Conscious or subconscious exposure of the consumer to certain media or messages, and the subconscious or active avoidance of others.

**Selective Perception.** See Selective Attention.

**Self-Designated Method.** A method of measuring some aspect of consumer behavior (such as opinion leadership) in which a person is asked to evaluate or describe his or her own attitudes or actions.

**Self Image.** The image a person has of himself or herself as a certain kind of person with certain characteristic traits, habits, possessions, relationships, and behavior.

**Self-Perception Theory.** A theory that suggests that consumers develop attitudes by reflecting on their own behavior.

**Self-Report Attitude Scales.** The measurement of consumer attitudes by self-scoring procedures, such as Likert scales, semantic differential scales, or rank-order scales.

**Self Reports.** Pen-and-pencil "tests" completed by individuals concerning their own actions, attitudes, or motivations in regard to a subject or product under study.

**Sensation.** The immediate and direct response of the sensory organs to simple stimuli (e.g., color, brightness, loudness, smoothness).

**Sensory Receptors.** The human organs (eyes, ears, nose, mouth, skin) that receive sensory inputs.

**Sensory Store.** According to information-processing theory, the place in which all sensory inputs are housed very briefly before passing into the short-term store.

**Sheth Family Decision-Making Model.** One of several comprehensive models of consumer behavior.

**Short-Term Store.** In information-processing theory, the stage of real memory in which information received from the sensory store for processing is retained briefly before passing into the long-term store or forgotten.

**Simplifying Decision Strategy.** A strategy whereby the consumer evaluates alternative brands in terms of one relevant criterion. (See also Optimizing Decision Strategy.)

**Single-Component Attitude Model.** An attitude model consisting of just one overall *affective*, or "feeling," component.

**Single Variable Index.** The use of a single socioeconomic variable (such as income) to estimate an individual's relative social class. (See also Composite Variable Index.)

**Sleeper Effect.** The tendency for persuasive communication to lose the impact of source credibility over time (i.e., the influence of a message from a high credibility source tends to *decrease* over time; the influence of a message from a low credibility source tends to increase over time).

**Social Character.** In the context of consumer behavior, a personality trait that ranges on a continuum from inner-directedness (reliance on one's own "inner" values or standards) to other-directedness (reliance on others for direction).

**Social Class.** The division of members of a society into a hierarchy of distinct status classes, so that members of each class have relatively the same status and members of all other classes have either higher or lower status.

**Sociocultural Segmentation.** The division of a total potential market into smaller subgroups on the basis of sociological or cultural variables, such as social class, stage in the family life cycle, religion, race, nationality, values, beliefs or customs.

**Social Marketing.** The use of marketing concepts and techniques to win adoption of socially beneficial ideas.

**Social Psychology.** The study of how individuals operate in a group.

**Socioeconomic Status Scores (SES).** A social class measure used by the United States Bureau of the Census which combines occupational status, family income, and educational attainment into one measure of social class standing.

**Sociology.** The study of groups.

**Sociometric Method.** A method of measuring opinion leadership whereby the actual pattern or web of person-to-person informal communication is traced.

**Source.** The initiator of a message.

**SRI Values and Lifestyle Program (VALS).** A research service that tracks marketing-relevant shifts in the beliefs, values and lifestyles of a sample of the American population that has been divided into a small number of consumer segments.

**Status.** The relative prestige accorded to an individual within a specific group or social system.

**Stimulus.** Any unit of input to any of the senses. Examples of consumer stimuli include products, packages, brand names, advertisements, and commercials. Also known as *sensory input*.

**Stimulus Discrimination.** The ability to select a specific stimulus from among similar stimuli because of perceived differences.

**Stimulus Generalization.** The inability to perceive differences between slightly dissimilar stimuli.

**Storage.** The stage in information processing in which individuals organize and reorganize information in long-term memory received from the short-term store.

**Store Image.** Consumers' perceptions of the "personality" of a store and the products it carries.

**Subculture.** A distinct cultural group that exists as an identifiable segment within a larger, more complex society.

**Subjective Measurement of Social Class.** A method of measuring social class whereby people are asked to estimate their own social class position.

**Sublimation.** The manifestation of repressed needs in a socially acceptable form of behavior; a type of defense mechanism.

**Subliminal Embeds.** Symbols implanted in print advertisements presumed to appeal to consumers below the level of their conscious awareness.

**Subliminal Perception.** Perception of very weak or rapid stimuli received below the level of conscious awareness.

**Superego.** In Freudian theory, the part of the personality that reflects society's moral and ethical codes of conduct. (See also Id and Ego.)

**Supraliminal Perception.** Perception of stimuli at or above the level of conscious awareness.

**Symbolic Group.** A group with which an individual identifies by adopting its values, attitudes, or behavior despite the unlikelihood of future membership.

**Targeting.** The selection of a distinct market segment at which to direct a marketing strategy.

**Theory.** A hypothesis (or group of hypotheses) that offers an explanation of behavior.

**Theory of Reasoned Action.** A comprehensive theory of the interrelationship among attitudes, intentions, and behavior.

**Three Hit Theory.** A theory which proposes that the optimum number of exposures to an advertisement to induce learning is three: one to gain consumers' awareness, a second to show the relevance of the product, and a third to show its benefits.

**Trait.** Any distinguishing, relatively enduring way in which one individual differs from another.

**Trait Theory.** A theory of personality that focuses on the measurement of specific psychological characteristics.

**Trial.** The fourth stage of the traditional adoption process in which the consumer tries the product innovation on a limited basis.

**Trialability.** The degree to which a new product is capable of being tried by consumers on a limited basis (e.g., through free samples or small size packages).

**Trial Purchase.** A type of purchase behavior in which the consumer purchases a product (usually in a small size) in order to evaluate it.

**Tricomponent Attitude Model.** An attitude model consisting of three parts: a cognitive (knowledge) component, an affective (feeling) component, and a conative (doing) component.

**Two-Step Flow of Communication Theory.** A communication model that portrays opinion leaders as direct receivers of information from mass media sources who in turn interpret and transmit this information to the general public.

**Unaided Recall Measures.** An advertising measurement technique in which respondents are asked to recall advertisements they have seen, with no cues as to the identity or product class of the advertisements to be recalled. Often used to measure the influence of timing on learning schedules.

**User Behavior Segmentation.** The division of a total potential market into smaller subgroups in terms of rate of usage or brand preference.

**Utilitarian Function.** A component of the functional approach to attitude-change theory that suggests consumers hold certain attitudes partly because of the brand's utility.

**Validity.** The degree to which a measurement instrument accurately reflects what it is designed to measure.

**VALS.** See SRI Values and Lifestyle Program.

**Value-Expressive Function.** A component of the functional approach to attitude-change theory that suggests that attitudes express consumers' general values, lifestyle and outlook.

**Value Instruments.** Data collection instruments used to ask people how they feel about basic personal and social concepts such as freedom, comfort, national security, or peace.

**Values.** Relatively enduring beliefs that serve as guides for what is considered "appropriate" behavior and are widely accepted by the members of a society.

**Variable.** A thing or idea that may vary (i.e., assume a succession of values).

**Venturesomeness.** A personality trait that measures a consumer's willingness to accept the risk of purchasing innovative products.

**Voluntary Simplifiers.** A small but growing segment of consumers that select lifestyles designed to maximize the amount of control they have over their own lives.

**Warner's Index of Status Characteristics.** See Index of Status Characteristics (ISC).

**Wear-Out.** The point at which repeated exposure to a stimulus, such as an advertising message, no longer has a positive or reinforcing influence on attitudes or behavior.

**Weber's Law.** A theory concerning the perceived differentiation of similar stimuli of varying intensities (i.e., the stronger the initial stimulus, the greater the additional intensity needed for the second stimulus to be perceived as different).

**Yankelovich Monitor.** A research service that tracks over fifty social trends, and provides information as to shifts in size and direction, and resulting marketing implications.

# Author Index

# Subject Index